The Persian Gulf States

The Persian Gulf States

A General Survey

ALVIN J. COTTRELL, GENERAL EDITOR

C. Edmund Bosworth, R. Michael Burrell,
Keith McLachlan, and Roger M. Savory, EDITORS

THE JOHNS HOPKINS UNIVERSITY PRESS   BALTIMORE AND LONDON

The Johns Hopkins University Press, Baltimore, Maryland 21218
The Johns Hopkins Press Ltd., London

Originally published, 1980
Second printing, 1981

Library of Congress Cataloging in Publication Data

Main entry under title:
The Persian Gulf States.
   Includes index.
   1. Persian Gulf region. I. Cottrell, Alvin J.
DS326.P48   953   79-19452
ISBN 0-8018-2204-1

EDITORS

Alvin J. Cottrell, Center for Strategic and International Studies, Georgetown University, Washington, D.C., *General Editor*

C. Edmund Bosworth, University of Manchester, Manchester, England.

R. Michael Burrell, School of Oriental and African Studies, University of London, London, England.

Keith McLachlan, School of Oriental and African Studies, University of London, London, England.

Roger M. Savory, University of Toronto, Toronto, Ontario.

STAFF

Frank T. Bray, Institute for Foreign Policy Analysis, Cambridge, Massachusetts.

Kimbriel Mitchell, London, England.

Marcia McMichael, Center for Strategic and International Studies, Georgetown University, Washington, D.C.

Michael M. Moodie, Center for Strategic and International Studies, Georgetown University, Washington, D.C.

CONTRIBUTORS

Gerald Blake, Centre for Middle East and Islamic Studies, University of Durham, Durham, England.

Heather Bleaney, Centre for Middle East and Islamic Studies, University of Durham, Durham, England.

Michael E. Bonine, University of Arizona, Tucson, Arizona.

C. Edmund Bosworth, University of Manchester, Manchester, England.

Frank T. Bray, Institute for Foreign Policy Analysis, Cambridge, Massachusetts.

R. Michael Burrell, School of Oriental and African Studies, University of London, London, England.

Brian D. Clark, Aberdeen University, Aberdeen, Scotland.

Alvin J. Cottrell, Center for Strategic and International Studies, Georgetown University, Washington, D.C.

James E. Dougherty, Saint Joseph's University, Philadelphia, Pennsylvania.

Michael M. J. Fischer, Harvard University, Cambridge, Massachusetts.

Robert J. Hanks, U.S. Strategic Institute, Washington, D.C.

Robert Hillenbrand, University of Edinburgh, Edinburgh, Scotland.

David Imrie, Centre for Middle East and Islamic Studies, University of Durham, England.

Bruce Ingham, School of Oriental and African Studies, University of London, London, England.

Richard Lawless, Centre for Middle East and Islamic Studies, University of Durham, Durham, England.

Ralph H. Magnus, United States Naval Postgraduate School, Monterey, California.

Keith McLachlan, School of Oriental and African Studies, University of London, London, England.

Kimbriel Mitchell, London, England.

Robert M. Rehder, Stirling University, Stirling, Scotland.

Roger M. Savory, University of Toronto, Toronto, Ontario.

G. M. Wickens, University of Toronto, Toronto, Ontario.

Malcolm Yapp, School of Oriental and African Studies, University of London, London, England.

Contents

TABLES

Foreword

The Persian Gulf—to some the very name is a political statement. The editors therefore have wisely included in this book a chapter on nomenclature, hardly necessary for other regions of the world. In Western Europe, at any rate, a man who speaks of "the Gulf" without qualification no longer means the Gulf of Mexico. These facts speak for themselves. They are perhaps the most eloquent signs of the surpassing importance of the Persian Gulf, which is defined in this book as Lorimer defined it in his great *Gazetteer*, though the names of many of the territories are different now: it includes Iran, Iraq, Sa'ūdī Arabia, Kuwait, Bahrain, Qatar, the United Arab Emirates, and Oman.

Thirty years ago, when I told my friends and acquaintances in an English provincial town that I was going to the Persian Gulf, I saw blank faces and heard those expressions of a lack of interest that sound like polite grunts. Only those who had served there during one of the two world wars had anything to say; and what they said was far from polite, for the Persian Gulf had a very bad name in those days.

I suspect it meant nothing at all to Americans and to other outsiders, for it was to the British alone that it had significance. It had been the road to India; not the most important road perhaps, at any rate after the opening of the Suez Canal, but it was in early imperial times the way the mails often took, and later the route of the telegraph. Even when its use for communications had declined, it was always regarded as an indispensable outpost of India. As Dr. Yapp shows in his chapter on British policy, Lord Curzon, the only viceroy to visit the Persian Gulf, had no doubt that British supremacy in the Persian Gulf was so closely bound up with British rule in India that the latter would not long survive the loss of the former. He was right, and the reverse was also true. Yet British power in the Persian Gulf not only survived the loss of the Indian empire by more than twenty years, but reached its greatest strength during that time. Trebizond had again outlived Byzantium.

It was not for strategic reasons that the British held on to the Persian Gulf when they had yielded their rule in India. That is not to say that considerations of strategy played no part in British policy after 1948: a mere glance at the map

xi

is enough to show the supreme strategic importance of Iran, for example. But for the first time in its modern history the Persian Gulf had become of prime importance not because of its position but for what it contained: no longer principally a route or passage, it was being rapidly transformed into the main source of the most valuable commodity in international trade. It is true that the British first took an interest in the Persian Gulf for commercial rather than imperial reasons, exchanging woolen goods for Persian silk and specie in the seventeenth century. This trade, however, was of small value to England or to her competitors from Western Europe. Nowadays the countries described in this book possess more than two-thirds of the world's published proved oil reserves. In the last few years, the importance of that trade has been brought home to the greater part of mankind.

Another significant change has taken place in the Persian Gulf with the recent withdrawal of the British. For the first time since the beginning of the sixteenth century, no outside power wields direct and decisive influence in the area. The Portuguese, the Dutch, the French, the Turks, the British—all have gone, and the Indian subcontinent, now divided among three major states, has neither the strength nor the will to inherit the power of the Raj. It is now therefore essential, as it has long been proper, that the outsider who visits or works in the countries of the Persian Gulf should take an interest in these countries and their peoples for their own sakes. All of them are now independent and all of them are courted in various ways by all the great powers.

The foreign visitor or resident who takes an interest in his hosts and his surroundings will not be disappointed. The region is rich in history: Sa'ūdī Arabia contains the original home of Islam, while Iraq and Persia were among its earliest conquests and exercised a decisive influence on its development. It was in the countries bordering on the Persian Gulf that the great battles within early Islam were fought and orthodox Islamic doctrine was hammered out. It is there too that all the centers of the greatest challenge to that orthodoxy are still to be found. It is there that Arab and Persian have always met, sometimes in destructive conflict but recently, and let us hope forever, in peace and cooperation.

But the greatest reward of knowledge and sympathetic interest is the response of the inhabitants. This is, of course, true everywhere. More than twenty-five years ago, in the Mediterranean, I came across one of the then capital ships of the United States Navy called *Valley Forge*. I do not think that I won many American friends by wondering aloud, and no doubt in a patronizing manner, why the Americans should give their ships such extraordinary names. Years later, a similar exposure of my ignorance of Irish history nearly cost me a black eye or worse.

The Americans and the Irish are perhaps more entitled than are Arabs and Persians to expect an Englishman to know something of their history and culture. But the Westerner who chooses to work with or live among Arabs and Persians will find his work easier and his private life richer if he pays his hosts the compliment that he would expect from them if the circumstances were reversed. Above all he will make good friends.

It is for this reason, above all others, that I commend this book. I read Sir Arnold Wilson's book *The Persian Gulf* thirty-five years ago and first felt the fascination of the area before I had seen much of it. In the last few years, numerous books, ranging from light novels to works of monumental scholarship, have been published on these countries; but this reference work is the first attempt, so far as I know, to bring together material on history, both tribal and international, geography, culture, religion, law, sociology, the arts, military affairs, agriculture, and economics. I hope it will tempt the reader to further reading and perhaps even to the arduous but rewarding study of the elements of the Arabic and Persian languages.

I found the time I served in these countries the most rewarding in my life. I think, or like to think, that I have more friends in them than anywhere else in the world. In some of them I feel more at home than anywhere, except my own country. As I write, I can think of several Western acquaintances who would, I know, say the same. It may not always be so, for these countries are exceptionally vulnerable, partly because of their very prosperity, to far-off events over which they have no control. They need the understanding of the West almost as much as the West needs them; and the foundation of that understanding must be the kind of knowledge that this book will go far to provide.

GEOFFREY ARTHUR, K.C.M.G.
Oxford University

Editors' Preface

As this book goes to press, the situation in the Persian Gulf region remains unsettled. When the editors planned this volume in the mid-1970s, we were acutely aware of the changing nature of events in the Middle East and realized that change would be part of the region's future. We consciously chose not to carry the material in these essays much beyond the middle of the twentieth century and to leave off discussing many of the unsettled controversies and problems facing the Persian Gulf states today. Thus, readers should not be disappointed if they do not find in these essays information about events or developments after the close of 1978. Still, at many points in this volume, we have sought to note this limitation and to correct passages that are clearly contrary to fact, especially as a result of the Iranian revolution of 1979.

Nevertheless, we believe that we have put together a scholarly, readable, and useable reference volume—one that for the first time treats the Persian Gulf region as a unit, with a common geography, history, economics, and culture, despite national and regional differences. Our intention is to provide the background information needed to understand the context in which change in the Persian Gulf region takes place. We hope we have accomplished this end.

A word is necessary concerning the always difficult and controversial editorial question of transliteration. Arabic, Persian, and other personal and place names abound in a book such as this. Wherever possible, the correct forms of these names have been ascertained; however, for common names like Tehran, Iraq. Riyadh, Hormuz, etc., the accepted English forms have been used. In some cases, an arbitrary decision had to be made concerning the demarcation of commonly accepted Western forms and the correct transliteration; hence, the adoption of *Saʿūdī* for *Saudi*, but *Sharja* for *al-Shāriqa*. Common sense and recognizability have seemed to be obvious guides.

The editors wish to thank all those who helped in the preparation of this volume. We would particularly like to thank Etta Pollock, who typed the entire manuscript—parts of it more than once. Mrs. Phoebe Howard also graciously assisted in the typing and other chores involved in preparing the manuscript for the publisher. Aileen Masterson worked closely with the editors in correcting galleys. We are deeply grateful to Dr. Elizabeth Sirriyyah for her work on the index.

Finally, the editors wish to thank Dr. Henry Y. K. Tom, Social Sciences Editor of The Johns Hopkins University Press, and his colleagues on the editorial staff, Nancy M. Gallienne and Jane Warth. They have been very patient, supportive, and helpful. They helped to make the long, and sometimes very complicated, process of editing this book a pleasure.

The Nomenclature of the Persian Gulf

The earliest historical references to the Persian Gulf appear to stem from the time of the Sumerian rulers of Mesopotamia in the third millennium B.C., when, for instance, the trade with Dilmun (on the western shores of the upper part of the Gulf) of Ur Nanše, King of Lagash (2494–2465 B.C.), is mentioned. The Gulf itself is specifically named in a historical text of Lugal Zagesi, King of Uruk (2340–2316 B.C.), where it is said that "then from the Lower Sea, by the Tigris and Euphrates, as far as the Upper Sea, [the god Enlil] provided him with clear routes"; and, in an inscription of Sargon of Akkad, it is said that Enlil gave him the Upper Sea and the Lower Sea. This contrasting in Sumerian of the Upper and the Lower Seas is carried over into Semitic Mesopotamia, for in Akkadian we have the term for the Lower Sea, *tâmtu šaplîtu*, frequently juxtaposed with the Upper Sea, *tâmtu elênîtu*, referring respectively to the Gulf and the Mediterranean; the combination of the two terms indicates in contemporary usage the breadth of the intervening lands, all under Mesopotamian control. In later times, i.e., in the first millennium B.C., the Gulf is referred to not only as a source of tribute brought to the rulers of Mesopotamia but also as a route for naval expeditions by the kings. Thus, Sennacherib (705–681 B.C.) mentions his campaigns across the Gulf to the land of Elam (i.e., southwestern Persia), referring to it as "the Great Sea of the East" (*tâmtu rabîtu ša sît šamši*, literally, "of the rising-place of the sun"), and he describes his impressions of it in detail.[1]

We know that maritime trade through the Gulf probably declined somewhat in the period of the Achaemenid empire in Persia, compared with its flourishing state during the Babylonian period. Achaemenid expansionism was essentially directed across the southwest Asian land mass, and the emperors lacked the wide vision of an Alexander the Great, who was to discern the complementary value

---

1. For the early texts, see D. D. Luckenbill, *Ancient Records of Assyria and Babylon* (Chicago, 1927), 2: 123, 246; and E. Sollberger *Inscriptions royales sumériennes et akkadiennes* (Paris, 1971), s.v. the rulers in question. For a general account of the Gulf in this ancient period, see Sir Arnold Wilson, *The Persian Gulf, an Historical Sketch from the Earliest Times to the Beginning of the Twentieth Century* (London, 1928), pp. 32–34.

of both land power and sea power and the importance of a brisk maritime trade with the further eastern parts of Asia. It may not, therefore, be entirely coincidence, or a reflection of our ignorance until the present time, that no special term designating the Persian Gulf is known to us either in Elamite or Old Persian; the extent of the emperors' conquests are proclaimed in their inscriptions, but the enumeration here is only of provinces on the land and not of coastlands and seas brought under Persian control.[2]

Classical authors, above all the Greek historians and geographers, displayed an interest in the Gulf both as a result of the Greco-Persian warfare of the fifth century B.C. and Alexander's journeyings to the lands beyond the Persian empire in the following century, and also as a consequence of commercial curiosity, i.e., an interest in the sources and habitats of the various luxury commodities, such as spices, aromatics, and dyestuffs, which were already reaching the eastern Mediterranean region from the semilegendary lands along the Indian Ocean shores, like Ophir and Punt.

Geographical conceptions of the Gulf were, however, only vague in the period before the epic voyage of Nearchus, in 325–24 B.C. Greek writers placed the Persian Gulf, the Arabian Sea, the Gulf of Aden, and the Red Sea under the blanket designation of *hē Erythra Thalassa* (Latin, *Mare Erythraeum*) "the Erythraean Sea." Various fanciful etymologies are given for this name in the early Greek sources. Thus, the late fourth century–early third century historian Dinon of Colophon says that it came from the son of Perseus, Erythras, left behind among the Persians when he traveled eastward, his name being then given to the sea down which he sailed. Other sources, such as the Ptolemaic official in Egypt Agatharchides (ca. 110 B.C.), in his *De Mari Erythraeo*, state that it was named after a noble Persian of the Median empire, Erythras son of Myozaeus, who lived by the Gulf coast (his grave on the island of Qarakhta being mentioned by Nearchus) and then extended his control over the then uninhabited islands lying off that coastland, colonizing them and giving his name to the whole sea; hence, so this author says, we speak of *hē Erythra Thalassa* "Sea of Erythras" and not *hē Thalassa Erythrē* "Red Sea." It is not impossible that a local prince with some name later interpreted by the Greeks as Erythras in fact existed, or that "Erythrean" simply means "red, oriental" in reference to the place of the rising sun, i.e., "the eastern sea." Agatharchides himself rejected the idea that the name arose because the sea itself was red, and, of course, the Persian Gulf, the Gulf of Aden, and the Red Sea are not particularly red in color—a medieval Chinese writer, Chau-ju-kua, in his work on Chinese and Arab trade during the twelfth and thirteenth centuries A.D., the *Chu-fan-chi*, calls the Persian Gulf "The Green Sea"—unless we have reference to the reddish-colored coral banks and reefs off certain coasts of the Red Sea and Persian Gulf, so that the name came to mean "Sea of the Red Lands," denoting all the Arabian peninsula coastlands.[3] At this time, and until early Christian times, as the very title *Periplus of the Erythraean Sea* (see below) shows, *hē Erythra Thalassa* referred to the whole

---

2. For the Gulf in the Old Persian Period, see Wilson, *The Persian Gulf*, pp. 34–36.

3. Various suggestions are reviewed by W. H. Schoff, "The Name of the Erythraean Sea," *Journal of the American Oriental Society* 33 (1913): 349–62; it seems impossible now, at a distance of 2,000 years or more, to discern the true origin of the name.

of the seas surrounding the Arabian peninsula, together with the Arabian Sea as far as the coasts of India, and only later was the designation "the Red Sea" restricted to that arm of the Indian Ocean running northward to Suez and Eilath.[4]

Herodotus (fifth century B.C.) and other early authors describe both the Red Sea and the Persian Gulf as gulfs (*kolpoi*) of the Indian Ocean or Arabian Sea. Herodotus calls the Red Sea *ho Arabios Kolpos* "the Arabian Gulf," although he does not use the term *ton Indikon Pelagos* "the Indian Sea"; and when he describes the course of the Euphrates he speaks of it as debouching into the *Erythrēn Thalassan* or Erythraean Sea.[5] Alexander the Great was very interested in the sea route to India (though potential activity here was cut short by his death), and the five months voyage of his general, Nearchus, from the Indus mouth to Charax, at the head of the Gulf, provided much information about the topography of the northern shorelines of the Indian Ocean, the Gulf of Oman, and the Persian Gulf, along which Nearchus sailed. Thus, his mariners hugged the inhospitable coasts of the Oreitai (the hinterland of the modern Sonmiyani Bay, in the former Las Bela state of British Baluchistan) and of the Ichthyophagi in Gedrosia (i.e., Makrān, the coastal region of Pakistani and Persian Baluchistan as far west as the Straits of Hormuz). They then sailed along the coasts of Carmania (modern Lāristān), passing the island of Oarakhta, or Qishm, described as 800 *stadia* (ca. 80 nautical miles) long, and then along the coasts of Persis (Fārs) and Susis (Khūzistān) to the mouth of the Pasitigrēs.[6]

Geographers of the subsequent period, such as Eratosthenes, with his world map, showed that they had a good idea of the topography of the coastlands of the Arabian peninsula and the hydrography of the surrounding seas. Valuable evidence for the Red Sea, South Arabian and Makrān shores and beyond, in both the Indian and the East African directions, is to be found in the *Periplus of the Erythraean Sea* (traditionally taken as having been compiled by an unknown Alexandrian Greek merchant and seafarer, perhaps as an official report, but conceivably a pastiche of various seafarers' accounts, and dating from a point between the closing years of the first century A.D. and the early third century A.D.),[7] but it contains little direct information on the Gulf of Oman and the Persian Gulf. The author describes, from his own experience, the coastlands of the "Frankincense country" (i.e., Zufār or Dhofar), the Zenobian Islands (i.e., the Kuria-Muria Islands), Sarapis Island (Masīra) and its Ichthyophagi, and the Colon Mountains of Oman (i.e., the Jabal Akhdar); but because of the closeness of Persian governmental control over navigation into the Gulf, he was unable to

4. The material of the classical period on the Gulf is gathered together in Pauly-Wissowa, *Realenzyklopaedie des klassischen Altertums*, vi/1, cols. 592–601, art. "Erythra thalassa" (Berger), brought up-to-date in *Der Kleine Pauly*, 2, cols. 366–67 (H. Treidler). This material is utilized in Wilson, *The Persian Gulf*, pp. 36–52, and in G. F. Hourani, *Arab Seafaring in the Indian Ocean in Ancient and Early Medieval Times* (Princeton, 1951), pp. 13–17.

5. Herodotus, *The Histories*, 1: 180.

6. The elucidation of many of the topographical problems here was undertaken by W. Tomaschek, "Topographische Erlaüterung der Küstenfahrt Nearchs," *Sitzungsber. der Kaiserl. Akad. der Wiss. zu Wien*, Phil.-Hist. Cl. 71, no. 8 (1890): 1–88.

7. Such are the views recently expressed by M. Rodinson, "Le Périple de la Mer Erythrée," *Annuaire de l'Ecole Pratique des Hautes Etudes, 1975–76. IVᵉ Section, sciences historiques et philologiques* (Paris, 1976), pp. 218–19.

describe the Gulf's topography and hydrography at first hand. He does, however, mention the importance of pearl fishing in the Gulf and the narrowness of the Straits of Hormuz, flanked on the south by the Asabon Mountains (i.e., the mountains of the Musandam peninsula) and on the north the Semiramis Mountain (perhaps, nevertheless, Ra's Musandam itself, or really on the northern shore of the Straits, the Kūh-i Mubārak, the Ra's al-Kūh of modern maps, where traveling westward, the Makrān coastline turns northward opposite the Musandam peninsula into the actual Straits of Hormuz). The author's description of the Gulf proper seems to depend on hearsay: that six days' sail beyond the Straits lies an important trading port under Persian control, Ommana (he seems to imply that this lay on the Persian coast of Carmania, but perhaps we should locate it on the former Trucial States' coast, toward Qatar); that on the eastern side of the Gulf lies the country of the Parsidae (i.e., Parthians or Arsacids); and that at the upper end of the Gulf is situated the trading center of Apologos (i.e., the early Islamic Ubulla), near Charax Spasinou. Only with his description of the Gedrosian coast does his information once more convey an impression of first-hand acquaintance with the region.[8]

Under Islam, the conquests of the Arabs in the decades after the Prophet's death early ensured that the Persian Gulf became a Muslim lake; already by 92/711 the general Muhammad b. al-Qāsim al-Thaqafī had raided through Fārs, Kirmān, and the Makrān coastland to the Indus mouth, thereby laying the foundations of the Muslim colony of Sind, for some three centuries the easternmost outpost of Islam in South Asia. The first century or so of the new world faith, corresponding roughly to the periods of the Orthodox or Patriarchal caliphs (11–40/632–61) and then of the Umayyad caliphs (41–132/661–750), was an age of rapid military expansion and the more gradual islamization of the conquered peoples. With the advent of the 'Abbasid caliphate in 132/750, the Arab empire approached territorial satiety; there arose for the first time an opportunity for cultivation of the arts of peace, and gradually a new Islamic culture was born of the fusion between the verve and enthusiasm of the desert Arabs and the older civilizations of Iran, Byzantium, Egypt, etc., many of whose territories were now under Muslim control. In particular, urban life began to develop, above all in Iraq, western Persia, Syria, and Egypt, with, for the first time, a leisured, moneyed class coming into existence and demanding a certain degree of luxury and ease. Such tastes and requirements were inevitably stimuli for internal agricultural development and industrial manufacturing (even if the latter was essentially that of small-scale production, the work of artisans and craftsmen) and for a concomitant desire for certain exotic products obtainable only outside the Islamic borders, although the Islamic world itself was, for all essentials of life, self-sufficient. The shift of the capital eastward from Damascus to Baghdad in the mid-eighth century and the political, military and cultural dominance in the early 'Abbasid caliphate of the peoples of Iraq and the Iranian world combined to develop in the Islamic heartland, and above all in Baghdad

---

8. The relevant passage of the *Periplus* (§§ 34–37) is translated in W. H. Schoff, *The Periplus of the Erythraean Sea: Travel and Trade in the Indian Ocean by a Merchant of the First Century* (New York, 1912), pp. 35–37; cf. commentary pp. 147–51; see also Wilson, *The Persian Gulf*, pp. 52–53, and Hourani, *Arab Seafaring*, pp. 15–18.

(founded in 145/762) and Sāmarrā (founded in 221/836), a demand for luxury goods, and this brought about a resumption of caravan trade with China via the lengthy and hazardous overland route through Central Asia; but, in terms of volume of trade, the maritime route down the Persian Gulf toward South Arabia, East Africa, India, Southeast Asia and China must have been more significant.

The origins and development of Islamic maritime trade with the South Asian and Far Eastern lands are only imperfectly known to us, but it seems that from the second half of the eighth century onward there was regular commercial intercourse with Southeast Asia and China, with Arab, Persian, and possibly Indian traders involved in the eastbound traffic, and almost certainly Chinese merchants involved in trade in the reverse direction, at least as far as Quilon (Kūlam or Kūlam-Malay in the Arabic sources) on the Malabar coast of southwestern peninsular India. And, of course, it is well known that certain Muslim traders must have penetrated to China before the 'Abbasid period, since in 758 the Ta-shih and Po-sse merchants (perhaps Malays, with an admixture of Arabs and Persians?) rebelled at Canton (Khānfū in the Arabic sources) against the T'ang government authorities.[9]

An analysis of this commercial traffic across the waters of the northern parts of the Indian Ocean lies outside the scope of this chapter, but its existence is sufficient to demonstrate that the configuration of the Persian Gulf and its hydrography, its hazardous rocks and shoals, and its tides, and the importance of the monsoons for navigation out of the Gulf and into the Arabian Sea and beyond, early became of interest to the flourishing school of Islamic geographers whose works are known to us from the mid-ninth century onward; it is these writers who first provide us with information on the Islamic conception of the Gulf and its nomenclature. While some of these geographers, and also the historians, may have been armchair travelers rather than practical explorers of the Islamic world and its neighbors (such as the anonymous author of the Persian geography, the *Hudūd al-'ālam*, who lived in what is now northern Afghanistan and who does not seem to have ever gone very far from his homeland), many of them were, on the contrary, indefatigable travelers, like Istakhrī, Mas'ūdī, Abū Dulaf al-Khazrajī, and Ibn Hawqal, or else possessed of a remarkably broad and sophisticated spirit of inquiry like Maqdisī (Muqaddasī). Such writers, when writing about regions where they had not themselves journeyed, sought out the best informants among the seafaring and mercantile communities, and in certain documents, such as the *Akhbār al-Sīn wa 'l-Hind* by an anonymous Indian Ocean

9. We lack a comprehensive history of medieval Islamic commerce, and, in particular, a work for the Indian Ocean and its shores comparable to W. Heyd's classic *Histoire du commerce du Levant*. Meanwhile, see on this trade through the Gulf and the Indian Ocean, the rather outdated work of A. Mez, *Die Renaissance des Islâms* (Heidelberg, 1922), *The Renaissance of Islam*, English tr. Khuda Bakhsh (Patna, 1936), pp. 505–17; Wilson, *The Persian Gulf*, pp. 56 ff.; the section "le commerce de l'Extrême-Orient" in the Introd., pp. 25–40, by J. Sauvaget to his text and French tr. of *Ahbār as-Sīn wa l-Hind, Relation de la Chine et de l'Inde, rédigée en 851* (Paris, 1948); Hourani, *Arab Seafaring*, pp. 61 ff.; and the relevant papers, those of B. Spuler, J. M. Rogers, G. T. Scanlon, R. R. di Meglio, M. A. P. Meilink-Roelofsz, and G. F. Hudson, in *Islam and the Trade of Asia, a colloquium*, ed. D. S. Richards (Oxford, 1970). That there was direct sailing between the Persian Gulf, under Sāsānid control, and China in the pre-Islamic period is more dubious; the evidence is reviewed by Hourani, *Arab Seafaring*, pp. 46–50.

trader, writing in 237/851, we have the verbatim information of someone who had obviously sailed up and down the Persian Gulf several times.[10]

Early Islamic geographers and cosmographers, when considering the position of the Persian Gulf, assumed that it was a "gulf" (khalīj) or a "tongue" (lisān) of the Great Sea, al-Bahr al-kabīr, i.e., the Indian Ocean, with which it, of course, connected. Such writers usually took the Indian Ocean for one of the two great seas of the world (the other being the system of the Mediterranean and the adjoining shores of the Atlantic Ocean), both of which connected ultimately with the "Encircling ocean" (al-Bahr al-muhīt), which itself surrounded the whole land mass of the inhabited world. The basis of these conceptions was ultimately Qur'anic, for the Qur'ān (xxiii: 102, xxv: 55, and lv: 19–22), speaks of the two seas of the world, separated by a barrier (barzakh).[11] This last term was often interpreted (e.g., by Maqdisī, see below) as being the isthmus of Suez, which separated the Red Sea–Indian Ocean system from the Mediterranean–Atlantic Ocean one. Concerning the parallel term hājiz "barrier, obstacle" (of xxvii: 62), the commentators state that there is an allusion here to the fresh waters of the Shatt al-'Arab that flow out into the Persian Gulf's salt water for a long way before they mingle, the impediment here being a law of nature immutably established by God.[12]

The opening pages of our earliest first-hand Islamic text on Indian Ocean seafaring, the Akhbār al-Sīn wa 'l-Hind, are unfortunately lost, and it must have been in these lost leaves that the author discussed the configuration of the Persian Gulf, which he subsequently calls by what became the most generally used term in medieval Islam for it, the Bahr Fāris "Sea of Fārs," describing it as the "First Sea." The "Second Sea" he calls the Bahr Lārwī, which cannot, as was perspicaciously discerned by the French orientalist Quatremère well over a century ago, refer to the southern Persian district of Lār or Lāristān, but must stem from an Indian name; it corresponds to the Arabian Sea. The "Third Sea" he calls the Bahr Harkand, a name that again seems to be of Indian origin, and since it is separated from the Second Sea by a multiplicity of islands, i.e., the Laccadives and Maldives, must be the Bay of Bengal.[13]

Hence the conception here delineated of the Persian Gulf, which must reflect the ideas of contemporary seamen, was that it formed the first of a string of seas stretching from Ubulla at the head of the Gulf right to the Malay peninsula and separated from each other by, first, the narrows of the Straits of Hormuz and beyond them the Sea of Oman, and, second, by the interposition across the route

10. For general analyses of this early Islamic geographical and travel literature tradition, see Encyl. of Islam², art. "Djughrāfiyā. I–V" (S. Maqbul Ahmad), and A. Miquel, La géographie humaine du monde musulmane jusqu'au milieu du XI° siècle: géographie et géographie humaine dans la littérature arabe (des origines à 1050) (The Hague, 1967).

11. In quotations from the Qur'ān, the verse numbering given first is that of the Flügel text, followed by that of the Egyptian "royal Qur'ān," where differing.

12. Cf. Maqdisī's discussion of the identification of the seas in his Ahsan al-taqāsīm², ed. M. J. de Goeje, Bibliotheca Geographorum Arabicorum, iii (Leiden, 1906), 15 ff., French tr. A. Miquel, La Meilleure répartition pour la connaissance des provinces (Damascus, 1963), pp. 43 ff., and also Encycl. of Islam², art. "Barzakh" (B. Carra de Vaux).

13. Sauvaget, Ahbār as-Sīn wa l-Hind, text § 4, commentary 35; Mas'ūdī, Murūj al-dhahab wa-ma'ādin al-jawhar, ed. and French tr. A. C. Barbier de Meynard and Pavet de Courteille (Paris, 1861–77), 1: 330, 332.

to the Far East of the two above-mentioned archipelagos and Sarandīb or Ceylon.
The author of the aforementioned *Akhbār* does not, accordingly, seem to have
an overall term for "the Indian Ocean." But as a practical mariner, he goes on
to discuss the ports of the Gulf and the distances between them. From Basra at
the head of the Gulf to Sīrāf on the Fārs coast (modern Bandar Tāhirī), the
greatest entrepôt of the middle reaches of the Gulf (the writer states that the
Chinese junks loaded and unloaded there, their cargoes being brought to Sīrāf
and subsequently distributed from there by local craft plying to Ubulla and
Basra, Oman, etc., since the shallow waters of the gently shelving western shores
of the Gulf and the alluvial deposits at the northern head made navigation away
from the Persian coast and beyond Sīrāf hazardous for ships like these of considerable draught) and a place where fresh water could be procured was 120
*farsakh*s, and from Sīrāf to Masqat was 200 *farsakh*s. That part of the northern
or eastern shoreland of the Gulf lying between Sīrāf and the island of Qishm was
known to the author of the *Akhbār* as the Sīf (= "coastland") Banī 'l-Saffāq, from
a component group of the great Arab tribe of Azd, which had crossed from Oman
and settled on the Persian side of the Gulf, being still important there, according
to the Arab philologist and genealogist Ibn Durayd, in the early tenth century.[14]

Qishm itself he calls by the Iranian name of Abarkāvān, one which subsequent Islamic authors deformed into names of a more Arabic-looking type such
as the Jazīrat Banī Kāwān of Ibn Khurradādhbih, Istakhrī and Mas'ūdī, and the
Jazīrat Ibn Jāwān of Ahmad b. Mājid. Among the hazards of the Gulf, stressed
by all authors, are mentioned in the *Akhbār* the two dangerous rocky islets of
Kusayr and 'Uwayr (= two of the modern Quoin Islands to the north of Ra's
Musandam), with a whirlpool (*durdūr*) between them. Only after having negoti-
ated these does one arrive at Suhār, the principal port of Oman and an old
Persian settlement, where fresh water could be taken on board and the sheep of
Oman purchased as food for the voyage.[15]

Among the authors of this period (i.e., the ninth and tenth centuries), the
most detailed discussions about the Gulf and the Indian Ocean are found in the
polyhistor and traveler Mas'ūdī (d. 345/956–57 or 346/957–58) who speaks of
these geographical concepts in both his *Kitāb al-tanbīh wa 'l-ishrāf* and his *Murūj
al-dhahab*. His favored term for the Indian Ocean is "the First Sea, the Abyssinian
Sea" (*al-Bahr al-Habashī*), for which he cites further names like "the Sea of China,
the Sea of India," etc. This he describes as the biggest sea of the inhabited part
of the world and as comprising within itself various seas deriving their names
from the adjacent coastlands—the Seas of Basra and Ubulla, of Fārs, of Kirmān,
of Bahrain, of Oman, of al-Shihr, of Yemen, etc. Off this Abyssinian Sea run
several gulfs, such as the Gulf of Barbarā (*al-Khalīj al-Barbarī*), i.e., the Gulf of
Socotra (Barbarā = Berbera, in modern Somalia); the Sea of Qulzum (*Bahr
al-Qulzum*), i.e., the Red Sea; and the Persian Sea or Gulf (*Bahr Fāris, Khalīj
Fāris*).[16]

The Persian Gulf itself is described in considerable detail. At the outset,

14. *Kitāb al-Ishtiqāq*, ed. 'Abd al-Sālam Muhammad Hārūn (Cairo, 1378/1958), p. 499.
15. Sauvaget, *Ahbār as-Sīn wa l-Hind*, text § 13, Commentary, pp. 41–42.
16. *Kitāb al-Tanbīh*, ed. de Goeje, Bibl. Geogr. Arab., viii (Leiden, 1894), pp. 51–56, French
tr. B. Carra de Vaux (Paris, 1896), pp. 76–84; *Murūj al-dhahab*, 1: 229.

Mas'ūdī states that in shape it is a triangle, with the apex at Ubulla; it is 1,400 miles long, and at its widest point is 500 miles across, narrowing to 150 miles. The Straits of Hormuz are actually only 29 miles across, and it is hard to imagine where he got these exaggerated figures from, unless that of 1,400 miles relates to the distance between Ubulla and the mouth of the Indus, extending right through what we now know as the Persian Gulf, the Sea of Oman, and the Arabian Sea. Later on, in fact, in the *Murūj al-dhahab* he gives some much more realistic figures for distances between internal points within the Gulf: from Basra to Sīrāf, 140 *farsakhs*; and from Sīrāf to Oman, 160 *farsakhs*, the distance from Suhār to Masqat being 50 *farsakhs*, with 50 more to Ra's al-Hadd—the total length of the Gulf being, accordingly, 400 *farsakhs*. These figures correspond, *grosso modo*, with those given by the author of the *Akhbār al-Sīn wa 'l-Hind*. Mas'ūdī then defines the boundaries of the Gulf in detail, from its head downward. He says that on its eastern shore it skirts the coasts of Ahwāz and Fārs by Dawraq, Mahrubān, Sīnīz, Jannāba, Najīram, the Sīf Ibn 'Umāra, the coastlands of Kirmān of Hormuz, and then Makrān and Sind. On the western shore, one passes the eastern Arabian coastal provinces of Bahrain (i.e., mainland Bahrain, medieval Islamic Hajar or al-Ahsā), the islands of Qatar (modern Bahrain Island, etc.), the coast of the Banū Judhayma (i.e., the former Trucial Oman coast), Oman, Ra's al-Jumjuma "the Cape of the Skull," and round to Mahra, al-Shibr and al-Ahqāf ("the sandhills," i.e., the desert interior of eastern Hadramawt). The "Cape of the Skull" might appear to correspond with Ra's al-Hadd, the easternmost tip of Oman, but it seems that, in reality, Mas'ūdī is expressing a curious view of his time that the coastal mountain chain of Makrān, on the opposite shore of the Gulf of Oman, had a submarine prolongation under that Gulf, reappearing in the mountains of Hadramawt and Yemen (even though he knew that the waters of the Gulf of Oman are in fact deep ones, in distinction from those of the Persian Gulf). Accordingly, we should probably localize the "Cape of the Skull" somewhere on the Makrān coast, perhaps the Ra's Jiwānī near Gwādar on the coast of modern Pakistani Baluchistan.

The islands of the Persian Gulf and the Straits of Hormuz are then detailed by Mas'ūdī: Khārg or Khārak, with its famed pearl fisheries; Uwāl (i.e., modern Bahrain Island), one day's sail from the Bahrain mainland and inhabited by such Arab tribes as the Ma'n and the Mismar; Qishm, here called Lāft (after the settlement of Lāft on the island's northern promontory facing the Clarence Strait); Hanjām Island off the south coast of Qishm, important as a source of fresh water; and the three dangerous rocks of Kusayr, 'Uwayr, and one other, with the nearby whirlpool of Musandam, called by the sailors Abū Khamīr "the place of whirling, ferment." These dangerous waters, where the adjacent coastland offers only bleak, inhospitable cliffs, had necessarily to be navigated by ships crossing from Sīrāf to Oman.[17]

The Gulf region held other dangers besides these. At the head of the Gulf, near 'Abbādān, the Muslim geographers mention the *Khashabāt* ("wooden constructions"), a timber platform in the sea on which was placed a beacon to guide ships through these dangerous waters. According to the Persian traveler Nāsir-i

17. Ibid., 1: 238–41.

Khusraw, who traveled down the Gulf to al-Ahsā on his way back from the pilgrimage in the middle years of the eleventh century (443/1052), the *Khashabāt* consisted of teak logs rising 60 feet above sea level, with a platform on them for the watchman and his illuminated, glass-shaded beacon. According to Mas'ūdī, there was near here, at a place called al-Bāsiyān along the coast between the Tigris mouth and Ahwāz, a spot where the roaring noise of the raging waters and the howling winds caused the terrified sailors to give it the name of al-Dhi'b, "the Wolf." This same author relates too that the Persian Sea has the peculiarity of being violent and disturbed when the Indian Ocean is tranquil, and vice versa, all this being attributable to the influence of the stars. Nevertheless, all these dangers and uncertainties did not inhibit pearl fishing, the banks off Khārg, Qatar, and Oman being specifically mentioned; the season for this ran from the beginning of Nīsān (or April) till the end of Aylūl (or September). Moreover, navigation between Basra and Oman was possible all the year round, whereas only the lightest-loaded craft of Oman dared to cross the Indian Ocean, beyond the sea of Oman, in midsummer (i.e., when the southwestern monsoons were blowing up the east coast of Africa and across the Arabian Sea to western India, reaching their peak in July–August); these light boats were accordingly called *tīrmāhiyya* (Tirmāh, Tīrmāh = the first summer month of the Persian calendar, the month of Sirius, i.e., June–July).[18]

The author of the Persian geography, the *Hudūd al-'ālam* or *Limits of the World*, displays a particular interest in physical geography, and above all in the mountains, seas, rivers, and islands of the Islamic world and the surrounding lands, although it would seem that his sources were literary ones rather than the first-hand accounts of contemporary travelers. He calls the Indian Ocean the *Bahr al-A'zam* "the Great Sea" and defines its northern boundaries as skirting China, Hindustan, Sind, and then the limits (*hudūd*) of Kirmān, Fārs, Khūzistān, and Saymara (actually in Luristān, *sic*), with its western limit as a gulf surrounding all the Arab country, i.e., the Arabian peninsula. This Great Sea has five gulfs: the Barbarā Gulf (= the Gulf of Aden); the Arabian Gulf, or Gulf of Ayla or Qulzum (= the Red Sea); the Gulf of Iraq (= the Persian Gulf from its head to the Straits of Hormuz); the Gulf of Fārs, extending from the narrows on the limits of Fārs to the borders of Sind (= the Gulf of Oman and the Arabian Sea); and the Indian Gulf (= the Bay of Bengal).

The designation of the Persian Gulf proper as that of Iraq and the use of the term "Gulf of Fārs" for the waters beyond Ra's Musandam is unusual and alien to the Arab geographers, whose cultural focus was Baghdad and Iraq and who had a more direct knowledge of the topography and hydrography of the Gulf region; as noted above, the author of the *Hudūd al-'ālam* was writing in the remote province of Gūzgān to the south of the upper Oxus valley. Probably explicable also by lack of direct experience is the writer's statement that the distance between the Gulf of Ayla and the Gulf of Iraq was only sixteen stages on swift riding camels (*jammāzāt*); in reality, the distance from 'Aqaba to

18. Ibid., 1: 255, 325 ff., Nāsir-i Khusraw, *Safar-nāma*, ed. Muhammad Dabīr-siyāqī (Tehran, 1335/1956), pp. 119–20; cf. *Encycl. of Islam*², art. "*Khashabāt*" (E. Wiedemann). The fame of the *Khashabāt* penetrated even to China, as mentions in the T'ang annals show; cf. Hourani, *Arab Seafaring*, p. 69.

Kuwait is ca. 800 miles across the extremely inhospitable Nefūd Desert of northern Nejd. He was, however, able to detail correctly some of the islands of the Persian Gulf, including Lāft or Qishm, with a flourishing town also called Lāft; Wāl = Uwāl, a port of call for ships; and Khārak-Khārg, described as a large and prosperous town with pearl fisheries.[19]

A much more practical geographer and a great traveler over all the Islamic heartlands, with an especial interest in what we would now call social geography and even sociology, was Maqdisī (Muqaddasī), who wrote his *Ahsan al-taqāsīm fī maʿrifat al-aqālīm*, undoubtedly the culmination of the medieval Arabic geographical tradition, in ca. 375/985. He himself had traveled by sea around the coasts of the Arabian peninsula, from Qulzum to ʿAbbādān, a journey that he estimated at ca. 2,000 *farsakhs*. In his description of the Great Eastern Sea[20] (in one place actually called the *Bahr al-Sīn* "Sea of [the route to] China"), he specifically names one of his sources. Thus, he describes his perplexity, after having seen various maps depicting the Great Eastern Sea, none of them the same shape and all with varying gulfs depicted. Hence, one day, when he was sitting by the seashore at Aden, a seasoned voyager and merchant, Shaykh Abū ʿAlī b. Hāzim, answered his queries and provided the relevant information, and it is presumably on this material that his account of the terrors of navigation in the Persian Gulf is based. Maqdisī accepted the Qurʾānic division of the waters of the world into two great seas, but was skeptical about an interpretation of the sacred book, based on *sūra* xxxi: 26/27, that there were eight seas in all; however, he says, if one has to find eight of them, they would comprise the seas around the Arabian peninsula, i.e., those of the Hijāz, Yemen, Oman, Makrān, Kirmān, Fārs, and Hajar. Most of what he says about the Persian Gulf relates to its perils. All of these waters are dangerous, and ships perish easily in them. The *Khashabāt* and the mouth of the Shatt al-ʿArab are the worst of all, to be equated with the Qurʾānic "great, overwhelming disaster," *al-tāmma al-kubrā*, of *sūra* lxxix: 34. One of the shifting channels of the Shatt al-ʿArab is called by Maqdisī *al-Sabuʿ* "the wild beast," a designation reminiscent of Masʿūdī's "the Wolf," see above. The port of Oman (not specified exactly) is "nasty and deadly," while the seas that one encounters when entering the Gulf of Oman are like "fixed, unmoving mountains," again a reminiscence of Qurʾānic phraseology, cf. *sūra* xxi: 32/31.[21]

After the great period of geographical writing in medieval Islam, spanning essentially the ninth and tenth centuries, we have no significant geographical works that bring anything new on the question of the Persian Gulf and its nomenclature. But, of course, maritime activity through the Gulf and the Indian Ocean continued to be intense, with the island of Qays continuing to be important as a fortress and trading center up to the fourteenth century, as descriptions by the Arab historian of South Arabia and Aden Ibn al-Mujāwir (d. 690/ 1291) and the Persian historian and geographer Hamd Allāh Mustawfī Qazwīnī

19. *Hudūd al-ʿālam*, tr. V. Minorsky, Gibb Memorial Series, N.S. xi, §§ 3–4, tr. 52–53, 56–57.

20. A name already used in the previous century by Ibn Khurradādhbih in his *Kitāb al-Masālik wa 'l-mamālik*, ed. de Goeje, *Bibl. Geogr. Arab.*, vi (Leiden, 1889), p. 61: *al-Bahr al-sharqī al-kabīr*.

21. *Ahsan al-taqāsīm*, pp. 10 ff., tr. Miquel, pp. 29 ff.

(d. after 740/1339–40) attest. However, these same intervening centuries saw the rise of Old Hormuz, the port on the mainland of Persia now marked by the modern town of Mināb, and the comparative eclipse of Qays. Hormuz had always been the natural entrepôt for Kirmān and Makrān and, indeed, the whole interior of southeastern Persia and was known even to Nearchus as Harmozeia. With the decline of order within Persia during the thirteenth century, the age of the Mongol invasions, the overthrow of dynasties like the Khwārazm-Shāhs and the ʿAbbasid caliphs in Baghdad, attacks of marauding tribesmen prompted the removal of the town to the island lying just off the shore, where [New] Hormuz was founded in 700/1300. The former name of the island, Jārūn, was transferred to the port on the mainland where goods in transit to or from New Hormuz were trans-shipped, and this name became corrupted on European tongues to the familiar Gombroon.[22] We owe to the Moroccan traveler Ibn Battūta (d. 770/1368–69 or 779/1377) a description of the lower Gulf in ca. 729/1329. He visited Qays and the opposite shores of Oman and al-Ahsā and describes at length the pearl fisheries of Bahrain (although his account here may be second-hand); he does not, however, mention specifically a term for the Persian Gulf.[23]

The later Islamic Middle Ages seem, indeed, to have been a period when writers and geographers took the Gulf largely for granted and were content to rely on the classic works of their predecessors of some four or five centuries before. G. R. Tibbetts has noted that except for one short poem on navigation in the Gulf, giving considerable detail, but in an obscure fashion, all the Indian Ocean navigators and pilots omit mention of the Gulf in their accounts. Thus, Ibn Mājid (see below) complains that the three outstanding compilers (he calls them "lions") of ca. 493/1100, Muhammad b. Shādhān, Sahl b. Abbān, and Layth b. Kahlān, were not practical navigators at all, but drew on material from two genuine pilots and navigators of ca. 990/1000, the Persians Ahmad b. Tabarūya and Khawāshir b. Yūsuf al-Arīkī; and these three, he says, had only sailed once between Sīrāf and Makrān. In any case, although their works were known to Ibn Mājid himself, they have not survived till our time; one would naturally expect such practical aids to sailing as charts and instructions to become quickly worn out in use and handling, unlike manuscripts deposited safely in libraries.[24]

Ahmad b. Mājid al-Najdī does, however, describe the Gulf in fair detail. He stemmed, it seems, from Oman (or conceivably, from al-Shihr in the Hadramawt) and wrote his treatise on Indian Ocean navigation, the *Kitāb al-Fawāʾid fī usūl al-bahr wa ʾl-qawāʾid*, in ca. 895/1489–90. He achieved considerable fame in Islamic circles as the authority par excellence on Indian Ocean sailing, though it seems improbable that he was the "Gujarati Moor" who gave the Portuguese Vasco da Gama guidance on the route from East Africa to India in 1498, since, as we have just noted, he came from eastern or southern Arabia and not western India. In the ninth chapter of his book, Ibn Mājid discusses the coastlands of the

22. See *Encycl. of Islam*², art. "Hurmuz" (L. Lockhart).

23. *Rihla*, ed. C. Defrémery and B. R. Sanguinetti (Paris, 1853–59), 2: 230 ff., tr. H. A. R. Gibb, *The Travels of Ibn Battūta, A.D. 1325–1354* (Cambridge, 1958–71), 2: 400 ff.

24. Tibbetts, G. R., *Arab Navigation in the Indian Ocean before the Coming of the Portuguese, Being a Translation of the Kitāb al-Fawāʾid . . . Together with an Introduction on the History of Arab Navigation . . .* (London, 1971), pp. 5, 7.

world, taking Ra's al-Hadd or Ra's al-Jumjuma as his starting point. He describes the *Fārsī* coast as stretching from Hormuz to Basra, along which are a number of islands by the "Cape of the Arabs," Ra's al-'Arab (presumably Ra's Musandam); this coast is a month and a half's sail in length. The southern shores of the Gulf are described in greater detail, with emphasis on the pearl fishing industry. About 1,000 ships were employed in pearl diving at Bahrain Island, facing the dangerous islands, treacherous currents, and ruffian Arabs of the Ra's Musandam region, until Masqat in Oman, "the best-known port in the world . . . the like of which cannot be found in the whole world" is reached. The succeeding, tenth chapter is on islands of the world, the eighth of which is given as Bahrain and the ninth as Qishm—the island of Ibn Jāwān or Burkhut (the later term explained by Ibn Mājid as referring to a settlement in the center of the island, which had a considerable population of weavers).[25] He does not, on the other hand, have a special section, as some of the Islamic geographers of the early medieval period had, on the gulfs of the world, and no special term for the Gulf as a whole is put forward. One concludes that the usage of such terms in Arabic as "Sea of Fārs" or "Gulf of Fārs" was so widespread and taken for granted that it was unnecessary to stress them.

With the opening years of the sixteenth century, the accounts of the Portuguese voyagers, beginning with that of Vasco da Gama around the Cape of Good Hope and up the east coast of Africa to South Arabia and eventually to Gujarat and the Malabar coast of peninsular India, become of significance in providing for the first time Western European information on the nomenclature of the Gulf. The question of whether the Portuguese navigators had extensively at their disposal charts used by the Muslim Indian Ocean mariners is not our concern here; but it may be safely surmised that it was from Islamic sources that they took over the universally used term "Persian Gulf." Thus, Fernão Lopes de Castanheda refers to it as the *Sino Persico*, echoing the *Sinus Persicus* of, for instance, Diego Ribero's *Mappa Mundi* of 1529, the so-called "Second Borgian Map."[26] João de Barros, in his monumental *Décadas*, generally uses the expression Mar Pérsio, and in regard to Afonso de Albuquerque's voyage from Socotra to Hormuz, he speaks of the two narrow entrances of the Gulf encompassing the Arabian peninsula, *dois estreitos do Mar Roxo, e Pérsio*. He shows some acquaintance with the internal hydrography and topography of the Gulf and its shorelands, for instance, describing *Catif* (Qatīf) as "a port on the Persian Sea facing the isle of *Baharem* (Bahrain), and these, with *Lahaçah* (al-Ahsā), are the best ports in all Arabia" (Qatīf was in fact important as the starting point for pilgrim and other caravans across Arabia via Yamāma to the Holy Cities). Speaking of a further journey of Albuquerque's from Socotra to Hormuz, he mentions the place called by Ptolemy *Metacuem* "situada além do Cabo Siagro, que he o do rosalgate contra o estreito Parseo" and of Bahrain Island, "Ilha

25. Ibid., pp. 212–14, 221–22, 447–48.

26. *História do descobrimento e conquista da Índia pelos Portugueses*, 3rd ed. by Pedro de Azevendo (Coimbra, 1924–33), 2: 365. The "Second Borgian Map" is reproduced in *The Book of Duarte Barbosa, an account of the countries bordering on the Indian Ocean and their inhabitants, written by Duarte Barbosa and completed about the year 1518 A.D.*, tr. M. Longworth Dames (London, 1918–21), 1: at end.

Baharem, que está no seio do mar da Pérsia pegada na costa do Arábia" (here, Rosalgate, also spelled Roscalgate by Barros = Ra's al-Hadd, described as the beginning of the ruler of Hormuz's dominions).[27]

The great port of New Hormuz, with its strategic position at the mouth of the inner Gulf, inevitably attracted the cupidity of the aggressive and expanding Portuguese. Albuquerque made an abortive attempt to seize the island in 1507, and in 1514 a permanent occupation was established, with the native ruler of Hormuz reduced to vassal status; not until a century later was Shah 'Abbās I of Persia able to dislodge the Portuguese from Gombroon on the mainland and then, with aid from the English East India Company's vessels, recapture Hormuz itself in 1622.[28]

Hence, Hormuz figures very prominently in the sixteenth century Portuguese accounts of voyages and conquests as one of the two points from which Portugal hoped to control the trade from India and the Far East into the central lands of the Islamic world, thus depriving the Mamlūk rulers of Egypt and Syria, and then their successors the Ottoman Turks, of exclusive domination there (the other point, Aden, was attacked by Albuquerque in 1513, with an inadequate fleet, but never taken by the Portuguese). Thus, Duarte Barbosa, who may have first come out to India with Cabral's fleet in 1500 and have had first-hand knowledge of the Indian Ocean and certainly of the Gulf of Oman as far up as Hormuz, and who wrote ca. 1518, gives a detailed description of Hormuz, which he describes as being at the entrance of the Persian Sea, i.e., the inner Gulf, detailing also many places along the coast of Oman, such as *Curiate* (Quryat, Qurayyāt), *Masqate* (Muscat, Masqat), and *Coquiar* (Suhār), and a few ports on the western coast of the Musandam peninsula, such as *Julfar* (Julfār) and *Recoyma* (Ra's al-Khayma), and also the islands dependent on the Arab nominal ruler of Hormuz, such as *Queixime* (Qishm), *Fomon* (read *Tomon*, Tunb), *Firol* (Farūr), etc. His account of the ports along both the shores of the inner Gulf proper is, on the other hand, confused, with names not in correct geographical order, and does not seem to have been written from personal knowledge. Some can be identified, such as *Lyma* (Linga, the mainland port to the west of Qishm), *Corgam* (probably Khārg Island and its immediate neighbor, the small island of Khārgū or Corgo, Khārg being an important trading center of the Dutch in the eighteenth century), and *Quongo* (the port of Kangun on the coast of Fārs to the east of Nakhilu Island), on the Persian shores of the Gulf; but others are quite unidentifiable.[29]

To the Portuguese period of hegemony in the waters of the Arabian Sea and the Gulf of Oman there succeeded an age when primacy there in trade passed to the maritime nations of Northwestern Europe, above all, to England and the Netherlands. The power of Portugal was weakened by the disastrous period of forcible union with Spain (1580–1640), and the beginning of their decline in Indian Ocean waters was signaled by the loss of Hormuz to the Persians in 1622 (as mentioned above). While the Portuguese had been all-powerful in those seas, English hopes for trade with the "Grand Sophy" in Persia

27. *Decadas, Selecção* . . . de Antonio Boião (Lisbon, 1945–46), 2: 228; 3: 14, 16; 4: 112–13, 121.

28. Lockhart, *Encycl. of Islam*[2], art. "Hurmuz."

29. *The Book of Duarte Barbosa*, 1: tr. 68–82, 90–105.

and with the Gulf region had had to concentrate on the possibilities of commercial intercourse either via Russia and the Caspian Sea route, or else through the Ottoman lands of Syria and Iraq to the head of the Gulf and thence on to the Iranian plateau and the Safavid capital of Isfahān. The first route was, accordingly, the concern of the Muscovy Company of London, founded in 1555, and the second that of the Levant Company, founded in 1581, which had one of its two most important factories situated at Aleppo, the Syrian terminus of the trans-Syrian Desert route to Iraq and the Gulf. It is from the travel accounts of merchants and agents of these two companies of merchant adventurers that we derive written information on the nomenclature of the Gulf during the later sixteenth and seventeenth centuries.

Thus, Geffrey Duckett, who, together with another of the Muscovy Company's agents, Thomas Banister, made the fifth overland journey through Russia to Persia in 1569, wrote in 1574 of "the Gulfe of Persia called Sinus Persicus, betweene the maine land of Persia and Arabia, etc.," and this same Latin translation of "Persian Gulf," familiar from many maps of the sixteenth and seventeenth centuries (see below), is the one used by Sir Humphrey Gilbert in his *A true report of the late discoveries . . . of the Newfound Lands*, where he describes the Portuguese conquests in the Indian Ocean, "they put off at the Cape of Guarda Fu, and past the great gulfe of Arabia, and the Indian Sea, East to Sinus Persicus, and the Island of Ormus."[30] The London merchant John Newberie, who made his second journey to the Middle East 1580–82, seems to extend the Persian Gulf into the Straits of Hormuz, for he speaks of "the Cities of Ormus in the Gulfe of Persia."[31]

A key point in the efforts of English merchants to develop trade directly with Safavid Persia, and also to secure a direct route up the Persian Gulf and through the lands of the Fertile Crescent for Indian silks and calicoes, was the port of Basra, where the East India Company (which had been founded in 1600) had a resident factor, as also at Bandar 'Abbās on the Gulf shore, the former Gombroon, after the Persian recapture of Hormuz, and at the capital Isfahān.[32] The London merchant Ralph Fitch traveled via Syrian Tripoli, Iraq, Basra, and Hormuz to India in 1583 and after, and says that "Basora standeth near the gulfe of Persia. I went from Basora to Ormus downe the gulfe of Persia in a certaine shippe made of boordes, and sowed together with cayro, which is threede made of the huske of cocoes, and certaine canes or straw leaves sowed upon the seames of the bordes which is the cause that they leake very much."[33] Those who were merchants and travelers in these regions knew the standard nomenclature for the waters in question and use these terms fairly consistently. A usage such as that of the historian of the Ottoman Turkish empire, Richard Knollys, who in one part of his writings on "the Gulf" describes Sultan Sulaymān the Magnificent's Indian Ocean naval operations in the middle years of the

30. R. Hakluyt, *The Principal Navigations, Voyages, Traffiques and Discoveries of the English Nation* (Glasgow, 1903–5), 3: 161; 8: 128.

31. S. Purchas, *Hakluytus Posthumus, or Purchas his pilgrimes, contayning a history of the world in sea voyages and lande travells by Englishmen and others* (Glasgow, 1905–7), 8: 450.

32. See A. C. Wood, *A History of the Levant Company* (Oxford, 1935), p. 103.

33. Hakluyt, *The Principal Navigations*, v. 371.

sixteenth century against the Portuguese in Goa, believes "the Gulf of Persia" to consist of part of the Arabian Sea, i.e., the waters outside the Straits of Hormuz, is somewhat unusual.[34]

In the seventeenth century, we have the appearance and increasingly frequent usage of an alternative term for the Persian Gulf, that of "the Gulf of Basra," an indication of the increasing commercial importance of that town. By the mid-eighteenth century, the East India Company merchants had established themselves with permanent factories in both places (the Bandar 'Abbās factory being abandoned, in the face of local Persian misgovernment and financial extortion, in 1763) so firmly that Basra had supplanted Aleppo as the main channel for the barter of English cloth and Persian silk, much to the chagrin of the Levant Company.[35] For a century or more it seemed as if the designation "Gulf of Basra" might prevail over the traditional one of "Gulf of Persia." In the *Discours sur l'histoire universelle* (1681), of the French ecclesiastic and historian Bishop Bossuet, one of the maps shows the Persian Gulf as "Golfe de Balsera" and the Gulf of Oman as "G[olfe] d'Ormuz (spellings like Balsara, Balsora, Balsera for Basra, Bassora, being common in the seventeenth and early eighteenth centuries, the intrusive *l* perhaps being the result of a metathesis from the Arabic complete form *al-Basra* or an attempt to represent the imperfectly heard thick "S"). The use of the second expression "Golfe d'Ormuz" shows that a parallel process in evolving nomenclature had taken place at the approaches to the Gulf, where the Gulf or Sea of Oman was being identified with the greatest port of the region familiar to westerners, Hormuz.[36] The evidence of the historian and theologian Peter Heylin in his *Cosmographie* or "universal history" (written in the 1650s) is especially interesting. He describes the Gulf on the basis of information from such classical authors as Ptolemy and Ammianus Marcellinus, using such classic terms as *Sinus Persicus* and "Gulf of Persia," and also *Sinus Carmanicus* "Gulf of Carmania," i.e., Kirmān, apparently meaning the waters around the Straits of Hormuz, and then he goes on to say: "Our late navigators have not added much but the change of names; the whole bay being now called Mare Elkarisse, and the entrances thereunto the Straits of Balsora; these last so-called because they opened the way to the town of Balsora, the most noted empory of these parts in the times foregoing."[37] The term *Mare Elkarisse* is curious and seems to be making here its first appearance in English travel and historical literature; unless we have in the second word here a reminiscence, through Heylin's classical and bookish sources, to the ancient city of Charax at the head of the Gulf, probably near the site of modern Muhammara or Mohammerah (which does not seem very likely), *Elkarisse* is possibly a somewhat strange deformation of the *Elcatif* of contemporary continental maps (see below). A series of common phonetic corruptions could also derive it from *al-Khalīj* = the Gulf. The designation "Gulf of Basra" or suchlike continues in

34. *The Turkish Histories*, 6th ed. (London, 1687), 1: 451.
35. See Wood, *The Levant Company*, p. 145; C. P. Grant, *The Syrian Desert: Caravans, Travel and Exploration* (London, 1937), p. 100; Abdul Amir Amin, *British Interests in the Persian Gulf* (Leiden, 1967), pp. 24 ff.
36. J. B. Bossuet, *Discours* . . . (Amsterdam and Leipzig, 1755), map no. 25.
37. Heylin, *Cosmographie* (London, 1669), p. 146.

use till the mid-eighteenth century—in Salmon's *A new geographical and historical grammar* of this period, there is still mentioned "the Gulf of Persia, or Bossora, and Ormus"[38]—but thereafter the usage declines. The old term had never gone out of use, in any case—for instance, the community of Carmelite Friars, established in Basra since 1623, recorded in their chronicle for the year 1675 the arrival of a letter from the admiral of the Portuguese navy in the Gulf, using here the phrase *in sinu Persico*—and from the late eighteenth century onward was to become virtually the sole phrase used to describe the Gulf until the most recent decade or so of the twentieth century.[39]

The evidence of cartography has been referred to on occasions, and one should now pause and look at the evidence presented by some of the great monuments of European map-making from the sixteenth to the eighteenth centuries. For the earlier period, the language of the legends on such maps was normally Latin, with vernaculars like English, French, and Dutch only coming in as the seventeenth century progressed. Ortelius, in his *Theatrum orbis terrarum* (1573), has two maps of relevance to our purpose here. The first one covers Persia and is called "Persici sive Sophorum regni typus," and here the Gulf is named as *Mare Elcatif, olim Sinus Persicus* (i.e., implying that the phrase "Sea of al-Qatīf" had replaced in common usage that of "Persian Gulf"), the Strait of Hormuz as *Bassora fretum* "Strait of Basra," and the Indian Ocean as *Mare Arabicum et Indicum*. Among the place names marked we have such forms as Bassora, Baram for Bahrain Island, Gamaroon for Gombroon, Insula Kisinis for Qishm, and Ormus for Oman (this last clearly confused with Hormuz, Ormus being also applicd in this map to the island). The second map covers the Ottoman empire and is called *Turcici imperii descriptio*; it includes the Arabian peninsula and gives the Red Sea as *Mare de Mecca et Bohar Corsun, olim Sinus Arabicus* (implying that the phrase "Sea of Mecca and Bohar Corsun," this last expression apparently from the Arabic *Bahr al-Qulzum*, had replaced in common usage that of "Arabian Gulf") and the Indian Ocean off the South Arabian coast as *Maris Rubri pars* "Part of the Red Sea," thus harking back to the classical designation of all the waters around the peninsula as the "Erythraean Sea" (see above). The phrase *Mare Elcatif* is new in the European geographical literature of this time, and it would be interesting to know if Ortelius's information came from an Arabic source that talked of the *Bahr al-Qatif* specifically, thereby designating the whole Gulf by the name of the province Qatīf on the Gulf shores of modern Sa'ūdī Arabia.[40]

Some ninety years later, Blaeu, in his monumental atlas (1662), followed Ortelius closely, with identical terms for the Gulf and the Hormuz Straits, with the Indian Ocean as *Mare Arabicum et Indicum* and with Oman again mistakenly called Ormus. But for the Red Sea he has *Mare Rubrum, Turcis Mare Mecca, olim Sinus Arabicus* "The Red Sea, known to the Turks as the Sea of Mecca, formerly Arabian Gulf," and for Bahrain Island the two spellings on his respec-

---

38. Salmon, *A new . . . grammar*, 9th ed. (London, 1764), pp. 398, 399, 408.

39. *Chronicle of events between the years 1623 and 1733 relating to the settlement of the Order of Carmelites in Mesopotamia (Bassora)*, ed. and tr. Sir Hermann Gollancz (London, 1927), Latin text, 15, tr. 344.

40. Abraham Ortelius, *Theatrum Orbis terrarum* (Antwerp, 1573).

tive maps *Arabia* and *Persia, sive Sophorum regnum* of Baram and Baharem (the latter form being that of the Portuguese sources, see above), with stress on the importance of pearl fishing there—*hic magna copia margaritarum.*[41] John Speed, in his *A prospect of the most famous parts of the world, viz, Asia, Africa, Europe, America . . .* (1626) simply marks "the Persian Gulfe" and "the Arabian and Indian Sea" on his small-scale map of Asia; and Raynal, in the atlas volume of his five-volume geography (1770) uses what was by then conventional nomenclature for his "Carte de l'Arabie, du Golfe Persique et de la Mer Rouge, avec l'Egypte, la Nubie et l'Abissinie, par M. Bonne," with terms like "Détroit de Moçandam" (Hormuz by now having fallen into ruins and the Musandam peninsula now supplying a name for the Straits), "Baharem" (again the Portuguese form), "Isle de Kismirche" (resembling the "Kichmichs" for Qishm used by the seventeenth-century French traveler in Persia, Chardin[42]), "Bassora," etc.[43] Thus, the standard nineteenth- and twentieth-century nomenclature was now taking shape, as is confirmed by the map of the *Sinus Persicus* compiled for the account of his travels by the Danish explorer of Arabia, Carsten Niebuhr (1765), where the names are largely the modern ones, with, e.g., the Gulf of Oman in Arabic form as "Bahhr Omân."[44]

There is little to add on the nomenclature of the Gulf in the last two centuries or so, for the term "Persian Gulf" was in universal use during this period. New administrative terms had, of course, to be invented as new political groupings came into being; thus, the term "the Trucial Shaikhdoms" seems to have been first used by Captain W. F. Prideaux in 1876, though J. B. Kelly thinks that the usage was probably older than this.[45] Not until the early 1960s does a major new development occur with the adoption by the Arab states bordering on the Gulf of the expression *al-Khalīj al-ʿArabī* as a weapon in the psychological war with Iran for political influence in the Gulf; but the story of these events belongs to a subsequent chapter on the modern political and diplomatic history of the Gulf.

C. EDMUND BOSWORTH

Selected Bibliography

Anonymous. *Hudūd al-ʿālam. The Regions of the World: A Persian Geography, 372 A.H.–982 A.D.* Translated and explained by V. Minorsky. London 1937.

Hourani, G. F. *Arab Seafaring in the Indian Ocean in Ancient and Early Medieval Times.* Princeton, 1951.

41. Johannes Blaeu, *Asia, quae est geographiae blauianae, pars quarta, libri duo, volumen decimum* (Amsterdam, 1662).

42. Cf. the Hon. G. N. Curzon, *Persia and the Persian Question* (London, 1892), 2: 410 n. 1.

43. John Speed, *A prospect of the most famous parts . . .* (London, 1668), p. 12; G. T. F. Raynal, *Atlas de toutes les parties connues du globe terrestre, dressé pour l'histoire philosophique et politique des établissements et du commerce des Européens dans les deux Indes* (Geneva, 1780), Atlas vol., map no. 14.

44. Map reproduced at end of Abdul Amir Amin, *British Interests in the Persian Gulf.*

45. Kelly, *Britain and the Persian Gulf, 1795–1880* (Oxford, 1968), p. 363 n. 2. However, J. G. Lorimer, *Gazetteer of the Persian Gulf, 'Omān, and Central Arabia. ii. Geographical and Statistical* (Calcutta, 1908), p. 1427 n., says that the term "Trucial Oman" originated with Captain F. B. Prideaux, political agent in Bahrain, in 1904.

al-Mas'ūdī. *Murūj adh-dhahab*. Edited by C. Barbier de Meynard and Pavet de Courteille. 9 vols. Paris, 1861–77.

Pauly-Wissowa. *Realenzyklopaedie des klassischen Altertums*, vi/1, cols. 592–601, art. "Erythra thalassa" (Berger).

Der Kleine Pauly. Vol. 2, 366–67, art. "Erythra thalassa" (H. Treidler).

Schoff, W. H. *The Periplus of the Erythraean Sea, Travel and Trade in the Indian Ocean by a Merchant of the First Century*. New York, 1912.

Tibbetts, G. R. *Arab Navigation in the Indian Ocean before the Coming of the Portuguese, Being a Translation of the Kitāb al-Fawā'id Together with an Introduction on the History of Arab Navigation*. London, 1971.

The Persian Gulf States

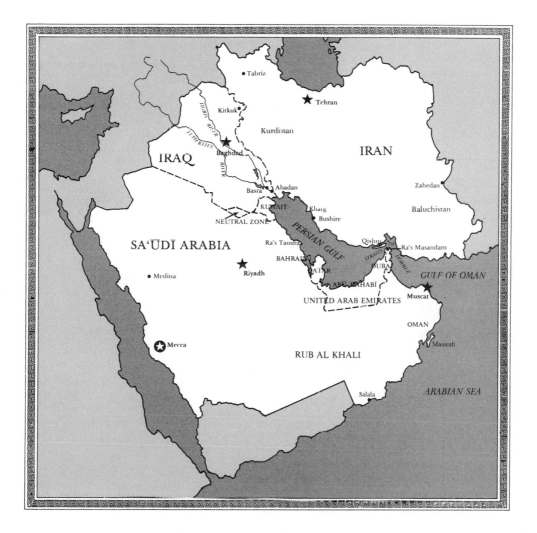

PART ONE

The History of the Persian Gulf

1. The Ancient Period ROGER M. SAVORY

"No arm of the sea has been, or is of greater interest, alike to the geologist and archaeologist, the historian and geographer, the merchant, the statesman, and the student of strategy, than the inland water known as the Persian Gulf."[1] So wrote Sir Arnold Wilson in his classic if not always very accurate history of the Persian Gulf in 1928. Today, half a century later, his words have as much validity as when he wrote them. Indeed, they have even greater validity, for, as a result of the massive intrusion of Western powers into the political and economic affairs of Middle Eastern countries during the ninteenth century and the first half of the twentieth century, and, more recently, as a result of the exigencies of the Cold War and of Great Power rivalries in the area and the dependence of Western powers on Middle Eastern oil, the Persian Gulf is still a principal focus of world attention.

The geographical position of the Persian Gulf, astride the main trade routes between Europe and the Indies and the Far East, has ensured its political and commercial importance since ancient times and has made it the rival of the Red Sea as a channel of communication between East and West. In this rivalry, the Red Sea obviously held great advantages. In the first place, its alignment was more suited to East-West trade. In this regard, the Persian Gulf has been called "a most perverse and inconvenient piece of water," since "it not only faces the wrong way; but it is on the wrong side of the Arabian peninsula. The sea mileage from anywhere in Europe to the head of the Persian Gulf is greater than to Bombay."[2] In the second place, the distance between the Mediterranean and Suez was much shorter than that between the Mediterranean and the head of the Persian Gulf, and the portaging of goods across the intervening land was consequently both quicker and cheaper by the Red Sea route. These geographical constraints meant that until the Portuguese rounded the Cape of Good Hope toward the end of the fifteenth century, thus by-passing the Red Sea and opening

1. Sir Arnold T. Wilson, *The Persian Gulf: An Historical Sketch from the Earliest Times to the Beginning of the Twentieth Century* (Oxford, 1928), p. 1.
2. Sir Roger Stevens, *The Land of the Great Sophy* (London, 1962), p. 4.

3

up a sea route to the Indian Ocean and the Persian Gulf, the Red Sea carried the lion's share of the European trade, while the bulk of the Persian Gulf trade was directed toward the Indies and China. This is not to say that, even in ancient times, there was no commercial communication between Europe and the Indies via the Persian Gulf. For its part, the Red Sea was far from being a perfect waterway for navigation and commerce; 1,200 miles long, it tended to isolate Arabia from Africa rather than to link the two, because it was flanked on both sides by hundreds of miles of waterless desert. In its northern reaches, the abundance of coral islands and reefs constituted both a hazard to shipping and an aid to piracy. There was a shortage of good harbors. In its northern reaches, too, rough seas and prevailing northerly winds made it difficult for large vessels to beat further north than Jar or Jidda.

Because of its strategic, mercantile, and political importance, the Persian Gulf has always been the scene of "simmering conflicts gripping numerous old and new, small and middle, great and super powers."[3] "It is scarcely possible to imagine a quarter of the globe of similar physical configuration that has had so romantic and varying a past, that contains more diverse nationalities and clashing interests."[4] Command of the sea has always been the prerequisite of political power in the Persian Gulf. In dealing with the history of the Persian Gulf, however, it is important to make the distinction between political hegemony in the area and control of the area's trade, for the power that exercised political hegemony was not necessarily the principal beneficiary of the Persian Gulf trade. This distinction has a special application to Iran in the post-Islamic period. After the Arab conquest of Iran in the seventh century A.D., there was no reassertion of Iranian political power in the Persian Gulf until Safavid times, until the early sixteenth century, yet for much of the intervening period Iranian ship's captains, sailors, and merchants had a large share of the trade between the Persian Gulf and the Indies, China, and Africa.

Western writers have made much of the alleged dislike of the Iranians for the sea. "The Persians seem to have an unconquerable aversion to the sea,"[5] is typical of their judgments. Lord Curzon roundly declared that: "Brave and victorious as the Persians have shown themselves at different epochs on land, no one has ever ventured so far to belie the national character as to insinuate that they have betrayed the smallest proficiency at sea. It would be difficult, and perhaps impossible, in the history of the world to find a country possessing two considerable seaboards, and admirably situated for trade, which has so absolutely ignored its advantages in both respects."[6] Various celebrated instances from the Iranian literary tradition are adduced in support of this generally unflattering view of Iranians as seafarers. The story recorded in Nizāmī 'Arūdī's *Chahār maqāla* of Muhammad b. Zakariyyā al-Rāzī's having to be bound hand and foot before he would consent to crossing the Oxus in a boat, the point being that he could not then be accused of having voluntarily placed his life in jeopardy, and

3. Rouhollah K. Ramazani, *The Persian Gulf: Iran's Role* (1972), preface.
4. G. N. Curzon, *Persia and the Persian Question*, 2 vols. (repr. London, 1966), ii: 398.
5. R. H. Major, *Introduction to India in the Fifteenth Century*, quoted in Hadi Hasan, *A History of Persian Navigation* (London, 1928), p. 142.
6. Curzon, *Persia*, 2: 388.

the story of the great lyric poet, Hāfiz, insisting on being returned to shore after embarkation at Hormuz for India because he was afflicted so badly by seasickness, support this view. On his return to Shīrāz, Hāfiz wrote a lyric containing the following lines:

> The waves run high, night is clouded with fears,
> And eddying whirlpools clash and roar;
> How shall my drowning voice strike their ears
> Whose light-freighted vessels have reached the shore?
>
> (Gertrude Bell, *Poems from the Divan of Hafiz* [London, 1928], pp. 85–86)

The story, quoted by Curzon,[7] of the mental agonies suffered by the ambassador 'Abd al-Razzāq when he was sent on a mission to India by the Timurid ruler Shāhrukh in 1442 further fosters this image. "As soon as I caught the smell of the vessel and all the terrors of the sea presented themselves before me, I fell into so deep a swoon that for three days respiration alone indicated that life remained within me."

It is quite true that the Iranians were, to begin with, "unskilled in maritime affairs," as Arrian put it, but this fact should occasion no surprise. The Aryans or Iranians were a seminomadic, pastoral, and agricultural people from the steppes of Central Asia. In 547 B.C., when Cyrus the Great defeated Croesus, king of Lydia, at Sardis, he reached the eastern shore of the Aegean Sea and found himself facing the sea power of Greece and Egypt. The Achaemenid monarch realized that he needed an immediate fleet, both to maintain his hold on his newly won territories in Asia Minor, where there were numerous and powerful Greek colonies that could be supplied and reinforced from the Greek mainland as long as Greece retained command of the sea, and also to make possible the future expansion of the Achaemenid empire either on the Greek mainland or in the direction of Egypt. The problem was solved when Cyrus enlisted the services of the Phoenicians, wooing them with semi-independent status and light taxation. Without building a single ship, "Persia bore undisputed sway in the Levant during the whole period of her existence as an empire,"[8] and from 525 to 480 the Achaemenids were masters of the Mediterranean Sea. At first, the only Persian element in the Persian fleet was the Persian "flag." "Later, Persian officers are found sailing, surveying and spying in the company of foreigners. Later still, Persians have risen to the rank of admirals and have begun to conquer the islands in the Mediterranean Sea. Eventually, the entire fleet is in the hands of Persian admirals, and is stiffened by the *epibatai* or marines,"[9] who were Persians, Medes, or Scythians.

Even in regard to naval power, then, Curzon's sweeping condemnation needs qualification, though it remains true as a generalization that, until very recent times, Iran has been primarily a land power whose excursions into naval operations have been infrequent and unsuccessful. The inferences that Curzon draws from Iran's lack of a navy, however, namely, that navigation in the Persian Gulf

---

7. Ibid., 2: 389.

8. Sir Henry Rawlinson, *The Five Great Monarchies* (London, 1879), 3: 194, quoted in Hasan, *A History of Persian Navigation*, p. 17.

9. Hasan, *A History of Persian Navigation*, p. 23.

"was entirely in the hands of Arab tribes, who had crossed over from the Arabian mainland and colonised the entire maritime border of Iran"; that these Arabs "were as venturesome as the Persians were timid"; and that "from the eighth to the sixteenth century they retained the trade of the seas,"[10] must be totally rejected as being contrary to the facts. As to the importance that should be attached to the literary evidence, it need only be said here that the instances already quoted of Iranian pusillanimity in face of the waves can be countered by numerous references to shipbuilding and maritime activity in the *Shāhnāma*, the Iranian national epic; the literary evidence, in other words, is inconclusive.

One important conclusion that does seem to emerge from the available evidence is that a clear distinction must be drawn between the Iranians living on the central Iranian plateau, the majority of whom had no more idea of the oceans of the world than had, say, a Canadian from one of the Prairie provinces or an American living in the Mid-West (at least until recent times), and those Iranians who lived along the Persian Gulf littoral. The latter were every bit as "venturesome" as their Arab counterparts along the southern shore of the Persian Gulf. Furthermore, one must make the same distinction between the Bedouin Arabs of central Arabia, who prior to the Islamic conquests had never seen the sea, and the Arabs living along the Arabian shores, in the Yemen, the Hadramaut, in Oman, and along the southern shore of the Persian Gulf. These coastal Arabs had a tradition of seafaring that existed prior to Islam, and it was they who supplied the crews and the navigators who shared the Persian Gulf trade with the Iranians. Finally, if the Iranians are to be castigated for their failure to develop naval forces, the Arabs were not exactly enthusiastic about the idea in early Islamic times. When Egypt was conquered by 'Amr b. al-'Ās in A.D. 640–41, Alexandria would have been impregnable by land but for internal dissensions among the Byzantine generals and the aid given by the Copts to the Arab invaders, and 'Amr had no navy. Indeed, when Mu'āwiya sought permission from the caliph 'Umar to embark his men on ships in order to attack the isles of the Levant, which lay so close to the Syrian shore, he said, that one "might almost hear the barking of the dogs and the cackling of the hens," the caliph refused his permission. 'Amr, the conqueror of Egypt, had advised him against naval operations: "The sea is a boundless expanse," said 'Amr, "whereon great ships look tiny specks; nought but the heavens above and waters beneath; when calm, the sailor's heart is broken; when tempestuous, his senses reel. Trust it little, fear it much. Man at sea is an insect on a splinter, now engulfed, now scared to death." This gloomy report confirmed the caliph's worst suspicions, and he replied to Mu'āwiya: "The Syrian Sea, they tell me, is longer and broader than the dry land, and is instant with the Lord, night and day, seeking to swallow it up. How should I trust my people on its accursed bosom? Nay, my friend, the safety of my people is dearer to me than all the treasures of Greece."[11] Clearly, the caliph 'Umar and his great general 'Amr were not numbered among Curzon's "venturesome" Arabs!

10. Curzon, *Persia*, 2: 390.
11. Sir William Muir, *The Caliphate: Its Rise, Decline and Fall* (Edinburgh, 1924), p. 205.

The Early History of the Persian Gulf

The very early history of the Persian Gulf is still largely conjectural. About 10,000 B.C., there seem to have been three races on its shores: Dravidians (in Makrān), Semites, and proto-Elamites. About 5,000 B.C., the Sumerians reached the Persian Gulf. It is possible that the Arabs made boats of skins or hollowed-out tree trunks, and paddled or punted their way across shallow waters; they fished, and dived for pearls.[12] Certainly, the geography of Arabia, with its long coastline stretching from the Gulf of Suez to the head of the Persian Gulf, encouraged the development of sailing, as did the fact that the most fertile parts of Arabia, the Yemen, the Hadramaut, and Oman lay near the coast. Trade with neighboring countries was similarly encouraged by the proximity of Iran along the northern shore of the Persian Gulf and of East Africa across the narrow but, as we have seen, not always benign, waters of the Red Sea. If one continued to follow the coast of Iran eastward, one reached India. From early times, therefore, the Persian Gulf constituted one of the natural channels for trade between the Mediterranean basin and Eastern Asia.[13] Shipbuilding, however, presented problems for the Arabs. Arabia possessed no wood suitable for ships, and all the wood for shipbuilding (teak was the preferred wood, but the wood of coconut palms was also used) had to be imported from India, Burma, Siam, and Indonesia. Arabia possessed no iron or copper from which nails could be manufactured, so the hulls of Arab vessels were carvel-built, the planks being stitched together.[14] Such a method of construction restricted the ability of the ships to venture into rough waters.

Between 3,000 and 2,000 B.C. Sumerian and Akkadian records bear witness to trade relations between the Tigris–Euphrates delta and Dilmun, Magan and Melukhkha. Sumerologists tend to identify Dilmun with the Bahrain islands; I. J. Gelb, for example, regards this as an "ironclad identification,"[15] but there is not unanimity on the subject. S. N. Kramer, for instance, is skeptical of the Dilmun–Bahrain equation, and favors "the region of southern Iran and the Indus valley."[16] During the later periods, beginning about the middle of the second millennium B.C., Magan/Makkan and Melukhkha are identified with Egypt and Nubia, respectively, and there are those who would make this identification apply to the third millennium B.C. also.[17] Gelb, however, regards Magan/Makkan as denoting in the earlier period the south shore of the Persian Gulf east to Oman, and gives strong reasons for identifying Melukhkha during the same period as the north shore of the Persian Gulf and the coast of Iran and India east to the Indus valley.[18]

12. G. F. Hourani, *Arab Seafaring in the Indian Ocean in Ancient and Early Medieval Times* (Princeton, 1951), p. 3.

13. Ibid., p. 4.

14. Ibid., pp. 88ff.

15. I. J. Gelb, *Makkan and Meluhha in Early Mesopotamian Sources*, in *Revue d'Assyriologie et d'Archéologie Orientale*, lxiv/1 (1970): p. 2.

16. S. N. Kramer, *The Sumerians* (Chicago, 1963), pp. 281–84.

17. Gelb, *Makkan and Meluhha*, p. 2.

18. I am indebted to my colleague Professor R. F. G. Sweet for the references to the works of Gelb and Kramer.

Between 3,000 and 2,000 B.C., Egyptian vessels were active in the Red Sea, trading as far south as the coast of Somalia. By the first millennium B.C., the Egyptians had been superseded as the principal mariners in the Eastern Mediterranean and Red Sea by the Phoenicians, who, Herodotus maintains, settled originally by the Indian Ocean, and whose early home, according to another ancient tradition, was Babylonia. Certainly, by the time of Solomon, the Phoenicians were both building and manning ships in large numbers for that king and, unlike the Arabs, they used nails of iron and of copper alloyed with iron.[19] For many centuries, the Phoenicians were the "universal mariners" of the region. The Assyrian king Sennacherib (705–681 B.C.) defeated the men of "Sealand" (Chaldaea) near the mouth of the Karun River, having sailed there in ships manned by sailors from Tyre and Sidon.[20] Nebuchadnezzar II, king of Babylon (604–561 B.C.), constructed a harbor and town at Teredon, west of the Euphrates, to protect Babylon from Arab raids.[21] Like the Arabs, the Babylonians imported teak from India for shipbuilding.

The Persian Gulf under the Achaemenids

With the founding of the first Persian empire by Cyrus the Great (550 B.C.), the history of the Persian Gulf becomes less fragmentary. The Achaemenids united the whole of Western Asia and Egypt into an enduring empire. As already noted, the establishment of this empire created an urgent need for an Iranian fleet, and this need was met by enlisting the services of their vassals the Phoenicians. After the conquest of Egypt by Cambyses in 525, the Achaemenid king again took great pains to conciliate the Egyptian naval commanders. Udjahorresne, the admiral of the Egyptian royal fleet, had already defected to the Iranians and had handed over to Cambyses the city of Saïs. He was rewarded by Cambyses with the office of head physician; "he was made to live with the king as a companion and was placed in charge of the palace."[22]

Darius the Great, after his accession in 521 B.C., took active steps to consolidate Achaemenid sea power with a view to extending Achaemenid trade. One of his most celebrated exploits was the completion of the great canal linking the Nile with the Red Sea that had been begun by the Pharaoh Necho, son of Psammetichus. Starting from a point on the Nile a little above the city of Bubastis, the canal passed by the city of Patumos and reached the Red Sea. By the construction of this canal, the predecessor by some 2,400 years of the present Suez Canal, Darius established direct communication between Iran and the Red Sea and thus opened up a cheaper trade route from Egypt to India and the Persian Gulf. The canal was one hundred and fifty feet wide and deep enough for merchant ships. Five huge stelae of red granite were placed at intervals along its banks, and their cuneiform inscriptions informed the traveler how the canal came to be built: "I, [Darius], am a Persian. From Parsa I seized Egypt. I com-

19. Hourani, *Arab Seafaring*, p. 3.
20. Ibid., p. 10.
21. Wilson, *The Persian Gulf*, p. 33.
22. A. T. Olmstead, *History of the Persian Empire* (Chicago, 1966), p. 91.

manded this canal to be dug from the river, Nile by name, which flows in Egypt, to the sea which goes from Parsa. Afterward this canal was dug as I commanded, and ships passed from Egypt through this canal to Parsa as was my will."[23]

About the same time that the Egyptian peasants were digging Darius's canal, the Great King sent a fleet down the Indus under the command of the Carian ship's captain Scylax of Caryanda. After reaching the mouth of the Indus, this expedition coasted along the entire southern shore of Iran, crossed to the southern shore of the Persian Gulf, and finally sailed all the way round Arabia and up the Red Sea to Suez. The *Periplus* or "Circumnavigation" written by Scylax after his return induced Darius to extend his dominions even further east, and before 513 B.C. he had conquered Western India, which he formed into the satrapy of Hindukush; the new satrapy consisted of the territory along the banks of the Indus and its affluents, and soon a brisk trade was established between it and other parts of the Achaemenid empire.

Alexander the Great and His Successors

After the death of Darius the Great, in 485 B.C., we hear little of maritime activity in the Persian Gulf until the arrival of Alexander the Great on the shores of the Indian Ocean in 326 B.C. From the mouth of the Indus, Alexander sent his officer Nearchus to sail along the north shore of the Persian Gulf, while he himself led the army through the arid wastes of Gedrosia (Baluchistan and Makrān). All the way to the Tigris, the Greek navigator carefully noted in his logbook "each island, and anchorage, and seaboard village."[24] In the year of his death (323 B.C.), Alexander was busy with ambitious plans for the conquest of Arabia, "a vast tract inconveniently interposed between his western and his eastern provinces."[25] A fleet under Nearchus was to proceed along the coast, and Alexander recruited Phoenicians to man this fleet and to colonize its shores. Ships were transported in sections from Tyre and Sidon to the Euphrates, where Alexander proposed to make Babylon the capital of his vast empire, and these ships were dispatched to the Persian Gulf to conduct preliminary surveys. "He hoped to establish a regular trade route from the Indus to the Tigris and Euphrates, and thence to the canals which connected the Nile with the Red Sea." Babylon was to be no ordinary capital. "It was to become a naval station and a centre of maritime commerce. Alexander set about the digging of a great harbour, with room for a thousand keels, and designed the building of shipsteads."[26] These plans died with Alexander in June 323.

After the death of Alexander, his empire was broken up among a number of "hard-headed Macedonians,"[27] who were capable rulers, but lacked Alexander's vision of a world empire uniting East and West. After more than a decade of

23. Ibid., p. 146.
24. Curzon, *Persia*, 2: 398.
25. George Rawlinson, *Ancient History from the Earliest Times to the Fall of the Western Empire* (New York, 1900), p. 175.
26. J. B. Bury, *A History of Greece* (London, 1938), pp. 818–19.
27. Ibid., p. 821.

incessant fighting among the rival claimants to the empire, the whole of the eastern half of Alexander's dominions fell to Seleucus Nicator. In 312 B.C., Seleucus declared himself king of Babylonia, Susiana, Media, and Persia, and a few years later he found himself master of all the territory lying between the Indus and the Euphrates. He transferred his capital from Babylon to Seleucia, on the west bank of the Tigris, south of the later city of Baghdad and virtually opposite the later capital of the Parthians and Sasanids, Ctesiphon. During the period of Seleucid rule, the city of Gerra or Gerrha, a Chaldaean town located on the northeast coast of Arabia slightly north of Bahrain, became the major emporium in the Persian Gulf for the trade of Arabia and India. It was the focal point of the caravan trade with South Arabia and of the trade both by land and sea with Seleucia, which was the terminus for westbound Persian Gulf trade. There were markets at Teredon, at the mouth of the Euphrates, and at Charax, at the junction of the Tigris with the Karun. In 205 B.C., the Seleucid king, Antiochus III, attacked Gerrha, but was bought off with tribute of silver, frankincense, and myrrh. Antiochus Epiphanes (176–164 B.C.) explored the Arabian shore of the Persian Gulf.

The Graeco-Roman Red Sea Trade in Parthian Times

From about 140 B.C., the rising power of the Parthians, essentially a land power with a lucrative overland trade with Central Asia and China, increasingly interfered with Graeco-Roman trade with the Orient via the Persian Gulf, and the Red Sea for several centuries became the primary line of communication between Europe and India. Egypt had laid the foundations for this commerce under Ptolemy II Philadelphus (283–247 B.C.), who founded two cities, both named Berenice, on the East African coast. From the more northerly of the two Berenices, which lay at about latitude 24 degrees N., a highroad was constructed to Coptus on the Nile, near Thebes. In addition to this river traffic, trade also flowed along the old canal link between the Nile and the Red Sea; Ptolemy reopened the canal and constructed the port of Arsinoë on the site of the modern town of Suez.[28] During much of the Hellenistic and Roman periods, the Persian Gulf trade was in the hands of small towns in which Arabs were prominent, such as Charax and Apologus on the Tigris-Euphrates estuary, or in the hands of semi-independent city-states like Palmyra, which flourished on the marches between the Roman and Parthian empires.

At some time during the first century B.C.,[29] the Greek navigator Hippalus developed the direct sea route from Arabia to India, taking advantage of the southwest monsoon. Hippalus brought back from India a typical cargo—gems and pearls, ebony and sandalwood, balms and spices, and, above all, pepper. Before the voyage of Hippalus, Arab and other seafarers had been in the habit of coasting along the shores of the Hadramaut from Aden and making as much

28. Rawlinson, *Ancient History*, p. 199.
29. Hourani, *Arab Seafaring*, p. 24, says "not later than 90 B.C."

northing as possible before "falling off" before the northeast monsoon, which blew during the winter months, in order to make an eventual landfall on the Indian coast somewhere between the mouth of the Indus and Baryagaza on the Gulf of Cambay. Following Hippalus, mariners sailed down the Red Sea before the northwest winds that prevail in the southerly reaches of that sea during the summer, and then, using the southwest monsoon, set a course north of Socotra to make an eventual landfall on the Malabar coast. This direct route to India was much faster, but the rougher seas of the open ocean were naturally more hazardous, particularly for Arab ships the planks of which were stitched together with coconut fiber.

When Octavian defeated Antony at the battle of Actium in 31 B.C., peace returned to the Eastern Mediterranean, and the early Roman empire represented the golden age of Graeco-Roman commerce, stimulated by the demand for oriental luxuries in the imperial cities of Rome and Alexandria. According to Strabo, there were about 120 sailings annually from the Red Sea to India. Archeologists have found evidence of the Roman presence in India in the form of coins and of monuments such as the temple of Augustus in Malabar. The Romans tried to protect this trade by means of a garrison at Aden and an alliance with the Himyarite rulers of Hadramaut and the Yemen. These Arab rulers were their commercial rivals both in regard to the Indian trade and also the East African trade to Thebes and Memphis in Egypt. This East African trade was brisk: the Africans exported rhinoceros horn, tortoise shell, and ivory, and imported items such as hatchets, awls, glass beads, and agricultural produce from India.[30]

Vigorous Roman activity continued into the second century A.D. In A.D. 106, Nabataea became the Roman province of Arabia Petraea, and a highway was built from the head of the Gulf of Aqaba to Damascus. The Emperor Trajan reopened the old canal from the Gulf of Suez, originally projected by Necho and put into operation by Darius and Ptolemy II, but its route, after passing Zaqaziq, swung in a southwesterly direction and joined the Nile at Cairo. In 116, a force sent by Trajan reached the Persian Gulf and temporarily subjugated Mesopotamia. By the second century A.D., Greeks were sailing to Ceylon, had reached the mouth of the Ganges in the Bay of Bengal, and even as far east as the Malay Peninsula. A Roman fleet was kept permanently on the Red Sea,[31] and in 166 a delegation of Romans sent by "An-tun" (the Emperor Marcus Aurelius Antoninus) reached Tongking and proceeded to the court of the Emperor Huan-Ti.[32]

The Revival of the Persian Gulf Trade under the Sasanids

In 226, Ardashīr overthrew the Parthians and established the second great Persian empire, that of the Sasanids. The Sasanid kings inherited and carried

30. Hasan, *A History of Persian Navigation*, p. 49.
31. Hourani, *Arab Seafaring*, pp. 34–36.
32. Hasan, *A History of Persian Navigation*, p. 54.

on the struggle with Rome that the Parthians had been waging for nearly three centuries, ever since the Romans discovered the existence in Asia of a power stronger and richer than Pontus or Armenia. With the accession of the Sasanids, the scales in the commercial rivalry between the Red Sea and the Persian Gulf routes to the wealth of the Indies gradually tipped again in favor of the latter. Of course, trade between the Persian Gulf and India had not ceased altogether during the Parthian period. Baryagaza on the Gulf of Cambay was the principal emporium for this trade. From it, cargoes of copper, sandalwood, teak, blackwood, and ebony were shipped to ports at the head of the Persian Gulf, such as Apologus and Charax; imports arriving at Baryagaza included purple [dye], clothing, wine, pearls, dates, gold, and slaves.[33] At Omana, now thought to be either Suhār or Muscat on the coast of Oman,[34] there was a flourishing shipbuilding industry.

The Sasanids not only gave a tremendous impetus to the Persian Gulf trade, but they were the first Iranian kings actively to encourage native Iranian seafaring. Ardashīr I founded, or refounded, cities with incredible industry during his short reign of fifteen years, and the most notable feature is that eleven out of some eighteen cities were sea or river ports. The most important of these latter were: Hormuzd Ardashēr (Ahvāz); Veh Ardashēr (Seleucia); Vahishtābādh Ardashēr (Basra); Astrābādh Ardashēr (Karkh Maysān, near Basra); Vahman Ardashēr (Bahmanshīr); Rēv Ardashēr (contracted to Rīshahr, 6 miles S. of Būshahr); Rām Ardashēr; and Bēth Ardashēr, on the coast opposite Bahrain. In 310, the Arabs crossed the Persian Gulf and raided the Sasanid provinces of Fars and Ardashēr Khurra, but in 326 Shāpūr II repaid the visit by attacking Bahrain and settling Iranian colonists there; Bahrain was annexed to the Sasanid empire and placed under the jurisdiction of a *marzbān* ("warden of the marches"). The sixth century A.D. marked the peak of Sasanid maritime activity, but once again it must be noted that this was purely commercial activity. The Sasanids had no navy, and this lack was a severe handicap in their wars with Rome. In 622, Heraclius crossed the Aegean unmolested, and in 623 he sailed from Byzantium across the Black Sea without opposition. Both voyages resulted in the defeat of a Sasanid army.[35]

By the beginning of the sixth century, Persian vessels were in active competition with those of Rome in Sinhalese ports. Under the great Sasanid king, Khusrau I Anūshirvān (531–79), Iranian influence had extended far beyond the river Indus, traditionally the boundary between Iran and India. Some Muslim sources say that Anūshirvān sent a fleet to Ceylon. Be that as it may, Ceylon was indubitably the meeting place for merchants from Western Asia and from China. The horizons of ship's captains no longer ended at India, or even at the East Indies; for many, China was now the goal, and for almost a thousand years the China trade was to constitute a major part of the Persian Gulf trade. From Ceylon westward, the trade was in the hands of Iranians and Axumites, from the South Arabian colony of Axum in East Africa; the western terminus of the China trade, at least as far as sea-going vessels were concerned, was Teredon, at the mouth of the Euphrates.

33. Ibid., p. 50.
34. Hourani, *Arab Seafaring*, p. 17.
35. Hasan, *A History of Persian Navigation*, p. 87.

The sea route to China provided an alternative to the ancient overland route through Central Asia, and the most valuable commodity brought from China in the sixth century was silk. Persian merchants seem to have largely excluded their rivals, particularly the Arabs, from this trade. South Arabia was in a state of decline, both politically and economically, during the sixth century. In 523, Dhū Nuwās, king of the Yemen, embraced Judaism and is said to have massacred 20,000 Christians from the neighboring province of Najrān who refused to do the same. The Emperor Justinian responded to an appeal by the Christians for retribution, and, at his instance, the Negus led an expedition from Abyssinia and overthrew the Himyarite regime, which was replaced by a Christian government under an Abyssinian viceroy (524–25). In 531, Justinian asked the Abyssinians to buy silk from India and sell it to the Romans; in this way the Romans hoped to avoid trading with their enemies the Sasanids. The Abyssinian merchants, however, found themselves quite unable to get the better of the Iranian merchants in Ceylon, who bought up whole cargoes of silk.[36] About the middle of the sixth century, the Romans' problem was solved by two Nestorian monks, who smuggled into the Byzantine empire from China silkworm's eggs, concealed in a hollow cane.[37]

The Sasanids, however, were not content with acquiring control of the Persian Gulf trade. About the year 570, Anūshirvān sent a force consisting of eight hundred condemned felons under the command of an aged commander Vahrīz on an expedition to the Yemen; clearly, the great king did not think the project worth the loss of any of his regular troops. The result of the expedition must certainly have exceeded his expectations. The Yemen was conquered and remained in Sasanid hands until 628; by its conquest, the Sasanids had achieved what the Romans had been unable to do and, as a result, the Red Sea trade between Egypt and India fell into Iranian hands. In Arabia, power shifted from the maritime kingdoms of South Arabia to the northern kingdoms of Hīra and Ghassan, and to the tribes of central Arabia; but the Bedouin had no ships. On the southern shore of the Persian Gulf, Arab maritime activity was severely restricted by Sasanid control of Bahrain and Oman. Even in the port of Ubulla, as the Arabs called Apologus, there was a strong Iranian element among the mercantile community.

36. Hourani, *Arab Seafaring*, p. 40.
37. Hasan, *A History of Persian Navigation*, p. 70.

2. A.D. 600—1800

ROGER M. SAVORY

Quinquireme of Nineveh from distant Ophir,
Rowing home to haven in sunny Palestine,
With a cargo of ivory,
And apes and peacocks,
Sandalwood, cedarwood, and sweet white wine.
                              John Masefield, *Cargoes*

The Persian Gulf in Early Islamic Times

 Within ten years from the date of the first border clash in 633, the Arabs had conquered the entire Sasanid empire, weakened by four centuries of struggle against Rome and Byzantium and torn by internal dissension. The Arabs reached the shores of the Mediterranean, but the latter, instead of being a highway unifying Europe and Asia, as in the past, now became the frontier across which the new and militant faith of Islam confronted Christendom. As a result of this development, the Red Sea and the Persian Gulf were no longer alternative and rival routes for the transit trade between Europe and the Far East, but the western termini of trade originating from the Far East, the Indies, and the Indian Ocean. In the Persian Gulf, center succeeded center as the principal emporium for this flourishing trade, its focal point moving ever southeastward toward the mouth of the Gulf: Hīra; Teredon; Ubulla; Basra; Sīrāf; Kīsh (termed Qais by the Arabs); Hormuz, on the northern shore; and Bahrain, on the southern shore. Behind these flourishing entrepôts stood, after its foundation in 762, the rich metropolis of Baghdad.

It has already been noted that a distinction must be drawn between the maritime Arabs and those of the central deserts; the latter had no more acquaintance with or experience of the sea than had the Iranians of the central Iranian plateau. In 655, only twenty years after the Arabs first reached the Mediterranean coast, they won a naval victory off the Lycian coast, but their fleet, probably

14

built at Alexandria, was manned by Copts, and the battle was won by the swords of the Arab marines rather than by naval tactics. George F. Hourani has characterized the maritime activity of the Arabs as confined to trade and piracy; their navies were manned by Greeks and Copts, never by Arabs. Instead, they extended to the oceans the Bedouin principle of the *ghazw*, or tribal raid, and Hourani has pointed out the significant fact that, in Arabic, the verb *rakaba*, meaning to "ride a camel," is also used of "sailing a ship."[1] The word *markab*, from the same root, means "mount," "vehicle," and "vessel." It is not by chance, therefore, that piracy became a way of life for many maritime Arabs from Bahrain to Oman.

Basra, founded in A.D. 638 and connected to the Shatt al-'Arab by two canals, grew with astonishing rapidity and gradually replaced Ubulla as the principal port of entry at the head of the Persian Gulf, just as Ubulla had replaced Teredon after the advent of Islam. From Basra, commodities such as antimony, cinnamon, saffron, and litharge were shipped upstream to Baghdad.

The Heyday of the China Trade:
Seventh to Tenth Centuries

Under the Umayyad caliphs (661–750), a unified empire, ruled from Damascus, extended over the vast region from Sind to Egypt and, along the southern shore of the Mediterranean, through North Africa to Spain. Although the 'Abbasid caliphs lost control of Spain in 756, they maintained conditions conducive to trade throughout their imperium until the devastating Zanj slave-revolt broke out in 869; in 871 the Zanj sacked Basra, and their forces ravaged southern Mesopotamia, Bahrain, and Khuzistan. In China, the T'ang dynasty maintained their rule from 618 to 907. With strong government ensuring security for merchants at each end of the route, the Persian Gulf–Canton run became the longest ocean trade route in regular use before the Portuguese rounded the Cape of Good Hope at the end of the fifteenth century.

In this lucrative trade, both Iranians and Arabs shared. In 758, Arabs (Ta-shih) and Persians (Po-sse; Po-ssu; Po-se) made a joint raid on the Chinese coast, sacked Canton, and went back to sea. This report is interesting not only because it identifies the Arabs and Persians as two distinct entities but also because it is the last time that the Persians are mentioned in the Chinese sources by the name Po-sse/Po-ssu.[2] From this, it has often been inferred that the Persians took no further part in the China trade after that date, but probably all that happened is that they lost their separate identity and were submerged in their Arab conquerors. Although Arab seafarers played an increasing part in the China trade during 'Abbasid times, the linguistic evidence suggests that they simply took over routes on which Iranian ships' captains already plied. If there had been an

1. G. F. Hourani, *Arab Seafaring in the Indian Ocean in Ancient and Early Medieval Times* (Princeton, 1951), pp. 52–53 [hereinafter referred to as "Hourani"].
2. Hadi Hasan, *A History of Persian Navigation* (London, 1928), p. 99 [hereinafter referred to as "Hasan"].

Arabic word in regular use for ship's captain, why would the Arabs have adopted the Persian term *nākhudā*, making from it the spurious broken plural *nawākhid*? Similarly, the regular word for a nautical manual was the Persian *rāhnāma*. The fifteenth-century Arabic work *Kitāb al-Fawā'id fi usūl al-'ilmī al-bahrī wa'l qawā'id*, compiled by the Hadramī navigators Ibn Mājid and Sulaimān al-Mahrī, refers to a *rahmānī* or *rahmānaj* dated 580/1184–85 and said to have been written by a certain Laith b. Kahlān and others, and there is an interesting reference in the twelfth-century *Iskandar-nāma* of Nizāmī of Ganja to the use of a *rahnāma*.[3] The form *rahmānaj* shows clearly that this is merely a metathesized form of *rahnāmak*, the lost Pahlavi original on which subsequent Persian nautical manuals were based and that were used by Arab navigators as well. Many other words of Persian origin were incorporated in the nautical vocabulary of the medieval Arabs. The fact that the Persian word for port, *bandar*, is found in many names used by the Arabs for ports from East Africa, round the coasts of Arabia, to the Indian Ocean, is surely conclusive evidence of a preponderant Iranian nautical and commercial influence in those areas before the upsurge of Arab maritime activity under the 'Abbasids.[4]

The fact seems to be that, after the Islamic conquests, ships' crews were recruited on both sides of the Persian Gulf, but among both shipbuilders and mariners the preponderant element seems to have been Iranian. According to al-Maqdisī, Iranian influence was also strong in the Red Sea and in Oman. Suhār, he said, was the "gateway to China"; "the Persians are masters in it. The bulk of the inhabitants of Aden and Jidda are Persians who speak Arabic; in Suhār, they speak Persian." Even in Jidda, the Persians constituted the ruling class and lived in splendid palaces. The list of ships' captains contained in the tenth-century *Kitāb 'Ajā'ib al-Hind* by Buzurg b. Shahryār of Rāmhurmuz consists mainly of Persian names, but, as G. F. Hourani has pointed out, this is not surprising because Buzurg collected much of his material in the Iranian port of Sīrāf.[5] Nevertheless, it does refute the commonly held opinion that Arab navigators totally superseded Iranians in the Persian Gulf after the Islamic conquests. Iranians not only became merchant princes in Oman and the Yemen, but colonies of Iranian merchants were established at Calicut on the Malabar coast, at Bengala in Bengal, at Cambay, and as far east as Malacca. At many places in East Africa, Iranians not only established merchant colonies but became the ruling princes; for instance, in Pemba and Zanzibar, Brava, Mogadishu, and Kilwa (on the site of the old Greek town of Rhapta).[6]

"This is the Tigris," said the 'Abbasid Caliph al-Mansūr"; there is no obstacle between us and China; everything on the sea can come to us on it."[7] From the middle of the ninth century, there were regular sailings from the Persian Gulf to China; whether Chinese junks penetrated the Persian Gulf before the fifteenth century remains an open question. The western termini of this trade had been successively Ubulla and Basra. Basra was at the height of its

---

3. Ibid., p. 129.
4. Hourani, p. 65.
5. Ibid., pp. 65–66.
6. Hasan, pp. 132, 144–45.
7. Hourani, p. 64, quoting Tabarī.

prosperity during the eighth and ninth centuries, when it flourished as a center of commerce and industry, financial activity, and also religious and intellectual inquiry. In 871, Basra was sacked by the Zanj, and the greater part of the city was burnt. In 923, it was again sacked, this time by the Carmathians. Basra never fully recovered from these two disasters, and its place as the leading emporium in the Persian Gulf was taken over during the tenth century by Sīrāf, situated 125 miles southeast of Bushire (Būshahr), on the coast of Fārs almost due south of Shīrāz, which city it for a short time rivaled in size and splendor. The wealthy merchants of Sīrāf built themselves handsome mansions of two or more stories, constructed of teak imported from Zanzibar and commanding fine views out to sea. Sīrāf was at the height of its prosperity between about 850 and 1000, during which period it was an entrepôt for trade both with India, Malaya, and China, and with the Red Sea and the East African coast.

It is noticeable that all the principal ports involved in the Persian Gulf–China trade from the sixth century to the sixteenth were on the northern shore of the Persian Gulf. The reason for this was that water along the northern shore was deeper than that along the southern shore. Even so, Sīrāf was little more than a roadstead; its harbor was liable to silt up, and in later centuries ships were obliged to lie as much as eight miles offshore. Some cargoes were transshipped at Sīrāf to smaller vessels that could negotiate the Shatt al-'Arab. From Sīrāf, eastbound ships would either coast along the northern shore of the Persian Gulf, calling at Kīsh island, Old Hormuz, Tiz (in the province of Makrān), Daibul (at the mouth of the Indus), and Mansūra (the capital of Sind), or else they would proceed to one of the ports of Oman, Muscat, or Suhār, take on supplies of fresh food and water, and strike across the Indian Ocean to the Malabar coast. Skirting Ceylon, ships would then set course due east to the Nicobar Islands, and thence to Kedah/Kalah Bār on the west coast of Malaya. From Kalah Bār it was a month's voyage to Sanf Fūlāw in IndoChina and another month's voyage from there to Canton. The total time taken for the voyage from the Persian Gulf to Canton was about six months. The favorite time for sailing from the Persian Gulf was September or October, using the northeast monsoon. Reaching Kūlam Malī on the Malabar coast in November or December, ships would wait until the end of the cyclone season in the Bay of Bengal. Reaching Kalah Bār toward the end of January, ships would await a favorite wind for the passage through the Malacca Straits, and then make use of the southern (summer) monsoon in the Sea of China; typhoons were also less prevalent in the Sea of China during April and May. Westbound ships sailed with the northeast monsoon to the Malacca Straits in October or December, crossed the Bay of Bengal in January, crossed to Raysut on the south coast of Arabia in February or March, and reached Muscat with the first breezes of the southwest monsoon in April.[8] In other words, the round trip Persian Gulf–Canton and back took about eighteen months.

The China trade began to decline in the tenth century. The T'ang dynasty never recovered from the revolt of Huang Ch'ao, who in 878 sacked Canton and is said to have massacred 120,000 Muslims, Christians, Jews, and Magians (i.e., Zoroastrians). Even allowing for inflation of the figures, this posits the existence

8. Ibid., pp. 69–75.

of a large foreign trading community at Canton. In the west, the Zanj revolt already mentioned started Basra on its path of decline and cut Baghdad off from the Persian Gulf. In the first quarter of the tenth century, the Carmathians ravaged eastern Arabia. Sīrāf itself was severely damaged by an earthquake in 977; and in 969 the Fāṭimids conquered Egypt, and Cairo replaced Baghdad as the most magnificent city in the Islamic world. The establishment of the Fāṭimid dynasty once again tipped the scales in favor of the Red Sea route, and trade from western Europe in particular used it. The port of Jidda in the Red Sea became the principal entrepôt both for trade with Egypt and the Mediterranean, and also for trade with the Indian Ocean ports and with Iran. In addition to the China trade, Oman and the Persian Gulf port of Sīrāf also shared during the tenth century in the lucrative trade in slaves, ivory, and ambergris from East Africa, and Muslim ships ventured as far south as Madagascar and Sofala in Mozambique.

After the end of the tenth century, trade between the Persian Gulf and China continued, but there were few direct sailings. In Sasanid times, Ceylon had been the meeting place of merchants from east and west Asia; from the tenth century onward, it was Kalah Bār in Malaya. In the eleventh century, Sīrāf was superseded as the chief emporium in the Persian Gulf by Kīsh (Qais), an island lying some twelve miles offshore about 120 miles southeast of Sīrāf, ruled by Arab amirs of the Banū Qaisar tribe. A large walled city was built on Kīsh island, and cultivation was carried on by means of *qanāts* or underground water channels. Extensive palm groves helped to mitigate the heat, but, nevertheless, said the fourteenth-century geographer and historian Hamdullāh Mustawfī Qazvīnī, it was hotter than the hottest room in a bathhouse. Kīsh maintained its preeminence until early in the thirteenth century, when the ruler of Hormuz, with the help of troops sent by his overlord, the *atabeg* of Kirman, captured the island in 1229. For almost the next three hundred years, until the advent of the Portuguese in the early sixteenth century, Hormuz was unchallenged as the chief commercial emporium in the Persian Gulf.

Hormuz: The "Pearl" of the Persian Gulf

Hormuz, situated on the banks of the Mīnāb creek about six to eight miles from the coast, is an ancient site first mentioned by Nearchus in 325 B.C. by the name Armuzia or Harmuzia. Early in the fourteenth century, a new city was established on the island of Hormuz, which also became known as Hormuz. To avoid confusion, the original mainland site will be referred to as Old Hormuz until its name was changed to Bandar 'Abbās by Shah 'Abbās I in 1622. By the tenth century, Old Hormuz had become the seaport for the provinces of Kirman, Sistan, and Khurasan. Indigo was its most important product, but it also exported gold, silver, copper, iron, cinnabar, and salt. Al-Maqdisī complained of its excessive heat; crops of wheat and barley were sown in November and harvested in March; after the end of March, everything became desiccated.[9] Early in the

9. Abbas Faroughy, *Histoire du Royaume de Hormuz* (Brussels, 1949), p. 7 [hereafter referred to as Faroughy].

tenth century, the 'Abbasid Caliph al-Mu'tadid sent the governor of Bahrain with an army to subjugate Oman; many Omanis fled to Old Hormuz, Basra, and Shīrāz. Among them was Mahmūd, the shaikh of Oman, whose descendants established, in *ca.* 1000, a small Arab kingdom based on Old Hormuz. These kings of Hormuz were vassals of the Seljuqs from 1041 until 1073, and of the Ghuzz from 1186 until 1200, when the Shabānkāra Kurds occupied Kirman and, in alliance with the ruler of Kīsh, killed the king of Hormuz. In 1203, however, the Shabānkāra Kurds were driven out of Kirman by the *atabeg* of Fārs, and this action preserved the semi-independent status of Old Hormuz. The intense rivalry between Old Hormuz and Kīsh for the position of principal entrepôt in the Persian Gulf was temporarily ended in 1229, when the Salghurid *atābeg* of Fārs, Abū Bakr, joined forces with the ruler of Old Hormuz, Saif al-Dīn Abā Nasr 'Alī, to subjugate Kīsh. Saif al-Dīn took prisoner most of the notables of Kīsh, and massacred them. Foolishly, Saif al-Dīn defaulted in the payment of tribute to the *atābeg* Abū Bakr, who promptly reoccupied Kīsh in 1230 and also annexed Bahrain. Not long afterward, however, Fārs came under the suzerainty of the Mongol Great Khan Ögedei and, subsequently, of the Il-khan Hülegü, and in 1270 the province came under direct Mongol rule. In 1272, Mahmūd, the ruler of Old Hormuz, took advantage of this situation to recover Kīsh; driven out by the Mongols, he again returned, and also invaded Oman and annexed the littoral as far as Dhufar.

By the beginning of the fourteenth century, raids by marauding tribes had become such a menace that the ruler of Old Hormuz, Ayāz, cast around for a suitable site to which to transfer the population of the town. In 1302, he moved the population to the island of Qishm, but he decided that Qishm was still too close to the coast to be secure, and about the year 1315 he selected a new site on the island of Jarūn, lying some four miles from the mainland and twenty-five miles west of the Mīnāb creek. On the north side of the island, a new port and city were constructed, known first as "New Hormuz," but subsequently simply as "Hormuz," a name that also superseded Jarūn as the name of the island. Since Jarūn had been a dependency of Kīsh, forces from Kīsh tried to oust the new settlers from Old Hormuz; the attempt failed and, although the invaders captured the king of Hormuz, he succeeded in escaping and making his way back to Hormuz. In 1331, Hormuz was visited by Ibn Battūta, who described it as "a fine large city, with magnificent bazaars, as it is the port of India and Sind, from which the wares of India are exported to the two Iraqs, Fārs and Khurasan."[10] Marco Polo is one of those who comments on the ready availability of wine at Hormuz, a fact that indicates the continuing strength of the pre-Islamic Iranian tradition there; indeed, the coastal region around Old Hormuz was still known as Mughistān, i.e., land of the Mugh or Zoroastrians, as late as the seventeenth century. From one important point of view, Hormuz Island was an astonishing choice as the site of a large city: there was absolutely no water on the island, and all drinking water (with the exception of what could be collected in cisterns during the meager winter rainfalls) had to be imported from the island of Qishm, which also supplied Hormuz with fruit and vegetables. Control of Qishm was

10. Sir Hamilton Gibb, Hakluyt Society Second Series, no. 117, p. 400.

therefore a vital necessity for the rulers of Hormuz. Hormuz island is about 12 miles in circumference and contains no natural products except salt, iron, red ochre, and sulphur. The hills are covered with a thick saline incrustation, under which they glisten white in the sun. As Master Ralph Fitch, the English merchant who was at Hormuz in 1583, succinctly put it: "it is the dryest island in the world, for there is nothing growing in it but only salt."[11] Nevertheless, in its heyday it is said to have supported a population of 40,000 people, and the Abbé Raynal has left this glowing account of Hormuz at the height of its prosperity:

At the time of the arrival of foreign merchants Ormuz afforded a more splendid and agreeable scene than any city in the East. Persons from all parts of the globe exchanged their commodities and transacted their business with an air of politeness and attention which are seldom seen in other places of trade. These manners were introduced by the merchants belonging to the ports, who induced foreigners to imitate their affability. Their address, the regularity of their police, and the variety of entertainments which their city afforded, joined to the interests of commerce, invited merchants to make it a place of resort. The pavement of the streets was covered with mats, and in some places with carpets; and the linen awnings which were suspended from the tops of the houses prevented any inconvenience from the heat of the sun. Indian cabinets, ornamented with gilded vases or china, filled with flowering shrubs or aromatic plants, adorned their apartments: camels, laden with water, were stationed in the public squares; Persian wines, perfumes and all the delicacies of the table, were furnished in the greatest abundance; they had the music of the East in its highest perfection. In short, universal opulence and extensive commerce, a refined luxury, politeness in the men, and gallantry in the women, united all their attractions to make their city the seat of pleasure.[12]

Portuguese Hegemony in the Persian Gulf:
1505–1622

As we have seen, for centuries before the coming of the Portuguese, the Persian Gulf had been one of the great highways of trade between the Far East and the Middle East, and, beyond that, Europe; westward flowed the products of India, China, and the Malay archipelago; eastward, the merchandise of Iran, the Arab countries, and Europe. Mercantile city-states rose and fell as events swept over them: Ubulla, Basra, Bahrain, Sīrāf, Kīsh, Rīshahr, Hormuz, but they were all, without exception, located on the Persian Gulf, and no one state had ever succeeded in imposing its hegemony over the whole area.

The advent of the Portuguese at the beginning of the sixteenth century totally changed this traditional pattern of trade. The Portuguese came not just as traders, but as conquerors. Their design was to establish a Portuguese imperium not only in the Persian Gulf, but throughout Asia. To this end, they set about seizing and holding the key strategic points in Asia. The Portuguese captain, General Afonso de Albuquerque, in his brilliant analysis of the strategic situation in the East Indies, had identified these key points as three: Aden, Hormuz, and the Straits of Malacca. "This city of Ormuz," he said, "is, according to my idea,

---

11. G. N. Curzon, *Persia and the Persian Question* (repr. London, 1966), 2: 415.
12. Quoted in ibid., p. 416.

the most important of them all. And if the King of Portugal had made himself master of Adem, with a good fortress, such as those of Ormuz and Malacca, and so held sway over these three straits, which I have specified, he might well have been called the lord of all the world—as did Alexander when he penetrated to the Ganges—for with these three keys in his hands, he might shut the door against all comers."[13] Until the advent of the nuclear age, nothing occurred during the intervening centuries to invalidate this analysis, and, even today, it is still valid in terms of warfare with conventional weapons.

The grand design of the Portuguese was thus to force all trade between Europe and the Indies to go around the Cape of Good Hope, by blocking its traditional outlets—the Persian Gulf, the Red Sea, and the Straits of Malacca. Since the Portuguese had obtained a headstart in the race to control the Indies trade, this meant that, initially at any rate, all trade would have to be carried in Portuguese bottoms. If, in addition, the Portuguese could acquire and fortify ports on the coasts of Arabia, the Persian Gulf, and the Indian Ocean, they would be in a position both to harass the shipping of rival European nations and to levy lucrative customs and port dues on foreign ships. The Portuguese Bartolomeu Dias rounded the Cape in 1487, and, in the same year, his compatriot Pedro da Covilhã sailed from Egypt to India. Da Covilhã visited Hormuz on his return journey and from Cairo sent to the Portuguese court a detailed report that was of great value in planning the voyage of Vasco da Gama ten years later. The dream of Prince Henry the Navigator of opening up a sea route from the Atlantic to the Indies had become a reality.

By this achievement, the Portuguese at one blow outflanked not only the Muslim countries of the Middle East, in whose hands lay most of the Indian and Far East trade, but also the other mercantile powers of Europe. Foremost among these was Venice, which had for some two and a half centuries been the supreme trading power in the Levant. The capture of Constantinople by the Turks in 1453 had already dealt a deathblow to Venetian trade; the establishment of the sea route to India by the Portuguese gave it the *coup-de-grâce*. The Venetians did all in their power to try and hamper Portuguese trade with the Indies via the Cape, but they failed. The establishment of Portuguese hegemony in the Persian Gulf and Indian Ocean was the logical culmination of the *Reconquista*, the reconquest by the Christians of Muslim Spain, a process that had taken more than four centuries. Although the primary goal of the Portuguese was the monopoly of the Indies trade, the emotional zeal of a holy war against the infidel was never far below the surface.[14] This zeal on occasion led the Portuguese to perpetrate atrocities, such as cutting off the ears and noses of prisoners.

After Vasco da Gama's second voyage (1502), the Portuguese decided to block the Red Sea to Muslim shipping. Dom Francisco de Almeida, the first Portuguese governor and viceroy of the Portuguese possessions in India, in 1505 captured Sofala, Kilwa, and Mombasa, on the East African coast.[15] The following year,

13. *Commentaries*, pp. iv, 185, quoted in A. T. Wilson, *The Persian Gulf* (Oxford, 1928), p. 153 [hereinafter referred to as "Wilson"].

14. R. B. Serjeant, *The Portuguese off the South Arabian Coast* (Oxford, 1963), p. 2 [hereinafter referred to as "Serjeant"].

15. Ibid., p. 14.

Almeida was succeeded by Afonso de Albuquerque, who seized the Island of Socotra, which enabled the Portuguese to control shipping entering or leaving the Red Sea. From Socotra, Albuquerque proceeded along the coast of south-eastern Arabia, forcing the governor of Qalhat, a dependency of Hormuz and therefore of Iran, to become a Portuguese tributary; sacking and burning Quryat and Muscat, seizing and making tributary Suhār; and sacking Khor Fakkan. Albuquerque's real objective, however, was Hormuz; possession of Hormuz, he thought, would give him control of the lucrative trade passing through that port and also enable him, with only a small number of ships, to establish Portuguese naval ascendancy in the Red Sea region. For these reasons Albuquerque, against the advice of his captains, decided to launch an attack on Hormuz, in 1507, with numerically inferior forces. After some hard fighting, Albuquerque took Hormuz and imposed on its ruler, the twelve-year-old Saif al-Dīn, a tribute of 15,000 xerafins (seraphins). Shortly afterward, an official arrived from the King of Hormuz's overlord, the Safavid Shah Ismā'īl I, demanding payment of the tribute due to the latter. Albuquerque threatened the young King of Hormuz that he would depose him if he paid any tribute to the Shah, and he sent the Shah's envoy some cannonballs, grenades, and guns, telling him to tell his master that this was the sort of coin in which the King of Portugal had commanded him to pay tribute.

The following year, a mutiny among Albuquerque's captains forced him, with the greatest reluctance, to weigh anchor and sail for India; before he left Hormuz, however, he had marked out a site for a future fort on the island of Hormuz. Albuquerque was away for seven years, during which time he made an unsuccessful attack on Aden, the second of the three keys to mastery in the East that he had identified. Repenting of his brusque reply to Shah Ismā'īl I in 1507, he sent Miguel Ferreira as an envoy to the Shah in 1513 with suitable gifts and a friendly message. In 1515, Albuquerque reappeared off Hormuz and re-occupied the city without fighting. Since Shah Ismā'īl had no navy, he was forced to accept the Portuguese occupation as a *fait accompli*. Albuquerque concluded a treaty with Shah Ismā'īl on the following terms: (1) the Portuguese would help the Iranians to recover the Bahrain Islands and Qatīf on the mainland from the Arab Jabrid dynasty; (2) the Portuguese would assist Shah Ismā'īl in suppressing a revolt in Makrān; (3) Iran and the Portuguese would form an alliance against the Ottoman Turks; (4) the Shah would recognize the King of Hormuz as a Portuguese vassal (*titulado*). After the conclusion of this treaty, Albuquerque sent with the returning Persian ambassador an envoy of his own, Fernão Gomes de Lemos, who bore to Shah Ismā'īl gifts double the value of those sent by the Shah. Based though it was on *force majeure*, this treaty represented a significant diplomatic achievement on the part of Albuquerque, but the latter did not live to exploit it; he sailed for Goa, but died en route, in December 1515.

Throughout the sixteenth century, Hormuz remained the key to Portuguese supremacy in the Persian Gulf. The King of Hormuz remained a Portuguese vassal, and all Portuguese trade with Basra, Muscat, and other Persian Gulf ports passed through Hormuz. A few years after the conclusion of the 1515 Treaty the Portuguese descended on the Bahrain islands and drove out the Jabrids, but their compliance with the treaty stopped at that point; instead of handing the islands over to Iran, as they were bound to do under the treaty, they claimed suzerainty over them for eighty years, although at times the ruler of Bahrain acknowledged Ottoman suzerainty. In 1522, Portuguese officials were placed in charge of the Hormuz customs, and their oppressive behavior caused revolts at Hormuz, Bahrain, Muscat, Quryat, and Suhār. In 1523, Portuguese suzerainty at Hormuz was confirmed by the Treaty of Mīnāb, concluded between Dom Duarte de Menzes and the thirteen-year-old king of Hormuz, Mahmūd Shah.[16] This treaty tightened the Portuguese grip on Hormuz, reducing it from the status of a Portuguese protectorate to that of a Portuguese colony; its terms provided for: (1) the grant of a site for a Portuguese factory; (2) exemption from customs duties for Portuguese ships calling at Hormuz; (3) payment of an annual tribute of 60,000 seraphins (four times the amount originally set by Albuquerque); and (4) a ban on the bearing of arms by Muslims, with the exception of the royal guards.[17]

The Portuguese commandants at Hormuz, having bought their office in Lisbon, had no thought but to enrich themselves at the expense of their subjects. Their refusal to pay tribute to the ruler of Lār interrupted internal trade between Hormuz and the rest of Iran. The Portuguese exacted ever heavier taxes from the people of Hormuz, arrested *vazīrs*, and even exiled the King to Goa. Thus, the maritime trade with Gujerat and the caravan trade with other cities in Iran, which were the bases of the prosperity of Hormuz, were both severely damaged by the actions of the Portuguese. Because of the decline in its commercial prosperity, Hormuz was unable to keep up its payments of tribute, and in 1542 the Portuguese Viceroy Afonso de Souza waived all arrears of tribute. The Portuguese resumed control of the Hormuz customs and became the *de facto* owners of Hormuz.[18] The kings of Hormuz were chosen by the Portuguese, and were virtual prisoners of the Portuguese commandants; they were not allowed to leave the island without the permission of the commandant, which was rarely granted.[19]

It was inevitable that at some stage the rival interests of the Ottomans, then in the phase of their greatest expansion under Sultan Sulaimān the Magnificent, and those of the Portuguese would bring the two powers into collision at the head of the Persian Gulf, as they had in the Red Sea. As early as 1529, the Portuguese had intervened militarily in the affairs of Basra; the Ottomans, after their capture of Baghdad from the Safavids in 1534, sought to expand their influence southward in the direction of Basra and the head of the Persian Gulf. In 1538, the name of the Ottoman sultan was stamped on the coinage and included in the *khutba* at Basra, and in 1546 Basra was formally incorporated into the Ottoman empire.[20] A dockyard was soon established there, and galleys were constructed with wood shipped down the Euphrates from the Mar'ash region of the

16. Wilson, p. 123.
17. Faroughy, p. 75.
18. Wilson, p. 124.
19. Faroughy, p. 87.
20. Salih Özbaran, "The Ottoman Turks and the Portuguese in the Persian Gulf, 1534–1581," *Journal of Asian History* vi/1 (1972): 52–54 [hereinafter cited as "Özbaran"]. The inclusion of the name of a secular ruler on the coinage and in the *khutba*, the address given in congregational mosques at the Friday noon-day prayer throughout the Islamic world, traditionally indicated one's allegiance to that ruler.

southern Taurus Mountains.[21] It was clear that it was the intention of the Ottomans to challenge Portuguese naval supremacy in the Persian Gulf. The first skirmish was indecisive. In 1550, the Ottomans occupied Qatīf in Hasā, on the mainland of Arabia opposite the Bahrain islands, but they were shortly afterward driven out by the Portuguese commander Antão de Noronha. In 1552, a strong Ottoman squadron consisting of twenty-five galleys and four galleons, together with one other ship containing 850 troops under the command of Pīrī Re'īs, appeared before Muscat and captured the Portuguese fort there without difficulty; the Portuguese commandant and the sixty men of the garrison were sent to the galleys. The principal objectives of the Ottomans, however, were Hormuz and the Bahrain islands.[22] In September 1552, Pīrī Re'īs laid siege to the Portuguese fort on the island of Hormuz without effect and, after ravaging the island of Qishm, withdrew. For his lack of success in this campaign, Pīrī Re'īs was subsequently executed. In August 1554, an Ottoman fleet under Seydī 'Alī Re'īs was virtually annihilated, in the second of two naval battles off Muscat, by the Portuguese under Fernando de Noronha. Seydī 'Alī's handful of surviving ships were driven by westerly winds on to the Indian coast, and Seydī 'Alī remained in Gujerat for some years, during which time he wrote his celebrated navigational guide entitled the *Muhīt*.[23]

Despite this reverse, the Ottomans had not abandoned their attempt to wrest control of the Persian Gulf from the Portuguese. In 1556, Mustafā Pasha, acting without orders from Istanbul, made an abortive attack on Bahrain, which was relieved by a Portuguese squadron from Hormuz; the Ottomans surrendered their arms to the Portuguese and paid an indemnity of 12,000 cruzados; in return for this, the Portuguese transported the Ottoman troops back to the mainland.[24] For the next quarter of a century, although the Ottomans continued to covet Bahrain, and although incidents between the rival powers occurred from time to time, on the whole, an uneasy truce prevailed in the Persian Gulf, and the flow of trade, which was to the advantage of both parties, continued. A final flurry of hostilities occurred in 1581, when an Ottoman corsair from the Red Sea sacked Muscat. Thus, by 1580, when the throne of Portugal was united with that of Spain, the Portuguese, as a result of their superior seamanship, had thrown back the Ottoman challenge in the Persian Gulf. The Ottomans had failed to take Hormuz, the key to the control of the Persian Gulf and the Bahrain islands. On the other hand, they had annexed Basra and Hasā and thus controlled the overland trade routes to and from Aleppo.[25]

The Ottoman challenge to Portuguese supremacy in the Persian Gulf had hardly come to an end before a new challenger appeared on the scene. Curiously enough, 1581, the date of the last Ottoman attack on a Portuguese possession in the region, was also the year in which the English Muscovy Company decided to abandon the sea route to Russia, Iran, and Central Asia round the north of Scandinavia, as too hazardous, and was the year in which an English merchant

21. Özbaran, p. 56.
22. Ibid., p. 60.
23. Ibid., p. 64.
24. Ibid., pp. 67–68.
25. Ibid., p. 70.

named John Newberie reached Hormuz, the first Englishman to travel by the overland route to the Persian Gulf. Impressed by the possibilities of trade with Iran and India, Newberie, on his return to London, contacted a group of merchants who had just formed the Levant Company and had obtained a charter giving their company the exclusive right to trade with Turkey for seven years. On hearing Newberie's news, these merchants decided to extend their operations to Iran and India, using the overland route through Syria and Mesopotamia. In 1583, Newberie returned to the Persian Gulf with three other merchants, Staper, Fitch, and Eldred, a jeweler named Leedes, and a painter named Storie. Eldred decided to stay at Basra, and the rest pressed on to Hormuz, intending to open up a factory or trading establishment there. A few days after their arrival at Hormuz, some local Venetian traders denounced them to the Portuguese authorities as heretics and spies, and they were thrown into jail and then transported for trial. It is evident that the effects of the Inquisition, established in Portugal in 1536, had spread to the Portuguese possessions overseas, and the Venetians had been able to make clever use of a charge of heresy to get rid of trade rivals. Fortunately for the Englishmen, they were released on bail at Goa through the good offices of an English Jesuit and two Dutchmen. The Portuguese had scotched, but not killed, the snake of English commercial rivalry. The capture of a Portuguese vessel by Drake in 1587 provided the English with much information on the profitable nature of the Indian trade, and the destruction of the Spanish Armada (1588) gave the English increased confidence in the power of their navy. The failure of the various attempts by English merchants to establish an overland trade route to the Persian Gulf had clearly shown that the Portuguese hegemony could be broken only by superior sea power, such as was now possessed by England. In 1600, Queen Elizabeth I established the English East India Company, an act that was to mean the end of Portuguese hegemony in the Persian Gulf.

Thus began the "era of the companies," companies chartered by European governments to carry on trade between Europe and Asia. Each company consisted of "a select group of merchants, corporately organized and given monopoly rights to trade in the seas east of the Cape of Good Hope and west of the Straits of Magellan."[26] The situation in the seventeenth century should thus be sharply distinguished from that obtaining in the sixteenth century, during which the East India trade had been a monopoly of the Portuguese crown and of private merchants licensed by the crown.

In 1588, Shah 'Abbās I, the greatest ruler of the Safavid dynasty, came to the throne. He inherited a kingdom that had been weakened by internal dissensions to such an extent that the traditional enemies of Safavid Iran, the Ottoman Turks to the west and the Özbeg Turks to the east, had been able to make substantial inroads into Iranian territory. In order not to have to fight on two fronts, and in order to have his hands free to deal with urgent domestic problems, Shah 'Abbās, shortly after his accession, concluded a peace treaty with the Ottomans by which he signed away large areas of Iranian territory. By 1602, the situation had so far improved that the Shah could think of trying to recover some of the most important provinces surrendered to the Ottomans. At the same time, he

26. H. Furber, *Rival Empires of Trade in the Orient, 1600–1800* (Minneapolis, 1976), p. 3.

began to take a closer look at the activities of the Portuguese, whose presence on Iranian territory had always been galling to the Safavid rulers; up to the accession of Shah ʿAbbās I, the Safavid monarchs, engaged in a life and death struggle with the Ottomans and, moreover, lacking a navy, had made no attempt to expel the Portuguese by force. In 1602, Shah ʿAbbās's forces, probably using small craft manned by Arabs subject to the Safavid crown, crossed to the Bahrain islands and drove out the Portuguese garrison. The Shah realized that he could not hope to capture the much stronger Portuguese position at Hormuz without naval assistance, and he shaped his policy toward the new intruders in the Persian Gulf, the English, with a view to enlisting their aid against the Portuguese.

Meanwhile, a series of untoward incidents clouded diplomatic relations between Shah ʿAbbās I and the Portuguese. Just before the turn of the century, a Portuguese Jesuit named Francisco da Costa, traveling from Goa to Rome, visited the court of Shah ʿAbbās. When he reported to Pope Clement VIII, he gave the Pope an exaggerated account of the position of the Christians in Iran, and also led the Pope to believe that the Shah might be persuaded to become a convert to Christianity, an event, said da Costa, that would facilitate an alliance between the Christian powers and the Shah against the Ottomans. The Pope sent da Costa back to Iran accompanied by a layman named Diego de Miranda, but the mission ended in disaster. Not only did the personal behavior of the two envoys affront the Shah, but the two envoys indulged in personal quarrels that ended in Miranda's succeeding in getting da Costa temporarily placed in chains.[27] The arrival of three Portuguese Augustinian friars, in 1602, led by the worthy Antonio de Gouveia, did much to erase the unpleasant memories of the da Costa–Miranda mission from the Shah's mind, and in 1609 Shah ʿAbbās dispatched de Gouveia to King Philip III of Spain, who also held the crown of Portugal. De Gouveia was accompanied by a *qizilbash* officer named Dengīz Beg Rūmlū. Again, the mission ended in disaster. When the envoys returned to Iran, in 1613, serious charges were laid against Dengīz Beg and he was put to death; at the same time, de Gouveia was charged with having made a gift to King Philip of some bales of silk that the Shah had instructed him to sell to that monarch. De Gouveia, in fear of his life, fled to Shīrāz and escaped via Hormuz.

These two experiences had given Shah ʿAbbās a jaundiced view of Catholic religious, and he asked Philip of Spain not to send him any more as ambassadors. "A religious man out of his cell was like a fish out of water," he said, and he would prefer the King of Spain to send him "some gentleman of note." King Philip agreed to the principle, but his choice of the person, the haughty hidalgo Don Garcia de Silva y Figueroa, was decidedly unfortunate. Don Garcia's patience was sorely tried by the attitude of the Portuguese authorities at Goa, where he arrived in October 1614. Because Don Garcia was a Spaniard (although he had some Portuguese blood in his veins), he was *persona non grata* to the Portuguese, who placed one obstacle after another in his way and delayed him at Goa for more than two years. Don Garcia reached Isfahan in 1617, but did not receive an audience with the Shah until 1619, five and a half years from the time he had left Spain. When, after such a long delay, he was finally ushered into the royal

---

27. *Chronicle of the Carmelites in Persia,* 1: 90–92.

presence his audience was brief. He infuriated Shah 'Abbās by his peremptory demand that Iran hand back to Portugal the Bahrain islands and Old Hormuz on the mainland (known as Gombrun to Europeans), which had been occupied by the Portuguese in 1612 and retaken by the Iranians in 1615; Don Garcia was at once given his congé.

This succession of diplomatic rebuffs administered to the Portuguese gave the English an opportunity to improve their prospects in Iran. Richard Steel, a factor of the newly formed English East India Company, had noted while traveling across Iran that Persian winters were cold and thought that Iran constituted a promising market for English cloth. In 1615, the English East India Company sent Steel and Crowther to Isfahan, where they had notable success. They obtained from Shah 'Abbās a *farmān*, dated 12 Ramadān 1024/5 October 1615, ordering his subjects "unto what degree soever . . . to kindly receive and entertaine the English Frankes or Nation, at what time any of their ships or shipping shall arrive at Jasques [Jāsk], or any other of the Ports in our Kingdome: to conduct them and their Merchandize to what place or places they themselves desire: and that you shall see them safely defended about our Coasts, from any other Frank or Franks whatsoever"[28]; in addition, the Shah authorized the company to establish factories in Iran. Sir Thomas Roe, "a gentleman of pregnant understanding, well spoken, learned, industrious, of a comely personage, and one of whom there are great hopes that he may work much good for the Company,"[29] who had just been appointed ambassador to the Mughal court by King James I, urged caution, on the ground that an immediate move to take advantage of this *farmān* might precipitate hostilities with Spain and Portugal. The English factors at Surat, however, overruled Sir Thomas and, in 1616, sent the *James* to Jāsk. On board was Edward Connock, who proceeded to open factories at Shīrāz and Isfahan and was cordially received by Shah 'Abbās, who dubbed King James I his "elder brother" and drank his health in wine, and promised Connock a free hand to build a factory at Jāsk or at any other port the company might think fit. At the same time, the Shah granted the company further privileges; this *farmān* is not extant, but the substance of it is probably embodied in the 1629 *farmān* of Shah Safī: permission was granted for the appointment of a permanent English ambassador to the Safavid court and, if necessary, a Safavid ambassador was to take up residence in London; English merchants had the right to buy and sell freely in Iran; they were guaranteed protection of their religion; they were granted the right to bear arms and use them in self-defense; the English ambassador, when appointed, was to have the power to appoint English agents and factors in Iran; and English nationals, if convicted on a criminal charge, were to be punished by their own ambassadors.[30] Extraterritorial rights for foreign nationals were, of course, part of the much hated system of "capitulations" contained in the Treaty of Turkomanchai concluded between Tsarist Russia and Iran in 1828, a system subsequently copied by many other foreign powers exercising political influence in Iran. The essential difference between the situation in 1616 and that

28. *Purchas his pilgrimes,* 4: 279.
29. Wilson, p. 135, n. 1.
30. Ibid., p. 139.

in 1828 was that, in 1616, the right of foreign nationals to be exempt from the law of the land was a privilege freely granted by the Shah that could be withdrawn at any time; in 1828, this privilege was extracted by force from an Iran that had been militarily defeated and was powerless either to deny the privilege or to rescind it. In 1618, the English merchants scored a further success when the Shah agreed not to export any silk to Spain or Portugal, or to Europe via Turkey. In addition, the Shah promised to supply the English East India Company merchants with a quantity of silk every year at a given rate, and this silk could be shipped from Jāsk free of duty.

Portugal did not intend to surrender without a fight the monopoly of the Persian Gulf and Indian Ocean trade that it had enjoyed for a century. Already, in 1612, the Portuguese were worried about the growing challenge from the English. The mission of Sir Robert Sherley, who had been sent to Europe by Shah 'Abbās I in 1608, had caused anxiety to the Portuguese authorities at Lisbon and Goa, and the Portuguese Viceroy at Goa was instructed to intercept Sir Robert on his return journey and to prevent him, by fair means or foul, from reaching Iran.[31] Dom Luiz da Gama, commandant-elect at Hormuz, was ordered to proceed to Laribandar at the mouth of the Indus and bribe the local governor to hand over to him Sir Robert, who had just arrived there, or to kill him. Sir Robert, however, had left Laribandar before da Gama arrived there, in January 1614, and made his way to Iran via Agra and Qandahār.[32]

In June 1620, a strong Portuguese naval squadron under the command of Ruy Freyre de Andrade appeared off Hormuz. Ruy Freyre and the English commander Shilling drank toasts to each other on their respective quarter-decks before fighting two naval battles off Jāsk, on Christmas Day or Boxing Day 1620 and on 7 January 1621. The second action was particularly bloody; as a result of Freyre's poor tactics, the Portuguese were exposed to the English broadsides for several hours, and lost 430 men as against 10 by the English.[33] In May 1621, Freyre landed troops on Qishm Island and constructed a fort there to protect the water supply for the island of Hormuz. Imām Qulī Khān, the governor-general of Fārs, initially failed to dislodge the Portuguese but, in February 1622, captured the fort with the assistance of the English, and Ruy Freyre was taken prisoner. The English discovered Freyre's commission from the King of Spain, authorizing him to attack English shipping in the Persian Gulf and, thus, considered themselves justified in engaging in hostilities against the Portuguese at a time when England and Spain were at peace in Europe.

Following the capture of Qishm, the way lay open for an attack on the island of Hormuz itself. Imām Qulī Khān sent two envoys to Captains Blyth and Weddel of the English East India Company, seeking their cooperation in such an attack. When the English captains demurred, Imām Qulī Khān told them plainly that failure to cooperate would mean the cancellation of all East India Company trading privileges in Iran. This threat led Edward Monnox, a former agent of

---

31. C. R. Boxer, "Anglo-Portuguese Rivalry in the Persian Gulf, 1615–1635," in *Chapters in Anglo-Portuguese Relations*, ed. Prestage (Watford, 1935), p. 53 [hereinafter referred to as "Boxer"].
32. Ibid., p. 54.
33. Ibid., p. 69.

the English East India Company in Iran, forcefully to advocate compliance with the Iranian request, and agreement on a joint operation was reached on the following terms: (1) all spoils were to be divided equally; (2) the English were to have the fort at Hormuz; (3) the English were to be entitled to import and export goods at Hormuz free of duty; (4) the English were to receive half the customs dues paid on other merchandise passing through the island; (5) Christian prisoners were to be handed over to the English, the rest to the Iranians; (6) the governor-general of Fārs was to defray half the cost of provisions consumed by the East India Company's ship's companies during the operation.

In February 1622, Safavid troops were transported to the island of Hormuz in ships of the English East India Company, and the Portuguese commandant and Mahmūd Shah, the nominal ruler of Hormuz, retreated within the fort. The English fleet anchored on the side of the fort where the walls ran down to the water, and Imām Qulī Khān's men gradually carried their breastworks up to the walls of the fort and commenced mining operations. In April 1622, charges of gunpowder were detonated beneath two of the towers, and the fort was stormed. The three thousand men of the Portuguese garrison surrendered their arms to the English. Of the Muslims found within the fort, those who had collaborated with or had fought at the side of the Portuguese were put to death; those who had been forced by the Portuguese to enter the fort against their will were released to return to their homes. Among the weapons that fell into Iranian hands were several large cannon and siege guns of various sizes "cunningly wrought by skilled Portuguese craftsmen and each one a masterpiece of the art of the Frankish cannon-founders."[34]

After the conquest of Hormuz, the inhabitants of the island were transferred to the mainland to Gombroon, which was renamed Bandar 'Abbās. The Safavid forces had borne the brunt of the assault on the fort at Hormuz and had lost a thousand men. The English had lost only twenty, but subsequently the heat and "rack," i.e., arrack (strong liquor) played havoc with the English sailors, and in September 1622 the fleet was forced to retire to Surat. Furthermore, the English East India Company had to bribe King James I and the Duke of Buckingham with £10,000 each, to persuade them to ward off the wrath of the King of Spain engendered by the company's acts of war at a time when England and Spain were officially at peace.

If the cost to the company was high, the benefits that accrued to it were substantial. The capture of Hormuz was the turning point in the struggle for power between the English and the Portuguese in the Persian Gulf. In 1625, and again in 1630, the Portuguese tried in vain to recapture Hormuz and succeeded only in gaining a foothold at Kung, a small town on the coast of Fārs 100 miles WSW of Hormuz. Under the terms of a treaty between Portugal and Shah 'Abbās in 1625, the Portuguese returned to Iran all its coastal possessions in the Persian Gulf, retaining only the pearl banks at Bahrain and a portion of the Kung customs.[35] With the transference of the population from the island of Hormuz to the mainland, Bandar 'Abbās succeeded Hormuz as the principal port of entry

---

34. Iskandar Beg Munshī, *Tārīkh-i 'Ālam-ārā-yi 'Abbāsī*, 2: 982.
35. Curzon, 2: 419.

in the Persian Gulf, a position it held for more than a century, until after the establishment of the English East India Company's factory at Basra in 1738. The privileges granted by Shah 'Abbās to English merchants in regard to Hormuz were transferred to Bandar 'Abbās. The transportation of the company's goods into the Iranian hinterland was facilitated, because the road from Bandar 'Abbās to Lār, Shīrāz, and Isfahan was better than the road into the interior from Jāsk.

After the loss of Hormuz, the port of Muscat on the coast of Oman assumed greater importance for the Portuguese. Muscat had been in Portuguese hands since 1506 and, between about 1550 and 1588, two forts had been built "on the summits of two craggy peaks" that commanded the town and harbor.[36] In addition, the Portuguese reestablished themselves at Ra's al-Khaima, on the west side of Cape Musandam, and concluded an alliance with the Shaykh of Qatīf, at that time a vassal of the Ottomans. From Qatīf, the Portuguese purchased the finest Arabian horses, which they sold at great profit in India, and also pearls; they paid for these commodities with cloth from Sind and Cambay and with Persian silver coins.[37] Muscat, the only harbor between Aden and the Persian Gulf and, next to Aden and Jidda, the best harbor in the Arabian Gulf, lies at the end of a horseshoe-shaped bay, sheltered from the winds by barren, multicolored volcanic rocks. Immediately behind the town rise mountain ranges, the highest peak of which, Jabal Akhdar, is 9,000 feet high and occasionally has a coating of snow in the winter. The chief defect of Muscat as a base was its vulnerability to attacks by the Arab tribes of the interior of Oman. In 1643, the forces of the Imām of Muscat recaptured Suhār, northwest of Muscat, which had been in Portuguese hands for some twenty years, and in 1650 Muscat itself capitulated to the Imām's troops after a two-month siege. All the Portuguese forts were destroyed, and the Portuguese evacuated Oman. After these successes, the Imām Sultān b. Saif declared a *jihād* or holy war against the Portuguese and carried the war across the Indian Ocean by attacking Portuguese bases at Diu and other places on the coast of Gujerat. The appearance of a Portuguese fleet off Muscat in 1652 was the last occasion on which the Portuguese flag was shown in the Gulf of Oman.[38]

The triumph of the English at the disappearance from the scene of the Portuguese, who during the sixteenth century had held a monopoly of trade in the Persian Gulf and Indian Ocean, was short-lived, because the ships of another great sea power from western Europe, Holland, arrived in the area to challenge English supremacy. Why had the Portuguese failed? Initially, they had taken the Indian and Far East trade out of the hands of the local merchants (Arabs from southwest Arabia and Oman, Persians, Jews, and Indians), because the Portuguese caravels were more seaworthy than Arab vessels designed only to run before the monsoon,[39] and because of the superior fire power of their ships' guns. Their master strategist, Albuquerque, had early identified the key points, possession of which would give the Portuguese mastery of the trade to the Indies, but his failure to capture Aden in 1513 had meant that possession of Hormuz was absolutely vital. When the Portuguese were evicted from Hormuz in 1622, the

36. Ibid., pp. 440 and n. 1.
37. Boxer, p. 127.
38. Wilson, p. 155.
39. Serjeant, p. 2.

final collapse of the Portuguese *imperium* in the Persian Gulf and Indian Ocean was only a matter of time. The low morale and bad discipline of their ships' crews placed them at a disadvantage in their naval battles with the ships of the English East India Company. In their dealings with local rulers, their behavior was often high-handed and they were, on occasion, guilty of bad faith; their racial pride and their fanatical anti-Muslim zeal were in large part responsible for this behavior. The arbitrary way in which they seized without payment, from whatever merchantmen came their way, any supplies that they happened to need, did not endear them to the mercantile populations of the region. Other sources of Portuguese weakness were their own internal jealousies and dissensions, the paucity of their numbers, the essentially military character of their presence in the region, their lack of capital, and, between 1580 and 1640, the antipathy between the Portuguese and the Spaniards. The successors to the Portuguese in the Persian Gulf, the English, Dutch, and French, came as merchant adventurers and did not seek to establish an *imperium* on the Portuguese model. For this reason, Kelly has rightly seen the sixteenth century as a deviation from previous political and economic patterns in the Persian Gulf.[40]

Dutch Supremacy in the Persian Gulf: 1630–1700

Until 1595, the Netherlands had been subject to Spain. In 1583, however, Jan Huyghen van Linschoten had made a pioneering voyage to India and, between 1598 and 1601, there were further such voyages. As a result, the Dutch East India Company was formed in 1602, only two years after the establishment of the English company of similar name. In 1599, the Dutch had signaled their entry into the commercial arena of the Indies trade by abruptly increasing the price of pepper from 3s. a pound to 6s. and then to 8s., an action that brought Holland into open conflict with England over the East Indies spice and pepper trade. At the same time, the Dutch vigorously attacked Portuguese positions in India and Southeast Asia. In 1602, a Dutch naval victory near Bantam opened the road to the Moluccas (the Spice Islands). It was the opinion of the Dutch that "the commerce of the Moluccas, Amboina and Banda should belong to the [Dutch East India] Company, and that no other nation in the world should have the least part." The massacre perpetrated at Amboina in 1623 resulted in the Dutch, in their turn, being accused of "inhuman acts, beastiality and ingratitude." In 1641, the Dutch captured Malacca, the third of the keys to the Indies identified by Albuquerque, from the Portuguese, and between 1638 and 1658 they expelled the Portuguese from Ceylon. In 1652, they established a colony on the Cape of Good Hope.[41]

It was inevitable that the Dutch would challenge the mercantile supremacy of the English in the Persian Gulf. In 1625, the Dutch cooperated with the English to frustrate a Portuguese attempt to recapture Hormuz, but the honeymoon was of short duration. Almost at once, the Dutch challenged the English

---

40. J. B. Kelly, *Britain and the Persian Gulf, 1795–1880* (Oxford, 1968), pp. 1–2.
41. Wilson, pp. 158–60, and 160 n. 1.

trading position in Iran itself. Under the terms of the 1622 agreement with Shah 'Abbās I, the English East India Company was to receive one-half of the customs dues levied on all merchandise passing through the port of Bandar 'Abbās. The Dutch refused to pay. Moreover, they took advantage of the death of 'Abbās I, in 1629, to make highly successful representations at the court of his successor, Shah Safī. The privileges of the English East India Company were not renewed and confirmed by Shah Safī until 1632. Meanwhile, the Dutch founded a factory at Bandar 'Abbās, and rapidly proceeded to establish a monopoly of the spice trade between the East Indies and Iran. The English traded in commodities such as cloth, tin, steel, indigo, and silks. The Dutch were prepared to sell some items at a loss in order to establish their market. In 1645, the Dutch attacked Qishm island, and obtained from Shah 'Abbās II a license to purchase silk in any part of Iran and to export it free of customs duty. In the same year, no doubt in an attempt to compensate for the increasingly dominant position of the Dutch at Bandar 'Abbās, the English East India Company started to move from Bandar 'Abbās to Basra, but the Dutch sent eight ships to Basra and virtually destroyed the English factory. By the middle of the seventeenth century, English trade in the Persian Gulf had been swamped by that of the Dutch; the value of the Dutch trade in the 1650s amounted to £100,000, a very substantial sum.[42] Thévenot, Fryer, and Chardin all testify to the supremacy of Dutch trade in the Persian Gulf in the second half of the seventeenth century.

Anglo-Dutch rivalry in the Persian Gulf was only one part of the fierce struggle for control of trade on the oceans of the world that these two powers were carrying on. The 1651 Navigation Act, designed to destroy the Dutch carrying trade, led to war in Europe in 1652, and the celebrated Dutch admirals Van Tromp and Ruyter tried to destroy the English fleet, led by the equally celebrated admirals of the Commonwealth, Blake and Monk. In 1653, and again in 1654, Dutch vessels sank or captured a number of the English East India Company's ships in the Persian Gulf and, on the conclusion of peace in 1654, damages of £85,000 were awarded to the English company.

In 1664, a third East India Company was established, by the French, under the title Compagnie Française des Indes. The establishment of the French company was the indirect result of the policies of Père Joseph and Cardinal Richelieu, who had taken note of the success achieved by the English and Dutch East India companies and had decided that France must follow their example. Moreover, both Père Joseph and Cardinal Richelieu disliked the fact that the Carmelite missions in Iran were staffed by Spaniards and Italians. In 1627, Cardinal Richelieu sent the Capuchin Père Pacifique de Provins to the court of Shah 'Abbās, to seek permission to found Capuchin missions in Iran, which would be exclusively French in character. Père Pacifique was successful in his mission, and the Superiors of the Capuchin Mission were regarded as representing the King of France and, thus, offsetting the Augustinians in terms of diplomatic status. The Superior of this Order in Iran was Père Raphaël du Mans, who arrived in Iran in 1644 and spent the rest of his life there, dying in Isfahan in 1696 at the age of ninety-three. He stood high in the favor of both Shah 'Abbās II and Shah

42. Ibid., pp. 161–64.

Sulaymān, and his *Estat de la Perse en 1660* was written for the guidance of the French Minister Colbert, when that minister was collecting information prior to the formation of the Compagnie Française des Indes, in 1664. Representatives of the Compagnie, and an ambassador from Louis XIV, were sent to the Safavid court. Despite the very unfavorable impression made on Shah 'Abbās II by quarrels that broke out between the members of the mission, he granted the Compagnie exemption from tolls and customs dues for three years and trading rights similar to those already granted to the English and the Dutch. Armed with this charter, the Compagnie also opened a factory at Bandar 'Abbās.

England and Holland were at war again 1665–67, but the independence of the Netherlands was assured by the Treaty of Nijmegen, in 1678, and England, after initially supporting France against Holland, switched sides and in 1688 was in alliance with Holland against France. Cromwell's government had strongly supported English commercial enterprise overseas, but the Stuarts, restored to the English throne in 1660, had shown a notable lack of interest in English trade with the Indies. For this reason, and because the Dutch government, on the contrary, gave its merchants strong support, the English East India Company was gradually forced to assume a more political role in order to maintain its commercial position. In 1687, the English East India Company moved its headquarters from Surat to Bombay, where it was given the authority to maintain troops. Another factor that seriously hampered the English East India Company in its struggle against its rivals was the creation of rival companies of merchant adventurers: the Merchant Adventurers (1654–57), the London Company (1701), and the English Company Trading to the East Indies. The conflicting interests and activities of these rival companies threatened to cause the ruin of all. Not until 1708 were all these companies united into a single company: The United Company of the Merchants of England Trading to the East Indies. The presidents of this company were invested with consular powers and rank, and an English ambassador was sent to the Mughal court.[43]

The Persian Gulf in the Eighteenth Century: The Rise of Local Powers; the Growth of Piracy; the Foundation of the British *Imperium*

The second half of the seventeenth century, which had seen the passing of the Portuguese *imperium* in the Persian Gulf, saw also the steady decline of the Safavid dynasty under Shah Sulaymān (1666–94) and Shah Sultān Husayn (1694–1722). Although the Safavids, lacking a navy, had required the help of the English in order to conduct large-scale operations from the sea, their strong land forces had exercised effective control along the northern shore of the Persian Gulf, and they had been able to make effective use of small local craft in order to mount attacks on various offshore islands in the Persian Gulf, such as the Bahrain islands and the island of Qishm. The Afghan incursions of the early

43. Ibid., pp. 166–69.

eighteenth century demonstrated the extent to which the Safavid military machine had decayed. The end of the Portuguese hegemony by sea, and of the Safavid control by land, enabled local rulers in the area gradually to assert their independence and extend their power. This process was but briefly interrupted by the short reign of Nādir Shah in Iran, and by his ill-fated attempts to create an Iranian navy.

During the Safavid period, the demand for Persian silk and the existence of a profitable market in Iran had encouraged foreign trading companies to expand their operations in the Persian Gulf. With the fall of the Safavids, this situation changed completely. In 1722, both the Dutch and the English merchants at Isfahan closed their houses and returned to Bandar 'Abbās, which for a century had been the principal port of entry in the Persian Gulf for foreign trade. By 1730, most European companies trading in Iran were operating at a loss.

In 1734, Nādir Khān Afshār, the *de facto* ruler of Iran, decided that the growth of lawlessness in the Persian Gulf could be checked only by the creation of naval forces to police the area. He had realized that the loan of ships from the East India companies, even when it had been possible to make such arrangements, was a totally inadequate means of controlling the Persian Gulf littoral. It is to Nādir's credit that he recognized the vital importance of sea power in maintaining security for trade in the region, but unfortunately the means employed to implement his plan to create a fleet were often impractical, and he made a series of disastrous mistakes in his choice of naval commanders.

In May 1734, he dispatched Latīf Khān to Bandar 'Abbās as "Admiral of the Gulph."[44] Latīf Khān tried to purchase two ships from the English and the Dutch as the nucleus of his fleet, but both the European companies were reluctant to sell and suggested that Nādir could place orders for new ships to be built at Surat. Surat-built ships, constructed of teak, were famous for their durability.[45] In the same year, Nādir selected as a naval base the port of Bushire, on the coast of Fārs, near the site of the ancient Sasanid port of Rīshahr (Rīv-Ardashīr). Bushire was renamed Bandar-i Nādiriyya, but the name did not endure. For the next one hundred and fifty years, however, Bushire superseded Bandar 'Abbās as the chief Persian port in the Persian Gulf.

The following year, in April 1735, Latīf Khān with three "grabs" (*ghurāb*) and a number of smaller vessels entered the Shatt al-'Arab and unsuccessfully threatened Basra. The local Ottoman commander commandeered two English ships, placed Turkish crews on board, and forced the ship's captains to engage the Persian flotilla. The English East India Company was so worried about the possibility of retaliatory action on the part of Nādir that it considered evacuating Bandar 'Abbās. However, Nādir's wrath was mainly directed at Latīf Khān for having attacked without waiting for the arrival of supporting land forces.[46]

In the spring of 1736, Latīf Khān redeemed himself to some extent by recapturing Bahrain, and, in April 1737, Nādir sought to extend his influence to Oman by intervening in local politics there. After the Imām of Muscat had

44. Lockhart, *Nadir Shah* (London, 1938), p. 78 [hereafter referred to as "Lockhart"].
45. Ibid., p. 79, n. 1.
46. Ibid., p. 93.

wrested Muscat from the Portuguese in 1650, the local tribes split into two bitterly hostile factions, the Hinawī and the Ghāfirī. In 1737, Nādir Shah sent an army to Oman at the request of Saif II b. Sultān, the Hinawī candidate, who had alienated many of his supporters by his dissolute habits. Nādir's forces, disembarked by Latīf Khān in northern Oman, defeated Saif's rival and reached Muscat. No sooner had Nādir's forces withdrawn, however, than the rebels once more drove the Imām out of Muscat.

In January 1738, Latīf Khān, this time accompanied by the *beglerbeg* of Fārs, Muhammad Taqī Khān Shīrāzī, again went to the assistance of the Imām, and again the Iranian forces occupied Muscat. Relations between the Imām and the Iranian commanders were far from harmonious, and the Imām eventually achieved a reconciliation with the rebels, who promised to aid him against his Iranian allies! This second Iranian intervention in Oman ended in a debacle, in May 1738, when Muhammad Taqī Khān had Latīf Khān poisoned and precipitated a mutiny among the Arab seamen by his niggardly treatment of them. Not content with this, Muhammad Taqī Khān went on to demonstrate his complete incompetence as a military commander both by land and by sea when he led an expedition from Makrān to Sind. His land forces were totally defeated by the Baluchis, in February 1740, and his fleet straggled back to Bandar 'Abbās in sorry shape. Muhammad Taqī Khān was dismissed from office, but only temporarily.[47]

The growing insecurity in the Persian Gulf led the English East India Company to establish a new factory at Basra in 1738 and to transfer to it much of the business formerly transacted at Bandar 'Abbās. In September 1740, the Arab seamen in the Iranian fleet again mutinied; this time, they murdered the Iranian admiral, Mīr 'Alī Khān, and all other Iranians who offered resistance, and they removed the Iranian fleet to Khor Fakkan. The new Iranian admiral, Mahmūd Taqī Khān, impounded two Dutch ships and attacked the mutineers, but was driven off. The Huwāla Arabs and the mutineers now had full license to raid any point they pleased in the Persian Gulf.

In an attempt to stabilize the situation, Nādir ordered eleven ships from Surat, in India, and the first one was delivered in May 1741. His dependence on the English East India Company irked him, since for each vessel supplied the company expected, in addition to payment in cash, the grant of a new privilege or the restoration of an old one. Nādir decided to build naval vessels himself at Bushire, but the traditional source of good timber for shipbuilding, India, was under the control of the English East India Company. Nādir therefore conceived the quixotic plan of having timber transported from Māzandarān to Bushire, a distance of over 600 miles, mainly on the shoulders of peasants, since there was a shortage of wagons. Not surprisingly, large numbers of these peasants died from exhaustion en route. To arm the new ships he hoped to build, Nādir established a cannon foundry at Bandar 'Abbās and ordered the casting of three hundred cannons.[48]

The unsuitability and incompetence of the officers appointed by Nādir mili-

47. Ibid., pp. 183–84.
48. Ibid., pp. 212–14.

tated against the success of naval operations. In June 1744, Imāmverdī Khān, who as Sardār-i Garmsīrāt ('Commander-in-chief of the hot regions') took precedence over the Admiral Mahmūd Taqī Khān, quarreled with the latter and imprisoned him at Kung. In October 1741, Imāmverdī Khān impounded two Dutch ships and attacked the mutineers at Kīsh. After sinking one of the mutineers' ships, Imāmverdī Khān was killed when a cannon exploded after he had ordered its charge doubled with the idea of increasing its range.[49]

By January 1742, the delivery of new ships from Surat had increased the size of Nādir's navy to fifteen ships, but, unaccountably, Muhammad Taqī Khān Shīrāzī was reinstated as admiral. In November 1742, Nādir's forces intervened in Oman for the third time on behalf of the Imām Saif b. Sultān. Muhammad Taqī Khān gained possession of the forts at Muscat by a stratagem, and the new Sardār-i Garmsīrāt, Kalb 'Alī Khān, captured Suhār in July 1743 after a lengthy siege that cost him three thousand casualties. The Imām Saif b. Sultān's principal rival, Sultān b. Murshid, was killed in the siege, and he himself died shortly afterward, an event that brought to an end the Ya'riba dynasty of Oman. Hearing reports of dissension between Muhammad Taqī Khān and Kalb 'Alī Khān, Nādir recalled them both, but Muhammad Taqī Khān murdered his superior officer and raised the standard of revolt in Fārs. Preoccupied with this revolt, and with renewed warfare against the Ottomans, Nādir was unable to reinforce his garrisons in Oman. As a result, the governor of Suhār, Ahmad b. Sa'īd, carried out a coup there in 1744 and founded the Āl Bū Sa'īd dynasty.[50]

Ahmad b. Sa'īd, a merchant and shipowner, was obliged to recruit Baluchi and African slaves as mercenaries in order to maintain his position. The death of Ahmad b. Sa'īd in 1783 was followed by more dynastic struggles, and also by the extension of Arab jurisdiction over areas of the northern littoral of the Persian Gulf. In 1793, the sultanate of Oman became a separate entity and a more important force in the politics of the Persian Gulf. Sultān b. Ahmad occupied Gwādar in Makrān, and Chāhbahār, and also the islands of Qishm and Hormuz, then held by the Banū Ma'in Arabs. In 1794, Sultān b. Ahmad obtained from the Banū Ma'in Arabs the lease of Bandar 'Abbās.

As a result of the increased power of local rulers in Oman and the decline of Iranian influence at the eastern end of the Persian Gulf, there was a marked shift in the focus of both commercial and political activities in the area from the entrance to the head of the Persian Gulf.

Nādir's campaigns in Oman had been a costly failure; they constituted a serious drain on the treasury, and more than 20,000 men were lost in battle and from disease. Exorbitant taxes had to be levied to defray the cost of these campaigns. Despite all his setbacks, however, Nādir did not abandon his dream of having a navy, and he continued to purchase ships built at Surat. In 1745, his navy numbered some thirty ships, but within a few years of his death, in 1747, this fleet had ceased to exist as a fighting force.[51]

In 1750, the anarchic state of affairs in Iran, as the Zands and Qājārs engaged in a bitter struggle for the succession to the Safavid empire, caused the English East India Company to close its Isfahan factory altogether. In 1759, the

49. Ibid., p. 215.
50. Ibid., pp. 215–19.
51. Ibid., p. 220.

French, during the Seven Years' War, bombarded the English East India Company factory at Bandar ʿAbbās and compelled it to surrender, and, a few years later (1763), the company abandoned Bandar ʿAbbās altogether in favor of Basra; the Dutch had already moved their factory from Bandar ʿAbbās to Basra (1759). The English East India Company vacillated between the choice of Bushire and that of Basra as their principal emporium in the Persian Gulf. Karīm Khān Zand granted the company a monopoly of the trade in woollen goods and extensive trading privileges at Bushire. Despite this, in 1769 the Company transferred its headquarters to Basra. In 1776, Karīm Khān Zand captured Basra from the Ottomans, but in 1778 the company brought its headquarters back to Bushire.

The general lack of security in the Persian Gulf region during the eighteenth century encouraged the increase of piracy. Piracy was nothing new in the Persian Gulf; it had existed since merchant ships first plied those waters and is mentioned by Pliny and Ptolemy. But never had it existed on the scale it had reached by the end of the eighteenth century. The Omanis were the pirates *par excellence*, but they were by no means the only offenders; there were English and American pirates, and the celebrated Captain Kidd operated in Indian waters. By 1771, the situation had become so bad that, for the first time, the English East India Company appealed to the Royal Navy to suppress piracy in the region; it is of some historical interest that on board H.M.S. *Seahorse*, which arrived at Bushire in May 1775, was a certain Midshipman Horatio Nelson.[52]

Another factor that contributed to the general insecurity of the area was the large-scale movement of Arab tribes from Najd to Khuzistan during the seventeenth and eighteenth centuries. In particular, the Banū Kaʿb, though attacked on numerous occasions by Karīm Khān Zand, established themselves firmly in the Tigris–Euphrates estuary and became a thorn in the flesh to Turks, British, and Persians alike. At the height of their power, in the second half of the eighteenth century, their sway extended from Basra to Bihbihān, in the province of Fārs, just east of the Khuzistan border. "Their effect on their neighbours was, however, out of proportion to their modest territorial domains: on land they could raid both the adjacent areas of Khuzistan and the Dashtistān owing allegiance to Karīm Khān, the ruler of Iran, and villages of the Ottoman governor of Basra's dependencies on both sides of the Shatt—and even Basra itself, with comparative impunity; their navy, comprising some eighty boats of various sizes, could not only ferry their forces around the rivers, creeks and channels of the estuary and coast, but could prey on shipping plying to and from Basra and close the Shatt to trade."[53] After 1788, some 17,450 families of the Banū Lām nomads migrated from the lower course of the Tigris into Iranian territory. The sharp decline in the prosperity of the province of Khuzistan in the eighteenth century may be attributed in large part to the activities of these Arab tribes, which raided trade caravans and caused extensive damage to agriculture and irrigation systems (Iranian tribes such as the Lurs and Bakhtiyārīs contributed to this damage), and whose shaikhs levied taxes at an extortionate level.[54]

Two factors that profoundly influenced the course of events in the Persian

52. Wilson, pp. 177–85.

53. J. R. Perry, "The Banu Kaʿb: An Amphibious Brigand State in Khuzistan," in *Le Monde Iranien et l'Islam* (1971), p. 131.

54. See *Encyclopedia of Islam*², art. "Khūzistān" (R. M. Savory).

Gulf during the nineteenth century were the French expedition to Egypt in 1798 and the rise of the Wahhābī power in Arabia; in 1800, the Wahhābīs captured Qatīf and the Buraimī oasis and threatened Oman itself. Although the French were soon driven out of Egypt, the great age of Western imperialism had begun, and the Middle East as a whole was increasingly subjected to the process often referred to as the "impact of the West."

The 1798 agreement between the English East India Company and the Imām of Muscat marks a turning point in the history of British involvement in the Persian Gulf. This agreement, dated 12 October 1798, was intended in part as a defensive measure against Napoleon's designs in the Middle East and India. Accordingly, most of the clauses of the agreement relate to the exclusion of the French from the territories of the Imām. There was, however, another reason why the British were anxious to conclude this agreement. The political vicissitudes of the eighteenth century, the destructive activities of the Banū Ka'b over a wide area of southern Mesopotamia and southwestern Iran, and increasing Ottoman pressure at the head of the Persian Gulf, had induced the company to return to its old base at Bandar 'Abbās, and to seek protection for this base by a political alliance with the most powerful ruler in the area at that time, the Imām of Muscat. Article 7 of the Agreement states: "In the port of Abassy (Gombroon) [Bandar 'Abbās] whenever the English shall be disposed to establish a Factory, I have no objection to their fortifying the same and mounting guns thereon, as many as they list, and to forty or fifty English gentlemen residing there, with seven or eight hundred English Sepoys, and for the rest, the rate on goods on buying and selling will be on the same footing as at Bussora [Basra] and Abushehr [Bushire]." No doubt the British had been encouraged to make overtures to the Imām of Muscat by the latter's refusal in 1785 to grant the French permission to build a factory at Muscat. The French had made sporadic and ineffectual attempts to increase their influence in the Persian Gulf. They had established a Residency at Basra in 1755, and had appointed a consul to that post in 1765. The 1798 agreement between the English East India Company and the Imām of Muscat "constituted the first of a series of acts which gradually placed most of the principalities along the eastern and southern littorals of the Arabian Peninsula in varying degrees of dependence on Great Britain."[55] A supplementary agreement dated 18 January 1800 stipulated that "an English gentleman of respectability, on the part of the Honourable Company, shall always reside at the port of Muscat, and be an Agent through whom all intercourse between the States shall be conducted." After the failure of Napoleon's grand design for the invasion of India via Iran,[56] the British captured the French headquarters on Mauritius in 1810, and thus put an end to what they regarded as the "vexatious" intrusion of the French into Eastern seas.[57]

55. J. C. Hurewitz, *Diplomacy in the Near and Middle East* (New York, 1956), pp. i, 64. Hurewitz gives the full text of the 1798 agreement, based on C. V. Aitchison, *Collection of Treaties* (5th ed., 1933), pp. xi, 287–88.

56. See Savory, "British and French Diplomacy in Persia, 1800–1810," in *Iran* (1972), pp. 31–44.

57. Wilson, p. 191.

Conclusion: The Persian Gulf at the End of the Eighteenth Century

Throughout the seventeenth century, the activities of the English East India Company in the Persian Gulf had been primarily commercial. Its merchants and factors had sought privileges from the rulers of Iran, and its military activity had been restricted to the defense of these privileges against those who, like the Portuguese and Dutch, sought to infringe upon them. It had not only not sought, but had tried hard to avoid political involvement in the area. The events of the eighteenth century had changed the whole scene: the disintegration of the Safavid empire, and the consequent political anarchy in Iran; the breakdown of security in the Persian Gulf, as numerous petty states contested among themselves for the dominant position in the region, and the concomitant increase in piracy; all these factors had led to a decline in the English East India Company's interest in the Persian Gulf. At the turn of the century, however, the repercussions of the French démarche in Egypt led the company gradually to establish a military and political imperium in the Persian Gulf, an imperium to which the 1820 General Treaty for suppressing piracy and slave traffic gave formal expression. By the signature of this treaty, concluded with the tribal shaikhs of the coast of Oman and with the shaikh of Bahrain, Great Britain assumed responsibility for the security of the Persian Gulf, a responsibility that it did not formally relinquish until 1971. The one hundred and fifty years of the British imperium in the Persian Gulf was regarded as one of the finest flowers of imperialism. As Lord Curzon put it, in his address to the Trucial Shaikhs on 21 November 1903: "We found strife and we have created order. . . . The great empire of India, which it is our duty to defend, lies almost at your gates. . . . We opened the seas to the ships of all nations, and enabled their flags to fly in peace. . . . We have not seized or held your territory. . . . We are not now going to throw away this century of costly and triumphant enterprise; we shall not wipe out the most unselfish page in history."[58]

Selected Bibliography

Boxer, C. R. *Anglo-Portuguese Rivalry in the Persian Gulf, 1615–1634. Chapters in Anglo-Portuguese Relations.* Watford, 1935.

Bury, J. B. *A History of Greece.* London, 1938.

Curzon, G. N. *Persia and the Persian Question.* London, 1966.

Faroughy, Abbas. *Histoire du Royaume de Hormuz.* Brussels, 1949.

Furber, Helden. *Rival Empires of Trade in the Orient, 1600–1800.* Minneapolis, 1976.

Gelb, J. J. "Makkan and Meluhha in Early Mesopotamian Sources." In *Revue d'Assyriologie et d'Archéologie Orientale* LXIV (1970): 1.

Hourani, George Fadlo. *Arab Seafaring in the Indian Ocean in Ancient and Early Medieval Times.* Princeton, 1951.

Hurewitz, J. C. *Diplomacy in the Near and Middle East.* New York, 1956.

58. Ibid., p. 192.

Kelly, J. B. *Britain and the Persian Gulf, 1795–1880*. Oxford, 1968.

Lockhart, Lawrence. *Nadir Shah*. London, 1938.

Major, R. H. *Introduction to India in the Fifteenth Century*. London, 1928.

Muir, Sir William. *The Caliphate: Its Rise, Decline and Fall*. Edinburgh, 1924.

Olmstead, A. T. *History of the Persian Empire*. Chicago, 1966.

Perry, John R. "The Banu Ka'b: An Amphibious Brigand State in Khuzistan." In *Le Monde Iranien et l'Islam*. Charlottesville, Va., 1971.

Ramazani, Rouhollah K. *The Persian Gulf: Iran's Role*. Charlottesville, Va., 1972.

Rawlinson, George. *Ancient History from the Earliest Times to the Fall of the Western Empire*. New York, 1900.

Rawlinson, Sir Henry. *The Five Great Monarchies*. London, 1879.

Serjeant, R. B. *The Portuguese off the South Arabian Coast: Hadrami Chronicles, with Yemeni and European Accounts of Dutch Pirates off Mocha in the Seventeenth Century*. Oxford, 1963.

Stevens, Sir Roger. *The Land of the Great Sophy*. London, 1962.

Wilson, Sir Arnold T. *The Persian Gulf: An Historical Sketch from the Earliest Times to the Beginning of the Twentieth Century*. Oxford, 1928.

3. The Nineteenth and Twentieth Centuries

MALCOLM YAPP

 The history of the Persian Gulf during the nineteenth and twentieth centuries may be viewed as the product of the relationship between three concentric circles of peoples and states. These circles were made up as follows: an inner ring representing the people of the Gulf coasts, including Oman; an intermediate ring made up of what it is convenient to term the regional powers—those countries whose rulers possessed or claimed to influence the shores of the Gulf and whose centers of power included Baghdad, Riyadh, and Tehran; and an outer ring comprising those powers whose international interests embraced, regularly or intermittently, the Persian Gulf. At various times this last ring of what may be termed the international powers included the Ottoman Empire, Egypt, the states of the Indian subcontinent, the European powers (including Russia) and the United States.[1] The eccentric movements of these circles and of the orbits of the powers within them produce a complex, fluctuating relationship that is the theme of this chapter. At the outset it will be convenient to comment on the broad features of that relationship under three headings: political, economic, and social.

The political links were provided by claims to political authority and by strategic concepts. The Sa'ūdī power in Najd claimed authority over areas of the Arabian shore, and it was through Najd that first Egyptian and later Ottoman claims to influence in the Gulf appeared during the nineteenth century. Ottoman claims also entered the region at the head of the Gulf through Basra in a tenuous chain stretching back through Baghdad to Istanbul. The sovereignty of the Iranian government on the Iranian shore was generally acknowledged. Other international powers were involved through strategic theory: France through a concern with the Indian Ocean and, subsequently, by a desire to put Britain under pressure in the interests of a greater diplomatic game; Russia by her

---

1. The distinctions are admittedly simplifications, and the situation of the Ottoman Empire and Egypt pose particular problems; both figure as international and as regional powers, and indeed it could be argued that the same is true of Britain. It is the old paradox of the paradigm; history destroys models but only models make it intelligible.

alleged quest for a warm-water port and by her undoubted concern with the fate of the Ottoman empire and Iran as the two great Muslim powers upon her southern frontier; and Britain through the problems of imperial defense deriving from the possession of India.

Economic links include those of trade and communications. The Gulf was an important route through which goods, especially exports from India, passed into the surrounding countries of Iran, Iraq, and Arabia. In the nineteenth century, this trade was too small to be of particular significance to the international powers, although Britain could not divest herself of concern for the trade of India. To the international powers, the Gulf was of more significance as a region through which passed imperial communications, particularly those of Britain with the east but also, with the prospective development of railways, Gulf communications became important to other powers. Trade with the outer world was of much greater consequence to the local powers who were heavily dependent on supplies of goods from India and, during the later nineteenth and twentieth centuries, on the export of pearls for sale on the world market. But during the twentieth century there grew up one great economic interest that bound the three circles together with a knot of unsurpassed strength; this was the oil industry.

Socially, the dominant link was provided by Islam. The people of the Gulf were overwhelmingly Muslims and were part of the great Islamic world. Islam bound the two inner circles together in a web of mutual understanding that was reinforced at particular points by bonds within Islam: the pilgrim routes that drew Shī'īs to the shrines of Iraq; and the peculiar inspiration of religious revivalism in Arabia. Differences within Islam, such as those of Sunnī and Shī'ī, Wahhābī and Ibādī, both divided the peoples of the Gulf shores and provided links that brought them into an intimacy with the people of the regional powers. Islam also formed a link with certain semi-international powers—the Ottomans and Egypt—and thereby legitimized their actions in the region in a manner denied to other international powers. For the European powers, Islam was an obstacle to a close relationship with the peoples of the Gulf area and even a source of active menace; one of the most enduring constraints that governed British attitudes toward the Gulf was fear of the effects of the Pan-Islamic appeal upon the loyalties of Muslims in India. However long the Europeans remained in the Gulf they would still be strangers in the land, disliking the customs and habits they feared to alter. The Europeans made no effort to subsume Islam within the universal religion of progress that they preached elsewhere; their civilizing mission was mainly confined to the waters of the Gulf, and, for a variety of reasons, they preferred that the Gulf should remain in cocooned seclusion.

It is conventional to emphasize the geographical isolation of the local powers of the Gulf from the regional powers, and there is some truth in this observation, for in the north the mountains of the Zagros and in the south the deserts of Arabia cut the Gulf coast off from its natural hinterlands. But the isolation can be overstressed and, historically, lack of interest rather than lack of facility has been a more powerful force for separation. On the Arabian side, key areas like Buraimi and Hufūf linked Najd with the coast, and the nomadic Bedouin, obstacles to outsiders, formed a valuable bridge for those who could command tribal support. On the Iranian side, there were passes through the mountains, and if communications were not easy they were not impossible; roads could be improved by a strong government and the tribes could be reduced to order. Nevertheless, during the twentieth century, a key factor in bringing the regional and local powers into closer contact has been the improvement of communications. At the head and the mouth of the Gulf were natural lines of communication, ready to be exploited, in the form of the waterways of the Tigris, Euphrates, Shatt al-'Arab, and the Kārūn at the one end and the Straits of Hormuz and the sea at the other. It was the early exploitation of the navigable possibilities of the sea and the waterways that contributed to the large role in the Gulf played by the powers that could master the water; but their prominence was a matter of technological history, and, in the course of time, the development of road, rail, and air communication overcame this advantage enjoyed by those powers, above all Britain, which could for long best exploit the waters. But in the nineteenth century the relative rate of technological development was to have a powerful influence on historical processes in the Gulf by strengthening the links between the inner and outer circles at the expense of the links between the inner and intermediate circles.

At the end of the eighteenth century, the Gulf was far from being a prosperous area.[2] Its population was small; certainly fewer than a million people lived around its coasts. Its agriculture was meager, the region lacked adequate and reliable supplies of good water, and the ingenuity of its *falājs* or *qanāts* (underground irrigation channels) was a palliative only. Cereal production was very rare; fruit, nuts, and vegetables were grown in a few favored locations, and the principal crop—dates—was confined to a select number of places—Buraimi, Liwā, Qatīf, Hasā on the Arabian shore, along the Mīnāb river on the Iranian side, and especially on the Batīna coast of Oman and around the Shatt al-'Arab at the head of the Gulf. The larger islands, Bahrain and Qishm, were also cultivated. Pastoralism was a feature of the economy, and its products—camels, horses, sheep, and goats—were exchanged for the products of cultivation. But the area as a whole required imports of foodstuffs, especially rice, from India. A major industry was fishing the rich waters of the Persian Gulf and the Gulf of Oman, and this pursuit was a principal occupation of many Arabs. Apart from a little weaving by the nomads and the collection of a few minerals, the only other industry of note was pearl fishing. Each year fleets gathered off Bahrain; in 1842, it was calculated that the industry employed 2,500 vessels and 30,000 to 40,000 men. Without doubt it was fishing and pearling that made the people of the Gulf so much at home on the sea and led them to become notable shipbuilders and the great carriers of seaborne trade, just as the desert and mountain skills of their pastoral neighbors made them the great carriers of goods on land. In 1800, the dhow and the camel were symbols of the Gulf as ubiquitous as oil derricks and

2. In this account as elsewhere, I have relied heavily upon J. G. Lorimer, *Gazetteer of the Persian Gulf*, 2 vols. (Calcutta, 1915). Lorimer's *Gazetteer* was based upon several summaries compiled from the British archives by J. D. Saldanha and others. A list of many of these summaries is given in J. B. Kelly, *Britain and the Persian Gulf* (Oxford, 1968), p. 860. I have also generally found Dr. Kelly's book of great assistance. See his summary of the position in the Gulf at the end of the eighteenth century, pp. 1–61. See also S. B. Miles, *Countries and Tribes of the Persian Gulf*, 2 vols. (London, 1919).

the oil tanker became in the latter part of the twentieth century. But significant as it was to the peoples of the Gulf, the size of their trade should not be exaggerated. It was estimated at £ 1.6 million in 1800, of which Muscat accounted for £ 1 million, but others criticized this estimate as too high.[3] Most trade was conducted with India, whither were sent pearls, horses, dates, and fruits, and whence came spices, coffee, woollens, and grain. Most of the imports from India were channeled to Iraq and especially Iran.

It is unnecessary to describe the social institutions of the people of the Gulf in detail. The great majority were Muslims, with a few Christians in Lower Iraq; also, a few Jews, Hindus, and Armenians engaged in trade. The commonest language was Arabic, spoken all along the Arabian shore and around the head of the Gulf, and by the fishermen of the Iranian shore. Primary loyalties were to the family, the clan, the tribe and confederacy, and social life was conducted in this context. Tribal customary law coexisted with the *sharī'a*; the authority of the family with that of the *qādī*; and feuds were endemic and prolonged. Educational provisions were minimal; a few schools taught the Qu'rān, but the great majority of people were illiterate. Housing was simple: the nomads had their black goat-hair tents; of town dwellers, a few had stone houses, a larger number dwellings of sun-dried mud brick, and the majority, lacking timber, built crude shelters from date palm branches. Destructive fires were frequent. Hygiene was primitive and epidemics common. Cholera was a frequent visitor, striking the Gulf in 1820–21 and again in 1830 when Iraq was reduced to a pitiful condition, and, in Arabia, related one chronicler, "the towns stank from the corpses of men."[4] In 1773, Basra had been struck by plague. Entertainments were unsophisticated: dancing, singing, and coffee-drinking at home; hunting, hawking, and camel- and horse-racing outside. It was a society whose public aspects were dominated by men.

The political structure of the Gulf in 1800 was but recently formed. In Oman, the Āl Bū Sa'īd dynasty had come to power in 1749 in the aftermath of the great civil war that racked Oman in the early eighteenth century and paved the way for an Iranian occupation, not terminated until 1744. With the consolidation of the power of the Āl Bū Sa'īd, the political shape of Oman altered and an effective partition was concluded.[5] The eye of outside observers was caught by the prosperity of the northern coastal area, particularly the ports of Matrah and Muscat, reported in 1790 to be the most flourishing ports in the Gulf.[6] These ports were the eastern pillars of the extensive trading empire in the Indian Ocean, of which the western pillar was Zanzibar, ruled by the great Āl Bū Sa'īd ruler known as Sayyid Sa'īd, who reigned from 1807–56. Within the Gulf this empire also included the islands of Qishm and Hormuz and Bandar 'Abbās and its de-

3. Malcolm to Mornington, 26 February 1800, Factory Records, Persia and the Persian Gulf, 22, 53. For a criticism by Harford Jones, see Jones to Malcolm, 10 October 1800, ibid., p. 23.

4. Quoted by R. Bayly Winder, *Saudi Arabia in the Nineteenth Century* (London, 1965), p. 91. For Iraq, see the description in A. N. Groves, *Journal of a Residence in Baghdad* (London, 1832).

5. Bertram Thomas, *Arab Rule under the Al Bu Sa'id Dynasty of Oman, 1741–1937* (London, 1938); R. G. Landen, *Oman since 1856* (Princeton, 1967); and G. P. Badger, *The History of the Imams and Seyyids of Oman* (London, 1871).

6. S. Manesty and H. Jones, "Report on British Trade with Persia and Arabia" 18 December 1790, in Landen, *Oman since 1856*, p. 62.

pendencies, which were leased from Iran, and, in the Gulf of Oman, the ports of Gwādur and Chāhbahār. In complete contrast was the interior of Oman, centered on the old capital of Rustāq, where the traditions of the Ibādī community continued unchanged in a largely subsistence economy made possible by the frugal benediction of the rains captured by the Jabal Akhdar mountains. Thus was reproduced the situation that had obtained when the Portuguese had ruled Muscat as part of their Indian Ocean empire, with the significant difference that an Omani dynasty now ruled in Muscat.

The political situation of what was to become known as Trucial Oman was also newly formed. The way of life of its Arab tribal inhabitants was old; settled along the small creeks that indent the coast, the Arabs took their living from the sea as fishers, traders, pearlers, and occasional pirates. During the eighteenth century, new dynasties had come to command these creeks. In the north, the Qawāsim, a branch of the Hawāla Arabs who had occupied both shores of the Gulf for many centuries, rose to power following the decline of Omani influence in the first half of the eighteenth century. The Āl Bū Saʿīd failed to subdue the Qawāsim and were compelled to recognize their independence in Sīr, Raʾs al-Khaima, and Sharja. The Qawāsim then extended their power to Lingeh, Khūnj, and Laft on the Iranian shore and briefly to Qishm, although here they were obliged to give way to the Āl Bū Saʿīd. It was the Qawāsim who, at the end of the eighteenth century, offered a major challenge to Muscati maritime preeminence. Curiously, the rule of the great Qawāsim Skaikh, Sultān ibn Saqr, (1803–66) even exceeded that of his great rival Sayyid Saʿīd. This Homeric figure perished as heroically as he had lived when, at the age of nearly one hundred years, he married a girl of fifteen and shortly afterward died of paralysis of the loins.[7]

In the southern part of the Gulf coast of Oman, another group also rose to prominence during the latter part of the eighteenth century. This was the Āl Bū Falāh, part of the previously largely nomadic tribe of Banū Yaʾs. The Āl Bū Falāh established their power at Abū Dhabī, but for some years their interests remained mainly pastoral and they did not exploit its possibilities fully until the 1830s, when they challenged the maritime power of the Qawāsim and thus inaugurated the long strife, by land and sea, which characterized relations between these two dynasties for many years. Factional disputes led to splits in the Banū Yaʾs and in 1833 one group, the Āl Bū Falāsa, settled in Dubai, thereby introducing a third force into the confused politics of the coast.[8]

Two other new Arab powers also challenged Muscati predominance in the Gulf. These were Kuwait and Bahrain. The elevation of Kuwait from its former situation as an obscure fishing village was connected with the arrival in the early eighteenth century of the ʿUtab, a branch of the great ʿAnaza confederation of central and northern Arabia. Under the leadership of the Āl Sabbāh family, the ʿUtab secured their independence from the Banū Khālid Arabs, who controlled the northern part of the Arabian coast. Aided by its geographic situation— an extensive bay at the terminus of the overland route from Syria—Kuwait was

7. Kelly, *Britain and the Persian Gulf*, n. 673.
8. Lorimer, *Gazetteer*, 1: 765–66, 772.

well placed to secure a share of the maritime advantages of the Gulf. During the
1760s, a branch of the 'Utab, the Āl Khalīfa, migrated from Kuwait to Qatar,
where they settled in 1766 at Zubāra. Their eventual destination, however, was
the fertile island of Bahrain, with its great pearl banks, the richest prize in the
Gulf, and after consolidating their power in Zubāra, the 'Utab wrested Bahrain
from Iranian sovereignty and from the rule of the Arabs of Bushire in 1783.
Their new wealth, trading skills, and sea power made the 'Utab a formidable
new element in the politics of the Gulf.[9]

The late eighteenth century also witnessed important changes in Najd in
the interior of Arabia. It is unnecessary to rehearse here the well-known story of
the rise of what became known to outsiders as the Wahhābī movement, for, like
the Ibādīs, the Wahhābīs regarded themselves only as good Muslims. It is
sufficient to note that the movement had two aspects, that of a puritanical religious
revival, a protest against the laxities that had crept into Muslim practice; and
that of a political revolution associated with the rise of a new dynasty, that of
the house of Āl Sa'ūd.[10] The combination proved irresistible, and the Wahhābī
expansion of the late eighteenth century was a major disruptive factor both in
Iraq and also on the Gulf coast, where the mild sway of the Banū Khālid,
which had comfortably screened the 'Utab, was broken in 1795 and replaced by
militant Wahhābism. In 1800, the Wahhābīs conquered Qatīf and by 1803
dominated the northern part of the Arab shore of the Gulf. Also, in 1800, they
occupied Buraimi, a key point from which to extend their influence from Oman.
Between 1807 and 1813, the Wahhābī governor of Buraimi, Mutlaq al-Mutairī,
encouraged the Qawāsim to intensify their campaign against Muscat and against
their other rivals. Like others, the Qawāsim espoused the Wahhābī doctrines,
which provided a convenient justification for their belligerency. Through conquest and voluntary submission, the Wahhābīs promised to bring the entire
Arabian shore under their hegemony.

The novelty of the political forms of the Arabian shore was duplicated on
the Iranian side of the Gulf. Under the rule of Nādir Shah, Iranian power in
the Gulf had increased during the second quarter of the eighteenth century and
Iranian control was extended over Oman and Bahrain.[11] Although Iranian power
in the Gulf waned during the second half of the eighteenth century, the Zand
dynasty, with its capital at Shīrāz, retained a close interest in the area and
asserted Iranian power on the Iranian shore and even at Basra.[12] It was with the
replacement of the Zands by the Qājārs, whose capital was now established far
to the north in Tehran, that Iranian concern about the Gulf diminished; preoccupied as they were with relations with the states of Transcaucasia and with the
advancing Russians, the Qājārs had neither the time nor the resources to maintain
Iranian power in the Gulf area. Indeed, the Qājārs were suspicious of the whole
of southern Iran, seeing it as a center of Zand support. The management of the
Gulf shore was entrusted to the governor of Fārs, and the customary confusion

9. See A. Abu Hakima, *History of Eastern Arabia, 1750–1800* (Beirut, 1965).
10. See G. S. Rentz, "Muhammad ibn 'Abd al-Wahhab and the Beginnings of Unitarian
Empire in Arabia," Ph.D. dissertation, University of California, 1948.
11. L. Lockhart, *Nadir Shah* (London, 1938).
12. A. Parsons, *Travels in Asia and Africa* (London, 1808).

between foreign relations and border policy insured an uneasy division of authority between Shīrāz and Tehran. In practice, the governor of Fārs often found his hands full with the old problems of the Bakhtīyārī and the Qashqā'ī tribes and was unable to exercise regular control over the Arab shaikhs who dominated the ports of the Iranian shore. In Khuzistan, the Banū Ka'b were already virtually independent since the middle of the eighteenth century; to the southeast, Bushire, the principal Iranian port on the Gulf, was ruled by the Nāsirī Arabs, who came from Oman; the extent of Qāsimī and Muscati influence on the remainder of the Iranian shore has been mentioned.

A new regime had also established itself in Iraq in the second half of the eighteenth century. Ottoman authority, never strong, had been shattered under the hammer blows of Nādir Shah, whose death, in 1747, left a vacuum that was filled in Iraq by a group of Georgian Mamlūks, slaves who had come to dominate the army and bureaucracy in the Iraqi provinces.[13] Although they maintained their allegiance to the Ottoman Empire, the Georgians were, for most purposes, autonomous rulers of Iraq. They ruled from Baghdad, and their authority over Basra was not always certain, while the power of the governors of Basra was limited by the need to conciliate the great tribes of the Muntafiq and the Ka'b. The Mamlūks had no power in the Gulf, since they had no navy, and they were obliged to pay the Muscatis to protect Basra from pirates. Once the great emporium of the Gulf, Basra declined in the last thirty years of the century, being struck by plague in 1773, occupied by Iran in 1776–79, and suffering from Kuwaiti competition. Even so, Basra remained second only to Muscat among Gulf ports in 1800.

One final political novelty in the Gulf remains to be mentioned. As a result of the political revolutions in India during the eighteenth century, the British East India Company had emerged as a powerful territorial power as well as a great mercantile one. The open sea-door of the Gulf now became the route through which this new factor entered the region.

The prosperity of the people of the Gulf depended upon trade and the pearl fisheries. In the early nineteenth century, persistent maritime warfare threatened to ruin both. Contemporary Britons described this maritime warfare as piracy, a term repudiated by modern Arab historians. Indeed, the distinction between the two terms is unclear, depending as it does on a discrimination between opponents and on a system of legalization that was essentially European; even in Europe privateering and the rights of neutrals raised questions about the connection between legitimate warfare and piracy to which there was no simple answer. Arguments about terminology, therefore, seem unproductive; more interesting is the question of the causes of maritime violence in the Gulf. According to one theory, it is explicable by the custom of centuries, even of millennia, and the natural consequence of the poverty of the pirates and the wealth of the trade that passed their doors. A second explanation sees piracy as the transfer of land conflicts to the sea by a people who were particularly at home on the water. A third view is that the peculiar violence that characterized the early nineteenth

13. S. H. Longrigg, *Four Centuries of Modern Iraq* (London, 1925); P. M. Holt, *Egypt and the Fertile Crescent, 1516–1922* (London, 1966), pp. 146–48.

century was the consequence of the Wahhābī revolution, which supplied a moral imperative to the pirates. "Their occupation is piracy and their delight murder," wrote one observer, "and to make it worse they give you the most pious reasons for every villainy they commit."[14] A more recent argument makes piracy, like Wahhābism itself, the consequence of the intrusion of Europeans bringing both innovations and their own wars and rivalries from Europe. No doubt each of these views has some merit, but a more convincing explanation is that which relates the outburst of maritime warfare to the competition of the Arab ports for a larger share of the trade then engrossed by Muscat, the efforts of Muscat to extend its power over a greater area of the Gulf, and the efforts of all concerned to dominate the pearl fisheries.

The pirates came from several ports in the Gulf. One of the most notable was Rahmān ibn Jabr of Qatar, who operated also from ports in al-Hasā and for whom Wahhābism was an excellent excuse to prosecute his bitter feud with Bahrain. In the light of the anti-European explanation of piracy, it is noteworthy that Rahmān never attacked British vessels and maintained friendly relations with British agents.[15] Bahrain itself was no innocent bystander, for it was a principal market for the sale of the spoils of piracy. But the principal marauders were the Qawāsim of the Gulf coast of Oman; in 1808, their fleet numbered 65 large vessels, 800 smaller boats, and 19,000 men. Their principal victims were Muscati vessels, but their ravages embraced other shipping, including British and Indian, and the British retaliated with punitive expeditions in force in 1809 and 1820. In the end, piracy was self-destructive, for the ravages of maritime warfare, by making pearling increasingly perilous and trade more and more unprofitable, impoverished the peoples of the Gulf and drove more and more of them to piracy. It seemed, however, impossible for the Arabs to achieve an agreement alone; some outside power was required to assume a regulating role, and that office was accepted—reluctantly, and after other modes had failed—by Britain, which, through the device of the Trucial system, achieved a voluntary cessation and eventual end to maritime warfare and to piracy.[16]

The Trucial system benefited the states involved because it ended the inconveniences and hardships caused by sea warfare. It also enabled Arab shipping to compete again with European vessels which, because of the insecurity in the Gulf, had been carrying a larger share of the region's trade. Trade itself expanded from the low point to which it had fallen in the mid-1830s when the Trucial system was introduced. Statistics are too imperfect to permit precise statements, but it is noteworthy that fluctuations in trade by no means varied inversely with the incidence of piracy, leading to the conclusion that piracy was certainly not the only constraint upon trade and perhaps not even the principal one. Factors such as outbreaks of plague and cholera in the surrounding areas and disturb-

14. Sir J. Malcolm, *Sketches of Persia* (London, 1861), p. 15. On piracy see Lorimer, *Gazetteer,* 1: 633–719; Kelly, *Britain and the Persian Gulf,* pp. 99–259; D. Hawley, *The Trucial States* (London, 1970), pp. 90–125; Sir Charles Belgrave, *The Pirate Coast* (London, 1970); H. Moyse Bartlett, *The Pirates of Trucial Oman* (London, 1966); Sir Arnold Wilson, *The Persian Gulf* (London, 1954), pp. 192–212.

15. Lorimer, *Gazetteer,* 1: 206–7. See the description of the death of Rahmān in C. R. Low, *History of the Indian Navy,* 2 vols. (London, 1877), 2: 198.

16. For the Trucial system, see Kelly, *Britain and the Persian Gulf,* pp. 354–409.

ances in Iraq and Iran during the 1830s also had their effect, and there may be connections with world trade patterns. Statistics show a marked rise in the amount of trade passing through the Gulf between the mid-1830s and 1860, although the estimated increase of more than 200 percent may be partly the consequence of selecting too low a base figure. Although it is reasonable to attribute some part of the undoubted increase in trade to improved security in the Gulf, the benefits accrued neither to Muscat nor to the Trucial states, but mainly to Bahrain, which was certainly aided by the greater security on the pearl banks, and, to a lesser extent, also to Kuwait, which now became a significant carrier of Gulf trade. Peace also benefited Iran and Iraq, since these countries were major participants in trade, although they did not carry it. A major beneficiary was Britain, not only because of the greater freedom of trade, but because she was able to reduce the expense of naval patrols. Some patrolling was still necessary because piracy was not wholly eliminated, and pirates continued to operate from ports outside the Trucial system.[17] Information about pirates operating from the Arab-controlled ports on the Iranian coast is deficient, but it is evident that there was some activity that the Iranian government was unable to regulate, although the Iranian authorities would not admit that this was so. In 1820, Iranian officials had refused to allow Britain to act against these pirates, and no satisfactory arrangement was made until 1846, when an unofficial agreement between the British resident and the governor of Fārs permitted Britain to act in the name of Iran.[18] A similar situation obtained in areas claimed by the Ottomans, and Bahrain represented yet another loophole that Britain dared not try to regulate by agreement because of the complications into which this might draw her. Finally, the persistence of land warfare, which was unrestricted, was still a potent cause of unrest.

Another well-established feature of Gulf life, and one which was also restricted during the nineteenth century, was the African slave trade.[19] The principal practitioner of this trade was Sayyid Saʻīd of Muscat, whose dominions in Zanzibar and Muscat were ideally positioned for carrying on the trade. By a series of treaties between 1838 and 1856, Sayyid Saʻīd bowed to British demands to restrict the trade. The Ottomans, the Trucial shaikhs, and Bahrain also agreed to forbid the carrying of slaves in their vessels, and in 1848 Iran went still further and prohibited the import of slaves into Iran by sea in any vessel. There were still loopholes in the arrangements, not least the lack of adequate forces to police the seas, and the agreement of some of the signatories was less than whole-hearted. Iran refused to allow Britain the right of search until 1852, although once commited to the abolition of the trade, Iran made determined efforts to eradicate it. A major problem was the continuation of the slave trade between the African mainland and Zanzibar, and this was not banned until 1873. Another problem was the existence of a second source of supply of slaves in Abyssinia, and this source tended to replace Zanzibar. But in the latter part of the nineteenth century, the pressure of international agreements, the European occupation of the

17. See ibid., pp. 249–51.
18. Ibid., p. 377. In 1832, the Governor of Fārs demanded British assistance against the Qawāsim pirates, Lorimer, *Gazetteer*, 1: 1954.
19. Kelly, *Britain and the Persian Gulf*, pp. 411–51, 576–637.

African coast, and more effective enforcement gradually extinguished the trade, although pockets of slavery in some form or other have survived until recent times.[20]

By the middle of the nineteenth century, the situation in the Gulf had materially altered. In the absence of an efficient regulator from the regional powers, Britain had been gradually drawn into the position of becoming the guarantor of maritime peace and had assumed also the task of ending the slave trade. The British intervention was already beginning to have a further effect, for stabilizing the area inevitably meant a freezing of the existing distribution of power. By obstructing the resolution of conflict through the emergence of a new powerful local state, Britain contrived to assist in the development of a situation in which a number of small powers coexisted under the British umbrella.

Of the regional powers, neither Mamlūk Iraq, nor the Ottomans, nor Iran had the resources with which to impose their control upon the area. For a time it seemed possible that Egypt might succeed in so doing. In 1817–18, the operations of Muhammad ʿAlī's forces against Najd smashed the power of the Wahhābīs for a short time, and Britain hoped to persuade the Egyptians to assume a larger role in the area.[21] Muhammad ʿAlī retired his forces to the Hijāz, but in 1837 his forces returned and under Khūrshīd Pasha became active in the Gulf region. Egyptian ambitions were reported to embrace Bahrain, Oman, Kuwait, and Basra, but Muhammad ʿAlī always disclaimed any intention of seeking power in the Gulf.[22] In any case, the Egyptian action came to nothing because the war in Syria caused Muhammad ʿAlī to withdraw his forces from Najd in 1840, and his defeat forced him to abandon all his claims in Arabia in favor of his suzerain, the Ottoman sultan. The Egyptian effort may, nevertheless, have been sufficient to prevent the emergence of another local regulator in the form of the Wahhābīs, who, at the beginning of the nineteenth century, had seemed most likely to impose their power on the Arabian coast. Their failure was partly due to the resistance of the Gulf states, partly to internal divisions within Arabia, but in no small degree to the devastating Egyptian invasions of Najd. The first Egyptian campaign in 1818 was an attempt to destroy the foundations of Wahhābī power, which the settled parts of the Ottoman world saw as a menace to the established political and social order. Wahhābī leaders were executed, date palms destroyed, and fortresses razed to the ground. The capital, Darʿiyya, was completely destroyed. "The first of it is rain, and the last of it is hail and lightning," remarked the Wahhābī chronicler Ibn Bishr concerning the Egyptian onslaught.[23] Although the Egyptian forces retired in 1819, they returned in 1820 to plant garrisons in the principal towns, and it was not until 1824 that the spirit of Najdi independence became too strong for them to withstand and the last Egyptian garrisons were withdrawn. After this severe blow, Saʿūdī power did subsequently revive from the new capital at Riyadh; their authority was re-established in the towns and their control over the Banū Khālid and al-Hasā resumed in 1830. The way seemed clear for the Saʿūdīs to impose their control on

20. Hawley, *The Trucial States*, p. 172.
21. George Sadleir, *Diary of a Journey across Arabia* (New York, 1977), p. 7.
22. H. Dodwell, *The Founder of Modern Egypt* (Cambridge, 1931), p. 143.
23. Quoted by Winder, *Saudi Arabia*, p. 124.

Oman, via Buraimi, and in 1833 Sayyid Sa'īd agreed to pay tribute to Riyadh. But just when it seemed that the Wahhābī power might be fastened upon the Arabian coast of the Gulf, internal dissension weakened Sa'ūdī purpose and in 1837 the Egyptians returned to complete the destruction of the Wahhābī hopes. When Wahhābī power rose for a third time, the British regulating system was already in operation. Also it is evident that by then the edge had been taken off Sa'ūdī ambitions. During the second reign of Faisal ibn Turkī (1843–65), the ruler concentrated mainly on internal consolidation and reorganization, although he maintained control over al-Hasā, extracted tribute from Oman, and kept up his claims to Bahrain. Nevertheless, the last chance that the Wahhābī state would assume a dominant position on the Gulf coast disappeared with his death and the subsequent dissension within the Sa'ūdī state.

The decline of the influence of Najd in the Gulf during the latter half of the nineteenth century was paralleled by an increase in the power of the other two regional powers: those based in Baghdad and Tehran. In Iraq, the hopes of independence seemingly cherished by Dā'ūd Pasha, the last of the Mamlūks, were frustrated by a devastating outbreak of plague in Iraq in 1830 and by the Ottoman resurgence under Mahmūd II. Ottoman power was reestablished in Iraq in 1831, and shortly afterward the movement of centralization and governmental and institutional reform known as the *Tanzīmāt* began to be applied in the area. Iraq remained a backwater of the Ottoman empire, and progress was less rapid in the Iraqi provinces than elsewhere; but there was some measurable development in communications through the use of steam navigation on the Tigris and Euphrates and the introduction of the telegraph, and some progress in increasing the authority of government over the tribes. The most eminent of the Ottoman governors in Iraq, Midhat Pasha (1869–71) decided to extend Ottoman authority along the Arabian shores of the Gulf, a move that complemented the similar Ottoman action in western Arabia that sought to advance Ottoman power into the Yemen.[24] Disputes within the Sa'ūdī family after the death of Faisal provided an opportunity when one claimant appealed to the Ottomans for assistance. In 1871, an Ottoman seaborne expedition from Basra landed on the Hasā coast, took Qatīf and pushed inland toward Najd. Although they were unable to complete the extension of their power in eastern Arabia, they remained in Hasā to represent a new factor in Gulf politics. As a European state, the Ottomans brought in the problems of European politics, and these complications were not made easier by the suspicious approach of Sultan 'Abd al-Hamīd II to all negotiations. A dormant, disregarded Ottoman claim had become a reality, and although the Ottomans lacked the power to enforce their claims, they were willing to bide their time. In the meantime, their presence affected the attitudes of factions throughout the Gulf area, not only in the northern part of the coast but in Qatar, Bahrain, and Trucial Oman. In Central Arabia, although they were not themselves able to assert direct control over Najd, they were able to do so partly by proxy through the power of the Āl Rashīd family of Hā'il. In the longer term, the Ottomans threatened to become a major power in the area through the con-

24. Longrigg, *Four Centuries*, pp. 277–324; Ali Haidar Midhat, *Life of Midhat Pasha* (London, 1903).

struction of the Baghdad railway. The railway line eastward from Istanbul was begun in 1889; in 1898 a plan was drawn up to extend it to the Gulf, and in 1903 the Ottoman government granted a concession for the construction of a line from Baghdad to Basra with a branch to the Gulf. Commonly regarded as an extension of German influence toward the Gulf, the Baghdad railway was in reality a device for the extension of Ottoman power; the chosen route was selected in accordance with Ottoman strategic requirements, even if these happened to coincide in large measure with German economic needs.[25]

The second half of the nineteenth century also witnessed a notable extension of Iranian influence in the area of the Gulf. For most of the early nineteenth century, the Iranian authorities had played a weak hand with much skill. They had maintained the appearance and style of a power that they could not, in fact, exercise, asserting their claims at every opportunity and protesting strongly at any supposed infraction of their rights. They resisted successfully several British efforts to obtain a base on Iranian territory and even secured a document (the so-called treaty of Shīrāz of 1822), which they implausibly claimed to constitute a British recognition of their claims to Bahrain. Contemporary Britons characterized this combination of weakness and verbal assertiveness as mere vanity, as they were also inclined to do many years later when the same technique was practiced by Charles de Gaulle; but it is not uncommon to resent in others behavior that in oneself is held to betoken a strong will and unyielding determination. The argument for intransigence was put in its bleakest form by the great Iranian minister Amīr-i Kabīr, in 1850, when he remarked that Iranians, lacking patriotism and becoming weak in religious solidarity, would be more inclined to seek foreign protection if they saw their own government bending to foreign pressure.[26] Nor was Britain the only European power concerned with Iran. Even if Iranians had been satisfied that Britain would not take advantage of any concessions to increase British influence among southern Iranian tribes (and Iran had some reason to doubt that Britain would not take such advantage), it was evident that any concessions to Britain in the Gulf would have to be matched by similar concessions to Russia in the Caspian region and elsewhere in the north.

Having survived the first half of the nineteenth century (including the British occupation of Khārg, 1838–42, and the Anglo-Iranian war of 1856–57, when Britain occupied Khārg, Bushire, and Muhammara) without conceding any ground in the area of the Gulf, Iran began to extend her power in that direction during the latter part of the century. Several strands contributed to this movement: the fears aroused by British intervention; the result of the consolidation of Qājār authority; the obstruction of the realization of Qājār ambitions in other directions, such as in Transcaucasia, Turkestan, Afghanistan, and Iraq; desire to protect a valuable trade (Iran always had the largest share of Gulf trade); and lastly a desire to increase customs revenues, which formed a very

25. E. M. Earle, *Turkey, the Great Powers and the Baghdad Railway* (New York, 1923); L. Ragey, *La question du chemin de fer de Baghdad 1843–1914* (Paris, 1936); M. K. Chapman, *Great Britain and the Baghdad Railway, 1888–1914* (Cambridge, Mass., 1948); H. S. W. Corrigan, "British, French and German Interests in Asiatic Turkey, 1881–1914." Ph.D. thesis, University of London, 1954.

26. Kelly, *Britain and the Persian Gulf*, p. 609.

substantial part of Iranian government revenue and which became particularly important because they could be increased more easily than could other sources of revenue and could be pledged against foreign loans.

Iran steadily reduced Arab influence on the Gulf coast. In 1856, the lease of Bandar 'Abbās to Muscat was renewed on more stringent terms, which included a high rental and the recognition of Iranian sovereignty over Qishm and Hormuz held by Muscat by right of conquest since 1798; and in 1868 the lease was canceled.[27] Iranian authority over Lingeh was also resumed; from 1874, Iran interfered increasingly, and in 1887 the Qāsimī ruler was arrested and replaced by an Iranian administrator of the Gulf ports.[28] On the Gulf of Oman coast, Iranian control over Baluchistan was extended after 1856, leading to the occupation of Chāhbahār, which was recognized as Iranian by the Boundary Commission of 1872. By this date, Arab influence on the coast of Iranian Baluchistan had disappeared. The Iranian claim to Bahrain, which had never been allowed to lapse, was asserted more loudly in 1860 and 1869. In 1889, there was some evidence of Iranian interest in the Trucial coast, although when challenged the Iranian government repudiated the former official responsible for proposing joint action to exclude British influence from Abū Dhabī and Dubai.[29] In 1900, another Iranian approach to Abū Dhabī (also probably unauthorized) was stopped after British protests.[30] In 1904, Iran emphasized her claim to Abū Mūsā and the Tunbs by setting up a customs house and guards, but these were withdrawn after British objections.[31] Britain eventually took the view that Abū Mūsā belonged to Sharja and the Tunbs to Ra's al-Khaima. Iranian administration in the Gulf area was also improved with a careful allocation of responsibility between the governors of Fārs (including Bushire), Lāristān (including Lingeh and Bandar 'Abbās), and Kirmān (the Makrān coast, including Chāhbahār). Weaknesses in Iranian control still remained in the north, in Khuzistan, where the Iranian governor in Shūshtar was obliged to acknowledge that real power was in the hands of the shaikh of the Muhaisin Arabs whose center was Muhammara (Khurramshahr), a town rebuilt in 1812, made a free port in the 1830s, and rapidly expanded following the opening of the Kārūn river to navigation.[32] Even so, it was the judgment of that acute observer, George Curzon, that the power of Tehran would also be confirmed in Muhammara.[33] Perhaps the most striking manifestation of the power of Iran in the Gulf was the activities of the reformed Iranian customs administration under Belgian control in the Gulf ports. Merchants complained bitterly about the conduct of the Belgians, but essentially they were complaining that slack Iranian control, easily avoided in the past, was replaced by an efficient organization anxious to collect as much revenue as possible for the Iranian government.[34] Perhaps the two most evident remaining weaknesses of the Iranian position on the Gulf by 1900 were the want

27. Lorimer, *Gazetteer*, 1: 2045–47.
28. Ibid., 1: 2063–65.
29. Ibid., 1: 737.
30. Ibid., 1: 744.
31. Ibid., 1: 745.
32. For the history of Khuzistan, see ibid., 1: 1625–1775.
33. G. N. Curzon, *Persia and the Persian Question*, 2 vols. (London, 1892), 2: 326–27.
34. Lorimer, *Gazetteer*, 2: 2594–2625.

of a railway and a navy; the first, to improve her internal communications in the south and to increase her control over the ports, and the second, to enable her to extend her power to the waters of the Gulf. The reasons why she had neither are too complex to analyze here; they were partly financial, economic, and political (the weakness of Qājār government), and partly diplomatic (the product of the conflict of British and Russian interests).[35]

The slow revival of Iranian power in the Gulf region came to an abrupt end in 1906 with the constitutional revolution, which was in part a struggle for power in Tehran and in part a struggle for provincial independence of control by Tehran. Along the Gulf coast, Iranian government power melted away and communications into the interior fell under the domination of the tribes.[36]

Just as there were significant changes in the relationships of the regional powers with the Gulf during the second half of the nineteenth century, so there were also changes in the position of the international powers. This change was partly the consequence of further developments in communications, i.e., steam navigation in the 1820s, its application to communications between Europe and the east in the 1830s and 1840s, and its upsurge after the opening of the Suez Canal in 1869 cut transport costs and helped to produce major changes in the economic relationships between various parts of the world, expanding trade, promoting specialization, and creating a world market in many commodities. The Gulf, as a mercantile outlier of the Indian system, was mainly affected when a steam service began between Bombay and Gulf ports in 1862, carried on by what became the British India Steam Navigation Company. These changes did not lead to a major increase in the trade of the Gulf; after a sudden jump in the 1860s inspired by the worldwide cotton boom caused by the American Civil War, the trade leveled off at between £5 and £6 million a year, where it remained for the last thirty years of the nineteenth century. But the changes did redistribute the trade. European steam vessels now monopolized the long-distance trade, and the Arab craft were confined (apart from their illegal employment in slaving or arms smuggling) to the interport trade in the Gulf itself. Because so many ports were unsuitable for use by steamers, this still left opportunities for the Arabs and some made use of them. Another effect of the use of steamers was to enhance the importance of the major Gulf ports of Bushire, Basra, and Muhammara; the former entrepôt system that had been the basis of the prosperity of Muscat and other ports declined.[37]

With the advent of the telegraph, the Gulf became an obvious area through which to link the European and eastern systems. Negotiations began in 1861 and construction in 1863. Between 1863 and 1905, a system of land and submarine cables was extended throughout the region. Economically its effect was to link the economy of the Gulf area more closely with the outside world; politically

35. See, in general, F. Kazemzadeh, *Russia and Britain in Persia, 1864–1914* (New Haven, 1968).

36. See P. Avery, *Modern Iran* (London, 1967); Sir F. C. O'Connor, *On the Frontier and Beyond* (London, 1931).

37. R. G. Landen, *Oman since 1856*, esp. pp. 79–81. On the telegraph, see Sir F. Goldsmid, *Telegraph and Travel* (London, 1974), and Lorimer, *Gazetteer*, 1: 2400–38. On communications generally, see H. L. Hoskins, *British Routes to India* (London, 1928).

the telegraph made it easier for the international and regional powers to operate in the Gulf area. Although it has rightly been observed that these technological developments increased European influence on the Gulf, it should be noted that the telegraph, like the new patterns of trade, also served to enhance the facility with which governments in Baghdad and Tehran could influence Gulf affairs. Iranian objections to the construction of the telegraph on the northern shore of the Gulf were not based on hostility to the telegraph as such, but on fears that its development under British control would hinder the extension of Iranian control in Makrān; instead, Iran wanted a line that would serve her purposes by linking Tehran with Bushire and connecting with the Ottoman and European systems at Khāniqīn. Indeed, in a long perspective it could be claimed that these developments were ultimately more important to the regional powers than to the international powers, for the Gulf remained an area that was relatively unattractive to Europeans until the discovery of oil. In a period of expanding world trade, the stagnant trade of the Gulf offered few allurements to European businessmen. Although the second half of the nineteenth and first years of the twentieth centuries saw novel activities by various European firms in the area—steamships, trading houses, railway projects, and the like—they appear of little consequence when judged by developments elsewhere, and became notorious more for their apparent political implications than for their economic promise. In relation to our theme of the relationship between circles of power, the chief importance of these developments affecting the international powers is that, like the increased activity of the regional powers, they contributed to diminish the independence of the local powers.[38]

Among the local powers the most dramatic event of the later nineteenth century was the decline of Muscat and Oman. Muscat lost its trading eminence, suffered a catastrophic fall in government revenues, and saw a striking fall in the population of its coastal towns; the population of Muscat and Matrah fell from about 70,000 in the 1850s to less than 20,000 in 1900. Several reasons for this decline have been propounded; European trade competition, inferior rulers after the death of Sayyid Saʿīd in 1856, Wahhābī inroads every decade until their expulsion from Buraimī in 1869, and currency problems arising from the decline in the value of silver. Nevertheless, two factors stand out. One is the division of Sayyid Saʿīd's empire after his death. The partition took from the ruler of Muscat the major source of his revenue and also his fleet. "I have been given the bone but Mājid [in Zanzibar] the flesh," complained Thuwainī ibn Saʿīd.[39] The second is partly a consequence of the resultant poverty of the Muscati state; a changed relationship between the coastal area and the interior of Oman. Saʿīd's wealth had enabled him to control the interior through subsidies, an expensive armed force, and control of access to the wealthy ports. These assets were denied to Thuwainī and his successors, and resentment of Muscati domination and its (to them) infidel styles increased, until it broke forth in a rising in 1868 that led

38. See Kazemzadeh, *Russia and Britain*; R. L. Greaves, *Persia and the Defence of India, 1884–1892* (London, 1959); J. B. Plass, *England zwischen Russland und Deutschland* (Hamburg, 1966), pp. 395–457; B. G. Martin, *German-Persian Diplomatic Relations, 1878–1912* (The Hague, 1959).

39. Quoted by Kelly, *Britain and the Persian Gulf*, p. 541; see also Landen, *Oman since 1856*.

to the installation of a new ruler, the Imam 'Azzān ibn Qais. Although the rule of the Sa'īd branch was restored in 1871, the sultans of Muscat never fully controlled the interior. A variety of devices, nevertheless, enabled them to influence it successfully until 1895, when a new general uprising broke out. The sultan survived in Muscat, but Ibādī contempt abided and led to a fresh uprising in 1914, which was beaten off only with British assistance. One would not wish to exaggerate the decline of the power of the sultans; even in the heyday of Muscat, they had never administered the interior, but they had maintained an influence that had enabled the two halves of Oman to live in fruitful harmony. It was this working relationship that broke down in the 1860s. Some compensation was found by the sultans in their extension of their power to Dhufar, which was annexed in 1879 and which, in a very minor way, was to play something of the same part formerly played by Zanzibar as a separate reservoir of power for the sultanate.[40]

One important effect of Muscat's decline was that the rulers became more and more dependent upon Britain. Britain controlled the payment of the Zanzibar subsidy (given to the Muscat rulers in compensation for the loss of revenues from the African empire), and in 1900 this subsidy was equal to one-fifth of the sultan's revenue; also, in the last analysis, the sultan was kept in power by British troops. Hence, although he was preserved from the formal loss of his independence by the circumstance of the joint Anglo-French declaration of 1862, he was obliged to admit increasing British control through a nonalienation agreement in 1891, British intervention to limit the arms traffic through Muscati ports, and British jurisdiction over the British–Indian merchants who controlled most of the trade of Muscat.[41]

Trucial Oman, which had never enjoyed the prosperity of Muscat, had less margin for decline. The most notable features of its internal development were the reduction of the power of the Qawāsim after the death of Sultan ibn Saqr in 1866, when the Qawāsim lands were divided; and the rise of the power of the rulers of Abū Dhabī. For this change in the balance of power, British influence may be held partly responsible, for the Qawāsim strength had always been greatest at sea, where it was restricted by the operation of the Trucial system, whereas the Banū Ya's strength was on land, where no limitations were placed on the use of force. The predominance of the Banū Ya's also owed something to the removal of the Wahhābī presence from Buraimī in 1869. One important factor was undoubtedly the ability of Shaikh Zaid ibn Khalīfa, who ruled Abū Dhabī from 1855 until 1908 and who slew the Qāsimī Shaikh Khālid ibn Sultān in personal combat in 1868. Although it was not undisputed, Abū Dhabī predominance endured into the twentieth century. A second significant development on the Trucial coast during the same period was the rise of Dubai, which by the late 1870s had become the largest port on the Trucial coast, profiting from the decline of the Qawāsim ports. During the last years of the nineteenth century and the first years of the twentieth, Dubai consolidated its position as the leading

40. See Lorimer, *Gazetteer*, 1: 589–601.

41. Landen, *Oman since 1856;* see also Ravinder Kumar, *India and the Persian Gulf Region, 1858–1907* (London, 1965), pp. 60–103; B. C. Busch, *Britain and the Persian Gulf, 1894–1914* (Berkeley, 1967).

commercial center on the coast; it attracted Arab traders from Lingeh, which had become less inviting to merchants after the resumption of Iranian control. The final development that should be noted here is the formalization of British control through a series of agreements concluded in 1887–92 and providing for non-alienation of territory and British control of foreign affairs.[42]

British influence also increased over Bahrain during the second half of the nineteenth century. The pearl-trade wealth of Bahrain always made it a tempting prize, and at various times it was coveted by Oman, Egypt, the Wahhābīs, Iran, and the Ottomans. Opportunities for outside intervention were enhanced by dissensions among the members of the ruling Āl Khalīfa family and by the continuing connection between the Āl Khalīfa and the settlement of Zubāra on Qatar. In 1854, Muhammad Āl Khalīfa's attempt to throw off the Wahhābī control imposed upon him in 1851 led to a Wahhābī attack upon Bahrain and compelled Muhammad to seek British help. The price was the acceptance of some measure of British control, which so irked Muhammad that he sought alternative protectors in the form of Iran and the Ottomans. "I shall be on the side of him who is stronger," he remarked with more circumspection than bravery.[43] Like most of us he wanted the impossible—a protector strong enough to protect but not strong enough to interfere. In fact, it was because Britain feared that Iranian or Ottoman protection would not be sufficiently strong, rather than because she feared a challenge to her own power, that she intervened to force Bahrain into the Trucial system. The danger was that a weak, uncontrolled Bahrain would disrupt the whole system of maritime peace of which Britain was the guarantor. Further British interventions inevitably followed; in 1880 and 1892 further agreements gave Britain control over Bahrain foreign relations and the alienation of Bahraini territory.

British control was also extended over Kuwait. Throughout the nineteenth century, Kuwait had developed steadily under the rule of the Āl Sabāh family. In 1862–63, the explorer, W. G. Palgrave, described it in glowing terms as the most active port in the northern Gulf.[44] Official British interest, however, was slight; Kuwait was regarded as an Ottoman dependency and approaches from its rulers were rejected.[45] The Ottoman expedition against Hasā in 1871 brought Kuwait more closely under Ottoman control, and from then onward the Āl Sabāh ruler seems to have been recognized as an Ottoman official (qā'im-maqām). Following the death of 'Abdallāh ibn Sabāh (1866–92), Kuwait appeared to drift closer to the Ottomans under the rule of his brother and successor Muhammad. In 1896, Muhammad was killed by his half-brother, Mubārak, who, to escape Ottoman control or vengeance, appealed to Britain for protection. After some discussion, an agreement was concluded that provided for nonalienation and British control of foreign affairs, in effect an informal protectorate. Seemingly, Kuwait had passed from the Ottoman to the British sphere of influence, but such

42. Hawley, *The Trucial States*, pp. 142–49.
43. Quoted by Kelly, *Britain and the Persian Gulf*, p. 516. On Bahrain, see also F. Adamiyat, *Bahrain Islands* (New York, 1955); and A. Faroughy, *The Bahrain Islands* (New York, 1951).
44. W. G. Palgrave, *A Year's Journey through Central and Eastern Arabia*, 2 vols. (London, 1865).
45. Lorimer, *Gazetteer*, 1: 1012–15.

was not entirely the case; in 1913, an Anglo-Ottoman agreement recognized that Kuwait was part of the Ottoman empire but exempted it from Ottoman administration and accepted the Anglo-Kuwaiti agreement. The ultimate fate of Kuwait was not then finally determined.[46]

To conclude this survey of the Gulf during the last years of the nineteenth and first years of the twentieth centuries, it is necessary to observe the recovery of the power of Najd after its long eclipse during the last thirty years of the nineteenth century. The decline of Sa'ūdī power was due to three factors. Dissension between the sons of Faisal led to prolonged civil war when, wrote the chronicler, Ibn 'Īsā, "the people were largely given over to famine, hunger, trials, plunder, killing, dissension, and rapidly stalking death."[47] Second, the Ottoman conquest of al-Hasā deprived the Sa'ūdīs of one of their richest provinces. Third, there was the rise of the power of the Rashīdī family of Hā'il in the north. The Rashīdīs had ruled Hā'il for the Sa'ūdīs since 1835. From 1872–97 they were led by the diminutive but very able Muhammad ibn Rashīd, who dominated the politics of eastern Arabia during his reign. Gradually he extended his power southward and in 1887 placed a Rashīdī garrison in Riyadh. In 1890, at the great battle of Mulaida, Muhammad ibn Rashīd crushed his enemies and forced the Sa'ūdī claimant 'Abd al-Rahmān ibn Faisal to flee to Kuwait with his son 'Abd al-'Azīz. Only after the death of Muhammad did Rashīdī control weaken, and in 1902 the young 'Abd al-'Azīz was able to recapture Riyadh. Still the Sa'ūdīs trod warily to avoid alienating Britain, the Ottomans, and the Rashīdīs. But in 1913 'Abd al-'Azīz took advantage of the Ottoman preoccupation with Europe to recover al-Hasā. Thus, although still heavily constrained and obliged to acknowledge Ottoman sovereignty, 'Abd āl-'Azīz was poised to play a major part in developments in the Gulf area. The long occlusion of the power of Najd was almost at an end.[48]

In terms of the circles of power, suggested at the beginning of this chapter, the half century that ended in 1914 had seen significant but inconclusive changes in the area of the Gulf. The local powers had maintained their existence, but had lost some freedom of action, partly to the regional powers and partly to Britain. For some time it had seemed that the regional powers might emerge as the dominant powers in the Gulf, but Iran and the Ottomans had not sustained their extended ambitions in the area and during the last decade their influence had waned. The causes of their failure must be sought in the internal problems of these two states: wars, revolutions, and inadequate modernization of their institutions left them too weak to assume the role of regulators of the Gulf. For most of the period, Najd was in eclipse. Accordingly, it was Britain who, having resisted the half-hearted challenges of the other international powers, was left as the only one with the capability to regulate affairs in the Gulf. Britain had not

---

46. See Busch, *Britain and the Persian Gulf*, pp. 330–47. See also P. Graves, *Life of Sir Percy Cox* (London, 1942), pp. 168–70. Text in *British Documents on the Origins of the War*, 10: 190–94.

47. Quoted by Winder, *Saudi Arabia*, p. 251.

48. See Winder, *Saudi Arabia*; H. St. J. B. Philby, *Saudi Arabia* (London, 1955). A copy of the treaty between Ibn Sa'ūd and the Ottomans of 15 May 1914 is given in G. Troeller, *The Birth of Saudi Arabia* (London, 1976), pp. 248–49. There are several descriptions of Hā'il, a favorite resort of many European travelers; see R. Bidwell, *Travellers in Arabia* (London, 1976).

sought this task, and the evidence suggests that the cabinet at least would have been willing to share it with others; British policy toward Ottoman and Iranian claims was generally conciliatory. But in the end Britain had been obliged to come forward, particularly on the Arabian shore where the weakness of Najd left a mighty vacuum. Britain had used her power to preserve the status quo and to try to support it by formal agreements of all those concerned, in effect, to preserve the Gulf in an internationally approved aspic jelly.

The Ottoman entry into World War I on the side of the Central Powers and the subsequent operations in the area transformed the political structure of the Gulf. By 1919, Britain was supreme in the region. Her international rivals, Russia and Germany, had gone down in defeat; so had the Ottoman empire, leaving Iraq securely in the hands of Britain. Iran was also seemingly at Britain's mercy, and 'Abd al-'Azīz was a British dependent. Thus, the regional powers were all dominated by Britain. British power was also predominant among the local powers of the Gulf: in Oman, Britain defended the sultan against his enemies and in 1920 mediated the Treaty of Sīb, which achieved an amicable agreement between Muscat and the interior; on the Trucial coast, there was no challenge to Britain; in 1916, Qatar had been incorporated within the Trucial system; British influence in Bahrain was paramount (in 1918, the Bahrain Order-in-Council of 1913 was brought into force, giving Britain control over the legal system and British pressure for reform forced the abdication of Shaikh 'Īsā in 1923). Kuwait was now formally a British protectorate, and British influence also prevailed in Muhammara, which was beginning to aspire to independence, in emulation of Kuwait.[49]

British supremacy in the Gulf in 1919 was a flash in the pan; not the inevitable result of a steady program of historic advance, but an accident of war. Within a few years it had disappeared; Britain could not retain control over the regional powers. In Iraq, Britain set up an Arab government in 1921, made treaties in 1922 and 1930, and relinquished her mandate in 1932. In Iran, the Anglo-Iranian agreement of 1919 was rejected by Iran and the British withdrew their troops from the country. In Arabia, 'Abd al-'Azīz emancipated himself from British control and secured recognition of his independence in 1927. The question that must be asked is why the regional powers did not at once proceed to assert their power more fully in the Gulf area, and why they left Britain to enjoy for some years the illusion of supremacy? The answer is to be found in the preoccupation of the regional powers with internal modernization.

Iraq faced the problem of constructing a state from the most recalcitrant materials, for few people in Iraq wanted an Iraqi state. Under the rule of the Hashimite kings, Iraq first developed an army to take over internal security duties from the British. Recruitment began in 1921 and limited conscription was introduced in 1934. By 1936, the army numbered 23,000 and, in addition, a strong

---

49. There is a very extensive literature on the war. See the notes to the article "British Policy in the Persian Gulf" and the bibliography in Busch, *Britain and the Persian Gulf*. For a survey of the situation in 1919, see *The Persian Gulf* (London: HMSO, 1920) (No. 76 of the Foreign Office Handbooks prepared for the Peace Conference). On Muscat, see Ian Skeet, *Muscat and Oman* (London, 1974), and on Bahrain, M. G. Rumaihi, *Bahrain: Social and Political Change since the First World War* (London, 1976).

force of 9,000 police was built up to share internal constabulary tasks. The army demonstrated its ability to suppress Arab tribal uprisings; the last great convulsion was crushed in 1936. Only in the Kurdish areas of the north was the army unable to achieve a final victory. It was this work of internal consolidation and the construction of an administrative apparatus suitable to the new tasks that consumed the energies of the Iraqi government; in so far as it had time for foreign policy, it was more concerned with projects for Fertile Crescent unity than with the Gulf, where it was content to allow Britain to safeguard the approaches to Basra.[50]

Iran was absorbed in similar tasks. The dominant personality in the new government that came to power in February 1921 was Rizā Khan, later Rizā Shah Pahlavi. As minister of war from 1921 to 1924, Rizā built a new Iranian army from the former Cossack Brigade and from remnants of the other military forces raised in Iran. The strength was raised to 40,000 and eventually, by 1941, to a nominal 80,000. With the aid of this army, Rizā was able to check separatist movements in the provinces and to crush tribal opposition to the power of the central government; in 1925, the Qashqā'īs and the Bakhtīyārīs were disarmed and pacified. In the same year, Rizā extinguished the hopes of independence cherished by Shaikh Khaz'al of Muhammara. Rizā Shah also gave considerable attention to economic modernization, seeing as the key to this the construction of a railway system; the Trans-Iranian Railway, built between 1927 and 1938 at a cost of £30 million, linked the Caspian Sea with the Gulf eventually (the terminus for some years was Ahwāz) through Tehran, and work was started on an east-west line to link Mashhad with Tabrīz. Such work consumed Iranian resources and left little to sustain an active policy in the Gulf, although Rizā Shah was quick to assert Iranian claims; the claim to Bahrain was regularly made from 1927 onward and a small naval force based on Khurramshahr was created. British freedom of action on the Iranian shore was more and more circumscribed, so as to make it desirable to move the political and naval headquarters to the Arabian shore.[51]

Sa'ūdī Arabia also developed as a state in the period between the wars, although without the aid of the oil revenues that contributed to the modernization of Iraq and Iran. In 1920, 'Abd al-'Azīz, often known as Ibn Sa'ūd, conquered 'Asīr, in 1921 Hā'il, and in 1926 the Hijāz. Much of this work was accomplished through the militant support of the Ikhwān ("Brotherhood"), in effect, the power of tribes harnessed by Muslim revivalism and directed both toward agricultural settlement and to war. Their unruly strength was well suited to the expansion of Sa'ūdī power, but much less to its consolidation within the frontiers of a settled state, and in 1930 Ibn Sa'ūd broke the power of the rebellious Ikhwān tribes. The kingdom of Sa'ūdī Arabia formally emerged in 1932. These tasks of building and consolidating his power preoccupied 'Abd al-'Azīz, and he was content to

50. See P. W. Ireland, *Iraq* (London, 1937); S. H. Longrigg, *Iraq, 1900–50* (London, 1953); M. Khadduri, *Independent Iraq, 1932–1958* (London, 1960).

51. H. Amirsadeghi, ed., *Twentieth Century Iran* (London, 1977); J. Bharier, *Economic Development in Iran, 1900–1920* (London, 1971); A. Banani, *The Modernization of Iran, 1921–1941* (Stanford, 1961); R. Ramazani, *The Foreign Policy of Iran, 1500–1941* (Charlottesville, Va., 1966).

remain loyal to his agreements with Britain concerning the areas of the Gulf and made no attempt to interfere in Bahrain, Qatar, and Trucial Oman, although he pursued a long and bitter quarrel with Kuwait.[52]

These developments within the regional powers were the most significant changes in the Gulf region during the interwar years. In different degrees, the three regional powers consolidated their states, centralized their governments, developed administrations and armies, and moved toward the time when they would assume leading positions within the Gulf. Their capability for action was transformed and, from this time onward, except under the peculiar circumstances of war, British power functioned within a framework of consent by the regional powers. It was within that framework that Britain continued to exercise a preponderant influence over the local powers of the Arabian shore, an influence chiefly confined to protecting them from external threats.

The Gulf saw three important economic developments between the wars. First was the search for oil throughout the area; its successful exploitation in Iraq, Iran, and Bahrain; its discovery in Kuwait, Qatar, and Sa'ūdī Arabia; and the effects of these events in bringing new wealth to and new interest in the area.[53] Second was the development of new forms of communications: motor roads, railways in Iraq and Iran, radio and airlines.[54] The effect of these innovations was to reduce the isolation of the Gulf region. The third economic change was the decline of the pearl fisheries, the major industry of the Gulf itself. This last event, caused by the rise of the Japanese cultured pearl industry, had a devastating effect upon the economies of all the small Gulf states, with the exception of Bahrain, which was saved by the development of its oil. Trucial Oman was especially badly hit; the governments were impoverished and the standards of life of the people fell. Only Dubai with its entrepôt trade, was able to maintain reasonable prosperity.[55]

World War II had significant economic and political effects in the Gulf region. Economically, it was a period of hardship. The war imposed a temporary halt on economic development, particularly of oil production. Oil production in Iraq and Iran was cut back and did not recover to the prewar level until 1944. Exports of oil from Sa'ūdī Arabia had begun in 1939, but remained almost static for the following four years, and only in 1944 did production begin to expand rapidly. In Kuwait, the newly developed oil wells were shut down and not reopened until 1946. Oil production also ceased in Qatar in 1940 for the duration of the war. Only in Bahrain did oil production continue unaffected and the refinery was expanded. The problems of the oil industry were those of steel and tanker shortages. The war also brought about other shortages, alleviated

52. Philby, *Saudi Arabia*; H. R. P. Dickson, *Kuwait and Her Neighbours* (London, 1956).

53. On the Kuwait Oil Concession, see A. H. T. Chisholm, *The First Kuwait Oil Concession Agreement* (London, 1975) and H. V. F. Winstone and Zahra Freeth, *Kuwait: Prospect and Reality* (London, 1972), pp. 132–63.

54. On air routes, see R. Higham, *Britain's Imperial Air Routes, 1918–39* (London, 1960).

55. R. Hay, *The Persian Gulf States* (Washington, 1959), pp. 51; Sir Charles Belgrave, *Personal Column* (London, 1966); R. Bowen, "The pearl fisheries of the Persian Gulf," *Middle East Journal* (1951): 161–80. For a late description of the pearling industry, see R. O'Shea, *The Sand Kings of Oman* (London, 1947), pp. 130–42, although the statistics quoted there differ from those given elsewhere.

in the case of Bahrain by rationing, and the economies of all the countries of the area were controlled by Allied demands and organizations. There was also severe inflation. Not until 1944 did the situation begin to improve.

Politically, the main effect was a renewed expansion of British power in the area. Fear of Axis influence in Iraq and Iran led to armed British interventions in both countries and the installation of new governments more friendly to the Allied cause. In Iran, British intervention was made jointly with Russia, and Iran became a corridor through which aid was directed to Russia.[56] In the early years of the war, British influence also increased in Sa'ūdī Arabia as a consequence of the economic pressures that made Sa'ūdī Arabia dependent upon British subsidies.[57] In the smaller Gulf states, British influence was unchallenged. But this ebullition of British influence in the Gulf area proved to be a swan-song. In Sa'ūdī Arabia, British influence was replaced by that of the United States before the end of the war; British troops were withdrawn from Iran in 1946 and from Iraq (except for the authorized base garrisons) in 1947. In both countries, it was soon to be made clear that British domination was a thing of the past: in Iran, by the nationalization of the oil industry in 1951, and in Iraq, by the rejection of the Treaty of Portsmouth in 1948 and finally by the revolution of 1958.

The first prominent feature of the postwar period was the decline in the importance of the international circle of powers in the Gulf area. In the reduction of the British role, an important element was the withdrawal from India in 1947, although the significance of this act should not be exaggerated, as the trend of events had been visible for a long time. Although other powers from the international circle came to play a larger part in the Gulf, none assumed the former British role. India and Pakistan were absorbed in nation building, economic development, internal political problems, and their own disputes, and took very little interest in the politics of the Gulf. Although individuals from these countries played important economic roles in the Gulf, India and Pakistan themselves had a diminishing economic influence; for example, in the 1920s 75 percent of Bahrain's imports came from India and in 1962 only 10 percent. The former economic dominance over the Gulf economy exercised by the Indian subcontinent was thus lost and the major trading partners of the Gulf states became the countries of Europe, the United States, and Japan. The influence of the United States increased, notably in Sa'ūdī Arabia and in Iran, through economic links and the supply of arms and other assistance; the Soviet Union entered the area through her program of assistance to Iraq after 1958, and through her association with revolutionary socialist groups such as the Tūdeh party in Iran; and as the leading Arab country and the standard bearer of Arab nationalism and radical change, Egypt came to exercise an influence in the Gulf area.[58]

But none of these countries enjoyed any influence comparable to the past economic and political eminence of Britain in the region. It is a curious fact that as the Gulf became, through the development of the oil industry, of so much greater consequence to the outside world, so the political influence of that world upon the Gulf declined.

56. R. Ramazani, *Iran's Foreign Policy, 1941–1973* (Charlottesville, Va., 1975).
57. J. Marlowe, *The Persian Gulf in the Twentieth Century* (London, 1962).
58. A recent study of Soviet interests in the Gulf is A. Yodfat and M. Abir, *In the Direction of the Persian Gulf* (London, 1977).

In contrast, the power of the regional states in the postwar world was much enhanced. This was to a considerable extent due to their growing wealth from oil. Iranian oil production was injured by the nationalization dispute of 1951–54, but following the settlement of that dispute and the stabilization of the political situation, Iran embarked upon ambitious projects of modernization. During the 1960s a fundamental transformation of Iran's social, economic, and political system was carried out under the name of the White Revolution.[59] These changes enabled Iran to pursue a more independent foreign policy and to play a larger part in regional affairs. Iran became more concerned about the security of the Gulf area after the Iraqi revolution of 1958 and the subsequent assertions of the claims of radical Arab nationalism, including the contention that Khuzistan was part of the Arab homeland. Confronted by possible threats to its security, to the free passage of trade (both exports of oil and imports of goods) through the Gulf, and to the major program of economic development in southern Iran which was planned, the Iranian government determined, after the announcement in 1968 of the intended British withdrawal, that no other international power would be allowed to replace Britain, and that the Gulf should become the preserve of the regional and Gulf powers. Her size, wealth, and military power marked Iran as a major regulator of Gulf affairs.[60]

Iraqi oil production grew slowly in the immediate postwar years and expanded rapidly only after the virtual cessation of Iranian production in 1951. During the 1950s, a program of long-term economic development was introduced, using oil revenues. The satisfaction of immediate wants and of the desire for social and political change was postponed, however. First, growing discontent, encouraged by the success of the Egyptian revolution of 1952, found expression in the Iraqi revolution of 1958, a major development in the history of the Gulf.[61] The revolution turned Iraq into the major exponent of radical Arab nationalism in the Gulf area; the existence of conservative or traditional regimes appeared both as an obstacle to the fulfillment of revolutionary Pan-Arab goals and as a menace to the security of the revolutionary regimes in Iraq. Second, the links immediately established with the USSR, culminating in the Iraq–Soviet treaty of 1972, gave the Soviet Union a position in the Gulf area and the use of Iraqi facilities. But in some respects the revolution weakened the ability of Iraq to act in the Gulf area: political instability led to the postponement of long-term economic development and a slower rise in oil wealth; existing internal discontents were not satisfied and opposition to the Baghdad government in the Kurdish areas became more violent and demanded a major military deployment in the north; Iraq's involvement in inter-Arab politics diverted her attention westward away from the Gulf.

59. H.I.M. Muhammad Rizā Shah Pahlavi, *Mission for My Country* (London, 1961), and *The White Revolution* (Tehran, 1967); A. K. S. Lambton, *The Persian Land Reform, 1962–1966* (Oxford, 1969); Ehsan Yar-Shater, ed., *Iran Faces the Seventies* (New York, 1971).

60. R. Ramazani, *The Persian Gulf: Iran's Role* (Charlottesville, Va., 1972). In his *Iran's Foreign Policy, 1941–1973*, p. 315, Dr. Ramazani argues that Iran's new, independent foreign policy predated the White Revolution and was a necessary precondition of reform, rather than the reverse. See also Amir Taheri, "Policies of Iran in the Foreign Gulf Region," in A. Amirie, ed., *The Persian Gulf and Indian Ocean in International Politics* (Tehran, 1975), pp. 259–78; and S. Zabih and S. Chubin, *Iran's Foreign Relations* (Berkeley, 1975).

61. M. Khadduri, *Republican Iraq* (London, 1969); U. Dann, *Iraq under Qassem* (London, 1969).

Most spectacular of all was the growth of Sa'ūdī Arabian oil production after 1944. Disputes about how the money should be spent characterized the reign of Sa'ūd ibn 'Abd al-'Azīz (1953–64), but under the direction of his brother and successor, Faisal (1964–75), the administration was modernized and a program of major development inaugurated. The army was reorganized and expanded, particularly after 1968. By 1971, the Sa'ūdī armed forces exceeded 70,000, of which 40,000 men were in the regular forces and 30,000 in the national guard, recruited mainly from the core area of Najd. The composition of the army reflected the continuing uncertainties about unresolved tensions within Arabia, but Sa'ūdī Arabia possessed a force and influence sufficient to enable her to play an important role in the Gulf, where she had major interests through her historic claims, the situation of her valuable Eastern province, and the passage of her oil exports.[62]

Contemplating the rise of the regional powers, one may detect two stages in their attitudes toward the Gulf. In the period before 1968, each was primarily concerned with resolving internal political and economic problems and with the assertion of national independence. Iran, Iraq, and Sa'ūdī Arabia were content to leave the regulation of the Gulf itself to Britain. The growth of oil wealth, the development of programs of internal modernization, and the disruptive force of radical Arab nationalism obliged them to give greater attention to the Gulf area, but so long as Britain remained in the area the full deployment of their influence was restrained. As soon as the decision to withdraw was announced by Britain in 1968, the regional powers found it necessary to assert themselves and to develop policies designed to secure their interests in the Gulf.

In the postwar period, rapid economic, social, and political changes took place within the territory of the local powers of the Gulf. The pace of these changes varied from one state to another; Bahrain and Kuwait took the lead, while Oman and Trucial Oman were slower to move—certain small Trucial states, 'Ajmān, Fujaira and Umm al-Qaiwain showed virtually no change. In this section, it will, however, be convenient to describe the main lines of change among the local powers as a group rather than to examine their development individually.[63]

The changes that took place were the consequence of the great increase of oil production and of the consequent inflow of money. Oil production in Bahrain had begun in 1934, developed gradually, and continued in the postwar period at a modest level. Production in other states began later, expanded much more rapidly, and reached far greater levels. Kuwaiti production began in 1946 and expanded very rapidly from 1949, helped by the cut in Iranian production during the Musaddiq period of nationalization; production in Qatar began in 1949 and developed steadily; in Abū Dhabī production began in 1962; elsewhere, oil began

62. See M. Abir, *Oil Power and Politics* (London, 1974).

63. This account is based upon the following: Hawley, *The Trucial States*; Hay, *The Persian Gulf States*; Skeet, *Muscat and Oman*; Rumaihi, *Bahrain*; Abir, *Oil Power*; Longrigg, *Oil*; Belgrave, *Personal Column*; Winstone and Freeth, *Kuwait*; K. G. Fenelon, *The United Arab Emirates, An Economic and Social Survey* (London, 1973); J. Daniels, *Abu Dhabi* (London, 1974); J. Daniels, *Kuwayt Journey* (Luton, 1971); R. O. Collins, *The Golden Bubble* (London, 1957); R. Hewins, *A Golden Dream* (London, 1963); J. D. Anthony, *Arab States of the Lower Gulf: People, Politics, Petroleum* (Washington, 1975); R. Moser, *Welcome to Sharjah* (Paris, 1974); M. T. Sadik and W. P. Snardy, *Bahrain, Qatar and the UAE* (Lexington, Mass., 1972).

to flow in the 1970s. With their small populations, the oil-rich Gulf states soon became the wealthiest-per-capita countries in the world. The development of oil production promoted other developments in construction, transport, and other forms of communication. There was considerable port development at Kuwait, Bahrain, Abū Dhabī, and Dubai. Bahrain benefited from the trade of Sa'ūdī Arabia, and the decision to improve Dubai's harbor, threatened by silting in the 1950s, left that state poised to play a major part in the greatly expanded trade. By 1968 its harbor had fifteen berths. Other industries were established in the wake of oil: the Bahrain refinery had opened in 1937 and that in Kuwait in 1949; other industries included petrochemicals, ship repairing and food processing. Economic expansion produced a rapid growth of population; at 8 percent per annum in 1969, that of Kuwait was the highest in the world; and between 1968 and 1972 the population of the area of the United Arab Emirates increased from 180,000 to 320,000. The greatest part of this increase was derived from the import of labor from abroad; in 1968, one-half of the population of Abū Dhabī consisted of immigrants and by 1975 two out of every three residents of Kuwait were not Kuwait citizens. A related feature of population change was the shift to towns; by 1973, three of every four Bahrainis lived in seven towns, the great majority in Manāma and its two connected towns.

Among social changes was a major improvement in health and sanitary conditions as a consequence of the attack on the malaria-carrying mosquito with insecticides after World War II, the development of medical and hospital services, and the general improvement in diet, housing, and water supplies that followed the investment of oil revenues. Another important social change was the expansion of educational facilities. The foundations of a modern school system had been laid in Bahrain and Kuwait in the 1930s, and in both states educational provision grew rapidly in the 1950s, leading to the inauguration of the University of Kuwait in 1969–70. There were also significant changes in legal organization. The traditional system that had divided jurisdiction between the ruler's courts, which dealt with his subjects, and British courts, which dealt with aliens, was gradually abandoned. British extraterritorial jurisdiction was finally terminated in Kuwait in 1960 and in Qatar and the Trucial states in 1971. The rulers' courts were reformed; new laws and legal codes were adopted and new, professional judges were appointed. There were also changes in the position of the family. In certain parts of the Gulf, the status of women improved with the spread of women's education and new job opportunities; and divorce, polygamy, and arranged marriages became less common. Changes also took place in the class structure; the expansion of industrial and government employment led to the creation of a new working class. The first state to undergo this experience was Bahrain, where two-thirds of the workers were Bahrainis: in other parts of the Gulf the largest part of the new working class was composed of immigrants. An educated middle class, employed in government offices, the professions, and business, also became important in Bahrain, Kuwait and Dubai and won a share of political power; in Bahrain the middle class entered the legislature, and in Kuwait the first cabinet included five men not from the Āl Sabāh family.[64] But

---

64. "The intelligentsia in the Gulf are a very small proportion of the population but they are now the people who matter," Belgrave, *Personal Column*, p. 237.

everywhere in the Gulf, the flow of new wealth reinforced the traditional leadership of the ruling families, such as the Āl Sabāh in Kuwait, the Āl Khalīfa in Bahrain, and the very extensive Āl Thānī family in Qatar. Such changes as took place within the ruling families often involved the displacement of rulers hostile to change by others to whom it was more congenial; such changes took place in Abū Dhabī (1968), Oman (1970), and Qatar (1972). A ruler favorable toward development, as was Rashīd of Dubai, could secure considerable advantages for his state in the flux of rapid change. More traditional factional disputes between branches of the ruling families also remained a feature of Gulf politics.

The economic and social changes had other political consequences. First, they led to a massive expansion of governmental activities; government became the chief employer of labor almost everywhere in the Gulf—in 1968–69 70 percent of Kuwaitis worked for the government. Only in Dubai did government hold back in favor of private development. Expansion took place in all departments of government, notably in the growth of security forces—police and military—for example, the first regular military force in Trucial Oman, the Trucial Oman Levies, was founded in 1951; by 1971, it numbered 1,700 and, in addition, Abū Dhabī's own defense forces then totaled 10,000.

Constitutional change was slow, but significant. In Bahrain the demand for a legislature was first advanced in 1938, and in the 1950s there was a marked increase in political agitation that grew out of Sunnī-Shī'ī rivalries and labor disputes. In 1954, the first political party in the local states of the Gulf was founded in Bahrain. Bahrain established an advisory council in 1956, a cabinet in 1970, and in 1972 a constituent assembly was elected, leading to the adoption of a constitution and the election of a national assembly in 1973. In Kuwait, a constitution was adopted in 1962 and a national assembly elected the following year. In Qatar a constitution was adopted in 1970, but a nominated consultative assembly established only in 1972. Although a tradition of municipal government dated back to the 1920s in Sharja, developments in Trucial Oman were generally stimulated only by the British decision to withdraw. Constitutional drafting began in the prospective United Arab Emirates in 1968 and led to the formation of a council of ministers and an appointed consultative assembly.

A feature of political development was the emergence of a new style of radical or ideological politics deriving especially from the influence of changes in Arab politics and the example and influence of Egypt from 1952, Iraq from 1958, and South Yemen from 1968. The role of radical Arabism was not wholly dissimilar in its effects to that of Wahhābism in the early nineteenth century. The influence of radical politics was most noticeable in Bahrain from the 1950s, in Kuwait, and especially in Oman, where the Dhufar Liberation Front emerged as the Popular Front for the Liberation of the Occupied Arab Gulf in 1968 and the National Democratic Front for the Liberation of Oman and the Arab Gulf in 1970. Radical Arab attacks were directed against traditional rulers and institutions and especially against the influence of Britain.

The decline of British influence within the local powers was an uneven process. The first major evidence of hostility to the British presence appeared in 1956, when the Anglo-French attack on Egypt led to demonstrations throughout the Gulf and especially in Kuwait. Kuwait became independent in 1961. Hostility to British influence was shown also in Bahrain during the 1950s, although Britain retained her base facilities there until 1971 and intervened in Bahrain politics in 1956 and 1965. Whereas in the northern part of the Gulf there was a gradual decline of British influence during the postwar period, in the southern part it increased; during the 1950s Britain intervened on land in Oman and Trucial Oman. Only shortly before the January 1968 announcement of Britain's intention to leave the Gulf did British control begin to loosen.[65] This decision performed the same office that Dr. Johnson believed to be served by the prospect of imminent hanging; it concentrated the minds of all concerned on the political structure that should follow.

Britain had already encouraged some measures of joint action among the Trucial states, such as the formation of the Trucial Oman Levies, the Trucial States Council (1952), and the Development Council (1965). These joint ventures pointed the way toward a federation. At first (25 February 1968) it was proposed that the federation should include Bahrain and Qatar as well as the Trucial states, but the first two states dropped out and the United Arab Emirates, which came into existence on 2 December 1971 under the presidency of Shaikh Zaid of Abū Dhabī, consisted only of six Trucial states (Abū Dhabī, Dubai, Sharja, 'Ajmān, Umm al-Qaiwain, and Fujaira); the seventh, Ra's al-Khaima, joined on 10 February 1972.

A second major problem posed by the British decision to withdraw from the Gulf area was the need to adjust certain disputes between states in the area.[66] The British presence had frozen disputes rather than solved them, for claimants were both deterred from pressing their claims and relieved of the necessity of resolving them. There was an obvious possibility that claimants might seek violent solutions. Traditionally, little attention had been paid to territorial boundaries in Arabia, as jurisdiction over men had been of much greater significance than jurisdiction over territory. Territorial disputes had been created by the introduction of the concept of the modern state and had been greatly magnified by the possible existence of oil deposits and extended to the sea bed of the Gulf itself. The first serious attempts to establish territorial boundaries in eastern Arabia followed World War I, but these frontiers were not fully demarcated. The dangerous possibilities of territorial disputes were revealed by the quarrel between Abū Dhabī, Oman, and Sa'ūdī Arabia concerning Buraimi, which began in 1952 and which in 1955 led to the expulsion of Sa'ūdī Arabian forces from the area by the Trucial Oman Scouts. This dispute and related issues were not finally settled until 1973. Another serious episode was the Iraqi claim to Kuwait, promoted when Kuwait became independent in 1961. Forces from Britain and the Arab League came to the aid of Kuwait, and Iraq recognized Kuwait in 1963. A longstanding and vexing problem was Iran's claim to Bahrain, which was finally relinquished in 1970. Iran's claim to the islands of Abū Mūsā

65. On the background to the British withdrawal see P. Darby, *British Defence Policy East of Suez, 1945–68*, London, 1973.

66. On the disputes see H. M. al-Baharna, *The Legal Status of the Arabian Gulf States* (Manchester, 1968); M. Burrell, "The Politics of the Arab Littoral States in the Persian Gulf Region" in Amirie, *Persian Gulf*, 227–48; J. Churba, *Conflict and Tension among the States of the Persian Gulf, Oman and South Arabia* (Montgomery, 1971); J. B. Kelly, *Eastern Arabian Frontiers* (London, 1964); E. Monroe, *The Changing Balance of Power in the Persian Gulf* (New York: AUFS, 1972); and M. Khadduri, "Iran's Claim to the Sovereignty of Bahrein," *American Journal of International Law* 45 (1957).

and the Tunbs was maintained, and these islands were occupied by Iranian forces in November 1971. Within Trucial Oman, Britain had begun the complicated process of demarcating the territories of the interlocked states, and some of the outstanding problems were decided before independence. The most noteworthy feature of the process of the settlement of disputes was the willingness of the Gulf powers, both local and regional, to seek peaceful negotiated settlements of their differences.

The political shape of the Persian Gulf region in 1971 was the product of the relationship between the three circles of power mentioned at the beginning of this chapter. The shape of the circle of local powers had been formed in the eighteenth century, but its survival owed much to the protective umbrella supplied by Britain and its final form to the interaction of the regional and international systems. To a considerable degree, the shape of the regional powers was also a consequence of the operation of the international powers: the frontiers of Iraq, Iran, and Sa'ūdī Arabia were defined in this way. But the geographical position, the resources and the energies and ambitions of the regional powers ensured that they could not be dominated by the international powers, and in the last analysis they could even determine the political structure of the Gulf. Habit, self-preservation, and the need to provide for the security of their greatest economic asset, oil, made them endorse the situation that had evolved since the eighteenth century. It was oil that had produced the economic shape of the Gulf in 1971; in seventy years it had transformed the region into one of the wealthiest in the world, and the citizens of the Gulf were exchanging the recklessness of those with nothing to lose for the caution of men of property. It was oil that had also transformed the social condition of the people of the Gulf, offering them a new life style and the challenge of bringing it into harmony with the forms of Islam as traditionally practiced in the region. No historical parallel exists for the speed and scale of the transformation of the Gulf in the last three decades; from an economic and political backwater to an Eldorado. Less remarkable than the dislocation that it suffered was the skill with which it has accomplished the change.

Selected Bibliography

Adamiyat, F. *Bahrain Islands*. New York, 1955.

Amirie, A., ed. *The Persian Gulf and Indian Ocean in International Politics*. Tehran, 1975.

Amirsadeghi, H., ed. *Twentieth Century Iran*. London, 1977.

Anthony, J. D. *Arab States of the Lower Gulf: People, Politics, Petroleum*. Washington, 1975.

Avery, P. *Modern Iran*. London, 1967.

Badger, G. P. *The History of the Imams and Seyyids of Oman*. London, 1871.

Bartlett, H. Moyse. *The Pirates of Trucial Oman*. London, 1966.

Belgrave, Sir Charles. *The Pirate Coast*. London, 1970.

Bidwell, Robin Leonard. *Travellers in Arabia*. London, 1976.

Busch, B. C. *Britain and the Persian Gulf, 1894–1914*. Berkeley, 1967.

Curzon, G. *Persia and the Persian Question*. 2 vols. London, 1892.

Daniels, J. *Abu Dhabi.* London, 1974.
———. *Kuwayt Journey.* Luton, 1971.
Dann, U. *Iraq under Qassem.* London, 1969.
Dodwell, H. *The Founder of Modern Egypt.* Cambridge, 1931.
Earle, E. M. *Turkey, the Great Powers and the Baghdad Railway.* New York, 1923.
Fenelon, K. G. *The United Arab Emirates, An Economic and Social Survey.* London, 1973.
Goldsmid, Sir F. *Telegraph and Travel.* London, 1974.
Graves, Philip P. *Life of Sir Percy Cox.* London, 1912.
Greaves, R. L. *Persia and the Defence of India, 1884–1892.* London, 1959.
Groves, Anthony N. *Journal of a Residence in Baghdad.* London, 1832.
Hawley, Donald. *The Trucial States.* London, 1970.
Hay, R. *The Persian Gulf States.* Washington, 1959.
Higham, R. *Britain's Imperial Air Routes, 1918–39.* London, 1960.
Holt, P. M. *Egypt and the Fertile Crescent, 1516–1922.* London, 1966.
Kazemzadeh, F. *Russia and Britain in Persia, 1864–1914.* New Haven, 1968.
Kelly, J. B. *Britain and the Persian Gulf.* Oxford, 1968.
Khadduri, M. *Independent Iraq, 1932–1958.* London, 1960.
———. *Republican Iraq.* London, 1969.
Kumar, Ravinder. *India and the Persian Gulf Region, 1858–1907.* London, 1965.
Landen, R. G. *Oman since 1856.* Princeton, 1967.
Lockhart, L. *Nadir Shah.* London, 1938.
Longrigg, S. H. *Four Centuries of Modern Iraq.* London, 1925.
———. *Iraq, 1900–50.* London, 1953.
Lorimer, J. G. *Gazetteer of the Persian Gulf.* 2 vols. Calcutta, 1915.
Low, C. R. *History of the Indian Navy.* 2 vols. London, 1877.
Malcolm, Sir J. *Sketches of Persia.* London, 1861.
Marlowe, John. *The Persian Gulf in the Twentieth Century.* London, 1962.
Martin, B. G. *German-Persian Diplomatic Relations, 1878–1912.* The Hague, 1959.
Miles, S. B. *Countries and Tribes of the Persian Gulf.* 2 vols. London, 1919.
Moser, R. *Welcome to Sharjah.* Paris, 1974.
O'Shea, R. *The Sand Kings of Oman.* London, 1947.
Palgrave, W. G. *A Year's Journey through Central and Eastern Arabia.* 2 vols. London, 1865.
Parsons, A. *Travels in Asia and Africa.* London, 1808.
Philby, H. St. J. B. *Saudi Arabia.* London, 1955.
Ramazani, R. *The Foreign Policy of Iran, 1500–1941.* Charlottesville, Va., 1966.
———. *Iran's Foreign Policy, 1941–1973.* Charlottesville, Va., 1975.
———. *The Persian Gulf: Iran's Role.* Charlottesville, Va., 1972.
Rentz, G. S. "Muhammad ibn 'Abd al-Wahhab and the Beginnings of Unitarian Empire in Arabia." Ph.D. dissertation. University of California, 1948.
Rumaihi, M. G. *Bahrain: Social and Political Change since the First World War.* London, 1976.
Sadik, M. T., and Snardy, W. P. *Bahrain, Qatar and the UAE.* Lexington, Mass., 1972.
Sadleir, George. *Diary of a Journey across Arabia.* New York, 1977.
Skeet, Ian. *Muscat and Oman.* London, 1974.
Thomas, Bertram. *Arab Rule under the Al Bu Sa'id Dynasty of Oman, 1741–1937.* London, 1938.
Winder, R. Bayly. *Saudi Arabia in the Nineteenth Century.* London, 1965.
Winstone, H. V. F. and Freeth, Zahra. *Kuwait: Prospect and Reality.* London, 1972.
Yodfat, A. and Abir, M. *In the Direction of the Persian Gulf.* London, 1977.
Zabih, S., and Chubin, S. *Iran's Foreign Relations.* Berkeley, 1975.

4. British Policy in the Persian Gulf MALCOLM YAPP

The political interest of Britain in the Persian Gulf began at the end of the eighteenth century. For two hundred years before that period British interests were dominated by commerce. Concern with the trade of the Persian Gulf had arisen as a by-product of the much more valuable British East Indian trade, to exploit which the English East India Company was founded in 1600.[1] From the outset, a major problem of the East Indian trade revolved around the circumstance that Indians wanted few British products and that bullion had to be exported to pay for British imports of Indian goods. Consequently, the English merchants sought markets for their woolen goods outside India, and they observed the potential of the cooler climate of Iran, which also offered the prospect of supplies of raw silk. Shah 'Abbās the Great was agreeable to their proposals, and in 1615 designated Jāsk as a suitable port for trade. But the Portuguese merchants, ensconced at Hormuz, did not like the prospect of a new competitor. In 1622, the English merchants aided 'Abbās in expelling the Portuguese from Hormuz. The British then established a new factory at Gombroon (Bandar 'Abbās), which became the company's commercial headquarters in the Gulf. From Bandar 'Abbās the company carried on its trade with Iran, and, from 1640, with Iraq, with varying success. There were difficulties in its dealings with the Iranian government and severe competition from the Dutch, whose preeminence in the Asian trade was undisputed in the seventeenth century. Only at the end of that century, when Dutch power was threatened in Europe, did the English company improve its trading position. The Gulf trade was not very large, but it was peculiarly valuable as a counter to mercantilist criticisms of the company's unfavorable balance of trade.

The position of the company in the Gulf altered during the course of the eighteenth century.[2] This was partly the consequence of disturbed political con-

---

1. On the early history of the British connection with the British Gulf, see: Sir W. Foster, *England's Quest of Eastern Trade* (London, 1933), esp. 295–313; and L. Lockhart, *The Fall of the Safavid Dynasty and the Afghan Occupation of Persia* (Cambridge, 1958).
2. See Abdul Amir Amin, *British Interests in the Persian Gulf* (Leiden, 1967).

ditions in Iran after the Afghan invasion of 1722, but primarily because of a significant change in the nature of the East India Company itself. This change was the outcome of the confused political situation in India that accompanied the decline of the Mughal empire and of the bitter conflict between Britain and France, a result both of local rivalries in India and of the wars between Britain and France in Europe. As a result, by 1765 Britain had become the dominant European power in India, and the East India Company had transformed itself from a trading company into a territorial power with important possessions in Bengal. The metamorphosis of the company had repercussions on its Gulf operations.

Insecurity in the Gulf was increasingly apparent after the death of Nādir Shah of Iran, in 1747, and for the company manifested itself in the form of disputes with the Iranian authorities and troubles with Arab pirates who operated from both shores of the Gulf. The company's agents were induced to seek other modes by which their buoyant trade could be pursued in a more satisfactory manner. One proposal was to find an island where British trade would be free from the menaces to which it was exposed at Bandar 'Abbās; at various times Bahrain, Qishm, and Hormuz were suggested as suitable sites. These suggestions were rejected by higher authorities in the company on the grounds that they would involve the company unnecessarily in local politics; territorial possessions in the Gulf were not wanted. Further, it was evident from the share of Iran in the company's trade that the company must continue to do the major part of its business on the Iranian coast whether it liked Iranian officials or not. A second proposal would have moved the company's headquarters to another coastal site, and in 1755–56 an attempt was made to locate at Bandar-i Rīg in the northern part of the Gulf, but the opposition of the Dutch, who were already based on the nearby island of Khārg, and the difficulties of dealing with the local potentate, the notorious pirate Mīr Muhannā, proved too great. It was only when the Bandar 'Abbās trade fell off markedly in the late 1750s and the local situation became especially difficult that, in 1763, the company decided to move to Basra, where there had been a permanent establishment since 1723. For security the company's agents would still have preferred an island base, but commercial considerations indicated a port that enjoyed a substantial trade. Economics therefore limited the choice to Basra and Bushire, and the former was chosen chiefly, it seems, because it was not in Iran. The advantages of Basra may have been a strong and stable government, a rapidly expanding trade, and convenience of communication. The western Asian route for communication between Britain and India had been used intermittently since the seventeenth century, but during the late eighteenth century the so-called overland route through the Syrian desert and the Gulf was developed systematically in response to the pressing need for a more rapid exchange of information, both information relating to market conditions and political news of developments in Europe that could affect the situation in India.[3] The company's Resident at Basra was well placed to handle the mails. In the early years, the desert route was most hazardous and many mails

3. See H. Furber, "The Overland Route to India in the Seventeenth and Eighteenth Centuries," *Journal of Indian History* 29 (1951).

were lost, but from 1761 on the use of the Baghdad route led to a marked improvement in the speed and reliability of the service. Basra therefore became the company's headquarters in the Gulf, and a subsidiary factory was established at Bushire in 1763, under very favorable conditions granted by Karīm Khān Zand, to look after the Iranian trade.

In the years which followed the move to Basra, the company's trade was profitable, and that of the company's agents even more so, for the company's factors were not only concerned with selling the company's goods but also with servicing the profitable trade between Bengal and the Gulf, which expanded greatly after the establishment of British control over Bengal and in which the company's servants' private interests were deeply involved.[4] The private trade has been estimated to have been ten times as great as the company's trade. Because of its maritime strength, the company was the recipient of attractive proposals from the Ottoman and Iranian authorities, who sought a naval arm with which to defend their trade and suppress the Arabs who defied them. The offers were seductive, holding out the prospect of new trading privileges and even the possession of a secure island base at Khārg. Local British agents recommended various proposals, but at higher levels of the company there was no agreement. It was foreseen that the company was likely to be extensively embroiled in local political rivalries to the detriment of its trade and its purse. In the end, the only decision taken was one to withdraw the company's factory from Bushire in 1769.

The importance of the company's Gulf trade declined in the last part of the eighteenth century because of competition, the shortage of specie in the Gulf with which to finance imports from India, and the disastrous outbreak of plague in Iraq in 1773, which hit Basra sorely and which was followed by an Iranian siege and occupation of the city in 1775–79. In consequence, the company's trade at Basra and also at Bushire, where the factory was reopened in 1775, languished and, indeed, became so unprofitable that its complete abandonment was contemplated. The trade of the Gulf was increasingly engrossed by Muscat, which became the principal entrepôt, and by other Gulf Arabs. In the absence of any important commercial or political interests, it is difficult to understand what sustained the company's establishments in the Gulf at the end of the eighteenth century. The maintenance of the overland mail provided one reason, but perhaps the principal reasons must be sought in the private interests of the company's servants and in simple inertia.

At the very end of the eighteenth century, the British situation in the Gulf was transformed by the injection of the question of strategy. This was the consequence of two events: the invasion of northern India by Zamān Shāh of Afghanistan, and the French expedition to Egypt in 1798. These events combined to create a new interest in the countries bordering the Gulf, first and foremost in Iran. It was envisaged that a political agreement between Britain and Iran might serve two purposes: first, that Iran, by threatening Afghanistan's western frontier,

4. See II. Furber, *John Company at Work* (Cambridge, Mass., 1951); P. J. Marshall, *East Indian Fortunes* (Oxford, 1976), pp. 76–105; A. Dalrymple, ed., *An Account of the Navigation between India and the Gulf of Persia* (London, 1786); P. Nightingale, *Trade and Empire in Western India, 1784–1806* (Cambridge, 1970).

might persuade Zamān Shāh to withdraw from India; and second, that Iran might serve as a buffer, protecting India from any chance that Bonaparte might march eastward to threaten the British possessions. Whether this formulation accurately reflected the true motives of those involved is a question that need not concern us; suffice it to note that in ostensible pursuit of them a treaty was made with Iran in January 1801. In the same context as the struggle with France, agreements were also formed with Muscat in 1798 and 1799, and the first British Resident established in Baghdad in 1798. Unlike the Basra Resident, the official at Baghdad had no commercial functions and was concerned with politics and communications alone.[5]

In any event, by the time these arrangements for erecting a defensive screen in the Gulf region were concluded Britain had lost interest in them; the dangers (if they ever existed) from France and Afghanistan had disappeared. The screen was allowed to decay and in 1806 the Indian government declined to assist Iran against Russia and suggested closing the Baghdad Residency. But immediately the French threat revived in the form of Napoleon's fresh overtures to the Ottomans and to Iran and the new fears were expressed for the security of British India. Missions to Iran were prepared simultaneously in London and in Calcutta, where the governor-general, Lord Minto, was peculiarly agitated by fears of a French attack on India.[6] It was Minto's initiative that led to the first clear formulation of a comprehensive strategic policy for the Gulf region. The author of this scheme was John Malcolm, who had led the mission to Iran in 1800–01, and who was chosen by Minto to lead the mission from India to the region in 1808.

Knowledge that a mission was being sent from London to Iran prevented Minto from sending Malcolm direct to Iran, and he was obliged instead to formulate a general mission to the Gulf region to warn all rulers who appeared to be contemplating alliance with France of the peril of their ways. Nevertheless, Malcolm was primarily concerned to break the alliance between Iran and France that had been formed at Finkenstein (May 1807). In this endeavor he failed and should reasonably have given way to the ambassador from London, Sir Harford Jones, who had been waiting patiently at Bombay. But Malcolm was unwilling to relinquish the mastery and instead proposed a new scheme to Minto.

Malcolm's new scheme hinged on the seizure of an island in the Gulf—Khārg—and its conversion into a British base. The idea of a Gulf base was not new; it has been shown how, during the eighteenth century, the company's agents frequently recommended the transfer of the company's headquarters to a Gulf island. But these earlier proposals had been couched in commercial terms, and commercial reasons had also predominated in an earlier proposal by Malcolm in 1800 to establish an island base on Qishm. In 1808, however, Malcolm hinged his proposal primarily on political and strategic considerations. Possession of

5. See J. W. Kaye, *Life of Malcolm*, 2 vols. (London, 1856), 1: 89–154; F. Ingram, "A Preview of the Great Game in Asia," Parts 1–4, *Middle East Studies* 9(1973) and 10(1974); M. E. Yapp, "The Establishment of the East India Company Residency at Baghdad 1798–1806," *Bulletin of the School of Oriental and African Studies* 30 (1967): 323–36.

6. Countess of Minto, *Life of Minto*, 2 vols. (London, 1875–80); G. J. Alder, "Britain and the Defence of India—the Origins of the Problem 1798–1815," *Journal of Asian History* 6 (1972); A. Majumdar, "Lord Minto's Administration in India (1807–13)," Ph.D. thesis, Oxford University, 1962.

an island in the Gulf would, given British control of the sea, enable Britain to strike against any of the countries on the periphery of the Gulf and thereby insure their deference to British interests. It was generally supposed that the tribes of southern Iran and Iraq could readily be persuaded to revolt against their governments.[7]

As it happened, Malcolm's plan failed, owing to the actions of Jones, who, disregarding Minto's instructions recalling him, pressed on to Tehran and negotiated a treaty—the Preliminary Treaty of 1809—which brought Iran back into the British camp. Jones's success led to a major clash between London and Calcutta over the correct policy to be pursued in the Gulf region. London supported the policy of the Anglo-Iranian alliance in which Iran would become a buffer for the defense of British India; Calcutta believed that the Iranian alliance was expensive and that it offered no worthwhile protection to India, and so supported Malcolm's Gulf strategy. Inevitably, the contest was won by London and the Gulf strategy disappeared from view. Yet the dispute did raise some interesting issues. The constitutional conflict between London and Calcutta does not concern this essay, but the political and strategic issues do. Although the conflict appeared to be about the best mode of defending India, such was not its true character; the reasons for which London supported the Iranian alliance had little to do with the defense of India, and much more to do with the politics of Europe and with the problems presented by the changing role of Russia in the war against Napoleon. It was European considerations that led the cabinet to override the policy of Indian defense upheld by the Indian government, and one reason why the Indian government advocated the Gulf policy was that it was a policy that seemingly could be carried out with the resources of that government alone, and that would reduce its dependence upon the London government and therefore the limitations upon India's freedom of action that were imposed by the problems of Europe. In the future, European diplomatic problems and the existence of the Anglo-Iranian alliance were to be major constraints upon the development of British policy in the Persian Gulf.[8]

The Indian government's commitment to the Gulf strategy should not be exaggerated. When the alleged French danger disappeared, so also did the Indian government's interest in any system of distant defense. Russian encroachments in northern Iran did not give rise to concern until after 1830. During the years 1810–30, strategy played little part in molding British policy in the Gulf area. In these years, the chief problem was once more seen to be the protection of trade from the depredations of the pirates of the Arabian coast. It was in this context that discussion of an island base revived.[9]

In 1809–10, a British expedition was sent against the pirate bases, and it was then suggested that the island of Hangām would be suitable for British purposes.

7. Kaye, *Malcolm*, 1: 432–35.

8. M. E. Yapp, "A Marriage of Inconvenience: The Anglo-Iranian Alliance 1809–38." Paper presented at the Anglo-Iranian Cultural Symposium at the Pahlavi University Shiraz, November 1977 (to be published in the forthcoming proceedings).

9. See J. B. Kelly, *Britain and the Persian Gulf* (Oxford, 1968). This magnificent work is by far the best study of British policy in the Persian Gulf ever written, and my debt to it will be evident to all who know it. I have differed from Dr. Kelly in the smaller emphasis that I have given to the role of strategy in the development of British policy.

But nothing was done and the pirate problem continued. In 1819–20, a second expedition was sent against the pirates and, after discussion, Qishm was occupied as a British base in the Gulf. But the island was unsuitable, and, moreover, the British action aroused Iranian resentment; in 1823, Qishm was evacuated, although the Gulf squadron continued to use its port of Basa‘īdū as their headquarters. However, British interest, emanating largely from the Gulf Residents and the Bombay government who were the parties principally concerned, still focused on the question of an island base, and in the early 1830s a new proposal to take Khārg was formulated but rejected by the authorities in England, who were still unconvinced that a Gulf base was necessary or desirable.

Throughout this period, British India was primarily concerned to find the cheapest and least inconvenient means of keeping order on the waters of the Gulf. The official position was well stated by both the Supreme Government in Calcutta and the Court of Directors of the East India Company in London in 1834. "Our concern," wrote the governor-general, Lord William Bentinck, "is only with the maritime commerce of the Gulf and as long as that is not molested it matters not to us whether one power or another holds dominion over its shores."[10] The court wrote in similar vein: "It is of little consequence to us what power predominates in the Gulf as long as commerce continues free and unmolested and the country remains tranquil."[11] These remarks were made in relation to proposals to aid the Sultan of Muscat against his various enemies. From time to time, this Muscati policy found advocates among British policymakers, chiefly because they hoped in this way to persuade the Sultan to do the work of maintaining peace on the waters of the Gulf and thus save Britain the trouble. Others, however, regarded the Sultan as himself a major cause of disturbances in the Gulf. The Sultan's efforts to secure continuous British support failed and the Muscat policy fell into oblivion.

In the end, piracy was suppressed neither by British expeditions, nor through an island base, nor by any Muscati agency, but by the novel device of the so-called Trucial system. In 1835, the pirate shaikhs were persuaded to sign voluntarily a truce forbidding maritime warfare during the pearling season. The truce was renewed annually, and its duration extended to the whole year. In 1843, it was converted into a ten-year truce, and in 1853 it was made permanent. The truce was superintended by the vessels of the Gulf squadron of the Indian navy, which was also responsible for the surveys of the Gulf and for other assistance to navigation in the area. The architect of this highly successful system was Samuel Hennell, the very capable Resident in the Persian Gulf who served in the area from 1826 to 1854.

The strategic problem again came to the fore during the 1830s, when important developments took place in Iraq, Iran, and Arabia. Since 1798, various possibilities for extending British influence in Iraq had been canvassed, but they had made little progress, partly because there was little interest in them and partly because the position of Iraq, as part of the Ottoman empire, involved European complications too embarrassing to Britain to make the venture worth

10. Quoted ibid., p. 235.
11. Quoted ibid., p. 238.

the risks. During the 1830s, however, there arose an interest in steam navigation and more rapid communication between Britain and India. In this connection, the use of the Gulf and the Euphrates River seemed to offer promising opportunities, and although the decision was taken to concentrate the main effort on the development of the Red Sea route, an expedition was sent to Iraq to test the suitability of the Euphrates route. The Euphrates expedition also became the vehicle for certain political ideas about the British position in the Gulf, for it was thought that through the expedition Britain might win support among the Arab tribes of the lower Euphrates and acquire influence generally in Iraq. Such influence, it was contemplated, could serve both to prevent Iraq falling under the control of Muhammad 'Alī of Egypt, or even, eventually, of Russia. But the Indian government had little enthusiasm for a project chiefly sponsored by the government in England and supported most vigorously by the company's agent in Iraq and by the expedition's leader, Francis Chesney. The interest of London derived chiefly from European political considerations, and waned after the expulsion of Muhammad 'Alī from Syria in 1840–41. The hopes of establishing a strong British political influence in Iraq disappeared.[12]

Renewed interest in Iran came as a consequence of fears that Russian influence would be extended over Iran and through Iran into the borderlands of British India. The Iranian siege of Herāt, in 1837–38, was regarded as being likely to result in the spread of Russian influence into Afghanistan and provoked a firm British response. Diplomatic pressure on Iran having failed to induce Muhammad Shah to desist from his attack on Herāt, the British minister, John McNeill, recommended that an expedition should be sent from India to the Gulf. In fact, he envisaged two expeditions: a small one to seize the island of Khārg; and, if that failed to achieve its purpose, a larger expedition to Bushire. Once more an opportunity to test the Gulf strategy was presented, but it was declined by the Indian government. The governor-general, Lord Auckland, sent the small expedition to Khārg, but, fearful of the possible effects on British relations with Russia of attacking the mainland of Iran, chose not to send the larger expedition to Bushire, but instead to concentrate his main efforts on building a buffer state in Afghanistan. His decision, which was fully supported by the government in England, led to the disastrous first Anglo-Afghan War of 1839–42.[13]

It was the expense of holding Afghanistan that induced Auckland to look again at the Gulf strategy, and the Indian government made a determined effort to be allowed to keep Khārg in any settlement with Iran. The stated reasons were partly strategic, partly for use as a base for operations against pirates, but chiefly for the sake of commerce. Khārg, wrote Auckland, could become "the Singapore of the Persian Gulph."[14] London was unimpressed; fearing the reaction of Russia and wanting a settlement with Iran, ministers ordered the Indian government to evacuate Khārg. Once more the Gulf strategy had been left untried.

12. On the Euphrates Expedition, see F. R. Chesney, *Narrative of the Euphrates Expedition* (London, 1968); H. Hoskins, *British Routes to India* (London, 1928); and M. G. Khan, "British Policy in Iraq, 1828–43," Ph.D. thesis, University of London, 1967.

13. Auckland to Hobhouse (personal communication) 23 August 1838 and 15 November 1838, Add MS 36473 ff. 304, 339.

14. Auckland to Hobhouse (personal communication) 15 August 1840, Add MS 36474 f. 338.

The third crisis of the 1830s in the Gulf region was the consequence of the possible threat that the Arabian coast of the Gulf and Bahrain might fall under the control of Muhammad 'Alī of Egypt, following the successful Egyptian conquest of Najd. On this occasion, it was the cabinet that pressed for sharp action to be taken by the Indian government to prevent this eventuality, and the Resident in the Gulf and the Bombay government joined in the plea. But Auckland refused to take vigorous action: India, he believed, lacked the resources for effective action in the Gulf; he did not want a protectorate over Bahrain, and he did not want any closer involvement in the area. If the cabinet believed Muhammad 'Alī should be stopped, they should do it themselves.[15] Although the foreign secretary, Lord Palmerston, procured orders to force Auckland to take action in the Gulf, by the time these orders reached India the Egyptian forces had begun to retire and the danger, if it had ever existed, disappeared. Bahrain was left independent.[16]

After 1842, the renewed British strategic interest in the Gulf lapsed. The interest had never been great. The acquisition of a base in the Gulf had been advocated by the Residents and by the Bombay government largely for local reasons; they were concerned with the maintenance of order on the Gulf waters. The Foreign Office in London had supported the base concept in the case of Bahrain, but opposed it in the case of Khārg for reasons connected with the politics of Europe; in the first case, to administer a rebuff to Muhammad 'Alī and, in the second, to conciliate Russia. The Supreme Government in Calcutta had supported taking Khārg partly for strategic but chiefly for commercial reasons and had opposed the acquisition of Bahrain. In general, one can say that there was little commitment to the development of a long-term Gulf strategy fashioned on Malcolm's proposals of 1808; Britain still wished to maintain satisfactory relations with the regional powers and to limit her involvement in the Gulf to the minimum compatible with the continuation of her commercial interests there.

The Gulf strategy reappeared during the Anglo-Iranian war of 1856–57.[17] Between 1842 and 1853, there were several periods of difficulty in Anglo-Iranian relations that were caused by British fears of the renewal of Iranian claims to Herāt. On each occasion, the London government gave thought to the possibilities of action in the Gulf—the seizure of Khārg—in the hope of deterring Iran. No action was found necessary until 1856, when a greater crisis occurred: a personal dispute led to the departure of the British envoy from Tehran, and Iran besieged Herāt and eventually occupied it in October 1856. Some British action was thought to be essential to assert British prestige. A reluctant cabinet ordered an even more reluctant governor-general, Lord Canning, to send an expedition to the Gulf. For once, thanks to the Crimean War, the Russian reaction could be disregarded. Canning did not want to send an expedition: India could not afford such wars, he said, and Herāt was not worth the trouble. Furthermore,

15. Auckland to Palmerston (personal communication) 16 February 1840, Add MS 37698 f. 25.

16. J. B. Kelly, "Mehemet Ali's expedition to the Persian Gulf, 1837–40," parts 1–2, *Middle East Studies* 1 and 2 (1965).

17. On the Anglo-Iranian war of 1856–57, see B. English, *John Company's Last War* (London, 1971); J. F. Standish, "The Persian War of 1856–1857," *Middle East Studies* 3 (1966); *Lieutenant General Sir James Outram's Persian Campaign in 1857* (London, 1860); and Kelly, *Britain*, pp. 452–99.

he believed that a small expedition would not work; "the talisman which we are supposed to have at our command by seizing the island of Khārg will be found to have lost its virtue and power," he prophesied correctly.[18] Iran, he thought, had too few interests on the Gulf coast to be responsive to such pressures. It was indeed found necessary to enlarge the action; first Khārg was seized, then Bushire occupied, and then Muhammara; and the news of peace found the British forces pushing far into Khūzistān. But at the same time, Britain was unwilling to fight an all-out war against Iran. From the beginning of the nineteenth century, the idea had prevailed that the tribes of southern Iran could be roused against the government in Tehran if Britain so chose, and this possibility was an essential part of Malcolm's Gulf strategy. It was, however, perceived that such action might topple the Iranian government, reduce Iran to anarchy, and invite Russian intervention. Britain wanted to end the war as soon as possible and to resume friendly relations with a stable Iran, and did not want to leave behind unfulfilled commitments to Iranian tribes. Accordingly, Canning forbade encouragement to the tribes, and although an impatient London government eventually overruled him, the war was terminated before anything was done. Negotiations were carried on throughout the war, and although the Gulf operations had some effect in alarming Iran, it is not clear that the eventual terms of the settlement were substantially different from those that might have been achieved without recourse to arms. The Gulf strategy was, therefore, not fully implemented in 1856–57, but it is evident that its implications frightened British policy-makers; like the nuclear bomb, it was a powerful weapon, but one that was insufficiently discriminating or controllable. It was certainly incompatible with good relations with the regional powers and the international powers. But it was also clear that without recourse to rousing the tribes there was little that Britain could do to coerce Iran from the side of the Gulf without incurring very great expense and without committing troops that she could not spare from India; as it was, the troops from Iran returned to India only just in time to save Britain during the Indian mutiny of 1857. Thus, under the most favorable conditions, i.e., in the absence of the Russian factor, the Gulf strategy was found wanting.

For some years after 1857, strategy was less important in Britain's Gulf policy. No European power threatened Britain's predominance and no clashes with the regional powers occurred. The period was marked by a steady increase in British involvement with the local powers of the Gulf area, notably with Muscat and Bahrain. This increased intervention was undertaken principally in order to protect the local arrangements in the Gulf previously sponsored by Britain. Disruption in Muscat and Bahrain invited possible intervention by the regional powers and threatened to open gaps in the British system of Gulf security. In consequence, Britain felt obliged to assert the independence of the two small states and to intervene in their internal affairs in order to prevent domestic dissension from subverting their independence. It has been argued that this increased scale of British intervention was also prompted by new developments in communications—the advent of the steamer service in the Gulf and the

18. Canning to Granville, 17 May 1856, quoted Kelly, *Britain*, p. 467; see also M. Maclagen, *"Clemency" Canning* (London, 1962), p. 51.

linking of the European and eastern telegraph systems through the Gulf—and by a new thrust of humanitarianism in British policy.[19] Neither of these new factors, however, seems to be either strong or especially novel. Interest in communications dated from the eighteenth century and the new forms did not materially change attitudes. Nor did the advent of steam navigation make the Gulf of much greater relative commercial worth to Britain; sales of British and Indian goods increased, but the Gulf area remained one of minor economic significance until the development of the oil industry. Nor was humanitarianism new, even if it became more fashionable, for it had been the main motive behind successive British attempts to regulate the African slave trade in the area since 1822. Increased intervention was undertaken to safeguard old interests rather than to advance new ones.

British influence in Bahrain was formalized in 1861. Factional disputes within Bahrain and claims to the island advanced successively by the Wahhābīs, Iran, and the Ottomans induced Britain to arrange a convention with Bahrain by which Britain recognized the independence of the Āl Khalīfa state and guaranteed it against external aggression—in effect, Bahrain was brought within the Trucial system. The consequences of the British undertaking were shortly made manifest when disputes in Bahrain menaced the peace of the Gulf. In 1868, Britain deposed Muhammad Āl Khalīfa and put his brother 'Alī in his place. The following year 'Alī was killed in a revolt led by his rivals, and Britain intervened again to set up another ruler, 'Isā ibn 'Alī. This episode inevitably led to renewed British difficulties with Iran, whose claim to Bahrain was reasserted.

In Muscat, British intervention was forced by the situation that developed after the death of Sayyid Sa'īd, in 1856, when his empire was divided between two sons, Mājid, who took the wealthiest area of Zanzibar, and Thuwaynī, who took Muscat and Oman. To avert a disruptive war between the two, Britain was compelled to mediate. By the Canning award of 2 April 1861 the governor-general upheld the division of Sayyid Sa'īd's empire, but to make up part of Thuwaynī's loss of revenue decreed that Zanzibar should pay 40,000 Maria Theresa dollars a year to Muscat. The partition of the empire was also recognized by France, in 1862, when Britain and France issued a joint declaration pledging themselves to respect the independence of the Sultans of Muscat and Zanzibar. Although Britain strove to resist the implications of the Canning award, it was evident that she was now committed to supporting the Āl Bū Sa'īd family in the Sultanate of Muscat, a circumstance that involved Britain in opposing the claims of the Sa'ūdīs and supporting the Sultan against his opponents in interior Oman. The Sa'ūdīs were warned off from Oman, and in 1866 a British vessel bombarded the Sa'ūdī fort at Dammān. As for the Omanis, British hostility to the regime of 'Azzān ibn Qais (1868–71) contributed to the fall of his government and the establishment of the rule of Sayyid ibn Turkī. Britain was suspicious of regimes dependent on the interior of Oman and mistakenly supposed them to be under Wahhābī influence.[20] In 1873, Britain acquired yet another source of influence

19. By R. G. Landen, *Oman since 1856* (Princeton, 1967).
20. Ravinder Kumar, *India and the Persian Gulf Region, 1858–1907* (London, 1965), pp. 24–51. See also J. Martineau, *Life of Sir Bartle Frere*, 2 vols. (London, 1895).

over the rulers of Muscat when she became responsible for the payment of the Zanzibar subsidy.

In retrospect, it is possible to descry a certain logical inevitability in these various British interventions. Such inevitability was not readily accepted at the time. For convenience, we talk about British policy as though there existed a consensus of British opinion, but this is a misleading simplification.

In studying British policy in the Gulf, as elsewhere, we are usually much more conscious of the conflicts between Britons involved in policy-making: between departments of government in London; between London and Calcutta; and between Calcutta and Bombay. Most of all, however, we become conscious of the importance of the role of the agents on the spot, the residents in the Persian Gulf, who, through their monopoly of information and their ability to act quickly in times of crisis, could often entice Britain into a policy that those above them would have preferred to have avoided. This leading role was played by Lewis Pelly, the agent chiefly responsible for the interventions in Bahrain and Muscat, but a similar part was taken by his predecessors and successors at different times and in varying degrees.

By 1871, the nature of the British position in the Persian Gulf had become clearer. In search of maritime peace, Britain had assumed a regulating role and, faced with the choice between abandoning that role or advancing it, she had moved forward to assume new obligations. By 1871, the basis of the British position was no longer questioned. "Whether our policy in the Persian Gulf rests on engagements contracted with the Arab chiefs of the littoral or on measures adopted for the security of our subjects and the protection of commerce," wrote the governor-general, Lord Mayo, "it is one which we have consistently pursued for the last fifty years with the happiest results as regards the peace of the seas. It is a policy from which . . . it is neither possible nor desirable that we should recede."[21] It was at this time also that the importance of the British position in the Gulf, and of the new problems created by the opening of the Suez Canal and the closer connection of Europe and the East, were recognized in a change in the direction of British policy in that region; direct control of the Residency was transferred from the subordinate Presidency Government of Bombay to the Supreme Government in Calcutta in 1873.

The truth of Lord Mayo's words was made plain during the next twenty years when, in response to fresh challenges to the British position, Britain assumed further formal control over Bahrain and the Trucial states. In this new forward movement, the major factor was the revival of Ottoman power in eastern Arabia, following the decline of the Sa'ūdī state in Najd and the Ottoman expedition to al-Hasā in 1871.

Britain had no legal right to complain of the Ottoman expedition. The British position in the Gulf, though strong in practice, rested on custom rather than law; there had been no need to define it more precisely because no international power had challenged it. The advent of the Ottomans, both an international power and, through possession of Iraq, also a regional power in the Gulf area, brought home the fact of this weakness in the British position. As one

21. Mayo to Argyll, 3 April 1971, quoted Kelly, *Britain*, p. 713.

British official remarked "we have no Treaty right nor are we under any Treaty obligation to prevent aggressive expeditions on the part of Turkey or Persia, nor have we any right to prevent any tribe, or even Bahrain from attacking Turkey or Persia."[22] Exclusive British supremacy in the Gulf could be ended at any time, and yet it was evident that the Ottoman expedition could lead to a war which, if it were extended to the sea, would make it impossible for Britain to maintain the maritime truce; or it could lead to clashes between the Ottoman pretensions and British obligations to Muscat, the Trucial states, and Bahrain. Fortunately for Britain, these greater menaces failed to materialize, for the Ottomans found Najd too much of a handful and were unable to do more than maintain themselves in al-Hasā; their wider claims were not pressed with any force. Nevertheless, their presence on the Arabian coast remained a challenge to British predominance that was magnified by the mysterious force that Britons were accustomed to attach to the appeal of Pan-Islamism. More particularly, the Ottoman presence prevented Britain from taking effective action against pirates operating from the coasts of al-Hasā and Qatar.

Britain debated what to do about the Ottomans. From an early period it was argued that she should seek a formal agreement dividing the Arabian shore of the Gulf into an Ottoman and a British sphere at a point roughly in the region of Qatar.[23] But while this might solve the problems of the mainland, with which Britain was not concerned, it left open the question of who should guard the waters of the Gulf: if Britain left the job of patrolling the northern Gulf to the Ottomans there would surely be Iranian objections; on the other hand, if Britain maintained her claim to patrol the whole of the Gulf there would be conflict over Ottoman territorial waters. Also, it was argued that the Ottomans lacked either the power or the will to keep any agreement. Another possibility, which was supported by the governor-general, Lord Lytton, in 1879, was to formalize the British position in the southern part of the Gulf by the establishment of protectorates over Muscat, Trucial Oman, and Bahrain. This was opposed by the foreign secretary, Lord Salisbury, on the grounds that the Ottomans were a European power and that he would not jeopardize his European policy of conciliation by quarreling with the Ottomans over their claims in remote Arabia. Also, the 1862 agreement with France made the establishment of a British protectorate over Muscat a difficult matter.[24]

These divided opinions reflected the lack of agreement about the importance of supporting the British position in the Gulf; the advent of the Ottomans meant that the constraints formerly imposed by European politics upon British dealings with the regional powers had now been extended to the Gulf itself, and the apparent freedom given by the Gulf strategy to the Indian government was shown to be illusory. The uncertainties engendered prevented the formulation of a coherent British response and it was left to the Resident, the able and experienced E. C. Ross, to produce *ad hoc* solutions. On 22 December 1880, he concluded a new agreement with Bahrain that possessed two features: British control of

22. Quoted Kelly, *Britain*, p. 804.
23. Kumar, *India*, p. 116.
24. Kelly, *Britain*, p. 805.

Bahrain foreign relations, and the exclusion of foreign diplomatic and consular agencies and coal depots without British agreement. This move was intended to strengthen the hand of the Shaikh of Bahrain in resisting Ottoman claims. The same motive and the same model informed new agreements negotiated with the Trucial shaikhdoms in 1887. In Muscat, as has been remarked, the situation was complicated by the 1862 agreement with France that prevented the assertion of British control over Muscati foreign relations. Instead, Britain was obliged to be content with an agreement, in 1891, by which the Sultan undertook to alienate no part of his territories without British consent. This nonalienation clause in the Muscati agreement was considerably wider that those contained in the earlier agreements with Bahrain and the Trucial shaikhs, and in 1892 the treaties with these states were remodeled to include similar nonalienation clauses. The agreements became known as the "exclusive agreements."[25]

As a consequence of the Ottoman intrusion, the British position had advanced considerably on paper. In practice, it might be argued, British power had not increased in the Gulf in the period, but had actually diminished. On the Iranian shore, Britain had never challenged Iranian sovereignty and had exercised influence only in the absence of effective Iranian authority. The strengthening of Iranian power on the Gulf shores during the second half of the nineteenth century diminished the freedom of British action on the northern shore of the Gulf. On the Arabian shore, Britain had always dealt with the powers that existed, but as long as these powers had consisted only of the small Arab states and the power of Najd she had enjoyed considerable freedom of action. The arrival of the Ottomans severely limited British freedom to operate in the northern part of the Gulf, notably in Qatar and on the al-Hasā coast. In the southern part of the area, British control was no stronger for being recorded on paper. The true area of British predominance remained the waters of the Gulf. In that sphere, Britain still played her former role, but now endured new constraints upon her liberty. During the process of formalizing the British positions between 1860 and 1892, the strategic argument for the British position in the Gulf had been notable mainly for its absence from the discussion. It was reinjected into the discussion largely by Lord Curzon, viceroy of India from 1898 to 1905. "Curzon," wrote one of his foremost contemporary apologists, "recalled both India and England to a sense of the supreme importance of the Persian Gulf." "British supremacy in India," he continued, "is unquestionably bound up with British supremacy in the Persian Gulf. If we lose control of the Gulf we shall not rule long in India."[26] To the older desiderata of the protection of trade and keeping the peace of the Gulf, he added the need to exclude European powers that might threaten India both by establishing fortified bases in the Gulf area or by their very presence, for no matter how innocent their activities, the proximity of other European powers would inevitably excite unrest within India, which would make that country more difficult to rule.

25. J. G. Lorimer, *Gazetteer of the Persian Gulf*, 1: 534, 628, 736–39, 786.

26. Lovat Fraser, *India under Curzon and After* (London, 1911), pp. 110, 112. For Curzon's own views, see his *Persia and the Persian Gulf*, 2 vols. (London, 1892), and his dispatch of 21 September 1899, in J. C. Hurewitz, *Diplomacy in the Near and Middle East*, 2 vols. (Princeton, 1956), 1: 101.

Two things may be said about this argument: first, that it seems very familiar because it was to be the stock-in-trade of later strategists who discussed the problems of the Gulf; and second, that in the context of the development of British policy in the Gulf it was very new to find strategy so prominently displayed. The resemblances of this doctrine to Malcolm's Gulf strategy are apparent, although there are also significant differences, but, as we have seen, the Gulf strategy had never been influential in shaping British policy in the Gulf. That the strategic arguments for the British presence in the Gulf now appeared as a focal point was very much the contribution of Curzon, but the new picture was very misleading. It seemed peculiarly well suited to the circumstances of the period because of the alleged attempts by European powers to exercise influence in the Gulf: France in Muscat, Germany in Kuwait, and Russia in Kuwait and in Iran. These supposed European intrusions gave rise to a number of crises in the Gulf between 1890 and 1914, and these must now be examined.[27]

In Muscat, there was new French activity in the 1890s as a consequence of the establishment of a French consul there, and of the support to French pretensions given by the colonial party in France and by those who saw the Franco-Russian alliance as operating against Britain in Asia. The Anglo-French dispute came to a head over two issues: the grant of a coal depot in Muscat to France and the shelter afforded to Arab slave traders and arms smugglers by the protection of the French flag. Curzon's answer to the problem was clear: a British protectorate should be established over Muscat and the French firmly told to go elsewhere. London, unwilling to quarrel with France over remote Muscat, was more conciliatory: The French depot concession was canceled, but France was offered other facilities; on the flags question Britain chose long negotiations, appeal to the International Court, and eventually a solution through compromise and compensation. In short, the London government rejected the blanket solution of the protectorate, adopted a discriminating policy supporting the Indian government's stand on specific issues and putting European relations first. Despite Curzon's pleas, London declined to include the question of Muscat in the Entente Cordiale negotiations with France.

The question of Kuwait became urgent because of fears that first Russia and then Germany might secure a railway outlet on the Persian Gulf at Kuwait. Once more, Curzon wanted a protectorate and the cabinet refused. Kuwait was traditionally considered to be under Ottoman suzerainty, and a protectorate would have upset European relations; ministers would accept only an exclusive agreement for Kuwait. In fact, the cabinet was willing to allow Germany an outlet for the Baghdad railway on the Gulf and was prevented from so doing only by a newspaper clamor in 1903. Even so, the cabinet remained committed to a negotiated solution and, in 1913–14, found one in agreements with the Ottomans and Germany that provided both for an outlet for the Baghdad

27. On these episodes, see Kumar, *India*; B. C. Busch, *Britain and the Persian Gulf, 1894–1914* (Berkeley, 1967); J. B. Plass, *England zwischen Russland und Deutschland* (Hamburg, 1966); Lord Ronaldshay, *Life of Curzon*, 3 vols. (London, 1928); P. Graves, *Life of Sir Percy Cox* (London, 1942); D. Dilks, *Curzon in India*, 2 vols. (London, 1969–70); J. B. Kelly, "Salisbury, Curzon and the Kuwait Agreement of 1899," in K. Bourne and D. E. Watt, eds., *Studies in International History* (London, 1967), pp. 249–90.

railway at Kuwait (although the Basra–Kuwait section was to be under British control) and for the recognition of Ottoman sovereignty (although not administrative control) over Kuwait. Thus, although the Kuwait exclusion agreement was very significant in extending British influence into the northern part of the Gulf, Curzon's wider hopes of extending the protectorate system to that region were defeated. By the Anglo-Ottoman Blue Line agreement of 1913, the demarcation of the British and Ottoman spheres of influence in Arabia (including the Gulf shore) followed roughly the lines envisaged in the 1870s, although Qatar was completely excluded from the Ottoman sphere.

The question of a Russian outlet to the Persian Gulf caused much controversy. Curzon was very hostile to permitting such a development, and the statement made on 5 May 1903 by the foreign secretary, Lord Lansdowne, that Britain would "regard the establishment of a naval base or of a fortified post in the Persian Gulf by any other Power as a very great menace to British interests, and we should certainly resist it with all the means at our disposal,"[28] was commonly regarded as a victory for Curzon's policy of determined resistance to Russian encroachment. Yet this view depends on a misreading of the situation: Lansdowne's statement related only to fortified bases, for which Russia had no desire, seeing them as potential hostages to fortune; at the same time, Lansdowne conceded that there would be no objection to a Russian commercial position, which from Curzon's viewpoint was almost as bad. And in the Anglo-Russian agreement of 1907 concerning Asia, the whole of the Iranian shore of the Gulf proper was left in the neutral zone in which the two Great Powers could compete freely, and there was no reference in the document itself to Britain's special position in the Gulf; this was ambiguously confined to other documents. Curzon regarded the 1907 agreement as a major defeat for his policy.

In each of the three issues considered, Curzon got some but not much support. The Indian government was also prevented from establishing greater control over Bahrain and Qatar. In short, although Curzon had advanced the British position in the Gulf, notably at Kuwait, he had failed to win acceptance for the doctrine of British supremacy. London had once more made it clear that British interests in the Gulf were not considered of sufficient importance to warrant assuming so exclusive a position at the price of European troubles. The true weakness of the position of the Indian government in this debate is seen most clearly in relation to Iran and Iraq from 1907 to 1914, when the Indian government was virtually excluded from decision-making.[29] In the years before 1914, British influence in the Gulf undeniably increased: trade expanded and new consulates were opened; the arms traffic was brought under control; navigation was improved by a new survey and the advent of new aids to navigation; and Britain remained the leading political power. But the Gulf was far from being a British lake.[30]

It was World War I that brought British power in the Gulf to its peak. This temporary apotheosis was the direct result of the Ottoman entry into the war in

28. *British Documents on the Origins of the War*, 4: 371.

29. On Iraq, see S. A. Cohen, *British Policy in Mesopotamia, 1903–14* (London, 1976); and on Iran, F. Kazemzadeh, *Russia and Britain in Persia, 1864–1914* (New Haven, 1968).

30. On the arms traffic, see Mahmood Ali Daud, "British Relations with the Persian Gulf, 1890–1902," Ph.D. thesis, University of London, 1957, and Lorimer, *Gazetteer*, 2: 2556–93.

1914 and the Russian departure from it in 1917. The Ottoman entry produced a British expedition to Basra, undertaken partly to protect the oil installations at Abadan from Ottoman attacks, partly to hold firm the Arab shaikhs of the Gulf, but principally to avoid the possibility that Ottoman successes in the Gulf area might influence Muslim sentiment in India against British rule. Certainly, the expedition was not intended to establish British political control over Iraq. It is true that Britain had long possessed interests in Iraq—commercial and political— and had recently shown especial interest in oil. Britain had striven to defend these interests, but not at the price of straining relations with the Ottomans and alienating Germany too far; in 1914, Britain still preferred to support the integrity of the Ottoman empire rather than to take her chances in a partition. But once planted in Basra, the temptations to advance further north proved irresistible, and shortly after the armistice Britain found herself in control of Basra, Baghdad, and Mosul. Under the direction of a large band of British officials led by Arnold Wilson, the work of transforming Iraq into a British-administered imperial showpiece began.[31]

The Ottoman involvement in the war also gave Britain a free hand on the Arabian shore of the Gulf. Ottoman influence there had already weakened before 1914: influence had been lost at Kuwait, and the revival of Sa'ūdī power in Arabia, under the direction of 'Abd al-'Azīz ibn Sa'ūd, culminated in 1913 in the expulsion of the Ottomans from al-Hasā. But Britain had not sought to exploit this situation; she had not supported Ibn Sa'ūd against the Ottomans and by the 1913 agreement had recognized Ottoman authority over Najd. In June 1914, the astute India Office official, Arthur Hirtzel, advised Captain W. H. Shakespear, the chief British advocate of a deal with Ibn Sa'ūd: "Please bear in mind the fixed policy of H.M. Government to assist the Turkish Government to consolidate itself in Asia. It is quite certain they will not do anything which they think tends in the opposite direction, and it is no use beating the air."[32] So the contrary view of the Residents in the Gulf and of the India government was overruled by the Foreign Office in the interests of European affairs. The British government's attitude was changed by the war, and in 1915 Britain formed a treaty with Ibn Sa'ūd, recognizing his independence. Ibn Sa'ūd agreed to accept British advice. In the short term, this treaty had little effect, for Ibn Sa'ūd was unable to play a significant role in the war and British interest in Arabia was principally focused on the Hijāz. But in the longer term, the treaty marked a major shift in British policy in the Gulf; the al-Hasā coast was at last brought into the area of British predominance, and British involvement was pulled away from the sea and deep into the problems of land frontiers in Arabia, of which she had previously fought shy. The new British position on the Arabian coast of the Gulf was rounded off by other involvements. In 1914, Kuwait was guaranteed independence under British protection, and in 1916 Qatar was brought within the Trucial system.[33]

British control on the Iranian coast was also increased as a consequence of

31. See Cohen, *British Policy*; F. J. Moberley, *The Campaign in Mesopotamia*, 4 vols. (London, 1923–27); Peter Sluglett, *Britain in Iraq, 1914–1932* (London, 1976); John Marlowe, *Late Victorian* (London, 1967): A. Wilson, *Loyalties, Mesopotamia, 1914–21* (Oxford, 1930), and *Mesopotamia, 1917–1920: A Clash of Loyalties* (Oxford, 1931).

32. Quoted H. V. F. Winstone, *Captain Shakespear* (London, 1976), p. 189.

33. See B. C. Busch, *Britain, India, and the Arabs, 1914–1921* (Berkeley, 1971), and G. Troeller, *The Birth of Saudi Arabia* (London, 1976).

the war. Since the Constitutional Revolution of 1906 there had been a considerable decline in the control of the Tehran government over the provinces, and Britain had increasingly resorted to local arrangements to safeguard her interests which, since 1908, had come to include oil. By a series of agreements with Shaikh Khaz'al of Muhammara, Britain had undertaken to support the Shaikh against encroachments on his power by the Iranian government, providing he honored his obligations to that government and accepted British advice. The Shaikh was given a renewed assurance in November 1914.[34] The disturbed conditions in southern Iran among the Tangistānī, Qashqā'ī, and Khamsa tribal groups also led to British intervention. In Bushire in 1909 and at Lingeh in 1910, British sailors were landed to defend the foreign community, and in 1911 consular guards were strengthened and Indian cavalry sent to Shīrāz and Isfahān. In 1913, the Swedish-officered Iranian gendarmerie had produced some order in the area and the cavalry were withdrawn, but World War I made the situation worse than it had ever been. The war turned Iran into an unofficial battleground between the Central and Entente powers. In the north, the decisive influence was exerted by Russian troops until they were withdrawn in 1917; in the south, including the neutral zone, which, by agreement with Russia, was incorporated into the British sphere of influence, the situation was very disturbed, as German agents instigated Iranian tribes to attack British positions—it was ironic that that element of the Gulf strategy which Britain had always shrunk from employing against Iran was now employed with such effect against herself. The gendarmerie being unreliable, Britain organized a force—the South Persia Rifles—to maintain order, but it proved only moderately effective, for the Iranian government refused it recognition, and in 1918 there were mutinies and desertions. After the collapse of Russia in 1917, the British situation became still more precarious. Britain tried to plug the holes left by the departure of the Russian forces by pushing troops into northwestern Iran from Iraq and into northeastern Iran from India. However, the collapse of the Central Powers in the autumn of 1918 left Britain with no rivals and well placed to impose her will upon Iran. This she sought to do through the Anglo-Iranian Agreement of August 1919, which would have given Britain effective control over Iranian finances and the Iranian army.[35]

By the summer of 1919, British power in the Gulf area was at its apogee. There were no international rivals; the regional powers—Iraq, Iran, and Sa'ūdī Arabia—were all linked to Britain, and Britain dominated the local states of the Gulf. This dominance lasted only a brief time. In Iraq, a rebellion broke out in the summer of 1919 that affected about one-third of the country and cost Britain forty million pounds to suppress. The rebellion was decisive in changing British policy. Strong doubts had already been expressed in the Foreign Office and in the India Office in London about the wisdom of the policy of the civil commissioner, Arnold Wilson. "The idea of Mesopotamia as the model of an

---

34. Graves, *Sir Percy Cox*, pp. 114–16, 120–22, 125.

35. See U. Gehrke, *Persien in der Deutschen Orientpolitik während des Ersten Weltkriegs*, 2 parts (Stuttgart, n.d.); Sir C. Skrine, *World War in Iran* (London, 1962); C. Sykes, *Wassmuss* (London, 1936); and Sir P. Sykes, *History of Persia*, 2 vols. (London, 1921).

efficiently administered British dependency or protectorate is dead," Hirtzel informed Wilson in July 1919.[36] The resources of men and money were lacking. Wilson could not accept this verdict. "Having set our hand to the task of regenerating Mesopotamia, we must be prepared to furnish men and money and to maintain continuity of control for many years to come," he wrote.[37] But the evidence of the Iraqi uprising confirmed the government in London in its view; the attempt to administer Iraq was abandoned; an Arab government under Faisal ibn Ḥusain was established in 1921 and an Anglo-Iraqi treaty signed the following year. Britain retained substantial influence in Iraq, for which she had been named as mandatory in 1920, but she relinquished detailed control over Iraqi affairs. In 1930, a new Anglo-Iraqi treaty paved the way for the relinquishment of the mandate in 1932; it gave Britain the use of Iraqi facilities in time of war and also permitted the continued use of the Royal Air Force bases at Shu'aiba, near Basra, and Habbāniyya, near Baghdad.[38]

In Iran, the collapse of British power was more rapid and more complete. The Anglo-Iranian Agreement was not ratified, and in 1920 it was decided to withdraw British forces from Iran. Britain then had no means with which to coerce Iran or to defend it against the threat posed by Bolshevik-supported insurgents in the north. It was even suggested that Britain might abandon northern Iran to anarchy and support the establishment of an independent power in southern Iran. But order was reestablished by the new Iranian government that emerged from the coup of February 1921 and that was dominated by Riżā Khan. There was, admitted Curzon, "a complete collapse of British prestige and influence."[39] The principal reason for the British debacle was the cabinet's unwillingness to provide the resources that were required to sustain British control in the face of Iranian opposition. In fact, neither the cabinet nor the Indian government thought Iran was worth the effort; just as Wilson had been the only real supporter of a British-administered Iraq, so Curzon had been the only convinced proponent of British dominance in Iran. Curzon still hoped to salvage Britain's position in the Gulf and urged the new ambassador to Iran to "never release or slacken our hold on the Gulf." But Riżā Khan was determined to bring the south under the close control of Tehran and directed his efforts against Shaikh Khaz'al of Muhammara.[40] Several Britons advocated support of Khaz'al because of the promises to him and because they feared disruption in the oil fields and refinery, but the ambassador, Sir Percy Loraine, decided that "Tehran is the ultimate criterion of our relations with Persia and that the cohesion of the Persian Empire as a whole is far more important to British interests generally and in the long run than the local supremacy of any of our particular protégés." Loraine's formulation was, indeed, in the main line of British policy in the region, for good relations with the regional powers had always been placed before domination of the Gulf. And Loraine won; after much wavering, Britain

36. Quoted Marlowe, *Late Victorian*, p. 165.
37. Quoted ibid., p. 195.
38. P. W. Ireland, *Iraq* (London, 1937).
39. Quoted G. Waterfield, *Professional Diplomat* (London, 1973), p. 62.
40. Ibid., p. 63.

did not support Khaz'al, although she attempted to dissuade Rizā Khan from an armed movement on Muhammara. However, Rizā pressed forward and established full control over Khuzistan at the end of 1924.[41]

There was also some deterioration in British influence in Sa'ūdī Arabia. British policy in Arabia had always suffered from the division between the Indian government, which, broadly speaking, wished to back the Sa'ūdīs of Najd because of the connection with the Gulf, and the Foreign Office in London, which, following the lead of British officials in Egypt and the Sudan, preferred to support Husain of the Hijāz. Inevitably, the Foreign Office won; British offers to 'Abd al-'Azīz ibn Sa'ūd had always little substance, for to have given him more might have helped him against his rival Husain or injured other British interests in the area. "Our policy is a Hussein policy," stated Curzon in March 1919.[42] But once again Britain's lack of will was demonstrated; in October 1924, Ibn Sa'ūd took Mecca and by the end of 1925 had dispossessed the Hashemites of the Hijāz. It was, declared the colonial secretary, J. H. Thomas, "out of the question that H.M.G. should in any case embark upon hostile action against Ibn Saud, whether direct or indirect, in defence of the Holy Places."[43] The ending of the subsidy paid to 'Abd al-'Azīz from 1917 until 1924 deprived Britain of that lever upon the Najdī leader, and the hostility of Indian Muslims was an important constraint. Britain opted for an agreement on frontiers with Ibn Sa'ūd in November 1925—the Hadda agreement, which settled those with Transjordan, and the Basra agreement, which settled those with Iraq. By the Treaty of Jidda, of 20 May 1927, Britain recognized "the absolute independence of the dominions" of Ibn Sa'ūd, while Ibn Sa'ūd undertook, *inter alia,* to respect British treaties with the Trucial states.[44]

Thus, although a strong British influence was retained in Iraq and a friendly relationship eventually reestablished with Sa'ūdī Arabia, Britain had failed to consolidate the dominant position that she had established during the war in the territories of the regional powers. This failure was not admitted. In January 1917, Curzon had written to Sir Percy Cox, the leading British official in the Gulf area and a former Resident in the Persian Gulf: "When the war is over we shall consolidate that Kingdom and see that no one snatches away the crown,"[45] and in May 1924 a British government spokesman declared that "our position in the Persian Gulf is at the present time absolutely untouched and unassailable."[46] But the last statement was untrue; the government had rejected Curzon's policy, and in considerable areas of the Gulf Britain had no freedom of action. It was only among the minor Gulf powers of the Arab shore that British influence was still dominant: in Muscat and Trucial Oman the British position established earlier was maintained; in Bahrain British interference in internal affairs became more pronounced; and in Qatar and Kuwait Britain had actually gained power compared to the prewar period. It was Britain who, at 'Uqair in 1922, negotiated

41. Ibid., p. 78.
42. Quoted E. Monroe, *Philby of Arabia* (London, 1973), p. 99.
43. Quoted Troeller, *Saudi Arabia*, p. 219.
44. See Sir G. Clayton, *An Arabian Diary* (Berkeley, 1969).
45. Quoted Graves, *Sir Percy Cox*, p. 231.
46. Hansard (House of Lords) 14 May 1924.

the frontiers of Kuwait with Sa'ūdī Arabia, signing away two-thirds of the territory claimed by Kuwait under the (unratified) Anglo-Ottoman agreement of 1913, apparently in part to compensate Ibn Sa'ūd for abandoning large areas to Iraq.[47]

It was only the preoccupation of the regional powers with the tasks of internal reconstruction and nation-building that diverted their attention from the Gulf and enabled Britain to preserve the illusion of dominance in the Gulf during the period between the wars. Britain's principal concerns in the area (apart from the maintenance of the tranquil navigation of the seas) were the development of communications, especially those by air, and the growth of the oil industry in the area. With regard to the first, Britain pioneered the development of the Imperial Airways route through the Gulf to the East. In 1929, a weekly flight began from Basra to Karachi. Until 1932, the route followed the Iranian coast, but for political reasons it was decided to switch to the Arabian coast. Ibn Sa'ūd refused to allow the route to follow the coast of al-Hasā, and an agreement was eventually made that provided for landing rights at Sharja in Trucial Oman. Iranian hostility to British control was also manifested in the transfer of the control of the Iranian telegraph from the Indian government to an Iranian organization.

The importance of the role of oil in shaping British policy in the Gulf area has been the subject of much controversy.[48] Oil was first discovered in commercial amounts at Masjid-i Sulaimān in Iran in 1908, and in the following year the Anglo-Persian Oil Company was formed to exploit it. In 1914, the British government acquired a majority shareholding in the company and a contract for the supply of fuel oil to the British navy was placed with the company. It was also evident before 1914 that deposits of oil existed in the Mosul region of Iraq, and there was keen competition between various oil interests for the concession to develop this oil. The agreement concerning Iraqi oil reached in 1914 was upset by the war and a new agreement was negotiated after the war. Commercial quantities of oil were discovered in Iraq in 1927. It is clear that oil was an important issue that demanded agreements between the oil companies and governments concerned, but there is no good evidence that the desire to control supplies of oil played a decisive part in the evolution of British policy toward Iraq during the immediate postwar period. Nor is there convincing evidence that British policy in the Gulf during the interwar period was strongly influenced by the desire to control oil resources. British oil companies had sufficient oil for their needs, and although they evidently wished to reserve possible deposits for the future, they were unwilling to invest the money needed to develop them. Hence, although British political agents in the area exercised their influence in favor of British companies, this influence was insufficient to secure a British oil monopoly, and the British government did not make use of its legal powers to exclude non-British companies. In consequence, although British interests prevailed in certain areas, such as Qatar, U.S. interests prevailed in Bahrain, and in

47. H. R. P. Dickson, *Kuwait and Her Neighbours* (London, 1956), pp. 345–51.
48. See J. E. Hartshorn, *Oil Companies and Governments* (London, 1967); a good recent study is Marion Kent, *Oil and Empire* (London, 1976); see also S. H. Longrigg, *Oil in the Middle East* (London, 1968).

1933 U.S. interests captured the important Sa'ūdī Arabian concession. Elsewhere, there was commonly a compromise between oil interests.

The rise of these new interests in air communication and oil did not bring about any radical change in British policy in the Gulf area, which continued to be administered on traditional lines. One important development was in response to Iranian self-assertion. This was the movement of the headquarters of the Gulf squadron to Bahrain in 1935, to be followed in 1946 by the transfer of the Persian Gulf Residency from Bushire. But this was a *pis aller*; there was no new strategic appreciation of the Gulf—indeed, it is striking how little it figures in the documents of the period. For example, although the formal justification of the British position in the Gulf was in terms of the British position in India, there was no consideration of the Gulf in the discussions of the implications of constitutional change in India, although the Simon report considered defense implications in other areas. Nor was there any detailed discussion of the role of the Indian army in imperial defense until 1937, when it became apparent that British forces might be heavily committed in Europe. The War Office then sought to persuade India to assume a more prominent role in Asian defense arrangements, including the western approaches to India. But there was no agreement on the subject, and in response to nationalist pressure the Indian government demanded a reduction in India's burden of military spending. In 1938, the Pownall Committee recommended that India should share in imperial defense and the cabinet appointed the Chatfield Committee to review the position of the Indian army. The Chatfield Committee recommended in 1939 a reduction in the number of European troops in India. At the same time the committee recommended that with the help of a subsidy from Britain the Indian government should contribute troops for use outside India. The possible areas of deployment included the Persian Gulf, where the main task was to protect the Anglo-Iranian oil fields. The brigade group envisaged, however, was evidently too small for major operations and the striking failure to examine the strategic implications of the British position in the Gulf was revealed during World War II.[49]

World War II resulted in a considerable demonstration of British power to command the Gulf area. During the first year of the war, the Gulf was largely ignored, but the repercussions of the entry of Italy into the war and the fall of France in June 1940 were quickly felt. It was envisaged that the best way in which Britain could reduce German power was to deny her access to oil. Although in 1940 Middle Eastern oil represented less than 5 percent of total world production, it was large enough to provide for German war-time needs. Accordingly, it was deemed especially important to deny Germany access to the oil of Iraq and Iran.[50] In fact, this strategy was misplaced, for Germany was never much interested in Middle Eastern oil.[51] Nevertheless, the rise of pro-Axis sentiment in Iraq apparently gave Germany an opening and thought was given to the problem of maintaining British control. As early as March 1940, a plan had been drawn up

49. See N. H. Gibbs, *Grand Strategy* (London, 1976), 1: 824–36; B. Prasad, ed., *Defence of India: Policy and Plans* (New Delhi, 1963), pp. 20–21, 34; P. J. Grigg, *Prejudice and Judgement* (London, 1948), pp. 293–94.

50. J. R. M. Butler, *Grand Strategy* (London, 1957), 2: 213–14.

51. G. Warner, *Iraq and Syria, 1941* (London, 1974), pp. 41–42.

for the occupation of Basra from India in case of a Soviet attack upon Iraq, and on 1 July the War Cabinet resolved to implement it as a safeguard against Axis influence. But in response to opposition from the Indian government and from the Middle Eastern Command, the military plan was dropped and diplomatic pressure on Iraq tried instead, although this device was pursued with very little energy.

On 1 November, another influential but mistaken appreciation by the British chiefs of staff was introduced into the consideration of British policy in the Gulf area. This was the vision of a giant pincer movement against the heart of the British position in the Middle East on the Suez Canal: one claw to be provided by the Germans and Italians in Libya, and the other by a German move through northern Iraq. This appreciation dominated British thinking in the first half of 1941 and accounts for the urgency with which they approached the Iraq problem. It was, however, mistaken, because Germany regarded the area as being reserved for Italy; she herself was committed to a prospective attack on Russia and regarded the Gulf area as merely a suitable direction in which to divert the attention of the USSR from Central Europe until the time came to strike.

Matters came to a head in Iraq in the spring of 1941. As Axis influence there increased, so the Indian government, prompted by the commander-in-chief, Auchinleck, changed its ground and became the ardent advocate of strong measures.[52] Wavell, in the Middle East, still opposed the diversion of troops to Iraq. On 31 March, the pro-British regent fled from Baghdad and on 3 April power was seized by the (to Britain) doubtful Rashīd 'Alī, supported by the army clique known as the Golden Square. The British chiefs of staff were now very concerned about the danger to Iraqi and Iranian oil, and on 11 April the cabinet ordered military action. On 17 April, Indian troops were sent to Basra, on 30 April Iraqi forces blockaded the British base at Habbāniyya; and on 2 May hostilities commenced. The still-reluctant Wavell was persuaded to send a force from Palestine to Baghdad, where the Rashīd 'Alī government was overthrown and a pro-British government installed. The episode resulted in the firm establishment of British influence in Iraq for the remainder of the war, but it also revealed the very divergent British views concerning the strategic significance of the area. Churchill's main concern was to secure Basra as a base through which U.S. and other supplies could reach the Middle East.[53] Auchinleck also thought control of Basra crucial to success in the Middle East in 1941.[54] The Indian government, with support from London, thought action was necessary to safeguard oil, as well as British power, in Bahrain and Kuwait, and in India itself. Just as in 1914, an important consideration was the effect of British inaction upon Indian Muslims. "The Arab world as such does not worry me," wrote Sir John Dill, chief of the imperial general staff, "but the Muslim world as a whole does—very much."[55] Wavell, on the other hand, believed that British interests in Iraq,

52. J. Connell, *Auchinleck* (London, 1959), pp. 192, 204–5; J. Glendevon, *The Viceroy at Bay* (London, 1971), p. 215.
53. W. S. Churchill, *The Second World War* (London, 1950), 3: 225.
54. Connell, *Auchinleck*, pp. 215–16.
55. Dill to Auchinleck 21 May 1941, quoted ibid., p. 237.

including Gulf oil and communications, were of minor importance compared to securing Egypt and Palestine.[56] In retrospect, one can see that Wavell's assessment of the war situation was nearer the mark than that of London; what he failed to allow for was the importance of maintaining British prestige both in the eyes of London and in the eyes of the government of India. Rashīd 'Alī had to go *pour encourager les autres.*

The second significant arena of British action was Iran, which became of importance after the German attack upon Russia in June 1941. This event gave rise to two problems. The first, which played a major part in British strategic thinking in the following year, was that a Russian collapse would pose a new German threat to British Middle Eastern oil supplies and to the port of Basra.[57] So grave did this danger seem that it was decided to build up ten divisions at Basra. After the Japanese entry into the war in December 1941, Britain feared an even greater Axis pincer movement in which the enemy claws would meet in the Persian Gulf. Such, however, were not Axis intentions and these fears evaporated in the latter part of 1942. The second problem concerned the desirability of supplying Russia through Iran. It was feared that Axis influence in Iran might obstruct this route, and so Anglo-Russian pressure was brought to bear on Iran. Dissatisfied with the Iranian response, the two powers invaded on 25 August, an event that was followed by the abdication of Rizā Shah and the formation of a new government in Iran. Britain and Russia were now in substantial control of Iran and dominated its economy.[58] In any event, it seemed that the Iranian corridor could not answer the needs of Russia; neither the port facilities at Basra nor the communications within Iran could handle the quantity of goods required before the end of 1943.[59]

The year 1941 marks both the peak of British influence in the Gulf region during World War II and the first signs of decline. Britain had contributed to the return of Russia to an area from which she had been virtually excluded as an important factor since 1917. Britain also helped to admit another international rival in the form of the United States. It was Americans who were brought into Iran to handle the transport of supplies and to serve as advisors to the Iranian government. British policy in Iran was criticized in a report by General Patrick J. Hurley, to the irritation of Churchill, who defined British interests in Iran as oil and strategy—the defense of India and Iraq.[60] In November 1943, at Tehran, Roosevelt suggested that a new free port should be established on the Iranian coast of the Gulf and that it and the Iranian railways should be run by inter-

56. Ibid., pp. 222–23, 227–28.
57. Butler, *Grand Strategy*, p. 460; I. S. O. Playfair, *The Mediterranean and the Middle East*, 5 vols. (London, 1954–73), 2: 248–50. The Oil Control Board reported that the loss of Abadan and Bahrain would be "calamitous." Michael Howard, *Grand Strategy* vol. 4 (London, 1972), p. 54. The instructions given to the commander of the British forces in Iran in August 1942 made it his first duty to safeguard oil in the Gulf area and only secondly to protect the route to Russia. (Ibid., p. 53.) For the views of the Chief of the Imperial General Staff, see Sir A. Bryant, *The Turn of the Tide* (London, 1958), p. 392.
58. See Reader Bullard, "Political Report for 1942," quoted in H. Amirsadeghi, ed., *Twentieth Century Iran* (London, 1977), pp. 55–56.
59. T. H. Vail Motter, *The Persian Corridor and Aid to Russia* (Washington, 1952); R. M. Leighton and R. W. Coakley, *Global Logistics and Strategy, 1940–1943* (Washington, 1955).
60. F. L. Loewenstein *et al.*, eds., *Roosevelt and Churchill: Their Secret Wartime Correspondence* (London, 1975), p. 499.

national trustees—presumably Americans. The rise of U.S. influence was also evident in Saʿūdī Arabia. In the early years of the war, it seemed that Britain might acquire an economic stranglehold upon Saʿūdī Arabia, and American oil interests persuaded Roosevelt to supply American aid. The ultimate effect was that U.S. interest supplanted that of Britain in Saʿūdī Arabia. The effective division of interest in the Gulf area was apparently delineated in an exchange of letters between Roosevelt and Churchill, "We are not," the President assured Churchill in 1944, "making sheep's eyes at your oil fields in Iraq or Iran," and the Prime Minister replied with an affirmation "that we have no thought of trying to horn in upon your interests or property in Saʿūdī Arabia."[61] But whether the United States was quite ready to show itself so disinterested over Iran is another matter, for in October 1946 the joint chiefs of staff declared Iran to be an area of major strategic interest to the United States as a source of oil.[62] By then it was evident that the United States was in a position to pick up some of the pieces in the Gulf region, if Britain could no longer hold them together.

In the post-war period, the major factor affecting British policy in the Persian Gulf ought to have been the withdrawal from the Indian subcontinent. As has been shown, the British position in the Gulf originated as an outcrop of the Indian empire. But from an early period, Indian interests alone had not been permitted to determine British policy. Britain's European interests had been increasingly important in decision-making, and from 1882 the British position in Egypt had provided another influence on policy-making throughout the Middle East. During both World Wars it is possible to see British policy in the Gulf as partly the product of the competing interests of Egypt and India, with the London government's decision embracing also Britain's greater strategic problems. In 1947, the Indian dimension was removed by virtue of the independence of India and Pakistan, and it might have been expected that this event would have led to a complete reexamination of the British position in the Gulf. In fact, no such examination took place and it is necessary to try to deduce the assumptions that underlay British policy in the postwar years from a variety of detached statements and actions. The problem has two aspects: what were believed to be British interests in the Gulf, and by what means were they to be upheld?[63]

Most prominent among British interests was oil. In the postwar years, Britain became heavily dependent upon Gulf oil. By 1949–50, more than 80 percent of Britain's crude oil imports came from the Gulf area. An interruption of supplies from the Gulf would have meant a severe loss of income, with a drain of foreign exchange, and would have jeopardized Britain's economic recovery. At the time of the Ābādān oil crisis, the responsible minister was advised that if the crisis were not resolved the Anglo-Iranian Oil Company would be ruined and the British economy crippled.[64] A second British interest was communications. Although India had gone, Britain still had substantial commitments in Southeast

61. Ibid., p. 459.
62. *Senate Foreign Relations (1946)* 7: 529–36. But, of course, this declaration was subsequent to the relation of Russian dealings with Iran over Azerbaijan, etc.
63. In what follows, I have relied heavily upon P. Darby, *British Defence Policy East of Suez, 1947–1968* (London, 1973).
64. J. Strachey, *The End of Empire* (London, 1959), p. 161.

Asia and the Far East and her forces in those areas had to be supported. Although the Red Sea route was the main supply line, the airway through the Gulf was an important supplement. The need to safeguard the use of Habbāniyya as a staging base made it important to reach a new agreement with Iraq to replace the 1930 Anglo-Iraqi treaty, which was due to expire in 1957. Britain failed to achieve a new agreement by the Treaty of Portsmouth (1947), but did so in the Baghdad Pact in 1955.[65] A third general motive for a continued British presence in the Gulf was supplied by the alleged threat that the USSR would seek to expand its power down to the Gulf, thus menacing the two direct British interests described above and, in a wider context, achieving an access of power that would pose a threat to the well-being of the Western alliance throughout the world. The defensive concepts of the Northern Tier, the Baghdad Pact and the Central Treaty Organization, can be seen in part as providing a screen for the defense of interests within the Gulf area. In turn, the British position in the Gulf, with its basis in custom and law, made it easier for Britain to play an important role in this defensive system and thereby to qualify for a higher place in the ranks of world powers than her economic and military strength might otherwise have warranted. In short, the British position in the Gulf (and in the Middle East generally) served as a ticket of admission to the White House. In a later formulation, which became popular in the 1960s, Britain's Gulf position was seen as making it possible for her to perform a unique peace-keeping role, preventing, by swift, decisive action or by the threat of such action, local disturbances from spreading and involving outside powers. It may be doubted, however, whether any of these three motives—oil, communications, or grand strategy—were so important in the British decision to remain in the Gulf after 1947 as the force of habit. Britain stayed in the Gulf because she was there and had been there for over a century, and also because there was no serious challenge to jolt her out of her habitual assumptions and responses.

The second question posed concerned the manner in which these interests could be protected and these various roles sustained. Diplomatic and political influence were not to be despised, but to have any real weight they had to be backed by force and by the willingness to use it. Formerly, India had supplied a base for action and troops that could be used in the Gulf, although, as the Iraq campaign in 1941 showed, the Indian contribution was not always sufficient. But without the Indian base, the Gulf position had to be supported from elsewhere and Britain had never found a suitable alternative base. Political developments in Egypt soon made it clear that the great Suez Canal base could not be maintained indefinitely. Palestine was closed to Britain after September 1947, and Britain turned half-heartedly to Kenya. The Egyptian base was finally lost in the 1950s: first came the Egyptian revolution of 1952, then the withdrawal of British troops from Egypt in 1953–54, and, finally, the disastrous Suez war of 1956. These events had a major effect on British policy in the Gulf area, for they not only resulted in the closure of the principal British base but led also to the creation of a hostile Arab block across British communications with the East,

65. J. C. Campbell, *Defense of the Middle East* (New York, 1960), pp. 39–62; Sir A. Eden, *Full Circle* (London, 1960), p. 220.

both those via the Red Sea and those via Syria, which made it impossible for Britain to operate successfully either from Britain or Cyprus. They led also to the development of a radical Arab nationalism that affected the Gulf states significantly in riots in Bahrain and Kuwait in 1956, which posed most serious threats to British supplies of oil from the Gulf; and most notably in the 1958 revolt in Iraq, which overthrew the pro-British Hashemite monarchy and inaugurated a series of unstable, professedly radical and nationalist regimes in Iraq, which looked to the USSR for support.[66] The loss of the Suez base led to a decision in favor of Kenya, but in 1960 a rapid change in British policy in Africa made the maintenance of a base in Kenya politically impossible. In 1961, it was decided to turn to Aden, but there too political events upset the decision. Aden became independent in November 1967 and the base was abandoned. The possibility then existed of building on the expanded facilities at Bahrain and Sharja, but this was never done because in January 1968 it was decided to leave the Gulf itself.

The principal factor in the British decision to relinquish its position in the Gulf was that of cost. Ever since the end of World War II, Britain had serviced her commitments frugally. The weaknesses were glaringly exposed in the Suez operation in 1956, and thereafter there were strong political pressures to find a cheaper and more efficient defensive system. The system adopted was that of the nuclear deterrent and a small mobile professional force. This option could not provide for British commitments east of Suez, particularly as it was decided not to proceed with a new aircraft carrier. So, despite the British government's manifest enthusiasm for its eastern role, military logic, political disenchantment, and financial exigency combined in the 1960s to force the cabinet to reconsider its commitments and made the eventual decision inevitable. There is a strong elasticity of supply and demand in regard to commitments; unlike the habit of smoking, habits of strategic thought are extremely vulnerable to changes in price. A blow in the pocket thrust Britain from the Gulf. For the final decision was not discriminating; all commitments east of Suez were abandoned, the seemingly inexpensive Gulf together with the extensive Far Eastern commitment with which, since 1962, it had been linked in a novel strategic concept, embracing the entire Indian Ocean area.[67]

Two questions remain to be answered: how effective was Britain in carrying out her ill-defined policy in the Gulf area between 1945 and 1968; and how far did Britain shape the structure that she left behind? Most obscure in discussions of British policy was the relationship between the interests that informed such policy and the means by which they should be protected; in particular, how British forces could be used to safeguard oil supplies. Developments in Iran and Iraq showed how reluctant Britain was to employ force. In the postwar period, an upsurge of Iranian nationalism found particular expression (after the repulse of the Russian military, political, and economic thrust in northern Iran) in an agitation against British domination of Iran's oil industry, culminating in the nationalization of 1951. The British government considered the use of force, but

66. On the Gulf riots, see J. Daniels, *Kuwayt Journey* (Luton, 1971), p. 46.
67. This is the argument of Philip Darby.

decided against it on the grounds that Britain could not mount an operation sufficiently quickly.[68] A negotiated settlement in 1954 eventually left Britain with a substantial but reduced share in the new oil consortium set up to organize production. In 1958, there was no question of intervention in Iraq—the memory of Suez was too sharp—and British bases at Habbāniyya and Shu'aiba were allowed to fall into disuse and were abandoned when Iraq withdrew from the Baghdad Pact in 1959.[69] In the following years, the British government avoided involvement in the negotiations between the Iraqi government and the oil companies. These negotiations eventually broke down, and in 1961 Iraq resumed all concessionary areas that were not actually producing oil, including most of the valuable Rumaila field.

The loss of British influence on the regional powers was not paralleled among the local states of the Arabian shore of the Gulf. In this area, British influence became more pervasive after 1945 than it had been before. Britain intervened more directly in the internal affairs of the states of Oman. This intervention was a consequence of the need to protect airline facilities and safeguard oil exploration parties; it also represented a resurgence of humanitarianism expressed in a desire to stamp out the remnants of the slave trade and slavery. Increased British intervention can be traced in general matters—a condition imposed upon new rulers, as the price of British recognition, that they should accept the advice of the political agent; the proliferation of political agents in the Gulf area; the creation of new institutions such as the Trucial Oman Levies (later Scouts) and of the Trucial States Council (1952); and, in specific instances, especially where intervention was made possible by the existence of the Levies, a locally recruited force under British and Jordanian officers.[70] Britain intervened to maintain law and order in the interior; to resist Sa'ūdī claims to Buraimī in 1955; and to extend the authority of the Sultan of Muscat into interior Oman in 1957–59.[71] In Muscat, British influence was strengthened by a new treaty in 1951, and in 1958 an agreement provided for the sending of British troops to Oman. In Bahrain, British troops intervened to suppress internal disorder in 1956 and 1965, and in Kuwait, British forces took part in an important operation in 1961, intended to safeguard the newly acquired independence of Kuwait against an apparent threat from Iraq. This last operation deserves greater attention, as it was commonly regarded as the clearest proof of Britain's ability to play an important peace-keeping role in the Gulf and to protect her oil interests.

Kuwait's rise to prosperity was a direct consequence of the cessation of the flow of Iranian oil in 1951. Within a short time, Kuwait became a major oil producer; production increased from 17 million tons in 1950 to 80 million in 1960. Kuwait was of especial importance to Britain, who drew over half of her oil from its fields during the years 1957 to 1960. The rapid development of Kuwait led to the end of the British protectorate in 1961 and its replacement by an agreement between Kuwait and Britain that allowed Kuwait to request British

68. H. S. Morrison, *An Autobiography* (London, 1960), pp. 281–82.
69. Humphrey Trevelyan, *The Middle East in Revolution* (London, 1970), p. 154.
70. Donald Hawley, *The Trucial States* (London, 1969), pp. 170–78.
71. James Morris, *Sultan in Oman* (London, 1957); J. B. Kelly, *Eastern Arabian Frontiers* (London, 1964).

assistance. It was recognized that Iraq might take the opportunity to revive old but unconvincing claims to Kuwait. The new agreement was signed on 19 June, and on 25 June President Qāsim laid claim to Kuwait. The question was, would Iraq support her claim by force? For some days nothing happened, but then evidence suggested that Iraqi troops were being mobilized against Kuwait. Kuwait had no force to resist an Iraqi attack and would have required British help. The British ambassador in Iraq advised his government not to commit ground forces until Iraqi forces actually moved on Kuwait, but the cabinet decided not to wait and on 1–2 July introduced 3,000 British troops into Kuwait in response to a request from the Shaikh.[72] It is noteworthy that the possible threat to Kuwait had induced Britain to maintain a vessel loaded with half a squadron of Centurion tanks permanently in the Gulf since 1960, and this factor made the rapid deployment possible. No Iraqi invasion took place and it was subsequently claimed that prompt British action had averted the threat. This view has been criticized on various grounds. First, it was contended that Qāsim never intended to pursue his claim by force and that there was no good evidence of troop movements against Kuwait.[73] Second, it has been argued that the decisive factor in securing the independence of Kuwait was not the British action but the support for Kuwait demonstrated by other Arab states, led by Sa'ūdī Arabia, which resulted in the admission of Kuwait to the Arab League on 20 July and the replacement of the British force by an Arab League force; another factor was the support of Iran. In many ways, the obtrusive British action was politically embarrassing, and although the authorities in London wished to retain the British force in Kuwait, claiming that the Arab force was inadequate, the Shaikh of Kuwait made it clear that he wanted an Arab not a British force.[74] Third, it has been argued that the British operation was militarily unconvincing; had Iraq pressed an attack, the British force would have been no match for the Iraqis, especially in armor, and but for the fortuitous presence of a British aircraft carrier in the area, there would have been no adequate air cover for the British ground forces for some days.[75] Finally, the operation cost £1 million. There are counters to each of these points, but it is nonetheless clear that the argument that the Kuwait operation demonstrated the effectiveness of British power in the Gulf cannot be accepted without serious question; if anything, the political and military problems argued the wisdom of attempting to repeat it.

After 1961, the area of British control in the Gulf had been reduced to Bahrain, Qatar, the Trucial states, and Oman. Her maritime power was still exhibited by four frigates usually retained in the Gulf, but naval power no longer rested on the sea alone, and there was serious doubt whether Britain could provide air cover against land-based aircraft in the area. Although the British position seemed not very different from what it had been before 1914, it was in fact much weaker.

72. Trevelyan, *The Middle East,* p. 190.
73. R. Hewins, *A Golden Dream* (London, 1963), pp. 280–305; M. Khadduri, *Republican Iraq* (London, 1969), pp. 166–73.
74. Trevelyan, *The Middle East,* p. 198.
75. Darby, *British Defence Policy,* p. 271.

There was no real advance consideration of what should follow the end of Britain's predominance, because its sudden termination had not been foreseen. It seemed evident that such small states could scarcely stand on their own and, therefore, despite Britain's dismal experience with federations, she decided to encourage the formation of a federation of the territories that she had controlled, the more enthusiastically as it appeared to be the wish of some of the rulers concerned; and to try to persuade the other states in the area to accept it. In this last brief period, Britain played a valuable role in assisting in the prior determination of certain disputed claims. But once she had announced her intention to go, Britain's predominant influence in the area was lost and the decisions made were essentially those of the Gulf states directly involved. Although the British role did not entirely cease when the legal foundation of British influence ended at the end of 1971, it was substantially the end of a chapter that had begun at the close of the eighteenth century.

It is common to describe the history of the British connection with the Persian Gulf in terms of the assertion and maintenance of British predominance in response to a recognition of the strategic importance of the area. Such is not the view that emerges from this review of that history. The Gulf found a place in a variety of British strategic theories, but none could be said to have consistently informed British policy in that region. The defense of India, the defense of the routes to the east, and the defense of economic interest each played some part in molding British policy, but none provided a conscious design; rather they were the means by which initial policy was rationalized. British predominance was primarily the consequence of a need for someone to keep the peace and the failure of the regional powers to do so. The British role in the Gulf was formed much more from the responses of local officers to local events than from the answers of cabinets and governors-general to questions of grand strategy. To the governors-general of India (with the exception of Curzon), and still more to the British government in London, the Gulf remained an area of minor importance, where the British position might be supported as long as it did not cost too much, and as long as it served or did not obstruct British purposes in areas of greater concern. But when those conditions were no longer met, the British position in the Gulf was readily compromised and quickly abandoned.

Selected Bibliography

Ali Daud, Mahmood. "British Relations with the Persian Gulf, 1890–1902." Ph.D. thesis, University of London, 1957.

Amin, Abdul Amir. *British Interests in the Persian Gulf*. Leiden, 1967.

Amirsadeghi, H., ed. *Twentieth Century Iran*. London, 1977.

British Documents on the Origins of the War, ed. G. P. Gooch and H. Temperley. Vol. 4. London, 1929.

Bryant, A. *The Turn of the Tide*. London, 1958.

Busch, B. C. *Britain and the Persian Gulf, 1894–1914*. Berkeley, 1967.

———. *Britain, India, and the Arabs, 1914–1921*. Berkeley, 1971.

Butler, J.R.M. *Grand Strategy*. Vol. 2. London, 1957.

Campbell, J. C. *Defense of the Middle East*. New York, 1960.

Chesney, F. R. *Narrative of the Euphrates Expedition*. London, 1968.

Clayton, Sir G. *An Arabian Diary*. Berkeley, 1969.

Cohen, S. A. *British Policy in Mesopotamia, 1903–14*. London, 1976.

Curzon, Hon. G. N. *Persia and the Persian Gulf*. 2 vols. London, 1892.

Dalrymple, A., ed. *An Account of the Navigation between India and the Gulf of Persia*. London, 1786.

Daniels, J. *Kuwayt Journey*. Luton, 1971.

Darby, P. *British Defence Policy East of Suez, 1947–1968*. London, 1973.

Dilks, D. *Curzon in India*. 2 vols. London, 1969–70.

English, B. *John Company's Last War*. London, 1971.

Foster, Sir W. *England's Quest of Eastern Trade*. London, 1933.

Fraser, Lovat. *India under Curzon and After*. London, 1911.

Furber, H. *John Company at Work*. Cambridge, Mass., 1951.

Gehrke, U. *Persien in der Deutschen Orientpolitik während des Ersten Weltkriegs*. 2 vols. Stuttgart, n.d.

Gibbs, N. H. *Grand Strategy*. Vol. 1. London, 1976.

Graves, P. *Life of Sir Percy Cox*. London, 1942.

Grigg, P. J. *Prejudice and Judgement*. London, 1948.

Hartshorn, J. E. *Oil Companies and Governments*. London, 1967.

Hawley, D. *The Trucial States*. London, 1969.

Hoskins, H. *British Routes to India*. London, 1928.

Howard, Michael. *Grand Strategy*. Vol. 4. London, 1977.

Hurewitz, J. C. *Diplomacy in the Near and Middle East*. 2 vols. Princeton, 1956.

Kaye, J. W. *Life of Malcolm*. 2 vols. London, 1856.

Kazemzadeh, Firuz. *Russia and Britain in Persia, 1864–1914*. New Haven, 1968.

Kelly, John B. *Britain and the Persian Gulf*. Oxford, 1968.

———. *Eastern Arabian Frontiers*. New York and London, 1964.

———. "Salisbury, Curzon, and the Kuwait Agreement of 1899." In Bourne, K., and Watt, D. E., eds., *Studies in International History*. London, 1967.

Kent, Marion. *Oil and Empire*. London, 1976.

Khan, M. G. "British Policy in Iraq, 1828–43." Ph.D. thesis, University of London, 1967.

Kumar, Ravinder. *India and the Persian Gulf Region, 1858–1907*. London, 1965.

Landen, R. G. *Oman since 1856*. Princeton, 1967.

Lockhart, L. *The Fall of the Safavid Dynasty and the Afghan Occupation of Persia*. Cambridge, 1958.

Lorimer, J. G. *Gazetteer of the Persian Gulf*. Calcutta, 1915.

Marlowe, John. *Late Victorian*. London, 1967.

Marshall, P. J. *East Indian Fortunes*. Oxford, 1967.

Minto, Countess of. *Life of Minto*. 2 vols. London, 1874–80.

Moberley, F. J. *The Campaign in Mesopotamia*. 4 vols. London, 1923–27.

Monroe, E. *Philby of Arabia*. London, 1973.

Morris, James. *Sultan in Oman*. London, 1957.

Morrison, H. S. *An Autobiography*. London, 1960.

Motter, T. H. Vail. *The Persian Corridor and Aid to Russia*. Washington, 1952.

Nightingale, P. *Trade and Empire in Western India, 1784–1806*. Cambridge, 1970.

Plass, J. B. *England zwischen Russland und Deutschland*. Hamburg, 1966.

Prasad, B., ed. *Defence of India: Policy and Plans*. New Delhi, 1963.

Ronaldshay, Earl of. *Life of Curzon*. 3 vols. London, 1928.

Skrine, Sir C. *World War in Iran*. London, 1962.

Sluglett, Peter. *Britain in Iraq, 1914–1932*. London, 1976.

Sykes, C. *Wassmuss*. London, 1936.
Sykes, Sir P. *History of Persia*. 2 vols. London, 1921.
Trevelyan, Humphrey. *The Middle East in Revolution*. London, 1970.
Warner, G. *Iraq and Syria, 1941*. London, 1974.
Wilson, A. *Loyalties, Mesopotamia, 1914–1921*. Oxford, 1930.
———. *Mesopotamia, 1917–1920: A Clash of Loyalties*. Oxford, 1931.
Winstone, H. V. F. *Captain Shakespear*. London, 1976.

5. Geographers of the Persian Gulf
GERALD BLAKE,
HEATHER BLEANEY, DAVID IMRIE,
AND RICHARD LAWLESS

Mediaeval Islamic Geographers[1]

 The earliest known works of Arabic-writing geographers date from the ninth century A.D., after the consolidation of the Islamic empire on both sides of the Gulf and beyond. The knowledge of the Indians, Iranians, and Greeks that they acquired formed the basis of these works, but their nature responded to the needs of empire and religious obligations. The traditional Bedouin empirical knowledge of the stars was corrected and expanded. Muhammad al-Khwārizmī,[2] the astronomer, produced a revised version of Ptolemy's "geography" in the middle of the ninth century A.D., and the exact positions of countries and, implicitly, their orientation from Mecca, became the subject of a number of works. At about the same time Ibn Khurradādhbih[3] com-

---

NOTE: The following abbreviations are used throughout the footnotes:
EI[1]—*Encyclopaedia of Islam*, first edition.
EI[2]—*Encyclopaedia of Islam*, second edition.
BGA—*Bibliotheca Geographorum Arabicorum* (third edition; Leiden: Brill, 1967).

1. Djugrāfiya, EI[2], (S. Maqbul Ahmad). R. Blanchère, *Extraits des principaux géographes arabes du moyen âge* (Paris, 1957). A. Miquel, *La géographie humaine du monde musulman jusqu'au milieu de 11e siècle*, Centre de Récherches Historiques, Civilisations et Sociétés 7 (Paris: Mouton, 1967). "Comment lire la littérature géographique arabe du moyen âge?" *Cahiers de Civilisation Médiévale* 15 (1972): 97–104. A. Sprenger, *Die alte Geographie Arabiens als Grundlage der Entwicklungsgeschichte des Semitismus* (Berne: Commissionsverlag von Huber & Co. 1875). J. H. Kramers, "L'influence de la tradition iranienne dans la géographie arabe," *Analecta Orientalia* (Leiden: Brill, 1954), 1: 146–58. Idem, "La littérature géographique classique des musulmans," pp. 172–204. J. Célérier, "Islam et géographique," *Hesperis* 39 (1952): 331–71.

2. al-Khwārizmī, EI[1] (E. Wiedemann). al-Khwārizmī, *Das Kitāb Surat al-'ard . . .* hrsg. von H. von Mzik, Leipzig, Bibliothek Arabischer Historiker und Geographen 3 (1926) (Arabic text). H. Daunicht, *Der Osten nach der Erdkarte al-Huwārizmīs: Beitrage zur historischen Geographie und Geschichte Asiens* Bd.1: *Rekonstruktion der Karte, Interpretation der Karte: Südasien*, Bonn, Bonner Orientalistische Studien, N. S. 19 (1968). J. Ruska, "Neue Bausteine zur Geschichte der Arabischen Geographie," *Geographische Zeitschrift* 24 (1918): 77–81.

3. Ibn Khurradādhbih, EI[2] (M. Hadj-Sadok). Ibn Khurradādhbih, *Kitāb al-masālik wa al-mamālik, Liber viarum et regnorum . . .*, ed. M. J. de Goeje, *BGA*, vol. 6.

posed a book of routes and realms (*Kitāb al-masālik wa 'l-mamālik*) that was really a list of the roads with their stages, with brief descriptions of the boundaries and topography of the various provinces. Books soon appeared describing the wonders of the world and curiosities about other peoples. On the whole, interest was confined to the Islamic world and its periphery, and the later descriptive geographies, which contained elements of all the above types, were composed for the entertainment of an educated general audience.

The Persian Gulf was, throughout this period, the scene of lively trading activity that was carried on principally from flourishing cities on the eastern side, such as Hormuz, and Sīrāf, the island of Kīsh (Kaish), and Basra. The western side is scarcely mentioned, except for Oman, long famous for the spice trade, and relatively fertile, and Bahrain with its pearl-divers. The inhospitable reaches of the desert inland are scarcely mentioned, beyond the names of tribes that controlled them. Information is often meager in the extreme, but the principal geographical writers and travelers are briefly described as follows:

al-Balkhī, al-Istakhrī and Ibn Hawqal; al-Maqdisī (al-Muqaddasī).[4] Abū Zaid Ahmad al-Balkhī was, according to al-Maqdisī, the author of a famous treatise on geography, as well as a variety of other subjects, including theology and astronomy, and founder of a "classical school" of Islamic geographers. He was born probably about A.D. 850 and died in A.D. 934, and his book, though lost, is generally thought to survive in the works of al-Istakhrī and Ibn Hawqal, of which it formed the basis, and in parts may be assumed to be virtually intact. It appears to have consisted of a series of maps accompanied by short explanatory texts and dealt with the whole Muslim world, divided into geographical regions.

Abū Ishāq al-Istakhrī, of Persian origin like so many of these writers, enlarged and corrected this work, in about A.D. 951 as another *Book of Routes and Realms*. He followed the same plan, but added considerably to the descriptions of the provinces, so that the maps became subsidiary to the text. Virtually nothing is known about his life, but he endeavored to verify his information by his own observations on his travels, in the course of which he encountered Ibn Hawqal, a geographer from Baghdad. His descriptions of Arabia, the Persian Gulf, and Fārs are virtually identical with those that appeared in the *Book of Routes and Realms* published by Abū 'l-Qāsim ibn Hawqal in about A.D. 971, and these passages are probably therefore much as al-Balkhī wrote them. Ibn

4. al-Balkhī, EI² (D. M. Dunlop). M. J. de Goeje, "Die Istahrī—Balhī Frage," *Zeitschrift der Deutschen Morgenländischen Gesellschaft* (1871) 25: 42–58. Anon. *Hudūd al-'ālam "The regions of the world" A Persian geography 372 AH–982 AD*, tr. and explained by V. Minorsky, with the preface by V. V. Barthold (tr. from the Russian), London, Gibb Memorial Series N.S. (1937) 11: 5–23. J. Kramers, "La question Balhi—Istahri—Ibn Hauqal et l'Atlas de l'Islam," *Acta Orientalia* (1932) 10: 9–30. V. Minorsky, "A false Jayhānī," *Bulletin of the School of Oriental and African Studies* 13 (1949): 93–94. al-Istakhrī, EI² (A. Miquel). *Kitāb al-masālik wa al-mamālik, viae regnorum*, ed. M. J. de Goeje," *BGA*, vol. 1. *The Oriental Geography of Ebn Haukal* (actually from the Persian version), tr. by W. Ouseley (London, 1800). *Das Buch der Länder von Schech Ebn Ishak el Farsi el Isstachri*, tr. A. D. Mordtmann (Hamburg: Akademie von Hamburg, 1845). Ibn Hawkal, EI² (A. Miquel). Ibn Hauqal, *Opus Geographicum . . .*, ed. J. H. Kramers *BGA*, vol. 2. *Configuration de la terre (Kitāb Sūrat al-ard)*, ed. J. H. Kramers and G. Wiet, 2 vols. (Paris: G. P. Maisonneuve, 1965). al-Mukaddasī, EI² (J. H. Kramers). al-Moqaddasī, *Descriptio Imperii Moslemici*, ed. M. J. Goeje, *BGA*, vol. 3.

Hawqal states that he was able to correct his friend al-Istakhri's maps and supplement his information, but it is doubtful that he himself traveled nearer to the Gulf than Basra. The descriptions are somewhat scanty, though Oman and the Persian cities are named as scenes of great commercial activity and the source of pearls.

A contemporary of Ibn Hawqal, from Jerusalem, Abū 'Abd Allāh Shams al-Dīn al-Maqdisī, wrote a substantial encyclopaedia that has been called the greatest of this particular genre. His work, composed during A.D. 985–90, is full of information concerning not only the topography but also the habits, religious beliefs, customs, and trade of the countries of the Muslim world. Unfortunately, the sections treating the Gulf are meager in the extreme and less full than those of Ibn Hawqal.

al-Mas'ūdī.[5] Abū 'l-Hasan 'Alī ibn al-Husain al-Mas'ūdī of Baghdad was one of the most wide-ranging writers of the tenth century A.D. His works are the only real source of information on his life, and we can trace his travels through Persia, India, Ceylon, Egypt, Spain, and Greece. He visited Basra twice and sailed down the Persian Gulf; he died in Egypt in A.D. 956.

It seems that it was the thirst for knowledge as well as a desire for adventure that propelled him across the length and breadth of the Islamic world. One of his extant works, *The Meadows of Gold* (*Murūj al-dhahab*) is a sort of geographical compendium, written in an interesting style that is wider in scope than the work of al-Balkhī's school. He has been criticized for his credulity, but it was part of his method to put down as much information as possible and let the reader decide. His narrative is therefore full of digressions, for instance, on the various theories concerning the formation of pearls and how the divers bring them up, as well as all manner of curiosities about the philosophy, politics, religious beliefs, and eating and drinking habits of the various peoples. Local legends are narrated along with astronomy and topographical features.

Yāqūt al-Hamawī.[6] Yāqūt al-Hamawī died in A.D. 1229. He was the author of a valuable *Dictionary of Countries* (*Mu'jam al-buldān*), in which are listed alphabetically the names of cities and islands, with a brief description. He was an Anatolian Greek, enslaved as a child and bought and brought up by a merchant in Baghdad.

He visited Basra several times, and also visited most of the commercial ports

5. al-Mas'ūdī, EI[1] (C. Brockelmann). *Kitāb al-tanbīh wa'l-ischrāf, indices et glossarium ad tomos 7 & 8,* ed. M. J. Goeje, *BGA,* vol. 8. *Les prairies d'or,* tr. C. Barbier de Meynard and J. Pavet de Courteille (Paris: La Société Asiatique, 1861–1877). *Les prairies d'or,* tr. rev. and corrected, C. Pellat (Paris: Société Asiatique, 1962). al-Mas'ūdī's historical encyclopaedia entitled, *Meadows of Gold & Mines of Gems,* tr. A. Sprenger, vol. 1 (no more published) (London, 1841). *Livre de l'avertissement et de la revision,* tr. B. Carra de Vaux (Paris: Société Asiatique, 1897). *L'Abrégé des merveilles,* tr. B. Carra de Vaux (Paris: Klinksieck, 1898).

6. Yākūt al-Rūmī, EI[1] (R. Blachère). Yāqūt, *Mu'jam al-buldān,* 5 vols. (Beirut: Dār Sādir Dār Beirūt, 1955–57). *Mu'jam al-buldān* (Leiden, 1959). *Jacut's Geographisches Wörterbuch . . .* hrsg. von F. Wüstenfeld, 6 vols. (Leipzig, 1866–70). *The Introductory Chapter of Yāqūt's Mu'jam al-Buldān,* tr. and annotated by W. Jwaideh (Leiden: Brill, 1959). R. M. N. E. Elahie, *The Life & Works of Yāqūt Ibn 'Abd Allāh al-Hamawī* (Lahore: Punjab Univ. Press, n.d.).

on the eastern side of the Gulf, and Oman and Qatīf on the western side. He used the best available written sources for his dictionary, supplementing them with additions and corrections based on his own observations.

al-Idrīsī.[7] One of the most famous Arab geographers, and the first to become known in the west, was Abū ʿAbd Allāh Muhammad al-Hammūdī, known as al-Idrīsī, who was born in Ceuta at the end of the eleventh century A.D. After studying in Cordoba, he traveled about Asia Minor, North Africa, and Spain, and then settled in Norman Sicily. He was commissioned by Roger II to make a planisphere of the seven climates of the earth with all the seas, rivers, cities, roads, etc., and he compiled a huge descriptive geography, named for his patron, to illustrate and complement it. He later rewrote this work in an expanded version for the next king, William I; he left Sicily toward the end of his life and died, probably in his native Ceuta, in 1166.

Except where he was able to use his own knowledge derived from his travels, he relied on previous authors, principally those mentioned above, where the Gulf was concerned; thus he adds little information on this area.

Ibn Battūta.[8] Abū ʿAbd Allāh Muhammad Ibn Battūta was born in Tangier in the early fourteenth century A.D. He was of Berber ethnic origin, but an Arab Muslim by religion and culture and, like so many other travelers, his first journey was a pilgrimage to Mecca, after which he took the opportunity to see some more of the world. He traveled over most of the Muslim world for the better part of twenty-five years, first setting out in A.D. 1325 and settling down in his native Morocco some twenty years before his death in A.D. 1377. He was an educated man, who sought out the learned theologians and jurors in the towns he visited, and even served as *qādī* (judge) for a time in India. On his return, he was commissioned by the sultan to set down an account of his adventures, and he dictated them to an amanuensis, Ibn Juzaiy, who seems to have inserted a certain amount of exaggeration and legend. Ibn Battūta admits to having lost his notes in the course of some of his more perilous adventures and having had to rewrite them from memory, but his *rihla* (journey) remains, nonetheless, a mine of information about the Islamic world from China to Timbuktu.

He visited Oman and the Persian Gulf in 1331–32 and again about fifteen years later. His narrative is at times dry and scanty of information, at others full

7. al-Idrīsī, EI[2] (G. Oman). *Opus Geographicum, sive ʿLiber ad eorum delectationem qui terras peragrare studeant' (Kitab nuzhat al-mushtak)*, ed. A. Bombaci et al. (Naples: Istituto Univ. Or. di Napoli, 1970–76). *Géographie*, tr. P. A. Jaubert (Paris, 1836–40). *Sūrat al-'ard*— Map drawn from that in Latin characters produced by Konrad Miller in 1931, ed. in Arabic by M. Bahjat al-Athari & Jawād Ali, comp. with 5 ill. MSS of al-Idrisi's Nuzhat al-Mushtak, Baghdad, Al-Majmaʿ al-ʿIlmī al-ʿIrāqī, 1370/1951.

8. Ibn Battūta, EI[2] (A. Miquel). *Rihla*—Dār Sādir-Dār Bairūt, 1379/1960. *Voyages,* texte arabe, tr. C. Defrémery & B. R. Sanguinetti, 4 vols. (Paris: Société Asiatique, 1914–22). *Travels of Ibn Battuta*, tr. H. A. R. Gibb, Hakluyt Society Series II, 1958, vol. 110; 1962, vol. 118; 1971, vol. 141. *Travels of Ibn Battuta, 1325–54*, tr. and selected by H. A. R. Gibb (London: Routledge, 1929). *The Travels* translated from the abridged Arabic copies by S. Lee, Oriental Translation Fund, 1829. H. F. Janssens, *Ibn Batouta, "Le voyageur de l'Islam," 1304–1369* (Brussels, 1948).

of the religions and peculiarities of the local inhabitants, their dress, food, etc., with anecdotes of his adventures among them. While not a geographer as such, his natural curiosity led him to acquire a wealth of information about his contemporaries to which we are much indebted.[9]

The First Europeans

The Portuguese Chroniclers. The Portuguese were the first Europeans since the time of Alexander to venture into the Persian Gulf, after their discovery of the sea route to India at the end of the fifteenth century. They came as soldiers and conquerors. Portuguese dominance of the Gulf, achieved at the beginning of the sixteenth century, was part of a grand design to capture the trade between Asia and Europe by securing control of the principal trade routes—the Persian Gulf, the Red Sea, and the Straits of Malacca—and then redirecting trade by way of the Cape of Good Hope. Following the Portuguese conquest, the Gulf ceased to be a major commercial highway, and its once prosperous city states, now under Portuguese suzerainty, fell into economic decline. The great fortress built at Hormuz, commanding the entrance to the Gulf, became the bastion of Portuguese power in the area for over a century; Portuguese ships commanded Gulf waters, and Portuguese governors controlled and regulated trade by decree.

The chronicles dedicated to the history of the Portuguese conquests in Asia and the Middle East provide a wealth of information about the lands bordering the Persian Gulf. Among the most distinguished Portuguese chroniclers were

9. *Minor Works of the Mediaeval Islamic Period:*

i) Ibn al-Fakīh (c. 900), EI[2] (H. Massé). Ibn al-Fakīh al-Hamadhānī, *Mukhtasar Kitāb al-buldān Compendium Libri Kitab al-buldān*, ed. M. J. Goeje *BGA*, vol. 5.

ii) Anon. *Hudūd al-'ālam "The Regions of the World" A Persian Geography 372 A.H.– 982 A.D.*, tr. and explained by V. Minorsky, with the preface by V. V. Barthold (tr. from the Russian), London, Gibb Memorial Series N.S. 11, 1937. *Hudūd al-'ālam min al-mashrik ilā al-maghrib*, ed. M. Sutūda (Tehran: Intishārāt-i Dānishgāh-i Tihrān, 1961), vol. 727, 1340/1961.

iii) Ibn Rustah (tenth century), EI[2] (S. Maqbul Ahmad). *Kitāb al-a'lāk an-nafīsa auctore Ibn Rosteh*, ed. M. J. Goeje, *BGA*, vol. 7. *Les atours précieux (Kitab al-a'lāq al-nafīsa)*, tr. G. Wiet (Cairo: Publs. de la Soc. de Geog. D'Egypte, 1955).

iv) al-Hamdānī, EI[2] (O. Löfgren). *Kitāb Sifat Jazīrat al-'arab*, ed. M. B. Balhīd al-Najdī (Cairo, 1953). M. J. De Goeje (ed.), *Selections from Arab Geographical Literature*, Semitic Study Series 8 (Leiden: Brill, 1907). al-Hamdānī, *Geographie der arabischen Halbinsel*, ed. D. H. Müller, 2 vols. (Leiden: Brill, 1884–91).

v) Qudāma Ibn Ja'far (d. 948 A.D.), EI[2] (C. Brockelmann). *Ibn Khorradādhbeh. . . . et excerpta e Kitāb al-Kharādj auctore Kodāma Ibn Dja'far*, ed. M. J. de Goeje, *BGA*, vol. 6. A. Makki, *Qudama b. Ja'far et son oeuvre*, thesis, University of Paris, 1955.

vi) al-Bīrūnī (d.c. 1050), EI[2] (D. J. Boilot). *Bīrūnī's Picture of the World*, ed. A. Zeki Velidi Togan (Memoirs of Archaeological Survey of India) 53 (New Delhi, 1941). J. F. Kramers, "Al-Biruni's determination of the geographical longitude by measuring the distances," *Analecta Orientalia*, 1: 205–22 (Leiden: Brill, 1954).

vii) Benjamin of Tudela (ca. 1170), *The Itinerary of Benjamin of Tudela*; critical Hebrew text, Eng. tr. and commentary by M. N. Adler (repr. New York, Feldheim, n.d.). *Die Reisebeschreibungen des R. Benjamin von Tudela . . .*, by L. Grünhut and M. N. Adler, 2 vols. (Jerusalem, 1903).

viii) Abu'l-Fidā (d. 1331 A.D.), EI[2] (H. A. R. Gibb). *Taqwīm al-buldān*, ed. J. T. Reinaud & MacGuckin de Slane (Paris, 1840). *Geographie d'Aboulféda*, tr. M. Reinaud and S. Guyard, 2 vols. (Paris: Impr. Nationale, 1883), with a good introduction on Arab geographers in Vol. 1.

João de Barros,[10] Fernão Lopes de Castanheda,[11] Gaspar Correa,[12] and Diogo do Couto,[13] all of whom wrote within a century of one another. With the exception of Barros, they all lived and worked in Portuguese India for many years, although only Correa and Couto appear to have visited the Persian Gulf; Couto may have seen action against the Ottomans in the region. In addition, because they were all officials of the Portuguese crown, their histories were based in part on the rich archival material of the Portuguese colonial administrations, to which they were given free access. Barros, for example, served from 1525 as treasurer and from 1532 to 1569 as crown agent in India House in Lisbon, while Couto became master of the arsenals at Goa and finally keeper of the records. In addition, both Barros and Couto were chosen to write official histories of the Portuguese in Asia. Access to the records of the Portuguese colonial government gives their chronicles a degree of accuracy and detail that earlier writers were unable to achieve, because of the almost total absence of written records in either Arabic or Persian in the indigenous city states of the Persian Gulf. Barros in his *Décadas,* for example, includes detailed financial statistics about local tax receipts and customs dues in the kingdom of Hormuz and its dependencies for the early sixteenth century, based on official documents of the period. Other sources of information, however, were not neglected. Books, maps, and manuscripts were gathered from all over Asia, and returning pilots, officials, and prisoners of war were sought out and questioned.

If Correa seems less a chronicler and more a historian, Barros's interest in geography is evident throughout his work. He is full of praise for the nautical achievements of the Arabs and is impressed by their maps and instruments; the accounts of both Arab and Persian geographers were used in his descriptions of the Persian Gulf. Unfortunately, although he wrote a full account of the produce and commerce of the East and an equally detailed geography of all the lands discovered by the Portuguese, both were lost after his death. Couto remembers him as "our great João de Barros, a man most learned in geography." Couto himself composed a treatise on Asian trade, but this work too has unfortunately been lost.

The weaknesses of the chronicles, however, should not be ignored. They all wrote within a particular historical context. Barros saw the discoveries and conquests as part of the Christian advance against the infidel, beginning in the twelfth century, and dwells with pride on the grandeur of the Portuguese achievements. Castanheda places even more emphasis on the theme of Christian against infidel, and only Correa questions Portuguese policy toward the Asian states and

---

10. João de Barros. *Asia. Dos feitos que os Portugeses fizeram no descobrimento e conquisto dos mares e terras do Oriente.* Sexta edição, actualizada na ortografia e anotada por Hernáni Cidade, 4 vols. (Lisbon, 1945–46).

11. Fernão Lopes de Castanheda, *História do descobrimento e conquista da Índia pelos Portugueses,* 3ª edição conforme à edição princeps, revista e anotada por Pedro de Azevedo, 4 vols. (Coïmbre, 1923–1924).

12. Gaspar Correa, *Lendas da Índia,* publicados . . . sobra direcção de Rodrigo Jose de Lima Felner, 4 vols (Lisbon, 1860–66).

13. Diogo do Couto, *Décadas,* 15 vols. (Lisbon, 1778–88); *Década Quinta,* ed. M. de Jong (Coïmbre, 1937). Cf. A. Bell, *Diogo do Couto* (London, 1924). J. B. Harrison, "Five Portuguese Historians," in *Historians of India, Pakistan & Ceylon,* ed. C. H. Philips (London, 1961), 156–69. C. R. Boxer, "Three historians of the Portuguese Asia (Barros, Couto & Bocarro)," *Boletim do Instituto Portugues de Hongkong* (Macau, 1948): 1–32.

their peoples. Furthermore, although they all describe events in great detail, little time is devoted to the analysis of cause and effect. Nevertheless, these chroniclers were extremely conscientious in their research and were careful to check their sources. Consequently, when their work is tested by modern scholars it is usually found to be reliable.

Until recent years, the value of the Portuguese chronicles to our understanding of the history and geography of the Persian Gulf has been almost completely neglected. Yet these sources contain much more than a mere list of conquests, battles, and political intrigues; nor are they just a sterile list of towns and tribes. They include invaluable information about the people and lands bordering the Persian Gulf during the sixteenth century. There are detailed descriptions of relief, climate, and vegetation, agricultural systems, pastoralism and the nomadic tribes. Special attention is devoted to the ports and urban centers, their morphology, architecture, defenses, trade and the urban economy, and the social, religious, and ethnic composition of the population. The political organization of these societies, and the relationship between Arabs and Persians, Sunnī and Shī'ī are also examined in some detail.[14]

A number of other Portuguese visited the Persian Gulf and wrote about their travels. They include Tenreiro,[15] Augur,[16] Barbosa[17] and Pires,[18] writing in the sixteenth century, and Figueroa[19] and Teixeira[20] in the early seventeenth century. Although less distinguished scholars than Barros, Castanheda, Correa, or Couto, their narratives are, nevertheless, useful sources of first-hand information on the lands and peoples of the Persian Gulf during the century of Portuguese rule. Several of these narratives were utilized by the major chroniclers in the compilation of their histories.

Particularly noteworthy is the work of Pires and Barbosa, probably the earliest Portuguese to visit and describe the newly conquered territories in the Indian Ocean. Tomé Pires (1468–1540), an apothecary, became an official in Portuguese India in 1511, and traveled on a variety of official business in South-

14. For example, they are used extensively in *Mare Luso-Indicum—études et documents sur l'histoire de l'Océan Indien et des pays riverains à l'époque de la domination portugaise*, ed. J. Aubin, 2 vols., Hautes Etudes Islamiques et Orientales d'Histoire Comparée 5 (Geneva, 1971 and 1973).

15. Antonio Tenreiro, *Itinerários da Índia a Portugal por terra*, ed. Antonio Baião, (Coïmbre, 1923), 3–127. Cf. J. Aubin, "Pour une étude critique de l'"Itinerário" d'António Tenreiro," *Arquivos do Centro cultural portugués* 3 (Paris, 1971): 238–52.

16. Augur, *Conquista de las Indias de Persia e Arabia que fizo la armada del rey don Manuel de Portugal e de las muchas tierras, diversas gentes, extranas riquezas e grandes batalhas que alla ovo* (Salamanque, 1512). Cf. J. B. McKenna, *A Spaniard in the Portuguese Indies—The Narrative of Martin Fernandez de Figueroa* (Cambridge, Mass.: Harvard University Press, 1967).

17. M. Longworth-Dames, ed., *The Book of Duarte Barbosa*, 2 vols. (London, 1918–21). (Works issued by the Hakluyt Society, 2nd series, nos. 44 and 49.)

18. T. Pires, *The Suma Oriental of Tomé Pires—An Account of the East, from the Red Sea to Japan, Written in Malacca & India in 1512 & 1515*, trans. and ed. Armando Cortesão, 2 vols. (London, 1944). (Works issued by the Hakluyt Society, 2nd Series, nos. 89 and 90.)

19. Figueroa, D. Garcia de Silva, *Commentarios de D. Garcia de Silva y Figueroa de la embajada que (. . .) hizo al rey Xa Abas de Persia*, 2 vols. (Madrid, 1903).

20. P. Teixeira, *Relaciones d'el origen, descendencia y succession de los reyes de Persia, y de Harmuz, y de un viage hecho por el mismo autor desde la India oriental hasta Italia por tierra* (Anvers, 1610). Cf. W. F. Sinclair, *The Journey of Pedro Teixeira from India to Italy by Land, 1604–1605, With His Chronicle of the Kings of Ormus* (London, 1901). (Works issued by the Hakluyt Society, 2nd series, no. 9.)

east Asia and the Far East. His major work, *Suma oriental*, written between 1512 and 1515, consists of six books, of which Book I is devoted to a description of the lands from Egypt to Cambay. Pires was especially interested in economic conditions and appears to have been a keen and honest observer, although his literary style is poor and sometimes compounded by errors in subsequent translation into English. It is unfortunate that his description of the Gulf is limited to Hormuz. Duarte Barbosa also saw service with the Portuguese government of India during the period between 1500 and 1516–17 and probably visited the Gulf in 1516. He was interested in the study of geography and the races of the world, and his narrative contains valuable descriptions of the lands, peoples, laws, and customs of the kingdom of Hormuz, the Persian shores of the Gulf, and the port of Basra.

The Ottoman Turks

Portuguese control over the Persian Gulf did not, however, go unchallenged. The Ottoman Turks, having conquered Egypt in 1517 and secured control of the Red Sea, later occupied Baghdad and toward the middle of the sixteenth century arrived at the head of the Persian Gulf. After the Ottoman occupation of Basra in 1546, and later the penetration of the Hasā region in northeastern Arabia, the Persian Gulf became the scene of conflict between the Portuguese and the Turks. The results were inconclusive. The Portuguese were unable to establish themselves in the Basra region or in al-Hasā, and the Ottomans failed to win control over Hormuz. The island of Bahrain remained a buffer zone, separating the two rival powers and marking the limit of their influence.[21]

Although a number of notable Turkish geographers—for example, Pīrī Re'īs and Seydī 'Alī Re'īs—saw action with the Ottoman naval forces in the Persian Gulf during the course of the sixteenth century, the Ottoman chronicles of this period are much less informative about the region than the great Portuguese histories. They made little use of the extensive Ottoman archives, which date from the mid-sixteenth century—a rich source of information on the Persian Gulf and one still neglected by scholars interested in this region. Court historians such as 'Ālī, the author of *Künhü 'l Akhbār*,[22] include very little original data on the region. They appear to have drawn extensively from a few more specialized accounts, like the work of Seydī 'Alī Re'īs the famous Ottoman naval commander and author of several books on navigation and marine geography. Seydī 'Alī Re'īs [Chelebi] fought against the Portuguese in the Persian Gulf in 1554, during an attempt to take the Ottoman fleet from Basra to its base at Suez, and wrote a vivid account of his travels and adventures entitled *Mir'ātu 'l-Memālik*.[23] The historian Kātib Chelebi, when dealing with the naval affairs of the Ottoman empire, also relied on the narrative of Seydī 'Alī Re'īs for his account of events in the Persian Gulf. The Ottoman chronicles contain further details about the wars between the sultans and the Safavid rulers of Persia, and some of these histories include information about Basra and the Persian Gulf.

21. S. Özbaran, "The Ottoman Turks and the Portuguese in the Persian Gulf, 1534–1581," *Journal of Asian History* 6, 1 (1972): 45–71.

22. 'Ālī, *Künhü 'lAhbar*, Üniversite Kütüphanesi, Istanbul; MS no. 2377.

23. Seydī 'Alī Re'īs, *Mir'ātü 'l Memālik* (Istanbul, 1895). C. Orhonlu, "Seydi Ali Reis," *Journal of the Regional Cultural Institute* 1, 2 (1967): 44–57.

Matraqchī Nasūh,[24] writing during the reign of Sultan Süleymān (1520–66) described the conflict between the Ottomans and the Bedouin tribes of the Jazāyir, while another chronicle, *Tawārīkh-i-āl-i ʿOthmān*[25] (which may have been the work of the Grand Vizier Rüstem Pasha) gives us some useful facts about the Ottoman occupation of Basra.

European Travelers of the Seventeenth and Eighteenth Centuries

Until the early seventeenth century, the only Europeans who had ventured into the Persian Gulf since the time of Alexander were the Portuguese. By the beginning of the seventeenth century, however, their fortunes were in decline and their control of the Gulf challenged by the Persians. In 1616, Shah ʿAbbās I had granted the English East India Company permission to trade in Persia, and English factories were later established at Shīrāz, Isfahān, and Jāsk. At the suggestion of the Persian ruler, the East India Company agreed to launch a joint attack on the Portuguese stronghold of Hormuz and, under the combined pressure of Persian land forces and English naval power, the fortress capitulated in 1622, thus ending a century of Portuguese domination in the Gulf.

In return for their cooperation, Shah ʿAbbās granted the English East India Company permission to establish a factory at Bandar ʿAbbās (on the Persian mainland opposite the island of Hormuz), which became the headquarters of the company's trade with Persia. In the eighteenth century, permanent factories were also established at Basra and Būshahr (Bushire), but the company's trade with the Gulf never became very lucrative and by the late eighteenth century it was running at a loss. Nevertheless, until the end of the eighteenth century British interests in the Gulf remained exclusively commercial, and the company had no political involvement in the region. However, ships of the Bombay Marine—the armed branch of the company's fleet—patrolled the waters of the Gulf and afforded naval protection to local shipping against attacks by pirates.[26]

A great wealth of information about the people and lands of the Persian Gulf is to be found in the archives of the British East India Company, which form part of the India Office Records.[27] Particularly noteworthy are the records of the individual factories, consisting of business transactions, correspondence reports and diaries prepared by the local resident and his staff for the government of Bombay and the company headquarters in London. They contain invaluable first-hand information about economic conditions and trading activities in the Gulf during this period.[28]

On the other hand, the narratives of independent travelers to the region,

24. Nasuh Matrakçi, *Süleymān-nāme*, Arkeoloji Kütüphanesi, Istanbul; MS no. 379.
25. Rüstem Pasha (?) *Tawārīkh-i Āl-i ʿOthmān*, Üniversite Kütüphanesi, Istanbul; MS no. 2438.
26. J. B. Kelly, *Britain and the Persian Gulf, 1795–1880* (Oxford: Clarendon Press, 1968).
27. P. Tuson, "Archival Sources for Arabian & Gulf Studies in the India Office Records," a paper presented at the Centre for Documentation & Research, Abū Dhabī, February 1977.
28. J. A. Saldanha, *Selections from State Papers, Bombay, Regarding the East India Company's Connection with the Persian Gulf, with a Summary of Events, 1600–1800* (Calcutta, 1908). (India Office) Persia & Persian Gulf Series, vol. 21, Samuel Manesty and Harford Jones (Joint Factors, Basra) to Governor-in-Council, Bombay, *Report on the Commerce of Arabia and Persia*, 18 December 1790.

particularly those of the seventeenth century, are disappointing. The majority were primarily concerned with either Persia or India, sometimes both, and little attention was devoted to the Persian Gulf.

One of the earliest travelers was the Italian, Pietro della Valle (1586–1652),[29] who arrived at the Gulf of Hormuz en route to India in 1622 during the seige of Hormuz by the Persians and British. Born into one of Rome's oldest families, he was well educated and became a member of the Academy of Umoristi—an Italian scientific and literary society. After entering military service and serving with Spanish forces in North Africa, he began his travels in the East, leaving Venice in 1614 and visiting Constantinople, Baghdad, and Persia before embarking at Bandar 'Abbās for India in 1623. On the return journey from India to Italy, he visited Muscat and Basra. Della Valle made only one journey to the Middle East and India and spent the rest of his life in Rome. His travels were described in a narrative divided into three parts devoted to Turkey, Persia, and India, respectively and composed from letters addressed to a friend in Naples. Only part one was published during his lifetime and the rest several years after his death. Della Valle was a skilled linguist, who claimed to know Turkish, Persian, and Arabic, and an intelligent observer. Unfortunately, although he traveled all through the Persian Gulf, his descriptions of the region are rather brief.

Later, in the mid-seventeenth century, another traveler to visit the Persian Gulf was the Frenchman Jean-Baptiste Tavernier[30] (1605–89). His father was a cartographer who owned a shop in Paris that sold geographical maps, and two of his uncles were well-known engravers and printers of maps. It was against this background that the young Tavernier developed an interest in distant lands and in travel. Already by the age of twenty-two he had visited most European countries. After military service in Bohemia, Hungary, and Germany he succeeded, through the good offices of Father Joseph, Richelieu's adviser and the director of French missionary activities in the Levant, in joining an embassy sent by the French king to Constantinople and Palestine. This was the first of six expeditions that Tavernier made to the Middle East and Asia between 1632 and 1668, when he returned to Paris and retired a wealthy man as a result of his commercial activities in the East. In 1684, at the age of seventy-nine years, Tavernier was invited to Berlin by the Elector of Brandenburg to establish an East India Company on the model of the British and Dutch companies. The project did not succeed, but the old traveler was undaunted and immediately set out on his first visit to Muscovy where he died in 1689.

The narrative of his adventures was published in 1677, entitled *Six voyages de Jean-Baptiste Tavernier*. Books 4 and 5 refer to his travels in Persia, which he visited nine times between 1632 and 1668. His knowledge of the lands bordering the Persian Gulf was limited to the region between Lār and Bandar 'Abbās, which he visited during a journey from Shīrāz to the island of Hormuz. Although his experiences were spatially limited, his brief description of the rural land-

29. E. Grey, *The Travels of Pietro Della Valle* (from the Old English translation of 1664 by G. Havers) 2 vols. (London, 1892). (Hakluyt Society, vols. 84, 85.)

30. J. B. Tavernier, *Voyages en Perse et description de ce royaume*, ed. Pascal Pia (Chartres, 1930).

scapes, agricultural activities, the ports and trade of this section of the Persian Gulf is based on careful and intelligent observation.

One of the few accounts by a British traveler is that by Dr. John Fryer,[31] who visited Persia and East India in the late seventeenth century. He states in the introduction to his work that it was written to draw attention to British achievements in this region. Most of his account, which is divided into eight letters, is devoted to his travels in India and Persia and, like Tavernier, his knowledge of the Persian Gulf was limited to Bandar 'Abbās and its hinterland, with a brief additional visit to Muscat. Fryer writes at length about his experiences, but his account is purely descriptive. As a medical doctor he was particularly interested in health hazards affecting the region, and special attention is devoted to the inhospitable climate and to problems of water supply. His work also contains detailed descriptions of the local wildlife, as well as some useful information about trading activity and shipping in the port of Bandar 'Abbās. Less satisfactory are his descriptions of the people of the region, and there is little effort to understand either their culture or their ways of life. This point is well illustrated by his comments on leaving the southern shores of the Gulf and arriving on the Persian mainland. He writes: "So strange an alteration in three hundred leagues as passes admiration! for whereas we left a sullen, melancholy, sunburnt nation; an open, jovial and clear complexioned race of mankind is offered in exchange." Fryer made only one visit to the Persian Gulf and returned from India to England by the Cape route.

Somewhat different from the other accounts by seventeenth century travelers to the Gulf is the work of Dr. E. Kaempfer.[32] He was born in Westphalia, but went to Persia in 1684 as secretary of a Swedish embassy to the Persian court. In 1686, he joined the Dutch East India Company at Bandar 'Abbās as chief surgeon—a post that he held for two years. During that time he made a detailed study of the natural history of the Bandar 'Abbās district, studying in particular the date palm, and published the results, together with illustrations, in his *Amoenitatum Exoticarum Fasciculi*, which appeared in 1712.

Accounts by eighteenth-century travelers provide information about much more of the Persian Gulf region than those of the seventeenth century, which focus almost exclusively on Bandar 'Abbās and its immediate hinterland. Nevertheless, once again the Persian Gulf is not a major region of interest in these narratives, but is generally referred to merely because of its function as a routeway on the journey to or from India. One of the earliest eighteenth-century travelers was Alexander Hamilton.[33] Born in Scotland, he became a ship's captain and traveled extensively in Europe, North Africa, and the West Indies before establishing himself in Bombay, where he became a merchant, trading with lands as far away as China. Hamilton made several visits to the Persian Gulf and five chapters of his narrative, published in 1727, are devoted to the region. He visited Muscat, Hormuz, and Bandar 'Abbās, and traveled along both the Persian

31. J. Fryer, *A new account of East India and Persia in eight letters being nine years travels begun 1672 and finished 1681* (London, 1698).

32. E. Kaempfer, *Amoenitatum Exoticarum Politico—Physico-Medicarum*, Fasciculi 5, Collectae Lemgoviae, Meyeri, 1712.

33. A. Hamilton, *A New Account of the East Indies*, ed. Sir William Foster, 2 vols. (London: Argonaut Press, 1930).

and Arabian shores of the Gulf as far as Basra. In the preface to the book, he states that friends urged him to place on record his observations and remarks to show that he was "no mercenary scribbler." His descriptions of the places that he visited in the Gulf are vivid and colorful, with detailed accounts of local costumes and cuisine. His work reveals some knowledge of the history of the region, but Lorimer, compiler of the great gazetteer of the Gulf, has found many inaccuracies in his narrative.

A later narrative referring to the mid-eighteenth century is that by Edward Ives,[34] a doctor who served with the British navy in India. He traveled back to England from India by way of the Persian Gulf and described his experiences in two books published in 1773. In the preface, Ives alleges that he was motivated to write down his experiences merely for his own amusement and to please his family and friends. The result is a highly personal account of his adventures and experiences in the form of a diary of events. The lands bordering the Persian Gulf are described in the final chapter of the first book and the opening chapter of the second. There are brief but useful descriptions of the places visited during the journey, which took place in 1758, i.e., Bandar 'Abbās, the island of Khārg, and Basra. He shows particular interest in the climate and its effect on the health of the residents, and the local population. Ives also discusses the troubled political conditions in Persia at that time, the leading personalities involved, and the strained relations between local rulers and European merchants.

Other British travelers to the Gulf during this period include Parsons[35] and Jackson,[36] but the most outstanding European to visit the region in the eighteenth century and to record his observations was without doubt the Danish geographer, Carsten Niebuhr.[37] He visited the Gulf during the course of a Danish expedition sent to Arabia in 1762 by Frederick V of Denmark (probably at the suggestion of the eminent Hebraist, Michaelis of Göttingen), to carry out biblical and geographical research. The expedition was composed of five members, each chosen for his special qualification; Niebuhr, the son of a farmer, was a trained surveyor, who had also spent some months learning Arabic before the journey; Peter Forskal, a doctor and botanist; Christian Cramer, a surgeon and zoologist; Frederick von Haven, philologist and orientalist, who with Forskal knew Arabic; and George William Baurenfeind, an artist. Of the six members, only Niebuhr survived. Sickness accounted for the others, either in Arabia, on the way to India after the expedition, or on arrival. Niebuhr remained in Bombay for fourteen months before returning to Europe by way of Muscat and the Persian Gulf, and to him fell the task of recording not merely his own observations but the discoveries made by the whole party. Niebuhr's *Description of Arabia* was first published in German in 1772 and in French two years later. His other book, *Travels in Arabia*, appeared in 1774–78, and the French edition in 1777–80. An abridged English version was published in 1775.

34. E. Ives, *A voyage from England to India in the year 1754 and a journey from Persia to England by an unusual route* (London, 1773).

35. A. Parsons, *Travels in Asia and Africa* (London: Longman, Hurst, Rees & Orme, 1808).

36. J. Jackson, *Journey from India towards England in the year 1797* (London, 1799).

37. K. Niebuhr, *Description de l'Arabie faite sur des observations propres et des avis recueillis dans les lieux mêmes* (Amsterdam, 1774). Idem, *Voyage en Arabie et en d'autres pays circonvoisins*, 2 vols. (Amsterdam, 1776–80).

His *Description of Arabia* begins with a general survey of the Arabian peninsula, the climate, people, religion, and customs, followed by a detailed account of each of the major regions—Yemen, Oman, the lands bordering the Persian Gulf, and the provinces of Najd and the Hijāz, incorporating not merely his own personal observations, because he visited only a small part of this vast region, but information gathered from conversations with local residents, especially educated Arabs and merchants. On the other hand, his second work, *Travels in Arabia*, is basically a diary of his journeys, containing descriptions of the places that he actually visited.

Yemen was the chief goal of the Danish expedition, even though it was already at that time the best-known in Europe of all the Arab lands. Much of Niebuhr's narrative is devoted to a description of this country and the results of the team's exploration. His knowledge of the Persian Gulf region was acquired during the journey from Bombay to Europe after the expedition's tragic end. He visited only a few places during his journey—Muscat, Būshahr (with an expedition to Shīrāz and Persepolis), Basra, and the Shatt al-'Arab—but supplemented his own observations with information received from conversations with local people.

Although not the major focus of his study, Niebuhr presents a rich and full account of the lands bordering the Persian Gulf, their topography, the people, their economy and ways of life. The principal towns are described, together with the main events in the region's recent history, the current social and political organization, and the leading personalities and important families. Above all, one is impressed by his tireless energy and spirit of adventure, and by the restraint and good judgement that characterize his work. Unlike the majority of contemporary travelers, he displays no trace of superiority in his attitude toward the local people. He traveled as a poor merchant without ostentatious display and did not seek out merely the wealthy and powerful. His knowledge of the Arabic language was sufficient to enable him to communicate with local people, and he had the ability critically to evaluate reports acquired from others. Consequently, his descriptions of the areas that he was unable to visit are extraordinarily detailed and accurate. His skills as a surveyor were also well employed. Niebuhr produced an excellent map of the Persian Gulf that remained in use for many years,[38] together with numerous useful plans and sketches of the region's major ports and urban centers.

The Nineteenth and Twentieth Centuries[39]

The important political factor in the nineteenth century was the emergence of British dominance in the Persian Gulf. Britain had originally taken an interest

38. In 1785, Lieutenant John McCluer of the Bombay Marine carried out a brief survey of the Persian shore of the Gulf correcting some details on Niebuhr's map. See *An Account of the Navigation between India and the Gulf of Persia at all Seasons* (London, 1786).

39. General references include: J. N. L. Baker, *A History of Geographical Discovery and Exploration* (London: George Harrap, 1931). D. G. Hogarth, *The Penetration of Arabia* (London: Alston Rivers, 1905). Jacqueline Pirenne, *À la découverte de l'Arabie* (Paris: Le Livre Contemporain, 1958). Sheik Mansur (pseud., V. Maurizi), *History of Seyd Said* etc. (London, 1919).

in the Gulf to safeguard her lines of communication with India from local pirates, and latterly from rival European powers. Throughout the nineteenth century, protection of the route to India was Britain's main concern, and this led her to increase her control of the Gulf shaikhdoms and Persian tribal groups in the southern Persian provinces.

As the century progressed, other interests were added—suppression of the slave trade, development of commerce, and the protection of British interests in Mesopotamia and Persia. These factors motivated European explorers (but principally the British) to find out more about the Gulf region and the interior of Arabia, to see what the possibilities were of extending political and economic influence, as well as protecting existing interests.

The explorers faced several problems. Arabia, with the exception of the Yemen, was inhospitable and barren, and the lack of water restricted the movement of travelers. Mountain regions on the peripheries and deserts in the interior posed physical barriers, while the hostile attitude of tribesmen, many of whom had never seen a European before, posed a barrier of a different kind. They resented foreigners, and this forced explorers to travel under disguise as locals, sometimes at night, and more often than not, protected by soldiers of the local rulers to guarantee them safe passage. Thus, their movements were restricted, and it was not always easy to record scientific observation. Added to this, was the spread—at the beginning of the century—of the fanatical Wahhābī movement. With their hatred of foreigners' influence, the Wahhābīs presented a hazard to travelers that greatly exacerbated the trials of one of the harshest climates in the world.

A foretaste of the difficulties awaiting travelers in Arabia was given in the *Journal* of Daniel Saunders (1794).[40] Saunders, a sailor on the ship *Commerce* from Boston, U.S.A., was wrecked near Ra's Mirbāt on the Zufār coast in July 1792. Only eight of the twenty-seven men who came ashore survived the month-long walk to Muscat. The appalling experiences of the party occupy much of the *Journal*, but useful observations are included on the coastal area of Oman and its people, forty years before the journeys of Wellsted and Whitelock.

Captain George Foster Sadlier[41] (1789–1859) was the first European to cross Arabia from east to west, and in so doing, described country that had not been explored before. He was appointed by the Bombay government in 1819 to proceed on a mission to meet the Egyptian Ibrāhīm Pasha, who was attempting to stop the spread of Wahhābī power in Arabia. The exact position of Ibrāhīm Pasha's camp was unknown, so Sadlier called at Muscat to tell the Imam of the intended expedition of the Egyptians inland to crush the Wahhābīs. On landing at Qahf in June 1819, however, Sadlier found that the Egyptians had already gone. He was determined to follow them, as he had been instructed to tell the Pasha that Britain would give him both military and naval support if he decided to capture Ra's al-Khaima. He left Qahf and began his journey of a thousand miles. It took eighty-four days to reach Yanbū' on the Red Sea, before going on to Jidda. Sadlier's *Diary of a Journey Across Arabia (1866)* contains details of his journey, and includes a very useful map. His description of the Hasā country

40. D. Saunders, *A Journal of the Travels and Sufferings of Daniel Saunders* (Salem, Mass.: Thos. Cushing, 1794).

41. G. F. Sadlier, *Diary of a Journey across Arabia* (Bombay, 1866).

to the north of Muscat is particularly valuable. His *Diary* gives a very modest account of a great journey, rich in detail and personal observation.

Captain W. F. W. Owen[42] of H.M.S. *Leven* was among the first British naval officers to gather information systematically about the coast of Oman. From Christmas Day 1823 until 11 January 1824 he traced all the most important navigation points between Muscat and Ra's Mirbāt, a distance of 450 miles. Previous knowledge of the coast was based on old (possibly sixteenth-century) Portuguese authorities still in use among Arab sailors, and on Horsburgh's *Directory*. Certain parts had been more recently surveyed by Captain Smith, R.N., in about 1780, Lieutenant Grub of the East India Company in 1820, and Captain Moresby in 1822. Many useful details of the coast were furnished by Captain Owen that were still worthy of publication in 1857, in the absence of a proper survey.

Captain S. B. Haines[43] of the East India Company undertook further exploration and survey of the coast of South Arabia in 1835. The results of his surveys, from Muscat to Ra's al-Hadd, were published in 1845. Some of his officers undertook expeditions inland, including Cruttenden and Wellsted. Lieutenant Wellsted returned from Bombay in November 1835 to begin his travels in Oman.

Lieutenant J. R. Wellsted,[44] F.R.C., served on the East India Company's vessel *Palinurus* (Captain R. Moresby) while undertaking a survey of the Red Sea in 1830, with a view to establishing a new steamship route from India to Great Britain. Also in 1830, he traveled from Muscat to Baghdad through the Persian Gulf and wrote an account of his journey that contains some interesting details, particularly on Bahrain island. Much of his description of the lower Gulf was, however, derived directly from Lieutenant Whitelock's work.

Between November 1834 and March 1835, Wellsted traveled in the interior of Oman, accompanied most of the time by Lieutenant Whitelock (whom he scarcely mentions in his book). Wellsted was frustrated in his aim of reaching Buraimī because of its occupation by Wahhābī tribesmen, but he visited 'Ibrī and Nizwa. His entertaining volumes include detailed and generally accurate information about the country, adding considerably to knowledge of southeastern Arabia and revealing the unexpected fertility of parts of Oman. Many of his observations on historic and political aspects may have been derived from V. Maurizi, an Italian adventurer who was medical adviser to the Imam Saiyid Sa'īd from 1809 to 1815. Saiyid Sa'īd greatly impressed Wellsted in 1834.

On a later survey of the coast of southern Arabia by the *Palinurus* (Captain S. B. Haines) in April–May 1835, Lieutenant Wellsted traveled in the Wādī Maifa'a with Midshipman Cruttenden, discovering the Himyaritic ruins of Naqab al-Haqar, some 50 miles inland.

42. W. F. W. Owen, "The Coast of Arabia Felix," *Nautical Magazine* (April, 1857): 180–91.
43. S. B. Haines, "Memoir of the South and East Coasts of Arabia," *J. Royal Geog. Soc.* 15 (1845).
44. J. R. Wellsted, "Narrative of a journey from the tower of Bá-'l-haff on the Southern Coast of Arabia, to the ruins of Nakab al Hajar in April 1835," *J. Royal Geog. Soc.* 7 (1837): 20–34. Idem, *Travels to the City of the Caliphs along the Shores of the Persian Gulf and the Mediterranean*, 2 vols. (London: Henry Colburn, 1840). Idem, *Travels in Arabia*, 2 vols. (London: John Murray, 1838).

In 1830, Lieutenant Whitelock[45] recorded valuable information about the islands and coasts at the entrance to the Persian Gulf. He visited Hormuz, Qishm, and the Great and Little Tunb Islands, noting that the former was well stocked with antelope. His observations provided a useful supplement to charts prepared by officers of the Indian navy between 1821 and 1829 and to the notes of Lieutenant G. B. Kempthorne.[46] Whitelock met Wellsted in Oman in 1834 and accompanied him on most of his journeys. After leaving Wellsted in March 1835, Whitelock traveled from Shinās on the coast of Oman to Sharja on the Persian Gulf. Three years later, the Frenchman Rémi Aucher-Éloy made a very different type of journey in a part of Oman already visited by Wellsted and Whitelock.

Rémi Aucher-Éloy[47] was possibly the most dedicated scientific explorer of the early nineteenth century. An enthusiastic botanist, he traveled in several parts of the Middle East between 1830 and 1839. In 1837, he set out to explore Oman, traveling overland through Persia to Bandar 'Abbās. Reaching Muscat in March 1838, he crossed the Jabal al-Akhdar to Nizwa, collecting 250 species of plants, some of which were hitherto unknown, and recording detailed observations on the country. Aucher-Éloy was dogged by ill-health, and a fever contracted in Oman led to his death at Isfahān in October 1839. Since 1836, he had sent over 15,000 plant specimens to the Natural History Museum in Paris.

If his account is to be believed, W. H. Palgrave's[48] journey in 1862–63 was remarkable indeed. Crossing Arabia from Gaza via Hā'il and Riyadh to the Persian Gulf at al-Qatīf, he continued by sea to Oman, where he was shipwrecked near Muscat, returning to Basra by sea via the Persian Gulf. His *Narrative of a Year's Journey through Central and Eastern Arabia* (1865) was widely acclaimed, being translated into French and German. Later travelers, however, found many inaccuracies in his writings, and it seems probable that Palgrave did not visit many of the places he describes. H. St. J. B. Philby, for example, has shown that the megalithic monuments Palgrave described at al-'Uyūn never existed. Philby believed that the journey was an elaborate alibi to cover Palgrave's activities as a political agent on behalf of the French, who had political ambitions in Arabia at the time. Palgrave attributed his lack of precision to the continuous need to preserve his native disguise and to the loss of some of his notes in the shipwreck of March 1863. Palgrave was able to fool most of the world because he probably knew more about the Middle East than any contemporary European. Living in Damascus, he almost certainly composed his travels from the second-hand reports of his Arab political agents. Palgrave was awarded the gold medal of the Paris Geographical Society, but was not similarly honored in Britain.

45. F. Whitelock, "Descriptive sketch of the islands and coast at the entrance of the Persian Gulf," *J. Royal Geog. Soc.* 8 (1838): 170–84.

46. G. B. Kempthorne, "Notes made on a survey along the eastern shore of the Persian Gulf in 1828," *J. Royal Geog. Soc.* 5 (1835): 263–85.

47. R. Aucher-Éloy, *Relation de voyages en Orient de 1830 à 1838* (annotated by M. Le Compte de Jaubert) (Paris: Lib. Encyclopédique de Roret, 1843).

48. W. G. Palgrave, *Narrative of a Year's Journey through Central and Eastern Arabia (1862–63)*, 2 vols. (London: Macmillan, 1865). H. St. J. B. Philby, "Palgrave in Arabia," *Geog. J.* 109 (1947): 282–85.

Shortly after Palgrave's alleged journey, it was suggested to Colonel Lewis Pelly,[49] the British Resident at Būshahr, that the Royal Geographical Society would be interested to know something of the country between the Persian Gulf and Riyadh, including the exact position of the oasis of al-Hufūf. Because of the increasing importance of Arabia to Britain, however, Pelly saw it as his duty to obtain information about the interior of Arabia for its own sake.

Pelly started his journey in Kuwait in 1865, traveled southwest by south through Thauj and Warī'a, passing through hundreds of Bedouin who had gathered for spring grazing. He then went across the Summān Desert and the Dahnā' sands to Najd. The most important aspect of Pelly's work is the scientific method he used to determine the exact position of Riyadh and al-Hufūf. He kept a journal describing each day's march, noting the points at which they started and finished, the number of hours actually on the move, and the general direction of movement. Together with stellar observations, Pelly was able to map his route both accurately and in detail. However, taken as a whole, Pelly's work is most useful as a supplement to that of Sadlier.

Colonel S. B. Miles,[50] British Resident and consul-general at Muscat, made two trips into the interior. The first was in 1870 with M. Werner Munzinger, a German who was making a strategic study of the area. The aim of the journey was to find any Himyaritic inscriptions, particularly at Habbān. The journey began at Aden, thence by sea to Hisn-Ghurāb, and then on to Nahab, the chief town of the Upper 'Aulāqī tribe's territory. They had a great deal of trouble with the Bedouin, and the guides wanted them to travel at night—a suggestion that they declined, as this would have defeated the whole point of the journey. As a result of this first journey, Miles severely criticized Palgrave's account of Muscat as inaccurate, notably in that he described villages that did not exist.

Because of the relatively peaceful state of the country, Miles made another journey in 1885, continuing his search for Himyaritic inscriptions. He proposed to travel through Oman and Dhahīra, which he had failed to reach in 1870–71 (although Wellsted and Whitelock had traveled there in 1835). Miles traveled through Samā'il and Izkī to Adam, then across the Najd al-Dharia to Obn and Shank, descending to the Wādī Huwāsina. He returned to Muscat through Rustāq.

Himyaritic letters were found at Shaa, and at Kathria, a high sandstone rock, they found one Himyaritic word. Miles made some extensive notes on the tribes between Bir 'Alī and Aden—principally the Wāhidi, the Du'aibī, the 'Aulāqī, and the Fādilī. He also proved that a practical route did exist from Nisāb and Harib to the Jauf of Yemen.

Theodore J. Bent[51] was in many ways unique among the western explorers in Arabia. Most Arabian explorers had adopted some form of disguise, but Bent traveled quite obviously as a foreigner (1894–95), on the assumption that this

49. L. Pelly, *Journal of a Journey from Persia to India through Herat and Candar* (Byculla: Bombay, 1866).

50. S. B. Miles, "Notes of a Journey through Oman and El-Dhahireh," *India Office Document* (R/15/6/18), 1886.

51. T. J. Bent, "Exploration of the Frankincense Country, Southern Arabia," *Geog. J.* 6 (1895): 109–33.

frankness gave him greater freedom to remain longer and to see more than his predecessors. He was also accompanied by his wife.

His aim was to travel from Muscat to Hadramaut, in an attempt to map the area. He adopted a piecemeal approach, producing a large number of small maps before putting them altogether. He had managed to penetrate Hadramaut in 1894, but tribal unrest had prevented him from traveling as far as he had wished. Bent waited until 1895, when there was a state of relative tranquillity, before advancing.

The main product of his journey was a description of the Dhufār (Dhofar) area. He began his journey at Dhufār by exploring the area and the Gaza mountains. The fertility of Dhufār contrasted sharply with the barren nature of the remainder of the Arabian coastline; he also noted the absence of suitable harbors.

From Dhufār, Bent traveled inland in a northeasterly direction from the coast at Raisūt to Takha, exploring the area behind the town. From this point he tried, unsuccessfully, to penetrate the Mahrī country and the Hadramaut. His courageous decision not to travel in disguise did not bring the freedom he had hoped.

Samuel Zwemer,[52] American missionary of the Dutch Reformed Church, had done a great deal of missionary work in Muscat with his brother Peter before they left the town in 1895 during a quarrel between the sultan and tribesmen of the interior.

Zwemer made three important journeys into the northern part of Oman in the period 1900–01. In 1900, he traveled from Sharja on the Persian Gulf to Shinās and Suhār on the Gulf of Oman, through Wādī Hitta. In February 1901, he traveled from Abū Dhabī to Sharja, and in May 1901, in the north of Oman via Buraimī to Suhār. While the prime motivation for his travels was his missionary zeal, his work *Arabia: The Cradle of Islam* contains some useful geographical details about northern Oman.

Major (later Sir) Percy Cox[53] was British Agent in Muscat from 1899 to 1904 and British Resident in the Persian Gulf from 1904 to 1913. He linked up the area explored by Zwemer with that explored by Miles. He spent much of his time trying to improve the relationship between the sultan of Muscat and the British authorities. In his role as British Resident in the Gulf, he was responsible for securing peace between the rival political factions in Arabia of Ibn Saʿūd and Muhammad ibn Rashīd.

He made his journey in 1902, from Abū Dhabī (which he reached on a gunboat), overland to Muscat, through the interior of Oman. He traveled east to Buraimī, then southeast across the Dhahira, through Dank and ʿIbrī to Gabrīn and Bahla. From here, Cox traveled northeast to the Jabal al-Akhdar, where he encountered some problems of safe passage that he finally overcame. He returned to Muscat via Samāʾit.

Captain W. H. I. Shakespear,[54] previously in the consular service at Bandar

---

52. S. M. Zwemer, *Arabia: The Cradle of Islam* (4th edition; London: Fleming H. Revell, 1912).

53. P. Cox, *Geog. J.* 19 (1902): 452.

54. D. Carruthers, "Captain Shakespear's Last Journey," *Geog. J.* 59 (1922): 321, 334, and 401–18.

'Abbās and Muscat, was appointed political agent at Kuwait in 1909. He extended his influence inland and on several excursions he filled in large blanks on the map. In 1909, he reconnoitered an area approximately 75 miles south of Kuwait, although he followed this in 1910 with a more extensive journey to Lisāfa, and then on to Hafar al-Bātin.

Shakespear made an extended tour to the south in 1911 to Nta, crossing unexplored country to the southeast. He returned to the region previously explored by Pelly in 1865. His principal finds were inscribed stones at the well of Hinna and the ruined site of Thaj. These were the first known monuments of the Sabaeans in northeast Arabia. Shakespear's journey of 1913 added 600 miles of new survey, as he penetrated as far as Majma'a, the chief town of Sudayr on the flanks of the Jabal Tuwaiq.

His most important journey was in 1914, when he crossed Arabia from the Gulf to Egypt, covering about 1,200 miles of largely unknown territory. Only about one-third of the whole route between Kuwait and the first Egyptian outpost in the Sinai at al-Kuntilla had been covered by Europeans. Shakespear had made a continuous route traverse to check latitude, and hypsometric readings for altitude gave a useful list of heights between the Gulf and the Hijāz railway. The journey took about three and one-half months and was important for producing reliable maps and details of routes in previously unexplored territory. Shakespear was killed during a tribal skirmish at Majma'a in 1915.

At about the same time, two other travelers were at work in the same region Captain G. E. Leachman,[55] of the Royal Sussex Regiment, traveled to the Najd in 1913–14 from the Syrian desert, to 'Ujair. He made his first expedition in 1909–10, when he studied the Wādī Khār, the great length of which he was the first to record. The journey of 1913–14 produced some useful notes on towns and general information about the country, but there was little opportunity for any surveying or mapping. The true importance was political, for it brought this British officer into touch with the leader of the Wahhābīs at Riyadh only two years before World War I. His previous journey (1910) had allowed him to make contact with the powerful shaikhs of the Amārāt and Muntafiq.

Early in 1912, the Dane Barclay Raunkiaer traveled in eastern Arabia on behalf of the Royal Danish Geographical Society to reconnoiter for a proposed Danish expedition into the southern desert. Various parts of Raunkiaer's route (Kuwait-Buraida-Riyadh-al-Hufūf-'Ujair) coincided with parts of the journeys of W. G. Palgrave (1862), Carlo Guarmani (1864), L. Pelly (1865), C. M. Doughty (1878), and W. H. I. Shakespear. Raunkiaer's scientific intentions were largely thwarted by practical problems, but his account of Kuwait in 1912 was praised by T. E. Lawrence, and he was the first European to visit Riyadh for fifty years. In Riyadh, he met 'Abd al-Rahmān Ibn Sa'ūd, father of 'Abd al-'Azīz Ibn Sa'ūd. While in Kuwait, Raunkiaer had become seriously ill; he never recovered and he died in 1915, aged twenty-five.

In 1923–24, Major R. E. Cheesman,[56] reached the unvisited oasis of Yabrīn, on the fringe of the great southern desert. He traversed 150 miles of unknown

55. G. E. Leachman, "Journey through Central Arabia," *Geog. J.* 43 (1914): 500–520.
56. R. E. Cheesman, *In Unknown Arabia* (London: Macmillan, 1926).

country and was able to fix the position of al-Hufūf accurately for the first time. A keen naturalist, his writings were a valuable introduction to flora and fauna in eastern Arabia.

One vital gap in European knowledge of Arabia thus remained: the Rubʿ al-Khālī or the Empty Quarter. This vast sandy desert was first crossed from south to north by Bertram Thomas[57] in 1931, and from north to south, in the following year, by H. St. J. B. Philby.[58] In 1946–47 and 1947–48, Wilfred Thesiger[59] made two remarkable journeys in little-known parts of the Empty Quarter. Although Thesiger added little to knowledge of the maps of Arabia, his observations of Bedouin life have become a classic. His travels were the last of their kind, providing a modern insight into the rigors of exploration on foot and camel-back.

Selected Bibliography

For the principal editions and translations of the texts of the *Islamic Geographers*, see both editions of the *Encyclopedia of Islam* (Leiden and London, 1913–34; new edition, 1958). For the principal editions and translations of *Western Geographers*, please refer to the notes.

Aubin, J., ed. *Mare Luso-Indicum—études et documents sur l'histoire de l'Océan Indien et des pays riverains à l'époque de la domination portugaise.* 2 vols. Geneva, 1971–73.

Baker, J.N.L. *A History of Geographical Discovery and Exploration.* London, 1931.

Bell, A. *Diogo do Couto.* London, 1924.

Blachère, R. *Extraits des principaux géographes arabes du moyen âge.* Paris, 1957.

Cheesman, R. E. *In Unknown Arabia.* London, 1926.

Daunicht, H. *Der Osten nach der Erdkarte al-Huwārizmīs: Beitrage zur historischen Geographie und Geschichte Asiens.* Bd. 1: *Rekonstruktion der Karte, Interpretation der Karte: Südasien.* Bonn, 1968.

Elahie, R.M.N.E. *The Life and Works of Yāqūt Ibn ʿAbd Allah al-Hamawī.* Lahore, n.d.

Harrison, J. B. "Five Portuguese Historians." In *Historians of India, Pakistan, and Ceylon,* ed. C. H. Philips, pp. 156–69. London, 1961.

Hogarth, D. G. *The Penetration of Arabia.* London, 1905.

Janssens, H. F. *Ibn Batouta, "Le voyageur de l'Islam," 1304–1369.* Brussels, 1948.

Miquel, A. *La géographie humaine du monde musulman jusqu'au milieu du 11ᵉ siècle.* Centre de Récherches Historiques, Civilisations et Sociétés 7. Paris, 1967.

Pirenne, Jacqueline. *À la découverte de l'Arabie.* Paris, 1958.

Sprenger, A. *Die alte Geographie Arabiens als Grundlage der Entwicklungsgeschichte des Semitismus.* Berne, 1875.

Thesiger, W. *Arabian Sands.* London, 1959.

Thomas, Bertram. *Arabia Felix: Across the Empty Quarter of Arabia.* London, 1938.

Togan, A.Z.V., ed. *Bīrūnī's Picture of the World.* New Delhi, 1941.

Zwemer, S. M. *Arabia: The Cradle of Islam.* 4th edition. London, 1912.

57. Bertram Thomas, *Arabia Felix: Across the Empty Quarter of Arabia* (London: Readers' Union, 1938).
58. H. St. J. B. Philby, *The Heart of Arabia,* 2 vols. (London: Constable, 1922).
59. W. Thesiger, *Arabian Sands* (London: Longmans, 1959).

6. The Political Geography of the Persian Gulf

R. MICHAEL BURRELL AND

KEITH McLACHLAN

Territorial Boundaries—Examples and Problems

 As with so many other features of the contemporary scene, the complex pattern of political boundaries around the Persian Gulf owes much to the existence of massive petroleum resources. Even in the recent past, boundaries were uncertain and were rarely defined. A former British Political Resident, Sir Rupert Hay, drew upon personal experience when he wrote: "Before the advent of oil the desert was in many ways similar to the high seas. Nomads and their camels roamed across it at will and, though there were vague tribal limits, there were few signs of the authority of any established government outside the ports and oases."[1] In the words of J. B. Kelly, what existed were "*frontières de convenance,* shadowy lines which serve to mark off the jurisdiction of one ruler from that of another."[2]

Kelly has explained why this was so.

Until recent years there was little disposition on the part of the rulers concerned to give these lines any more substance. The concept of territorial sovereignty in the Western sense did not exist in Eastern Arabia. A ruler exercised jurisdiction over a territory by virtue of his jurisdiction over the tribes inhabiting it. They, in turn, owed loyalty to him and not to the shaikhdom, amirate or sultanate in which they dwelt. Political allegiance to a territorial unit, such as is implicit in the European states system, is unknown to the Arabian tribesman. His loyalty is personal to his tribe, his shaikh, or a leader of greater consequence, and not to any abstract image of the state. In so far as he conceives of a territorial loyalty, it is to his domestic abode, his wells, his gardens, his palm trees, or, in the case of the nomad, his *dirah,* or tribal grazing ground. A claim to jurisdiction over him, therefore, amounts to a claim to jurisdiction over the land he occupies. In the case of the settled populations of the seaports or oases such claims do not normally give rise to any difficulties. Applied to nomadic tribes, however, they almost inevitably produce complications.

1. R. Hay, *The Persian Gulf States* (Washington, D.C., 1959), pp. 3 and 4.
2. J. B. Kelly, *Eastern Arabian Frontiers* (London, 1964), p. 17.

While the pattern of movement of a nomadic tribe is normally fixed, it may alter slightly, or even dramatically, with changes in the grazing brought about by drought or other causes. For a ruler to claim possession of the area over which a tribe roams, on the grounds that it owes loyalty to him, is tantamount, in theory, to his claiming possession of an area not only of considerable size but also one whose limits may fluctuate, sometimes to a large degree. In practice, however, such claims are usually limited to the tribe's home range, or *dirah*, to which it may or may not possess exclusive rights. But a tribe's loyalty is not always constant. It may be, and sometimes is, withdrawn from one ruler and transferred to another, or even withheld completely. Where it is transferred, the tribe's new ruler is as likely as not to lay claim to its *dirah*. Since it is just as likely that the tribe's former ruler will refuse to recognize its defection or relinquish his claim to its *dirah*, the territory in question becomes an object of dispute.[3]

Under such circumstances, traditional rulers disliked, and if possible they avoided, the creation of firm boundaries for their states. H. St. J. B. Philby reported that Ibn Sa'ūd "was by no means enamoured of Sir Percy Cox's ideal of a fixed frontier, owing to the traditional Badawin [Bedouin] situation in the area concerned,"[4] when that British official was trying, in 1922, to set limits to Sa'ūdī expansion to the northeast. Simple, but sound, reasoning lay behind this opposition to fixed frontiers. Tribal folk and, in particular, their leaders could see little sense in the drawing of apparently arbitrary lines across almost feature-less desert. Frontiers that paid little or no attention to patterns of migration, and to possible changes in those patterns resulting from shortage of forage or the drying up of wells, were unlikely to be regarded as sacrosanct, and they could only give rise to quarrels. When the areas in question were poorly surveyed, if surveyed at all, and where the location of important wells was in doubt, then disputes were even more likely to occur.

The European mind was, however, reluctant to accept this reasoning and instead sought the reassurance of established frontiers. The first country to have to meet the wishes of the European powers in this respect was Persia, and it is appropriate to see how complex this process could be.

Warfare between Persia and the Ottoman empire was not uncommon, and the cessation of hostilities was sometimes marked by the signing of documents that resembled peace treaties, but rarely was the frontier fixed. The so-called "Treaty of Peace and Frontiers" between Turkey and Persia, for example, which was signed in May 1639 at Dhuhāb, followed a period of prolonged warfare between the two states, but it could not be said to have established a frontier line; rather, it described that strip of land in which the authority of both sultan and shah was weak and disputed.[5] Somewhere within that zone lay the boundary and, in the absence of reliable maps and modern means of transportation, communication, and political control, little else could be expected.

Such a treaty could not bring to an end frontier disputes between the two states, and in 1842 it seemed likely that major hostilities would once again erupt between Persia and Turkey. This would not have been in the interests of the two Great Powers Britain and Russia, which had now begun to pay increasing

3. Kelly, *Eastern Arabian Frontiers*, pp. 18 and 19.
4. H. St. J. B. Philby, *Saudi Arabia* (London, 1955), p. 284.
5. British and Foreign State Papers (London, 1912), 105: 763–66.

attention to that area of the world. They were able to persuade the potential enemies to establish a joint boundary commission and to sign the Treaty of Erzerum of 1847, which reaffirmed the 1639 treaty; but it also appointed a commission of delimitation to survey the disputed area and to determine where, on the map, the actual frontier lay. It should be noted that this treaty allocated the whole of the Shatt al-'Arab (i.e., up to the low water mark on the eastern bank), from Muhammara to the point of entry into the Persian Gulf, to the Ottoman empire. This provision does not appear to have been contested at the time by the Shah, but it was to be a source of future disputes.[6]

The commission of delimitation began its work in 1849, and it had first to survey the 700 miles of terrain that lay between Muhammara in the south and Mount Ararat in the north. The outbreak of the Crimean War interrupted progress, and when the English and Russian surveyors finally compared their maps in 1865 they discovered no less than 4,000 discrepancies in the names and locations of places on the first half of the survey sheets alone. After what the secretary to a later boundary commission described as "some surprising feat of cartography," a *carte identique* some 60 feet long and over 2 feet wide was produced.[7] Persia and Turkey reasserted their belief that the frontier did indeed lie somewhere within that zone, but further progress toward a frontier line was slow and was seriously interrupted by the outbreak of the Russian–Turkish war of 1890. Border skirmishes and incursions continued to occur, but by 1911 the two European powers had even greater interests at stake. The existence of an infant oil industry in the southwest of Persia was a focus of British attention, while Russia had now gained a large and recognized sphere of influence in northern Persia. London and St. Petersburg resolved therefore to delimit the frontier on the map and to demarcate it on the ground by the erection of boundary pillars. A new commission of delimitation was appointed in 1913, but on this occasion the British and Russian members were authorized to arbitrate, and not merely to mediate, between Persia and Turkey. The determination of the Great Powers to see an end to this dispute was reflected in the fact that the new commission completed its survey and constructed the boundary pillars in less than twelve months. Even so, the task was finished only weeks before the outbreak of World War I.

Although the work of the 1913 boundary commission did not put an end to quarrels about Persia's western boundaries (control of the Shatt al-'Arab remained a matter of dispute until 1975),[8] pressure exerted by the Great Powers had been responsible for the considerable degree of progress that had been achieved. In like manner, it was London that was largely responsible for sustained attempts to delimit and demarcate a fixed frontier on Persia's eastern boundaries with Afghanistan and the British protected states in Baluchistan. Work on this frontier began in 1870, and the fact that only one Great Power was involved meant that progress was less difficult, albeit not easy to achieve.

6. V. J. Sevian, "The Evolution of the Boundary between Iraq and Iran" in C. A. Fisher (ed.), *Essays in Political Geography* (London, 1968), pp. 211–23.

7. G. E. Hubbard, *From the Gulf to Ararat* (Edinburgh, 1916), pp. 10–12.

8. For the texts of the Iraqi-Iranian treaty and protocols of June 13, 1975, see *Le Matin/An-Nahar Arab Report*, Beirut, vol. 6, no. 26, 30/6/75; and vol. 6, no. 28, 14/7/75.

These efforts in eastern Persia were again not entirely successful: part of Persia's frontier with Afghanistan had to be demarcated again in 1934-35, and the complex question of the division of waters in the Helmand River between Afghanistan and Iran was still a matter of some dispute in the late 1960s; but in the east as in the west, Persia's boundaries had been established with a considerable degree of certainty before the outbreak of World War I.

On the Arabian side of the Gulf, however, matters were very different. On that side, there were few if any territorial borders that could be regarded as established and accepted. One of the reasons for this, i.e., the desire of tribal leaders to retain maximum flexibility, has already been mentioned. A second important factor was the lack of pressure from the Great Powers. Here the contrast with the situation in Persia was very marked. On the Arabian side of the Gulf, throughout the nineteenth century the British government, and particularly British officials in India, sought to avoid territorial commitments. It was believed both that Britain's interests could be met by maintaining peace at sea, and that that task could be accomplished by the navy alone.[9] To be drawn into the complexities of the internal politics of the Arabian peninsula was something to be avoided like the plague. One result was that only Bahrain—an archipelago—was to receive a guarantee of external defense by Britain, for that ruler's defense could be secured by maritime power alone. The other rulers could receive no such promises about the preservation of their territories, for to have made such commitments would have involved the possible use of land forces. In the nineteenth century, Britain had no wish to concern herself with the delimitation of boundaries in eastern Arabia. It was only after receiving the mandate for Iraq, and realizing that the growing power of the new Sa'ūdī state appeared to threaten that country's southern fringes, and later to threaten the borders of the shaikhdoms of the Trucial coast, that Britain began to take a sustained interest in such matters.

With the creation of new Arabian states in the twentieth century, the likelihood of border disputes increased greatly. Perhaps the best-known quarrel concerned Sa'ūdī Arabia's claim for a major extension to her southeastern boundaries. This issue is generally known as the Buraimi oasis dispute, but in fact the area involved was immensely larger than that occupied by that collection of small villages. The claim advanced by Sa'ūdī Arabia in 1949, for example, would have involved the loss of some 80 percent of the territory of Abū Dhabī.[10] The claim was last revived by Riyadh, albeit in a modified form, during 1971, after oil had been discovered in the disputed area. In July 1974, it was reported that the two rulers had reached an agreement and that the resources of the oil field would be shared between the two states. It was also reported that Sa'ūdī Arabia had gained an outlet to the waters of the Persian Gulf at the base of the Qatar peninsula, but the full details of the agreement do not appear to have been made public.[11]

9. For the history of Britain's involvement in the Persian Gulf in the nineteenth century, see J. B. Kelly, *Britain and the Persian Gulf, 1795–1880* (Oxford, 1968).

10. For details, see Kelly, *Eastern Arabian Frontiers.* Both the British and Sa'ūdī Arabian governments published documents concerning the dispute, which are discussed in Kelly's book.

11. J. D. Anthony, *Arab States of the Lower Gulf: People, Politics, Petroleum* (Washington, D.C., 1975), pp. 148–49.

Another well-known territorial dispute is the claim by Iraq to the whole of Kuwait's territory.[12] That claim was pursued actively in the summer of 1961, when British troops were used to assist in the defense of Kuwait's borders. Since that time, the Iraqi claim has been revived intermittently, but on a modified basis. At the heart of the current dispute is Baghdad's claim to the Kuwaiti islands of Būbiyān and Warba; the claim to the whole of Kuwait now seems to have been dropped. The Iraqi government has said that it needs those two islands in order to be able to improve, by deepening, the approaches to its port at Fāō. In fact, however, if the islands were to be gained by Iraq then that state would have a much better claim to offshore areas that are believed to be very rich in oil. (For a discussion of the general issue of submarine boundaries, see below.)

The greatest concentration of potential disputes occurs, however, at the opposite end of the Gulf, within the United Arab Emirates. Only two of the seven members of that federation, Abū Dhabī and Umm al-Qaiwain, possess contiguous territory. All the others consist of a main territory and several outlying enclaves. Some of the latter are small indeed and may comprise only part of a village or a small clump of date palms. The seven states also have diverse political histories. The most northerly shaikhdom, Ra's al-Khaima, seems to have had an independent existence in the late nineteenth century, but it was incorporated within Sharja in the early years of the present century, before being recognized by Britain as an independent entity in 1921. Kalba, on the Batīna coast, was recognized as an independent shaikhdom by Britain between 1936 and 1951; in the latter year, it was incorporated within Sharja. The most recent change occurred in 1952, when Fujaira was recognized by Britain as an independent shaikhdom.[13]

Diverse patterns of tribal settlement and migration, combined with a complex and often obscure political history, have therefore resulted in an extremely complicated patchwork of territorial holdings within the United Arab Emirates, and very few of the frontiers have ever been demarcated. The small size of some of the holdings involved should not, however, be taken as an indication of the degree of importance attached to them. When the ruler of Fujaira tried, in 1972, to give a date garden in his emirate to the ruler of Abū Dhabī, the shaikh of Sharja objected to the transfer on the grounds that the water within the date garden had, he believed, traditionally been used by some of his subjects as well as by those of the shaikh of Fujaira. The suggested transfer involved a piece of land covering approximately a quarter of an acre, but in the fighting that resulted, more than twenty people were reported to have been killed.[14]

Lord Halifax had pointed to one of the origins of such problems in January 1939, when, as British secretary of state for foreign affairs, he wrote to Lord Zetland, the secretary of state for India: "One of the main causes of the frontier difficulties which have arisen in this part of Arabia in recent years has been the

12. H. M. Al Baharna, *The Legal Status of the Arabian Gulf States* (Manchester, 1968), chapter 15.
13. See Anthony, *Arab States of the Lower Gulf;* M. M. Abdullah, *The United Arab Emirates: A Modern History* (London, 1978); and R. S. Zahlan, *The Origins of the United Arab Emirates* (London, 1978) for the political history of those shaikhdoms.
14. Anthony, *Arab States of the Lower Gulf,* pp. 214–15.

fact that His Majesty's Government and the Government of India have in the past given undertakings to local rulers recognizing them as the possessors of certain territories, when those rulers had in fact little hold over the territories in question, or have since lost such influence there as they formerly possessed."[15] It was precisely this giving of undertakings that the makers of British policy in the nineteenth century had sought to avoid.

Two factors were to cause Britain to change this policy in the twentieth century. One was the creation of the new state of Sa'ūdī Arabia, part of whose territory had in the nineteenth century been under the nominal control of the Ottoman empire. The British government felt that its continuing interests in the Red Sea and Persian Gulf routes to India meant that limits had to be set to the expansion of the new Sa'ūdī state before it endeavored to control the whole of the peninsula. A second and contemporaneous cause of British involvement was that oil concessions were beginning to be sought and granted in Arabia. In Persia, the D'Arcy oil concession had been signed in 1901, and oil was discovered seven years later. In the Ottoman empire, the Turkish Petroleum Company had been formed before World War I to begin exploration in what is now northern Iraq. The extension of oil exploration ventures into Arabia proper did not begin until the 1920s, but when it did occur it meant that rulers who had previously been reluctant to allow the delimitation of boundaries now became keen to establish them as advantageously as possible.

The ruler of Bahrain granted an oil concession in 1925, and oil was discovered seven years later. In Sa'ūdī Arabia, the first concession was granted in 1923, but exploration did not begin until after a second concession had been signed in 1933, and it was a further five years before commercially viable oil reserves were discovered. The ruler of Kuwait had granted his first concession in 1934, and oil was discovered in 1938. Qatar had granted its first concession in 1935, and oil was found four years later. No discoveries were made in the Trucial states before 1939, but the possibility of oil being found in that region had been recognized as early as 1922, when the six shaikhs had promised the British Political Resident in the Gulf that they would not grant exploration concessions to persons other than those acceptable to the British government.[16]

Although important oil discoveries had been made in the Arabian peninsula before 1939, major commercial development of those fields did not take place until after World War II, when a further very important change occurred—the claim by riparian states to the resources of the sea-bed of the Gulf. This meant that submarine boundaries were soon to assume an importance as great as those on land. The existence of oil reservoirs on both sides of the Gulf had led to earlier speculation that oil was also likely to be found under the waters of the Gulf, but in the late 1930s adequate techniques for undersea oil drilling were not yet available. Some of the concessions that had then been granted included exploration rights in territorial waters, but in 1945 the legal situation was altered when

15. Quoted in R. M. Burrell, "Britain, Iran and the Gulf: Some Aspects of the Situation in the 1920s and the 1930s," in D. Hopwood, ed., *The Arabian Peninsula: Society and Politics* (London, 1972), p. 163.

16. The six shaikhs were the rulers of Sharja, Ra's al-Khaima, Dubai, Abū Dhabī, 'Ajmān and Umm al-Qaiwain; see Al Baharna, *Legal Status of the Arabian Gulf States*, pp. 316–17.

President Truman claimed, for the United States, possession of the natural resources of the sea-bed and subsoil of the continental shelf of the United States. Four years later, the king of Sa'ūdī Arabia, followed by nine other rulers of the Arab coast, issued similar declarations about the offshore resources of the Gulf. An Iranian law that made corresponding claims was drafted in 1949 and passed by the parliament in Tehran in 1955.

A major difficulty concerning these declarations arises from the geographical fact that the waters of the Persian Gulf are very shallow—rarely over 50 fathoms —and the internationally accepted depth for the edge of the continental shelf is 100 fathoms. In other words, what could be described as the continental shelf of the Arab states extends up to the low-water mark on the Persian shore and vice versa.[17] This meant that the whole floor of the Gulf was open to conflicting claims, and as the necessary oil drilling techniques soon became available, many of these claims were pursued with vigor.

Although the problems were complex, they resolved themselves into two basic issues—the division of the sea-bed between Iran and the states of the Arabian peninsula on the one hand, and the division of any agreed Arabian zone among the Arab riparian states on the other. With the object of seeking the maximum amount of submarine territory, the Iranian government argued that the median line should be drawn equidistant between outlying Persian islands (for example, that of Khārg) and the Arabian shore, and not equidistantly between the two coastlines. As the island of Khārg lies over 20 miles off the Persian coast, such an arrangement would have been greatly to the advantage of Tehran. The Gulf, however, is dotted with many islands, and Arab governments were quick to claim similar treatment for their off-shore possessions. In those agreements that have been reached, few islands have been allowed the advantage of their full distance from the mainland, and in cases where the existence of islands has affected the drawing of the median line, those islands have usually been allowed the advantage of only half their off-shore distance. After long and complex negotiations, an agreement was reached between the governments of Iran and Sa'ūdī Arabia in 1968, and that agreement was ratified the following year. For much of the central section of the Gulf, there now exists an agreement concerning undersea delimitation, and even though the line drawn may follow an apparently tortuous course, serious disputes are less likely in this zone. At the head of the Gulf, however, and for some of the waters off the United Arab Emirates, there are no such binding agreements. In the latter case, both sets of problems, namely, the division between Arab and Persian zones, and the division within the Arab zone, persist. Iranian claims to the islands of the Tunbs and Abū Mūsā have added a further complication to the issue.[18] The British government recognized Abū Mūsā as being territory belonging to Sharja, while the two Tunb islands belong to Ra's al-Khaima. In 1971, the Iranian government managed to reach an agreement with the shaikh of Sharja about the island of Abū Mūsā, but no such agreement was possible between Tehran and the shaikh of Ra's al-Khaima, and the two Tunb islands were occupied by a small Iranian invasion

17. See Al Baharna, *The Legal Status of the Arabian Gulf States*, Chapter 17.
18. On claims to Abū Mūsā and the Tunbs, see Abdullah, *United Arab Emirates*, Chapter 4 (II) and 4 (IV), and Zahlan, *The Origins of the United Arab Emirates*, Chapter 8.

force in early November 1971. The dispute around Abū Mūsā did not concern only Iran and Sharja, for in 1970 an inter-Arab disagreement had occurred over that island's territorial waters. The shaikh of Sharja had claimed a twelve-mile radius zone of territorial waters; whereas the shaikh of Umm al-Qaiwain, while accepting that Abū Mūsā belonged to the shaikh of Sharja, believed that only a three-mile radius of territorial waters was acceptable. As well as involving Umm al-Qaiwain and Sharja, the dispute also involved the intermediate shaikhdom of 'Ajmān, which claimed that its rights in the offshore zone had been infringed by the declaration of a twelve-mile limit of territorial waters around Abū Mūsā.[19]

With regard to the division of zones between the Arab riparian states, much depends upon how the offshore boundaries are projected. To simplify a very complex matter, it can be said that if they are extended at that angle at which the territorial boundaries meet the coastline, then some of the riparian states feel themselves to have been deprived of potential oil-bearing areas; in these cases such states tend to argue that the offshore line of division should be drawn tangentially to the point of contact between the land frontier and the coastline. The existence of many islands, and indeed the definition of the term island as opposed to a tidally covered shoal or sandbank, has given rise to further complications. Not all problems, however, are insoluble, and some of the inter-Arab boundaries have been settled; for example, that between Bahrain and Sa'ūdī Arabia was agreed upon in 1968.

A further complication arises when oil fields are discovered that straddle either proposed or agreed lines of demarcation. Under such circumstances, geological conditions could make it easier for one state to extract oil and thereby gain greater revenues. Even if the geological conditions do not favor either partner, differences in patterns of drilling or in extraction techniques can allow one of the states to "capture" a greater share of the oil than the line of demarcation would appear to permit. Examples of this problem occur in the Safaniyya field, which is shared between Sa'ūdī Arabia and the Sa'ūdī Arabia/Kuwait neutral zone. At the opposite end of the Gulf, the Bunduq field straddles the offshore boundary between Qatar and Abū Dhabī. In the latter case, the two states have agreed to share the revenues derived from the field.

Thus, in brief, the territorial and submarine boundaries in and around the Gulf are a reflection of very complex historical and geographical factors. The fact that Iran was the subject of such intense Anglo–Russian rivalry at the end of the nineteenth century was, in this respect at least, of advantage to her, for she was the first country to acquire anything resembling established boundaries. The creation of new states in the Arabian peninsula during this century, and the expanding pattern of oil exploration, have together meant that territorial boundaries have taken on a new significance. Although some disputes have been resolved by patient negotiations, there are still several cases where serious conflict could occur.[20]

19. See *Oil and Gas Journal*, 8 June 1970.
20. See Al Baharna, *Legal Status of the Arabian Gulf States*, pp. 298–300.

The Changing Pattern of Economic Power

If the quest for the discovery of oil reserves has given a new importance to the drawing and location of international boundaries in the Gulf region, then the exploitation of those reserves and the resulting patterns of international trade have recalled earlier eras in the region's history. Lebon described the area as "a ganglion of world routes"[21] situated at the heart of the Old World, and it is this crucial location that has given the area repeated importance since the emergence of the earliest civilizations in the Middle East.

With the epoch of the great discoveries made by the European powers from the end of the fifteenth century, a second factor in the geopolitics of the Gulf— rivalry by external powers for influence within and over the region—began to emerge. Toward the end of the eighteenth century, that rivalry began to intensify, and after the defeat of France in the Napoleonic Wars, the major contestants were Britain and Russia.

Discovery of oil in commercial quantities at Masjid-i Sulaimān in southern Iran in 1908 brought into play a third geopolitical factor. Nothing could illustrate this new importance more clearly than the purchase by the British government in 1914 of a major interest in the oil company operating the Iranian concession. From this time, rival economic interests focused on petroleum. In the early years of the twentieth century, it became apparent that the Persian Gulf area offered a cheap and plentiful supply of oil products for the industrialized and industrializing nations of the world. Within the last half century, it has been established that this region held the largest single accumulation of crude oil reserves in the world. By the 1960s, Japan and Western Europe were largely dependent on the Persian Gulf for oil supplies, while the United States of America had developed an international oil business heavily dependent upon ownership of oil concessions in this area.

A natural result of the production and export of oil from the Persian Gulf was a return flow of foreign exchange income to the governments of the respective states, and the growth of enclaves of intensive but isolated industrial activity associated with the oil industry in the oil fields, refineries, and export terminals of the region. Differences, often appreciable, grew up between the economic standards of those countries with oil and those without; and, moreover, similar discrepancies developed between those provinces or areas where the operations of the oil companies had an impact and those regions of the same country where traditional activities continued unaffected by the new industry. An imbalance in regional and intraregional economic development has a profound influence on political relations between the littoral states and between the states of the Persian Gulf and other powers.

The balance of economic power between the littoral countries of the Persian Gulf has been of greater international concern since the United Kingdom began its protracted military withdrawal from the area. British monopoly of petroleum

21. J. H. G. Lebon, "South-West Asia and Egypt" in W. G. East, O. H. K. Spate, and C. A. Fisher, eds., *The Changing Map of Asia* (5th edition [revised]; London: Methuen, 1971), p. 53.

resources in the region was lost much earlier, beginning with the 1928 Red Line agreement, accelerated by the signature of the Sa'ūdī Arabian concession by Standard Oil of California in 1933, and it culminated in the nationalization of the Anglo-Iranian Oil Company in 1951.

In a changing situation, there have been a number of constant factors. In terms of surface area, only three of the states bordering the Persian Gulf are large—Sa'ūdī Arabia, with 873,000 square miles (2,260,000 square kilometers); Iran, 636,363 square miles (1,648,000 square kilometers); and Iraq, 167,567 square miles (438,446 square kilometers). If the entire area of modern Oman is taken into account, then this, too, could be considered among the major territories of the region with 105,000 square miles (272,000 square kilometers). The smaller states of the Persian Gulf represent an opposite pole with extremely limited surface areas (Table 6–1).

The existence of co-adjacent states of vastly differing sizes presents specific political problems. With few exceptions, the tiny national entities of the Persian Gulf region are difficult to defend. Generally, open terrain and lack of scope for defense in depth have fostered a degree of insecurity since British military withdrawal. Amalgamation of the former Trucial states within the United Arab Emirates (UAE) has been one form of response to problems of scale. But even within this unit, problems of relative size cannot be ignored, and to some of its smaller members the UAE appears—and is sometimes described as—"Greater Abū Dhabī." The small countries have tried, as another form of defense, to maintain good relations with as many of their larger neighbors as possible.

Polarization between the large and small states is even more apparent when population size is taken into account. Iran is outstandingly the main area of demographic strength, with more than 35 million people, and no other state approaches this total; indeed, the Iranian population is half as big again as the combined population of all other countries of the region. Only Iran has a market of sufficient size to offer economies of scale and the potential for development of industries with viable home markets. All other states suffer the adverse effects of restricted domestic markets, including absence of economies of scale, limited scope for division of labor, and a poor labor supply for the industrial

TABLE 6–1. AREAS AND POPULATIONS
OF THE PERSIAN GULF STATES

Country	Surface area sq km	1976 population	Persons per sq km
Iran	1,648,000	33,592,000	21
Iraq	438,446	11,505,000	21
Kuwait	16,900	1,093,000	65
Oman	272,000	770,000	3
Qatar	5,200	182,000	35
Sa'ūdī Arabia	2,260,000	9,260,000	4
United Arab Emirates	32,000	656,000	21
of which: Abū Dhabī	25,000	236,000	9

Sources: United Nations yearbooks; official country reports; *Europa, Middle East and North Africa 1976/77*; Economist Intelligence Unit, *Quarterly Economic Reviews*.

sector.[22] Insofar as military strength is a function of population size, and in the Persian Gulf area this is a relevant consideration, Iran is an unequal regional power, with more men under arms than the total populations of many of the smaller states.

The Persian Gulf has long been an area of easy and relatively unimpeded movement. Until recent times, the waters of the Persian Gulf offered passage between opposite shores that was more easily accomplished than travel from the coast to centers inland in the Arabian peninsula and the Iranian plateau. In consequence, there has been intermingling of Iranian and Arab groups across the waters of the Persian Gulf.[23] Iranians, in particular, have moved at various times to the shore of the Arabian peninsula, where they constitute an appreciable minority in a number of the states and have become important members of the trading communities in their adopted countries. A second movement by Iranian migrants to the shaikhdoms came in the period after 1951, when Iranian labor participated in the expansion of the oil industry on the southern shores of the Persian Gulf and especially in Kuwait. Recent migrants have tended to be short-stay, and have not in general been absorbed into the societies in which they have worked. Although the position of the communities of Iranian origin in the Arab states of the Persian Gulf can be overemphasized, it is not without geo-political importance that economically strong, and to an extent culturally discrete, Iranian groups exist in relatively privileged circumstances among the Arab so-cieties of the peninsula.

The 1960s and 1970s have witnessed a most significant change in the distri-bution of population. The southern provinces of Iran, including Khūzistān, Fārs, and Kirmān, have become among the fastest growing regions, with growth rates in the 1966 to 1976 period of 3.0, 3.4, and 3.5 percent, respectively, against an average national population growth rate of 2.67 percent. By 1976, the Persian Gulf provinces and districts of Iran, including Khūzistān, Fārs, Kirmān, Chahār Mahāl, and Bakhtīyārī, Būshahr, Hormuz, and Kūhgīlūya and Boyir Ahmadī, contained more than 20 percent of the total Iranian population. In demographic, as well as in other terms, Iran became increasingly powerful on the Persian Gulf littoral from the mid-1960s.[24]

The Balance of Industrial Power

The main industry in the Persian Gulf area is petroleum; and the modes of ownership of reserves of crude oil and natural gas, of installed productive ca-pacity, and of the means for transport and export of hydrocarbons, have all established a virtual hierarchy among the oil-rich exporting states. The level of reserves of oil and natural gas has an implicit influence on the relative standing of the various states, in the future, which cannot be underestimated.

22. F. 'Abd al-Razzaq, "The Marine Resources of Kuwait," Ph.D. thesis, University of London, 1979.

23. M. T. Razavian, "The Communities of the Persian Gulf," Ph.D. thesis, University of London, 1978.

24. Preliminary report on the results of the national census of population and property, Aban Mah 2535.

As expressed through production of crude oil, Iran had long held the center of the stage and was without rival in the period from 1908 to 1951. Since that time, with the exception of the years of crisis 1951–54, Iran has regained importance, but has never risen again to a position of complete preeminence. Between 1954 and 1972, Iran, Kuwait, and Saʿūdī Arabia vied for shares in incremental output, though from 1966 Kuwait lost ground to the other two producers. From 1972, Saʿūdī Arabia has emerged as the major regional producer of crude oil, a position that, by virtue of installed capacity and strength in reserves, no other regional state can challenge.

The hierarchy set by oil output, reinforced by the corresponding earnings through oil revenues,[25] was led in 1976 by Saʿūdī Arabia and Iran, which together accounted for 24.5 percent of total world production in that year. Iraq, Kuwait, and Abū Dhabī formed a second tier in the league of Persian Gulf oil producers, with an aggregate output of 9.8 percent of the world's total, while a group of small producers, including most of the other states bordering the Persian Gulf, accounted for a further 2.8 percent of world crude oil production in that year. The relative importance of the Persian Gulf producers in their regional and international contexts is shown in Table 6–2.

Flows of foreign exchange revenues have given opportunity for the states of the Persian Gulf to develop both oil-related industries, such as petrochemicals, and new industry entirely separate from the operations of the petroleum sector. There has been a growing discrepancy between the regional states in degree of dedication to, investment in, and success with industrialization. To an important extent, there are variations in resource endowment by way of population-size and quality, and of physical factors including land, water, and minerals, that have

25. For more detail on the hydrocarbons resources of the Persian Gulf states, see Part III, Section 4, Oil.

TABLE 6–2. RELATIVE IMPORTANCE OF PERSIAN GULF OIL PRODUCING STATES IN 1976

	% of Persian Gulf output	% world output	Oil revenues 1976—$ million
Saʿūdī Arabia	38.8	14.3	33,200
Iran	26.9	9.9	22,500
Iraq	10.4	3.8	8,200
Kuwait	8.9	3.3	8,400
Abū Dhabī	7.2	2.7	7,200[a]
Qatar	2.2	0.8	2,000
Neutral Zone	2.1	0.8	[b]
Oman	1.6	0.6	1,340
Dubai	1.4	0.5	[a]
Bahrain	0.3	0.1	330
Sharja	0.2	0.1	[a]

[a] Total revenues for the United Arab Emirates.
[b] Divided between Saʿūdī Arabia and Kuwait.
Source: BP Statistical Review of the World Oil Industry 1976; Middle East Economic Survey.

contributed to growing disparities in the economic development of countries bordering the Persian Gulf.

Iran has a comparative advantage in the industrial field over all other countries bordering the Persian Gulf. Its resource base is large and diverse. Apart from possessing the second largest oil reserves and the largest natural gas reserves in the area, Iran has major iron ore, coal, and copper resources. A wide range of other minerals occur in less abundance, including chromite, manganese, antimony, borax, lead, zinc, and barytes. Large-scale commercial exploitation of iron ore, coal, copper, and chromite was well-established by 1978, when copper and chromite were actually being exported.

In the remaining states of the area, mineral endowment is currently believed to be less rich. Iraq began the commercial exploitation of natural sulphur deposits in 1973 and phosphates were mined in 1978. Limited deposits of iron ores, ceramic clay, and glass sand exist, but exploitation is on a modest scale. The Arabian peninsula, which came under close scrutiny for minerals other than hydrocarbons only in the mid-1970s, has reserves of phosphates, iron ore, copper, and gold, but exploitation has been slow and only small quantities of salt and construction materials were being extracted by 1978.

Great strength in traditional craft industries has assisted the development of modern industry in Iran, whereas the rest of the region is relatively weak in craft skills. It is estimated that Iran has some 130,000 persons engaged in carpet-weaving alone, while metal-working, tile-making, and jewelry manufacturing are important employers of labor in most Iranian cities and large towns. In addition to providing exports, the craft industries provided a training ground for employees who were later absorbed by modern industrial plants. For the most part, the Arabian peninsula was devoid of carpet-weaving and bazaar crafts; and Iraq's main traditional manufacturing center, Baghdad, was reliant on Jewish capital and skill, which have moved away on an increasing scale since 1948.

The growth of Iranian industry outside the traditional crafts predates the development of modern industry elsewhere in the Persian Gulf region. During the reign of Riżā Shāh Pahlavī (1926–41), the government set up modern factories for textiles, sugar-beet processing, and munitions manufacture. Improvements in transport and educational facilities did much to strengthen this early Iranian drive to industrialization. Despite setbacks during World War II, the Iranian manufacturing industry increased its capacity slowly to 1963–64, after which rapid and more or less continuous expansion has characterized this sector.[26] As elsewhere noted in this volume, Iran has developed a very substantial capacity in iron and steel, petrochemicals, aluminum, metal fabricating, and machine-building, as well as a sophisticated light industrial capacity, mainly in the hands of the private sector.[27]

In comparison, the other states of the Persian Gulf remained, other than in the petroleum sector, altogether lacking an elaborated industrial fabric. The government of Iraq attempted to develop industry through a series of economic development plans beginning in the 1950s, but progress was severely inhibited

26. H. Amirsadeghi, *Twentieth Century Iran* (London, 1977), p. 130.
27. See Part III, Section 3, Manufacture and Industry.

as a consequence of frequently changing political circumstances, which brought inconsistency in policy and unsure financial provision for projects in the industrial sphere. Some success was achieved in light industry and a number of large-scale, state-sponsored textile and chemical companies were established, but the virtual exclusion of the private sector and inefficiencies in the state industries retarded progress toward creation of a competitive and expanding industry.

In the other oil exporting states of the area, constraints deriving from small-ness of scale and high costs of production have imposed an economic isolation on industrial plants catering for a protected domestic market. In Bahrain, where a limited oil resource has given urgency to the establishment of alternative export capability, seriously sustained measures were taken from the late 1960s to set up industry. Aluminum-smelting and development of a ship-repairing facility were the main elements of this industrialization program.

The discrepancy between the industrial achievements of the states of the Persian Gulf is shown by comparison with the 600,000 tons/year actual produc-tion from Iranian steel mills in 1977. Apart from Iran, only Sa'ūdī Arabia, with an installed capacity of 45,000 tons/year, produced iron and steel in 1977. Iran also led by a large measure in capacity under construction for the iron and steel industry, with 2,200,000 tons of new plant contracted for. Iraq was in the process of setting up an iron industry of 400,000 tons/year capacity in the southern part of the country, and first steps were being taken by 1978 for the establishment of a steel plant in Qatar, ultimately planned to be of 400,000 tons/year capacity also. In the longer term, Iran was already making provision for further iron and steel production, with 3,700,000 tons of new capacity to be begun during the 1970s. More tentative plans for development of the iron and steel industry sug-gested that Sa'ūdī Arabia would expand its Jidda plant and set up a 4,500,000 tons/year mill at Jubail. In Iraq, the economic development plan adopted by the government proposed increasing the capacity of the steel industry to 1,000,000 tons/year, and in the United Arab Emirates initial planning of a 2,000,000 tons/year mill had been attempted. Iranian regional supremacy in basic industry was well established by the late 1970s and, given the strength of the domestic market, the elaboration of steel fabricating and processing industries within the country, and a growing indigenous work force, the Iranian position appeared increasingly more favorable than that of its neighbors.

The Persian Gulf area has become dependent on external food supplies on a steadily increasing scale since 1950. The area had never been entirely self-sufficient and had imported foodstuffs during periods of drought, pestilence, and political disorder. As oil exports grew, revenues enabled food imports to be augmented, while domestic demand inevitably expanded as incomes of the mass of the population rose. To cater for the expatriate communities associated with the development of the oil industry, and—of increasing importance—to provide for changing domestic patterns of demand, there was resort to imports of food-stuffs with growing frequency through the 1960s. The effects of the boom in oil incomes after 1973 included an appreciable surge in food imports by the oil states. By 1975, only Iran, Iraq, and Oman were able to feed their populations from domestic resources to any significant extent.

Every oil-exporting state of the Persian Gulf was import-dependent for foodstuffs by 1975. Excluding reexports, all the regional states imported more food-stuff per head than they exported as nonoil exports—that is, none of the countries could sustain their basic food imports without oil income. The degree of reliance on food imports varied considerably from Iran, where $30 worth of foodstuffs and agricultural products was imported in 1975 for every man, woman, and child, to $60 per capita in Iraq, and $90 per capita in Oman. At the other end of the scale, the United Arab Emirates imported $300 of agricultural goods per head, Kuwait $330, and Sa'ūdī Arabia no less than $1,100, indicating a total reliance on imports of food items, mainly from the more temperate latitude producers such as the United States, Australia, and Canada. Whereas there are no cartels of grain- or meat-producers in any way comparable to the Organization of Petroleum Exporting Countries, it remains the case that the main customers for crude oil shipped from the Persian Gulf tend to be the major world suppliers of foodstuffs. This relationship heightens the economic and political consequences of the position of the Persian Gulf as the main world suppliers of crude oil and makes unilateral action against suppliers a less easily used weapon than it might otherwise be.

Dependence on imports of agricultural goods and a more general wish for improvement in productivity and income in the agricultural sector has en-couraged the governments of the regional states to invest in agricultural de-velopment programs. Environmental constraints are considerable, especially in the Arabian peninsula, and only a small contribution toward total food supply can ever be expected from domestic resources in this area. Iran and Iraq are better endowed with land and water for agriculture, and there are good prospects for a large measure of self-sufficiency, which will add to strategic strength in both a regional and international context (Table 6–3).

The transport and communications infrastructures of the states of the Persian Gulf area reflect the fact that modernization has begun in comparatively recent times. For the countries with large surface areas, characterized over much of their territory by scattered and isolated human settlements, geography militates against a rapid and total solution to problems of land communications. In Iran, Riżā Shah ordered the construction of the Trans-Iranian Railway during the 1930s and began the process of setting up an all-weather road network, but Iran had far

TABLE 6–3. AGRICULTURE IN THE PERSIAN GULF AREA

Country	Surface area square kilometers	Proportion of land cultivated (%)	Proportion of land under irrigation (%)
Bahrain	662	5	100
Iran	1,648,000	14	20
Iraq	438,446	18	50
Kuwait	16,900	1[a]	80
Oman	272,000	1[a]	—
Qatar	5,200	5	100
Sa'ūdī Arabia	2,260,000	1[a]	80
United Arab Emirates	32,000	5	100

[a] Less than 1.

Source: Issues in the Middle East (Washington: U.S. Government Printing Office, 1973), p. 13.

from completed its basic transport system by the late 1970s. Elsewhere, traditional means of transport prevailed, except where external military power, mainly British–Indian, intervened for its own strategic purposes, as, for example, in the case of the Basra–Baghdad railway.

Consolidation of the authority of the independent nation-states that have emerged in the Persian Gulf area has demanded the linking of all parts of the provinces to the center, especially where tribal or religious affiliations exist between the periphery and the outside world. Despite considerable allocation of financial and physical resources to the expansion of the transport and communications networks, Iran, Iraq, Oman, and Sa'ūdī Arabia have much to do before many of their remote and/or mountain areas are effectively commanded by the national road and rail services. Inadequacies in the port and distribution facilities within the Persian Gulf oil-exporting states exacerbated the economic difficulties experienced in the period after 1973, when the area was unable to absorb either financial allocations to the various development plans or to cope with the increasing physical volume of imports required to satisfy demand for capital and consumer goods. Domestic price inflation, resulting in part from constraints on imports as a result of the poverty of the transport infrastructure, was a matter of political importance in all regional states in the period 1973 to 1977.

The nature of oil revenues in the Persian Gulf area, regardless of whether income was earned as taxes, royalties, or profits on direct sales to oil companies, is such that moneys accrue in the form of foreign exchange. Oil exporters in the Persian Gulf region have had the ability to import goods and services, at least to the combined value of oil income, overseas earnings, and foreign credits. Borrowing capacity of the oil-exporting states has been enhanced by virtue of the dependable future income from oil. Growth of income, and specifically oil income, in the Persian Gulf area saw a corresponding increase in the volume and value of imports. Boom conditions for the oil-exporting states in 1973, 1974, and 1975 fostered a large expansion in imports, making the Persian Gulf states the largest consuming center of imports in the Third World of Asia, Africa, and Latin America. Intense rivalry among the industrialized nations of the world to supply the goods demanded in the Persian Gulf gave added geopolitical importance to the region as a center for external interest.

At the time the oil boom was in full swing in 1974, total imports by the states of the Persian Gulf amounted to $16,610 million.[28] In 1970, the same area had imported only $4,200 million-worth of goods. As oil revenues augmented during the 1970s, so imports rose and the trading position of the area increased in importance. The relationship between the Persian Gulf and the industrialized nations of the world, the one supplying oil and the other supplying goods and services, was further exaggerated in the years after 1973. The industrial nations of Western Europe, North America, and Japan, comprising fourteen countries in all, supplied the Persian Gulf area with some two-thirds of its imports and purchased the bulk of its oil exports. The interdependence of the Persian Gulf states and the major industrialized nations has profound implications for mutual

28. Economic Research Institute for the Middle East, *Middle East Imports, 1970–74* (Tokyo, 1976).

interests in regional security in the Persian Gulf and Indian Ocean, through which the oil tankers carrying crude to the international markets have to pass.

Comparative Economic Development
in the Persian Gulf Area

It will be apparent that, for the most part, the countries of the Persian Gulf area have economies that are immature. Without exception, these states are fundamentally reliant on crude oil exports for foreign exchange income, for the generation of goods and services for domestic consumption, and for the provision of government revenues. Differences between the regional states arise from the degree of dependence on the oil sector or, conversely, the degree of development of the industrial and agricultural bases of production.

Earlier discussion of the patterns of industrial and agricultural development in the states of the region indicated that Iran is an appreciably more mature economy than any other in the Persian Gulf area. Substantial contributions are made to employment and to national income by the nonoil sectors of the economy. Particularly significant is the participation of the manufacturing industries in the national income. No other state in any way approaches Iran in this respect.

The contribution of manufacturing industry to gross domestic product (GDP) in Sa'ūdī Arabia in 1975 was 0.7 percent and of agriculture 1.2 percent. With the sole exception of Oman, the states of the Arabian peninsula reflect similar characteristics of economic structure. Iraq, with a strong resource base, shows more maturity, and here manufacturing industry accounted in the mid-1970s for 8.6 percent of GDP, against 15.5 percent for agriculture. As already indicated, the most mature state in the region by way of economic structure is Iran, where the role of agriculture had diminished to a contribution of 10 percent and manufacturing industry had increased to 11.3 percent.

But in all the economies of the Persian Gulf region, deep imbalance affects the sources of national income, since the oil sector plays such a large role. Fluctuations in the supply and demand situation for oil and its products can have an immediate and damaging effect on the economic welfare of even the most sophisticated of the regional states.

Iran clearly has a more diversified economy than all other countries in the Persian Gulf. It also had strength in depth in the basic sectors of industry and agriculture. By value of output in all sectors of the economy, even including petroleum, Iran was similarly the most powerful of states in the area in the mid-1970s. Assessment of national income in the Persian Gulf is open to a number of technical difficulties, but it would appear from the most considered estimates[29] that Iran had a gross domestic product of some $52,000 million in 1975, while Sa'ūdī Arabia, its nearest rival, had $42,000 million, and Iraq, third by size, had $13,000 million. In terms of national income, the United Arab Emirates was the

---

29. Estimates of national income are drawn from the International Monetary Fund (IMF), *International Financial Statistics*, IMF, *Yearbook of National Accounts Statistics*, various central bank reports and official statistical abstracts on the individual states of the Persian Gulf area.

fourth strongest country of the area with $7,000 million, followed by Kuwait at $5,000 million, and Oman with $1,250 million.

Given wide variations in population size and national income, there were differences in income per head between the states of the Persian Gulf. A contrasting hierarchy emerges from examination of per capita income, in which the United Arab Emirates appeared in the mid-1970s as leaders, with an estimated average of $10,500 for every man, woman, and child. Kuwaitis had approximately half the average income of those in the United Arab Emirates, while the population of Sa'ūdī Arabia earned an average of some $3,200 each per year. Iran, Iraq, and Oman all came within a narrow range, spreading from $1,600 in the case of Iran and Oman to $1,200 in the case of Iraq.

Special geopolitical problems arise from the concentration of wealth in the Persian Gulf states. Most countries of the region found difficulties in absorbing the flow of revenues, especially after 1973; and, lacking the means to utilize all their funds within the domestic economy, surpluses were placed abroad. One or two countries, notably Sa'ūdī Arabia, had financial surpluses on so large a scale that changes in the Sa'ūdī Arabian position could affect the financial health of world currencies and other states. The Persian Gulf countries came, therefore, under considerable pressures of a financial, economic, and political nature as a result of their ownership of reserves of foreign exchange and other assets overseas.

More influential for the longer-term, the high incomes enjoyed by the populations of the Persian Gulf states contrast starkly with those of adjacent regions. Inequalities of income distribution, where the poorer states of the Arabian peninsula enjoy an average income of one-tenth of the richest of the Persian Gulf countries, tend to foster political problems for both sets of states. Economic gravity sets in motion rapid population movements from poor to rich areas, leaving the poorer countries without their best-trained manpower, and the richer countries with problems of housing and of controlling a vigorous, young, and politically radical immigrant community. Political polarization between relatively conservative oil states and radical socialist poor countries has been a result of large variations in economic status between the Persian Gulf states and their neighbors.

Conclusion

The international role of the Persian Gulf has long been established on the basis of its strategic location. The emergence of the area as the world's main source of petroleum and natural gas, the main supplier to the world's largest industry and the main beneficiary of trade in crude oil, has added a new and overwhelming dimension to the economic and political importance of the Persian Gulf area. Relations between that area and the industrialized nations of the world have been enhanced considerably as interdependence has grown in commercial and financial spheres.

Within the Persian Gulf zone itself, there are appreciable differences growing up between states based on oil income. Much more important, Iran has expanded and diversified its economy, and brought to maturity its economic structure; by the late 1970s it had taken on a character more analogous to an industrial economy than to an oil economy. In virtually every way, Iran has become a larger economy than any other in the Persian Gulf area. In most dimensions, Iran is equal to all other states together. The only clear exception to this is in the petroleum sector, where the preeminence of the Sa'ūdī Arabian position is absolute.

International and interstate cooperation and conflict in the Persian Gulf area were intensifying during the 1970s and, given reliance by industrialized and developing countries on oil for some time into the future, the geopolitical position of the Persian Gulf should become increasingly sensitive with the passage of time.

Selected Bibliography

'Abd al-Razzaq, F. "The Marine Resources of Kuwait." Ph.D. thesis, University of London, 1979.

Abdullah, M. M. *The United Arab Emirates: A Modern History*. London, 1978.

Al Baharna, H. M. *The Legal Status of the Arabian Gulf States*. Manchester, 1968.

Amirsadeghi, H. *Twentieth Century Iran*. London, 1977.

Anthony, J. D. *Arab States of the Lower Gulf: People, Politics, Petroleum*. Washington, D.C., 1975.

Economic Research Institute for The Middle East. *Middle East Imports, 1970–74*. Tokyo, 1976.

Hay, R. *The Persian Gulf States*. Washington, D.C., 1959.

Hopwood, D. (ed.) *The Arabian Peninsula: Society and Politics*. London, 1972.

Hubbard, G. E. *From the Gulf to Ararat*. Edinburgh, 1916.

Kelly, J. B. *Eastern Arabian Frontiers*. London, 1964.

Lebon, J.H.G. "South-West Asia and Egypt," in *The Changing Map of Asia*. W. G. East, O.H.K. Spate, and C. A. Fisher, eds., 5th ed., rev. London, 1971.

Razavian, M. T. "The Communities of the Persian Gulf." Ph.D. thesis, University of London, 1978.

Sevian, V. J. "The Evolution of the Boundary between Iraq and Iran," in Fisher, C. A., ed., *Essays in Political Geography*. London, 1968.

Zahlan, R. S. *The Origins of the United Arab Emirates*. London, 1978.

7. Military Affairs in the Persian Gulf ALVIN J. COTTRELL, ROBERT J. HANKS, AND FRANK T. BRAY

 This chapter considers the defense establishments of the Persian Gulf states: Sa'ūdī Arabia, Kuwait, Iraq, Iran, Oman, Bahrain, Qatar, and the United Arab Emirates (UAE). The three largest Persian Gulf states in terms of armed forces, population and territory will be treated first. While some attention is given to the historical evolution of the armed forces of the Persian Gulf states, primary emphasis is placed on the development of military capabilities from 1968 to the present; this last decade has been an era of stark transition in their security policies.

In 1968, Britain announced its decision to withdraw all military forces east of Suez before 1971. Prior to 1971, Britain, through treaties and other less formal arrangements, had assumed responsibility of the Foreign affairs and defense requirements of the Persian Gulf states. In many respects, the defense efforts outlined below represent subsequent local attempts to fill the military vacuum that resulted from the rundown of Britain's military presence in the region. The military programs of the Persian Gulf states are examined in terms of defense expenditures, manpower and weapon system aggregates, the quality of equipment, organization, and the degree of reliance on foreign sources for assistance.

The Larger Persian Gulf States

Sa'ūdī Arabia. Sa'ūdī Arabia's military establishment traces its formal beginning to 1944, when King 'Abd al-'Azīz ibn 'Abd al-Rahmān Āl Sa'ūd established the Ministry of Defense. It became the Ministry of Defense and Aviation in 1952 under the Council of Ministers. Command and control within the armed services is centralized in the hands of high-ranking members of the Royal House of Sa'ūd. The Council of Ministers and the Ministry of Defense and Aviation share the administration of defense matters, with the king exercising ultimate authority.[1]

1. Richard F. Nyrop, et al., *Area Handbook for Saudi Arabia* (3rd edition; Washington, D.C.: U.S. Government Printing Office, 1977), p. 311.

Much of the country's military tradition—particularly the relationship among the services—is rooted, however, in King Sa'ūd's long struggle, launched at the turn of the century, to bring the present-day borders of Sa'ūdī Arabia under his rule. He completed this task in the mid-1920s with the help of an armed force recruited primarily from Bedouin tribes fervently loyal to the House of Sa'ūd. These Bedouin were successful in defeating the last remnants of opposition to the House of Sa'ūd and ever since have enjoyed an autonomous position within the country's defense framework. Today they constitute the National Guard (the White Army). Answering solely to the King, the National Guard is charged with protecting the Royal Family, as well as watching over the nation's other armed services: The Royal Sa'ūdī Army, Navy, Air Force, and paramilitary groups. The National Guard's "special" position in Sa'ūdī Arabia was eclipsed for a brief period in the 1960s as King Faisal concentrated on developing the other armed services. By 1978, the Guard, however, appeared to have regained much, if not all, of its former influence, particularly in the wake of King Faisal's assassination in 1975. It is generally believed that following Faisal's death the National Guard played an instrumental role in insuring a smooth transition of power to King Khālid. As *Strategic Survey* noted in 1976, "the armed forces—so often a potential threat to the political leadership in developing countries—did not figure in succession politics because it had long been the practice to maintain two separate and distinct forces: the regular armed forces and the White Army—a 'family army' intensely loyal to the regime and a formidable obstacle to would-be usurpers."[2]

In 1964, King Faisal launched a campaign to modernize the country's armed forces. Faisal's decision was based, in large part, on the perceived need to shore up his country's ability to meet the challenges to established monarchical governments, emanating from within and outside the region. These challenges had already proven too formidable for several royal households. In 1958, the Iraqi royal family was overthrown and most of its members executed. Egypt's King Fārūq fell from power in 1952. A civil war in Yemen led to the overthrow of that country's traditional rulers (i.e., the Imam), and to the establishment, in the mid-1960s, of a left-wing socialist government. 'Abd al-Nāsir deployed 70,000 Egyptian troops to Yemen, and Sa'ūdī Arabia became involved on the side of the Royalists in that civil war. Throughout this period of upheaval the House of Sa'ūd found itself under frequent and hostile criticism from the Egyptian government, as well as from other countries that had deposed their traditional governments. Superimposed upon these concerns was the protection of the country's major economic asset—oil.[3]

The air force was the major beneficiary of Faisal's initial modernization efforts. This is evident from the major arms orders placed by Sa'ūdī Arabia between 1964 and 1968. During this period, the Royal Sa'ūdī Air Force placed orders for almost 100 Hawker Hunter FGA-9s, BAC Lightnings, and BAC Strikemasters. Major procurement for the army was limited to Panhard AML-90 armored vehicles. Air defense, however, was enhanced by the acquisition of addi-

2. *Strategic Survey* (London: International Institute for Strategic Studies, 1976), p. 89.

3. Alvin J. Cottrell, "Iranian and Saudi Arabian security interests," *Washington Review of Strategic and International Studies* (May 1977): 50–51.

tional BAC Thunderbird I surface-to-air missiles (SAMs).[4] No major weapon systems were procured for the navy.

Faisal's attempts to modernize the armed forces were just beginning to bear fruit when Britain announced its intention to withdraw from the Persian Gulf. Sa'ūdī Arabia had the third largest standing armed forces in the region. Approximately 36,000 men were in uniform. The country's land forces were about 30,000 strong, with manpower divided equally between the National Guard and the Royal Sa'ūdī Army. The navy had 1,000 men in service, the air force, 5,000.[5]

Much of the equipment ordered by Faisal, however, had not yet entered service. The army's five brigades were armed with M-24 light tanks, Vigilant antitank wire-guided missiles, and smaller arms and munitions. The air force had twenty combat aircraft (four Hunters, four Lightnings, and twelve F-86s), a dozen transport aircraft (four C-130s, six C-47s, and two Alouette III helicopters) as well as forty trainer aircraft, which, if required, could have lent limited ground support. Air defense was provided by a modest number of Thunderbird SAMs. The navy consisted of one former U.S. patrol boat and a number of smaller craft.[6]

Britain's decision to terminate its treaties and other arrangements with the littoral states of the Persian Gulf heightened Sa'ūdī Arabian interest in improving its defense capabilities. In 1968, Sa'ūdī Arabia devoted $171 million to defense. By 1973, this figure had climbed to $988 million.[7] An even more dramatic increase in Sa'ūdī defense expenditures came in the wake of the rise in oil prices that followed the 1973 Middle East War. Between 1973 and 1974, Sa'ūdī Arabian oil revenues rose from a previous all-time high of $4.34 billion to $23.2 billion (figures are rounded off to the nearest tenth unless otherwise noted). Oil revenues for 1975 brought more than $32 billion into the Sa'ūdī treasury.[8] That same year, Sa'ūdī Arabia allocated $6.9 billion to defense—almost forty times the amount allocated to the 1968 defense budget.[9] The defense budget for 1978 was estimated to be about $9.63 billion.[10]

The jump in oil prices, however, has permitted Sa'ūdī Arabia to augment its defense capabilities without skewing the ratio of defense spending to total government expenditures. Between 1974 and 1977, defense spending fluctuated between 20 and 29 percent of the total national budget.[11] During the same period, defense expeditures in the United States, Israel, and Switzerland claimed, respectively, an average of 26, 54.5, and 19.5 percent of total yearly government expenditures.[12]

4. Nyrop, et al., *Area Handbook*, p. 334.

5. *The Gulf: Implications of British Withdrawal* (Washington: Center for Strategic and International Studies, 1969), p. 82.

6. Ibid.

7. Jan Nolan, "Notes On: The Interaction between the Growth of Oil Revenues and Military Expenditures: Libya, Kuwait, and Saudi Arabia, 1968–1974/75," paper prepared for *Conference on Implications of the Military Build-up in Non-Industrial States*, International Security Studies Program, The Fletcher School of Law and Diplomacy, May 6–8, 1976, p. 12.

8. Ibid.

9. *The Military Balance, 1978–79* (London: International Institute for Strategic Studies, 1977), p. 41.

10. Ibid.

11. Ibid.

12. Ibid.

Estimates of Sa'ūdī Arabia's population vary from 5 to 8 million, with foreign nationals accounting for a significant percentage. It is generally accepted, how ever, that Sa'ūdī Arabia spends more per capita on defense than any other Arab country. In 1978, with a total military force of 93,500 men under arms, Sa'ūdī Arabia had a higher percentage of its total population in the armed services than even Iran, which had a population of 35 million and armed forces of 300,000.

By 1977, manpower in the Sa'ūdī armed forces had increased by over 70 percent since 1968. According to the 1978–79 *Military Balance*, 58,500 men served in the regular armed forces: 45,000 with the army, 1,500 with the navy, and 12,000 with the air force.[13] Manpower in the air force had tripled since the late 1960s. Calculations of Sa'ūdī Arabian manpower, however, must also take into consideration the strength of the country's paramilitary forces, particularly that of the National Guard, which numbered 35,000.[14] Late in 1978, while the National Guard's primary duties were devoted to internal security, in case of an external threat the Guard would prove an invaluable mobilization agent and a complement to the country's regular armed forces.[15] This is true, although to a lesser extent, of the country's other two paramilitary groups—the frontier force and the coast guard, which in 1978 had a combined manpower strength of 35,000.[16]

Military service is voluntary and, not surprisingly, the Sa'ūdī armed forces suffer from a shortage of available and trainable manpower. Manpower problems have affected both the structure of the country's armed forces and the type of weapon systems the Sa'ūdī's procure. In modernizing the army, the Sa'ūdī government has shown a sensitivity to its manpower limitations. As one analyst has noted, for example, "rather than increasing the number of brigades, it is improving existing ones."[17]

The regular armed forces are drawn from a fair cross section of the population, as recruitment for these services is undertaken nationwide. The National Guard, however, is more parochial in make-up. Recruits for the Guard are largely from Bedouin tribes living in the areas closest to National Guard installations.[18]

In 1978, the Royal Sa'ūdī Army was organized into one armored brigade, one mechanized division, four infantry brigades battalions, two parachute battalions, one Royal Guard battalion, three artillery battalions, six antiaircraft artillery battalions, and ten SAM batteries.[19] Until 1977, Sa'ūdī Arabia had one brigade stationed in Jordan, a holdover from the 1967 Arab–Israeli War, and one brigade in Syria, sent in reaction to the 1973 Middle East War. In addition, Sa'ūdī Arabia contributed 750 men to the Arab peace-keeping force stationed in Lebanon.

The country's major air force bases are located at Dhahran, opposite the island shaikhdom of Bahrain, Khamīs Mushait, Tabūk, Jidda, Riyadh—the country's capital—and Tā'if. Dhahran and Khamīs Mushait are the principal

---

13. *Military Balance, 1978–79*, p. 40.
14. Ibid.
15. Nyrop, *Area Handbook*, p. 320.
16. *Military Balance, 1978–79*, pp. 41–42.
17. Dale R. Tahtinen, *National Security Challenges to Saudi Arabia* (Washington, D.C.: American Enterprise Institute for Public Policy Research, 1978), p. 15.
18. Nyrop, *Area Handbook*, p. 324.
19. *Military Balance, 1978–79*, p. 41.

bases from which Lightning air defense operations originate. Saʿūdī Arabia's F-5Es are based at Dhahran, Tāif, and Tabūk. Three F-5E squadrons (comprising sixty aircraft) have reached operational status, with two additional squadrons expected to become operational by 1979. In 1975, Saʿūdī Arabia's F-5s participated in exercises near the Golan Heights, with elements of the Syrian and Jordanian air forces.[20]

Saʿūdī naval efforts are concentrated at two facilities: a small hovercraft base near Jidda on the Red Sea and another at Jubayl on the Persian Gulf. Naval headquarters are located in Damman. The present and planned Saʿūdī naval inventory reflects a preoccupation with coastal security. At the present time, Saʿūdī naval capabilities are quite limited. In 1978, the Saʿūdī naval order of battle consisted of twelve vessels: three Jaguar-class fast patrol boats (FPB), two utility landing craft (LCU), two yard tugs (YTB), four small landing craft (LCM), and one large patrol craft—a former U.S. Coast Guard cutter.[21] Saʿūdī Arabia, however, is planning to acquire a limited regional naval capability through the acquisition of fast attack patrol gun boats (PGGs) and patrol chase ships (PCGs), all the latter with guided missiles.

Saʿūdī Arabia concluded an agreement in 1972 with the United States for the procurement of a wide variety of naval vessels, including four 700-ton PCGs, nine 300-ton PGGs, four MSC-322 class coastal mine sweepers, and eight smaller craft. These ships will variously be fitted with reasonably sophisticated ordnance and equipment (e.g., Harpoon antiship missiles, 76 mm rapid fire guns, MK 46 torpedoes, MK 92 fire control systems, and AN/SPS 60 surface search radar). To date, it is known that the largest Saʿūdī craft will not exceed 1,000 tons.

The National Guard has installations near most important cities and at some border locations. The Guard is complemented by an undetermined number of irregular members stationed in smaller communities, who are paid by the government to meet once a month. The system has proven quite effective, as it provides, according to one source, "for a direct dispersal of the country's wealth to local communities," thereby facilitating the Guard's ability to deal effectively with internal threats to security almost anywhere in the country.[22] The Guard is presently undergoing a modernization program that is scheduled to be completed by 1980. Under the program, four of the Guard's infantry battalions will be mechanized. Each mechanized battalion will include one artillery battery. In addition, the Guard is expanding its infrastructure, while improving its management, training, and support facilities. Traditionally, the Guard has been armed with lighter arms than the country's regular ground forces. Its basic combat vehicle is to be the V-150 wheeled armored personnel carrier. Air defense weapons are to be limited to antiaircraft guns. TOW missiles are on order, which will give the National Guard an antitank capability.[23] It must be emphasized, however, that traditionally the Guard's real power has stemmed less from its equipment than from the status afforded it by the monarch as well as by its widespread presence throughout the country.

20. "Arab air power," *Air International* 13 (September, 1977): 145.

21. "Saudi Arabia Embarking (Modestly) at Sea," *Arabia and the Gulf*, October 10, 1977, p. 4; and *Military Balance, 1978–79*, p. 42.

22. Nyrop, *Area Handbook*, p. 320.

23. Tahtinen, *National Security Challenges*, p. 17.

The most tangible improvements have been made in the weapon inventories of the regular armed forces. The army's small force of M-24 light tanks have been retired, and Sa'ūdī armor has been upgraded significantly. In 1978, the Sa'ūdī army had a total of 250 highly sophisticated AMX-30 tanks. The AMX-30, armed with the effective 105 mm gun, is well protected and mobile. In addition, there were 75 Scorpion tanks, 75 of the older M-47 Patton and modern M-60 medium tanks, and 60 M-41s in the Sa'ūdī arsenal. Other major pieces of Sa'ūdī equipment included Staghound and Greyhound armored cars, Ferret and Fox scout cars, M-113s, M-113 and Panhard M-3s, Commando armored personnel carriers, and a variety of artillery weapons, as well as TOW antitank missiles.[24] Six batteries of improved Hawk SAMs along with 175 M-60 medium tanks were ordered from the United States.[25]

In 1978, there were 171 combat aircraft in the Sa'ūdī air force—almost nine times the number in the 1967 inventory.[26] The Sa'ūdī's intend to develop an air force of fourteen squadrons, with six first-line combat squadrons.[27]

The 1978 combat arm of the Sa'ūdī air force was broken down as follows: three fighter-bomber squadrons with sixty F-5Es, two counterinsurgency training squadrons with thirty-five BAC-167s, and one interceptor squadron with sixteen Lightning F-53s.[28] The British-made BAC-167 is a light tactical support aircraft. The F-5E is a late version of the F-5 series, with improved flexibility. In 1978, the United States agreed to sell Sa'ūdī Arabia sixty U.S. F-15 fighters—marking the first transfer of such a sophisticated American-made aircraft to an Arab country. Deliveries will begin in the United States in 1981, full operational capability being achieved in 1985, with the total cost to Sa'ūdī Arabia estimated at $2.5 billion.[29] The F-15s will replace Sa'ūdī Arabia's aging Lightnings, which are scheduled for retirement in the early 1980s.[30] They will provide the country with an all-weather, extended-range air defense fighter. Sa'ūdī Arabia has placed an order for 2,000 U.S. Sidewinder air-to-air missiles, which will in all probability be fitted to the F-5E, as well as Sa'ūdī Arabia's F-15s.

By 1978, the transport arm of the Sa'ūdī air force also had been expanded to include two squadrons with thirty-five C-130 aircraft and two helicopter squadrons with sixteen AB-206 and twenty-four AB-205s. There were also four KC-130 tankers, one Boeing 707, two Falcon-20s, two Jetstars, twenty-two Alouette III helicopters, and an inventory of nine sizable trainer aircraft in service.[31] Sa'ūdī Arabia plans to create two assault helicopter battalions, an attack helicopter battalion, as well as two air cavalry helicopter battalions. Approximately 440 helicopters are scheduled to be procured for these purposes.[32]

The structure of the Sa'ūdī armed forces has been influenced heavily by that of the British and the U.S. armed forces, reflecting the close association the three military establishments have enjoyed over the years. Sa'ūdī Arabia traditionally

24. *Military Balance, 1978–79*, p. 41.
25. Ibid., p. 41.
26. Ibid., p. 42.
27. "Arab air power," p. 121.
28. *Military Balance, 1978–79*, p. 42.
29. "Middle East aircraft sales," *GIST* (March 1978).
30. Tahtinen, *National Security Challenges*, p. 11.
31. *Military Balance, 1978–79*, p. 42.
32. "Arab air power," p. 146.

has relied on foreign advice in the development of its military infrastructure. Having no indigenous defense development and production capability of its own, Saʿūdī Arabia also has had to rely on foreign suppliers for its weapons systems. Saʿūdī Arabia, however, has joined Egypt, Qatar, and the United Arab Emirates in the formation of the Arab Military Industries Organization (AMIO), which is aimed at making these countries more self-sufficient in weapons production. The organization has already produced helicopters and jeeps under French and British license. Most of these, however, have gone to Egypt. Saʿūdī Arabia, and other members of the AMIO, however, are likely to remain dependent on foreign sources for sophisticated weapons for some time.

For a time, Britain was Saʿūdī Arabia's chief military supporter. By the late 1940s, however, the United States had assumed this position due, in large part, to the "successful relations between the United States and Saʿūdī Arabia, as experienced through the Arabian–American Oil Company (ARAMCO), as well as new tensions in Saʿūdī Arabian–British relations over the Buraimī Oasis dispute."[33] United States–Saʿūdī Arabian relations became even closer after the United States dispatched a squadron of F-100s to Saʿūdī Arabia after Egypt's bombing raid on a Saʿūdī border village during the Yemeni civil war.

American assistance is provided to Saʿūdī Arabia in a number of ways: through the U.S. Department of Defense—primarily the U.S. Military Training Mission (USMTM) at Dhahrān—its civilian contractors, the U.S. Army Corps of Engineers based in Riyadh and private U.S. firms contracted directly by the Saʿūdī government. The U.S. Corps of Engineers, for example, is presently involved in the construction of the Khālid military city project. The town will house three brigades, an air force squadron, and an engineer's depot. In the early 1970s, the U.S. Department of Defense assisted Saʿūdī Arabia in the development of the Peace Hawk Program, designed to make Saʿūdī Arabia relatively self-sufficient in the use and maintenance of the F-5.[34] Increasingly, however, U.S. support assistance originates from the private sector, reflecting the desire of both countries to keep the number of U.S. military personnel stationed on Saʿūdī territory to a minimum. In 1975, there were only 500 U.S. government personnel stationed in Saʿūdī Arabia at USMTM and with the Corps of Engineers. Approximately 300 of these were carrying out military-related tasks. In contrast, there were an estimated 16,000 employees of American firms (and their dependents) in Saʿūdī Arabia constructing military bases.[35]

The Vinnell Corporation is constructing facilities for the National Guard and is involved in the training of Guard personnel. Northrop Corporation is building new facilities for the Royal Saʿūdī Air Force. Lockheed has contracted to assist in the upgrading of the country's air defense force. Raytheon is overseeing the installation and maintenance of Saʿūdī Arabia's Hawk missiles, and Bendix is training the Saʿūdī Ordnance Corps. A total of 3,000 Saʿūdī military personnel has been trained in either the United States or Europe.[36]

33. Nyrop, *Area Handbook*, p. 331.

34. "News Review on West Asia," Institute for Defence Studies and Arabia (New Delhi) March 1978, p. 775; and Tahtinen, *National Security Challenges*, p. 10.

35. Nyrop, *Area Handbook*, pp. 332–33.

36. David Lynn Price, unpublished memorandum to Alvin J. Cottrell, January 6, 1978.

Sa'ūdī Arabia's military training academies are under the supervision of the Army School Command and include the Military Preparatory School, the Royal Military College, the King Faisal Air Force College, and a number of smaller basic military schools. The National Guard has its own training center. There are also plans to establish a naval academy.[37]

Sa'ūdī military sales orders placed with the United States have increased considerably—from $4.6 million in 1968 to $7.2 billion in 1975. Sa'ūdī purchases from the United States quadrupled between 1973 and 1974, and nearly tripled between 1974 and 1975.[38]

In 1974, the United States and Sa'ūdī Arabia established a Joint Commission on Security Cooperation (JCSC), and Sa'ūdī Arabia remains one of the largest purchasers of arms from the United States. In recent years, however, Sa'ūdī Arabia has been placing greater emphasis on diversifying its sources of arms and other military supplies and services.[39]

Sa'ūdī Arabia's flexibility in choosing arms supplies has been enhanced by the startling increases in its oil revenues. This wealth has already allowed Sa'ūdī Arabia to terminate its previous dependence on foreign military assistance grants. Between 1950–65, for example, the United States extended $31.7 million in military assistance to Sa'ūdī Arabia. As Table 7–1 indicates, however, U.S. aid extended to Sa'ūdī Arabia began to taper off in the late 1960s, dropping dramatically after 1974.

At present, Sa'ūdī Arabia receives no aid from the United States and, in fact, not only pays for all the military equipment and service it receives but also now

37. Ibid., p. 326.   38. See Nyrop, *Area Handbook*, p. 322.   39. Ibid., p. 340.

TABLE 7–1 SA'ŪDĪ ARABIA, UNITED STATES IMPORTS AND U.S. MILITARY ASSISTANCE, U.S. FISCAL YEARS, 1950–75 (IN THOUSANDS OF U.S. DOLLARS)

Date	Military assistance	Military sales orders	Military sales deliveries	Commercial sales deliveries
1950–65[a]	31,663	2,140,494	20,450	n.a.
1966	667	8,494	12,220	856
1967	768	49,324	48,854	14,902
1968	756	4,654	36,854	33,580
1969	536	4,213	32,086	35,481
1970	520	44,878	51,937	6,253
1971	632	95,954	63,774	12,723
1972	427	227,263	49,854	8,200
1973	179	625,895	108,030	5,649
1974	173	2,539,408	216,481	18,031
1975	38	7,224,588	316,070	n.a.

n.a.—not available
[a] combined total
Source: Richard F. Nyrop et al., *Area Handbook for Saudi Arabia* (Washington, D.C.: U.S. Government Printing Office, 1977), p. 336.

provides military aid to several of its neighbors: Yemen (San'ā), Oman, Egypt, Jordan, and Somalia.

Iraq. Iraq achieved full independence in 1932. The country's armed forces, however, were formed in the early 1920s, after Iraq came under British mandate. By independence, Iraq had established, with British assistance, an army of 11,500 men, which rose to 23,000 by 1936. Internal security is maintained by the army, acting in conjunction with the mobile force—a paramilitary organization founded in the 1930s. The Iraqi air force was established in the early 1930s as a subordinate organization to the army, as is the navy, founded several years later. The navy, in fact, is considered a specialized integral part of the army. The chief of the general staff is also the chief of staff of the army.

The army is not only the country's predominant armed service, but over the years it has exercised considerable influence on Iraqi politics. In 1938, the army, in association with the Ahālī—a reformist group—carried out a successful coup d'état, forcing the then prime minister, General Yāsīn al-Hāshimī to resign. Over the next five years, several other Iraqi governments were deposed and formed in succession by the army.[40] Such precedents have led to a *de facto* institutionalization of the coup as a technique for effecting political change in Iraq.

Perhaps the most dramatic change resulting from an army coup came in 1958, when the country's pro-Western Hashemite monarch, King Faisal, was overthrown and the country declared a nonaligned republic, under Brigadier 'Abd al-Karīm Qāsim. King Faisal and other members of the royal family and government were executed. The Qāsim government was overthrown and Qāsim himself executed in 1963 by pan-Arab elements of the army and their supporters. The army's continued predominance in political affairs is demonstrated by the fact that many of the most influential members of the Revolutionary Command Council (RCC)—Iraq's chief governing body—have been drawn from its ranks.

In 1968, when Britain announced its planned withdrawal from the Persian Gulf, Iraq's armed forces had a total manpower strength of approximately 82,000, apportioned as follows among the country's three services: army, 70,000; navy, 2,000; and air force, 10,000.[41] The army was organized into one armored division and four infantry brigades. Equipment included between 400 and 600 tanks and smaller armaments. Most of the tanks were Soviet T-34 and T-35s. Some vintage British Centurions, however, were still operational. Naval capabilities were quite limited. Only nineteen small craft were in service—four British-built patrol craft, three Soviet-made submarine chasers, and twelve Soviet-made torpedo boats.[42] By Persian Gulf standards, Iraq's air force was relatively large, with 170 combat and 40 transport and support aircraft. The Iraqi inventory of combat aircraft included: six IL-16 medium bombers, ten IL-28 light bombers, fifty MIG-21 interceptors, 50 Hunter MK-9s, thirty-four MIG-17s and MIG-19s, and twenty T-52 Provost ground attack aircraft.[43]

40. Harvey H. Smith, et al., *Area Handbook for Iraq* (2nd edition; Washington, D.C.: U.S. Government Printing Office, 1969), pp. 41, 340, 343.
41. *The Gulf: Implications of British Withdrawal*, p. 81.
42. Ibid., pp. 81–82.
43. Ibid., p. 81.

In many respects, the 1968 inventory reflected the crossroad Iraq had reached with respect to arms procurement. Without an indigenous defense industry of its own, Iraq relied, and must for the foreseeable future continue to rely, on foreign sources of weapons for most of its military supplies. During Iraq's tenure as a British mandate, and for the first years following independence, Britain was Iraq's primary source of arms supply. With the fall of the pro-Western monarchy, the Soviets gradually began to assume the position of Iraq's principal weapons supplier. Hence the situation reflected above, where, in the 1968 inventory, most of Iraq's older equipment was British and its newer and more sophisticated weapons were Soviet in origin. It must be emphasized, however, that unlike Egypt and some other Arab states, Iraq did not become completely dependent on Moscow for arms. France agreed in 1968, for example, to supply Iraq with weapons, including armored gun-carriers, tanks, mortars, and Mirage jet fighter aircraft. As one source has noted, by the mid-1960s—a time of global polarization—Iraq enjoyed a somewhat unique position: "Iraq had not only become the third largest recipient of Soviet aid in the Arab world, after the United Arab Republic and Algeria, but had also continued to receive aid from Western nations."[44]

In the late 1960s, Iraq launched a concerted effort to upgrade its military capabilities. This move was prompted by several factors. Britain's decision to withdraw from the region played a part. Even though Iraqi-British relations were not particularly close after 1958, Iraq, like other Persian Gulf countries, appreciated the stability London's presence had injected into the Persian Gulf area. Iraq, however, had pressing security concerns that demanded improved military capabilities. Iraq's pan-Arabism had drawn it into the Arab-Israeli controversy on numerous occasions. Iraqi forces participated in the Arab-Israeli wars of 1948, 1956, 1967, and 1973. Over 12,000 Iraqi troops participated in the 1948 Arab intervention against Israel. Iraqi involvement in 1956 was on a small scale. In 1967, however, Iraq became more heavily involved and numerous losses were incurred by their forces.[45] In 1973, Iraq committed three divisions to help Syria in the Golan Heights.

The losses incurred in 1967, in particular, hardened Iraqi resolve to strengthen its position. In addition, Iraq was faced with a separatist movement, launched in the early 1960s by the Kurds, inhabiting the north and northeast regions of the country. The Kurdish rebellion flared to civil war proportions in 1974, skewing the peacetime organization of the armed forces. In fact, at the height of the rebellion more than 80 percent of the total Iraqi armed forces were involved in meeting the Kurdish threat.[46]

The growth in Iraq's armed forces over the last decade is reflected in almost every commonly used indicator of military strength. In 1968, Iraq devoted approximately 9 percent of its GNP to defense. In the 1960s, defense spending claimed on the average 25 percent of total yearly government expenditures. By 1974—the last year for which accurate figures on GNP exist—Iraqi defense expenditures represented 18.7 percent of the country's GNP and 59.5 percent of the

44. Smith, et al., *Area Handbook*, p. 203.
45. Ibid., p. 341.
46. Ibid., p. 342.

total national budget. Defense consumed 43.7 percent of the national budget in 1975. More recently, defense spending has accounted for a smaller proportion of national expenditures, claiming in 1978, for example, only 17.6 percent of the national budget.[47] In 1978, Iraq spent $1.66 billion on defense.[48]

Between 1968 and 1970, overall manpower strengths in the armed forces increased by almost 10 percent to 91,000. Since 1970, manpower levels have more than doubled. In 1978, Iraq had 212,000 men in uniform divided as follows among the three services: the army, 180,000; the navy, 4,000; and the air force, 28,000.[49] Manpower levels are maintained through conscription. Every physically fit male is subject by law to two years military service. The ethnic composition of the Iraqi armed forces is representative of that of the total population—43 percent Sunnī (which includes 18 percent Kurdi) Muslim, 46 percent Shī'ī Muslim, 8 percent Christian Arab and Armenian, and 3 percent others.

The Soviet Union has been extensively involved in the training of Iraqi forces. As of January 1978, there were an estimated 2,000 Soviet advisors in Iraq training army special forces and armored divisions, air force combat, bomber, transport, and helicopter squadrons, and navy submarine chaser and missile patrol boat crews.[50] Czechoslovakia, East Germany, India, Pakistan, Egypt, France, and Cuba have also maintained military missions in Iraq.

Improvements in the army have been aimed at creating armored, infantry, and specialized support units. According to one source, in the late 1960s, Iraq's "military establishment was not a balanced force. . . . The preponderance of ground forces, with the principal emphasis on infantry, limited its overall combat effectiveness."[51] This was evident not only in Iraq's 1967 operations against Israel but also in its counter-insurgency operations in the 1960s against the Kurds, which, as noted, nearly became the full-time mission of the Iraqi armed forces.

In 1978, the army comprised four armored divisions (each with two armored and one mechanized brigade), two mechanized divisions, four infantry divisions, one independent armored brigade, one independent infantry brigade, one special forces brigade, and the Republican Guard mechanized brigade. Under normal conditions, the combat elements of the Iraqi army are deployed in the northern, central, and southern areas of the country.

According to the 1978–79 *Military Balance*, there were 1,700 T-62, T-54, and T-55 tanks in the Iraqi inventory, as well as 100 T-34 and AMX-30 medium tanks and 100 PT-76 light tanks.[52] (The T-62 is the standard tank of the Soviet army.) Iraq had ordered an undisclosed number of additional T-62 tanks and SCUD surface-to-surface missiles (SSMs), with delivery set for 1979.[53] Other equipment included 1,600 armored fighting vehicles of varying vintages; over 900 artillery pieces ranging in size from 75 mm to 152 mm, as well as numerous 120 and 160 mm mortars, SU-100 and ISU self-propelled guns (SPG), BM-21 rocket launchers,

47. *Military Balance, 1978–79*, p. 37.
48. Ibid., p. 37.
49. Ibid., 37–38.
50. Price (footnote 36).
51. Smith et al., *Area Handbook*, p. 343.
52. *Military Balance, 1978–79*, pp. 37 and 38.
53. Ibid., p. 38.

TABLE 7-2. IRAQI AIR FORCE UNITS

1 Bomber squadron, with 12 TU-22s

1 Light bomber squadron, with 10 IL-28s

12 Fighter ground attack (FGA) interceptor squadrons: 4 with 80 MIG-23Bs, 3 with 60 SU-7Bs, 3 with SU-20s, 2 with 20 Hunter FB59/FR10s

5 Interceptor squadrons, with 115 MIG-21s

1 Counterinsurgency squadron, with 12 Jet Provost T-52s

2 Transport squadrons with 12 AN-2s, 6 AN-12s, 10 AN-24s, 2 TU-124s, 13 IL-14s, 2 Heron, 2 Islander

7 Helicopter squadrons, with 4 MI-1s, 35 MI-4s, 14 BI-6s, 80 MI-80s, 47 Alouette IIIs, 10 Super Frelons, 40 Gazelles, 3 Pumas

Trainers: 30 MIG-15/-21/23, SU-7U, Hunter T-69, Yak-11, L-29, L-39

Source: 1978–79 *Military Balance* (London: The International Institute for Strategic Studies, 1977), p. 38.

Sagger and SS-11 antitank guided weapons 1,200 AA guns plus SA-7 SAMs and FROG-7 and SCUD-13 SSMS.[54]

In 1978, the combat wing of the Iraqi air force included about 339 aircraft. Significant improvements were made in 1977, when seventy additional combat aircraft entered service. Iraq also had a total of eighty MIG-23Bs and sixty SU-7Bs. The MIG-23 is one of the USSR's most advanced aircraft. Its transfer to Iraq continued Soviet practice, initiated in 1958, of supplying Iraq with sophisticated fighter aircraft. The SU-7, while an "old timer" in a NATO/Warsaw Pact context, is still a very capable aircraft for operations in the Persian Gulf region.

As can be seen in Table 7–2, by 1978 the vast majority of Iraq's air inventory was Soviet in origin. France, however, now appears to have made some inroads into the Iraqi market. Iraq signed an agreement with France in the fall of 1977 for the purchase of thirty-six Dassault-Breguet Mirage F1 with Matra Magic air-to-air missiles. Iraq was also believed to be interested in the Mirage 2000.[55] Major Iraqi airbases are located at Shu'aiba, Kirkuk, Basra, Habbāniyya, Rashīd, and Mosul. Air force headquarters are situated in Baghdad.[56]

To date, the most significant addition to the Iraqi navy has been the delivery of fourteen OSA-class fast patrol boats equipped with Styx surface-to-surface missiles from the Soviet Union. The Iraqi navy also includes three submarine chasers, ten torpedo boats, two Poluchat-class patrol craft, six small coastal patrol boats, five minesweepers, and three Polnocny-class landing ships. Iraq has reportedly granted Moscow full control over major bases at Qurna and Hurriyya, as well as partial control over the naval complex under development at Umm Qasr (built mainly with Soviet assistance), and partial control and land access to other bases. The agreement also allowed the number of Soviet advisors in Iraq to be increased.[57]

*Iran.** Iran's present day military are proud descendants of the "10,000 Im-

54. Ibid., p. 38.
55. "Air scene: Military affairs," *Air International* 13 (September, 1977): 109.
56. Smith et al., *Area Handbook*, p. 343.
57. *Defense and Foreign Affairs Digest* (November 1976): 44.

* *See also Epilogue*

mortals" whose exploits in the sixth and fifth centuries B.C. were largely responsible for the creation of the Persian empire, as well as for Persian forays westward into Europe and southward into Africa. Twentieth-century Iranian military tradition, however, begins in 1921, when Riẓā Khān removed Russian officers from the Persian Cossack Brigade and later led a successful coup against the Qājār dynasty. As minister of war, Riẓā Khān then planned a national army of 40,000 men, and in 1925 assumed the throne.[58] After the overthrow of the Musaddiq regime in 1953, Riẓā Khān's son and then Iran's next ruler, Muhammad Riẓā Shāh, focused much of his attention on modernizing his country's armed forces, which had rallied to his side.

The Imperial Iranian Ground Forces (IIGF) received first priority. The Shah, deeply concerned about Iran's internal security problems and her vulnerability to pressures from the Soviet Union, was determined to improve his country's military strength. The ground forces were steadily upgraded until, in the mid-sixties two basic developments combined to bring about a reexamination of Iran's broader strategic interests.

One event was the Indian–Pakistani War of 1965. It did not escape the Shah's attention that the United States had in effect abandoned her ally in favor of neutral policy. While Washington had frozen its arms shipments to both belligerents, the American action basically affected only Pakistan, whose armed forces depended largely on American equipment and spare parts. A second development was the growing influence of radical Arab movements along the periphery of the Arabian peninsula.

These trends drew the Shah's attention to upgrading Iran's other military services. The major upgrading and build-up of the Imperial Iranian Air Force (IIAF) began in the mid-1960s, with the expansion of the Imperial Iranian Navy (IIN) gaining momentum in the late 1960s and early 1970s.

In this respect it is important to note that while Britain's decision to withdraw its military presence in the Persian Gulf moved the Shah to take steps to fill the inevitable power vacuum that would be left in the wake of London's withdrawal, it was not the prime motivating factor for Iran's military build-up, which had begun in earnest well before Britain's 1968 announcement. In fact, by 1968, Iran already had a total armed force of 180,000. The IIGF, 164,000 strong, consisted of seven infantry divisions, one armored division, and an independent armored brigade. The IIN had 6,000 men, two U.S. destroyer escorts, two former British escorts of World War II vintage, two U.S.-built minesweepers, and a variety of smaller patrol craft, landing craft, and maintenance ships.[59] The IIAF had 10,000 men and 166 combat aircraft, including approximately 75 F-86Fs, 75 F-5s, and 16 RT-33As.

Defense spending in 1968 accounted for 5.6 percent of Iran's GNP. In 1976, the last year for which both figures have been published, Iran spent $9.5 billion or 12 percent of its GNP on defense. Defense spending tapered off to $7.9 billion in 1977.[60]

58. Smith et al., *Area Handbook for Iran* (second edition; Washington, D.C.: U.S. Government Printing Office, 1971), p. 580.

59. *The Gulf: Implications of British Withdrawal*, p. 81.

60. *Military Balance, 1978–79*, p. 37.

In many respects, the IIAF has undergone the most impressive changes since the late 1960s. Between the mid-1960s and the mid-1970s, in fact, the number of combat aircraft doubled, to include the most sophisticated vintage of American combat aircraft. The IIGF have not increased in numbers as have the other services, but they have been transformed from a largely infantry-based force to an army built around armor, helicopter, and mechanized elements. The IIN, with its primarily coastal orientation, is being upgraded markedly and expanded to provide a deep-water capability.

Iran's growing defense establishment numbering approximately 300,000 men under arms represents clearly the largest as well as the most modern military force in the Persian Gulf area. Yet this is not an excessive force level for a country with a population of 35 million, nor is the ratio at all high for the region. Iraq, Syria, Turkey, and Israel are all keeping a proportionately larger number of men under arms. Egypt retains a force of comparable size. Sa'ūdī Arabia, whose security problems are less serious than Iran's, could afford to keep a considerably smaller volunteer force. The Iranian conscription period of two years is less than that of Israel and Egypt (three years) or Syria (thirty months), and the same as Iraq's. Rather than relying upon the sheer number of military personnel, the Shah preferred to stress quality of personnel and weapons. The ethnic composition of Iran's armed forces is representative of that of the country as a whole, i.e., 64 percent ethnic Persians, 24 percent Turkish-speaking Iranians, and 12 percent nonethnic Persian tribes.

A developing country cannot modernize its military establishment without a good deal of technical training assistance from outside. The rapid acquisition of increasingly sophisticated weapons and other equipment therefore adds an additional dimension to the military problem. By 1976, the development and upgrading of Iran's armed forces was being supported by a large number of foreign military and civilian advisors. Most of these were Americans, but there were also some British and French. There were approximately 209 U.S. officers attached to the U.S. Army Mission and Military Assistance and Advisory Group (ARMISHMAAG). This was only about half the number in the MAAG a decade previously. In 1975, there were, however, about 2,728 American civilian technicians in Iran for the purpose of training Iranians to use their new complex systems, aircraft, missiles, destroyers, communications, and other equipment.[61] The civilian companies and the number of civilian personnel doing defense-related work in Iran in 1975 are listed in Table 7-3. The number of American civilians doing defense-related work in Iran is expected to increase to "at least 34,000 including dependents by 1980."

Grouped into three field armies, the ground combat forces include three armored divisions, four infantry divisions, and four independent brigades (one airborne, one special forces, and two infantry). In 1977, the infantry forces were equipped with modern rifles and machine guns and had more than 2,000 armored personnel carriers at their disposal.[62] The artillery units contributed about 30

61. Price (footnote 36).
62. Many of the American-supplied personnel carriers were armed with advanced wire-guided antitank missiles. Iran also had French antitank missiles. See R. D. M. Furlong, "Iran—a power to be reckoned with," *International Defense Review* (June 1973): 724.

TABLE 7–3. U.S. COMPANIES AND PERSONNEL CONDUCTING DEFENSE-RELATED TASKS IN IRAN, 1975

Company and major field of activity	Number of personnel
AAI Corp. (aircraft electronics)	3
Agusta Bell (aircraft maintenance)	10
Avco Corp./Lycoming (aircraft engine maintenance)	13
Bell Helicopter International (flight training)	1,424
Booz Allen & Hamilton (program management)	7
Bowen-McLaughlin-York (tank rebuilding)	35
Brown & Root E. & C. (shipyard construction)	16
Cessna Aircraft Co. (aircraft)	1
Collins Radio (communications electronics)	4
Computer Sciences Corp. (computers software)	264
Emerson Electric (armament maintenance)	1
Epsco Inc. (electronics)	1
General Dynamics (missiles)	11
General Electric (engines and armament)	15
General Motors/Allison (aircraft engine maintenance)	3
Grumman Aerospace Corp. (aircraft maintenance)	19
Hazeltine Corp. (electronics)	1
Hughes Aircraft (aircraft electronics and munitions)	7
ITT (communications electronics)	4
International Technical Product (communications)	85
Itek Corp. (electronics)	3
Kaman Aerospace Corp. (aircraft maintenance)	3
Litton (electronics)	7
Lockheed (aircraft maintenance)	123
Logistics Support Corp. (aircraft maintenance)	160
Martin-Marietta (electronics)	4
McDonnell Douglas (aircraft maintenance)	41
Northrop (missiles/aircraft maintenance)	29
Page Communications (communications)	5
Philco-Ford (electronics)	35
Pratt-Whitney (aircraft engine maintenance)	4
Raytheon (missiles)	126
RCA Corp. (electronics)	7
SDC (air defense systems training)	4
Singer Co. (electronics)	1
Stanwick (shipyard construction)	107
Sylvania Corp. (electronics)	3
Texas Instruments (armaments)	2
Westinghouse (electronics)	140
Total	2,728

Source: United States Arms Policies in the Persian Gulf and Red Sea Areas: Past, Present and Future. Report of a Staff Survey Mission to Ethiopia, Iran, and the Arabian Peninsula, U.S. House of Representatives (Washington, U.S. Government Printing Office, 1977), p. 145.

percent of the army's personnel and had undergone a major upgrading. They were for the most part equipped with Soviet and American antiair guns and surface-to-surface gun systems.[63]

In the armored divisions, some of the M-47 and M-60 American tanks had been replaced with the newer and more advanced British Chieftains and Scorpion tanks. The medium-weight Chieftain, armed with 120 mm guns, will be fitted with laser range finders. Iran, in 1973, began to take delivery of her order of some 760 Chieftains.[64] In May 1975, Iran reportedly ordered another 1,200 Chieftains. Of the lighter Scorpion tanks, some 250 were being acquired. Additional plans called for a tank force approximately comparable in total number to the forces of Egypt and Israel combined and about one-quarter to one-third larger than those of Syria and Iraq. Iran's projected tank force is nearly equal to that of France and double the size of the British tank force.[65]

To service and maintain the Chieftains, Iran has built a Military Industrial Complex (MIC) intended to produce Chieftain spare parts and ammunition, as well as replacement parts for Iran's armored vehicles, and thus complement the Royal Armaments Factory in northern Tehran, which produces small arms and ammunition.

Iran has also developed an airborne brigade, as well as a special forces brigade along American lines for counterinsurgency operations. These forces offer a capability for suppressing insurgencies in the Gulf region. To provide them with a rapid deployment capability, the army is developing an aviation command, with headquarters at Isfahān. The core of the Army Aviation Command is to be some 600 helicopters, which will provide transport, command, and close-fire support elements to the Sky Cavalry Brigade.[66]

Iran's ground forces are for the most part stationed along the border with Iraq. Army troops, however, are also deployed in the southeast, near the Pakistani frontier, to prevent the crossing of insurgents from Pakistan into Iran. Some 1,500 combat troops were deployed in Oman to assist the Sultan of Oman in containing the insurgency of the Dhufār Liberation Front. From the time the Shah answered Oman's request for support up to 1976, some 25,000 troops had been rotated through Oman. These forces have now been withdrawn.[67]

Although the Imperial Iranian Air Force (IIAF) did not receive separate

63. Ibid., p. 726. The Soviet systems included the dual-purpose twin 23 mm towed cannon; the ZSU-23-4 self-propelled radar-controlled antiair guns are still on order. The ZSU-57-2 antiair tanks, mounting twin 57 mm cannon, and the 85 mm M-44 towed gun are part of the artillery equipment. The American artillery systems ranged from the small 75 mm MIA1 mountain pack howitzers, the 105 mm M101's and the 203 M-115's—both towed—to the more modern self-propelled 175 mm M103 and 203 mm M110's. There were two relatively new Soviet surface-to-surface systems: the M-46 130 mm towed gun and the 40-tube 122 mm BM-21 version of the truck-carried Katyusha rocket family.

64. International Institute for Strategic Studies, *Military Balance, 1975–76*, p. 90.

65. Henry Stanhope writes that Iran's number of Chieftain tanks is "more than twice as many as Britain itself can afford to buy or to man." See his "Iran's defence budget," *Defence Journal* (Karachi) 2 (April–May 1976): 42.

66. Richard Burt, "Power and the Peacock Throne," *Round Table*, December 25, 1975, p. 354. Helicopter systems included the 202 Bell Sea Cobra, armed with the TOW missile; the Bell Isfahan twin-turbine troop assault chopper; and the Agusta Bell Jet Rangers.

67. D. L. Price, "Iran's Military Role," paper for the Institute for the Study of Conflict, p. 13.

service status until 1955, it had been organized as a branch of the army before World War II.[68] After the war, and especially after Iran had joined the Baghdad Pact in 1955, the U.S. military aid program enabled Iran to develop her air force with the F-86 fighter as its workhorse. The primary mission of the air force was to provide air defense and close air support for the ground forces. Still, it was not until 1965, when the government in Tehran allocated some $400 million to its defense build-up, that the expansion of the IIAF began to make rapid strides. Much of the impressive modernization of the air force bears the stamp of its former commander, General Muhammad Khātimī, by whose untimely death in 1975 the IIAF lost one of its most illustrious leaders.

With more than 100,000 personnel in 1977, the IIAF is patterned on the American model. It had an established strength of approximately 450 combat aircraft, including F-4 Phantoms, F-5 Tiger fighter bombers, and F-14 Tomcats. All of these aircraft are equipped with air-to-air missiles.[69] The most spectacular item among Iran's latest purchases, the swing-wing F-14 Tomcat, equipped with long-range Phoenix missiles, provides an effective counter to the Soviet MIG-23 or even, should the Iraqis acquire it, to the MIG-25. It offers a good capability to protect Iranian air space from possible intruders. In deciding to acquire the U.S. F-14 aircraft, the Shah was clearly concerned about Iraq's possession of the MIG-23, which was superior to Iran's F-4.

For inflight fueling, the Iranian fighter-bomber force relies on a squadron of Boeing 707 tankers, which could increase the combat radii of the F-4s and F-5s to 1,400 miles, thereby enabling them to cover the northwestern sector of the Indian Ocean region.[70] The upgrading of Iran's fighter and bomber capabilities has been matched by the expansion of her transport forces.[71] Air defense missiles have also been installed.[72]

Domestic air force training is conducted at the Air Force Training Center in Tehran. Instruction is in English; this facilitates further training that usually occurs in the United States, and occasionally in Pakistan.[73] Even more so than in the army, the air force places a premium on skilled manpower. But, as in the army, the acquisition of technically trained personnel poses a major problem. This does not mean, however, that Iran lacks qualified pilots. By criteria prevailing in the Persian Gulf–Middle East–Indian Ocean area, which is the environment in which the Iranian air force would have to be tested, the IIAF clearly ranks among the superior forces.

Iran's air force of 1978 consisted of about 450 combat aircraft. But Iran's

68. Iranian Ministry of Information, *Iran* (Iran: The Ministry, 1969), p. 103. As early as 1925, the Iranian government sent officers abroad for pilot training, and by 1950 some forty fighters formed the core of the army's air arm.

69. International Institute for Strategic Studies, *Military Balance, 1975–76*, p. 33. Several of the F-4E versions were fitted with the AIM-7 Sparrow long-range intercept missile. For ground strikes, the F-4E's were armed with Maverick air-to-surface missiles, of which Iran in 1973 bought some 2,500 from the United States. An order for close to 260 F-4s and another 180 F-5s had been placed.

70. Furlong, "Iran—a power to be reckoned with," p. 728.

71. Ibid., p. 729. Air transport units included six transport squadrons of C-130s and two light squadrons of the Fokker-72, the Beech C-45, the Douglas C-47, and the Beaver. Helicopter carriers counted the Super Frelons, Chinooks, Jet Rangers, and Huskies.

72. Ibid., pp. 728–29.

73. Ibid., p. 729.

projected air force of at least 500 or more combat aircraft previously contracted for would have roughly equaled the number and exceeded in quality the air force of Egypt in the late 1970s (612, including 100 in storage) or that of Israel (543). Iran's air force is considerably larger than that of Iraq (339), and vastly superior to the Sa'ūdī Arabian combat force, which currently numbers 171 and will grow to 231 with the delivery of the F-15s. Compared to West European air forces, Iran's would have approximated those of the British (511), West Germany (484), and the French (471). It is significantly larger than those of Turkey (290) and Italy (279). These figures, of course, indicate only quantitative equivalents. If we consider qualitative equipment factors, we must conclude that the Shah's determination to purchase the most modern and sophisticated aircraft available eventually should give Iran, on a selective basis, at least, technological superiority over many of those air forces mentioned above.

The Imperial Iranian Navy traces its origin to 1927, when the Ministry of War ordered two frigates for its Southern Command. The two gunboats delivered in 1932 were followed in subsequent years by several other ships until, in 1941, the Southern Command had four squadrons at its disposal. Each squadron included one frigate and at least two sloops.[74] In the years after the war, Iran received a number of torpedo boats, minelayers, and minesweepers from the United States, and some reconditioned destroyers from Britain.

More recently, the IIN has undergone a major modernization. While, in terms of manpower, still easily the smallest among Iran's armed services, the navy nevertheless has become a respectable ocean-going force. It already constitutes by far the most impressive fleet in the Persian Gulf; no combination of forces of the littoral states can offer the IIN a serious challenge.

In 1978, the IIN included one former British battle class destroyer, the 2,325-ton *Artemis*; and two former U.S. 2,250-ton destroyers, the *Babr* and the *Palang*. The latter have been extensively modernized and armed with Standard missiles. The navy also included four newly built Vosper Thornycraft, gas-turbine fast frigates equipped with British surface-to-surface and surface-to-air missiles. Four U.S. patrol frigates supplemented the larger units.[75]

To help protect the sea lines of communication through the Indian Ocean to the Persian Gulf, Iran ordered three Tang-class diesel submarines from the United States. Four modified U.S. Spruance-class destroyers, fitted with multiple missile launchers, and a new U.S. Harpoon antiship missile, also were ordered, with delivery set for the 1979–82 period.

As of 1978, the light naval forces included six large P-3 Orion patrol aircraft, which are operated by the air force and can stay aloft for seventeen hours, and thus could be used for maritime missions well beyond the Persian Gulf. Fourteen hovercraft, a number of support ships, three former U.S. coastal minesweepers and two U.S. inshore minesweepers further rounded out the Iranian naval capability. The light forces underwrite the Iranian navy's mission of supporting the Iranian army in local interventions when necessary. Important in this respect are the military hovercraft. Iran, in fact, operates the world's largest fleet of military hovercraft for patrol purposes. The craft, first used when Iranian forces were

74. Iranian Ministry of Information, *Iran*, p. 103.
75. *Jane's All the World's Fighting Ships, 1975–76*, p. 179 et seq. The destroyer Artemiz was armed with a quadruple Seacat antiair missile launcher, with 4.5-inch and 40 mm antiair guns.

landed on Abū Mūsā and the Tunb islands in November 1971, are based in the northern part of the Gulf and are generally used for coastal defense and logistic missions.

As of this writing there were more than a dozen other smaller British patrol craft in the Iranian inventory. Several of these were fitted with surface-to-surface missiles. Twelve fast attack missile patrol boats of the La Combattante type were ordered from France,[76] five having been delivered by mid-1978.

In addition, the Iranian navy had an air arm of some sixty-five operational aircraft of various types, fixed-wing and helicopter, which were used principally for antisubmarine warfare (ASW) operations, Iranian marine corps operations, and for the escort of tankers sailing through the Shatt al-'Arab.[77]

To support the Iranian navy, a network of bases is being built. Fleet head-quarters are at Bandar 'Abbās, with Bushire and Chāhbahār planned as main subsidiary operating bases. The base at Chāhbahār was designed to accommodate the Spruance class destroyers and the diesel submarines ordered from the United States. Chāhbahār could also provide an excellent air base for giving air cover with F-4 Phantoms and for the antisubmarine warfare and surveillance capa-bilities made possible by the Orion P-3 aircraft.[78] This arm of the navy is to operate in deep water, patrolling the sealanes and routes of access and egress to and from choke points and other strategic passages east and south of the Persian Gulf. It is thus vital to Iran's Indian Ocean policy. Light naval forces are based at Khurramshahr. Bandar 'Abbās is also the site of the fleet maintenance unit. Bandar Pahlavī, on the Caspian Sea, is the headquarters of the Northern Com-mand, which has primarily a training mission.

The IIN currently patrols Iran's nearly 2,000 miles of coastal waters, as well as islands over which she exercises sovereignty in the Persian Gulf, and also large portions of the northwestern Indian Ocean, extending down to ten degrees north latitude. Provided sufficient logistical support ships are procured, the U.S. Spruance class destroyers would have enabled Iran to extend her patrol of the sea lanes as far southward in the Indian Ocean as South Africa.

The projected Imperial Iranian Navy of the late 1970s with over 15,000 personnel and 30 principal combat vessels, would be comparable to the Egyptian navy (20,000 and 50, many of the latter older), somewhat larger than the Israeli navy (8,000 and 24), and much larger than the Iraqi navy (2,000 and about 20 smaller vessels, several of less than 100 tons). Iran is the only Middle Eastern country in possession of modern missile destroyers and missile frigates. The IIN, however, is not on a par with the naval forces of several European NATO coun-tries, such as Britain, France, West Germany, Italy, and Turkey. Even the Nether-lands, with a population only two-fifths that of Iran, maintained an equivalent navy.

Recently there has been discussion in the West about the prospect of a

76. Ibid.

77. International Institute for Strategic Studies, *Military Balance, 1975–76*, p. 33. These latter were armed with the Harpoon surface-to-surface cruise missiles. Six of the British patrol craft were Wellington Bn-7s, and the rest were Winchester Sr-N6s.

78. The naval air force consisted of 6 fixed-wing Strike Commanders, 5 AB-205 Hueys, 14 AB-206 A Jet Rangers, 6 AB-212s, and 10 Agusta-Sikorsky SH-3D Sea Kings.

nuclear weapons option for Iran. Speculation along this vein has been prompted, in large part, by the rise in oil prices that has given Iran the wherewithal to purchase nuclear technology. In 1975, Iran arranged the purchase of eight 1,200 Mwe reactors from the United States. In addition, Iran concluded an agreement with France for the purchase of two 900 Mwe reactors which are scheduled to be completed by 1983.[79] Kraftwerk—a West German firm—has signed a contract with Iran to construct two 1,200 Mwe reactors, which should be operational by 1981. Iran, according to official sources, plans to acquire a nuclear generating capability of 23,000 Mwe by 1990.[80]

The Iranian government, however, has steadfastly denied having a desire to develop nuclear weapons. The Shah, in fact, has shown his preference for a strong conventional rather than nuclear defense and has publicly stated that Iran's large-scale conventional arms program contributes adequate evidence of its interest to counter local conflict with conventional means. Iran has stated that it is seeking nuclear reactors for purposes of economic development and, unlike India and Pakistan, which are often cited as potential nuclear states, has signed the Nuclear Nonproliferation Treaty (NPT). Tehran has also voiced strong support for a nuclear free zone for the Indian Ocean area.

Smaller Persian Gulf States

Oman. Oman's armed forces have undergone considerable expansion and modernization over the last decade. In 1968, Oman's armed forces consisted of only 1,400 men.[81] By 1970, it had developed an army of 4,000, a small air force with Provost, Caribou, and Beaver aircraft, and a navy with two armored dhows. In 1978, Oman devoted $787 million to defense and, according to the 1978–79 *Military Balance*, had a total armed force of 19,200.[82] Native Omanis, however, constitute only about 50 percent of the country's armed forces. Baluchis and Yemenis each account for 20 percent, with the remainder drawn from persons ethnically tied to the United Arab Emirates (UAE).

The army, 16,200 strong in 1978, received the bulk of the increase in manpower. At that time it was organized into eight infantry battalions, one Royal Guard regiment, one artillery regiment, one signal regiment, an armored car squadron, one parachute regiment, one engineer regiment, and "strong and efficient ancillary services."[83] The army was equipped with thirty-six Saladin armored cars, thirty-six 105 mm guns, plus a number of 80 mm and 120 mm mortars.[84]

The air force consisted of 2,100 personnel and had thirty-six combat aircraft, of which twelve were Jaguar Internationals. There were also twelve Hunter FGA

79. Frank Bray and Alvin J. Cottrell, "The Armed Force of Iran, India, and Pakistan; A Comparative Assessment," *Brassey's Defence Yearbook* (London: Brassey's Publishers, 1977), pp. 36–37.
80. Ibid.
81. *The Gulf: Implications of British Withdrawal*, p. 83.
82. *Military Balance, 1978–79*, p. 41.
83. Donald Hawley, *Oman and Its Renaissance* (London: Stacey International, 1977), p. 243.
84. *Military Balance, 1978–79*, p. 41.

and eight BAC Strikemasters in the Omani air combat inventory. Oman's Hunters were transferred from Jordan. The Beavers and Caribous used in the 1960s by the Omanis have been sold or retired. Other aircraft in the Omani inventory included twenty Skyvans, three BAC-111, one VC-10, one Gulfstream, and two AS202 Bravo trainers; twenty-seven helicopters (twenty AB-205s, two AB-206s, and five AB-214s) complete the inventory. Air defense capabilities have been enhanced with the recent delivery of 28 Rapier SAMs and Blindfire SAM radars that have been integrated with the country's new Jaguars. As of 1977, the air force was organized into two fighter ground-attack squadrons, a counterinsurgency training squadron, a tactical transport squadron, two transport squadrons, and a helicopter squadron.[85]

Oman's navy is geared toward coastal defense, but, despite additions to the fleet, its capabilities remain quite limited even in this respect. The navy, in 1978, had 900 men and eighteen vessels, the most important of which are three patrol craft (one the Royal Yacht, two ex-Netherland Weldevank-class minesweepers), seven fast patrol boats (three being armed with Exocet missiles), one training ship, and four coastal patrol and three small landing craft. Oman's navy, however, was scheduled to undergo a period of modest expansion with the delivery of two minesweepers, three fast patrol boats, and one support ship, currently on order.[86] Omani naval operations originate from Muscat and Matrah, which are strategically located south of the approaches to the Straits of Hormuz.

Two factors must be kept in mind when assessing Oman's efforts to enhance its military capabilities. First, Omani forces traditionally have relied on British and other foreign nationals for leadership and training. In 1958, for example, Britain signed an agreement with Oman to provide training for Omani soldiers and to assist Oman in the development of its air force. In fact, until the accession of Sultan Qābūs, in 1970, Omanis were not permitted to hold ranks above the level of lieutenant.[87] Higher ranks were reserved for British, Pakistani, or other foreigners who were either seconded to Oman or under direct contract to the Omani government. Sultan Qābūs, however, has made a concerted effort to bring more Omanis into the higher levels of the officer corps. In 1977, for example, the chief of staff, previously a post held by a British officer, was held by a native Omani. Approximately 100 Omani officers a year are now commissioned from the ranks. Officer training is initiated in Oman. Promising candidates receive further training abroad, either in the United Kingdom or Jordan.

Like many smaller Persian Gulf countries, Oman remains heavily dependent on foreign assistance, not only for weapons systems, but for officers and training as well. The foreign military influence in Oman is summarized in Table 7–4. The United Kingdom, Pakistan, Iran, Jordan, and India maintain military missions in Oman.[88]

Second, Oman's military effort has been geared, in large part, toward meeting an internal threat, i.e., the Dhufār separation movement, which at the height of

85. Ibid.

86. *Defense and Foreign Affairs Handbook, 1976–1977*, p. 345.

87. Hawley, *Oman*, p. 243.

88. Conversation with Rear Admiral Robert J. Hanks, former Mid-East force commander, 1972–75.

its rebellion in the early 1970s posed a formidable challenge to Sultan Qābūs. The need to quell the rebellion, which was finally brought under control in the mid-70s, helps to explain Oman's inventory of helicopters and transport aircraft, which provided mobility for counterinsurgency operations.

According to one source, the rebellion, in fact, "had caused as much as 50 percent of Oman's national budget to be devoted to defense."[89] This level of effort alone, however, proved insufficient to contain the rebels, who were receiving assistance from and had been granted sanctuaries by the People's Democratic Republic of Yemen (PDRY). While Omani forces performed well, gradually gaining a foothold in the mountain areas of the south and in coastal areas, it was only after 1973 (when Iran, at the request of the Sultan, intervened militarily in Oman) that the tide of battle clearly began to turn in favor of the Sultan's forces. Iranian troops were instrumental in driving the Dhufār rebels back from the city of Salāla, with its strategically important airport, and in regaining control of the critical Midway Road between Salāla and Muscat. Most importantly, perhaps, the Iranians achieved great success in sealing off the border between Oman and the People's Democratic Republic of Yemen (PDRY) and in the establishment of what they named the Damāvand Line. This action sharply reduced the supplies the Dhufārīs were receiving from the PDRY. In 1977, Iranian troops still patroled the Damāvand Line. As noted above, by 1976 some 25,000 Iranian troops had been rotated through Oman. Jordan and the United Kingdom also had sent troops to Oman, British officers playing a key role, but did not become as heavily involved numerically as Iran.

Qatar. Before gaining independence in 1971 Qatar, like many of the smaller Gulf shaikhdoms, trusted its defense against external aggression to the British task force stationed in nearby Bahrain and Sharja. The task force was composed of approximately 8,400 men drawn from the British army, navy, and air force. The army component of the force consisted of 4,700 men. The British deployed three frigates, six coastal minesweepers, helicopters, and a small contingent of Royal Marines in the region. In addition, the air force attached two jet fighter

89. Hawley, *Oman*, p. 243.

TABLE 7-4. FOREIGN PERSONNEL PERFORMING
MILITARY-RELATED TASKS IN OMAN

Function	Unit	Number
i) Counter-insurgency	Special Air Service (UK)	15
ii) Military construction	Royal Engineers (UK)	63
iii) Health care	Royal Army Medical Corps (UK)	20
iv) Seconded officers	British Army	200
v) Contract officers	Freelance	465
vi) Water engineering	Jordan	45
vii) Counterinsurgency	Iran	1,000
Air Force		
i) Air defense	Iran	500

Source: David Lynn Price, unpublished memorandum to Alvin J. Cottrell, January 6, 1978.

squadrons to the task force, one based at Bahrain, the other in Sharja.[90] Internal security was maintained by a small security force under the supervision of Qatar's Public Security Department which, after Britain's withdrawal from Bahrain, evolved into a very modest defense force, headquartered at Dōha.

In 1978, Qatar's ruler, Shaikh Khalīfa ibn Hanad al-Thānī, became the supreme commander of the country's armed forces. He is assisted by a Defense Council that is authorized to advise the ruler on all matters concerning defense.[91] Qatar's defense budget for 1974–75, the last year for which accurate figures are published, was $53.7 million, representing approximately 12 percent of the country's GNP.[92] Qatar has no defense production capability of its own and purchases all its weapons abroad. Qatar, however, has agreed to join Egypt, the UAE, and Sa'ūdī Arabia in the formation of a cooperative arms and ordnance production organization. In 1978, Qatar's armed forces totaled 4,000, divided as follows among the three services: the army, 3,500, the navy, 200, the air force, 300.[93]

The army was organized into two armored car regiments, a Guards infantry battalion, and a mobile regiment. Equipment included twelve AMX-30 tanks, thirty Saladin and twenty Cascauel armored cars, ten Ferret scout cars, twelve AMX-10P mechanized infantry combat vehicles, eight Saracen APCs, four 25-pounder guns and a number of 81 mm mortars.

The air force was organized into a fighter unit, with three HS Hunter FGA-78s and IT-79s; and a transport squadron, with one Islander. In addition, there were eleven helicopters in service: two Whirlwind IIIs, two Gazelles, four Westland Commandos, and three Lynx. The two Gazelles normally used for police work would be detached to the air force in case of external threat.[94]

The navy had six large Vosper-type patrol craft and thirty-one small, assorted coastal patrol craft. The prospects for a modest expansion of the navy seem good in the near future.[95]

Officers in the Qatarī armed forces are primarily British and Pakistan seconded to Qatar or under contract to the government. A limited number of Qatarīs, however, do serve as officers. In general, the ethnic composition of the armed forces representative of the Qatarī population, is 56 percent Arab, 14 percent Iranian, and 7 percent Pakistani.

The British firm, Hillbank Technical Services, has provided training assistance to Qatar in coastal defense operations. The extent to which other foreign businesses or governments have performed military-related tasks in Qatar is not clear. The United Kingdom, Jordan, Pakistan, and Egypt, however, have foreign military missions in Qatar.

United Arab Emirates. The United Arab Emirates (UAE) is composed of seven shaikhdoms that were granted independence by Great Britain in 1971, namely, Abū Dhabī, Dubai, Sharja, Ra's al-Khaima, 'Ajmān, Umm al-Qaiwain, and Fujaira. The Provisional Constitution of Union, adopted in December 1971,

90. *The Gulf: Implications of British Withdrawal*, p. 79.
91. Richard F. Nyrop et al., *Area Handbook for the Persian Gulf States* (Washington, D.C.: U.S. Government Printing Office, 1977).
92. *Defense and Foreign Affairs Handbook, 1976–1977*, p. 373.
93. *Military Balance 1978–79*, p. 41.
94. Ibid., p. 41.
95. Ibid., p. 41.

envisaged a united defense effort by the seven shaikhdoms. Initially, however, individual sheikhdoms were permitted to maintain their own security forces.[96] These forces were considered separate entities from the all Union Defense Force (UDF), which was founded at independence and based on the Trucial Oman Scouts—a 1,600 man force that had carried out internal security functions under British rule.[97]

In 1975, the UDF numbered approximately 3,500 men and was organized into six mobile squadrons and an air detachment with seven helicopters. Three of these helicopters had been donated by Abū Dhabī, as a first step toward the creation of a union air force.[98] Ground forces were equipped with light tanks, armored cars, and mortars.

The UDF, however, paled in comparison to some of the shaikhdom forces. In 1975, for example, Abū Dhabī had a total armed strength of 10,000 men apportioned as follows among three branches: the army, 8,600; the sea wing 200; and the air wing, 1,200. Abū Dhabī's army was equipped with heavy and light armored cars, 25 pounder artillery, and Vigilant antitank missiles. The sea wing of the Abū Dhabī defense force had nine small patrol craft and patrolled the entire UAE coast, including that on the Gulf of Oman. In addition, the shaikhdom's defense force had an air wing of twenty-six combat aircraft (fourteen Mirage V and twelve Hawker Hunter jet fighter bombers).[99] Dubai also chose to maintain a separate armed force and by 1975 had 1,500 men at arms organized into three infantry battalions, one armored car battalion, a support battalion, and an air wing with ten light aircraft. Ra's al-Khaima and Sharja had defense forces of 300 and 250 men, respectively.[100]

On May 6, 1976, the Supreme Defense Council of the UAE unified the land, sea, and air forces of the federation under a central command and divided the country into western, central, and northern regions.[101] The Supreme Defense Council also named the president of the UAE, Shaikh Zāyid, supreme commander of the armed forces. The minister of defense, however, has day-to-day responsibility for the armed forces. He is assisted by a chief of staff. In 1978, the UAE devoted $661 million to defense, with Abū Dhabī contributing the largest share of the federation's defense budget.[102]

The integration of the emirate forces into the UDF, as well as subsequent programs, has increased the UDF's total manpower and capabilities considerably. According to the 1978–79 *Military Balance* the UDF had a manpower strength of 25,900. This figure represents an increase in manpower of more than 60 percent over the combined UDF and emirate force total of 16,000 in 1975. Approximately 23,500 men serve in the army, 600 in the navy, and 1,800 in the Union Air Force.[103] Abū Dhabī contingents account for roughly 80 percent of army manpower.[104]

While the constitution provides for conscription, the customary practice of

96. Nyrop et al., *The Persian Gulf States*, p. 325.
97. Ibid.
98. "Arab air power," p. 277.
99. Ibid.
100. Nyrop et al., *The Persian Gulf States*, p. 325.
101. Ibid., p. 330.
102. *Military Balance, 1978–79*, p. 43.
103. Ibid.
104. "Arab air power," p. 276.

contracting foreigners into the UDF has not made conscription necessary. The Abū Dhabī contingent of the UDF, for example, is composed of approximately 50 percent "foreign" personnel. Other emirate contingents are ethnically about 72 percent Arab, with the rest recruited from foreigners residing in the UAE or from abroad.

Foreign personnel fill many posts in the UDF's officer corps. At independence, the UAE's noncommissioned and commissioned officers were mostly British and Pakistani in origin. Recently, however, more Jordanians appear to be serving [as officers] in the UDF. This trend is quite evident with respect to the army which, in 1977, had about sixty Jordanian commissioned and noncommissioned officers.[105] Like other smaller Persian Gulf states, the UAE is making a concerted effort to bring more nationals into the officer corps.

The UAE depends on foreign assistance for training purposes. The British firm Hillbank Technical Service, for example, has assisted the UAE in the training of armored car squadrons. The United Kingdom, Jordan, Saʻūdī Arabia, the Sudan, Egypt, Lebanon, and Pakistan maintain military missions in the UAE. Of these, the UAE perhaps has closest ties with Pakistan. In 1972, UAE president, Shaikh Zāyid, and former president of Pakistan, Bhutto, reached an agreement whereby Pakistan took over the training of Abū Dhabī's personnel and seconded pilots and maintenance crews to the emirates air force. Abū Dhabī reportedly consented to make its Mirages available to Pakistan on a "lease in emergency basis."[106]

In 1978, UAE land forces were organized into one Royal Guard Brigade, three armored and armored car battalions, seven infantry battalions, three artillery battalions, and three air defense battalions. Equipment included thirty Scorpion light tanks, eighty-six Saladin, Shortland, and Panhard armored cars, sixty Ferret Scout cars, plus a force of armored personnel carriers, 25-pounder guns, AMX 155 mm self-propelled howitzers, and a number of 105 mm guns, 81 mm mortars, and 120 mm recoilless rifles constitute the artillery strength. Vigilant antitank guided weapons as well as Rapier and Crotalle SAMs were also in the UAE arsenal.[107] UAE land forces are deployed chiefly within the country. The UAE, however, has attached 700 troops to serve in the Arab Peace Keeping Force in Lebanon.

Sea wing forces consisted of six large Vosper-type and nine small patrol craft. In addition, the police force had a complement of fourteen patrol craft that could be used, if necessary, in conjunction with naval forces.

The 1978–79 *Military Balance* notes that there were forty-six combat aircraft in the Union Air Force: thirty-two Mirages, seven Hunter FGAs, two T-77s, and four MB-326 counterinsurgency aircraft. Other aircraft included two C-130H, one Boeing 727, one G-222, four Islander, one Falcon, three DHC-4, one DHC-5D, and one Cessna 182 transport aircraft. In addition, the Union Air Force had thirty-seven helicopters on hand: eight AB-205s, six AB-206s, three AB-212s, ten Alouette IIIs, and ten Pumas. The UAE has placed orders for two additional G-222 transports and three DHC-5D transports. The Union Air Force, as con-

105. Nyrop et al., *The Persian Gulf States*, p. 332.
106. "Arab air power," p. 277.
107. *Military Balance, 1978–79*, p. 43.

figured in 1978, was basically an amalgamation of the former Abū Dhabī and Dubai shaikhdom air forces. Abū Dhabī preferred aircraft of French origin, Dubai aircraft of Italian origin. In the past, Dubai's relationship with Italy has included assistance in training. Dubai's pilots, for example, underwent a "conversion" course for the MB-326 in Italy.[108] The UAE is presently trying to standardize its sources of arms. While Abū Dhabī did place a follow-up order for the Mirage V before the formal merging of shaikhdom forces, until procurement preferences are rationalized the combat wing of the Union Air Force is unlikely to undergo significant expansion. Most of the Mirage Vs now on order, for example, are intended to make up for attrition losses incurred by the first squadron of Mirage Vs. Air defense surveillance radar, basic trainers, and anti-armor helicopters appear to be the types of equipment the UAE is most interested in procuring.

Kuwait. Kuwait became completely independent in 1961. Until then, Kuwait's foreign and defense policies had been controlled by the British. For a time after independence, however, Kuwait's security continued to be tied closely to the British presence in the Gulf. This was made quite clear when, in its first week of independence, Kuwait was threatened by Iraq, which promptly resurrected historic claims. Britain, deploying troops, ships, and aircraft to Kuwait, blocked the Iraqi threat.

In 1968, Kuwait had an army of between 6,000 and 8,000 men organized into one brigade group armed with small British guns, Vigilant antitank weapons, and a very limited number of Centurion tanks.[109] Britain's withdrawal from the Persian Gulf in 1971 brought the limitations of Kuwait's own military force into sharp focus. Kuwait was virtually defenseless against those who might covet its immense oil wealth or against radical elements dedicated to the overthrow of established conservative governments throughout the Persian Gulf.

The small shaikhdom moved to shore up its security position in two ways. First, it began to share its wealth with its neighbors, extending, for example, substantial amounts of aid to national and regional development programs. Kuwait has also assisted Arab countries in recovering from the devastation of repeated war with Israel. Kuwait, in fact, is one of the world's foremost donors of foreign aid.

Second, Kuwait began to expand its own military capabilities. Since 1971, Kuwait has devoted more than $3.5 billion to the expansion and modernization of its military. In 1977, $428 million was spent on defense. This figure was expected to increase by slightly less than 18 percent in 1978. Defense expenditures for 1978 probably accounted for about 35 percent of Kuwait's total national budget.[110]

In 1977, Kuwait had a total armed force of 12,000 men. The army numbered 10,500; its air force, 1,000; and its navy, 500. Kuwait's army was organized into one armored brigade and two armor-infantry-artillery brigades. It possessed 124 medium tanks, with 129 on order. In addition, the Kuwaiti army order of battle

---

108. "Arab air power," p. 291.
109. *The Gulf: Implications of British Withdrawal*, pp. 82–83.
110. *The Middle East* (September 1977): 18.

TABLE 7–5. KUWAITI NAVAL INVENTORY

Navy: 500 (coast guard)
5 fast patrol boats
12 inshore patrol boats
16 patrol launches
3 landing craft

Source: The Military Balance, 1978–79, p. 38.

included 100 Saladin armored cars, 130 Saracen APCs, ten 25-Pdr guns, 200 155-mm howitzers, SS-11, 40 T, TOW, and Harpon antitank weapons. In 1977, Kuwait agreed to purchase SA-7 (Strela) surface-to-air missiles from the Soviet Union. Later that same year, however, an announcement from the Defense Ministry stated that "western arms would be sufficient for the country's needs."[111] The break with Moscow was based, in large part, on Kuwaiti reluctance to allow Soviet technicians in Kuwait to instruct Kuwaiti soldiers in the weapon's operations and maintenance. This reluctance stemmed from U.S. refusal to proceed with the sale of sophisticated American arms if Soviet advisors were to be allowed in the country.

Kuwait's air force consisted of forty-nine combat aircraft in 1977. It hopes to raise manpower in the air force to 8,000 over the next few years. According to the 1978–79 *Military Balance*, the combat wing of the Kuwaiti air force was organized into two fighter bomber squadrons forming around twenty A-4M Sky-hawks; one interceptor squadron, with twenty Mirage F-1 B/Cs; and one counter-insurgency squadron, with nine BAC-167 Strikemaster MK 83s. Kuwait also had two Lockheed L-100 20s, two DC-9 VIP transport aircraft, and about forty-two helicopters, of which twenty were Gazelles and twelve Pumas. Some of the Gazelles were armed with TOW missiles. An order had been placed for fourteen A-4KU and four TA-4KUFGAs.

A small navy of light patrol craft has been developed, with modest plans for expansion. Kuwait's naval inventory is listed in Table 7–5. Some of Kuwait's craft may ultimately be fitted with SSMs in the near future. Finally, a new naval base is currently being constructed in southern Kuwait with Japanese, Yugoslav, and Pakistani assistance. In early 1978, some consideration had been given in Kuwait to the formation of a joint naval force with Qatar and Bahrain, but, as of this writing, this had not materialized.

Kuwait's armed forces are under the command of the country's constitutional emir, whose powers are quite comprehensive. The minister of defense exercises authority directly under the emir. To date, military service has been voluntary, but the government now appears set on introducing conscription in the very near future. Conscription is being considered in order to fill the government's man-power goals as well as to bring more Kuwaiti nationals into the country's armed forces. According to one source, Kuwait has had difficulty securing enlistees from "the ranks of better educated young Kuwaitis who are more attracted by business opportunities . . . Kuwait is not anxious to fill its upper military ranks with mercenaries."[112] Nor does the ruling Sabāh Family wish to see those ranks domi-

111. *Defense and Foreign Affairs Digest* (September 1977): 38 and 263.
112. Joe Alex Morris, Jr., "Kuwait prepares to draft soldiers, updates weapons," *Los Angeles Times*, April 15, 1978, p. 2.

nated by Kuwait's huge Palestinian minority. About one-third to one-half of Kuwait's army, for example, is comprised of poorly educated Iraqi or Sa'ūdī tribesmen. Information indicates that the remainder of the armed forces is ethnically representative of the overall Kuwaiti population, which is 87 percent Arab, 12 percent Iranian, Indian or Pakistani, and 1 percent others.

Skilled manpower is particularly lacking in the air force. In 1977, approximately 80 British personnel were training Kuwaitis to use the sophisticated aircraft and other equipment that had been ordered in the past few years. Other countries were also providing technical assistance and advice to Kuwait, most notably, Pakistan (re: coastal defense), Syria (re: conscription) and Egypt (re: special forces and general training). Egypt signed an agreement with Kuwait, in August 1977, to train 300 Kuwaitis in the use of the SA-7, which was subsequently turned down. India had been selected by the Kuwait Defense Ministry to construct a military camp outside Kuwait City. These countries all maintained military missions in Kuwait, as did Jordan.

Bahrain. Bahrain served as the nodal point of the British military and political presence in the Persian Gulf. British military facilities in Bahrain included naval headquarters, a refueling depot, joint services headquarters, housing for 650 dependents, and an airfield capable of accommodating the largest aircraft then in the British inventory. At the height of British operations in the Persian Gulf, the airfield at Bahrain handled approximately 250 aircraft per month.[113]

This impressive military infrastructure was bequeathed to Bahrain incident to Britain's departure in 1971. For years, a small portion of Britain's former facilities on Bahrain were used by the United States Navy to support its operations in the region. The American presence in Bahrain, however, has been significantly curtailed. Bahrain has decided not to allow the United States to continue the practice of home-porting its Middle East Force flagship at Manāma. United States manpower levels in Bahrain have therefore, been reduced from about 125 shore-based personnel, plus 500 dependents, to 75, with only a few dependents. Except for Middle East Force ships, U.S. naval vessels, contrary to past practice, must now make a formal diplomatic request to call in Bahrain.[114] Such requests are almost certain to be granted, barring some crisis such as another Arab-Israeli war.

In 1975—the last year for which accurate figures have been published—Bahrain devoted $14.05 million, or 4.3 percent, of its total national budget to defense. In 1978, Bahrain maintained only a small defense force of 2,300 men organized into one infantry battalion and one armored car squadron, as well as administrative and support units.[115] Service is voluntary. Equipment included eight Saladin armored cars, eight Ferret scout cars, six 81 mm mortars, and six 120 mm recoilless rifles. In addition to its defense force, Bahrain also had a small coast guard and an air police force, with a combined manpower of 100.

---

113. *Gulf: Implications of British Withdrawal*, p. 80.
114. Alvin J. Cottrell and Thomas H. Moorer, "U.S. Overseas Bases: Problems of Projecting American Military Power Abroad," in *The Washington Papers* 47 (Sage Publications, 1977), pp. 31–32.
115. *Military Balance, 1978–79*, pp. 35 and 36.

The coastal force had twenty patrol launches at its disposal. The air police force has two Scout helicopters.[116]

Conclusions

Britain's withdrawal east of Suez left the Persian Gulf states with a wide variety of security dilemmas. For years, Britain's presence in the Persian Gulf had served to contain tensions among the Gulf countries. As was noted at the time, disputes among the various Persian Gulf states were not pursued, in great part, "because the parties concerned recognized that while the British were present, temporary silence over a claim did not imply its forfeiture."[117] Britain's withdrawal, Persian Gulf leaders feared, could result in an outbreak of hostilities among Gulf states over old rivalries and territorial claims or in the development of new disputes over territorial or resources issues.

Equally disturbing, many Persian Gulf leaders felt that Britain's absence from the area would entice other external powers to bid for positions of dominance over the region. Sa'ūdī Arabia, Iran, and other traditionally ruled states of the Gulf became concerned that external forces would move to take advantage of the void left by Britain's withdrawal. Added to these concerns was the possibility that insurgents would be encouraged to directly challenge the historic rulers in the Gulf. More recently, the world's seemingly insatiable thirst for energy has made the Persian Gulf, with its vast oil resources, an attractive arena in which to play out superpower rivalries. To varying degrees, many of these fears have proven well founded, adding further impetus for the Persian Gulf nations to improve their military postures.

The increase in the size and sophistication of Persian Gulf military forces has been taking place at a time when many of the traditional rulers of the area, having witnessed Britain's withdrawal, see little hope that their security will be ensured by any great power. Relatively speaking, the military capabilities of the Persian Gulf states have improved considerably. In some countries, the number of men under arms has more than doubled, and the quantity and quality of most Persian Gulf weapons inventories bear little resemblance to those on hand in the immediate aftermath of Britain's withdrawal.

Primary emphasis has been placed on shoring-up defensive as opposed to offensive capabilities. This is reflected in the various national procurement programs cited above. Fighter and counterinsurgency aircraft, helicopters, improved radar, and other defense systems appear to be the items most sought after by Persian Gulf air forces. SAMs and antitank weapons are becoming prevalent in the arsenals of Persian Gulf armies. Persian Gulf navies, just beginning to come to the fore, are focusing primarily on coastal defense. For the most part, procurement is being geared toward light, fast patrol boats armed with precision-guided munitions (PGMs). For the foreseeable future, Iran appeared to be the only Persian Gulf state moving toward a full-fledged blue-water capability.

116. *Defense and Foreign Affairs Handbook, 1976–1977*, p. 27.
117. *The Gulf: Implications of British Withdrawal*, p. 8.

Despite their substantial progress, however, the Persian Gulf states have a long way to go before they will be capable of fending for themselves in defense matters—even against a medium power threat. This is true on the battlefield as well as in the areas of training, weapons development, production, and even maintenance. Manpower shortages pose a most serious constraint on military capabilities in some Persian Gulf states. The lack of a skilled or trainable labor force, as well as the absence of a high-technology-oriented industrial base, has placed crucial limitations on the military programs of every Persian Gulf state, particularly with respect to "staying power" in regional conflicts. In any drawn-out military action, all Persian Gulf nations would find themselves dependent on foreign supplies to replenish their arsenals. This presents a problem that will take a long time to alleviate, notwithstanding the immense concentration of oil wealth throughout the region.

Epilogue

In January 1979, revolution wracked Iran and, thereby, drastically altered the existing and projected Iranian military forces discussed in the foregoing chapter. The future configuration and size of the military forces that will evolve in Iran under whatever new government eventually emerges, are thus still not clear. What is clearly evident, however, is the certainty that Iran will no longer remain the leading military power in the Gulf, with respect to quantity and quality, as it was before the revolution. This power position will now fall to Iraq, which never was far behind Iran in the size and quality of its forces and equipment, and which will surely become the principal Persian Gulf military power.

Iran's military forces are likely, henceforth, to be little more than a third of the 400,000 total which the Imperial Iranian Armed Forces heretofore boasted: a new total of about 150,000. If current statements by the new Iranian leadership prove accurate, the army will be reduced from 285,000 to about 100,000—or slightly less—the air force from nearly 100,000 to about 35,000, and the navy from around 30,000 to about 15,000. Iraq's present and developing overall military strength based on current estimates, would be roughly 217,000. Total Iraqi forces would comprise 185,000 in the army, 4,000 in the navy, and 28,500 in the air force.

One must assume that the quality of Iran's armed forces will have suffered severely since all officers of the Imperial Iranian armed forces above the rank of brigadier general have been retired, arrested, or executed. Even the ranks of brigadier general have been badly decimated. Not more than 40 percent of the army has heeded the new authorities' call to return to duty. Thus, a serious question remains as to whether the military forces can be reconstituted in the near future into anything approaching an effective force for maintaining domestic stability, let alone one capable of defending against external threats to the country. Moreover, the revolutionary leaders have stated that, unlike Imperial Iran, they do not intend to play any role as a regional policeman in the Persian Gulf area.

Decisions still must be taken on whether foreign military technicians will be retained or called back to help with the training of Iranian military personnel to use the very sophisticated weaponry Iran procured in the United States and elsewhere in the West. There have been discussions of selling back to the United States the more sophisticated weaponry procured under the Imperial regime, particularly the very advanced F-14 Tomcat aircraft with its Phoenix missile, which the United States hopes will not fall into enemy hands. Iran still has seventy to eighty left. The Khomeini officials also are canceling many weapons systems that had been ordered from the United States, such as the F-16 aircraft, the Spruance destroyers, submarines, and the Boeing AWACs airborne early warning and command aircraft.

The changed regional security role now projected by the new leadership will, of course, reduce the requirement for much of the equipment as well as the size of the armed forces originally projected. In sum, as a result of the revolution, Iran will have to rebuild and redesign the command structure of its armed forces as well as restructure and reconfigure the army, navy, and air force for a much diminished domestic and regional role.

Selected Bibliography

Bray, F., and Cottrell, A. J. "The Armed Forces of Iran, India, and Pakistan: A Comparative Assessment." In *Brassey's Defence Yearbook*. London, 1977.

Burt, R. "Power and the Peacock Throne." *Round Table,* December 25, 1975.

Center For Strategic and International Studies. *The Gulf: Implications of British Withdrawal*. Washington, D.C., 1969.

Chubin, S. "Iran's security in the 1980s." *International Security* (Winter, 1978).

Copley, G. R. *Defense and Foreign Affairs Handbook, 1976–1977*. Washington, D.C., 1978).

Cottrell, A. J. "Iranian and Saudi Arabian Security Interests." *The Washington Review of Strategic and International Studies* (White Paper, May 1977).

Cottrell, A. J., and Moorer, T. H. "U.S. Overseas Bases: Problems of Projecting American Military Power Abroad." In *The Washington Papers* 47. Beverly Hills, 1977.

Defense and Foreign Affairs Digest (November 1976).

Furlong, R. D. M. "Iran—a Power to Be Reckoned With." *International Defense Review* (June 1973).

GIST. (State Department document) *Middle East Aircraft Sales*. Washington, D.C., March, 1978.

Hawley, D. *Oman and Its Renaissance*. London, 1977.

Institute for Defence Studies and Analyses. *News Review on West Asia*. New Delhi, 1978.

International Institute for Strategic Studies. *Strategic Survey*. London, 1976.

———. *The Military Balance, 1975–76*. London, 1976.

———. *The Military Balance, 1977–78*. London, 1977.

———. *The Military Balance, 1978–79*. London, 1978.

Iranian Ministry of Information. *Iran*. Teheran, 1969.

Jane's All the World's Fighting Ships, 1975–76, New York, 1976, 1977 and 1978.

Nolan, J. "Notes On: The Interaction between the Growth of Oil Revenues and Military Expenditures: Libya, Kuwait, and Saudi Arabia, 1968–1974/75" (unpublished).

Nyrop, R. F., et al. *Area Handbook for the Persian Gulf States*. Washington, D.C., 1977.

————. *Area Handbook for Saudi Arabia*. 3rd ed. Washington, D.C., 1977.

Price, D. L. "Iran's Military Role." Paper for the Institute for the Study of Conflict, 1977.

Smith, H. H., et al. *Area Handbook for Iran*. 2nd ed. Washington, D.C., 1971.

————. *Area Handbook for Iraq*. 2nd ed. Washington, D.C., 1969.

Stanhope, H. "Iran's defence budget." *Defence Journal* (April/May 1976).

Tahtinen, D. R. *National Security Challenges to Saudi Arabia*. Washington, D.C., 1978.

8. International Organizations in the Persian Gulf RALPH H. MAGNUS

 This chapter examines the various international organizations that Persian Gulf nations have joined. The international organizations to which they belong can be classified into five categories, using a mixture of two criteria: issue area and membership. In many cases, questions might well be raised to the proper category for a given organization, since many are in fact multifunctional in nature. Our solution is to look at their central theme in the first instance and also to discuss their other functions. Similarly, subordinate specialized and functional organizations related to larger umbrella-type organizations, such as the League of Arab States, will be discussed along with their parent organization. Some major organizations that no longer exist, such as the League of Nations, will be examined as well. Five categories of international organizations will be considered: universal organizations, regional political/security organizations, regional economic organizations, petroleum organizations, and religious organizations.

Universal Organizations

The League of Nations. The League of Nations was founded in 1920, growing out of the desires of the victorious allies to assure the *status quo* of the World War I peace settlement, and out of the idealism of the final point of President Wilson's famous Fourteen Points: "A general association of nations must be formed under specific covenants for the purpose of affording mutual guarantees of political independence and territorial integrity to great and small states alike."[1] Iran was one of the founding members of the League and was for twelve years its only Middle Eastern member. It was joined in 1932 by Iraq and Turkey, in 1934 by Afghanistan, and in 1937 by Egypt. The lack of Middle Eastern membership,

1. "United States War Aims: President Wilson's XIV Points Speech to Congress (excerpts), January 8, 1918," in Ralph H. Magnus, ed., *Documents on the Middle East* (Washington, 1969), p. 27.

of course, was a reflection of the domination of the area in the interwar years by Great Britain and France. The remaining two fully independent Middle Eastern states, Saʿūdī Arabia and Yemen, were not members. The Hashemite kingdom of the Hijāz, which had been one of the victorious allied powers, was offended by the establishment of foreign mandates in Palestine and Syria. It did not ratify the Treaty of Versailles nor did it join the League.[2]

Both Iran and Iraq were deeply involved with the League of Nations and pursued active diplomatic policies there. They seemed to view acceptance in the League as a "seal of approval" of their fully independent status and to take the Wilsonian ideals of an international guarantee of the independence and territorial integrity of small states at face value. Iran's first experience with the machinery of the League might well have given it second thoughts, however. One of the first international disputes to be considered by the League was an appeal of Iran on 19 May 1920 in the case of the invasion of the Caspian Sea province of Gīlān by Bolshevik forces, which had landed at the port of Enzelī the previous day. The League Council delayed, recommending that Iran wait to see if the assurances of the Bolshevik foreign minister that the forces would be withdrawn would be honored.[3] More than a year later the troops were withdrawn, but not until after the Soviet–Iranian Treaty of Friendship and Non-Aggression of March 1921 had given them the right to return, should the Soviets feel threatened by foreign forces in Iran.[4]

As a conquered Arab province of the Ottoman empire, Iraq was assigned as a mandate to Great Britain by the Supreme Allied Council, meeting at San Remo, Italy, on 25 April 1920. Iraqi nationalists, however, were firmly opposed to the mandate, and Britain acceded to their demands to the extent of exercising its mandatory powers through a treaty with the Iraqi government. This arrangement was approved by the League Council.[5] Britain sponsored the termination of the mandate and the admission of Iraq to the League of Nations on 3 October 1932. Iraq, however, had to agree to conditions stipulated by the Permanent Mandatory Commission for safeguarding the rights of minorities and foreigners, guaranteeing economic equality for all League members and the respecting of international conventions.[6]

Even before its admission to the League, Iraq was involved in a serious boundary dispute before the League over the status of Mosul province. The final peace treaty between the Allies and the Turkish republic, the Treaty of Lausanne of 1923, left Mosul's status clouded and open for bilateral negotiations between Britain and Turkey. When no agreement was reached, the matter was placed before the League Council in 1924 by Great Britain. Although not yet a League member, Turkey also presented its case. Following a Commission of Enquiry on the spot and an opinion by the Permanent Count of International Justice, the Council awarded the province to Iraq in late 1925. Turkey was unhappy with the

2. George Lenczowski, *The Middle East in World Affairs* (3rd edition; Ithaca, N.Y., 1962), p. 543.
3. Peter Avery, *Modern Iran* (New York and Washington, 1965), pp. 220–21.
4. Ibid., p. 246.
5. Abid A. Al-Marayati, *A Diplomatic History of Modern Iraq* (New York, 1961), p. 21.
6. Ibid., p. 44.

outcome, but an Anglo-Turkish Treaty of 5 June 1926 finally settled the matter. Turkey was guaranteed 10 percent of Mosul's oil production for its needs.[7]

The Syrian–Iraqi boundary was another dispute resolved by the League in 1932, largely in Iraq's favor. Internally, the League was involved in the questions of Iraq's treatment of its Assyrian minority, most of them refugees from Turkey and Iran, who wished for autonomous status under their Patriarch. An Assyrian uprising in 1933 was put down with brutality by the Iraqi military.[8] The League considered the Assyrian question a number of times between 1932 and 1937, both in the Council of the League and in a special committee. Eventually, Iraq agreed to contribute to the cost of a settlement established in Syria by the Assyrians who had been interned by Iraq during the uprising. Iraq assured the Council that those Assyrians wishing to remain as a minority within Iraq would be allowed to do so, and the special committee was terminated in September 1937.[9]

A further dispute in this period involved both Iran and Iraq; this was the famous Shatt al-'Arab river boundary.[10] Iraq placed the issue before the League Council in 1934. The Council appointed a rapporteur to bring the two parties together. However, private negotiations, aided by the good offices of Turkey, caused both parties to recommend that the League postpone its consideration of the matter. These negotiations led to the signing of a new treaty between Iran and Iraq on 4 July 1937.[11]

In November 1932, Iran canceled the concession of the Anglo-Persian Oil Company, originally granted to D'Arcy in 1901. Britain protested this action and brought the case before the League. Iran held that it was not a proper matter for League consideration, since it involved a company and not a government. However, Iran did present its case before the League Council. The two parties agreed to the suggestion of the Council's rapporteur (Dr. Beneš, later president of Czechoslovakia at the time of the Munich agreement) to resume bilateral discussions. A revised oil concession agreement was reached and signed in Tehran on 30 April 1933.[12]

The United Nations. It would be impossible in a study of this length to do more than touch on the highlights of the activities of the United Nations and its related agencies in the Persian Gulf. Only the most prominent issues, especially those involving the relations of the states of the area to each other, can be mentioned here. Like its predecessor, the League of Nations, the United Nations grew out of the combination of a wartime alliance and an idealistic vision of an organization that would, unlike the League, prove successful in the preservation of world peace.[13] All three of the independent states of the region at the time of

7. Lenczowski, *The Middle East*, p. 131.
8. Ibid., p. 267.
9. Al-Marayati, *Modern Iraq*, pp. 65–69.
10. The background of this controversy can be found in Majid Khadduri, ed., *Major Middle Eastern Problems in International Law* (Washington, 1972), pp. 88–94.
11. Abbas Khalatbary, *L'Iran et le Pacte Oriental* (Paris, 1938), p. 76.
12. Lenczowski, *The Middle East*, p. 188.
13. For a comparison of the League and the United Nations, see Stanley J. Michalak, Jr., "The United Nations and the League," in Leon Gordenker, ed., *The United Nations and International Politics* (Princeton, 1971), pp. 60–105.

the San Francisco Conference in 1945, Iran, Iraq, and Saʿūdī Arabia, became charter members of the new universal organization. Kuwait gained its independence in 1961, but its admission to the United Nations was initially blocked by the Soviet Union, anxious to maintain good relations with Iraq. It was not until after the overthrow of the Qāsim rēgime in Iraq, in 1963, and the dropping of the Iraqi claim to Kuwait, that the Soviets dropped their opposition and Kuwait gained admission on 7 May 1963. Bahrain, Oman, Qatar, and the United Arab Emirates were all admitted in 1971, following the withdrawal of the British from the area.

Just as Iran's complaint to the League of Nations over Soviet aggressive actions had been one of the first cases brought before the League in 1920, one of the first issues brought before the United Nations Security Council was the January 1946 complaint of Iran over the interference of the Soviet Union in its internal affairs. Perhaps remembering its earlier experience, Iran was careful to keep the matter on the agenda, despite its bilateral negotiations with the Soviet Union. The eventual withdrawal of Soviet troops from Iran in May 1946 was the result of a combination of circumstances, including the bilateral negotiations and pressure from the United States. It was clear, however, that the USSR was concerned also about the public airing of its dispute with a weak neighboring country in the United Nations forum.[14]

In 1959, the United Nations became involved in the Buraimi oasis dispute. Parts of the oasis were claimed by Saʿūdī Arabia, Abū Dhabī, and Oman. The latter two states, of course, were under British protection. Diplomatic relations between Britain and Saʿūdī Arabia were broken following the occupation of the area by British-officered troops of the Trucial Oman Scouts in 1955. Talks were resumed at the United Nations in the presence of Secretary General Dag Hammarskjöld in 1959 and 1960. In August 1960, the Secretary General sent a representative to the area. The Secretary General continued his mediation efforts even after the resumption of Anglo-Saʿūdī relations in 1963.[15] The dispute was not finally resolved until after British withdrawal from the area and the establishment of the United Arab Emirates through an agreement reached on 29 July 1974.[16]

Iraq's involvement with the political/security functions of the United Nations brought back echoes of the League of Nations in the issues of minorities and the Iraq–Iran border. The minority this time was the Kurds rather than the Assyrians: between 1961 and 1975 there was a series of Kurdish rebellions interrupted by reconciliations between various Iraqi regimes and the Kurdish nationalist leader, Mustafā Barzānī. The Kurds maintained an observer delegation at the United Nations and made numerous appeals to various United Nations organs.[17]

14. Rouhollah K. Ramazani, *Iran's Foreign Policy, 1941–1973* (Charlottesville, Va., 1975), pp. 132–43.

15. J. B. Kelly, *Eastern Arabian Frontiers* (New York and London, 1964), pp. 266–68.

16. John Duke Anthony, *Arab States of the Lower Gulf: People, Politics, Petroleum* (Washington, 1975), pp. 148–49.

17. Several of these are mentioned in C. J. Edmonds, "The Kurdish National Struggle in Iraq," *Asian Affairs, The Journal of the Royal Central Asian Society* 58 (New Series, vol. 6), part 2 (June 1971): 147–58.

The Iraq–Iran border dispute in the Shatt al-'Arab region, supposedly settled in 1937, escalated into a serious conflict in 1969. Iraqi interference with Iranian shipping resulted in the provision of armed escorts and led to Iran's formal denunciation of the 1937 treaty on 19 April 1969.[18] Armed clashes became frequent and were extended to the areas of the Kurdish rebellion in the north; each side complained to the United Nations over various incidents. In February 1974, the dispute came before the Security Council, which sent an investigator to the area. On 28 May 1974, the Security Council endorsed a tentative settlement reached by the two parties. This agreement did not hold, and it was not until March 1975, following the Algiers OPEC summit meeting, that the final settlement was put in motion.

Another dispute reaching the United Nations was the question of the three islands in the Straits of Hormuz at the entrance to the Persian Gulf. These islands, Greater Tunb, Lesser Tunb, and Abū Mūsā, were historically Iranian before the entry of the British.[19] Iran had been content with the status quo while the British were in control, but doubted the abilities of the shaikhs of Sharja and Ra's al-Khaima to defend such a vital waterway. On 30 November 1971, the day before the end of the British protectorates, Iranian forces occupied the islands. Iraq, Algeria, Libya, and South Yemen protested to the United Nations Security Council, but to no avail. Their protest, no doubt, was weakened by the fact that neither Sa'ūdī Arabia nor Egypt would join them.[20]

An effective example of the function of the United Nations in the peaceful resolution of international disputes was its role in the Bahrain controversy. This was another case of an Iranian claim of an historical right to a territory with a predominantly Arab population which had been under British protection for more than a century. Iran claimed that Britain could not give Bahrain its independence, since it had never been independent prior to the British occupation, but had owed allegiance to various Iranian rulers. In January 1969, the Shah announced that Iran would not use force and would listen to the wishes of the people of Bahrain as to their future. In March and April 1970, the special representative of the secretary general of the United Nations visited Bahrain and concluded that the overwhelming sentiment of the people favored independence. This finding was endorsed by the Security Council. Iran relinquished its claims and recognized the independence of Bahrain.[21]

The Persian Gulf states are members of most of the thirteen specialized agencies of the United Nations. Iran, Iraq, and Sa'ūdī Arabia, for instance, are all members of every specialized agency except the GATT (General Agreement on Tariffs and Trade). An interesting case revealing the different orientations of Iran and the Arab states of the area can be found in their membership in different regional economic commissions affiliated with the United Nations Economic and Social Council. These regional commissions have been, in fact, some of the most

18. Shahram Chubin and Sepehr Zabih, *The Foreign Relations of Iran* (Berkeley and Los Angeles, 1974), pp. 185–86.

19. The historical basis of Iran's claims is given in R. M. Burrell, "Britain, Iran and the Persian Gulf: Some Aspects of the Situation in the 1920s and 1930s," in Derek Hopwood, ed., *The Arabian Peninsula: Society and Politics* (London, 1972), pp. 171–79.

20. Ramazani, *Iran's Foreign Policy*, p. 425.

21. Ibid., pp. 415–16.

effective of the institutions of the United Nations. Iran was an original member of the Economic and Social Commission for Asia and the Pacific (ESCAP), founded in 1947, with its headquarters in Bangkok. (It was known originally as ECAFE, or the Economic Commission for Asia and the Far East.) The Arab states of the area, however, are all members of the Economic Commission for West Asia (ECWA), the newest of the regional commissions founded in 1974, with its headquarters at Baghdad. ECWA might well have come into being much earlier but for the Arab-Israeli conflict.

Regional Political/Security Organizations

The Sa'dābād Pact. The Sa'dābād Pact of 8 July 1937 between Turkey, Iran, Iraq, and Afghanistan was the first regional international organization involving Persian Gulf states.[22] Signed at the Shah's palace north of Tehran, the pact looked to the creation of a regional grouping strong enough to counter aggression from outside of the region. This was a question of great importance in the wake of Italian aggression against a fellow member of the League of Nations, Ethiopia. At the same time, it was a treaty of friendship and nonaggression between neighboring states that had but recently freed themselves from foreign domination, loosely shared a common cultural heritage, and wished to settle a number of their own regional disputes. In addition, it was intended to act as a voting bloc in the League of Nations. Of all these motivations, the most important was mutual nonaggression.

The draft of the pact had been initialed at the League of Nations in Geneva in the course of discussions over the Shatt al-'Arab boundary dispute between Iran and Iraq in 1935. It was not signed until after the solution of this dispute in the Iranian–Iraqi Treaty of 4 July 1937. The text of the pact did not contain any obligations for collective self-defense. Instead, there was the negative obligation to abstain from any aggressive action, either individually or in concert with outside powers, against any other member.[23]

The organization of the pact was covered in a separate protocol. It was to be headed by a Council of the Pact, consisting of the foreign ministers of its members. The presidency of the council was to rotate annually, and it was to meet at least annually in conjunction with the meetings of the League of Nations. A permanent secretariat was established, but its location and *chef de bureau* were to rotate along with the council's presidency.

Three meetings of the Council of the Pact were held, but its only positive accomplishment was the agreement to support Iran for election to the semi-permanent "Asiatic" seat on the Council of the League of Nations as Turkey's replacement. In April 1939, Turkey announced to the Council of the Pact its

22. The best sources for the Sa'dābād Pact are Khalatbary, *L'Iran;* D. C. Watt, "The Sa'dabad Pact of July 9, 1937," *Journal of Royal Central Asian Society* 49 (July–October, 1962): 296–306, and in the *Survey of International Affairs* of the Royal Institute of International Affairs (London) in various articles written by Arnold J. Toynbee; see especially the volumes for 1928, 1934, 1936, and 1937.

23. Khalatbary, *L'Iran,* p. 104.

intention of signing a treaty of alliance with France and Great Britain and invited Iran and Afghanistan to join them. (Iraq, of course, was already an ally of Great Britain.) The other two members declined, but it was decided that Turkey's new alliance would not contradict its alignment with its Sa'dābād neighbors, since it would be signed in Turkey's capacity as a European state, while Sa'dābād dealt with Turkey's "Asiatic" relations.[24]

Although attempts were made, especially by Turkey, to revive the pact following the outbreak of World War II in September 1939, these efforts proved futile. Any attempt to revive it would obviously arouse the hostility of both the Axis powers and the USSR, which was now Germany's ally. However, the pact was not formally renounced in accordance with the procedures of Article 10, and is thus technically in force. Nūrī al-Sa'īd, the Iraqi prime minister who had been the leading architect of the pact, still wished to revive it in 1945.[25] The government of Afghanistan in 1972 continued to consider the pact as valid and binding.[26]

The League of Arab States. The League of Arab States was established on 22 March 1945 by the seven independent Arab states: Egypt, Iraq, Lebanon, Sa'ūdī Arabia, Syria, Trans-Jordan, and Yemen.[27] Discussions had been under way for years among the Arab states, and there was a great deal of sentiment in favor of Arab unity or, at least, for a confederation. In its final form, however, the Arab League (as its formal name implies) stressed the voluntary cooperation of sovereign states. The decisions of the League are binding only upon those members who vote for them.

Today, The Arab League consists of twenty-one member nations, including all of the Arab states of the Persian Gulf region. Its headquarters is in Tunis. There the secretary-general, appointed by a two-thirds vote, heads a large secretariat. The supreme authority is the Council of the League, which meets at least twice annually; additional meetings may be called on the application of two members. There are a number of committees attached to the Council, as well as an Economic Council and a Joint Defence Council. A number of specialized agencies form an integral part of the organization. Cooperation with the United Nations is based upon a memorandum between the two secretaries-general in 1960, but long before there began quite close cooperation between the specialized agencies of the two organizations, with formal agreements being signed with UNESCO, ILO, FAO, and the WHO.[28]

Arab League actions in the Persian Gulf have been limited by several factors. The first of these has been the fact that most of the Arab states in the area did

24. Watt, "The Sa'dabad Pact," p. 304.

25. Lord Birdwood, *Nuri al-Said, a Study in Arab Leadership* (London, 1959), p. 304.

26. Interview, H. E. Dr. Abdul Ghaffar Rawan Farhadi, then deputy foreign minister of Afghanistan, Kabul, 1972.

27. Robert D. Macdonald, *The League of Arab States* (Princeton, 1965), is the standard work for the history and functioning of the organization until that date. A recent work dealing with the organization's role in intra-Arab conflicts and the Arab-Israeli conflict is Hussein A. Hassouna, *The League of Arab States and Regional Disputes: A Study of Middle East Conflicts* (Dobbs Ferry, N.Y., and Leiden, 1975). See also Lenczowski, *The Middle East*, pp. 633–52.

28. Macdonald, *League of Arab States*, p. 271.

not attain their independence from various forms of British protection until 1971. Second had been the almost constant hostility, either latent or overt, between the two largest Arab states of the area—Sa'ūdī Arabia and Iraq. Before 1958, this had a dynastic basis, since then there has been an ideological clash between the "radical revolutionary" régimes in Iraq and the strongly religious and conservative Sa'ūdī monarchy. Finally, there is the fact that the Persian Gulf political and security issues have involved, in most cases, the interests of non-Arab states, regional and nonregional, including Iran, Great Britain, the United States, Turkey, Pakistan, and the USSR.

One of the few instances in which the Arab League did play a major role in a political/security issue in the area was the Kuwait–Iraq confrontation in 1961–63. Britain ended its protectorate of Kuwait in 1961, and Kuwait applied for United Nations and Arab League membership as an independent state. A few days later, Iraq's leader, General Qāsim, laid claim to all of Kuwait as a part of the Ottoman province of Basra, which had been stolen by the British imperialists. Kuwait immediately requested the return of British troops under a mutual security treaty just concluded with Great Britain. These were provided with alacrity by the British.

The Arab League admitted Kuwait to membership on 20 July, and on 10 September a 3,000-man Arab League military force from Sa'ūdī Arabia, the United Arab Republic, the Sudan, Jordan, and Tunisia, under the command of a Sa'ūdī general, began to arrive to replace the British forces. They remained until 1963, when Iraq, following the overthrow of the Qāsim régime, withdrew its claim and recognized Kuwaiti independence.[29]

The Baghdad Pact and CENTO. The Baghdad Pact was formed on 24 February 1955 as a bilateral pact of mutual cooperation between Iraq and Turkey.[30] It invited the adherence of other members of the Arab League, or any other state actively concerned with the peace and security of the region that was recognized by both Iraq and Turkey. (This provision excluded Israel from membership.) Later in the year, it was joined by Great Britain, Pakistan, and Iran, and a permanent organization was set up in Baghdad. Following the *coup d'état* of 14 July 1958 in Iraq and the overthrow of the Hashemite dynasty, the Qāsim régime suspended its membership, but did not formally denounce the treaty until March 1959. The headquarters of the Pact had moved to Ankara, where on 19 August 1959 its name was changed to the Central Treaty Organization (CENTO). The United States has had a close association with the Baghdad Pact and CENTO, being a member of all the Pact's committees and functional groups and, in fact, being a full member in all but name. However, despite re-

29. Macdonald, *League of Arab States*, pp. 235–37.
30. The text of the Baghdad Pact may be found in Ralph H. Magnus, ed., *Documents*, pp. 81–83. A full history and analysis of the Baghdad Pact and CENTO remains to be written. The best treatments to date are Guy Hadley, *CENTO—The Forgotten Alliance* (Brighton, 1971: Institute for the Study of International Organization, Monographs, First Series, No. 4); W. M. Hale and Julian Bharier, "CENTO, RCD and the Northern Tier: A political and economic appraisal," *Middle Eastern Studies* 8 (May 1972): 217–26 and Alvin J. Cottrell, "Iran and the Central Treaty Organization," in the Royal United Services Institute and *Brassey's Defence Yearbook, 1976–77* (London, 1977), pp. 68–83.

peated appeals from the members, the United States had never signed the treaty itself, and its closest legal connection remains in the form of three bilateral executive agreements to promote the independence and territorial integrity of the three regional members, as well as to aid their economic development. The agreements are identical in language and were signed at a Baghdad Pact meeting in Ankara on 5 March 1959. The legal basis for the United States' executive action, as cited in the agreement's preamble, lay in the Mutual Security Act of 1954 and the Joint Resolution to Promote Peace and Stability in the Middle East (The Eisenhower Doctrine) of 1957.[31] The fundamental reason why the United States has never formally adhered to the treaty is that the obligations of the treaty are general cooperation for security and defense, while the interests of the United States as stated in the two acts of Congress are limited to the defense of those nations in the area threatened by "armed aggression from any country controlled by international communism."[32]

The regional members of CENTO have hoped, since its inception, to use it as a vehicle to enhance their security against regional threats. In this way, it is a direct successor to the Sa'dābād Pact, which is hardly surprising, since Nūrī al-Sa'īd was the principal author of both treaties. Nūrī Pasha had hoped that other Arab states would join the Baghdad Pact and would thus acknowledge the leadership of Iraq and the Hashemites among the Arab states. What transpired was exactly the opposite, Gamal 'Abd al-Nāsir (Nasser) used opposition to the Baghdad Pact as a rallying cry establishing his own leadership of the Arab states and, especially, his charismatic image as a popular, nationalist, anti-imperialist leader of "progressive" Arab public opinion.

At the same time, however, the Pact was inspired by genuine and justifiable fears of aggression and subversion from the USSR. After the unfortunate experience of the Sa'dābād Pact in facing the challenge of World War II, the regional members realized that their only effective security against such a powerful neighbor would require the cooperation of the other Great Powers, the United States and Great Britain. The regional CENTO members continue to feel that even the limited formal commitment of the United States to their independence and territorial integrity is valuable enough to their security to make the continuation of the organization useful to them.

The regular meetings of foreign ministers in the supreme policy-making body of the organization, the Ministerial Council, the meetings of their chiefs-of-staff in the Military Committee, as well as the continuous day-to-day contact within the secretariat, and the establishment of permanent military deputies, combined military planning staff, an economic committee, a liaison committee, and a countersubversion committee, all tend to create an atmosphere of cooperation and informal opportunities for influencing the other members.[33] At the same time, a number of valuable economic, technical, educational, and scientific projects have been planned and carried out through the organization, including the construction of the railroad link between Turkey and Iran opened in 1971.

31. The text of the United States–Iran Agreement can be found in Magnus, *Documents*, pp. 83–85. For the text of the Eisenhower Doctrine (Public Law 85–7), see also ibid., pp. 93–94.
32. Ibid., p. 93.
33. Interview, Admiral Thomas H. Moorer, former chairman of the joint chiefs of staff, Washington, 1977.

It is impossible in practice to separate some of the aspects of regional security against regional threats from those of regional security against threats from the Soviet Union. The regular joint military, naval and air training and exercises carried out under CENTO (normally, six exercises annually) enhance the effectiveness of the military forces of the regional members against any potential foe, Communist or otherwise.[34] With the withdrawal of Great Britain from its special security role in the Persian Gulf in 1971, there has been an increasing emphasis from Iran on using CENTO as an active force in support of Iranian policy in the region.[35] The United States responded to this desire in a statement by Secretary of State Rogers made before the meeting of the CENTO Ministerial Council in Ankara in 1971: "We believe that it is proper that, following the British action, the states of the region should exercise primary responsibility for security in the Gulf, as the distinguished Foreign Minister of Iran has pointed out."[36]

Regional Economic Organizations

Regional Cooperation for Development (RCD). This organization was established on 21 July 1964 at the conclusion of a summit meeting in Istanbul of the leaders of Iran, Pakistan, and Turkey. It was aimed at the promotion of closer economic, technical, and cultural cooperation between the states of the region, and the participation of other states was specifically invited.[37] To date, no other state has joined, although the question of Iraq's joining was raised during negotiations between Iran and Iraq in 1966.[38]

As is the case with most international organizations, a variety of motivations and aspirations have led to the formation and continued existence of RCD. The organization is an off-shoot of CENTO. This is true in both a positive and a negative sense. It is positive in that the successful cooperation on economic and technical matters among the three regional CENTO members created a friendly atmosphere among both individuals and organizations that they wished to expand even further on their own. Negatively, the regional members of CENTO all had reason to feel slighted in the lack of political support they were receiving from their Western allies, especially from the United States. The United States, of course, had made it clear that its participation in CENTO did not involve support for purely regional issues involving the regional members. Although this was accepted on the official level, it was by no means popular among them. The regional members felt, regardless of technicalities, that as allies of the United

34. Interview, Major General Hamilton A. Twitchell, former commanding general, USMAG, Iran, Washington, D.C., 1977.

35. Ramazani, *Iran's Foreign Policy*, pp. 355–59.

36. "Statement before CENTO ministerial meeting, April 30," *U.S. Department of State Bulletin* 44 (May 31, 1971): 652.

37. RCD Secretariat, "Regional Cooperation for Development, Eighth Anniversary" (Tehran, 1972), pp. 3–5. RCD has received even less scholarly attention than its sister organization, CENTO. The article by W. M. Hale and Julian Bharier ("CENTO, RCD and the Northern Tier") is good, but tends to overemphasize the political aspects. An excellent short study is William E. Culbert, *Regionalism in the Northern Tier: The Implications of RCD* (Department of State, Foreign Service Institute, Eleventh Senior Seminar in Foreign Policy, Washington, 1968–69).

38. Interview, H. E. Abbas Aram, former foreign minister of Iran, Tehran, 1972.

States *they* were entitled to better than "even-handed" treatment from the United States in matters of great concern to *them*.

The RCD is an organization formally limited to "nonpolitical" economic, social, technical, and cultural cooperation. There is a genuine sentiment in favor of the recommendations of the United Nations Conference on Trade and Development (UNCTAD) concerning the need for the less developed countries to cooperate on a regional basis.[39]

RCD is headed by a Ministerial Council of the foreign ministers of the members, but most of the actual decision-making is done in the Regional Planning Council, made up of the heads of the economic planning organizations. In addition, questions as to the fundamental orientation of the organization are discussed at periodic meetings of the heads of state. There is a permanent secretariat, located in Tehran, headed by a secretary-general nominated on a rotating basis. Each member provides one deputy secretary-general. There are six specialized committees and a general coordinating committee. In addition, there are four specialized agencies: the RCD Chamber of Commerce and Industry (Tehran), the RCD Cultural Institute (Tehran), the RCD Insurance Center (Karachi), and the RCD Shipping Services (Istanbul).

Close relationships have been maintained with the specialized agencies of the United Nations. Experts from UNCTAD and UNIDO (United Nations Industrial Development Organization) have been brought in to study regional problems and advise the organization. Close relationships are also maintained with the economic, technical, and scientific agencies of CENTO. In some cases, the infrastructure and technical projects begun or constructed by CENTO have been taken over for operational purposes by RCD.

Originally emphasis in the RCD was placed upon economic cooperation through the development of joint purpose enterprises. The logic of these was to have large industrial establishments that could produce efficiently for a regional market. Regional trade, however, has remained a very small percentage of the total volume of trade, hovering around 1 or 2 percent in the case of Iran, for example.[40] In an effort to boost these percentages of regional trade and, more importantly, to demonstrate that they are truly serious in their efforts toward regional cooperation, the three heads of state, meeting in Izmir, Turkey, in April 1976, adopted the goal of the creation of a free-trade zone in ten years. The treaty to achieve this goal was signed in Tehran on 12 March 1977.[41]

The Colombo Plan for the Economic Development of South and South-East Asia (Colombo Plan). The Colombo Plan is a regional organization for economic development created after a conference of British Commonwealth foreign ministers in Colombo, Ceylon (Sri Lanka) in January 1950. Its charter members were

39. RCD Secretariat, "Regional Cooperation," p. 1. The same sentiments were expressed to the author by Hassan Parviz, director, RCD Trade Committee, in an interview at RCD headquarters in 1972.

40. Jahangir Amuzegar, *Iran, An Economic Profile* (Washington, 1977), table XI. 2, p. 151. For figures in the years 1962–68, see Hale and Bharier (footnote 38), p. 223.

41. See the comments of the three foreign ministers at the treaty signing as broadcast over the radio Tehran domestic service in Persian and reported under the headline "Turkish, Pakistani ministers arrive from RCD meeting," *Foreign Broadcast Information Service, Daily Report, The Middle East and North Africa* (15 March 1977).

Australia, Canada, Ceylon, India, New Zealand, Pakistan, and the United Kingdom. The organization, with its headquarters in Colombo, began operations on
1 July 1951.[42] Today its membership reaches from Egypt to Japan, while the
United States has been a member since 1951. Iran is the only Persian Gulf state
to join, being admitted in 1966, but neighboring Afghanistan has been a member
since 1963.

It is headed by a ministerial-level Consultative Committee, but its organization is very loose. The emphasis is on functioning as a clearing house for bilateral
development cooperation. The members make their development needs known
and the organization attempts to match these with available resources from other
members. Through 1975, however, some $45 million (three-quarters provided by
the United States) of capital aid has gone out as well, in the form of loans and
grants. The Colombo Plan works with governments, private businesses, private
organizations, and international organizations, especially with the United Nations
Economic and Social Commission for Asia and the Pacific.

The Arab Common Market. Iraq and Kuwait are the two regional states
that have ratified the 1964 agreement establishing the Council of Arab Economic
Unity within the framework of the Arab League. The other states ratifying this
agreement are Egypt, Jordan, Morocco, the Sudan, Syria, and the Yemen Arab
Republic. Decision number 17, adopted by the Council in August 1964, called
for the establishment of an Arab Common Market as of 1 January 1965. In its
first stage, the Arab Common Market was to work to establish a free-trade area;
five years were allowed to establish free trade in agricultural and mineral products
and ten years for industrial products.[43] The second stage called for the establishment of a customs union. These ambitious goals aimed at eventual total economic
unity "presupposing a unity of view extending into social and political fields."[44]

Only four states have joined the Arab Common Market; these are Egypt,
Iraq, Jordan, and Syria. Even on this limited basis, there has been little increase
noted in the scale of regional trade within the Arab Common Market, and most
of this has been attributed to specific bilateral agreements. Four reasons have
been given to explain the lack of progress of the organization:
a) the unwillingness of the members to limit their independence;
b) opposition from vested interests fearing foreign competition;
c) fear on the part of the less developed that they will lose new industrial development projects to the more developed, and;
d) problems stemming from the existence of different economic systems.[45]

Petroleum Organizations

The Organization of Petroleum Exporting Countries (OPEC). OPEC was
established at a meeting in Baghdad, on 14 September 1960, with a membership

42. W. Howard Wriggins, *Ceylon: Dilemmas of a New Nation* (Princeton, 1960), pp. 412–13.
43. "Economic co-operation and integration efforts in selected countries of Western Asia,"
Studies on Development Problems in Western Asia, 1974 (United Nations, ECWA, 1975), p. 36.
44. "Institutional framework of the Arab common market," *Studies on Development
Problems in Selected Countries of the Middle East, 1972* (United Nations, 1973), p. 1.
45. Ibid., p. 10.

of four Persian Gulf states—Iran, Iraq, Kuwait, and Sa'ūdī Arabia—and Venezuela. At the time of its establishment, these five states accounted for 38 percent of the world's petroleum production, including 90 percent of the petroleum involved in international trade, and held some 67 percent of the world's proven reserves of petroleum.[46] The Arab League had long been concerned with oil issues, and a Petroleum Bureau was established in 1954. In 1959, the First Arab Petroleum Congress met in Cairo, with invited observers from Venezuela and Iran. The formation of a permanent organization grew out of informal discussions at this meeting.

OPEC today has thirteen member states, including Iran, Iraq, Kuwait, Qatar, Sa'ūdī Arabia, and the United Arab Emirates. The qualifications for membership are that a state must be a net exporter of crude oil in substantial quantities, and that its petroleum interests are fundamentally similar to those of the other members. States are admitted on a three-fourths vote, providing that the five original members all vote in favor of admission.[47] Its supreme authority is the conference, consisting of the ministerial-level representatives of the members (usually, the ministers for petroleum affairs). Meetings are normally held semiannually, with the venue rotating among the capitals of the members, at the OPEC headquarters in Vienna, or, occasionally, at another site. Decisions of the conference are taken on the basis of unanimity. Great effort is made to reach a compromise. If unanimity cannot be obtained on an issue, it is often postponed rather than being put to a divisive vote.

A board of governors, consisting of representatives of all of the members, oversees the execution of the decisions of the conference, draws up the budget, and, in general, supervises the operations of the secretariat. It also meets semiannually. Finally, there is a permanent secretariat headed by a secretary-general appointed for a term of three years. Prior to 1970 this was a one-year appointment rotating among the members.[48] The headquarters of OPEC moved from Geneva to Vienna in 1965, where its offices and personnel have the equivalent of diplomatic status under an agreement with the Austrian government.[49] Following the oil price increase of 1973–74, the heads of state of the OPEC members at their First Summit Conference, in Algiers in March 1975, agreed to the establishment of an OPEC Special Fund to give concessional financing to developing countries.[50]

OPEC was formed and has maintained its existence on the basis of shared economic interests. Despite differences among its membership over political, religious, or ethnic issues, they have a fundamental common interest in their relationships with the major international oil companies.[51] These companies, under the concessionary system that had developed in the Middle East since the inception of its petroleum industry, unilaterally established prices and rates of pro-

46. Fuad Rouhani, *A History of OPEC* (New York, 1971), p. 77. This book by the first secretary general of OPEC is the standard work on the organization. Another excellent study is Zuhayr Mikdashi, *The Community of Oil Exporting Countries, A Study in Governmental Cooperation* (Ithaca, N.Y., 1972).

47. Rouhani, *History of OPEC*, p. 86.

48. Mikdashi, *Oil Exporting Countries*, pp. 98–99.

49. Rouhani, *History of OPEC*, pp. 135–37.

50. Organization of Arab Petroleum Exporting Countries, *OAPEC News Bulletin* 4 (January 1978): 14–20.

51. Interview, His Excellency Dr. Fuad Rouhani, former secretary general, OPEC, Tehran, 1972.

duction. OPEC thus developed a long-range goal and a short-range objective. In the long range, it wished to safeguard the common interests and coordinate the petroleum policies of its members. In the short term, it wished to halt and reverse the downward trend in the prices received from the international oil companies.

The basic problem of the OPEC states was the fact that there was a glut of crude oil on the international market. In this situation, the oil companies (and hence, the producing states) were forced to compete with one another for market shares, and the competition took the form of lowering prices. In the first ten years of its existence, due to the fact of oversupply, OPEC could achieve only limited gains. Their protests did manage to halt the fall of oil prices, and their revenues were aided by an agreement with the companies to count the per-barrel royalties as a business expense, instead of being considered part of the 50–50 profit-sharing split with the host governments. However, repeated efforts to establish a true cartel through the limiting of production on a pro-rata basis were failures.[52]

In the late 1960s, OPEC entered a more active phase. In 1968, a "Declaration of Petroleum Policy" asserted the "permanent and inalienable" sovereignty of the producing nations over their natural resources. It also asserted the doctrine of changing circumstances, in which the earlier concession agreements (normally, quite long in term) could be unilaterally altered when they no longer met the interests of the producing states. It also called for the participation of the host governments in the equity of the international companies.[53]

Beginning with the confrontation between Libya and the oil companies in 1970, OPEC began to give effective support to the efforts of individual members to achieve greater control over their oil resources. They pledged that they would not allow the oil companies to compensate for the loss of Libyan oil by increasing their production in other states. The new stance was possible only because of the rapidly rising world demand coupled with the fall in non-OPEC production, especially in the United States. Politically, the United States did not wish to antagonize the oil-producing states to the detriment of its overall policy in the Middle East. The structure of the oil industry also has changed. The new "independent" companies in the OPEC states were much more vulnerable to the pressure of a single state than were the "majors," who had diversified sources of supply.[54]

In this new situation, the Persian Gulf members of OPEC, under the personal direction of the Shah of Iran, concluded the first of a series of agreements between OPEC members and a group of sixteen oil companies who produced in the Persian Gulf area. This agreement was signed in Tehran on 14 February 1971. Libya followed later in the year with an even more advantageous agreement. Finally, two general agreements were concluded at Geneva in 1972 and 1973 between OPEC and the oil companies.

In October 1973, however, after the start of the Arab–Israeli War, the six

52. Mikdashi, *Oil Exporting Countries*, pp. 111–36.

53. Edith Penrose, "International Oil Companies and Governments in the Middle East," in John Duke Anthony, ed., *The Middle East: Oil, Politics, and Development* (Washington, 1975), pp. 7–8.

54. These factors are discussed in George Lenczowski, *Middle East Oil in a Revolutionary Age* (Washington, 1976), pp. 7–8.

Persian Gulf members of OPEC, meeting in Kuwait, unilaterally set the price of their oil at $5.119 per barrel for the benchmark of Sa'ūdī Arabian light crude, a rise of 70 percent. On 22 December, encouraged by spot prices of over $17 per barrel being realized for some sales in the panic conditions created by the Arab oil producers' politically motivated production cutbacks and embargo, they raised their price to $11.651 for the benchmark crude.[55]

More important than the prices themselves, dramatic though the increases undoubtedly were, was the fact that the OPEC states had completely reversed the situation that had faced them at the inception of their organization. Instead of accepting the unilateral setting of prices by the oil companies, they now set their own prices in a unilateral manner. Formidable problems still remained. With the lessening of the role of the companies, the pricing issue now became a matter of producer-government to consumer-government confrontation and emerged as openly political in nature. Economically, OPEC had to face the fact that the new price levels had discouraged consumption, increased conservation, and led to the opening of new sources of supply, including the North Sea and Alaska. In the face of oversupply, OPEC was unable to agree on a plan for reducing their production (although, in practice, Sa'ūdī Arabia did reduce its own production and thus absorbed a good deal of the burden of oversupply). The OPEC states were unable to agree on a single set of prices for all different grades of crude oil. Each member has its own policies with regard to production, pricing, credit terms, bilateral deals with consumers, conservation, and their relationships with the oil companies. Within the OPEC structure, these differences have led to serious splits, especially over the issue of prices.

All things considered, however, OPEC has managed to maintain its fundamental solidarity in the face of economic and political differences. This was demonstrated at the North–South Conference on International Economic Co-operation (CIEC) held in Paris in 1977.[56] Regardless of political differences, some of the cooperation among OPEC members spilled over into purely political fields. This was clearly demonstrated at the First OPEC Summit Conference in Algiers in March 1975. Here, with the mediation of the Algerian president, an agreement was set in motion between Iran and Iraq for the final settlement of their boundary dispute on the Shatt al-'Arab, as well as other outstanding differences.[57]

The Organization of Arab Petroleum Exporting Countries (OAPEC). OAPEC was established by Kuwait, Libya, and Sa'ūdī Arabia at a meeting in Beirut on 9 January 1968.[58] Initially, membership was restricted to Arab states where oil forms the main source of national income and whose application is approved by the three founding members. In 1971, this was changed so that Arab states where oil forms only an important source of the national income are eligible as well. There are ten members at present, including the Persian Gulf states of Bahrain,

55. Ibid., pp. 26–27.
56. John C. Campbell, "Oil Power in the Middle East," *Foreign Affairs* (October 1977): 89–110.
57. Rouhollah K. Ramazani, "Iran's Search for Regional Co-operation," *Middle East Journal* 30 (Spring 1977): 177.
58. Organization of Arab Petroleum Exporting Countries, *Basic Facts about the OAPEC* (Kuwait, 1976), p. 1. See also Mikdashi, *Oil Exporting Countries*, pp. 103–10.

Kuwait, Iraq, Saʿūdī Arabia, Qatar, and the United Arab Emirates. Dubai had been a member between 1970 and 1972, when it withdrew over the decision of the organization to build a dry-dock at Bahrain instead of Dubai.

The functions of OAPEC are the coordination of the petroleum policies of its members, the exchange of information and training, and the establishment of joint projects in fields connected with the petroleum industry.[59] The supreme authority is the Council of Ministers, consisting of the petroleum ministers of the members. Regular meetings are on a semiannual basis. Substantive matters require a three-fourths vote, while nonsubstantive matters can be decided by a simple majority. However, substantive votes must be ratified to be binding and, hence, in practice binding decisions require unanimity.[60] An executive board composed of under-secretaries of the oil ministries performs the same supervisory function as the OPEC board of governors. A permanent secretariat, headed by a secretary-general, has its headquarters in Kuwait. The organization provides for the establishment of a judicial board to arbitrate disputes between member states, but this has yet to be formed. OAPEC membership is not intended to conflict with the obligations of OPEC membership. Indeed, OAPEC members are bound by the decisions of OPEC, even though they are not themselves members of OPEC in all cases.[61]

As an organization of states bound together by political and cultural ties, as well as common economic interests, OAPEC is overtly both a political and an economic organization. In fact, it grew out of the failure of the Arab states effectively to coordinate their oil policies during the 1967 Arab–Israeli War. In a meeting of OAPEC oil ministers in Kuwait on October 17–19, 1973, following the outbreak of the October War between Israel and Syria and Egypt, the policy of successive production cutbacks and a total embargo of the United States and the Netherlands was agreed upon. The supply of oil to consuming nations was made contingent upon their policies toward the Arab–Israeli conflict.[62] Even in this case, however, unanimity could not be achieved, as Iraq refused to support the production cutbacks but agreed to the embargo decision. The implementation of the decisions was left to the individual member states.

In its political aspects, therefore, OAPEC has a broader scope than does OPEC. Its economic aspects are both broader and narrower than OPEC's. They are broader in the sense that OAPEC has several joint projects in operation designed to bring its members into the "downstream" operations of the oil industry and oil-related industries. These joint projects include an Arab maritime petroleum transport company, an Arab shipbuilding and repair-yard company, an Arab petroleum investments corporation, and an Arab petroleum services company.[63] In this aspect, OAPEC resembles a regional economic development organization, such as RCD.[64] The economic impact of OAPEC is, at the same time, narrower, since its limitation to Arab states alone limits its worldwide impact.

59. *Basic Facts about the OAPEC,* p. 7.
60. Mikhashi, *Oil Exporting Countries,* p. 106.
61. *Basic Facts about the OAPEC,* p. 12.
62. The best source for the details of the operation of the Arab oil embargo and production cutbacks in 1973–74 is George Lenczowski, *Middle East Oil,* pp. 12–24.
63. *Basic Facts about the OAPEC,* pp. 14–17.
64. Mikdashi, *Oil Exporting Countries,* pp. 205–7.

Religious Organizations

The Islamic Conference. The Islamic Conference was established in May 1971 as an outgrowth of the First Summit Conference of Islamic Heads of State held in Rabat, Morocco, in September 1969 (called to consider the response of the Islamic states to the burning of the al-Aqsā Mosque in Israeli-occupied Jerusalem). Its forty-two members include all of the states of the Persian Gulf region. In 1976, it was given official observer status by the United Nations.

The aims of the conference are the promotion of Islamic solidarity, the safeguarding of the Holy Places, the support of the Palestinian people, the elimination of racial segregation and colonialism, and the promotion of cooperation between the Islamic states and other countries.[65] The secretariat is located in Jidda, Sa'ūdī Arabia. It has established an International Islamic News Agency and an Islamic Development Bank. Regular conferences of foreign ministers have been held, and a Second Islamic Summit Meeting was held in Lahore, Pakistan, in February 1974.

Observations on the Future of International Organizations in the Persian Gulf

One cannot but be struck by the fact that among all these organizations involving Persian Gulf states there is no regional international organization dealing exclusively with the Persian Gulf itself, as a political, economic, cultural, or ecological unit. Indeed, it is striking that apart from the universal organization of the United Nations the only international organization to which all Persian Gulf states belong is the Islamic Conference.

After the announcement of the planned British withdrawal in early 1968, there was a flurry of activity concerning the possible creation of an international organization in the area. The United Arab Emirates is itself a successful effort to avoid the maximum fragmentation of which the area was capable. However, both Qatar and Bahrain opted for independence rather than carrying out the broader Federation Agreement they had entered into on 25 February 1968.[66]

The United States attempted to encourage a broadly based regional security organization as well. In an interview over the Voice of America on 19 January 1968, Under Secretary of State Eugene Rostow supported the idea: "As to the Persian Gulf area, some very strong and quite active and stable states are interested in assuming responsibility for regional security . . . Iran, Turkey, Pakistan, Saudi Arabia and Kuwait would certainly be a nucleus around which security arrangements could hopefully be built, and we hope that in the long run the policy of Iraq will orient itself in a co-operative direction so that it can join in such efforts."[67] This trial balloon was not supported by the states concerned, but

65. Europa, *Europa World Yearbook* (London, 1975), p. 234.
66. Anthony, *Arab States of the Lower Gulf*, p. 98.
67. "The USSR and the Persian Gulf," *Mizan* (March–April 1968): 51.

it resulted in a charge by the Soviet News Agency *Tass* that the United States and Britain were attempting to create a military bloc in the Persian Gulf aimed at the southern frontier of the USSR.[68]

The issue of a regional organization for the area had been discussed at a series of meetings of the foreign ministers of the region. At such a meeting in Muscat (Oman) in November 1976, specific working papers on the design of a regional political/security organization were discussed, but no agreement could be reached. The Omani foreign minister expressed the hope that discussions would continue at a later date, but regretted that the present situation did not allow for joint cooperation.[69] In an interview given to a Kuwaiti newspaper on 29 January 1977, the Shah of Iran commented on the Muscat conference failure. Previously, he said, popular sentiment in the states of the area had been against cooperation. Now he felt that popular sentiment had changed, but there was a new reluctance on the part of governments. He said he could give no explanation for this.[70]

Prospects are still not hopeless. Bilateral relations among the states of the area have improved in many cases. Iran and Iraq reached an agreement to settle their differences through negotiations after being on the brink of war. The rebellion in Dhufār province of Oman, which led to the Sultan's calling for and receiving military aid from Iran, has been substantially put down and most of the Iranian forces withdrawn. Most recently, Sa'ūdī Arabia and Iran have adopted similar stands on pricing policy within OPEC. Cooperation within OPEC, both in the Conference on International Economic Cooperation and in the delicate negotiations leading to the Tehran agreement of February 1971, has shown that under certain circumstances cooperation among the Persian Gulf states over important matters can be successful. Should relationships among the states of the region continue to develop along peaceful and cooperative lines for a sufficient length of time, it is possible that one day we will have to add to our list a regional organization of all Persian Gulf states.

Postscript

Following the establishment of the Provisional Islamic Revolutionary Government in Tehran in February 1979, it was soon clear that the structure of international organizations in the Persian Gulf would not escape major changes. The imperial government of Iran had been the key regional member of both the CENTO (Central Treaty Organization) regional security alliance and the RCD economic cooperation organization. It had remained committed to CENTO, despite frequent criticisms of its effectiveness, for reason of its value as an Ameri-

68. Ibid., pp. 51–52.

69. "Continued Reportage on Gulf Foreign Ministers Meeting," *Daily Reports, The Middle East and North Africa* (Foreign Broadcast Information Service), 29 November 1976, p. C-1, as reported over the Kuwait domestic service broadcast on 26 November.

70. "Shah Interviewed by Kuwait's As-Siyasah Editor," *Daily Reports, The Middle East and North Africa* (Foreign Broadcast Information Service) 3 February 1977, p. R-1, as reported over the Tehran domestic Persian service, 2 February 1977.

can security guarantee against the potential of Soviet aggression and as a means of keeping Iran's security formally linked to its eastern and western neighbors. RCD had, in practice, been of even less effective value than CENTO. However, it was highly regarded by Pakistan and had the potential of becoming a more significant regional economic organization should the goal of a free trade zone within ten years, as envisaged by the Tehran Treaty of March 1977, be attained.

Early in March 1979, Pakistan announced its intention of withdrawing from CENTO. Agha Shahi, principal foreign affairs adviser to the president and chief martial law administrator of Pakistan, was sent to confer with his Iranian and Turkish colleagues. Both Dr. Karim Sanjabi of Iran and Gunduz Okcun of Turkey issued statements in agreement with the Pakistani position that CENTO should be dissolved, but that, simultaneously, RCD should be strengthened and, if possible, expanded. The Iranian foreign ministry formally notified its allies that its withdrawal from CENTO would be effective as of 27 March.

Since its inception in 1964, Regional Cooperation for Development has represented a common sentiment of its member governments in favor of strengthening their mutual ties in an organizational framework independent of Great Power involvement. Nevertheless, as long as CENTO remained it tended to overshadow its understudy organization and make it virtually impossible for RCD to attract other members from among the largely nonaligned states of the area. With demise of CENTO and the emergence of RCD as the principal remaining link between Turkey, Iran, and Pakistan, it is much more likely that this regional organization will become more effective and might serve as the basis for expanded cooperation among the states of the Persian Gulf region.

Selected Bibliography

Amirie, Abbas, ed. *The Persian Gulf and the Indian Ocean in International Politics.* Tehran, 1975.

Anthony, John Duke. *The Middle East: Oil, Politics, and Development.* Washington, D.C., 1975.

Chubin, Shahram. "Iran's security in the 1980's." *International Security* 2: 51–80.

Chubin, Shahram, and Zabih, Sepehr. *The Foreign Relations of Iran: A Small State in a Zone of Great Power Conflict.* Berkeley, 1974.

Cottrell, Alvin J. "Iran and the Central Treaty Organization." In *Royal United Services Institute and Brassey's Defence Yearbook, 1976–77.* London, 1977.

Cottrell, Alvin J., and Dougherty, James E. *Iran's Quest for Security: U.S. Arms Transfers and the Nuclear Option.* Cambridge, Mass., 1977.

Hadley, Guy. *CENTO—The Forgotten Alliance.* Brighton, 1971.

Hale, W. M., and Bharier, Julian. "CENTO, RCD and the Northern Tier: A Political and Economic Appraisal," *Middle Eastern Studies* 8: 217–26.

Hopwood, Derek, ed. *The Arabian Peninsula: Society and Politics.* London, 1972.

Kelly, J. B. *Eastern Arabian Frontiers.* New York and London, 1964.

Khadduri, Majid, ed. *Major Middle Eastern Problems in International Law.* Washington, D.C., 1972.

Khalatbary, Abbas. *L'Iran et le Pacte Oriental.* Paris, 1938.

Lenczowski, George. *Middle East Oil in a Revolutionary Age.* Washington, D.C., 1976.

————. *The Middle East in World Affairs*. 3rd ed., Ithaca, N.Y., 1962.

Long, David E. *The Persian Gulf: An Introduction to Its People, Politics and Economics*. Boulder, Colorado, 1976.

Macdonald, Robert W. *The League of Arab States*. Princeton, 1965.

Magnus, Ralph H., ed. *Documents on the Middle East*. Washington, D.C., 1969.

Nakhleh, Emile A. *Arab-American Relations in the Persian Gulf*. Washington, D.C., 1975.

Ramazani, Rouhollah K. *The Foreign Policy of Iran, 1500–1941: A Developing Nation in World Affairs*. Charlottesville, Va., 1966.

————. *Iran's Foreign Policy, 1941–1973: A Study of Foreign Policy in Modernizing Nations*. Charlottesville, Va., 1975.

————. "Iran's Search for Regional Co-operation." *Middle East Journal*. 30: 173–86.

Rouhani, Fuad. *A History of OPEC*. New York, 1971.

Survey of International Affairs. London, 1928, 1934, 1936, and 1937.

Watt, D. C. "The Sa'dabad Pact of July 9, 1937." *Journal of Royal Central Asian Society* 69: 296–306.

PART TWO

Economics and Urban Development in the Persian Gulf

9. Oil in the Persian Gulf Area   KEITH McLACHLAN

The Physical Basis of the Oil Industry

 The great sedimentary basin of which the Persian Gulf is the center contains within it geological structures that encase the richest known reserves of crude oil and natural gas in the entire world. This vast structural depression is bounded to the north by the Taurus Mountains in Turkey, to the east by the mountain rims of Iran and Oman, and to the west by the uplands of the Levant. The Arabian block in the heartland of Saʻūdī Arabia forms a marked boundary on the southern perimeter. Underlying the basin is a deep basement of volcanic rocks continuous throughout, with the exception of faulting through the central plateau of Iran (see Fig. 9–1). Sedimentary zones of the Arabian peninsula present a relatively straightforward geological sequence, which in Saʻūdī Arabia is exemplified by a succession of Jurassic carbonates, Lower Cretaceous carbonates or limestones, Upper Cretaceous and Eocene carbonates, with the Upper Jurassic providing the major oil-bearing strata. Iran presents a rather different case, with a complex geological history. The main oil field region is circumscribed by a discontinuous major line of overthrusting from the Kīrmānshāh area to Mīnāb on the north and east. Iran's principal oil fields lie in the main Zagros in the Asmari and Oligo-Miocene limestones. Significant oil fields also occur in the less contorted zone under and adjacent to the Persian Gulf where, as in the Arabian peninsula, oil is found in the Jurassic and Cretaceous levels, though less abundantly than in either the Iranian Zagros or the Arabian peninsula.

Of the other oil states of the Persian Gulf area, Iraq possesses geological structures analogous to the Iranian Zagros in the northern fields of Kirkuk, Ain Zalah, Bai Hassan, and Jambur, but has access to the Cretaceous series in the south at Rumaila and Zubair in the Basra region. Geological characteristics of the other Persian Gulf oil-producing states tend to be similar to those experienced in Saʻūdī Arabia, with the oil-bearing strata of Jurassic or Cretaceous date. A generalized geology of the area is shown in Figure 9–1, and the key elements of stratigraphy

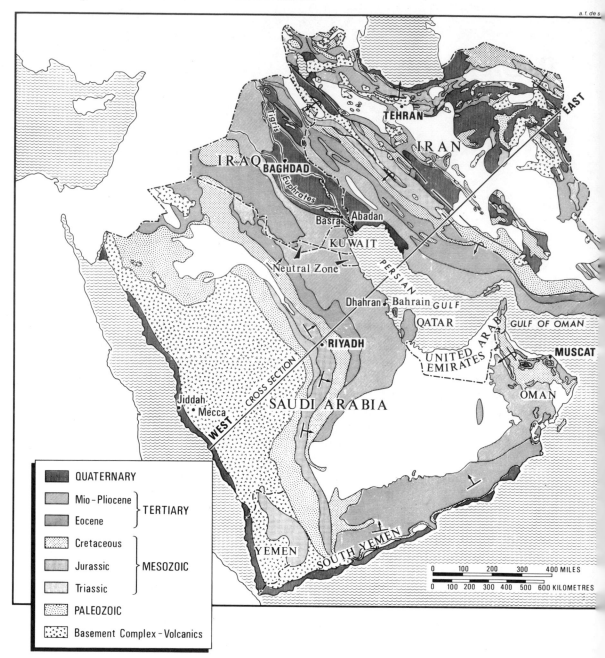

FIG. 9–1. (*Above*) Generalized geology of the Persian Gulf states. (*On facing page*) Diagrammatic cross-section of the Persian Gulf states (west to east) (after *ARAMCO Handbook*).

relating to eastern and western zones of the sedimentary basin disposed about the Persian Gulf appear in the cross section on the same figure.

A close relation exists between the features of geology and the nature of the oil reservoirs lying in the Persian Gulf region. Oil structures in the Zagros zone, including Iran and the northern Iraqi fields, tend to be elongated, but of narrow cross section, while the oil fields to the south are broader and, especially in the case of the Ghawar reservoir, tend to be oriented north to south. Ghawar structure is estimated to have an axis of 250 kilometers and a breadth ranging between 25 to 40 kilometers, stretching between Fazran in the north and Haradh in the south, in Saʿūdī Arabia. The regional distribution of oil fields is shown in Figure 9–2.

Influences of geology determine not only the distribution of oil fields but also the yield and quality of the crude oil and natural gas contained in them. Regional differentiation of wealth in hydrocarbons is acute, varying with the volume of reserves, the recoverability of those reserves, and the quality of the oil and gas within them. Distribution of oil fields around the Persian Gulf should be related to the characteristics of geology, the specific gravity of crude oil as

measured by the American Petroleum Institute: gravity $= (\dfrac{141.5}{\text{specific gravity at } 60°\text{F}}$

$- 131.5$), and the productive capacity of the individual oil fields. A summary of data on established oil fields in the states bordering the Persian Gulf is given in Table 9–2. The outstandingly prolific fields are Burgan in Kuwait, Kirkuk in Iraq, Ghawar in Saʿūdī Arabia, and Marun in Iran, all of which have produced consistently at well over 1 mn b/d. A number of oil fields have been exploited over long periods and are ending their productive life, as, for instance, the Masjid-i Sulaimān field in Iran.

The states of the Persian Gulf region are rich not simply in crude oil but also in the range of crudes they possess. Highly prized light oils are present in the region, though not on a large scale. Qatar has reserves of 41.4° API in the Dukhan, Iran 41.4° in Naft-i Shah, and Iraq 42.0° in Naft Khana fields. At the other end of the scale, heavy crudes down to 18.0° in the Wafra field in the Neutral Zone and 19.2° in the Cyrus field of the Iranian offshore zone provide a not always profitable source for production of asphalt and other heavy products. The important Ghawar field in Saʿūdī Arabia produces oil with 34.0° API, while the Iranian Marun field produces 32.9° crude (see also Table 9–2).

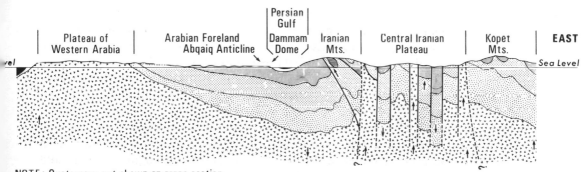

NOTE: Quaternary not shown on cross section

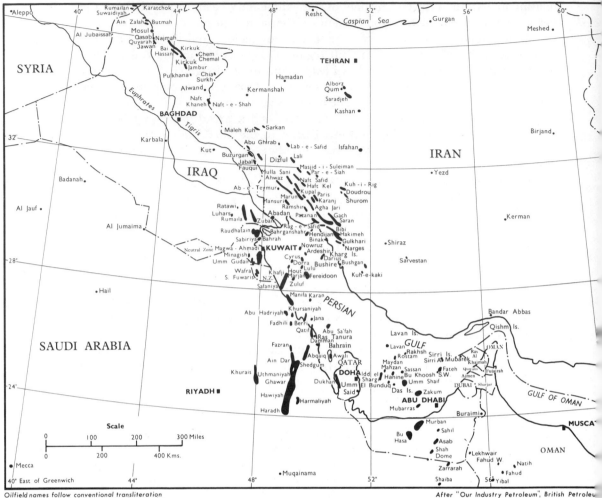

FIG. 9–2. Oil fields of the Persian Gulf states

Crude oil production in the Persian Gulf area may be prolific, but it is largely of crudes that have a relatively high sulphur content, in comparison with the medium sulphur crudes of Venezuela or the much-valued low sulphur crudes of North Africa and North America. A number of oil fields in the Persian Gulf states possess heavy sulphur crudes that in untreated form tend to be polluting and corrosive during refining. On the other hand, the great bulk of crudes originating in the Persian Gulf oil-exporting states possess only modest wax contents in the range 5 to 7 percent weight on crude and are also moderate in vanadium and nickel content, which characteristics are valued in transport and refining activities, respectively.

History of the Oil Industry

The founding of the oil industry in the Persian Gulf area dates back to 1908, when oil was discovered by the D'Arcy concessionaires at Masjid-i Sulaimān in southwest Iran. D'Arcy was granted his concession by the Iranian government in 1901 and by 1911 operations were taken over by the Anglo-Persian Oil Company, which was renamed the Anglo-Iranian Oil Company in 1935. The company was responsible for both the extraction of oil and the Ābādān refinery. In 1914, the company signed a contract with the British Admiralty for the supply of fuel oil to the British navy and, at the same time, the British government bought a controlling interest in the Anglo-Persian Oil Company.

Iranian oil facilities were rapidly expanded during World War I and production rose from 654,409 metric tons in 1917 to 1,124,170 tons in 1919. The D'Arcy concession was revoked in 1932 and a new agreement drawn up with Anglo-Persian in 1933, under which the concession area was limited to some 260,000 square kilometers in the south and changes were made in the level of royalty payments by the company to the Iranian exchequer. Naft-i Shah oil field was brought into production in 1935, and, further south, oil fields at Haft Kel and Gach Saran began production in 1929 and 1940, respectively. Important oil discoveries were made at Naft Safid, Agha Jari, and Pazanan during this same period.

Immediately preceding World War II, production in Iran exceeded the ten million ton mark, but output fell sharply in the early years of the war, with military constraints bearing on the supply routes to the United Kingdom. Recovery began from 1943, and by 1944 production was running at 13,492,172 metric tons. Development of the Iranian oil industry was accelerated in the later years of the war, and the Agha Jari field brought on stream in 1945, together with Naft Safid, both connected to the Ābādān refinery by pipeline. An important shift in the geographical alignment of the industry occurred in 1948, when the increasingly productive Agha Jari field was linked by pipeline to the export terminal at Bandar Ma'shur (now renamed Mahshahr), with Ābādān thereafter concentrating on the export of refined products. Net production of crude oil in Iran amounted by 1949 to 27,247,933 metric tons, of which 24,632,589 tons were exported. Production in 1950 amounted to 32.3 million tons, by which time Iran was the main oil exporter in the Persian Gulf area.

Political difficulties between the Anglo-Iranian Oil Company and the Iranian government were exacerbated in the postwar period by the monopoly position enjoyed by the company and its close relationship with the British government. There was growing dissatisfaction with the financial terms of the concession. In 1948 and 1949, negotiations between the Iranian government and the Anglo-Iranian Oil Company produced an agreement supplementary to the 1933 concession agreement, offering improved financial terms to Iran, though allowing little scope for the assertion of Iranian sovereignty over its oil resources. The Iranian *majlis* rejected the agreement and a breakdown in relations between state and company led to nationalization of the oil industry on May 1, 1951.

Oil production dropped steeply to 16.8 million tons in 1951, to 1.4 million tons in 1952, and 1.3 million tons in 1953. The rapid development of alternative oil sources in the Persian Gulf area dates from this time, as the international oil companies sought to make good the loss of supplies from Iran.

Rupture of the relations between the Iranian cabinet, led by Dr. Musaddegh, and the Anglo-Iranian Oil Company represented a major turning point for the Iranian oil industry. Only in October 1954 was compromise reached, when an agreement was signed between the Iranian government, from which Dr. Musaddegh had been removed, and a group of oil companies, including British Petroleum (formerly the Anglo-Iranian Oil Company) acting under the name of Iranian Oil Participants, though generally known as the Consortium. The Consortium was initially made up of eight major oil companies, but was later augmented by eight small U.S. companies to give a composition of: BP 40 percent; Royal Dutch/Shell 14 percent; Gulf, Mobil, Standard of New Jersey, Standard of California, and Texaco each 7 percent: Compagnie Française des Pétroles 6 percent; and the Iricon Agency, comprising eight U.S. independent oil companies, 5 percent.

Exploration and production were managed by the Iranian Exploration and Production Company, while refining was controlled by the Iranian Oil Refining Company. Exploitation and marketing rights were assigned to the Consortium, but it was recognized that the National Iranian Oil Company remained the sole owner of all fixed assets of the Iranian oil industry. The National Iranian Oil Company took over all service and amenity functions formerly undertaken by Anglo-Iranian, together with property used for these nonbasic activities. In principle, the oil agreement of October 29, 1954 recognized Iranian nationalization of the oil industry and provided what amounted to a 50–50 share of profits.

The 1954 Supplemental Agreement was modified in 1966 when the Consortium relinquished 25 percent of its agreement area. A further modification to the agreement came into force on March 20, 1973, under which the National Iranian Oil Company assumed control over oil production and refining in the agreement area. The Consortium was granted a five-year contract for servicing its former area, and the national company was given access to stated volumes of crude oil from the agreement area to dispose of on its own account. Effectively, from 1973, Iran took comprehensive charge of its oil industry, though even before then the National Iranian Oil Company had allocated areas for exploration and development under joint arrangements with overseas oil companies and had granted service contracts to companies. Among successful joint-venture companies set up by the National Iranian Oil Company are Sirip, in association with Agip of Italy; Ipac, in association with Pan-American; Lapco, in association with a group led by Atlantic Richfield; and Iminoco, in association with a consortium led by Phillips Petroleum. The National Iranian Oil Company also expanded production from its own fields in the period from 1954.

Creation of the oil industry in Iraq began later and was pursued at a slower pace than in Iran. Oil was first struck in commercial quantities at Naft Khana, adjacent to the Iranian frontier, in 1923. The strike was made by the Khanaqin Oil Company, a subsidiary of the Anglo-Persian Oil Company. The concession included only the area immediately surrounding the Naft Khana field and was ultimately relinquished to the Iraqi government in 1958. In 1925, the Turkish

Petroleum Company was confirmed in its concession covering northeastern and central zones of Iraq, but excluding the Khanaqin oil field. In 1928, the composition of the company was changed, and in the subsequent year it was renamed the Iraq Petroleum Company, with shareholdings allocated 23.75 percent each to Anglo-Persian, Royal Dutch/Shell, Compagnie Française des Pétroles, and Near East Development Corporation and with 5 percent to Participations and Explorations Corporation (the Gulbenkian Estate). In 1932, British Oil Development was granted a concession in the Mosul area. The concession was taken over by Mosul Petroleum in 1941, with ownership the same as Iraq Petroleum Company. Basra Petroleum Company, again with Iraq Petroleum Company participants, was awarded a concession over the south of the country in 1938.

The most important of oil discoveries was made in 1927 by the Turkish Petroleum Company, an Anglo-German established consortium that had received a concession from the then Ottoman government. German interest in the company had been removed during World War I and, with French and U.S. involvement, the company maintained operations and found oil at Kirkuk. Kirkuk has remained the main source of Iraqi crude oil, though export of crude from Mosul began in 1952 and from Basra in 1951.

The Iraqi government and the Iraq Petroleum Company were engaged in prolonged negotiations between 1947 and 1952 leading to the adoption of the 50–50 profit-sharing principle and the underwriting by the Iraq Petroleum Company of a guaranteed level of income for the government. The Iraqi government was also permitted to take up to one-eighth of oil produced for disposal either on its own account or for resale to the company. The agreement was ratified in 1952.

The monopoly position of the Iraqi Petroleum Company in Iraq and the concession terms were subject to much criticism in Iraq after 1952. With the coming of the 1958 revolution, pressure grew for the renegotiation of the 1952 agreement. Terms for the relinquishment of parts of the concession and improved financial arrangements in favor of Iraq were discussed by the government and the company, but before an agreed solution was reached the Iraqi government issued Decree Law 80 of December 11, 1961, which limited the Iraq Petroleum Company to an area of 1,938 square kilometers, representing a mere 0.44 percent of the former concession. A change of government in Iraq in 1963 did little to relieve the impasse between the two sides, and further negotiations came to nothing, since political instability and the position of oil at the center of Iraqi political sensibilities precluded ratification of a proposed agreement.

In August 1967, Law 97 reconstituted the Iraq National Oil Company, which had existed since 1964, but without a clear role, and assigned all but small areas to the Iraq National Oil Company to operate on its own behalf or using partners. Service contracts for this area were concluded in 1968 with the French state company Erap and in 1972 with Petrobras of Brasil and the Indian Oil and Natural Gas Commission. New oil finds were made by Erap and Petrobras. North Rumaila oil field, discovered by the Basra Petroleum Company, was developed by the Iraqi authorities with technical and other aid from the Soviet Union.

A final solution to the conflict with the Iraq Petroleum Company was imposed on June 1, 1972, when the northern oil fields were nationalized. Iraq Petroleum Company acknowledged this step in February 1973, when the Mosul Petroleum Company was also nationalized. Takeover of the Basra Petroleum Company took place in stages and was finalized in December 1975.

Between 1972 and 1976, the Iraqi Company for Oil Operations operated the facilities formerly owned by the Iraq Petroleum Company and its subsidiaries. New legislation in September 1976 consolidated authority for the oil sector in the hands of the Ministry of Petroleum, which reported only to the Revolutionary Command Council, the highest body in the state. Iraq National Petroleum Company was attached to the Ministry of Petroleum and assumed responsibility from the Iraqi Company for Oil Operations for managing day-to-day operations in the oil fields, while general organizations of state under the national oil company handle exploration, marketing, and other aspects of the oil industry.

The first concession granted to the international oil companies in Kuwait came as late as 23 December 1934, when the mainland of Kuwait and a six-mile offshore zone was allocated to Kuwait Oil Company, equally owned by the Anglo-Persian Oil Company and Gulf Oil Corporation of the USA. Discovery of oil in commercial quantities was made in 1938, but delays arising from World War II and the Anglo-Iranian Oil Company vested interests in Iran retarded development. It was not until 1946 that the first exports of Kuwaiti crude oil were made. Dramatic expansion of the Burgan oil field and the Magwa-Ahmadi field, the latter discovered in 1952, took place after 1952 with the virtual close-down of the Iranian oil industry at the time of the Musaddegh crisis. In the decade 1948 to 1958, production rose from 806,616 metric tons to 69,275,952 million tons. By 1953, Kuwait was the main producer in the Persian Gulf region, a position held until 1965. Further discoveries of new oil fields were made by Kuwait Oil Company at Raudhatain, Sabriya, Minagish, and Umm Gudair.

The Kuwait government's agreement with Kuwait Oil Company was reviewed in 1951, when a 50–50 profit-sharing arrangement was introduced. Adjustments were made to the agreement in 1955, under which royalties were paid on a percentage rather than flat rate basis, while extended discussions on the agreement between 1964 and 1967 led to a revision of terms in May 1967, mainly affecting access to crude supplies for the Kuwaiti government, royalty payments, and arbitration on disputes. Negotiated provisions for Kuwaiti participation in the production operations of the Kuwait Oil Company led to the transfer of 25 percent of facilities in 1973, a further 35 percent in 1974, and a complete takeover of the Kuwait Oil Company position within Kuwait in 1975.

In the Kuwaiti-Sa'ūdī Arabian neutral zone, a concession was granted in 1948 to the American Independent Oil Company, later known as Aminoil, to explore the Kuwait half-share of the area. Oil was discovered at Wafra in 1953 and at South Fuwaris in 1962. Both fields were operated by Aminoil, which ultimately included eight U.S. independent oil companies led by Phillips Petroleum with 37.30 percent and Signal Oil and Gas with 33.54 percent of the company's equity. In 1970, Aminoil was bought by R. J. Reynolds of the United States, but subsequently was taken over by the Kuwaiti state.

An offshore concession was awarded to the Arabian Oil Company in 1958. Arabian Oil was a consortium of sixty Japanese interests that also gained the concession for working the Sa'ūdī Arabian portion of the offshore Neutral Zone. The company struck oil in the Khafji field in 1960. In the Kuwait offshore zone, Shell was awarded a concession in 1960, but little progress has been made in this area, pending a settlement of the boundaries in the Gulf separating Kuwait, Iran, and Iraq.

Although Sa'ūdī Arabia rose to prominence as a state rich in oil reserves later than others in the region, it has since achieved a preeminence in global terms as the largest single holder of oil in the world. In conditions of rivalry between the established British and the incoming U.S. oil companies, King Ibn Sa'ūd granted a concession to the Arabian American Oil Company (Aramco) in 1933. Aramco was the operating company for Standard Oil of California and Texaco, who were joined by Socony Mobil and Jersey Standard in 1948, with the three main partners holding 30 percent each of the shares and the minor partner, Mobil, holding 10 percent.

Early exploration drilling in Sa'ūdī Arabia was not successful and, although the first well was completed in 1935, it was not until March 1938 that oil was struck in commercial quantities in the Dammām structure. First exports of oil took place in 1938, and continued at very modest levels until after World War II, the bulk of oil being transferred to Bahrain for refining. New fields were found at Abqā'iq and Abū Hadriyya in 1940 and at Qatif in 1945. But the discovery that transformed prospects for the oil industry in Sa'ūdī Arabia was undoubtedly the discovery of the Ghawar field in 1948, which with later development proved to be one of the largest single oil-bearing structures in the world, and includes the Fazran, Ain Dar, Shedgum, Uthmaniyya, Hawiyya, and Haradh oil fields, originally thought to be separate fields. Important discoveries were made in 1949 at the Fadhili field, in 1956 at the Khursaniyya field, and in 1957 at the Khurais field. Continuing exploration activity revealed the Harmaliyya and Mazalij fields in 1971 and the Airdi and Abu Jifan fields in 1973.

Sa'ūdī Arabia's offshore zone has also proved to be well endowed with oil resources. The Qatīf field, discovered in 1945, and the Berri field, discovered in 1964, underlie both the land and offshore areas. The world's largest offshore field lies in Sa'ūdī Arabian waters of the Persian Gulf at Safaniya, while other important offshore fields include Manifa, Abu Sa'fa, and Berri. The Zuluf offshore field came on stream in 1973, together with the Marjan field, slightly to the east.

In December 1950, the Sa'ūdī Arabian government and Aramco reached agreement on a modified system of profit-sharing, which introduced the notion of the 50–50 division between host country and concessionaire. Following the establishment of a national oil company in 1956, to supervise the exploration and development of oil resources outside the Aramco concession, Aramco itself began to relinquish parts of the 673,000 square mile (1,743,063 square kilometer) concession, including 588,000 square miles, though the residual 85,000 square miles included the most prolific oil-bearing areas of the kingdom.

From 1 January 1973, the General Petroleum and Minerals Organisation (Petromin), the Sa'ūdī Arabian state oil company, took a 25 percent share in the Aramco concession. One year later this participation was increased to 60 percent, with the objective of total takeover of the Aramco concession shortly after.

Petromin granted a concession to Erap of France in 1965 for three blocks of territory along the Red Sea coast, where a natural gas and condensate field was discovered in 1969. Other onshore ventures by Petromin have not yet revealed significant oil finds. In the Sa'ūdī Arabian part of the Neutral Zone an exclusive concession was awarded to the Getty Oil Corporation in 1949. In the offshore area of the Neutral Zone the concession is held by the Arabian Oil Company, which also works the Kuwaiti section. Sa'ūdī Arabia holds a 10 percent share in the operation.

Exploration for oil along the Trucial Coast was first taken up by the Iraq Petroleum Company through a subsidiary, Petroleum Concessions Ltd., which became Petroleum Development (Trucial Coast) in 1936. Petroleum Development eventually arranged concession terms with the rulers of Dubai, Kalba, Ra's al-Khaima, and Sharja by 1938, and Abū Dhabī signed a separate agreement in the following year. Little was achieved in the early years of the concession and serious geophysical survey did not get under way until 1947; drilling was begun only in 1950 in Abū Dhabī, Dubai, and Sharja. Oil was struck in Abū Dhabī at Murban in 1953, but it was not until the third well at this site was completed in 1960 that oil was acknowledged to be present in commercial quantities.

Onshore exploration by the Abū Dhabī Petroleum Company, under which name Petroleum Development later operated, revealed the Bu Hasa extension to Murban oil field. Bu Hasa came into production in 1965 as the emirate's main production area, while a third oil field at Asab came on stream in 1973. A minor field at Sahil was exploited from 1975. Abū Dhabī Petroleum Company was owned by the constituent members of the Iraq Petroleum Company (British Petroleum, Royal Dutch/Shell, Compagnie Française des Pétroles, and the Near East Development Corporation with equal shares and Participants and Explorations Corporation with a 5 percent holding), of which 25 percent was acquired by the Abū Dhabī National Oil Company in 1973.

In the offshore zone, exploration began in 1954 and a first well drilled in 1958 struck oil at Umm Shaif, from which export commenced in 1962. A second offshore oil field was discovered in 1964 and named the Zakum field. Both offshore finds were made by Abū Dhabī Marine Areas, a company that was set up in 1953 and made up of British Petroleum with two-thirds and Compagnie Française des Pétroles with one-third of the shares. British Petroleum disposed of part of its shares to Overseas Petroleum Corporation of Japan in 1972, while the Abū Dhabī National Oil Company took over 60 percent of the company as a result of the participation agreements of 1973 and 1974. Abū Dhabī Marine Area discovered the al-Bunduq field in 1965, though this oil field underlay both Abū Dhabī and Qatar territory and was not brought into production until 1975. A similar situation affects the Abū 'l-Bakush field, which is shared with Iran, though this has been developed by a consortium, without the participation of Abū Dhabī Marine Areas. The latter company discovered the Sa'ath al-Razbut field in 1969, though this will be brought into operation by Compagnie Française des Pétroles for the national company.

Early exploration activity in Dubai in the period from 1937 under the auspices of Petroleum Development (Trucial Coast) yielded no positive results and the concession was given up. Reallotment of the concession gave Dubai Petroleum Company, made up of Continental Oil and two partners—Sun Oil and

Deutsche Erdöl who joined later—the onshore zone in 1963. No commercial oil finds were made. The offshore zone was allocated to British Petroleum and Compagnie Française des Pétroles in 1952. They operated as Dubai Marine Areas until a half-interest was taken up in their holding by the Dubai Petroleum Company, BP withdrew, and further partners were found. Oil was struck at the Fateh field in 1966, and production commenced in 1969. Meanwhile, small-scale finds of oil were made in the Rashid oil field in 1973 and the Falah oil field in 1977.

Intensive exploration of the territories of the other members of the United Arab Emirates took place in the late 1960s and the 1970s. In Sharja, the first discoveries of oil in commercial quantities were made offshore in an area close to the island of Abū Mūsā. The field is operated by Crescent Petroleum for a group of five independent oil companies, but revenues are shared with Iran, which has a 50 percent holding, and Umm al-Qaiwain, which has 15 percent. Small quantities of oil have been found offshore in Umm al-Qaiwain and Ra's al-Khaima.

Bahrain was among the earlier of oil producers in the Persian Gulf area, with oil struck in commercial quantities in 1932 at Awali. The Bahrain Petroleum Company is jointly owned by Standard Oil of California and Texaco, though since 1976 the Bahrain National Oil Company has taken up a 60 percent share in operations. Intensive exploration in the Bahrain offshore area has failed to reveal new oil reservoirs, though Bahrain shares in the revenues of the Abu Safah oil field, which is actually operated by Aramco, and also takes delivery of crude oil from Sa'ūdī Arabia for processing in Bahrain.

Exploration for oil in Oman began as early as 1925, when Petroleum Development (Oman) undertook initial surveys in the period to 1937, when a new concession was awarded. Drilling between 1956 and 1960 was generally without success, and all oil companies other than Shell and Participations and Explorations Corporations (Partex) withdrew. Exploratory drilling in the northern provinces eventually located oil at Yibal in 1962, Natih in 1963, and Fahud in 1964. Meanwhile, the Compagnie Française des Pétroles had bought 10 percent of the Partex share and the Oman government acquired a 60 percent holding in the whole operation. Exploration offshore in the Persian Gulf and Gulf of Oman by consortia led by Wintershall Aktiengesellschaft and Sun Oil, respectively, has not proved profitable in its early phases. Evaluation of Dhofar is in the hands of Petroleum Development (Oman), while French and Japanese interests are appraising the areas in the vicinity of the Straits of Hormuz.

The Qatar Petroleum Company, owned by the participants in Iraq Petroleum Company, was awarded a 75-year concession in Qatar in 1935. Although oil was struck by the first well drilled at the Dukhan oil field in the years immediately preceding World War II, development was not completed until 1949. Further exploration by Continental Oil in the period 1963–68 was not successful, and the Qatar Oil Company, with Japanese participants, failed to find oil in commercial quantities. Royal Dutch/Shell was granted a concession for offshore exploration in 1952 and struck oil at Idd al-Shargi field in 1960, at Maydan Mahzam in 1963, and at Bul Hanine in 1970. The Qatar government took over a 25 percent share of operations in 1973, acquired a further 35 percent in 1974, and in 1977 became the owner of the entire assets of Shell Qatar. Qatar shares the revenues of the Bunduq oil field equally with Abū Dhabī.

Oil Installations

The Persian Gulf oil-producing states present the most concentrated areas of investment in the oil industry in the world, where fixed assets created over the period since 1908 enable production, processing, transport, storage, refining, and export of crude oil, refined products, and natural gas in a variety of forms. Each oil-producing state has its own special history of development of oil facilities and, with only few exceptions, oil operations are exclusive to the nation in question. There have been a number of important changes in the pattern of oil installations since the inception of the oil industry in the Persian Gulf area. The dominant axis of activity in the regional oil industry until 1951 lay in Iran, approximately on lines between the inland oil fields of Masjid-i Sulaimān, Lālī, and Agha Jari and the refinery and terminal center at Ābādān.

Virtual closure of the Iranian oil industry during the crisis in relations between the Iranian government and Anglo-Iranian Oil Company accelerated changes that were already taking place in the Persian Gulf oil states. Not only was exploration in countries other than Iran stepped up, but rapid development of known alternative oil resources also took place. The center of gravity of the oil industry in the region swung rapidly to the western side of the Persian Gulf, as oil resources in Kuwait, Sa'ūdī Arabia, and the United Arab Emirates (formerly the Trucial States) were exploited. The single most important area of oil activity lies in the area south and west of Ra's Tanūra, where Ghawar, Abqā'iq, Qatīf, Dammām, Khurais, and Harmaliyya oil fields are linked via pipeline systems to the main oil terminal and oil refinery at Ra's Tanūra, by submarine pipeline to the Bahrain refinery and to the Trans-Arabian pipeline, which connects to the eastern Mediterranean coast at Sidon, but which has been little used since 1975. This complex encompasses two of the world's largest oil fields, Ghawar and Abqā'iq, and is the most significant by volume of crude oil export systems worldwide. The offshore oil fields of the northern zone are also tied in to Ra's Tanūra. A pipeline link connects Safaniya field and the smaller offshore oil fields around it with Ra's Tanūra, collecting production from minor onshore oil fields on its route. The southern offshore fields, including Abu Safah, are linked to Ra's Tanūra separately.

Second only to the Ra's Tanūra complex of Sa'ūdī Arabia is the Iranian crude producing, gathering, and exporting system that centers on Khārg Island in the Persian Gulf. The crude oil processing, storage, and export facilities at Khārg Island service four main groups of oil fields. Prime among these is the light oil producing area, including Agha Jari, Karanj, Paris, and Pazanan oil fields, which is linked by a large diameter pipeline through Ganāva on the mainland to Khārg Island via submarine pipelines. Iranian heavy crude fields include Gach Saran and Bibi Hakima, which are tied into Khārg Island via Ganāva. A legacy of oil development in the earlier part of the twentieth century remains in the central fields areas, where the Masjid-i Sulaimān, Haft Kel, Lālī, Naft Safīd, and Kupal fields remain aligned toward Ābādān, where most crude is refined. The Ahrāz oil field in the central area is both tied in to Abādān and the Khārg Island systems. In the offshore zone, there are a number of small producing fields with a variety of terminal facilities. Fields close to Khārg Island make use of its facilities. Feridun, Darius, Cyrus, and Ardeshir fields are joined by submarine pipelines to Khārg Island, while to the north the Bahragan, Nawruz, and Hendījān fields have a separate export terminal at Imam Hasan. An oil terminal at Lavan Island, further south in the Persian Gulf offshore zone, serves the Sassan, Rustam, Raksh, and Alpha fields. In the region of Bandar 'Abbās, the Sirri oil field is linked by pipeline to a terminal at the town.

Although Iraq occupies an important position at the head of the Persian Gulf, the country was for many years of little significance as a producer of oil on the Persian Gulf. Only the Basra Petroleum Company's fields at Rumaila and Zubair were serviced by the Ra's al-Bakr oil terminal. Development of the North Rumaila oil field enhanced the flow of Iraqi oil to the south, and a new oil terminal was constructed at Fāō. In the north of the country, Kirkuk was the center of the oil industry to which other fields belonging to the Iraqi Petroleum Company were linked. Oil fields in the Mosul area were connected to the Kirkuk export pipeline system that led to the Haditha area and thence to the Mediterranean coast at Banias and Tripoli, carrying the greater part of Iraqi oil exports. A strategic oil pipeline was constructed to enable oil from the northern oil fields to be transported to the Persian Gulf export terminals. This line runs from Kirkuk to North Rumaila and was opened in 1976. A new export pipeline was commissioned in 1977, running from Kirkuk to the Turkish Mediterranean port of Dörtyol, thereby decreasing considerably the reliance of Iraq on the goodwill of its neighbors to the west for transit facilities.

The pattern of oil installations in Kuwait centers on the Ahmadi area. The northern fields of Raudhatain, Sabiriyah, and Bahrah are transferred by pipeline to Ahmadi and exported mainly through the North Pier, while the southern fields of Burgan, Magwa, and Minagish are linked to Ahmadi and the oil terminal at Mina al-Ahmadi. Umm Gudair oil field is connected to the oil refinery at Shu'aiba. In the Neutral Zone, exports by Aminoil are carried via Mina Abdullah and Getty exports through Mina Saud.

In the United Arab Emirates and other smaller oil-producing areas of the Persian Gulf, only two important and complex oil transporting and exporting systems are worthy of special note and both are in Abū Dhabī. On shore, an extending pipeline system feeds oil from the scattered fields to Jabal Dhanna terminal. More remarkably, offshore facilities have been built up as a web centering on Das Island, which caters for the processing of oil from Umm Shaif, Zakum, and al-Bunduq offshore fields.

The disposition of the main oil facilities in the Persian Gulf area is shown in Figure 9–3. There has been a notable increase in the number of oil refineries in the region. By far the largest increase in refinery capacity has been to cater for rapidly increasing domestic demands within the oil-producing states themselves. This is especially true of Iran, where the consumption of refined products rose from 12,201 million metric tons in the 1971–72 Iranian year to 21,803 million metric tons in 1975–76. Although there has been a great desire in the oil-producing states of the Persian Gulf to refine a greater volume of oil exports within the region, few export refinery projects have been begun. Growth of refining capacity in the region is shown in Table 9–1.

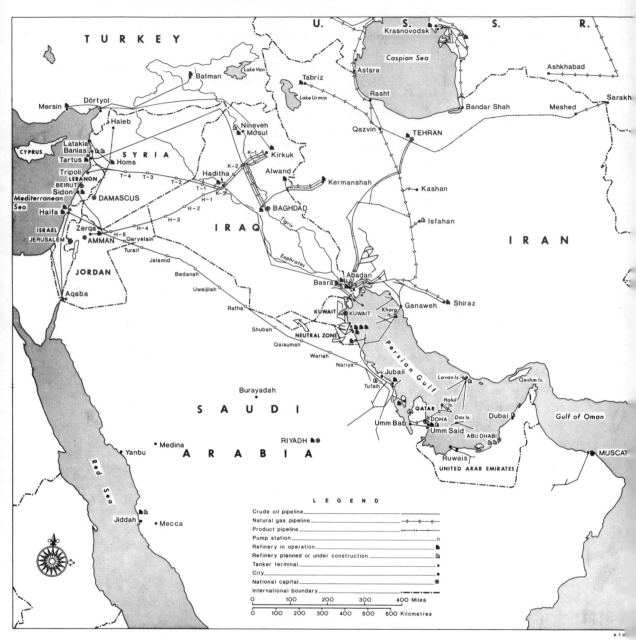

FIG. 9–3. Oil installations in the Persian Gulf area

Oil Reserves

Estimates of the reserves of crude oil in the Persian Gulf area suggest that, with available engineering skills and in foreseeable economic conditions, the region possesses between 55 and 60 percent of world proved oil reserves. Indeed, the next largest holder of oil reserves, the USSR, has less than one-quarter the

TABLE 9-1. REFINING CAPACITY IN THE PERSIAN GULF
AREA (IN MILLIONS OF TONS/YEAR)

Country	1966	1968	1970	1972	1974	1976
Bahrain	10	10	10	12	12	12
Iran	26	30	30	30	33	38
Iraq	4	5	5	6	9	9
Kuwait	18	22	23	26	26	28
Neutral Zone	4	4	4	4	4	4
Sa'ūdī Arabia	14	14	21	21	23	23
Others[a]	4	6	6	6	8	9
Total	80	91	99	105	115	123

[a] Estimated.

Source: BP Statistical Review of the World Oil Industry 1976 (London, British Petroleum).

reserves thought to lie in the Persian Gulf area. A general estimate of the distribution of world crude oil reserves is given in Table 9-2. The outstanding characteristic of the distribution of oil reserves in the Persian Gulf states is the great concentration in the single country, Sa'ūdī Arabia, which has no less than 23 percent of world resources. The remaining important holders of oil reserves are Kuwait, Iran, Iraq, and Abū Dhabī. Reserves elsewhere are minor in importance, though in aggregate still of international interest. The dominant position of the Persian Gulf in the Middle East is shown by the very low estimates of reserves in other countries of that region, which are put at a mere 0.3 percent of the world total.

Concentration of reserves in the Persian Gulf states is likely to become more rather than less pronounced with the passing of time. It is expected by geological opinion that the countries bordering the Persian Gulf will reveal the greatest addition to reserves into the 1980s, with the sole exception of the USSR. The strength of the crude oil reserves of the Persian Gulf oil producers is shown by the fact that should no further oil be found, existing reserves would sustain output

TABLE 9-2. WORLD CRUDE OIL RESERVES AT END OF 1976

Country/area	Billion barrels	Share of total %	Country/area	Billion barrels	Share of total %
Persian Gulf	365.1	55.9	Other Middle East	2.2	0.3
Sa'ūdī Arabia	151.4	23.2	North America	45.1	6.9
Kuwait	67.4	10.3	Latin America	33.6	5.1
Iran	63.0	9.7	Western Europe	24.9	3.8
Iraq	34.0	5.2	Africa	60.6	9.3
Abū Dhabī	29.0	4.4	USSR	78.1	12.0
Neutral Zone	6.3	0.9	Eastern Europe	3.0	0.5
Oman	5.8	0.9	China	20.0	3.1
Qatar	5.7	0.9	Others	19.4	3.0
Dubai	1.5	0.2	Total	652.0	100.0
Sharja	0.7	0.1			
Bahrain	0.3	0.1			

Source: Oil and Gas Journal; BP Statistical Review of the World Oil Industry 1976.

FIG. 9–4. Ra's Tanūra Refinery, Sa'ūdī Arabia (Courtesy of ARAMCO and the American Petroleum Institute)

for more than forty-five years, at least, at present-day levels of production. There is wide variation in the strength of the reserves of the individual states. Whereas Kuwait could produce at 1976 levels for almost a century, Qatar could continue to sustain output for only thirty more years and Bahrain for a mere fifteen years.

Natural Gas Reserves

For many years natural gas produced in association with crude oil was flared off in most of the states surrounding the Persian Gulf, since demand for it and the means of converting it into a transportable material were generally lacking.

TABLE 9–3. ESTIMATED PRODUCTION TO RESERVES RATIOS FOR
PERSIAN GULF OIL STATES—1976 DATA[a]

Sa'ūdī Arabia	1:50	Oman	1:45
Kuwait	1:95	Qatar	1:30
Iran	1:30	Dubai	1:15
Iraq	1:40	Sharja	1:50
Abū Dhabī	1:50	Bahrain	1:15
Neutral Zone	1:40	Persian Gulf states—average	1:45

[a] The figures estimate the period for which output could be sustained at
present rates without additions to reserves.

With improving technology and growing demand for natural gas, it is increasingly
being used rather than wasted. The Persian Gulf oil states have less of a monopoly
of natural gas reserves than they do of crude oil, but none the less control 23
percent of estimated world reserves. Full exploitation of associated gas and
natural gas from purely gas fields could add very substantially to the hydrocarbon
wealth of the Persian Gulf states. Table 9–4 indicates the relative importance of
the area in world terms.

Crude Oil Production

Of the oil-producing states of the Persian Gulf region, only Iran has a long
history of involvement in petroleum affairs. There have been dramatic changes
in the level of production in that country, coinciding with periods of world crisis
or local disruption, most notably during the period of World War II and at the
time of the Anglo-Iranian confrontation in the years 1951–53.

Important expansions of oil production in the area came above all after 1951,
when the potential of Kuwait and Sa'ūdī Arabia in particular began to be exploited. By the 1960s, the oil-producing states were virtually vying with one another to augment their rates of oil output, and this is reflected clearly in the very
rapid increase in production in the decade 1963–73, when the average increase in
production for the Persian Gulf area was in excess of 11.5 percent each year against
a world average of 7.7 percent.

TABLE 9–4. WORLD NATURAL GAS RESERVES AT END OF 1976

Country/area	Trillion cubic feet	Share of total %	Country/area	Trillion cubic feet	Share of total %
Persian Gulf[a]	523.1	22.5	USSR	918.0	39.5
Other Middle East	12.8	0.5	Eastern Europe	10.0	0.4
North America	274.3	11.8	China	25.0	1.1
Latin America	90.3	3.9	Others	120.0	5.2
Western Europe	142.4	6.1	Total	2,325.0	100.0
Africa	209.1	9.0			

[a] In mid-1977, Iranian reserves were estimated at 90–100 billion barrels of oil equivalent.
Sources: BP Statistical Review of the World Oil Industry 1976. Outlook for Natural Gas, Shell
Briefing Service, 1977.

TABLE 9–5. CRUDE OIL PRODUCTION BY PRODUCERS IN THE PERSIAN GULF AREA ('000 BARRELS/DAY)

Year	Abū Dhabi	Dubai	Iran	Iraq	Kuwait	Neutral Zone	Oman	Qatar	Saʿūdi Arabia	Sharjah	Bahrain
1913			5								
1914			8								
1915			10								
1916			12								
1917			19								
1918			24								
1919			28								
1920			33								
1921			46								
1922			61								
1923			69								
1924			88								
1925			96								
1926			98								
1927			109								
1928			119	2							
1929			115	2							
1930			126	2							
1931			122	2							
1932			135	2							
1933			149	2							
1934			158	22							1
1935			157	76							3
1936			171	84							12
1937			213	89							21
1938			215	90					1		22
1939			214	83					11		20
1940			181	53					14		19
1941			139	33					12		19
1942			198	54					12		17
1943			204	75					13		18

Year											
1944		279		87					21		18
1945		358		97					58		20
1946		402		98	16				164		22
1947		425		99	44				246		25
1948		520		72	127				391		29
1949		561		85	246			2	477		30
1950		664		136	344			33	547		30
1951		340		181	561			49	760		30
1952		20		390	750			69	820		30
1953		30		580	860			85	840		30
1954		60		630	950	16		100	950		30
1955		330		690	1,090	24		115	970		30
1956		540		630	1,085	30		125	975		32
1957		730		445	1,140	65		140	985		40
1958		825		725	1,395	80		175	1,005		45
1959		940		850	1,380	120		160	1,100		45
1960		1,060		955	1,620	135		175	1,245		45
1961		1,195		990	1,645	175		175	1,390		45
1962	15	1,330		995	1,830	245		190	1,525		45
1963	55	1,475		1,160	1,930	315		195	1,630		45
1964	185	1,710		1,255	2,115	360		215	1,730		49
1965	280	1,910		1,315	2,170	370		235	2,025		56
1966	360	2,110		1,390	2,275	420		290	2,395		63
1967	380	2,605		1,230	2,290	415	55	325	2,600		69
1968	495	2,840		1,505	2,420	405	240	340	2,830		78
1969	600	3,375	10	1,525	2,575	420	330	355	2,995		79
1970	695	3,845	85	1,565	2,735	505	330	370	3,550		79
1971	935	4,565	125	1,700	2,925	545	285	430	4,500		74
1972	1,050	5,050	155	1,465	3,000	565	280	485	5,730		70
1973	1,305	5,895	220	2,020	2,755	535	295	570	7,345		68
1974	1,410	6,060	240	1,975	2,275	540	290	520	8,350	30	67
1975	1,400	5,385	255	2,260	1,840	500	340	435	6,970	40	61
1976	1,595	5,920	315	2,280	1,950	465	365	485	8,525	35	58

Sources: BP Statistical Review of the World Oil Industry; S. H. Longrigg, *Oil in the Middle East,* 1968; C. Issawi and M. Yeganeh, *Economics of Middle Eastern Oil,* 1962; De Golyer and MacNaughton, *Twentieth-Century Petroleum Statistics;* oil companies' annual reports.

The position changed after 1971. As prices of oil went up, culminating in the unprecedented quadrupling of oil prices in the period from October 1973, the producing governments faced a much more constrained demand in the international markets and output ceased to grow as fast as in the preceding period. The years 1971–76 witnessed a rate of growth in output averaging 6.4 percent, though this was still well above the world average of 2.5 percent.

The very recent emergence of the oil producers of the Persian Gulf, with the exception of Iran, is illustrated in Table 9–5. Such a late and rapid rate of development of the petroleum industry in societies that were often traditional in social and political structure and economically adjusted to simple forms of agriculture has inevitably led to immaturity in the oil industries in these countries. Trained cadres in technical, managerial, and sales aspects of oil are almost universally lacking throughout the Persian Gulf countries, with the sole exception of Iran. Despite the takeover of the productive factors relating to the oil industry in the states of the area through various participation agreements and nationalization of the assets of the international oil companies in the period since 1970, there is heavy and continuing reliance by the oil producers of the Persian Gulf on imported expertise, not least from the international oil companies, to ensure the maintenance and expansion of the indigenous operating structures. Other than the National Iranian Oil Company, few national oil companies have successfully developed integrated oil operations overseas through extensive direct selling of oil in the international market.

Fluctuations in production from individual countries have occurred in response to outside events, as noted in the case of Iran and as acts of policy on the part of the regional governments. Iraq has experienced greater vicissitudes than most other producers. Early exploration met difficulties of a legal and technical kind, and production got under way only slowly. In consequence, although production in Iraq began earlier than in all Persian Gulf states other than Iran, the rate of increase has been slow. Gains made in the level of production in Iraq during the Anglo-Iranian crisis, when Iraq became the third largest oil producer in the Persian Gulf area, were later lost as Iranian output recovered. In the period 1961–66, annual production in Iraq rose at a steady rate of 7 percent, but there was a marked fall in output in 1967 as a result of the closure of the Mediterranean pipeline, and the rate of growth of output in the period 1966–76 ran at only 5.1 percent each year as a consequence of further disruptions of exports in 1972 and 1974.

Kuwait, too, has experienced a varying level of output. Steady expansion of production characterized the period to 1972, and the decade 1962–72 saw the output from Kuwait rise by an average of 5.1 percent each year to 3 million barrels/day. Fears in Kuwait of an overrapid erosion of the reserves position, together with a reduction in the attractiveness of rather sulphurous crudes on the world market, led after 1973 to a decline in Kuwaiti production to 1.95 million barrels/day by 1976. Less dramatically, though for similar reasons to those in Kuwait itself, production in the Neutral Zone slipped back from 1972.

Quite the most consistent expansion in output has been witnessed in Sa'ūdī Arabia. This is indicated in Table 9–6 for the four main oil producers in the Persian Gulf expressed as percent annual growth rates. Sa'ūdī Arabian oil production rose above one million barrels/day average in 1958, and by 1972 the country established clear supremacy as major producer in the Persian Gulf area and became the third largest oil producer in the world, a position that by way of reserves and installed production capacity it will be able to retain for a considerable period into the future.

Abū Dhabī began as a producer much later than the other major oil exporters of the Persian Gulf, but has displayed the most rapid rate of growth over the last decade, with 16.1 percent average annual increase in 1966–76. Production in 1976 averaged 1.595 million barrels/day. Output by the smaller producers is shown in Table 9–7, and whereas Dubai, the Neutral Zone, Oman, Qatar, Sharja, and Bahrain are small producers, their aggregate contribution to total output enhances the dominant position of the Persian Gulf area in an international context.

In 1976, the oil-producing states bordering the Persian Gulf accounted for 37 percent of total world output and almost 99 percent of production from the Middle East. This compares with 27 percent of world output derived from the Persian Gulf in 1966, 24 percent in 1961, 19 percent in 1956, and 15 percent in 1951. The growing importance of the Persian Gulf oil producers is illustrated in Table 9–7.

The important position of the Persian Gulf producers arises from the high proportion of crude oil exported. Only small, though increasing, volumes of oil and natural gas are consumed within the producing states, enabling the Persian Gulf to be the world's largest exporter of crude oil. Total exports of crude oil and refined products from the Persian Gulf area in 1976 amounted to 19,800 and 1,000 barrels/day, respectively. In the oil sector, the Persian Gulf provided no less than 68.4 percent of crude entering international trade in 1976 and 18.6 percent of refined products. This contrasts with 59.0 percent of crude and 27.7 percent of products entering international trade in 1966.

Exports of crude oil and refined products are dispatched from the Persian Gulf to most consuming areas of the world. Two areas have heavy and long-standing dependence on oil from the Persian Gulf—Western Europe and Japan. Table 9–8 shows that Western Europe alone absorbed 45 percent of all oil exports from the Persian Gulf area in 1976, while Japan took 19 percent. The United States became an increasingly important customer for Persian Gulf oil during the period 1971–76, when its share of exports rose from less than 3 to more than 9 percent.

TABLE 9–6. ANNUAL GROWTH RATES OF
OIL PRODUCTION FOR FOUR MAIN OIL PRODUCERS
IN THE PERSIAN GULF AREA

Period	1956–61	1961–66	1966–71	1971–76
Iran	17.0	12.0	16.5	5.4
Iraq	9.5	7.0	4.1	6.1
Kuwait	8.5	6.5	5.2	—7.7
Sa'ūdī Arabia	7.0	11.5	13.5	13.5

Source: BP Statistical Review of the World Oil Industry, various years.

TABLE 9-7. CRUDE OIL PRODUCTION IN THE PERSIAN GULF STATES AND ITS CONTRIBUTION TO WORLD OUTPUT, 1951-76

Country/area	1951 Output mn b/d	1951 % share of total	1956 Output mn b/d	1956 % share of total	1961 Output mn b/d	1961 % share of total	1966 Output mn b/d	1966 % share of total	1971 Output mn b/d	1971 % share of total	1976 Output mn b/d	1976 % share of total
Persian Gulf	1.860	15.1	3.410	19.4	5.600	23.9	9.255	26.9	16.080	31.9	21.893	36.8
Iran	0.340	2.8	0.540	3.1	1.195	5.1	2.110	6.1	4.565	9.1	5.920	9.9
Iraq	0.181	1.5	0.630	3.6	0.990	4.2	1.390	4.0	1.700	3.4	2.280	3.8
Kuwait	0.561	4.6	1.085	6.2	1.645	7.0	2.275	6.6	2.925	5.8	1.950	3.3
Saʿūdi Arabia	0.760	6.2	0.975	5.6	1.390	5.9	2.395	7.0	4.500	8.9	8.525	14.3
Neutral Zone			0.030	0.2	0.175	0.7	0.420	1.2	0.545	1.1	0.465	0.8
Qatar			0.125	0.7	0.175	0.7	0.290	0.8	0.430	0.9	0.485	0.8
Oman									0.285	0.6	0.365	0.6
Abū Dhabi							0.360	1.0	0.935	1.9	1.595	2.7
Dubai									0.125	0.2	0.315	0.5
Sharja											0.035	0.1
North America	7.060	57.5	8.670	49.4	9.135	38.9	10.595	30.8	12.745	25.3	11.330	19.0
Latin America	2.000	16.3	2.845	16.2	3.610	15.4	4.640	13.5	5.185	10.3	4.575	7.7
Western Europe	0.090	0.7	0.210	1.2	0.330	1.4	0.435	1.2	0.425	0.8	0.905	1.5
Africa	0.050	0.4	0.035	0.2	0.500	2.1	2.845	8.3	5.810	11.5	5.850	9.8
South East Asia	0.260	2.1	0.375	2.1	0.510	2.2	0.570	1.7	1.110	2.2	1.865	3.1
USSR	0.780	6.4	1.680	9.6	3.340	14.2	5.335	15.5	7.470	14.8	10.315	17.3
Eastern Europe and China	0.110	0.8	0.285	1.6	0.400	1.7	0.580	1.7	0.875	1.7	1.900	3.2
Others	0.080	0.7	0.030	0.3	0.060	0.2	0.195	0.4	0.625	1.5	0.917	1.5
World	12.290	100.0	17.540	100.0	23.485	100.0	34.450	100.0	50.325	100.0	59.555	100.0

Sources: BP Statistical Review of the World Oil Industry, various years; Middle East Economic Survey; Oil and Gas Journal.

Energy Consumption

While the strength of the export position of the oil-producing states of the Persian Gulf area has long rested on the fact that production ran at high levels, while domestic consumption was small or even negligible, changes have been taking place in this pattern, especially in Iran and particularly since 1973. The Iranian situation is, however, by no means typical of the area as a whole. Estimates for local consumption put domestic use of petroleum products in Sa'ūdī Arabia, for example, at a mere 120,000 barrels/day in 1976, while even Iraq, with a larger population and a greater degree of nonoil economic activity, reported domestic consumption of slightly more than 100,000 barrels/day. The level of oil use in the smaller states is equally small, both at the national and per capita level. In Kuwait, average domestic consumption ran at 26,000 barrels/day in 1976, while in Bahrain the comparable figure was 3,300 barrels/day.

Iran, with far the largest population of the region, naturally utilizes a greater proportion of its oil production domestically, though with consumption reported at 417,000 barrels/day in 1976 (or 450,640 barrels/day in the Iranian year 1976–77), it is apparent that Iranian use of oil within the domestic economy is also a function of rapid industrialization.

Despite the abundance of hydrocarbon resources in the Persian Gulf area, there has been a degree of diversification in the use of energy and investment for the future. This is particularly true of Iran. Hydroelectric power has been used with increasing effect since the inauguration of the great reservoir dams on the Dez, Safid Rud, and Karaj rivers in the 1960s. By 1976–77, 23 percent of all electricity produced in Iran was from hydroelectric installations. Work began in 1977 on the construction of a number of nuclear power stations in Iran.

Oil Revenues

Oil revenues accruing to the oil exporters of the Persian Gulf in the period before 1951 were limited both by the small number of exporters at that time—Iran, Iraq, Kuwait, Sa'ūdī Arabia, and Bahrain—and by the comparatively disadvantageous terms available to the oil states. Of importance in lifting the revenues of the Persian Gulf states, was the introduction from 1950 onward of the 50–50 split of profits between host countries and international oil companies

TABLE 9–8. DISTRIBUTION OF PERSIAN GULF OIL EXPORTS (PERCENT)

Country/area	1966	1971	1976	Country/area	1966	1971	1976
Western Europe	50.7	50.4	45.1	Africa	5.8	3.4	2.4
Japan	19.1	24.9	18.9	Canada	1.7	1.9	1.9
USA	3.7	2.6	9.2	Australasia	3.9	2.1	1.2
Latin America	3.4	3.1	8.3	Others	11.7	11.6	13.0

Source: BP Statistical Review of the World Oil Industry and *Oil in the Middle East*, Economist Intelligence Unit.

that followed the agreement in Venezuela in 1948 of the *impuesta adicional*. From the early 1950s, profit division was based on posted prices at the export terminals. Posted prices were set by the oil companies and a reduction in posted prices in 1960 led to the formation of the Organization of Petroleum Exporting Countries (OPEC), in which the Persian Gulf producers have traditionally played a commanding role.

During the 1960s, further improvements in the level of payments made by the oil companies arose from the 1964–65 OPEC settlement on discount expensing, which reduced by stages the ability of companies to attribute the costs of discounts to customers to the host countries. The status of concessions and contracts allotted to the oil companies increasingly favored the Persian Gulf producers during the late 1960s by way of bonuses on award of concessions and other nonfiscal benefits. The total effect of augmenting output and improved financial terms led to an increase in oil revenues of the Persian Gulf states from $1,497 million in 1961 to $4,189 million by 1970, distributed as shown in Table 9–9.

The receipts of the Persian Gulf oil exporters for each barrel of oil exported improved from an average of 77.7 cents in 1963 to 87.4 cents by 1970. A major renegotiation of the unit price of oil exports was undertaken in 1970 and 1971, leading to an agreement between the OPEC states of the Persian Gulf, led by the Shah of Iran, and the oil companies and signed in Tehran in February 1971. Posted prices for Persian Gulf crude were raised by 9 cents/barrel, effective from 14 November 1970, the posted price of 40° API crude was raised by 33 cents/ barrel from 15 February 1971, and other modifications made to the rate of company payments. A commitment was made by the oil companies for future rises in the period to 1975, to adjust oil prices to any deterioration in terms of trade with the industrialized nations. As a result of the Tehran agreement, and other related modifications to the oil price, the unit payments for crude oil exports for the Persian Gulf states rose to $1.255 in 1971 and to $1.407 per barrel in 1972.

Conditions of the Tehran and subsequent agreements were entirely overthrown on 16 October 1973, when the Persian Gulf oil exporting states unilaterally raised the posted price of crude oil by more than 70 percent. A general meeting of OPEC in Geneva on 1 January 1974 raised posted prices again. The impact of

TABLE 9–9. OIL REVENUES OF PERSIAN GULF EXPORTERS,[a] 1961–70 ($ MILLION)

Year	Iran	Iraq	Kuwait	Saʻūdī Arabia	Qatar	Abū Dhabī	Others	Total
1961	301	265	464	400	53	—	13	1,497
1962	334	267	526	451	56	—	13	1,649
1963	398	325	557	502	60	6	13	1,861
1964	470	353	655	561	65	12	14	2,131
1965	522	375	671	655	68	33	16	2,342
1966	593	394	707	777	92	100	18	2,682
1967	737	361	718	852	102	105	24	2,898
1968	817	476	766	966	109	153	83	3,370
1969	938	483	812	1,008	115	191	118	3,660
1970	1,076	513	896	1,200	122	231	150	4,189

[a] Discrepancies due to rounding.
Source: Petroleum Press Service; IMF publications.

the increase in posted prices in the period 1973 and 1974 was, to say the least, dramatic. In the case of Arabian light crude, posted prices rose from $3.011 on 1 October 1973 to $11.651 by 1 January 1974, a gross increase of some 280 percent in the course of three months. Unity in pricing arrangements lasted until 15 December 1976, when an OPEC meeting in Dōha saw a split between Persian Gulf producers. Iran, Iraq, Kuwait, Qatar, on the one hand, increased prices by 10 percent on 1 January 1977 and provided for a further rise of 5 percent in the following July. Sa'ūdī Arabia and the United Arab Emirates, on the other hand, declined to raise the unit price of their export crude.

A most significant trend, quite separate from the price issue, was followed by the Persian Gulf oil producers in the years from 1974, as the nation states asserted their full sovereignty over domestic oil operations. The process of participation, in which the production operations of the oil companies were taken over piecemeal by the indigenous national oil companies, began in Qatar effective from 1 January 1974. Other Persian Gulf exporters have followed similar agreements that will see all domestic aspects of the oil industry in national ownership, though interim arrangements in most regional states call for a continuing but contractual role for the international oil companies in day-to-day operation of installations and handling of sales for the national companies. In the case of Iran, the National Iranian Oil Company has since the early 1960s represented a large and sophisticated organization, acting in many ways as an international oil company in its own right. From March 1973, the National Iranian Oil Company took over all functions of the Iranian Oil Operating Company.

The various national oil companies in the Persian Gulf area are differently constituted by legal definition and by degree of government involvement, but all are characterized by an ability to make contracts with third parties for exploration and development, to enter joint-venture arrangements in exploration and production, and to act independently as producers, distributors, and exporters of oil and oil products. Most complex of the state companies, the National Iranian Oil Company, has established interests in the equity of overseas refineries, exploration interests outside Iranian territory, and an expanding marketing function in downstream areas.

A consequence of the rise in oil prices, not least since 1973, was a large increase in the total revenues flowing to the governments of the oil-exporting states. Whereas oil revenues for all Persian Gulf producers in 1973 amounted to $8,747 million, it is estimated that by 1976 revenues were some $83,170 million (Table 9–10). The real purchasing power of revenues earned by the Persian Gulf states was eroded by both domestic price inflation and by deteriorating terms of trade vis-à-vis the industrialized nations. *De facto* devaluation of the U.S. dollar, in which most oil revenues were paid, also had an adverse impact on the value of apparently rising levels of oil revenues.

The Oil Industry and the Local Economies

Large sums of foreign exchange accrue to the governments of the Persian Gulf oil-exporting states on account of oil sales, and the effects of the use of these financial resources are discussed elsewhere in this volume. In addition to earnings from royalties, taxes, and bonuses, a secondary flow of foreign exchange has been earned by the oil states through purchases of local currencies for foreign oil companies to pay for their site operations. Historically, the level of purchase of local currency has exceeded the level of oil revenues, as in Iran in the period 1946–47 to 1951–52, taken as a whole. The foreign exchange acquisitions through purchases of local currency were only part of the impact on the domestic economy, since actual disbursements by the oil companies on labor, materials, and services created albeit localized areas of economic activity. Indeed, in the period before 1952 and in some Persian Gulf states as late as the 1970s, the concessionaire oil companies were among the largest consumers of local goods and services.

Although there was a tendency in the early period for the international oil companies to import their requirements of materials, leading to a rather enclave nature of the oil industry, with a deliberately minimized impact upon local economy and society, economic and political considerations in Iran, Iraq, and Kuwait, in particular, encouraged the companies to procure goods locally with increasing vigor. Total expenditures by the oil companies in Iran, for example, were valued at $101 million in the Iranian year 1961–62, at $125 million in 1971–72, and $183 million in 1976–77.

Oil exploration, development, and, to an extent, operation provided a significant element of employment in the economies of the states of the Persian Gulf. Since the oil industry grew up in countries where economic activity was above all based on cultivation, livestock herding, pearling, and trade, for many years and for most regional states, petroleum was the dominant modern sector industrial employer. During the early stages of the growth of the oil industry in Iran and Iraq, the oil companies pursued a deliberate policy of employing large numbers of local people as a means of acquiring influence and articulating paternalistic policies, some with genuine considerations of welfare for the local peoples.

Employment in the Iranian oil fields and the Ābādān refinery grew from 12,076 at the beginning of 1935 to 38,812 by 1949, when there were 4,477 foreigners in the labor force. In 1957, no less than 63,303 persons were engaged in the Iranian oil industry, but since that time there has been a gradual reduction in employment in this sector. Similar trends were present in Iraq, where, with many

TABLE 9–10. OIL REVENUES OF PERSIAN GULF EXPORTERS, 1971–76[a] ($ MILLION)

Year	Iran	Iraq	Kuwait	Sa'ūdī Arabia	Qatar	UAE	Oman	Bahrain	Total
1971	2,167	928	1,395	2,160	221	481	115	35	7,502
1972	2,380	909	1,657	3,107	255	625	122	36	9,091
1973	5,500	1,700	1,900	5,500	409	798	177	36[b]	15,014
1974	17,500	5,700	7,000	22,574	1,362	4,245	857	178	59,416
1975	18,500	7,600	7,500	25,675	1,690	6,100	1,100	287	68,452
1976	22,500	8,200	8,400	33,200	2,000	7,200	1,340	330	83,170

[a] Most figures represent best estimates.
[b] Bapco only.
Sources: Oil in the Middle East, Economist Intelligence Unit, London; Oil and Gas Journal; company reports.

fluctuations, employment rose to 15,000 persons in 1948, but has since run in the range 11,000 to 14,000 persons. Estimates by the United Nations suggest that by 1954 the oil industry in the Persian Gulf area employed as many as 150,000 persons. Despite reductions in employment in the Iranian oil industry, the proliferation of smaller producers in the Persian Gulf has sustained relatively large-scale job creation in the sector. By the mid 1970s, it is estimated that some 52,000 were directly engaged in the oil industry.

A feature that has been notable in all the oil states of the Persian Gulf was the provision of welfare facilities by the international oil companies. This was particularly the case in the earlier decades of the twentieth century, above all in Iran, and this form of benevolent paternalism on the part of the oil companies vanished only after 1954, as the host states asserted their sovereignty in areas of domestic concern. In Iran, the Anglo-Iranian Oil Company had set up more than thirty schools and handed them over to the local education authorities in the oil fields areas. Apprentice training schools were opened as early as the late 1920s and more than 3,000 Iranians were enrolled as apprentices by 1951. A technical institute of international stature was opened in Ābādān in 1939, and an elite of managers and technicians was trained by the oil company in Europe. After accomplishment of full Iranian control over nonbasic oil services in 1954, training programs were much expanded to take in most professional, artisan, and craft skills. As the Iranian economy picked up momentum from the Shah's reform program of 1962, the cadres trained in the Iranian oil industry formed a valuable resource for use in new and expanding areas of industry, commerce, and administration. The international status of the National Iranian Oil Company, more sophisticated in most operations than any other national oil company in the Persian Gulf area, owes no little to the long-standing training of Iranians by and experience in the domestic oil industry.

For other oil-producing states in the area development of the oil industry was less continuous and occurred when the oil companies were increasingly seeking a purely commercial role. Even so, the national oil companies and the agencies of governments concerned with petroleum have attempted to develop training and educational programs that have benefited the economy and the society as a whole.

Although mainly geographically specific to the areas of oil operations, activities by the national and international oil companies in the creation of transport infrastructure, public services (including electricity, gas, and water supply), housing and health programs have had a direct impact on the local areas involved and have set standards applicable throughout the nation.

Directly related to the growth of the Persian Gulf oil industries has been a trend toward diversification of the type of hydrocarbon export. Crude oil sales overseas earn lower returns than refined products or petrochemical materials and create lower levels of local employment than up-graded items. At the same time, production of fertilizers can be made to have an immediate and positive impact on the productivity of domestic agriculture.

Iran made an early start in the petrochemical field. A nitrogenous fertilizer plant was set up near Shiraz in 1961, and from 1965 on the country began development of a large-scale, export-oriented petrochemical industry mainly located in the south of the country within easy reach of the Ābādān refinery, the oil and natural gas fields, and the country's main ports. By 1978, Iran possessed one of the largest petrochemical industries outside the OECD states and expansion was proceeding.

Other Persian Gulf states have followed the same path as Iran. Kuwait, Iraq, the UAE, Saʿūdī Arabia, and the smaller producers are embarking on development of oil-related industry, and there is optimism that in time the Persian Gulf could become the world's major petrochemicals manufacturing region.

The Persian Gulf area was estimated in 1976 to possess only slightly less than one-quarter of the world's natural gas reserves. Utilization of this resource to an economically significant extent began only in 1966, when the National Iranian Gas Company was set up to manage the Gach Saran to Marv Dasht gasline. A turning point was also reached in 1970, when Iran succeeded in exporting natural gas to the USSR through the Igat trunkline. A second parallel gasline was negotiated with the USSR in 1977. Under this latter scheme, Iranian natural gas supplied to the southern republics of the Soviet Union was compensated for by deliveries of Soviet natural gas to East and West Europe in the north.

Rates of utilization of natural gas produced in association with crude oil in other Persian Gulf oil states remained low as late as 1978. Modest use of this resource in electricity generation, oil reservoir reinjection, and consumption or export as liquid natural gas remained the pattern on the Arabian peninsula, awaiting investment in pipeline facilities and suitable economic conditions. In any case, Iranian gas reserves represent some three-fifths of total reserves of the Persian Gulf states.

A related consequence of the emergence of a large oil industry and increasing local control over production and marketing of oil was the involvement of the exporting states in oil tanker ownership. This trend has developed only slowly. In 1968, the Iranian tanker marine comprised two tankers of 33,000 d.w.tons and two of 53,000 d.w.tons each, while Iraq had a negligible tonnage at that time. All the oil-exporting countries of the Persian Gulf significantly expanded their ownership and lease of tankers in the period after 1970, though their aggregate tonnage by 1977 was less than 2 percent of the world total.

In all, the direct effects of the oil industry in the oil field, refinery, storage, processing, and terminal areas of the littoral states of the Persian Gulf are less apparent than the indirect impact of the oil industry by way of oil revenues accruing to the central governments. But, spread over a number of years, the local operations of the oil industry created pressures for change and development within the regional society and economy that often had appreciable repercussions on the wider community, many of them of a positive and valuable nature.

Conclusions

The oil-producing and -exporting states of the Persian Gulf area alone are the owners of the world's largest oil reserves. With reassessment of Iranian natural gas reserves, the area could also prove to control if not the largest, at least the second largest of world gas reserves. At the same time, the Persian Gulf producers are currently, and will remain for many years, low consumers of their oil and gas resources, with a consequently unequaled potential for producing oil and gas for disposal on the international market. Such a position gives the Persian Gulf area a unique importance in both energy and political terms, especially in relation to the economies of the United States of America, Western Europe, Japan, and much of Africa, Asia, and Australasia.

Within the oil sector there are established and strong relations with outside areas that enhance the position of the Persian Gulf countries. Through the Organization of Petroleum Exporting Countries, the Persian Gulf oil-producing states have a structured international link for cooperation that proved effective during the later 1960s, and particularly during the period 1970 to 1974, in uniting oil producers that supplied the international market to their mutual benefit. OPEC increasingly became an articulation of the Persian Gulf states from the early 1970s, as the comparative advantages of the producers in that area by way of reserves and current production capacity became evident in commercial and political spheres.

Internationally, the Persian Gulf oil fields rose to early importance with the signature of the British Admiralty agreement to purchase Iranian oil in 1914. The economic and strategic position of the area has suffered vicissitudes, but its dominance has been asserted in oil affairs with growing effect in the last decade. In a period of expanding energy demand, the Persian Gulf producers and exporters of crude oil, refined products, and natural gas would appear to be in a strong position for some time into the immediate future. For the more distant future, the oil states are preparing for a world that will no longer absorb and pay for large volumes of crude oil. The struggle for the strongest oil economies in the world to convert themselves into viable nonoil economies is at the heart of the paradox inherent in development of the Persian Gulf states dealt with elsewhere in this volume.

Selected Bibliography

Arabian American Oil Company. *ARAMCO Handbook*. Damman, undated.

Arabian American Oil Company. *Annual reports*.

Bénard, A. *Prospects for Oil and Gas to End of the Century*. Shell, 1977.

British Petroleum. *Our Industry Petroleum*. London, 1977.

De Golyer and MacNaughton. *Twentieth Century Petroleum Statistics*.

Economist Intelligence Unit, *Oil in the Middle East*. London.

El Mallakh, R. *Economic Development and Regional Co-operation: Kuwait*. Chicago, 1968.

Europa. *The Middle East and North Africa*. London, 1977.

International Monetary Fund. *International Financial Statistics*.

Iranian Oil Operating Companies. *Annual reports*.

Issawi, C., and Yeganeh, M. *Economics of Middle Eastern Oil*. London, 1962.

Kuwait Oil Company. *Annual reports*.

Longrigg, S. H. *Oil in the Middle East*. London, 1968.

McLachlan, K. S., and Ghorban, N. *Oil Production, Revenues and Economic Development*. London, 1974.

Middle East Economic Review. London, 1977.

Middle East Economic Survey. Beirut.

National Iranian Oil Company. *Chairman's reports.*

National Iranian Oil Company. *Iran Oil Journal.*

Oil and Gas Journal.

Petroleum Press Service.

Shell International Petroleum Company. *Outlook for Natural Gas.* London, 1977.

Shell International Petroleum Company. *Oil and Gas in 1976.* London, 1977.

10. The Urbanization of the Persian Gulf Nations MICHAEL E. BONINE

 The twentieth century has witnessed vast changes among the urban areas of the developing world, with the transformation of preindustrial cities to large and complex metropolitan areas sprawling over the landscape. Traditional society, with its emphasis on family, kinship, and residential propinquity, becomes integrated into a wider society in the new urban environment. Urbanization accelerates as mortality rates decline in both the city and countryside, and rural migrants flock to cities for economic betterment or survival. Cities expand in population, size, function, and importance. New towns and cities are established.

Rapidity is a characteristic of this process, and in the fast transformation, the structure and morphology of the traditional city has been greatly modified. Wide avenues, rectangular asphalted grids, single detached houses, high-rise apartment and office buildings, and sprawling suburbs all become part of the urban scene. Older sections of cities are contemptuously razed by planners, the compact traditional residences being viewed as anachronistic, dirty, and not amenable to the new appliances, automobiles, and life styles.

But rapid urbanization creates problems. Essential services such as electricity, sewage systems, piped water, and garbage collection cannot keep up with the great expansion. In older neighborhoods, these amenities have to be imposed upon structures ill-suited for modernization. Housing shortages result for the swelling urban population, and residential densities increase considerably. Shanty towns arise in response to these shortages and are a blight on the master plans. Planners attempt to implement blueprints for reasonable and logical urban development with deficient staff, insufficient funds, and inadequate authority.

In the Middle East, urbanization has followed these patterns. Yet, the transformation here has occurred in a region in which an urban tradition has been an integral part of the society. Cities have existed in various areas of the Middle East since the end of the fourth millennium B.C., when the lowlands of Mesopotamia were the focus of such centers as Ur, Uruk, and Lagash. These cities were the focal points for surrounding hinterlands with their storehouses, temples, literati, and ruling élites. In cities, the great tradition of these ancient civilizations passed from one generation to another. The recent development of cities in the Middle East, then, is built upon a long urban heritage. However, the scale of urbanization in the twentieth century is unprecedented, and vast changes and modifications in society are reflected in the burgeoning urban environment. One of the most dramatic transformations, not only in the Middle East, but in the entire developing world, has occurred among the countries surrounding the Persian Gulf.

The Persian Gulf urbanization exemplifies a pattern that is unique in the annals of urban development. The pace of urbanization, with its drastic altera- tions in such a short period of time, has not been duplicated for any other major region of the world. The reason for the extremely rapid urban development is, of course, oil. Although petroleum was discovered in Iran at the beginning of the twentieth century and in a few other Persian Gulf nations in the 1930s, it is the developments since World War II, and specifically within the last two decades, which have provided the revenues for industrialization and concomitant city growth. Also, the four-fold increase in the price of oil in 1973 furnished the final impetus for runaway urban growth for many of these countries.

The following essay is a brief examination of the recent urbanization of the nations of the Persian Gulf. It looks at the rapid urbanization and the growth of cities within the last several decades and assesses the factors influencing this de- velopment. Problems engendered by the accelerating expansion of urban areas are brought out, stressing the issues of the urban housing situation. Attempts to direct and control urban growth focus on city planning, and the myriad problems that the planners encounter are emphasized.

The present essay, however, is only a preliminary analysis of the phenomenal urban growth in the Persian Gulf region. Statistics on city growth and urbaniza- tion are inadequate, inaccessible, or simply nonexistent. Few studies have focused on the city or related subjects for the region, hence there are many lacunae and problems in attempting to assess the process. This deficiency must be kept in mind when one examines the urbanization of the Persian Gulf.

Iran*

Urbanization and City Growth. Iran has a greater population than any na- tion of the Persian Gulf. The 1976 total of 33.6 million represents more inhabi- tants than all the other Gulf states combined.[1] In that year, one out of every three Iranians lived in a city larger than 50,000 persons, while almost half (46.7 percent) lived in an officially defined urban settlement of 5,000 inhabitants or larger. Most

* Editors' note: This material was written prior to the Iranian Revolution of January 1979.
    1. The discussion of population in Iran is derived from the three national population censuses held in 1956, 1966, and 1976. See Ministry of Interior, *National and Province Statistics of the First Census of Iran: November 1956*, vol. 1: *Number and Distribution of the Inhabitants for Iran and the Census Provinces* (August 1961); Plan Organization, Iranian Statistical Center, *National Census of Population and Housing, November 1966*, no. 168: *Total Country—Settled Population, March 1968*; *Iran Almanac and Book of Facts, 1977* (16th ed.; Tehran: Echo of Iran, 1977). (This latter source must be used for 1976 statistics, because the official publications of the census have yet to be published.)

of Iran's population and urban settlement are concentrated in the inland western and northern areas of the country. The four largest cities, Tehran, Isfahān, Mashhad, and Tabrīz, account for 41 percent of the official urbanites and 57.2 percent of persons in cities over 50,000 (Table 10–1). The official urban population has increased from 10.6 million in 1966 to 15.7 million in 1976, an annual growth rate of 4 percent. The number of urban places increased from 223 to 365 in this ten-year period. In contrast, the rural population grew at a rate of 0.82 percent, increasing only from 16.5 million to 17.9 million. Migration from rural areas to the towns and cities, and the fact that many rural settlements reached 5,000 persons and hence became "urban," account for the great difference between rural and urban growth rates.

Forty-two cities had at least 50,000 persons in 1976 (Table 10–1). These cities have been growing at an annual rate of 5.3 percent, which is almost double the 2.7 percent per annum rate of the country for 1966–76. Seven of these settlements are within the sphere of the Persian Gulf, located in Khūzistān and the newly named Hurmuzdgān provinces. Ahvāz and Ābādān are Iran's sixth and seventh largest cities, while the remaining cities are somewhat lower ranked (Table 10–1). These urban concentrations constitute 44.1 percent of Khūzistān's population and 31.7 percent of Hurmuzdgān's, indicating that the former province is considerably more urbanized than the country as a whole (33.5 percent) and is, in fact, one of the most urbanized provinces in Iran.

The growth of these Persian Gulf cities (Table 10–2) indicates interesting, contrasting patterns. Ābādān has the slowest annual growth rate (0.8 percent) of any of the forty-two major Iranian cities, and Masjid-i Sulaimān is the third lowest (1.8 percent). Būshahr and Bandar 'Abbās, on the other hand, are the fastest growing major cities in Iran. With annual growth rates of 9.3 percent and 9.9 percent respectively, only the burgeoning complex of Karaj within the sphere of Tehran's influence grew faster in 1966–76 (12.1 percent).

The great contrast between the growth of these cities represents the different stage of development in Khūzistān province compared to Hurmuzdgān. Urban development in the former was largely due to the expansion of the oil industry in the first half of the twentieth century, and the economies of Ābādān and Masjid-i Sulaimān have not become substantially diversified. Ahvāz and Khurramshahr have grown at about the national urban rate, although it is significant that even in these two cities the annual growth rate in the 1966–76 census period is less than their rates in the 1956–66 period.

The phenomenal growth of Būshahr and Bandar 'Abbās represents responses to the great expansion of the Iranian economy. Imports into Iran increased 500 percent from 1972–77,[2] and as much as three-fourths of the total has been coming through the southern ports of the Persian Gulf. Bandar Shāhpūr and Khurramshahr handle over half of all the imports, but Bandar 'Abbās and Būshahr are becoming more and more important as their port facilities expand. Bandar 'Abbās's port facilities will more than double with the construction of a new port complex 15 kilometers west of the existing one, and it should soon rival Bandar Shāhpūr as Iran's largest Persian Gulf commercial port, except that this port

2. *Iran Economic News* 3 (July 1977): 4.

TABLE 10–1. POPULATION OF MAJOR[a] CITIES IN IRAN, 1956–76

Rank[b] and city	1956	1966	1956–66 % annual growth	1976	1966–76 % annual growth
1. Tehran[c]	1,512,082	2,980,044	7.0	4,496,159	4.2
2. Isfahān	254,708	424,045	5.2	671,825	4.7
3. Mashhad	241,989	409,616	5.4	670,180	5.1
4. Tabrīz	289,996	403,413	3.4	598,576	3.9
5. Shīrāz	170,659	269,865	4.7	416,408	4.4
6. Ahvāz	120,098	206,375	5.6	329,006	4.8
7. Ābādān	226,083	272,962	1.9	296,081	0.8
8. Kirmānshāh	125,439	187,930	4.1	290,861	4.5
9. Qum	96,499	134,292	3.4	246,831	6.3
10. Rasht	109,491	143,557	2.7	187,203	2.7
11. Rezā'iya	67,605	110,749	5.1	163,991	4.0
12. Hamadān	99,909	124,167	2.2	155,846	2.3
13. Ardabīl	65,742	83,596	2.4	147,404	5.8
14. Khurramshahr	43,850	88,573	7.3	146,709	5.2
15. Kirmān	62,157	85,404	3.2	140,309	5.1
16. Karaj	14,526	44,243	11.8	138,774	12.1
17. Qazvīn	66,420	88,106	2.9	138,527	4.6
18. Yazd	63,502	93,241	3.9	135,978	3.8
19. Arāk	48,998	71,925	2.0	114,507	4.7
20. Dizfūl	52,121	84,499	5.0	110,287	2.7
21. Khurramābād	38,676	59,578	4.4	104,928	5.8
22. Burūjird	49,186	71,486	3.8	100,103	3.4
23. Zanjān	47,159	58,714	2.2	99,967	5.5
24. Sanandaj	40,641	54,578	3.0	98,834	5.8
25. Zāhidān	17,495	39,732	8.5	92,628	8.9
26. Bandar 'Abbās	17,710	34,627	6.9	89,103	9.9
27. Gurgān	23,380	51,181	6.1	88,348	5.6
28. Kāshān	45,955	58,468	2.4	84,545	3.8
29. Masjid-i Sulaimān	44,651	64,488	3.7	77,161	1.8
30. Najafābād	30,422	43,384	3.6	76,236	5.8
31. Sārī	26,278	44,547	5.4	70,936	4.8
32. Khoy	34,491	47,648	3.3	70,040	3.9
33. Sabzavār	30,545	42,415	3.3	69,174	5.1
34. Āmul	22,251	40,076	6.1	68,782	5.6
35. Bābul	36,194	49,973	3.3	67,790	3.1
36. Shāhī	23,055	38,898	5.4	63,289	5.0
37. Marāgha	36,551	54,106	4.0	60,820	1.2
38. Gunbad-i Qābūs	18,347	40,667	8.1	59,868	3.9
39. Nīshāpūr	25,820	33,482	2.6	59,101	5.9
40. Būshahr	18,412	23,547	2.5	57,681	9.3
41. Bandar Pahlavī	31,349	41,785	2.9	55,978	3.0
42. Kāzarūn	30,641	39,758	2.6	51,309	2.6
Total	4,436,083	7,339,740	5.2	11,262,383	4.4
Total 50,000+	3,683,498	6,738,258	6.2	11,262,383	5.3
Total Urban (5,000+)	5,449,161	9,794,246	6.0	15,715,338	4.8
Total Iran	18,954,704	25,788,722	3.1	33,591,875	2.7

[a] Cities over 50,000 population in 1976.
[b] Rank based on population in 1976.
[c] 1956 and 1966 figures for Tehran include Tajrīsh and Shahr-i Ray for comparability with 1976.
Source: Iranian Census of Population for 1956, 1966, and 1976; the latter in *Iran Almanac, 1977.*

is being greatly expanded as well.[3] The tonnage through Būshahr has increased fifteen-fold in a decade, and the capacity of the port is expected to increase 50 percent during the Sixth Development Plan (1978–83).[4]

Considerable construction and industrialization are occurring in these two port cities. Two nuclear power plants are being built at Būshahr, and these will power Iran's first two desalination plants, which will have a combined daily capacity of 200,000 cubic meters of potable water. Bandar 'Abbās is one of the nine development poles designated for industrializing the country (and to counter the excessive growth and industrial concentration around Tehran). A steel-rolling mill is to be completed by 1982, and a major power station is being constructed that will help supply the Sarchashma copper complex near Kirmān. A 460-kilometer, double-track, electrified railroad from the port to Kirmān also is to be built during the Sixth Plan, and the railroad will provide an export outlet for the Sarchashma copper.[5] Bandar 'Abbās is emerging as a major tourist center, and recently the former Italian luxury liner "Raffaello" was brought to the city to serve as a floating hotel. The development of tourism is, in fact, becoming important for many of Iran's cities, especially for such cultural centers as Isfahān and Shīrāz. The latter city also is important as a summer residence for Arabs from the Gulf; approximately 30,000 Arabs spend an average of 2½ months per year here.[6]

Ahvāz also is one of the industrial development poles and steel mills, pipe

3. Ibid., 3 (November 1977): 5; *Iran Almanac*, pp. 290–91; *Middle East Economic Digest*, Special Report on Iran (February 1977): 21.
4. *Iran Economic News* 3 (June 1977): 3.
5. Ibid. 3 (May 1977): 4.
6. Eckart Ehlers, "Some geographic and socio-economic aspects of tourism in Iran," *Orient* 15 (September 1974): 101.

TABLE 10–2. MAJOR[a] IRANIAN PERSIAN GULF CITIES, 1956–76

	1956	1966	1956–66 % annual growth	1976	1966–76 % annual growth
Khūzistān Province					
Ābādān	226,083	272,962	1.9	296,081	0.8
Ahvāz	120,098	206,375	5.6	329,006	4.8
Khurramshahr	43,850	88,573	7.3	146,709	5.2
Dizfūl	52,121	84,499	5.0	110,287	2.7
Masjid-i Sulaimān	44,651	64,488	3.7	77,161	1.8
Total	486,803	716,897	4.7	959,244	3.1
Hurmuzdgān Province[b]					
Bandar 'Abbās	17,710	34,627	6.9	89,103	9.9
Būshahr	18,412	23,547	2.5	57,681	9.3
Total	36,122	58,174	4.7	146,784	9.6
Grand total	522,925	775,071	4.0	1,106,023	3.6

[a] Cities over 50,000 population in 1976.
[b] Formerly the ports and islands of the Persian Gulf and the Gulf of Oman Province (also known as the Coastal Province).
Source: Iranian Census of Population for 1956, 1966, and 1976; the latter in *Iran Almanac, 1977.*

plants, nuclear power plants, thermal power plants, and many other industrial projects that have been recently completed or will be constructed in the near future. Because of its previous development, size, and greater diversification the city has not been affected in terms of statistical growth rates as greatly as Būshahr or Bandar 'Abbās. Such development has kept Ahvāz growing at about the same rate as most of Iran's larger cities and has prevented the stagnation that has affected some of the Khūzistān cities.

The remaining cities for which industrial development is to be concentrated are Isfahān, Mashhad, Tabrīz, Shīrāz, Kirmānshāh, Qazvīn, and Arāk. These include the largest cities of Iran outside Tehran and help explain why they continue to expand rapidly. Many of the smaller major cities are expanding at very fast rates (Table 10-1), partly due to the smaller absolute numbers, and, therefore, modest additions cause relatively great rates—which is the case for Būshahr and Bandar 'Abbās. This is exemplified even more by the great increase in the number of small urban places (less than 50,000 but more than 5,000 persons). These towns increased from 196 in 1966 to 323 in 1976 and were increasing at a remarkable 9.9 percent growth rate during 1966–76. Yet, the absolute numerical increase is only 1,393,627 persons, compared to the 4,980,420 increment for the major cities. Tehran by itself increased by more persons than the total growth of the small cities.

The capital of Tehran dominates the country demographically and economically, and in 1976 this primate city of 4.5 million persons comprised over a quarter of the official urban population and 39.9 percent of the inhabitants in cities over 50,000. In fact, almost one out of every seven Iranians lives in Tehran, amounting to 13.4 percent of the nation's 33.6 million persons. The Tehran region's economic importance can be realized by the fact that approximately 30 percent of Iran's labor force in industry and services, one-third of all productive investments, and 60 percent of value-added for industry, are found in Central (Markazī) Province.[7] In the first six months of the Iranian year 2535* (1976/77), the Iranian private sector invested about $1.7 billion in construction activities in urban areas. Tehran accounted for 46.5 percent of the total investment.[8]

The changing cities of Iran are accelerating the differences between the urban and rural areas. The new appliances, modern houses, and automobiles are urban phenomena, and the great consumption and changing urban life style become more and more distant from the peasantry. The widening urban-rural income distribution gap was estimated to be 1:5 or 1:6 in 1972 and has tripled within the last decade, as agriculture stagnates. In urban areas, there has been at least a six-fold rise in per capita income within the last decade, whereas the income levels in rural areas probably have not doubled.[9] The low and inadequate prices for agricultural commodities, the rampant inflation for other goods, and

---

7. Bernard Hourcade, "Teheran: Evolution récente d'une métropole," *Méditerranée* 1 (1974): 25.

* During 1978, due to the political protests, the calendar reverted to the Iranian solar calendar, i.e., 2535 = 1355.

8. *Iran Economic News* 3 (February 1977): 6.

9. *Middle East Economic Digest*, Special Report on Iran (February 1977): 8, 17; James A. Bill, "Iran: Is the Shah Pushing it Too Fast?" *Christian Science Monitor* (November 9, 1977): 17.

the financial opportunities of the city leave few incentives to stay in the countryside, especially for the younger, economically active population.

The rural exodus has created an additional burden on the cities, for these migrants seldom have the needed skills for which there have been chronic labor shortages. In 1977, the labor shortage was estimated to be 600,000 skilled workers, although such shortages may be overestimated.[10] The most critical shortages have been in the construction trades due to the extensive building activities. Because of these shortages, the average wage rise was 48 percent in 1975–76 for construction workers. No large numbers of foreign workers have been brought in to fill the gap. In 1978, only about 55,000 long-term foreign employees and 15,000–20,000 temporary ones were in Iran.[11]

Urban Planning and Housing. Municipalities in Iran derive their legal and administrative structure from a law enacted in 1949, and during the first two development plans the emphasis was to provide Iran's major cities with the most basic facilities and infrastructure: electricity, piped water, and paved streets.[12] Most major cities earlier had had a few major streets driven through the compact clusters of houses by Riza Shah, the legal basis being a "Street Widening Act of 1933." Contrary to the wide belief that these streets were indiscriminately superimposed upon the old pattern of streets and alleyways, the grid pattern usually was aligned in conjunction and in the same direction as the major traditional streets, which also were basically in a grid system.[13] Roundabouts (traffic circles) and squares were also built at this time, as well as numerous governmental buildings.

Master plans of Iranian cities were not begun until the Third Development Plan (1962–68). A High Council for City Planning was established to oversee the preparation and to give final approval of the master plans. Seventeen cities had plans prepared by consulting firms. During the Fourth Development Plan (1968–73), more master plans were prepared and a few specific projects of the existing plans were completed. However, during this period the majority of the town plans ran into problems. The machinery and authority to implement the plans did not exist. This inability to execute the designed frameworks caused the discontinuation of making new master plans, even though forty-six more municipalities had applied for these plans to the High Council for City Planning.

The failure of these first master plans resulted from a number of factors. The plans were made by consulting firms to please the High Council of Town Planning, and so the individual requirements and actual needs of each city were

10. *Middle East Economic Digest,* Special Report on Iran (February 1977): 5; Walter Elkan, "Employment, education, training and skilled labor in Iran," *Middle East Journal* 31 (Spring 1977): 175–87.

11. *Middle East Economic Digest,* Special Report on Iran (February 1977): 5. Foreign workers include a substantial number of technicians. Filipino doctors and nurses, Indian and Pakistani doctors, and South Koreans are some of the more recent foreign arrivals.

12. Manootchehr Mozayeni, "City planning in Iran: Evolution and problems," *Ekistics* 38 (October 1974): 264–67. Much of the discussion of the planning through the Fourth Development Plan comes from this article.

13. Michael E. Bonine, "The morphogenesis of Iranian cities," *Annals of the Association of American Geographers* 69 (June 1979): 208–24.

ignored. The regional context, the wider framework in which to properly understand the role and growth of the city, had been disregarded. For instance, for
many of the cities in the arid central plateau the availability of water is a most
acute problem for future growth. Yet, the proper assessment of water resources,
and the effect and rate of decline of the water table had not been considered. The
imposition of the master plans from the central government caused mistrust and
a lack of cooperation by the local urbanites, including the town councils. This
lack of proper communication from Tehran meant that a plan was viewed as
something to be put on the shelf, and was not considered a program to influence
the process of urban development. In any case, most cities did not have the
financial structure or the technical staff to implement the plans. Rivalries between
various governmental agencies for approving projects, providing funds, supervising expenditures, and implementing projects impeded any proper urban
planning.

Recognition of many of these problems led to some attempts at corrective
measures during the Fifth Development Plan (1973–78). Studies were instituted to
provide the proper regional setting and more qualified town planners and
technical staff were trained. However, many problems remain. The municipalities do not have the financial structure to take care of the actual problems that
have beset their expanding cities, hence few funds are available for planning. The
most critical problem remains the lack of local authority to coordinate and implement planning activities. The centralization of decision-making leaves the cities
without sufficient ability to control the activities of the myriad agencies and
governmental offices which receive their directives from Tehran. This hinders
cooperation with the planners, and often basic statistics and data which are collected by one agency are not made available to the municipality. On the other
hand, the great land speculation since 1973 shows that any master plan, with its
restricted land use and boundaries, is an instrument that can be easily abused
by individuals for their personal gain. This certainly is a problem even in the
West, but somewhat effective controls and checks on developers exist in the
West that have yet to evolve in Iranian cities. Urban planning and directed
growth and development of cities will continue to be a major problem for Iran
as it emerges into a modern industrial state.

The expansion of the Iranian economy has largely affected the cities. The
influx of rural and some foreign migrants, and the increased purchasing power
of the urbanites, has created a great consumer demand for goods and services. One
of the primary demands that has been created is housing. This is not only because
of the burgeoning urban population but also due to the desire of the traditional
urbanites to obtain better and new housing. The older mud-brick structures are
not perceived as conducive to a modern life style with its electrical appliances,
lights, piped water, and garages for automobiles. These forces have created such
a demand for housing that chronic shortages exist, and the cost of housing has
been the primary ingredient of the rampant inflation.

During 1976–77, the average price of housing in urban areas increased 33.9
percent, the principal component of the 16.6 percent price increase in urban consumer goods and services. Shortages of building materials, especially cement and
bricks, a scarcity of manpower, and a 39.4 percent rise in construction wages,

contributed to a 46.7 percent increase in housing costs.[14] These fantastic inflationary rates of housing costs began to drop slightly from the fall of 1977,[15] although the rise in costs is still a major problem for the inhabitants of Iran's cities.

Land prices and speculation have been one of the major components of the rise in the cost of housing in Iran. In the 1970s, and especially after 1973, urban land prices rose so swiftly that prices could be quoted only daily. In some instances, land was bought and sold the same day—at a considerable profit. Land in south Tehran was selling for $600 a square meter, while in the northern, prestigious part of the city it was much higher, sometimes over $4,000 a square meter. Lots for average-sized houses cost several hundred thousand dollars in the north of Tehran. All the major cities were affected similarly: land increased in value 1,000 percent in Tabrīz from 1971 to 1974; 700 percent in Shīrāz in three years; 800 percent in Kirmān in five years; 1,000 percent in residential areas and 2,000 percent in commercial areas of Rasht in five years, and so forth. In the latter city, some land increased 100 to 200 times from 1969 to 1974.[16] The difference between the provincial cities and Tehran is only one of scale; good houses cost hundreds of thousands of dollars in the provinces, millions in the capital. Rents have been correspondingly affected by the rising cost of housing. An older two-bedroom or even one-bedroom apartment in central Tehran rents for at least $500 per month; newer apartments and homes in north Tehran (if available) may rent for several thousand dollars per month.

Despite the fact that the average Iranian urbanite is being priced out of the housing market by these costs, the demand for housing still far exceeds the supply. A 1973 survey indicated a shortage of 1,134,000 housing units in urban areas and an occupancy level of 1.8 families per housing unit—over eight persons per unit. The Ministry of Housing and Urban Development has estimated that if one housing unit for each Iranian family is to be achieved by 1993, at least 7.8 million new housing units (in both urban and rural areas) will have to be constructed in the twenty-year period beginning in 1973.[17] The goal during the Fifth Plan (1973–78) was to construct about one million new housing units, about four-fifths of these in the urban areas. A similar number of units has been proposed for the Sixth Plan (1978–83).

Attempts to relieve the pressing housing shortage includes encouraging the construction of medium and low-priced housing by the private sector, which generally avoids these less profitable projects. Unfortunately, the government has not invested heavily in low-priced housing for the lower classes, but has concentrated on housing for office and industrial workers where specific projects are being built. For instance, in the 1977–78 budget of $1.28 billion for government housing construction, 65 percent is for office-worker housing and 23 percent for industrial-worker housing.[18] Standardizing and mechanizing house construction

14. *Iran Economic News* 3 (July 1977): 1.
15. Ibid., 4 (January 1978): 1.
16. *Iran Almanac*, pp. 246–47.
17. Ibid., p. 249; Ministry of Housing and Urban Development, Imperial Government of Iran, *Twenty Year Housing Program*, n.d.
18. *Iran Almanac*, p. 250.

has led to the establishment of a dozen prefabricated housing plants throughout the country and more in the planning stage.[19]

Several other hindrances continue to plague the Iranian building industry. Red tape in obtaining the proper building permits, especially in Tehran, is usually measured in months, and in some cases even in years. Construction materials still are insufficient in number, hence cement, plaster, bricks, and steel often have to be bought on the black market at three or four times the official rate. Some materials cannot be obtained in sufficient quantities anywhere, and this causes long delays in construction. Laborers are insufficient in number and certainly in skill. Many of the rural migrants have had no training in the type of construction or use of the materials being used in these urban structures. Shoddy workmanship is the norm.

One of the most pressing problems for the housing industry, especially in regard to the lower priced housing, is the extremely inadequate financial structure for house purchases. Unlike the generous loan conditions available for the citizens on the Arab side of the Gulf (see below), the ordinary Iranian finds it most difficult to get a bank loan for building or purchasing a house. High rates, enormous security as collateral, short-term repayment schedules, and even duplicity by the banks inhibit the granting of loans for housing. A mortgage requiring a monthly payment of several thousand dollars is not uncommon.[20] Lower-income residents in cheaper apartments in Tehran in the early 1970s often were paying half of the household head's income for rent or loan payments. Hence, several families and wage earners may occupy such a house, one or more families renting from the household head, or (if close relatives) all wage earners contributing to the funds for the loan payment or rent.[21]

The housing shortages and high costs should be most conducive to the development of squatter settlements. However, extensive shanty towns have not formed and are not a major problem in Iran. An equivalent of the hundreds of thousands of *gecekondu* settlements in Turkey or the *bidonville* agglomerations in Morocco has not developed in this country.[22] Even in Tehran it was estimated in 1972 that there were only 4,000 squatter families, and these were living mostly in single-room houses of either brick or secondhand materials,[23] shelter conditions that are perhaps somewhat better than those of the inhabitants of many squatter settlements elsewhere in the developing world.[24] Shanty towns are generally absent from the other major Iranian cities, except for Shīrāz, where many nomads have recently settled around the outskirts of the city. Illegal squatter houses also exist

19. *Iran Economic News* 3 (April 1977): 6.
20. *Iran Almanac*, p. 248.
21. Ministry of Housing and Urban Development, Imperial Government of Iran, *A Survey of Residents in Naziabad Apartments (First Series)*, 1350 (1971/72); *Survey of Residents in Naziabad (Second Series)*, 1353 (1974/75).
22. For example, see Kemal H. Karpat, *The 'Gecekondu': Rural Migration and Urbanization* (Cambridge: Cambridge University Press, 1976).
23. Ministry of Housing and Urban Development, Imperial Government of Iran, *Survey of Squatter Settlements in Tehran*, 1351 (1972/73).
24. For example, see United Nations, Department of Economic and Social Affairs, *Improvement of Slums and Uncontrolled Settlements* (New York: United Nations, 1971).

to the north of Karaj on the hills of Murād Āb, and this is part of the extreme growth of Karaj as a residential suburb for Tehran.[25]

Some housing projects have been built to relocate and house squatters in Tehran, such as the project of Nuhum-i Ābān located near the railroad station in south Tehran. Completed in 1970, this housing scheme has 3,750 units with its own post office, police station, clinic, park, shops, schools, and social-work centers. The original design of the two-room units was poorly suited to the needs of the inhabitants or the extremes of the climate, and so the occupants altered the housing considerably. The project generally was a failure, either because over 2,000 units were sold at a considerable profit by the original squatter owners within the first five years to soldiers and lower-income government employees, or else because they rented out their house or rooms to lodgers. Nuhum-i Ābān was a failure in the eyes of the government because it provided the squatters with too high quality housing and too valuable an asset relative to the rest of their possessions and earning capacity.[26]

Iran's "shanty towns" are the decaying residences of the old quarters of the cities. The desire to obtain new housing and now the widespread means to buy this housing, in spite of the great costs, have enabled many inhabitants of old districts to move to the new suburbs. Permanent migration from the major cities to Tehran also has vacated much of the housing in the older parts of these provincial settlements. Some of these mud-brick houses stay empty and become dilapidated, although the majority are inhabited by either rural or small-town migrants, or lower classes moving from more dilapidated quarters within the city. This process has been going on for several decades because of the constant migration to the national capital. Ethnic or religious quarters especially have been affected because a greater percentage of these groups have moved to Tehran or have emigrated to other countries. As exemplified by the Jewish and Zoroastrian neighborhoods of Kirmān and Yazd, poor Muslims take the place of these minorities and the spatial cohesion of the minority community no longer exists.[27]

Deterioration of the traditional quarters is inevitable. Although this housing is most practical for the climate and the traditional Iranian style of life, it is incompatible with rapid modernization. The government views these neighborhoods as impediments to a modern industrial society. If a new wide avenue is deemed necessary, the appropriate sections of the old neighborhoods are destroyed without considering the wishes or alternative housing needs of the inhabitants. Modernizing the cities often has aggravated the shortage of housing.

In the largest cities, and especially in Tehran, large apartment complexes have been built, and many of these new residential areas are for wealthier groups. Housing projects often have occupants from one single profession, such as em-

25. H. Bahrambeygui, "The Urban Problems of Karaj," in Günther Schweizer, ed., *Beiträge zur Kulturgeographie Irans, Beihefte zum Tübinger Atlas des Vorderen Orients, Reihe B. (Geistewissenschaften)* (Wiesbaden: Dr. Ludwig Reichert, forthcoming).

26. Ministry of Housing and Urban Development, Imperial Government of Iran, *Study of Nine Residential Districts in Tehran*, n.d.

27. For example, see Paul Ward English, "Culture Change and the Structure of a Persian City," in Carl Leiden, ed., *The Conflict of Traditionalism and Modernism in the Muslim Middle East* (Austin: The Humanities Research Center, The University of Texas at Austin, 1966), pp. 32–48.

ployees of a specific ministry, teachers, or doctors. Lower-income groups tend to be segregated in low-density, semitraditional housing located on the outskirts of the cities.

A number of housing developments and even entire towns have resulted from the government's attempt to relieve the population pressure on the Tehran region. Tax incentives are offered to locate industry away from the capital, for new industries have to pay much higher taxes within a 120 kilometer radius of Tehran[28]—although this incentive has not been very effective. Large industrial zones are being developed in the provinces by the Industrial Development and Renovation Organization, offering complete infrastructure facilities, including both the industrial complex and the housing. One $1.2 billion project is planned for Khurāsān and will create 15,000 jobs; a $3 billion project, the Shahrizā site near Isfahan, is expected to provide housing for 150,000 persons; and the huge petrochemical complex at Bandar Shāhpūr includes a $17 million housing project for employees in nearby Bandar Māhshahr.[29] Similar in concept is the completely planned city of Āryāshahr, built to house the employees and families of the new Āryāmehr Steel Plant southwest of Isfahan. Over 10,000 persons already live in the city, and it is presently being rapidly expanded for a future population of several hundred thousand persons.

Within the last few years there has been some reaction against the homogeneous professional or employee developments within cities and, accordingly, many of the new housing projects are designed to include a mixture of building types and different socioeconomic and income groups. The new towns of Lavizan and Kan in eastern Tehran represent this policy.[30]

The most ambitious Iranian urban project is the Shāhistān Pahlavī, a development aimed at providing Tehran with a planned prestigious city center. Located on 222 undeveloped hectares in north-central Tehran (north of 'Abbāsābād), the project will include residential areas, commercial offices, shopping centers, government ministries, hotels, and parks, all built around the Shah-and-Nation Square, an area as large as Moscow's Red Square. A resident population of 36,000 is planned, and a massive cultural complex, the National Cultural Center, will have museums, theaters, headquarters of the Pahlavi National Library, and many other cultural amenities. An estimated 200,000 employees and civil servants will commute daily to the center, and to help alleviate the movement there will be the planned underground metro that will run from south Tehran. Many of the government and commercial offices, as well as some of the housing projects, are to be completed by 1980; the public buildings are not planned to be finished for about twelve years and some of the private sector development may take up to twenty years for completion.[31] Although the gigantic model community will serve as a national symbol, this planned center will not unify Tehran around one commercial focus, but may only intensify the bipolar

28. Ann T. Schulz, "Iran's new industrial state," *Current History* 72 (January 1977): 16.
29. *Iran Economic News* 3 (March 1977): 3.
30. For example, see Abdol Aziz Farmanfarmaian and Associates, *The New City of Lavizan, Preliminary Plan*, prepared for the Ministry of Housing and Urban Development, n.d.
31. *Middle East Economic Digest*, Special Report on Iran (February 1977): 26–27; *Profile on Iran* (November 1975): 7–10.

development of the capital, the traditional sector around the bazaar and the newer, modern city to the north.[32]

Iraq

Urbanization and City Growth. The October 1977 Iraqi census enumerated 12.17 million inhabitants,[33] which represents an average annual increase of 3.5 percent since the previous census of 1965. However, due to the unavailability of details from this latest census, earlier population estimates and the 1965 census have to be relied upon for a discussion of the cities of Iraq.[34]

Similar to the position of Tehran in Iran, the capital of Baghdad is a primate city that dominates the country. In 1975, about one-fourth of all Iraqis lived in the capital, and the total for Baghdad has been increasing steadily over the decades: 10.7 percent of total population in 1947; 16.7 percent in 1957; and 21.7 percent in 1965. In this latter year, Baghdad contained 35 percent of Iraq's industries, which included some of the largest and most efficient enterprises.[35] The percent annual growth of Baghdad, however, has been decreasing (Table 10–3), which is not surprising considering the increasing size of the city. The primacy of the city in relation to the next largest cities also has been decreasing within the last decade, because of the phenomenal growth of Mosul and Basra. Whereas Baghdad had been four to five times larger than the second ranked city earlier, by the 1970s it was only about three times larger than either of these two cities (Table 10–3). Since 1965, Mosul has been growing at an annual rate of 15.0 percent and Basra at 11.8 percent, rather remarkable rates for these large cities, which now have over one million persons each. In 1975, over two-fifths of the country's inhabitants lived in one of these three largest cities, and if these metropolises continue to grow at similar rates, half of Iraq's population will soon be contained in the three settlements.

Iraq was officially predominantly an urban country even in 1965, for 51.3 percent of the population were classified as urban according to the official definition of urban as 5,000 persons or more (including a few smaller settlements that were designated urban for administrative purposes). Yet, besides the three metropolises previously mentioned, only two other cities, Kirkuk and Najaf, had over 100,000 persons, while seven cities were between 50,000–10,000 (Table 10–3). Iraq does have a great number of smaller towns; in 1965, there were 29 settlements between 10,000–50,000. In that year, 32.3 percent of Iraqis lived in a city over 100,000; 38.9 percent in a settlement over 50,000; and 46.3 percent in one larger than 10,000.

32. Martin Seger, "Strukturelemente der Stadt Teheran und das Modell der modernen orientalischen Stadt," *Erdkunde* 29 (March 1975): 21–38.

33. Economist Intelligence Unit, *Quarterly Economic Review of Iraq* (4th Quarter 1977): 7.

34. Much of the discussion of Iraqi cities in 1965 relies upon the excellent article, R. I. Lawless, "Iraq: Changing Population Patterns," in J. I. Clarke and W. B. Fisher, eds., *Populations of the Middle East and North Africa: A Geographical Approach* (New York: Africana Publishing Corporation, 1972), pp. 97–129.

35. United Nations, Department of Economic and Social Affairs, *Urban Land Policies and Land-Use Control Measures*, vol. 5: *Middle East* (New York: United Nations, 1973), p. 12.

Estimates in 1975 of the urban population were 7.08 million (63.7 percent), and of the rural population 4.04 million (36.3 percent).[36] The country's growth per annum has been 3.5 percent; but the urban population has increased at an annual rate of 5.5 percent and the rural sector at a rate of only 0.25 percent. Of course, it must be remembered that the lack of growth of the rural population not only represents migration to the cities but also the attainment of urban status (5,000 persons) by many rural settlements—which is part of the process of urbanization by whatever definition.

The growth of Iraq's cities can be attributed to the same factors that are affecting most of the developing nations, including industrialization, employment opportunities, greater life spans, lower infant death rates, and rural-urban migration. The latter factor, however, is especially important in the case of Iraq. Before the 1958 revolution, an oppressive land tenure system had been worsening

36. Republic of Iraq, *Annual Abstract of Statistics, 1975.*

TABLE 10-3. POPULATION OF MAJOR[a] CITIES IN IRAQ, 1947–76

Rank[b] and city	1947	1957	1947–57 % annual growth	1965	1957–65 % annual growth	1976 est.[c]
1. Baghdad	515,411	1,056,604	7.4	1,745,000	6.5	3,100,000
2. Basra	101,535	164,623	5.0	313,327	8.4	1,070,000
3. Mosul	133,625	179,646	3.0	243,311	3.9	1,130,000
4. Kirkuk	68,308	120,593	5.8	167,413	4.2	263,000
5. Najaf	56,261	88,809	4.7	128,096	4.7	212,000
6. Arbil	27,036	34,751	2.5	90,320	12.7	175,000
7. Sulaimāniyya	33,510	48,450	3.8	86,822	7.6	194,000
8. Hilla	36,577	54,095	4.0	84,717	5.8	158,000
9. Karbala	44,150	60,804	3.3	83,301	4.0	128,000
10. Amāra	36,907	53,311	3.7	64,847	2.5	85,000
11. Dīwāniyya	19,878	33,204	5.3	60,553	7.8	139,000
12. Nāsiriyya	24,038	39,060	5.0	60,405	5.6	110,000
13. Kut	16,237	26,524	5.0	42,116	6.0	80,000
14. Zubair	17,884	28,699	4.8	41,408	4.7	69,000
15. Falluja	10,981	20,009	6.2	38,072	8.4	92,000
16. Tel Afar	19,951	25,543	2.5	36,837	4.7	61,000
17. Ba'qūbā	10,511	18,527	5.8	34,575	8.1	81,000
18. Kufa	13,700	21,880	4.8	30,862	4.4	50,000
19. Ramādī	n.a.[d]	17,747	—	28,723	6.2	56,000
Total	1,186,500	2,093,099	5.8	3,380,705	6.2	7,253,000
Total 50,000+	875,140	1,778,485	—	3,128,112	—	7,253,000
Total Iraq	4,816,000	6,298,000	2.7	8,220,000	3.4	11,750,000

[a] Cities over 50,000 population in 1976 (estimated).
[b] Rank based on population in 1965.
[c] Estimated from 1965 population using the 57–65 percent annual growth rate projected to 1976, except for Baghdad, Basra, and Mosul, whose 1976 estimate is based upon official 1974 estimates and projections from the 65–74 percent annual growth rate and Arbil whose rate is based upon the 57–65 average of 6.2 due to an unrealistic total using 12.7 percent.
[d] n.a. = not available (less than 10,000 population).
Source: Iraqi Census of Population for 1947, 1957, and 1965, in R. I. Lawless, "Iraq: Changing Population Patterns," in J. I. Clarke and W. B. Fisher, eds., *Populations of the Middle East and North Africa* (1972); *The Middle East and North Africa, 1975–76.*

since a 1932 law enabled tribal shaikhs to register the land in their own name. The extremely depressed condition of the peasants, especially in the south, as well as floods and droughts, prompted many to leave the land and attempt to eke out a better existence in the cities. Although land reform gave the land to the peasants in 1958, there were considerable delays, uncertainties, and general confusion. Rival parties, such as the Baathists and Communists, made promises of employment, public housing, cars, and other urban amenities—which, of course, could not be met, but did further induce the flight from the countryside.[37]

Baghdad has been the recipient of most of the migrants over the decades, although other cities, and particularly Basra for the southern migrants, have become more frequently an alternative. The southern provinces of Dīwāniyya, Nāsiriyya, Basra, and particularly Amāra have had a very high rate of migration, and these provinces had an absolute decline in rural population from 1957 to 1965. The flight from these provinces became so great after 1958 that the government took measures, largely ineffectual, to attempt to prevent their depopulation.

The rapid growth of Iraq's cities within the last decade has largely been due to industrialization and the multifaceted ramifications and multiplier effects of this process. The Kurdish conflict in the north has resulted in some depopulation of the countryside, and this migration has contributed to the rapid growth of some northern cities, such as Mosul. Yet, the southern part of the country has been the focus for much of the industrial investment. This region has been receiving half of the industrial development by value (the other half being divided about equally between the north and the central or Baghdad area).[38] Basra and nearby Zubair have been the recipients of most of these new developments. In Basra, several projects are being built, such as a $1 billion petrochemical complex, power stations, more jetties, more oil refineries, a urea plant, a lube oil plant, a paper mill, expansion of Basra University, and major hotels (e.g., the Basra Sheraton). Twenty kilometers to the southwest at Zubair, the major iron and steel complex is being completed as well as an export refinery, petrochemical complex, power stations, more jetties, more oil refineries, a urea plant, a lube doubled from the original forecast, largely due to growth of industry in the Basra area and the rapid expansion of urban areas.[39] The great labor supply needed for the already existing completed industrial projects, as well as the employees involved in construction and in accompanying services, creates the great attraction of the Basra area for migrants and has been responsible for the phenomenal growth of the city.

Urban Planning and Housing. Urban planning in Iraq was confined largely to Baghdad before the oil revenues of post-World War II enabled plans to be applied to other cities as well. Hence, a glance at the development of the capital represents the major planning efforts in the twentieth century.[40]

37. Fuad Baali, "Agrarian reform in Iraq: Some socio-economic aspects," *American Journal of Economics and Sociology* 28 (1969): 61–76.

38. Economist Intelligence Unit, *Quarterly Economic Review of Iraq* (3rd Quarter 1977): 7.

39. Ibid., p. 14.

40. Much of the discussion of planning in Baghdad comes from John Gulick, "Baghdad: Portrait of a city in physical and cultural change," *Journal of the American Institute of Planners* 33 (July 1967): 246–55; William C. Fox, "Baghdad: A city in transition," *East Lakes Geographer* 5 (December 1969): 5–23.

Major changes had begun in Baghdad shortly before World War I, when German military advisors stressed the need for wider streets in the city to facilitate the movement of artillery. During World War I, a number of streets were cut through the compact Old City (Rusāfa). Following the war, the British colonial administration continued street construction, as well as introducing such amenities as a piped water supply, street lights, and sanitation measures. They provided a new flood protection measure (the Eastern Bund), and the city could now expand in areas previously frequently under water.

The British also introduced a new type of residential unit, a detached house without any inner courtyard and with windows (barred) on the ground floor, looking out on the street. New residential areas were constructed around rigid gridiron street patterns. One area, south of the *madīna*, was at first inhabited mainly by the British and other Westerners, but soon wealthy native Christians and Jews began to move out of the Old City to these new residences. Well-to-do Sunnī Muslims moved to new residences north of the Old City, where the King had built a compound, and many high government officials also had moved to this district (Wazīriya).

In the 1930s, more wide streets were cut through the Old City and built in outer areas, continuing the suburbanization of Baghdad. In such areas, the inner courtyard often was given up and replaced by a two-story detached house with a surrounding walled garden to maintain the household's privacy. These detached houses took four times as much land as the traditional structures.

In the 1950s, the availability of oil revenues enabled numerous urban projects to be implemented or at least planned. Street paving, better street lighting, sewage systems, and industrial areas were initiated not only for Baghdad, but in many of Iraq's other major cities. The most important project for Baghdad, however, was the completion in 1956 of the Wadi Tharthar flood-diversion project, which included a large barrage on the Tigris at Sāmarrā, 110 kilometers north of Baghdad. Since this provided complete flood protection for the city, the bunds became obsolete and were ignored and even knocked down as the city could now expand beyond these protective dikes. Many of the squatters had been living in these areas, which had been periodically flooding, and so the diversion project enabled their shanty towns to take on more permanence.

Baghdad's first master plan was put into effect in 1956. It covered 500 square kilometers and conceived the capital as developing in a semicircular pattern. However, there were no specific details for implementing the plan, and the great extension of the municipal region produced a wave of land speculation that raised the cost of housing for the middle and lower classes.[41]

Another plan, prepared by the Greek firm of Doxiadis Associates in 1958, envisaged a city of three million focused on four major commercial-industrial zones, each surrounded by residential communities. Although some low-cost housing was eventually built in western Baghdad based upon this plan, the 1958 revolution generally thwarted any attempts to implement the new design. Hence, the 1956 plan has remained the official plan, but without specific guidelines or

41. United Nations, Economic and Social Office in Beirut, *Studies on Social Development in the Middle East, 1971* (New York: United Nations, 1973), p. 50.

stages of development the capital has continued to grow haphazardly. The government did confiscate much of the periphery city land after 1958, which ended some of the land speculation.[42]

Although there has been less reliance on outside consultants since 1958, in 1967 a Polish city planning firm drafted a 25-year master plan for Baghdad that included high-rise apartments, heterogeneous neighborhoods of professional and working people, monorail systems, and freeways—all seeming to be an imposition of Western values and showing a lack of understanding of Baghdad's environment or the cultural values of typical Islamic Middle Easterners.[43] Fortunately, the plan was never implemented due to disagreements over the costs of carrying out the various projects.[44]

The other major cities of Iraq also have had master plans, a total of thirteen plans having been completed as of 1971. Their implementation and positive effectiveness however is uncertain. As with Baghdad, the great expansion of the municipality boundaries was wider than necessary. Although this was intended to increase revenues, the opposite occurred due to overextension of the municipalities and the inclusion of many villages, which put an extra burden on the budget. Land speculation became more prevalent and the government has had to confiscate much of the surrounding land, as in Baghdad.[45]

After a visit to Baghdad and Basra in 1967, the Arab city planner, Saba George Shiber, lamented the destruction and the lack of proper planning in these cities. He condemned the "chop-up" approach and reliance upon bulldozers as one of the main instruments of the planners. He notes (in 1967) that "the 'planning' of Baghdad during the past eight to nine years is, perhaps, the most tragic example of that type of abject planning that is the epitome of the vacuity and insensitivity [that] Arab cities . . . have been wilfully subjected to, thereby destroying their character, cohesiveness, harmony."[46] The mentality of the planners, however, is exemplified by the testimony of the director general of planning and design of the Iraqi Ministry of Municipalities (and lecturer in planning and design, University of Baghdad and former head of the Planning Section, Ministry of Housing). He decries the use of brick and stone for Iraq's cities, on the grounds that such housing and cities will not last (the reason no ancient Mesopotamian cities have survived!). He advocates cities of aluminum and steel, and asserts that "the importance of reinforced concrete to the future of Iraqi cities is . . . easy to appreciate."[47]

Urban planning in Iraq has been somewhat ineffectual due to the lack of authority, manpower, and funds committed to this important function. In 1960, the municipality of Baghdad had only one planner and a few assistants and draftsmen to oversee the planning of a bursting city, with already more than a

42. Ibid.; Gulick, "Baghdad," p. 253; United Nations, *Urban Land Policies*, p. 13; Kahtan H. J. Al-Madfai, "Baghdad," in Morroe Berger, ed., *The New Metropolis in the Arab World* (New Delhi: Allied Publishers, 1963), p. 47.

43. Fox, "Baghdad," pp. 22–23.

44. United Nations, *Urban Land Policies*, p. 13.

45. United Nations, *Studies on Social Development in the Middle East, 1971*, pp. 50–51.

46. Saba George Shiber, *Recent Arab City Growth* (Kuwait: Kuwait Government Printing Press, 1968), p. 546.

47. Al-Madfai, "Baghdad," pp. 40–41.

million inhabitants.[48] The preparation of master plans for all of Iraq's cities, except Baghdad, is the responsibility of the Directorate General of Municipalities. In 1970, the directorate had only two qualified town planners for this gigantic task.[49] The instability and changes in government since 1958, as well as an understandable preoccupation with the Kurdish problem in the north and the Shī'ī dissatisfaction in the south (and in the capital), have left a low priority for city planning. Although improvement of Iraq's cities is progressing slowly, as in other Middle Eastern countries, a national governmental ministry oversees its particular investments and construction within a city, and any overall coordination by a municipality for the proper development of its city gets lost in the centralization. Water systems, sewage systems, electricity, industry, housing, and many other activities fall under the control of various national góvernmental agencies and ministries—with resultant overlaps, conflicts, and gaps. Yet, not even one of these sectors is coordinated. For instance, although a Ministry of Housing exists, the housing problem is not exclusively its concern. Other ministries, departments, government controlled banks, municipalities, and semi-autonomous agencies in the public sector have their own programs, and there is not one agency that can examine the housing problem as a whole and coordinate the necessary projects.[50]

The urban housing situation is more critical in Iraq than any of the other Persian Gulf countries. Rapid urbanization has created a housing shortage that had reached catastrophic proportions by 1970 and was becoming worse annually.[51] In 1956, there were half a million unacceptable houses in the country. With the deterioration and obsolescence of some housing each year and with the increasing population, the total needed housing in 1968 was calculated to be 1,274,689 units. In the late 1960s, about 23,000 houses were being built annually, making absolutely no inroads on the housing shortage. In the economic development plan for 1965–69, for instance, provision was made only for the construction of industrial housing projects.[52]

A major form of housing in Iraqi cities, especially in Baghdad, results from cooperative housing societies. Begun in 1944, these societies provided their members with housing at cost until 1958, and after this date they supplied them with the land and some loans for the construction costs. The confiscation and nationalization of the royal family's land and some other large private estates in 1958 allowed large tracts around Baghdad to be developed for the professional cooperatives, which numbered about 120 in 1965 in the capital. The municipality of Baghdad, in cooperation with the Ministry of Housing, subdivided and distributed more than 65,000 plots of land to the housing cooperatives in the period 1964–68.[53]

These projects, called "cities" (mudun), are named after the type of cooperative society developing the land: Doctors' City, Lawyers' City, Engineers' City, and so forth. The size of the plots are uniform: 200 square meters for workers

48. Ibid., p. 61.
49. United Nations, *Urban Land Policies*, p. 13.
50. United Nations, *Studies on Social Development in the Middle East, 1971*, p. 59.
51. United Nations, *Improvement of Slums and Uncontrolled Settlements*, p. 80.
52. United Nations, *Studies on Social Development in the Middle East, 1971*, pp. 44–45, 56.
53. Ibid., p. 62.

and 600 square meters for government officials and civil servants. The prices in the late 1960s were usually less than one-tenth of the market values, ranging from 50 fils ($0.14) per meter for the workers to 250 fils ($0.70) per meter for the government officials.[54] In the 1960s, the members could obtain a loan of $1,400 at 10 percent interest from the cooperative for building a house, although each person contracted individually for the actual construction of the house.[55]

The housing in these areas, two-storied houses surrounded by gardens, is mass-produced in a very standardized style and superficially resembles cheaper tract housing developments in the United States.[56] One major problem of this housing is that the design and materials make use of unnecessarily sophisticated building technologies: reinforced concrete, complex plumbing and electrical fixtures, electrical cooling systems, and so forth. Most individuals have to obtain excessive loans beyond those from the cooperative to finance such costly housing,[57] and perhaps only the sense of acquiring a certain status of modernity compensates for the financial hardships and a housing design that may not be too suitable for the climate of Iraq or the life styles of Iraqis.

The residential explosion in the cities was so great in the 1960s and 1970s that, even though the government provided paved streets, sewage lines, electricity, and public transport, they could not keep up with the expansion. The lack of adequate commercial centers in the suburbs has been a major problem for the residents, and lengthy trips must be taken not only to places of employment but for much of the shopping for goods other than the basic daily necessities.

In the newer suburban cities, the residences are based on modern occupations or classes, replacing the kinship and religious-based quarters that had traditionally comprised the city. The professional cooperative cities provide a homogeneity of neighborhoods that generally is not found in the industrial societies of the West. However, the homogeneity of the professional cities is being somewhat diluted due to the selling or renting of houses by the original owners, although there are usually a minimum number of years residence required before a house can be sold or rented.

The rural migrants in Baghdad usually have lived in squatter settlements in houses made of mud, tin cans, or reeds (sarīfas). Some migration had begun in the 1930s, and in 1947 about 11 percent (57,000) of the capital's population were living in these shanty towns, whose temporary dwellings comprised 17 percent of the total housing in Baghdad.[58] By 1956 there were 16,413 sarīfas and 27,491 mud huts, which accounted for 44 percent of the total dwellings and about one-fourth of the population.[59] In 1957, squatters constituted 57 percent of the industrial workers in Baghdad.[60] Most of the squatters were Shī'ī Muslims from the southern provinces, particularly from Amāra province where the land tenure conditions were the most intolerable.

In the shanty towns, there generally were no potable water, electricity, or

54. Ibid.
55. Besim Selim Hakim, "Co-op housing, Baghdad: An evaluation and recommendations," Ekistics 36 (March 1972): 166–72.
56. Fox, "Baghdad," pp. 20–21.
57. Hakim, "Co-op housing, Baghdad," pp. 167–68.
58. Fox, "Baghdad," p. 14.
59. Ibid., p. 17.
60. Gulick, "Baghdad," p. 252.

sanitation facilities; health conditions were quite bad, hence various diseases were common. Although an Iraqi Development Board had been set up in 1951 to implement, among other things, housing projects with revenues available from the growth of the oil industry, little was done for the squatters. Recommendations by international agencies to build suitable housing for the *sarifa* dwellers and other low-income people were never followed, and, in fact, in the 1950s several attempts were made by the government to force the squatters back to their villages—which always failed. The Development Board did construct new flood protection measures, but this enabled new squatter settlements to develop in areas that previously often had been flooded. After the 1958 revolution, the shanty town problem was officially recognized by the government and some education and health services were provided. However, after the fall of Qāsim in 1963, most of the *sarifa* dwellings were torn down by the government—not least of the reasons being Communist sympathies among the squatters and the attempted coup by the Communists in the summer of 1963.[61]

More than 65,000 *sarifa*s were eradicated, and on the east bank of the Tigris a new city was established for the squatters, called Madīnat al-Thawra ("Revolution City"), and later another project, Madīnat al-Nūr ("City of Light"), was also built on the west bank. It is definitely questionable whether the government-built housing in Thawra was any improvement over the *sarifa*s. Composed of row upon row of small, overcrowded concrete and brick homes, the designs did not provide the inhabitants with air and sunlight, which at least had been available in their own constructions. Also, services such as piped water, sanitation, and paved streets were not generally provided, and one outside water faucet served many houses. In the second project on the west bank, the government was somewhat wiser, and the people were provided with materials and advice, but were allowed to build their houses more or less as they wanted, as long as the structures met certain standards.[62]

Implementation of urban projects in the 1970s in Iraq has been hampered by the lack of skilled manpower. Unlike many of the nearby Persian Gulf countries, Iraq is attempting to rely upon its own population instead of importing large amounts of foreign labor. This has meant a huge investment in education to train the required skilled and educated manpower. In 1977, there was an 84 percent rise in public spending on education, reaching $275 million.[63]

Yet, despite the manpower problems and shortages of materials, especially cement, housing construction has had to be emphasized to keep up with the industrial and urban growth. A special housing board has been set up to supervise the construction of housing in the new industrial areas being developed under the 1976–80 Five-Year Plan. About 6,000 prefabricated houses are to be erected in such areas by this board, while the State Organization of Housing also is responsible for financing conventional and prefabricated housing in other major projects.[64] As the cities continue to grow at the expense of the rural areas, as in

61. Fuad Baali, "Social factors in Iraqi rural-urban migration," *American Journal of Economics and Sociology* 25 (1966): 362.

62. Fox, "Baghdad," pp. 20–21; Gulick, "Baghdad," p. 252; United Nations, *Improvement of Slums and Uncontrolled Settlements*, p. 9.

63. *Middle East Economic Digest* 21 (September 30, 1977): 7–8.

64. Economist Intelligence Unit, *Quarterly Economic Review of Iraq* (4th Quarter 1977): 15.

Iran, the rural-urban gap increases.[65] Yet, in contrast to Iran, the increased consumer demand in Iraqi cities appears to be remaining unfulfilled.

Kuwait

Urbanization and City Growth. The urbanization of Kuwait is one of the most spectacular transformations in the history of urban development. Kuwait Town and its immediate suburbs constitute the vast majority of the population of this small country; hence, we have the evolution of a city-state. At the turn of the century, the town had an estimated 35,000 inhabitants (plus 13,000 Bedouin in the rest of the country),[66] and this size had approximately doubled by World War II.[67] Oil exports began in earnest immediately after the war and the population began expanding due to immigrant labor. In the first census in 1957, the country's population was already 206,473,[68] and this more than doubled by the 1965 census and doubled again by the 1975 census. The 994,837 total of that year represents a 9.1 percent per annum increase since 1957, one of the greatest national growth rates in the world. The 1977 population is at least 1.1 million; Kuwait's inhabitants have increased more than five-fold in two decades.

Almost all of Kuwait's population is urban, not only because the vast majority of the population resides in larger settlements but also because even the smaller settlements, such as those of less than 5,000 persons, are basically urban in function instead of being agricultural villages.[69] Although it is rather difficult to compare city populations over time, because of boundary changes from one census to another, most of the inhabitants live in one large conurbation, in what might be called Kuwait City.[70] In 1975, this area had a population of 763,524, comprising 76.8 percent of the nation's total. By 1979 or 1980, the metropolis will have over a million persons.[71] Except for about 12,000 persons in the desert, the remaining population in Kuwait is to the south in Ahmadī Governorate, where in 1975 the cities of Fahāhil (32,417) and Ahmadī (19,137) were the largest of many

65. *Middle East Economic Digest,* Special Report on Iraq (June 1977): 8. Outside of the major cities conditions continue to be rather primitive and about 45 percent of the Iraqis still live in villages without electricity.

66. J. G. Lorimer, *Gazetteer of the Persian Gulf, 'Oman, and Central Arabia,* vol. 2:B, *Geographical and Statistical* (Westmead, England: Gregg International Publishers, 1970 reprint of the 1908 edition), pp. 1051, 1074.

67. Naval Intelligence Division, *Iraq and the Persian Gulf* (London: H.M. Stationery Office, 1944), p. 149.

68. And this number may be understated. See A. G. Hill, "The Gulf States: Petroleum and Population Growth," in Clarke and Fisher, *Populations,* p. 244.

69. In 1970, only about 200 hectares of agricultural land were being utilized in the country. See Colin Buchanan and Partners, *Kuwait: Studies for National Physical Plan and Master Plan for Urban Areas: The Long Term Strategy* (London: Colin Buchanan and Partners, 1970), p. 28.

70. As opposed to Kuwait Town, the old *madīna* within the Old City.

71. Central Statistical Office, Ministry of Planning, Kuwait, *Annual Statistical Abstract, 1976,* pp. 28–30. The total has been calculated by adding the populations of the governorates of Capital and Hawālī, after subtracting individuals from Jahra, Dōha, Ushairij, and the desert in the former governorate. Most statistical yearbooks identify only the "principal towns" of Kuwait City (=Kuwait Town), Hawālī and Salīmiyya and, hence, entirely miss an assessment of the size of this large, contiguous metropolis. For example, see *The Middle East and North Africa, 1975–1976* (London: Europa Publications, 1975), p. 478.

small towns that comprised the bulk of the 141,256 persons in the governorate. The urban development around Ahmadī, the center of operations for the Kuwait Oil Company, and the nearby industrializing coast and port facilities, may within the next decade or two be joined by the expanding suburbs from the north. A preliminary master plan developed in 1970 by Colin Buchanan and partners suggested that the development strategy should be with a southern node, and so the country's projected population of two million in 1990, or three million in 2000, will indeed be almost entirely in the metropolis of Kuwait City.[72]

Kuwait's spectacular growth is perhaps one of the most vivid examples of the effects of vast oil revenues on a nation attempting to modernize overnight. Foreign laborers poured into the country and the great increase in population has been largely due to this immigration. In the early 1960s, the foreign population became larger than the native Kuwaitis, a trend that has continued to the present day, although the percentages of Kuwaitis and non-Kuwaitis has remained approximately the same since 1965 (Table 10–4). In 1975, the foreign population was 522,749, constituting 52.5 percent of the nation's total. However, more significant statistics are that for the total of 298,415 economically active persons, 70.9 percent were not Kuwaitis (Table 10–5). Kuwaitis were more numerous only in agriculture, hunting, and fishing, on account of the Bedouin population, while aliens comprised as much as 84.0 percent of the workers in trade and restaurants, 90.8 percent in manufacturing industries, and 94.6 percent in construction.

These foreigners work principally in the urban areas, not only because most of the population, including the aliens, are classified as urban, but because it is in such areas where most services, construction, restaurants, hotels, and industry are located. In 1975, Arabs constituted about 80 percent of the foreign population, about half of these being Palestinian and Jordanian, their presence being largely the result of the establishment of Israel and its continued expansion.[73] In 1961,

72. Colin Buchanan and Partners, *Kuwait*, pp. 127–81.
73. Geoffrey E. Ffrench and Allan G. Hill, *Kuwait: Urban and Medical Ecology, A Geomedical Study*, Geomedical Monograph Series, no. 4: Kuwait (Berlin: Springer–Verlag, 1971), p. 23.

TABLE 10–4. KUWAITI AND IMMIGRANT POPULATIONS, 1957–75

	Kuwaitis			Immigrants			Total	
Census date	Number	% of total	% annual growth	Number	% of total	% annual growth	Number	% annual growth
February 1957	113,622	55.0	—	92,851	45.0	—	206,473	—
May 1961	161,909	50.3	8.7	159,712	49.7	13.6	321,621	11.0
April 1965	220,059	47.1	8.2	247,280	52.9	11.8	467,339	10.0
April 1970	347,396	47.0	9.6	391,266	53.0	9.6	738,662	9.6
April 1975	472,088	47.5	6.3	522,749	52.5	6.0	994,837	6.1

1957–75 percent annual growth = 9.0.
1957–75 Kuwaiti percent annual growth = 8.2.
1957–75 Immigrant percent annual growth = 10.0.

Source: Kuwaiti Census of Population for 1957, 1961, 1965, 1970, and 1975, in A. G. Hill, "The Gulf States: Petroleum and Population Growth," in J. I. Clarke and W. B. Fisher, eds., *Populations of the Middle East and North Africa* (1972); *Kuwait, Annual Statistical Abstract, 1976.*

half of the Jordanian population living outside that country was in Kuwait. The non-Arab twenty percent was composed mainly of Iranians, Indians, and Pakistanis (Table 10–6). The Iranians are probably the second largest group of aliens after the Palestinians and Jordanians because of the great number of illegal Iranians who get into Kuwait through a well-developed smuggling system.[74] In 1970, when the official number of Iranians was enumerated to be 39,129, about the same number of illegal Iranians were also estimated to be in the country.[75] In the four years of 1969–72, for instance, 23,139 illegal Iranians were deported from Kuwait.[76]

The great immigration into Kuwait is for employment, which is a reflection of the lesser economic opportunities in the countries of origin—although this has begun to change in some of the nearby countries since 1973 because of the tremendous revenues available for investment and development. The workers do not come from all regions of their various countries, but represent emigrants from more economically depressed areas. For instance, most of the Iranians come from southern Iran, especially from southern Fārs and the coastal areas,[77] while Iraqis are mainly from the depressed agricultural areas of the southern part of that country. The rural origins of these Iranians and Iraqis are perhaps stressed by the rather high illiteracy rates of the aliens in Kuwait, 81 percent for the former and 67 percent for the latter in 1965. As might be expected, the Iranians and Iraqis tend to be manual laborers or engage in other low-skilled occupations. Similar positions are held by the largely illiterate Arab groups from Oman and the Yemens. In contrast to these are the highly literate Jordanians (16 percent illiterate in 1965), Lebanese (17 percent illiterate), and Syrians (26 percent illiterate).[78] These Arabs tend to be in the higher-paying technical and skilled jobs, and as the Kuwaiti economy matures these individuals are more in demand than the laborers.

74. Mohammad Taghi Razavian, "Iranian Communities of the Persian Gulf: A Geographical Analysis," Ph.D. thesis, University of London, 1975, pp. 147–302.
75. Ibid., p. 296.
76. Statistics from the Kuwait Ministry of Interior, in ibid., p. 295.
77. Ibid., pp. 147–302.
78. Ffrench and Hill, Kuwait, p. 23.

TABLE 10–5. KUWAITI AND IMMIGRANT ECONOMICALLY ACTIVE POPULATIONS, 1975

	Kuwaitis	%	Immigrants	%	Total
Agriculture, hunting, and fishing	3,983	53.0	3,531	47.0	7,514
Mining and quarrying	1,779	36.6	3,080	63.4	4,859
Manufacturing industries	2,258	9.2	22,209	90.8	24,467
Electricity, gas, and water	2,034	28.0	5,237	72.0	7,271
Construction	1,756	5.4	30,500	94.6	32,256
Trade and restaurants	6,327	16.0	33,232	84.0	39,559
Transport, storage, and communications	4,567	29.1	11,118	70.9	15,685
Financial institutions, insurance	1,377	21.1	5,146	78.9	6,523
Services (including defense)	62,888	39.2	97,391	60.8	160,279
Total	86,969	29.1	211,444	70.9	298,415

Source: Kuwaiti Census of Population for 1975, in The Middle East and North Africa, 1977–1978.

Kuwait also has attracted immigrants due to its policy of providing free education and free health services at a standard generally above the nearby states. Yet, such facilities, especially for education, are becoming more restricted for foreigners, and the increasing population puts pressure on these services.[79] Kuwait's low import duties are also attractive, and so emigrants return to their country with radios, televisions, cameras, and other luxury goods (often smuggled into the homeland for resale).

Urban Planning and Housing. In 1952, the British city planning firm of Minoprio, Spencely, and Macfarlane produced a master plan for Kuwait City that was to drastically alter and provide for subsequent development of the metropolis.[80] A series of four concentric ring-roads were built around the old *madīna* (Kuwait Town), with a green belt 250 meters wide around the old wall. Roads radiating out from this city crossed the ring-roads at right angles. Industrial areas were developed along the coast to the west, while within the concentric zones formed by the roads seventeen major residential superblocks were built by the government. Each neighborhood included services such as mosques, schools, and shops for local needs. The residential blocks were reserved only for Kuwaitis, while the nearby settlements of Hawālī, Salīmiyya, and other outlying areas were developed for non-Kuwaitis.[81] The old *madīna* was partly leveled and was de-

79. Ibid.
80. Much of the discussion of the early planning of Kuwait City comes from ibid., pp. 33–43, and Colin Buchanan and Partners, *Kuwait*, pp. 3–12.
81. Ffrench and Hill, *Kuwait*, note that this segregation of Kuwaitis and non-Kuwaitis was not in the original plan, but was established as policy by the Kuwaiti government in its implementation. Ibid., p. 37.

TABLE 10–6. IMMIGRANT NATIONALITIES IN KUWAIT, 1975

Nationality	Number	% of total population	% of immigrant population
Jordanian/Palestinian	204,178	20.5	39.0
Egyptian	60,534	6.1	11.6
Iraqi	45,070	4.5	8.6
Syrian	40,962	4.1	8.0
Other Arabs	67,843	6.9	13.0
All Arabs	419,187	42.1	80.2
Iranian	40,842	4.1	8.0
Indian	32,105	3.2	6.1
Pakistani	23,016	2.3	4.4
All Others	2,599	0.8	1.3
Non-Arabs	103,562	10.4	19.8
Total	522,749	52.5	100.0

Source: Kuwaiti Census of Population for 1975, in *Kuwait, Annual Statistical Abstract, 1976.*

signated to be the central business district, as a focus for the whole metropolis. A number of roads were put through the old residences, and blocks of land were purchased by the government to be razed and developed as modern shopping districts and the location of public buildings.

By the 1960s, many phases of the 1952 plan had been completed, but it was evident that it was inadequate to deal with the continued development of Kuwait City. In 1960, the energetic Arab planner, Saba George Shiber, was recruited to advise the Town Planning Department of Kuwait, and he developed plans for some new residential areas and some projects within Kuwait Town. His large volume, *The Kuwait Urbanization*,[82] is based upon his experience with the planning process in Kuwait and throughout the book he laments the reckless speed at which everything had to be planned and built. He stresses that most of the myriad foreign consultants (and Kuwaiti planners) had no appreciation of the Arab Islamic culture, of the practical, indigenous Middle Eastern architecture, or of the harsh climatic conditions that make many of the Western buildings and architectural styles so impractical in the desert.

During 1965–68, many town-planning experts were brought in for advice, and they suggested that, except for the coastline to the southeast, development should be contained within the fourth ring-road, filling in the open spaces (including graveyards). Such advice was ignored and, following the general outlines of the 1952 plan, two more ring-roads were added and the radial streets were extended to the new roads.

There are some problems in the implementation of urban plans in Kuwait. Interorganizational conflicts, the inadequate control by one agency over planning, as well as the changing constituency and the lack of expertise in the existing bodies all hinder effective planning. The Kuwait Municipal Council, which is in charge of running the metropolis, consisted of twelve members (plus a president), in 1960, appointed by the Emir. These council members all belonged to the Kuwaiti elite (traditional merchant families) and were not planning experts or engineers. This council was involved in planning, although the Kuwaiti Planning Board and numerous ministries also had various planning powers. A new council was to be elected for the first time in January 1963, but the elections were postponed until June 1964, and during this one and one-half years the business of the Kuwait municipality had to be carried on by a specially appointed central committee. The newly elected council attempted to tackle the problem of land registration and land acquisition in the city in order to assure that proper land sites would be available for public development projects. It was soon evident that the needed communication and coordination between the municipality and other governmental agencies was lacking. There were no clear policy lines, and the duties and authority of agencies were too general and vague to be operational. When the council attempted to have various governmental agencies justify their excessive land requests and overpricing of land payments, the delays this caused in implementation of projects resulted in such a public outcry that the Emir dissolved the council in May 1966. He then appointed a central committee presided over

82. Saba George Shiber, *The Kuwait Urbanization* (Kuwait: Privately published, 1964).

by the Ministry of State to handle the affairs of the municipality. Any corrective measures for the land acquisition and overpricing were never implemented.[83]

An entirely new city, Ahmadī, was built by the Kuwait Oil Company for its employees. In 1949, 9,000 employees and workers were housed in tents and temporary buildings, but by 1952 over 1,000 houses had been built and most of the Western style housing was completed by 1954. Ahmadī's city structure reflected a policy of separation from the rest of the country and within the city itself. The different cultures and nationalities not only had separate residential areas, but their facilities were separate as well. The Anglo-American neighborhoods with their schools, clubs, and churches were in the northern part of the town, the Indians and Pakistanis were grouped in the south with their clubs and schools, while the Kuwaiti and other Arabs were in another section of the south with their facilities. In the early 1960s, about 6,000 Kuwait Oil Company employees and their families lived in the city and in 1975 the population was 19,137.[84]

The implementation of the 1952 Plan included acquisition of land by the government, mainly within Kuwait Town. The owners of land and property were offered deliberately inflated prices, not only to induce the Kuwaitis to move to the new suburban neighborhoods but also as a means of providing capital for investment in the private sector. By 1967, about $1.5 billion had been spent in this government land-purchase scheme. Land prices rose by a multiple of 32 from 1952–60, while housing costs increased 15.4 times between 1953–66. The scheme provided large blocks of state-owned land that the government used for the transformation of the old *madīna*. However, the capital investment aspect of the program was not too successful because much of the money released to private interests was invested outside of Kuwait and was therefore of little benefit to the state.[85]

In January 1970, there were approximately 111,600 housing units in Kuwait, comprising five separate types (Table 10–7). The housing in the new neighborhoods between the fourth ring-road and the old *madīna* constituted the majority of the single, detached houses. The government sold plots by lottery at nominal

83. Saif Abbas Abdulla, "Politics, Administration, and Urban Planning in a Welfare Society: Kuwait," Ph.D. thesis, Indiana University, 1973, pp. 259–93.
84. Kamal S. Sayegh, *Oil and Arab Regional Development* (New York, Frederick A. Praeger, 1968), pp. 128–34; *Kuwaiti Digest* 3 (January/February 1975): 28–31.
85. Ffrench and Hill, *Kuwait*, pp. 35–36.

TABLE 10–7. URBAN HOUSING CATEGORIES IN KUWAIT, 1970

Housing category	Number[a]	Percentage
Detached houses on distributed plots	9,000	8
Low-income group houses	12,500	11
Traditional houses	17,600	16
Shanties	28,000	25
Apartments and other dwellings	44,500	40
Total	111,600	100

[a] Estimates in January 1970.
Source: Colin Buchanan and Partners, *Kuwait: Studies for National Physical Plan and Master Plan for Urban Areas, the Long Term Strategy* (March 1970).

prices (below market values) to Kuwaiti citizens who: (1) had lost property through expropriation and government purchasing in Kuwait Town; or (2) were government employees; or (3) were persons of low or no income. The large payments for the property in Kuwait Town, plus interest-free loans up to KD 15,000, helped to finance the construction of the houses, which were mostly individually designed and built and which in the late 1960s were costing from KD 40,000 to KD 80,000 each. Plots are either 750 or 1,000 square meters and the average gross floor area of these detached "villas" is about 800 square meters, with a garden comprising the remaining area. Each neighborhood in 1970 consisted of about 900 houses, comprising only one-third of the area, while wide internal roads and numerous open spaces were provided. A neighborhood center was planned with shops, a police station, mosque, and government offices; and ample schools also were provided.[86] Table 10–8 indicates the typical land use in a neighborhood.

The housing in the new neighborhoods, despite the great costs, was often poorly built and many of the houses constructed in the early 1950s were already deteriorating and had to be repaired by the late 1960s. In these neighborhoods, more than anywhere else in Kuwait, there is strict control over the site layout, building height, peripheral walls, and setbacks—which imposed a Western style house surrounded by a garden, instead of the traditional house with its internal courtyard. Only Kuwaitis can own land in the country, and so non-Kuwaitis have been kept out of these planned neighborhoods. Also, unlike other areas, these units generally cannot be rented.[87]

Low-income housing has received some attention by Kuwait and up to 1971 a total of 12,000 units had been built by the government, despite considerable confusion, overlaps, and changes in authority over such housing.[88] These one-story dwellings were sold to low-income Kuwaitis[89] for monthly payments of from

86. Colin Buchanan and Partners, *Kuwait*, pp. 39–50.

87. However, Colin Buchanan and Partners, *Kuwait*, p. 41, estimated that one-quarter of the population in these neighborhoods were, in fact, non-Kuwaitis. This is due to non-Kuwaiti houseboys, maids, and other servants who also resided in the houses.

88. Abdulla, "Politics, Administration, and Urban Planning," pp. 325–29, 335.

89. Generally before 1970 low-income was defined as earning less than KD 150 monthly. Colin Buchanan and Partners, *Kuwait*, p. 41.

TABLE 10–8. LAND USE IN A TYPICAL KUWAITI
PLANNED NEIGHBORHOOD

Land use	Percentage
Residential	33
Educational	10
Commercial	3
Roads and parking	23
Public open space and playing fields	6
Other uses	3
Vacant land	22
Total	100

Source: Colin Buchanan and Partners, *Kuwait: Studies for National Physical Plan and Master Plan for Urban Areas, the Long Term Strategy* (March 1970).

KD 3.50 to KD 15,000, according to the size of the house and the income of the occupant.[90]

Much of the traditional housing has been destroyed, because the majority was located in Kuwait Town. Only about 4,000 traditional houses remained in the Old City in 1970. This housing generally was constructed before 1950 and is built of traditional materials such as mud, gatch (lime-plaster), and coral, and it is arranged around a courtyard. Many of these houses have unsatisfactory sewage disposal facilities and most are in poor structural condition. Especially within the old *madīna*, the majority of these houses are rented to foreign immigrants. Even the dilapidated structures are rented for extreme amounts (compared to wages), which are split between many immigrants in most instances. Much of this housing still occupies prime land for redevelopment, and hence continues to be purchased by the government and demolished.

Most apartments are rented by non-Kuwaitis in Kuwait Town and the nearby suburbs of Hawālī and Salīmiyya, and these areas have much greater densities than the Kuwaiti neighborhoods. In 1970, the average residential densities of Hawālī and Salīmiyya were 215 and 136 persons per hectare, respectively, while it was 65 persons per hectare in the Kuwaiti neighborhoods.[91] Much of the housing in Hawālī and Salīmiyya has been built without the benefit of detailed planning. In the late 1960s, the predominant form of these residences was of four-story apartment buildings over ground-floor shops.[92]

A continuing embarrassment for the Kuwaiti government is its inability to solve the problem of shanty towns in this progressive, modern welfare state. In 1970, estimates of the numbers living in shanties varied from 12.3 percent to 25 percent of the population, such differences probably being due to definitions of these dwellings.[93] Most of the shanty dwellers are Bedouin, and in 1975 they constituted 80 percent of the total shanty population of 131,257.[94] These Bedouin not only came from Kuwait, but from many of the surrounding deserts.[95] Even though the shanty town population has increased over the decades, it has not grown as fast as the annual growth of the total population.

The shanties have been illegally built on government or private land and hence are squatter settlements. Because space is not a problem in this arid region, the shanty dwellings are built at considerable distances from one another, and this pattern, in effect, reproduces the spatial arrangements of the Bedouin tent

90. The houses usually are one-story, with a gross floor area of 250 to 350 square meters on a plot of 600 square meters. They are either L-shaped semidetached houses, with a courtyard, or the detached Western style surrounded by a garden, both having a walled roof area and the outer wall eight feet high. Ibid., pp. 41–42.

91. Ibid., p. 44.

92. Ibid., p. 50.

93. Abdulla, "Politics, Administration, and Urban Planning," p. 331, mentions the 12.3 percent figure with 14,500 Kuwaiti families residing in the shanties from Planning Board Memo No. MT/44/1, 1972, while Colin Buchanan and Partners, *Kuwait*, p. 43, give a figure of one-fourth from a Kuwaiti Credit Bank estimate.

94. Abdulrasoul A. Al-Moosa, "Bedouin Shanty Settlements in Kuwait: A Study in Social Geography," Ph.D. thesis, University of London, 1976, p. 94

95. However, not only the Bedouin, but all the people in the shanty towns are classified as Kuwaitis by the Census—even though some of these people do not have Kuwaiti citizenship, as evidenced in problems they encounter in obtaining other housing and various benefits reserved for citizens. Ibid.

encampments. Hence, the densities of the shanty towns are less than the urban areas, a pattern rarely found among squatter settlements elsewhere in the developing world. In 1975, there were about 19,000 shanty dwellings found in six major shanty areas, and at least ten to fifteen smaller areas.[96] By 1975, about 6,000 Bedouin had been moved to special housing. These improved squatter settlements were at first called Bedouin (Badū or Bādiya) housing, but the term was changed to "popular" housing. Every family that was allocated a house at a rent of KD 7 per month had to vacate their shanty to permit its demolition by the government. This was to insure that the shanty was not used by any other Bedouin, and to prevent the family from staying in the shanty and renting out the popular housing. Even though alterations were not allowed, all the families made changes because the houses were poorly designed for the Bedouin needs. Walls and screens were put up to provide greater privacy and to hide front doors, houses were painted, floors tiled, pens made for animals, and extra rooms were built. A guest room (dīwāniyya) was a special necessity for these tribal people, and for this there had been no provision. However, many of the alterations were demolished by the government, and this lack of understanding of the social needs of a people in providing them with housing caused great resentment.[97]

Sa'ūdī Arabia

Urbanization and City Growth. The urbanization of Sa'ūdī Arabia has been very rapid within the last several decades, due to the exploitation of oil and the industrialization and construction resulting from the vast petroleum revenues. Problems, however, exist in assessing this urbanization, because of the lack of accurate statistics. The first census of 1962–63 was officially repudiated and many details never disclosed, while the census of 1974 has never been officially approved or released. Hence, population and city statistics must be viewed cautiously.

In the 1930s, the population of Sa'ūdī Arabia is estimated to have been 1.5–2.0 million persons. About one-fourth or one-fifth of this total were in urban settlements, while half were villagers and the remainder nomadic pastoralists. All the cities were rather small, and Mecca was the largest, with perhaps only about 50,000 permanent inhabitants.[98] The 1962–63 census recorded 3,302,330 persons, and although the figures for all settlements were not released, one scholar estimates that 24 percent of the total were urban (located in settlements of 20,000 persons or more).[99] Six cities were larger than 50,000, comprising 20.6 percent of the total population (Table 10–9). The royal capital of Riyadh had by this time displaced Mecca as the largest city, and the administrative capital and port city of Jidda was now almost as large as the Holy City.

96. Ibid., pp. 105–16. Also, for another excellent analysis of the Bedouin settlement patterns in Kuwait, see Fred Scholz, "Sesshaftwerdung von Beduinen in Kuwait," *Erdkunde* 29 (1975): 223–34.

97. Al-Moosa, "Bedouin Shanty Settlements," pp. 118–30.

98. R. McGregor, "Saudi Arabia: Population and the Making of a Modern State," in Clarke and Fisher, *Populations*, p. 221.

99. McGregor, "Saudi Arabia," pp. 226–27, estimated that 21 percent were nomadic and 55 percent rural settled. However, since McGregor's urban category was 20,000+, the urban population would be larger if a lower figure were used (e.g., 5,000+).

The 1974 census recorded 7,012,642 inhabitants, including about 1.9 million (26.9 percent) nomads. Ten cities were over 50,000, comprising 34.6 percent of the total population (Table 10–9), while six other cities were also over 30,000, bringing the total percentage in cities of this size close to 38.2 percent.[100] If urban is defined as 5,000 inhabitants or larger, then Sa'ūdī Arabia's urban population in 1974 was probably somewhere between 40 and 50 percent. Riyadh continued to be the largest city, although unlike most of the Middle Eastern countries there has yet to be a primate city in Sa'ūdī Arabia. Jidda is not far behind Riyadh and the other large cities, such as Mecca, Madīna, and, surprisingly, Tā'if, are growing very fast as well.

The annual growth rates (Table 10–9) are spectacular; the country's growth has been 7.1 percent since 1963, while the rates for some of the largest cities are in the double digits. However, it must be remembered that the 1974 census has never been officially released. The major reason appears to be that the Sa'ūdī population was much less than had been anticipated (or desired), and various

100. Kingdom of Saudi Arabia, Ministry of Finance and National Economy, Central Department of Statistics, *The Statistical Indicator* (First Issue, 1976), p. 112.

TABLE 10–9. POPULATION OF MAIN[a] CITIES IN SA'ŪDĪ ARABIA, 1962/63–1974

City	1962–63	1974	1963–74 % annual growth
Riyadh	197,800	666,840	11.7
Jidda	147,811	561,104	12.9
Mecca	158,641	366,801	7.9
Tā'if	53,954	204,857	12.9
Madīna	71,998	198,186	9.6
Dammām	n.a.[b]	127,844	—
Hofūf	50,000	101,271	6.4
Tabūk	n.a.	74,825	—
Burajda	n.a.	69,940	—
al-Mubarraz	n.a.	54,325	—
Khamīs-Mushait	n.a.	49,581	—
al-Khobar	n.a.	48,817	—
Najrān	n.a.	47,501	—
Hā'il	n.a.	40,502	—
Jīzān	n.a.	32,812	—
Abhā	n.a.	30,150	—
Total		2,675,356	

[a] Cities over 30,000 population in 1974.
[b] n.a. = not available.
Source: Department of Statistics, Sa'ūdī Arabia, "Survey of Population and Establishments," 1963, in R. McGregor, "Saudi Arabia: Population and the Making of a Modern State," in J. I. Clarke and W. B. Fisher, eds., *Populations of the Middle East and North Africa* (1972); Kingdom of Sa'ūdī Arabia, Ministry of Finance and National Economy, Central Department of Statistics, *The Statistical Indicator*, 1976.

figures from 3.5 to 5.5 million are mentioned by foreign consultants and other informed individuals who supposedly have inside information. Related to the problem of the low Sa'ūdī population is the great number of immigrant workers, comprising at least 1.5 million individuals, and probably more. Sa'ūdī Arabia is very fearful of a situation like that of neighboring Kuwait, where the immigrants outnumber the nationals, and so the Sa'ūdīs are reluctant to admit there are great numbers of foreigners in their country. Based upon the 1962–63 population and an annual rate of increase of 2 percent that rises to 2.9 percent due to a declining mortality rate, McGregor estimated that the population would be 3.90 million in 1970 and 4.46 million in 1975. He also projected the population increase as calculated on the basis that the 1962–63 census was about 10 percent under-estimated, and his revised figures were 4.28 million in 1970 and 4.90 million in 1975.[101] These estimates might be used instead of the suspect census figures, except for the fact that McGregor underestimates the great number of foreign workers that will come into the country in the 1970s.[102]

Hence, in 1974 the Sa'ūdī population may well have been 4 to 4.5 million, while the total population was about 5.5 to 6 million persons—or even higher if there were more immigrants. The major discrepancy in the official 1974 census seems to be in the nomadic Bedouin population. The 1974 figure is 1.88 million, more than a million persons greater than the approximate 700,000 nomads enumerated in 1962–63. But the nomadic population is declining, not increasing. Employment opportunities in the cities and in the industrializing regions, such as the Eastern Province, have attracted the Bedouin (as well as foreign immigrants) and many nomads have settled down. Hence, it appears that the nomad population may have been greatly exaggerated in an attempt to bolster the Sa'ūdī population percentage. The major urban population statistics, on the other hand, possibly may be fairly accurate, especially considering that large numbers of foreigners constitute part of the urban population. Therefore, no adjustments will be attempted with the 1974 city totals, but the unreliability of these statistics must be kept in mind.

The factors that have affected Sa'ūdī Arabia's cities are similar to those in the other countries of the Persian Gulf, except for the fact that the magnitude of the Sa'ūdī oil revenues since 1973 is so great that development seems to have no financial constraints. The growth of Jidda on the Red Sea and the urban explosion in the Eastern Province on the Gulf represent a direct response to the tremendous investments. The complex of Dhahrān, al-Khobar, Dammām, and Qatīf is a major urban-industrial region, one which began to develop in the 1930s with Aramco and oil production. A new industrial center and completely planned city is being built north of the complex on the coast at Jubail. This will become the major industrial node of Sa'ūdī Arabia, including refineries, petrochemical plants, an aluminum smelter, desalination plants, a steel mill, and other related industries. A modern city of 175,000 spread out over 600 square kilometers will be built in conjunction with the industrial area. A temporary city is first needed for this

101. McGregor, "Saudi Arabia," p. 236.
102. Ibid., p. 239, estimated 150,000 immigrant workers in 1962–63 and 400,000 in 1969–70, increasing at about 15 percent per annum.

gigantic industrial and urban project, for about 40,000 workers will be engaged in the construction. A similar industrial complex, although not quite as large, is being developed on the Red Sea at Yanbū'.[103]

Another large urban project is the construction of King Khālid Military City at Hafar al-Bātin, south of the neutral zone with Iraq. The U.S. Army Corps of Engineers, which is developing most of the military facilities in Sa'ūdī Arabia, has contracted with an American consortium to build the $1 billion city. Slated to be completed by 1985, the city will have a population of 70,000 persons. An entire new port has had to be constructed at Ra's al-Mishab to supply the building materials for this inland city.[104]

The labor shortage in Sa'ūdī Arabia has required the importation of considerable foreign labor, even though the Sa'ūdī government refuses to acknowledge the great numbers needed. Yemenis constitute the largest single group, numbering perhaps even a million persons, while Omanis, Egyptians, Pakistanis, and other nationalities comprise the remainder of the foreigners. More recent foreign workers include thousands of South Koreans, most of whom work on projects on the Gulf coast and live in floating barges.

The great growth of the cities in Sa'ūdī Arabia cannot be attributed entirely to the influx of foreign laborers, however. Rural-urban migration within the country has been great, including many nomadic Bedouin who have settled on the outskirts of the cities. The greatly expanding ports and industrial complexes, such as Jidda and Dammām, are the recipients of many of these indigenous migrants. However, as in other developing countries, it is the capital itself that is a magnet for its own countrymen. A 1968 household sample survey in Riyadh estimated that 85 percent of the city's household heads were born outside the capital, and only 21 percent were foreigners from other Arab countries.[105]

The spontaneous settling of Bedouin nomads has resulted in the creation of numerous shanty towns in the cities of Sa'ūdī Arabia. These spontaneous settlements (hilal), are found on the outskirts of the urban areas, unless the city has expanded and engulfed them. The largest number of hilal can be found in Riyadh and the oil towns of the Eastern Province, although most cities have some of these sedentarized-nomad settlements. For instance, in north-central Sa'ūdī Arabia in the Qasīm region, as of 1972, eighteen separate hilal were located around seven cities: eight at 'Unaiza, two at the regional capital of Buraida, and the remainder in smaller towns.[106] Many of the hilal were founded during drought years when these nomadic Bedouin lost most of their livestock, although settling for economic opportunities in the urban areas is becoming more common.

The hilal usually are comprised of families from specific tribes. For instance, in the Qasīm region the Harb, Mutair, 'Utayba, Suluba, 'Anaza, and Shammar

103. "Focus on the Eastern Province," The Times (London), Special Report (November 21, 1977).
104. Ibid., p. 1.
105. Saleh Abdullah Malik, "Rural Migration and Urban Growth in Riyadh, Saudi Arabia," Ph.D. thesis, University of Michigan, 1973, p. 7.
106. Ahmed A. Shamekh, "Spatial Patterns of Bedouin Settlement in Al-Qasim Region, Saudi Arabia," Ph.D. thesis, University of Kentucky, 1975, pp. 219–46. Two hilal had been established in 1943, nine in the 1950s, five in the 1960s, and two in 1970.

tribes constitute the *hilal*, the inhabitants being either entirely from one tribe or sometimes from two or three.[107] In three shanty towns around Abqā'iq, the inhabitants are predominantly from the Āl Murra tribe. In the Jidda and Mecca area, however, most of the shanty towns have resulted from pilgrims staying in Sa'ūdī Arabia after visiting the Holy City, a centuries-old Islamic practice. Shacks of tin and wood can be found on the urban peripheries of these cities, and a number of the occupants are from West Africa and other regions of the Islamic world.[108] The problem has been aggravated in Mecca because in the mid-1950s a large area around the Masjid al-Harām (the Holy Mosque) was demolished and thousands of families had to move to the suburbs of the city.

Hilal are located on the periphery of cities not only because of the availability of cheap or free land but also because the settled Bedouin do not want to live in the crowded urban areas. Hence, they are not too far from the jobs and *sūqs* (markets) of the cities, but, equally important, the Bedouin have preserved the open spaces that they so highly prize. Although some may live in an improvised shack, they often continue to live in their black tents. The *hilal* settlement is therefore a transition stage between nomadism and integration into an urban society. The newly settled Bedouin keep many of their ties with their nomadic kinsmen, often acting as middlemen in the livestock trade and being hosts to their relatives during visits. Few Bedouin are ready for the urban environment until after a long transition period, and this is the dilemma for the government. Low-income housing and squatter resettlement may improve the landscape, but seldom does it provide a viable alternative for a people whose life-style and spirit are in tune with the open desert.

Urban Planning and Housing. Urban planning in Sa'ūdī Arabia has progressed considerably within the last decade. During the First Development Plan (1970–75), the number of settlements endowed with municipality status rose from 54 to 85, and this number is slated to reach 162 by the end of the Second Plan in 1980. Municipalities are classified into four categories according to their importance (and size); of the 85 municipalities in 1975 there were 4 A (Riyadh, Jidda, Mecca, and Madīna), 14 B, 18 C, and 49 D municipalities. The 77 settlements to acquire municipality status assumedly will be D municipalities, but whether or how the existing municipalities can change status is not clear.[109]

Master plans were designed under the First Development Plan for the principal cities, and one for Riyadh was actually implemented. Beautification studies were conducted for the cities of Mecca, Madīna, Jidda, and Tā'if, and there were studies and designs for public parks in 11 major cities. During the Second Development Plan, comprehensive master plans will be made for 66 cities, and a great many projects are to be continued or implemented, such as asphalting of streets, sewage systems, rainwater drainage systems, street lighting, construction of municipality buildings and facilities, parks and gardens, and so forth. Entirely

---

107. Ibid., pp. 303–04.
108. United Nations, *Improvement of Slums and Uncontrolled Settlements*, pp. 80–92.
109. Kingdom of Saudi Arabia, Central Planning Organization, *Development Plan, 1395–1400 (1975–1980)* (Springfield, Va.: Reproduced by National Technical Information Service, U.S. Department of Commerce, 1975), pp. 559–76.

new projects include public transportation, cultural centers, guest-houses and hostels, public zoos, and the development of model communities. Green-belt recreational areas are to be established near the major cities, including areas totaling 10 and 12 kilometers in Riyadh and Jidda, respectively. In cooperation with the Central Planning Organization, a national urban policy is to be formulated to guide planning and development policy. This will include a land-use classification system, building codes, traffic control, and a land development policy.[110]

Water supply is a most critical need in this arid peninsula, and the construction and operation of urban water supply systems has been under the control of the Ministry of Agriculture and Water. A major goal is to provide the municipalities with sufficient piped water for all the inhabitants. Numerous schemes for drilling wells, building dams, constructing desalination plants, and providing the pipe networks in the cities are contemplated for the Second Development Plan. It is also planned for the municipalities to "assume gradually" from the Ministry of Agriculture and Water the responsibility for the construction and operation of the urban water supply systems.[111]

As the last statement implies, conflict of authority and responsibility is one of the major difficulties facing urban planning in Sa'ūdī Arabia. There is inadequate coordination between the separate agencies and organizations responsible for the various facilities and services in the cities. National agencies in charge of electricity, water, industry, labor, education, health, communications, and so forth, must have their programs coordinated for an orderly development of the urban environment. The municipalities, however, not only have insufficient authority, but their manpower is inadequate to carry out their programs. Qualified persons are difficult to find, especially for the smaller cities and towns in remoter areas. But even Riyadh cannot find adequate workers or the needed expertise. In 1977, the capital handed over its entire city-cleaning operation to a foreign subsidiary. A five-year, $240-million contract includes bringing in 2,000 Egyptians, Pakistanis, and/or South Koreans as well as 300 compactors, trucks, and other vehicles to collect the estimated 100,000 tons of rubbish generated annually.[112]

The lack of skilled workers and planners is recognized by the Sa'ūdī government. A major effort is being made to train more personnel at such schools as the Institute of Public Administration and a newly created Institute of Training for Municipal Affairs in Riyadh.[113] Yet inadequate staff will continue to be a major hindrance for urban affairs and effective city planning.

Housing shortages remain quite acute in Sa'ūdī Arabia, because of the rapid urbanization and the fact that the government has generally ignored the housing problem. Contractors and employees of the major construction projects must now provide not only their own work force but also accommodation for them, and so a major expense of most projects involves constructing housing, albeit often temporary in nature. Aramco built an entirely Western style city, Dhahrān, as the headquarters for its company and employees, as well as smaller company towns at Ra's Tanūra and Abqā'iq. More recently, Aramco has embarked on a program of

110. Ibid., pp. 559, 565–66, 573–74.
111. Ibid., pp. 99–113, 561.
112. *Middle East Economic Digest* 21 (February 11, 1977): 11.
113. Kingdom of Saudi Arabia, *Development Plan, 1395–1400 (1975–1980)*, pp. 559, 561, 576.

office, warehouse, and housing construction connected with the world's largest gas gathering scheme, which will provide much of the energy for the new industrial projects such as Jubail and Yanbū'.[114]

The Saʿūdī government assumed responsibility for direct financing of housing construction for civil servants in the 1950s. By the early 1970s, there had been 717 houses and 96 apartment units financed by the government. No fees are charged for the cost of the land or for designing and supervising the projects. The cost of each house is financed with a no-interest, 20-year loan and the monthly payments are collected from the employee's salary. Aramco also inaugurated a house-ownership plan in the 1950s in which the loans are interest-free and repayable only up to 80 percent of the total, the company subsidizing the remaining 20 percent. By 1970, over 8,000 Saʿūdī employees had bought houses through this plan.[115]

In 1971, a general Housing Department was organized under the Ministry of Finance and National Economy, and this department has been responsible for implementing a public housing program. In 1975, there were 2,500 public housing units under construction, mainly in Dammām, al-Khobar, Jidda, and Riyadh. These houses are for low- and moderate-income households, and are available to qualified individuals through interest-free 25-year loans. During the present Five-Year Plan (1975–80), construction of 52,500 public housing units is planned, as well as the creation of 44,300 serviced plots. The latter are allocated to low-income households for self-help housing construction and are part of the effort to get rid of shanty dwellings.[116]

During the First Development Plan (1970–75), approximately 75,000 housing units were constructed, although this was only half of the projected need for new houses or replacements in this period.[117] Land speculation has been prevalent and land prices have been rising considerably in recent years. This has tended to promote urban sprawl, as lower land costs on the perimeter of cities cause development there before the more expensive land nearer the center is purchased. Capital for housing also is in short supply and most new residences have to be financed privately. As the cost of a new house for middle- and moderate-income households is now from 50,000 up to the hundreds of thousands of dollars (and rising), such financing is becoming more and more difficult.

An indication of the progress in housing, however, is shown by the increase in the Real Estate Development Fund, which is responsible for financing many of the private housing projects. When it started in July 1974, it had a capital of only $70 million, but by the 1977–78 financial year its capital had grown to $6.7 billion. Huge housing projects are being contemplated in the major cities. A $622-million project was begun in 1977 in Jidda; in Dammām, 32 blocks of apartment buildings, each 18 stories, were under construction, while over 4,000 housing units were being provided in al-Khobar and 500 units in Qatīf.[118] Although 122,100 housing units are to be built by the private sector during the

114. "Focus on the Eastern Province," p. 3.
115. United Nations, *Studies on Social Development in the Middle East, 1971*, pp. 49, 60.
116. Kingdom of Saudi Arabia, *Development Plan, 1395–1400 (1975–1980)*, p. 580.
117. Ibid., p. 577.
118. "Focus on the Eastern Province," p. 8; Economist Intelligence Unit, *Quarterly Economic Review of Saudi Arabia, Jordan* (2nd Quarter, 1977): 13.

Second Development Plan, an estimated 338,000 new urban housing units are needed. It is recognized that housing needs cannot be met during the five-year period and that it will be "some years" after 1980 before the goal of adequate housing can be achieved.[119]

The Lower Gulf Shaikhdoms

Urbanization and City Growth. The Arab shaikhdoms of the lower Persian Gulf have undergone some of the most dramatic growth that has ever propelled a society into the twentieth century. The recent growth rates of these countries and cities (Tables 10–10 and 10–11) are the highest in the world. The population of the United Arab Emirates increased from 178,700 in 1968 to 655,937 in 1975, a phenomenal growth rate of 20.4 percent per annum.[120] The new population has concentrated in the cities, helped by indigenous rural-urban migration, and so the growth of the urban areas is even higher. Abū Dhabī City increased from 22,023 in 1968 to an estimated 200,000 in 1975, an annual growth rate of 37 percent!

Qatar, increasing at about a 13 percent per annum rate, had an estimated population of 80,000 in 1969 and 190,000 in 1976.[121] The capital, Dōha, was only a small fishing town of 20,000 before the first exports of oil from Qatar in 1949, with no electricity, no local water supply, and not even a single paved road. By 1976, Dōha had an estimated population of 140,000.

Bahrain, with a population of 266,078 in 1975,[122] presents something of a contrast to the other small Arab states of the Gulf. The population certainly is increasing rapidly by world standards, but the 4 percent per annum increase from 1959 to 1975 is modest for this region (although the rate of growth has been slightly higher in the 1970s). Oil was discovered comparatively early in Bahrain, but not in quantities of its neighbors. With production and exports beginning in the 1930s, the industry has long since peaked. The gradual and more orderly growth of the petroleum industry there also is responsible for another unusual characteristic for this area, the fact that Bahrainis are the great majority in their own country. Ever since the first census of 1941, aliens usually have comprised slightly less than one-fifth of the total population (Table 10–12). In 1971, of the total of 216,078 persons, 82.5 percent were Bahrainis and 17.5 percent foreigners. The vast majority of these foreigners live in the capital area of Manāma and Muharraq or in Awālī, the BAPCO town, and nearby Riffa.[123] Omanis have been the predominate aliens, while Iranians, Indians, and Pakistanis are the next largest groups (Table 10–13).

119. Kingdom of Saudi Arabia, *Development Plan, 1395–1400 (1975–1980)*, p. 580.

120. Trucial States, Census of Population, 1968, and United Arab Emirates, Census of Population, 1975, reported in *Arab World File*, March 1976 and *Middle East Yearbook, 1977* (Durham: Middle East Documentation Centre, University of Durham, 1977), p. 269.

121. Ibid., p. 214; Hill, "The Gulf States: Petroleum and Population Growth," p. 263.

122. *The Middle East and North Africa, 1977–78* (London: Europa Publications, 1977), p. 243.

123. Emile A. Nakhleh, *Bahrain: Political Development in a Modernizing Society* (Lexington, Mass.: D.C. Heath and Company, 1976), p. 18.

Bahrain has been predominately urban for many decades, and at least since 1959 the urban population has comprised almost four-fifths of the population. It has a large indigenous Shī'ī population, and although they traditionally have occupied the villages and rural areas, recent rural-urban migration has increased their numbers considerably in the lower ranks of the urban labor force.[124] In actuality, three-fourths of the urban population live in only two cities, Manāma and Muharraq (Table 10–11), and this capital area's total also is more than half of the inhabitants of the country (58.6 percent in 1971). By the mid-1970s, Manāma had passed the 100,000 mark and together these twin cities had over 150,000 inhabitants.

Statistically, the smaller shaikhdoms of the Persian Gulf are some of the most urbanized countries of the developing world. By 1975, some of these states were at least three-fourths urban (Table 10–10), and even then many of the rural

124. John Duke Anthony, *Arab States of the Lower Gulf: People, Politics, Petroleum* (Washington, D.C.: The Middle East Institute, 1975), p. 65.

TABLE 10–10. CITY AND NATIONAL POPULATION GROWTH IN UNITED ARAB EMIRATES, 1968–75, AND QATAR, 1969–76

United Arab Emirates	1968	Urban pop. as % of 1968 Emirate pop.	1975	1968–75 % annual growth	Urban pop. as % of 1975 Emirate pop.
Abū Dhabī	46,375		235,662	26.1	
Abū Dhabī City	22,023	47.5	200,000[a]	37[a]	85[a]
Dubai	58,971		209,231	19.8	
Dubai City	57,469	97.5	200,000[a]	20[a]	96[a]
Sharja	31,668		88,188	15.8	
Sharja City	19,198	60.6	75,000[a]	21[a]	85[a]
Ra's al-Khaima	24,387		57,282	13.0	
Ra's al-Khaima Town	5,244	21.5	25,000[a]	25[a]	44[a]
Fujaira	9,735		26,498	15.4	
Fujaira Town	777	8.0	5,000?[a]	30[a]	19[a]
'Ajmān	4,246		21,566	26.1	
'Ajmān Town	3,725	87.7	20,000?[a]	27[a]	93[a]
Umm al-Qaiwain	3,744		16,879	24.0	
Umm al-Qaiwain Town	2,928	78.2	10,000?[a]	19[a]	59[a]
	179,126		655,937[b]	20.4	
	111,364	62.2	535,000[a]	25[a]	82[a]
Qatar	*1969*	*1969*	*1976*	*1969–76*	*1976*
Qatar	80,000[a]		190,000[a]	13[a]	
Dōha	60,000[a]	75[a]	140,000[a]	13[a]	74[a]
Umm Sa'īd	?		6,000[a]	—	3[a]
			146,000[a]		77[a]

[a] Estimates.
[b] Includes 631 inhabitants whose emirate of residence has not been determined.
Source: Trucial States, Census of Population, 1968; United Arab Emirates, Census of Population, 1975, in *Arab World File* (March 1976); *The Middle East Yearbook, 1977.*

inhabitants are near urban areas, being "rural" only due to administrative boundaries and statistical enumerations. Even in 1968, the three cities of Dubai, Abū Dhabī, and Sharja comprised 54.6 percent of the total population of the Emirates (then, the Trucial States). Although the absolute numbers are relatively small compared to the nearby larger nations, the concentration of urban population is one of the outstanding characteristics of the Arab side of the lower Gulf and its economic transformation.

The development of the oil industry within the last several decades, and earlier in Bahrain, has provided the capital for industrialization and urban growth. These developments have required great amounts of labor, especially during construction phases, and this could be supplied only by bringing in large numbers of immigrant workers. These laborers had to be housed and provided with necessary services, which meant more construction—and more workers. The cities have expanded at unbelievable rates, and were it not for some of the revenues available from the petroleum industry to invest in housing and urban

TABLE 10-11. POPULATION OF CITIES IN BAHRAIN, 1959–71

Rank[a] and city	1959	1965	1959–65 % annual growth	1971	1965–71 % annual growth	1971 % of urban population
1. Manāma	61,726	79,098	4.4	88,785	1.9	52.6
2. Muharraq	27,115	34,430	4.2	37,732	1.5	22.4
3. Jidhafs	5,591	7,941	6.3	11,152	5.8	6.6
4. Riffa	6,623	9,403	6.3	10,731	2.2	6.4
5. Isa Town	—	—	—	7,501	—	4.4
6. Sitra	3,926	5,071	4.6	6,663	4.7	3.9
7. Hidd	4,440	5,230	2.9	5,269	0.1	3.1
8. Awālī	3,123	2,097	—7.2	984	—13.4	0.6
Total	112,544	143,270	4.3	168,817	2.8	100.0
Rural Areas	30,591	38,933	4.3	47,261	3.3	
Total Bahrain	143,135	182,203	4.3	216,078	2.9	

[a] Rank based upon 1971 population.
Source: Bahrain, Ministry of Finance and National Economy, Statistical Abstract, 1972.

TABLE 10-12. BAHRAINI AND IMMIGRANT POPULATIONS, 1941–71

Census date	Bahrainis Number	% of total	% annual growth	Immigrants Number	% of total	% annual growth	Total Number	% annual growth
January 1941	74,040	82.3	—	15,930	17.7	—	89,970	—
March 1950	91,179	83.2	2.3	18,471	16.8	1.6	109,650	2.2
May 1959	118,734	83.0	2.9	24,401	17.0	3.1	143,135	2.9
February 1965	143,814	78.9	3.4	38,389	21.1	8.2	182,203	4.3
1971	178,193	82.5	3.6	37,885	17.5	—0.2	216,078	2.9

Source: Bahrain, Ministry of Finance and National Economy, Statistical Abstract, 1972.

development, they would be in a most critical situation—similar to much of the developing world. As it is, there are housing shortages, neglect of the needs of the foreign workers, inadequate city planning, and insufficient funds allocated to properly alleviate many of the problems resulting from the great expansion.

Rural-urban migration within the Gulf shaikhdoms also has increased the urbanization. Many Shī'ī villagers in Bahrain have migrated to the capital region, while in the rest of these states Bedouin nomads have begun to settle in the cities. Often the nomads are induced to settle with numerous benefits in order to help counter the growing foreign population. In Qatar, the ruling Āl Thānī family have settled entire nomadic tribes around their numerous palaces, subsidizing them and having them available to help defend the regime if needed.[125] These settled nomads, as elsewhere in the Gulf, live in tents or in flimsy palmfrond dwellings (barastis). Often these are located in shanty towns on the outskirts of the cities. Being employed in the low-status unskilled jobs, they are only marginally integrated into the urban society.[126]

The foreign workers who have swelled the population of the cities of the lower Gulf come from many Arab and non-Arab countries. As with Kuwait, the immigrant population includes higher-status, white-collar workers, principally from Palestine, Lebanon, Egypt, Iraq, Pakistan, and India, holding jobs such as engineers, foremen, storekeepers, and accountants. This class is quite well off compared with the local majority. At the other end of the social scale are the greater number of unskilled foreign laborers, composed principally of Arabs from Oman and Yemen and of Iranians, Indians, and Pakistanis.[127] In fact, in 1968 in Abū Dhabī, when 26,023 aliens constituted 56.1 percent of the state's population,

125. Ibid., p. 85.   126. Ibid., p. 11.   127. Ibid., p. 127.

TABLE 10–13. IMMIGRANT NATIONALITIES IN BAHRAIN, 1971

Nationality	Number	% of immigrant population	% of total population
Omanis	10,785	28.5	5.0
Yemenis	1,538	4.1	0.7
Jordanians/Palestinians	1,338	3.5	0.6
Sa'ūdīs	1,332	3.5	0.6
Other Arabs	2,008	5.3	0.9
All Arabs	17,001	44.9	7.8
Indians	6,657	17.6	3.1
Pakistanis	5,377	14.2	2.5
Iranians	5,097	13.4	2.4
British	2,901	7.7	1.3
All others	852	2.2	0.4
Non-Arabs	20,884	55.1	9.7
Total	37,885	100.0	17.5

Source: Bahrain, Ministry of Finance and National Economy, Statistical Abstract, 1972.

42 percent were Iranians and 34 percent from India and Pakistan.[128] Many of the Indians and Iranians in the shaikhdoms are merchants, and in these states Persian is often the commercial *lingua franca*.[129]

The great number of foreign workers has become an embarrassment and even a potential sociopolitical danger to many of the lower Gulf nations. In 1968, the foreign population of the Emirates (Trucial States) comprised 36.7 percent and the native citizens 63.3 percent. By 1975, the indigenous Arab populations of the Emirates formed an even smaller minority than in Kuwait, with perhaps only about one-fourth of the total being native inhabitants.[130] In Qatar, only 30,000 to 50,000 (16 to 26 percent) of the estimated 190,000 persons in 1975 were indigenous citizens. The foreign population is actually higher than the official count in the shaikhdoms because of the number of illegal aliens working in these states.

In order not to dilute the indigenous Arab population (and disregarding the Iranian ancestry of many of these natives), citizenship and many other rights usually are denied to foreigners. They cannot own land or housing and are not allowed certain free educational, health, and other benefits. In Qatar, nationality can be extended only to a maximum of ten persons annually, who must have resided in Qatar for ten years in the case of Arabs and fifteen years for others. Even when granted nationality, for a period of five years the new citizens are not equal to native-born Qataris with regard to certain types of employment.[131] In Bahrain, only 432 aliens were naturalized between 1948 and 1969.[132]

A major dilemma faces the shaikhdoms. There is the need for an industrial infrastructure, but in order to develop this sector more foreign labor must be imported. A recent exhaustive survey of the industrial future of the United Arab Emirates by a Swiss consulting firm estimated that to support the needed industry, the Emirates' present population of three-fourths of a million would have to increase to three million by 1985.[133] Yet, severe social problems and inadequate facilities already exist. In Abū Dhabī, 73 percent of the population in 1975 were men and 73 percent also were foreigners. This state had the highest rate of inflation in the world between 1972–75, and compared with other major cities of the world the wages are the highest or second highest for nearly every range of skill. But there are still few manufacturing industries in production or under construction in Abū Dhabī.[134]

On the other hand, Bahrain has been able to successfully diversify its economy. With the oil industry almost half a century old there, and relatively small by Persian Gulf standards, the Bahrainis have had to rely upon other industries and services. The establishment of a major aluminum smelter (Alba) in 1971, which employs about 2,300 workers, represents this strategy. The BAPCO refinery, which gets crude from Sa'ūdī Arabia, is the second largest refinery in the Persian Gulf. The main port is Mīnā Salmān, 3.5 kilometers south of Manāma,

128. Hill, "The Gulf States: Petroleum and Population Growth," p. 267.
129. Anthony, *Arab States*, p. 17.
130. *Middle East Yearbook, 1977*, p. 269.
131. Hill, "The Gulf States: Petroleum and Population Growth," p. 264.
132. Ibid., p. 259.
133. *Middle East Economic Digest* 21 (August 5, 1977): 5.
134. Ibid., 21 (September 23, 1977): 3; 21 (August 5, 1977): 5.

and it has become one of the biggest and most important ports in the Gulf, handling a considerable trade and, more recently, becoming a major ship-repairing and service center with the completion of the OAPEC-financed Arab Shipbuilding and Repair Yard (ASRY). The island has become an offshore entrepôt service center for the Arab side of the Gulf, and this has been a major impetus for the growth of Manāma and Muharraq.[135]

Helped by the collapse of Beirut, the capital has become a major international business center for the Middle East. Excellent communication via satellite transmission and major non-stop flights to the Muharraq airport, including the Concorde, are some of the attractions for the business community. Bahrain allows "offshore companies" (businesses whose transactions are largely external to the country, but who can operate in Bahrain free from taxation by paying only a modest annual registration fee). In 1977, for instance, there were thirty-two offshore banks with assets of $13.2 billion.[136] Also, there is a free zone at Mīnā Salmān to attract small industries, exempting them from import duties on raw materials and most capital goods. Further impetus for the growth of the capital will result from the completion of a causeway with a four-lane highway between Bahrain and the Sa'ūdī Arabian mainland at al-Khobar. To be completed in the early 1980s, the causeway is expected to lead to the building of more hotels in the capital. More apartments might be added as well, in order to attract weekending Sa'ūdī Arabians and Kuwaitis away from their strict environment.

In the United Arab Emirates, an important pattern of urban growth is the gradual coalescence of several of the major cities, as well as the lack of cooperation and even the competition between urban areas, because they are located in different states of the federation. Dubai and Sharja are the best examples that have duplicate, adjacent major port facilities, international airports, and urban functions. The construction of a $765-million, 74-berth port 15 kilometers north of Dubai represents an example of this pattern. If 'Ajmān and Umm al-Qaiwain ever start to develop at the pace of the other states, urbanization will affect the entire coast for approximately 50 kilometers, from Dubai to the city of Umm al-Qaiwain.[137]

Urban Planning and Housing. The rapid urbanization of the shaikhdoms has placed an extreme strain on the facilities and infrastructures of the cities. Municipalities exist in all these cities, but these agencies often must struggle with inadequate authority and funding. City planning, in an attempt to control the rampant construction and sprawl, often runs into conflict with the national goals of growth and industrialization.

In the United Arab Emirates, master plans have been prepared for most of the major cities, including Abū Dhabī, Dubai, Sharja, and Ra's al-Khaima. City planning departments are responsible for implementing these plans, which emphasize the building of elaborate street systems with numerous roundabouts; street

135. Nakhleh, *Bahrain*, p. 4.
136. "Focus on Bahrain," *The Times* (London), Special Report (December 16, 1977): 7.
137. Although it is doubtful that these two northern cities will grow as rapidly as Dubai or Sharja, Japanese consultants are currently working on the design of a new township for 'Ajmān to accommodate 30,000 inhabitants. See Economist Intelligence Unit, *Quarterly Economic Review of the Arabian Peninsula: Shaikhdoms and Republics* (1st Quarter 1977): 40.

improvements; zoning of urban land into residential, commercial, industrial, and other uses; furnishing a potable water supply and distribution system; providing sewage systems; and selecting and developing suitable sites for schools, parks, and playing fields.[138]

The Abū Dhabī city plan has directed development around a rectangular street pattern linked together by 170 roundabouts. The active city planning department has attempted to control the growth by approving plans and preventing buildings from rising higher than twelve stories. In 1976 more than 400 construction licenses were granted for multistory apartment and office blocks in the city.[139] A major project of the planners has been a drainage scheme to prevent surface water from flooding the street-level floors and stagnating in the alleys of Abū Dhabī. Although the planning department is responsible for zoning in the city, in 1974 a decision on the national level was made to move all the factories to Mafraq. Located some 30 kilometers inland to the southeast of the capital, a new town will be constructed at this industrial site.[140]

In Dubai, one of the most important government institutions is the Municipal Council of the capital, made up of sixteen members appointed by the Emir from among the merchant community. The Council, assisted by a small bureaucracy, administers the municipality and is responsible for its town planning. It has been very active and successful, partly due to its director, Kamal Hamza, a Sudanese national.[141] Dubai had a master plan designed as early as 1960 by British planners. It included the creation of a town center, the establishment of outlying residential areas, and the preservation of the focus on Dubai Creek that divides the city into two halves.[142] In 1969, the heights of buildings were restricted to nine stories, depending upon their location. However, this regulation was abandoned in the 1970s and higher apartment and office buildings are under construction, including a 33-story trade center that not only will be the tallest building on the Persian Gulf, but will have a full-size skating rink and a revolving restaurant on top.

Within the old sections of Dubai, redevelopment has been largely confined to buildings of mixed commercial and residential use on privately owned land, although some of the best traditional houses, as in the Bastakiyya quarter, are being preserved.[143] In these older areas, there is an increasing tendency for plots to be developed for rental rather than for owner occupation. On the main-road frontages, many multistory buildings have been constructed, with the upper floors often given over to offices. Along Dubai Creek there has been some land reclamation and land values are becoming very high, with growing pressure for

138. K. G. Fenelon, *The United Arab Emirates: An Economic and Social Survey* (2nd ed.; London: Longman, 1976), p. 113; Ragaei El Mallakh, "The challenge of affluence: Abu Dhabi," *Middle East Journal* 24 (Spring 1970): 143.

139. "Partners in growth: The Gulf," *Aramco World Magazine* 28 (January/February 1977): 7.

140. Michael Tomkinson, *The United Arab Emirates: An Insight and a Guide* (Hammamet, Tunisia: Michael Tomkinson Publishing, 1975), p. 91.

141. Anthony, *Arab States*, pp. 154, 162.

142. John R. Harris, Architects and Planning Consultants, *Dubai Development Plan: Review, May 1971* (London: John R. Harris, 1971).

143. Annes Coles and Peter Jackson, *A Windtower House in Dubai* (London: Art and Archeology Research Papers, 1975).

the multistory buildings. In the new suburbs, the development has been largely single- and two-story residential units, although even here there has been an increasing demand for multistory apartment buildings.

In Sharja, the agency responsible for administering and planning the city is the municipality of Sharja, which was incorporated almost fifty years ago. Its activities have expanded slowly and it is a well-established, well-recognized body. The executive apparatus is probably the most formal and elaborate of any cities of the Emirates.[144] Similarly, the municipality of Ra's al-Khaima is important and even has had responsibility for overseeing much of the state's modest development program in recent years. Most of its income is derived from various taxes and licensing fees, supplemented by subsidies from the Ruler.[145]

Dōha, the capital of Qatar, was the object of extensive city planning, beginning in the 1960s. The old city of Dōha was redeveloped by the government purchasing land in the city center, making generous payments to the Qatari landowners. Extensive residential areas were developed in the suburbs, and many of the individuals who had received payments for the land in the center built their houses with that capital.[146] More recently, emphasis has been on land reclamation, filling in the western part of Dōha Bay, and creating residences for 10,000 persons. Included in this area is a wealthy, self-contained development that will have a tower with restaurants and observation decks, a shopping plaza and arcade, a hotel and conference complex, and housing for senior officials and diplomats.[147]

Unlike Qatar (or Kuwait), Abū Dhabī has avoided any large land purchase scheme in which the government buys land from private citizens at highly inflated prices and gives or resells it to qualified nationals below the market price. The Kuwaiti experience of many individuals lacking productive economic incentives because of the high payments has been one of the major deterrents for a similar program in Abū Dhabī. On the other hand, this policy of preserving a work ethic has alienated many of the urbanites and businessmen, who lack the capital to open or expand a business.[148]

As in Iran and the other larger states of the Persian Gulf, a number of new towns have been constructed in the shaikhdoms in conjunction with industrial complexes. In Bahrain, the town of Awālī was built to house the employees of the BAPCO refinery and the adjacent industrial area, while Isa Town was built just south of Manāma to help solve the housing problem of the capital. Begun in the mid-1960s, the land was donated by the Emir and the houses were built with low-interest mortgages. By the mid-1970s, there were over 15,000 persons living in this self-contained city, with its shops, schools, mosques, community centers, and other facilities. Also, near Isa Town a sports city is being constructed, which includes a 30,000-seat stadium and an Olympic-size swimming complex.[149]

144. Anthony, *Arab States,* p. 172.

145. Ibid., pp. 192–93.

146. Hill, "The Gulf States: Petroleum and Population Growth," p. 263.

147. *Gulf Handbook, 1976–77* (1st edition; Bath: Trade and Travel Publications Ltd., 1976), p. 394.

148. El Mallakh, "The challenge of affluence," pp. 142–44; Anthony, *Arab States,* p. 136.

149. *Middle East Economic Digest,* Special Report on Construction (August 5, 1977): x; "Focus on Bahrain," p. 8.

Umm Saʻīd is a new town 25 kilometers south of the Qatari capital designed to house the labor force of the industrial complex being developed there. A radial pattern of mixed high-rise and low-rise housing around a central commercial core is planned, and in 1977 foreign contractors began 1,400 housing units in the town.[150] In Abū Dhabī, plans are to set up a petrochemical industry in a new town at Ruwais, 100 miles west of the capital. The city is expected to house 40,000 to 80,000 persons, although as of 1977 financial problems have prevented much progress on the project.[151]

Housing shortages in the burgeoning cities of the lower Gulf are inevitable. The situation is especially acute among the immigrant workers, who continue to flow into the cities for employment. Many of these workers live in shanty towns or rent the older houses and apartments at exorbitant rates. Sometimes fifteen to twenty males will share one housing unit, although part of the overcrowding is voluntary, because the immigrants want to save as much money as possible to take back to their homeland.[152]

Within the United Arab Emirates cement-block houses and reinforced concrete, multistory apartment buildings are quickly replacing the date-palm *barasti* structures, which had constituted some 40 percent of the housing in the late 1960s. In Abū Dhabī, from 1968 to 1971, the percentage of stone or concrete houses increased four-fold and the number of *barasti*s fell by 20 percent.[153] In the cities of Abū Dhabī, Dubai, and Sharja, the trend is toward large blocks of centrally air-conditioned apartments, rising four or more stories. These blocks usually have shops or offices on the ground floor, with apartments in the upper stories.

Low-cost housing for lower-income families has been erected by all the governments of shaikhdoms, although the effectiveness of the program varies. These houses are usually one-story and built in the suburbs. They are referred to as low-cost housing not because of their actual costs, which can be quite high due to the cost of materials and wages,[154] but because the occupants (citizens) often pay either nothing or only nominal fees for them. In other instances, similar to the programs in Kuwait and Saʻūdī Arabia, long-term (20 to 25 year) interest-free government loans form the basis of such housing. In Qatar, such a low-cost or "popular" housing scheme was begun in 1964 under the Ministry of Labor and Social Affairs. Repayment of the long-term loan was either related to the financial capacity of the recipient (but to be repaid only to 70 percent of the value) or completely waived. Disabled or elderly Qataris also could rent these units for nominal amounts. By 1975, over 650 units had been handed over free, most of the newer units being constructed were to be free, and many of the existing loans were simply being canceled after nonpayment.[155]

150. *Gulf Handbook, 1976–77*, p. 394; Economist Intelligence Unit, *Quarterly Economic Review of the Arabian Peninsula: Shaikdoms and Republics* (1st Quarter 1977): 26; *Qatar: A Forward Looking Country with Centuries Old Traditions* (Paris: Delroisse, for the Ministry of Information, Qatar, n.d.), p. 151.

151. *Middle East Economic Digest* 21 (August 5, 1977): 5; 21 (September 23, 1977): 3.

152. Anthony, *Arab States*, p. 16.

153. Fenelon, *The United Arab Emirates*, pp. 110–11.

154. For example, some low-cost units built in Abū Dhabī recently cost about $24,000 per unit. See *Essays: United Arab Emirates* (Zug, Switzerland: T.R.P. Ltd., for Ministry of Information and Culture, U.A.E., 1976), p. 88.

155. *Gulf Handbook, 1976–77*, p. 394.

In Abū Dhabī, all unused land is owned by the Emir and he allocates plots to nationals who have requested property. A native can sell or exchange his plot for another piece of land only with the consent of the Emir. Foreigners are not allowed to own property and can lease land from a citizen for a maximum of eight years only, after which the land together with any buildings or improvements made by the tenant revert to the original owner. The short leases have obvious drawbacks, in that tenants are reluctant to improve or even fully maintain the properties, especially toward the end of the period of the lease.[156]

In spite of the problems in housing, the inhabitants of Abū Dhabī are generally better off than those of the other states of the Emirates. Public housing is especially inadequate in the other states. On the other hand, immigrants have found it much easier to purchase land and even obtain citizenship in Sharja than in the other lower Gulf shaikhdoms. This less restrictive policy has been an attempt by Sharja to counteract the phenomenal growth of Dubai and Abū Dhabī.[157]

Bahrain underwent a housing boom in the mid-1970s. Construction costs tripled between 1973 and 1976 and land values rose at least six-fold. Expensive apartments, which may rent for several thousand dollars per month, were built in conjunction with multistory office buildings. For the less wealthy, five-story blocks of apartments and prefabricated houses were being constructed. Although the construction boom slackened in 1977, the urban areas of Bahrain still need about 15,000 more housing units to reduce the overcrowding.[158]

Oman

Urbanization and City Growth. Oman has never had an official census, and population estimates for the country (by informed individuals) vary from 350,000 to 1.25 million persons.[159] The great majority of the people are in the northern part of the country, and traditionally most of the inhabitants have lived in permanent settlements, including many larger towns on the coast such as Suhar, Sīb, Matrah, Muscat, and Sūr. Interior towns also have been prominent historically, such as Nizwa, Izkī, and Bahla. Inhabitants of the interior have been principally followers of the strict Ibādī sect, while the coastal towns have "orthodox" Sunnīs and even large numbers of Shī'īs, especially among merchants. The coastal towns also traditionally had large minorities of Indians, Baluchis, Iranians, Pakistanis, and even Africans.[160]

Changes began in Oman essentially only after 1970 because of the accession of Sultan Qābūs ibn Sa'īd and the fact that oil exports did not begin until 1967. The oil revenue, although modest compared to most of the Persian Gulf countries,

156. Fenelon, *The United Arab Emirates*, p. 111.
157. Anthony, *Arab States*, p. 181.
158. "Focus on Bahrain," p. 5; *Middle East Economic Digest* 21 (June 17, 1977): 18.
159. J. S. Birks, "Some aspects of demography related to development in the Middle East, with special reference to the Sultanate of Oman," *British Society for Middle East Studies Bulletin* 3 (1976): 79–80.
160. Donald Hawley, *Oman and Its Renaissance* (London: Stacey International, 1977), pp. 73–107, 165–75.

in combination with the ruler's modernization programs, has begun to transform the urban environment. This is particularly true for the capital, Muscat, and its twin city, the commercial center of Matrah. Whereas their population was about 30,000 at the end of the 1960s, the population had at least doubled and perhaps tripled by the later 1970s.

The expansion of the capital region is due to migration from the interior and the return of many Omanis who have been working in the nearby countries with their oil-inflated economies. There is, in fact, a shortage of labor in Oman, although much of it is for skilled occupations that the largely unskilled Omanis cannot fill. For instance, about 85 percent of the teachers in the country come from other Arab states, such as Egypt, Jordan, and Sudan, while most of the doctors are Indians and Pakistanis. The lack of trained Omanis is certainly understandable when one considers the fact that in 1970 for the entire country there were only three schools with 900 male students, one hotel, five kilometers of paved road, 800 cars, and one hospital, run by American missionaries. By 1976, there were 207 schools with 65,000 pupils of both sexes, 22,000 cars and taxis, 12 hospitals, 32 modern clinics, and 2 maternity centers.[161]

Urban Planning and Housing. Oman's national development policy has the stated goal of erasing the differences between the coast and the more backward interior. This policy includes the development of towns in the interior with an eye to preventing further rural-urban migration and establishing good road links to the capital. The capital area is to be built up, and, in fact, it is this region of Muscat–Matrah–Sīb that is getting most of the attention. Recently, 55 percent of the development budget went to the capital area. Interior projects also have been primarily economically nonproductive, concentrating on the provision of such essential services as schools and hospitals.[162]

It is the coastal cities that are getting the functions most conducive to economic and population growth. Suhār and Sūr are to be the major fishing centers, and the former is to have a new harbor and a major copper-smelting plant. In the capital area, Muscat is being built up as the administrative center of Oman, Matra-Ruwi as the center of trade and commerce, and Wutayya as the cultural center. Mīnā al-Fahal, Matrah's new harbor, is to be the headquarters for the exporting of oil. Major housing developments have been completed at Qurm, Ruwi, and Madīnat Qābūs, the latter being a prestigious, model development combining traditional and modern architectural styles. The capital area is broken up by hills and mountains, but eventually the capital region may fill many of the valleys and the seacoast from Muscat to Sīb, 40 kilometers to the west.[163]

Yet, much of the urban development in the capital has resulted from hasty and unwise decisions. The development in the Ruwi valley, part of the "Greater Matrah Development Plan," was rushed through by the Interim Advisory Council

161. Ibid., pp. 222–32; "Focus on Oman," *The Times* (London), Special Report (November 18, 1977): 1.

162. Fred Scholz, "Sultanat Oman: Ein Entwicklungsland im Südosten der Arabischen Halbinsel," *Die Erde* 108 (1977): 23–74; Economist Intelligence Unit, *Quarterly Economic Review of the Arabian Peninsula: Shaikhdoms and Republics* (1st Quarter 1977): 44.

163. See the map in Scholz, "Sultanat Oman," p. 39.

of the Sultan in six weeks, "with no thought given to alternative locations, with inadequate planning, no thought to likely water requirements and their source, or the likely cost, or the likely population growth."[164] Ruwi is in a land-locked valley without cooling sea breezes and has very limited room for future expansion. As a result of this poor decision, "Oman is now saddled with an untidy and badly located new town development, a development which will dictate the shape of the whole capital area for probably many generations."[165]

The Omani government is attempting to direct and control the rapid development of the capital; many foreign consultants were employed in the early 1970s. A Ministry of Lands was established in 1972 and titles to property in Muscat, Matrah, and the nearby developing areas were systematically registered. Grants were made through this ministry to qualified individuals and all construction had to fit into the zoning plans. But the control was seen to be inadequate, and in 1976 a Ministry of Land Affairs was organized that grouped municipal affairs, planning, and lands under one ministry.[166]

More recently, three British consulting firms have prepared long-range power and water requirement programs, with projected needs for the urban areas from 1977 to 1995. Included in these studies are recommendations for improvements in the structure, organization, finance, operations, and maintenance of the power and water systems of Muscat and the other major cities and towns.[167]

Although Muscat and Matrah had had a sort of municipal status for several decades prior to 1970, the achievements and effectiveness of these municipalities were modest, being confined to elementary public cleaning. A single municipal council for the entire capital area was established after the change in government. However, because the government itself was undertaking so much work and development in the capital region, the municipality was never certain of its responsibilities. Also, the municipal council was formed of prominent businessmen who were on many councils and committees, and who had always to consider their businesses. Its principal duty has been rubbish-disposal and public cleaning, but slowly some people are getting experience in local government. Municipalities also have been formed, from 1973 onward, in a number of the smaller towns such as Nizwa, Suhār, and Sūr. With modest funds provided through the government and a small income from market stall-holders' licenses and fees, these nascent organizations have often made some dramatic changes, especially in the field of clearing rubbish and providing a healthier environment for the community.[168]

Housing has been one of the most immediate problems of the rapid urbanization, especially in the capital region. The government has built many housing units and apartments itself, as well as commissioning low-cost housing. Over 1,000 of the latter units had been built by 1975. The private sector also has been encouraged to build housing, headed by the Oman National Company for Housing Development, a joint venture between banks and the government that provided

164. John Townsend, *Oman: The Making of a Modern State* (London: Croom Helm, 1977), p. 81.
165. Ibid.
166. Hawley, *Oman*, pp. 214–21.
167. "Focus on Oman," p. 8.
168. Townsend, *Oman*, pp. 161–62.

loans for private individuals. More recently, the formation of the Oman Housing Bank has been specifically for encouraging investment in housing for Omani nationals. However, the housing shortage is not as critical as in many other Gulf countries, such as the Emirates or Sa'ūdī Arabia. In fact, foreign companies are forbidden to build housing for their own employees so as to stimulate rentals from Omanis.[169]

Conclusion: The Oil Urbanization and its Comparisons

Urbanization is occurring throughout the developing world as cities grow faster than the rural countryside. The Persian Gulf region, however, is distinguishable because of the extreme rapidity of the urbanization. Vast oil revenues have provided the means to finance gigantic industrial schemes and the construction of entire cities. Existing cities have expanded enormously, resulting in some of the fastest growing cities in the world.

Comparisons with other world regions show that the countries of the Persian Gulf constitute one of the most urbanized areas of the developing world (Table 10–14). Slightly more than half of the inhabitants (53 percent) can be classified as urban in 1975. This percentage actually may vary by several percentage points due to lack of accurate statistics in some of these countries (see Table 10–15), but in any case it would remain at least half urban. Only tropical South America and Central America have higher percentages of urban population of the less developed regions, although the developed world certainly is more urbanized, ranging from 56.6 percent to 85.5 percent. In the Middle East, the regions of North Africa and Southwest Asia (including the Persian Gulf countries) have urban percentages of 39.5 percent and 43.7 percent, respectively.

The urbanization levels within the Persian Gulf region show considerable variations (Table 10–15). Oman is definitely the least urbanized, and the estimate of 20 percent urban is probably too high for this basically rural, traditional society. On the other hand, there are the small Arab shaikhdoms whose urban percentages are similar to or greater than most of the developed regions of the world. Kuwait is the most urbanized and, indeed, is a city-state, although some of the individual states of the United Arab Emirates are similar (Table 10–10). In 1975, the small shaikhdoms, with slightly more than two million persons, were approximately 86 percent urban. With Iraq and Sa'ūdī Arabia included, the Arab side of the Gulf was about 65 percent urban.[170] Iraq is, in fact, the most urbanized of the more populous Persian Gulf countries.

Except for peripheral Oman, Iran is the least urbanized of the Persian Gulf nations.[171] Its urban population was 38 percent in 1966 and 46.8 percent in 1976, somewhat less than the average for the region. But the country's total popula-

169. "Focus on Oman," pp. 2, 6; Hawley, *Oman*, pp. 214–21.
170. This excludes Oman, although even with the estimates of Oman included the total of the Arab side equals 64 percent.
171. It is possible that Sa'ūdī Arabia is less urbanized than Iran, if the urban populations are much smaller and the total much larger than estimated. However, it is doubtful if this is the case.

tion is so much greater than the other nations that it is the main component of the aggregate totals and percentages. Iran's population of 25.8 million in 1966 and 33.6 million in 1976 constituted 67 percent and 62 percent, respectively, of the calculated estimates of the region's total population.

Even though Iran may be the least urbanized, it certainly has more urbanites than any of the other Gulf states (Table 10–15). In the mid-1960s, Iran had more than half (62 percent) of the urban population of these countries, but with the faster urbanization of the Arab states by the mid-1970s, this percentage had dropped to about 55 percent. In the earlier decade, Iran also had more than half of the cities over 50,000 and over 100,000 (and over half of the total population in these size cities). The percentages in these categories also had dropped by the mid-1970s, although approximately half of the urbanites in these larger cities still reside in Iran.

The faster growth of larger cities also is indicated by Table 10–15. Whereas, urban population had not quite doubled in this decade, the total number in cities of 50,000+ was twice the amount and the total of 100,000+ had more than doubled. In the mid-1960s, there were respectively 49 and 22 cities in these two categories, while the total had reached 78 and 45, respectively, by the mid-1970s. This allometric growth (more rapid growth of larger cities) is especially common in the developing world and is further emphasized by the great growth of the metropolises of the region; the total in cities over 500,000 increased from two cities (Tehran and Baghdad) with 4.7 million to ten cities with 13.7 million in the same period.

The allometric growth and concentration of government, industry, services,

TABLE 10–14. URBAN PERCENTAGES OF PERSIAN GULF COUNTRIES AND OF MAJOR WORLD REGIONS, 1975

Less developed regions	1975 % urban[a] of total population	More developed regions	1975 % urban[a] of total population
Tropical South America	59.3	Australia and New Zealand	85.5
Middle America	57.1	Temperate South America	80.8
PERSIAN GULF[b]	53.0	Western Europe	77.1
Southeast Asia	50.0	North America	76.5
Caribbean	48.2	Japan	75.2
Southern Africa	46.2	Soviet Union	60.5
Southwest Asia	43.7	Southern Europe	59.2
North Africa	39.5	Eastern Europe	56.6
Middle Africa	24.6		
China	23.5		
South Asia	23.0		
West Africa	18.5		
East Africa	12.3		

[a] Urban defined by each nation; 5,000+ used for Persian Gulf.
[b] c. 1975–76, see Table 10–15.
Source: Richard Hay, Jr., "Patterns of Urbanization and Socio-Economic Development in the Third World: An Overview," in Janet Abu-Lughod and Richard Hay, Jr., eds., *Third World Urbanization* (1977); Persian Gulf calculations by author.

TABLE 10-15. URBAN POPULATION COMPARISONS OF THE PERSIAN GULF COUNTRIES, 1965-69 AND 1974-76

	Total (thous.)	Urban (5,000+) (thous.)	% of national total	50,000+ (thous.)	% of national total	No. of cities	100,000+ (thous.)	% of national total	No. of cities
ca. 1965–69									
Iran (1966)	25,789	9,794	38.0	6,738	26.1	27	5,667	22.0	12
Iraq (1965)	8,220	4,217	51.3	3,128	38.1	12	2,597	31.6	5
Saʻūdī Arabia (1962–63)	3,302	1,100?	33.3?	680	20.6	6	504	15.3	3
Kuwait (1965)	467	453	97.0	386	82.7	1	386	82.7	1
U.A.E. (1968)	179	104	58.1	57	31.8	1	—	—	—
Qatar (1969)	80	60	75.0	60	75.0	1	—	—	—
Bahrain (1965)	182	141	77.5	114	77.5	1[a]	114	77.5	1[a]
Oman (1965)	500?	100?	20?	—	—	—	—	—	—
Total (rounded)	39 mil.	1.6 mil.	41	11.2 mil.	29	49	9.3 mil.	24	22
ca. 1974–76									
Iran (1976)	33,592	15,715	46.8	11,262	33.5	42	9,800	29.2	22
Iraq (1976)	11,750	8,000?	68?	7,253	61.7	19	6,679	56.8	11
Saʻūdī Arabia (1974)	5,750?	3,000?	52?	2,426	42?	10	2,227	39?	7
Kuwait (1975)	995	946	95.1	764	76.8	1	764	76.8	1
U.A.E. (1975)	656	535	81.6	475	72.4	3	400	61.0	2
Qatar (1976)	190	146	76.8	140	73.7	1	140	73.7	1
Bahrain (1975)	266	187	70.3	137	51.5	1[a]	137	51.5	1[a]
Oman (1976)	750?	150?	20?	60	8?	1[b]	—	—	—
Total (rounded)	54 mil.	29 mil.	53	22.5 mil.	42	78	20.1 mil.	37	45

[a] Manāma and Muharraq as one city.
[b] Muscat and Matra as one city.
Source: Computed by author from numerous sources. See Tables 10–1, 10–3, 10–4, 10–9, 10–10, and 10–11.

and population in a few of the largest cities of the Middle East has led a number of writers to suggest that there is an overconcentration of population in these centers. Overurbanization has occurred and the lack of an articulated urban hierarchy is part of the malady.[172] This belief further implies that "under-urbanism" has resulted because of the lag in the economic and qualitative aspect of urbanites in comparison to the cities of the developed world. Hence per capita GNP, daily calorie intake, number of telephones and a myriad of other indicators are given as evidence of the lack of a true "urbanistic modern life-style"[173] in these cities.

Although it already has been shown that economic development and urban hierarchies certainly are not synonymous,[174] the concept of hierarchies has even less applicability in the Persian Gulf region. Within the Arabian peninsula, agricultural land is scarce and cities did not evolve primarily as marketing centers to support local hinterlands. Premodern cities were located on major trade routes or were ports on the coasts. More recently, the fortuitous location of oil fields has been the catalyst for the phenomenal urban development along the Arab side of the Persian Gulf, as well as in southwest Iran. Accessibility of water transport on the Gulf has logically led to industrialization and city development along this coast.

In Iran and Iraq, on the other hand, the urban growth induced by petroleum actually is helping to counteract the primacy of the capitals of these two countries. Specific decentralization programs have been adopted and diversification of industrialization outside of the primate cities has begun. The development of Basra, Mosul, Ābādān, and Ahvāz represents the direct influence of the petroleum industry and its revenues, although programs in all the cities are affected by these funds. But the revenues also are increasing development in the capitals themselves, and so the dominance of Baghdad and Tehran will continue, and urban planners will continue to be faced with formidable problems in these metropolises.

City planners, indeed, have a most unenviable task in dealing with the bursting, sprawling cities of the Persian Gulf region. Most of the problems have been previously identified: the lack of authority, funds, and manpower for implementing any rational plan of urban growth and development. What is needed is more local autonomy and authority for the municipalities to attempt to coordinate and control the evolution of their urban environment. Presently, the centralization of decision-making at the national level has led to duplicate programs, conflict of interests, and gaps. The lack of knowledge or interest in a city's problems shown by individuals living in a distant capital, whose agencies are appraised in terms of national goals and statistics, is understandable.

City planning is hindered by the fact that there are national plans for everything except the cities. Although Sa'ūdī Arabia has proposed to formulate a national urban policy during its Second Development Plan (1975–80), until this

---

172. For example, see Saad E. M. Ibrahim, "Over-urbanization and under-urbanism: The case of the Arab world," *International Journal of Middle East Studies* 6 (January 1975): 29–45.

173. Ibid., pp. 40–41.

174. Brian J. L. Berry, "City size distributions and economic development," *Economic Development and Cultural Change* 9 (July 1961): 573–88; Brian J. L. Berry and Frank E. Horton, *Geographic Perspectives on Urban Systems* (Englewood Cliffs: Prentice-Hall, 1970), pp. 64–93.

is brought to fruition it can be stated that none of the nations of the Persian Gulf have specific national policies or goals for their urban environment. Growth, GNP, industrialization, imports-exports, and balance of payments dominate the goals of these countries. Few resources are allocated, and little thought is placed upon the environment in which the people live.

Urban housing shortages have resulted partly from this lack of emphasis and ineffective city planning, although many of the shortages result simply from the fact that these cities have expanded at such incredible rates. No amount of planning could have foreseen or immediately solved the shortages of cement, bricks, and manpower, or the congestion of the port facilities that kept ships waiting six months during the mid-1970s. The sudden four-fold increase in oil prices at the end of 1973 provided such an increase in revenues for investment that shortages were inevitable. Presently, however, more and more attention is being placed on housing, as previously discussed. Although inadequacies and insufficient housing still exist and problems such as the escalation of prices and financing continue to occur, as compared with the metropolises of South Asia, Southeast Asia, and much of the developing world, the Persian Gulf states do have the funds and the ability to solve their urban housing problems. Whether or not the housing shortages are ended depends upon the priorities established by these nations.

In solving housing needs, however, another problem is being created in the new urban environment. What is happening to the cultural identity—to the culture of this society being transformed overnight into one inhabiting multistory apartment buildings, detached houses, courtyard-less structures of reinforced concrete? A society that had been organized by small neighborhoods, villages, or nomadic tribal groups, and where mutual kinship relationships and obligations were fundamental, has suddenly been thrust into cooperative housing, professional housing projects, and new industrial towns. Residences that enable some of the traditional values to be kept, such as shanty dwellings, are deemed a blight by authorities and are replaced by sterile rows of ill-designed houses. Traditional residences in the old *madina*s are seen as antiquated and fit only for demolishing. The story of Kuwait Town and its redevelopment exemplifies this regrettable attitude.

The new cities of the Gulf are evolving into massive high-rise office buildings and apartments. The skyline of Sharja or Dubai would make some Western city administrators envious. But as Janet Abu-Lughod has so aptly stated: "It will little benefit a country to achieve glistening cities and elegantly appointed dwellings and even massive industrial strength if the moral fibre of that society erodes and if the basic human needs for security, social connectivity and personal worth and significance go unmet."[175]

The nations of the Persian Gulf have given little thought to such considerations. Yet, it is these wider, long-term consequences by which the rapid urbanization of the Persian Gulf and the spectacular growth of its cities finally must be judged.

175. Janet Abu-Lughod, "Problems and Policy Implications of Middle Eastern Urbanization," in United Nations, Economic and Social Office in Beirut, *Studies on Development Problems in Selected Countries of the Middle East, 1972* (New York: United Nations, 1973), p. 61.

Selected Bibliography

Abdulla, Saif Abbas. "Politics, Administration, and Urban Planning in a Welfare Society: Kuwait." Ph.D. thesis, Indiana University, 1973.

Abu-Lughod, Janet. "Problems and Policy Implications of Middle Eastern Urbanization." In *Studies on Development Problems in Selected Countries of the Middle East, 1972,* pp. 42–62. United Nations, Economic and Social Office in Beirut. New York, 1973.

Al-Moosa, Abdulrasoul A. "Bedouin Shanty Settlements in Kuwait: A Study in Social Geography." Ph.D. thesis, University of London, 1976.

Anthony, John Duke. *Arab States of the Lower Gulf: People, Politics, Petroleum.* Washington, D.C., 1975.

Baali, Fuad. "Social factors in Iraqi rural-urban migration." *American Journal of Economics and Sociology* 25 (1966): 359–64.

Bonine, Michael E. "The morphogenesis of Iranian cities." *Annals of the Association of American Geographers* 69 (June 1979): 208–24.

Clarke, J. I., and Fisher, W. B., eds. *Populations of the Middle East and North Africa: A Geographical Approach.* New York: 1972.

Ehlers, Eckart. "Some geographic and socio-economic aspects of tourism in Iran." *Orient* 15 (September 1974): 97–105.

El Mallakh, Ragaei. "The challenge of affluence: Abu Dhabi." *Middle East Journal* 24 (Spring 1970): 135–46.

Fenelon, K. G. *The United Arab Emirates: An Economic and Social Survey,* 2nd ed. London, 1976.

Ffrench, Geoffrey E., and Hill, Allan G. *Kuwait: Urban and Medical Ecology, A Geomedical Study,* Geomedical Monograph Series, no. 4. Berlin, 1971.

Fox, William C. "Baghdad: A city in transition." *East Lakes Geographer* 5 (December 1969): 5–23.

Gulf Handbook, 1976–77, 1st ed. Bath, 1976.

Gulick, John. "Baghdad: Portrait of a city in physical and cultural change." *Journal of the American Institute of Planners* 33 (July 1967): 246–55.

Hakim, Besim Selim. "Co-op housing, Baghdad: An evaluation and recommendations." *Ekistics* 36 (March 1972): 166–72.

Hawley, Donald. *Oman and Its Renaissance.* London, 1977.

Hay, Richard, Jr. "Patterns of Urbanization and Socio-Economic Development in the Third World: An Overview." In *Third World Urbanization,* pp. 71–101, ed. Janet Abu-Lughod and Richard Hay, Jr. Chicago, 1977.

Hill, A. G. "The Gulf States: Petroleum and Population Growth." In *Populations of the Middle East and North Africa: A Geographical Approach,* pp. 242–73, ed. J. I. Clarke and W. B. Fisher. New York, 1972.

Ibrahim, Saad E. M. "Over-urbanization and under-urbanism: The case of the Arab world." *International Journal of Middle East Studies* 6 (January 1975): 29–45.

Iran Almanac and Book of Facts, 1977. Tehran, 1977.

Lawless, R. I. "Iraq: Changing Population Patterns." In *Populations of the Middle East and North Africa: A Geographical Approach,* pp. 97–129, ed. J. I. Clarke and W. B. Fisher. New York, 1972.

Lorimer, J. G. *Gazetteer of the Persian Gulf, 'Oman, and Central Arabia.* Vol. 2:B: Geographical and Statistical. Westmead, 1970.

McGregor, R. "Saudi Arabia: Population and the Making of a Modern State." In *Populations of the Middle East and North Africa: A Geographical Approach,* pp. 220–41, ed. J. I. Clarke and W. B. Fisher. New York, 1972.

Malik, Saleh Abdullah. "Rural Migration and Urban Growth in Riyadh, Saudi Arabia." Ph.D. thesis, University of Michigan, 1973.

Mozayeni, Manootchehr. "City planning in Iran: Evolution and problems." *Ekistics* 38 (October 1974): 264–67.

Nakhleh, Emile A. *Bahrain: Political Development in a Modernizing Society.* Lexington, Mass., 1976.

Naval Intelligence Division. *Iraq and the Persian Gulf.* London, 1944.

Razavian, Mohammad Taghi. "Iranian Communities of the Persian Gulf: A Geographical Analysis." Ph.D. thesis, University of London, 1975.

Scholz, Fred. "Sultanat Oman: Ein Entwicklungsland im Südosten der Arabischen Halbinsel." *Die Erde* 108 (1977): 23–74.

Seger, Martin. "Strukturelemente der Stadt Teheran und das Modell der modernen orientalischen Stadt." *Erdkunde* 29 (March 1975): 21–38.

Shamekh, Ahmed A. "Spatial Patterns of Bedouin Settlement in Al-Qasim Region, Saudi Arabia." Ph.D. thesis, University of Kentucky, 1975.

Shiber, Saba George. *The Kuwait Urbanization.* Kuwait, 1964.

————. *Recent Arab City Growth.* Kuwait, 1968.

Tomkinson, Michael. *The United Arab Emirates: An Insight and a Guide.* Hammamet, Tunisia, 1975.

Townsend, John. *Oman: The Making of a Modern State.* London, 1977.

United Nations. Department of Economic and Social Affairs. *Improvement of Slums and Uncontrolled Settlements.* New York, 1971.

————. *Urban Land Policies and Land-Use Control Measures.* Vol. 5: *Middle East.* New York, 1973.

United Nations. Economic and Social Office in Beirut. *Studies on Social Development in the Middle East, 1971.* New York, 1973.

PART THREE

Culture: Religion, Language, and Literature

11. Religion and Law

JAMES E. DOUGHERTY

 The Persian Gulf is an integral part of what used to be called Asia Minor or the Near East and what is now referred to as the Middle East. No matter what they call it, authorities agree that this geographic region has played a uniquely important role in the religious and moral history and consciousness of mankind, for it is the land of Abraham, Moses, Jesus, and Muhammad, and thus the home of three great monotheistic religions of universal outlook—Judaism, Christianity, and Islam. All three of these religions have survived within the region as a whole, but one has been clearly dominant. "For the last thirteen and a half centuries the Middle East has been pre-eminently the land of Islam, the geographical and spiritual center of the Islamic world, where the civilization of Islam received its first, classical formulations."[1] Generally speaking, the dominance of Islam is even more pronounced in the areas adjacent to the Persian Gulf than in those Arab countries of the Middle East—i.e., Egypt, Lebanon, and Syria—where several other large religious communities survive from ancient times, and where the total cultural, political, economic, and religious, as well as secularizing, impact of the West in modern times has been more noticeable.

Islam is the youngest and the most "historical" of the three monotheistic religions mentioned in the sense that it came to birth in the full light of history. The circumstances of its origins are more readily accessible to the research scholar. Judaism and Christianity preceded Islam, and elements of those religions influenced Muslim belief. "Historically," wrote Philip K. Hitti, "Islam is an offshoot of these other two, and of all faiths it comes nearest to being their kin. All three are the product of one spiritual life, the Semitic life."[2] Islam had to

1. Bernard Lewis, *The Middle East and the West* (Bloomington, Indiana: Indiana University Press, 1964), p. 16.
2. Philip K. Hitti, *The Arabs: A Short History* (Chicago: Regnery–Gateway Editions, 1943), p. 5.

establish itself in the face of the two older and more developed faiths and, like them, to meet the challenge of Greek philosophy, adopting the latter's intellectual tools to strengthen its own self-consciousness.

Jewish and Christian communities had long existed on the Arabian peninsula. It seems certain that the Prophet had come into contact with them, as well as with Christian traders who came to Mecca and Medina from Syria and Abyssinia. Reference is made in the Qur'ān to three religious groups: heathens (or pagans), Jews, and Christians. Prior to Muhammad's preaching, many inhabitants of Arabia would have known about Christian churches and monasteries, and probably had a vague conception of some basic Christian beliefs, but they were never strongly attracted to the Christian faith, even though some accepted it perfunctorily. It is clear from the teachings embodied in the Qur'ān, however, that several fundamental ideas concerning the nature of God, man's relation to God, and the implications of that relationship for the moral behavior of human beings to each other are common to Jews, Christians, and Muslims.[3]

Islam deeply permeates the life of all the societies bordering on the Persian Gulf. In several of these societies, the processes known as modernization, Westernization, and secularization have not been carried as far as in such countries as Egypt, Syria, Lebanon, and Turkey. Charles J. Adams has referred to the gap between the two Islams—the "high Islam" of the intellectual theologians and the simpler, more emotional Islam of the common people.[4] Generally speaking, it can be said that throughout the Persian Gulf area, and especially in Sa'ūdī Arabia, Muscat, and Oman, and the shaikhdoms and emirates, the forms of Islam adhered to by both learned religious elites and popular masses are somewhat more traditional than those that prevail in the more urbanized and Westernized Muslim states to the northwest, closer to the Mediterranean. This, of course, is a matter of degree, not of kind, and should not be exaggerated. For a religious-cultural system dispersed over a wide geographical area—from Morocco to the Philippines—Islam has maintained a remarkable degree of unity and homogeneity of basic beliefs, even though specific religious practices and even certain doctrines differ markedly from place to place or from sect to sect.

Muslims everywhere live in a universe of faith in the existence of a supernatural order beyond time for which life in this world is but a prelude. The laws governing the conduct of human affairs and even certain customs regulating diet, dress, and social amenities have their origin in the will of the Divine Creator. These laws and customs are to be preserved at all costs because they have been prescribed by God Himself. "To change these things deliberately," Charles Adams has written, "is not simply to give up what is familiar; it is also to forsake what is known to be right and true . . . to forsake the way of the fathers."[5] The fundamental distinction between a spiritual and a temporal jurisdiction to which human life is subject—historically and theologically characteristic of Christianity

---

3. P. M. Holt, Introduction to *The Cambridge History of Islam* (hereafter referred to as *CHI*), P. M. Holt, Ann K. S. Lambton, and Bernard Lewis, eds. (Cambridge: Cambridge University Press, 1970), 1: xi.

4. Charles J. Adams, "Islamic Faith," in R. M. Savory, ed., *Introduction to Islamic Civilisation* (Cambridge: Cambridge University Press, 1976), p. 33.

5. Ibid., p. 35.

—has no counterpart in Islam, which does not separate the religious order from the order of politics and the law. The devout Muslim does not look to a "Church" or priesthood that regulates some aspects of life and to a "State" that regulates others, but rather to a community of faith (*umma*) in which all law and policy should conform to the Divine Will. Before we can fully understand the implications of this all-pervasive religious faith for the life of the Persian Gulf peoples in the twentieth century, we must turn to history to see how Islam came to be.

The Pre-Islamic Period

Before the rise of Islam, i.e., during the period known as the Jāhiliyya or "time of ignorance," most Arabs could be called heathens, pagans, polytheists, and animists who venerated stones, trees, wells, and other objects thought to be the dwelling place of deities. Each group of tribes had its favorite god and felt bound to a particular sacred enclave or *haram* that it was obliged to defend by force of arms. Among the gods worshipped by Bedouin tribesmen on the peninsula were *al-Lāt* (associated with the sun), *al-'Uzzā* (the planet Venus), *al-Manāt* (fate), and *al-Ilāh* (the moon). According to Islamic tradition, Muhammad as a youth sacrificed a white sheep to the goddess *al-'Uzzā*, who was for the people of Mecca "the mighty one." The practice of undertaking a pilgrimage to a certain settlement or oasis to do homage to a god residing in a holy place is readily traceable to pagan times. Stones or rocks served as altars for blood sacrifices. According to Herodotus, tribesmen smeared the victim's blood on the stone while dancing around it, and then licked the blood or dipped their hands in it to establish brotherhood ties among themselves.[6] The Qur'ān condemned as unclean and satanical the blood rites at sacred stones. The Prophet also gave orders for the destruction of pagan idols and images. But just as the early Christian Church had "baptized," as it were, certain familiar feasts, symbols, and ceremonial rituals associated with the pagan religion of the Roman empire, so Muhammad would, in sympathy with the customs of his people, reserve a place in the religious culture he was fashioning for such pre-Islamic traditions as the pilgrimage to a holy city (Mecca) and the veneration of the ancient sacred places that Mecca housed—the *Ka'ba* (containing the Black Stone), and a pantheon of various deities that Islamic tradition associates with Adam, Abraham, Hagar, Ishmael, and others.[7]

6. Thomas W. Arnold noted that "Islam knows of no priesthood, of no body of men set apart for the performance of religious duties which the general body of the faithful are not authorized to perform." *The Caliphate* (London: Oxford University Press, 1924), p. 15. H. A. R. Gibb argues that the learned doctors (*'ulamā'*), corresponding to the "scribes" of Judaism, became for all practical purposes a clerical class with social and religious authority and prestige similar to those of the Christian clergy. *Mohammedanism: A Historical Survey* (New York: New American Library, 1955), p. 77. But while the *'ulamā'* can interpret doctrine, they do not perform rituals or act as priestly intermediaries between God and man. The Caliph and other *imāms* usually lead the community in public prayer, but any "acceptable" Muslim can perform that function.

7. For the pagan Arab background, see Hitti, *The Arabs*, pp. 23–26; Alfred Guillaume, *Islam* (Harmondsworth: Penguin Books, 1954), pp. 6–10; and R. B. Serjeant "Historical Review," in A. J. Arberry, ed., *Religion in the Middle East* (Cambridge: Cambridge University Press, 1979), 2: 4–6.

A great world religion arises out of a historical past and within a specific cultural environment. Some elements from the historical-cultural background are reacted against and rejected; other aspects may be appreciated for their enduring human value and incorporated into the new faith and moral practice. But the most important truth about a new religion is that it is new. It contains a message of revelation that people have never heard before—a message that touches them at the deepest core of their being, furnishing an insight into the meaning of reality that henceforth becomes, for both the individual and the society, a central organizing principle of life.[8] The Arabs were, for the most part, polytheists (*mushriks*), but the time was ripe for their acceptance of monotheism. (Some Arabs were *hanifs*, who believed at least vaguely in the God of Abraham.) The Jews were a people of the Book. The Christians, too, had both an old and a new scripture. It was Muhammad's historic achievement that he gave to the Arabs and to countless generations of Muslims their own Book of Revelation.

Muhammad and the Qur'ān

The account of Muhammad's life is well known and requires no retelling in detail. He was born about 571 A.D. into the house of Hāshim of the Quraish tribe, the senior or "holy" kinship group of Mecca. The Quraish controlled the lucrative offices associated with the sacred enclave or *haram* surrounding the *Ka'ba* shrine, including the guardianship of the temple keys, the collection of taxes to supply food and water to the pilgrims, and the care of the council chamber and the banners. Gradually, these various functions had come to be divided between the Quraish branches of 'Abd al-Dār and 'Abd al-Manāf. The latter had further subdivided into the houses of Hāshim (which had responsibility for feeding the pilgrims) and of Umayya. By the time of Muhammad's birth, Mecca was not only a religious shrine but also a thriving caravan center along the route between the Indian trade ports in the south and the Syrian markets in the north.

Muhammad (whose name means "highly praised") was orphaned at an early age and was raised by an uncle, Abū Tālib. When he was in his mid-twenties, he married the wealthy widow Khadīja, who was several years his senior. Khadīja was an astute businesswoman engaged in the conduct of her late husband's caravan commerce. Muhammad had been in her employ, and it is probable, given her wealth, that the proposal was made by the woman. While Khadīja lived, Muhammad would take no other wife. They had four daughters who survived to maturity, and several sons, none of whom survived.

8. All of the great world religions, writes Wilfred Cantwell Smith, are quite literally infinite. "There is no end to their profundity; nor to their ramification, their variety. For each religion is the point at which its adherent is in touch, through the intermediary of an accumulating tradition, with the infinitude of the divine. . . . Manifestly Islam never could have become across the centuries one of the four or five great world religions had it not, like the others, had the quality of having something profound and relevant and personal to say directly to all sorts and conditions of men, of every status, background, capacity, temperament and aspiration." *Islam in Modern History* (Princeton: Princeton University Press, 1957; New York: New American Library, 1959), pp. 15–17.

For four decades there was nothing extraordinary about the life or accomplishments of Muhammad—nothing to attract the attention of Arabs in Mecca or elsewhere. His was a routine existence, lived according to the cultural and religious traditions of his tribe. But he was a man of thought and meditation, endowed with a special gift in the understanding and use of words. His marriage to a woman of means provided greater opportunity for leisure in which the mind could turn away reflectively from the world. It became Muhammad's custom to retreat for meditation to a hillside cave on the outskirts of Mecca. Tradition has it that it was here, in the year 610, that he received his call to preach the truth concerning God—*Allāh*—to his fellow Meccans.[9]

"Recite thou in the name of thy Lord who created, created man from a clod; recite thou that thy Lord is most generous." This command that Muhammad heard is found in the opening verses of chapter 96 of the Qur'ān. Muhammad was commanded to preach, to recite, not to write. Indeed, Muslims have often pointed to his alleged illiteracy (a matter of dispute among scholars) as additional evidence of the divine origin of the message he preached. But whether he was illiterate or not, whether he wrote down parts of the Qur'ān or whether—as is traditionally and more commonly held—the Qur'ān was not finally and authoritatively committed to writing until two decades after his death, it is certain that the fundamental meaning of Qur'ān is "recitation."[10]

The Book consists of more than six thousand verses arranged in one-hundred and fourteen chapters (*sūras*). The language of the Qur'ān is, of course, Arabic. It is the great classic of a people for whom verbal expression has always been the principal artistic medium and over whom the recitation of truth in carefully articulated form could always cast an irresistible spell.[11] The beauty of the Qur'ān can perhaps be fully appreciated only in Arabic; if Western readers find it formidable or tedious, it is usually because they know it only in translation. For nearly thirteen centuries, non-Arab Muslims in such countries as Turkey and Iran were able to read the verses of the Qur'ān, for ritual purposes, only in Arabic. (The first "authorized" translation into a non-Arabic tongue was published in Turkish in 1926 as part of Mustafa Kemal Atatürk's program of nationalism, modernization, and secularization.)

The author of the Qur'ān is believed by all devout Muslims to be Allāh himself—whose name is a combination of the definite article *al-* (meaning "the") with the Arabic word *ilāh* ("god"). Muhammad was not merely inspired to utter his message, as the Jewish prophets and Christian authors of the New Testament had been. Islam contains no formal doctrine of inspiration. The Qur'ān embodies

9. See Alfred Guillaume, *The Life of Muhammad* (Oxford: Oxford University Press, 1955); and W. Montgomery Watt, *Muhammad: Prophet and Statesman* (London: Oxford University Press, 1961). See also the latter's article, "Muhammad," in *CHI*, 1: 30–56.

10. See Guillaume, *Islam*, pp. 55–62; Gibb, *Mohammedanism*, Chapter 3.

11. Hitti, *The Arabs*, pp. 23–25. The importance of the Arabic language for the evolution of Islamic culture cannot be too greatly emphasized. Irfan Shahid has observed that Arabic, instead of remaining an obscure language of the desert, became the sacred language for the Muslim peoples. Arabic emphasis on poetry in pre-Islamic times made it likely that literature would become a prominent constituent of Islamic civilization. Its intimate association with the Qur'ān not only ensured the dominance of Arabic as the Latin of the Muslim world but also enabled the language to maintain its original structure for thirteen centuries and to become the most important single factor in the rise of modern Arab nationalism. "Pre-Islamic Arabia," *CHI*, 1: 28–29.

the dictation of Allāh's own Truth, communicated through the "Spirit" or through a voice at first thought to be God's, but later identified as that of Gabriel, and "taken down" verbatim in the memory of Muhammad. Except for a few passages, the speaker throughout is Allāh in the first person plural.[12]

The Islamic Faith

There is no god but God, *Lā ilāha illa-allāhu!*, Muhammad is His Messenger, His Apostle, the "one sent" (*rasūl*). There had been authentic prophets before, of whom the Jewish and Christian scriptures told, but Muhammad is the "Seal of the Prophets," and with him revelation comes to an end. He is not a divine person; he performs nothing; his only function is to preach what Allāh commands him to preach. The only miracle with which he was willing to be identified was the Qur'ān itself, the first great and unmatchable classic of the Arabic language. His own basic message concerned the oneness of God, creator of world and man. The first man was Adam, whose descendants led to Noah and his son Shem, progenitor of the Semitic peoples. Later came Abraham, called to serve the one true God. Abraham was specially blessed because of his readiness to offer to God the supreme sacrifice of faith—the life of his beloved son Isaac. Abraham's act of submission or surrender is referred to by the verb *aslama* (Qur'ān, 37:103), with which term it is generally taken that the name of Islam is associated by a normal process of Arabic grammatical "generation."

It is possible that Muhammad did not originally intend to found a new religion, but only to call the Arabs back to the worship of the God of Abraham, who was all-powerful, but sternly just to the proud, arrogant, and impious who had no feeling either for Allāh or for their fellow creatures. Muhammad saw his own role as one of fulfilling and completing the mission of the divinely ordained prophets of the Jewish and Christian scriptures. At times the Qur'ān explicitly linked his own message to the older revelations. "All this is written in earlier scriptures, the scriptures of Abraham and Moses" (Qur'ān, 87:18). There is full acceptance of the Mosaic account (Genesis, 16, 21) concerning Abraham's paternity of Ishmael by the Egyptian slave Hagar and of Isaac by his wife Sarah. When Sarah demanded that Hagar and Ishmael be expelled, God said to Abraham: "Be not distressed on account of your boy and the slave-girl; heed all that Sarah says to you, for through Isaac shall your descendants be called. But I will also make the son of the slave-girl a great nation because he is your offspring" (Genesis, 21:12–13). According to Genesis, 25:12, the tribes of northern Arabia are listed as the offspring of Ishmael. Islam believes that the descendants of both Isaac and Ishmael are inheritors of God's promise to Abraham. The Qur'ān refers, directly or indirectly, and with varying frequency, to Moses, Abraham, Isaac, Ishmael, Jacob, Saul, David, Solomon, Elijah, Job, and Jonah.

Nor did the revelation dissociate itself from the other "People of the Book"—

---

12. The Prophet said he found the messages in his heart, but he did not regard them as products of his own mind. M. W. Watt writes: "He believed that he could easily distinguish between his own thinking and these revelations. His sincerity in this belief must be accepted by the modern historian, for this alone makes credible the development of a great religion" (*Muhammad*, p. 31).

the Christians. It respected John the Baptist and treated Mary and Jesus with reverence. It also accepted that Jesus Christ was conceived by the Holy Spirit and born of the Virgin Mary. But strict monotheism prevented any countenancing of the doctrine of the Trinity. There was no room for belief that Jesus could be the "Son of God" as Christians understood that term, because it implied physical generation. In the eyes of Muslims, God is such a transcendent being that He cannot have a son who walks the earth with other men. In fact, the Qur'ān does not speak of Allāh as "Father"; Jesus, the son of Mary, was an apostle—not the Word of God Incarnate, but a "word from Him." According to the Qur'ān, Jesus was not really crucified, but only appeared to die on the cross. But it is believed that Jesus ascended into heaven and will, according to Islamic tradition, reappear before the Judgment Day.

The Qur'ān placed great emphasis upon the almighty power of Allāh and man's obligation to recognize his utter dependence upon the Creator. It taught the doctrines of the goodness and unbounded power of God, the immortality of the soul, resurrection and the Day of Judgment, when each one will be called to account for the good and evil in this life. For some, the Day of Judgment will be a day of wrath and retribution, when the wicked will be cast into hell (the Fire), while the good are led into Paradise (the Garden). But Allāh is the "Compassionate and Merciful One," as the formula that opens every *sūra* of the Qur'ān (except no. 9) proclaims. Through his Messenger He has given to human creatures all the guidance that they need and that they must follow if they are to be saved. This guidance is to be found in the Qur'ān and in the traditional utterances and practices traceable to the Prophet (*hadīth*, somewhat comparable to Tradition in Judaism and Christianity), including the important admonition that the believer will be given judgment in the same measure as he has treated the poor and the oppressed with mercy, kindness, and aid.[13] It is designed to enable man to follow the path of goodness, to seek forgiveness for sins, and to attain everlasting bliss. Orthodox Jews and Christians would have no quarrel with most of the fundamental religious and moral doctrines preached by Muhammad on the relations between God and man. But the Prophet was scandalized by the fact that Jews and Christians could not agree on the meaning of the scriptures that they held in common. *Sūra* 2, verse 107 contains this passage: "The Jews say the Christians have nothing to stand on, and the Christians say the Jews have nothing to stand on, and yet they both read the Book." Despite significant doctrinal differences, however, Jew, Christian, and Muslim should experience no great difficulties in understanding what each means by God, creation, man, revelation, prophecy, sin, forgiveness, justice, prayer, compassion, judgment, and immortality.[14]

The Five Pillars of Islam,[15] which spell out from the Qur'ān and the Traditions (*hadīth*) the basic religious duties (*'ibādāt*) of the Muslim, are:

13. For further discussion of the teachings contained in the Qur'ān, see Hitti, *The Arabs*, pp. 38–45; Guillaume, *Islam*, pp. 63–77; Gibb, *Mohammedanism*, Chapter 4.

14. For a sensitive and insightful analysis of the relationship of Judaism, Christianity, and Islam, especially in their conceptions of the divine intervention in history, territory, ethnic exclusivism, the mission of the universal salvation, and the role of Messiah, see 'Abd al-Tafāhum, "Doctrine," in Arberry, ed., *Religion in the Middle East*, pp. 365–412.

15. For more detailed treatment of the "Five Pillars," see Hitti, *The Arabs*, pp. 45–49; Guillaume, *Islam*, pp. 66–71; Gibb, *Mohammedanism*, pp. 54–57.

First, the *Profession of Faith* (*shahāda*). "There is no god but God; Muhammad is the Messenger of God." No other words are heard or repeated more frequently throughout the life of the devout Muslim. They occur in the summons of the muezzin (*mu'adhdhin*) to prayer, chanted several times each day from the minaret of the mosque.

Second, *Prayer*. The Muslim is enjoined to pray regularly and often in order to keep his life in proper prespective and to acknowledge his creaturely dependence upon the greatness and goodness of Allāh. Although the Qur'ān apparently prescribes only three times for prayer each day, Islamic tradition calls for five—beginning at sunset, followed by night, dawn, noon, and afternoon prayers. The worshiper, after performing a minor ablution, faces toward Mecca (the Prophet changed the direction from Jerusalem), carries out a ritual prostration, and recites the opening chapter (*fātiha*) and other passages of the Qur'ān, in addition to set prayer formulas. The Friday noon prayer service, conducted by a leader (*imām*) who intercedes for the political ruler, is the only public prayer ceremony in which all adult males are obliged to take part. Women attended public prayer in the time of the Prophet, but it became traditional for them to pray at home. In the modern era, many mosques reserve places for women.

Third, *Almsgiving*. Alms are of two kinds—obligatory or legal (*zakāt*) and voluntary (*sadaqāt*). These two terms were incorporated into Islamic tradition from the Jewish law. The former is similar to the tithe and was fixed in the law books at an average of one-fortieth of the annual revenue in money or in kind (cattle, grain, fruit, merchandise, etc.). Although there was a legal requirement to make the contribution, which in earlier times was collected by public officials to support the poor, prisoners, and wayfarers, and to build mosques for the community (*umma*), it was not a tax, strictly speaking. "Rather," according to H.A.R. Gibb, "is it to be regarded as a loan made to God, which he will repay many-fold." (Both Jews and Christians hold similar beliefs.) In modern times, the duty of almsgiving has come to be looked upon as a matter for the conscience of the individual believer, who performs the act as an outward sign of faith and piety in expiation for sins.

Fourth, *Fasting*. The Qur'ān prescribes fasting, "as it was prescribed for those who were before you"—i.e., for the Jews and Christians. Fasting is a form of spiritual self-discipline; it enables one to control appetites and passions; it helps the believer to advance in compassion for the poor by experiencing deprivation and hunger. The Muslim is obliged to abstain from all food, drink, and smoking between approximately sunrise and sunset, and refrain entirely from sexual relations, during the ninth month of the Islamic calendar—*Ramadān*, the month in which Muhammad received the first revelations. Since the calendar is based on the lunar cycle, the season of the year in which *Ramadān* falls varies. When it comes in the winter, the fast is bearable, but when *Ramadān* coincides with the summer months (as it does on the average of nine times every twenty-five years), the effort to avoid all food and liquid, even a single drop of water, during the hours of daylight entails considerable hardship.

Fifth, the *Pilgrimage* (*hajj*). Once in a lifetime every male Muslim who can afford it and who is physically capable is expected to undertake a holy visit to Mecca, normally in the twelfth month of the year (*Dhu'l-Hijja*). There is an element of voluntariness where women are concerned. Women should not be prevented from undertaking a pilgrimage, but they must be accompanied by a proper male escort. The pilgrim must be ritually cleansed, must discard ordinary clothing and don two plain unsewn sheets before entering Mecca, must abstain from sexual relations, circumambulate the *Ka'ba*, kiss the Black Stone on one of its walls, go to the hill of 'Arafāt (twelve miles east of Mecca), and sacrifice a sheep or camel at Minā on the return to Mecca.

These are the Five Pillars of Islam, which provide clear guidance to the Muslim on what is required for salvation. Many in the West who have difficulty remembering the Five Pillars accurately sometimes include within the list the duty of waging a holy war (*jihād*) in the "Way of God." Actually, this duty has been elevated to a sixth pillar by only one Islamic sect—the Khārijīs (see section on "The Caliphate and Schism in Islam" below). In theory, the *dār al-Islām* (the abode of Islam, i.e., the abode of those who have submitted themselves to the will of Allāh) is involved in a perpetual war or struggle with the *dār al-ḥarb* (the abode of war). *Sūra* 2, vv. 186 ff. directs believers to fight in the way of God until allegiance is rendered to God alone, but this appears to apply only to pagan peoples, for *sūra* 9 has been interpreted to exempt the people of the Book (i.e., Jews and Christians) from having war waged against them. Where the obligation of *jihād* did exist—and this was something to be proclaimed by the caliph—it fell upon the whole community, not upon individual Muslims, as the Five Pillars did.[16]

16. It is necessary to stress that the duty of *jihād* is not considered a "pillar of Islam" by most Muslims, since the formulation of the duty appears in the Qur'ān between the regulations for the Fast and the Pilgrimage. "Fight in the Way of God against those who fight against you, but do not commit aggression. . . . Fight against them until sedition is no more and allegiance is rendered to God alone; but if they make an end, then no aggression save against the evildoers." *Sūra* 2:186 ff., as quoted in Gibb, *Mohammedanism*, pp. 57–58. It has often been suggested that Muhammad, while originally formulating the duty of the *jihād* as a means of extending the frontiers of Islam against nearby Arab enemies, foresaw its applicability in the not too distant future to foes beyond the peninsula. Cf. Watt, *Muhammad*, p. 50. In any event, the Prophet has usually been credited with having substantially attenuated the ferocity of intra-Arab tribal warfare in the form of raids by directing Arab fighting energies outward against infidels beyond the "territory of Islam." During the early centuries of the dynamic expansion of Islam, the *jihād* was an important policy instrument. In theory, the *dār al-Islām* was in a state of permanent war with the *dār al-ḥarb*, and Islamic political authority (i.e., the caliph, whose duty it was to wage the *jihād* on behalf of the *umma*) refused to recognize the coexistence of any non-Muslim communities except in a subordinate status. Contrary to the old belief that Islam offered its enemies the stark choice of "Allah or the sword," Muslim conquerors actually presented three alternatives—conversion to Islam, payment of taxes, or death. The state of war, though permanent, did not have to be continuous; even in theory it could be interrupted by treaties of peace not to exceed ten years in duration. Majid Khadduri compares the *jihād* to the Christian concepts of "Crusade" or *bellum justum* (just war). "The Islamic Theory of International Relations and Its Contemporary Relevance," in J. Harris Procter, ed., *Islam and International Relations* (New York: Praeger, 1975), p. 29. The former would appear to constitute a more appropriate comparison than the latter, since the Crusades were a form of religious-ideological warfare, while the "just war" theory was designed to deal with conflicts arising out of a violation of juridical rights. Writing about the *jihād*, Khadduri says: "To Muslim publicists it was an 'exertion' of one's own power to make the sword of Allah supreme over the world, and the individual's recompense would be the achievement of salvation, because participation in the *jihād*, especially by martyrdom, was Allah's direct way to Paradise. This participation might be fulfilled by the heart, by the tongue, by the hands, and by the sword. The *jihād* was accordingly a form of religious propaganda carried out by spiritual as well as by material means" (ibid., p. 29). As early as the beginning of the fifteenth century, Ibn Khaldūn held that Islam had by then progressed to a

Beyond the basic religious doctrines and moral practices summarized above, the Muslim believes in predestination, angels, and *jinn* (a class of beings in between men and angels, some of whom are good and helpful to humans, and some of whom are diabolical). The Muslim is forbidden to drink wine, eat pork, gamble, charge usury, commit fraud, perjury or slander, or make an idolatrous representation of any living creature (although the portrayal of a human or animal form is of long standing, and may be tolerated in modern times so long as it is clear that idolatrous intention is not present). The teachings of the Qur'ān also condemn lying, stealing, and murder. Thus, although there is no formal Decalogue (or Ten Commandments) in Islam, the Muslim lives under a moral code essentially similar to that of the Jew or Christian except in regard to marriage.

In order to ensure the propagation of children, the Qur'ān permitted a man to have as many as four wives at any one time. So long as Khadīja lived, the Prophet would take no other woman as a wife. The Muslim is enjoined to treat his wives with kindness and impartiality; if he cannot do that he should limit himself to one (*sūra* 4, v. 3). Divorce proceedings may normally be instituted only by the man and not by the woman, except with difficulty; but if a husband divorces a wife he is not allowed to take her back until she has remarried and been divorced again. (The practice of polygamy is in long-range decline throughout the Islamic world, in both urban and rural areas, partly for economic reasons and partly because of changes in the social status of women. Most cases of contemporary polygamy involve husbands with no more than two wives. See the section on "Islamic Law," below.)

The *Hijra* and Subsequent Expansion of Islam

The Prophet's earliest converts were found among his closest relatives—his wife Khadīja, his cousin 'Alī, a former slave Zaid, and his father-in-law, Abū Bakr. His preaching also attracted a number of young men in Mecca—a few from well-to-do families, but most of no particular social status. Sydney N. Fisher has characterized Muhammad's initial followers not as "consciously frustrated men seeking solace in religion," but rather as "conservatives reacting against the abandonment of traditional virtues."[17] In the beginning, Muhammad made an effort to come to terms with the polytheism prevalent in the Arabian peninsula by treating the lesser gods as intercessors for man before Allāh. But as his mono-

---

higher stage of civilization than that in which the *jihād* had played a prominent part. In 1914, when *jihād* was officially proclaimed—by the Ottoman Sultan-Caliph Muhammad Rashād against the Allies—it failed dismally, partly because a true *jihād* cannot be waged successfully for political purposes only slightly related to Islam, and partly because Arab nationalists, including the Protector of the Holy Places of Arabia, concluded that their cause had more to gain by tilting toward the Western infidels and away from Ottoman Turkish oppression. In December 1971, the World Muslim League, meeting in Mecca, called for a *jihād* against India because of its role in the Bangladesh War, but the call produced no concrete results.

17. Sydney N. Fisher, *The Middle East: A History* (New York: Alfred A. Knopf, 1959), pp. 32–33.

theistic vision became purer, the Prophet came to look upon some of the earlier passages as "satanic verses." From that time onward, his uncompromising message posed a threat to the social privileges of those who stood to profit from the pilgrims coming to worship the lesser deities of Mecca. It quickly became apparent that Muhammad's condemnation of idols could ruin Mecca. Therefore, he had to be subjected to economic boycott and other forms of persecution. His revelations were ridiculed and the Banū Hāshim were forbidden to intermarry with other Quraish tribes. Acceptance of Islam was out of the question for the established leaders, for that would have been tantamount to recognizing Muhammad's preeminent position in the city.[18]

After his wife and uncle died, conversions to Islam dropped off. Muhammad looked elsewhere, and found that the recently warring Arab tribes of Yathrib, 200 miles to the north of Mecca, were willing to offer him protection and embrace Islam if he would bring peace to the city, later called Medina (or "City [of the Prophet]"). When twelve clan heads (naqībs) promised to worship Allāh and no other gods, the Prophet's followers began to leave Mecca and headed for Medina. The Quraish allegedly plotted to have Muhammad killed and force the Banū Hāshim to take blood-money in compensation. Muhammad and Abū Bakr then fled to Medina. This hijra ("flight" or "migration") occurred in the year 622, from which time the Islamic calendar begins.

Upon arriving in Medina, Muhammad concluded treaties and agreements that gradually brought into existence a theocratic confederation (umma) of which he was the religious and political head and to whom, under Allāh, all disputes were to be referred as the authoritative interpreter of customary law. Except where the Qur'ān required the establishment of new precedents, the Prophet upheld tradition and resisted innovations and novelties.[19] At Medina, the life of Muhammad shifted from the contemplative to the active, or, as we would see it, from prophet to political leader and diplomat.

Historians question the extent of the influence of Islam on the Arabian peninsula before the death of Muhammad in 632. When the Prophet died, he was succeeded in all his functions except the prophetic one—i.e., as lawgiver, religious leader (Imām), chief judge, commander of the army, and civil ruler of the state—by his father-in-law, Abū Bakr, who was invested with the title Khalīfa Rasūl Allāh ("Successor of the Apostle of God"), later abbreviated to Khalīfa (caliph). During the caliphate of Abū Bakr, Khālid b. al-Walīd became the outstanding military leader of Islam, and he and other commanders subdued the tribes of central Arabia. Within two or three years of Muhammad's death, Islam was carried to the southern and western shores of the Persian Gulf, including Bahrain and Oman.[20]

Under the second caliph, 'Umar, Islamic armies within a period of less than ten years completed the conquest of Mesopotamia (Iraq) to the north and east, and of Syria, Palestine, and Egypt to the north and west. Within twenty years of the Hijra, Islam was dominant in all the lands around the Persian Gulf. But

18. Ibid., pp. 34–36.
19. Serjeant, "Historical Review," p. 12.
20. See the chapters, "Islam on the March," in Hitti, The Arabs; "The Islamic Empire," in Guillaume, Islam; and "The Expansion of Islam," in Gibb, Mohammedanism.

Islam has three levels of reality—those of religion, culture, and political community (eventually state). It was the Arabian Islamic political community that first extended its sway over the inhabitants of Mesopotamia, Persia, and the other littoral lands of the Persian Gulf. The Arabian tribes that originally conquered the professional troops of the Persians in Mesopotamia and Iran were not religious zealots. More than a century was required—probably closer to two centuries—for the religious message of Islam to be communicated to really large numbers of people. The first authoritative written version of the Qur'ān (according to the most general view) was not completed until nineteen years after the death of the Prophet, under the supervision of the third caliph, 'Uthmān. From that time on, new written copies in the Arabic language were produced, but they were highly precious and far too few to keep pace with the rapid expansion of Islam. Since the principal means of transmitting Allāh's revealed word was through the memorization of the Qur'ān's more than six thousand verses (āyas), the process of genuine religious conversion was necessarily slow.

When Islam came to the Persian Gulf area it did not, of course, enter a religious vacuum. In Mesopotamia (Iraq), there were Christianity and Zoroastrianism; in Bahrain, Christianity, which had been carried from the Nestorian centers at Hīra from the fifth century onward; in Yemen, both Monophysite Christianity and a Judaism, from which Muhammad could have derived some knowledge of the older scriptures. In its initial confrontation with Christianity, Islam had the advantage of a relatively high degree of internal cohesiveness, whereas the Christian churches had already lost their solidarity as a result of numerous heresies and schisms. Both Christians and Jews in the newly conquered countries found Islamic rule more tolerant and less oppressive than Byzantine rule, with its emphasis on elaborately defined orthodoxy.

At first, the Muslims did not seek to propagate Islam except among the Arabs themselves, but as time went on their proselytizing zeal grew. Toward the end of the first Islamic century, the caliphs became more severe in dealing with the Christian churches. Later, European Christians were often to misinterpret Arab expansion as involving a crude choice between Islam and the sword. Actually, Muslims were ordered by the Qur'ān (9:29) to make war upon the "People of the Book" only until they should pay tribute. Non-Muslims who paid taxes were allowed to live according to their own laws and customs—the origin of the later *millet* system of the Ottoman empire—and were not compelled or even allowed to bear arms.[21] The caliph 'Umar enforced the dictum attributed to Muhammad (but in variance to Muhammad's actual policy) that in Arabia itself, because of the Holy Places, there should be no religion except Islam. This decree fell more heavily upon the large urban Christian population, which could be easily expelled, than upon the smaller, more widely scattered and economically better integrated Jewish communities. Outside the Arabian peninsula, Christians, Jews, Manichaeans, Zoroastrians, and Buddhists enjoyed a good deal of freedom.

Islam developed into a more coherent religious system partly as a result of intellectual interaction with a Christianity that had been profoundly influenced by Greek philosophy. At the 'Abbasid court in Baghdad, Christian and Muslim

21. Hitti, *The Arabs*, p. 51. See also footnote 11 above.

theologians debated their religious beliefs with mutual tolerance.[22] Both had to face the question of the relationship between religious faith and philosophical reason—the wisdom of the believer and the wisdom of the Greeks. The Christian Fathers had begun to think about that relationship in the first few centuries of their history. Four or five centuries later, Arabic-using philosophers and theologians would elaborate Greek philosophical ideas and transmit them through Spain to the Schoolmen of medieval Europe who were analyzing anew the relationship of faith and reason.

Tradition

The revelation contained in the Qur'ān constitutes the unshakable foundation of the Muslim's religious belief. This always remains the final authority, the ultimate criterion of doctrinal certainty. It is much more important than the "Five Pillars," which together constitute one practical mark of "Muslimness." But a religion based essentially upon a scriptural text invariably develops historically by way of custom and tradition. The religious text requires authoritative interpretation; and questions concerning individual conduct and social organization are bound to arise, for which the written word does not provide a readily apparent answer. Such had been the experience of the other People of the Book— Jews and Christians. The experience of Muhammad's followers proved to be no different in this respect.

The Book tells what is to be believed and indicates in a general way some of the things that are to be done for salvation. Only about 10 percent (or 600) of all the verses in the Qur'ān take the form of legal prescriptions and, of these, only about 80 can be regarded as legislation in the strict sense.[23] The body of religious legal duties in their meticulous detail is developed through custom, precedent, tradition, the rulings of judges (qādīs), and the intellectual interpretations of theologians. How did this corpus of Islamic law for the whole community develop? While Muhammad was living, he made the rulings whenever matters of dispute were referred to him. He himself distinguished between what Allāh had revealed and the precepts or guidelines that he, as a supreme secular judge, was obliged to lay down. But within a few years of the Prophet's death, Arab armies had conquered a vast area from Egypt to Iran and from the Mediterranean coast to the Hadramaut. Within this territory, tribal custom (sunna) varied considerably from one locality to another. Questions immediately arose concerning the relationship between immemorial ways of doing things and the duties imposed by the new faith. In the Qur'ān, the Meccans are reproached for adhering to the sunna of their ancestors when they should embrace the unchanging sunna of Allāh.

Gradually, the term sunna came to mean for most Muslims the "usage of the Prophet and the Community," handed down by oral transmission. Obviously, however, there was a difference between those sayings and rulings traceable

22. Serjeant, "Historical Review," p. 21.
23. R. M. Savory, "Law and Traditional Society," in Savory, ed., Islamic Civilisation, p. 55.

to the Prophet and the broader spectrum of customs and traditions belonging to all the peoples who comprised Islam. The *sunna* of Muhammad was transmitted in the form of narrative statements, each of which is called a *hadith* (verbal report). The principal early sources of the *hadith* were 'Ā'isha, wife of the Prophet, and the Companions of Mecca and Medina. Within a few generations of Muhammad's death, hundreds of thousands of *hadith*s were in circulation throughout the lands of Islam. Each religious sect and political party accepted certain traditions that conformed to its own predilections and rejected others as spurious. It eventually became clear that fabrication and forgery had been practiced on a large scale. The Prophet was often quoted on opposite sides of the same question—marriage and divorce, money-lending and artistic representations, eating and drinking, praying and fasting, what kind of clothes and ornaments should be worn, and whether to fight wars or avoid them for the sake of the peaceful life. Unless these contradictions could be resolved, there was a danger that the ideological cohesiveness of Islamic society might dissolve in anarchy.[24]

The problem was to devise a method by which genuine traditions could be authenticated and false ones sifted out, by carefully tracing the statement back to the Prophet through his Companions (i.e., those of the Prophet's own generation), Followers (i.e., those of the succeeding generation), and other sources. Authenticity depended upon the character of the first person who told the narrative about what the Prophet had said or done, as well as the reliability of the chain of persons (*sanad* or *isnād*) by whom the tradition was handed down. (The process of authenticating the chain is also called *isnād*.) During the second and third centuries of the Islamic era, a complex science of *hadith*-criticism emerged among scholars. Biographical dictionaries appeared in which sources were classified as Muslims of the first generation (Companions), of the second generation (Followers), of the third generation (Followers of the Followers) and so forth. As a result of various investigations and comparisons concerning the trustworthiness of sources, traditions were divided into such categories as "genuine" (*sahih*), "good" (*hasan*), and "weak" (*da'if*). The most authoritative collection of reliable traditions was the *Sahih* compiled by al-Bukhārī (816–78), who was said to have employed such rigorous criteria that he reduced a total of more than 200,000 (some say 600,000) statements to fewer than 3,000 *hadith*s. The *Sahih* of al-Bukhārī became the most important book in Islam, next to the Qur'an, and played a significant role in the development of both theology and sacred law. A second collection of traditions was compiled by a man usually referred to simply as Muslim, a contemporary of al-Bukhārī. Four additional collections of the next generation—by Abū Dāwūd, al-Nasā'ī, al-Tirmidhī, and Ibn Māja—were granted canonical status. Among the subjects dealt with in the traditions were: opposition to pictures of human and animal forms; divorce; the forgiveness of bodily injury; the condemnation of money-lending; the kind treatment of orphans; the punishment of crime; and injunctions against the fabrication of false traditions, and warnings against observing the letter while ignoring the spirit of traditions.

---

24. For the discussion of the *sunna* and *hadith* and the subsequent discussion of the four legal schools, the author relied upon Savory, *Islamic Civilization*, and the chapters on tradition in Gibb, *Mohammedanism*, and Guillaume, *Islam*.

Gradually there developed within Islam a body of orthodox tradition or *sunna*, from which the followers derive the name Sunnīs. The Sunnīs constitute a majority throughout the Islamic Middle East, but not in the two most populous states of the Persian Gulf region—Iran and Iraq. Other Islamic sects to be discussed below adhere to their own traditions.

Within Sunnī Islam, it is possible to distinguish four principal schools or "ways" (*madhhab*): Hanafī, Mālikī, Shāfi'ī, and Hanbalī. These cannot properly be regarded as sects, because each is tolerated as orthodox by the others. Every Sunnī Muslim belongs to one of these schools, which differ from each other principally in respect to the importance they attach to various ways of interpreting the Qur'ān, Tradition, Islamic Law, the consensus (*ijmā'*) of the Islamic Community, and the relationship between faith and reason—especially *qiyās* or analogical reasoning. The oldest school is the Hanafī, named after the Iraqi scholar Abū Hanīfa (d. 772), who emphasized the part to be played by well-informed individual interpretation (*ijtihād*) of the Qur'ān and tradition where no general consensus had yet been reached. The second, named after Mālik b. Anas (d. 801), accepted as authoritative the consensus of the Medina community but not the consensus of the Islamic community. The third school was founded by al-Shāfi'ī (d. 826), the "father of Islamic jurisprudence," who taught that *ijmā'*, or the general consensus of the Islamic community, should override the interpretation of a particular school, and who also held that reasoning by analogy could never be used to contradict a rule founded on the Qur'ān, the *sunna* of the Prophet or *ijmā'*. Ahmad b. Hanbal (d. 855), who had been a student of al-Shāfi'ī, objected to individual interpretation, reasoning by analogy and the validity of general consensus. His followers insisted that Islamic law (*sharī'a*) must be based on the Qur'ān or on the traditions of the Prophet (see the section on "Islamic Law" below).

Today, so far as the Persian Gulf area is concerned, the Sunnī minority in Iraq is, for the most part, of the Hanafī school. Shāfi'īs are found in western, eastern, and southern Arabia. There are also prominent Mālikī communities in the Eastern Province of Arabia. Although Hanbalism virtually disappeared after the Ottoman conquest, this most austere of all orthodox Sunnī doctrines was revived on the Arabian peninsula during the eighteenth century by the religious leader Muhammad b. 'Abd-al-Wahhāb, born into a line of Hanbalite *qādīs* (religious judges). Disturbed by the decay of popular faith and by the reverence paid to saints and their tombs, as well as by the superstitious worship of trees and stones, he sought to bring Muslims back to the pure Islam of the Prophet. Wahhābism—Hanbalism in its modern spirit of spiritual reform—became the official religion of Sa'ūdī Arabia. Hanbalism is the most conservative and least tolerant of all the orthodox Islamic schools.

The Caliphate and Schism In Islam

Muhammad as Prophet could have no successor. But the continuity of Islam as a political-social community made succession imperative for his functions as head of state, law-giver, adjudicator of disputes, and commander of the military forces. Immediately upon Muhammad's death in the year 10 A.H. (632 A.D.), his father-in-law, close associate and substitute prayer-leader at the mosque during the Prophet's final illness—Abū Bakr—was proclaimed *Khalīfa Rasūl Allāh* ("Successor of the Apostle of God"). Sydney Fisher finds nothing unusual in the decision: "Chiefs in Mecca and Medina, as well as in Arab tribes, were chosen by the heads of families meeting more or less openly. Leadership often passed to another in the same family, but without any idea of inheritance or legal claim; the power and prestige of a family prejudiced the decision in its favor."[25]

There had been other aspirants to the office of *Khalīfa* from Mecca and Medina, but the early military successes achieved under Abū Bakr's leadership throughout Arabia helped to curtail dissension. Abū Bakr, who ruled for only two years before his death, was succeeded by 'Umar, noted (as Abū Bakr had been) for his piety, justice, patriarchal simplicity, and zeal for the faith. Islam continued its remarkable rate of expansion under 'Umar, who ruled for ten years until he was assassinated by a Christian slave with a personal grudge against him. The third caliph was the elderly 'Uthmān, a Companion of the Prophet and a member of the Umayyad family of the Quraish tribe that had earlier opposed Muhammad. Although a pious Muslim, 'Uthmān was criticized for his weakness and inaction, his religious innovations, and his nepotism and restoration of pre-Islamic Arab tribal ways. Rebellion against 'Uthmān's policies broke out in Iraq and Egypt among the followers of 'Alī, the husband of Muhammad's daughter Fātima. A group of rebels from Egypt, led by Abū Bakr's son, stormed 'Uthmān's residence in Medina, killed the Caliph and forced the election of 'Alī.[26]

It is from the caliphate of 'Alī that the most fundamental divisions of Islam are traced. 'Alī was widely recognized as caliph throughout the Islamic world, except in Syria, ruled by Mu'āwiya—of the Umayyad family and nephew of the murdered 'Uthmān. Mu'āwiya accused 'Alī of being implicated in the murder of his uncle, at least by granting immunity to the killers, if not more directly. The Prophet's widow 'Ā'isha also opposed 'Alī and gathered an insurgent army against him. 'Alī defeated that insurgent force near Basra in the famous "Battle of the Camel," and this marked the first serious occasion when Muslim was pitted against Muslim. 'Alī thereupon established himself as caliph at Kūfa, Iraq—the fourth and last of the so-called "Rightly Guided Caliphs." From that time onward, no caliph ever resided in Medina. Mu'āwiya proved to be a more formidable opponent than 'Ā'isha. Deposed by 'Alī, the governor of Syria refused to step down, and 'Alī had no choice but to engage him militarily at Siffīn on the

---

25. Fisher, *The Middle East*, p. 44. Laura Veccia Vaglieri writes: "The caliphate lasted for centuries, and many things were subsequently changed, but the idea that the appointment of the caliph was a kind of contract imposing reciprocal obligations on the man elected and on his subjects gained ground, and became a fundamental concept once the Muslims had developed a juridical mentality" ("The Patriarchal and Ummayed Caliphates," in *CHI*, 1: 57). Vaglieri notes that fortuitous circumstances became important principles for the orthodox: The caliph had to be a member of the Prophet's tribe (Quraish) and should be chosen by the leading members of the community, with the people ratifying their choice (ibid., pp. 57–58).

26. For an account of the long rivalry between 'Alī and 'Uthmān and the scandal that the murder of 'Uthmān caused within the Arab world, as well as the ensuing schism, see Vaglieri, ibid., pp. 67–72.

Euphrates. After inconclusive skirmishing, the Syrians are said to have brought the fighting to an end by fixing leaves of the Qur'ān on their lances (though this seems improbable), demanding that the issue be decided by Allāh in arbitration. 'Alī felt compelled to shift from the indecisiveness of the battlefield to negotiations that were also to prove inconclusive.

A group of Mesopotamian religious extremists, scandalized that the caliph should agree to submit his claim to arbitration, parted company from him. They became known as the "Seceders" (*Khawārij* or *Khārijīs*), contending that the partisans of 'Alī and of Mu'āwiya were pursuing an unholy compromise path and that they themselves were the only true Muslims. 'Alī defeated them, but in the meantime the arbitration apparently went against 'Alī. The zealots attempted to assassinate the two rivals for the caliphate, but succeeded only in killing 'Alī early in the year 661. Iraq recognized as the legitimate successor al-Hasan, the son of 'Alī and of the Prophet's daughter Fātima. But al-Hasan proved no match for the politically talented Mu'āwiya, in whose favor he soon abdicated. The latter established the Umayyad caliphate in Damascus. It was founded on the principle of dynastic succession rather than election, and this introduced stability into the caliphate during the Umayyad period (661–750), which saw thirteen caliphs. When al-Hasan died in 669, his brother Husain became the head of the house of 'Alī. The Arabs of Kūfa in Iraq remained at peace with Mu'āwiya, but upon his death in 680 they agitated for the restoration of the caliphate to the descendants of 'Alī. The "party" (*shī'a*) of 'Alī formulated, in opposition to the orthodox doctrine of the community (the followers of the *Sunna*), a distinctive doctrine concerning the exclusive right of the house of 'Alī to the caliphate. According to the Shī'īs, 'Alī should have been chosen as the immediate successor to the Prophet; Abū Bakr, 'Umar, and 'Uthmān were regarded as usurpers. The Shī'īs in Kūfa refused to accept the Umayyad successor Yazīd I and invited al-Husain from Mecca to Kūfa to assume the caliphate. Enroute to Kūfa, al-Husain and a small band of followers were defeated by a Umayyad force. Al-Husain lost his life, and his head was cut off—first to be sent to Damascus and later to be buried with his body at Karbalā', one of the leading religious shrines of the Shī'a, where the anniversary is commemorated on the fateful date, the tenth of Muharram, with a sacred play.

Although the Shī'īs had their origin in a political dispute with the Sunnīs over the succession to rule, the division between the two bodies of Islam soon came to be distinguished by theological, legal, and ritual differences.[27] The Shī'a adhered to the *Sunna* of the Prophet, but regarded the subsequent conduct of the community to have been wrongful inasmuch as the "Imamate" (their term for the caliphate) had been transmitted outside the house of 'Alī. The Shī'īs believed that succession to the Prophet, and the accompanying responsibility for sound theological guidance, could not be determined by vote, but had been preordained by the will of Allāh to remain with 'Alī and his direct descendants. According to H.A.R. Gibb, Shī'īsm attracted to itself several strands of oriental religious be-

27. See the chapter on "Sects" in Guillaume, *Islam*, pp. 111–25; and Gibb, *Mohammedanism*, pp. 85–87 and 94–97. For a complete history, see Dwight M. Donaldson, *The Shi'ite Religion: A History of Islam in Persia and Irak* (London: Luzac, 1933).

lief—Babylonian, Persian, and Indian—which placed emphasis on the importance of esoteric knowledge, and thus it attributed to the *Imām* a spiritual function of interpreting the Qur'ān and defining dogma that the orthodox or Sunnī branch of Islam had denied to the caliph.[28] Not all Shī'īs stressed the supernatural qualities of *Imāms*, as if they were alone capable of revealing the true meaning of the Qur'ān under the changing circumstances of history. One group that survives in the Yemen, the Zaidīs (named for Zaid, a great grandson of 'Alī) continues to focus principally upon the legitimacy of the claim of 'Alī's descendants, while otherwise remaining close to the Sunnī concept of the powers of the caliph or *imām*. Zaidism remains the most moderate form of Shī'ism.

The Shī'a or legitimist party of 'Alī (the 'Alids) began as an anti-Umayyad party. The Shī'īs and Khārijīs flourished in Iraq and Iran and tended to make common cause against the Umayyads ruling from Syria. The 'Alids appealed both to Arabs and also elements of the population (*mawālī*), who were "clients" recently converted to Islam and supposedly under the protection of Arabs, yet who felt themselves treated unfairly by the Arab aristocracy. To this day, Iran and Iraq remain the two Islamic countries in which Shī'īs constitute the majority of the population. In Iran, where 98 percent of the people are Muslim, more than 90 percent of these are Shī'īs. In Iranian history, Shī'īsm had long been favored by such dynasties as the Buwaihids and the Safavids. Adherence to Shī'īsm has enabled Iran to maintain an identity separate from that of the predominantly Sunnī Arabs, and it has been the official religion of Iran since the beginning of the sixteenth century. Shī'īs are also to be found in Kuwait, the Gulf states—particularly, Dubai and Bahrain, and eastern Arabia, as well as in the Zaydī regions of the Yemen. The Khārijīs have survived most prominently in Oman.

The Shī'īs themselves have divided into sects. The two most important groups are the Imāmīs, also known as the "Twelvers," and the Ismā'īlīs, or the "Seveners." Members of the first sect believe that there were twelve imams in the line of Fātima that ended with the so-called Hidden Imām, Muhammad al-Muntazar, who disappeared at a very young age in the year 878 and who is expected to return at the end of time as *Mahdī* (Savior or Messiah) to establish the reign of truth and justice throughout the world. The twelfth or, again, Hidden Imām is believed to be spiritually alive but invisible and continues to be the leader of the faithful until the time of his return at the Last Judgment. In the meantime, the Twelvers have looked upon some of their leaders as deputies of the Hidden Imām. The Twelvers are popularly known for two practices unique to them—temporary marriages, and the practice of dissimulation (*taqiyya*), by which any member of the community could invoke the right to deny his adherence to the Shī'ī faith when in danger of persecution by Sunnis bent upon punishing Shī'īs for denying the authority of the caliph.

The Ismā'īlīs or Seveners constitute a smaller and more extreme sect. This group broke off in the ninth century from the Imāmīs as the result of a disagreement over the identity of the seventh Imām. Both sects concur on the first six Imāms, including Ja'far. Ja'far disinherited his eldest son Ismā'īl as being unworthy of the office and named a younger son, Mūsā, as his successor. The

28. Gibb, *Mohammedanism*, pp. 95–96.

Seveners were shocked by the substitution, which they considered impossible, and claimed that Ismā'īl was the last rightful Imām. In the ninth century, the Ismā'īlīs became significant in the western part of the Muslim world. From the tenth to the twelfth centuries they supplied the backing for the Fāṭimid dynasty in Egypt, from where they penetrated as far east as Persia. Subsequently, the Seljuk Turks, who were adherents of Sunnī orthodoxy, suppressed the politically troublesome Ismā'īlīs in Persia, thereby leaving the more moderate Imāmīs as the dominant Shī'a group. The practice of *taqiyya* enabled the Twelvers to survive under Seljuk rule. Ja'farī Shī'ism became the official religion of Iran at the beginning of the sixteenth century under the Safavids. Until 1979, the Pahlavi Constitution provided that the article in which the faith is proclaimed shall remain in effect until the coming of the Mahdī.[29] Ismā'īlī minorities have survived in eastern and northwestern Iran, as well as in the Yemen.

Historically, the Sunnī caliphate was the most important office in Islam. Traditional Islam did not distinguish, as Western Christianity did quite sharply, between a spiritual-religious realm and a temporal-political realm, between *sacerdotium* and *imperium*, between Church and State. Philip K. Hitti's warning is pertinent: "We should guard against the common fallacy that the Caliphate was a religious office. In this regard analogies drawn from the headship of the Holy Roman Empire and from the Catholic Church are misleading."[30] It was not until the latter part of the eighteenth century that Europeans ceased to look upon the (then) Ottoman caliph as a kind of Muslim pope with spiritual jurisdiction over the followers of Muhammad.

The caliphate became an office of hereditary succession, held by either the most competent son or the most qualified kinsman under the 'Abbasids and thereafter, although it was always maintained in Islamic political theory that the office was an elective one.[31] The Sunnī caliphate was situated first at Medina, later at Damascus, still later at Baghdad, then (in reduced form) at Cairo, and finally at Constantinople. The caliph was "Commander of the Faithful" (*Amīr al-Mu'minīn*), upholder of the *Sharī'a*, and leader of the faithful in prayer (*Imām*). The ruler was expected to be the benefactor of schools, hospitals, and mosques, as well as military chief, administrator of justice, and guardian of public morals. At times he also became in fact the patron of literature and the arts, though such fields have no official recognition in Islamic society.

In theory, there was supposed to be only one caliph ruling over the entire *umma*. But early in Islamic history, as we have seen, religious schism set the stage

29. Before ascending to the throne, the Shāhanshāh swore on the Qur'ān that he would propagate the *Ithnā 'Asharī* religion (Article 39). The constitution guaranteed freedom of the press and of publication, except for antireligious writings harmful to the Islamic faith. E. I. J. Rosenthal, *Islam in the Modern National State* (Cambridge: Cambridge University Press, 1965), pp. 307, 308.

30. Hitti, *The Arabs*, p. 69. See also George Stewart, "Is the Caliph a Pope?" in J. Stewart-Robinson, ed., *The Traditional Near East* (Englewood Cliffs, N.J.: Prentice-Hall, 1966), p. 137.

31. See Arnold, *The Caliphate*, pp. 22–23, and the article "Khalifa," in *Encyclopedia of Islam* (London: Brill, Leiden and Luzac, New Edition, 1954–60), 2: 884. To qualify for election, a candidate had to be not only a member of the tribe of Quraish but also "a male of mature age, of spotless character, without physical or mental infirmity, a man of sound judgment; he must, in addition, possess knowledge sufficient to adjudicate cases at law and must possess courage and energy in the defense of Moslem lands." Stewart, "Is the Caliph a Pope?" pp. 141–42.

for the eventual emergence of rival dynasties and centers of political power. From the late tenth to late twelfth century A.D., the "Sevener" Shī'īs supported the Fātimid caliphate in Cairo (this was before the orthodox caliphate was transferred to that city from Baghdad). Rival caliphs to the 'Abbasids in Cairo appeared in Tunis, Iraq, and elsewhere. Eventually, the title was assumed by the Ottoman sultans (but not by Selīm or Süleymān), although no Turkish sultan could ever claim descent from the tribe of Quraish.[32] Turkey became a republic in 1922, and the government of Kemal Atatürk declared the office of caliph abolished in 1924. Devout Muslims, however, believe that a decree of a secular government can have no effect upon the office of *Khalīfa Rasūl Allāh*, and they look toward the day when a single ruler will apply, throughout a united Islam, the law of the Qur'ān and the Traditions of the Prophet.

Sūfism

No discussion of Islam, however summary, would be complete without reference to Islamic mysticism—Sūfism. Sūfism had its origins in the Persian Gulf region, probably in Kūfa, Iraq, in the second century of the Islamic era. The Sūfis took their name from the humble garment of undyed wool (*sūf*) that was their distinguishing mark, but the designation came to apply to all Islamic mystics who, in reaction against the excessive theological abstractionism and legalism of the *'ulamā'*, sought a more direct, intuitive experience and withdrawal from the materialism and vanity of the world. They stressed a life of simplicity, voluntary poverty, prayer, and meditation. Above all, the Sūfis aspired to lose themselves and to achieve the extinction of self-identity (*fanā'*) in loving communion with God by following a mystical path—graded phases of contemplation, and illumination not unlike those that medieval writers of Christian mystical literature called *via purgativa, via contemplativa*, and *via illuminativa*. Not merely through the observance of external rules but also through an active interior life of love and self-sacrifice the Sūfī aimed at the ecstasy of union with Allāh.[33]

According to H.A.R. Gibb, Sūfism implied a protest against the social and political abuses that seemed to be tolerated by the official Sunnī *'ulamā'*, and the latter felt threatened by the fact that the Sufīs enjoyed a reputation as among the most zealous missionaries of the Islamic faith. Fearful of the gradual disintegration of orthodox control, the *'ulamā'* looked upon the Sūfī movement with suspicion. The Sūfī developed their own distinctive liturgical litanies (*dhikr*) based in part on the Qur'ān. Sūfī novices placed themselves under a spiritual director (*shaikh* or *pir*). Throughout the Muslim world in the medieval period, religious brotherhoods of *faqīrs* (Arabic) or *darvīshes* (Persian), poor men or beggars, sprang up everywhere—comparable to the monastic and fraternal orders of European Christendom. Orthodox theologians, concerned about their posi-

32. Stewart, "Is the Caliph a Pope?" pp. 142–45.
33. See Martin Lings, "Sufism," in A. J. Arberry, ed., *Religion in the Middle East*, 2: 253–54; Guillaume, *Life of Muhammad*, pp. 141–45; Reynold A. Nicholson, *The Mystics of Islam* (New York: Schocken Books, 1975), pp. 3–4, 10–11.

tions of religious leadership, inevitably felt threatened by the Sūfīs and feared that Sūfī religious exercises might replace the prayer services in the mosque. The *'ulamā'* and the authorities they supported attempted to question the orthodoxy of the Sūfīs on two grounds: (1) that whereas the Qur'ān enjoined marriage, some of them preached celibacy as a spiritually more exalted mode of life; and (2) that whereas, in the orthodox tradition, the worship of saints was condemned as a vestige of primitive polytheism, Sūfism taught that there are certain persons who through extraordinary spiritual discipline have penetrated to the secrets of the Divine Reality, possess an aura of holiness and carry within their being a special power or blessedness (*baraka*), and that these "friends (of God)" (*awliyā'*) deserve to be reverenced by the faithful.[34]

All efforts to suppress Sūfism ended in failure. The movement had too firm a foundation in the spiritual doctrines of the Qur'ān to be dismissed as an aberration. The orthodoxy of Sūfism was ardently defended by the Persian Abū Ḥāmid al-Ghazālī (b. 1059), widely renowned as the greatest authority of his day on Sunnī Islamic theology and law. Indeed, al-Ghazālī himself, at last repelled by the casuistry of many theologians and the spiritual aridity of their doctrines, found satisfaction only in the personal mystical experience of God through the Sūfī path, and this enabled him to carry out a "revival" of Islamic theology. As a result of al-Ghazālī's work, Gibb concludes, "Sufism swept over the whole body of Islam and rode roughshod over, though it could not entirely stifle, the resistance of the scholastic theologians."[35] Orthodox Islam acquired a new power to attract the masses, and Shī'īsm, which had formerly appealed so strongly to the religious emotions of the people, lost much of its influence, except in the Persian Gulf region.

In recent centuries, the Sūfī orders (*turuq*, sing. *tarīqa*) have carried on through their convents important charitable activities, such as feeding the poor.[36] Whereas Islamic theologians and canonists have stressed the external obligations of all Muslims, the Sūfīs have continued to emphasize the inward mystical aspect of religion, the path of perfection and sanctification that is an ideal not for the whole community but for a spiritual elite.[37] At various times Sūfīs have been looked upon as pantheists because of their doctrine of the Oneness of Being, but this is a misinterpretation of the mainstream of Sūfism, which adheres to the orthodox Islamic belief in God as the all-else-excluding Infinite One.[38] Throughout the Islamic world today, and especially in the Persian Gulf countries, except for Sa'ūdī Arabia, one can still encounter saintly *shaikhs* with thousands of devout followers, men and women who recite their litanies and practice their special fasts. In Sa'ūdī Arabia, the Sūfī orders are officially proscribed because they are not considered sufficiently conservative, and because the Wahhābī tradition objects to Sūfism, both for the practice of visiting tombs of saints and for teaching that there is a Special Path for the elite beyond those obligations that

34. Gibb, *Mohammedanism*, pp. 104–6; Adams, "Islamic Faith," pp. 43–44; Nicholson, ibid., Chapter V.
35. Gibb, *Mohammedanism*, p. 111.
36. *CHI*, 1: 476–77.
37. Lings, "Sufism," in Arberry, *Religion in the Middle East*, 2: 254–55.
38. Ibid., p. 255.

devolve on all members of the Islamic community. But Sa'ūdī Arabia does not interfere with the right of Sūfīs to make pilgrimages to Mecca and Medīna. In other Middle East countries, the Sūfīs are sometimes criticized by the more secular elites for being too conservative and for being uninterested in economic modernization. The Sūfīs are frequently criticized for failing to "move with the times." But by brotherhoods primarily concerned with the achievement of mystical union with the Divine after overcoming the allurements of this world, such an accusation is taken for praise.[39]

Islamic Law

The Qur'ān is the guide to what the Muslim believes; his external actions are regulated by Islamic law. "In the Muslim view," writes Roger Savory, "the law is virtually as much the revealed will of God as is the Qur'ān itself. . . . In Islam, the religious law of Sharī'a (literally, the 'straight path') theoretically governs the life of every Muslim in all its aspects. Since the Sharī'a constitutes the will of God, any Muslim who violates it not only commits a crime, but also a sin. In other words, law and morals are aspects of religion, and jurisprudence is not only based on theology but has subsumed numerous elements which, from a western viewpoint, would belong to theology rather than to law."[40]

Early Islam was a system of religious beliefs and ethical norms, not a code of law in any strict sense. The Islamic community expanded so rapidly throughout a wide area, encompassing peoples diverse in cultural and ethnic backgrounds, that it was not possible to develop a uniform code of law. There was no alternative in most cases but to incorporate the existing legal institutions and customary legal practices ('ādāt) of the locality, and to work for their gradual modification according to Qu'rānic moral norms. The Sunnī and Shī'ī branches of Islam disagreed over the relationship between customary tribal law and the Qur'ān, the former holding that custom remained in effect unless explicitly abrogated by the Prophet's revelation, while the Shī'īs contended that customary law had no validity unless specifically sanctioned by the Qur'ān.[41]

The Sharī'a, or body of Islamic religious law, began with Muhammad's judicial decisions at Medina, but did not develop into a coherent legal system for two centuries. Under the Umayyad caliphs, the qāḍīs, or religious judges, had been given considerable latitude, in handing down judgments on questions where the Qur'ān was silent or unclear, to rely upon their ra'y, personal opinion, based on precedent and common sense. The 'Abbasids set about purifying Islamic jurisprudence according to the norms of the Qur'ān, and these efforts gave rise to the four legal schools mentioned earlier (Hanafī, Mālikī, Shāfi'ī, and Hanbalī).[42]

---

39. Lings, ibid., p. 268–69.

40. R. M. Savory, "Law and Traditional Society," in R. M. Savory, Islamic Civilisation, p. 54. See also Joseph Schacht, "The Law," in Gustave von Grunebaum, ed., Unity and Variety in Muslim Civilization (Chicago: University of Chicago Press, 1955), pp. 65–86; and "Law and Justice," CHI, 2: 539–68.

41. Savory, ibid., p. 55.

42. Savory, ibid., pp. 55–56. See also p. 295 of this chapter.

As we have seen previously, all four orthodox schools assigned an indubitable primacy to the teachings contained in the Qur'ān. They disagreed substantially, however, in their emphasis upon or willingness to tolerate other criteria. All, of course, accepted the *Sunna* of the Prophet, although there were different ways of authenticating it. The Mālikīs placed a heavy stress upon the traditions of Medina in contrast to those of the whole *umma*, while the Shāfi'ī, and to a lesser extent the Hanafīs, were willing to abide by *ijmā'* (the consensus or agreement of the Islamic community)—based upon a *hadīth* of the Prophet ("My people will never agree on an error")[43]—and *qiyās*, or analogical reasoning from a comparable norm accepted on the basis of revelation or tradition. In addition to the codes of the four principal schools, another supplementary body of law developed out of the judicial practice of submitting complex legal questions to a learned jurisconsult (*muftī*), whose reply constituted an indication of the correct decision known as a *fatwā*.[44]

Historically, the Islamic community looked upon itself as a theocracy in which the *Sharī'a* was supposed to govern all areas of conduct. Originally, neither written nor circumstantial evidence was admissible in Islamic courts. Only the oral testimony of two Muslims of unimpeachable reputation was permitted, and there was no procedure of cross-examination. In practice, the *Sharī'a* was never a fully comprehensive system of ethical, religious, and legal duties. Even in earlier 'Abbasid times, certain *Sharī'a* rules were set aside by the caliphs (who were primarily responsible for defending and preserving the religious law), and another system of courts (called *Mazālim*, or "complaint" courts) developed. The *Sharī'a* courts were principally concerned with regulating the details of ritual laws, oaths and vows, marriage and divorce, inheritance, and criminal law. Even in these areas their jurisdiction did not remain exclusive. There were only a few crimes for which the Qur'ān provided specific penalties: unlawful sexual relations, false accusations of unchastity, theft, wine-drinking, armed robbery, and apostasy. In general, says Schacht, the law aimed at securing arbitration with justice, the giving of true evidence, the fulfillment of contracts, restricting the laxity of sexual morals and strengthening the marriage tie, improving the position of women, orphans and the weak in general (including slaves and servants), and curtailing private vengeance and retaliation.[45]

Because of the variety of problems not covered by religious law, the rigidity of procedures in *Sharī'a* courts, and the slow pace at which the law of those

43. The Shāfi'īs regard *ijmā'* as the highest and safest authority for making new law in Islam. Some commentators have suggested that placing greater reliance on *ijmā'* would facilitate the modernization of law, but that the orthodox resist such a trend. Others contend that *ijmā'* was traditionally and remains today more a conservative than an innovative force. See Guillaume, *Life of Muhammad*, pp. 101, 166–86; Morroe Berger, *The Arab World Today* (Garden City, New York, 1962), p. 36; and H. A. R. Gibb, *Modern Trends in Islam* (Chicago: University of Chicago Press, 1947), pp. 11–13.

44. Cf. Guillaume, *Life of Muhammad*, pp. 102–3.

45. See Joseph Schacht, "Law and Justice," *CHI*, 2: 541–42. For the list of penalties prescribed in the Qur'ān, see R. M. Savory, "Law and Traditional Society," p. 58. According to Schacht, the penalty for wine-drinking was not specified in the Qur'ān, but was fixed later by law. "Law and Justice," p. 541. Again, according to Schacht, law is more important than theology in Islam. Islamic law is a system of duties, of ritual, legal and moral obligations. "Law and Justice," *CHI*, 2: 541.

courts could be developed to meet changing social conditions, the gap between the religious-legal ideal of Islam and its political-legal reality gradually widened, even during the centuries of traditional stability and continuity.[46] Under the impact of European political, economic, and cultural influence in the nineteenth and twentieth centuries, there was an acceleration in the rate of social change throughout Islam, and many aspects of life came to be regulated by secular legal codes imported from Europe.[47] There has been an increasing tendency to ignore, by-pass, or formally modify the *Sharī'a* in regard to such matters as polygamy, child marriage, the seclusion of women, the inheritance of land, the taking of interest, and the forms of criminal punishment prescribed under traditional Islamic law (such as cutting off the hand for theft).

The abrogation in Turkey in 1926 of the *Sharī'a*-based legal system known as the Mejelle, and its replacement by an adaptation of the Swiss Civil Code, with a penal code based on the Italian model, constituted the most extreme case of modernizing secularism in the Middle East. Since World War II, most countries have adopted new legal codes that incorporate a combination of Western and Islamic concepts. Law has not changed as fundamentally in the conservative political systems bordering on the Persian Gulf—i.e., Sa'ūdī Arabia and the shaikhdoms—as in those states that have experienced revolutionary republican movements—such as Egypt, Syria, and Iraq.

Iran may serve as an example of the general pressure for legal reform. In 1906, there erupted a movement of popular protest that blamed the breakdown of Persian society partly on the neglect of the *Sharī'a*, while simultaneously calling for a new system of law to be equated with the *Sharī'a*. In the mid-1920's, Rizā Shah, carrying out a program of Westernization and modernization, reformed the systems of education and law. Many categories of law were transferred to the jurisdiction of civil courts, and a secular law degree was made a minimum qualification for holding judicial office—a requirement that rendered most religious judges ineligible.[48] But secularization led to serious strains.

It was virtually inevitable that the traditional religious law of Islam, as of other religions, should undergo change in the face of modern democratic ideas, scientific-technical knowledge, economic-industrial forces, and sociocultural life styles. Only in Sa'ūdī Arabia, guardian of the Holy Places and still influenced by Wahhābī puritanism, and in a few Persian Gulf shaikhdoms can it be said that the legal system is still based on the Qur'ān, but even in these states the more

---

46. Muslim lawyers sought to rationalize the dual system of administering justice in the Middle Ages by acknowledging the right of the sovereign to formulate policy in the public interest and by resorting to the fiction that the ruler was acting within limits permitted by the *Sharī'a*. On the necessity of medieval Islam to develop administrative, criminal, civil, and commercial law apart from the *Sharī'a*, and on the need of political rulers and *'ulamā'* to cooperate with each other, see Manfred Halpern, *The Politics of Social Change in the Middle East and North Africa* (Princeton, New Jersey: Princeton University Press, 1963), pp. 15–17. Halpern quotes the great medieval theologian al-Ghazālī: "The concessions made by us are not spontaneous, but necessity makes lawful what is forbidden. . . . We should like to ask: which is to be preferred, anarchy and the stoppage of social life for lack of a properly constituted authority, or acknowledgement of the existing power, whatever it be? Of these two alternatives the jurist cannot but choose the latter" (ibid., p. 17).

47. Morroe Berger, *The Arab World Today*, p. 164. See also Majid Khadduri, "From Religious to National Law," in Ruth Nanda Anshen, ed., *Mid-East: World Center* (New York: 1956), p. 232.

48. R. M. Savory, "Modern Persia," in *The Cambridge History of Islam*, 1: 603–4.

severe applications of strict *Sharī'a* law have been somewhat modified in recent decades, harsh decisions (such as stoning to death for adultery or cutting off the hand of a thief) being reserved for occasional exemplary purposes.

With regard to traditional family relationships, perhaps the area in which the most striking changes have occurred pertains to the rights of women. Throughout Islam, including all the Persian Gulf states, the status of women has improved in recent decades—more noticeably, of course, in urban than in rural areas, and among the wealthier and middle classes than among the peasant and poorer classes, although it should be added that peasant and poor women are hardly worse off than their male counterparts. Polygamy has declined markedly, although it is still legally permitted. Child marriages and easy divorces by husbands (who under traditional law could separate from their wives by repudiating them three times, for any or no reason) have been curtailed by legislated discouragement and complication, while women have been accorded wider grounds (e.g., ill-treatment, disease or physical disability, desertion or failure to support) for seeking dissolution of a marriage. In all countries, women's schools have been established in this century, with schooling for both sexes compulsory up to the age of twelve in some states. Women have enjoyed not only the benefits of education but also the opportunity to set aside the veil and to pursue occupations in manufacturing and business or professional careers in teaching, the arts, law, medicine, and other fields. Women, however, do not play a major role in business, the professions, and public life (even where they are allowed to vote), and veiling remains common throughout many parts of the Arabian peninsula and along the Persian Gulf. Abortion and sterilization are still considered contrary to Islamic law, and in many areas of the Persian Gulf the sale of contraceptives is prohibited. Generally speaking, the pattern of social life throughout the area is more traditional than modernized, and there are and will continue to be recurring impulses among people, *'ulamā'*, and political leaders to re-infuse secular law with the spirit of the *Sharī'a*. A prolonged and forceful drive for modernization almost inevitably produces some backlash, as it did recently in Iran.

Contemporary Islam in the Persian Gulf Region

More than 98 percent of all the peoples who inhabit the Persian Gulf region profess the religion of Islam. (This includes most of the Iranian and Arab elites whom sociologists would call "secularized.") Although probably more than 80 percent of all the Muslims in the world (estimated in excess of 500 to 600 million) adhere to Sunnī Islam, most of the 55 million Muslims in the Persian Gulf region are Shī'īs. This is due to the fact that nearly all the Muslims in Iran (by far the most populous state),[49] and slightly more than half of the Muslims in Iraq (the second most populous state),[50] are followers of the caliph 'Alī and his

---

49. In Iran, the Kurds, Turkomans, and Baluch are for the most part Sunnī.

50. In Iraq, Sunnī Muslims had an overwhelming influence in the Cabinet and the making of Cabinet policy until 1958. Following the coup against King Faisal and Prime Minister Nūrī al-Sa'īd in that year, the Shī'īs came into greater prominence. Under the Law for Personal Status of 1959, the government of Iraq made a start toward integrating Shī'īs and Sunnīs in a single legal system without regard to sect or legal school. Nevertheless, Sunnīs remain the preponderant element in all the executive and policy-making arms of government.

descendants. Thus, there are about 35 million Ithnā 'Asharī ("Twelvers") Shī'īs who believe that none but those in the line of the Prophet's son-in-law can be designated Imāms. The principal Holy Cities of the Shī'a—Najaf, the burial place of 'Alī and Karbalā', where the third Imām al-Husayn was killed, are visited each year by many thousands of pilgrims from Iran.

Apart from Iran and Iraq, Sunnī Muslims constitute a majority of the populations of Persian Gulf states (including Sa'ūdī Arabia). Persians, however, whose ancestors emigrated to Kuwait, Bahrain, and the United Arab Emirates and eastern Sa'ūdī Arabia have for the most part continued to adhere to Shī'ism. Sa'ūdī Arabia, with a population of possibly more than 8 million, is by far the largest of the Sunnī states in the Persian Gulf region. Its official religion, to which the royal family and most of the people belong, is the very orthodox, puritanical Wahhābism, propounded by the late eighteenth century shaikh, Muhammad b. 'Abd al-Wahhāb, who allied himself with the House of Sa'ūd.[51] Since then, all the kings have claimed direct descent from Muhammad b. Sa'ūd and this shaikh. It is not surprising that the strictest of all Sunnī Muslims should predominate in the country that guards the holiest shrines of Islam. Non-Muslims are forbidden under any circumstances to cross the frontiers of the *haram*, the sacred sanctuary that surrounds Mecca from three to eighteen miles from the *Ka'ba*. The governing authorities of Sa'ūdī Arabia are the most religiously conservative in the entire Muslim world, and the most zealous in resisting secularization in the areas of law and social life. But Wahhābism has become more tolerant of other Islamic sects in recent decades. "The school system supplements the traditional Islamic curriculum with many courses in the Western sciences and humanities leading up to and including the university level. Girls' schools are becoming increasingly popular."[52] Nevertheless, a pronounced Wahhābī strain persists in Sa'ūdī Arabia and, to a lesser extent, in Qatar.

Oman has long been split along religious, ethnic, and political lines. Ever since the eighth century the country has known schism between its Ibādī and Sunnī inhabitants. The Ibādīs, named for 'Abdullāh b. Ibād, an Iraqi theologian, trace their history to the seventh century Khārijī secession from orthodox Islam mentioned earlier. The Khārijīs were fundamentalists who believed that no other guides to spiritual, social, and political life were needed except the Qur'ān and the life of the Prophet. After breaking with 'Alī, because he had been willing to submit his claim to the caliphate to arbitration, they became fragmented into a number of sects, of which one of the more moderate, the followers of Ibād, migrated from Iraq to Oman in the eighth century to escape persecution by the Sunnī Umayyad caliph. The Ibādīs elected their first Imām in 749.

The Ibādī ideal was to restore Islam to its pristine condition at the time of the Prophet. In contrast to Sunnī and Shī'ī Muslims, the Ibādīs did not believe that there must necessarily be a permanent, visible head of the *umma*, but that if a suitable person is not available, the leader remains hidden and the community might have to conceal its beliefs. Ibādism eventually became the ideology of Omani particularism, and today is the official religion of the state. In the eight-

51. See George Rentz, "Wahhabism and Saudi Arabia," in Derek Hopwood, ed., *The Arabian Peninsula: Society and Politics* (London: George Allen and Unwin, 1972), pp. 54–61.

52. Ibid., p. 65.

eenth century, a struggle developed between the Hināwī tribe and their allies (mostly Yemenī and Ibādī) and the Ghāfirī tribe and their allies (mostly Nizārī and Sunnī). The Ghāfirī tribes, many of whom are Sunnīs, predominate in the northwest; the more staunchly Ibādī Hināwī are stronger in the southeastern parts of Oman. The Ibādīs, noted for their prayer and piety, resemble the Wahhābīs in their tendency to look upon other Muslim sects as religiously lax compared with themselves. The Ibādīs are sometimes regarded unjustifiably as puritanical because their mosques are simple and generally devoid of ornament, and because music is not permitted in the Ibādī interior. But they are not an intolerant people, and they are capable of making commonsense exceptions to their own moral rules—for example, the faithful who live in cold, mountainous regions are given a medical dispensation to drink wine.[53]

Throughout the Persian Gulf region, Islam remains a vital force in all societies. Its significance in the belief and behavioral patterns of the great majority of the people cannot be too greatly emphasized. Even in Iran, where the modernizing effects of industrialization, education, and political-social-economic reform have had the most pronounced effects upon national life, most of the people remain keenly aware of the religious dimension of human existence and convinced of the binding character of the *Sharī'a*. In areas where the secular law may be silent or permissive, deeply ingrained religious attitudes continue to affect conduct in the economic order—e.g., in regard to such matters as usury, even where it is justified by legal fictions. In the most modern elementary and secondary schools, religion comprises part of the curriculum—albeit separate from secular subjects. The study of traditional Islamic philosophy still thrives in Iran,[54] and traditional religious sentiment is still evident in artistic and cultural expression. For example, there lingers in less modernized regions an aversion to representing animal or human figures in art, though less so than in many other parts of the Islamic world. The Islamic revival is bound to bring stricter rules.

Devout Muslims faithfully prostrate themselves to say their prayers—the Sunnīs five times each day, the Shī'īs usually three—after ritual washing of hands, arms, feet, and face. Shī'īs place less emphasis on public congregational prayer than do the Sunnīs. Women for the most part pray in private rather than in public. Iranian and Arabic radio broadcasting services normally include the chanting of the Qur'ān in their daily programs. In Sa'ūdī Arabia and the conservative shaikhdoms, alcoholic beverages are legally prohibited, according to *Sharī'a* tradition; but they can usually be imported under license for sale to non-Muslims. There was no ban on their sale in Iran until 1979. Besides the drinking of spirits, Muslims are expected to shun gambling (although this is widespread) and the eating of pork, as well as the importation of meat from non-Muslim countries (because the animals are not ritually slaughtered). Even in those areas of life where the *Sharī'a* has been superseded by modern secular legislation, many Muslims prefer to abide by the traditional rules.

Many devout Muslims fast in a spirit of repentance several times during the

53. See J. B. Kelly, "A Prevalence of Furies: Tribes, Politics and Religion in Oman and Trucial Oman," in Hopwood, *The Arabian Peninsula*, pp. 107–41; and Donald Hawley, *Oman and Its Renaissance* (London: Stacey International, 1977), pp. 167–69.

54. Seyyed Hossein Nasr, "Ithna 'Ashari Shī'ism and Iranian Islam," in Arberry, *Religion in the Middle East*, 2: 102–11.

year, especially at the beginning, middle, and end of each month. But the observance of fasting laws is most widespread during the month of Ramadān, when the whole rhythm of social life changes. The dawn-to-dusk fast makes the days quiet, but the pace of social life picks up markedly in the evenings. The altered pattern affects even the modern secularized elites, but not as much as traditional Muslims. Every year scores of thousands of Muslims from the Persian Gulf states join the throng of faithful—numbering at least from a half million to a million— who undertake the pilgrimage (*hajj*) to Mecca.

Within the last few decades, Western scholars have paid a good deal of attention to the secularization of elites, the process of social change and modernization, and the passing of traditional society in the Middle East. While some Western-educated elites have been inclined to regard Islam as a conservative obstacle along the road to socioeconomic progress, political leaders have had to refrain from criticizing Islam, even though they may have regarded specific Islamic institutions or customs as obstacles to their plans for modernizing their countries.[55] They have found a variety of ways to circumvent or weaken Islamic opposition to change: supporting secular rather than religious schools, suppressing the religious brotherhoods, favoring persons of secularist attitudes in governmental appointments, etc. Yet it would be an exaggeration to say that Islam is in long-term decline as an influential factor in the societies of the Middle East. As Wilfred Cantwell Smith has observed, secularism in the Islamic world has not produced an antireligious theoretical literature *à la Voltaire*, and the secularist attitude is not so much an indigenous outlook as an importation from the West.[56] Thus, even the "secularists" in the Middle East (and this is particularly true of the Persian Gulf countries) feel obliged to remain loyal to Islam as a great religious-cultural heritage under erosive attack from foreign forces—cultural, philosophical and economic. Since the Iranian Revolution of 1979, Islam has generally undergone a revival throughout the region. (See the Epilogue below.)

For the Muslims of the Persian Gulf region, the community of Islam remains the all-important social reality. Modern technical media of communication make it more possible than ever for them to identify with the fate of suffering co-religionists, e.g., in Kashmir, Bangladesh, and the Philippines. Within recent years, Persian Gulf governments have been among the forty or more that take part in the Pan-Islamic Conferences, where religious, political, and cultural considerations combine to promote Islamic unity and interests on those issues that touch the deep-rooted sentiments of those who still follow the teachings of the Prophet—sentiments that political leaders, far from wishing to ignore, may deem it appropriate to kindle.

Other Religions in the Persian Gulf Region

Prior to the rise of Islam, several beliefs flourished in Iran and the Persian Gulf region (see pp. 292–93 above). Among these, the ancient Iranian religion of

55. See Halpern, *Politics of Social Change*, pp. 129–33. "The word for 'innovation' in the religious sense," writes Morroe Berger, "is 'bid'a,' meaning also heresy and something generally bad" (ibid., p. 417). See also the landmark study by Daniel Lerner, *The Passing of Traditional Society* (Glencoe, Ill.: The Free Press, 1958).
56. Smith, *Islam in Modern History*, pp. 112–13.

Zoroastrianism accepted a dualistic view of the universe. It recognized good and evil as eternally subsisting principles, stressed the importance of moral duties in man's struggle for salvation, and looked toward a life beyond death. Iranian religious thought interacted with and had an impact upon Judaism, Christianity, and Islam—regardless of whether its elements were accepted, rejected, or modified by the three great world religions that originated in the Middle East.[57]

Zoroaster (Zarathustra) was an Iranian prophet whose life-dates probably fall somewhere close to the sixth century B.C. He taught that a totally good and orderly universe, including man, was created by Ahura Mazda, the spirit of life and light (later to be called Ohrmazd). Eternally opposed to the creator of goodness is the evil Ahriman (Satan), author of death, darkness, disease, calamities, disorder, and moral vices. In the conflict between goodness and evil, waged in the soul of man (who has free will), the individual allies himself with Ohrmazd by every good thought, word, and deed, and with Satan by every evil one. The teachings of Zoroaster are contained in the sacred books called the *Avesta*.[58] The Zoroastrians developed a priesthood and a system of spiritual direction, penance, and ritual sacrifice. Since they were forbidden to bury or cremate their dead, because this would pollute the earth, air, fire, or water created by Ohrmazd, they exposed their corpses to birds or beasts of prey. Zoroastrianism was the national religion of Iran and reached the zenith of its spiritual and social influence in the Sāsānid empire from the third to the seventh centuries A.D. Persecuted by the invading Muslims for their ostensible polytheism, many Zoroastrians fled to India, where they became known as Parsees. In modern Iran, Zoroastrianism is officially tolerated. Recent estimates of their numbers have ranged from 7,000 to 35,000 concentrated mainly in Tehran, Yazd, and Kirman.[59] Within the last decade, Zoroastrianism has become an object of growing interest among some Iranian nationalists—a tendency comparable to various "atavistic" movements in Egypt, Syria, and Turkey.

Islam, from the time of the Prophet, has always been more or less tolerant of the "People of the Book"—the Jews and the Christians; however, despite the autonomy they enjoyed, these peoples were in an "unquestionably inferior judicial condition" during the medieval period before discriminatory legislation was alleviated during the Ottoman period and began to disappear in the nineteenth century.[60] Both groups are legally permitted to maintain synagogues, churches,

57. Christian, Jewish, and Zoroastrian communities were allowed to elect their own representatives to the Majlis, but members of these groups could not occupy command positions in the armed services or major decision-making positions in the government under the Shah, and are less likely to be given a public role in the new Islamic Republic.

58. See A. V. W. Jackson, *Zoroaster, Prophet of Ancient Iran* (New York: Gordon Press, 1976); W. B. Henning, *Zoroaster* (London: Oxford University Press, 1951); R. C. Zaehner, *The Dawn and Twilight of Zorastrianism* (London: Weidenfeld and Nicolson, 1961); and Richard N. Frye, *The Heritage of Persia* (New York: New American Library, 1963), pp. 49–65.

59. Estimates of the numerical strength of the various non-Islamic religious communities in the Persian Gulf region are drawn from recent editions of *Encyclopaedia Britannica Books of the Year*, *The Oxford Map of Arabia* (London: Oxford University Press); *The Middle East and North Africa* (London: Europa Publications, Ltd.), and Peter Mansfield, ed., *The Middle East: A Political and Economic Survey* (4th ed.; London: Oxford University Press, 1973). For an excellent general survey of the background and history of many of these groups, see Albert H. Hourani, *Minorities in the Arab World* (London: Oxford University Press, 1947).

60. Y. Linant de Bellefonds, "Law," in A. J. Arberry, *Religion in the Middle East*, 2: 413–20. The author notes that in earlier times Jews and Christians were obliged to live in special dis-

and schools, publish religious periodicals, and conduct worship services openly in all Persian Gulf states, except Saʻūdī Arabia, where private enclaves only are permitted. Since the creation of the state of Israel in 1948, Jewish communities have all but disappeared in Saʻūdī Arabia and the smaller states along the Persian Gulf. Although some 50,000 Jews have emigrated from Iran, approximately 70,000 remain in that country, principally in Tehran, Isfahān, Kāshān, Hamadān, and Shīrāz. About 5,000 Jews are estimated to be still in Iraq.[61]

It should not be necessary in a work of this nature, designed primarily for Western readers, to explain the religious beliefs and theological doctrines of Judaism and Christianity—subjects better covered in many other readily accessible publications. Nor is it possible within an article of this compass to examine the complexities of Christian theological disagreements and ecclesiastical schisms, along with their repercussions upon the history of the Persian Gulf. Such a task would require delving into the East-West rivalry of Eastern (Byzantine) Orthodox Christianity and Western (Roman, Latin) Christianity, as well as the theological subtleties of Iconoclasm, Monophysitism, Monothelitism, Nestorianism, Armenian and Syrian Christianity. Here no more can be done than to note in passing the adverse effects of the Crusades and the expulsion of the Muslims from Spain upon Islamic-Christian relations, the interests of Christian churches as a motive or pretext for Great Power interventions in the Middle East since the latter part of the eighteenth century, and the role played by Christian intellectuals in modern nationalist movements within the area.[62]

Today Christians in the Persian Gulf region number 550,000 to 600,000. About half of these are in Iran (190,000 Armenians, 35,000 Roman Catholics, 26,000 Protestants, and 25,000 Assyrians), concentrated mainly in Tehran and Isfahān. Another quarter of a million Christians (145,000 Chaldeans, 35,000 Syrian Catholics, 30,000 Jacobites, 23,000 Nestorians, and 18,000 Armenians) live in Iraq. Approximately 30,000 Christians are to be found in Kuwait and the other Persian Gulf States. Catholic and Anglican Churches, as well as missions of the Dutch Reformed Church of America, are located in Ahmadī, Kuwait City, and Manāma. Within recent years, both Catholic and Protestant Christians have im-

---

tricts, whereas today coreligionists tend to congregate as a matter of preference (ibid., p. 415). Jews and Christians antedated Muslims in that area, and therefore never felt like strangers. H. Z. Hirschberg writes: "In actual fact most of the special laws concerning Christians and Jews were at first almost ignored. From time to time devout, zealous caliphs confirmed their validity. . . . The caliphs themselves infringed the prohibition of admitting 'unbelievers' to high government office, and the latter did not willingly submit to discriminatory measures." "The Oriental Jewish Communities," in A. J. Arberry, *Religion in the Middle East*, 1: 128. See also W. H. C. Frend, "Christianity in the Middle East: Survey Down to A.D. 1800," ibid., pp. 239–96.

61. For a history of Jewish-Islamic relations, see Nehemiah Robinson, *The Arab Countries of the Near East and Their Jewish Communities* (New York: Institute of Jewish Affairs, 1951); and E. I. J. Rosenthal, *Judaism and Islam* (London: T. Yoseloff, 1961).

62. See L. E. Browne, *The Eclipse of Christianity in Asia* (Cambridge: Cambridge University Press, 1933); Steven Runciman, *A History of the Crusades*, 4 vols. (Cambridge: Cambridge University Press, 1951–58); Pierre Rondot, *Les Chretiéns d'Orient* (Paris: Peyronnet, 1955); and Donald Attwater, *The Christian Churches of the East*, 2 vols. (Milwaukee: Bruce, 1947–48). The role played by Catholic and Protestant educators in the formation of the nineteenth-century forerunners of Arab nationalism is treated in George Antonius, *The Arab Awakening* (Beirut: Khayat's, 1936; Philadelphia: Lippincott, 1939); and A. L. Tibawi, "The American Missionaries in Beirut and Butrus Al-Bustani," in Albert Hourani, ed., *St. Antony's Papers*, No. 16, *Middle Eastern Affairs* (Carbondale: Southern Illinois University Press, 1959), pp. 137–84.

proved their relations with Islam as the result of an intensified dialogue, this despite the strains caused by the political-religious civil war in Lebanon.

The Baha'i movement had its origin in an eighteenth century offshoot of Shī'ī Islam in Iran. Shaikh Ahmad Ahsā'ī taught that it was possible, through a human intermediary known as the *Bāb* (Door or Gateway), to make contact with the creative force of the Hidden Imām. In 1840, Mīrzā 'Alī Muhammad gained a considerable following by proclaiming himself to be the *Bāb*. The Bābī movement was persecuted by the official Shī'ī leaders as well as by the state, and Mīrzā 'Alī Muhammad was put to death in 1850. One of his disciples, Husain 'Alī Bahā' Allāh, declared himself the Messiah of all religions. The modern Baha'i movement takes its name from him. The Baha'is now claim a world membership of a half million. Within the Persian Gulf area, they are found in substantial numbers only in Iraq and Iran. They are still regarded as a deviant religious group by the Shī'īs. Although not legally recognized, they are tolerated.

Epilogue on Religion and the Iranian Revolution

Religion played a role of crucial significance in the Iranian Revolution of 1978–79, in which the pro-Western government of Shah Rizā Pahlavi was overturned by a coalition of disparate elements, ranging from Marxists to liberal reformist intellectuals and devout Muslims. All those who were opposed to the Shah for a variety of reasons united at least temporarily in support of the religious leader, the Āyatullāh Rūhullāh Khumainī, who had been exiled from Iran fifteen years earlier for opposing, on religious grounds, some of the Shah's fundamental reforms, such as the Land Reform Law of 1962 and the enfranchisement of women. The coalition, of course, was a fragile political expedient; few observers expected the advocates of secular modernization, whether Marxist or Westernized liberal, to be able to cooperate enthusiastically or long with the leaders of a profound Islamic revival.

In order to understand the religio-political situation in Iran, we must draw a few summary lessons from the history of Islam, described above. In theory, it will be recalled, Islam recognized no clear distinction between "Church" and "State" as the Christian West gradually came to do. For Muslims, all aspects of society are governed by the Qur'an and the *Sharī'a*. But, as we have seen, there was a progressive differentiation between the religious and the political authorities in the history of Islam. Moreover, the Sunnis—who comprised by far the dominant branch of Islam—were generally ready to accept those political institutions (under the Caliphate) capable of preserving order and to blink at political policies (such as the toleration of sinful practices) that did not conform to the teachings and traditions of the Prophet.

Throughout history, the Shī'īs have displayed a stronger tendency than the Sunnīs to resist political authority, and much less readiness to accommodate the imperatives of the faith to the practical compromises that political rule requires. Thus Shī'īsm never recognized the legitimacy of the Caliphate. The earliest Shī'īs were Arabs, but once Persia had become the stronghold of Shī'īsm, this religious sect—a persecuted minority throughout Islam as a whole—emerged gradually as an appropriate vehicle whereby the Persians could put distance between themselves and the Arabic institution of the Caliphate, preserving a non-Arabic Islamic identity by forging a link between Islam and traditional Iranian political institutions. Shī'īsm was disposed to regard monarchy as the preferred form of government in the interval between the Twelfth Imam and the *Mahdī*, so long as the ruler accepted guidance from the *'ulamā'* in defending Islam and upholding the *Shari'a*. The shahs of the Safavid dynasty, which assumed power at the beginning of the sixteenth century, were able to assert their authority over the *'ulamā'* by a variety of ingenious policies, but during the nineteenth century, under a succession of weak Qājār rulers, the power of the *'ulamā'* steadily increased.

The fundamental problem of sovereignty in a Shī'ī state came to a head early in the twentieth century, before the accession of the Pahlavi dynasty. Western-educated intellectuals who sought to modernize the country looked upon traditional Islam as an obstacle to progress. In their efforts to obtain the promulgation of a liberal Constitution in 1906–07, they realized that they could not reach their goal without at least the grudging acquiescence of the conservative elements—the *mujtahids*, the *'ulamā'*, and the bazaar merchants. The result was a precarious and uneasy truce. Both sides were agreed in their opposition to bureaucratic repression by the Qājār regime and the exploitative presence of foreign influence in Iran. But the liberals had to mute their enthusiasm for democracy and the secularization of education and law, and to accept a constitutional arrangement establishing a group of five *mujtahids* to make certain that all legislation passed by the *Majlis* conformed to the sacred laws of Islam. Once the religious authorities realized the extent to which the liberals were determined to bring about social change, many withdrew their support from the new Constitution; others went along reluctantly, but only to preserve some religious influence in the state. *Mujtahids* and reforming intellectuals have been basically suspicious of each other ever since.

When Rizā Shah came to power in 1925, the religious leaders at first tolerated him because, among other reasons, they thought he was "safer" than Kemal Atatürk of Turkey. Nevertheless, he speeded up the process of modernizing and secularizing the Islamic society of Iran. This meant undermining the traditional power of the *mullahs*—curbing their power over education and the settlement of legal disputes. Devout Moslems were scandalized by his decisions to allow foreigners to enter mosques and to encourage women to put aside the *chador* in favor of Western dress. The Shah ordered the admission of girls to school and finally banned the wearing of the veil in 1936. In recent decades, his son carried the policies of Westernization even further, using the oil revenues to build a modern industrial economy and a modern military force. The gap widened steadily between the religious world of Qum and minarets on the one hand and the technological-commercial world of Tehran with its office buildings, hotels, shops, theaters, and night clubs on the other. Muhammad Rizā Pahlavi carried out a "White Revolution" in an agrarian society that reduced the landholdings of the religious leaders. He also replaced the Islamic calendar with one dating back to the ancient monarchy of Cyrus. The Āyatullāh Khumainī, first from Iraq and later from Paris, galvanized the resentment of the faithful against the monarchy and in favor of an Islamic republic.

Whether or not genuine religious belief was a more important factor in the revolution than political considerations is a question over which historians will long argue. But there was little doubt that neither the middle-class liberal reformers alone, nor the Marxists alone, nor the two groups in combination, could have brought about the overthrow of the Pahlavi dynasty had it not been possible to organize the widespread discontent of the Muslim faithful. The removal of the Shah from the scene, however, was not likely to resolve the underlying tensions in Iranian society between traditional religion and the forces of modernization and secularization. Both Marxists and liberals were quick to enter a tactical alliance with religious authorities toward whose outlook they would normally be unsympathetic. Religious belief was probably the most effective wedge that could be driven between a military officer corps loyal to the monarchy and regular soldiers who had been raised as Muslims. But as soon as the old structures had collapsed, it became apparent that the more modern sectors of Iranian society found themselves seriously at odds with certain manifestations of revived Islamic zeal—in the area of women's rights, freedom of the press, the summary administration of harsh justice, and in regard to the basic right of all citizens, whether Muslim or non-Muslim, to have equal status before the law.

The Islamic revival associated with the Iranian Revolution seemed likely to have far-reaching repercussions, both internal and external. Internally, it set the stage for protracted tension between a sophisticated secular modernism and a puritanical religious zeal, and between those interested in continued industrialization and those committed to a reduced rate of Western-style economic growth. Because both Kurdistan and Baluchistan are predominantly Sunnī, the Shī'ī revolution in Iran may increase separatist tendencies on the part of the Kurds and Baluchis. It was expected or feared that throughout the Muslim world sentiments of religiously inspired nationalism would be stirred, that pro-Western monarchs and shaikhs might come under increasing pressure, and that the cause of Palestinian liberation would receive emotional and perhaps political reinforcement, complicating the efforts of diplomats to work out practical compromises in the Arab–Israeli conflict. But all projections into the future should take into account the differences between Sunnī and Shī'ī in their basic approaches to religio-political matters.

Selected Bibliography

Arberry, A. J., ed. *Religion in the Middle East*. Cambridge, 1979.

Gibb, H. A. R. *Modern Trends in Islam*. Chicago, 1946.

———. *Mohammedanism: A Historical Survey*. New York, 1955.

Guillaume, Alfred. *Islam*. Harmondsworth, 1954.

———. *Life of Muhammad*. Oxford, 1955.

Holt, P. M., et al., eds. *Cambridge History of Islam*. Cambridge, 1970.

Nicholson, Reynold A. *Mystics of Islam*. New York, 1975.

Rosenthal, E. I. J. *Islam in the Modern National State*. Cambridge, 1965.

Savory, Roger M., ed. *Introduction to Islamic Civilisation*. Cambridge, 1976.

Smith, W. C. *Islam in Modern History*. Princeton, 1957.

von Grunebaum, Gustave, ed. *Unity and Variety in Muslim Civilization*. Chicago, 1955.

Watt, Montgomery W. *Muhammad: Prophet and Statesman*. London, 1961.

12. Languages of the Persian Gulf BRUCE INGHAM

 The two main languages of the Persian Gulf are Arabic and Persian; by these terms one includes both the standard languages and the colloquial dialects. A Turkish dialect is also spoken in areas of the province of Fārs in Iran. These three are etymologically of quite separate linguistic stocks. Arabic is a Semitic language akin to Hebrew, Maltese, and Amharic, to give the most well-known examples. Persian is Indo-European and related to the majority of the languages of Europe, while Turkish is a member of the Ural-Altaic group, the majority of whose members are in northern and central Asia. Arabic is the standard language of the emirates, Saudi Arabia and Iraq, Persian the language of Iran. Some overlap also occurs in terms of the colloquial dialects and as a result of emigration. In the plain of Khūzistān in southwestern Persia, Arabic is the speech of the indigenous population; pockets of Arabic-speaking immigrant groups were also,[1] and perhaps still are, to be found along the Persian coast of the Persian Gulf and Arabic may also be spoken by some nomadic groups in Fārs.[2] A Persian dialect is spoken on the Ra's Musandam peninsula of Oman, and there are large Persian-speaking émigré populations in Kuwait and Bahrain, and also in the Holy Cities of Najaf and Karbalā in Iraq, though many of the latter have returned to Iran recently. In Khūzistān, immigration from the Persian-speaking areas of Iran connected with the oil industry has recently increased the use of Persian in the towns, particularly Ahvāz and Ābādān. Historically, contact between the two languages has always been considerable. Prior to Islam, Arabic adopted many Persian words connected with Persian culture, in particular material culture. With the expansion of Islam, Persia adopted the Arabic alphabet and a large amount of Arabic vocabulary connected with Islam, with the world of learning, and with administration. Further, the whole Arabic morphological framework has been adopted into Persian together with the original Persian framework and exists, rather as Latin does with the European languages, as a

1. See J. G. Lorimer, *Gazetteer of the Persian Gulf*, II, A and B articles on Lingeh and Bandar Abbas.
2. See F. Barth, *Nomads of South West Persia* (Oslo, 1961), pp. 1, 2.

314

source of vocabulary for technical and administrative fields. Turkish also has borrowed similarly from Arabic and Persian. As a continuing process, Arabic has continued to borrow Persian words of the type mentioned above, connected with manufactured items and processes originating in Iran or beyond. This is heaviest in Iraq and the Persian Gulf states, but penetrates quite deeply into the Arabian peninsula in some instances. Turkish also has furnished a certain amount of new vocabulary and even, strangely enough, some syntactic and grammatical elements, but the influence of Turkish on Arabic is now minimal. Certain other languages have been and still are present in the Persian Gulf, such as Urdu, Baluchi, English, and Portuguese. However, their effect on the general language situation is in no case comparable with that of the two main languages.

The following are illustrative examples of cross-language borrowing in the area:

Central Asian Loans in Persian. These examples are taken from Doerfer[3] and marked according to his classification as wmmo (westmittelmongolisch), tü (Turkic), or m (Mongolian). The form given is the current Persian form:

bājināq	sister-in-law's husband	tü		qāb	frame	tü
				qāblama	pot	tü
bahādur	hero	tü/m		qadaghan	forbidden	wmmo
bushqāb	plate	tü		qāz	goose	tü
chāq	fat, healthy	tü		qaychi	scissors	wmmo
chāqū	knife	wmmo		qāyiq	canoe, small boat	tü
īl	tribe	wmmo				
jādū	magic spell	wmmo		qū	swan	tü
kākul	haarschopf	wmmo		qushūn	army	wmmo
khān	chief	tü		qūti	box	tü
kumak	help	tü		sawqāt	present, gift	wmmo
kūch	migration	tü		yaqa	collar	tü
kūchik	small	tü		yaylāq	summer camp	tü
urdū	camp	wmmo				

Persian Loans in the Arabic Dialects of Iraq, Khūzistān, and the Persian Gulf. The Persian Gulf material is taken mostly from Johnstone,[4] while the Iraqi and Khūzistānī material is from my own notes. As most Persian loans in the Persian Gulf dialects are also present in the Mesopotamian dialects, exclusively Mesopotamian items will be marked here as M. The material here consists of words that would seem to have entered Arabic through Persian, although some of them are of ultimate central Asian origin. They are, nevertheless, regarded as Persian in this area:

bardāya	curtain		charakh	wheel
byāla	cup		chingāl	fork
chāra	trick, stratagem M.		daftar	notebook
			darīsha	window
chāy/shāhī	tea		darwāza	gate

3. G. Doerfer, *Türkische und Mongolische Elemente im Neupersischen* (Wiesbaden, 1963).
4. T. M. Johnstone, *Eastern Arabian Dialect Studies* (London, 1967), pp. 56–57.

dahlīz	alcove	sardāb	cellar
finjāl/finyāl	cup	shākha	canal M.
jām	glass	shīsha	water-pipe
mēwa	fruit	turshī	pickle
khōsh	good	ghand	lump, sugar
rōshna/rōzna	window,	ghāshūgha	spoon
	alcove	ghūri	pot, kettle
shikar	sugar	ghūti	tin, box
sira	queue,	khurda	small change
	station	yākha	collar

Local differences in pronunciation are not considered in the above list and the form of the word given is in some cases not universal to the whole area. Nevertheless, the item itself will be present.

Turkish Loans in Arabic Dialects of the Area. Turkish loans are more common in the speech of Iraq and Khūzistān than in the Peninsula. However, even there some loans can be found. Turkish loans were far more prevalent following the Ottoman period, especially in military and administrative fields. The Turkish suffixes -*chi*, and to a less extent -*siz*, occur in the dialects of Iraq in a number of examples. Examples that are mainly Mesopotamian are marked M:

adabsiz	ill-mannered	chākūch	hammer
	M.	janta	suitcase
bērag	flag	chōl	desert M.
burghi	screw	gahwachi	coffee-maker
burghul	chick-peas	gēmar	skimmed milk
kalakchi	trickster M.	dundurma	ice cream
sūch	fault M.	ghandara	shoes
sakhtachi	trickster M.	'ōdha	room

Arabic Loans in Persian and Turkish. Arabic loans in Persian and Turkish are in far greater number than in the other direction, both as a result of the long use of Arabic as the language of learning in the Islamic community, and also as the vehicle of the Islamic religion. Personal names, place names, titles, salutations, politeness formulae of Arabic origin are common in both languages. Although recently nationalistic movements have led to a reduction of these, nevertheless, Arabic is present in all lexical fields to a great extent. The great number of these makes it unnecessary to give examples.

In the following description of the languages of the Gulf, only Persian and Arabic are considered. Although Turkic is admittedly a language of the Persian Gulf area, little is known about the particular dialect spoken there except that it seems to be a dialect of the Oghuz branch akin to Āzerī and Osmānlī.[5] Unlike the Persian and Arabic dialects that exist within larger Persian and Arabic

5. P. Oberling, *The Qashqai Nomads of Fārs* (The Hague, 1974), p. 27. Karl H. Menges, "Research in the Turkic dialects of Iran," *Oriens* 4 (1951): 273–79. It seems that these dialects are more highly assimilated to Persian than those of the north in terms of phonology and lexis. This information I have from Dr. R. Tapper, who has worked among the Shāh-savan of Northern Iran and is in a position to compare the two. This is backed up by an informant from Mālīcheh in the 'Alīgūdarz district of Arāk in Western Iran, where a Turkic dialect is spoken also. The informant (M. Tavakkoli) reports that this dialect also is very similar to Persian in its phonology.

language areas, the Turkic dialect of Fārs is isolated from the main Turkic area and does not function within a Turkic code matrix. There is, therefore, little that one can say about it from a sociolinguistic or dialectological point of view that is relevant to the Persian Gulf area. The accounts of Persian and Arabic differ somewhat in approach. This is because of the different linguistic situation (see below) and also the state of our knowledge of the two. For Arabic we have some detailed descriptions of the dialect groups around the Persian Gulf. For Persian, we have only one account of the village dialects of Fārs, which seems to present a picture of a fairly homogeneous group. We have rather more for Lurī. Therefore, for Arabic a survey of the dialect geography of the area is given, while for Persian the description is in terms of a comparison of the Fārs dialects with dialects of other areas and with standard Persian.

Language Communities of the Persian Gulf

In the two main language communities of the Gulf, namely, the Arabic and Persian communities, great language divergence exists mainly as a result of the great distances over which they are spoken and the difficulty of communication within the area. Arabic is spoken as a national language throughout North Africa, Egypt, Sudan, the Levant, Iraq, and the Arabian peninsula. Persian is spoken as a national language in Iran and as an important second language in Afghanistan, Baluchistan, and parts of Central Asia.[6] Within the area of the Persian Gulf, we will consider for the purpose of this article the Arabic dialects of Southern Iraq, Khūzistān, Najd, Eastern Arabia, and Oman, the Persian dialects of Fārs (including Lurī); and briefly the Turkic dialects of Fārs, since these can be said to impinge upon the Gulf in some form or other.

There are considerable differences between these three communities in terms of the total code matrices[7] that they involve. Within the Arabic area, excluding Khūzistān, the written language and the language appropriate to formal situations is literary Arabic. This is a modern development of classical Arabic, a standardized form of Arabic spoken in the north-central Arabian peninsula at the time of the Islamic expansion in the seventh century and differing from literary Arabic only in minor details of vocabulary and style. In interdialect communication, in the area considered here, total mutual intelligibility obtains in cases where contact normally occurs. However, in cases of difficulty the choice is open to the speaker to modify his dialect in the direction of that of the interlocutor or in the direction of literary Arabic, which is generally known, in some degree, at least among educated speakers. In the Persian area, the situation is rather different.

Modern Persian, the national language of Iran, is a development of one of the dialects of Fārs, adopted as the general language of communication in the main towns of Iran, also in certain rural areas such as Khurasan and western Afghanistan. The written language differs only minimally from this spoken form. However, the dialects of the rest of the countryside differ considerably from modern Persian and from each other. For interdialect conversation, modern

6. I. M. Oranskij, *Die neuiranische Sprache der Sowjetunion* (The Hague, 1975).
7. For the use of this term, see J. Gumperz, "Types of linguistic community," *Anthropological Linguistics* 4, 1 (1962): 28–40.

FIG. 12–1. Arabic dialects of the Persian Gulf

Persian is normally used, hence the frequent reference in older works to Bāzārī, i.e., the language of the bazaar, where people of different dialect backgrounds may meet. There are therefore important differences between the Arabic and Persian speech communities. In the Arabic area, we have a situation of "diglossia," as defined by Ferguson[8] where the contrast is between a formal written variety

8. C. Ferguson, "Diglossia," *Word* 15, 2 (1959).

and informal spoken varieties, and where the formal variety represents an earlier form of the language and as such is associated with the history and culture of the area as a whole. Naturally, with the spread of modern communications, standard dialects are growing up so that one may speak of standard Baghdad colloquial for Iraq,[9] standard Gulf Arabic for the Persian Gulf.[10] For Saʿūdī Arabia the situation is more complex, since both the urban speech of the Ḥijāz[11] and the dialects of Najd have some prestige. However, it seems likely that the Riyadhi dialect will emerge as a standard form. In the Persian area, on the other hand, we have a situation mainly of an urban standard variety vs. nonstandard rural varieties. The Turkic speech of Fārs again differs from both the above in being an enclave of Turkish speech within the Persian language area isolated from the main Turkish-speaking areas to the north, i.e., Turkey, Azerbaijan, and Central Asia. Turkic, within this area, is purely a 'spoken' form,[12] the standard language for speakers of Turkic within Fārs, as also for the Arabs of Khūzistān, being modern Persian. These different code matrices are illustrated in Tables 12–1 and 12–2.

9. C. Erwin, *Short Reference Grammar of Iraqi Arabic* (Washington, D.C., 1963).

10. Hamdi A. Qafisheh, *A Basic Course in Gulf Arabic* (Tucson, Arizona, 1976).

11. See M. Sieny, "The Syntax of Urban Hijazi Arabic," Ph.D. thesis, University of Michigan, Ann Arbor, 1972.

12. It is, of course, not unknown for these "purely-spoken" forms to be written down and used in correspondence among rural groups or less educated classes. This is true also of the Arabic dialects in the area. However, no common form of spelling is known, although nowadays interest in folklore and collections of colloquial poetry is leading to a certain amount of standardization in the writing.

TABLE 12–1. THE PERSIAN SPEECH COMMUNITY

	Standard	Modern Persian		
Codes	Regional	Persian dialects (including Kurdish and Lurī)	Khūzistānī Arabic	Turkic

TABLE 12–2. THE ARABIC SPEECH COMMUNITY

	Formal	Modern literary Arabic				
		Standard	Standard Riyādhi or urban Hijāzī	Standard urban Gulf colloquial	Standard Baghdad colloquial	
Codes	Informal	Regional	Speech of the rest of Saʿūdī Arabia	Speech of the nomadic population of the Gulf states, akin to Najdī speech in the main	Other Arabic dialects of Iraq	Kurdish

The above model does not include the speech of émigré groups, such as the Persian communities of the Persian Gulf, who can be considered to be members of both speech communities.

Arabic Dialect Geography

INTRODUCTION

The Arabic dialect geography of the region is described in terms of the main dialect areas that impinge on the Persian Gulf itself, some of which extend fairly far inland.[13] The term "dialect area" is used here to mean an area from which a set of dialect features radiates. We distinguish this central core area, which exhibits all the features characteristic of the area, from a periphery zone that will show only some members of the set. Where two such periphery zones overlap there will occur dialects that show features characteristic of both areas. However, since our task is not to present a rigid classification, but to describe the dialect geography of the area, this is not a problem, merely a complication. A further complication of the model in this area is that we must consider two dimensions that are related but not coextensive; that of the sedentary and that of the nomadic populations. Demographically, the Arabian peninsula and Mesopotamia present a picture of concentrations of settlement in specific areas separated by large intervening areas of little or no sedentary population.[14] These concentrations form the core of the sedentary dialect areas and are tied to sources of water for irrigation or coastal settlements dependent originally on fishing,

13. The materials are drawn from the following sources. For southern Iraq and Khūzistān, including the north Arabian type dialects of the Humaid and Rufai', my own notes were used, obtained on visits to the area in 1969, 1971, 1973, and 1977. See also my "Urban and rural Arabic in Khūzistān," *BSOAS* (*Bulletin of the School of Oriental and African Studies*) 36, 3 (1973): 633–53; and "Regional and social factors in the dialect geography of Southern Iraq and Khūzistān," *BSOAS* 39, 1 (1976): 62–82. For the Arabian peninsula the following published and unpublished sources were used: J. Cantineau, "Etudes sur quelques parlers de nomades arabes d'Orient," *AIEO* (*Annales de l'Institut des Etudes Orientales*) 2 (1936): 1–118; and 3 (1937): 119–227; P. A. Abboud, "Syntax of Najdi Arabic," Ph.D. dissertation, University of Texas, 1964, dealing with the dialect of Hā'il; W. Diem, *Skizzen Jemenitischer Dialekte* (Beirut, Wiesbaden, 1973); J. J. Hess, *Von den Beduinen des Inneren Arabiens* (Zurich, Leipzig, 1938), for the dialect of the 'Utaiba; T. M. Johnstone, "Some characteristics of the Dōsiri dialect of Arabic as spoken in Kuwait," *BSOAS* 24, 2 (1961): 249–97, "Further studies on the Dōsiri dialect as spoken in Kuwait," *BSOAS* 28, 1 (1964): 77–113; "Aspects of syllabication in the spoken Arabic of 'Anaiza'," *BSOAS* 30, 1 (1967): 1–16; *Eastern Arabian Dialect Studies* (London, 1967); C. Landberg, *Etudes sur les dialectes d'Arabie méridionale*. Vol. 1, *Hadhramout* (Leiden, 1901), Vol. 2, *Datînah* (Leiden, 1904–13); *Langue des bédouins 'Anazeh* (Uppsala, 1940); A. M. il-Hazmi, "A Critical and Comparative Study of the Spoken Dialect of the Harb Tribe in Saudi Arabia," Ph.D. thesis, Leeds University, 1975; S. M. M. Badawī, "An Intonational Study of Riyadhi Arabic," Ph.D. thesis, University of London, 1965; R. Montagne, "Contes poétiques Bédouins (récueillis chez les Šammar de Géziré)," *BEO* (*Bulletin d'Études Orientales*) 5 (1935): 33–119; N. Rhodokanakis, *Die vulgärabische Dialekt im Dofâr* (Zfâr), *I Prosaische und poetische Texte, Übersetzung und Indices* (Vienna, 1908); *II Einleitung Glossar und Grammatik* (Vienna, 1911); J. G. Wetzstein, "Sprachliches aus den Zeltlagern der syrischen Wüste," *ZDMG* (*Zeitschrift der Deutschen morgenländischen Gesellschaft*) 22 (1868): 69–194; on the dialects of the Arabian peninsula in general and for the speech of Najrān, Hofūf, and Sudair in particular, much useful information was obtained from an as yet unpublished manuscript by T. Prochazka, Jr., "Studies in the Dialects of the Arabian Peninsula." Work was also carried out with informants in Kuwait in 1977 on the speech of the 'Aniza (Sba'a section), Shammar, 'Awāzim, Rashāyida, Mutair, and 'Ajmān tribes, also the area of al-Qasīm and Dhahrān. This was with the help of the Arabic Department of Kuwait University. Particular thanks are due to Sayyār Rādhi al-'Anizī, Mamdūh Rādhi al-'Anizī, Lāfī ibn Slēmān al-'Anizī, and 'Ayidh Tu'ma Hamdān al-Dhafīrī. Much useful help and advice also was provided by the Kuwait Radio and Television services, particularly by Sālih Mansūr al-'Alayyān and Talāl Sa'īd. Work was also done in London on the dialect of the Harb with Hamza Muzainī. The Dhafīr and Shammarī material was checked during a visit to Sa'ūdī Arabia in 1978.

14. See A. Musil, *Northern Neğd* (New York, 1928), pp. 256–57.

pearling, and trade. As regards the inland settlements, in Iraq and Khūzistān these follow the lines of the rivers and irrigation channels, reaching their densest along the banks of Shatt al-'Arab, the confluence of the Tigris, Euphrates, and Kārūn rivers, an area of intensive palm cultivation. In Arabia, concentrations of wells and cultivable basins occur along the central scarp of the Jabal Tuwaiq, around the Jabal Shammar[15] and in the area of al-Hasā. Connected with these foci are nomadic groups concentrated near wells in the summer, but ranging far out into the grazing grounds between the settlements in the late winter and spring.[16] In most cases the nomads speak a dialect closely linked to that of the settlers of the area.[17] In others, however, where the nomads are newcomers, they speak an intruder dialect related to their original home,[18] which may or may not have begun to blend with the language of the settlers of the area. The areas isolated for the purpose of this study are the following:

1) *Southern Mesopotamia:* the valleys of the Tigris and Euphrates up to about Baghdad and the areas in between. The Shatt al-'Arab and the rivers Kārūn and Jarrāhī and most of the plain of Khūzistān. Here the core is formed by the river valleys, while the periphery is the surrounding plain. In some areas of the plain or *bādiya*, to give it its Arabic name, the influence of the north Arabian type is evident, especially in the case of the nomads.

2) *North Arabia:* an area centered on the Jabal Shammar in northern Arabia and spreading south to al-Qasīm and north and east into the Syrian Desert and the Shāmiyya to the west of the Euphrates and the Shatt al-'Arab.

3) *Central Arabia:* an area centered on the settlements of the Jabal Tuwaiq of central Najd and spreading west toward the Hijāz and east toward al-Hasā and the Persian Gulf, also overlapping with area 2 in al-Qasīm.

4) *Southern Arabia*[19]*:* an area whose northern borders are here only vaguely defined, but centered on the Yemen and Najrān, and spreading up through the areas to the north and east of the empty quarter, also including the speech of Hadramaut and Oman.[20]

It has always been recognized by dialectologists that divisions such as the above are to a great extent subjective, since the choice of feature determines the area. This is, course, true here, and other divisions are possible. Other investigators have made more general divisions, such as Mesopotamia vs. Arabia proper, or

15. Ibid., pp. 236-37, 256-57.

16. Harold R. P. Dickson, *The Arab of the Desert* (London, 1949), pp. 50–51; D. P. Cole, *Nomads of the Nomads* (Chicago, 1975), pp. 39–51.

17. This is true of the 'Awāzim, Rashāyida, and Mutair of central and eastern Arabia, also of the shepherd tribes of southern Iraq, such as the Budūr.

18. Examples of this type are the Murra and 'Ajmān of eastern Arabia, who speak a dialect of the southern type; the 'Aniza tribes of the Syrian desert, who speak a dialect of the central Arabian type; and the Shammar of northern Iraq, who speak a north Arabian dialect.

19. Southern Arabia as a dialect area should be kept separate from South Arabian as a language group separate from Arabic itself and including Mehri, Socotri, Sheri, and Harsūsi. See Sabatino Moscati, ed., *An Introduction to the Comparative Grammar of the Semitic Languages* (Wiesbaden, 1969), pp. 13–15.

20. The exact nature of the relationship of the Yemeni dialects to the dialects of Hadramaut and Oman is not gone into here. For our purpose, the delimitation of a "southern type" is sufficient in the context of the Persian Gulf.

Najdī (combining our 2 and 3) vs. South Arabian on the basis of certain major criteria.[21] The present classification is chosen here because it reflects the aerial relationship of the groups, which is one of a continuum in which southern Arabian is allied to central Arabian by one set of features, the central to northern by another, and northern to Mesopotamian by yet another, while the main dialect areas are nevertheless easily distinguishable.[22] It is also relevant that we are here looking at these dialects from the focus of the Persian Gulf, and from their direction these four main types present themselves, whereas, in terms of the dialectology of Arabia and the Middle East as a whole, the division into Najdī (our 2 and 3) vs. Hijāzī is important.

DIALECT DIFFUSION IN ARABIA AND MESOPOTAMIA

In examining the history of dialect diffusion in an area, two main factors have to be considered: (i) wave action and (ii) population movement. The first of these is the process by which a linguistic feature or set of features may spread across an area being adopted by one locality after another. The second is that a group may move from one locality to another, taking their original dialect with them as an intruder dialect. The factors affecting the spread of a feature by factor (i) or the persistence of an intruder dialect introduced by factor (ii) are social in the widest sense, and depend upon the prestige attached to the type concerned. In the area of Arabia and Mesopotamia, large-scale population movements have occurred throughout recorded history from southern Arabia upward to central Arabia and eastward to the Persian Gulf or north to Mesopotamia. The relationship of the four areas can be explained in terms of the spread of linguistic features out from central Arabia to southern Mesopotamia due to the movements of nomads in that direction and the adoption by the sedentary population of a nomadic type of dialect.[23] In the past, also, the tribes of southern and central Arabia have pushed northeast and east toward the Persian Gulf, so that the two types have come to coexist along the coast.[24] This constant flow is expressed in the Arabic saying al-yaman rahim al-'arab wa l-'irāq qabruhum, i.e., "Yaman is the womb of the Arabs and Iraq their grave."[25] A reverse process has, it seems, also occurred along the gulf coast where the coastal settlements, particularly Kuwait and Bahrain, have undergone immigration from Mesopotamia, but the

21. An alternative division grouping my 2 and 3 as submembers of a large Najdī group is given in Johnstone, *Eastern Arabian Dialect Studies*, p. 1.

22. The ethnographic side of this picture is well summed up by W. G. Palgrave, *Central and Eastern Arabia* (London and Cambridge, 1866), 1:247. "The boundary lines of the kingdoms of Oman, Nejed, of Yemen, of Shomer and of Hijaz—are scarcely more political than ethnographical and being such must always subsist, at least in tendency and often in fact, with slender modification. Certain anomalies may it is true occur. Thus Hasa and Kaseem, nearer allied by race the one with Oman, the other with Shomer, then either with Nejed, have yet for some years past become incorporated with the latter owing to superior strength and the events of war."

23. See H. Blanc, *Communal Dialects in Baghdad* (Cambridge, Massachusetts, 1964), pp. 165–66, and the author's "Regional and social factors in the dialect geography of southern Iraq and Khuzistan," *BSOAS* 39, 1 (1976):63–65.

24. See Cole, *Nomads of the Nomads*, p. 106, for the northward expansion of the Murra, H. St. J. B. Philby, *The Heart of Arabia* (London, 1922), pp. 203–4, for the Dawāsir and 'Utaiba; p. 297 for the 'Ajmān, also Dickson, *Arab of the Desert*, p. 284.

25. Philby, *Heart of Arabia*, p. 22.

nature of this movement is less well documented.[26] This would seem to have been mostly a matter of individual or family emigration, as has also happened from central Arabia out to the Gulf.

1. The South Mesopotamian Type. This type includes the speech of the settled areas of the valleys of the Tigris and Euphrates up to the area of Baghdad, and also the valleys of the Kārūn and Jarrāhī. This includes both settled cultivators and the seminomadic marsh-dwellers of the Haur al-Hammār and Haur al-Huwaiza region, also the Kāwliyya or gypsies of Iraq. With some exceptions, namely, in respect of features 2 and 5, they would seem to occur in the speech of the Shāwiya, semi- or fully nomadic[27] shepherd tribes of the Euphrates, known in Kuwait as the *hakar* or *hukra*. With regard to these exceptions, the Shāwiya resemble the Arabian populations in their speech.[28] All these can be regarded as Mesopotamian communities. Although the shepherd tribes migrate southward in late winter to northern Arabia and Kuwait, they spend the summer along the Euphrates, where many of their number are permanently settled and where their main ethnic ties are.

Certain groups of camel-herding Bedouin known in Arabia as the *Ahl al-shimāl*, "people of the north," or *Ahl al-Furāt*, "people of the Euphrates," namely, the Sā'da, Humaid, Rufai', and Bu'aij, also show feature 4, but in the main show a north Arabian type of dialect. These also spend the summer along the Euphrates and were previously associated with the Muntafiq confederation, often grouped together as the Ghizya.[29] The main features of this type are the following:

A) Final consonant clusters are always separated by an anaptyctic vowel "i" or "u," which in many cases contrasts with the speech of Arabia: *chabid* (liver), *chalib* (dog), *'abid* (slave), *chidhib* (lie), *sidig/sidij* (truth), *ghanid* (lump sugar), *wilid* (children), *zibid* (butter), *'ishib* (grass), *wakit* (time), *gilit* (I said), *shifit* (I saw), *rimidh* (a type of grass), *libis* (clothes), *'iris* (wedding), *galub* (heart), *shurub* (drink), *shifitha* (I saw her), *gilitla* (I said to him).

Compare the following examples of the Arabian type from the speech of the 'Awāzim, Mutair, and 'Aniza: 'Awāzim *tsabd tsalb 'abd tsidhb, wagt, sidg/sidz* Mutair *wild, zibd, rimdh, libs, ghand* 'Aniza (Sba'a), *shiftaha, giltilih, shift, gilt.*

In the Arabian type, anaptyctics of a similar type do occur in association with the final voiced continuants *r, l, m, n, y.* The following examples are general to most of the area of Arabia considered here, with minor modifications: *nijir* (coffeepot), *sagur* (falcon), *mithil* (like), *gabul/gabil* (before), *tibin* (straw), *jifin* (eyelash), *samin* (fat), *dihin* (grease), *khashim* (nose), *hatsiy/hachiy* (talk), *tiliy* (lamb), *dhabiy* (hyena), *baduw* (bedouins), *ghazuw* (raid), *ghiruw* (girl), *garuw* (well-trough), *ra'iy* (grazing).

26. But see also M. T. Razavian, "Iranian Communities of the Persian Gulf," Ph.D. thesis, University of London, 1975, pp. 63–68, for emigration from Khūzistān.
27. For further information on the shepherd tribes, see Dickson, *Arab of the Desert*, pp. 545–66; Musil, *Northern Neğd*, pp. 167–69; Philby, *Heart of Arabia*, 1: 245.
28. My information for the speech of shepherd tribes is mainly from the Budūr; however, informants suggested that the speech of the other tribes resembled them in most features.
29. See 'Abbās al-'Azzāwī, *'Ashā'ir al-'Irāq* (Baghdad, 1955), 3: 54–56; 4: 79–86.

B) Reflexes of Old Arabic[30] *ai* are realized as a falling diphthong [iɛ] or [iə] symbolized here as *ie* in environments where it follows consonants other than the pharyngeals, emphatics, gutturals, or *r, w, h*. In the other dialects, it is realized either as a half open front vowel [ɛ:] or a diphthong [ɛi] generalized here as *ē*: *biet* (house), *shiex* (shaikh), *liel* (night), *zien* (good), *ties* (goat), *bien* (between), *ligiet* (I found), *sintien* (two years). Compare Arabian *bēt, shēx, lēl, zēn, tēs, bēn, ligēt, santēn.*

C) The first person singular imperfective of verbs may show a suffix *-an* (*n*) that seems to be a contraction of *-ana* (I). This is not found in other areas. *arūhan* (I go), *ashūfan* (I see), *amurran* (I pass), *ashūfanna* (I will see him), *ashūfanhin* (I will see them [f.])

D) The basic form of the prefixes of the imperfective are yi-, ti-, ni-,[31] with all verbs in contrast with the speech of north and central Arabia, which has ya-, ta-, na- in some cases:[32] *yimshi* (he walks), *tibchi* (she cries), *niksir* (we break), *tibti* (she delays).

E) The perfective may show a stem in final *-ē* preceding the consonant initial suffixes *-t, -ti, -tu, -tan, -na* alongside the more usual type of stem. This represents a simplification of the verb system whereby all verbs fall into line with the final weak class: *kitbēt* (I write), *nāmēt* (slept), *kitbēna* (we wrote), *wislēna* (we arrived).

Compare Arabian *kitabt, nimt, kitabna, wisilna.*

F) Certain lexical features of high frequency of occurrence distinguish the Mesopotamian area from Arabia in general. In some cases, these are also found in the dialects of Kuwait and Bahrain.[33] However, it seems that they are of Mesopotamian origin. Many of the examples given here are words of grammatical function, i.e., pronouns, conjunctions, etc.: *rād/yrīd* (to want), *aku* (there is), *māl* (belonging to) [possessive particle], *hnā* (here), *shin-* (what), *yā* (which), *yāhu* (who), *yamta* (when), *lō* (or, either), *hādhanni* (these [fem.]), *chaffiyya* (head cloth), *dishdāsha* (robe), *fad/farid* (a) [indefinite pronoun].

Compare Arabian *bagha/yabi, fīh/bih, hagg-, hni/hnayya, wish-, ayy-, min, mita, walla* (or), *yā* (either), *hādhōlīts/hādhōlints, ghutra, thōb.* No equivalent of the Mesopotamian *fad/farid* exists.

2. *The North Arabian Type.* This includes the speech of the Jabal Shammar and al-Qasīm the Shammar and Dhafīr tribes of the southern desert west of the Euphrates and, according to informants, the previously mentioned Muntafiq Bedouin tribes of the Euphrates, namely, the Humaid, Rufai', Bu'aij, and Sā'da,

30. The term Old Arabic is used here to denote the antecedent of these dialects, which was probably not classical Arabic, itself an ancient Koine or Lingua Franca of the Arabian peninsula. See the article " 'Arabiyya," *Encyclopedia of Islam,* vol. 1 (Leiden, 1960); pp. 573–74.

31. The symbol i here symbolizes the height of the vowel; however, the quality varied between i, u, and ə, depending on the nature of the initial root consonant. See the author's "Urban and rural Arabic," pp. 535–37.

32. Here the facts differ from area to area. Some dialects, such as those of the Shammar and 'Aniza, show ya-, na- in all verbs, while yi-, ti-, ni- mark the passive. Some dialects of the central group, such as that of Sudair and most dialects of Eastern Arabia, show dissimilation of prefix and stem vowel, i.e., *yisma'* (he hears), *yishrab* (he drinks), *yaktib* (he writes), *yamshi* (he walks). For further examples refer to T. Prochazka, *Studies.*

33. Particularly *aku, shin-, māl-, dishdāsha,* feature 5 is also found in Bahraini.

although I have material only from the Humaid and Rufai'. These last are, according to some authorities, of Shammar origin, as also are some elements of the Dhafīr.[34] As many other tribes of southern Iraq are also of Shammar origin, it may be that features of this type of speech are more widespread in the area than was previously thought. Informants from the Banī Khālid also indicated that their dialect was of a similar type. This type stands out as very idiosyncratic when compared with the speech of surrounding areas as a whole, a fact generally recognized by the speakers themselves and by their neighbors. One can perhaps attribute this idiosyncratic type to the very isolated position of its center, the Shammar plateau. Although geographical isolation is no obstacle to nomadic movement, it may have a more marked effect on immigration and contact with the sedentary population of surrounding areas. To the north, the Nafūd separates it from Mesopotamia, while to the southeast it also separates it from the settlements of the Jabal Tuwaiq. Perhaps more important than this is the fact that in contrast to neighboring areas, the Shammar plateau was traditionally a center of nomadic activity,[35] ruled by nomads. In the central area, on the other hand, although large nomad tribes were to be found, they do not seem to have been in such a powerful position and the area was, it seems, ruled from the settlements.[36] It may be that a certain geographical and ethnic isolation of this type has allowed the speech of the area to develop independently along its own lines.[37] Nomad dīras or tribal areas of the region also reflect this general communication pattern, dividing it into an area facing north to the Syrian desert and the Euphrates and one facing east to the Persian Gulf. The Shammar tribes range over the Shammar plateau and al-Qasīm and north to the Euphrates, the Dhafīr also occupy the area between them and the Euphrates. The tribes of eastern Arabia, such as the Murra and 'Ilwa Mutair, extend east from the central plateau to the gulf.[38] Generally, the north-facing tribes speak a north Arabian type of dialect, while the rest speak a central or southern type.

The core dialects of the group showing all relevant features are the speech of Hā'il and the Shammar tribes. Fringe types showing only some features are the speech of al-Qasīm, the Dhafīr, and the Euphrates tribes mentioned above (1, 2, and 3 with, in some cases, hesitation as regards 1. The Dhafīr also show 4).

34. Musil, Northern Neğd, p. 169; Dickson, Arab of the Desert, p. 545.

35. Palgrave, Central and Eastern Arabia, 1: 75, 98; and generally chap. 3; Musil, Northern Neğd, appendix 8 particularly p. 237.

36. Musil, Northern Neğd, appendix 9; Philby, Heart of Arabia, 1: 12–13, 250; Cole, Nomads of the Nomads, pp. 98–100.

37. It seems that these characteristics have been present for some time and that some at least were remarked by the Arab grammarians, Cantineau, "Etudes," p. 21. The fact that the 'Aniza tribes of the Syrian desert, who occupy an equally isolated and traditionally independent position, speak a dialect of the central type, less idiosyncratic in its main characteristics, may seem to contradict this. However, we know that the 'Aniza are comparatively recent arrivals to the area, coming originally from central and western Najd in the eighteenth and nineteenth centuries. See Philby, Heart of Arabia, pp. 108, 249, 288; Musil, Northern Neğd, p. 112; Montagne, Contes, p. 40.

38. Cole, Nomads of the Nomads, p. 31, states further that the Dahnā' separates nomad dīras in the area. This is not borne out by Dickson's description of the Mutair dīra, which spans the Dahnā' but nevertheless stops roughly at the Nafūd as its western border (Arab of the Desert, p. 47). Both accounts support the basic picture of the division as given here. See also Dickson's statements on the musābila or nomadic provision expeditions, Arab of the Desert, p. 49, Kuwait and Her Neighbours, p. 266.

Feature 4 was also present in the speech of the Banī Khālid informants inter-viewed and of some seminomadic or recently settled *bādiya* groups of Southern Iraq and Khūzistān.[39] These testify to the overriding influence of the Shammar in the area in previous centuries, as suggested by Cantineau.[40]

Characteristics isolated for this type are the following:

A) The form of the first person singular object suffix is *-an* postconsonantally, *-n* or *-nan* post vocalically rather than *-ni*.[41]

shāfan (he saw me), m'alliman (having taught me), nshidan (he asked me), shāfōn/shāfōnan (they [masc.] saw me), 'atan (give me!).

B) The form of the 3rd person masculine singular object and possessive suffix is *-uh* postconsonantally and *-w* after *a* rather than *-ih* or *-ah* and *-h*.

shiftuh (I saw him), ibnuh (his son), shāfuh (he saw him), shfuh (look at him!), khadhāw (he took it [m.]).

C) The form of the 3rd person feminine singular object and possessive suffix is *-ah* rather than *-ha*.

shiftah (I saw her), shfah (look at her!), ibnah (her son), sigwah (you [masc. plur.] drive her away), sāgwah (they [masc.] drove her away), 'alyah (upon it [fem.]).

D) The form of the 2nd and 3rd masculine plural object suffixes, and in some cases the 2nd masc. plural subject suffix, have *a* rather than *u* as in other areas, giving *-kam*, *-ham*, *-tam*, rather than *-kum*, *-hum*, *-tum*.

shāfaham (he saw them [masc.]), shiftakam (I saw you [masc. plur.]), salamatkam (your [masc. plur.] health), shiftam (you [masc. plur.] saw).

E) Fronting of certain feminine suffixes has occurred, giving *-ih* for the feminine singular nominal, *-e* for the feminine singular verbal, and *-āy* for the feminine plural nominal, rather than *-ah*, *-at*, *-āt* as in other areas. Of these, the first occurs it seems in a wider area than the other two, being attested for 'Anaiza in al-Qasīm and also for the Euphrates tribes mentioned above.

Examples: dīrih (tribal area), dōlih (state), khēzarānih (riding stick), mihīlih (drought), thalāthih (three), sam'e (she heard), nhaje (she went away), witsle (it [fem.] was eaten), banāy (girls), shjarāy (trees), tsithīray (many [fem. plur.]).

3. The Central Arabian Type. Material is available for the speech of Riyadh, Sudair, Hofūf, Dhahrān, Zubair in southern Iraq and the Persian Gulf states, and also for certain large Bedouin tribes of the area, namely, the Mutair, 'Awāzim, and Rashāyida of eastern Arabia, and the Harb, 'Utaiba, and Wild 'Alī of central Najd. The speech of the 'Aniza tribes of the Syrian desert is also basically of this type, with certain north Arabian features in some cases.[42] The speech of the nomads, though spread over a very wide area, is surprisingly homogeneous, while

39. For further details, see the writer's "Regional and social factors," pp. 77–80.
40. "Etudes," p. 233.
41. For a more detailed description of the morphological characteristics of the north Arabian type, see Cantineau, "Etudes," 2: 229–33.
42. The use of *-ak* rather than *-ik* as the second person masculine singular suffix, also *-ham*, *-kam*, *intam*, *-tam*, rather than *-hum*, *-kum*, *intum-intu*, *-tum*, *-tu-*, *hīts* rather than *tsidha* for "thus." These examples are taken from Prochazka's Ruweli material, *Studies*, and Landberg *'Anezeh*, p. 27.

the speech of the towns shows more variation. The coastal area in particular has some special developments, namely, the shift of OA /j*/ to /y/, and in the area of al-Hasā, the collapse of the OA distinction /d*/ and /dh*/ to /d/ and /t/ and /th/ to /t/, and in Bahrain the shift of initial /sh/ to /ch/. However, on the evidence of informants and in view of the general homogeneity of the nomad dialects, it seems likely that this type of dialect is general to central Najd, i.e., the Jabal Tuwaiq region and eastern Arabia. Features 1 and 2 are also found in the speech of al-Qasīm. As mentioned earlier, this type is less idiosyncratic in terms of its general characteristics than the north Arabian type, and is in fact extremely conservative in preserving what we presume to be the OA forms. Exclusive characteristics are therefore difficult to pinpoint; nevertheless, it represents a well-defined type when contrasted with the neighboring north and south Arabian types. The following features are general:

A) The basic form of the 2nd person masculine singular objective suffix is -ik rather than -ak, as in most of the area.

'indik (you [masc. s.] have), agūllik (I say to you [masc. s.]), sōtik (your [masc. s.] voice), ajībihlik (I bring it [masc. s.] to you).

B) In certain environments, the object suffixes of the 2nd person singular and the 3rd person masculine singular appear without their initial vowel, giving -k, -ts (or -ch) and -h rather than -ak, -its (or -ich), -uh as in other areas.

mink (from you [m.s.]), minh (from him), salamatk (your [m.s.] health), salāmatts (your [fem.s.] health), and often by assimilation salāmakk and salāmatsts, shālh (azza'al) ([anger] took him away), jābh (alla) ([God] brought him).

C) In nonverbal negative sentences, a structure mā b- may occur to mark the negative rather than the more usual mā.

mā hi b-hi (it is not her), mā hu b-zēn (it is not good), m-anta bjāy (you [m.s.] are not coming).

D) In the 3rd person masculine plural of the perfective and the masculine plural imperative the suffix may have a final -m in contrast to the -aw more usual in the area.

gālam (they [m.] said), shāfam (they [m.] saw), jam (they [m.] came), rabba'am (they [m.] had a good spring), mudham (they [m.] passed), tifadhdhalum (come in [m. pl.]).

The core features of this type are 2 and 3 attested for Riyadhi and for all the nomad tribes considered, with 2 spreading also into the southern region to Najrān and Dhofār. Feature 1 is also noted for all dialects considered except Harbī, while Hess's 'Utaibi material gives both -ik and -ak. This feature also spreads south to Najrān. Feature 4 is attested for the 'Anazi tribes and for the 'Awāzim, Rashāyida, Mutair, and Harb. It would seem likely on this basis that it would be found in the rest of central Najd, but I have no evidence for this. Also unlike the other Central type features it is a departure from the OA type, which may be the reason why it does not occur in standard Riyadh speech.

4. The South Arabian Type. Within the area of the Persian Gulf, the speech of Oman and the area to the north of the Empty Quarter is sharply differentiated from the areas to the north. The 'Ajmān and Murra and Manāsīr tribes who originate in the south, but whose *dīra*s extend up to the area of al-Hasa are also said to share this type of dialect. Some scanty material is available on the speech of Najrān and the 'Ajmān; however, my information on the rest is from informants of other tribes in Kuwait.[43] These characteristics are in turn generally shared with the Yemen and the rest of South Arabia. This southern dialect area correlates to a great extent with an ethnic and communication area looking away from the Gulf toward the Indian Ocean and so is, strictly speaking, outside the purview of this article. Oman is, of course, marginal in this. However, the aforementioned 'Ajmān, Murra, and Manāsīr tribes are now Persian Gulf tribes in terms of their main centers of influence and attention.[44] The main distinctive characteristics of this type are the following:

A) OA *kāf* and *qāf* are realized in all positions as *k* and *g* (or *q* in the case of Omani) and are not fronted palatalized alveolar affricates *ts* and *dz* or palato-alveolar affricates *ch* and *j*, as in the areas to the north, i.e., our areas 1, 2, and 3. Examples:
   Omani   *kīs* (purse), *kidheh* (thus), *bākir* (tomorrow)
   'Ajmī   *kalb* (dog), *rikab* (he mounted), *kān* (he was), *kabdi* (my dear [lit. "my liver"]), *gidirin* (a pot), *galīb* (well), *gid* [perfective particle]
   Murra   *'agīd* (tribal war leader)
   Najrān   *gibīlah* (tribe), *rikib* (he mounted)
   Compare the following examples taken from the Central type. These are from the speech of Riyadh and from the Mutair and 'Awāzim tribes, which agree in this feature. These would also be true of the northern group in general.
   tsīs, tsidhah, bātsir, tsalb, ritsib, tsān, tsabdi, dzidir, dzilīb, dzid.

B) The form of the second person feminine singular object suffix is *-sh*, rather than *-its* or *ich* as in the north.
   Omani   *sāhibish* (your [f.s.] friend), *'andish* (you [f.s.] have)
   'Ajmī   *wishkhubūrish* (what is your [f.s.] news?).

C) The definite article may have the form *im-* rather than the more usual *al-* or *-il*.
   'Ajmī   *im blād* (the town)
   Omani   *im haid* (the hill)
   Yamani   *im bait* (the home), *im hajar* (the stone).

D) Speakers of central type dialects generally regard the southern type as being markedly different in terms of vocabulary. This fact is also mentioned by Johnstone, *Further Studies on the Dōsiri Dialect*, p. 85; and H. R. P. Dickson, *Kuwait and Her Neighbours* (London, 1956), p. 169. In illustration of this, a number of items are presented here tentatively that were given by a Mutairī informant in Kuwait as 'Ajmī and generally characteristic of the Southern type. The more normal Central type is given in contrast as by the informant:

43. for further examples of the 'Ajmī type of dialect, see Johnstone, "Some characteristics of the Dōsiri dialect" and "Further studies on the Dōsiri dialect," from whom some of these examples are taken. The Najrān examples are from Prochazka, the Omani, from Landberg, *Dialectes méridionales*.

44. For details of these nomad areas, see Cole, *Nomads of the Nomads*, pp. 28–29, 106–108; Philby, *Heart of Arabia*, 2: 297; Dickson, *Arab of the Desert*, pp. 47–49, 264.

al-shima'	tree, contrast	*shjarah*	*ālās*	chewing gum	*'ilts*
al-gidah	pot	*tāsah*	*tawwi*	beside me	*jambi*
shbihih	look at it	*shifih*	*j'ari*	dog	*tsalb*
asāylik	I ask you [m.s.]	*as 'alk*	*hantūr*	can	*sayyārah*
gurus	bread	*xubz*	*tēk*	there it is	*hāk*

The Persian Language Area of the Persian Gulf

The Persian dialects of Iran are divided into three main groups, a central one comprising the dialects of the Caspian Sea littoral and the area bounded roughly by Tehran, Isfahān, and Yazd, a southwestern one comprising the Kurdish dialects, and a southern one comprising the dialects of Fārs and the Lur dialects.[45] The term "Persian" is used here in contrast to Turkic or Arabic and does not take into account the question of separate language identity for Lurī and Kurdish, since the main considerations here are ethnic rather than strictly linguistic. Kurdish and, to a lesser extent, Lurī are often spoken of as separate languages. However, Kurdish is not markedly more different from standard Persian than are the other Persian rural dialects, and Lurī is in fact closer to it than most of them. The reason for the separate language status often given to these forms is the fact that in the past speakers of these varieties have often been independent of the Iranian central government in a way in which speakers of the other dialects have not. The dividing line between separate language and separate dialect status is not often easy to make,[46] and one can give "purely linguistic," "sociolinguistic," or "ethnic" definitions. One common criterion is that of mutual intelligibility, but here also the "Persian" dialects are a marginal case. They are mostly unintelligible at first acquaintance to a speaker of the standard. However, some level of mutual intelligibility is possible if the conversation is restricted and most dialect speakers have acquired a knowledge of standard Persian. Further, a speaker of standard Persian can acquire a receptive competence in a dialect within a short time if necessary. In general, a situation of partial mutual intelligibility or one-way intelligibility exists. However, Kurdish is a written form and regarded as the vehicle of the culture of the Kurdish people, so in this ethnic respect can be regarded as a separate language.

For the purpose of this study, we are concerned with the dialects of Fārs and the Lur dialects,[47] which are spoken as far north as Khurramābād, which can be

---

45. A. Christensen, *La dialectologie iranienne* (Copenhagen, 1930), 1: 1.

46. For a general discussion of these points, see Martinet, "Dialect" in *Romance Philology* 8, 1 (1954); J. J. Gumperz, "Types of linguistic communities," *Anthropological Linguistics* 4 (1962): 28–40.

47. The main sources for these are Oskar Mann, *Die Tâdjik-Mundarten der Provinz Fârs, Kurdische-Persische Forschungen I* (Berlin, 1909): *Die Mundarten der Lur-Stämme in Südwestlichen Persien, Kurdische-Persische Forschungen II* (1910), *Kurze Skizze der Lurdialekte, Sitzungsberichte der Akademie der Wissenschaften zu Berlin* 39 (1904); D. L. R. Lorimer, *The Phonology of Bakhtiari, Badakhshani, and Madaglashti Dialects of Modern Persian* (London, 1922). Much useful material on the dialect of Bihbihān was obtained from M. Tabātabā'i in London. This dialect seems to be basically of the same type as the Fārs dialects described by Mann; Bihbihān also comes culturally within the area of Fārs, it would seem. However, in order to

regarded as strictly speaking within the area of the Gulf. As mentioned earlier, standard Persian is a development of a dialect of Fārs, hence its name Fārsī, and stands in a very close relationship to Lurī.[48] It has a written history in the present alphabet of about 1,000 years, emerging under the Saffārid and Sāmānid dynasties and adopted since then as the language of the main urban centers. The Lur dialects are spoken by the Southern Lur tribes, the Bakhtīyārī, Māmāssanī, and Kūhgilūi in Fārs, and by the other Lur tribes of Luristān. The following description of the dialects of Fārs will be in terms of a three-way contrast between the Fārs dialects and Lurī, standard colloquial Persian (SCP) (Tehran pronunciation), and some representative dialects of the central group.

1.   The main characteristics distinguishing the southwestern dialects from the central group are given below. Examples from the central group are taken from Natanzī and Yazdī.[49]

A)   *b* contrasts with *v* in initial position in a wide area.
SCP	*mibīnam* (I see), *bīd* (willow), *barf* (snow), *bād* (wind), *bārūn* (rain), *bāzār* (bazaar), *bachche* (child)
Lurī	*ibīnum, bēdh, barf, bād, bachcha*
Fārs[50]	*mibunum*

Bihbihān	*bīd, barf, bād, bārū(n), bāzār, beche*
Natanz	*vīnūn, vī, varf, vāy, vārān, vāchār, vacha*

B)   *z* contrasts with *zh, j, ch* or the absence of a consonant in many places.
SCP	*rūz* (day), *zan* (woman), *tāze* (new), *za-* (to hit), *bāzār* (market), *sūzan* (needle), *zīr* (under)
Lurī	*rūz, zan, zai-*
Fārs	*rūz, zan, zai-*
Bihbihān	*tāza, bāzār, sūzen, zīr*
Natanz	*rū, jan, tāja, jan-, vāchār, jīr*
Yazdī	*sijin*

C)   *d* contrasts with *z* in the verb "to know."
SCP	*mīdūnam* (I know)
Lurī	*īdhōnum*
Fārs	*mīdhānam*
Natanz	*zunōn*

D)   The dialects of Fārs and standard Persian show a prefix *mī-* or *ma-* (*ī* in the Lur dialects of Bakhtīyārī and Māmāsanī[51]) in the present tense, while the dialects of the central group show either no prefix or a variety of other prefixes.

---

distinguish between these examples and those of Mann, the examples will be marked separately. A simplified transcription system is used here for all examples, which does not substantially affect the accuracy of the data, except perhaps in the vowels, since it is difficult to reconcile the notation systems of different writers.

48. Mann, *Kurze Skizze*, p. 17.

49. The examples for the central group are taken from Christensen, *La dialectologie iranienne*.

50. The Fārs dialects investigated by Mann are Somghūnī, Māsarmī, Pāpūnī, Būringūnī, and Lārī. For the purposes of this article, examples are drawn indiscriminately from these. Where important differences occur these are mentioned.

51. Mann, *Kurze Skizze*, p. 12.

SCP	*mīām* (I come), *mīuftam* (I fall), *mībaram* (I carry), *mīdam* (I give)
Lurī	*īyum, īuftum, ībarum, īdhum*
Fārs[52]	*mayam, mīftam, mīdhayum*
Natanz	*yūn, uftūn, burūn, hādūn*

2. Features separating the southwestern dialects from standard Persian.

A) The dialects have *ī* in a number of cases, where the standard has *ū*.

Lurī	*pīl* (money), *bīdh* (was), *ballī* (oak), *rī* (face), *hīn* (blood), *sīzan* (needle), *dīr* (far), *mī* (hair), *dī* (smoke)
Fārs	*bī* (was), *arīs* (bride), *tī* (in), *tīt* (mulberry), *sīlākh* (hole), *shī* (husband)
SCP	*pūl, būd, ballūt, rū, khūn, sūzan, dūr, mū, dūd, arūs, tū, tūt, sūrakh, shouhar* (or *šū*).

B) The dialects show *dh* as a variant of *d* or as a fully fledged sound unit, while this is absent in the standard. In some cases, this corresponds to *d* in the standard, in others, to *-kht*.

Lurī	*gudhum* (I said), *bēdh* (willow), *dōdhan* (to sew), *furōdhan* (to sell), *poudhan* (to cook), *soudhan* (to burn)
Fārs	*ish-dādh* (he gave), *ādham* (man), *ish-barrī* (he cut)
SCP	*guftam, bīd, dūkhtan, furūkhtan, pukhtan, sūkhtan, dād, ādam, burid.*

C) The dialects show *au* or *ou* for *āb* or *āf* in the standard in many places.

Fārs	*kutau* (book), *shau* (night), *lou* (lip), *āu* (water)
Lurī	*aur* (cloud), *benaush* (violet), *sauz* (green), *aftau* (sun), *zaur* (rough)
SCP	*kitāb, shab, lab, āb, abr, banafsh, sabz, āftāb, zibr.*

D) The dialects have a plural morpheme *-gal, -yal,* or *-al* in place of the standard *-hā*.

Fārs	*mīshgal* (ewes), *ādamyal* (men), *harfal* (words), *bachial* (children)
Lurī	*ūngal* (those), *īngal* (these), *zangal* (women), *hōnayal* (houses), *vazīral* (ministers)
SCP	*mīshhā, ādamhā, harfhā, bachchehā, ūnhā, inhā, zanhā, khūnehā, vazīrhā.*

In general, apart from the facts mentioned here and also the difference in the verb system mentioned below, the southwestern dialects, especially Lurī, differ from the standard in surface phonology. While standard Persian has been stabilized by writing, linguistic drift in the form of metathesis, elision, vowel shift, and consonant assimilation[53] and merger has been allowed to proceed unhindered in the dialects. Therefore, in many cases the dialect form is an eroded form of the standard. In some cases, the spoken form of the standard has also undergone these changes and agrees with the dialects while differing from the written form. The clearest example of this is in the shift of *ā* to *ū* before *n*, and to lesser extent *m*. This is widespread in the dialects, slightly less so in the spoken standard, and unrecognized in the written form.

52. The form of the suffix of the first person is basically *-am* in Somghūnī and Pāpūnī *-om* in Māsamī and Būringūnī. Mann, *Die Tajik Mundarten*, p. 24.

53. For examples in Lurī, see Lorimer, *Phonology of Bakhtiari, Badaskhsani, and Madaglashti Dialects*, pp. 94–100.

Lurī *sultūn* (Sultan), *natōna* (he cannot), *dōnes* (he knew), *ūvayt* (he came), *dūmā* (bridegroom)

Spoken
Standard *sultūn, natūne, dānist, ūmad, dāmād*

Written
Standard *sultān, natavānad, dānist, āmad, dāmād*

A further example is the form of the 3rd person singular suffix *-a* in the dialects, *-e* in the spoken standard, but *-ad* in the written form.

Fārs *mīga* (he says), standard colloquial *mīge*, written form *mīgūyad*.

3. The verb systems of the southwestern group.

As mentioned above, standard Persian stands in a very close relationship to Lurī. Indeed, as Mann himself states this is one of the few cases of an old-established nomadic tribe in Persia with no independent language of their own.[54]

The most striking feature of this relationship is in the formation of the preterite of the transitive verb. The old Iranian verb system showed a formal division into transitive and intransitive verbs. The intransitive type formed its preterite by adding the personal pronoun suffixes to the verb. In the transitive type, however, the suffixes are attached to the object or, in the absence of an object, to the subject pronoun, in what is in fact a basically passive formation. This system is retained in the rural dialects of Iran generally, including the Fārs dialects as exemplified in Mann's material. In modern Persian and Lurī, however, the intransitive pattern has been generalized for all verbs, and the old passive type of construction has been dropped. Further, in the Fārs dialects the subject suffixes can be prefixed to the verb, where no object is present. Also, a further development of this system has evolved, namely, that intransitive verbs are also declined in this way.

In the following examples, the subject pronoun element is underlined.

Fārs dialects *u̲m̲ chard* (I grazed [animals]), *mi̲m̲ dā* (I gave), *mā-s̲h̲ū̲ lū kī* (they robbed us), *kōhemū̲ gasht* (we went around the mountain), *ya mīsh-e̲s̲h̲ gīrī* (he took a sheep)

Bihbihān *te̲m̲ dī* (I saw you), *ketāb-a̲m̲ xund* (I read a book), *u-m̲ dī* (I saw him), *u-s̲h̲ me-dī* (he saw me)

SCP *turā dīda̲m̲, kitābrā khūnda̲m̲, charūnda̲m̲, dāda̲m̲, ūnhārā lukht karda̲n̲d, kūhrā gashtī̲m̲, yak mīsh giri̲f̲t*

Lurī *kashīdhu̲m̲* (I pulled), *burrīdhu̲m̲* (I cut), *a̲n̲dākhtu̲m̲* (I threw), *āvurdi̲n̲* (they brought).

Further differences also occur where the object of the verb is pronominal. In the old passive system, this may be attached to the stem of the verb directly. In the new system, it may precede the verb or follow the subject pronoun affix.

Fārs dialects *shū burd-a̲m̲ a khūna* (they took me home), *shū kushsay-a̲m̲* (they have killed me), *shū a pushta kerd-a̲m̲* (they took me on their backs)

54. Mann, *Kurze Skizze*, p. 17.

Bihbihān   *ush ū-she*[55] *mebō khūne* (they took me home), *shumā-tē mēbō khūne* (you [pl.] took me home)

SCP   *burdīmeshūn* (we took them away), *burdandimūn* (they took us away), *dīdamat* and *tura dīdam* (I saw you)

Lurī   *zadhumash* (I hit him), *eshkenaimeshnū* (we defeated them).

Selected Bibliography

Barth, F. *Nomads of South West Persia.* Olso, 1961.

Blanc, H. *Communal Dialects of Baghdad.* Cambridge, Mass., 1964.

Christensen, A. *La dialectologie iraniènne.* Copenhagen, 1930.

Cole, D. P. *Nomads of the Nomads.* Chicago, 1975.

Dickson, Harold R. P. *The Arab of the Desert.* London, 1949.

Diem, W. *Skizzen Jemenitischer Dialekte.* Beirut, 1973.

Doerfer, G. *Türkische und Mongolische Elemente in Neupersichen.* Wiesbaden, 1963.

Erwin, W. *Short Reference Grammar of Iraqi Arabic.* Washington, D.C., 1963.

Hamdi, A. Qafisheh. *A Basic Course in Gulf Arabic.* Tucson, Arizona, 1976.

Hess, J. J. *Von den Beduinen des Inneren Arabiens.* Zurich, 1938.

Johnstone, T. M. *Eastern Arabian Dialect Studies.* London, 1967.

Landberg, C. *Etudes sur les dialectes d'Arabie méridionale.* Leiden, 1901.

Lorimer, D.L.R. *The Phonology of Bakhtiari, Badakhsani, and Madaglashti Dialects of Modern Persian.* London, 1922.

Mann, Oskar. *Die Mundarten der Lur-Stämme in Südwestlichen Persien, Kurdische-Persische Forschungen II.* Berlin, 1910.

———. *Die Tâdjik-Mundarten der Provinz Fârs, Kurdische-Persische Forschungen I.* Berlin, 1909.

———. *Kurze Skizze der Lurdialekte, Sitzungsberichte der Akademie der Wissenschaften zu Berlin.* Berlin, 1904.

Moscati, Sabatino, ed. *An Introduction to the Comparative Grammar of the Semitic Languages.* Wiesbaden, 1969.

Musil, A. *Northern Neğd.* New York, 1928.

Oberling, P. *The Qashqai Nomads of Fārs.* The Hague, 1974.

Oranskij, I. M. *Die Neuiranische Sprache der Sowjetunion.* The Hague, 1975.

Rhodokanakis, N. *Die vulgararabische Dialekt im Dofār.* 2 vols. Vienna, 1908, 1911.

55. In Bihbihānī, a further morph— *-she, -me, -te*—occurs in the plural to mark the subject.

13. Literature in Arabic G. M. WICKENS

A large proportion of Arabic literature bears no relation to the Gulf area at all, other than that of ultimate linguistic (and, less certainly, racial and cultural) descent: it has been produced in Syria, Egypt, North Africa and Spain, Turkey, northern and eastern Iran, Central Asia, and northern "India"—to mention only some of the most peripheral examples. This was the case throughout the medieval period (say, until A.D. 1500), and in great measure into modern times. Moreover, in the postmedieval and modern periods, the Gulf area itself has been a virtual wasteland, where Arabic literary creation became stunted by several factors, often acting in combination: first, by an Ottoman-dominated status as a provincial outpost; later by a semicolonial or post-colonial psychology; by religious and/or political puritanism and "thought control"; and, until very recently, by a low standard of living for all but a (usually philistine) few, particularly after the late medieval destruction or deterioration of the large-scale irrigation systems and trade routes. New technological prosperity has brought its own priorities, and literature is not likely to be accorded a front rank.

It is, therefore, a very fortunate chance that two great literary eras *are* Gulf-related: the age of the immediately pre-Islamic poetry (sixth century A.D.), centered notionally—and probably in reality—in the Arabian peninsula for the most part; and the classical age of the 'Abbasid dynasty, based on Baghdad and Iraq generally (A.D. 750–1258). This chapter will address itself to these two eras and their immediate locations in the Gulf area, but with incidental reference as necessary to Arabic literature in general.

Arabic Literature: Some Idiosyncratic Features and Associations

The Western reader cannot approach Arabic literature, even in a good translation, in the same "direct" manner as he would French, German, or Russian literature. Even the Arabic-speaker has no great advantage in this respect. Whether as seen within its own culture or as traditionally regarded from outside, certain idiosyncrasies and associations must be clarified in advance of any meaningful discussion of literary activity in Arabic, both in respect to the Gulf area and generally.

Intrinsic Characteristics. When the relatively small Arabian forces of Islam gained control of the Middle East, North Africa, and part of Central Asia, between A.D. 640 and 750, they did not bring with them any literature as such; and they took small account of the various literatures they found in place in the sophisticated cultures they now dominated and with which they would eventually merge. They had a form of writing, but it was inexact, unserviceable as anything more than an aid to the memory, and they regarded the art of writing and recording generally with the customary contempt of a warrior élite. With the growth of their administrative and commercial responsibilities, they quickly recognized the importance of professional "writers"; but they held firm to the belief that writing was no fit occupation for Arabian aristocrats—which is what even the poorest were apt to consider themselves. With the passage of time, the absorption of a non-Arab majority into Islam, the increasing urbanization of the culture as a whole, and the rise of a leisured, literate middle-class, these attitudes would come to seem barbaric. Moreover, by preoccupation with the written Word of God (the Qur'ān/Koran), and with the recorded personal sayings and doings of the Prophet (known as *hadīth* = Tradition), this would become one of the most literate cultures in history. But it was not so at the beginning, and the early preeminence of the oral and the personal left its mark in many ways. Toward literature as such, official Islam would always remain indifferent, often even hostile.

What the conquering "Arabians" did bring with them were strong oral traditions in poetry and rhetoric, both genres being highly stylized and idiosyncratic. The poetry was in set form as to length and subdivisions, categories and themes, style, and imagery: it was enormously rich in vocabulary, and in evocative allusions to places, persons, and events. The rhetoric was terse, paratactic, gnomic, often semimetrical and loosely rhymed and, again, rich in vocabulary and allusive. Neither genre was couched in any of the normal everyday dialects of Arabic, but in an apparently generally understood high-culture speech, suitable for important occasions. This was (and in great measure still is) Arabic *par excellence:* [*al-lughat*] *al-'arabiyya, lisān al-'arab.* It became the core of the written, literary language; was studied laboriously and preserved for centuries in nearly all its pristine purity; and, even where changed by distance or time or practical necessity, remained largely homogeneous and remote from the spoken forms, often to the point of total unintelligibility to the uneducated. At the present day, a somewhat less formal Arabic, sometimes modified by local features, is taught in schools and used in writing and for all "educated," public purposes. It is still largely beyond the reach of the illiterate majority, but seems destined to prevail in the long run, rather than to succumb to some written form of a prestigious colloquial such as that of Egypt.

Such a language "gap" would naturally tend to make any written material, let alone literature, the preserve of an élite. But there were also reinforcements of the situation from other sides. The writing system, though gradually improved (and capable, in absolute necessity, of full phonetic representation), remains difficult and time-consuming to learn and is normally used in a shorthand form. Furthermore, the two oral genres from which Arabic literature derived, though rooted in a very specific Arabian milieu, continued in great measure to dominate its character through all the changing circumstances of the succeeding ages and places. There were adaptations, diversified uses, and even innovations, but they were accidental, very rarely essential. Not only did the old material, as preserved in written form, need extensive commentary for later generations, but it was no uncommon thing for fresh compositions to be provided with a commentary by the author himself or a close associate; and, in important instances, an unbroken succession of commentaries might continue for centuries. Finally, at the social and economic level, a high proportion of Arabic literature was traditionally written to commission by the powerful, or at least in hope of their patronage; this inevitably ensured not only conservative attitudes but also much artificiality and insincerity. (While the same holds true to some extent for such other Islamic literatures as Persian and Turkish, these never entirely lost touch with the living language in which, essentially, they were written, however "flowery" an individual author's style might be.)

Because written Arabic and its literature had to be learned systematically, it was little more difficult for non-Arabs than for Arabs themselves: just as easy, if they began early enough. So long as Arabic fully retained its "international," multicultural prestige (say, A.D. 700–1200), it was a commonplace for many of the most learned and skilled practitioners of the Arabic literary arts, particularly in the Gulf area, to be not Arabs by race or native language, but Persians, Assyrians, Turks, Jews, and people of mixed descent. The Persians in particular were influential in developing a true Arabic prose literature, i.e., prose directly composed onto paper, not oratory copied down as spoken. Such discourse, naturally having longer grammatical periods, and capable of more complex and subtle articulation, was indispensable for discursive reasoning, as opposed to the pithy, but often superficial, aphorisms of early Arabic wisdom. The Persians also led in experimentation with Arabic poetic forms and in the sophisticated application of music to poetry (as is shown by the high proportion of Persian musical terms).

By Western standards, the literary genres in both prose and poetry often seem confused (mechanical criteria of length, meter, rhyme, figures, and imagery are often the essential yardsticks of differentiation); and, until modern times, there is no real notion of literature as a whole. Basically, Arabic writing (outside practical documents, and even there in some cases) remains either poetry (*shi'r:* technically, verse is referred to as *nazm* = ordered discourse) or studied prose (*adab:* prose as such is called *nathr* = scattered discourse). *Adab* absorbed and refined the earlier rhetorical tradition, but the terse and epigrammatic style never entirely lost its prestige. Whatever purposes prose served—historiography, biography, philosophical writing, even geography—it would tend to remain deliberate, not to say near-literary. Poetry was eventually used for a wide range of purposes besides the original tribal boasting, self-advertisement, descriptions of natural phenomena, and complaints against fate; and the longer early forms were broken up to serve the new needs: lyrical, elegiac, panegyric, and even didactic. But, as with prose, an unmistakable "flavor" remained, which would both leave a broad gulf between Arabic and other Islamic poetry and also make Arabic poetry more than usually difficult to translate effectively into any other language. In all manner of writing, prose and poetry often alternated. Western genres, such as the novel and the drama, were virtually unknown; and the epic (a favorite with Persian and Turkish speakers) never established itself explicitly and firmly.

Arabic Literature as Seen from the Outside. Because of its homogeneity and its at least quasi-literary flavor in most instances, there has been a tendency in Western scholarship to treat *all* deliberate writing in Arabic as literature, at least up to the end of what was seen as the medieval period (i.e., broadly 550–1500, more narrowly 700–1250). Thus, virtually all "histories of Arabic literature" produced throughout the nineteenth century, and most of those in the present century, include studies of works on history, philosophy, science, mathematics, medicine, geography, and many other fields, together with treatment of those works that indisputably rank as literature by any standards. Furthermore, the latter are often dealt with in a sadly unprofessional manner, showing either the mere dilettante interest of "men of general culture" or the somewhat heavy-handed approach of the classical historian-philologist. While it cannot be denied that taste and a sense of culture, together with a sound grounding in history and language, are essential to the study of Arabic literature, the particular combination applied in most cases has produced work that is impossibly cumbersome and unattractive to the outsider. Some of the literature can never be made truly accessible in translation or paraphrase or analysis, but much can: one has to decide which is which, and then bring to bear on the items chosen sound scholarship, a "disciplinary" understanding of literature in its own terms, and some gift for the work of transference to members of other cultures.

We shall here concern ourselves primarily with literature only in the obviously creative, artistic sense, though considering "near-literature" in passing or where special circumstances warrant closer scrutiny.

Pre-Islamic Poetry on the Arabian Peninsula and on Its Northern Margins

There is in existence a large corpus of Arabic poetry that is commonly designated pre-Islamic, i.e., it is held to have been composed ("uttered" would render the various Arabic terms) in the Arab heartland in the period approximately A.D. 500–630. Most of the corpus is scattered and unrelated, and the items run from single couplets or short fragments to full-scale poems of twenty to fifty couplets and upward. Some of the material is anonymous, and even where a name is ascribed little or nothing is known of the poet in most cases.

From time to time (and most dramatically under the influence of the famous Egyptian scholar and man of letters Tāhā Husayn 1889–1973) it has been asserted that much of this poetry is spurious, having been composed long after its notional date in great metropolises like Baghdad. There is no doubt that, throughout Islamic history, considerable forgery and plagiarism have taken place, largely because of excessive reverence for earlier models and earlier times generally, though defective memory also bears some responsibility. In the case of poetry in particular, forgery was also widely practiced in the seventh–ninth centuries for a more esoteric reason. The commentators on the Qur'ān and the Traditions of the Prophet, and their colleagues the grammarians, found themselves in difficulties when they came to explain and justify particular usages and constructions in a language that was already no longer really their own. In such circumstances, recourse was had to the supposed custodians of pure Arabic, the Bedouin of "Arabia" (the connection was sometimes rather remote): if a Bedouin could be persuaded to put his seal on a linguistic item as also occurring within the matrix of his own speech habits or in a poem he remembered, he might be handsomely rewarded. Undoubtedly, as with the collection of human data the world over, the temptation to invention in necessity was overwhelming: many contemporary observations confirm this. But Tāhā Husayn was much influenced by nineteenth-century Western skepticism and the Higher Criticism, and his dismissals are unquestionably too sweeping. Such all-or-nothing approaches no longer carry weight, at least outside politics. Moreover, whatever its genuineness on some absolute scale, some of this poetry is unquestionably of a very high standard and must be accepted as mature art. What we do not have, in the nature of the case, is any original or early manuscript evidence, and we must take the material as it comes to us from the eighth century and later.

What sort of poetry is this in its full classical form? The standard is a poem of some 20 to 50 couplets or more, called a *qasīda*. (The term has been interpreted, perhaps by a process of popular etymology, as meaning "purpose poem," i.e., one composed to elicit some favor or to achieve some specific effect. In Western languages it is often rendered as "ode," but this introduces false associations with Greek and Latin traditions.) The individual lines are couplets, long lines of two, more or less equal, halves or hemistichs. The first pair of hemistichs have a twin rhyme, which thereafter appears only at the end of each full line (thus, *aa, ba, ca, da.* . . .). It should be mentioned that the Arabic language has a very high proportion of standard word patterns and grammatical terminations, so that prolonged rhyming or assonantal near-rhyming is infinitely easier than in a heterogeneous language like English (indeed, at times, almost unavoidable). For the same reason, metrical effect is an almost inescapable feature of all Arabic discourse, let alone of poetry. The niceties of the criteria governing rhyme and meter need not be discussed here at any length, but something must be said of the influence of the latter on the poetry as such. There are some sixteen principal meters (all capable of several set variations); they are based on syllable-length (*la: lā*) and consonant-closure (*lam*) rather than, as in English, on stress—which, to the untrained Western ear, makes the "beat" in many cases difficult to detect. Theoretically, a full couplet-line could contain some forty syllables (though most run between twenty and thirty). An impression of ponderousness is accordingly bound to affect ears accustomed to lines at most only half as long; and this impression is only reinforced by the sonorous, measured contrast of the long vowels with the short and the doubled consonants with the single. But while all this is but one factor making adequate translation almost impossibly difficult, it must be understood that for the Arabic-speaking connoisseur it is part of the very essence of Arabic poetry at its best.

There are other features of pre-Islamic Arabic poetry that make appreciation difficult for the Western student. We have already referred to the richness of the language (though the grammatical structure is usually very simple); and to the allusions to persons, places, and events long lost, in many cases, to all but the most inventive commentator. There is also the arbitrary-seeming, ritual division into three broad components. First comes a so-called "erotic prelude" (nasīb), which the poet may open by addressing companions (two is a preferred number) amid the debris of a camp where he once knew his beloved—a sort of Romeo and Juliet predicament is a standard cliché of such poetry; sometimes, but not always, he describes the beloved in some detail. Then he will pass to an account of his steed and the experiences they have shared; this provides an opportunity to speak of other animals, landscapes, storms and various natural hardships, feuds, night raids, ambushes, and the like. Finally, he comes to his main "purpose," which may be satire, menace and/or boasting (on his own account or that of his tribe), panegyric, entreaty, solicitation, or whatever. The final line will often seem to come abruptly and inconclusively. Indeed, despite all the elaborate criteria of structuring mentioned above, and although some groups of lines necessarily belong together, there is an overall impression that each line—like the gnomic statements of the classical rhetoric—is crafted separately and put into place like a piece of mosaic or a pearl on a string. The total effect may be striking enough, but there seems no inherent necessity for any one item to be where it is rather than elsewhere. There are some remarkable exceptions, but the general principle holds, particularly in the longer poems.

Perhaps the greatest difference between the typically Arab appreciation of this poetry and a Westerner's expectation would lie in content, in respect of both mood and ideas. This is poetry with an extremely keen eye for physical detail. It is also generally pagan (whatever the nominal religious allegiance of the poet), rooted in life in this world, but life in an idealized Arabian version: it speaks of reckless generosity, courage, endurance, honor, pride, loyalty, the implacable cruelty of fate, and the cold finality of death. But it offers no profound and rounded criticism of life on a universal scale. It is this, above everything else, which renders all translations disappointing (indeed, many are a total failure): when one has avoided or successfully overcome some or all of the many technical problems, if the content fails to "register," little or nothing avails. Nor is this difficulty confined to Western readers: this poetry has never been successfully rendered into other Islamic languages, or for long been written or enjoyed by other Islamic peoples.

The most famous group of pre-Islamic qasīdas is known as the Golden (or Suspended = Mu'allaqāt) Odes. (We need not discuss what are generally agreed to be picturesque but fanciful explanations for these names: the essential point is that this collection is uniquely preeminent in the long tradition of Arabic poetry as a whole, and remained a general model even in the short-lived periods when poets or critics attacked it and consciously tried to break away from what they saw as its deadening limitations.) The number of qasīdas in the group is usually set at seven, but one or two more are sometimes included, and there is general agreement only on five. The best known names are probably those of Imru'l-Qais, Labīd, 'Amr b. Kulthūm, Tarafa, and Zuhair: despite the constraints of form, style, and theme, each of these poets has left a marked imprint of "character" on his poem. The generally agreed corpus has been several times "introduced" and translated into the main Western languages, and some serviceable and accessible English versions are indicated in the bibliography following.

There are several other groupings of pre-Islamic poetry, as well as collections of poems (the technical name is *dīwāns*) by individual poets, and innumerable quoted items scattered throughout verse anthologies and prose works of all kinds. Since these were, like the *Mu'allaqāt*, recorded long after the event, but have much less importance than the latter, we will refer to them only briefly in the discussion of Arabic literature during the 'Abbasid Caliphate (750–1258). Again, much of this material has been translated, but it is usually scattered in general literary histories or specialized monographs and articles.

A.D. 632–750

The first century and a half of Islam was not a distinguished period in Arabic literature; nor was it one in which the Gulf area enjoyed any literary preeminence, or indeed any real literary status at all. It may best be seen as a period of preparation, during which the new religious culture was establishing itself over its maximum area of domination: from Spain to the Chinese borders, from Africa to Central Asia. It was a period, too, in which that culture was deciding, in the different regions of the "empire," where the balance would lie as between religion and secular concerns, i.e., to what extent society would be religiously inspired or religiously controlled. On the whole, a felicitous balance was achieved, and literature was able to come to birth and grow.

For the first thirty years or so, a small theocracy ruled from the City of the Prophet, Medina. It dealt efficiently with immediate matters of material, administrative, and military significance; it was generally pragmatic and tolerant, especially toward non-Muslims; but it had a simplistic view of the essential pattern of Islamic life, which apparently took little account of the vast changes, amalgamations and adaptations that must inevitably come about if the new society was to maintain its hold on the older, highly sophisticated cultures of the various non-Arab peoples who had now joined Islam. To such a theocracy, the literary aspects of culture meant little or nothing. Poets still composed, their reciters (when not the poets themselves) delivered their "odes" and "fragments"; and orators still coined their telling phrases, terse, linguistically rich, and allusive; but little of this material was put directly into writing. Above all, whatever happened in practice, officialdom (following the alleged example of the Prophet)[1] denounced poetry as a frivolous, and even dangerous, relic of paganism; likewise, oratory was downgraded in favor of prayer and the study of the Qur'ān and the Prophetic Tradition. Both poetry and rhetoric were seen not only as vehicles of unacceptable moral attitudes (pride, vengeance, agnostic hedonism, pessimism, and the like) but as divisive forces in Islamic society. Nor was this apprehension groundless, for both were freely used by several of the violently clashing "sects"

---

1. The Prophet's reported attitudes to poetry are ambivalent: at one extreme he is said to have deeply resented being classified as a poet, at the other he is said to have encouraged his own poetic following, principally Hassān b. Thābit.

that sprang up after the Prophet's death. Even in "secular" verse, a new note of vicious stridency was being heard.

After A.D. 660, the great Meccan family of the Umayyads came to power, and the capital of the Islamic world was moved to Damascus, where it would remain formally for some ninety years. This was the most "Arab" period in all Islamic history, but Arabia itself now entered on its long life as a cultural backwater, important in the strictly religious sense, and for the activities associated with the Pilgrimage, but in virtually no other respect. The Gulf area generally was growing in importance, but its significance was still primarily military and commercial rather than cultural or literary. Linguistic studies were being undertaken there for the first time, but their fruit would only appear later.

Nearly all the Umayyads are regarded by posterity as lukewarm Muslims, so aristocratic and secular in attitude as to be virtually pagan. They were naturally at odds with the relics of the Medina theocracy and with other zealots, and their outlook was certainly rather broad, sophisticated, and cosmopolitan. There were poets and orators at their court and in the great centers; but their own interest was less in literature and ideas than in material and social amenities—palaces, summer residences, and other buildings; art, hunting, and love; the enjoyment of wealth, health, and good-fellowship. It was a golden age for Jewish and Christian physicians, architects, artists and craftsmen, and purveyors of choice clothes, foods, and wines; and such people, to the scandal of Arab tribalists and pious Muslims alike, often had great influence in public affairs. The Umayyad world was essentially an updating, a more polished and luxurious "Islamic" version of the way of life that had flourished in the century before Islam in the petty Arab kingdoms that lay north of Arabia and owed allegiance to Byzantium or Sasanid Iran.

The downfall of the Umayyads was brought about partly by their own ultimate incompetence to lead the "state" into the future, but largely by the opposition of important, quite diverse, groups who found themselves permanently excluded from the power and dignity to which they believed they were entitled: the great non-Arabian majority of "new" Muslims, the pious Muslims of orthodox belief and practice, and the nonorthodox groups of varying views on the choice and the proper role of successors to the Prophet. Eventually, by a skilful propaganda—which played on all these and other resentments without ever really satisfying them—the 'Abbasid family overthrew their relatives the Umayyads (wiping out all but a tiny remnant that escaped to Spain and established a new caliphate there). For their support they relied heavily on Iranians, and the great days of Iranian cultural influence had now arrived.

The 'Abbasid Caliphate and the Gulf Area,
A.D. 750–1258

The 'Abbasids moved the capital of the Islamic "empire" to the area of Baghdad, where (with minor interruptions) it would remain for over 500 years. This move is often described as a necessary piece of symbolism, a clear break with the former regime, and a triumph of the Arab tribes settled in Iraq over those of Syria and elsewhere. While there is some truth in this assessment, the real reasons are much more pragmatic and important for the long term. The administrative, communicational, commercial, and cultural center of gravity in the Islamic world had shifted from western Arabia and the Mediterranean toward Iraq and Iran, and Iran itself was closely tied with Central Asia, India, and the Far East. Baghdad was in an immense area of permanent fertility; and its strategic position—on an extensive waterway system, and on caravan routes of which the most famous was part of the Great Silk Road—made it an ideal center from which to administer the Islamic world as it had by then taken shape. It was no accident that it was in virtually the same location as the long-time capital of another great international state, that of the Iranian Sasanids, to which Islam had succeeded more fully than to any other. With its millennia of history at the cross-roads of the development of Middle Eastern civilization, Iraq was well fitted to be the matrix of the most recent of them all, for it was peculiarly open to new things, and new ideas and methods: it was in this matrix that the religious culture of Islam would blend alchemically with virtually all that Iran had to offer and with the philosophical and scientific thought of Greece. Though the "empire" itself would soon fragment politically, and the caliphate as an institution become largely ineffectual, Baghdad would remain for five centuries the commercial and cultural capital of the Islamic realm and one of the few great cities of the medieval world.

It was in this rich and variegated intellectual locale that Arabic literature—whether considered generally or from the standpoint of the Gulf area in particular—came to full maturity in its various genres. Once more it should be emphasized that while most of the writers had some Arab blood, and some might consider themselves "pure" Arabs, Arabic literature in this region was for centuries a multicultural product. In varying degrees, the same holds true of the Arabic literature written further afield. This latter, incidentally, apart from some attractive innovations in Spain, was largely a reflection of the metropolitan models fashionable at various times in Iraq.

Arabic Literature in 'Abbasid Times: Prose. As already pointed out, written prose was not an original literary genre in Arabic. One primary genesis of prose, like so much else in Arabic literature, lay in scholarly and religious, not in artistic, concerns. Within a few years of the Prophet's death, simple oral transmission of the Qur'ān, even had it remained physically possible, was no longer adequate. The original reciters were growing old and dying, their recollections conflicted or overlapped, and the text was no longer fully meaningful to those who heard and uttered it. It thus became necessary to standardize, and to record in sufficient copies for use over a great and growing empire, one inhabited by vastly more non-Arabs than Arabs. This led first to improvements in the writing system, so as ultimately to guarantee phonetic completeness if required. It also resulted in the development of exegesis, lengthy explanatory commentary ranging from linguistic details to historical identification and theological justification. This, in turn, required the study of all materials, "literary" or otherwise, that might have a bearing on such matters and, particularly, the specialized study of the life, the sayings and the actions of the Prophet himself. The sheer weight of new material thus called into being inevitably demanded the use of written prose on an unprecedented scale, though oral processes still played a large part. Much of this work remained centered in Medina, but Iraq–Iran soon began to play a leading role, doubtless in part because the newer Muslims, whether Arab or non-Arab, genuinely needed or desired to go more deeply into what the older Muslims took for granted. The most important Gulf centers first engaged in such activities were the military garrison towns and commercial centers of Kufa and Basra, which became the respective locations of rival "schools" of language and other learned pursuits.

Prose also developed for very practical reasons, having nothing to do with the Qur'ān and all its satellite areas of study. The professional secretaries and scribes who controlled the administration of the lands taken over by the Muslims needed scarcely to break step at the time of the conquests, for (as was said earlier) their new masters were quick to grasp the importance of keeping the machines running smoothly so as to preserve order and assure the continuance of revenue. But for nearly a century more this work was done in the original languages (of which the most significant was Persian), the conversion to Arabic being completed only a few years before the 'Abbasid revolution. It is not clear to what extent this conversion demanded the recruitment of new personnel (officially, non-Muslims were henceforth excluded), but it is virtually certain that many of the hereditary civil-service families would by this time be Muslim and more than sufficiently skilled in Arabic to continue in office under the new dispensation. Equally certain is that their matrilingual and cultural traditions would affect their use of Arabic, more perhaps in the innovative field of prose than in poetry. In some communities such people had long been among the chief proponents of literary activity: indeed, many official documents (e.g., diplomatic exchanges, petitions, decrees, grants, and the like) traditionally had a literary flavor of their own because they were drafted by people with such a bent. This style (later technically known as *inshā'* = composition) would always be an important component of Arabic prose, though in the course of time other elements would be introduced by other classes of people as well. At its height, Arabic prose was cultivated by all manner of writers, professional and amateur, and could handle, with superb precision and functional elegance, virtually any topic in any field. At its best it can still make the English into which it may be rendered seem clumsy and wordy, since it is often almost twice as long as the original.

Medieval Arabic prose from the Gulf area, even that amount that has survived the ravages of time and countless natural and human disasters, is of such vast extent that any attempt to survey it in short compass would be pretentious and absurd. Even if one limited one's purview to the strictly literary (as distinguished earlier) the task would still be self-defeating. The most that can usefully and interestingly be done is to discuss briefly one or two key figures.

The nominal, but clearly identifiable "father" of Arabic prose was an 'Abbasid Persian secretary named Ibn al-Muqaffa', who was executed (in somewhat confused circumstances involving charges of relapse from Islam to Zoroastrianism) in 757. Most of his literary writing was in fact translation and adaptation from Persian models, some of which were themselves of Indian derivation. With him one can see the first clear delineation of the essential features of theme and style in this new genre, which would become known under the general term *adab* (= manners, polish, discipline, culture—and, by extension, the prose literature embodying such concepts). These features were: entertainment combined with "uplift," i.e., advice to rulers and the educated public, illustrated with interesting and attractively told anecdotes; and the material to be couched in carefully articulated and balanced periods, often with parallelisms and antitheses. Though much of his work has been subsequently adapted and interpolated, and no original manuscripts now exist, the difficulties he experienced with the new vehicle still show through clearly in places. Even he seems sometimes more at ease with the old forms in their brevity and their epigrammatic character, but they are, of course, ultimately inadequate to his purpose. His most famous contribution was an early rendering of the originally Indian animal fables of Bidpai (Pilpai), always known in Arabic and other Islamic literatures as the tales of Kalīla and Dimna, after the two central animals in the narrative complex.

Incontestably, the greatest writer of Arabic prose is a Gulf figure in the fullest sense of the word, being associated almost exclusively with his native city of Basra and his adopted home of Baghdad: 'Amr b. Bahr, best known by his nickname of al-Jāhiz ("Popeye"). He seems to have been of African-slave descent, but took inordinate pride in his Arab affiliations and was a sworn foe of the non-Arabs, particularly of the Persian or Persianized secretarial corps (on whom he wrote a famous satire). Jāhiz is a figure of great interest from many points of view—personal, social, political, religious, literary, scientific, to name only some of the most important. Born about A.D. 776 and dying about 869, his long life more than covers the greatest days of the 'Abbasid caliphate: the era of Hārūn al-Rashīd and his son Ma'mūn, a period not only of political and material greatness, but one of enormous intellectual and spiritual vigor also. Though he enjoyed little or no formal instruction at any level, and displayed scant aptitude for academic or any other discipline, he educated himself (from life and books and discussion) to the point where he became the finest stylist and one of the most remarkable polymaths of his time. His originality, eccentricity, and sense of humor were equally unusual in the writing of the period; and for that reason he has, until recently at least, often tended to be dismissed by the graver elements in Islam as a lightweight or a clown. Nor was he a mere intellectual, or a "personality," living on the easy fringes of everyday happenings: he was deeply embroiled in the public and the social life of his time, and in political, religious, and ethnic controversy. He seems never to have held a steady, much less an important position, though he is said to have served briefly as a tutor and even more briefly as a civil servant. His livelihood, which fluctuated considerably, came from his writings, in two ways: in the special sense that he wrote propaganda briefs more or less to order, and in the more general sense that, in the new age of paper production on a mass scale, his writings were bought by a wide public. There was nothing about him of the well-organized, objective scholar; not only did his character unfit him for such a role, but the very circumstances of his life—his early poverty, his constant struggles, his mixed racial origins, his notorious ugliness, and his public failures—conspired to nurture his pet prejudices and preoccupations.

Of some 200 titles commonly ascribed to him, only about 30 survive entire and another 50 in part. Some are books (one, the *Book of Animals*, being multi-volumed), but the majority are essays (or, as one might say, epistles or shorter monographs). It is this latter form that Jāhiz brought to perfection, and even his longer works could be regarded as a series of essays or an essay indefinitely prolonged. The Arabic name for the genre is *risāla* (pl. *rasā'il*), i.e., a written message, a letter. Whatever prejudices Jāhiz may have had against the secretary corps, such a name betrays the early association of his chosen genre with these writers. But Jāhiz put his own seal on the *risāla* in a way no other writers ever achieved, however accomplished might be their work in itself. Before his time it had not really found its character, and after his day it tended toward blandness or to a wide range of specializations in learned fields. Jāhiz, whether or not a given *risāla* is a genuine reply to someone's questions or comments, writes in a highly personal tone. The satire on secretaries begins: "God keep and preserve you, and give you enjoyment! I have read your book, in which you praise the character and conduct of secretaries, and describe their virtues and their prodigious feats—and I understand what you say. However. . . ." Sometimes he is urbane, sometimes aggressive, but rarely crude. As may not be readily obvious in this example, his style is usually too florid for modern Western tastes, full of near repetitions, fine-spun "developments," and manifold quotations. In all this, of course, he can fully display his fantastic knowledge of the Arabic language, and of poetry and rhetoric. He is also given to frequent and extensive digressions, prompted by recall from his enormous stock of information on people, events, facts, and ideas of all kinds: the present was as interesting to him as the past, and he went on learning and observing all his life. To take just one example, his *Book of Animals* does not belie its title, inasmuch as it contains a vast and disorganized store of commonplace or curious information about real and legendary beasts; but it is also possible to lose oneself completely for long passages in nonzoological material or in discussions with only a remotely zoological reference.

His obsession with animals was part of his overall interest in scientific and pseudoscientific matters, but it also meshed with his preoccupation with race and evolutionary breeding at the human, social level. Two other concerns that interacted were his support of the 'Abbasids against their foes and his espousal of the rationalist school of Mu'tazilite theology (he even founded his own subsect!), which for a time enjoyed the Caliph's "moral" support—as did the great translation movement of the Greek texts that stimulated rational attitudes. Jāhiz's "sincerity" in much of this is difficult to estimate; but his *interest* is not in doubt, and it is this quality of keen interest that makes so absorbing his many general studies of the quirks of human behavior—avarice, envy, indiscretion, pride, crooked dealings, confidence tricks, and the like. Unlike so many Arabic authors, he considered no idea or activity or event beneath his notice so long as it could be made into "good copy."

Jāhiz remains unique, or at least uniquely great. But his chosen vehicle, the *risāla*, with all its capacity for elegance and delight, was to become the workhorse of Arabic literature—apt to bear serious philosophical argument, scientific and medical exposition, biographical analysis, and the like, as well as lighter discussion of all manner of topics natural and contrived. As with Jāhiz, its original nature was often disguised by its organization, at greater length or in series, in book form. (Books with an obvious organic unity of their own, something beyond the sum of their parts, are not the general rule in Arabic literature.)

This versatility does not hold for the other principal genre of Arabic prose in the 'Abbasid era, the *maqāma* (pl. *maqāmāt*: with a rather wooden and un-informative literalness, the term is usually rendered "session," "seance," or "assembly"). This too was very much a Gulf creation, elaborated in Iraq and owing a great deal to Persian influences. The *maqāmāt* exhibit what Western taste would tend to regard as a grotesque discrepancy between content and style: they consist of a loose series of quasi-dramatic, social-satirical anecdotes, by or about a witty and erudite rogue; but they are couched in recherché, heavily ornamented and highly polished rhymed prose, interspersed with occasional verses. It is a self-contained, artificial form, devised entirely for entertainment—possibly "live," in the sense that the episodes were often read aloud and acted out. But its style and format made it an entertainment open only to the highly educated, not to say the learned; and commentary on the most famous *maqāmāt* proliferated through the ages. Nevertheless, they were an immediate and long-lived success with the bourgeois and professional classes and became (like Jāhiz's *Book of Animals*) a favorite vehicle for lavish illustration. Western taste might prefer a simpler prototype by the Persian Badī' al-Zamān al-Hamadhānī (d. 1008), but it is the work by al-Harīrī of Basra (d. 1122) that incontestably holds the pride of place for this genre in Arabic. Indeed, it has been said that for perfection of language it stands second only to the Qur'ān. It is a remarkable fact that a work so idiosyncratically Arabic should have been one of the earliest to engage Western attention: there are laborious, and sometimes practically incomprehensible, versions in the main Western languages.

A charming, rather underrated, piece of late prose literature—which masquerades as political philosophy and history—is a book by an Iraqi judge, Ibn al-Tiqtaqā, which is known as *al-Fakhrī*, after the ruler to whom it was dedicated. It was written near the end of the thirteenth century, some forty years after the caliphate at Baghdad had been extinguished by the Mongols; the author professes to be conducting a retrospective review, in a detached spirit, at the end of an epoch, though the book does not really live up to such pretensions. Apart from its elegant and easy style and manner, what does lend it special interest (if we accept his explanation that he wrote it more or less from memory, while snowed-in in northern Iraq) is that it may be taken as a short statement of the "myth" of Islamic history and culture as seen by an educated, but not necessarily learned, person at the end of the "Classical Age." It deserves more sympathetic study than it has hitherto received at the hands of "serious" historians: it also merits more sensitive translation than that of the current English version.

What most Western readers would recall as the most famous work in Arabic prose associated (if rather in subject matter than in actual composition) with the Gulf area, the *Arabian* (or *Thousand and One*) *Nights*, is not officially rated as part of Arabic literature at all. This vast and indeterminate collection belongs to the oral/folk tradition and derives ultimately from all parts of the ancient Middle East, including "India" and Iran. It was probably not written down in anything like its present form before the fifteenth century A.D.; and where the texts have not been updated, or "corrected" to conform to literary Arabic, the language would suggest that the more or less final versions were made in Mamluk Egypt. But the dominant inspiration is Gulf-oriented not only by the placing of some tales in the Baghdad of Hārūn al-Rashīd or in Iran, but by the whole rich social and commercial life, centering on the Gulf trade with India and the Far East, that forms the background of such tales as those of Aladdin and Sindbad. Even in the Middle East, where literature has for so long been associated with élitism in attitudes, interests, and the use of language, the *Nights* are now engaging the study of scholars as a fundamental document of Arabic expression.

Arabic Literature in 'Abbasid Times: Poetry. In literature, the major creation of the 'Abbasid era was prose. The West does not always appreciate that the culture of Islam is essentially urban and commercial, not desert or rural;[2] and prose was the most natural expression of society in the great Gulf centers and (once established) the form best capable of surviving through all vicissitudes and for most purposes. With poetry matters seem otherwise ordained.

With a few exceptions, 'Abbasid poetry was written to commission or in hope of favor or reward; and this meant that the envisaged audience was not primarily one of scholars or cultured professionals (and certainly not the general public), but the powerful and the wealthy: either a ruler himself or his high officials, or the courts generally. Much of the verse was outright panegyric or elegy, in which the formality and insincerity are either obvious or may well be suspected. But even where it strikes an ostensibly fresher and more personal note, such poetry is still written for recital at courts, for the most part, and very much with the (probably conservative and overblown) tastes of the patrons in mind. Even where disappointed sycophancy turns sour, and the poet (at a safe distance) ridicules or viciously attacks his audience that might have been, the result gains no more validity and integrity in human terms, however interesting it may be linguistically and psychologically.

The two greatest names in Arabic poetry during the 'Abbasid era, al-Mutanabbī (d. 965) and al-Ma'arrī (d. 1057), have only brief and tenuous associations with the Gulf area, being normally reckoned as belonging to the so-called Syrian school. The former—chief of the "Moderns" (see below), a latter-day, self-appointed "desert hero"—wrote poetry that it is difficult not to see as overladen, strained, and bombastic, and sometimes technically faulty: many Arabic critics have themselves said as much, but it has remained in generally high favor, no doubt in part because it is a great source of "quotable quotes." Al-Ma'arrī was a tortured genius, blind, an agnostic, a vegetarian, a celibate, fiercely independent, and even quarrelsome, but possessed of a self-critical, if pessimistic, sense of humor. Of all Arabic poetry, his (and also his prose)—despite often heavy learning and a tendency to obscurity and virtuosity—may strike the non-Arabic reader as having the most universal significance. Some contemporaries seem to have esteemed him greatly, but his highly personal reactions to religion and other important societal touchstones have contrived to keep him, over the

---

2. This is, of course, not to deny the agricultural and pastoral bases of the economy; the survival of tribes in several areas; or nostalgia for the desert ideal as a permanent element in Arabic poetry.

centuries, under something of a cloud. A critical study (in Arabic) published in 1944 was significantly entitled *Al-Ma'arrī: The Unknown Man* (= *dhālika al-majhūl*).

Since virtually all 'Abbasid poets are considerably inferior to these two, and as their numbers are no fewer than those of the prose writers, it will be most useful to discuss the main features of content, structure, and style during this period, mentioning individual names only where particularly relevant.

Unlike prose, Arabic poetry came into the 'Abbasid era fully matured and continued to be cultivated without any essential break. However, while—as indicated earlier—the old *qasīda* genre never really died, there were sufficiently dramatic innovations in theme, structure, and style to justify the recognition of distinct additional categories (none of which would correspond precisely to Western expectations). Urban life naturally affected the *themes*: much of 'Abbasid verse is clearly no longer the "natural" poetry of supposed primitives, but sophisticated material written for the pleasure and edification of a cultured audience in a great metropolis, or at least a fair-sized city. The rigid *qasīda structure* was broken down so as to give its component sections virtual independence; new categories were also devised from, or created in addition to, these; the poet could always call his poem a "fragment" (*qit'a*), i.e., something that approximates the ancient, more or less genuine fragment, but cannot be fitted into any obvious category. Apart from the ubiquitous panegyric, poems might now be wholly devoted to hedonistic themes of love and wine; they might mock not just individuals or other tribes, but society and even organized religion itself; they might contain references to the new ideas of science and philosophy; they might also be so topical and "political" as to be nowadays virtually unintelligible. An individual note, together with subtle humor and a delicate irony, were particular features of the "modern" genres. The innovations in *style* were no less marked than those in theme and structure. In place of, or in addition to, the old richness of near-synonyms and proper-name allusions, there now appeared a whole range of complex artifices (the technical name is *badī'*: "original," "newly invented"— though the fact of their being unprecedented has long been disputed, no doubt partly out of unwillingness to admit that 'Abbasid Arabic literature was greatly indebted to foreign influences). These artifices related to imagery and figures of all kinds, parallel or opposed phrases, word-plays, assonance and alliteration. If Islamic urban life dictated the new themes and instances, it seems to have been above all Persian influences that affected structures and style: a sort of short lyrical *qasīda* (about six to fifteen double lines, set in the sprightlier meters), known as the *ghazal*, though possibly not of Persian origin, is a very foundation stone of classical Persian poetry, and it was during this period that it enjoyed its greatest popularity in Arabic; in addition, the whole *badī'* style reflects very faithfully what has nearly always been most popular in extant Persian poetry, whereas its hold on Arabic poetry has never been fully assured.

It should not be assumed that all these features developed evenly or ever became universal. Some poets made no use of them at all, while others selected from them, generously or to a limited extent as the case might be. There were fashions, too, with so-called Neo-classicism making a strong comeback from time to time. Women poets, who had been well represented in pre-Islamic and early

Islamic times, became less numerous in the 'Abbasid era, though accomplished singing-girls continued the old function of the "reciters." The development of sophisticated musical accompaniment to much of the poetry is one of the most striking Persian contributions. (In fact, "accompaniment" is not an appropriate term for a musical component that was an organically integrated part of such compositions.)

Though little of this poetry has been translated into English, and even less has been translated well, some of the best known poets of the 'Abbasid era are worth mention by name, as being characteristic of these various trends. Bashshār b. Burd, the "blind Persian," was the first major Arabic poet of his people, and the first to use the *badī'* style, albeit in an as yet restrained form. Like the prose innovator, Ibn al-Muqaffa', he was executed (in 784) on charges involving heresy, and his general antinomianism was a byword. A half-Persian, Abū Nuwās (d. ca. 810), was the epitome of the brilliant, cynical court-poet familiar in English literature from the Elizabethan period. He was supreme in poetry inspired by wine, love (as often as not homosexual), and the hunt; and his preferred form was the *ghazal*. Though a brilliant master of the Arabic language (not least in his shocking satires), he worked with apparently effortless ease, bound neither by the chains of philology nor caught in the webs of *badī'*. His contemporary Abu'l-'Atāhiya (d. ca. 828) presents a complete contrast: he was the originator of Arabic ascetic poetry, as conceived on a grand moral and didactic scale, and he judged his effect would be best achieved by a virtual abandonment of linguistic, metrical, and structural complications, thus coming closer than any of his contemporaries or successors to popular folk verse. He was in receipt of a sizable official stipend from the court in recognition of his "good influence," a fact that has led some to cast doubt on both his affected simplicity of life style and the sincerity of his verse itself. Ibn al-Rūmī (d. 896) was, as his name would suggest, of Byzantine origin: his innovations lie in two areas, his pointedly introspective themes and the degree of unity manifested in each poem, in contrast with the usual atomicity of construction referred to on p. 339. One of the most original poets was Ibn al-Mu'tazz, who was himself a very short-lived caliph, being assassinated in 908. He was able to spend all his time, up to his final unlucky venture, on his poetry and on critical study of the work of others; and he was a master of the traditional, the traditional-adapted, and the *badī'* style simultaneously. Perhaps his best poetry was his hedonistic verse, a rather more measured utterance than that of Abū Nuwās. But he also developed descriptive verse for its own sake, he wrote a mini-epic on the reign of a cousin, and he experimented with a verse form of the *risāla*. His most valuable legacy, particularly to the posterity of Western scholars, is his critical study of the canons and conventions of the new styles of poetry. Self-conscious analyses are not common in the culture of Islam, which was usually able to take itself very much for granted; where they are found in relation to literature they are usually the work of philologists or latter-day pedagogues, so that there is a rare value to one written by a working poet of outstanding ability. Its basic deficiencies are its tendentious attempts to establish the "Arabicity" of the *badī'* style and its apparent unawareness of its reliance on (and partial misuse of) such Greek models as Aristotle's *Rhetoric*.

In many ways, the great achievement of the 'Abbasid era in poetry was one of retrospection and collection. As indicated on pp. 337–38, we shall never know how much of what was allegedly collected from former ages and recorded was in fact forged; but in view of the bulk involved, and the obvious quality of much of the material, it can hardly have been the greater part. The most remarkable collection, still practically untranslated and only lightly tapped for its riches in literature, history, biography, social comment, and musical information, is the *Book of Songs* (*Kitāb al-Aghānī*), a work in twenty-odd large volumes, by Abu 'l-Faraj al-Isfahānī (d. 967). Largely compiled in Syria, it nevertheless included much Gulf material and played a crucial part in the literary life of the Gulf area (as it did wherever Arabic literature flourished); and its author—though a descendant of the Umayyads—was associated on another side with Iran. Two other famous, but much smaller and more selective, anthologies both share the same name, *al-Hamāsa* ("Valor," after the name of the topic around which the initial section of the earlier work is arranged). One is by Abū Tammām (d. ca. 845), the other (somewhat inferior) by al-Buhturī (d. 897). Both were at one time or another court poets in Baghdad, and their poetry enjoys a certain esteem in its own right. Abū Tammām's *Hamāsa* in particular remained highly popular for centuries, being a classical example of a work regularly commented on for the benefit of successive generations of students and poets. The term *hamāsa* soon became generic for all such collections (for a brief period in modern times it was also used as the Arabic word for "epic").

The Postmediaeval and Modern Period, 1258–Present

Arabic literature in the 'Abbasid era was running down in Iraq as early as the eleventh century (and had virtually died in Arabia long before that). This was not merely because the caliphate was no longer effective as a political institution, for this had been the case since the middle of the ninth century, when foreign mercenaries began to control affairs, with the caliph relegated to the role of a symbolic figurehead. Nor was Baghdad yet eclipsed as the great metropolitan center of commerce and culture. But with the loosening of political control overall and the recurrent threats to civil peace in Baghdad itself, men of letters began to look to the attractions of the many new courts that had sprung up on the periphery of the Baghdad-centered Islamic world—in Iran, Central Asia, Syria, Egypt, North Africa, and Spain. This was one of the inevitable results of the universally heavy dependence on patronage. Moreover, in the particular case of Iran—the external area most closely associated with the Baghdad caliphate—the many talents that had for some four centuries been drawn to Baghdad, and composed Arabic literature there, now tended to stay at home to write, or increasingly to compose once again in their native tongue. Persian literature began to revive strongly a little before A.D. 1000, and Turkish literature was eventually to develop with greater dependence on Persian than on Arabic. (Arabic still retained a supremacy for some centuries to come, in most parts of the Islamic world, as the language of religion, religious argument, and thought generally.)

As far as the Gulf was concerned, the disaster of the Mongol invasions came to a climax in 1258, with the sack of Baghdad and the murder of the last clearly legitimate caliph. While these invasions did not wreak all the destruction commonly ascribed to them (the Baghdad markets were functioning again within a few days, for example), they did dislocate the great machines—commercial, agricultural, and intellectual—which, though sadly in need of overhaul, were still geared to a wide world far beyond the Gulf itself. The center of gravity of the Islamic world began to shift erratically, finally pluralizing and settling down in Asia Minor, in Iran and Central Asia, in Egypt, and in northern "India." Only in Egypt and North Africa did any considerable literary activity in Arabic continue, and even there it was not of the first rank. (A great historian and thinker like Ibn Khaldūn [d. 1406], for example, wrote a notably turgid, unattractive Arabic style: at times it is even completely lacking in the classic Arabic quality of lucidity. The decline in the "literary" quality of nonliterary works was, as in our own age, one of the best indicators of the decay of humanistic education and literary sensibility throughout the Arabic-writing world.)

By the mid-sixteenth century, the Gulf area had passed into the jealously divided and disputed control of the Ottoman Turks and the Safavid dynasty of Iran, and (with changes of rule in Iran) this was to remain the case until World War I. Iran, though sporadically open to European, Indian, and Far Eastern influences, grew steadily in self-definition as a Persian-speaking, Persian-writing cultural unit. The Ottomans too were developing their own literature, vastly more under Persian than under Arabic "tutelage." In both empires, written Arabic had virtually ceased to be used for all but religious purposes, and Persian and Turkish were increasingly employed for these as well. Arabia had long been a region where literature was regarded as a distracting and dangerous frivolity, a situation that more or less continues to this day—at least as far as the *creation* of literary works is concerned. Most good minds in the area are, in any case, now too busy with technology and finance.

Once-great Iraq remained for nearly four centuries an Ottoman outpost ruled from Istanbul, and a Shī'ī religious center controlled from Iran. This divided authority exacerbated religious conflicts and tribal v. urban hostilities. Iraq was not without commercial and strategic importance, and it sometimes enjoyed efficient administration, as under the remarkable Midhat Pasha (d. 1884). But in matters of literature and culture generally it was no longer of any significance. Even the Arabic renaissance (*nahda*) of the mid-nineteenth century, which so powerfully affected Syria–Lebanon and Egypt as they came under Western influences, left Iraq relatively untouched until much later. While admittedly rather long-lived, the two best-known Iraqi poets of this period, al-Zahāwī and al-Rusāfī, died as late into the twentieth century as 1936 and 1945, respectively.

The British regime, which lasted effectively from the end of World War I until after World War II, did much to raise the level of Iraqi material and intellectual prosperity (not, of course, without an eye to Britain's own commercial and strategic interests); but this was slow to bear fruit in literature, partly because the Iraqi intelligentsia were more concerned with politics, professional education, and technology, partly because promising writers tended to look and move westward. Recent regimes have been radically and dictatorially left-wing: their policies have neither encouraged literature in any broad, humanistic sense nor permitted outsiders to assess the country's present literary and intellectual developments. It may never prove possible to write a satisfactory account of Iraqi Arabic literature, even in the first half of this century, for—even more than with most Middle Eastern countries—much of the material, both original and critical, appeared in short-run books or in obscure and ephemeral journals. Practically nothing has been translated.

It is customary to say, with a great deal of justice, that all Middle Eastern writing of the last hundred years or so tends to become less interesting to the outsider as it approximates ever more closely Western models. This may well prove true of Arabic literature written in Iraq. However, there has always been, in Iraq's rich and complex society, a strong streak of originality and specificity, a trait that seems to have manifested itself, in the long period of high-cultural stagnation, in the composition of popular and dialectal literature, particularly poetry. To judge from the keen sense of daily life displayed in, for example, the short stories of the mid-century writer Ja'far al-Khalīlī, Iraqi Arabic writing may yet prove to have a distinctive character of its own. This assumes, of course, that literature generally will again become important in the modern Iraqi scheme of things.

Selected Bibliography

A. GENERAL WORKS

Cambridge History of Islam. 2 vols. Cambridge, 1970. Useful background material and a chapter on Arabic literature.

Encyclopaedia of Islam (1913–38); 2nd ed. 1954–. Individual articles on topics, persons and important works: entries under Arabic terms (Latinized), but good cross references to English.

Hitti, P. K. *History of the Arabs.* Macmillan (and paperback) 1967 (9th ed.). A "classic," and somewhat old-fashioned in scholarship. Tends to "Arabic" chauvinism.

Legacy of Islam (Oxford "Legacy" Series). Oxford, 1931; new edition 1974. The two editions are, in fact, different works, and both are invaluable.

Levy, R. *A Baghdad Chronicle.* Cambridge, 1929.

Longrigg, S. H. *Four Centuries of Modern Iraq.* London, 1925 (and reprinted). A standard work, a little outdated.

Pearson, J. D. *Index Islamicus 1906–55.* Cambridge, 1958. The standard bibliography for periodical articles. Updating supplements appear regularly.

Savory, R. M., ed. *Introduction to Islamic Civilisation.* Cambridge, 1976. A good introduction by several hands: substantial literary component.

von Grunebaum, G. E. *Medieval Islam: A Study in Cultural Orientation.* London, 1953— several printings, including Penguin. A profound, often difficult, book on the classical Islamic world-view: many references to literature.

B. HISTORY AND BIBLIOGRAPHY OF ARABIC LITERATURE

Altoma, Salih J. *Modern Arabic Literature: A Bibliography of Articles, Books, Dissertations and Translations—in English.* Indiana, 1975 (Asian Studies Research Institute Occasional Papers No. 3).

Brockelmann, C. E. *Geschichte der Arabischen Litteratur.* 5 vols. Weimar/Berlin/Leiden, 1898–1942 (and reprinted). The standard bibliography: now much in need of revision and updating.

Gibb, H. A. R. *Arabic Literature: An Introduction.* Oxford, 1963. Compact and useful, but much on near- and nonliterature.

Lichtenstadter, I. *Introduction to Classical Arabic Literature.* New York, 1974. Reliable and well-written, but too much on near- and nonliterature, as with the older studies.

Nicholson, R. A. *Literary History of the Arabs.* Cambridge, 1953 (3rd ed.). A "classic," but despite frequent reprinting now out of date by some seventy years. Much on near- or nonliterature.

C. AUTHORS AND WORKS

Arabian Nights (1,001 Nights), many translations into English and other languages, all with different merits. The latest two Penguin selections (by N. J. Dawood) are excellent.

Arberry, A. J. *Arabic Poetry: A Primer for Students.* Cambridge, 1967 (also in paperback). A useful introduction.

———. *Poems of al-Mutanabbī.* Cambridge, 1967.

Beeston, A. F. L. *Selections from the Poetry of Baššar* (Bashshār b. Burd). Cambridge, 1977. Has an introductory sketch on Arabic poetic structures.

Al-Harīrī. *Maqāmāt (Assemblies),* vol. 1, tr. T. Chenery. London, 1867. Vol. 2, tr. F. Steingass. London, 1898. Both reprinted 1969.

Ibn al-Tiqtaqā, *al-Fakhrī,* tr. C.E.J. Whitting. London, 1947. Reasonably accurate, but insensitive and poorly produced.

Kritzeck, J. *Anthology of Islamic Literature (. . . to Modern Times).* London, 1964. Several printings, including Penguin and Mentor.

———. *Modern Islamic Literature from 1800 to the Present.* New York, 1972.

Muʿallaqāt and other "pre-Islamic" poetry: Sir C. Lyall, *Translations of Ancient Arabic Poetry,* London 1885, 1930; W. S. Blunt, *Seven Golden Odes of Pagan Arabia,* London, 1903; A. J. Arberry, *The Seven Odes: First Chapter in Arabic Literature,* London/New York, 1957.

Nicholson, R. A. *Eastern Poetry and Prose.* Cambridge, 1922.

———. *Studies in Islamic Poetry.* Cambridge, 1921 (especially for Maʿarrī).

Pellat, C. *The Life and Works of Jahiz.* London, 1969. Very readable, with much translation by the acknowledged expert on this writer.

Prendergast, W. *The Maqāmāt of Badīʿ al-Zamān.* Madras/London, 1915; reprinted 1973.

Wightman, G. B. H., and al-Udhari, A. Y. *Birds through a Ceiling of Alabaster (Three Abbasid Poets).* Harmondsworth, 1975.

14. Persian Literature

ROBERT M. REHDER

 Persian is an Indo-European language spoken in the area between the Indus in the east and the Zagros in the west, between the Caucasus and Jaxartes in the north and the Persian Gulf and Indian Ocean in the south. The language seems to have been introduced into the Iranian area from the north sometime after 2000 B.C. Persian is divided into Old Persian (ca. 600–300 B.C.), Middle Persian (ca. 300 B.C.–A.D. 900), and New Persian or Farsi (ca. A.D. 900 to the present).

Persian literature is one of the great literatures of the world and perhaps no other great literature has been so little studied. So far most of the work has been on textual and historical questions. Studies of texts as literature virtually do not exist, and it is not possible to speak with any certainty about the development of Persian literature as a whole. The old overall notions are no longer satisfactory, but we do not know enough to put anything new in their place. Any general statements can only be extremely tentative.

The problems of Persian literature begin with the fundamental tools of research. There is neither an adequate grammar of classical Persian that includes the language of poetry nor a good, modern dictionary of the older language. There is no etymological dictionary of Persian and nothing comparable to the *Oxford English Dictionary*, a dictionary on historical principles with extensive illustrative citations. There is no adequate dictionary of the spoken language.

For Persian literature there is no series like the *Oxford English Texts* or *Les Classiques Français du Moyen Âge* or the *Bibliothèque de la Pléiade*. There are, in fact, extremely few good texts, even of major authors, an extremely small number of critical editions, and an even smaller number of texts with extensive commentaries and notes. There are almost no concordances. Some of those that exist are incomplete or based on imperfect texts. Prose texts are commonly not indexed or are provided with defective indexes. Many important works and important authors remain in manuscript, despite the very large number of texts that have been published in Tehran in the last twenty years, and many printed editions are produced in such small editions that to all effects these works are still in manuscript. In addition, many large collections of Persian manuscripts in Turkey and Iran have yet to be catalogued.

There has been almost no literary criticism of Persian by the writers themselves. In general, the best literary criticism has been written by poets, and it is unusual to find good literary criticism written by anyone who is not a writer. Such criticism is invaluable in helping us to understand not just the individual works but also the minds of writers and how they think about literature. We need only to consider how much can be learned about Greek literature from Aristotle's Poetics or about English poetry from the criticism of Dryden, Johnson, Coleridge, and Blackmur to appreciate what the absence of such work means to the study of Persian literature. There is virtually nothing in Persian like Sidney's *Defence of Poesy*, Wordsworth's preface to the *Lyrical Ballads* or Henry James's prefaces to the New York editions of his works. Not only is criticism by the writers themselves lacking, but there is very little of the other varieties of literary criticism. The *tadhkirāt* (collections of biographies) of poets contain usually only very general remarks about their poetry. The Persian books of rhetoric, imitated from Arabic models, define the rhetorical figures to be used in poetry, describe the different meters, and discuss rhyme, but beyond this, literary criticism is not a common form in Persian literature. Modern Persian literary criticism is an imitation of European criticism.

Moreover, in addition to the many specific problems presented by the literature as such, the present state of Persian studies makes it extremely difficult to place the work of any Persian author in the context of his culture. The history of the Iranian world has yet to be written in any detail, and our knowledge of most periods is general and uncertain. A better understanding of Persian literature waits upon a better understanding of the culture as a whole.

The greatness of Persian literature until the modern period rests upon the greatness of its poetry. The major subject of this poetry is love, both secular and religious love, sometimes treated separately, sometimes together. It is, on the whole, a learned poetry, part of a conservative written tradition and characterized by an interest in rhetorical figures, elaborate metaphors, and rigorous forms. The poets took pleasure in using the same forms over and over, reworking the same subjects and varying the same metaphors.

The basic units of Persian poetry are the *misrā'* and the *bait*. Each *bait* is composed of two *misrā'*s and consists of between eighteen and thirty-two syllables, depending on the meter. Neither the *misrā'* nor the *bait* exactly corresponds to the line in European poetry. All the *misrā'*s in a given poem are metrically identical, but all the feet in a given meter may not be the same. For example: ∪-∪-/∪∪--/∪-∪-/∪∪- is a common meter and constitutes one *misrā'*. The *bait* is the building block of most of the verse forms and the unit of thought, but the meter is defined in terms of the *misrā'*.

The Persians eventually adopted the Arabic system of quantitative meters after the Arab invasion (633), although the meters most commonly used in Arabic are not those most commonly used in Persian. The Persian system, like all quantitative systems, is a matter of convention and there are many syllables that may be either long or short depending on the meter. The division of the *misrā'* into syllables for the purposes of scansion ignores word boundaries.

The three most important poetic forms are the *qasīda*, *ghazal*, and *masnavī*. The *qasīda* and *ghazal* have the same rhyme scheme: the end of the first *misrā'* rhymes with the end of the second *misrā'*, but after this the rhyme occurs only at the end of the second *misrā'*. The same rhyme is used throughout, and sometimes in the *ghazal* the identical word or phrase is repeated. Most *qasīdas* are substantially longer than most *ghazals*, although there is no fixed length for either form. *Qasīdas* are usually between 10 and 200 *baits* and normally less than a 100 *baits*, while *ghazals* are rarely longer than 15 *baits*. The *qasīda* is the form of most of the archaic Arabic poetry and is commonly composed of two parts: an introduction and a panegyric. The early Arabic *qasīdas* usually open with a lament for something lost, the early Persian *qasīdas* are more often celebrations, but in time both become more and more taken up with the praise of rulers and their victories or other actions. Of the three forms, it is the *qasīda* that is most apt to make a specific reference to actual persons and events.

The *ghazal* is essentially a love lyric, although it is used for meditations on other subjects. It has a longer known history in Arabic than in Persian literature, but it is not certain that it is of Arabic origin. The form appears to enter Arabic literature after the Arab invasion of Persia, and although the actual word, *ghazal*, is Arabic, its first recorded use to mean a love song is in a poem attributed to Waddāh (d. ca. 705–15), who was probably a Persian. *Ghazals* rarely contain identifiable references to specific historical events of any kind; instead, they are occupied with emotion. They are intimate without being autobiographical. As the *ghazal* developed, it became a convention for the poet to name himself in the final *bait*. Thus, the poet's dialogue with himself becomes part of the form of the poem and the end of the poem is as clearly marked as the beginning.

The *masnavī* is the form of all very long Persian poems, as the monorhyme of the *qasīda* and *ghazal* imposes a certain limit on length. The rhyme scheme of the *masnavī* is: aa, bb, cc . . . , the end of every first *misrā'* rhyming with the end of every second *misrā'*. The rhyme is within the *bait* rather than between *baits*. The *masnavī* appears to have started as a narrative poem, and then to have absorbed an increasing amount of philosophical and/or religious material. As narratives they tend to be episodic and fantastic. They are journeys in the imagination rather than in the world, as if the poets found it difficult to expand any description by including more reality.

From the Arab Invasion to Nizāmī, 650–1200

The invasion of Persia by the Arabs, beginning with the capture of Hīra in 633, started a very complex process of change. The cultures of the Iranian world and of its invaders were transformed. The Islamic culture that resulted was a new creation, born out of the process of the Arab conquests.

To judge by such evidence as we have, the Persian language did not undergo any important changes in its phonology or basic structure between 600 and 900, and generally the rate of linguistic change over the past thousand years has been relatively slow. The poetry of Rūdakī (d. 940) is closer to the Persian spoken in

Tehran today than the poetry of Chaucer (d. 1400) is to the English being spoken in London. Although after the conquest the Persians adopted the Arabic script, New Persian is, in many ways, very close to Middle Persian.

The Persian language did, however, absorb an enormous Arabic vocabulary, as well as some syntactic forms, and the Persians adopted Arabic literature, which obviously means a significant change in how they thought about the world. The process is especially complicated because Persians writing in Arabic contributed so much to Arabic literature and because Persian literature may have affected Arabic literature in the pre-Islamic period.

Very little is known about the pre-Islamic poetry of Iran, but Persian poetry appears to have been transformed after the Arab conquest. The old meters were discarded in favor of an adaptation of the Arabic system, and poets composed using a new set of forms. None of the stanzaic forms of New Persian resemble those of Old and Middle Persian, and, perhaps more important, none of the most popular New Persian forms is stanzaic.

Arabic became the language of scientific work and of everything to do with religion. There were, however, many translations and summaries in Persian, especially after the tenth century, and there were always some specialists in these subjects who felt the need to compose in Persian, but, even so, until the last century, to be considered an educated person in Persia it was necessary to know Arabic.

Most of the earliest New Persian poetry can be dated between 800 and 900 and consists of fragments. Very few whole poems have survived. Most of the extant texts are citations in biographical works, books of rhetoric, dictionaries, and histories. They present many problems of authenticity, attribution, and interpretation. The richest source is 'Awfi's *Lubāb al-albāb* (1221/22), one of the oldest Persian biographical works and significantly about poets. The only major poet of the early period who can be identified is Rūdakī (d. 940), of whom about a thousand *baits* survive. The first poets by whom a substantial body of work exists are Firdawsī (d. ca. 1020), 'Unsurī (d. 1039/40), Farrukhī (d. 1037/38), and Manūchihrī (d. 1040/41). With the exception of Firdawsī, they are all known for their *qasīdas*.

The oldest surviving prose works of any extent in New Persian date from the tenth century. These are the preface to the prose *Shāhnāma* (957–58), all that remains of the work, made for the governor of Tūs, Abū Mansūr Muhammad; Bal'amī's adaptation of Tabarī's *History*; and the collective adaption of Tabarī's Qur'ān commentary (the last two made between 961 and 976). According to Lazard, the systematic employment of symmetrical phrases and striving for ornamentation that characterizes so much Persian prose does not become common until the end of the eleventh century. Among the more important early prose works are Nāsir-i Khusraw's account of his travels (1045–52), the *Safarnāma*; Abu'l-Fadl Muhammad Baihaqī's brilliant history of the Ghaznavids, known as *Tārīkh-i Baihaqī* (written ca. 1059–60); Nizām al-Mulk's discussion of the art of government, the *Siyāsatnāma* (1091–92); Kai Kā'ūs's advice to his son on how to live, the *Qābūsnāma* (1082–83); and Nizāmī 'Arūdī's collection of anecdotes, the *Chahār maqāla* [*The Four Discourses*] (ca. 1155–57).

The *Shāhnāma* [*The Book of Kings*] of Firdawsī has remained probably the most popular poem in the history of Persia. There are references to it throughout Persian literature, and it has been performed for hundreds of years by professional reciters, *shāhnāma-khvāns*. This immense work, a *masnavi* of over 60,000 *baits*, in a somewhat monotonous meter, is a combination of myth and history. It tells the story of Persia from the first man to the Arab invasion in terms of its kings and heroes. The kings are grouped in four dynasties: the Pīshdādī, Kayānī, Ashkānī, and Sāsānī. The first two are mythical, the last two historical. Although the story is told in chronological order, it is a loosely connected series of episodes and about a fifth of the poem is devoted to the reign of the Kayānid, Kay Khusraw. The heroes struggle against demons and dragons, and against their fate. The fatalism of Firdawsī is evident on virtually every page of the poem.

Next to nothing is known about Firdawsī's life. He was probably born about 934 and was an impecunious small landowner near Tūs. He knew the scholars and translators whom the governor of Tūs, Abū Mansūr Muhammad, summoned in 957 to collect the written and oral traditions necessary to make a New Persian version of the Middle Persian text (or texts) of the history of Iran, and he obviously shared their enthusiasm for the Iranian past. The prose *Shāhnāma* that they prepared seems to have been Firdawsī's major source, although he also appears to have relied on the oral tradition, as he mentions some of the scholars by name in his poem. Firdawsī probably began work on the *Shāhnāma* in about 975–76 and completed it in 1009–10. The poem, however, was started by another poet of Tūs, Daqīqī (d. between 976 and 981), and Firdawsī incorporates about a thousand *baits* of Daqīqī's work.

The greatest writer of *masnavīs*, after Firdawsī, is Nizāmī (1141–1209), who spent virtually his whole life in his birthplace, in Ganja (Azerbaijan S. S. R.). His mother and father died when he was a child; nevertheless, he received, on the evidence of his poems, an excellent education. Instead of composing one long poem like Firdawsī, Nizāmī wrote five separate poems, each in a different meter. These came to be known as the *Khamsa* [*The Five*]. They are *Makhzan al-asrār* [*The Treasury of Secrets*], a philosophical poem in imitation of Sanā'ī's *Hadīqat al-haqīqa* [*The Garden of Truth*] (1141?); *Khusraw u Shīrīn*, a reworking of one of the stories in the *Shāhnāma* (117–81); *Laylā u Majnūn*, the old Arabic love story, a subject chosen for the poet by a patron (1188–9?); *Haft paykar* [*The Seven Portraits*], which describes Bahrām Gur's wooing of seven princesses, each of whom tells him various stories (1197); and the *Iskandarnāma*, the story of Alexander the Great, also found in the *Shāhnāma* (1191?, 1200–1?). The last four poems contain about 7,000, 4,000, 5,000, and 10,000 *baits*, respectively.

There are a number of changes that take place in lyric poetry at about this time. The *qasīdas* of Anvarī (d. ca. 1169/70) and Khāqānī (d. ca. 1199) are more ornate, more complicated and more difficult than those of Farrukhī and Manūchihrī. These poems show a serious use and deliberate display of learning that is absent in the work of most earlier poets. Sūfism becomes widely diffused through Persian poetry—and Persian culture as a whole—after Sanā'ī (d. 1141?), who is said to be the first major Sūfi poet. Sūfism offers a set of terms with which to order and map the inner world. It furnished poets with new metaphors and opened up new areas of fantasy at the same time that it encouraged greater emotion and greater abstraction.

There was also a change from the *qasīda* to the *ghazal*. Farrukhī, Manū-chihrī, Anvarī, and Khāqānī are known for their *qasīdas*. The great poets who follow them, Rūmī, Sa'dī, and Hāfiz, wrote hundreds of *ghazals* and very few *qasīdas*. This change can be observed in the *Dīvān* [Collected Poems] of Nizāmī, where there are 194 *ghazals* and 17 *qasīdas* (although a substantial number of poems may have been lost). This shift is from a longer to a shorter form. It represents a preference for condensation and terseness, for the abstract and the lyrical. There are less physical descriptions, fewer references to historical events, and less emphasis on knowledge. Poets appear to become more inward looking and to concern themselves more directly with feeling.

Rūmī to Hāfiz, 1200–1400

The new interest in Sūfism is exemplified in the works of 'Attār (d. 1220). He is best known for his long poems and his biographies of mystics, the *Tadhkirat al-awliyā*, although he composed many lyric poems and made a selection of some of his own best quatrains, the *Mukhtārnāma*. His *Dīvān*, even more than that of Nizāmī, shows the turning away from the *qasīda* in favor of the *ghazal*: it contains 27 *qasīdas* and 794 *ghazals*. Recent work by S. Nafīsī (1941) and H. Ritter (1939 and 1955–61) has rejected as spurious most of the many works attributed to 'Attār and has established him as the author of at least six *masnavīs*: the *Khusrawnāma*; the *Mantiq al-tair* [*The Language of the Birds*], probably his most famous poem, a work of over 4,600 *baits*; the *Ilāhīnāma* [*The Book of God*]; the *Musībatnāma* [*The Book of Affliction*]; the *Asrārnāma* [*The Book of Secrets*]; and the *Pandnāma* [*The Book of Advice*]. 'Attār's major subject in these poems, as in all his works, is the search for religious experience.

Perhaps the three greatest Persian lyric poets are Rūmī (d. 1273/74), Sa'dī (d. 1292), and Hāfiz (d. 1389/90). Rūmī's career spans the Iranian world, showing the wide diffusion of Persian culture and the openness of the Islamic culture as a whole at that time. He was born in Balkh in 1207, the son of a well-known preacher who allegedly had to emigrate in 1217 because of the anger of the Khwārizmshāh. The family lived in various towns in western Turkey, and finally in 1228 settled in Konya. Rūmī devoted himself to religious studies and became a Sūfī master with many disciples. An extremely prolific poet, he is the author of 5,498 poems. This includes his famous long poem of 27,000 *baits* that is known simply as *the Masnavī*. Composed with the *masnavīs* of Sanā'ī and 'Attār in mind, it is an amorphous work made up of many short sections, combining anecdotes of different kinds, philosophic passages, and lyric passages. His short poems are full of the longing for the other world and his love for his master and friend, *Shams al-Dīn Tabrīzī*. They are reworkings of fantasies and what happens in them happens according to the laws of fantasy.

The chronology of Sa'dī's life, like that of 'Attār, presents many problems and has been radically revised in recent years. He is now thought to have been born in Shīrāz, probably between 1213 and 1219, and to have died there in 1292. As a young man he studied at the famous theological college, the Nizāmiyya, in Baghdad, and it is possible that he may have traveled extensively in the Near

East before returning to Shīrāz in 1257. Upon his return, he composed the *Būstān* [*The Garden*] (1257), a *masnavī*, and the *Gulistān* [*The Rose Garden*] (1258), the latter a series of very short anecdotes narrated in a terse and elegant prose, alternating with apposite and summary *baits* of poetry. A good proportion of the stories advocate a distrust of other people and a morality of ruthless self-interest in the name of survival. The *Gulistān* is perhaps the most widely known and often quoted of all Persian prose works and is still held up as a model of good style. Sa'dī's uncomplicated and melodious *ghazals* show the same love of simplicity and elegance as his prose. They are love poems that are wholly within the conventions of the tradition.

The greatest Persian lyric poet is Hāfiz (d. 1389–90). Unlike Rūmī, he is a poet of this world rather than of the world of fantasy, and both his hate and his love are fiercer than the passions of Sa'dī. His sense of the transience of things is a passion, and yet whatever his losses or his fears, they seem mitigated by the completeness of his pleasures. He often combines a number of subjects in a single *ghazal*, as if he took pleasure in the rigors of the *ghazal* as a form, but wished to test all of its possibilities. The energy, the timing, and the feeling of his poems are unmatched in Persian poetry.

Hāfiz appears to have spent virtually the whole of his life in Shīrāz and to have been known as a professional Qur'ān reader. The friend who collected his poems tells us that the poet was too preoccupied with his studies to gather them together himself. Hāfiz's poems were popular throughout the Iranian world during his lifetime (or soon after), and even today in Iran his *Dīvān* is the only book, besides the Qur'ān, used to tell fortunes.

Jāmī to Sā'ib, 1400–1700

The poets before Hāfiz are greater than those after. There is a certain uniformity about the work of those who follow Hāfiz, a sameness that persists until the modern rejection of classical models. They appear more concerned to imitate the tradition than to re-create it, although many of the poets of the so-called Indian style, what Bahār calls *sabk-i hindī*, seem to want to go beyond the tradition by their extravagance and by the sheer elaborateness of their fantasies. When, at the end of the eighteenth century, the poets in Isfahan urged a *bāzgasht* or a return to the poetry of the earliest periods down to Hāfiz, it was almost as if they realized that after Hāfiz something important had been lost.

Between 1370 and 1405, Tīmūr conquered virtually the whole Iranian world. He put an end to the rule of the Chagata Mogols in the east, to the Muzaffarids in the south, and to the Jalāyirids in the west. He is said to have been responsible for an enormous amount of destruction, and certainly his armies were destructive, but as yet it is impossible either to estimate the total amount of damage and disorder that was caused or its effect on his contemporaries.

There was a large amount of literary activity at the brilliant Timurid courts of Samarqand and Herat during the rule of Tīmūr's son, Shāhrukh (1405–47) and his son Husain Bāyqarā (1469–1506), but only one great poet, 'Abd al-Rahmān Jāmī (1414–92). The idea that Jāmī is the last great classical poet derives from

Dawlatshāh's *Tadhkirat al-shuʿarā* (ca. 1474–86). He is the last major poet discussed by Dawlatshāh. Jāmī, who was very famous in his lifetime and had a high opinion of himself, was an extremely prolific author and wrote on a great variety of subjects. He spent most of his life in Herat and was a member of the Naqshbandī dervish or mystical order. He is called Jāmī after the town Jām in Khurasan where he was born, but *jām* is also the ordinary word for a wine cup in Persian poetry, and Jāmī obviously enjoyed playing with his own name in his lyrics. He seems to take for granted the existence of two worlds. His *ghazals* on mystical subjects lack the passion of Rūmī.

Jāmī's self-interest gave him some notion of his own development, as he recorded, unusually, the dates when most of his works were composed and collected his shorter poems into three *dīvāns*, according to whether they were composed during the beginning, middle, or end of his life. These *dīvāns* were edited in 1479/80, 1489, and 1490/91, respectively.

He also wrote seven long poems known as the *Haft awrang* [*The Seven Thrones*], one of the names of the constellation of the Great Bear; *Silsilat al-dhahab* [*The Chain of Gold*], the first part composed in 1468–72; *Salāmān u Absāl*; *Tuhfat al-ahrār* [*The Gift of the Noble*] (1481); *Subhat al-abrār* [*The Rosary of the Pious*] (1482); *Yūsuf u Zulaikhā* (1483), perhaps his most popular work; *Lailā u Majnūn* (1484); and *Khiradnāma-yi Sikandar* [*The Book of the Wisdom of Alexander*] (1485). This group of poems was written in imitation of Nizāmī's *Khamsa*, although only in the *Tuhfat al-ahrār*, *Layla u Majnūn*, and *Khiradnāma-yi Sikandar* does Jāmī take up the same subjects as Nizāmī. Jāmī appears to have felt that the great writers of the past were his rivals and to have imitated them in order to compete with them. He may have written seven *masnavīs* in order to show that he could surpass Nizāmī.

During this period, Nizāmī's long poems were imitated more than those of any other poet. The *Khamsa* shaped everyone's notions of what a long poem should be and presented the idea of a set of long poems as a goal to which every poet should aspire. Kātibī Turshīzī (d. ca. 1485) completed two of his five poems. Hātifī (d. 1520) wrote four, Hilālī (d. 1529), three, and ʿUrfī (d. 1590/91) two, while Faidī (d. 1595) wrote a complete set.

Jāmī's two best known prose works are the *Nafahāt al-uns* [*The Breath of Friendship*], a collection of Sūfī biographies composed in 1480, and the *Bahāristān* [*The Garden of Spring*], an imitation of Saʿdī's *Gulistān*, composed in 1487.

Many of the most important prose works of this period are histories and collections of biographies. They include: Nizām al-Dīn Shāmī's history of Tīmūr's reign, the *Zafarnāma* [*The Book of Victory*] (1401/02–04), which is remarkable for its straightforward style and its use of primary sources; Hāfiz Abrū's *Majmaʿ al-tavārīkh* [*The Collection of the Histories*], a history of the world up to 1416 (completed in 1427); Mīrkhvānd's *Rawdat al-safā* [*The Garden of Purity*], until recently perhaps the most widely read of the Persian world histories; Khvānda-mīr's *Tārīkh-i Habīb al-siyar* [*The History of the Friend of Biographies*] (1521–24), another world history, and Iskandar Munshī's *Tārīkh-i ʿĀlamārā-yi ʿAbbāsī* [*The World-adorning History of ʿAbbās*], a history of the Safavids to the death of Shāh ʿAbbās. Husain Vāʿiz's reworking of *Kalīla u Dimna* in his *Anvār-i Suhailī* [*The Lights of Canopus*] is famous for its elaborate ornateness. Vāʿiz, who died in 1504–05, describes a mouse squeaking as "raising its outcry to the aetherial sphere." The most important writer on philosophical subjects is probably Mullā Sadrā (d. 1640–41).

The literature of the Safavid period (1501–1722) is now rarely read, and Browne speaks of "the extraordinary dearth of notable poets in Persia" during this time. The standard explanation of this phenomenon is that given by Qazvīnī in 1924: that the Safavid rulers "devoted the greater part of their energies to the propagation of the Shī'a doctrine and the encouragement of divines learned in its principles and laws." He argues that their persecution of Sūfism, because of its close connection with literature in Persia, also meant the destruction of literature, and especially of poetry. The period remains, however, largely unknown. Rypka, looking at its poetry in 1959, finds "an endless variety of names. The works of those poets have unfortunately not yet been thoroughly studied, so that for the present the names remain practically without significance."

Many Persian poets and men of letters emigrated to India in order to enjoy the patronage of the Mughal court. The most notable poet of the period is Sā'ib (d. 1677/78), who, although he did go to India, returned to spend most of his life in Isfahan and to be the chief poet of Shāh 'Abbās II. His *ghazals* represent his best work.

Modern Literature, 1700 to the Present

All modern literature is essentially European literature, and it has come into being in non-European cultures as the result of deep and radical changes that are still continuing and that involve the very nature of those cultures. The development of modern Persian literature is not simply a Persian phenomenon, but part of the whole history of the absorption of European culture by the Islamic cultures of the Near East. From about 1500 until about 1800, the Near East was virtually a closed system, but Bonaparte's invasion of Egypt demonstrated the weakness of the Ottoman Empire and marks the end of this self-isolation.

The advent of European ideas represents the greatest change in Persian culture since the Arab invasion, a change so great that the Persians briefly adopted (1905–21) a form of democratic government for the only time in their history. The process of Europeanization, however, was intensified after Riza Shah's coup d'état in 1921, and the rate of change in the last two generations probably has been more rapid than at any time in the last two thousand years. Europeanization was not forced upon Iran by European nations, but has been chosen by the Persians themselves; and when force has been used it has been used by the Persian government to impose European ways on the Persian nation. The appeal of European culture has been primarily to the best educated and the most powerful, and to the majority of them it has been irresistible.

The Persian awareness of Europe is graphically portrayed in the paintings in the main room of the Chihil Sutūn, one of the garden pavilions of the Safavid palace complex at Isfahan. The scene of Shah Tahmāsp (1523–76) receiving the Mughal Emperor Humāyūn is balanced by one of Shah 'Abbās (1581–1629) receiving a European ambassador. Thus are presented the two major powers on the peripheries of the Iranian world. That this is not simply a confrontation is revealed by the figure of a prince in another painting. He is shown hunting in European dress, and this is an image of the future. The realism of later Safavid painting, with its greater attention to individual figures, developed under the influence of European pictures. Persians were starting to look at the world through European eyes.

The beginnings of the reform of Persian institutions on European models is associated with 'Abbās Mīrzā (d. 1833), the son and heir of Fath 'Alī Shah. As governor of Azerbaijan, he sent men to London to learn printing and to St. Petersburg to learn lithography. He established a printing press in Tabrīz in 1816/17 and soon afterward another was set up in Tehran. The first printing business was opened in Tabriz in 1824/25 and in Tehran about 1837/38. Printing was slow to become popular, because lithography was at first preferred to print (perhaps because it had the look of handwriting). This attachment to the tradition can also be seen in the first lithographed book produced in Tehran, the *Kulliyyāt-i Hāfiz*, the poet's collected works.

More changes were introduced in the reign of Nāsir al-Dīn Shah (1848–96): the telegraph, a postal service, regular newspapers (from 1851; the first seems to have appeared for a short time in 1839) and a system of roads—a new network of communications that fostered a new sense of national unity and provided the means of widely diffusing new ideas. The Shah founded in Tehran in 1851 his own center for the study and creation of European ideas: the Dār al-Funūn, an Ecole Polytechnique with a European curriculum and a number of European teachers. The teachers at the school, European and Persian, and subsequently their students, were the authors of the first wave of translations and adaptations of European books into Persian. The first recorded dramatic performances, other than the Shī'ī passion plays were staged in the Dār al-Funūn.

The government at this time also started to provide scholarships for students to study in Europe and others were sent by their families. Not only did young people desire to do this, but their parents wanted them to go. There are new attitudes in both young and old. The Shah's own visits to Europe in 1873, 1878, and 1889 indicated the direction in which the country was looking for the future.

The transformation of Persian literature can be said to begin with the generation of Nāsir al-Dīn Shah (b. 1831). Mīrzā Malkum Khān (1833–1908), who helped to create a simpler, discursive prose style and the modern Persian vocabulary by writing about the need for reform, is typical of the new writers. Born of Armenian parents, he was educated in Europe, taught at the Dār al-Funūn, published a Persian newspaper in London that was banned by the government, and composed many essays, mostly on political subjects (the four plays that have been attributed to Malkum Khān are in fact by Mīrzā Āqā Tabrīzī, see H. Algar, *Mirza Malkum Khan* [Berkeley 1973], pp. 264–77). The author of the first Persian novel, *Siyāhatnāma-yi Ibrāhīm Beg* [*The Travels of Ibrāhīm Beg*] Hājj Zain al-'Ābidīn (1837–1910), lived most of his life in Russia and Turkey, and his novel was banned because of its criticisms of the conditions in Iran. 'Abd al-Rahīm Najjār-zāda (1855–1910), who wrote under the names of Tālibov and Tālibzāda, made his reputation by writing popular books about European science and political ideas. He lived most of his life in the Caucasus. Thus, all three men were in some sense outsiders, and thereby especially prepared to act as interpreters between the old culture and the new.

Riẓā Shah (1878–1944) made his country break with the immediate past and find a new identity. The life of every individual was changed. This was literally a new time: instead of the Islamic religious calendar, one based rather on ancient Iranian practice was adopted. The months received Persian rather than Arabic names, and a solar rather than a lunar year was employed. The old Qājār titles were abolished and the European style of personal names was introduced. Everyone had to choose a surname, and men and women were addressed as *Āqā* and *Khānum* [Mr. and Mrs.]. Riẓā Shah decreed in 1928 that European clothes were compulsory for men, and in 1936 that women should no longer wear a veil. He established a national system of primary, secondary, university, and adult education, a new code of laws and a secular judiciary. He had a railway built from the Caspian Sea to the Persian Gulf, and drafted a plan for the economic development of the country.

The major literary consequences of this process of Europeanization are as follows: The old poetry has been almost entirely abandoned, and although a new poetry has not been able to fully establish itself, most of the best poetry is now being written in free verse and in various stanzaic forms. Perhaps the first major poet to make a radical break with the tradition is Nīmā Yushīj (1895–1960), although during the period of the Constitution the multitude of political poems, mostly published in the newspapers, meant that the old forms were overwhelmed by new content. Instead of accepting the traditional style, each poet now seeks his own personal style.

The most important authors of the last two hundred years have been prose writers, not poets. Compared with most of the earlier prose, modern Persian prose is simpler, less ornamental, more colloquial and contains a large number of new and foreign words. *Saj'* [rhymed prose] is rarely written now and Arabic words are not a staple element in the same way as they were formerly. The great Islamic scholar, Sir Hamilton Gibb, has stated that "the part played by journalism in the development of modern Arabic literature is almost impossible to over-estimate," and the same is true of modern Persian literature. The article, the essay, and the nonfiction book are all forms that have emerged with journalism and, together with newspapers themselves, have been adopted from Europe; moreover, the discursive prose created to argue for reform has also been employed in the writing of fiction.

Perhaps the most important achievements of modern Persian literature have been in the short story and in the novel. Both are European forms, although Persian literature has a very long and rich tradition of story-telling and the modern works can be seen as a continuation of this tradition in other terms. Here, unlike poetry, it has been easier to maintain continuity and fruitful contact with the old.

This connection is clearly demonstrated by the title of one of the most important modern books of short stories, *Yakī būd yakī nabūd* (1921) by Muḥammad 'Alī Jamālzāda. It is the Persian equivalent of "Once upon a time" and is the traditional beginning of the Persian story-teller, which Jamālzāda uses to present satiric, realistic stories of everyday life in Persia and, according to

Kamshad, "to introduce the techniques of European short-story writing" into Persian literature. Jamālzāda's work is characterized by his effort to have his characters speak authentic colloquial Persian and to include its wealth of idioms. The bringing together of the written and spoken languages was one of the major purposes and achievements of modern Persian writers, and it has happened in poetry as well as in prose.

The greatest modern Persian writer is Sādiq Hidāyat (1903–51). He was a member of a rich and powerful family that held some of the highest places in the Qājār administration. His father was Dean of the Military Academy, his grandfather was a minister and his great-grandfather, Riżā Qulī Khān (1800–72), was the poet laureate, the tutor of Muzaffar al-Dīn Shah, and the director of the Dār al-Funūn. As a young man, Sādiq Hidāyat studied in France, and it was to Paris that he returned at the age of forty-eight and finally killed himself. He is the author of short stories, novels, plays, essays on a variety of subjects, translations from the French, and studies of Middle Persian texts. Hidāyat writes with great economy and lucidity, and there is no Persian writer with a better ear for speech. He is a sharp observer, particularly interested in the lives of the poorest people and in those who are somehow isolated. He has a great empathy for other people, but most of his stories are studies of loneliness. Even when it is neither sardonic nor blackly pessimistic, his work has an aura of sadness and its realism is frequently allied with horrific fantasies.

Among contemporary writers, the most important are probably Buzurg ʿAlavī (b. 1907), Sādiq Chūbak (b. 1916), Jalāl Āl-i Ahmad (1923–69), and ʿAli Muhammad Afghānī (b. 1925). The first three are known for both their short stories and their novels, while Afghānī's reputation so far rests on his very long novel about life in Kirmanshah, *Shawhar-i Āhū Khānum* [*The Husband of Āhū Khānum*] (1961), which has been called by some "the greatest Persian novel."

Selected Bibliography

E. G. Browne's *A Literary History of Persia*, 4 vols., Cambridge, 1902–24, is still the best history of Persian literature, but also valuable are Shiblī Nuʿmānī, *Shiʿr al-ʿAjam*, Persian translation by M. Gīlānī, 5 vols., Tehran, 2nd edition, 1956; Z. Safa, *Tārīkh-i adabiyyāt dar Irān*, 3 vols. to date, Tehran, 1953–; A. Pagliaro and A. Bausani, *Storia della letteratura persiana*, Milan, 1960; and the articles on literature in *The Cambridge History of Iran*, 4 and 5 to date, Cambridge, 1975–. J. Rypka's *History of Iranian Literature*, Dordrecht, 1968, contains a useful bibliography and can serve as a work of reference, but the historical interpretation is very unsatisfactory. The best general reference work is the *Encyclopaedia of Islām*. The new edition, Leiden, 1954–, has not yet superseded the old one (4 vols. and Supplement, Leiden, 1913–42).

C. A. Storey's unfinished *Persian Literature*, London, 1927–39, provides short biographies of authors and lists the MSS and editions of their works (excluding poetry). Yu. E. Bregel and Yu. E. Borschchevsky are preparing a revised and corrected Russian translation, with additional material to bring the work up to date, 3 vols. so far, Moscow, 1972–. Khān Bābā Mushār's *Fihrist-i Kitābhā-yi chāpī fārsī*, 3 vols., Tehran, 2nd edition, 1971–73, is a list of Persian printed books. Articles in European langauges on specific subjects can be located with the help of J. D. Pearson's *Index Islamicus, 1906–1955*,

Cambridge, 1958, and supplements (1962–); and in Persian with Iraj Afshār's *Index Iranicus*, 1, 1910–58, Tehran, 1961; and 2, 1959–66, Tehran, 1969.

On poetry, see G. Lazard, *Les premiers poétes persans*, 2 vols., Paris and Tehran, 1964; J. W. Clinton, *The Divan of Manūchihrī Dāmghānī*, Minneapolis, 1972; Hellmut Ritter, *Über die Bildersprache Nizāmīs*, Berlin, 1927; and his study of 'Attār, *Das Meer der Seele*, Leiden, 1955; and R. M. Rehder's "The Style of Jalāl al-Dīn Rūmī," in *The Scholar and the Saint*, P. Chelkowski, New York, 1975, pp. 275–85, and his "The Unity of the Ghazals of Hāfiz," *Der Islam* 51 (1974): 55–96. On prose, see M. Bahār, *Sabkshināsī*, 3 vols., Tehran, 1958; and H. Kamshad, *Modern Persian Prose Literature*, Cambridge, 1968.

PART FOUR

Arts and Society in the Persian Gulf

15. Societies and Social Change in the Persian Gulf RALPH H. MAGNUS

Societies in the Persian Gulf reflect to an exaggerated degree the duality of the contemporary Middle East. They encompass, at one and the same time, some of the most "modern" aspects of technologically advanced Western civilization—most notably, of course, in the petroleum industry—alongside some of the strongest examples of religiously oriented conservatism, tribalism, and "traditionalism" still extant in the Middle East. The concepts of "traditionalism" and "modernity," however, need to be much more clearly defined before they can be used without physical or mental quotation.[1]

The broadest possible system of classification of Persian Gulf traditionalism involves at least four different forms of societal organization, each an equally valid and distinct representative of the general category of "traditionalism": desert patriarchal systems, urban imperial systems, tribal city-states, and theocratic communities.

Traditionalism in the region was thus a very complex phenomenon even before the impact of Western political, economic, and social forces. Since that time, and especially in the last few decades, Persian Gulf traditionalism has become still more complex as it has absorbed and integrated into its structure a number of modern innovations, while remaining essentially traditional at its core. Formal constitutional arrangements are certainly not, in themselves, a true measure of the strength of traditionalism in a Middle Eastern state. However, one cannot but be impressed by the fact that outside of the Persian Gulf there are but two monarchies remaining in the Middle East (Morocco and Jordan), while around it there is but a single republican regime—Iraq. This suggests that, at least to date, the traditional political leadership of the Persian Gulf states has been much more successful in adapting, integrating, and controlling the often disruptive forces of change in the areas than have other traditional Middle Eastern leaders.

1. An excellent discussion of this issue can be found in S. N. Eisenstadt, "Convergence and divergence of modern and modernizing societies: Indications from the analysis of the structuring of social hierarchies in Middle Eastern societies," *International Journal of Middle East Studies* 8 (1977): 1–27. See also Carl Leiden, ed., *The Conflict of Traditionalism and Modernism in the Muslim Middle East* (Austin, 1969). A more general discussion can be found in S. N. Eisenstadt, *Tradition, Change and Modernity* (New York, 1973).

The Persian Gulf region maintained its traditionalist characteristics in the early years of the modernization process through being a region of little significance to either Middle Eastern reformers or foreign imperialists. Once it became an area of increasing importance, especially following World War II, both the traditional rulers and the Western oil concessionaires had powerful incentives and common interests in preserving the existing political, economic, and social order, or at least in seeing that the inevitable changes brought about by the development of the industry did not upset their political control. Through their oil revenues, provided they were wisely used, they had the resources to carry out programs designed to ensure these results.

Throughout the Arab world there has been an increasing distaste for empty revolutionary rhetoric and, indeed, a turning back toward its Islamic heritage (Libya, however, since its revolution in 1969, has attempted to combine Islam and revolution). This has been accompanied by an appreciation of the successes of the traditional rulers of the Persian Gulf states in the transformation of their countries in a peaceful and evolutionary manner into societies that were in many respects simultaneously Islamic, national, and "modern" in the Western sense. Through an extraordinary combination of circumstances, the Persian Gulf states, preserved as a "quaint museum" of traditionalism in the midst of the waves of rapid political, economic, and social change sweeping the Middle East in the twentieth century, began to emerge in the 1970s as a plausible model for the Middle East of the future—a Middle East that would preserve and reconcile its traditional heritage with its contemporary problems and opportunities.

Major Social Groups and Institutions

Religions. Due to its comprehensiveness (it is simultaneously an intellectual system of thought, a religious system of belief, and a sociolegal system for the detailed and proper ordering of society), Islam must be studied closely for the understanding of Persian Gulf societies. In the words of one scholar: "Any attempt to 'diagnose the situation' within Muslim Middle Eastern societies without taking into account the ubiquitous influence of Islam would produce only sterile and distorted images of social reality."[2]

This very comprehensiveness, however, makes it difficult for Westerners, in particular, to assess its social impact. In the West, even at the zenith of the societal influence of the Christian church during the Middle Ages, a distinction between the legitimate spheres of authority of secular and religious institutions ultimately was preserved.[3] The ideal of the Islamic community, the *umma*, was to deny any such division of authority. It was, rather, to achieve a community embracing all believers in a brotherhood as closely knit and perfectly regulated as was the medieval Christian monastery for its monks.

The well-known characteristics of Islam: its universalism, uncompromising

---

2. Richard Pfaff, "Technicism vs. Traditionalism: The Developmental Dialectic in the Middle East," in C. Leiden, ed., *Traditionalism and Modernism*, p. 102.
3. Otto von Gierke, *Political Theories of the Middle Ages* (Boston, 1958), pp. 10–11.

monotheism, simplicity of fundamental doctrines, lack of a priestly hierarchy, and its transmission through a series of prophets, ending in the revelation to the Prophet of the Qur'ān as the final word of God, have made it highly resistant to overt change. Yet these very characteristics assure that its concrete forms, inevitably, will vary. "The very comprehensiveness of the vision of Islam as it is unfolded has insured that it can never be quite the same from one place or one time to another . . . Islam and its associated lifeways form a cultural tradition, and a cultural tradition by its nature grows and changes, the more so, the broader its scope."[4] To the Muslim, however, these changes are seen only as further manifestations of the universality and timelessness of Islam, and thus are integrated into its cultural tradition.

In the social sphere, Islam holds to an ideal of a universal community of equal believers, differentiated only by degrees of their individual piety. Despite all of the real social divisions between tribes, classes, and nations, the ideal of the *umma* has served as a powerful force for equality. The religious duty of the *hajj*, or pilgrimage to Mecca, incumbent once in a lifetime on all Muslims having good health and sufficient means, each year serves as a reminder of the egalitarian and communal nature of Islam. Pilgrims from every corner of the globe assemble at the same place and perform the same ritual, while wearing identical garments, demonstrating their devotion and equality before God.

As a literate religion, based upon written revelation amplified by traditions (*hadīth*) of the Prophet, Islamic religious institutions developed around the *'ulamā'*, a class of pious and learned scholars who studied, maintained, interpreted and transmitted its written word from generation to generation, thus providing authoritative guidance to the Muslims as to the correct behavior required of them. They have been the key group maintaining Islam as a more or less unified system of beliefs and behavior and rejecting all deviation and innovation. Perhaps more than any other social group, the *'ulamā'* have benefited from the nonhierarchical nature of Islam. An elite based upon scholarship, with a relatively open recruitment process and diverse sources of training and self-regulating in its discipline, it has remained generally beyond the control of any particular political, social, or economic group that has sought to use it for its own ends.

A necessary, and at times unfortunate, corollary of this independence of the *'ulamā'* has been the splitting of Islamic unity into competitive and at times violently hostile sects. As Islam was unable to conceive of the idea of a secular state, political disputes came to be argued in religious terms and religious arguments took on the aspects of political conflict and violence. Most of the major religious schools and sects of Islam are represented in the Persian Gulf region, and, in particular, the division between the Shī'ī establishment of Iran (the state sect of Islam since the sixteenth century) versus the predominantly Sunnī governments and populations of the Arab states constitutes a fundamental cleavage in the region. In the mountains of Oman, the majority are members of a branch of the Khārijite sect, the Ibādīs, who have repeatedly established their own communal religious state under an elected *Imām*. Around the Persian Gulf, therefore,

4. Marshall G. S. Hodgson, *The Venture of Islam*, vol. 1, *The Classical Age of Islam* (Chicago, 1974), p. 79.

there are representatives of the three major branches of Islamic thought to develop during the first century of its existence: the Shī'īs, who believe that the only true successors to the Prophet as leader of the Islamic community are his nephew and son-in-law, 'Alī and his descendants; the Sunnīs, who believe that the successors of the Prophet must be elected from among his tribe, the Quraish, by the pious and learned leaders and scholars; and the Khārijites, who believe that the successors of the Prophet are to be elected from the entire body of the community, regardless of their relationship to Muhammad.[5]

Sectarian differences have had important political and social, as well as religious, consequences within the Islamic community from its earliest days to the present. Nevertheless, Islam has maintained its essential unity as a religion and way of life. The *'ulamā'*, of whatever school or sect, taught that Islam remains united; to do otherwise would be un-Islamic. The average believer finds that the similarities perceived between the fundamental religious beliefs and practices of all Muslims cause them to feel at home in any Muslim country, and to disregard the finer points of theological disputes.

Despite their crucial role as carriers of Islamic civilization, the *'ulamā'* were forced to compromise upon two fronts. The first challenge came from what we would define as secular power. Powerful military and political leaders, often of non-Arab origin (Turkish and Persian), but sometimes of rival Arab families ('Abbasids and Umayyads), contended for the leadership of the community. In order to preserve the theoretical unity of the *umma* and to check the excesses of the *de facto* political rulers, the *'ulamā'* began to legitimize whoever happened to be the effective ruler at a given time and place. This view was explained by the great theologian al-Ghazālī (A.D. 1058–1111). He held that some government was necessary to provide order in the community and that any form of order was to be preferred to anarchy. Thus, any ruler who professes Islam and protects Islamic law and institutions must be considered to be legitimate, regardless of his origins.[6]

The second challenge came from the opposite pole of society—from the masses rather than the elites. Popular religious feeling and enthusiasm demanded its own channels of expression, apart from the dry, legalistic scholarship of the *'ulamā'*. Often this expression took the form of mysticism in organized groups of *Sūfīs*.[7] Another form of popular involvement in religion came from reform and

5. The essence of *Khawārij* theory is given in H. A. R. Gibb and J. H. Kramers, eds., *Shorter Encyclopedia of Islam* (Leiden, 1961), p. 248. The article "Khāridjites" explains ". . . they declare every believer who is morally and religiously irreproachable to be capable of being raised by the vote of the community to the supreme dignity of the inamate 'even if he were a black slave'." There were, to be sure, other issues dividing the sects of Islam, but the question of the legitimate leadership of the *umma* was one of the most divisive.

6. E. I. J. Rosenthal, *Political Thought in Medieval Islam* (Cambridge, 1962), pp. 38–42. The fullest exposition of al-Ghazālī's political thought in English can be found in Leonard Binder, "Al-Ghazzali's Theory of Islamic Government," *The Muslim World* (1955) 45: 229–41. See also F. R. C. Bagley, translator and editor, *Nasīhat al-Mulūk: Ghazālī's Book of Counsel for Kings* (London, 1964).

7. Sūfism has performed a myriad of different social functions at different times and places. At times, certain Sūfī orders (*tarīqas*, Ar.: path, road, way) following the teachings of a particular *shaikh* would become the allies of the *'ulamā'* and, virtually, part of the state. Fundamentally, however, they represented a mystical and popular reaction to the legalistic formalism of the establishment *'ulamā'*. See J. Spencer Trimingham, *The Sufi Orders in Islam* (London, 1971).

revival movements, which sought to recapture the purity and enthusiasm of the earliest Islamic community through the strictest application of the *Shari'a*. Sometimes the leaders of these revival movements would claim to be the Mahdī, an individual especially sent and "guided" by God to restore the true faith.

The predominant pattern for the traditional Islamic state in the Middle East was for a political leader to proclaim himself as the protector of Islam and then be accorded religious legitimacy by more or less independent *'ulamā'* through the mentioning of his name in the *khutba* (the sermon given before Friday service). Secondarily, there were rulers whose legitimacy stemmed from their leadership of a religious order or reform movement or from personal religious status (such as the Shī'ī Imams).

Family. The basic characteristics of the family and family life have remained stable in Islamic societies throughout the Middle East from the earliest times. Indeed, these characteristics often predate Islam and have been only slightly modified by it. "With few exceptions," writes Raphael Patai, "the traditional family exhibits identical basic characteristics all over the Middle East."[8] These characteristics and their codification in the *Shari'a* have been the most persistent of traditional social institutions to the present day. Family law has been the least modified of all legal codes by modern legislation, and the general practices can hardly be said to keep up with even the changes in the codes. This isolation of the family from political interference and control is probably the most important single characteristic of the Middle Eastern family and has given it immense strength and persistence from generation to generation. Only in this century have some Persian Gulf governments presumed to interfere in the regulation of family life; these efforts have been hesitant and of dubious effect at best.

The traditional family is generally an extended unit, with several generations living together, often in the same house. Married sons with their wives and children live there, as well as unmarried sons and daughters. The extended family forms a single economic unit, property being held in common. This extended family is patrilineal; a person belongs to the family of his father. Daughters, however, marry into the family of their husband. However, since the preferred marriage is between first cousins born of brothers, this often means that the husband and wife are of the same extended family.[9] The family also is patrilocal. Upon marriage, the sons bring their brides to live with or near (at least in the same village as) their father, thus strengthening the extended family.

Another important social characteristic of the traditional family is that it is patriarchal. The undisputed head of the family is the eldest male of the senior generation. At times, this authority of the head of the family extends to the power of life and death over family members. In any case, it means that the approval of the patriarch must be obtained before any important family decision, such as the choice of a school, the change of an occupation, foreign travel or, especially, a marriage by a member of the family.

---

8. Raphael Patai, *Society, Culture and Change in the Middle East* (3d edition; Philadelphia, 1971), p. 84.
   9. Reuben Levy, *The Social Structure of Islam* (Cambridge, 1965), p. 102.

The traditional family is endogamous, preferring marriages within a restricted group. As already mentioned, the most highly preferred marriage is the closest possible permissible by law—between the children of brothers. But in general, closer ties within the extended family, tribe or, at least, ethnic group, are preferred over more distant groups as marriage partners. (One prominent exception to this is the practice of political marriages sealing the alliance between two tribes.) Although all Muslims are in theory equal, there is a preference for marriage within one's own social class and resistance to marriage of a woman into an inferior class or group.[10]

Finally, polygyny is legal and socially acceptable, if not actually prevalent, in the traditional family. As is well known, the Qur'ān permits simultaneous marriage to four wives, provided that they are cared for equally. One of the major Islamic changes in the traditional social structure was the limitation of polygyny to four wives, while the provision for equal treatment made its practice an expensive proposition. Undoubtedly, one of the reasons for polygyny has been the desire for large families. As the family is the basic economic unit, an advantage was seen in increasing its size. For women, one of the surest means for increasing her standing in the family was the bearing of children, especially males. Within a family with several wives there would be a natural rivalry to bear the most sons. All of these considerations, of course, are reinforced by the high rates of infant mortality in traditional society.

Ethnic and Tribal Groups. Traditional societies of the Persian Gulf region were a mosaic of racial, ethnic, and linguistic strains. There was less of a religious complexity than elsewhere in the Middle East. Iran and Iraq, however, had Christian, Jewish, and even (in Iran) Zoroastrian minorities. Under the *Sharī'a*, as well as according to Middle Eastern custom, these were each isolated and largely self-contained communities, under their own religious leaders.

The Persian Gulf region had long maintained extensive commercial dealings with India and Africa; some extending at times to Southeast Asia and the Far East.[11] There was some racial mixture stemming from these ties, especially in the case of Africa. The connection of the region with Africa extended to the establishment of political control over the East African littoral through the Omani dynasty of the sultans of Zanzibar.[12]

The most important ethnic-linguistic division in the Gulf area was between the Arabs and Iranians. Following the initial Arab conquest of Iran in the seventh century A.D., Persian language and culture were largely submerged by the literary and official use of Arabic. However, the language and culture (but not the religion) of ancient Persia had a renaissance in a new Islamic context in eastern and northern Iran. The 'Abbasids, although an Arab dynasty, were strongly supported by the Iranians of Khurasan, from where they had launched their successful revolution to overthrow the Umayyad caliphate. In the eleventh century, there was the definitive revival of the Persian language by Firdawsī through

10. Patai, *Society, Culture and Change*, p. 90.
11. John O'Kane, *The Ship of Sulaiman* (New York, 1972), presents a translation of an account by Iban Muhammad Ibrāhīm of a seventeenth-century Persian embassy to Siam.
12. Anthony Law and Alison Smith, eds., *The Oxford History of East Africa*, Vol. 1 (London, 1962), has several chapters dealing with the sultans of Zanzibar.

his creation of the national epic, the *Shāhnāma*.[13] In the sixteenth century, the cultural-linguistic differences between Arabs and Iranians were reinforced by the establishment of the Ithnā 'Ashariyya (Twelver) sect of the *Shī'īs* as the state religion of Iran by the Safavid Shah Ismā'īl (1501–24). The third major ethnic group in the region, the Turks, first appeared in the area as slave soldiers of the 'Abbasids, at times even usurping the caliph's political power. But in the eleventh century there began a series of Turkish tribal invasions. These Turkish tribes, newly converted to Islam but still strongly influenced by their Central Asian culture, soon gained political control over both Iran and Iraq. However, as good Sunnīs they acknowledged the theoretical sovereignty of the 'Abbasid caliph of Baghdad.

Two centuries after this Seljuk Turkish invasion came the infinitely more disruptive Mongol invasions of the mid-thirteenth century, resulting in the final overthrow of the 'Abbasids and the temporary political detachment of Iran from the Islamic world. The Mongols in Iran, far from their homeland, eventually adopted the Persian language and culture and, finally, Islam as well.[14]

Following the decline and eventual break-up of the Mongol empire, a number of Turkish dynasties came to be established in the area. The most prominent of these were the Ottomans of Anatolia. Several Turkish tribally based dynasties ruled in Iran, but at the beginning of the sixteenth century a unique empire was established by Shah Ismā'īl, the head of a Sūfī religious order supported by an alliance of Shī'ī Turkish tribes.

Important as these fundamental ethnic-linguistic differences are to the understanding of the Middle East, it should not be supposed that Arabs, Iranians, and Turks felt anything like modern nationalistic feelings, although Iranians most certainly had a sense of national identity. All of the Turkish and Iranian groups, as well as the Arabs, subscribed to Islam. Indeed, those of the earlier period often claimed that the protection and advancement of Islam was the sole aim of their seizure of political power. Arabic remained as the language of Islamic religion and culture, and, of course, it also remained the basic language in areas predominantly Arab in population.

An additional basis for traditional group solidarity has been tribalism. Tribes are based upon allegiance to an assumed common ancestor. They were the dominant form of social organization in pre-Islamic Arabia, especially among the Bedouin (*Badw*) peoples. However, they were prominent also in cities, and the Prophet was a member of the noble Meccan tribe of the Quraish. Islam established a wider basis for solidarity in the community of all believers, but it did not, in fact, succeed in completely replacing earlier tribal loyalties. Tribes have tended to be dominant among nomadic peoples, Arab and non-Arab, but in the historical, geographical, and cultural context of the area they have played a vital role in the life of settled agricultural communities and cities as well. In particular, they have often formed the nucleus for the foundation of territorial states and empires.[15]

---

13. The *Shāh-nāma* is available in a condensed English translation, with an introduction by Reuben Levy, *The Epic of Kings, Shah-nama* (London, 1967).

14. The Mongol Īl-Khān Ghāzān Khān (1295–1304) effected the permanent conversion of his dynasty to Islam.

15. Ibn Khaldūn, *The Muqaddimah* (Franz Rosenthal, trans.) three vols. (Princeton, 1958).

Tribes have varied widely in their organizations, from the closely knit ones (*tāmma*), under the authority of the paramount *shaikh*, to loose confederations of almost autonomous clans. Although most tribes boast of their ancient lineage, tribalism has been a continuous and dynamic process in the area; new tribes have been formed and older ones disintegrated.[16] Internally, the tribal leader (Arab *shaikh*; Iranian *khān*; Kurdish *agha*; Turkish *bey*) is elected from among the members of a particular family by the tribal elders and can be deposed by the same procedure. Tribal "dynasties" do tend to be established, but rarely is there a simple hereditary succession. Once accepted, the tribal leader takes on the patriarchal authority of a family head for all of his kinsmen—always provided that he does not violate tribal customs and keeps on relatively good terms with the tribal elders. Not all persons in a tribal society are members of tribes; some groups are affiliated to a tribe as clients but not as free members, and other classes and occupations (tinkers, blacksmiths, entertainers, and, of course, slaves) are outside the system.

Contrasting Life Styles

Urban, Village, and Pastoral. Three distinct patterns of social organization have coexisted and interacted in the traditional societies of the Persian Gulf. Both their distinctiveness and their interaction must be borne in mind to gain a true picture of society as a whole. One of the most widespread and consistent themes in Middle Eastern history is the interaction between two social groups— the nomadic pastoralists and the rich, cultured, and politically crucial urbanites. Ibn Khaldūn found the central dynamic of history in the cyclical rise and fall of nomadic tribes conquering urban states, only to be destroyed in their turn when their group solidarity and primitive virtues were undermined by luxury and vice.[17]

The third form of society, the villages, were too bound up in the harsh routine of their existence to have much time for either attack or defense. There are few, if any, examples of successful peasant armies or revolts in the Middle East. Characteristically, the villagers were alternately plundered by the nomads and milked by the urban-based landlords and tax collectors. The actual management of the villages was left in the hands of subordinate officials, and there was very little of the medieval European pattern of a feudal lord living on his fiefdom.

Tribal organization was strongest among the nomads, but was present also in both villages and cities. Nomads were dependent on their flocks and herds, but at times they engaged in both trade and agriculture. The line between nomad and villager was not impenetrable. In some cases, especially in Eastern Arabia, tribes became established in coastal cities, engaged in commerce, and took their nomadic

16. J. E. Peterson, "Tribes and politics in Eastern Arabia," *Middle East Journal* 31 (1977): 199, contains several contemporary examples of tribal formation and disintegration.

17. This thesis is expressed most vividly by Ibn Khaldūn: "The things that go with luxury and submergence in a life of ease break the vigor of group feeling, which alone produces superiority. When group feeling is destroyed, the tribe is no longer able to defend or protect itself, let alone press any claims. It will be swallowed up by other nations." Ibn Khaldūn, *The Muqaddimah*, 1: 287.

raiding customs to sea with them.[18] Although the nomads were probably no match for regular military forces in the service of the urban-based rulers, it is probably true also that nomadic life was the best natural training ground for a soldier.[19]

Urban life was the ideal of Islamic civilization. It was in the urban setting alone that one could have great religious, cultural, educational, and governmental institutions. Of course, cities were the centers of commerce and manufacture as well and provided these services to their surrounding villages and nomadic neighbors. The governmental function was probably the most vital of all. Cities were military garrisons, centers of bureaucracies, and residences for the royal courts. Thus it was in the cities that the various strands of Middle Eastern society converged and were held together by political-cultural elites.[20]

Cities were crucial in both European and Middle Eastern historical development. In Europe, the cities were centers of relative freedom and vigorous corporate civic life. Islamic cities never developed the autonomous municipal institutions of the European cities.[21] Their guild organizations had no role in the city government. Voluntary organizations, with the exception of religious orders, were virtually nonexistent. Despite the lack of powerful corporate groups, the traditional city was not easily governed. Often, there was great turbulence, communal violence, and virtual internecine war between factions, residential quarters, and criminal gangs. However, there were so many mutually hostile, diverse groups that the rulers could pit one against the other and intervene in a series of shifting alliances. "The Mamlūks," writes Ira Lapidus concerning medieval Syrian cities, "governed not by administration but by holding all of the vital social threads in their hands."[22]

Traditional Societies

The crucial social distinction evident in all three forms of traditional societies in the Middle East—nomadic, village, and urban—was the steepness of the gradient and the depth of the division separating the elites from the masses. Although there might well be some intermediate groups possessing wealth and corresponding to our Western ideas of a "middle class," particularly in urban settings, these groups did not truly represent a social mid-point between the elites and the masses.

Every society must reach a compromise between the demands of the society as a whole and the distinctiveness of its component parts. Middle Eastern societies have been heavily weighted toward the separateness of their various constituent elements, especially at the lower and middle ranges of society, and, by the convergence of the separate group elites, at the very top levels of society. The

18. Robert Geran Landen, *Oman since 1856* (Princeton, 1967), pp. 24–25.

19. Carleton S. Coon, *Caravan: The Story of the Middle East*, rev. ed. (New York, 1964), p. 193.

20. C. A. O. Van Nieuwenhuijze, *Social Stratification and the Middle East: An Interpretation* (Leiden, 1965), p. 63.

21. V. F. Costello, *Urbanization in the Middle East* (Cambridge, 1977), pp. 8–9.

22. Ira Marvin Lapidus, *Muslim Cities in the Later Middle Ages* (Cambridge, Mass., 1967), p. 187.

most important, stable, and persistent of these constituent groups were those connected with primordial loyalties to the family, tribe, or ethnic group. "In this part of the world, there is a high degree of suspicion of the efficacy of membership in or attachment to large or mass institutional groups. Personal ties based upon kinship, friendship, religious, and regional affiliation have been among the best means of insuring effective individual effort."[23]

Much of the literature of Western sociology is concerned with the analysis of social classes. In the Middle East, particularly when discussing traditional societies, the concept of social class is of limited utility, in all probability leading to confusion rather than to clarification of social reality.[24] This underlying social reality consisted of a pervasive pluralism of groups, each jealously guarding its separate and distinct existence. Instead of horizontal classes stretching across the societies, there were parallel vertical groups maintaining their distance from each other, except for their tendency to converge at the top around a common core of cultural-religious beliefs and in a ruling power elite composed of the higher elites of the various societal groups.[25]

The ruling elite, estimated by two recent authors at no more than two percent of the total population,[26] once having attained its position of political dominance, sought to consolidate and expand its position through its access to the surplus wealth of the society. The major components of the traditional elite were the following: (1) the ruler; (2) the ruling family; (3) tribal nobility; (4) native landlords; (5) high members of the 'ulamā'; and (6) the military elite.[27] Three traditional groups composed a middle stratum: the bureaucrats, the traditional bourgeoisie of bazaar merchants, and the bulk of the 'ulamā'. The wealth of the merchants and bureaucrats often might equal or surpass that of members of the elite, but they were in a subordinate position to the political power of the elite groups, and their wealth was in constant danger of confiscation. The 'ulamā', through their control over the educational system, formed an invaluable link between the elite groups and the rest of society. The elites patronized the educational system, as did the bureaucrats, while most of the merchants and the overwhelming majority of the masses had little or no education. However, they had an immense respect for the 'ulamā' as representatives of religion *per se*. In urban-based imperial systems, the position of the bureaucracy at times approached that of a hereditary political and clerical caste, exercising great political power through their control over access to the rulers and their professional knowledge of how things worked. But in the absence of the attributes of a true bureaucratic system (as described by Max Weber), such as a regular and formal system of training, employment, tenure, salaries, and ranks, they lacked legal protection

23. James A. Bill and Carl Leiden, *The Middle East: Politics and Power* (Boston, 1974), p. 63.

24. For an illuminating discussion of the problems of class analysis in the Middle East, see Marvin Zonis and James A. Bill, "Classes, elites and Iranian politics: An exchange," *Iranian Studies* 3 (1975): 134–65. See also Van Nieuwenhuijze, *Social Stratification*; Eisenstadt, "Convergence and divergence of modern and modernizing societies"; and James A. Bill, "Class analysis and the dialectics of modernization in the Middle East," *International Journal of Middle East Studies* 3 (1972): 417–34.

25. Van Nieuwenhuijze, *Social Stratification*, p. 53.

26. Bill and Leiden, *The Middle East*, p. 79.

27. Bill, "Class analysis and the dialectics," p. 428.

from the whims of their political masters, even though as a group they were indispensable.

The immense bulk of the population consisted of three lower groups: traditional workers and artisans, peasants, and tribal nomads. The workers and peasants had little power, wealth, or political influence. Of course, there was some recognition of the practical fact that there was a limit to the exploitation that these groups could bear before the law of diminishing returns began to apply. But despite their oppression, there were few, if any, examples of popular rebellions. The tribal nomads, however, occupied a somewhat ambiguous position. In the first instance, many of the traditional Persian Gulf societies were purely and simply tribal societies. In these, there would be a much more simple form of social organization, almost exclusively based upon kinship, without the elaboration of landlords, military, high 'ulamā', and bureaucracies. Although tribal societies had their own distinctions of ruling families, noble tribes, subordinate tribes, and clients, the idea of a common tribal ancestry and the practical fact that each tribesman was a valuable warrior made for a certain degree of egalitarianism. In addition, many of the traditional societies of the region, down to the contemporary Saʿūdī state, have been tribal in their origin. In these cases, when the tribal leaders and the ruling family of the empire were one and the same group, their fellow tribesmen enjoyed a position somewhat more elevated than the ordinary nomad. It was common practice, however, for a tribally based elite to attempt to shift the basis of its power from fellow tribesmen to more easily subordinated military and bureaucratic groups once they obtained imperial status.

Apart from these groups, there were additional categories of non-Muslim communities—Christians, Jews, and Zoroastrians—who were tolerated under Islamic law and custom in a subordinate social position, but who were given a substantial degree of communal autonomy. Slaves were an additional social category, but were largely attached to the family system. In fact, although the lowest category in theory, slaves attached to ruling families often could become an important component of the ruling elite, as witnessed by the famous Mamlūks of Egypt and Syria.

The autonomy, diversity, and multiplicity of a bewildering variety of social groups thus constituted the traditional social structures of Persian Gulf societies. Neither their common adherence to one of the sects of Islam nor the political impositions of their various secular rulers could alter this fact. Each group, down to and including individual families, operated as an independent unit in its dealings with the rest of society. In principle, each maintained its own autonomy through the avoidance of other groups insofar as possible. The ability of the rulers to integrate these societies was severely limited by the fact that they shared in these values of group autonomy, as well as by the fact that they lacked effective instruments of communications and control. Institutions of social control prominent in other societies, such as organized churches, educational systems, legal systems, and bureaucracies, were either nonexistent or were themselves constituted as autonomous groups.

These societies were in a continual state of tension and flux caused by the interaction of so many different autonomous groups in competition with one another. Although none of the constituent groups could be eliminated as a category of society, any particular group or even an individual member of a group was in constant peril of falling or in hope of rising within the social universe of his day. All pervasive uncertainty led to the formation of informal networks of personal contacts, temporary alliances, obligations from and duties to other individuals. These informal networks of personal cliques, of which the Iranian *dawra* is a prime example, acted to support and promote the interests of their members.[28] In a highly complex and personalistic society, an individual could not have too many personal contacts. Even though one's own kinship group (including, in the broadest sense, ethnic and tribal groups) was undoubtedly the most reliable support in the long run, the individual was well advised to attach himself in informal and more temporary groups based upon personal friendship, mutual support and reciprocal obligation. These ties might be weaker, but they afforded additional flexibility and hence a form of social insurance.

The traditional social system was remarkably stable, adaptive, and resistant to basic changes, even though its individual components were in a continual state of flux. The spectacular rise of an individual, family, tribe or nation from the most humble of circumstances to the most exalted positions, and the simultaneous decline of other individuals and groups to lower status, were commonplace. Each society had an easily identifiable and very powerful elite at its core, but it lacked a closed, hereditary aristocracy. Its common mode of operation was much more informal than in contemporary European feudalism, lacking the strictly hierarchical structure of social orders, with mutual obligations binding both lord and master, and, especially, the corporate representation of classes in the estates of the kingdom. Middle Eastern traditional elites centralized and monopolized the political and economic power of society to a high degree, often through naked, brute force. They did not, however, attempt to alter the structure of society itself. Certainly, there were individuals and groups who ranked, on the basis of their wealth, somewhere in the middle between the elites and the masses. But they did not constitute a "middle class." The basis of social class in the Middle East (if, indeed, it can be called "class" at all) was political power. And political power was the exclusive preserve of the elite groups.

Variations of Traditionalism

We have, thus far, been examining the social characteristics of traditionalism as if the Persian Gulf were a single social unit. To be sure, there are some general characteristics, such as Islamic culture and institutions, the central importance of the family, and the domination of political elites, held in common throughout the area. Concrete examples of specific societies, however, tended to conform to one of several subtypes of Middle Eastern traditionalism. Two subtypes represent the opposite ends of a spectrum of social organization from the most highly elaborated urban imperial systems to most simple desert patriarchal societies.[29]

28. Bill and Leiden, *The Middle East*, p. 66.
29. See George Lenczowski, "Changing patterns of political organizations in the twentieth-century Middle East," *Western Political Quarterly* 18 (September 1965): 669–88.

Two other variations, the tribally based city states of the eastern Arabian peninsula and the theocratic community of the Ibādī Imāms of Oman, are almost unique, at least in comparatively modern times, to this region. In addition, it might be argued that an intermediate and generally short-lived type of social organization is the desert imperial system, i.e., an empire based upon the domination of a nomadic tribe or tribal confederation.

Urban imperial traditional societies have existed most commonly in Iran and Iraq. They exhibit the greatest variety of social organizations in the most fully elaborated institutional frameworks. The city dominates over the countryside as the residence of the ruling elite, including the sultan or shah, his family, his court bureaucracy, and high 'ulamā' officials. Also represented at the royal court would be the elites of the landlords and the nomadic tribes. It was within and for the benefit of these imperial courts that the greatest cultural, artistic, and literary creations of Islamic civilization were executed. The 'Abbasid, Great Seljuk, Safavid, and Ottoman empires all conformed to this general pattern.

Iran experienced the rise and fall of several dynasties, interspersed with periods of interregnum, foreign invasions and internal disunity. It served as a buffer-state for the Middle East against invasions from the north and east and was thus generally less effectively organized as a centralized empire than was its Ottoman/Turkish imperial rival, which maintained the same dynasty for more than six centuries. The power of the great landlords was more absolute and that of the tribal leaders more independent than was the rule in the Ottoman provinces. "All except the strongest governments (in Iran) have delegated responsibility in the tribal areas to the tribal chiefs," writes A.K.S. Lambton.[30] Even more importantly, most of the ruling dynasties were themselves tribal in origin or depended upon tribal support. Once in power, of course, the rulers would strive to free themselves from this dependence, but it was a difficult and not always successful effort. The last of these traditional tribally based dynasties, the Qājār (1779–1925), were in fact more dependent upon the tribal system than some of their predecessors.[31] With a more uncertain and less effectively centralized administration and political leadership, coupled with the greater independence of the high Shī'ī 'ulamā', the social patterns of Iran exhibited a more variegated aspect than was normally the case in an urban imperial society. The rulers had to depend more on the manipulation of rival individuals and groups than upon bureaucratic control. Even in the cities, traditionally the centers of royal authority, there was a considerable degree of local autonomy based on well-organized craft guilds and supported by the 'ulamā'.

Ottoman society conformed more closely to the ideal type of an urban imperial society. The bureaucratic, military and religious elements were more highly centralized and rationally organized than in any previous or contemporary Islamic

---

30. A. K. S. Lambton, "Islamic Society in Persia," reprinted in Louise E. Sweet, ed. *Peoples and Cultures of the Middle East*, Vol. 1, *Depth and Diversity* (Garden City, N.Y., 1970), p. 77.

31. Ervand Abrahamian, "Oriental despotism: The case of Qajar Iran," *International Journal of Middle East Studies* 5 (1974): 13. p. 11. "The *ilkhans* were virtual kings within their own tribes, governing without the intervention of outside authorities, administering their own laws, collecting their own taxes, and being only 'nominally' subject to the central government."

state. The degree of control from the center in provincial government varied in the Ottoman Empire, and, unfortunately for Iraq, it was one of the more distant provinces of the empire. This meant, in practice, that the province was given over to exploitation by a succession of rapacious governors sent out from the capital.[32] The major mitigating circumstance was the resistance of the local elites, of land-lords, tribal leaders, and the remnants of the Mamlūk class. Iraq also suffered the effects of its being one of the major battlegrounds in the long series of wars between the Ottoman and Safavid empires.

Examples of desert patriarchal societies in the Persian Gulf region are, typically, found among nomadic tribal peoples. However, all of the major ethnic groups in the region, Arabs, Iranians, Turks, and Kurds, have some portion of their populations living as nomads, while others are farmers or townspeople. In fact, there is no hard and fast dividing line between tribal/nomadic societies and sedentary farming and urban societies in the Middle East. There is rather a broad "in-between" category of seminomadic villagers and semisedentary nomads. The Bakhtiyārīs, for example, are usually counted as one of the major tribal groups in Iran, but all of them practice some combination of agriculture and pastoral-ism.[33] Nomadic tribes do settle into permanent communities on a voluntary basis and still manage to maintain a good portion of their tribal social structure. The ruling families of Kuwait and Bahrain, for example, the Āl Sabāh and the Āl Khalīfa, are both part of the Banī 'Utba clan of the powerful noble 'Anaza tribal confederation of the Syrian Desert; they did not settle on the shores of the Persian Gulf until the eighteenth century.[34]

The social and political organizations of Middle Eastern tribes are based upon kinship, although often affected by purely political considerations as well. The Bakhtiyārī khans were not only tribal leaders, for example, but were the tax farmers and military leaders of their region for the central government under the Qājār dynasty.[35] Among the Arabian tribes in particular, but also present in other Middle Eastern tribal groups, there is an elaborate distinction between noble and tribute-paying vassal tribes.[36] Since kinship is the basis of social organization, it is only natural that "The noble tribes generally show a much greater organizational coherence than the vassal tribes."[37] The prime basis of nobility is an ancient lineage coupled with freedom from being dependent upon any other tribe. The fundamental division is two-fold; a tribe that is a vassal is

32. Stanford J. Shaw, *History of the Ottoman Empire and Modern Turkey*, Vol. 1, *Empire of the Gazis* (Cambridge, 1976), p. 122, points out the distinction between the government of the central Ottoman provinces in Rumelia and Anatolia, which were more regularly organized along bureaucratic lines and the distant provinces, including Iraq, which were essentially tax farms held by the governor. Phillip K. Hitti, *The Near East in History* (Princeton, 1961), p. 341, mentions the case of Syria, which had 133 governors in its first 180 years as an Ottoman province.

33. Abraham Rosman and Paula G. Rubel, "Nomad-sedentary interethnic relations in Iran and Afghanistan," *International Journal of Middle East Studies* 7 (1976): 550.

34. Emile A. Nakhleh, *Bahrain* (Lexington, Mass., 1976), p. 8.

35. For the position of the Bakhtiyārī tribe in nineteenth century Iran, see Gene Garth-waite's excellent article "The Bakhtiari Khans, the government and the British 1846–1915," *International Journal of Middle East Studies* 3 (1972): 24–44.

36. Patai, *Society, Culture and Change*, p. 251.

37. Ibid.

considered inferior to all noble tribes, even though it is formally a vassal to a single noble tribe. Only very rarely does a vassal tribe have a still more inferior tribe as its own vassal. These distinctions among tribes are widely accepted by all involved, both nobles and vassals. A tribe can change its status by throwing off the conditions of vassalage, but it would retain some of its inferiority through the fact of *ever* having been in the condition of vassalage. The clearest distinction between noble and vassal tribes is the refusal of noble tribes to permit inter-marriage with their inferiors, a prohibition that covers both men and women of the tribe.[38]

Leadership in a desert patriarchal society rests with a particular family that provides from among its adult males, through an informal process of family consultation, an able and respected person to serve as its leader. The leadership is thus an elective position, with the leader holding office and ruling with the consent and consultation of his peers as a *primus inter pares*.[39] The leader's actions must not violate tribal custom, although the custom itself may allot certain leaders more power than others. Even more important than the selection of the ruler and his exercise of authority is the fact that the leader can be deposed through the same process and be replaced by a more able member of his family, as witnessed in modern times by the deposition of King Sa'ūd of Sa'ūdī Arabia and his replacement by King Faisal.

All free tribesmen are from a single class by birth, although they may acquire individual distinction through exceptional bravery or wisdom. The crucial social and political difference between desert pastoral societies and Islamic urban im-perialistic societies is that the ruler in the former is not detached from the bulk of society, surrounded with elaborate ritual, and shielded from the easy access of his fellow tribesmen by court and state bureaucracies.

In a desert empire the authority of a particular tribe and its leader becomes extended to a number of different tribes as well as to nontribal urban and rural populations. However, the ruler does not develop the formal political structures associated with Islamic urban empires, but rather remains as a more powerful leader still within the tribal tradition of patriarchal authority, combined with proven ability. As one scholar has written, "There have always been the rich and the poor, but until recently they were not far apart. The ruler built his modest mansion out of the same sundried brick his subjects used for their huts, he wore much the same garb as they did and he and they spoke with each other on a first name basis."[40] The ruler governs through the processes of informal consulta-tion both within his own family and with the leaders of the major tribes. Sa'ūdī Arabia is the prime example of a desert empire, with the interesting addition of the unique alliance between the family of a noted religious reformer, Shaikh Muhammad ibn 'Abd al-Wahhāb (the Āl Shaikh) and a traditional family of tribal leaders descended from Shaikh Muhammad ibn Sa'ūd, who in 1744 made a compact to establish a reformed and purified Islamic state to replace the tribal

38. Ibid., p. 258.
39. Peterson, "Tribes and politics," p. 297.
40. George Rentz, "Saudi Arabia: Desert island," *Journal of International Affairs* 19 (1965): 79.

anarchy and irreligion to which the Arabian peninsula had fallen.[41] The Sa'ūdī dynasty, with an ability rare in desert empires, managed to revive its fortunes in spite of defeats. The current revival dates from this century (1902) with the reconquest of their traditional capital of al-Riyadh by a small band of Sa'ūdī exiles led by Shaikh 'Abd al-'Azīz ibn 'Abd al-Rahmān Āl-Faisal Āl Sa'ūd. Beginning in 1912, the Sa'ūdī leader strengthened and extended his rule through the formation of agricultural colonies of dedicated coreligionists, the *Ikhwān* (brethren). These formed the backbone of the armies through which the House of Sa'ūd conquered its present territory. In 1921, 'Abd al-Azīz adopted the secular title of Sultan of the Najd, while following the conquest of the Hijāz he took the title of King of the Hijāz in 1926. Finally, in the late 1920s the *Ikhwān* had to be suppressed, since they disregarded royal authority and continued their original mission of spreading their faith through force of arms into the neighboring British mandated states of Trans-Jordan and Iraq. They also questioned the acceptance of "secular" innovations by the Sa'ūdī rulers (such as telephones and motor vehicles).[42]

The Sa'ūdī Arabian kingdom thus represents a varied and composite type of desert empire. Its origin was certainly in traditional tribal society, but it gained immense prestige and staying power through its alliance with the Wahhābī religious reformation. Since the 1920s, at least, it has undergone a gradual process of secularization in which it has adopted some of the formal institutions of an Islamic urban imperial system, along with increasing amounts of modern secular organization.

The history of the tribally based traditional shaikhdoms centered around the cities of the eastern Arabian littoral resembles, on a smaller scale, the career of the Sa'ūdī kingdom.[43] In each case, a Bedouin tribal shaikh came to rule over a settled coastal community. The population of the coastal cities (often, in reality, little more than villages) represented a mixture of ethnic, social, and religious origins, engaging in commerce, fishing, pearling, and, on occasion, piracy. In these societies, the ruler's tribe constitutes an elite, with the original inhabitants providing the merchant, *'ulamā'*, and laboring classes. Some of them developed great seafaring traditions and even overseas empires, such as the Āl Bū Sa'īd dynasty of Oman. Occasionally, the ruling shaikh became involved personally in commerce.[44]

Society is essentially desert-patriarchal, with the ruling family and tribe still adhering to tribal custom, governing through consultation with the other members of the family and leaders of the tribe. By no means all of the tribal population settled in the coastal cities; many remained as desert nomads and provided a reserve of loyal supporters. Only in Bahrain was the nomadic life style completely abandoned. The merchants, farmers, and common laborers (including sailors) composed the other significant social groups. Leading merchant families composed

---

41. George Rentz, "Wahhabism and Saudi Arabia," in Derek Hopwood, ed., *The Arabian Peninsula, Society and Politics* (London, 1972), p. 56.

42. Ibid., p. 64.

43. The best English language source for the tribal backgrounds of the present Arab Shaikhdoms is John Duke Anthony, *Arab States of the Lower Gulf: People, Politics, Petroleum* (Washington, 1975). Peterson, "Tribes and politics," pp. 299–304, discusses the process of state formation out of tribal origins.

44. Anthony, *Arab States*, pp. 155–56.

a kind of subelite, often consulted by the rulers on commercial and even political matters.[45] The cosmopolitan character of the traditional Gulf city-states set them apart from the remainder of the Arabian peninsula—almost wholly Arab in population. Iranian, Balūchī, Afghan, Indian, and even Jewish communities all coexisted along with Arabs from the ruling tribe and other Arabs from neighboring cities and tribes.[46] While these societies were at least partially urban, and the rulers had their principal residence in the urban setting (albeit they often maintained an interior residence as well), they did not develop a bureaucratic structure or professional military organizations characteristic of urban Islamic empires. Even the 'ulamā', despite the fact that some of the rulers were followers of Wahhābī doctrine, did not develop the powerful political influence they exercised in the neighboring Sa'ūdī state.[47]

The final variant of traditional society in the area is the Ibādī imamate of Oman. Ibādism is a branch of the movement of the Khawārij, founded by 'Abd Allāh ibn Ibād in Basra in the later seventh century. They believed in the rule of an elected imām, selected in secret by the religious shaikhs and prominent laymen from among the entire body of the community. The elected imām could be deposed by the same means, should he refuse to rule in accordance with the strict interpretation of the Sharī'a, as agreed to by the 'ulamā'; but they did not go to the extreme measures as did some other branches of the Khawārij, such as calling all of their opponents unbelievers, forbidding intermarriage with non-Ibādīs, or endorsing assassination.[48]

Oman became a stronghold of Ibādī doctrine as early as the second century of the Islamic era, although there were always Sunnīs as well, especially in the coastal areas. The interior mountain and plateau area have been the particular stronghold of Ibādism down to the present day, where the religious divisions between Ibādī tribes and Sunnī tribes have been superimposed upon still older tribal divisions and feuds. "The rigid adherence to the sharī'a along with the somewhat egalitarian principles of the Khawārij in general has largely determined the social and economic organization of the country."[49]

The whole structure of the imamate government derived from tribal society. Real power, including control over the military, rested with the local tribal leaders. The extreme democracy of the imamate and its politico-religious elected leadership made it virtually inevitable that the course of various "dynasties" of imāms would follow the classical theory of cyclical change of Ibn Khaldūn. An outburst of religious enthusiasm would unite the Ibādī tribes into a strong imamate government, which would expand to dominate the country. In time, however, tribal-religious solidarity would be undermined by splits between the rulers and their supporters. In the nineteenth century, there was a split between the conservative imamate and the secularly oriented sultanate of the Āl Bū Sa'īd

45. Sir Rupert Hay, The Persian Gulf States (Washington, 1959), p. 38.

46. The Bahrain census of 1950 listed 18,471 foreigners, nearly 7,000 of whom were Iranians, to 9,179 Bahranis. The Jewish community, well established there for several hundred years, numbered about 250 persons. See Fahim I. Qubain, "Social classes and tensions in Bahrain," Middle East Journal 9 (1955): 270–74.

47. Hay, The Persian Gulf States, p. 35.

48. "Ibadiya," Shorter Encyclopedia of Islam, p. 143.

49. J. C. Wilkinson, "The Origins of the Omani State," in Hopwood, ed., The Arabian Peninsula, p. 76.

dynasty (who had earlier themselves combined the offices of *imām* and sultan). The imamate lapsed from 1871 to 1913, when it was revived in the interior. The sultan, however, continued to hold the coast. After years of intermittent warfare, a compromise was reached in the Treaty of Sīb in 1920. The imamate agreed to confine its rule to the interior and the sultan to the coast. This lasted until 1955, when the sultanate absorbed the *imām*'s territory and drove the reigning *imām* into exile in Sa'ūdī Arabia.[50]

Forces of Change and Persistence

As has been the case elsewhere in the Middle East (and in the non-Western world in general), the initial impetus for current patterns of social change in the traditional societies of the Persian Gulf region has come from the West. This is not to deny that social changes that are unrelated to Western influences have occurred and are now occurring in the traditional context. With both of these sources of change, however, it may be stressed that the traditional social institutions and cultural patterns have proven to be highly flexible, so much so that they have been able to incorporate vast changes, while at the same time denying to themselves that any change had in fact taken place. "The Near East is thus perhaps not so much a categorically static or stagnant area as one the cultural pattern of which implies accentuation—particularly to outside observers—of that which persists, rather than of things disappearing or newly appearing."[51]

This emphasis on the persistent, no doubt, antedates Islam; one can point to the ancient Hebrew idea of divine law and of a chosen people as a powerful statement stressing the persistent over the transitory. But Islam, certainly, reinforced this pattern of thought. The centrality of the revelation of Islam puts all subsequent "facts" of social change into a very subordinate position. One cannot improve upon perfection, thus Islamic thought has sought to retain its perception of the spirit and, insofar as possible, the practice of the social patterns established by the Prophet and his immediate successors as the ideal for mankind at all times and places. It is accepted as unfortunate but inevitable that man will stray from the correct patterns of the *Sharī'a*. It is then the task of a religious reformer to renew the true faith as a *mujaddid*: "Once in every century somebody will be endowed with the special gift—not to say charge—to renew, revivify religion."[52]

Within the perfect community of Islam there can be no place for change that is seen as change. When changes do appear, they are seen as divine manifestations of God's will and are thus accommodated into the existing pattern. The ruler was the head of the most powerful elite group and the coordinator of the "top" elites representing all of the groups in a pluralistic society, including the *'ulamā'*. Most rulers were content to leave the regulation of society to the traditional elites, and especially to the *'ulamā'*. In turn, the *'ulamā'* generally would

---

50. Landen, *Oman since 1856*, pp. 418–22.

51. C. A. O. Van Nieuwenhuijze, *Cross Cultural Studies* (The Hague, 1963), p. 231.

52. Ibid., p. 234. In Shī'ī doctrine, this function is a continuous process, since the *mujtahids* are the living representatives of the Hidden Imam. There is some dispute as to the frequency of the appearance of a *mujaddid*, some holding that it could be once in an "age" or in a "generation."

cooperate in the extension of religious sanction to the actions of the ruler taken for "reasons of state." Even though some actions might be doubtful, to say the least, under the *Sharī'a*, they could be justified under the ruler's general charge to defend and extend the community against its enemies. In the Ottoman empire, this position became highly institutionalized; official religious doctrine held that the *qādīs* derived their authority from the monarch and were thus bound to apply the *Sharī'a* in accordance with his directives.[53]

There was little reason for the political leader to challenge religious authority. Far from exercising a practical restraint upon any policy he could conceivably adopt, it rather provided religious legitimacy for his actions. Neither the *'ulamā'* nor the ruler had any thought of changing or interfering with the fundamental institutions of social and religious life. And in traditional Middle Eastern societies only they would have had the authority and power to do so.[54]

Persian Gulf societies, despite their being strongly Islamic and traditional, thus provided in practice for considerable leeway in their acceptance of changes that we would consider as "modernizing." Gradual and indirect changes, by far the most prevalent changes in practice, would be accommodated intellectually through the Islamic belief that nothing could exist that was not subject to the universal laws of God. They would be accommodated socially by the social plurality of traditional societies. Each social group was compartmentalized from all other groups and enjoyed a high degree of autonomy, except at the very highest levels, where their elites converged about the person of the ruler. Changes affecting one group did not, in the short term at least, affect them all. Certainly, changes did not affect them all at the same rate.

Those changes that affected the rulers and the ruling elites, *in the actual historical context of their introduction to the Persian Gulf region*, were also those changes that tended to enhance their power. Most changes have been accommodated and absorbed into the existing traditional social patterns. The net result, thus far, has been persistence and stability. Of course, instability and fundamental change cannot be ruled out as more drastic changes come to affect more social groups more deeply, so as to strain the accommodating institutions to the breaking point. We shall see that this was in fact the case in the Iraqi revolution of 1958.

Character of Historical Change in the Persian Gulf

With the exception of a brief period of military government in Iraq during and after World War I, no Persian Gulf state ever has been under the direct administration of a foreign (non-Middle Eastern) power. Even the mandate of Iraq, assigned to Great Britain by the San Remo Conference of 1920, was actually

---

53. Hodgson, *Gunpowder Empires*, p. 116.

54. A possible exception to the rule of noninterference by the rulers in the fundamental institutions of religious and social life might be made for the Mughal Emperor Akbar (1556–1605), who is credited with having proclaimed his own religion in the year 1582, see S. M. Edwards and H. L. O. Garrett, *Mughal Rule in India* (New Delhi, 1962), pp. 31–32. Hodgson, however, disputes this and states that Akbar "continued to be what we must call a Muslim," see Hodgson, *Gunpowder Empires*, p. 73.

exercised by means of a treaty with the Iraqi government.[55] British imperialism and, in the case of Iran, a combination of British and Russian imperialism, began to have a major impact on the political and economic organizations of the region, beginning in the early years of the nineteenth century. For the most part, however, social structures remained in their traditional molds. In the British view, their Persian Gulf interests were directly related to their imperial role on the Indian subcontinent and were strictly limited in character.

The hierarchy of British interests in the region was first and foremost political; second, economic and; finally, humanitarian. All of these goals could be accomplished most effectively and economically through indirect means. The most common method was through treaties with local rulers. Where direct means were necessary, a small naval force was usually adequate for the suppression of piracy and the slave trade. Once political security had been established, the economic benefits would be reaped through the "natural" actions of laissez-faire economic policy. The somewhat limited resources of the area would be exchanged for the manufactures of Great Britain and the exports of India.

The most important direct consequence of European imperialism on the region was the preservation and stabilization of the existing traditional political systems of the area. This meant that the social changes that eventually followed in the late nineteenth and twentieth centuries were mediated through the existing traditional elites. This stability, in fact, brought an end to the traditional pattern of cyclical sociopolitical change in Middle Eastern societies for the past thousand years. Britain and Russia between them (although most often as rivals) stabilized the remaining Middle Eastern empires; no more could a great conqueror sweep out of Central Asia to devastate the area and found a new empire. Never again would these empires be allowed to expand against their neighbors in the Balkans, the Ukraine, the Caucasus, or India. Nor would they be allowed seriously to alter their boundaries with each other. British protection of the Omani sultanate and the minor Arabian shaikhs accomplished the same ends on a more modest scale on the Arabian peninsula. Only in the interior of Arabia, with the rise of the Sa'ūdī desert empire, did the old pattern reassert itself for the last time. But here, as well, it was the British protection of the littoral states and, eventually, of the Transjordanian and Iraqi mandates, which set limits to Sa'ūdī expansionism.

All of our examination of subsequent social changes in the region (some examples of which, undoubtedly, have had a disruptive effect on these societies) must be prefaced by an understanding that many of them have immeasurably enhanced the power and stability of their ruling elites. They have been protected from foreign conquest, from each other, and from the revolutionary consequences of some of their internal changes. As Nikki R. Keddie has remarked: "Although several observers noted the great unpopularity of the Qajar dynasty and predicted its early demise, the knowledge that Great Britain and especially Russia would back the legitimate dynasty by force of arms was a deterrent to any move to overthrow the Qajars or to force upon them revolutionary concessions."[56] Looking to the opposite shore of the Gulf, another scholar has observed: "Indeed, by 1900

55. Lenczowski, *The Middle East in World Affairs* (third edition; Ithaca, 1962), pp. 270–71.
56. Nikki R. Keddie, "The Iranian power structure and social change 1800–1969: An overview," *International Journal of Middle East Studies* 2 (1971): 7.

Britain's friendship and support had become an even more important prerequisite to a ruler's continuance in power than popularity among his own subjects."[57]

Beginning with the discovery of the first commercial quantities of petroleum in Iran in 1908, the concerns of both the outside world and the local rulers in the area began to shift. For the first time in many centuries, the Persian Gulf region became valuable in its own right and not merely because of its strategic geographical position. For the first time also, large numbers of non-Middle Eastern foreigners came into the area. Some of the most modern aspects of Western industrial technology were installed. Local personnel were employed, at first in menial tasks, but increasingly rising to supervisory and even technical positions.[58]

Social change in the area now became, for the first time, a dual process. From the bottom, ripples of change spread from the development of the modern oil sector of the economy. Some of these changes became evident quite early. In 1913, the British political officer and scholar Sir Arnold Wilson noted: "In places where no Europeans save an occasional Consul was ever seen, employees of the Oil Company can not only travel freely but look forward to a welcome. Tribesmen who used to stone or shoot at me, a few miles from the oil fields, are becoming skilled mechanics. We are witnessing here a new 'Industrial Revolution' which is quietly transforming this part of Persia."[59]

The oil industry had even more profound effects, at least immediately, in its impact at the top of society. One of the most immediate of these was to hasten the resolution of territorial boundaries—itself a revolutionary change from the traditional vagueness of territorial claims among the Persian Gulf states. Oil companies hardly could be expected to drill in areas of uncertain sovereignty.[60] Simultaneously, it provided a powerful incentive to the central governments to assert their effective political control over outlying areas; areas that had traditionally been more or less autonomous in practice. The first Middle Eastern oil strike, for instance, took place in an area of Iran that had long been under the *de facto* control of a local Arab tribal leader, Shaikh Khaz'al ibn Jābir of Muhammara, who maintained his own independent relations with the British and refused to pay any taxes to the Shah's government. It was only in 1924 that the Iranian army, under the command of Rizā Khan (later Rizā Shah the Great), established the control of the central government over the oil fields.[61]

Underlying all of these changes were the financial benefits accruing to the central governments in the form of oil revenues. Direct oil revenues in Iran, for example, in the 1930s were about 25 to 30 percent of the total budget.[62] And it was precisely in these years that Rizā Shah's programs of political, economic, and social change were being pushed. Similarly, the "White Revolution" socio-

57. Robert G. Landen, "The Modernization of the Persian Gulf: The Period of British Dominance," in T. Cuyler Young, ed., *Middle East Focus: The Persian Gulf* (Princeton, 1968), p. 15.

58. Lenczowski, *Oil and State in the Middle East*, (Ithaca, 1960), pp. 253–311.

59. Quoted from Sir Arnold Wilson, *Southwest Persia* (London, 1941), p. 264, by George Rentz, "Development of the Oil Industry in the Persian Arabian Gulf, 1901–1968," in T. Cuyler Young, ed., *Middle East Focus*, p. 42.

60. Lenczowski, *Oil and State in the Middle East*, pp. 137–52.

61. Donald N. Wilber, *Riza Shah Pahlavi: The Resurrection and Reconstruction of Iran* (Hicksville, N.Y., 1975), pp. 89–100.

62. Julian Bharier, *Economic Development in Iran, 1900–1970* (Oxford, 1970), p. 159.

economic reforms of the 1960s were supported by even larger oil revenues. In 1968, for example, oil revenues provided 50 percent of the budget, and 80 percent of them were allocated to the Plan Organization for development expenditures.[63]

Consideration of the social changes wrought by the oil industry in the region must, however, be put in its proper perspective. First, although oil production began quite early in this century, its rate of growth was really quite slow until the post-World War II era. Before World War II only Iran (1912), Iraq (1927), Bahrain (1934), and Sa'ūdī Arabia (1939) had actually exported oil (and Sa'ūdī exports were really nominal).[64] Many more concessions had been granted and more oil had been discovered in commercial quantities, but the great boom in Persian Gulf oil did not start until the 1950s. Second, for the most part, these industries developed as enclaves in a society and economy that were still traditional and underdeveloped; they were not really integrated into the local scene.

In a purely physical sense, as well, the industry developed as an enclave. In each of the three largest countries in the area (Iran, Iraq, and Sa'ūdī Arabia), the major oil fields were located in areas distant from their political and population centers. Thus, although the country as a whole was eventually affected by the rise in government revenues, improved governmental efficiency, and the beginning of programs of socioeconomic development, only a relatively few people had direct experience with the operations of the industry. The social impact of the oil industry was largely indirect. In effect, this provided an additional cushion of time for the local rulers to adjust their policies to the disruptive social, economic, and political consequences which, inevitably, did come in the wake of the new industry.

Forces of Social Change

Many observers have identified the most important Western influence for social change in the Middle East as the introduction of new psychological and intellectual attitudes. There was a willingness and, indeed, an eagerness to accept certain elements of Western society as superior and to adopt them for themselves. "The restlessness and impatience of the educated elite has impelled them to espouse, plan and institute social changes more profound than those the Western powers ever dared to bring."[65]

There has certainly been some of this type of social change in Persian Gulf societies, but first it was necessary to have an educated (Western-educated) elite. From where did this new elite spring? Beginning with the nineteenth-century reforms of the *Tanzīmāt* period of the Ottoman Empire (1839–76), social change

63. Ibid., p. 168. The contribution of oil revenues to the budgets of most of the Arab oil producers was even greater. In the 1960s, it amounted to between 85 and 90 percent of the revenues in Sa'ūdī Arabia; in Iraq it was about two-thirds.

64. Zuhayr Mikdashi, *A Financial Analysis of Middle East Oil Concessions, 1901–1965* (New York, 1966), Table 39, p. 318.

65. Morroe Berger, *The Arab World Today* (Garden City, N.Y., 1962), p. 391.

began to filter down to the outlying provinces of the Persian Gulf, including reforms in education. In the Hijāz, there were some seventy-eight state elementary schools in 1915, the year before the Arab Revolt against Ottoman rule.[66] Midhat Pasha, one of the most notable of the *Tanzīmāt* reformers, was the governor of Baghdad from 1869 to 1871. His establishment of the power of the state, the ending of tribal disorders, the institution of a new tax system, land reform, public works, and new agricultural methods have led some modern historians to credit him as, "in truth, the founder of modern Iraq."[67]

Educational reforms, however, were few and far between in Qājār Persia, as was any other type of social, economic, or political reform. But even here a modern school for the training of civil servants on the European model known as the *Dār al-Funūn* (Polytechnic) was established in 1851. Still earlier, some American missionaries had opened schools. At first these were attended by local Christian minorities, but Persians came as well in increasing numbers.[68] In the smaller Arab states of the region, educational change was even slower— in the 1920s in Bahrain, the 1930s in Kuwait, and the 1950s in the United Arab Emirates (Sharja).[69]

The aim of state-supported modern education was to provide for a more efficient administration and military, hence for a more powerful state. The immediate and most persistent beneficiaries of the new educational institutions, as well as the other social changes of Westernization, were the rulers and the local elites: "The rich native upper class had the most opportunity for firsthand and close contact with Westerners, had the financial means necessary to acquire the trappings of Western civilization, and was the first to succumb to the lure of the West."[70] The most important social result of this change (if we consider that the strengthening of the power of the state was more of a political result) was the widening of the already yawning gap between the upper strata of society and the masses. Traditional Middle Eastern society had been always unified by its convergence on a cultural core linking nomad, peasant, and craftsman with shah, sultan, and scholar. All shared in the same culture, even though the shares were disturbed in a very uneven manner. Now, however, Western contacts created an alternative culture that only the elites could hope to achieve. For one thing, only they had the necessary education.

Social changes, thus, came about not because of any great desire for change per se, but rather as an unintended consequence of changes in the political systems, economies, bureaucracies, or communications systems that the local rulers were either powerless to resist (since they represented the fundamental interests of the more powerful Westerners), or that they saw as being worth some measure of social strain (since they simultaneously enhanced the power of the rulers). Despite a century and a half of Western influence and social change, each of the

66. Richard F. Nyrop et al., ed., *Area Handbook for Saudi Arabia* (Washington, 1977), p. 98.

67. Stanford J. Shaw and Ezel Kural Shaw, *History of the Ottoman Empire and Modern Turkey*. Vol. 2, *Reform, Revolution and Republic: The Rise of Modern Turkey 1808–1975* (Cambridge, 1977), p. 68.

68. Donald N. Wilber, *Iran: Past and Present* (eighth edition; Princeton, 1976), pp. 202–3.

69. K. G. Fenelon, *The United Arab Emirates: An Economic and Social Survey* (second edition; London, 1976), p. 98.

70. Patai, *Society, Culture and Change*, p. 371.

Arab states, from Kuwait to Oman, today has the same form (albeit modernized) of tribal-monarchical government as they possessed at the beginning of the period. With the advent of Riẓā Shah to the Peacock throne in the 1920s, the Iranian state became an increasingly active agent for social change in a society highly resistant to such change. But here again, partially due to the depth of society's resistance to change, it was dictated from the top.[71] Although Iraq has undergone a national revolution overthrowing its foreign-imposed monarchy, the new leaders remain a small minority, attempting both to increase the power of the state and to impose their version of social change upon society.

Economic and technological innovations, rather than deliberate policies promoting social change, have been the main motive force behind the societal changes in the region, at least until very recent times. Simultaneously, governments have increased their capacity both to promote change and to deal with the potentially disruptive consequences of economic and technological change. The extent of their achievement can be gauged through an examination of the degree of urbanization and industrialization that these societies have absorbed.

In almost all of the Persian Gulf states, there has been a shift from a predominantly rural society toward one that is increasingly urban. In Iran's national census in 1956, less than one-third of the population was found to be urban; only two decades later the figure was 48 percent.[72] In Iraq, the urban population had remained at a relatively constant 25 percent from the 1860s to 1930; it is estimated today (1974) at 63 percent.[73] Saʿūdī Arabia is still predominantly rural, but it is now becoming urban at the same rate as Iran and Iraq, with its urban population increasing in less than a decade by more than 10 percent, reaching an estimated 33 percent in 1970.[74] For the smaller Arab states the percentages of urbanites must, certainly, be among the highest in the world; Kuwait, for instance, was 94 percent urban in 1965.[75] Only Oman is an exception to the rule, with an urban population of but 4.9 percent in 1970.[76]

Within the overall pattern of rapid urbanization two distinct subpatterns can be seen. The first of these is the concentration of urban growth and of economic activities in a few, or even in a single urban area—almost always the capital city. In 1960, Tehran had 56 percent of the industrial workers of the nation, at the same time Baghdad had 70 percent. This overconcentration has been recognized by the governments concerned as a problem, and official programs are promoting decentralization of both population and industry.

The second trend is the large number of foreigners in the populations of the Arabian peninsula states. These come from both within and outside of the Middle East. The desire for rapid economic growth, the presence of an abundance of surplus wealth from oil revenues and the small size of the local populations have resulted in the importation of foreign professional, technical, clerical

71. Roger M. Savory, "The principle of homeostasis considered in relation to political events in Iran in the 1960s," *International Journal of Middle East Studies* 3 (1973): 283.

72. Jahangir Amuzegar, *Iran: An Economic Profile* (Washington, 1977), p. 15.

73. Costello, *Urbanization*, pp. 31 and 111.

74. Ibid., p. 32.

75. Ibid.

76. Peter Beaumont, Gerald H. Blake, and J. Malcolm Wagstaff, *The Middle East: A Geographical Survey* (London, 1976), Table 6.2. p. 205.

workers, and even of common laborers. In Qatar, Kuwait, and the United Arab Emirates, the indigenous populations are in a minority. Even in Saʻūdī Arabia, which was traditionally a remarkably homogeneous society, foreigners now constitute an estimated 30 percent of the population.[77] With a population of 33.5 million, the largest in the region, it would seem that Iran would have little need to import foreign workers. But here as well the desire for rapid growth has strained the national educational facilities and resulted in the importation of many thousands of foreign technicians and skilled workers. It seems obvious that large numbers of foreign workers would cause serious social problems, as have much smaller percentages in certain European nations. From a purely political standpoint, the local governments are understandably worried about the fact that their own nationals are in a minority. Kuwait hopes that the extremely high national birth rate of 4.5 percent and the admission of a small percentage of the permanent foreign residents to citizenship (1 percent per annum) will give Kuwait a majority of nationals in ten years time.[78] In all of the Arabian peninsula states it is government policy to encourage a high rate of population growth. On the other hand, while Iraq has no explicit policy of limiting population growth, government policies do tend to promote this goal. Iran, however, has an active program of family planning, considered to be one of the most imaginative and widely known in the Islamic world, aimed at reducing the rate of growth to 2.4 percent in 1978 and to 1 percent in 1990.[79]

Social change induced as a necessary but disruptive consequence of economic and technological change has been contained and channeled through government planning and social policies. Education, health services, and social security are generally provided free to nationals. Governments also subsidize housing and basic foodstuffs. The United Arab Emirates even provides camelbreeders a subsidy of 250 dollars per camel. To encourage education, parents are paid for each of their children who attend school.[80]

Social customs, moreover, are not changed automatically by the factors of urban living and industrial employment. Urban living has been one of the traditional life styles of the Middle East. It is nothing new, although now it is much more frequent, for a villager or nomad to move to the city. "Traditional social patterns have been well preserved or even reinforced among some migrant groups, as evinced by the tribal Amara migrants in Baghdad, who worked in the city and were thus subject to the rhythms and pressures of urban employment, but whose social, tribal and religious life remained largely untouched by the city."[81] Information on the size of urban households, a good indicator of the persistence of traditional patterns of family structures in urban settings, show no clear pattern toward smaller families. In an Iraqi study in 1957, the national average size of a household was 5.60 persons, while Baghdad registered 6.16 persons per house-

77. Peter Martin, "Arabia, Economist Survey," *The Economist* (December 10, 1977), pp. 25–26.

78. Ibid., p. 33.

79. Melvyn C. Thorne and Joel Montague, "Special characteristics of population policy in the Middle East and North Africa," *International Journal of Health Services* 3 (1973): 783 (Table 1), 786.

80. "United Arab Emirates: Special report," *Middle East Economic Digest* (July 1977): 32.

81. Costello, *Urbanization*, p. 106.

hold.[82] Another recent study of traditional Arab patterns of family honor (although not including data from the states in our region) concluded that urbanization had no effect on these values.[83]

Economic and social change, of course, are not confined to urbanites. Studies in Iranian society have noted significant changes due to the spread of a national market economy. The demand for meat in urban areas, the consequence of rising incomes, has resulted in changes in the economy of nomadic pastoralists, for example.[84] Even the traditional Iranian villagers, long assumed to be virtually immune to change, have become successful peasant entrepreneurs as contractors and have shifted from farming to employment as store keepers, government employees, teachers, and migrant laborers. Local wages are almost as high as in the towns, and standards of living are visibly rising.[85]

Ever since the pioneering work of Daniel Lerner in the 1950s, *The Passing of Traditional Society in the Middle East*, the role of communications has been stressed as an agent of social change in the Middle East. In countries where illiteracy is still high, it is the media of mass communications that are best able to transmit an awareness of new social institutions and values, as well as a sense of national identity. This has been the case even in Sa'ūdī Arabia, where the conservatism of the religious establishment delayed its development. Since the opening of the first radio station in 1949 by King 'Abd al-'Azīz, the government has strongly supported radio and television broadcasting. The first television station was opened by King Faisal in 1965, and now television covers all the population centers of the kingdom. Public cinemas, however, are still banned, although private, noncommercial showings are allowed.[86] Religious programs, of course, are featured prominently in Sa'ūdī broadcasting; communications can reinforce tradition as well as change. Foreign radio broadcasts are popular and listened to with regularity, with significantly higher percentages of the better educated listening with greater frequency. It has been estimated that one-third of the urban population in two cities surveyed in Sa'ūdī Arabia in 1975 (Jidda and Dammām) listened to foreign radio broadcasts with regularity.

Modern channels of communication are becoming widespread throughout the Persian Gulf region. But they are largely channels under the control of the government and are not balanced by the development of channels for the citizens to communicate with the rulers. Communications developments only serve to confirm the general pattern and process of social change in the region. The greatest change of all has been in the creation of a type of modern governmental organization, which in turn has been able, through its monopoly of power and the utilization of vast oil revenues, to dominate the other processes of socio-economic change.

82. Kahtan A. J. Madfai, "Baghdad," in Morroe Berger, ed. *The New Metropolis in the Arab World* (New Delhi, 1963), p. 51. See also, Fuad Baali, "Social forces in Iraqi rural-urban migration," *American Journal of Economics and Sociology* 25 (1966): 357–64.

83. Peter C. Dodd, "Family honor and the forces of change in Arab society," *International Journal of Middle East Studies* 4 (1973): 49.

84. Michael Fisher, "Persian Society: Transformation and Strain," in Hossein Amirsadeghi, ed., *Twentieth Century Iran* (London, 1977), p. 177.

85. Reinhold L. Loeffler, "Recent economic changes in Boir Ahmad: Regional growth without development," *Iranian Studies* 4 (1976): 266.

86. Nyrop, ed., *Area Handbook*, pp. 193–204.

Patterns of Societal Response to Change

Four overall patterns have characterized the responses of Persian Gulf societies to those forces of social change that have influenced developments since the early decades of the nineteenth century. These patterns are: homeostatic responses, unplanned change, planned partial change, and planned total change.

Homeostatic responses have been defined as the tendency of a society to "maintain as much of its former condition as is practically possible however determined the attempts to alter its shape."[87] The resilience and flexibility of traditional Middle Eastern societies have been truly remarkable over a long period of time. Any disturbance in the traditional social equilibrium arouses countervailing forces in opposition to change in general and in defense of their traditional privileges in particular. In Iran, these forces have been identified as the monarchy, the 'ulamā', the bazaar merchants, the tribal khans, and the landlords.[88] Similar lists could no doubt be drawn up for all Middle Eastern societies.

In his examination of the response of Islam to the forces of Western modernization, the Pakistani scholar Fazlur Rahman has illuminated the intellectual roots of this attitude.[89] The great Islamic modernists of the nineteenth century, including Sir Sayyid Ahmad Khan, Shaikh Muhammad 'Abduh, and Jamāl al-Dīn al-Afghānī, saw the challenge of the West to Islam in intellectual terms. They adopted a comprehensive view of Islamic reform, one which would emphasize the intellectual, moral, and spiritual revival of Islam and not just political, legal, and social reforms. However, the attitude of the dominant establishment of the 'ulamā', which had been antirationalist for many centuries, was to brand any criticism of the moral and spiritual realities of contemporary Islam as an attack on its fundamental beliefs. Moreover, such criticism had a divisive effect on the solidarity of Islamic communities in the face of the challenge of the West. It was this attitude, rather than that of the reformers, which triumphed.

The denial of any need to respond to the changes of Westernization, except through repudiating them and attempting to limit their effects, did not prevent the West from exerting a profound, if unplanned, change in traditional societies. The establishment of steamship lines altered the traditional maritime economies of the Gulf city-states without asking the permission of either the 'ulamā' or the local political leaders. Certain individuals and groups within the traditional social order, usually but not always the rulers, saw that it was in their own self-interest to cooperate with the West in certain matters. In the founding of the Dār al-Funūn, Nāsir al-Dīn Shah Qājār, gave little, if any, thought to the potential social impact of Western education upon Iranian society; he wanted a more efficient and better-trained group of bureaucrats, diplomats, and soldiers to enhance his own position in dealing with both his traditional domestic foes and with the powerful West. The impact of this kind of unplanned change upon society was none the less profound for being unplanned, as the Shah himself was to

87. Savory, "The principle of homeostasis," p. 283.
88. Ibid., pp. 283–84.
89. Fazlur Rahman, "Islamic modernism: Its scope, method and alternatives," *International Journal of Middle East Studies* 1 (1970): 317–33.

find out when his insatiable demands for money led to the granting of the tobacco concession to a foreign company in 1890.[90]

The predominant mode of social change in the area has been that of planned partial change, almost always under the direction of the local rulers and political elites. This process prompts the separation of the processes of change into a number of distinct categories, such as economic, legal, educational, military, and political. Emphasis is usually placed upon the economic category as the least controversial and the most immediately helpful in enhancing the power of the state and its ruler. It represents an advancement over the pattern of un-planned change (although unplanned change, of course, still goes on in the midst of the best-laid planned change), since it does take into account the side effects that will be produced in society. The rulers and planners will either attempt to contain the social impact of their actions or arrive at a rough cost-benefit analysis that will convince them that the benefits of change will outweigh their social costs. Changes of this type are more acceptable to both rulers and the ruled. They make it possible for the rulers to continue their age-old game of balancing one group against the other. The 'ulamā' feel that this is the same type of control that they long ago conceded to be within the realm of "secular" rulers. As long as the strictly "religious" spheres of faith, morals, and family life are left alone, along with the special privileges of the 'ulamā', such change may even work to strengthen Islamic communities in the face of more dangerous foreign aggressions.

The final pattern of social change to be found in the area is that of a compre-hensive system of planned total change. This is an effort to create a new man and a new society, not merely to reform a few of the more glaring social weak-nesses and abuses of the existent society. This involves a bold, frontal attack on the homeostatic forces of society which, thus far, only a few leaders have been able to mount. In the Middle East, the earliest example of such a program is undoubtedly the Kemalist Revolution in Turkey. Despite its continued problems, this is probably also still the most successful example. In the Persian Gulf area the beginnings of such an attack can be found in the programs of Rizā Shah in the 1920s and 1930s.[91]

Unfortunately, Rizā Shah lacked the advantage of more than a century of planned partial change under the Ottoman reformers, as well as the immense prestige gained by Kemal Atatürk through his leadership in the War of Inde-pendence (1919–23). He also lacked Atatürk's education and knowledge of the wide world. Rizā Shah's ultimate aims were clear and his actual achievements considerable, but the strength of the homeostatic forces in society forced him to compromise with the 'ulamā' in his desire for a republic and with the traditional system of land tenure.[92] After his removal as a result of foreign invasion and exile, the homeostatic forces in Iranian society reasserted themselves. It was not until the 1960s that his son, Muhammad Rizā Shah, was able to institute an even more comprehensive and uncompromising program of political, social, and economic

90. Nikki R. Keddie, *Religion and Rebellion in Iran: The Iranian Tobacco Protest of 1891–1892* (London, 1966), gives a fascinating account of this prelude to the Iranian constitutional revolution.

91. The most complete study of the reforms of Rizā Shah is that of Amin Banani, *The Modernization of Iran, 1921–1941* (Stanford, 1961). See also Wilber, *Riza Shah Pahlavi*.

92. Peter Avery, *Modern Iran* (London, 1965), p. 267.

reforms. This "White Revolution" or "Shah-People Revolution" finally took on the homeostatic forces of society, including the landlords and the *'ulamā'*. The process, however, is not yet completed. The development of a truly national and representative form of participation for all classes of society, versus the present heavy emphasis on reform from the top and bureaucratic control, is still a matter of intense debate and controversy.[93]

Since the Iraqi Revolution of 14 July 1958 overthrowing the foreign-imposed Hashimite dynasty, Iraq has had a number of régimes bent upon the application of some form of "Arab Socialism" as a program of planned total change for the nation. Like its more conservative Arab neighbors, Iraq has had the advantage of large oil revenues. But in the first ten years following the 1958 revolution, these advantages were dissipated by a succession of short-lived régimes, all of them dependent upon the army and based upon a small group of radical political leaders. These leaders showed no more competence at implementing their grandiose plans for social development than they did in staying in power.[94] Since 1968 there has been a greater degree of internal stability provided by the Ba'th party régime, but the divisions in Iraqi society between Shī'ī and Sunnī, Kurd and Arab, as well as the involvement in quarrels with Iraq's neighbors, have continued to hinder Iraq's revolutionary social programs. "While claiming to espouse radical ideologies, the new leadership has introduced radical reforms only spasmodically and often for political, nonideological reasons."[95] With the defeat of the Kurdish Revolt in 1975, coupled with the spectacular rise in oil income after 1973, Iraq would seem to have the greatest potential of all of the radical "Arab Socialist" states to actually achieve its stated goals of a total transformation of society.

Our final example of a program of planned total change must consider the somewhat surprising case of Sa'ūdī Arabia. The present Sa'ūdī state is founded upon the basis of an Islamic ideology calling for the return to the fundamental purity of early Islam. If this were to be achieved, few would doubt that it would be a revolutionary change. Islam is certainly one of the most successful revolutionary movements in world history, while the achievement of King 'Abd al-Azīz on the twentieth-century Arabian peninsula deserves to be termed, as it is termed today by the present generation of Sa'ūdī leaders, a "revolutionary and reformist" success.[96] The scope of Sa'ūdī Arabia's present five-year development plan adopted in 1975 and calling for the expenditure of $143 billion in a country of less than seven million population cannot but have a revolutionary impact on society.[97] The present leaders realize this, but do not seem particularly worried. With its continued emphasis on the contemporary validity of Islamic values,

93. For an excellent discussion of this process of debate, see James A. Bill's article, "Iran: Is the Shah Pushing Too Fast?" *Christian Science Monitor* (November 6, 1977).

94. Phoebe A. Marr, "The Political Elite of Iraq," in George Lenczowski, ed., *Political Elites in the Middle East* (Washington, 1975), pp. 119–49.

95. Ibid., p. 149.

96. This is the term used by Crown Prince Fahd of Sa'ūdī Arabia to describe the policies of both King 'Abd al-'Azīz and of King Khālid. See the extensive interview given to a Kuwaiti newspaper editor as reported in "Kuwait's As-Siyasā Interviews Crown Prince Fahd." *Middle East and North Africa Daily Reports* (Foreign Broadcast Information Service) April 21, 1977, pp. C-2 and C-3.

97. Donald A. Wells, *Saudi Arabian Development Policy* (Washington, 1976), p. 11.

along with a firm commitment to change at a rate believed to be impossible only a few years ago, it would seem that the Sa'ūdī experiment deserves to be considered within the category of planned total change, even though its goal of the new society and the new man is the timeless goal of Islam itself.

Emergence of a New Social Structure

We have characterized traditional Persian Gulf society as one in which a number of distinct social groups existed with a considerable degree of autonomy. It was an integrated society only to the extent that most of these groups shared in the same culture and religion. Developments since the nineteenth century have created, if not yet a new type of class basis for society, at least a number of new elements to be accounted for in our appraisal of the contemporary societies of the Persian Gulf. Some of these new elements seem to be wholly new to the experience of the area. Others appear to be substantial variants of traditional social groups. But, whether totally new or variant elements are considered, clearly the new social structure of the Persian Gulf contains strong elements of its traditional groups as well, and especially strong elements of its traditional patterns of articulation and integration.

Industrial Workers. Industrial workers are a totally new group in the experience of the area. Statistics as to the numbers of this new group are notoriously unreliable. Most contain employment in traditional crafts, along with modern industrial employment. Still, industrial employment is definitely increasing, while traditional crafts are declining. In only five years between 1966 and 1971, the industrial work force of Iran rose from 20 percent of the total labor force to 28 percent.[98] If anything, the trend toward industrial employment is accelerating; the Fifth Development Plan (1973–77) aimed at the creation of 40 percent of the new employment opportunities within the industrial sector.[99]

As a social group, the industrial workers occupy an anomalous position. Their origins seem to be among traditional lower-status groups, especially former villagers attracted to the city.[100] However, it would be difficult indeed to attempt to equate their social position with that of European or American industrial workers at a comparative stage of the West's industrial revolution. Compared to many of their countrymen they are relatively well off economically. "In the oil shaikhdoms," writes John Duke Anthony, "even the lowest paid unskilled indigenous worker is very well off by Middle Eastern standards. He may earn from five to six dollars a day."[101] Generally, they have excellent job security. In 1968, Aramco's work force was 82 percent Sa'ūdī Arabian nationals, with a norm of eighteen years of continuous service.[102] No Kuwaiti ever need worry about un-

98. Firouz Tofigh, "Development in Iran: A Statistical Note," in Jane W. Jacqz, ed., *Iran: Past, Present and Future* (New York and Aspen, 1976), p. 59.

99. F. Aminzadeh, "Human Resources Development: Problems and Prospects," in Jacqz, ed., *Iran*, Table 47, p. 191.

100. Costello, *Urbanization*, p. 82.

101. Anthony, *Arab States*, p. 12.

102. Powell Ownby, "The Development of Human Resources," in Young, ed., *Middle East Focus*, p. 113.

employment; he is entitled to a government job if no other employment is available.[103]

Industrial employment is the subject of numerous laws and government regulations. Although sometimes not too well enforced, especially in the early years, such regulation gave the workers considerably more protection than other sectors of the population. Industrial workers have been among the first and most consistent beneficiaries of governmental actions in the fields of health, education, welfare, and social services (including wage and hour legislation and unemployment insurance). Despite their economic position and the numerous government-provided or guaranteed benefits, they are still looked down upon socially. "The social stigma attached to virtually any type of manual labor is a chief reason for the reluctance of students to select technical training. In Iraq, the typical young person aspires to become a lowly paid clerk rather than a prosperous mechanic or television repairman," write two Iraqi educators.[104]

The industrial worker is thus relatively well off economically, but still of low social standing; additionally, he is closely watched politically. The first labor unions in Iran were founded in 1921 by leaders trained by the Communist party of the USSR. In 1929, the labor unions were closed by the government and about fifty of their leaders imprisoned. At this time they had an estimated 7,000 members.[105] The trade union movement was resurrected under the auspices of the *Tūdeh* (Masses) party in 1942 under Soviet protection. They remained a powerful element in the *Tūdeh*'s structure (with some of the same leaders who were released from prison following the occupation of northern Iran by the Soviets in August, 1941) until the party itself was banned in 1949.

Iran today has more than 900 labor syndicates and 20 labor confederations under the provisions of the Labor Law of 1959. Collective bargaining is practiced, but labor disputes are settled by compulsory government arbitration, should collective bargaining fail.[106] Iraq has a national labor federation, the Iraqi Confederation of Trade Unions, but, like all such groups in Iraq, it operates under close governmental surveillance.[107]

Labor unions are generally banned in all of the Arabian peninsula states. However, in Bahrain the workers have displayed an amazing tenacity in demanding the right to organize. This tenacity has been matched by the equal determination of the government to prevent the organization of trade unions. "Labor unions have been viewed as a negative force whose long-range objective was to dismantle the Khalīfa régime, and therefore such a force could not be tolerated."[108] The first strike in Bahrain was directed against the Bahrain Petroleum Company, in 1938, and led to an increase in the number of expatriate workers, who were deemed to be less likely to strike. In 1965, another strike against the oil company turned into a national uprising, suppressed after several months by

103. "Special report, Kuwait," *Middle East Economic Digest* (August, 1977): 38.
104. Abdul Jalil Alzobaie and Mohammed Ahmed El-Ghannam, "Iraqi student perceptions of occupations," *Sociology and Social Research* 52 (1968): 231.
105. Wilber, *Iran: Past and Present*, pp. 312–13.
106. Amuzegar, *Iran*, pp. 234–35.
107. Richard F. Nyrop, et al., eds., *Area Handbook for Iraq*, 2d printing (Washington, D.C., 1971), pp. 299–300.
108. Nakhleh, *Bahrain*, p. 75.

a state of emergency and numerous arrests.[109] Today, despite the provision in the 1973 Constitution, guaranteeing the right to form labor unions "on a patriotic basis, for lawful ends, and by peaceful means," there are no legal unions; the Labor Law of 1976 does not even mention them.[110]

Clearly, the industrial worker belongs to a new social group, but his ultimate position in the social structure is still clouded. He is alternately pampered and suppressed by the government. He is of lowly social status, but he is well-off economically. With the possible exception of Bahrain, the workers have yet to demonstrate that they are a "working class" in the Western sense of that term. Rather, as one scholar has written: "If anything, the industrial workers of the Middle East seem to become the base of some sort of bourgeois category."[111] They are still suppliants, albeit often successful suppliants before their governments. Their material condition is improving due to a combination of economic and political factors. Simultaneously, two major factors work against the development of a greater degree of class consciousness. First, in countries with large populations there remains a tremendous reservoir of potential industrial workers who are willing and eager to obtain the benefits of steady wage labor. Second, in the smaller oil-rich states there is the pressure of immigrant workers available for lower wages and few, if any, benefits.

The New Middle Class. A second new social group, the so-called "New Middle Class," is even more fascinating than is the industrial working group. "The question whether there exists, yes or no, a (budding or, as some say, new) middle class in the Middle East is perhaps more, and more hotly debated than any other social issue in the area."[112] Western sociologists who describe this class tend to identify it too closely with Western ideas of the middle class. Its major components are the modern secular educated and salaried "military, organizers, administrators and experts."[113] The revolutionary potential (as distinguished from the coup-making potential—admittedly very high) is exaggerated, as is the degree of their commitment as a group to progress and social reform.

Observers of the new middle class agree that its social position is based largely upon its mastery of secular, technical, and nontraditional knowledge. Its members commonly occupy positions in the bureaucracy, professions, and intelligentsia, and these positions are obtained more through merit and individual achievement than through membership in ascriptive groups or through personal/familial influence.[114] The term used by James A. Bill to describe this group in Iran is instructive: "the professional-bureaucratic intelligentsia."[115] It is growing rapidly in size and political influence. Between 1956 and 1966, its members increased from 322,000 to 513,000, or 8.6 percent of the employed population.[116] In

109. Ibid., p. 79.

110. Emile A. Nakhleh, "Labor markets and citizenship in Bahrayn and Qatar," *Middle East Journal* 31 (1977): 147.

111. Van Nieuwenhuijze, *Sociology of the Middle East*, p. 731.

112. Ibid., p. 581.

113. Halpern, *Politics of Social Change*, pp. 52–53.

114. James Alban Bill, *The Politics of Iran: Groups, Classes and Modernization* (Columbus, Ohio, 1972), pp. 53–72.

115. Ibid., p. 53.

116. Ibid. Tables 4 and 6, pp. 65 and 67. In the same decade, the bourgeois middle class grew at the rate of 2.3 percent to total 471,500 or 7.9 percent of the employed population.

his study of the same group in Saʻūdī Arabia, William Rugh does not attempt to give its numerical total, rather characterizing it as small, but increasingly influential. The examination of the educational background of the top two grades of the civil service in the government in 1969 revealed that only 31 out of a total of 189 had traditional education, 45 had Western education, while the rest had a secular Arab education.[117]

The crucial question to be examined regarding these groups is not their exact numerical strength, but rather the extent to which their behavior differs from that of other social groups and tends to disrupt the traditional social structure. We identified the components of the traditional "middle strata" in the Middle East as the bureaucracy, the traditional bourgeoisie, and the bulk of the ʻulamāʾ. The largest employer of the present new middle class is the bureaucracy, while the modern intelligentsia would seem to correspond in function (especially in its educational function) to the traditional ʻulamāʾ. There thus seems to be some potential for the new group to model itself after its traditional predecessors. In their power relationship, the new group remains subordinated to the political elites. Social mobility is another characteristic of the new middle class. However, in the Middle Eastern social structure, the middle strata were inferior to the landlord, nomad, religious, military, and even slave elites gathered about the person of the ruler. It is thus possible that the upwardly mobile member of the new middle class will seek elite status on an individual basis, instead of middle status as a group. The European bourgeoisie was in fact a revolutionary class. It grew up outside of the traditional feudal social order, but was able to gain recognition and influence as a separate class because it was economically independent and because medieval ideology accepted the idea of corporate groups. In contrast, the new middle class in the Persian Gulf is emerging in a society with a strong tradition of centralized political control, and one in which they lack economic independence, since most are state employees.

In practice, as Bill points out, only a portion of the new middle class attempts to challenge the basis of the traditional social order; he terms these "the uprooters." Others seek to perform their modern roles in a competent and politically neutral manner—"the technocrats." Still a third group become active players in the traditional social game and supporters of the traditional social order; these are termed "the maneuverers."[118] In Saʻūdī Arabia, the new middle class has obtained a more important economic position in society, but conforms to the social and political aspects of the traditional social order. It has welcomed the changes introduced by the Saʻūdī political elite, but it did not demand them. "As long as economic development and some social change have occurred, it has eschewed demands for political change."[119]

The Iraqi experience should provide some clues as to the direction and potential of the new middle class in power. Since the 1958 revolution, the ruling elites in Iraq have all come from the middle class and, increasingly, from the lower middle class.[120] There has been a great gap, however, between revolutionary

---

117. William Rugh, "Emergence of a new middle class in Saudi Arabia," *Middle East Journal* 27 (1973): Table 14.

118. Bill, *The Politics of Iran*, pp. 70–72.

119. Rugh, "A new middle class in Saudi Arabia," p. 20.

120. Marr, "Political Elite of Iraq," p. 134. However, as the author points out, many of the leaders under the Hashimites were also of middle class origin, including Nūrī al-Saʻīd.

slogans and actions. The traditional categories of ethnic and religious origins are far more important than are socioeconomic class in the composition of the revolutionary leadership. Of the three basic divisions in Iraqi society, Sunnī Arab, Shī'ī Arab, and Kurd, it is the Sunnī Arab (25 percent of the population) who have dominated the leadership of postrevolution Iraq, just as they dominated society under the monarchy. The Shī'ī community has held only 29 percent of the political leadership positions, and but 16 percent of the top positions, despite being the majority of the population.[121]

The new middle class has yet to justify the hopes, or fears, of those who have seen it as a force for progressive social change in the area.[122] It has been rent by internal strife, based upon both traditional social divisions and upon its orientation toward programs of modernization directed from above by the rulers and ruling elites. The traditional rulers have not been idle; they themselves have introduced many of the social reforms desired by the new groups. The new middle class, or at least some members of it, have been put in charge of the execution, planning, and, increasingly, the initiation of vast programs of socioeconomic reforms.

Changes in the international situation have eased pressures from the new middle class on Persian Gulf rulers. A large measure of the opposition of the new middle class to the traditional and bourgeois liberal leadership of Middle Eastern governments stemmed from the perception that they were not sufficiently nationalistic.[123] Direct Western imperialism in the Middle East was a very live issue in the 1950s and 1960s. On the Arabian peninsula, however, Western imperialism was a more indirect influence. By the time that significant groups of the new middle class had been formed, the British imperialist had withdrawn voluntarily. In the case of Iran and Iraq, where imperialist pressures upon local governments were more direct, the leaders were weakened by charges of their subjection to foreign control. The withdrawal of Western imperialism and the weakening of the danger of Soviet expansionism have allowed the local governments to adopt independent national foreign and economic policies. The rise in oil revenues, which has done so much to strengthen the hands of the local rulers in a purely economic sense, has served also to demonstrate that they are just as capable (or even more so) as are the "revolutionary" governments of the Middle East in advancing their common national goals of control of their natural resources, foreign policies, and economic policies.

Rural Change: Landlords, Peasants, Nomads, and Officials

A major focus of social change in the Persian Gulf societies has been in the rural sector. Traditionally, two social groups controlled the countryside—the nomads and the landlords. In addition, the top elites of these two groups formed a part of the ruling elite of society, indeed, the rulers themselves often came from

121. Ibid., p. 137.
122. Bill and Leiden, *The Middle East*, pp. 87–88.
123. Arnold Hottinger, "How the Arab bourgeoisie lost power," *Journal of Contemporary History* 37 (1968): 116.

among the nomadic tribes. Today, both the landlords and nomads have declined in importance as social groups, or have been virtually eliminated. Simultaneously, the actual cultivators of the land are becoming transformed from their former status as the most oppressed social group of the whole society into something approaching the status of an independent owner-operator of their own farms. Tribal nomads, who formerly established imperial dynasties, now find themselves politically under the firm control of the government and see their economic basis being transformed by the development of communications and national markets. All governments in the area encourage the settlement of nomads. Today, the nomadic population of Iran is estimated at only 1 percent, Iraq at 2.8 percent, Saʿūdī Arabia at 11 percent, and the United Arab Emirates ranging from 5 to 15 percent.[124]

One social factor remains unchanged; it is the center that dominates the periphery in both traditional and modernizing societies. In the traditional societies, however, the central governments lacked the military, administrative, and technical means to control the countryside directly; they had to depend upon the cooperation of the landlords and tribal chiefs. Contemporary changes have made it possible for the governments to establish direct control. First came the establishment of security through military campaigns and gendarmerie posts. Then, in the past two decades, came efforts to replace the traditional rural power structure of tribal chiefs and landlords with a combination of government officials and some newly established rural social and political institutions. In the major agricultural development project at Qazvīn, Iran, one observer noted that "government bureaucrats and engineers became the functional equivalents of the landlords, excluding the peasants from decision making."[125] Among the nomads, however, the traditional tribal chiefs were likely to be turned into government functionaries and intermediaries between their tribesmen and the bureaucracy.[126]

The displacement of the traditional rural social groups has been more successful than has the creation of a vigorous new class of independent farmers. This is hardly surprising. The impetus for change came from the rulers and elements among the ruling elites anxious, above all, to break the rural basis of power of these traditional groups who opposed all change in the traditional social order. The reorganization of rural society on a new basis was, if not exactly an afterthought, at least a secondary consideration. A. K. S. Lambton has observed, in connection with Iranian land reform: "Its aims were in the first instance political and social. It was intended first to break the political and social influence of the landowning class, and secondly, so far as Dr. Arsanjani, its main architect, was concerned, to bring about the emergence of an independent peasantry."[127] The Iraqi land reform following the 1958 revolution had substantially the same objectives.[128] Its effects on the Iraqi government are clear. Since 1958 only one percent of the ministers and members of the RCC (Revolutionary Command

124. Beaumont, Blake, and Wagstaff, *The Middle East*, Table 5.6, p. 87.
125. Fisher, "Persian Society," p. 184.
126. Philip Carl Salzman, "Continuity and change in Baluchi tribal leadership," *International Journal of Middle East Studies* 4 (1973): 428–39.
127. A. K. S. Lambton, *The Persian Land Reform, 1962–1966* (Oxford, 1969), p. 64.
128. Nyrop, et al., eds., *Area Handbook*, p. 258.

Council) have been of merchant or landlord origins, while previously some 16 percent of the top elites came from such a background.[129]

The economic and social effects of land reform have been varied. Iraq suffered a 25 percent drop in the production of wheat, barley, and rice in the first three years following land reform. Although cooperatives were encouraged, they suffered from a lack of trained and competent administration, and agricultural credit facilities were lacking.[130] Evaluations of the land reform's social effects in Iran are mixed, but generally positive in their belief that the social life of the countryside is being genuinely transformed by the creation of a new group of independent farmers. Nikki R. Keddie estimates that this new group consists of between 14 and 15 percent of the former tenants.[131] Ismail Ajami, however, estimates that between 40 and 50 percent of the cultivable land has been transferred to some 70 percent of the rural population.[132] This difference may be explicable by the fact that some of the land is now registered in the name of its former tenants, but they are continuing to make payments to the former landlords. In any case, there remains a considerable group of landless farm laborers.

In Iran the new social and political institutions established in the villages, such as the cooperatives, village councils, and houses of justice have had difficulty in obtaining competent administrators and in dealing with the higher levels of the bureaucracy. The education and health corps, however, have been successful in their mission of providing services to rural areas and in creating a new progressive atmosphere.[133] Traditional social attitudes are being transformed as the villagers begin to demand better government services. A recent village study refers to this development as: "A process which is filling them with new expectations for the future, but which is also changing basically the structure of their traditional way of life."[134] Another author noted that the former tenants are reluctant to perform the traditional "services" due to their former landlords and that a few have even challenged the right of former landlords to a particular plot of ground.[135] But here, as elsewhere in our study of Persian Gulf society, elements of the old social structure still remain: on ritual occasions the ex-tenants defer socially to their ex-landlords, and they still continue to refer to them, among themselves, as "landlords."[136]

Status of Women

One could scarcely refer to women as a distinct social group or class, yet their position in traditional Persian Gulf societies (and, to some extent, their

129. Marr, "Political Elite of Iraq," p. 129.
130. Beaumont, Blake, and Wagstaff, The Middle East, p. 147.
131. Nikki R. Keddie, "Stratification, Social Control, and Capitalism in Iranian Villages: Before and After Land Reform." In Richard Antoun and Iliya Harik, eds., Rural Politics and Social Change in the Middle East (Bloomington, Ind., 1972), p. 394.
132. Ismail Ajami, "Agriculture and Rural Development in Iran," in Jacqz, ed., Iran, p. 146.
133. Fisher, "Persian Society," p. 185.
134. Loeffler, "Recent economic changes," p. 266.
135. Richard Antoun, "The Gentry of a Traditional Peasant Community undergoing Rapid Technological Change: An Iranian Case Study," Iranian Studies (1976), 4: 7.
136. Ibid.

position in contemporary society as well) is perhaps more distinctive than that of any social group. Traditionally, men and women live in two different realms with different life styles. "Nor were there any grounds for talking about lack of equal rights because men and women in Kurdistan each have their own pattern of life," writes Henny Harold Hansen. "One might as well say that a man had not the same rights as a woman because he was unable to follow her pattern of life. The worlds of men and women were simply divided, more or less (mostly more) from the cradle to the grave."[137]

The position of women is probably the least investigated aspect of Middle Eastern societies. This is especially true of contemporary social change. There are a number of excellent studies of women in traditional communities, but few indeed of women in modern, urban conditions. An obvious reason for all this is, of course, the difficulties of associating with women in the Middle East, even for women foreigners. In many ways it is harder to do so in modern urban settings than it was in villages. In his influential work, *The Politics of Social Change in the Middle East and North Africa*, Manfred Halpern acknowledges that, for reasons of time and space, he has been forced to omit the entire subject of women from his study.[138] Donald N. Wilber's encyclopedic *Iran: Past and Present* contains no topical heading on women in its contents, nor are they mentioned in the index.[139] With rare exceptions, women have not been worked into the broad discussions of the processes of social change in the Middle East. C.A.O. Van Nieuwenhuijze's *Social Stratification and the Middle East* does consider the role of women, but the title of the chapter is suggestive of his views—"A Category Aside."[140]

Such evidence that we do possess would seem to suggest that women are among the strongest supporters of the persistence and flexibility of the traditional social order. For this is a system which, above all, is based upon ties of personal and familial influence rather than upon formal institutions. It is precisely this area which is the particular sphere of women, i.e., family relationships and inter-family communications. Women have their own communications networks, and constant visiting between households is their characteristic occupation. Through these family relationships, they can achieve remarkable influence and power over men, both husbands and sons. Relationships between mothers and sons are especially strong and have had major social and political consequences.[141]

Unfortunately, probably 99 percent of this influence remains hidden behind "the veil," even where veils themselves are no longer worn. On rare occasions, however, a public manifestation of this power becomes visible and causes one to wonder how one's evaluation of these societies would be changed were we to know the full extent of women's societal role. The political career of Shaikha Hassa bint al-Murr, mother of Shaikh Rashīd of Dubai, is instructive. She was publicly acknowledged for many years as the real power in the state, engaging in commerce and property development, holding public *majlis* for men, and even,

137. Henny Harold Hansen, *The Kurdish Woman's Life* (Copenhagen, 1961), p. 178.
138. Halpern, *Politics of Social Change*, p. xiii.
139. Wilber, *Iran: Past and Present*, pp. vii, viii, and 369.
140. Van Nieuwenhuijze, *Social Stratification*, pp. 69–76.
141. Nyrop, et al., eds. *Area Handbook*, pp. 153–54.

reportedly, leading the army in a war against Sharja.[142] It is perhaps significant that in a civil war in 1939–40 she played a leading role in the defeat of the reformist party: "Modern education, street cleaning and the like, had to wait for another twenty years."[143]

A fundamental social change in the contemporary Persian Gulf is the emergence of women into the previously exclusively male world of public affairs. Modern education is the first and most visible component of this change. Women are being educated through university levels, but there is still a wide gap between the percentages enrolled at the different educational levels. During the decade of the 1960s, Iran had 34 percent of the 5 to 14-year-old age group enrolled in school, but only 13.9 percent of the 15 to 19-year-old group and 3.3 percent of the 20 to 24-year-old university level students.[144] In 1967, Sa'ūdī Arabian girls' schools enrolled 72,584 primary pupils, 2,206 intermediate, and only 494 at the secondary level. Teacher training institutes, however, enrolled 1,718 and technical institutes a further 158.[145] Less than a decade later, in 1975, the absolute numbers had multiplied in all categories, but the gaps between the different levels remained substantial: 214,641 elementary, 34,061 intermediate, 7,616 secondary, 4,561 teacher training, and 550 technical.[146]

Education is often in separate schools for girls and boys, but coeducation is becoming more common, especially in elementary schools. All Bahrain's state schools are coeducational, as are Iranian schools. Iraqi schools are coeducational at the primary levels; there is some indication that university education may become coeducational in Kuwait. Overall, Kuwait offers the most extensive educational opportunities for women. In the decade of the 1960s it had the highest rate of female literacy in the area (and, indeed, in the Muslim world), some 42 percent. In the same period, Bahrain's female literacy rate was 37 percent and Iran's 25.3 percent (data for 1971 in both cases).[147] Kuwait was in another unique position, due to the fact that women were a majority of its university students, although this might be explained by the fact that many male students go abroad for university education.[148]

Outside of education, the participation of women in the male world of economic, social, and political affairs is much less dramatic. Given the traditional system, however, any such participation must be counted as being significant. Many of the women who participate in "modern" institutions, such as hospitals, schools, and welfare institutions, do so in institutions that deal with women exclusively. Still, only an estimated 2 percent of Sa'ūdī Arabian women have any employment outside of the home.[149] In Iran, the employment of women rose from

142. Anthony, *Arab States of the Lower Gulf*, pp. 156–58.
143. P. A. Lienhardt, "Some Social Aspects of the Trucial States: The Position of Women in the Society of the Trucial Coast," in Hopwood, ed., *The Arabian Peninsula*, pp. 230.
144. Nadia H. Youssef, "Education and female modernism in the Muslim world," *Journal of International Affairs* 30: 2 (Fall/Winter 1976–77): Table 3.
145. Abd-el Wahab Abd-el Wassie, *Education in Saudi Arabia* (London, 1970), Table 11.
146. Nyrop, et al., eds., *Area Handbook*, Table 1.
147. Youssef, "Education and female modernism," p. 193, Nakhleh, *Bahrain*, p. 19, and Mamideh Sedghi and Ahmad Ashraf, "The Role of Women in Iranian Development," in Jacqz, ed., *Iran*, p. 207.
148. "Special Report, Kuwait," p. 37.
149. Nyrop, et al., eds., *Area Handbook*, p. 154. Legal restrictions above, such as the banning of women drivers, undoubtedly makes the employment of women very difficult.

9.2 percent of the population in 1956 to 11 percent in 1971, and was expected to reach 25 percent in 1992.[150]

Politically, only Iran (1963) and Iraq (1967) have granted the right to vote to women. In 1972, however, in a step almost without precedent in the area, the women's organizations of Bahrain petitioned the ruler to grant them suffrage under the new constitution. They cited their educational achievements, Bahrain's position as "the cultural, social and civilizational leader of the Gulf," and the Charter and Universal Declaration of Human Rights of the United Nations as reasons why their petition should be granted. They did not achieve their goal.[151]

Socially, the custom of veiling (the actual form of the veil varies from place to place) is seen as a key indication of both governmental and societal attitudes toward women. This is complicated, however, by the fact that veiling is not universal in traditional societies of the area, and in some places it is practiced as a result of custom, while in other places it is legally enforced. For instance, it was not until 1926 that the veiling of women was made legally compulsory in Sa'ūdī Arabia.[152] Iran, in 1936, was the first Gulf state to enforce the banning of the veil.[153] But even here there was a resurgence of the veil following the exile of Riżā Shah in 1941.[154] There is some evidence that there might be a return to the veil today, even among educated, urban women.[155] On the other hand, women have become very active in the programs of the White Revolution, especially through service in the Education and Health Corps. Some serve also in the regular armed forces. The legal status of women had begun to change with the reforms of Riżā Shah, and this has continued until the present day. Divorce is now a civil procedure, with equal rights for men and women; polygamy requires official permission; and the right of women to work without their husband's consent is guaranteed.[156] Both the Shāhbānū (Empress) Farah and H. R. H. Princess Ashraf, the twin sister of the Shah, occupied positions of prominence in Iranian public life. In 1967, an amendment to the constitution provided for the Shāhbānū to assume the regency during the reign of a minor shah.*

Clearly, women are participating to an increasing degree in the social, economic, and political activities of Persian Gulf societies. These participants are most likely to be the younger, better educated, urban, and relatively more wealthy women. With the exception of education, actual levels of participation lag behind comparable groups of men. It would appear that the governments concerned have an excellent opportunity for enlisting the support of this emerging new force. On the other hand, the emergence of a new public social role for women will affect their traditional role within the social system. As they become

---

150. Sedghi and Ashraf, "Role of Women in Iranian Development," pp. 205 and 209.

151. Nakhleh, *Bahrain*, pp. 143–44, gives the text of this petition.

152. Levy, *Social Structure of Islam*, p. 129.

153. Avery, *Modern Iran*, p. 292.

154. Ibid. He suggests that part of the return to the veil in Iran during the years after 1941 may have been due to economic conditions, which made it a less expensive form of dress.

155. Bill, "Iran, Is the Shah Going Too Fast?"

156. Sedghi and Ashraf, "Role of Women in Iranian Development," p. 204. See Banani, *Modernization of Iran*, pp. 8–84, for a summary of the legal reforms in the status of women in the reign of Riżā Shah.

* Editors' note: This paragraph predates the Iranian Revolution of January 1979.

formal participants in an organized and institutionalized manner, they may fail to maintain their informal dominance over the sphere of familial and personal relations.

Immigrant Populations

Immigrant workers must be considered as an important new social group for two reasons. First, it is a unique social fact for the native population of a country to be greatly outnumbered by aliens. Second, it seems to be increasingly accepted as a semipermanent fact of life, given the small populations, vast wealth, and desire for rapid economic and administrative modernization in the area. In general, the smaller, wealthier, and less developed the state, the greater the role of the immigrant population.

The sociopolitical effects of this extraordinary situation have been mitigated by a number of factors. Traditionally, Persian Gulf societies have maintained extensive contacts with foreign peoples as a consequence of both commercial ties and religious pilgrimage (such as the *Hajj* or pilgrimage to Mecca and the pilgrimages to the Shī'ī shrines of Iraq and Iran). These societies were built also from a number of separate and virtually autonomous social groups who maintained their distance from one another and from the government. Indeed, one might say that the societies were aggregations of "foreign" communities, with only limited and specific areas of interaction.

Immigrant populations extend across the entire social and occupational spectrum, and from all parts of the globe. Some of the Indian and Pakistani Muslims, as well as Iranian communities, in Kuwait, Bahrain, Dubai, and Muscat are old and well established. Other groups of Western businessmen, technical advisors, and petroleum engineers, as well as the Egyptian and Palestinian professionals and technicians, date from the period of British domination and the growth of the petroleum industry. Finally, there are large numbers of recent immigrants, often low-wage laborers, who have been attracted by the spectacular economic boom of the current decade. The greatest number of these come from the poor states of the Arabian peninsula, especially from the Yemen Arab Republic. These latter immigrants are likely to be unskilled, poorly paid (typically at half the rate of native-born workers), and lacking in any form of social or legal protection. Their housing conditions in the United Arab Emirates have been compared unfavorably with those of Palestinian refugee camps in Jordan.[157]

There is understandable resentment among the immigrants, but this has yet to take on the dimensions of widespread organized activity. Conditions are even worse where they came from, so they keep a very low social and political profile. On the other hand, there has been some active resentment by groups within the native-born populace. This had been evident in Bahrain, where the tensions between the Arab Shī'ī and Sunnī groups is aggravated by the presence of the Iranian Shī'ī community. In Bahrain as well, following the strike against the

157. Anthony, *Arab States of the Lower Gulf*, p. 16.

Bahrain Petroleum Company in 1938, the company began a deliberate policy of hiring more docile (and cheaper) Indian and Iranian workers.[158]

There seems to be nothing inherently destabilizing to the local societies in accepting the services of foreign workers. The difficulty would come if this were to be accepted as a permanent state of affairs and hinder the development of needed skills within the native-born population. Should the presence of immigrant groups be seen as a permanent condition, more liberal standards of naturalization might well be adopted.[159]

Changing Elites

The key both to the direction of social change and the continuation of social stability in the Persian Gulf region continues to lie with their political elites. In this area, the present situation resembles the traditional state of affairs. Since the end of the reign of Sultan Sa'īd ibn Taimūr of Oman, at the start of this decade, all of the rulers of the area have accepted the necessity of guiding progressive programs of planned change. With the exception of Iraq's revolutionary leadership, all have emphasized the continuity of their programs with their traditional religious, cultural, and social systems. Results have been mixed; economic and even political changes have proven easier to induce and control than has social change. We have seen the "traditional" Shah acting as a revolutionary, while serious doubts have been expressed as to the "revolutionary" character of the Iraqi Revolutionary Command Council.[160] By any standard of measurement, the socioeconomic reforms of Iran have proven to be more successful than those of revolutionary Iraq.[161] Within Iraq itself, however, the leadership appears to be adopting a much more pragmatic and nonideological approach to social and economic issues.[162]

Persian Gulf elites have broadened and expanded their horizons in two directions. In the first instance, those members of the traditional elites and ruling families who are better educated (in the modern sense) and more receptive to change have come to dominate the loosely woven inner politics of the traditional family councils. Thus, King Faisal replaced King Sa'ūd in Sa'ūdī Arabia, Sultan Qābūs replaced Sultan Sa'īd in Oman, and Shaikh Zāyd replaced Shaikh Shakhbūt in Abū Dhabī. The traditional political systems of the area allow a great degree of flexibility in the location of the actual power and influence within the ruling families, so that the most able and vigorous members of the family will occupy

158. Nakhleh, *Bahrain*, p. 77.

159. Yusif A. Sayigh, "Problems and Prospects of Development in the Arabian Peninsula," *International Journal of Middle East Studies* 2 (1971): 51. The reverse, as in the case of Great Britain, is also possible.

160. Marr, "Political Elite of Iraq," p. 149.

161. See Howard S. Ellis, *Private Enterprise and Socialism in the Middle East* (Washington, D.C., 1970), for interesting comparisons of the performance of the two countries. Also valuable is J. C. Hurewitz, "Soldiers and Social Change in Plural Societies: The Contemporary Middle East," in V. J. Parry and M. E. Yapp. eds., *War, Technology and Society in the Middle East* (Oxford, 1975), pp. 402–403.

162. See Ian Seymour, "Iraqi oil policy in focus," *Middle East Economic Survey*, Supplement (June 20, 1975).

the most important positions in the government. Within Sa'ūdī Arabia, for instance, with its ruling family numbering in the thousands, it is not enough to be a prince to be influential; one must be competent as well.

The elites have broadened themselves also by accepting new members from other educated and competent social groups, particularly from the "new middle class." Roger Savory describes them as "younger technicians and civil servants who implemented both the development schemes prepared by the Plan Organization, and the sweeping reforms induced by the land reform legislation."[163] Many of these are former members of the National Front opposition, and even of the Tūdeh party. The Shah does not hesitate to use their expertise and advice: "We don't fear these technocrats, our programs are prepared in a rational manner and they have ample opportunity to debate and voice their objections."[164] In Sa'ūdī Arabia, the first breakthrough of educated commoners into key governmental positions came in 1960. Throughout the 1960s and into the 1970s, their numbers have swelled from a trickle to a stream.[165] Given their present progressive leadership and the extraordinary wealth at their disposal, there seems no inherent reason why the present and future generations of the political elites of the region cannot continue to adapt to changing social conditions.

Persian Gulf Societies: Challenge, Innovation, and Tradition

The traditional plural societies, based upon the coexistence of varied ethnic, religious, occupational, and tribal groups, have persisted in the Persian Gulf. Modern innovations have been, in the main, incorporated into the system as additional groups in the social fabric, or have modified rather than eliminated the existing plural groups. "In plural societies we may not simply speak of the middle class. We must first ascertain whose middle class we are talking about," writes J. C. Hurewitz.[166] New elements in these societies, especially those connected with economic development and Western education, have tended (although not always consciously) toward the creation of modern-style class cleavages. More importantly, however, they tend to add a further dimension to the existing social structure, instead of fundamentally alternating its nature. Thus, the vertical group social structure continues to unite shaikh and tribesmen more than their class distinctions divide them. In this situation, few of the "new middle class" are either so bold or so foolish as to repudiate entirely the advantages of the system of group, family, and personal influence. This does not create a static social structure. On the contrary, it is a structure in constant motion, and the flexibility and mobility it offers to successful and ambitious groups and individuals provides it with its basic strength.

163. Savory, "The principle of homeostasis," p. 300.
164. Audience with H.I.M. The Shahanshah of Iran, Tehran, May 1970.
165. Rugh, "A new middle class in Saudi Arabia," p. 177. For a fascinating portrait of the career of one of these men, see Stephen Duguid, "A Biographical Approach to the Study of Social Change in the Middle East: Abdullah Takiki as a New Man," *International Journal of Middle East Studies* 1 (1970): 195–220.
166. Hurewitz, "Soldiers and Social Change," p. 403.

In these societies, the impetus for change usually comes from the top, rather than the middle or bottom. It is in the nature of the processes of social change that not even the most comprehensive systems of "planned total change" can affect all groups in society to the same degree, even though the direction of change may be broadly the same. Any permanent change in such societies is a difficult accomplishment; what Savory refers to as the "homeostatic" forces are always present. Fifty years after the Kemalist revolution in Turkey, we see that they are still alive and vigorous, and yet this is generally agreed to have been the most successful example of "planned total change" in the Middle East.

Change does come, however, when the rulers and ruling elites decide in favor of it. Does this mean that change is completely subject to the whim of the ruler? Can its course be reversed overnight? Can it become self-sustaining? The answers to these questions would seem to depend on the degree to which the forces of social change have affected a sufficient number of social groups and individuals. Groups and individuals, acting through complex and informal networks of intergroup and interpersonal relationships, have a fundamental autonomy in the societies of the Persian Gulf. When enough of them become convinced that social change should or will come—whether they believe it to be in their own self-interest, because the ruler wills it, because it is in accordance with the will of God, or with the historical forces of dialectical materialism—no direction or force from above will be able to stop it. The Shah of Iran, for one, believes this to be the case. In speaking at a ceremony distributing land titles to the farmers at Arāk in September, 1962, he stated that not even he could reverse the direction of the land reform program: "Those who still do not understand the meaning of this work should know that nothing can stop the Land Reform movement. If I do not want this or if it is said that it is only the Minister of Agriculture (Dr. Arsanjānī) who is carrying out this work and, should he leave, the program would not be carried out, this is not so. It is impossible for this program to change. Even if I, who have been the originator of this idea and who have put all my force behind this movement, were to change my mind, this program would not stop."[167]

Selected Bibliography

Abrahamian, Ervand. "Oriental despotism: The case of Qajar Iran." *International Journal of Middle East Studies* (1974).

Amirie, Abbas, and Twitchell, Hamilton A., eds. *Iran in the 1980s*. Washington, D.C., 1978.

Amirsadeghi, Hossein, ed. *Twentieth Century Iran*. London, 1977.

Anthony, John Duke. *Arab States of the Lower Gulf: People, Politics, Petroleum*. Washington, D.C., 1975.

Antoun, Richard, and Harik, Iliya, eds. *Rural Politics and Social Change in the Middle East*. Bloomington, Ind., 1972.

Avery, Peter. *Modern Iran*. London, 1965.

Banani, Amin. *The Modernization of Iran, 1921–1941*. Stanford, 1961.

167. *Kayhan International* (Tehran), 17 September 1962.

Barth, Fredrik. *Principles of Social Organization in Southern Kurdistan.* Oslo, 1953.

———. *Nomads of South Persia. The Basseri Tribe of the Khamseh Confederacy.* London, 1961.

Beaumont, Peter, Blake, Gerald H., and Wagstaff, J. Malcolm. *The Middle East: A Geographical Survey.* London, 1976.

Berger, Morroe. *The Arab World Today.* Garden City, N.Y., 1962.

Bharier, Julian. *Economic Development in Iran, 1900–1970.* London, 1970.

Bill, James A. "Class analysis and the dialectics of modernization in the Middle East." *International Journal of Middle East Studies* 3. (1972): 417–34.

———. *The Politics of Iran: Groups, Classes and Modernization.* Columbus, Ohio, 1972.

Browne, E. G. *A Year amongst the Persians.* Cambridge, 1927.

Coon, Carleton S. *Caravan: The Story of the Middle East.* New York, 1964.

Costello, V. F. *Urbanization in the Middle East.* Cambridge, 1977.

Eisenstadt, S. N. "Convergence and divergence of modern and modernizing societies: Indications from the analysis of the structuring of social hierarchies in Middle Eastern societies." *International Journal of Middle East Studies* 8 (1977): 1–28.

English, Paul Ward. *City and Village in Iran: Settlement and Economy in the Kirman Basin.* Madison, Wis., 1966.

Fenelon, K. G. *The United Arab Emirates: An Economic and Social Survey.* 2nd ed. London, 1976.

Gibb, H.A.R., and Kramers, J. H., eds. *Shorter Encyclopedia of Islam.* Leiden and London, 1961.

Halpern, Manfred. *The Politics of Social Change in the Middle East and North Africa.* Princeton, 1963.

Hay, Sir Rupert. *The Persian Gulf States.* Washington, D.C., 1959.

Hodgson, Marshall G. S. *The Venture of Islam.* 3 vols. Chicago, 1974.

Hopwood, Derek, ed. *The Arabian Peninsula, Society and Politics.* London, 1972.

Ibn Khaldūn. *The Muqaddimah, An Introduction to History.* 2 vols. Translated and edited by Franz Rosenthal. Princeton, 1967.

Jacqz, Jane W., ed. *Iran: Past, Present and Future.* New York and Aspen, Colo., 1976.

Keddie, Nikki R. "The Iranian power structure and social change 1800–1969: An overview." *International Journal of Middle East Studies* 2 (1971): 3–20.

———. *Religion and Rebellion in Iran: The Iranian Tobacco Protest of 1891–1892.* London, 1966.

Lambton, A.K.S. *The Persian Land Reform, 1962–1966.* Oxford, 1969.

Landen, Robert Geran. *Oman since 1856.* Princeton, 1967.

Leiden, Carl, ed. *The Conflict of Traditionalism and Modernism in the Muslim Middle East.* Austin, Tex., 1969.

Lenczowski, George, ed. *Iran under the Pahlavis.* Stanford, 1978.

———. *Oil and State in the Middle East.* Ithaca, N.Y., 1960.

Levy, Reuben. *The Social Structure of Islam.* Cambridge, 1965.

Nakhleh, Emile A. *Bahrain.* Lexington, Mass., 1976.

Nieuwenhuijze, C.A.O. Van. *Social Stratification and the Middle East: An Interpretation.* Leiden, 1965.

———. *Sociology of the Middle East.* Leiden, 1971.

Nyrop, Richard F., ed. *Area Handbook for Saudi Arabia.* Washington, D.C., 1977.

Pahlavi, H.I.M. Mohammad Reza, Shahanshah of Iran. *Mission for My Country.* London and New York, 1961.

———. *The White Revolution.* Tehran, 1967.

Parry, V. J., and Yapp, M. E., eds. *War, Technology and Society in the Middle East.* Oxford, 1975.

Patai, Raphael. *Society, Culture and Change in the Middle East.* 3rd edition. Philadelphia, 1971.

Peterson, J. E. "Tribes and politics in Eastern Arabia." *Middle East Journal* 31 (1977): 297–312.

Philby, H. St. John. *Arabian Jubilee.* London, 1952.

Quabain, Fahim I. "Social classes and tensions in Bahrain." *Middle East Journal* 9 (1955): 268–80.

Rentz, George. "Saudi Arabia: Desert island." *Journal of International Affairs* 19 (1965): 77–86.

Rosenthal, E.I.J. *Political Thought in Medieval Islam.* Cambridge, 1962.

Rugh, William. "Emergence of a new middle class in Saudi Arabia." *Middle East Journal* 27 (1973): 9–20.

Savory, Roger M. "The principle of homeostasis considered in relation to political events in Iran in the 1960s." *International Journal of Middle East Studies* 3 (1973) 282–302.

Sayigh, Yusif A. "Problems and prospects of development in the Arabian peninsula." *International Journal of Middle East Studies* 2 (1971): 40–58.

Smith, Wilfred Cantwell. *Islam in Modern History.* Princeton, 1957.

Sweet, Louise E., ed. *Peoples and Cultures of the Middle East.* 2 vols. Garden City, N. Y., 1970.

Trimingham, J. Spencer. *The Sufi Orders in Islam.* Oxford, 1971

Upton, Joseph M. *The History of Modern Iran: An Interpretation.* Cambridge, Mass., 1960.

von Grunebaum, G. E. *Modern Islam: The Search for Cultural Identity.* Berkeley, 1962.

Wells, Donald A. *Saudi Arabian Development Policy.* Washington, D.C., 1976.

Wilber, Donald N. *Iran: Past and Present.* 8th ed. Princeton, 1976.

Young, T. Cuyler, ed. *Middle East Focus: The Persian Gulf.* (Twentieth Annual Near East Conference, Princeton University.) Princeton, 1968.

Zonis, Marvin. *The Political Elite of Iran.* Princeton, 1971.

16. Art in the Persian Gulf

ROBERT HILLENBRAND

Early Developments

The earliest significant and large-scale manifestations of the visual arts in the areas bordering the Persian Gulf occur in Mesopotamia. For many years the southern part of the country was held to be the cradle of civilization, but recent discoveries have established the prior development of the northern cultures, beginning with that of Neolithic Qal'at Jarmo, where the sequence begins ca. 6750 B.C. Among the northern Chalcolithic cultures that followed in close succession, those of Sāmarrā, and especially Tell Halaf, produced fine pottery. Monumental architecture of this period included carefully planned temples at Tepe Gawra and *tholoi* with stone foundations at Arpachiya. During the sixth and fifth millenniums, amidst the marshland of southern Mesopotamia (Sumer), there was developing a proto-urban culture, exemplified at Eridu, which in the course of the fourth millennium grew into a full-scale urban civilization. This development was largely accomplished during the Uruk culture, which flourished throughout Mesopotamia. This so-called protoliterate period saw the first crude pictographs on clay tablets and the earliest carved cylinder seals, perhaps the most typical art form of early Mesopotamia, the function of which was to identify property and to authenticate messages. These seals took the form of a small cylinder usually about 3 or 4 cm in length and 1 to 3 cm in diameter, and could thus be worn round the wrist or the neck. Their designs were carved as a negative which, when rolled in moist clay, would produce a positive version of the design. Unlike the stamp seal, the format permitted a continuous design restricted only by the upper and lower horizontal borders. The personal nature of these seals helps to explain why they were buried with their owners. Their designs show a developed religious symbolism apparently linked to a fertility cult.

This early phase of Sumerian civilization produced such monumental architecture as the precinct of Inanna (E-Anna) and the ziggurat and temple of Anu, both excavated at the important religious center of Erech or Uruk (modern Warka). The latter temple had a stone foundation bearing a raised brick platform approached by steps and was perhaps—like the even older al-'Ubaid temple at

Eridu—an embryonic ziggurat. Its material, given the scarcity of stone in Meso-potamia, was clay, but this was decorated internally by frescoes. Temples dating from the Uruk period have colored stone and terra-cotta cone mosaics forming reed-mat patterns. This decoration experimented with the effect of shadow on a brick façade; in later periods niches and buttresses served much the same purpose. Temples were indeed the earliest major buildings of Sumerian civiliza-tion. They rose high above the alluvial plain by means of platforms that came to be arranged in as many as eight successive stages of diminishing size. They may have taken this stepped form more as a result of constant rebuilding on one site than because of a deliberate plan. Eventually, the design was formalized. Thus was created the ziggurat or temple-tower, the distinctive hallmark of religious architecture in Mesopotamia for three millenniums. These temples, which could be hundreds of feet high and extend to about 50,000 square meters, were always of mud brick and mud mortar sometimes faced and paved with baked brick. Temples were built on increasingly high platforms that may have expressed a religious symbolism invoking the concept of the god on a mountain. Despite the humble material used, the Sumerians well knew how to impart monumentality to their buildings. The origin of certain features in reed-built houses is recalled by clustered engaged columns in brick, while regular reveals and buttresses articulate the long façades. Doorways are arched, while the flat roofs were reached by stairways.

Usually, the temple had a central courtyard with rooms grouped around it, and this simple plan was gradually refined by the addition of a vestibule, ante-cella, and cella all laid out on the same axis. The same crucial period of ca. 3500 to 3000 B.C. saw the invention of writing, the development of metallurgy, and a

FIG. 16–1. Ziggurrat of Ur, c. 3000 B.C.

host of other technological improvements. The earliest Sumerian sculpture includes the so-called "hunting stele" and an alabaster vase, both from Uruk and both datable ca. 3200 B.C. The vase shows a theme that was often to recur in ancient Near Eastern art—a ceremonial procession of men and animals toward a divinity (in this case the goddess Inanna). This theme was to remain typical of Mesopotamian art for three millenniums. It is this fidelity to the theme of priestly or kingly worship afforded to a powerful deity that lends ancient Mesopotamian art a unity that far transcends the stylistic variations from one dynasty to another and remains independent of the political organization of a given state, be it city or empire. The primacy of the king as representative of his people, and his god-like status, were not seriously questioned throughout this period. The politico-religious bias of ancient Mesopotamian art proved a more potent unifying agent than did geographical or racial factors. Even a cursory comparison with classical art will show how limited this concept of art and its function was, and how Mesopotamian art entirely ignores huge tracts of human experience. But its very limitations were also its strength. Even more celebrated than the vase depicting a procession to Inanna is the marble head (ca. 3200 B.C.), known as "The Lady of Warka," in which the precious imported material is modeled with great restraint and subtlety. Also from predynastic Uruk come a remarkable variety of cylinder seals showing processional, sacrificial, and other religious scenes. Shortly before 2600 B.C., Sumerian sculpture took a new turn, becoming preoccupied with dynamic subjects of struggling and menacing animals. Cylinder seals of the time show a curious breakdown of the earlier styles into a rapid and abstract idiom of wavy lines, termed the "brocaded" style. This brief era came to an end with the First Dynasty of Ur, commonly dated ca. 2600 B.C. This city was now one of the major cities of Sumer, though fine work continued to be produced all over the country. Indeed, a large copper relief from al-'Ubaid, almost 2½ meters in breadth, is perhaps the masterpiece of the period. It depicts a widespread theme—the benevolent lion-headed eagle god, Imdugud, spreading out his wings protectively over two ad-dorsed creatures that are apparently stags. The heraldic symmetry of the design finds echoes in the repertoire of cylinder seals and may have expressed some apotropaic intention. The work at Ur is on a smaller scale. Excavations in the vast royal cemeteries there have disclosed among other grave goods a series of spectacular masterpieces of high technical proficiency, using gold and lapis lazuli and dating between ca. 2700 and ca. 2500 B.C.: a rearing ram in a thicket—probably an offering stand—a bull's head decorating the front of a lyre, golden helmets and beakers, and the jewelry of Queen Pu-abi. Inlay work is especially fine in many of these objects and is found in architectural friezes on the walls of temples at al-'Ubaid and Kish. Unique is the so-called "Standard of Ur," a box that depicts scenes of war and banqueting in processional form, using shell, red limestone, and lapis lazuli inlaid into a bitumen base. These objects are too varied in form and style to permit ready classification, but roughly contemporary with them is a group of votive stone statuettes from Tell Asmar with a highly distinctive style. They depict men and women at prayer, their hands clasped over their chests, and were probably intended for permanent display in temples. Greatly enlarged eyes give these tall figures an intense expressiveness that is accentuated by the contrasting simplicity of their pose and dress. In quite a different style is a sculptured head found at Lagash and datable to ca. 2500 B.C. This lacks the

FIG. 16–2. Impressions from Sumerian cylinder seals. (top) 89137 Seal of Ibil-Ishtar. Hunting scene, about 2250 B.C. (middle) 89538 Hero and animals, about 2750 B.C. (bottom) 89115 Liberation of the sun-god, about 2250 B.C. (Reproduced by Courtesy of the Trustees of the British Museum)

formal hieratic quality and the false beards of the Tell Asmar figures, and instead is strongly and semirealistically modeled. Its large almond eyes, set wide apart, and heavy, bald, round skull recur in a contemporary monumental painted basalt sculpture of a seated figure from al-'Ubaid. These early dynastic works mark the early prime of Sumerian sculpture, and they are complemented by votive relief plaques from Lagash that show scenes of temple building and war, and others from Nippur depicting domestic and pastoral scenes and banquets. The Lagash plaques merit study quite independently of their artistic quality, for they represent the earliest examples of reliefs depicting historical events, a type that was to enjoy great popularity throughout the Near East. But they are quite eclipsed by the work of the Akkadian dynasty, which founded an extensive Mesopotamian-based empire in ca. 2340 B.C. Very little large-scale Akkadian sculpture survives, and it is therefore difficult to determine whether the rarity of certain typical forms of Sumerian sculpture, such as votive statuettes or processional scenes, is significant or merely a matter of chance. In general, only war monuments have been found, perhaps because so few monumental buildings with associated finds have been excavated.

Preeminent among surviving works of Akkadian sculpture is a bronze head, thought by some to be that of King Naram-Suen. The details of headdress and hair style are rendered with smooth precision, but this same quality also distinguishes the features and lends them an impersonal, formal air. This remoteness is no doubt deliberate. It emphasizes the dignified and exalted quality of kingship. A sandstone stele, also of Naram-Suen, is datable to ca. 2300 B.C. and is equally official. It depicts a victorious military expedition. But, whether because of its explicit propagandist intent, its logically integrated composition, or its narrative quality, this stele has a directness and a force that the head lacks. The king is shown as divine, for he wears the horned headdress of the gods and stands, well over life-size, directly before the sacred mountain. He tramples fallen enemies underfoot, while diminutive soldiers, their heads raised toward him, ascend the path below. Such major examples of Akkadian sculpture are rare, although they suffice to indicate that official art was taking new directions. A more comprehensive, if necessarily limited, view of the period may be gained from its numerous cylinder seals. Mythological scenes dominate, often depicting dramatic combats between hybrid creatures and fearsome beasts. The meaning of such scenes remains for the most part enigmatic. A comparatively new feature is the presence of framed inscriptions. The treatment is remarkably precise and detailed, with a bent toward naturalism that is hard to parallel in the previous period.

The Akkadian empire was overthrown in ca. 2150 B.C. by the Guti, barbarians from Iran, and the Sumerians reestablished their power in numerous cities, notably Lagash and Ur, now ruled by its empire-building Third Dynasty. Temples, palaces, and three-stage ziggurats, the latter incorporating ancient features and reusing ancient sites, were built in great numbers. Sculpture has positive links with Akkadian work, but it also shows a return to the traditions of early Sumerian art. This demonstrates not only the longevity of Sumerian modes of artistic expression but also a sense of cultural and ethnic unity that in our day would be termed nationalism. Political motives may thus have contributed to this Sumerian revival. The most memorable creations of the period evoke with remarkable success the

FIG. 16–3. Statue of Gudea, Sumerian, c. 2000 B.C. (The Louvre, Paris)

mood of simple devotion that marked cult statues of the early dynastic period. The statues of Gudea, the governor of Lagash, illustrate this. In them the ruler is conceived in the Sumerian style as priest, not as king. Executed in polished diorite, an intractable black stone, they conform to a traditional schema: a frontal depiction of the large-eyed worshipper, smiling enigmatically and standing with his hands folded across his chest. A remarkable sense of contained power and dignity pervades these statues. Their simple planes and wide expanses uncluttered by detail are brought to life by subtle, restrained modeling that exploits the play of light. A highly intellectual abstraction simplifies and generalizes Gudea's features, which for extra clarity are rendered with the utmost smoothness. Apart from the eyebrows, no hair or wrinkle disturbs the face. Steles—such as that of Urnammu of Ur—also favor religious themes and introduce a new motif that was later to gain great popularity: the worshipper introduced to his deity by a lesser god.

Neo-Sumerian cylinder seals reject the rich mythological subject matter of Akkadian seals in favor of traditional themes of worship that often echo those of contemporary reliefs. Figures are serially deployed in a vertical scheme to which the inscriptions, which now play an increasingly important role, also conform. Their monotonously repeated compositions bear the mark of mass production.

Babylon

The Sumerians and Akkadians were finally replaced by the Semitic Amorites from the west, and their cities were sacked by the Elamites, who struck from Iran. At first local city-states such as Isin and Larsa filled the power vacuum. This period is best known from the site of Mari, now in Syria, though the important temple of Ishtar Kititum has been excavated at Ischali. It was only after a period of Larsa rule that Mesopotamia was gradually welded into a single state under the domination of the strongest of these Semitic powers, Babylon, which thereafter remained the major city in the land. The key figure in this unification was the Amorite Hammurabi (1792–1750 B.C.?). But the Babylonian civilization and religion of his time was largely dependent on that of Sumer, and perhaps its only important innovation was the replacement of Sumerian, which sank to the level of a liturgical language, by Akkadian, a Semitic tongue. Perhaps the most celebrated monument of the time is the stele of Hammurabi inscribed with his laws and crowned by a relief of the king saluting the enthroned Sun God. Far less formal in tone is a bearded and hatted portrait head found at Susa, thought by some to depict Hammurabi, and by others to date about two centuries earlier. The immaculate smoothness of the Gudea statues is here discarded in favor of the highlighting of eyes and mouth. It is a living face marked by age—haggard and weary—and this personal quality sets it apart from standard official art. Old Babylonian seals are cruder in finish than their predecessors, though their traditional Sumerian iconography is enlivened by Syrian themes.

Recent excavations have clarified our picture of Old Babylonian palaces. Their basic element is a courtyard, apparently containing groves of trees and gardens. This is surrounded by rooms, several of which are combined. The main reception and ceremonial chambers are on the ground floor. The sparse survivals of Old Babylonian art and architecture may reflect a readiness to reuse earlier artifacts or a preference for wood and metal, materials that are less likely to survive than stone. Plentiful inscriptions have however been found stamped on bricks, terra-cotta wall cones, and other architectural and decorative features, including brick façades decorated with spiral columns and others imitating palm trees (Tell al-Rimah and the "Bastion of Warad-Sin" at Ur). Many terra-cotta plaques of the time survive and their genre and mythological scenes throw much light on Bablyonian life, but they scarcely enter the category of official art.

Kassite Dominion, ca. 1600–ca. 1100 B.C.

After the Hittites had brought the Old Babylonian empire to an end, political control passed to the Kassites, Iranian tribes from the Zagros who were thereby following a cyclical pattern illustrated by the Guti and Sumerians before them. The five centuries of Kassite dominion (ca. 1600 to ca. 1100 B.C.) revitalized Mesopotamian art. Their capital, Dur Kurigalzu ('Aqar Qūf, near Baghdad) has yielded a quite well-preserved ziggurat, its mud brick reinforced by reed matting. Approached by three stairways, it originally rose to several hundred feet. But the most original monument of Kassite architecture is probably the small temple of the goddess Inanna built by King Karaindash at Uruk in ca. 1420 B.C. Its façade is not only broken up by numerous recesses in the traditional manner but also bears applied, vigorously stylized sculpture built up of specially shaped bricks. These sculptures depict the gods. A similar technique is found in a slightly later temple at Susa. Such work, which is first found in the Isin–Larsa period, presages the glazed relief sculpture of later Babylonian times; indeed, glazed terra cotta makes its first appearance in Mesopotamia in this period. Free-standing painted terra-cotta sculptures from Dur Kurigalzu partake of the same lively quality. Molded plaques of this material, used for religious offerings, abound. The cylinder seals of the period, though of limited subject matter, are remarkable for their long and erudite Sumerian inscriptions.

Perhaps the most distinctive feature of Kassite art, however, is the boundary stone (*kudurru*). Though these were known earlier, their popularity dates from this period. Their function was to mark and protect territory or property, indeed they served as a kind of title deed. Varied in form—many are just boulders, others are cylindrical—they bore relief sculptures of the ruler, details of the property concerned, occasional religious inscriptions, and symbols—not figures—of the gods. Their compositions are uncluttered, with a single dominant figure and a remarkable sensitivity to empty space. Similar features characterize Kassite cylinder seals.

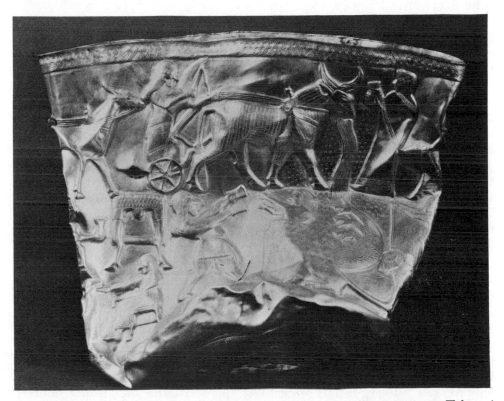

FIG. 16–4. The Hasanlu Cup, Azerbaijan, c. 1000 B.C. (Iran Bastan Museum, Teheran)

FIG. 16–5. Ivory plaque for inlaying furniture, Nimrud (Fort Shalmaneser), Iraq, eighth century B.C. (Ashmolean Museum, Oxford)

The Assyrians

The later Kassite period saw the reemergence of another Semitic power in northern Mesopotamia—the Assyrians. The name derives from Ashur—at once their land, their capital, and their god. In the late second millennium, important survivals include the wall paintings of Kar-Tukulti-Ninurta and the governor's residence and wall paintings at Nuzu, as well as numerous incised ivories. But it is clear that the area was at least as much influenced by Anatolia and Syria as by southern Mesopotamia. In architecture, such features as crenellated walls or double ziggurats and double cellas (temple of Sin and Shamash at Assur, ca. 1500 B.C., or the later temple of Amu and Adad there) are foreign to Babylonian tradition. A distinctively Assyrian glyptic style can also be distinguished from ca. 1500 B.C. onward, expressing itself in cylinder seals of marked naturalism and also in incised ivories. The much later palaces of Nimrud, Nineveh, and Khorsabad (eighth century B.C.) are conceived on a massive scale. They display careful planning and a taste for military display expressed by walls more than 20 meters thick, heavily buttressed and with fortified gateways. Internally, their central elements were frequently large rectangular throne chambers entered from a courtyard. Polychrome narrative relief sculpture in stone is the principal expression of Assyrian art. Military, religious, ceremonial, and mythical scenes abound. Reliefs of tribute-bearers placed near throne rooms no doubt reflected actual ceremonies there. These reliefs ornamented numerous rooms in the royal palaces. Several square miles of them have survived. They were supplemented by frescoes for the ceilings and higher parts of the rooms, while some rooms bore only frescoes. Military themes are entirely appropriate for the greatest military power of the time, and they came to dominate Assyrian art. Sieges, massacres, torture, and deportations are chronicled with unsparing accuracy and a grim realism hitherto absent from Mesopotamian art (reliefs depicting the capture of Susa and Lachish). This same minutely detailed technique is extended to the equally bloodthirsty hunting scenes shown on the reliefs of Ashur-bani-pal at Nimrud, datable between 887 and 859 B.C., perhaps the most famous sculptures of the ancient Near East. They too exalt the ruler, this time as hunter rather than warrior or vice-gerent of the national god. But these reliefs are also imbued with a sympathy for the animals that adds an unexpected dimension of pathos. The wounded and dying animals are especially moving. Strict profile convention governed the depiction of movement, but this scarcely fettered the artists' treatment of animals, even though it made their figures seem wooden. Quite apart from their aesthetic value—they exploit a delicate low relief to a degree unknown earlier in the region—they constitute the only extensive record of royal pastimes in ancient Mesopotamian art. The high level of technical accomplishment displayed by these reliefs remains unbroken throughout the Assyrian period, but certain stylistic changes may be noted. In the narrative manner just described, the carving continues across the joins of the slabs and the inscriptions consist of relevant captions. An increasingly bold use of empty space may also be discerned. In contrast to this, the reliefs of Ashur-nasir-pal are essentially hieratic. They are solemn and immobile renditions of ritual scenes, especially sacrifices. Their arrangement is processional, their inscriptions standard and repetitive. The figures move with a measured tread; they lack the verve of the hunting scenes. They have a ponderous, official quality and a precision of finish that renders them lifeless. A novel sidelight is shed on their contemporary significance by the wide bands of inscriptions glorifying the king that are sometimes carved in a wide swathe across them, regardless of aesthetic and narrative concerns. Freestanding sculptures of the Assyrian kings perpetuate this formal idiom with its obsessively accurate detail, accentuated modeling, and emphasis on musculature, features that make these sculptures remarkably precise and more three-dimensional than those of any preceding periods, as do the hybrid bulls and lions with bearded human heads which, sculpted partly in the round, acted as guardian figures at the principal doorways of palaces of Nineveh and Nimrud. Some of the carved gilded ivories, as well as the bronze bowls found at the latter site, are commonly attributed to deported Phoenician and Aramean craftsmen using their native styles, but other ivories employing an incised technique rather than modeled relief are also found. These ivories were used in furniture and chariot and harness trappings. The presence of alien influences was a natural consequence of the Assyrian domination of most of the Near East. Evidence suggests that the bare, white-washed walls of neo-Assyrian and later palaces were covered with tapestry hangings, carpets, and rugs.

The unbridled expansion of the last Assyrian rulers undermined the stability of the empire, and it fell to the resurgent Babylonian state in 612 B.C. An unparalleled spate of building activity, lasting a mere seventy years or so, now began. Nebuchadnezzar II restored many Sumerian cities and above all Babylon itself, which was rebuilt on a colossal scale. Within its double tier of fortified walls, the city contained a raised processional avenue the walls of which were decorated with rows of lions, bulls, and dragons in bas-reliefs formed of glazed and unglazed brick. These animals were respectively the emblems of the deities Ishtar, Adad, and Marduk. The Ishtar gate, now in Berlin, was entirely decorated

FIG. 16–6. Assyrian relief of a bird-headed genius fertilizing a date palm, Nimrud (north-west palace), Iraq, ninth century B.C. (Ashmolean Museum, Oxford)

FIG. 16–7. Column capital, Persepolis, c. 500 B.C.

in this style. The huge royal palace measured some 350 by 200 meters and contained the celebrated "hanging gardens," honored in antiquity as one of the Seven Wonders of the World. The walls of its great courtyard are frescoed with illusionistic columns on a base of lions *passant*; this was probably influenced by Median palaces. The city's seven-story ziggurat (*Etemenanki*) became identified in later tradition with the Tower of Babel itself. Its crowning temple was enameled in blue-glazed bricks, a fitting symbol of the heavens. In 539 B.C., Babylon was peacefully taken over by Cyrus, the first Achaemenid, and for several centuries thereafter remained an artistically unproductive satellite of Persia. The art of Mesopotamia in the Parthian and Sasanian periods is so closely linked with that of Iran under these same dynasties that the two areas will be treated together in this account, in the section devoted to Iran.

The Advent of Islam

Little survives of the architectural and artistic achievements of early Islamic Iraq. Literary sources describe the mosques at Kūfa and Basra erected in the first decades of Islam and indicate that these obeyed what subsequently became the classic formula of the Arab-style, enclosed, rectangular mosque. A deep, flat-roofed sanctuary gave on to an open courtyard. Excavations have revealed the *Dār al-Imāra* (i.e., governmental buildings) of Kūfa, dated 639, as a cruciform structure with a central throne room, a model clearly dependent on Sāsānid antecedents. But these fragmentary ruins are entirely dwarfed by the first significant surviving work of Islamic architecture in Iraq, the fortified palace at Ukhaidir. Datable to ca. 780, its structure expresses both the despotic and the pleasure-loving character of the royal 'Abbasid house. The flamboyant isolation of its setting is unmatched by any earlier Umayyad palace. So too is its size—it measures ca. 175 by 169m—while its luxurious amenities, seemingly intended for a nobleman rather than for the ruler himself, yield little to the most sumptuous Umayyad caliphs' palaces in Syria. Although the somewhat cramped living quarters perpetuate Arab tradition, the ceremonial aspect of the palace is strongly Persian in flavor, notably in the use of *īwāns* (open bays) in conjunction with large courtyards. This formal aspect of the palace is oddly inconsistent with its remote and inhospitable site. It is hard to conceive of occasions when the ceremonial rooms would have been put to full use. Indeed, the whole function of the complex presents serious problems. The surrounding area does not seem to have been cultivated, so Ukhaidir was not the center of an agricultural estate on the Syrian pattern. Indeed, it must have posed major problems of supply. The decorative details of the palace, such as ornamental brickwork

FIG. 16–8. Statue of a ruler, Hatra, second century A.D. (Iraq Museum, Baghdad)

in the *hazārbāf* style, and the numerous small domes and ingenious vaults, again display marked Persian influence, presaging many Seljuk forms. The military technology of Ukhaidir is also remarkably advanced for its time and includes such features as continuous machicolation and a portcullis. Along the route linking Ukhaidir to Kūfa, the nearest major urban center, are two structures probably built in association with the palace: the fortified *khān* or caravanserai of 'Atshān, probably intended as a stopover, and a minaret, Manāra al-Mujida, with geometric patterns in brick, which may have served as a landmark.

Much more important than these isolated early 'Abbasid structures are the buildings of Sāmarrā. As the caliphate capital for half a century, from 836 onward, Sāmarrā exerted unique prestige in matters of art and architecture, and its influence extended throughout most of the Islamic world. Moreover, unlike Baghdad, the celebrated circular city built from 762 onward by the caliph al-Mansūr, it has been extensively excavated and thus provides a detailed picture of certain aspects of 'Abbasid material culture at its peak. The architectural remains fall into four categories: the Great Mosque, the palaces, a mausoleum, and the stucco decoration that is virtually synonymous with the city. The Great Mosque strikes the note of gigantism that characterizes the entire site. It is the largest mosque in the world, closely approached only by the nearby mosque of Abū Dulaf, which is a contemporary copy of it. A buttressed rectangular enceinte encloses a courtyard surrounded by successive bays clustered deepest on the *qibla* (direction of prayer) side. These formerly carried a flat roof without the intermediary of arches. The entire effect was probably somewhat oppressive. The mosque measures some 240 by 156 meters internally, thus obeying a ratio of 3:2 that was standard for much 'Abbasid architecture. Little remains of its mosaic and stucco decoration, but no ornament could have disguised entirely the rather humdrum and repetitive nature of the building. None of the expedients devised in the mosques of Damascus, Cordoba, or Qairawān are here employed to vary the standard formula enunciated by Muhammad's house at Medina, the first mosque. Apart from its vastly expanded proportions, the building is a routine descendant of the Umayyad mosques of Kūfa and Basra. Only its huge minaret, placed outside the enclosure on the axis of the *mihrāb* (prayer niche), departs radically from precedent. Its helicoidal shape, incorporating an external ramp, was derived from the spiral ziggurats of ancient Mesopotamia.

The palaces of Sāmarrā are again of gigantic scale, measuring as much as a mile in length. In most of them, the formal reception rooms and private living quarters with gardens are supplemented by vast administrative complexes, barracks and arsenals, polo grounds and hunting preserves, while one of them even has a clover-leaf racecourse within its walls. Such palaces were strung out along the banks of the Tigris in a ribbon development stretching for miles. The larger ones were self-contained, functioning as miniature cities well suited to the isolated and despotic nature of 'Abbasid royal life. The Jausaq al-Khāqānī—palace of Mu'tasim—for example, has a triple-arched entrance gate whose central *īwān* may well have functioned as a public hall of audience. Within the palace a series of courts and antechambers funneled visitors toward a great throne room, probably domed, with a basilical hall opening on each arm. The disposition of the various elements of the plan was subordinated to a dominant axiality inherited from Umayyad and Sāsānid architecture. The sole surviving mausoleum at Sāmarrā,

FIG. 16–9. Sasanian silver plate: Shapur II hunting, Persia, fourth century (Courtesy of the Smithsonian Institution, Freer Gallery of Art, Washington, D.C., no. 34.23)

and the earliest extant in the Islamic world, is the Qubbat al-Sulaibiyya datable to ca. 862. It is a remarkably original building with no parallel in Islamic mausoleums outside India, though it owes something to the Dome of the Rock in Jerusalem. Three caliphs were interred within it. It comprises an inner domed octagon separated by an ambulatory from an outer octagon, the whole being built of artificial stone in the form of large bricks.

The decoration of the palaces is found also in the private houses of Sāmarrā. It is of a kind new to Islam, though long familiar in Sāsānid Iran. Entire walls are coated with plaster, which is worked into ornate repetitive designs of foliate inspiration. Three major styles have been isolated; their chronological order is disputed. In the first, the surface is divided into polygonal compartments, with borders of pearl roundels. Each compartment is filled with vine stems bearing lobed leaves or with fancifully curved leaves or vegetal elements too stylized to equate with any actual plant. In the second style, this tendency is accentuated to the point where recognizably natural forms disappear. The borders become plain and the compartments themselves more varied. The Chinese motif of *yin* and *yang* becomes a standard feature. Finally, in the third style, the decoration is applied not by carving but by molds that are executed in a beveled style with ancient Central Asian antecedents. The motifs themselves are more loosely and flowingly arranged, and are more varied—spirals, lobed designs, bottle-shaped forms, and other motifs no longer dependent on vegetal life. This style quickly established itself in eastern Islam and was still full of life five centuries later. The labor-saving properties of the molded beveled style were ideally suited to the mushroom growth of Sāmarrā, and the humble mud brick of which even the palaces were mostly built was cheaply and effectively disguised by this mass-produced decoration.

After Sāmarrā, there is a period of some three centuries from which very little work remains. Only in the later twelfth century do buildings again survive in some quantity. Several Syriac churches near Mosul, notably Mār Behnam, Mār Shem'ūn, and Mār Adudh-Immī contain figural relief carving closely related to local Atabegid sculpture, as does the Yazīdī shrine at 'Ain Sifnī. Among other Muslim buildings, this figural carving appears on a *khān* and a niche (conceivably a *mihrāb* [prayer niche] from a *madrasa* [college]!) at Sinjār, the palace of Qarā Sarāy at Mosul built by Badr al-Dīn Lū'lū', the door of the *turba* (mausoleum) of Imām Bāhir, and city gates at Mosul, 'Amadiyya, and Baghdad. Griffins, lions,

FIG. 16–10. Minaret of the Great Mosque of Sāmarrā, Iraq, after A.D. 836

FIG. 16–11. Inlaid marble slab in the name of the Atabeg Zangī, Iraq, early twelfth century (Mosul Museum)

serpents, and dragons are the favorite animal motifs of this style and they seem to have served an apotropaic function. Similar designs, augmented by heraldic and astrological motifs that often refer in punning fashion to the ruler himself, appear on Atabegid coins. This emphasis on figural ornament was not echoed elsewhere in Iraq or in Iran, but it was a standard feature of medieval art in Anatolia. Very few medieval mosques remain in Iraq. The major example that survived into modern times was the *jāmi'* (Friday mosque) of Nūr al-Dīn in Mosul, completed in 568/1172 and comprising a *musallā* (oratory) with an array of small vaults in the sanctuary, a major dome over the *mihrāb*—which is also marked by a wider central aisle—and a large courtyard. Other mosques with similar plans include the Jāmi' al-Mujāhidī at Mosul (572–76/1176–80) and the *masjid* (mosque) at Dhu'l-Kifl. The Kūfa Jāmi', though mostly of modern construction, retains part of an elaborate Jalāyirid gateway decorated in terra cotta and a vaulted octagonal substructure also of fourteenth-century date underneath the courtyard and known as al-Safīna; this may have served for prayer or for retreat. Strangely enough, Iraq is richer in pre-Timurid *madrasas* than Iran, for apart from the Mustansiriyya (631/1233) and Mirjāniyya (758/1357) in Baghdad and some ruined *madrasas* of twelfth-century date in Mosul, the evidence suggests that the buildings in Baghdad and Wāsit, each known as al-Sharābiyya, are in fact *madrasas*. No standard plan was followed in these structures, though all those in central Iraq are on two floors and feature monumental portals and a number of rooms opening off a central courtyard. One or two *īwāns* pierce the inner façades. The most elaborate exterior is the ineptly restored two-minaret façade at Wāsit, closely rivaled by the Mirjāniyya *madrasa*. The latter structure is notable for one of the longest *waqfiyyas* or dedicatory and foundation inscriptions ever to be inscribed on a medieval Islamic building; indeed, no building in Iraq has inscriptions of comparable length. Its domed *musallā*, a hall with a triple arched façade opening onto the courtyard, is the only Iraqi example of a common Syrian type. It is also one of the rare surviving examples of the *madrasa* with a *turba* attached; such funerary *madrasas* were very common in the eastern Islamic world. Internally, the masterpiece of these buildings is the Sharābiyya of Baghdad (formerly known as the 'Abbasid palace), with its narrow corridors crowned by multiple tiers of steeply-stilted stalactite vaulting arranged in diminishing perspective toward a distant vanishing point. These are the finest pre-Ilkhānid *muqarnas* vaults in the eastern Islamic world, and they exploit illusionistic devices in an entirely novel way. They are covered in lacy terra-cotta carving of remarkable precision and intricacy. Minarets are preserved in greater numbers than any other buildings in Iraq. Many are firmly within the orbit of contemporary Iranian minarets and exhibit the same tall cylindrical form embellished by decorative brickwork (e.g., Mosul, Sinjar, Irbil, and Ta'ūq). A few are short and stumpy, with domical heads and deep balconies on single or multiple stalactite corbels (minarets of Jāmi' al-Khaffāfīn, Jāmi' Qumriyya, and Jāmi' al-Khulafā'). These features are prophetic of much later Iraqi minarets. The minaret at 'Āna is exceptional in its rectangular form and its preference for a plaster decoration of blind arches. Mausoleums, too, follow the Iranian pattern, though they are exclusively of the domed square or octagonal rather than the tomb tower type. All but half a dozen or so were built for Shī'ī *imāms*. Representative examples of such buildings are the *turbas* of Muhammad al-Sakrān at al-Jadīda and of Dhu'l-Kifl, both of Ilkhānid date.

Around Mosul, during the thirteenth century, rather squat square tombs with pyramidal roofs and façades in decorated brick were the rule (Imām 'Awn al-Dīn, Imām Yahyā ibn al-Qāsim, both apparently converted Christian structures); while the Baghdad area produced at the same time some notable mausolea, with sugar-loaf domes of pine-cone type decorated internally with ambitious steep *muqarnas* vaults (the so-called tomb of Zubaida; the tomb of 'Umar al-Suhrawardī). The earliest of this genre is the tomb known as Imām Dūr near Takrīt, dated by inscription to 1086. The masterpiece of secular architecture in later medieval Iraq is without doubt Khān Mirjān, built in 1359 in conjunction with the Madrasa Mirjāniyya and a now-vanished hospital. The revenues of the Khān were intended to help finance the *madrasa* and the hospital. It served as a hotel and commercial center, with numerous adjoining shops, rather than as a caravanserai. Its two floors provide forty-five cells for sleeping quarters, while a gallery carried

FIG. 16–12. Baghdad, al-Madrasa al-Sharābiyya (the so-called " 'Abbāsid Palace"):
muqarnas vault, early thirteenth ccntury

on stalactite corbels encircles the first floor. The ensemble is roofed by eight bold transverse arches alternating with smaller high-crowned vaults pierced by numerous windows. These smaller vaults not only solve the problem of lighting a potentially oppressive enclosed space but also impart a rhythmical undulation to the external roof-line. But the glory of the building remains its internal vaulting system, which must rank as the finest of its kind in Islam. Among the notable medieval bridges of Iraq are the Kirī Si'da (possibly fifteenth century), the Harba bridge (1228), both built of brick, the latter with a magnificent, lengthy, high-relief inscription in *naskh* script, comparable to that on the lateral wall of the Mustansiriyya, and, finally, in northern Iraq, four Seljuk bridges: Kisik Köprü, Eski Mosul, 'Amadiyya, and al-Jisr al-'Abbāsī.

In its decorative techniques, the architecture of Iraq after the Sāmarrā period is generally closer to Iran than to Anatolia or Syria. But Anatolian influence can be detected in the short-lived popularity of figural carving during the Atabegid period, while the ancient Syrian tradition of marble carving may be seen as early as the Khāssakī *mihrāb* (ninth century). Distinctively local techniques include polychrome inlaid marble, used for inscriptions and abstract patterns in the Mosul area during the twelfth century, and a style of minutely carved terra cotta that flourished in central Iraq in later 'Abbasid and Īlkhānid times. Its closest analogies are, curiously enough, with work from Central Asia rather than Iran proper.

It will be clear from this survey that after the period of Sāmarrā, the architecture of Iraq came to depend for inspiration either on Anatolia—as in the case of some of the Atabegid architecture of the Mosul area—or on Iran. This dependence continued after the rise of the Ottoman and Safavid empires, though the lack of building stone meant that the brick and tile architecture of Iran was the

FIG. 16–13. Baghdad, al-Madrasa al-Mustansiriyya: interior façade of entrance block, early thirteenth century

principal inspiration. Thus, the great Shī'ī shrines of Karbalā', Najaf, Sāmarrā, and Kāzimain exhibit a style much more Persian than Iraqi. From the seventeenth century onward, the domes of these shrines were embellished with plates of gilded copper. The domes at Najaf and Karbalā' were the work of Nādir Shāh, while Āqā Muhammad Khān Qājār and Fath 'Alī Shāh respectively were responsible for those at Kāzimain and Sāmarrā. This Iranian influence is equally marked in later caravanserais (e.g., Khān al-Mashāhida, Baghdad) or in the many minarets of Ottoman date, which differ from Iranian models principally in their stumpy shafts and domed apices girdled by balconies, but otherwise display tiled decoration of geometric patterns and stylized square Kufic inscriptions. No major masterpieces date from these later periods.

Early Islamic Pottery

In Iraq, the ninth century sees the beginning of the long and distinguished tradition of Islamic pottery. Strangely enough, there is no feeling of hesitation in these early styles; the technique and decoration are equally assured, and at least half a dozen major varieties of ceramics are encountered in this first century. It is not easy to explain this immediate maturity, especially since no fine pottery of Umayyad date has yet come to light, and since glazed pottery—into which category virtually all the quality medieval ware belongs—though known in ancient Egypt and Parthia, did not achieve the status of a fine art in the ancient world. The earliest Arab pottery, being simply for domestic use, continued this utilitarian bias and was sparsely decorated with simple incised or relief designs. But ample literary references testify that a great deal of pottery was imported from China, both by the overland route that ran through Persia and by the sea route via India, and imported Chinese wares have been found in nearly all excavations on Islamic sites. In the early centuries of Islam, Chinese art had a peculiar cachet, and in the field of ceramics, China was held to be supreme. In the late classical world and in early Islam, pottery was used only for utensils; in China alone it was cultivated as an art. Given the prestige of Chinese art, it would be natural for the 'Abbasids to try to supplement the always insufficient imports of choice pottery by establishing a local industry. This seems the most likely explanation for the sudden burgeoning of the ceramics industry in the ninth century. Theological prohibitions may also have contributed in slight measure, for various hadīths (Islamic Traditions) condemn the use of gold and silver vessels. The development of pottery with a sheen imitating precious metals lends some credence to this view. Finally, the advent of Islam led to a much-reduced output in certain well-established media—notably sculpture—which depended on figural motifs. It seems likely that the burgeoning of a quality ceramic tradition was an attempt, whether conscious or not, to develop an alternative means of expression for this type of subject matter. Unglazed wares, though produced in greater quantities than glazed pottery, offered far more limited scope for decoration. They are deliberately omitted from this account, though they were made uninterruptedly throughout the Islamic period.

Among imitations of Chinese ware, the most common—perhaps because it

FIG. 16–14. Ardistān, Iran, Masjid-i Jami', epigraphic frieze, c. 1158

was also the cheapest—is the so-called splashed ware that imitates the mottled decoration of certain Chinese ceramics of the contemporary T'ang period and later. This lead-glazed ware is also known as "egg and spinach" after its predominant colors; sometimes it was lightly incised. Chinese celadon, much prized because it was thought to shatter when poisoned food was placed in it, was also widely imitated. Nor were these the only types of Chinese ware to provide inspiration for Islamic craftsmen. Lack of suitable raw material meant that the 'Abbasid potters could not reproduce the stone-hard body of Chinese porcelain, but they copied this much-admired and coveted monochrome ware by applying an opaque white glaze to ordinary earthenware. Typically, they did not rest content with this, but began to decorate such tin-glazed ware, which was painted and glazed in one firing. In this technique, the color is absorbed into the glaze and spreads like ink in blotting paper. This running of the glaze betrays a lack of technical expertise, a deficiency here turned to good account. But the potters were soon able to devise glazes that would not run and that therefore allowed a controlled precision in the application of paint. Much more complex designs were thus made possible. It was in the ninth century that the Islamic potters developed a difficult technique entirely new to ceramics, that of luster, which was used for tiles as well as for pottery. In this type of pottery, sulphur and metallic oxides are combined with ochre and vinegar and the mixture is painted onto an already glazed vessel. It is then lightly fired in a reducing kiln in which the metal oxides are reduced to an iridescent metallic sheen on the surface. It seems clear that the intention was to copy the splendor of precious metals. The details of the technique were a closely guarded secret, and the process was difficult: the vessels were liable

FIG. 16–15. Isfahān, Iran, Madrasa-yi Imāmī, courtyard, c. 1325

to overfire, underfire, or crack during the second firing. 'Abbasid luster has been found as far afield as Samarqand, Sind, Egypt, Tunisia, and Spain; presumably it was usually the pottery that was exported rather than the craftsmen. The commonest colors are brown and yellow, and at first decoration is extremely simple, consisting mainly of spots, squares, and dashes. But after about 900, animal and human figures with a dotted background enclosing the central design became popular. These figures are often grotesquely, almost frighteningly, distorted.

In all these varied types of pottery, whose secular bias requires emphasis, the intention of the potter is clearly to devise colorful and stimulating decoration. He was able to use figural motifs, often with a pronounced courtly flavor, as well as geometric designs, epigraphy, and a whole range of vegetal ornament. With this *embarras de choix* in the field of decoration, it is not surprising that his interest is not focused on technical refinements of body or glaze or on the shape of the pottery itself. In these respects, Islamic pottery departs radically at the very outset from the Chinese tradition. 'Abbasid luster was the last major ware associated almost exclusively with Mesopotamia. In later medieval times, primacy in ceramics passed to other Islamic countries and Mesopotamian production remained in the orbit of Syria and Iran.

Metalwork in Medieval Iraq

The medieval metalwork of Iraq is synonymous with the name of Mosul, for numerous inscriptions on major pieces bear the names of craftsmen from that city (e.g., Ahmad al-Dhakī), and thus substantiate the literary evidence that this town was renowned above all other Islamic cities for its brass metalwork. Its specialty was smoothly finished inlay work in red copper, silver, and even gold. The sequence of some thirty signed or dated pieces begins in the early thirteenth century and lasts for about a century. A hallmark of Mosul work is the dense background of interlocking T-shapes, while animated scripts in Kufic and *naskh* scripts are of unequaled fantasy. Astrological designs, especially those representing the moon, are a leitmotif, while another common theme of decoration is a series of lobed medallions depicting the cycle of scenes from court life—music, banqueting, the hunt, and other spectacles—first developed at Sāmarrā. Bowls, vases, ewers, and candlesticks are the most popular objects of Mosul metalwork, rather than the boxes popular further west. The unique prestige of Mosul helped its craftsmen to set up metalworking centers in other Islamic cities, such as Cairo, and it is sometimes difficult to distinguish between the work of Mosul and that of such other centers.

Painting in Iraq

The *floruit* of Iraqi painting is barely a century long, and comes to an abrupt end soon after the Mongol invasion. But in that brief space it was the dominant school of the Islamic world. One major center was Mosul. In such works as the *Kitāb al-Diryāq* (1199; now in Paris; another related copy is probably early thirteenth century), the royal and cosmological symbolism employed in the frontispieces finds ready parallels in the contemporary sculpture and coinage of northern Iraq. The facial types with their slant eyes and heavy jowls are those familiar from Seljuk pottery, while some of the figures are best paralleled in *minā'ī* work. The surviving frontispieces from a multivolumed manuscript of the *Kitāb al-Aghānī* firmly establish the connection with Mosul, for they depict Badr al-Dīn Lū'lū', the ruler of the city from 1218. Despite the strong Seljuk strain in this style, the Byzantine elements are legion. They range from iconographic motifs such as angels or victories and the symbolic use of drapery, to stylistic details such as the imitation of Byzantine enamelwork and chrysography. The content of some of these books again follows an ancient classical and Byzantine tradition, for they are treatises on agriculture and other practical subjects.

A more celebrated school of painting developed slightly later at Baghdad. Here again the books chosen for illustration were frequently of a practical or scientific nature—the *De materia medica* and the *Properties of Plants*, both by Dioscorides, come to mind. In this school, too, Byzantium was a potent influence, possibly through the mediation of the Jacobite Christians of northern Mesopotamia, who seem to have overlaid the Byzantine element with such ancient Near Eastern traditions as strong outline drawing, exaggeratedly large eyes, and an interest in surface patterning, especially the technique of rendering drapery by "scroll-folds." Nevertheless, the "author" portraits in these treatises clearly derive their immediate inspiration from the Byzantine evangelist portrait, itself a reworking of the classical prototype. Hence the gold background, the omission of the author's muse, and the system of white highlights. Details of costume and architecture alone betray the Islamic context. In other aspects, however, the paintings of the Baghdad school owe little to Byzantium or even to Persia. The distinctive facial types, for example, with their black brows, hook noses, and projecting crania, owe nothing to the moon face that was the popular Persian convention of the time. And the book that was most often illustrated by the painters of Baghdad was quintessentially Arab: the *Maqāmāt* of al-Harīrī, an episodic and picaresque text expressed in rhymed prose, each *Maqāma* fashioned by a wordsmith exploiting the full resources of the language. Together they constitute a thesaurus of curious and recondite terms; but the illustrations mirror daily life with an extraordinary gusto. The artist favors scenes of intrigue, fraud, disputation; he loves to group his many figures in tight bunches and is at his best in depicting processions. His painting relies primarily on precise draftsmanship, rather than on modeling or bright color or elaborate landscape. The action is always crammed into the frontal plane and the background in the neutral color of the paper itself. Architectural settings are rendered with a notable precision, although without any attempt at perspective. Indeed, laborious spatial devices are consistently avoided. A few fleshy plants do duty for a landscape and the sky is rarely indicated. The masterpiece of the school is without doubt the *Maqāmāt* illustrated by Yahyā ibn Mahmūd al-Wāsitī in 1237. Late examples of the style are furnished by the *'Ajā'ib al-makhlūqāt* of al-Qazwīnī, dated 1278, and the *Rasā'īl ikhwān al-safā'* of 1287. Later Mesopotamian painting petered out in a stale imitation of this style, though court painting in the Persian manner was occasionally practiced in Baghdad.

Art in Ancient Iran

Turning now from Iraq to the Iranian world, man's development from roving hunter to settled farmer is amply documented in Iran, and as early as the ninth millennium B.C. the site of Ganj Dara Tepe, near Kirmānshāh, probably the winter quarters of a seminomadic community, actually displays permanent architecture. Though this comprises no more than clusters of primitive houses, the technique is curious, employing mud plano-convex bricks nearly one meter long and laid between mud mortar, as well as alternate layers of mud and fine plaster. Among the small finds were small clay sculptures of animal and "Venus" figurines. Crude pottery of ca. 7000 B.C., perhaps the earliest in Iran, was also found here. But it is not until the sixth millennium B.C. that the first evidence of man's ability as an artist begins to emerge. This coincides within a thousand years or so with the earliest considerable villages and the first evidence of irrigation. From this period—and also from sites in the Zagros mountains, as well as Tell-i Bakūn near Persepolis—date the earliest painted ceramics in Iran, which many regard as the earliest in the world. But it was slightly later, in the early levels at Sialk (near Kāshān) and Susa, that extremely fine pottery was produced, of a quality that in some respects was not matched for millenniums. Thin elegant beakers were a favorite form, and they often bear animal designs in which the natural form is wilfully abstracted to the very limits of recognition. But an intuitive understanding of nature controls the potter's artistic license. The designs are monochrome, usually executed in chocolate against a buff ground. The fourth and third millenniums were periods in which trading and cultural links between wide areas flourished with little restriction, so it is not surprising to find comparable images—possibly, indeed, of earlier date—farther west. During the fourth millennium, the earliest cities began to spring up, and in Iran as elsewhere the so-called "urban revolution" encouraged such crucial developments as writing and public administration. In Iran as in Egypt and Mesopotamia, the preferred sites for the earliest cities were fertile river valleys like that of the Hilmand in eastern Iran, where enough food could be grown to support a considerable population. In such centers, great wealth was soon amassed and thus were created the conditions of stable patronage that have so often been a prerequisite of great art.

By 4000 B.C., the Iranians had begun to learn about metallurgy, for evidence of copper smelting has been found in the area of Kirmān (where, by 3100–2700 B.C., bronze was also being made) at Tepe Yahyā. The same site has yielded some of the earliest inscribed clay tablets yet found in Iran. Datable to ca. 3000 B.C., they are in a script that suggests that this area was in the orbit of Anshan and Susa, Iran's first great city-states forming the kingdom of Elam. Much of Elam extended into Mesopotamia, of which the Khūzistān plain is a natural geographical extension. Indeed, as early as the fourth millennium B.C. there were close links between Iran and Mesopotamia, as is evident at Choga Mish, near Susa, a sizable city that is contemporary with the Uruk period in Mesopotamia (ca. 3500 B.C.) and that has produced many clay cylinder seal impressions. These depict military, musical, and domestic activities and various scenes of animal life. Throughout its long history, then, Elam straddled Iran and Mesopotamia. Yet surprisingly little of major artistic significance survives of Elamite civilization during the third and much of the second millennium B.C. Instead, recent discoveries at Banī Surma and elsewhere in Luristān suggest that in some fields of achievement this area was ahead of Elam. Corbel-vaulted tombs have yielded superb metalwork of Sumero-Akkadian type. From the same area comes Iran's earliest major bas-relief, that of King Annubanini of the Lullubi tribes, datable to ca. 2100 B.C., which depicts investiture and triumphal scenes. Only from the latter part of the second millennium do major Elamite buildings survive, though some Elamite bas-reliefs,

FIG. 16–16. Two hares from a *Kalīla wa Dimna* manuscript, probably Baghdad, c. 1230 (British Library, London, Or. 2784, f. 166v.)

such as one at Kurangun, may be rather earlier. At Haft Tepe, two tombs for collective burial, with elliptical vaults constructed of bricks laid slantwise, have been excavated, as have a temple and a massive brick building, possibly a ziggurat.

But the finest Elamite monument, also in Iran, is without doubt the four-stage ziggurat of Choga Zanbil, the center-piece of an extensive walled sacred precinct that housed storerooms and quarters for the priests, as well as other cultic structures. Begun by the Elamite ruler Untash-Napirisha(?) ca. 1250 B.C. in the later stages of Elamite power, the ziggurat was built as a series of hollow square towers placed one inside the other, reaching above 26 meters in height, and thus was constructed quite differently from the rectangular or spiral ziggurats found in Mesopotamia. The mud-brick core was faced with baked brick, and glazed brick was used for the façade of the topmost tower. A huge zebu of baked clay is the major sculptural find from the site. Contemporary finds from Susa include a bronze statue of Queen Napirasu.

The last centuries of the first millennium saw the heyday of perhaps the most distinctive metalwork in pre-Achaemenid Iran: the so-called "Luristān bronzes" of southwestern Iran. A few bear cuneiform inscriptions, but most are anepigraphic. Weapons, standards, jewelry, and personal ornaments like belt buckles are all outnumbered by horse and chariot gear. The prosaic function of these bits, rein rings, pins, and so on did not inhibit their creators from adorning them with an entire bestiary of Iranian fauna. Wild sheep, gazelles, lions, and bulls are among the many animals depicted, very often in profile. Human figures also occur frequently and are subject to even more severe stylization. The more ambitious pieces have complex figural scenes of unguessed but probably magical significance and feature mythical animals like griffins and winged human-headed bulls. Since virtually all the Luristān bronzes currently known were the fruit of clandestine excavations, their full context is lost, but it can safely be said that they were made between ca. 2600 and ca. 500 B.C., probably by settled craftsmen. Of the various groups that can be identified, the latest may have been produced for a civilization of Cimmerian, Median, or Iranian nomadic horsemen in the Zagros mountains; they probably served practical as well as funerary, ritualistic, and votive purposes. Many of the themes are of ancient Mesopotamian origin, such as the man between rearing felines or affronted or addorsed animals. Contemporary architecture in Luristān is best represented at Bābā Jān Tepe, where the principal occupation dates to the ninth and eighth centuries B.C. Its main feature was perhaps a fort-like building with such refinements as a spiral staircase, recessed doorways, built-in benches, and a central hall the flat roof of which rested on four columns. Most remarkable of all, however, was a chamber in which were found fragments of nearly 200 tiles painted with cruciform and square designs. These tiles probably decorated the ceiling.

Urartian and Median Art

Northwestern Iran at this period was part of the empire of Urartu, which extended into modern Turkey and Soviet Armenia. The major Urartian site yet excavated in Iran is Bastām, near Mākū, which has yielded massive gates and a great hall formerly carried on columns, while at Haftavān Tepe on Lake Urmiyya, a stone-built structure of the eighth century B.C., laid out on a regular plan, may have served as the residence of the local governor. Spectacular metalwork, this time in gold and silver, marks the almost contemporary Mannean civilization of western Iran, whose apogee can be dated to the beginning of the first millennium B.C. Hasanlū, the probable capital of the Manneans, has yielded a solid gold bowl decorated with numerous human and animal figures of enigmatic meaning. From nearby Ziviyya comes an undated treasure, including a great gold pectoral with designs of mingled Assyrian and Scythian inspiration and a silver dish with concentric circles of animals and animal heads, again of Scythian type. Lastly, at Marlik near Rasht was found a treasure of gold beakers dating from 1000 B.C. and a gold bowl decorated with a double row of horned animals in high relief. The finds from these three sites all testify to a mingling of races and cultures in northwestern Iran that coincide with the arrival in this area of new peoples, including the Medes and the Persians. Their wider horizons are hinted at in the iconography of their metalwork, in which the influences of Assyria and Urartu, the great powers immediately to the west, mingle with those of nomadic tribes from the northern steppes and others from Anatolia, Syria, and even Egypt. By the eighth century B.C., the Medes had become a powerful force in northwest Iran. Their capital at Ecbatana/Hamadān is as yet unexcavated, but at Tepe Nūsh-i Jān, some 45 miles south of Hamadān, a Median temple and fort with multiple walls and a large columned hall, dated to ca. 750 to 600 B.C., have been uncovered. These buildings are mainly of mud brick. The temple offers valuable evidence for a pre-Zoroastrian fire cult in Iran, complete with a curious triangular sanctuary containing a stepped altar. The nearby Median sites of Godin Tepe and Bābā Jān Tepe complement many of the architectural findings of Tepe Nūsh-i Jān.

Achaemenid Art

Although disappointingly little remains of Median art and architecture, this situation is entirely reversed in the case of the Achaemenids, who succeeded to and vastly expanded the Median empire. No pre-Christian civilization in Iran has left such abundant traces. The sequence begins with Pasargadae (the Achaemenid Pasragada), founded probably after 547 B.C. by Cyrus, the first great Achaemenid ruler (559–530 B.C.). In the renowned tomb of Cyrus, comprising a single gabled chamber set on a stepped plinth, the Achaemenid architects hit on a formula of noble and arresting simplicity. Scattered in a wide arc around it are numerous other buildings, whose original garden and parkland setting is now lost. They include a rectangular audience hall whose central reception chamber was carried on two rows of four columns. The stonework technique is impeccable and makes much play of an effective contrast of black and white limestone. Reliefs decorated the doorways and their remains suggest that they depicted apotropaic composite monsters. A trilingual inscription in Elamite, Babylonian, and Old Persian identifies the building with Cyrus himself. A residential palace nearby has a more complex plan partitioned into small units by mud-brick walls, while at the extreme northeastern end of the site is the citadel, whose stone-faced platform bore numerous structures, including a palace. Nearby is a ruined tower known as "the prison of Solomon" of which a better-preserved variant exists at Naqsh-i Rustam near Persepolis. In the latter building, the rectangular façade is broken by rows of narrow slots and blank windows with black stone frames that accentuate the white limestone of the structure. A single doorway reached by a wide staircase leads to an empty chamber. These towers seem, to judge from Urartian parallels, to have functioned as temples, though they have also been interpreted as tombs or as repositories for sacred books or royal relics.

The site's masonry techniques prove that Greek stone-cutting methods (known from Lydia and Ionia) were already being employed, but the small size and light proportions of the buildings seem more of an original product. Although Pasargadae was the earliest Achaemenid capital, this loose conglomeration of buildings—unfortified and innocent even of an enclosing wall—was clearly on too modest a scale to merit that title. It dates, too, from a time when the Achaemenid empire had still not reached its full extent. Within a generation, the Achaemenids were dominating almost the entire civilized world west of India, and in this new situation something grander than Pasargadae was required. The slightly later Achaemenid palace at Susa was, by contrast, ideally suited by size and location to become the nerve center of the largest empire of the time. Several Achaemenid palaces attributed to Darius I and Artaxerxes (II?) have come to light here, with halls of which the square stone plinths and the lotus-flower, bell-shaped bases formerly holding columns remain. Susa has also produced glazed bricks of Assyrian and Babylonian type that were joined to form large-scale processional scenes of archers and animals (lions, bulls, and griffins) decorating the palace walls. Mural paintings, dedicatory tablets, and a notable statue of Darius I decorated with Egyptian hieroglyphics are the most important recent discoveries here. Such work reveals official Achaemenid art as essentially composite, a synthesis of the major artistic traditions of the time. It draws impartially on the artistic traditions of alien peoples, whether free or conquered. This judgment applies as much to iconography as to materials and techniques.

The Achaemenid rulers followed a seminomadic life style in that they moved from one capital to another, according to the season. Susa served as a winter capital, and Hamadān—as yet unexcavated—for the summer, while at least part of the spring was spent at the most evocative of all Achaemenid sites, Persepolis (the Achaemenid Parsa; mostly built ca. 500–460 B.C.). The comparatively small surface area of the site indicates that Persepolis was used principally by the court and its officials, yet it was not entirely administrative, and the beautifully preserved reliefs provide the necessary clues to its purpose. The recurrent theme of the lion attacking the bull dovetails with the extended scenes of tribute to suggest that Persepolis was the site where the New Year was ritually celebrated. Probably then as now, this was celebrated in Iran at the time of the vernal equinox—about 21 March—when the constellations of Leo and Taurus were at their zenith. Sited at the foot of a mountain range, Persepolis comprises a massive artificial platform, 60 feet high in places and faced with huge blocks of smooth limestone. Switchback staircases, with deep, low treads suitable for horses, lead to the top of the platform and to the Portal of All Nations, a ceremonial entrance guarded by winged human-headed bulls of Assyrian type. The four-square form of this portal was perhaps intended as a reference to Achaemenid rule over the four quarters of the earth. Numerous palaces and administrative buildings of markedly rectilinear type take up the rest of the platform. Their architecture is hypostyle in plan and trabeate in elevation, though all trace of the wooden ceilings perished in the fire of 330 B.C., which destroyed the site. The beams rested on limestone columns with gigantic composite capitals depicting addorsed protomes of bulls, lions, griffins, and other creatures. Major architectural features, such as door jambs, lintels, and window frames, were of limestone, but the curtain walls, now perished, were of mud brick. The typical layout of these palaces was to surround the central columned hall by a series of small rooms. Curvilinear architecture was restricted to the mud-brick buildings adjoining the great platform, and even here it is found only occasionally. But architecture is secondary to the wealth of relief sculpture at this site. Tablets reveal that this work was executed by paid craftsmen, many of them foreigners. The central scene of the Apadana sculptures is the so-called Treasury relief, showing Darius enthroned, accompanied by his son Xerxes and court officials. But the largest single section depicts the New Year ceremony at which representatives of the twenty-three satrapies present the offerings appropriate to their lands. No doubt this ceremony was intended as an official reaffirmation of their loyalty to the great king. This lengthy narrative is completed by reliefs of the Immortals, the Praetorian guard of the Achaemenid court, and of the astrologically potent theme of a lion bringing down a bull. Door jambs frequently depict the king killing a composite monster in hand-to-hand combat, presumably an apotropaic motif. The carvings were originally embellished with paint (as was the woodwork) and with applied metal. Although their precision and modeling owe much to Assyrian models, scenes of war and carnage are noticeably absent. In the Bīsitūn reliefs Darius is shown in triumph over his defeated enemies, but there the specific purpose is to emphasize the legitimacy of Darius, not simply to proclaim his success in battle. Other Achaemenid rock reliefs (notably those at Naqsh-i Rustam) deploy the familiar themes of enthronement and worship.

The minor arts of the Achaemenid period again owe much to earlier traditions. This is especially true of the rhytons, bowls, and other containers executed in precious metals. Such vessels use the millennial iconography of pacing lions or other fearsome beasts familiar from Ziviyya, Hasanlu, and elsewhere. The hoard of late Achaemenid gold and silver jewelry uncovered at Pasargadae, on the other hand, is remarkably varied in type and design and many of its elements are unique.

The Parthian Period

After the death of Alexander, the veneer of Greek culture worn by the people of Mesopotamia and Persia became increasingly thin. Much of this area fell under the sway of Seleucus, one of the many generals who parceled up the heritage of Alexander. He founded a dynasty ruled from two capitals, both named Seleucia: one on the Orontes, the other on the Tigris. Surviving monuments of this period (323–223 B.C.) are scarce. In western Iran, they include the terraced shrine of Bard-i Nishanda and the fragmentary remains of a temple at Khurha, with two columns bearing capitals of a debased Ionic style. The temple at Khurha, however, is quite inadequate to serve as a yardstick of Seleucid architecture. Perhaps the most that can be hazarded is that within a generally classical context an indifference to the precise reproduction of Greek architectural vocabulary coexisted with an enthusiasm for sheer scale that was quite un-Greek in concept. Much of the sculpture that survives from this period also bears an Iranian stamp, despite superficial classicism (e.g., the sculpture of the reclining Herakles at Bisutun). The subjects are principally religious and show that Greek cults, such as that of Dionysus, were practiced alongside Iranian ones. A few rock-cut tombs survive from this period; the most important of these is that known as Dukkān-i Dā'ūd in Luristān.

The Seleucids were finally swept away by a dynasty that must have owed much of its appeal to its Iranian descent. The Parthians originally came from the steppes that bordered Iran to the northeast, and they were at first noted horse breeders. It could be argued, therefore, that they were only partly Iranian and that to see them as the Iranian reaction to Hellenism could be misconceived. Their artifacts show them deliberately aping classical styles, and an early Parthian ruler even termed himself Philhellene. Only gradually did Iranian values reassert themselves. The uninterrupted series of Parthian coins makes it possible to trace this evolution in detail. The earliest specimens are typically Hellenistic in their fully modeled, realistic, convex portrait heads. By degrees such coins are replaced by issues in which the face is simplified and attention focuses on the clothes and headgear that in oriental tradition have always been the proper appurtenances of kingship. Occasionally, a portrait head is depicted frontally, in violation of Greek numismatic canons. Finally, all pretense of portraiture is abandoned and the coin becomes a symbol of abstract kingship.

It is hard to generalize about Parthian architecture, because the styles vary considerably throughout the extensive territory of the empire, and because very little has survived. The largest single body of Parthian architecture is in Syria, in Palmyra, and it differs fundamentally from Parthian work further east in its heavy reliance on classical models. The Parthian city of Hatra in northern Iraq was, as its art reveals, firmly in the orbit of Palmyra, but eastern influences are more apparent here. Its numerous mausoleums are provincial versions of the domed square that was a standard form of classical tomb, but many of them incorporate novel variants. Some have two stories, others have crypts, yet others are furnished with staircases. As a group they depart decisively from classical types. Clustered together in a restricted area, and comprising a series of deliberate variations on a single basic type, they foreshadow the mausoleums of medieval Islam. The temples of Hatra are recognizably classical in their detailing, but their bold use of arches, while not unusual in Roman architecture generally, is hard to parallel in Syria and seems rather to indicate Iranian influence. The deep vaults within a rectangular frame (īwāns) that are such a hallmark of the site were certainly to become a distinctively Iranian feature. Theatrical masks adorn the blank façades of these buildings; though they are Roman in type, their haphazard setting—a random scatter around a side door—is itself a major solecism within this classical vocabulary. A similar penchant for external sculpture used in an unclassical way can be seen at Palmyra. Other Parthian buildings in Mesopotamia are more frankly Iranian in type or decoration. In the 1840s, Loftus discovered much geometric stucco decoration at Warka, which boldly exploited contrasts of light and shade and seems to have been carved rather than molded like much subsequent work. The function of the building itself was not established.

In contrast, a Parthian palace excavated at Assur is interesting largely because of its ground plan and its stucco façade. Grouped around a diminutive courtyard are four large rectangular openings in roughly cruciform disposition. These *iwāns* were to become a major space-defining agent in later Iranian architecture. They help to create a varied architectonic inner façade, imposing order on a warren of living and reception rooms. Single *iwāns* of dominating proportions were used as monumental entrances in the Parthian palace at Nippur, again foreshadowing Islamic architecture. In Iran proper, Parthian architecture is notably varied and far-flung. Certain fire temples, such as that of Bāz-i Hūr or the massive Ribāt-i Safīd, both in Khurāsān, have been attributed to the Parthian period, but they are far outnumbered by secular buildings. Perhaps the most spectacular of these is the kiosk known as Qal'a-yi Zahhāk in Kurdistān. Sited in lonely splendor at the far edge of a spur projecting over a deep chasm, its function is a riddle. Too elaborate for a lookout post, too cramped for official use, it seems to answer some commemorative purpose. So eclectic were Parthian funerary practices that it could be interpreted as an Iranian version of the Palmyrene or Hatran tomb towers; or, alternatively, as some kind of victory monument, for which both Sāsānid and Islamic parallels exist. It was so clearly intended as a dominating landmark that some public function must be assigned to it. Its decoration appears to be virtually unique and makes much play with polychrome borders of simple alternating geometrical shapes. The basic layout has much in common with the Sāsānid *chahār tāq* ("four arches") or fire temple: a square ground plan punctuated by four axial arches crowned by a dome. But here the stilted profile of the dome and the pronounced ellipsis of the arches discounts a Sāsānid identification. No other Parthian building in Iran can approach this kiosk for elegance and lightness of touch. At Shahr-i Qūmis near Dāmghān, the elliptical arch recurs, this time in mud brick, an indication that the form is rooted in the Iranian vernacular tradition. Perhaps its most ambitious use is in the vaulted palace of Īwān-i Karkha near Susa, which seems to be late Parthian or early Sāsānid in date. Here transverse barrel vaults further strengthen the structure. The largest Parthian site excavated to date is at Kūh-i Khvāja in Sīstān, where frescoes showing three gods and a king with his consort have been found. The site has long been a holy place and has been in continuous occupation since Parthian, if not Achaemenid, times. Little but the massive circular enclosing wall survives of the Parthian settlement at Takht-i Sulaimān; this wall uses columns as applied decoration in a bastardized classical style and its main gateway, too, has a classical flavor.

Parthian sculpture in Mesopotamia and Iran falls far short of the heights it reached at Palmyra. Hatra has yielded the largest quantity of fine statuary in these areas. Though the style of these sculptured figures is clearly related to that of Palmyra, it also has certain idiosyncrasies that make it difficult to confuse the two schools. Votive figures are the rule. A rigid convention governs the pose. The worshipper is shown frontally, standing with the right hand raised, palm outward, in a gesture of adoration. Faces betray no emotion, but their impassive, withdrawn expression suggests that these people are in touch with another world. This deliberate spirituality is, of course, a feature of the imperial image in the late antique classical world. In their aloof, hieratic quality, these figures inhabit a different world from that of the self-confident merchant princes of Palmyra. Although these figures are often in the round, the sculptors were apparently not fully emancipated from the techniques of relief sculpture. Thus, the frontal plane dominates and there is an almost fussy concern with the surface detailing of hair and costume. Numerous Hatran reliefs survive and they show that identical modes were used in these two essentially different techniques. Above all, the freestanding statues do not exploit mobility. The same wooden poses recur constantly and the variety of poses and scenes found in Palmyrene statuary is conspicuously absent, yet their nobility and latent spirituality are adequate compensation. Only one piece of sculpture from Iran proper can rival the work at Hatra. This is a freak survival of a more than life-size bronze figure of a chieftain found at Shāmī in Luristān. It is impressive enough technologically, but perhaps even more interesting is the evidence that it offers as to the existence of a court style of Parthian sculpture that could be found in a remote site like Shāmī, as well as in Palmyra. Moreover, the figure rejects decisively the classical vocabulary that permeates Palmyrene sculpture. The chieftain's costume is a long belted tunic over baggy trousers, and the dominant feature of his impassive face is his heavy moustache. Nothing in Parthian relief sculpture is of comparable quality. Typical examples at Bīsutūn, Susa, and Tang-i Sarwak have varied subjects—battle, investiture, worship, and the hunt—but are alike in their preference for low relief or incision and their deliberate disregard of natural proportion. Elaborate late Parthian stucco sculpture, expressing a remarkably mixed iconography in which images of classical Iranian and nomadic origin occur, has been found at Qal'a-yi Yazdigird in Persian Kurdistān.

Sāsānid Art

Parthian rule was finally terminated by the Sāsānids, a noble family of priestly descent whose power centered on the province of Fārs, the traditional heartland of Iran from Achaemenid times onward. The Sāsānid kings exploited to the full the link with their illustrious predecessors. They left inscriptions on Achaemenid monuments—as at Naqsh-i Rustam, where, beneath the cliff tombs of the Achaemenid kings, they laid out an immense picture gallery of rock reliefs with exclusively royal themes. Thus, they revived on the grand scale the forgotten glories of Achaemenid relief sculpture, employed some of the same subject matter, such as investitures and victories, and like their predecessors flaunted trilingual inscriptions of propaganda content. They too drew artistic inspiration from the classical world, though this was more evident in their relief sculpture than in their architecture. Above all, they emphasized the primacy of Fārs, and it is here that nearly all their reliefs and much of their architecture may be found. The language of these reliefs, of which about thirty are known, is generally inflated, for their content is political and propagandist. Muscle-bound kings un-horse their enemies in a crashing mêlée of shattered lances and sprawling limbs. These single combats presage medieval tournaments, even to the use of personal devices on the armor, but their flavor is as much political as heroic. Their sequel makes this clear, as defeated enemies are trampled by mounted emperors or cringe before them. Sometimes the king sits enthroned amidst his standing courtiers, his sword planted between his knees, his body in aggressively frontal pose—the very image of martial power. Moreover, the setting of these images is more carefully calculated than was previously the case. Most are sited with an eye to drama, at the foot of lowering cliffs or in echoing grottoes. Dwarfed as they are by nature, they are nevertheless far above life-size, and since they are seen at eye level the viewer cannot help being awed. Thus both god and man are served. Unique among these reliefs in scale, variety and content are the hunting panoramas that unfold within the grotto of Ṭāq-i Būstān, near Kirmānshah. Here a Sāsānid *firdaws* (*paradeisos* or game park) is depicted in arresting detail. Despite the conflicting systems of perspective the artist contrives to present the story with the utmost clarity. His favorite device is to emphasize the might of the ruler by making him much larger than those around him, whose individuality is denied by their treatment as a rhythmical sequence of monotonous identical figures. Sometimes the ruler is surrounded by empty space as by an aura, in marked contrast to the busy, jostling activity of his entourage or to the closely packed animals that he hunts. The quantity of incident that is packed into the boar and stag hunts suggests that these reliefs depend on Sāsānid wall paintings, which are known to have favored similar subjects. At the back of the grotto, beneath a typically Sāsānid investiture scene, towers a mounted warrior in three-quarter relief. Horse and rider alike are covered in intricately detailed body armor; even the visor is clamped shut. This relief vividly evokes the fearsome Persian cataphract of late antiquity.

Sāsānid minor arts present a much more impressive picture than comparable Parthian work. An unbroken series of coins has permitted a firm political chronology to be established. The Sāsānid silver *dirham* was the "dollar" of late antiquity, penetrating far beyond the borders of the Persian empire. For this—as in the more recent case of the Maria Theresa *thaler*—its distinctive format was no doubt at least partly responsible. Large and thin, it bore the obtrusive bust of the current ruler, identified by his crown. Each ruler adopted a different variety of crown; indeed, this was true even of a king ruling for the second time. This built-in dating control not only identifies coins with illegible inscriptions but also the numerous seals and cameos produced in this period. Above all, it helps to classify the magnificent silver display plates conventionally dubbed "Sāsānid." Many of them are betrayed as early Islamic copies by their slight irregularities of detail in the depiction of crowns. As a group, these silver plates irresistibly recall the lavish ostentation of later Roman and Byzantine plate, which became increasingly charged with political meaning (e.g., the early seventh-century plates depicting scenes from the life of David). Their themes frankly express the legendary splendor of the Sāsānid court, in that the king is shown in full regalia hunting, feasting, listening to music, and giving audience. Ewers with voluptuous dancing girls belong to the same courtly cycle, though they may also express latent religious symbolism. Cosmic symbolism has also been suggested for the hunting scenes, which could be interpreted as images of the successive seasons—hence the carefully selected species of animals depicted—while other plates depict scenes of royal apotheosis that still await full explanation. No doubt the propagandist intent of these plates explains why so many of them were exported to Iran's neighbors. They exhibit a wide range of techniques—chasing, engraving, gilding, and niello among others. Several royal busts have been found, but no full-length figure in metal like that from Shāmī.

Many of the themes found in Sāsānid reliefs and silverware recur in the stucco ornament that was the preferred decorative medium in Sāsānid buildings. But other motifs were commoner. They include repetitive geometric and floral designs of a rather stereotyped character and also a very varied selection of small figure plaques. These have much in common with the *emblemata* of classical floor mosaics and their descendants in Coptic textiles, and they include such familiar types as the woman at the window, peacocks, boars, and even monograms. Their freshness, vigor, and capacity to seize on essentials all place them in quite a different class from the floral and geometric decoration. Work of this kind has been found at Ctesiphon, Chahār Tarkhān, and Dāmghān. A freak example of full-scale stucco sculpture, the figure of a woman, has recently turned up at Khunj in Fārs; but even at that site it was the only such find. The undoubted masterpiece of free-standing, large-scale Sāsānid statuary is the colossal image of Shāpūr I (8 meters high and carved from a stalactite) at Bīshāpūr, which dates from the late third century. In later times, the Sāsānid tradition, though virtually extinguished in Persia and Iraq with the coming of Islam, lived on in the stucco sculpture of the Umayyad residences in Syria. Indeed, Sāsānid iconography as a whole became a potent repository of themes and anecdote in later Islamic art. Byzantine art, which at the time of the Islamic conquest offered the major alternative artistic tradition, was the product of an unconquered and hostile civilization, and thus could not exert the same degree of influence. Moreover, with the fall of the Umayyads in 750 the center of gravity in the Islamic world moved eastward to Baghdad, in former Persian territory. At the 'Abbasid court, Persian ways became fashionable, and Persian officials wielded immense power. Thus the situation favored the survival and revival of pre-Islamic Persian traditions in art as in other fields.

But it is principally in architecture that the Sāsānid artistic achievement dominated the Muslim imagination. This was due principally to the survival, uncomfortably close to Baghdad, of the most spectacular of all Sāsānid palaces—Ctesiphon or Tāq-i Kisrā (the Arch of Chosroes). Much of the palace has vanished, but until a flood in 1887 the façade remained substantially intact. Its blind arcades in superposed tiers recall the Hellenistic *scenae frons*, but the gigantic arched opening in the center of the façade has no classical parallel. It is the largest unsupported brick vault ever built, 29 meters high and 43 meters deep. Muslim rulers tried in vain to demolish or to surpass it; it remained an ideal of excellence throughout medieval times and (like Tāq-i Būstān) became a *topos* of Islamic literature. No other Sāsānid building of comparable splendor survives, but the principles of curvilinear rather than trabeate architecture inspire all Sāsānid building. The materials are often crude—rubble masonry veneered with plaster,

poor quality baked brick and even mud brick. Sometimes the bricks are remarkably large, twice the size of medieval Islamic bricks, and are laid in vertical
or radial bond. Rubble and brick were readily available throughout the country
and this no doubt facilitated the growth of a standard, rather unambitious provincial architecture, as exemplified in the many small fire temples of Fārs. The
value of these buildings is that they ensured that an architecture dependent on
arches, vaults, and domes became thoroughly acclimatized in Iran. This curvilinear
emphasis infused even small and simple buildings with monumentality. Since
the building material was somewhat crude, the Sāsānid architects preferred wide
safety margins, and their work does not give evidence of the same precise calculations that were made in the erection of later Islamic domes. But their importance
lay in establishing such elements as the squinch, the domed square, and the *iwān*.
Moreover, their buildings have a pronounced sense of axiality, a feature also
much refined by later Islamic architects. Even their round cities, such as Gūr and
Hirakla, provided inspiration for such later creations as Baghdad and Raqqa.
By far the most widespread type of Sāsānid architecture was the fire temple, the
chahār tāq ("four arches"); of which a classic example survives at Niyāsar. This
square-domed chamber pierced by an arch at each of the four cardinal points
proved a model capable of being repeated on many scales, and it gained a new
lease on life when it was adopted for the sanctuary chambers of medieval Iranian
mosques. Devoid of axial emphasis, and of an open plan dictated by the open-air
ceremonies of Zoroastrianism, this admirably simple building type also influenced
the designs of later mausoleums and garden pavilions. Other types of cultic
structure have been found, such as the high-walled sanctuary at Bīshāpūr or the
rock-cut fire altars at Naqsh-i Rustam, but these exceptions serve only to under-
line the prevalence of the free-standing domed square. In a class by itself is the
impressive late Sāsānid temple at Kangavār. The deity to which it was dedicated
is not known, though Artemis and Anahita have been suggested. A drawing
made in the 1840s shows many of the columns enclosing the massive *cella* still
standing, but since that time the temple has fallen victim to that greatly accelerated pace of destruction that has characterized the Near East for the past 150
years. Recent excavations have shown that formal access to the temple was by a
pair of lateral staircases strikingly reminiscent of those at Persepolis. With their
broad treads and low risers they suggest that here too, despite the very different
functional context, access for riders was intended. Numerous masons' marks
afford valuable evidence of the distribution of labor and the number of teams at
work. The Kangavār temple, with its massive scale and careful stereotomy,
represents a final echo of the golden age of Achaemenid architecture. Sāsānid
palaces are much more varied than the cultic structures of the period; indeed
there is no standard palatial type. At Fīrūzābād (the ancient Gūr) the central
triple-domed complex, surrounded by narrow wall passages, is flanked to north
and south by courtyards giving on to living quarters and articulated by *iwān*s.
Multiple domes are also a feature of the notably compact palace at Sarvistān,
which rejects courtyards in favor of a series of covered corridors and chambers of
varied scales. No overall symmetry holds the plan together and indeed its status
as a palace has recently been questioned. By contrast, symmetry is the keynote
of the extensive palace with attendant gardens laid out along a ceremonial axis

by Khusraw II at Qasr-i Shīrīn. The climax of the whole was an immense domed chamber with axial *iwāns* serving as exedrae, a device reminiscent of the great audience hall at Bīshāpūr. Outside the mainstream of Sāsānid architecture lie the mysterious tower at Fīrūzābād and the victory tower put up at Pāikulī by Mihr Narseh. Significant public works of the dynasty include the piers of the Shahristān bridge at Isfahān and the barrages at Dizfūl and Shustar, built, so it is said, by Roman prisoners of war in the third century.

Iranian Islamic Architecture

Iranian Islamic architecture flourished from the Arab conquest in the seventh century to the fall of the Safavid dynasty in the eighteenth century. In this period of over a millennium, it developed a remarkably consistent vocabulary of basic forms. In this respect, it can be compared with classical architecture, to which it otherwise owes so little, but which also drew inspiration from a few simple forms. In the Islamic architecture of Persia, the key elements were the dome, the *iwān*, and the courtyard. The trabeate tradition of Achaemenid architecture had already been rejected by the Sāsānids, and it fell to Muslim architects to refine and diversify Sāsānid forms. The forum for their many experiments was the mosque; indeed, its history is that of Iranian Islamic architecture in miniature.

Very little architecture survives from before the tenth century. Literary sources state that the Arabs often converted the existing cultic buildings of Sāsānid Persia, the fire temples, into mosques; but no incontrovertible archaeological evidence for this practice has yet been found (though the mosques of Yazdīkhvāst and Qurva may be examples). These fire temples, with their square-domed chambers broken by four axial arched entrances, were often placed in the center of a large open enclosure. This model conformed admirably to the major liturgical need of Islamic worship, namely, a large open space for prayer. The early mosques that the Arabs built in Iraq, Egypt, and elsewhere usually consisted of large open enclosures surrounded by arcades that were deeper on the *qibla* side. Early Iranian mosques of this "Arab plan" are at Sīrāf and Fahraj. This plan did not maintain currency for long, though small village mosques, consisting exclusively of a covered sanctuary, continued to be built into modern times. Soon the single-domed chamber of local tradition replaced the extra aisles of the sanctuary. Sāsānid architecture provided another feature that was adapted for cultic purposes—the *iwān* commonly used in palaces. This too replaced the aisled sanctuary of the Arab plan. Thus, from the early centuries of Islam onward, local traditions modified an alien building type and assimilated it to familiar forms. It was in the development and combination of these three features —the square-domed chamber, the *iwān*, and the courtyard—that the future of Persian architecture was to lie. It is possible that originally each of these features was used by itself as a mosque.

The Tārī(k) Khāna at Dāmghān, perhaps the earliest mosque in Iran, illustrates how the Persians quickly modified the Arab plan. The arcades surrounding the courtyard are executed in huge bricks of Sāsānid type, the round piers are stumpy and massive and the arch profiles are elliptical. Above all, the central arch of the north façade, on the axis of the *mihrāb*, rises higher than the other arches and is encased in a rectangular frame—an embryonic *iwān*. The mosque had a square minaret, as at Sīrāf, and a deviant *qibla*—a feature that is not rare in Iranian mosques. Its use of mud brick is paralleled by the Fahraj mosque. The lack of decoration in the Dāmghān mosque means that the late eighth century date normally accorded to it must be regarded as tentative. It certainly cannot be sustained for the whole mosque, since the lateral arcades display typically Seljuk arch profiles. Another mosque type comprised a single *iwān* on the *qibla* side, facing a courtyard with arcades on the other three sides (Nīrīz; Firdaws). It is not certain when the first attempts to combine the various types were made, but among surviving monuments the process of development can be traced most clearly in the incomparable Friday mosque of Isfahān. The original mosque was probably of Arab plan, and underwent a major reshaping in the Būyid period. The arcaded courtyard was retained, but was now graced by multilobed piers and subtle geometric brick ornament exploiting contrasted planes. At the end of the eleventh century, two square-domed chambers were introduced into the north and south sides. Both chambers are masterpieces, but the northern one is an outstanding example of the structural finesse of Seljuk architecture and its capacity to subordinate rich ornament to clarity of form. A single arch form repeated on many scales is the leitmotif of the building and lends it a formidable concentration. The octagonal zone of transition between the dome and the square chamber is here accorded a marked prominence, notably by the sculptural emphasis of its trilobed squinches. Henceforward, this zone was aesthetically integrated into the elevation and became a focus of decoration in its own right. A fire destroyed much of the Isfahān mosque, except for the two domed chambers, in 1121, and it was probably soon after this disaster that four *iwān*s were added on the axes of the mosque. Thus the sequence of courtyard-*iwān*-domed chamber, so popular in later periods, was established. Considerable variation was possible within this basic schema, for example, in the size of the courtyard or the number of *iwān*s.

On occasion, mosques that had previously consisted of an isolated domed chamber or were of Arab type had *iwān*s added to them. Such modifications document the extensive influence of this new articulation of the mosque, which presumably enjoyed active official support. The Seljuks introduced other types of mosques too: in Khurāsān, for example, a courtyard mosque with an *iwān* on the north and south side and no domed chamber was popular (Gūnābād), and small, domed mosques of square plan abound (Sangān-i Pā'īn; 'Abdullāhābād) as do mosques consisting simply of a low-columned arcaded hall with a flat roof (Simnān; Zarand). After the Seljuk period, no major innovations in mosque plans were made. The Mongols, who built mainly in the fourteenth century, added much to existing mosques (prayer hall and *madrasa* in Isfahān Friday mosque). When they built new mosques, they favored established types, such as the four-*iwān* plan (Varāmīn; Hafshūya), the covered sanctuary (mosques at Quhrūd and the Friday mosque of Barzūk), or the isolated domed chamber (Dashtī; Azīrān). The mosque of 'Alī Shāh at Tabriz is atypical, for it consists only of a courtyard and *qibla iwān*. It illustrates the huge scale of some Mongol foundations. The Mongol contribution lay principally in a refining and attenuation of Seljuk forms: one may compare the relationship of Gothic to Romanesque. The Timurids also added to existing mosques rather than building anew (Abarqūh). Their winter prayer hall in the Isfahān Friday mosque comprises multiple aisles of massive pointed arches springing directly from the ground. Alabaster windows admit a "dim religious light." Their most ambitious foundations are in Transoxiana and Afghanistan and, therefore, outside the scope of this survey, but large Timurid mosques surviving at Mashhad, Gurgān, and Nīshāpūr show that sheer size characterizes Timurid foundations within Iran proper as well as outside it. Khurāsān, in particular, also has many modest mosques of this period (e.g., Handūvālān). Perhaps the most important and unusual mosque of this period is the Blue Mosque at Tabrīz (1465), a large domed octagon surrounded by lesser domed chambers.

Few major mosques in the country lack traces of Safavid work, but the number of important new mosques erected under this dynasty is surprisingly small. The finest are in Isfahān, which the Safavids made their capital under Shāh 'Abbās (1588–1629). His two most famous mosques, the Lutfullāh Mosque and the Masjid-i Shāh, again repeat familiar schemas—the domed square chamber and the four-*īwān* plan, respectively. Their exceptional size and splendid decoration make it easy to overlook their essential conservatism. The façades of both open onto the great square or *maidān*, which was the center of the new city, and both have bent entrances, so that the mosques themselves are correctly orientated but do not compromise the regularity of the façades defining the square. The high officials of the Safavid court built numerous mosques in Isfahān (e.g., the Masjid-i Hakīm), but as a group these do not display any marked originality. Even more than in earlier times, some of the finest mosques formed part of much larger complexes, whether these were shrines (Ardabīl, Qum, Māhān, Mashhad) or institutions that were both religious and secular (Isfahān, complex on the Chahār Bāgh; foundations of Ganj 'Alī Khān at Kirmān).

During the subsequent centuries, standards remained high (Wakīl mosque, Shīrāz; Sipahsālār mosque, Tehran), especially when the architect had ample space at his disposal (Nūshābād). Perhaps the most interesting of Qājār mosques is the ingenious split-level Masjid-i Āqā Buzurg at Kāshān, but this flouting of tradition is exceptional. As at Khiva in Transoxiania, medieval formulas have lasted into modern times.

The earliest minarets in Iran seem to have copied the square form current in early Islam (Dāmghān, Sīrāf). But with the eleventh century a striking new type of tall cylindrical minaret, usually set on a polygonal plinth, was introduced. These minarets were usually built of high-quality baked brick and thus have often survived, even though all trace of the mosque to which they belonged has vanished. A few remain standing even though they are of mud brick (e.g., Fahraj). The existence of an earlier mosque can often be deduced from the presence of a door well above ground level; many minarets were entered from the roof of the mosque. Gradually, structural variations were introduced. These included complicated flaring corbeled balconies just below the summit of the minaret (Sarabān minaret, Isfahān); single and double internal spiral staircases, both with and without a central column (Simnān; Samīrān); an elevation with flanges or alternating engaged columns and flanges (Zarand; Nigār); and, finally, a division of the elevation into three stages, each more tapering than the last (Ziār). Double minarets flanking a portal were introduced late in the twelfth century and became very popular in the Mongol period (Ashtarjān); later they were also used to emphasize the *qibla īwān* in mosques (Masjid-i Shāh). Some rather puzzling minarets were apparently intended to be free-standing, perhaps as signal towers or commemorative monuments (Karat; Mīl-i Nādirī). In the case of minarets, as in so many other building types, the innovations of the thirteenth to fifteenth centuries were limited to architectural decoration; indeed, far fewer minarets were built than in previous periods.

The basic forms of mausoleums were also established in early medieval times. Despite religious prohibitions, mausoleums were apparently built even in the first years of Islam. In Iran, two basic types may be distinguished: the domed mausoleum of square plan and the tomb tower. The former type is common throughout Islam, while the latter is distinctively Iranian, though it later inspired similar structures in Anatolia. In many respects, the domed square scarcely differs from a Sāsānid fire temple, but the early examples in Iran (Sangbast, Tūs) are markedly larger in scale and embody such refinements as an arcaded gallery or a *pishtaq* (a projecting rectangular *īwān* serving as a portal). In Timurid times, the bulbous, ribbed dome and the double dome were often used for mausoleums. The domed mausoleum allowed for considerable variation in size and ground plan: the tomb of Öljeitü at Sultāniyya, built after 1307, illustrates another popular type, the octagon with a deep niche on each side. A novel feature here is a corona of eight cylindrical minarets encircling the dome. The octagon, especially when combined with a galleried second story, allowed more interpretation of exterior and interior space than did the domed square, which was often closed on three sides. The tomb tower was, if possible, an even more outward-looking building; few examples attempt to exploit interior space. Its origins are obscure, but are perhaps rather to be sought in Central Asia than in the Near East. These monuments were built from the tenth century onward and are found principally in northern Iran. Some are diminutive structures no more than 30 ft. high (mausoleums of Māzandarān); others tower nearly 200 ft. (Gunbād-i Qābūs, 1006). Few postdate the fifteenth century. Their purpose was at first usually only commemorative, but the presence of *mihrābs* indicates that later some were used for prayer. They are sited outside settlements, in cemeteries or on hills, and are intended to be seen from all sides. Some are incorporated into shrines (Bastām, Natanz, Ardabīl), while the literary sources abound with references to funerary *madrasas* and mosques, both with attached mausoleums. With the Mongol period, a major shift of emphasis occurs, with most tomb towers being built to serve religious (specifically Shī'ī) purposes rather than secular ones. Their ground plans are extremely varied—circular, polygonal, square, lobed, or flanged. They can be distinguished from domed square mausoleums not only by these plans but also by their much lower ratio of width to height and by their roofs, which are conical or pyramidal rather than domed. Blank niches, flanges, and engaged columns articulate the shafts of these towers. Under the Timurids, a third type of funerary structure, the *hazīra* or open courtyard, often with a tall *īwān*, gained popularity.

The principal early medieval Persian palace is the remotely sited Ribāt-i Sharaf, which served also as a caravanserai. Its unusual plan has two four-*īwān* units of unequal size joined by a narrow thoroughfare. Monumental *pishtāqs* characterize the Mongol palace at Takht-i Sulaimān, which also includes free-standing kiosks. Several Safavid palaces survive in Isfahan. They include the 'Alī Qāpū, an arched portico crowned by a flat-roofed balcony on wooden columns, from which the Shah and his entourage could watch spectacles in the *maidān* below. Like several other Safavid pleasaunces, it was designed to be seen frontally or at an angle, but not from behind. The formal gardens and watercourses into which it leads were once scattered with courts, two-story, open-plan kiosks, and pavilions, of which one, the Chihil Sutūn, has a flat-roofed portico on wooden columns, like an Achaemenid *tālār*, preceding the Shah's throne room. The sculpture in the surrounding garden may also be intended to evoke ancient imperial memories. The Chahār Bāgh, an avenue nearly a mile long lined with trees and streams, gave access to the new capital from the south, while massive bridges, e.g., the Khvājū Bridge, featuring not only sluice gates but also pavilions for the royal party, linked Isfahān with some of its suburbs.

Medieval Persian architecture is dominated by mosques and mausoleums. They are therefore emphasized in this account. Many more types of building were erected, but often too few have survived to permit generalizations about their characteristics. In other cases, the building type, though widespread, displays less variety than does the mosque or the mausoleum. It is significant that many buildings of very different functions rely on the same basic elements that occur in the architecture of the mosque—the domed square, the *iwān*, and the courtyard. This can be explained as much by the versatility of these elements as by the conservatism of Persian architects. In the *madrasa*, for example, the four-*iwān* plan, though often contracted, is modified only by the addition of cells for students; these are disposed in two stories around the courtyard and broken by the axial *iwān*s, here used for teaching purposes (Khargird; Madrasa Imāmī, Isfahān).

Darvīsh or Sūfī oratories adopt the plan of the square-domed chamber, and bazaar entrances use the monumental *iwān* flanked by two-story screen walls with arched recesses. Caravanserais are another case in point. Though octagonal (Dihbīd) and circular (Zain al-Dīn) examples are known, most follow the four-*iwān* plan, while the space in the corners is used for stables. A monumental *pishtāq*, separated from the court by a domed vestibule, defines the major axis. It usually contains an entrance high enough to admit a loaded camel. Features common to many caravanserais are a fountain or well in the center of the courtyard; a single massive portal, with an entrance high enough to admit a loaded camel; kitchens in the corners; and, especially in the case of small caravanserais, adjoining enclosures for tethering animals. Caravanserais in the open country were often built at intervals of a day's journey—about 25 km—along the major trade routes. Those in the towns (often very numerous; Isfahān, for example, had nearly 2,000 in the seventeenth century) served not only to house and feed travelers but also as warehouses and centers for a particular trade or group of merchants.

Traditional elements predominated even in Safavid Isfahān, one of the most ambitious and novel schemes of town planning in Islamic history.

Building Styles and Construction Methods

The large public buildings of Iran display a notable preference for inner enclosed space at the expense of the exterior. Even major buildings often have no exterior façade to speak of. This trend probably originated, in part, in the early mosques, which were usually built in the midst of bazaars on irregular sites that discouraged carefully planned façades. Even when an unencumbered site was available, the Iranian architect rarely made full use of the opportunities for large-scale external display, as numerous caravanserais show. At most he would add a monumental *pīshtāq* (Varāmīn mosque; Masjid-i Shāh). In the major public buildings, there is less an interaction of exterior and interior space than a complete divorce between the two. It is rare for the larger urban buildings to be treated as a unity. Much care will be lavished on a highly decorated portal, but this portal is apt to be conceived separately from the rest of the façade, while the rear of the building, and perhaps even its sides, will be neglected—devoid of decoration and marred by an irregular silhouette. This piecemeal approach meant that Iranian architects rarely operated on the grand scale familiar, for example, in much Roman architecture or in European palaces from Renaissance times onward. In contrast to the unavoidably haphazard nature of ground plans, interiors are usually governed by a strict sense of symmetry and balance. The façade has, in effect, moved into the building. The result is not often subtle, but the juxtaposition of powerfully defined masses—domes, vaults, *iwāns*, arcades—and the strong contrasts of light and shade which these produce, infuse this architecture with energy and monumentality. At its best it can well do without decoration.

Although building stone is available in much of the country, brick is the almost exclusive medium of construction for large buildings, rather than rubble as in Sāsānid times. No satisfactory reason has yet been adduced for this, though the desire to refine the somewhat crude proportions of Sāsānid vaulted architecture was probably a potent factor. As building units, bricks had a precision that rubble lacked, and their lightness allowed architects to experiment with fewer and less ponderous supports and with more daring spans. Thus the versatility of this high quality baked brick soon made itself felt in the development of a wide range of vaults and domes of a scale and complexity difficult to match elsewhere in the medieval Islamic world. Much of the technical expertise that made such vaulting possible was acquired in the humble milieu of village architecture. To this day, mud-brick and even pisé structures display elegant and probably ancient solutions to numerous structural problems, and some forms of vernacular architecture, such as cisterns and ice-houses, achieve real monumentality. In baked brick, the forms included fluted and double domes and a highly complicated system of stalactite vaulting for concave spaces, such as the semi-domes of *pīshtāqs*. These honeycomb vaults lost their structural function as they gained in complexity and ended as geometric *tours de force* of plaster supported by an intricate hidden framework of struts and ropes. The four-centered arch was a basic element of construction, and combinations of such arches were used to articulate whole interiors. Iranian architects preferred the squinch to the pendentive and used it in the octagonal and hexadecagonal zones of transition in their great domes. The numerous varieties of the trilobed squinch, a leitmotif of Seljuk architecture, illustrate the Iranian virtuosity in vaulting. In Timurid times, the squinch shrank drastically and generated instead a smooth continuous network of arched ornamental profiles that formed a suave transition to the base of the dome. The builders dispensed with centering, using instead canes bent to the desired shape, encased in plaster and then set into place once this had hardened. The "ribs" thus formed produce a superficially Gothic effect, but the lack of centering precludes any close connection between the two traditions. This remarkably simple technique partly accounts for the speed with which large building works were executed. Even the largest domes might be no more than one brick in thickness at their crowns. This daring vaulting is best exemplified in the scores of different domes in the Friday Mosque at Isfahān.

Use of Applied Decoration in Architecture

Abstract and epigraphic decoration is a major component of Iranian Islamic architecture. It seems likely that from the very beginning applied decoration was regarded as a vital component of this architecture, and the few striking exceptions (principally tomb towers) only prove the rule. Three basic media were used— baked brick, carved stucco, and glazed tilework. From the tenth century and probably earlier, brick was laid in decorative bonds that were sunken, flush, or in high relief and formed geometric patterns. Although it was usually a revetment applied to a plain core it was indistinguishable from the building material in color or texture. It thus blended admirably with the structure itself and with surrounding buildings, and altered its character with the changing shadows. Its durability made it ideal for external ornament. For more refined and detailed work, where the innate angularity of the bricks was a disadvantage, it was supplemented by carved terra cotta. Stucco, a still more flexible medium, permitted the development of curvilinear designs, whether carved, molded, or precast. It often employed several contrasting planes. It was often painted, but was usually not robust enough to decorate exteriors. Glazed colored tilework was used tentatively from the eleventh century as a means of enhancing decorative brickwork and making inscriptions more easily visible, but gradually its scope extended to the whole building. Entire bricks glazed light and dark blue were supplemented by simple polygonal and stellar shapes in glazed terra cotta, used principally in borders. Glazed brick was succeeded by tile mosaic and then by entire glazed tiles of several colors, with large- and small-scale patterns often reminiscent of carpet motifs. In the late Seljuk and Mongol periods, tiles with a wide range of animal and figure designs, including courtly and legendary scenes, were produced. The most popular media for such tiles, which were a luxury decoration for houses and palaces, were luster, *lājvardīna*, and *mīnā'ī* (see next section). *Lājvardīna* ware took its name from the luscious deep blue of lapis lazuli (*lājvard*), its ground color, though turquoise was also thus used. Similar luster tiles, with predominantly abstract and floral ornament, were widely used in Shī'ī mausoleums. The incandescent colors of such fifteenth-century buildings as the mosque of Gawhar Shād at Mashhad and the Blue Mosque at Tabrīz mark the apogee of glazed tilework. This became a prestigious art, as is shown by the quantity of signed and dated examples that survive. In tile mosaic, small fragments cut from larger tiles, each color being fired at its optimum temperature, were fitted together like the pieces of a jigsaw puzzle. This expensive and time-consuming technique is still practiced, but it was largely superseded in the sixteenth century by large multicolored tiles produced in the *cuerda seca* technique. A whole range of Zand and Qājār figure tiles of this kind survive. They draw on traditional epic themes, but also display marked European influence; many are bizarre rather than beautiful. They form a fascinating epilogue to a millennial tradition.

The Development of Ceramics in Iran

The earliest Islamic pottery in Iran frequently copies the products of Umayyad Syria and 'Abbasid Iraq, though a few original types occur, such as a category of heavily potted pieces, with molded relief decoration of rosettes and palmettes. None of these early pieces, however, gives the least hint of the consummate masterpieces soon to be produced by Sāmānid potters, notably at Samarqand and Nīshāpūr, though similar wares have been found at numerous other sites in Soviet Central Asia, Iran, and Afghanistan. The hallmark of this slip-painted ware is its stylish epigraphy, which unfolds in majestic rhythm around the surface of the dishes. This manner owed nothing to China or Mesopotamia; its interest is less technical than decorative. The inscriptions are all in Kufic, and this choice of hand itself imparts a certain formality to these pieces, implying that they were intended to be treated as serious works of art. The numerous varieties of script encountered share an almost wilful complexity, as if they were meant to elude ready decipherment. The oracular quality of the aphorisms that they express is thus entirely appropriate. As decorative ensembles, these wares are remarkable in their appreciation of void space as a positive factor of the design. Human figures are never found, and birds and animals occur only in severely stylized form. A comparable austerity usually restricts the color range to cream and dark brown, purple or red, thereby highlighting the starkness of the inscriptions. A clue to the origin of this decoration may perhaps be sought in the close resemblance of some of the scripts used to the Uighur script of Central Asia. These dishes apparently offer the first examples in Islamic art of Arabic script being used as the major element in surface decoration, if one excepts coins where the epigraphy has a mainly utilitarian function. The virtuoso calligraphy and its nonreligious content is adequate evidence of a purely aesthetic preference for this kind of decoration.

Other contemporary work at Nīshāpūr did not share this cerebral quality. Of outstanding interest is a group of wares distinguished by sprawling, cluttered compositions and violent color contrasts, usually involving a bright mustard-yellow. Here the designs are simplified almost to the limit of recognition, but they maintain the directness and vitality of an unsophisticated folk art. Birds, rosettes, and scattered Arabic inscriptions calling down blessings on the owner are all used as space-fillers. Sometimes the design is a bastard survival of the Sāsānid royal iconography of the banqueting scene or the hunt, and astrological themes are also found. Such pottery belongs to the so-called "ceramic underworld of Islam," a category represented by wares from numerous provincial centers. Thus, Sārī may have been the center of production for a type of ware closely akin to folk art in the primitive vigor and garish coloring of its stylized animal drawing. The commonest category of provincial pottery, however, unlike the wares associated with Nīshāpūr and Sārī, is of *sgraffiato* type. It is so called after the technique of incising the design into the body before or after glazing and is found widely distributed in northwest Persia. Its decoration frequently apes metalwork, even to the use of the incised lines to prevent colors from running, as in cloisonné enamels. A particular class of champlevé ware, in which the white slip is gouged away to form the design, is associated with the Garrūs area in Kurdistān. These varied provincial schools were independent of influences from the court and from abroad, though reminiscences of Sāsānid iconography are common. Their subject matter favors single figures of animals and monsters or bold abstract designs.

Such wares fill the chronological gap between Sāmānid epigraphic pottery and the late twelfth century, which inaugurated the golden age of Persian pottery. But they offer no clue as to the stimulus that was responsible, and it remains a puzzling paradox, also applicable—though in a lesser degree—to metalwork, that this artistic flowering dates from the decline of Seljuk power and a time of marked political instability. The sheer quantity of pottery that has survived argues a considerably wider range of patrons than had hitherto existed; possibly one should think in terms of a wealthy mercantile class eager to ape the fashions of the court.

Pottery was now firmly established as a major art form, with the city of Kāshān as the principal—perhaps the only major—center, and many new techniques were devised. The body of these fine wares, which survive in remarkably large quantities, is a very hard composite material commonly termed soft-paste porcelain, in recognition of the potter's ambition to emulate Chinese wares. Although some pieces are utilitarian, others seem to have served as souvenirs, gifts, or symbols of rank, while yet others imitate the most prestigious metalwork. The consequent higher status of potters may explain the quantities of signed and dated pieces that now appear. The themes are greatly expanded: they include scenes of religious ceremonies, the varied cycle of court life, themes from epic poetry (especially the exploits of Bahrām Gūr as recounted in the *Shāhnāma*), heraldic and zodiacal forms, fabulous animals, and, of course, the decorative and abstract motifs that are always commonest in Islamic art. Apart from the luster and slip-painted pottery that the 'Abbasids had introduced and a wide range of under-glaze painted ceramics, the scenes with courtly associations dominate: enthroned or equestrian rulers, often shown with their consorts or with groups of courtiers, constitute perhaps the most popular theme. The physical features of these people conform to the "moon face," which is a stereotype of Persian poetry and for which an ultimately Buddhist origin has persuasively been canvassed. Bland fleshy faces with slanting eyes and minute mouths are framed by long plaits of hair. Lengthy inscriptions in Persian verse that supplement the more conventional Arabic benedictory phrases are a novel feature of these luster pieces, many of which are signed and dated. In the more ambitious examples, the whole design is unified by the spirals, lines, and dots that cover virtually every free space and contrive to make a genre scene into an abstract pattern. No distinction is made between the main theme and the background. This, together with the facial types, subject matter, and fine drawing, suggests that such pottery may reflect contemporary book painting.

Such wares were expensive and rare, not only because of the difficult technique but also because of their elaborate decoration. A much more popular ware was the black slip silhouette ware. In this pottery, a thin slip of black clay was spread over the surface, and those parts that were to be left void were removed with a knife. Although the technique did not allow for much freedom of drawing, the quality of some of these dishes is such that one may suggest that master painters and master potters worked closely together. Striding sphinxes, elephants, and other exotic creatures are favored subjects on this ware and exploit its dramatic color contrasts to the full.

Apart from luster, the most precious pottery made under the Seljuks was the so-called *minā'ī*, a word meaning enamel. It is a purely Persian invention. Certain colors were fixed in a first firing and others, which could not withstand great heat, were fired at a lower temperature. This technique of overglaze painting, used also for the so-called *lājvardīna*—of rather later date—allowed the artist considerable freedom of drawing, and *minā'ī* ware excels in small-scale figures rendered in bright colors against a white or buff ground. Sometimes it is combined with gilding, relief ornament and even luster. That it may, like luster, offer some clues to the nature of Seljuk book and wall painting is suggested by a unique dish in the Freer Gallery, which seems to reflect a fresco in some Seljuk palace. Typical of the extravagant techniques in which the Seljuks excelled is the so-called double shell ware, in which the outer shell was perforated to achieve a complete openwork pattern—a technique clearly derived from metalwork. The decoration is further enriched by additional underglaze painting and by an overall glaze in turquoise and cobalt. The willowy scroll pattern and the style of figure drawing suggests that such pieces were made in Kāshān, a city so famous for its pottery that a common name for architectural tilework is *kāshī*. Chinese influence is attested by another type of carved ware, the white, hard body of which was intended to rival porcelain. The decoration and the shapes of this ware too sometimes depend on Chinese prototypes. Yet another type of Seljuk pottery tried to reproduce the translucency of Sung porcelain by the ingenious device of piercing the body with a network of small holes that were filmed over by the glaze.

The vigor of the ceramic industry in late Seljuk times is expressed not only in the wide variety of techniques employed but also in the forms themselves. Shapes like inkwells and aquamaniles were borrowed from metalwork, while figurines displayed a monumentality remarkable in such small-scale work and also bear witness to the potter's innate affinity with free-standing sculpture, a medium that Islamic tradition discouraged. Models of houses and furniture and ornamental figurines are common, but some full-scale objects of practical use, like well-covers and tabourets, are also known. But it was in the tiles used as wall decoration that late Seljuk potters were able to extend their scope most effectively. Luster tiles were produced in great quantities, especially at Kāshān, where, as inscriptions show, the tradition was sometimes handed down from father to son for generations. Several entire *mihrābs* composed of these rectangular tiles have survived. The production of such tiles seems actually to have increased during the Mongol period, though even in this area a hiatus of about twenty-five years (ca. 1230–1255) is apparent and was presumably caused by the chaotic aftermath of the Mongol invasions. Luster tiles of star or cross shapes, often set off by interlocking monochrome glazed tiles to act as a foil, composed huge shimmering dadoes in cultic buildings and palaces. Very often the individual tiles would

FIG. 16–17. Lustre plate, Kāshān, Iran, thirteenth century

each bear a Persian inscription rendered in a hurried scrawl all along its outer edge. Floral or animal motifs are the staple decoration of these tiles, which again were mostly made in Kāshān. In the larger rectangular tiles in which living creatures dominate the design, an effective combination of relief and luster painting was devised.

Many other wares of Seljuk type continued to be made under the Īlkhānids. A few minor innovations occur—such as a group of vases and tiles with relief decoration under a blue glaze, or the use of applied gold leaf—but only two major new types of pottery appear. *Lājvardīna* is a simplified successor of the *mīnā'ī* technique. The courtly scenes of the earlier ware are replaced by geometric and epigraphic themes and, at Takht-i Sulaimān, by dragons and phoenixes. Gold overpainting set against a deep, royal blue makes *lājvardīna* ware one of the most spectacular ever produced in Persia. The other new Īlkhānid ware is dowdy by comparison. Traditionally associated with the Sultānābād region, it is heavily potted and makes frequent use of a grey slip with thick outlines, while another type displays black painting under a turquoise glaze. The drawing is of indifferent quality, but the ware as a whole has a special interest in that it provides a *locus classicus* of the invasion of the Persian ceramic tradition by Chinese motifs. Earlier, Chinese techniques and shapes alone had inspired the Persian potter; but from now on his iconographic repertoire drew widely on Chinese sources. Dragons, phoenixes, mandarin ducks, cloud bands, peonies, and lotuses are all standard Īlkhānid themes, and they are treated with a new naturalism also inspired by China. Meager though the surviving tally of Timurid pottery may be, it is enough to show that this trend continued. Side by side with such traditional techniques as luster, the quality of which was appreciably lower than in earlier centuries, the Persian potter now produced blue and white wares inspired by imported porcelain of Ming type. The ultimate origin of these wares is disputed, but reciprocal influences between China and Persia are certain. Timurid copies of this Chinese porcelain body are also known.

Quite different in style is a category of pottery made in northern Iran from at least the 1460s until the seventeenth century. These ceramics were all found in the Caucasian village of Kubachi, a famed metalworking center; presumably they had been exchanged for local metalwork. The earlier pieces of this school are painted in black under a bluish green glaze and eschew figural designs in favor of floral cartouches or scrollwork and epigraphic motifs. The scarcity of high quality Timurid pottery may well be a direct consequence of the great expansion of the tile-making industry at this time.

Not until the last decades of the sixteenth century was there a revival of the pottery industry. Chinese influence became if possible even stronger, and some of the vases made in Kirmān and depicting swirling dragons are a passable pastiche of Chinese work, a comment that applies equally to their semiporcelain body. Much of this "chinoiserie" pottery was produced in response to European demand. More Iranian designs, however, also appear on such pieces. More subtle references to Chinese originals include the so-called Gombroon ware, which depends for its effect on distinction of form and on its translucent body, often of celadon color. Luster enjoyed a revival under Shāh ʿAbbās and was produced in great quantity, but it has a rather brassy sheen which, combined with an emphasis on underglaze blue, results in pieces inferior to earlier luster in aesthetic quality. The decoration is restricted to vegetal motifs. Polychrome ware was produced in great quantities in Kirmān. Figural designs on Safavid pottery that avoids chinoiserie echo the mannered style of the painter Rizā-i ʿAbbāsī and, more generally, of Safavid carpets and textiles. Later Kubachi ware has a much wider and brighter color range than the earlier pieces and often has a central medallion enclosing a portrait bust executed in typical late Safavid style. The Safavid pictorial idiom lingered long after the fall of the dynasty and in an enfeebled state remained the staple of Qājār potters. This staleness, combined with the widespread popularity of cheap European ceramics from the eighteenth century onward, brought about the final demise of fine wares in Iran, though Mashhad and Kirmān continued to produce blue and white ware with black outlines into the nineteenth century. Only in architectural tilework did the Safavid tradition continue with undiminished vigor and a new emphasis on relief, though in this field too European influence exerted a decisive role.

The Art of the Book in Iran

Persian painting before the Safavid period is almost exclusively confined to books, and even in the sixteenth and seventeenth centuries book painting maintained its traditional primacy over the arts of fresco and easel painting.

Among the various traditions of Islamic manuscript painting—Arabic, Persian, Turkish, and Indian—Persian painting must take pride of place on several scores. For diversity and sheer output it is without parallel in Islam—and although the Arab world can boast slightly earlier work it cannot match the continuity of the Persian tradition. The origins of that tradition are probably destined to remain obscure. Virtually nothing survives that can be dated before the end of the thirteenth century, though textual evidence establishes the continuity of this art from the Sāsānid period. Thus, Iranian book painting for the first five centuries of Islam is an almost total blank and must be reconstructed with the help of painted pottery and a few wall paintings from Sāmānid Nīshāpūr and Ghaznavid Lashkar-i Bāzār. The first really useful clues are provided by the late Seljuk painting practiced in Iraq. This probably reflects contemporary Persian work to judge by the painted Persian pottery of that time, just as the paintings of Bīrūnī's *al-Āthār al-Bāqīya* dated 1307 echo the style of the Baghdad school. In the period under discussion, both Iran and Iraq were frequently part of the same political unit, so these close links are to be expected.

The Bīrūnī manuscript is, like other illustrated manuscripts of its time, a fortunate survival, for it documents the invasion of the established pictorial idiom of eastern Islam by totally alien influences, especially from the Far East. But the resultant degree of flux in fourteenth-century painting is, nevertheless, surprising. Several distinctive styles flourished, some of them owing little to each other and quite remote in spirit and in style from the pre-Mongol pictorial tradition. Several of these early Īlkhānid manuscripts reflect contemporary conditions. The Bīrunī manuscript, with its emphasis on non-Islamic faiths, especially Christianity, its astrological content, and its choice of key Shī'ī themes, is a case in point. The Pierpont Morgan *Bestiary* (dated 1290–91 and produced at Marāgha) and the manuscripts illustrating Rashīd al-Dīn's *World History* share the stress on biblical themes. In content, the *Bestiary*—of which several other contemporary versions are known—belongs firmly within the tradition of those practical treatises long popular in Mesopotamia and issuing from an ancient Byzantine and classical tradition. But it inhabits a different imaginative world from that of its Arab equivalents. The clue lies in the artists' partiality for drama. They invest essentially undramatic subjects with a portentous power wholly at variance with the stiff, woodenly articulated animals of Arab bestiaries. Some of the painters obey the formulas of Mesopotamian painting for details of plants, landscape, drapery, and facial features. Other miniatures are infused with a new Chinese spirit expressed in the treatment of landscape details and especially in the overlapping planes that lend depth to a composition. But, as in later times, the Persian artists were never fully attuned to the artistic ideals that underlie Chinese painting. They preferred to borrow, and frequently to use out of context, eye-catching individual motifs like exotic creatures (phoenixes, dragons), plants (peonies, lotuses), and the conventions for rendering water, fire, and clouds. The manuscripts illustrating the *World History* of Rashīd al-Dīn were produced in Tabrīz, then the most cosmopolitan city in Asia, in the first two decades of the fourteenth century. This provenance guaranteed the paintings a remarkably mixed ancestry in which Chinese, Byzantine, and Uighur elements mingle with Persian and Arab strains. Their large oblong format allowed the artists ample scope for scenes expressing the savage lust of battle as well as for solemn tableaux of enthroned monarchs. One manuscript is prefaced by dozens of stereotyped royal portraits that are pastiches of Chinese models even to details of dress and pose. The same obedience to formula governs the many court scenes in a contemporary codex of the *Dīwān* of Mu'izzī. But whether the scenes depicted are inventive or merely

FIG. 16–18. Enthroned ruler, *Kitāb-i Samak ‘Ayyār*, Iran, c. 1340 (Bodleian Library, Oxford, MS. Ouseley 381, f. 94v.)

routine, the hybrid style associated with the atelier by Rashīd al-Dīn is instantly recognizable. So muted are the tones and so dominant is the role of line that many of the paintings resemble tinted drawings.

This style disappeared virtually without trace on the death of Rashīd al-Dīn. The next major manuscript, an ambitious illustrated version of the *Shāhnāma* or *Book of Kings*, the national epic, is named after the dealer Demotte, its former owner. Its date is disputed, but the second quarter of the fourteenth century seems the most likely date. Its multiple styles seem to indicate a style in flux. It is notable especially for the dense design and spatial complexity of many of its paintings, their subtle gamut of colors, and their wide emotional range, within which a marked predilection for drama and violent action can be discerned. No subsequent version of the epic matched its heroic stature. But numerous leaves from lost manuscripts (such as those from a magnificent *Kalīla wa-Dimna*) later bound together in albums permit a tentative reconstruction of the court style from ca. 1340 onward. These paintings, which are mostly in Istanbul and Tübingen, are sometimes still under the spell of the Demotte *Shāhnāma*, especially in their generous scale, but many of them attest much more vigorous Chinese and Central Asian influences than that manuscript.

Provincial Mongol work is typified by the so-called "small *Shāhnāma*s" variously associated with Baghdad, Tabrīz, and Shīrāz. These feature a strip cartoon style enlivened by bright—even garish—colors and by assertive little figures. The summary drawing and vigorous rather than careful application of color sometimes justifies a comparison with folk art. But such work was more in harmony with the fundamental approach of Persian painting than were the grander products of Īlkhānid painting. These "small *Shāhnāmas*," with their very numerous illustrations, familiarized Persian painters with the concept of diminutive pictures and—perhaps more significantly—with the concept of reducing the range within which the artist operates. In a word, they popularized the miniature. Later Iranian painting, even when executed within a large picture space, customarily retains a miniature-like character absent from Īlkhānid court painting.

Court painting of the very late fourteenth century illustrates this new approach. The central masterpiece is the *Kulliyyāt* of Khvājū Kirmānī produced for a Jalāyirid patron at Baghdad in 1396. The experimental manner of the previous decades is here replaced by a notable sureness of touch. The artist is entirely at home within the self-imposed limitations of his style, and that style maintained currency for some 250 years. It is marked by small figures, high horizon, fanciful vegetation, and a luxurious palette. Man himself has become smaller, subordinated to his surroundings, and these tend to reflect moods (especially violent moods) less than they did earlier. The picture size decreases, and with it the scale of all elements shrinks; detail may challenge the mastery of the grand design, and the sense of drama evaporates in a dreamlike fantasy world. Colors are no longer used to evoke bleakness, menace, horror. This is by and large

FIG. 16–19. The sages of China bringing books on history to Ghāzān Khān. Leaf from Hāfiz-i Abrū, *Majma' al-Tawarīkh*, probably Herat, c. 1425 (Reproduced by Courtesy of the Trustees of the British Museum, London, no. 1966. 10–10.013)

a smiling world, its inhabitants privileged and precious. The intrusion of script into the picture space becomes more varied and playful. Chinese elements no longer occur in their pristine starkness, but have been absorbed into the new idiom. Persian painting has found itself and henceforth generations of artists strove to achieve perfection in this style.

Early Timurid painting reached its peak in the work of the academy founded at Herat by the celebrated bibliophile Prince Bāysunghur b. Shāhrukh, who in the intervals of the dissipation that plunged him into an early grave found time to oversee the production of fastidiously choice illustrated copies of the great classics of Persian literature. The hallmarks of this style are an unflagging attention to detail, a preference for slender, elegant figures and a clear design that gains extra strength from intense purity of color. A high rectangular format permits an uncluttered arrangement of numerous spatially distinct figures. The Herat style became a standard of excellence for later painters, and as late as the reign of Shāh ʿAbbās I it was sedulously imitated. Its courtly bias is reflected in its subject matter—picnics, hunts, banquets, performing musicians, and dancers (Saʿdī, *Gulistān,* 1426), though a much wider thematic range can be seen in the illustrated versions of the *Shāhnāma* and the *Khamsa* of Nizāmī.

Other styles of the early fifteenth century include a simplified recreation of the style of the Rashīd al-Dīn manuscripts, employed in historical manuscripts, and a vigorous, bold style associated with Shīrāz. Once again an enthusiastic patron, in this case Ibrāhīm Sultān, a brother of Bāysunghur, seems to have been the key figure in the formation of a local school. The figures of this Shīrāz school are sketchily drawn. They wear tight-fitting caps above long melancholy faces and their narrow torsos are inflexibly straight. The same stiffness seems to permeate their movements and the design itself, for they are disposed woodenly in tight groups, peering over the horizon in serried ranks. Such figures claim more than their normal share of attention, because they are set within a ruthlessly simplified landscape (Berlin *Anthology,* 1420–21; *Zafarnāma,* 1436).

Later in the century, Shīrāz became a major center of production for one of the most appealing schools in Persian painting, the Turkoman style. Once again, this style, serviceable and well suited to large-scale production, coexisted with the more ambitious painting produced in the orbit of the court. It is generally on a small scale and can be recognized by such features as an obsession with greenery, a detailed linear rendering of the vegetation, and a preference for squat, jowly figures. Rosy cheeks add a delicate charm to many of these figures, but the variety of facial types and the peculiar resonance of color that characterize contemporary Herat painting are quite absent.

The climax of fifteenth-century painting, if not of Persian painting in general, is indeed reached in Herat at the Timurid court of Husain Bāyqarā, from ca. 1480–ca. 1500, a time when Bihzād, the most famous of all Persian artists, was at the height of his powers. These decades usher in the age when the names and achievements of individual painters begin to attract the notice of chroniclers. But controversy has flourished as scholars attempt to attribute paintings to given artists. It seems likely that painters to some extent pooled their talents and that training in a royal atelier encouraged a high degree of uniformity among the pupils. Hence the difficulty of isolating the works of Bihzād from those of his closest rivals. But if his personality remains elusive, the style associated with his

FIG. 16–20. The King of the East with two ladies. Leaf from the *Khavār Nāma* of Maulāna Muhammad b. Husām al-Dīn, Iran, 1477 (Chester Beatty Library, Dublin, Ms. 293, no. 4; photograph, PDI)

school is unmistakable. Once again, the determining influence of the Bāysunghur academy can be detected, as in a singular intensity of color heightened by vibrant contrasts. But other elements are new: the delight in devising spatial complexities and an unexpected interest in various poses and in individual types. In depictions of the human body in movement, too, the school of Bihzād greatly enlarged the existing repertory. But none of these innovations really deserve the term "realistic." Persian painting customarily favored the general at the expense of the particular, and even the work most commonly associated with Bihzād (*Bustān* of Sa'dī, 1488; *Khamsa* of Nizāmī, 1494) testifies as much to intellectual abstraction as to patient observation. Figures are sharply differentiated, but the sense of a living, unique personality is generally absent. The same sharp focus combined with idealization is applied to landscape and to architecture.

The Herat style did not entirely vanish after the fall of the Timurids, for many of its most gifted masters, including Bihzād himself, made new homes in Tabrīz under the patronage of Ismā'īl, the first Safavid shah. His successor, Shah Tahmāsp, even expanded the royal atelier. In the first two decades of his reign, Persian artists achieved a rare perfection within their chosen style (the Houghton *Shāhnāma*, 1537–38; *Khamsa* of Nizāmī in The British Library, 1543). Tabrīz painting owes much to the Turkoman school, but its lissom, eternally youthful figures are apparently an original creation. Perfection proved hard to sustain and before long artists were overreaching themselves, for in many works of this school so much detail is crammed into the composition that its fastidious precision fails to make its full effect. Similarly, the color range may be so kaleidoscopic that the very richness confuses the eye. It could be argued that the manuscript page had too limited a scope to accommodate the increasing complexity of these compositions.

The dependence of this art on the whim of the monarch is made abundantly clear by the fate of the Tabrīz court style. In his middle and later years, Shah Tahmāsp became a religious bigot. He turned his back on painting and his atelier was disbanded. The court style associated with Qazvīn, which became the capital in 1548, is marked, despite certain exceptions (like the *Haft Awrang* of Jāmī in the Freer Gallery of Art in Washington) by a palpable decline in quality. Compared with the best Tabrīz work, landscape becomes simpler, with large areas given up to a single color (*Shāhnāma* of Ismā'īl II, 1576). Figures tend to increase in size and they exhibit a curious stiffness. Yet in courtly tableaus youths and maidens are rendered with a consistently suave line. No trace remains of the vigorously differentiated types of the school of Bihzād, and the earlier obsession with detail gradually disappears. In the later sixteenth century, the enforced change of patronage led the best artists to produce single leaves that were eagerly collected by connoisseurs and bound into albums. Figure studies—of pages, prisoners, and princes among others—became a popular subject for such leaves, many of them tinted drawings rather than paintings. These drawings became the forte of the Qazvīn school, and their subjects came to include genre scenes of the utmost delicacy, with pastel shades forming the grace notes of the composition.

The major school of provincial painting throughout the sixteenth century was at Shīrāz. These paintings display tolerably rich color, and many compositions are crowded with well-executed detail. But individual figures and even entire compositions were blithely reused (by pouncing) from one manuscript to the next

FIG. 16–21. Court scene from Amīr Khusrau Dihlavī, *Intikhāb-i Dīvān*, probably Tabrīz, 1536–37 (Nationalbibliothek, Vienna, Cod. Mixt. 356, f. 50 r.)

as if they were stencils. This practice lends Shīrāz painting a rather hackneyed air, and these provincial artists seem to have made no major breakthrough in style or content. But patrons as far afield as Turkey and India, to say nothing of those in Persia itself, provided a ready market for this somewhat mass-produced art.

Less numerous and ambitious than Shīrāz paintings are those of Khurāsān in the later sixteenth century. Perhaps their most attractive feature is their unerring use of bright, cheerful colors. Simplified drawing and design allow these colors to make their full effect. The figures owe something to the later style of Qazvīn in their elongation and in their peaky, rather vapid faces.

New Developments in Persian Painting

The accession of Shah 'Abbās I in 1588 brought to power an enthusiastic patron of painting, and in theory he ought to have been able to repeat the success of Bāysunghur and Shah Tahmāsp. But the fashion for single leaves had become entrenched, and artists therefore had an attractive alternative to working in semiobscurity in the royal atelier. Unquestionably the most celebrated and sought-after painter of the day, Riżā-i 'Abbāsī, specialized in single leaves and was generally ill at ease as a book illustrator. The Shah was therefore powerless to emulate his great predecessors; Persian painting had taken a different turn. From the all too fluent brush of Riżā-i 'Abbāsī flowed an endless succession of languid, sleepily erotic youths and ladies. He had so many imitators that this precious style, with its trite subject matter, came to dominate seventeenth-century painting; no significant provincial schools have been identified in this period. In the courtly scenes, the line is smooth and full-blown, but in genre subjects Riżā and some of his imitators display an acutely satiric bent expressed in nervous, energetic draftsmanship. As a result of the vogue for single leaves, dozens of Safavid artists are known from signatures, attributions, and contemporary texts. Often a leaf will bear a long and detailed inscription, giving such information as the name of the artist, the date, and the reason why the subject was chosen. Mu'īn Musavvir is the outstanding exponent of this practice. The emphasis on calligraphic line may have led directly to a falling off in the quality of color. Colors now tended to be mixed rather than pure, and the intrusion of these hybrid shades changed the subtle color harmonies of earlier work. Nevertheless, this period produced a few outstanding illustrated manuscripts in which these new colors are used with great verve and assurance (Shāhnāma of 1648 at Windsor Castle).

As the seventeenth century progressed, Persian painting was subjected to increasingly strong European influences, partly resulting from the international outlook of the Safavid court. In earlier centuries, Chinese influences had been absorbed and their effect had been to enrich, not to impoverish, the native style. But in the seventeenth-century, Persian artists, unlike their Mughal colleagues, were not able to preserve their own values intact under this onslaught of alien influences. Late seventeenth-century painting is replete with examples of traditional themes transformed and weakened by such European features as modeling, perspective devices, and realistic landscapes. This hybrid style persisted throughout the eighteenth century, but Qājār times witnessed a fascinating dual reaction to European art. At one extreme is the deliberate primitivism of the many official portraits of Fath 'Alī Shah surrounded by his courtiers, and the highly stylized oil paintings of tumblers and other entertainers, as well as comely youths and girls. Some of the court scenes evoke, it seems deliberately, the formal idiom of Sāsānid art. But at the other extreme lay a whole-hearted acceptance of European traditions of realistic portraiture. The gallery of searching character studies of Qājār notables produced by Abu'l-Hasan Ghaffārī (who had visited Italy) and Yūsuf Khānzāda, among others, is unique in Persian painting and even seems to owe something to photography. Faces and hands are treated with a careful modeling largely denied to costume and background. But such paintings are outside the mainstream of Persian book illustration in subject matter and technique. In Qājār painting, then, as in Qājār tilework, the references to earlier traditions serve principally to emphasize how far the artist had strayed from them.

Iranian Islamic Metalwork

The consistently high level of achievement reached by the Sāsānid silversmiths only gradually declined with the coming of Islam. Many plates and other silver objects continued to be produced, and in iconography and technique they often retained a recognizably Sāsānid air. Indeed, in many cases it is hard to be certain whether they are Islamic or earlier work. Occasionally, inscriptions permit a closer identification, such as the hoard that belonged to Valgīr ibn Hārūn. This notable, like several others whose names are inscribed on this transitional silverware, probably came from the Caspian region where Sāsānid customs died hard. In the more thoroughly Islamicized parts of Iran, the religious depreciation of vessels of precious metal may well have been more respected, while the perennial demand for bullion must have made steady inroads on the stock of gold and silver objects. Presumably fine pottery was used instead; it has certainly survived in massive quantities from the pre-Seljuk period, often in shapes that seem to owe much to prototypes in silverware. The limited quantity of precious metalwork datable before 1200 is rendered still more difficult to assess by unsettled disputes about the authenticity of precisely the most remarkable pieces, such as the two gold ewers inscribed with the names of Būyid princes, the Alp Arslān salver and the candlestick with the name of Sultan Sanjar. Given the wide time span between the Arab conquest and the end of the Seljuk period—over five centuries—it is only to be expected that this early metalwork illustrates disparate styles and themes. It seems premature, also, to try to differentiate between Sāmānid, Būyid, and early Ghaznavid work. But attention should be drawn to the wide range of shapes (e.g., in incense burners) produced in this creative period. A common motif in this early metalwork is a boldly delineated animal, treated in heraldic fashion—sīmurgh, griffon, duck, or cockerel. The designs are executed in repoussé work or engraving rather than in the inlay so popular in later periods. Floral and geometrical designs are drawn on a bold, spacious scale; they lack the intricate detail of later work. Pierced palmette patterns and stylish Kufic inscriptions are the standby of the artist. Large areas of the design are blank or, at most, lightly chased. In view of the small quantity of Iranian metalwork securely datable before 1100 that survives, the high proportion of silver objects among these pieces is especially notable.

The twelfth century saw the burgeoning of the metalworking industry in Iran, with major centers in Khurāsān and Azarbāijan. Bronze was the material of choice, though silver objects seem to have provided the inspiration for the more adventurous designs. Decoration was more ambitious and elaborate than hitherto, while by means of inlay and overlay the chromatic range of a given piece could be greatly extended. In such works as the Leningrad pen-case (1148), the Bobrinski bucket (1163), or the ewer in Tiflis (1181) the inlay is in copper and silver, which when combined with black mastic and the bronze ground of the piece results in a remarkably colorful display. Side by side with these inlaid bronzes were produced many types of pieces with engraved or relief decoration. The body itself was often cast. Mirrors, mortars, candlesticks, and other utilitarian objects are the most frequently encountered types. Incense burners and aquamaniles were also very popular and took the form of animals or birds, both real and mythical. This varied bestiary may owe something to the ancient nomadic traditions of the Eurasian steppe. Though treated as free-standing sculpture, these sculptures also bear the minutely worked surface ornament of other contemporary metalwork. Although the techniques in which all these post-Seljuk pieces are executed are so varied that they demand detailed classification, the pieces form *in toto* a readily recognizable group. It can be distinguished from earlier work first by the smaller scale and more refined detail of its decoration. No longer does a single motif dominate the surface. Instead, small figures or floral motifs are set within cartouches that are arranged rhythmically over the object, or continuous decoration unfolds across the surface in a series of superimposed tiers. The nonfigural decoration is more often floral than geometric; it is supplemented by openwork ornament. Second, multiple inscription bands divide the figural motifs. In these, Kufic is supplemented by *naskh* and by a variety termed "animated script," which was developed exclusively in metalwork and seems to have originated in Iran. In this ductus (more often *naskh* than Kufic), the shafts of the letters end in human or animal heads. The idea was further exploited until the letters themselves were formed by a continuous band of human and animal bodies, a device that rendered such inscriptions all but illegible. These Arabic inscriptions generally call down blessings on the owner in a series of stereotyped litanies, but occasionally seem to contain some esoteric religious significance. Only a few are signed or dated. No other works of Islamic art, apart from other objects in metal, habitually present such lengthy and unspecific inscriptions. No satisfactory explanation for this has yet been adduced. Third, the forms of this post-Seljuk metalwork are extremely varied; many of the aquamaniles and incense burners take the forms of animals and birds, both real and mythical, while the mortars and candlesticks have a compact, chunky quality that vaguely evokes architectural forms. Lobed, fluted, and polygonal shapes are common and are often of great distinction in themselves. The capacity to draw seemingly endless variations from a few basic shapes sharply distinguishes Seljuk from earlier Islamic metalwork in Iran. It seems likely that this daring and innovative approach to form inspired a comparable virtuosity in ornament and forestalled any stagnation in design.

The patrons for whom these objects were made are not easily identified. Occasionally, an inscription will mention a merchant or high official, but the anonymity of the inscriptions suggests rather that such metalwork was not usually made for a specific person, though the artist may well have had a certain class of people in mind. These are perhaps more likely to have been high officials and members of the ruling class than wealthy merchants, for the quality of the work is in no way inferior to the Ayyūbid and Mamlūk metalwork made for high *amīrs*. The comparatively sudden disappearance of silver can be explained by reference to the widespread silver shortage from the late eleventh century onward, which first made itself felt in coinage and eventually led to the production of copper *dirham*s in the eastern Iranian world. Bronze metalwork is not, therefore, in itself a factor suggesting a lower social level of patronage for these objects. But the large quantity of bronze metalwork produced in stereotyped shapes in the twelfth and thirteenth centuries does suggest the advent of mass production for a wide market.

In metalwork as in ceramic production, the Mongol invasion fatally disrupted a flourishing industry. It is now generally agreed that some of the artists who fled westward from Khurāsān made their homes in Mosul and there founded the most renowned school of metalworking in Arab lands. In Iran itself, though, the ravaged province of Khurāsān never again supported a major metalworking industry. After a gap in production of almost a century, which can be paralleled closely in architecture and painting, the industry revived—but in new centers. Southern Iran now came to the fore. This area had been spared Mongol devastation, but was, of course, open to Mongol stylistic influences. Hence, there appear in the metalwork of Fārs such features as the peony, the lotus, flying ducks, *ju-i* heads, and Chinese phoenixes. The figures, slim and narrow-waisted, have something of the elegance that characterizes the figures of late fourteenth-century Persian painting, a link that extends also to their costume. A general readiness to adopt alien fashions would explain the presence of geometrical patterning of Mosul type and of the bold elongated *naskhī* inscriptions that were the hallmark of contemporary Mamlūk metalwork. But this same school seems to have popularized the use of Persian poetry on metalwork, and its epigraphic formulas celebrating Solomon are rooted deep in the Persian tradition.

With the irruption of Timur and his hordes into Iran at the end of the fourteenth century, the desolation of the Mongol conquest repeated itself. Craftsmen were once again transported, but this time to Transoxiana, where some notable metalwork was produced at Turkistān by artists from Isfahān and Tabrīz. Of outstanding interest is a huge cauldron some six feet high, closely paralleled by a cauldron of roughly the same date in the Great Mosque of Herat. The closest analogies for these huge and impressive vessels, which are virtually undecorated apart from their inscriptions, are in the metalwork of Dāghistān in the Caucasus.

Very little high quality Timurid metalwork has survived, though miniatures of the period show that ewers with long curved spouts were developed at this time. The Seljuk and Mongol motif of a figural scene within a cartouche seems to have been definitively superseded by closely knit floral designs. A new style heavily dependent on manuscript illumination is found on Khurāsānī inlaid metalwork in the later fifteenth century, while the same province generated simultaneously a style of engraved metalwork that leads without a break into the Safavid period.

Safavid metalwork has long been neglected, even though it made significant innovations. These include a type of tall octagonal torch-holder on a circular plinth, a new type of ewer of Chinese inspiration, and the almost total disappearance of Arabic inscriptions in favor of Persian poetry. Dense arabesques and floral designs were more to contemporary taste than figural motifs, perhaps because they provided a more low-key background for inscriptions, which were allotted a greater surface area than ever before, in bold zigzags and cartouches as well as the more conventional encircling bands. A few pieces commissioned by Armenian patrons juxtapose lines from Persian mystical poets with Armenian inscriptions. Brass was apparently often tinned to simulate silver, though the most luxurious metalwork, of which only a few pieces are known, was inlaid with gold and incrusted with jewels. Other lost types of Safavid metalwork can be reconstructed with the help of ceramic copies. But some of the best Islamic armor, fashioned in iron and steel, was produced by Safavid smiths (e.g., the helmet of Shah 'Abbās and a group of *shamshīr*s from Khurāsān). Damascening and openwork were perhaps the most common decorative techniques used for such objects, which often bear lengthy inscriptions. Safavid metalwork remained the standard for subsequent artists, and Zand and Qājār work perpetuates its shapes and decorative conventions, though the execution tends to lose itself in a meaningless intricacy.

Applied Art in Textiles

In Persian textiles, as in metalwork, Sāsānid iconography persisted long after the fall of the dynasty. The favorite themes of the silks usually identified as Sāsānid were large roundels with pearled borders enclosing heraldic beasts, such as the griffon, the cock, or the sīmurgh. The survival of these motifs into Islamic times makes it difficult to date the objects they decorate, since these are almost all devoid of any archaeological context. Apart from one small group of excavated textiles, all "Sāsānid" textiles have been found beyond the frontiers of Iran.

Literary sources show that Iran had numerous centers making so-called *tirāz* fabrics. These garments, which were for ceremonial wear, commonly bore no ornament except narrow bands of closely packed Kufic inscriptions across the sleeves or along other parts of the garment. These *tirāz* fabrics differ little from those produced in Egypt and Mesopotamia and form a distinctive group.

Very occasionally an inscription allows the precise dating and provenance of a pictorial silk to be established, as in the case of the St. Josse silk woven in Khurāsān before 960 for the Sāmānid *amīr* Abū Mansūr Bukhtagīn. Affronted elephants whose aberrant form betrays Chinese rather than Indian influence take up the field, while Bactrian camels and peacocks pace the borders, supplemented by a benedictory Kufic inscription in lapidary style. This silk is typical of many formal pictoral silks from Sāsānid and Islamic Iran, Syria, and Byzantium, which found their way westward and were preserved in church treasuries because they were used to wrap relics.

Only slightly later in date than the St. Josse silk is the large group of so-called "Būyid silks." Unfortunately, the excavations that produced them were clandestine and no reliable inventory of what was found or of its exact context is available. But it is generally accepted that they were found in the crypt of a ruined tomb tower, datable to ca. 1000, in ancient Rayy. Unlike "Sāsānid" silks, they employ a restricted range of somber colors, and the same austerity dictates the design. Perhaps the funerary purpose of these silks, itself unusual in Islamic textiles, is sufficient explanation for this solemnity. In place of the roundels and multiple small motifs of "Sāsānid" silks, the Būyid weavers preferred a measured succession of dominant, large, single images, usually heraldic creatures such as the lion or the eagle. Stately Kufic inscriptions, whose formality matches that of the designs themselves, provide a fit framework for these ceremonial images. Inscriptions and images alike are closely packed and intricately decorative. The technique is of an unrivaled finesse. These silks invite a detailed iconographic and technical study. In them, the Sāsānid tradition has been absorbed and refashioned into something distinctively Islamic, which has a commanding presence not found in other contemporary art forms. It is too early to say whether the iconography is a deliberate revival of Sāsānid themes in the full consciousness of what they mean, or whether the images were chosen for their Sāsānid appearance, even though they had lost their meaning for contemporary society. It is less likely that in their new Islamic context they had acquired some new significance, for the basic themes are shared with Byzantine and Syrian fabrics.

No comparably large body of material has survived from Mongol or Timurid times, but what remains shows that Chinese influences became important in the fourteenth century and that Timurid silks conform to the decorative style common to the minor arts in this period, with a preference for finely detailed arabesques and floral designs rather than for animal or figural motifs. The result is an all-over pattern with no marked focus of interest.

Safavid textiles, by contrast, survive in great quantities. The most important centers for this art seem to have been Yazd, Kāshān, and later Isfahān. Many of these textiles are signed. In general, they display a much more varied iconography than earlier silks. The themes are clearly dependent on book painting and, as in so much of Safavid art, figural subjects dominate. Embroidered brocades and velvets (fine examples of the latter are found in Rosenborg Castle in Denmark and Karlsruhe in Germany) supplement the more traditional plain silk weaves. Their themes include, beside the large-scale floral motifs familiar from contemporary carpets and tilework, which became more naturalistic from the early seventeenth century onward, courtiers relaxing in gardens, hunting scenes, and images drawn from the epic and lyric poetry that was the staple of illustrated manuscripts. The composition is often stiffly arranged in repetitive rows. Although most of them were used as robes, sashes, or other garments, some of these fabrics functioned as wall hangings, tent decoration, cushions, or covers for presents; some were even used as carpets. Metal thread was widely employed. Embroideries with double darning or cross stitch on a linen ground continued to be produced in quantity in subsequent centuries, the finest work being reserved for women's trousers embroidered with diagonal bands of floral patterns. Patchwork filled out with papier-mâché was also common. From Qājār times onward, block-printed cottons (qalamkār) became fashionable, and they are made to this day, though the details of the designs are no longer separately painted by hand.

Carpet Making

It is generally agreed that carpet making is an art of high antiquity in central and western Asia, even though no material evidence earlier than the sixteenth century survives in most of this area. But the finds from Pazyryk in Siberia, where the tomb of a nomadic chieftain buried in the fourth century B.C. was excavated in 1949, included a knotted pile rug of superb quality and fineness, with themes of pacing animals related to the iconography of metalwork and sculpture in the Iranian world of the first millennium B.C. The Pazyryk carpet, whose developed technique implies long experience of rug making, establishes that the traditionally close connection between the Eurasian nomad and carpet making dates back to the earliest recorded appearance of the craft. That same link is maintained in the earliest carpets that survive from the medieval Iranian world: the group of rugs found in the Great Mosque of Konya and datable in the early thirteenth century. Their date and their Anatolian provenance associate them with the Seljuks, whose immediate origins were nomadic and Central Asian.

Only literary accounts bridge the immense time span of some two thousand years between the Pazyryk and Konya carpets. They are rarely helpful. But amid the many casual references to "carpets" (perhaps tapestries or other textiles) in classical and early Islamic sources one specific masterpiece is repeatedly singled out for attention: the Sāsānid imperial carpet known as "The Springtime of Khusraw." Measuring an unparalleled 35 by 30 meters, it graced the royal palace at Ctesiphon. Its design reflected a whim of the ruler, for this carpet, intended for use in winter-time, depicted—in deliberate contrast to its surroundings—a lush blossoming garden. Unnumbered jewels were woven into its fabric and served to represent the fruits of the garden, while the plants and trees were executed in silver and gold as well as silk. It may well have had a symbolic function as a vast advertisement for a way of life as unattainable as it was lavish. A significant portion of the royal treasury was, so to speak, on permanent public display. A faint memory of this legendary carpet is preserved in the numerous "garden" carpets produced from late Safavid times onward. When Ctesiphon fell to Islam, the Arab soldiery hacked the carpet into small pieces and many a warrior bought a sizable property with his fragment. The valuta aspect of this carpet, which was thus so quickly and rudely realized, recurs in much later carpets, again produced for a particular sovereign (Fath 'Alī Shah), who used them as an instrument of crude political (and financial?) propaganda.

Virtually no carpets datable to the Mongol and Timurid periods survive. But the exiguous fragments and the laconic and rather ambiguous literary evidence can be augmented by the depictions of carpets in Western easel paintings and in Persian manuscripts. These visual clues establish that the severely geometrical style of the Seljuk carpets, in which animal motifs—when they occur— are abstracted almost beyond recognition, continued for more than two centuries. These paintings do not offer sufficient grounds to distinguish categorically between Anatolian and Persian carpets. But most scholars assume that the carpets shown in Western paintings were of Anatolian provenance; and in fact the trade in such carpets was between Italy and Asia Minor. The carpets shown in Persian paintings of the fourteenth and early fifteenth centuries show that the Iranian style of the time had far more in common with contemporary Anatolian work than with later Persian carpets. Colors were rich but few in number, the field was customarily geometrical, and the border consisted of Kufic inscriptions that were often entirely devoid of meaning. The later fifteenth century, to judge by miniatures of the school of Bihzād, saw a fundamental change in Persian carpet designs and the first appearance of what were to be characteristically Safavid types. Angular geometric motifs give way to flowing arabesques and floral compositions.

The golden age of the Persian carpet was shortlived, extending as it did from the early sixteenth to the later seventeenth centuries. For many tastes, indeed, the Persian carpet must be judged as already past its prime by about 1600, and in this respect it is no different from the other "minor" arts of the period. Part of the reason—it might be argued—may be the undisputed prevalence, in certain carpets as in other art forms, of an unchanging "house style" whose prestige prevented the concomitant growth of provincial styles that could provide an alternative. But while such an argument may hold in the case of carpets with animal and figural designs, which are clearly in the orbit of court art, it is more difficult to sustain this contention in the case of carpets with abstract designs. Rather does the great variety of such designs point to the continued vigor of numerous local traditions. Nevertheless, the finest and most ambitious carpets were those made for the court, and it is precisely these that betray symptoms of decline after ca. 1600. It is hard to avoid the conclusion that this decline spread by degrees throughout the rest of the country, to such an extent that by ca. 1700 the great days of carpet making were—it seems irrevocably—at an end.

Traditionally, the study of Safavid carpets has been focused rather too closely on questions of provenance and dating that cannot now be resolved unless substantial new information becomes available. Only four dated carpets of major significance survive, and unambiguous information on provenance that can be linked to specific carpets is even more scanty. Perhaps the most sensible course, therefore, is to classify carpets on iconographic and technical grounds. Such a classification must take account of the fact that fine carpets were produced not only in the manufactories attached to the court—which moved successively from Tabrīz to Qazvīn and, finally, to Isfahan—but in numerous other cities (Kāshān, Yazd, Herat, and Kirmān) and villages (such as Jūshāqān). No doubt the various nomadic groups also continued to produce carpets, but their work was never of the finest quality. Unfortunately, most categories of Safavid carpets cannot be associated with a specific rug-producing center.

So many different themes coexist in the repertoire of early Safavid carpets that a lengthy prior development must be postulated for them. It is therefore difficult to identify what was new. Perhaps the major change was an unprecedented dependence on the arts of the book. Earlier Islamic carpets and contemporary ones from elsewhere in the Islamic world had remained faithful to a restricted range of rectilinear geometrical designs whose stiffness and angularity were well attuned to the technique of weaving. Thus, a decorative vocabulary evolved, which—even in such details as the form taken by Kufic inscriptions—was peculiarly suited to, and identified with, the medium. Possibly as a result of the growing prestige of book painting throughout the Timurid period—a process that culminated in the adulation accorded to Bihzād—and of the relative decline in pottery and metalwork, it gradually became more natural for carpet designers to seek inspiration from the themes of painting, bookbinding, and manuscript illumination.

Moreover, the Timurid period foreshadowed Safavid times in that it saw the development of an immediately recognizable generalized style of ornament that was widely applied in architecture and in the so-called "minor" arts.

For these reasons it is quite possible that some carpets currently classified as "early Safavid" are in fact late Timurid, though the evidence of the very different carpets depicted in early fifteenth-century Persian painting makes it impossible to propose a substantially earlier date for them. It seems, therefore, that a remarkably short preparation period of rather less than a century preceded the great Safavid masterpieces. But it should also be emphasized that the major landmark was the "policy decision" to transfer painting and bookbinding themes onto carpets. These themes did not require adaptation; their internal harmony and consistency had been attained in their original medium and could be reproduced ready-made on carpets; the hard work of design had been done. Moreover, both media employed the same vertical rectangular format, so that in many cases the task of the artist was confined to the appropriate expansion of the motif. The real difficulty facing the weaver was, therefore, a technical one: that of executing patterns far more complex than those he had previously encountered in his craft. One important change was however imposed by the tradition, well established in the art of weaving, of using repetitive patterns. Thus, in many Safavid carpets, the essential composition is laid out on half the carpet and echoed in mirror image on the other half. This repetition is commonly disguised not only by the apparently artless, even random, arrangement of the various motifs but also by lavish use of filler ornaments (arabesques or plants) and by rendering the key elements of the design in different colors. The charge frequently leveled at Safavid hunting carpets, that they are paintings in wool or silk, is therefore not entirely just. It is more true of the parts than of the whole. The poses of figures and animals echo their manuscript originals with mechanical fidelity, indeed they seem stenciled; yet the recondite harmonies of these repetitive designs were devised entirely for carpets. But it seems likely that these compositions, too, were the work of painters—a theory that would account for their subtle orchestrations of color that stand in such marked contrast to the few strong colors frankly juxtaposed in the earlier carpets of Anatolia.

Color is indeed a potent factor in the overall harmony of the great Safavid carpets; the weavers deployed a wide range of tones, like Safavid painters, but were more consistently successful in avoiding a distracting farrago of bright colors, all competing for attention. Pastel shades of grey, cream, or brown set off the more powerful tonalities of red and blue. It is noticeable that these carpets avoid the massed expanses of a single color that characterize Chinese carpets. Instead, they display that busy quality that became a marked feature of Persian decoration in Timurid times. Even when a single motif dominates the field, the corners and borders are alive with closely packed figures, arabesques, or other ornaments.

If the distinctive coloring of Chinese carpets finds no echo in Persian rugs, China nevertheless provided the inspiration for many typical motifs of Safavid rugs: dragons, phoenixes, cloud collars, *yin-yang* roundels, peonies, and lotuses. Such features had long passed into the repertoire of the Iranian "minor arts," but only in certain kinds of pottery were they so often allotted a central role. The explanation for this is not far to seek. These motifs were not tied to specific iconographic meanings, even though many of them had such meanings in the culture of their origin. They could therefore be used in a neutral fashion as a series of independent images. As such they were ideally suited to the compartmental layout of so many Safavid carpets. In paintings, by contrast, the narrative emphasis was apt to be so strong that such motifs were demoted to the level of ornamental accessories, and the composition was to be seen as a whole rather than as an amalgam of numerous, equally important parts. The narrative mode was not attempted in Safavid carpets of animal and figural type, although it was practiced in certain Mughal rugs. In the discrete layout followed in so many Safavid carpets, it was therefore possible for minor motifs to acquire major importance.

A few Safavid carpets are signed as well as dated, notably the Ardabīl carpets of 1539, which carry the name of Maqsūd al-Kāshānī. But in these cases, as elsewhere in Islamic art, the *nisba* should not be taken in isolation as positive proof of the craftsman's place of origin. These signatures are, in any case, too few to constitute firm evidence associating a certain type of carpet with a given locality. The status of the craftsman—whether designer, overseer, or weaver—is not revealed in these inscriptions, nor do they shed any light on workshop organization.

Although the 1500 or so fine Safavid carpets that survive can be classified according to various categories, they share certain significant features. The base (i.e., the warp and the weft) is customarily of wool, though cotton is used in cheaper rugs, and silk in the very finest. The knots, which can be as fine as 800 per square inch, are usually of silk, which may have gold or silver thread wrapped around it. This fineness allows such precise rendering of detail that the concept of a "woven painting" is clearly justified. The field itself is usually enclosed by multiple borders, as many as ten in number, none of them identical. This device accentuates the choiceness of the main design and permits a wide range of subsidiary colors to be deployed. Earlier carpets had far fewer borders. Whatever the main motif, a remarkable sense of balance rules the design. This ensures that even a partial view of the whole allows the spectator to sense the underlying unity of the composition, and that the carpet may be seen to advantage from several viewpoints.

Symbolic meanings are often proposed for Persian carpets, but so far no unequivocal supporting evidence has yet been put forward. Indeed, the use of visual symbols in Islamic art is a study still in its infancy. At the most general level it seems reasonable to interpret the garden carpets as paradigms of paradise and to see in the hunting carpets a reference to royal pleasures. Certain vegetal themes, too, seem to have connoted concepts of immortality, of death, or of paradise (e.g., the cypress). Some medallion rugs, like the Ardabīl carpet, irresistibly evoke the image of a starry sky, but whether a more deliberate and detailed cosmic symbolism—perhaps drawing on Chinese sources—is intended in such works as the Sanguszko carpet is open to doubt. The basic weakness of such theories seems to be the lack of contemporary literary sources to show that carpet designs were interpreted in these deeper terms in the society for which they were made. A distinction should be made here between the many primitive pictographs, stylized almost beyond recognition, which could be termed "symbols" of plants or of creatures like the dragon or the phoenix, and the use of a carpet design to express some broad symbolic theme by means of several related images. Generally speaking, the former case seems as common as the latter seems rare. No vocabulary of religious symbolism seems to have evolved, beyond the obvious image of the *mihrāb* and *qandīl* on prayer rugs. Yet a prime function of carpets was to serve as the floor covering in cultic buildings. Some were woven specifically for that purpose, for example the Ardabīl carpets or a rug at Qum whose twelve-sided form may be a reference to the Twelve Shī'ī creed. There appears to be no evidence that carpets with figural scenes were used in cultic buildings; indeed, a common floor covering was the homely *zīlū*, with a flat weave, a repetitive (often grid) pattern, and a date woven into the border.

The basic categories of Safavid rugs may quickly be summarized. Among the most spectacular are the hunting carpets, which resolve themselves into a single motif repeated with numerous variations: a horseman fighting a feline or shooting a deer. But within this overall grid the layout is fluid and irregular, while the many different animals and colors mask the underlying regimentation. These rugs were prestigious export pieces and many bearing Polish coats of arms were commissioned by nobles of that country. Hunting carpets and the related "animal" carpets reached a peak of achievement in the sixteenth century and thereafter declined. By contrast, the finest garden carpets date from a century later and were even being produced in the early eighteenth century. They mirror the formal arrangement of the traditional Persian garden, crisscrossed by watercourses marking out rectangular plots filled with flowers, trees, or shrubs. Such carpets are designed essentially as ground plans enlivened by a primitive notation for water and plants. Perhaps the most typical Safavid carpets are those with floral patterns. These are often associated with medallions or with vases from which the plants issue. The sheer quantity of vegetal motifs in these carpets gives them a remarkable opulence; indeed, their decoration can be indigestibly rich. In designing such carpets, the weaver could draw on the centuries of experience accumulated by Persian artists in the rendering of vegetal forms, whether in painting, stucco, tilework, or other media. The flowing rhythm is unfaltering even when the blossom or tendril has to accommodate itself to an irregular space. Sometimes animals and birds disport themselves amidst the trees and plants. A final category is that of geometric or simply repetitive designs. In the former, of which outstanding examples come from the area of the Caucasus, a strong tribal element is manifest, with loud colors and strong, angular forms. Sunburst designs are especially common. The carpets with repetitive patterns are somewhat monotonous in that a single motif, perhaps insignificant in itself, becomes dominant simply by virtue of apparently endless repetition. As specimens of design, these carpets are the least distinguished of the whole series.

Although many carpets were finely woven of costly materials and intended for distribution as gifts, even these shared with other, lesser, carpets the primary function of a floor covering. It is this utilitarian purpose that has inevitably led to the destruction of much fine work. The present account has had to concentrate on Safavid carpets simply because wear and tear has removed virtually all earlier Persian specimens. Nevertheless, the circumstantial evidence for an unbroken tradition of rug manufacture dating back for nearly three millenniums is very strong. Safavid carpets should therefore be seen simply as one facet of this rich tradition.

The Art and Architecture of the Arabian Penninsula

Since the present account is confined to the art and archaeology of those states bordering the Persian Gulf, it cannot include material from either Yemeni state. Yet any discussion of the art and archaeology of the Arabian peninsula that omits this area is most seriously defective, and has the same unreal quality as a history of Renaissance art that excludes Italy. The material culture of pre-Islamic Arabia is largely concentrated in the area of Yemen, the ancient Arabia Felix. At best, a few reflections of its successive sophisticated cultures can be found elsewhere in the peninsula. Although these scattered monuments, artifacts, and inscriptions have been found in most areas of Arabia, the important material outside the Yemen is concentrated in four areas: the Najrān valley, which is historically and geographically an extension of the south Arabian cultural sphere; the southeast, for which the same generalization holds; the east; and the northwest. It will be most convenient to deal with the pre-Islamic monuments of each area in turn.

Inscriptions attest that the people of Ma'īn (the major state in ancient South Arabia) had a colony in northern Arabia, and a dependence on alien influence remains characteristic of the art of this latter area. Indeed, the form of the Thamūdic and Lihyānite inscriptions scattered over much of central and northern Arabia and dating from the early first millennium B.C. onward derives from South Arabian prototypes. A stele with an Aramaic inscription found at Taima and datable to the fifth century B.C. is executed in Assyrian style. Animal carvings from Dedan (al-'Ulā), notably those of seated guardian lions in relief and a frieze of ostriches and ibexes, have a Hittite flavor; they date from the period of Minaean colonization (after the fifth century B.C.). Lihyānite sculptures of the first century B.C. from the same site betray Egyptian and Syrian influence. The artists of the area were therefore thoroughly eclectic in outlook, though the foreign stylistic traits that they copied were frequently centuries out of date.

These scattered artifacts testify that for most of the first millennium B.C. northwestern Arabia was culturally a satellite of more advanced civilizations and they suggest that civilization itself was little more than a veneer. But with the establishment of the Nabataean empire in the first century B.C. this area became a cultural center in its own right, with Madā'in Sālih, Rām, and al-'Ulā among its major settlements. Great quantities of monuments datable between the first century B.C. and the second century A.D. survive. Most are executed in the hybrid Romano-Nabataean style that reached its peak in Petra. The cultural orientation was therefore northward rather than southward as hitherto. Rock-cut mausoleums with frontages imitating house façades are especially common, though rock-cut sanctuaries are also known (Madā'in Sālih). Egyptian features, like the use of pylons or decorative grooving, coexist with a predominantly classical vocabulary of columns, capitals (the latter decidedly original and often almost baroque in spirit), pilasters, cornices, and architraves. But, as in Umayyad art a few centuries later, the artists take bizarre liberties with these classical forms and employ them in a markedly unclassical spirit. Frequent Nabataean inscriptions, some very stylish and refined, show that almost all the stone masons had Nabataean names. Figural carvings of lions, eagles, or other creatures sometimes adorn the lintels of the tombs, and the coping may be stepped or crenellated. Behind such elaborate façades there is commonly a chamber with tomb niches in the walls and the floor (Madā'in Sālih; Madyan). Free-standing temples were commonly rectangular (Ruwāfa; Rām, temple possible dedicated to the goddess Allāt), or square (Qasr Qurayyim Sa'īd) and had such classical features as tetrastyles, colonnaded portals, and raised cellas. In the temple at Rām, wood and stone were used together in the walls, a technique familiar in the Yemen and originally of Ethiopian origin.

The area of Dhofār, now the southwestern part of the sultanate of Oman and formerly an important incense-producing center, was in pre-Islamic times a cultural offshoot of southern Arabia, and was indeed colonized from Ma'īn. Four major ruined cities have been investigated in this area: al-Balīd, Rūbāt, Tāqa, and Khur Ruri. The first two possess temples no earlier than the second century B.C. and characterized by rectangular plans. Columns are cylindrical, concave, octagonal, or rectangular; their capitals are of reversed stepped type and thus still innocent of any Hellenistic influence. These columns are arranged in three pairs in the sanctuary. The Rūbāt temple has a remarkable ribbed arch consisting of stone slabs. Khur Ruri has yielded a square temple with cyclopean masonry.

In the monuments of the Najrān valley immediately to the north of Yemen, the incompatability between historical and modern political boundaries is most manifest, for these buildings can only be understood in the context of ancient South Arabian art. At al-Ukhdūd, a vast ruined city some twenty acres in extent, the principal remains comprise a ruined paved processional area centered on a sacred stone, an arrangement that immediately recalls the Ka'ba and the Dome of the Rock; an extensive precinct, possibly a *temenos*; and a massive rectangular structure, possibly a castle or a palace, articulated by projections. The whole is datable no later than the fifth century A.D., though the building technique employing stepped buttresses is far more ancient, being found in Babylonian buildings.

It is in the northeast, in the area of Bahrain, that the most ancient vestiges of civilization in Arabia have been found. Bahrain itself, possibly the ancient Dilmun, was apparently a Sumerian trading post around 3000 B.C. and serviced the trade to India. At the temple of Barbar, dating from ca. 2500 B.C., was found a bronze statue of a man whose arms were folded across his chest in typically Sumerian style. The temple itself was set within an elliptical enclosure and was reached by a ramp. This arrangement echoes southern Mesopotamian temples at al-'Ubaid and Khafāja and recurs much later at the Awwām temple (the so-called Haram Bilqīs) near Marib in the Yemen, datable to the eighth century B.C. Babylonian gods were apparently worshipped in Dilmun, and it seems clear that in some ways this area of Arabia was culturally an extension of Mesopotamia, forming a bridge between that area and Southern Arabia. Unfortunately, the distinctive qualities of this civilization are still imperfectly known, since only a few of the ca. 100,000 funerary mounds scattered throughout Bahrain and dating between ca. 2300 B.C. and the Parthian period have been excavated. Many pre-historic artifacts have been discovered on the island of Qātar and in the province of al-Hasa. A headless limestone statue of a man in Parthian style found near al-Qatīf is the most important find from the latter province. Near Bahrain, the finds in the necropolis of ʿAin Jawān, which date from the centuries immediately before and after the coming of Islam, testify to the trade relations between Eastern Arabia and the Sabaeans of the Yemen at this period.

Despite the central importance of Arabia in the history of Islam, the tally of significant Islamic monuments in the area, apart from Mecca and Medina, is remarkably small. This disappointing situation certainly reflects, at least partially, the dearth of serious published work on Islamic archaeology and art history in this area. Of the Great Mosque at Medina, for example, it is possible to say that the Umayyad foundation of 706 was continually remodeled in later times, espe-cially after a fire in 1256; but how much of this structure survives within the present mosque, whose form dates from a thorough rebuilding in 1853–54 under Sultan ʿAbd al-Majīd, is debatable. Similarly, in the case of the Great Mosque of Mecca, the alterations undergone by the structure that Muhammad founded in the year 8/630 have yet to be traced in a detailed monograph, using the extremely rich literary sources. In its present form, a parallelogram measuring roughly 170 by 110 meters internally and provided with seven minarets, the mosque dates largely to the years 1572–77, in the time of Sultan Selīm II. From this rebuilding, date the multiple small domes of the covered area surrounding the courtyard. Among several earlier features of the mosque that survive is the important late Mamlūk *madrasa* of Qāʾit Bey. As for the Kaʿba itself, the focal point not only of this mosque but also of Islamic architecture in general, it still retains the roughly cubic form that it seems to have had in pre-Islamic times, but periodic restorations have in this case too made it a palimpsest whose component elements defy precise identification.

A freak survival of the early international Sāmarrā style is provided by the Shīʿī mosque of Manāma on Bahrain Island, datable to the eleventh century. It is interesting primarily for its decoration, notably the carved teakwood pillars and the two stone *mihrāb*s with their fine floriated Kufic inscriptions. Rectangular in plan, the mosque has a narrow courtyard bordered by columns that bear a flat roof without any intermediary arches.

Mecca, like Jidda and Tāʾif, has much splendid domestic stone architecture dating largely from the Ottoman period. Such houses rise to several stories and are studded with corbeled balconies, *mashrabiyya* work of Egyptian type, and decorative arches. The entire external surface is thus incrusted with rich decora-tion.

It will be clear from this brief outline that the heritage of medieval Islamic architecture in Saʿūdī Arabia and the Gulf states is extremely sparse, though systematic surveys, excavations, and restoration work are certain to provide further material. Such new evidence is unlikely, however, to alter the picture radically. As in the case of pre-Islamic antiquities, nearly all the significant medi-eval monuments are in the Yemen. This area also has perhaps the finest and most varied vernacular architecture of the peninsula. The influence of these structures extends beyond the Yemeni frontier. In the Najrān valley, for instance, the most impressive building by far is the undated high stone palace of the Makārima in Khushaiwa. Its round corner towers echo the arrangement of the Roman frontier forts in the Provincia Arabia, but such details as the triangular crenellations, or the square windows that regularly punctuate the sheer mass of deeply coursed masonry, seem to draw rather on local precedents. While this building is probably of medieval date, there is little doubt that the more modern vernacular architecture reproduces ancient patterns. Examples are the round helmet-shaped straw huts of the Tihāma or the more ambitious cylindrical or pylon-shaped buildings at Hijla near Abhā, whose walls comprise alternating courses of brick and slate. These slates project at a slight slope and thus protect the building from rain. This traditional South Arabian feature is of Ethiopian origin. Sometimes these "pylons" comprise two or three stories, the lowest one of stone; but in the Asir area east of Abhā they are entirely of mud brick and rise to five stories. Their bold painted polychromy, relying on red mud, white lime, and similar natural materials, is again a Yemenī feature.

Conclusion

This survey has attempted to highlight some of the outstanding features of the arts of the Persian Gulf from the earliest times to the present day. The variety of cultures and artifacts encompassed in such a survey renders any generalization hazardous and forbids any attempt to see the area as an unbroken cultural whole. Nevertheless, two characteristics of the output of this vast region over the millenniums may be noted. First, the area of Mesopotamia and Iran exhibits a remarkable continuity in its production of art and architecture over the entire historic period. This has made these countries the cultural heartland of western Asia. No natural or manmade calamity could quench the inspiration of their artists, who have repeatedly proved their ability to absorb alien influences and transmute them into something that was original and yet rooted in their own traditions. Second, these cultures shared with much ancient and medieval art in the West the notion that art had a religious rather than a purely aesthetic function. This is what links the temple to the mosque and the votive statue to the luster tile. The exceptions, such as most Islamic painting, only emphasize that art existed principally to express and to serve the transcendental. Most ancient Mesopotamian and Iranian art was produced in the orbit of the temple, while Islamic architecture is predominantly religious in function. In these two senses, then— continuity and religious inspiration—it is perhaps permissible to treat as a single entity the artistic production of the states bordering the Persian Gulf over the centuries.

Selected Bibliography

Barrett, D. E. *Islamic Metalwork in the British Museum.* London, 1949.

Bunt, C.G.E. *Persian Fabrics.* Leigh-on-Sea, 1963.

Creswell, K.A.C. *A Bibliography of the Architecture, Arts and Crafts of Islam.* Cairo, 1961; *Supplement.* Cairo, 1973.

Doe, D. B. *Southern Arabia*. London, 1971.

Edwards, C. E. *The Persian Carpet*. London, 1953.

Ellis, R. S. *A Bibliography of Mesopotamian Archaeological Sites*. Wiesbaden, 1972.

Erdmann, K. *Die Kunst Irans zur Zeit der Sasaniden*, repr. Mainz, 1968.

————. *Seven Hundred Years of Oriental Carpets*. Ed. H. Erdmann, tr. M. H. Beattie and H. Hertzog. London, 1970.

Ettinghausen, R. *Arab Painting*. Geneva, 1962.

Frankfort, H. *The Art and Architecture of the Ancient Orient*, paperback ed. Harmondsworth, 1970.

Ghirshman, R. *Persia: From the Origins to Alexander the Great*. Tr. S. Gilbert and J. Emmons. London, 1964.

————. *Iran. Parthians and Sassanians*. Tr. S. Gilbert and J. Emmons. London, 1962.

————. *Iran from the Earliest Times to the Islamic Conquest*. Tr. M. Munn-Rankin, D. Kirkbride and M.E.L. Mallowan. Harmondsworth, 1951.

Godard, A. *The Art of Iran*. Ed. J. M. Rogers, tr. M. Heron. London, 1965.

Grabar, O. *The Formation of Islamic Art*. New Haven, 1973.

Gray, B. *Persian Painting*. Geneva, 1961.

Grohmann, A., and Nielsen, D. *Handbuch der Altarabischen altertumskunde*. Copenhagen, 1927.

Grube, E. J. *Islamic Pottery in the Keir Collection*. London, 1976.

Herrmann, G. *The Iranian Revival*. Oxford, 1977.

Hill, D., and Grabar, O. *Islamic Architecture and Its Decoration, A.D. 800–1500*. 2nd. ed. London, 1967.

Lane, A. *Early Islamic Pottery*. London, 1947.

————. *Later Islamic Pottery*. 2nd ed., rev. R. H. Pinder-Wilson. London, 1971.

Lloyd, S. *The Archaeology of Mesopotamia from the Old Stone Age to the Persian Conquest*. London, 1978.

Melikian-Chirvani, A. S. *Le Bronze Iranien*. Paris, 1973.

Moortgat, A. *The Art of Ancient Mesopotamia*. London, 1969.

Pearson, J. D. *Index Islamicus*. London, 1955 to date.

Pope, A. U., and Ackerman, P., eds. *A Survey of Persian Art from Prehistoric Times to the Present*. London and New York, 1939.

Pope, A. U. *Persian Architecture*. London, 1965.

Porada, E. *Ancient Iran*. London, 1965.

Sarre, F., and Herzfeld, E. E. *Archäologische Reise im Euphrat- und Tigris-Gebiet*. Berlin, 1911–20.

Seher-Thoss, H. and S. *Design and Color in Islamic Architecture*. Washington, D.C., 1968.

Spuhler, F. *Islamic Carpets and Textiles in the Keir Collection*. London, 1973 .

Spuler, B., and Sourdel-Thomine, J. *Die Kunst des Islam*. Berlin, 1973.

Woolley, C. L. *The Art of the Middle East*. New York, 1961.

17. Tribes of the Persian Gulf

BRIAN D. CLARK

The word tribe is often used as a descriptive term to delineate social groups. Generally, tribes are differentiated from each other on the basis of unique social, cultural, and political features. The definition of a tribe is usually dependent upon who is doing the defining, i.e., the criteria for using "tribe" could be on the basis of language or religion or dress, or an enforced term given by the administration because of a common locality, or a term accepted by a group because of common descent. It has been suggested by several authorities that political parameters are probably the most important factors in defining a "tribe" in the Middle East. In the states bordering the Persian Gulf, the political aspects of tribes are of considerable importance. Tribes in this area have often been in conflict with the nation-state and its centralizing and bureaucratic tendencies. On the other hand, in several countries bordering the Persian Gulf, tribal dynasties have provided not only the ruling shaikhs but also the power base to maintain them, as in the United Arab Emirates, Bahrain and Qatar.

It may be helpful to think of the tribes of the Gulf as part of a continuum in time and space. At one end of the continuum are the tribesmen of the desert and rural areas who live in an organized system of traditional social relations; while at the other extreme, one finds in the growing urban areas of the Gulf, tribal identity will usually, over a period of years, decline, although, in some situation in which the position of tribes on this continuum may change as a result of a large number of processes. These may include one or more of the following, although it should be stressed that the list is by no means exhaustive:

1) Environmental processes, such as revaluation of the resource base, drought, and shortage of pasture.
2) Political processes, of which conquest of new territory, forced transfer of tribes, and sedentarization have all been important.
3) Economic processes, such as the attraction of oil-related or urban employment

and decline in the demand for services (protecting the desert caravans) and products (the camel).
4) Social processes, of which decline in the power of tribal rulers, break-up of tribes, and growth of the welfare state in some of the Persian Gulf countries can be cited.

In some instances, these processes may be in conflict: at other times, they may work together. Drought, for example, may force a section of a tribe to sell its stock. As stock is the main source of capital for a nomadic tribe, its members may be forced to seek employment in an urban area. Having acquired capital, the tribal group may again buy stock and return to their former nomadic life. On the other hand, all or some of the members of the tribe may remain employed, thus becoming gradually absorbed into the urban system. When this happens, tribal identity will usually, over a period of years, decline, although, in some recorded cases, it may be strengthened.

It is my purpose to select certain key topics in order to analyze the tribes of the Persian Gulf. Initially, a brief overview of the economic structure and social and political organization of the tribes will be made, and this will be followed by a study of their numbers and broad spatial distribution. Individual countries will then be examined. At the country level, different themes will be emphasized to show the great variety of contrasting situations that can be seen among the tribes of the Gulf.

The Economic Structure of Tribes

It is only possible here to highlight certain features of the relationships between the economic systems of the countries bordering the Persian Gulf and the tribes. Until the discovery of oil in several of the countries, an event which is radically altering their economic structure, the agricultural patterns, strongly conditioned by the often harsh physical environment, have been of primary importance. Three major types of physical area can be identified, and within these areas distinctive systems of response have evolved. In all cases, the availability of water, both in quantity and seasonality, together with the climatic variations and their effect on the growing season, must be stressed as important factors. First, one has the various desert areas, with a limited number of oases, where water and pasturage are scarce and where pastoral nomadism provides the basis for a viable economy. Areas covered by this type of regime include most of South Arabia, the southwestern parts of Iraq, and parts of Khūzistān, and certain coastal regions in southern Iran. It is the lack of grazing, resulting from the climatic constraints, which has led to such extensive nomadism. The second area is the marshlands of southern Iraq; the third area is the intermontane valleys and ranges of the Zagros mountains of Iran.

In the desert areas of the Arabian peninsula, pastoral nomadism, as personified by the Bedouin, is traditionally believed to have occurred as a result of either forced or natural movement of tribes from the cultivated lands of southwest Arabia to the bordering desert. To survive, these tribes had to establish a sensitive socio-ecological balance. The result was the development of pastoralism as the main land use system; a system that was maintained and controlled in part by raiding; natural disasters, such as drought; intertribal hostilities; alliances; conquests; and the possibility of finding a more suitable habitat. Over the years there have been great migrations of Bedouin tribes across the deserts in a move toward the potentially more favorable north. One result of this is that all Iraqi Arab tribes appear to have migrated from Arabia.

Until recently the human response to the environmental constraints in Arabia saw the development of two types of community. First, the people of the *bādiya*, or pastoral nomads, herding camels, sheep or goats, who claim membership in a specific tribal group and not a specific settlement; and second, the people of the *hadar*, or settled communities comprising mainly cultivators settled in oases growing dates and certain other crops or vegetables. Historically, the peoples of the *hadar* and the *bādiya* were spatially and culturally different, often political rivals but economically interdependent. Within the *hadar*, allegiance to the tribes may be equally as strong as among the *bādiya* population. Overall, the various tribes that make up the people of the *bādiya* represent the most economically viable adaptation to desert conditions. The livelihood of the tribes is based upon livestock, livestock products, and by-products. Animal husbandry of camels, and to a lesser extent, sheep and goats, constitutes the principal land use, provides the tribes' main source of income, and, apart from dates and grain bought or bartered from the settled population, provides the staple diet.

There is little general agreement as to a definition of the people of the *bādiya*, or *badw*. Glubb defines them as "pure desert dwellers . . ., the breeders of camels," while Arbos stressed "an entire human group accompanying the herds and flocks in their migration." According to Peppelenbosch, true Bedouin pastoral nomadism should refer to the nonsedentary animal husbandry of nomads in search of pastures, with the entire human group accompanying the flocks and herds that roam seasonally over winter and summer grazing grounds, following more or less fixed routes on tribal land, but still without necessarily being self-sufficient.

To avoid overcrowding of water sources and pastures, tribal nomads normally travel in groups of between twenty to thirty tents and may travel over an area of some 500 square miles in a complex seasonal cycle. Many tribes may travel more than this, for example the Ruwāla, who journey over 1,500 miles. During the winter months, herds and tents change grounds approximately every ten days, until by May all nomad households and their animals are once more beginning to converge on the summer grazing area around the tribal wells.

As well as these nomadic tribes, there are a number of social groups who lead a seminomadic existence. They may be sections of fully nomadic tribes, or distinctive tribes in their own right. Usually they comprise ex-nomads who have lost some, but not all, of the basic traits of nomadism. It is often a stage in the process by which a Bedouin tribe evolves to a sedentary mode of life. Usually, they own and breed sheep, keep fewer camels, and may practice some form of cultivation, usually in an oasis or on irrigated land at a village. Several of these seminomadic tribes live in huts built of mud and straw, although they move to fresh pastures and water in spring and winter.

The final type is the settled tribes that are found in parts of the Arabian peninsula, Iraq, and Iran. The different processes by which sedentarization has occurred will be considered when the tribes are analyzed in selected Gulf countries. Likewise, the second major physical land-use type, the marshlands of southern Iraq, will also be evaluated under the section on that country. It is, however, important to comment on the third major physical area, the Zagros mountains of Iran. Here the pattern of pastoralism, including a strong nomadic tribal component, while having some similarities with the Arabian peninsula, has certain distinctive features.

In the central and southern Zagros mountains of Iran and in Baluchistan, rainfall, as in the Arabian peninsula, fluctuates greatly in amount and in the times at which it falls. Also, as in the Arabian peninsula, the agricultural system that is practiced is a response to a complex set of physical factors. Nomadic, semi-nomadic, and settled tribes are all found in the Zagros mountains. The main form of nomadism practiced in southern Iran involves a twice yearly movement of flocks from the warm low-lying areas near the Gulf to the higher mountain slopes and upper valleys of the Zagros. Winters are spent in the warmer areas (*garmsīr* or *qishlāq*), and as the *garmsīr* pastures dry up in the late winter or early spring the tribes move northward, up into the Zagros, to take advantage of the rich summer pastures in the higher cooler areas (*sarhadd* or *yailāq*). As autumn approaches and the higher pastures become cooler the return descent is made. As can be seen from Figure 17–1, the winter and summer quarters of some of the Iranian tribes are separated by land that is occupied by a settled population, often of a different tribe and in many cases of a different ethnic background.

By custom, some of the tribes follow a well-defined migration route (the *il rāh*) or tribal road. Each subgroup of the tribe has by tradition the right to pass through certain defined areas. Where several different tribes use the same route to pass between summer and winter quarters, there is a need for careful phasing, and increasingly this is being controlled by government officials in conjunction with the tribal khans or chiefs.

The groups in the Zagros that are nomadic pastoralists keep a wide variety of animals, cows, camels, horses, donkeys, and hens, but their main wealth is derived from sheep and goats. Much of the carpet weaving that is done takes place in the summer pasture areas. In the case of many tribes in the Zagros, cultivation occurs in both the *garmsīr* and *sarhadd*. In the *garmsīr*, fruit production is of increasing importance. As sedentarization increases there is a tendency for the tribes to settle in the *garmsīr* and to develop more permanent agricultural activities.

As in the Arabian peninsula, there is a complex system of interaction between the nomadic tribes and the settled population. Exchange of goods and services, meat for grain, grazing on stubble of tribes' flocks in return for labor, labor of tribesmen in harvesting crops in return for cash, which is used to purchase tea, sugar, and other necessities, can be cited as examples of the interactions that occur. Indeed, as industrialization occurs in Iran, the nomad becomes more dependent on items supplied by towns and villages. With increased sedentarization, either forced or voluntary, many changes are occurring in the agricultural systems of virtually all the major tribes of the Zagros.

FIG. 17–1. General location of tribes in the Persian Gulf area

Social and Political Organizations

Although there are similarities between the social structure of the tribes in the Arab countries of the Gulf and Iran, there are certain differences that need to be indicated. These partly result from the patterns of nomadic activity that have evolved because of contrasting systems of pastoralism, horizontal migration in the Arabian peninsula and vertical migration in Iran, and partly because of the different historical circumstances of the tribal groups.

The main feature of Bedouin social structure is that it is based on kinship, real or putative, from the smallest unit to the largest federation of tribes. However, the tribe is the prevailing political unit. The unification of tribes into a more closely organized unit was, in the case of Sa'ūdī Arabia, a rare occurrence until the establishment of the kingdom in the 1930s.

The classification of Bedouin society into its units, and the names and sizes of these units, differ widely from tribe to tribe and region to region. According to Baer, however, the main units into which Bedouin tribes can be divided are as follows:

1) The extended family (*ahl*).
2) A group of families that trace descent back five or seven generations to a common ancestor (*hamūla*). The *hamūla* generally move and camp together.
3) The tribe. The tribal unit is mainly political, although members of a single tribe do consider themselves to be related. It may contain refugees, emigrants from other tribes, and persons under its protection. At times, the whole tribe camps together during the summer near a group of wells. The tribe is headed by a shaikh; this is usually a hereditary position. The shaikh takes responsibility for decisions relating to migration, war, and internal and intertribal disputes. He is usually advised by a council of tribal elders (*majlis*).
4) In some areas, an association of tribes exists, headed by a shaikh of one of the stronger tribes.
5) Coalitions of these associations of tribes, such as the Shammar or 'Unaiza, were formed under stress of war.

This hierarchy is flexible and undergoes continual modification. The complete set of units does not exist in all Bedouin tribes, and there are big differences between the size of any two parallel units.

Among the nomadic tribes of Iran, a similar structure exists. The names given to different tiers varies from tribe to tribe, but the situation among the Qashqā'ī can be taken as representative.

1) The individual family (*khānavāda*).
2) A descent group, comprising six to ten tents, which camps together, in both the summer and winter quarters, shares resources and herds together (*baila*).
3) A descent group made up of several *baila*s that normally migrate together and share the same pasture land. It may consist of up to fifty families (*boskuh*) and is led by an elder.
4) Tribal section or subtribe (*tīra*). The *tīra* is the main unit of identification for the individual Qashqā'ī and has a territorial basis, with most of its members sharing common pasture areas. The average size of nomadic *tīra*s appears to be eighty tents, or approximately 500 people. It is also a political unit headed by a *kadkhudā*.
5) The main tribes (*tā'ifa*) are collections of from twelve to seventy-one *tīra*s. The nomadic branches of the tribes average 3,000 families. The *tā'ifa* is controlled by a chief (*khān*) who is responsible for maintaining order and organizing the affairs of the tribe.
6) The Qashqā'ī confederacy (*īl*) is made up of five or six *tā'ifa*s, divided into approximately 250 *tīra*s. The confederacy is controlled by a paramount chief (*īl-khān*).

The hierarchical structure of most Gulf area tribes clearly demarcates social behavior, and the conflict between tribe and state is often a result of the interference by the state in this hierarchy.

The Number and Distribution of Tribal Populations

Several major difficulties are encountered when attempting to make a quantitative assessment of the tribes of the Gulf. In some countries there are no reliable published statistics of the total population, let alone of the tribal components. Where tribal figures are included in census data, they have been shown to be unreliable, often equating the tribal population with the nomadic or, to use the Iranian term, "nonsettled," population. This hides those people living in villages and towns who consider themselves part of a tribal group. Any figures quoted, either for countries or individual tribes, must at the best be no more than approximations. While detailed data and information are available on some individual tribes, much of this is now dated, being the result of studies undertaken many years ago. Indeed, of the hundreds of tribes and tribal sections that are found in countries bordering the Gulf, many have never been studied at all. Also, in several countries, studies of tribes made by government officials are not made publicly available, being used for internal security and other official purposes. This partly reflects the view held in some countries that tribes are now an anachronism, that their existence should be played down and that their study should not be encouraged. In sum, any analysis of the tribes of the Gulf must rely heavily on what is qualitative, often historical, evidence, the contemporary reliability of which it is difficult to verify.

Tribal populations are found in all the countries that surround the Persian Gulf. The first feature to be noted is that in eastern Sa'ūdī Arabia, southern Iraq, and the Gulf shaikhdoms, nearly all of the tribal populations, whether they are now nomadic, seminomadic, or settled, claim Bedouin ancestry. The exceptions, such as the remnants of small Baluch tribes found in Sa'ūdī Arabia, are statistically insignificant. In Iran, however, the position is far more complex. There are a great number of tribes having neither ethnic nor linguistic unity. The principal elements are Persian (including Kurd and Lur), Turkish, Baluch, and Arab.

A second feature is that the tribal population of the Gulf littoral is distributed in a wide range of physical environments. In Sa'ūdī Arabia and the Gulf shaikhdoms, the predominantly desert environment, with a number of oasis settlements, and a growing number of urban and industrial nodes, helps to explain both the numbers and distribution of the tribal population. Areas with a deficient resource base, whether rural or urban, see a small number of tribal groups, whereas areas of better pasture, selected oases, and oil-dominated urban centers show a higher tribal population density. The movement to certain major nodes (urban and oil-related centers) or linear developments (pipelines, new communication routes) also helps to explain the continuing transformation of the population from a nomadic to a more sedentary state.

In southern Iraq, there are marked contrasts in the environment in which the tribal population are located. On the one hand, there is a high density of tribal population in the area near Basra and in the marshlands and regions bordering the Tigris and Euphrates rivers. Many of these tribal groups claim Bedouin ancestry, but most now live in settled communities. In contrast, areas to the south and west of the Euphrates have a low population density, with nomadic and semi-nomadic tribes practicing traditional pastoralism. Details of the distribution of the tribal population in Iran will be considered when the various tribal groups are analyzed, although it should be emphasized that the area bordering the Persian Gulf, particularly the Zagros mountains, is, in terms of numbers, the most important area of tribal population in the country.

In terms of their total numbers, Bedouin tribes must be considered as the most important tribal group on the Gulf. For reasons already stated, it is difficult to give precise tribal figures. Abu el-Ula (1972) has calculated that there are some 300 tribes on the Arabian peninsula, and that 75 percent of the total population of Sa'ūdī Arabia belong to, or claim ancestry, real or imaginary, from one or other of these tribes. He further estimates that there are 11 million people in these tribes, of whom approximately 2 million persons are still nomadic. This figure applies to the whole of the Arabian peninsula. For Sa'ūdī Arabia, Fisher (1970) estimates that there were three-quarters of a million nomads, with a further 300,000 in Iraq.

For Sa'ūdī Arabia, three semiofficial estimates of the Bedouin population have until 1974 been considered by demographers to be reasonably accurate approximations. In 1932, 3 million were defined as Bedouin. In 1962–63, it is estimated that there were 694,013 Bedouins, of whom 40 percent were concentrated in and around urban areas and villages and hence could be considered as semi-Bedouins, while the rest, 60 percent, were clustered around water holes throughout the country. A 1970 survey suggests a figure of 423,000. These very approximate figures suggest that in the last forty years the decline of the nomadic Bedouin has been substantial, dropping from 58 percent of the population in 1932, to 21 percent in 1962, and to 15 percent in 1970. Since 1970, it has been estimated that the decline in the number of nomadic Bedouin is 1 percent per annum. However, the reliability of these figures must now be questioned, if one is to believe the results of the population census carried out in Sa'ūdī Arabia in 1975. According to these figures, 1,883,987 of a total population of 7,012,642 are nomadic, a figure far in excess of other recent surveys and estimates. It is still too early to comment on the reliability of these figures, but it does illustrate the very real problems of attempting to analyze the demographic trends of the tribal and nomadic population. In the Eastern province of Sa'ūdī Arabia, the area bordering the Persian Gulf, 79,460 of the total population of 769,648 are said in 1975 to be nomadic tribesmen.

In 1974, the total population of Bahrain and Qatar and the seven United Arab Emirates was estimated to be 550,000 persons. Excluding the immigrant population, which has rapidly increased in recent years, most of the population are from Bedouin tribes. The majority of the population are concentrated on the barren seacoast, mainly in growing urban centers and usually in the Emirate capital or in oasis settlements. The population of 'Ajmān, Bahrain, Dubai, and Umm al-Qaiwain is almost entirely settled, as are 85 to 95 percent of the inhabitants in the other five states. The remaining 5 to 15 percent are nomadic or seminomadic tribesmen.

In Iraq, the nomadic population has declined from approximately half-a-million in 1867 to 65,000 in 1957, a decline from 35 percent to just over 1 percent of the total population, although these estimates are believed by many authorities to be too low. For example, another study in the 1950s estimated that 8 percent of the population were nomads, 48 percent were Bedouin tribesmen living in villages, 22 percent were a settled rural population, and 20 percent lived in communities with a population of more than 20,000. The decline in the nomadic population has been greatest in the central and southern parts of the country, where between 1947 and 1957 it decreased from 180,000 to 26,660. In 1957, almost two-thirds of the nomads, who belong to two main groups, the 'Unaiza and Shammar tribes, were in the province of Mosul, with the remainder found in the desert provinces of Ramādī and Dīwāniyya forming 6.7 and 1.9 percent of the total population, respectively. Again, it should be stressed that many people, although now settled, still live in a strong tribal organization.

Population figures of the total population in Iran are difficult to ascertain. Curzon, in 1892, stated that there were 2 million in the nomadic state, and an estimate of 1910 quotes 2.65 million, which is believed to include a settled tribal component. By 1932, it was estimated that the number of tribal nomads had declined to 1 million, and numbers continued to decline until 1940, as a result of Riżā Shah's policies. According to the last national census of Iran (1966), 240,000 are said to be "nonsettled population." Even as a figure for the nomadic population it appears to be too low and excludes many tribesmen who are seminomadic or settled in villages. According to Firoozi, there are approximately 3 million tribal members living a nomadic life in Iran, a figure that would appear to be more realistic.

Sa'ūdī Arabia

In considering the tribes of Sa'ūdī Arabia, emphasis will be placed on an analysis of the various factors leading to their sedentarization, together with brief comments on the individual tribes that are located on the Gulf littoral. There will be no need to evaluate the tribes' economic, social, and political structure, as this has already been referred to in earlier sections. It is worth reiterating, however, that until the discovery of oil a pastoral economy dominated the history of Sa'ūdī Arabia and provided the main economic activity. In this the Bedouin tribes have played a key role. Tribal settlement can be thought of as being both planned and spontaneous. Planned refers to the official government policy of encouraging Bedouin tribesmen to settle. It involves what el-Farra has described as a policy of detribalization. Implementation of this policy began as early as 1912, with the creation of a confraternity by Ibn Sa'ūd of tribal warriors who were called "the Brethren" (Ikhwān). They were bound together by the Wahhābī concept of a purified Islam. They were established in permanent military colonies (hijras), with populations of from 2,000 to 10,000 persons, around a water source that was to be used to cultivate land. The aim was mainly a political one and an attempt to break down Bedouin individualism and tribal alliances. By transforming a large part of the Bedouin population into a settled agriculture society, it was hoped to end the "tribes' archaic particularism." Each settlement was to contain a tribal group, and between 1912 and 1927 over seventy colonies were established. By 1932, there were approximately 200 *hijra*s, with an estimated population of a quarter of a million. With strong military, political, and social objectives behind their establishment, many have flourished while others have failed. After 1932, as a result of the unification of the country, enthusiasm for creating *hijra*s declined.

Droughts in the 1950s revived the idea of settling Bedouin tribesmen in selected parts of the country. A great deal of money has been invested in a number of agricultural schemes which, it was hoped, would prove attractive to nomadic tribesmen. The success of these schemes has been mixed, but they have not done very much to sedentarize further the nomadic population. Instead, this has been largely achieved by spontaneous settlement.

The spontaneous settlement of Bedouin tribesmen throughout much of Saʿūdī Arabia appears to be accelerating, and results from a combination of environmental, political, economic, and social factors, all of which are putting pressure on the Bedouin to leave their traditional way of life for a new one. Some Bedouin tribal groups are now totally sedentarized, and many of them live in tent and hut encampments that have sprung up around urban centers, while others are permanently established as cultivators in oases. In both these cases, they still may retain some animals. Many of these groups also still retain a tribal organization, although this appears to be weakening. In a great number of cases, those who have become settled in urban areas follow occupations not far removed from their traditional way of life in nomadic Bedouin society, such as soldiers, policemen, or security guards.

Of environmental factors leading to sedentarization, it is perhaps the major droughts of the 1930s and 1950s that have been most important. These droughts led to a reduction of grazing lands and overgrazing of those that remained. The introduction of pump-wells in recent years has led some tribes to increase their number of animals and this has also led to a deterioration of the ranges by overgrazing.

Perhaps the most important political factor affecting sedentarization is that the modern bureaucratic state is not compatible with tribal organization. While tribal Bedouin institutions thrived on raids, imprecise boundaries, clan alliances, and mobility, the modern state is based upon fixed international and internal boundaries and on treaties and bilateral agreements. Consequently, the traditional movement of the nomadic tribesmen has been curtailed. Tribal territories and rights were abolished in 1925, and this eliminated, at least in theory, the self-government of tribes and subjected them to state control.

When considering economic factors, it is the discovery and exploitation of oil that has had the greatest impact on the Bedouin. It has been estimated that up to 35 percent of the oil work force are Bedouin tribesmen. Of perhaps greater importance is the fact that government investment as a result of oil revenue has led to an improved transport network and the provision of an economic and social infrastructure that not only requires a labor force but also has actively encouraged many Bedouin to seek regular employment. Specifically, many of the new urban areas that have sprung up as a result of oil development have attracted Bedouin tribesmen.

Finally, important cultural changes have also affected the Bedouin. Raiding, the caravan trade, and hunting all used to provide supplementary income and are largely no more. The herding of camels (which in the past was an important status symbol) and sheep is increasingly market-oriented. The camel in its traditional role as the main vehicle of transportation has largely been replaced by the motorized vehicle. The size and make of car or truck is now the new status symbol of the tribesmen. It is also the means whereby animals are transferred to new pastures, and this itself is creating new patterns of tribal mobility and environmental degradation of pastures.

Other Tribes

In the area bordering the Persian Gulf, there are found a number of major tribal groups. Some have been largely sedentary for many years, while others still practice traditional systems of pastoral nomadism. A brief comment on the major tribes of the eastern part of Sa'ūdī Arabia helps to show some of these contrasts.

Shammar. Sections of the Shammar confederation are found today in Sa'ūdī Arabia, Iraq, and Syria. Until their defeat by Ibn Sa'ūd in 1921, they were a very powerful group. In the nineteenth century, they controlled large parts of the Arabian peninsula from their power base Hā'il. Four major subdivisions of the tribe now live in Sa'ūdī Arabia. These are the 'Abda, Āl Tūmān, Sinjara, and Aslam tribes, whose tribal pastures (*dīra*) are found in the hill country near Hā'il, extending into the Great Nafūd and in a belt of land of over 400 miles along the Tapline. By 1928, the Shammar had formed 9 *hijra*s, of which Jubba on the edge of the Great Nafūd was the most important. In 1960, the date of the latest statistics on this tribe, half of the 5,000 Shammar families were believed to be sedentary.

Dhafīr. The tribal area of the Dhafīr lies on both sides of the Sa'ūdī Arabia/Iraq border and includes part of the Neutral Zone. This tribe faced considerable intratribal conflict as a result of the fixing of the Sa'ūdī Arabian–Iraq boundary by the Treaty of Muhammara in 1922. The main settlement of the tribe is al-Shu'ba, a former *Ikhwān* colony. There are two subtribes, and in total they number approximately 2,000 families, of whom the majority are still nomadic.

'Awāzim. The 'Awāzim were originally a subtribe of the Mutaim. They live in the north of the Eastern Province, including the Sa'ūdī Arabian–Kuwait Neutral Zone. The great majority of the tribe were sedentary before the start of World War II, when they were said to number 1,300 families. The tribe are now almost entirely settled and live in Kuwait or in *hijra*s, of which Thāj is the most important.

Harb. This important tribal group migrated to the area between Mecca and Medina from south Arabia in the ninth century. During the period of the great tribal movements in the eighteenth and nineteenth centuries, the Harb once more became mobile and extended their territory from the Hijāz toward the east. Their modern tribal area is a thin strip of land extending across the Arabian peninsula from Medina in the west to east of the sand desert near Qiba. While the Harb in the west of the country near Medina and on the coastal lowlands near Rabigh have been sedentary for a long period, the groups of the tribe in the Najd and toward Qiba have until recently been largely nomadic. Under the war-like Harb, the *Ikhwān* movement gained many supporters, and in total 27 *hijras* were founded.

Mutair. Like the Harb, the Mutair were originally located on the west of the Arabian peninsula and migrated to their present tribal area in northeastern Sa'ūdī Arabia in the latter part of the nineteenth century. Their *dīra* extends from al-Qaisūma on the Tapline across the desert to al-Artawiyya. By 1928, this tribe had established 18 *hijras*, several of which grew in importance through being on the main inland route from Kuwait to the west. Today only a very small percentage of the estimated 5,000 Mutair families are nomadic, although several groups are seminomadic. The most important centers around which settlement has occurred are 'Unaiza and Buraida.

'Ajmān. Originally part of the Yām tribe, who were located in southwestern Arabia, the 'Ajmān tribe moved to the Eastern Province in the eighteenth century. Their tribal pastures were in the area between Hufūf and Riyadh. As a warlike tribe, the 'Ajmān succeeded in uniting with the Khālid tribe who had formerly controlled this area. Fourteen *hijras* had been established by 1928, including the town of Hanidh between Hufūf and the Tapline. As a result of the rapid development of this area in the past fifteen years, many 'Ajmān tribesmen have become sedentary and are now employed in the oil industry.

Banī Khālid. In pre-Wahhābī times, this tribe was one of the most powerful in the Eastern Province of Arabia, with the shaikh of the tribe ruling an extensive empire from the Gulf into central Arabia. In the eighteenth century, they were greatly weakened as a tribe through their struggle with the Wahhābīs. The tribe was one of the first to become sedentarized and are now found in the oases of al-Hasā and Qatīf.

Banī Hājir. This tribe originated in Qahtān and moved to the east coast of Arabia at the start of the eighteenth century. Their main tribal territory was the peninsula of Qātār and the area near Abqaia. This latter place, now an important oil town, was originally a *hijra* colony. Today most members of the tribe live in the rapidly growing towns and associated villages in this area.

The Āl Murra. The Āl Murra is one of the most powerful tribes of camel nomads living in Sa'ūdī Arabia. They have one of the largest tribal areas in the country, which extends over the vast, almost vegetationless desert of the Rub' al-Khālī or Empty Quarter. In good years, some groups penetrate as far as the south of this desert. Although the Āl Murra are located in the Eastern Province, whose economic potential is particularly attractive for settlement, well over half the tribe are still nomadic. Pressure on the tribe from the *Ikhwān* movement to establish colonies was resisted, as they had no desire to give up their nomadic

life. The few *hijra*s that were in fact established in the 1920s were largely abandoned by the 1930s, with the tribe returning to its former ways. In recent years,
however, government irrigation projects in Haradh have encouraged some of the
Āl Murra to settle.

The United Arab Emirates. The decision of the British government in 1971
to end the defense treaties that had existed since the early nineteenth century
with the nine shaikhdoms of the Lower Gulf, and their proclamation as independent states, marked the end of an era, an era that had sustained a complicated tribal dynastic structure. Nowhere in the Persian Gulf is this tribal structure
more important for an understanding of the contemporary problems of the shaikhdoms than in the seven that combined to form the United Arab Emirates. Until
petroleum was discovered, the conflicts were those normally associated with
tribal competition for scarce resources and limited income, such as fishing and
pearling rights, access and control of restricted grazing land and water holes.
Since oil has been discovered in some but not all of the Emirates, the conflicts
that now exist more often relate to boundary disputes over prospecting and
drilling rights as a function of the inevitable jealousy between those that have a
buoyant oil economy and those that have not. Intradynastic tribal rivalry is still
of major importance, and although many of the ruling families come from the
same tribe, tribal status between shaikhdoms is still a cause of conflict.

Most tribal confederations in the area are divided into distinctive tribes,
which in turn are subdivided into clans, sections, and families. The rulers of the
seven Emirates are drawn from the most prominent tribal clans of the shaikhdom.
The chief of the confederation is chosen by, and is a member of, the family recognized as the ruling family, which is equivalent to a dynasty. This dynasty is the
most important unit of the tribal organization under its chief, who stands at the
apex. Tribal chiefs are normally elected by the elders of their various clans and
sections and are generally considered first among equals, for the tribesmen consider themselves to be full partners. The size of the tribes ranges from several
thousand to only a few hundred families, although the largest tribes are not always the ruling dynasty.

Abū Dhabī. Abū Dhabī, with a population of approximately 95,000 in 1974,
is the largest, richest, and arguably the most important member of the Emirates.
More tribes are still nomadic than in any of the other shaikhdoms, and some of
them still move into neighboring states. Those that are settled are found in the
capital and the Buraimī and Liwā oases.

The tribes are the most important source of local political power for the
ruling family, and this has been the case since the early nineteenth century, when
the Āl Nuhayyān ruling family forged an alliance among the four major tribes,
the Banī Yās, the Manāsir, the Āl Jawāhir, and the 'Awāmir. Of these, the Banī
Yās are most important and include all the main branches of the Āl Nuhayyān
family. A loose federation of some fifteen tribes, they dominate Abū Dhabī town,
the Liwā oasis, and some of the villages in Buraimī oasis. Unlike many of the other
tribes found throughout the Emirates, who pride themselves on their nomadic
traditions, the Banī Yās have had a long history of being semisettled or sedentary.

The Manāsir tribes have sections who are date cultivators and other sections who are still nomadic. As the most important tribe of al-Dhafra, they have been important to the ruling family as the tribe that controls the western territory of the shaikhdoms bordering Sa'ūdī Arabia. The Dhawāhir tribes, comprised of fifteen subtribes, are most strongly represented in the Eastern Province. Allied with the Banī Yās for over one hundred years, they, of all the nonruling tribes, have benefited most from oil exploitation, as a large percentage of the development budget of the state has been used for infrastructure development in their tribal areas. The 'Awāmir are found to the west of Buraimī oasis and south of al-Dhafra. Many sections of this tribe still seasonally migrate with their flocks into the Oman and Sa'ūdī Arabia. In addition to these four major tribes, there are a number of other important tribes. These include the Nu'aim, related to the ruling Nu'aim tribe, the 'Ajmān, and a Balūch tribe that migrated to the Buraimī area over one hundred years ago.

Dubai. Dubai, as the leading commercial center in the Emirates, had an estimated population of 100,000 in 1974. The country has an almost entirely settled tribal population. Most of them live in Dubai town or are fishermen and farmers producing dried fish, dates, and limes. Shaikh Rāshid, the ruler, is also paramount shaikh of the Āl Bū Falāsa section of the Banī Yās, the most important tribal group in Dubai.

Sharja (al-Shāriqa). With an estimated population of 55,000 in 1974, Sharja has only recently, as a result of the discovery of oil, been able to embark on a range of development programs. These programs have been difficult to establish, as a result of the fragmented enclaves that make up the shaikhdom. The most important tribal group in Sharja are the Qawāsim, who provide the ruling shaikh and whose members hold most of the key government positions. Traditionally, great rivals of the Banī Yās, the Qawāsim controlled most of the Musandam peninsula, including the area of Abū Dhabī and Dubai, until well into the nineteenth century. Members of the Qawāsim tribe, and certain of the other small tribes who are found in the territory, are engaged in agriculture, particularly date cultivation, although some clans still practice pastoral nomadism.

Ra's al-Khaima. Although lacking oil, this shaikhdom, with a population estimated in 1974 to be 45,000, has a reasonably balanced economy, with a well-developed system of agriculture and extensive fishing resources. The Ra's al-Khaima ruling family belong to the same Qawāsim tribe that rules in Sharja, but unlike Sharja they are one of the smaller tribes in the shaikhdom. According to the 1968 census, which indicated that 18,000 of the estimated population of 28,000 were of tribal origin, four other tribes were larger. These tribes were the Shihuh (5,845), the Za'b (2,455), the Āl 'Alī (1,445), and the Mazārī' (1,062).

'Ajmān, Umm al-Qaiwain and Fujaira. These three smaller Emirates are the most traditional and tribally oriented of the Lower Gulf States. Their economic position is a function of their lack of oil and their very poor resource base. With an estimated population in 1974 of 8,000, 7,000, and 15,000, respectively, they

are heavily dependent on the oil-producing shaikhdoms for financial assistance. Generating little income from their own physical resources, the Emirates claim *zakāt*, or Islamic tax, from the nomadic tribes that pass through or use their territory for grazing. The most important tribes of the three shaikhdoms are the Nu'aim, the Āl 'Alī, and the Āl Sharqī, who according to the 1968 census had 2,329, 5,058, and 8,729 members. These three tribes are not geographically confined to the shaikhdom of their paramount chiefs. The Nu'aim, for example, while dominant in 'Ajmān, are also found in Ra's al-Khaima, Abū Dhabī, and Oman.

According to the 1968 census, 96 percent of the population of Fujaira were tribally oriented, and of these 8,300, or 90 percent, of all tribesmen in the shaikhdoms were members of the Āl Sharqī tribe. The rest were believed to be Shihuh tribesmen. In Umm al-Qaiwain, 87 percent of the population were members of the Āl 'Alī tribe; in 'Ajmān, fewer claimed tribal affiliation, but of those that did, 44 percent belonged to the ruling Nu'aim tribe.

Bahrain. A traditional society less than half a century ago, Bahrain is acknowledged by many as the Lower Gulf's most advanced state, both socially and economically. The Āl Khalīfa are the ruling tribal dynasty and occupy the most important posts in the country. As the population of Bahrain is now largely settled, and there is an initial absence of a nomadic Bedouin population, tribal groups, apart from the ruling Āl Khalīfa family, do not play an important role. The close connections between Bahrain and Sa'ūdī Arabia are partly rooted in tribal ancestral links with the Āl Khalīfa and Āl Sa'ūd, both tracing their origins to the Banī 'Utūb of the famous 'Unaiza tribal confederation of north central Arabia.

Qatar. According to Lorimer, there were a great many small tribes in the area of Qatar at the turn of the century. Many of them were nomadic pastoralists, but today only approximately 10 percent of the total population are nomadic Bedouins. However, the most important tribal influence in Qatar is the Āl Thānī family of the Ma'ādid tribe, who are now said to number 20,000 persons out of an estimated population in the mid-1970s of 190,000. As well as providing the ruler, members of the Āl Thānī family hold most of the important positions in government.

Kuwait. Prior to the development of oil in Kuwait, the area was used by Bedouin tribes in search of pasture and water. There were seven major summer camping grounds in the area. The first settlers were tribesmen from the 'Unaiza tribe who were one of the largest groups of north central Arabia. The most important subtribes in the area were the Āl Khalīfa, the Jalahamar, and the Āl Sabāh. The latter tribe now provides the ruling family. The 'Awāzim and Rashā'ida, Dhafīr and Mutair tribes either had their tribal headquarters in this locality or utilized water holes and pastures. The 'Awāzim tribe were particularly important in fishing off the coast, an occupation that was combined with nomadic herding.

After the discovery of oil, many Bedouin tribesmen were attracted to employment in the industry from the 1930s onward. They acted as guards and drivers, although many left to return to the desert for certain periods of the year. At first, members of one particular tribe refused to work for members of another tribe, but this problem was gradually resolved. Increasingly, members of the tribes who have joined the oil company and taken other urban employment are now prepared to take a wider range of jobs, but the qualities established by life in the desert have helped them to obtain employment, particularly as guards, military personnel, or policemen.

Although houses were built for the tribesmen by the Kuwait Oil Company, many preferred to live in their traditional black tents. In time, more permanent houses, or what are described locally as shanty dwellings, some of a very sophisticated design, were built by the Bedouin tribesmen who had settled in and around Kuwait. A study of shanty dwellers undertaken in the mid-1970s by Al-Moosa, suggests that up to 60 percent of the occupants of these were Bedouin tribesmen who had come from the desert. These shanty areas are constantly being cleared by government planners, as the land is required for more permanent building purposes. One interesting feature of these shanty areas is that the layout takes its form from the arrangement of Bedouin tents in the desert, i.e., there is an accepted distance between tents within the tribal unit and greater distances between the tents of subtribes, and this has been transferred to the arrangement of dwellings in the shanty areas. In 1975, it was estimated that the number of shanty-dwelling Bedouin was 104,703, or 80 percent of the total shanty population. All Bedouins in shanty areas represent 22.3 percent of the total Kuwaiti population, and 10.6 of the total Kuwait and non-Kuwait population. Many Bedouin also now live in "people's housing" areas that have been built. The sites are isolated from the main city, and only houses and little infrastructure have been provided. They have not proved attractive to the Bedouin who, in many instances, prefer to remain in a shanty area.

In the shanty areas, and to a lesser extent in the "people's housing" areas, strong tribal organization is still maintained among the different groups of the Bedouin tribesmen. As a group that is clearly not integrated into Kuwaiti society, many of the Bedouin, whether in shanty or "people's housing" areas, have kept many aspects of their tribal structure. One example of this is that the space for a guest, which was a fundamental feature of the tent, has now been transferred to a separate guest room, which in the shanty areas is separate from the rest of the dwelling. Although tribal shaikhs do not live in the shanty areas, they visit them regularly to look after the interests of members of their tribe.

Tribal influence in shanty settlements is also strong with regard to the social structure. In the sample study of shanty areas already referred to, it was shown that 95 percent of husbands and wives came from the same tribe. Tribal activity is also seen by the way in which members of the tribe are important in influencing social patterns, for example, in arranging marriages, helping members of the tribe who are unemployed to find jobs, and helping to solve disputes. In over 85 percent of the sample cases, individuals choose to live in the area because members of the same tribe lived there. The pastoral element, however, is still shown by the fact that in the shanty areas, and indeed in the "people's housing" areas, 53 percent and 33 percent of population kept animals, usually goats or sheep. Some of the dwellers had members of the family who took the animals into the desert at certain periods of the year. However, the main pattern now is of members living in these shanty settlements only going into the desert for recreational purposes at certain periods of the year. Overall, it is a pattern of the Bedouin tribesmen gradually abandoning their nomadic life and visiting the desert with diminishing frequency.

Throughout Kuwait one witnesses some conflict between the Kuwaiti population, many of whom have tribal ancestry, and the new workers coming into the community, of whom Bedouin tribesmen are a major component. The Bedouin find it difficult to adjust in a new environment, and many problems arise. In sum, the Bedouin is torn between traditional tribal habits and the attraction of Kuwait's urban society. There is some evidence that incomers from the desert, who settle in the shanty towns or in "people's housing" areas, tend to reinject traditional values of the desert, but it is debatable how long this will last.

Iraq. Although Iraq has been dominated for a great part of its history by Persian and Anatolian empires, the main element in its population has been recruited continuously from tribes of the Arabian peninsula.

In much of the period of Ottoman rule, the Turkish influence on the towns was ineffective or nonexistent, with tribes being virtually independent. The Bedouin tribes, having encroached on the settled land over the past three centuries, continued to do so, being replenished by the entry of fresh tribes from Arabia in periods of weak control. This process continued in the seventeenth century when the great Shammar tribe entered Iraq. Forcing out the Muwali tribe from the west bank of the Euphrates, they themselves were then forced into the Jazīra by the 'Unaiza. By the eighteenth century, it is possible to see that the loosely defined tribal distribution was taking place. For example, the Muntafiq was created by the uniting of several smaller tribes to the south of the Samāwa. Strengthened by the creation of a new tribal dynasty founded by Shaikh Sadūm in 1738, they often aligned with the Mamlūk Pashas. At the same time, the Banī Lām, a new group founded by Shaikh Hāfiz, took the land between Shaikh Sa'd and al-Amāra, while the Banī Ka'b established themselves in the Shatt al-'Arab by dominating the river. After 1800, the new religions and tribal movement of the Wahhābīs threatened Iraq from Arabia. Several of the major tribal groups however, such as the Muntafiq, Shammar, and 'Ubaid, joined forces to resist them.

The period of the reformed Ottoman administration (1831–1914) saw the new Turkish *walīs* or governors trying to force the tribes into submission without much success. It was decided by Midhat Pasha that the best way to bring the troublesome tribes to heel was by settling them on irrigated lands with security of tenure. To this end, the *Tapu* office was set up, together with a policy of Ottomanization of the tribal shaikhs by offering them Turkish titles and administrative positions. The policy met with some success, and as a result many sections of the Ka'b, Shammar, Toqa, Dulaim, and Zubaid tribes were settled in their present locations. This process also broke the unity of the powerful Muntafiq confederation through internal conflict between the various tribal sections.

In the mandate period after World War I, several of the leading tribal shaikhs were given ministerial positions in the Council of State, a fact that greatly assisted in the pacification of the country, although local tribal unrest was a common feature of the 1930s. Perhaps more serious were the attacks made on the tribes of Iraq, such as the 'Unaiza, Dhafir, and Muntafiq, by tribesmen of Arabia at the time of the expansion policies of Ibn Sa'ūd. After a period of much brutality, a treaty was signed between Iraq and Ibn Sa'ūd in 1931. It provided measures to prevent raiding from either country and established the rights of tribes of either country to have complete freedom of movement in the other's territory for grazing or for purchasing provisions.

Since World War II, Iraqi society, as a result of social, economic, and political change, has been evolving rapidly. While the marked distinction between city and tribe that existed in Iraq is now slowly breaking down, it is still an important feature of life. When thinking of the tribal population of Iraq, one thinks of both nomadic tribesmen and settled cultivators, their differences being essentially of function. The vast majority of Iraqi peasants are of tribal origin, and this tribal organization has often survived their transformation from nomadic to sedentary life. It has been the policy of Iraqi governments in recent years to attempt to sedentarize for reasons of security, including the need to reduce the power of the shaikhs and to facilitate conscription, taxation, and other administrative measures.

Pure camel-raising nomadism, confined to the Arabs of Iraq's western and southwestern deserts and the Jazīra, is rare and is becoming rarer. The nomadic tribes that survive conform to the patterns of economic activity and social structures that have already been defined. Many of the seminomadic tribal groups continue agriculture, combined with sheep and goat breeding. Most of the sections of these tribes are settled, but some move their flocks to pasturage in spring and early summer and later return to their settlements.

The majority of the Arab tribes in Iraq are now completely sedentary, and by far the greater part of the tribal population is settled in villages. Its tribal coherence is less marked than in the nomadic tribes.

One very distinctive aspect of the tribal position in Iraq has been the development of groups of Marsh Arabs, or Ma'dan, who inhabit a vast area of marshland in southern Iraq, where the Tigris and Euphrates rivers meet in the area to the north of Basra. The inaccessibility of the marshland made it a refuge for defeated tribes and persecuted minorities, who have intermarried for centuries, but are of diverse origins and include Arabs, Iranians, and Africans. Arabic is the main language. The Marsh Arabs have retained the values of their desert ancestors and offer hospitality in the same manner as the Bedouin. Tribal status is conferred by lineage rather than by wealth. It was estimated in the 1960s that there were 60,000 Marsh Arabs.

A typical marsh village consists of low houses made of reeds standing on damp, man-made islands; canoes provide transport. The Ma'dan can be divided into two occupational groups: water buffalo breeders and those who fish and make mats. The former are nomadic and move according to their animals' needs, while the latter are settled, but keep buffalo for their milk and dung. Although the marshmen have a contempt for commerce and trade, they must sell mats in order to buy essential imports from the outside world.

In recent years, there has been a drift of population from this area to the cities and oil fields. The government now exerts more control over the marshes, and a money economy is being introduced. There are now plans that in the future much of the marshland will be drained, and this is likely to have a great impact on the tribal structure and lead to forced sedentarization.

Iran. The great historical nomadic movements into Iran help to explain much of the ethnic diversity that still exists. During the last fourteen centuries, at least three major movements have occurred: the Arabs came in the seventh century, to be followed by the Seljuks in the eleventh century; the last group were the Mongols, who occupied much of the territory. To these major movements must be added what Field calls "minor incursions and slow infiltrations." It is these movements that help us to understand the contemporary tribal map of Iran. There is no doubt that tribes have been one of the most persistent elements in Iranian society. As Lambton has said: "The most widespread group organizations in time and place are the tribal group and village group, both of which have played an immensely important role in Persian history." When Riżā Khan came to power in 1925, and started on the rapid modernization of his country, it was inevitable that the tribal confederations would come into conflict with the Shah. The settled population regarded the tribes as a threat to their society, and Riżā Shah felt that nomadic tribesmen were an anachronism in his policy of modernization and creation of a nation-state. During his reign, from 1925 to 1941, he attempted to destroy tribal organizations, prevent seasonal migration, and by policies of enforced sedentarization to convert the tribal nomads into agriculturalists. Many were settled, others were transferred to different parts of the country, and many were killed either directly, or indirectly, when they were stopped moving from winter to summer quarters. It can be argued that the tribal policy was ill-conceived and badly executed and resulted in a heavy loss of livestock and a general impoverishment of the tribes. Tribal uprisings in the period were common, but, in general, the central government managed to impose its will, being able to make movement through tribal areas more safe and also to introduce government officials into areas where previously the tribal khans had been almost exclusively in administrative control.

After the abdication of Riżā Shah in 1941 and a weakening of control of the central government, many tribesmen who had been forced to settle reverted to a nomadic or seminomadic existence. Tribal rebellions started, particularly among the tribes of Kurdistan and in Bakhtiyārī and Qashqā'ī territory.

By the early 1950s, the government was in a position to attempt greater control over tribal activity, and a Higher Tribal Council, under the direction of the Ministry of Court, was established in 1953. Its aim was to encourage sedentarization and increase the economic contribution of the tribes to the national economy. Through policies of economic planning, land reform, and infrastructure planning of health and welfare facilities, there can be no doubt that far greater control of tribes is now exerted. One result has been increased sedentarization, but it will be more appropriate to consider the current status of tribes by an examination of the main tribal groups found in the Iranian Gulf littoral.

The Bakhtiyārī. The Bakhtiyārī were estimated in 1976 to number 600,000. The majority are now sedentary, but it is estimated that 150,000 migrate annually.

Of the two main divisions, the Haft Lang and the Chahār Lang, the former are the most numerous, and it is their members who still annually migrate. Most members of the Chahār Lang have been sedentary for many years. The major tribes of the Haft Lang are Durakī, Dinārī, Babadī, and Bakhtiyārwand-i Jānakī, while the main tribes of the Chahār Lang are the Mahmūd Sālih, Mumzai, Sahunī, and Hihawand. The Bakhtīyārī are found in the mountains and foothills of the Kārūn basin and the region between the northern tributaries of the Kārūn and the Āb-i Diz. Their summer grazing (*sarhadd*) is in the intermontane plains in the highest ranges of the Zagros, while their winter quarters (*garmsīr*) are in the outer foothills from Malāmir and Kuh-i Mungasht toward Dizfūl, Shushtar, and Rām Hormuz. Initially, sedentarization of the Bakhtīyārī occurred in the *garmsīr*, but now it is also occurring in parts of the *sarhadd*, particularly in the district of Chahār Mahāl.

Kūhgīlūya. The Kūhgīlūya are one of the four groups (Failī Lur, Bakhtiyārī, and Mamassānī) that make up the loosely defined Lur confederation. There are three main tribes, the Jaki, Babuli, and Agajari. The Jaki include a number of subgroups, of which the most important clans are the Chahār Bunicha (Boyir Ahmadī and Liravī). They are located to the south of the Bakhtiyārī country and to the west of the Qashqā'ī summer quarters in the district, which consist of the Marun basin, the Zuhra basin, and the upper valley of the river Kārūn. The Boyir Ahmadī were the main nomadic element, with their *sarhadd* in the village east of Kūh-i Dīnār and near Basht, while their *garmsīr* was in the plains and valleys near Bihbihān.

Mamassānī. Little is known about the current status of this tribal group, who are part of the Lur confederation. The Mamassānī inhabit the southeastern part of the Zuhra basin and the upper basin of the Hilla Rūd. There are four tribes, all now sedentary or semisedentary, and in the 1950s they were believed to number 6,000 families (30,000 in total).

Qashqā'ī. The Qashqā'ī are one of the best-known tribal groups found in Iran. The first mention of the name Qashqā'ī is in the time of Shah 'Abbās the Great (1587–1629), when a certain Jāmī Āqā Qashqā'ī was given authority over the many Fārs tribes. The loose confederation of tribes developed considerable power, but they lost much of their influence with the decline of the Zand dynasty and also with the rise of the Qājārs, who moved their power base from Shīrāz to Tehran.

The number and names of groups affiliated to the Qashqā'ī have been varied over the years. Tribal sections have disappeared and, as the power of the Qashqā'ī leaders has fluctuated, so has their political allegiance. At the present time, seven major groups are said to exist. In 1972, the Department of Tribal Education stated that there were 141,000 individuals, of whom one-third were now sedentary. The Qashqā'ī confederation was officially disbanded by the government of Iran in 1956. The *garmsīr* of the Qashqā'ī is enclosed by the upper River Zuhra on the north and the encircling Mand on the south, east, and northeast. Westward it stretches to the coastal plain of Dashtistān and Burāzjān. A tongue of Mamassānī territory separates the Qashqā'ī *garmsīr* into a larger southern and smaller northern area. The *sarhadds* of the Qashqā'ī are found in adjoining but distinct regions; first, in the Nirīz basin, and second, on the plateau between Ābāda and Shāhrizā. These two towns act as tribal centers, while in the *sarhadd* and *garmsīr*, centers are Kaz and Fīrūz. The length of the migration varies, with the average distance being 150 miles, but some cover 320 miles and take from seven to eight weeks.

Khamsa. This confederation, based on the Arabic word for "five," consists of five separate tribal groups. Two of these, the Ainallū and the Bahārlū, are Turki-speaking; two are Arabic-speaking, the Arab Shaibānī and the Arab Jabbāra; and one is Farsi-speaking, the Basseri. The confederacy came into being in 1865, at the instigation of the British, the Qājār monarchs, and the Shīrāz family of the Qavāms, as a military and political balance to the growing power of the Qashqā'ī.

Located to the northeast and southeast of Shīrāz in Fārs province, their *sarhadd* is in the Nirīz basin, and their *garmsīr* extends from the Upper Mand and Āb-i Fasā east to Furg and Tārum on the Rūd Shūr and south to the open plains of Lār.

Given the different backgrounds of the tribes that make up the confederacy, and because it was essentially a political alliance, the ways of the different tribes vary. The Arab tribes are now largely settled, with only a limited number annually migrating. Until recently, additional income was made by hiring of mules and camels for transport. As good rug weavers they produce many of the best Fārs carpets. The Nafars, a subgroup of the Basseri, were still nomadic until the 1920s, but since then have become sedentary. Declining in importance, they live in a barren area of Lāristān. The Bahārlū live in the Dārāb region, and in 1957 it was estimated that they numbered 4,000 individuals. The other Turki-speaking tribe, the Ainallū, had estimates of population ranging from 5,000 to 1,400 families in the 1950s, and today they are largely sedentary, living near Fasā. The Basseris, like many of the nomadic tribes of Fārs, were forcibly settled in 1931, but most of them resumed their migration following the abdication of Riżā Shah in 1941. Approximately 300 miles separate their winter quarters, which are found to the south of Jahrān and west of Lār, and the summer quarters of the upper Kur River and the Kūh-i Bul area.

Balūch Tribes. In the bleak, inhospitable mountainous area of southeast Iran are found numerous Balūch tribes. While most of the estimated 1.1 million Balūch tribesmen live in the Balūchistān area of Pakistan, half-a-million live in Iran, from the Gulf of Oman to Sīstān on the Afghan border. Apart from a few cultivated oases, much of the land in this area is dry and inhospitable. Most of the Balūch tribes, of whom there are great numbers of small sections, are pastoral nomads, but increasingly they are becoming settled. Others are soldiers, policemen, or rent collectors for big landlords growing wheat or dates. The low rainfall throughout the region leads to a low density of population and their wide dispersal, and many of the small tribes are commonly intermingled with alien tribes and clans.

Arab Tribes of the Gulf. It is estimated that approximately 0.5 million Arabs live in Iran. Of these the great majority live in Khūzistān, although some are also found in Fārs and in coastal areas of the Persian Gulf. The majority of the Arab population, whether settled, semisettled, or nomadic, are tribally organized. In northern Khūzistān, the two most important tribes are the Āl Kathīr and the Banī Lām. The former are now largely a settled tribe, holding land in the district between the rivers Karkha and Kārūn, while the latter are found between the Iraq frontier to the Karkha north of the Havīza area. Formerly sections of the Banī Lām used to migrate to north of al-Amāra in Iraq. The Banī Sālih and Banī Turūf are the two major sedentary tribes of the Havīza district, while the Banī Tamīm, who used to be nomadic, ranged from the Karkha to east of Ahvāz. The Muhassin and Durais Nisar tribes are found on the banks of Shatt al-'Arab and Khurramshahr. The Muhassin tribe played an important role in the development of the oil industry, for until the disposition of the Shaikh of Muhammara by Riẓā Shah, they were overlords of most of southern Khūzistān, a position from which they had ousted the Ka'b in the nineteenth century. It was Shaikh Khaz'al who in 1910 concluded an agreement with Britain, allowing construction of a pipeline from Masjid-i Sulaimān to Ābādān and granting them the site for the oil refinery. With lack of control by the central government, this tribe also policed the pipelines. The Ka'b, now much reduced in size and significance, are settled around Shedegan and grow cereals, rice, and dates, and herd cattle and sheep. Other Arab tribes include the Jarrāhī Arabs, who are found near the Gulf ports and in the neighborhood of Ramhurmūz, comprising the Āl Khamsīn.

Conclusion

By selecting certain aspects of the tribal situation in the Gulf littoral, it has been shown that tribes have played an important role in the history and development of the various countries, a role that has had significant economic, social, and political implications. Given the very wide variations that exist within and between countries, it is difficult to make generalizations, but certain major trends do seem to be occurring. Most significant, perhaps, has been the decline of the tribe as the principal political unit. Decentralized and egalitarian in nature, the tribe has now been replaced, particularly in the Lower Gulf, by a number of nation-states, which have ultimate political control. Of importance in this process of transformation has been a marked shift from a largely nomadic population to a seminomadic or sedentary population in most of the Gulf countries. As has been shown, however, tribal structures may persist, whether in the shanty dwellings of Kuwait or the planned new settlements in Iran, although control by the tribal rulers is declining. Reasons for this are many, but include new economic stimuli, such as oil, political pressures to settle the population, and the introduction of health, welfare, and education facilities that can be best administered by the government among a sedentarized population.

It is now realized, however, by many governments in the Gulf littoral that previous policies to settle the nomadic tribal population were at times ill-conceived and often damaging to the economic well-being, not only of the tribesmen but also the country at large. In Saʿūdī Arabia, for example, initial policies of sedentarization were primarily political in motive. Now the government aims at the modernization of tribal society rather than its elimination and recognizes the value of preserving those aspects that are positive, such as social solidarity and economic potential. In this process of transformation to a more settled society, Saʿūdī officials have learned that it is more useful to try to improve sectors of the Bedouin economy that tribesmen are familiar with, such as livestock rearing, rather than to try to introduce them to crop raising, which in the past has led to economic hardship and failure. Present schemes under the current five-year development plan envisage the improvement of Bedouin livestock and grazing land and the setting up of marketing cooperatives. At the same time, a system of boarding schools for Bedouin children is being established. All the evidence suggests that the government now realizes that tribesmen know best to what degree they should become settled and what type of farming they can most profitably adopt.

In Iran, a similar situation appears to be occurring. Until recently, development plans gave a lower priority to nomadic pastoralists than to the sedentary population. In some planning quarters, the view is still held that sedentarization of nomadic tribesmen is the only solution. Increasingly prevalent, however, is the view that as a great deal of the southern Zagros is natural range land, it can only be economically exploited by a pastoral nomadic system. Others argue that tribes reflect cultural diversity and need not be thought of as an anachronism. Despite many attempts to reduce the number of nomadic tribesmen in Iran, they survive as an important social and economic, if no longer political, entity. Much of this is due to the work of organizations such as the Tribal Education Office, which is responsible for the provision of 1,400 mobile schools in tribal areas and who are now setting up vocational training centers and a handicraft center in Shīrāz.

Selected Bibliography

Al-Moosa, A.A.S. "Bedouin Shanty Settlements in Kuwait." Ph.D. thesis, University of London, 1977.

Anthony, J. D. "The Union of Arab Emirates." *Middle East Journal* 26 (1972).

————. *Arab States of the Lower Gulf: People, Politics, Petroleum*. Washington, D.C., 1975.

Arfa, H. *Under Five Shahs*. London, 1964.

Awad, M. "Settlement of nomadic and semi-nomadis tribal groups in the Middle East." *International Labour Review* 79 (1959).

Baer, G. *Population and Society in the Arab East*. London, 1964.

Barth, F. *The Land Use Pattern of Migrating Tribes of South Persia*. Norsk Geografisk Tidsskrift, Band XVII. Oslo, 1959.

————. "Nomads of South Persia." *Universitets Etnografiske Museum, Bull. 8*. Oslo, 1961.

————. "Nomadism in the Mountain and Plateau Areas of Southwest Asia." UNESCO, *The Problems of the Arid Zone*, Arid Zone Research, vol. 18. Paris, 1962.

Beaumont, P., Blake, G. H., and Wagstaff, J. M. *The Middle East: A Geographical Study*. London, 1976.

Caskell, W. "The Bedouinization of Arabia. In *Studies in Islamic Cultural History*, Am. Anth. Assoc., Memo. No. 76. New York, 1954.

Clarke, J. I., and Fisher, W. B., eds. *Populations of the Middle East and North Africa*. London, 1972.

Curzon, G. N. *Persia and the Persian Question*. Hyderabad, 1892.

Dickson, H.R.P. *The Arab of the Desert: A Glimpse of Badawin Life in Kuwait and Saʿūdī Arabia*. London, 1949.

Dostal, W. *Die Beduinen in SüdaArabien*. Vienna, 1967.

Echo of Iran, Iran Almanac. Tehran, 1977.

Evans-Pritchard, E., ed. *Western and Central Asia*, vol. 15; *The Arab World*, vol. 17. In *Peoples of the Earth*. New York, 1973.

Farvar, M. T., and Milton, J. P. *The Careless Technology*. London, 1972.

Field, H. "Contributions to the anthropology of Iran." Anthropological Series. *Field Museum of Natural History* 29 (1939).

Fisher, W. B., ed. *The Cambridge History of Iran*. Vol. 1, *The Land of Iran*. London, 1968.

————. *The Middle East*. London, 1970.

Fried, M. H. *The Notion of Tribe*. New York, 1975.

Garrod, O. "The nomadic tribes of Persia today." *Journal of the Royal Central Asian Society* 2, 33 (1946).

Hawley, D. F. *The Trucial States*. London, 1970.

Helaissi, A. S. "The Bedouins and tribal life of Saudi Arabia." *International Social Science Bulletin* 11, 4 (1959).

Irons, W., and Dyson-Hudson, N., eds. *Perspectives on Nomadism*. Leiden, 1972.

Johnson, D. *The Nature of Nomadism. A Comparative Study of Pastoral Migrations in Southwestern Asia and Northern Africa*. Dept. of Geography, Res. Paper 118. Chicago, 1969.

Lambton, A.K.S. *Landlord and Peasant in Persia*. Oxford, 1953.

Longrigg, S. H. *Iraq, 1900–1950*. London, 1953.

Longrigg, S. H., and Stoakes, F. *Iraq*. London, 1958.

Lorimer, J. G. *Gazetteer of the Persian Gulf*, vol. 2, Geographical and Statistical. Calcutta, 1908.

Lutfiyya, A. M., and Churchill, C. W., eds. *Readings in Arab Middle Eastern Societies and Cultures*. The Hague, 1970.

Marsden, D. *The Qashqāʾi Nomadic Pastoralists of Fars Province*. Manchester, 1975.

————. "Qashqāʿi." In *Family of Man*. Vol. 6, part 82. London, 1976.

Marx, E. "The tribe as a unit of subsistence: Nomadic pastoralism in the Middle East." *American Anthropologist* 79 (1977).

Miles, S. B. *The Countries and Tribes of the Persian Gulf*. London, 1919.

Monteil, V. *Les Tribus du Fârs et la Sédentarisation des Nomades*. Paris, 1966.

Naval Intelligence Division. *Iraq and the Persian Gulf*. London, 1944.

————. *Persia*. London, 1945.

————. *Western Arabia and the Red Sea*. London, 1946.

Oberling, P. *The Turkish Peoples of Southern Iran*. Columbia, 1960.

————. *The Qashqāʾi Nomads of Fars*. The Hague, 1974.

Osborne, C. *The Gulf States and Oman. The Impact of Oil*. London, 1977.

Peppelenbosch, P.G.N. "Nomadism on the Arabian Peninsula: A general appraisal." *Tijdschrift. Econ. Soc. Geogr.* (Nov./Dec. 1968).

Petersen, J. L. "Tribes and politics in Eastern Arabia." *Middle East Journal* 31 (1977).

Philby, H. St.J. *Saʻūdī Arabia*. London, 1955.

Raswan, C. R. "Tribal areas and migration lines of the North Arabian Bedouins." *Geog. Rev.* 20 (1930).

Salim, S. M. *Marsh Dwellers of the Euphrates Delta. L.S.E. Monographs on Social Anthropology*, no 23, 1962.

Salzman, P. C. "National integration of the tribes in modern Iran." *Middle East Journal* 25 (Summer 1971).

Schweizer, G. *Saudi-Arabien. Natur, Geschichte, Mensch und Wirtschaft*. Tübingen, 1976.

Singer, A. "Some Problems of Adaptive Nomadic Pastoralism in Western Iran." B. Litt., University of Oxford, 1969.

Sweet, L. E. *Peoples and Cultures of the Middle East*. New York, 1970.

Thesiger, W. *Arabian Sands*. London, 1959.

———. *The Marsh Arabs*. London, 1964.

18. Competing Ideologies and Social Structure in the Persian Gulf MICHAEL M. J. FISCHER

Introduction

 The Persian Gulf region provides a pastiche of social and cultural formations potentially of extraordinary theoretical interest. Although detailed accounts of the geography, politics, and political history of the region are gradually being made available, only minimal systematic work on the social anthropology of the region has been attempted. Among the theoretical issues of interest are the various formations of hierarchy; the variety of politico-religious ideologies (Ibādism, Wahhābism, Sunnīsm, Shī'īsm); the evolution of social formations (liturgical monarchies or patrimonialisms, tribal confederations, merchant city-states); local level community forms (village communal organizations, nomadic production strategies); the curing cults of possession with their implications for psychodynamic organization; gender definitions and styles of interpersonal relations; and the creation of a precarious industrial class structure, using personnel from the entire Middle East, as well as elsewhere, with the concomitant implications for sociopolitical development.

These theoretical issues relate in part to anthropological work done in other parts of the world. They, however, also fall broadly into two immediate questions facing the peoples of the Gulf: the choosing of strategies of development, and the preservation of a cultural heritage. While most thought about development in the Gulf tends to be in narrow strategic and political terms (the maintenance of power by the shaikhs, king, or Baath party leaders; the maintenance of stability and access to oil for the industrial world; and the demands of socialists and nationalists for power and independence), the greatest threat to long-term development may be the overwhelming of local level initiative and self-confidence by large-scale industry and centralized control. Some of the more pessimistic Kuwaiti social thinkers, for instance, worry that when the oil runs out, not only will Kuwait disappear as a political unit, but more seriously, most Kuwaitis will not be prepared for the modern world. Similarly, Iranians worried that the huge agricultural development program in Khūzistān would make enormous numbers of peasants idle burdens on the state, with all the associated problems of depression and sociocultural disorganization. The problems posed by centralized control are not new ones in the region. Scholars have long speculated about cycles of rise and fall of oriental despotisms. But never in the past has there been the modern capacity to implement the ideology of centralized control, nor the promise of breaking through to a new threshhold of qualitatively higher standards of living for the entire population.

Similarly, the claims for cultural heritage and integrity must not be confused with any romantic assertion of an idyllic past. The Gulf is an area full of mythological and symbolic potential. As a major ancient trade conduit between East and West, it raises associations of pearls, myrrh, and frankincense; of Sinbad the Sailor; of the ports of Ur, Dilmun, and Gerrha; of the shifting influences and needs of the great civilizations (Egypt, Mesopotamia, Iran, India); of the rise and fall of petty states (Oman, Bahrain, Lār, Hormuz); and of a changing mix of ethnic groups. Today the Gulf is again becoming cosmopolitan, after a period of parochialism and reduction to two main ethnic populations: Arab and Persian. Oil, smuggling (gold, appliances, small industrial goods), and development contracts have replaced pearls, myrrh, and frankincense; but the work force is a more international mixture than ever before, with people from as far as Korea, the Philippines, Taiwan, Europe, and America. The questions of balancing the pressures of industrial demands, desires for better standards of living, keeping up with modernization in the world at large, and protecting cultural and personal integrity—these are modern challenges requiring new and creative syntheses.

Two laws may guide discussion of the scattered empirical work that can illuminate these issues. The first, formulated by Sa'ūdī Arabia's former oil minister 'Abdullāh Tāriqī, says that "Rags to riches can happen to individuals, but not to nations," and is a decidedly cautious view of social development in the Persian Gulf region: it takes time to build skills and institutions; modernization is an ideology imposed upon a nation in order to speed development, but one that has clear political risks. The second law leads to a more positive view of the chaos and intricacy of culture and human relations in the Gulf: the economy of honor, the theater of manners and self-control, the art of hospitality, and the private pursuit of purity makes everything at least twice as complicated as it appears.

Socioeconomic Reorganization

While space does not allow a survey of the available studies on reorganization of the entire framework of local economic activity over the past half-century, a few patterns should be noted as grounding for any consideration of ideological and cultural reorganization. The traditional economies of half a century ago were composed of five main strategies in varying proportions: date palm cultivation (with export to both East Africa and India); nomadic pastoralism; fishing and pearling; wheat and vegetable irrigated agriculture; and trade (dates for slaves, building materials, etc.).

Investigation of the integration of these strategies has provided fertile material for a number of major issues in social evolution: (a) political organization where centralized states do not exist (through hierarchical tribal ranking from the *sharif* or noble camel-raising, militarily independent tribes claiming pure descent from one of the pre-Islamic Arab ancestors and engaging in raiding competitions, to tribes forced into marginal areas and into paying a brotherhood tax [*khuwa*] to the sharif tribes for access to water and pasture, to noncamel breeders, the sheep and goat herders who could not range as far, the gypsy-like Sulabah, who were tinkers and smiths, and the settled breeders of buffalo and donkeys; through the balance of opposed forces as when different tribes provided protection for oases and trade routes on different days and extracted dues for their services; and through the creation of small emirates by tribal sheikhs settling in oases as amirs); (b) using the wheat, vegetable, and rice agricultural systems of the Gulf peripheries—especially Mesopotamia, Khūzistān, and the Iranian plateau, but also the mountains and Batinah coast of Oman—to experiment with centralized control and liturgical monarchies; (c) the evolution of trade forms and their contribution to social stratification.

The Gulf ports of the seventeenth and eighteenth centuries had clear aspects of what Max Weber called merchant-aristocratic city-states: a dominant class of lineages emphasizing purity of high blood, owning slaves or serfs, ruled by a sheikh who was either elected or merely *primes inter pares*, drawing surrounding peasants and marine labor into debt slavery and existing in the interstices between monarchies that used administered trade monopolies for fiscal rather than economic motives (that is, rather than trying to maximize profits on trade, trade was used to translate taxes and tributes paid in kind into goods that could be used to pay soldiers, bureaucrats, and royal retainers). In the seventeenth century, the East India Companies came to the Gulf and, in competition with local trade forms, slowly evolved into the forerunners of modern multinational firms. The evolution was from peddling trade with nontransparent distribution chains and high protection costs, to internalization and control of protection costs, to eventual control of the entire market from production to final sale.

The development of the oil industry has allowed the emergence of states financially independent of their citizens. The social effect of the oil industry is structured further by two paradoxes: direct employment in the oil industry is not great; yet labor immigration for construction, shopkeeping, professional services, technical advice, and military support has overwhelmed the local populations. Furthermore, the direct multiplier effect of the oil industry on economic development is relatively slight; yet the funneling of funds from the oil industry through the governments of the area is vast and unprecedented. These funds contain the promise of more rational, efficient, and purposeful spending on social development; but the reverse side of the coin contains dangers of developing highly patrimonial, bureaucratically top-heavy, inefficient, corrupt, and repressive social systems.

All the Gulf states have responded to Tāriqī's Law by investing in education, health, and social welfare, and also by increased attention to maintaining control. The contrast with development in the West is striking. In the West, development was thought to depend on the expansion of enfranchisement of ever larger portions of society so as to give more people a stake in the stability of society; i.e., development was linked to a political ideology of contractual law, democracy, free enterprise. In the Gulf, as in much of the third world, development is explicitly linked to a different ideology: "revolution from above," "tutelage of the masses," a-democratic organization "to prepare society," single party "command structures," and the inculcation of discipline (as opposed to the internal, anxiety-generated discipline of the Western "protestant ethic"). The saving grace of the Arab and Persian world is the theater of manners, duality of personality, and individualistic suspicion of government that prevents the realization of efficient dictatorial models. Before considering further questions of control, political evolution, and modern ideologies, a quick survey of traditional religious ideology is in order.

Religion and Ideological Competition

The ideological drama of the Persian Gulf is often portrayed as that of Western-trained technocrats attempting to steer a steady course between reactionary Islam and revolutionary Marxism. Reality is both more complex and interesting. At least four varieties of Islam have been associated with competing states in the Gulf: Twelver Shī'īsm with Iran, Wahhābism with Sa'ūdī Arabia, Sunnīsm with the Ottomans, and Ibādism with Oman. Still, today the Gulf littoral is a checkerboard of different confessional communities. Previously, of course, the pattern was complicated by merchant groups of Jews, Hindus, Ismā'īlīs, and others. With the current labor influx, some of the cosmopolitan character is returning. Islamic rhetoric is often conservative and opposed to atheistic modernism, but it also is a potent protest idiom against imperialism, occasionally melding with similar Marxist rhetoric. Further, the uses to which the political elite, the religious leadership, and the local populations put these rhetorics are often in contradiction (as a class analysis would suspect). As always in the Middle East, the arabesques of intention are intricate.

Twelver Shī'īsm and the Gulf

The clearest example of the continuing potency of religion, as well as the above-mentioned contradictions, is provided by the 1977–79 revolution in Iran. With respect to the Gulf, two sorts of questions need commentary: Sunnī-Shī'ī relations, and the dynamics of Shī'īsm as a living interpretive tradition.

Towns on the Persian side of the Gulf tend to be Shī'ī with hinterlands of Sunnī villages; inversely, Bahrain and the al-Hasā oasis have Sunnī towns with hinterlands of Shī'ī villages. This has led not only to economic structures of unequal opportunities, but to complex communication networks among confessional groups across the Gulf; and in the past, when violence broke out, it often used a religious idiom. G. H. Sa'īdī's story "Killing Omar" vividly describes the violence of Shī'ī celebrations of 'Id-i 'Umar (the anniversary of the Caliph 'Umar's assassination) in Bushire, when it was under the temporary rule of an Ottoman governor. Neighborhoods competed to construct the grossest effigies of

'Umar out of sticks, cloth, donkey turds, and fireworks. The effigies were ridden about backward on donkeys and reviled with competitive obscene versifications. They were then ignited in front of the governor's office. Fights and bloodshed between Shī'ī and Sunnīs on the 'Id-i 'Umar are still fondly remembered by old-timers up and down the Persian littoral. In elections during the 1960s and 1970s in the town of Lār, troops were called in to prevent violence between Sunnī villagers and Shī'ī urbanites suspecting manipulation in the others' favor; and in Bahrain, Sunnī-Shī'ī tension was an aggravating factor in the labor unrest of 1953–54. In al-Hasā, Vidal notes (1964: 80–85), where land, trade, education, and administration are Sunnī controlled, Shī'ī did not send their children to school in the fifties and sixties, and did not feel free to openly celebrate Muharram, the greatest ritual of the Shī'ī year. Indeed, Shī'ī in al-Hasā suffer the position of non-Muslims in the traditional Islamic world: they are not recruited into the army and pay an extra tax; they are referred to with disparaging names, are used as scapegoats to explain disease and impotency, and are said to have outrageous rites. In recent years, however, Shī'ī have come to supply the bulk of Sa'ūdī Arabia's oil labor force, and during the 1977–79 Iranian revolution felt strong enough to stage public demonstrations in support of their coreligionists across the Gulf.

Lest an impression be left of dualistic antagonism, it should immediately be pointed out that communal distinctions also operate in other directions to which we shall return: the zār cults on the margins of Islam; the opposition within Shī'ism of the majority Usūlīs and the Shaikhī sect (the latter strong in the Hofūf town of al-Hasā, whence came the founder of Shaikhism and whose center is now on the Iranian plateau in Kirmān); and the distinctions between, say again in al-Hasā, the ruling Wahhābīs (strict Hanbalī Sunnīs), the Mālikī Sunnī land-owners, the Hanafī Sunnīs, said to be remnants of the Ottoman administration, and the Shāfi'īs, said to be the oldest legal school in the oasis. What is of greater importance is to take dramas such as 'Id-i 'Umar and the Muharram rites and explore the dynamics of understanding that motivate their participants.

Most Iranians are Ja'farī or Twelver Shī'ī because in 1501 Shāh Ismā'īl Safavī declared Shī'ism to be the state religion in opposition to the Sunnī Ottoman empire to the west. Prior to 1501, the four Sunnī legal schools, the several Shī'ī sects, and the various popular Sufi movements, competed for followers and achieved temporary and localized dominance. The Safavids endowed shrines and religious colleges and used 'ulamā in official positions to promote a standardized state religion. Sufīs, Sunnīs, and non-Muslims were at various times severely persecuted. Many 'ulamā, however, were not integrated into the state. This position of independence contributed importantly to the development of the Persian Constitutional Revolution and continued as the most general and vocal opposition to the Pahlavi shahs, leading ultimately to their overthrow in 1979. The idiom of opposition was analogous with the events of the Battle of Karbalā on 10 Muharram 61 A.H./A.D. 680, when Husain, the grandson of the Prophet, was, in Shī'ī eyes, cruelly and deliberately martyred by the armies of the caliph Yazīd I. Yazīd is thus for Shī'īs the archetypical tyrannical king, and the details of his cruelties to Husain and the family of Husain were used as metaphors for contemporary oppression. The analogy was made dramatically potent through passion plays during the first ten days of Muharram, re-creating the events of Karbalā, and in similar but restricted form through the *rauza* (preachments) held throughout the year, in which the subject of the sermon was always linked first to the Qur'ān and then to dramatic verses about Karbalā intended to elicit tears and rededication to the ideals of Shī'īsm, despite any adversities the authorities might place in the way. The 'Id-i 'Umar fitted into the Karbalā paradigm because in the Shī'ī version of Islamic history, the caliph 'Umar was a leading figure in structuring the events leading up to the Battle of Karbalā, by denying the proper succession from the Prophet to his descendants.

While the Karbalā story provided a unifying paradign for Shī'ī, it is an extremely flexible and multivocal language. Because it was the only political protest idiom more or less allowed by the Pahlavi monarchy, various groups with different interests utilized it, and thus different styles of religious behavior within Shī'īsm provided an extremely useful guide to cleavages in the social structure. While the 'ulamā had grievances against the Pahlavi state, their most important function during the 1977–79 revolution was to articulate the grievances of more important sectors of society; eventually, they had to fight for their right to authoritatively interpret Islam for a modern nation. Two groups that have long disputed the 'ulamā's right to authoritatively interpret Islam are Sūfīs and modernists.

Sūfism—Islamic mysticism—depends on a distinction between esoteric understanding of the intent of the religious scriptures and exoteric following of the letter of the scripture. A similar distinction is used by Shī'ī 'ulamā against Sunnīs, and has also been used among Shī'ī in the dispute between the Akhbārīs and Usūlīs in the eighteenth century. But Sūfīs tend toward vagueness and to rule them out of court; the 'ulamā draw a distinction between *tasawwuf* (Sūfism) and *'irfān* (gnosis). Anyone who claims direct divine inspiration belongs in the former category and is to be regarded with suspicion. Sūfīs are denigrated as unclean because they place little importance on rituals of purity, irrational because some of their mystic exercises are ecstatic, and heretical because they do not adhere to the letter of the law. Sūfīs respond by charging the 'ulamā with mindless adherence to external forms. Similar disputes separate Twelver Shī'ī from Ismā'īlīs (so-called "Sevener Shī'ī") and Shaikhīs. It is unclear how much, if any, hold Sūfism has today in the Gulf region. In Iran, in general, most towns have a sedate group of Ni'matullāhī, a few areas have other orders; but Sūfism as a general orientation is all pervasive: the poetry of Rūmī, the love of music and art (frowned on by the 'ulamā), the play between outward corruptibility and inner purity in moral self-evaluations, and the celebration of the moral qualities of 'Alī, the son-in-law of the Prophet and source of most chains of Sūfī esoteric knowledge: strength, humility, generosity, treating all as equals.

Modernists have long posed a similar challenge to the 'ulamā's desire to be recognized as the authoritative voice of Islam. In the 1930s, Ahmad Kasravī attempted to debunk the superstitions of the popular Shī'īsm preached by the 'ulamā; he was denounced as a Wahhābī, one who has no use for shrines and other psychological aides to faith. But others, both within and outside the ranks of the 'ulamā, have kept up the attempt to break the traditionalist orientation to past authorities, most importantly in the 1970s Dr. Ali Shariati. Despite the attempt by the head of the 1977–79 revolutionary movement, Āyatullāh Khumayni, to write into September 1979 draft constitution provisions for a theocratic head of state, traditionally the 'ulamā have only been able to claim a right, based on knowledge and study, to advise and guide governments. Modernizing governments thus have grounds to challenge the moral expertise of the 'ulamā insofar as they can show that they make decisions based on self-interest, blind traditionalism, or perversion of Islamic values (e.g., that the 'ulamā misused religious endowment funds, that modern education, land reform, welfare systems promote Islamic values of equality). Insofar as the Pahlavis chose to argue on these grounds, the 'ulamā responded by charging arbitrary dictatorship, corruption, torture, and misappropriation of wealth. Insofar as the 'ulamā take on government functions in the course of the revolutionary process, they will become subject to the same moral critique as other governments.

How much of these dynamics affect the Gulf is known only through casual observation. In Kuwait, the young Shī'ī shopkeepers, mechanics, bakers, and laborers kept up with the religio-political events of Iran; how far they were organized into *dasta* groups, listened to *rauzas*, had *majlis madhhabī*s or Sūfī *khānaqāh*s, however, is unclear. A Shī'ī leader annually visited al-Hasā from Najaf; a second rank *marja'-i taqlīd* (highest religious authority) resides in Kuwait; and periodic missions are sent out from Qum to Bahrain and the other Gulf communities.

Wahhābism

As Shī'ism unified Iran, Wahhābism unified Sa'ūdī Arabia. In both cases, what began as a tool of state consolidation became a conservative brake on state policy. But while Shī'ism utilizes a rich array of dramatic, physical, visual, and psychological devices—passion plays, poetic chanting, rhythmic flagellation, shrines, banners, and portraits—Wahhābism is starkly iconoclastic, rejecting shrines, pictures, and music as idolatry. Further, the leadership of Wahhābism is much more tied to a hereditary family allied to the large but also family-controlled political system. Technically, it is wrong to refer to the religion of the Sa'ūdī state as Wahhābism. Muhammad ibn 'Abd al-Wahhāb (1703–92) began a reform that his followers call *al-da'wa ilā 'l tauhīd* ["return to the unity of God"]. As a unifying movement, it had two major phases: one in the eighteenth and early nineteenth century, and one in the twentieth century.

In the eighteenth century, the towns of the Arabian Peninsula had leaderships with various religious leanings: Najrān was Ismā'īlī Shī'ī, highland Yemen was Zaidī Shī'ī, Oman was Ibādī, al-Qatīf was Twelver Shī'ī, al-Hasā was Shāfi'ī Sunnī, 'Uyaina was Hanbalī Sunnī. Ibn 'Abd al-Wahhāb, after being banned from his home town 'Uyaina at the request of the Banū Khālid, made a political and marital alliance with the Āl Sa'ūd of the town of Dir'iyya. Beginning with raids on caravans, much as had Muhammad from Medina twelve centuries earlier, the Wahhābīs gradually gained control of Riyadh (1773), al-Qatīf (1792), Mecca (1803), Medina (1805), and made forays as far afield as Damascus, Yemen, and the Buraimī oasis on the border of Oman. Local Hanbalī populations along the

Gulf aided their advance in that direction, and the Banū Bū ʿAlī joined in their cause, remaining faithful to the present. (The Wahhābīs follow the Hanbalī legal school.) When they took a city, but also in their temporary forays, they destroyed shrines, musical instruments, and water pipes. Shīʿī still bitterly remember the destructive attack on the shrines of Karbalā in 1802. The early expansion, however, was broken by Ottoman-Egyptian advances into the Hijāz, and Ottoman-Iraqi advances into the Eastern provinces (taking administrative control for a time of al-Hasā, if having little control on the roads outside). In the middle, the Āl Rashīd expanded from Hāʾil and took Riyadh. The Saʿūd family retreated to Kuwait.

In 1902, ʿAbd al-ʿAzīz ibn ʿAbd al-Rahmān Āl Faisal Āl Saʿūd began the consolidation that created the Saʿūdī Arabian state in 1932, by taking Riyadh (1902), al-Hasā and al-Qatīf (1913), and, in the 1920s, ʿAsīr, Jabal Shammar (the homeland of the Āl Rashīd) and the Hijāz (1925). He organized his tribal followers into a fighting brotherhood (*Ikhwān*), and attempted to settle the bedouin in some two hundred agricultural colonies. The Ikhwān rapidly became an embarrassment by raiding across the borders of Iraq and Transjordan on the ideological grounds of jihād against the unbelievers who needed to be returned to true Islam. ʿAbd al-ʿAzīz had to defeat them with nontribal troops, and tribal levies are now only one component of the state's military. But the other arm of Wahhābism—the influence of the ʿulamā—is still in a process of negotiation. Indeed, to outsiders this latter is a drama of absorbing interest: reports of public beheadings at noon on Friday by hereditary executioners; objections to radio, television, and cinema; segregation even of university women; a special police to enforce attendance at mosque; bans on liquor and music; and female veiling.

From the beginning of the modern Saʿūdī state, the rulers have moved steadily, if slowly, to moderate Wahhābism without destroying its ideological force. In the 1930s, when oil prospecting was hampered by the ban on telephone and radio communication, Ibn Saʿūd is said to have convened the ʿulamā and by reading the Qurʾān over the air convinced them these new devices were aids to the propagation of Islam. In 1965, when television was introduced, large amounts of air time were devoted to religious programming for similar reasons; nonetheless, King Faisal's nephew, Khālid ibn Musāʿid, led an attack on the transmitter that had to be put down by troops. Troops were also required to open the first schools for girls. Until 1970, the Muftī and chief Qādī was of the Āl Shaikh (family of Ibn ʿAbd al-Wahhāb); when the last Muftī died, the post was not filled, but a Ministry of Justice was created and a Jeddah judge raised to be the first minister. The old Muftī was a champion of the Morals Police, and now, except during Ramadān, the month of fast, they have become less intrusive; as Rugh (1973) puts it, "they no longer enter private homes, stop people from smoking or playing music or get them to go to the mosque," but they are still around. The minister of education was still a member of the Āl Shaikh, but he had a secular education (local degree) and in 1971 had been given two deputies, one with a B.A. and the other a Ph.D. from the United States. The first secular high schools were financed by Hijāzī merchants, but by 1957 there was a secular university in Riyadh, and university education is being expanded rapidly both at home and by sending students abroad. Women are taught in separate facilities. But plans to have international hotels with separate entrances for men and women were scrapped when the Intercontinental Hotel in Riyadh was built in 1971. There are no public cinemas or films shown on television, but films are shown on international flights of Saʻūdī Airlines, and private films and cassette televisions abound. In 1975, a ban on contraceptives was imposed officially because of a decision of the World Muslim League, but more likely on the basis of a calculated need for more Saʻūdī labor.

The dynamics of Wahhābism are poorly described in the literature. As a puritanizing force, it clearly met much resistance, and is currently held in check by a leadership that still finds it a useful tool in the delicate attempt to modernize without losing control. Ibn ʻAbd al-Wahhāb's cutting down of sacred trees, razing a revered tomb, and stoning an adulterous woman in his hometown led to his expulsion. The cosmopolitan Hijāzīs and the non-Wahhābi Hasawīs have chafed under his successors. Their brandishments of the Protocols of Zion, preachings against alcohol, tobacco, music, and so on, are respected in public but ignored as much as possible in private, except when politically useful. The Āl Shaikh are heavily intermarried with the Āl Saʻūd and they have a weekly Thursday audience with the king, but their influence is clearly being dampened. With the death of the religious but pragmatic King Faisal, a more modern, technocratic leadership seems to be forming, though speculation is still rife about what could happen if there was an army coup, as in Libya, and whether the Jordanian-trained bedouin National Guard would resurrect a Wahhābi counter to any Western, socialist-inspired ideas. Clearly, a good anthropological study of the dynamics of Wahhābism is needed, and as the pace of change increases, such a study will become ever more interesting.

Ibādism

Ibādism today occurs in the interior of Oman and displays some sociological patterns not yet discussed: a living Iman, and a moeity factionalism, as arbitors in a tribalized society. Wilkinson has suggested (1972) also that Ibādism is productive of egalitarianism in an area of the Muslim world where hierarchy is well developed, almost to caste-like form.

Omani society has developed through a fascinating interplay between maritime commerce, coastal irrigation agriculture, and mountain mixed husbandry and agriculture. The ancient Persians (both Achaemenids and Sasanians) colonized the coast, constructing underground irrigation canals (qanāts), appropriating the coastal spice trade, and exacting tribute from the mountain folk through the Julandā vassal family. In the second century A.D., a great influx of Arab tribes came into the area, divided between the southern, or Qahtānī, tribes coming from the Hadramaut via Dhofār, and the northern, or ʻAdnānī, tribes coming via the Buraimī oasis. Islam and the rule of the Ummayyad Caliphate used Omani troops to conquer Khorasan and put down revolts. When the Ummayyads fell and the troops returned home, they brought a new brand of Islam, an off-shoot of the Khawārij (those who rejected both Sunnī Ummayyad and ʻAlid (Shīʻī) claims to the caliphate). This Omani offshoot was called Ibādī, after the reformer

'Abdullāh ibn Ibād of Nizwa; an important characteristic was open election of the Imām. Julandā hegemony was overthrown, and the first Imām was elected in the ninth century.

Coastal colonization from across the waters occurred periodically by the Abbasids (called in during a factional dispute; they destroyed much of the irrigation system), Carmathians, Buwayhids, and Seljuks. In the sixteenth century, the coastal trade was controlled by the Portuguese (the Ottomans briefly took Muscat; the Persians, with English aid, took Suḥār and Khār Fakkān). But in the seventeenth century there was an Omani renaissance under Imāms of the Ya'rubī mountain tribes, who, using the Ibādī banner to mobilize, retook Suḥār and Muscat and put the Portuguese on the defensive everywhere in the Indian Ocean.

The financial basis of the Imāmate decisively shifted from the mountains to taxes from the maritime trade. This was not accomplished without a serious civil war led by conservative Ibādīs of the Banū Hinā protesting the luxuries and worldliness of the Imāms. The two sides of the civil war were called Hināwī and Ghāfirī, after two leading tribes on each side; interestingly, the Hināwī-Ghāfirī split roughly falls along both the old Qahtānī-'Adnānī lines and an Ibādī-Sūnnī split. The victorious Āl Bū Sa'īd dynasty in the nineteenth century gave up the title Imām for that of Sultan. As a result, mountain opposition could continue to be organized under the banner of an elected Imām.

Part of the impetus for a renewal of the Imāmate came from opposition to Wahhābī advances, and part from opposition to the Sultan. In the mid-1950s, the Imām Ghālib ibn 'Alī became the center of a rebellion, with Sa'ūdī and Egyptian aid, declaring an independent state (1954), an Oman Liberation Army (1957–59), and eventually, when defeated by British and Omani forces, guerrilla warfare. There were serious reasons for revolt both in the highlands and in Dhofār, where rebellion broke out in 1963, aided first by the Sa'ūdīs, then by the U.S.S.R., Iraq, and China. Among these reasons were the refusal of Sultan Sa'īd ibn Taimūr (r. 1932–70) to open schools, medical facilities, or economic development programs. Omanis went abroad to universities in Iraq, Syria, Egypt, and Algeria; while Dhofārīs, who had been recognized as industrious and quick-learning workers in the Gulf, also went abroad for training.

Just why a previously mercantile-oriented, and throughout British-advised, sultanate was allowed so to stagnate and regress has yet to be satisfactorily explained. With the overthrow of Sultan Sa'īd in 1970, the expansion of development programs made possible by oil production from 1967 on, the military aid of Iran, Sa'ūdī Arabia, and Jordan against the Dhofār rebellion, and the assignment of important ambassadorships to the Imām Ghālib's nephews, the new regime of Sultan Qābūs appears set on a reasonable path toward modernization and relief of the worst of past complaints.

Three observations are in order here about religion, about the vocabulary of factional feuding, and about stratification. First, in regard to religion: while political details of the above sketch can be found in various accounts, as can a few details on commerce and Ibādī doctrine, practically no accounts exist of how Ibādism organized community life or contemplative thought. An elective Imām clearly is different from the hereditary but occulted Imām of the Twelver

Shī'īs, and from the hereditary but living Imām of the Ismā'īlīs; but to treat it as merely a political office surely is inadequate. In the Shī'ī case, the 'ulamā became an important deliberative and guiding body; in the Ismā'īlī case, a remarkably effective, hierarchical organization was created; what can one say of Ibādism as a religious community, not merely as a religious doctrine?

Second, regarding politics and factionalism. Accounts of Omani history (e.g., Wilkinson 1972) use an uneven mixture of feudalism, Ibn Khaldūn's cyclical model of tribal power, and moeity-factional designations (Qahtānī-'Adnānī, Azd/Yemenī-Nizārī, Hinawī-Ghāfirī, Ibādī-Sunnī). Wilkinson attributes feudal elements to the decay of Sasanian organization, but basically describes the history of the first Ibādī Imāmate in terms of Ibn Khaldūn's cyclical scheme: decentralized military power unified under a leadership crystallizing into a hereditary power with consequent lessening of ideological attention, and, in turn, a weakening of commitment to the leadership; struggle for power, civil war; and then a new cycle of centralization and decay. The decay and civil war came as a dispute between regions (coastal and mountain), between an Azd confederation and a confederation in the north. The northern confederation called in the Abbasids, presenting the issue as a fight between Yemenī and Nizārī factions. In the aftermath, as Ibādī power was reconsolidated, members of the northern confederation were declared heretics and, in consequence, a number of 'ulamā in the north began to subscribe to Sunnī legal schools and to convert the northern tribesmen. Further consideration of the factional names invoked may prove interesting. Qahtān, 'Adnān, Nizār, and Azd are all genealogical names of Arab ancestry; they and other names from the legendary past are repeatedly used in Islamic history to define sides.

Furthermore, in many parts of the Islamic world, there is an ill-understood pattern of dividing communities or localities into opposing groups so as to maintain peace through competition or balance of power: thus, cities in Iran were until recently divided into Haidarī and Ni'matī halves; in the Atlas mountains of Morocco, Berber villages are arranged in checkerboard fashion between two *leff* (parties); in Kabyle society of Algeria a similar arrangement is called *soff*; in Palestine landed families allied themselves as Qaysī or Yemenī; in Yemen, the mountain Zaidīs are divided into Hashid and Bakin, and all Zaidīs together are opposed to the Shāfi'īs along a social division going back to pre-Islamic times; and, in Yemen, 'Adnānī meant "sayyid" (both northerner and descendant of the Prophet and thus kin with the ruling Imām), while Qahtānī meant "indigenous" (in the post-royalist era, no one is a sayyid or 'Adnānī any more). In other words, if a similar localized pattern exists in central Oman, then a clearer understanding of the tribal dynamics of the area may be defined than the attempt to identify the names with inflexible kinship units, economic areas, and hsitorically continuous ethnic groups, i.e., we may have a flexible vocabulary of feud and competition.

Third, in regard to stratification. It appears that Ibādī central Oman was much more egalitarian than either northern Oman or the almost caste-like Sunnī Dhofār and the Hadramaut. Dhofār has two dominant confederations: the Āl Kahtīr on the coast and the Qāra in the mountains (some of whom are said to be only partially Islamicized, in that prayers are said facing the sun rather than Mecca). In the Qāra area there is an aristocratic class of sayyids (Hāshimīs) and a servile class called Shahara. Kelly (1976) too simply attributes the rigid stratification to intercourse with India. Wilkinson somewhat more subtly contrasts the use of the terms *bayāsir* (servant, client, but not slave) and *bayādir* (laborer, free but property-less) in Ibādī central Oman and in northern Oman, where they are more degrading, as reflecting differential decay of an original Sasanian feudal organization into more and less egalitarian tribal hierarchies. Bayāsira, he speculates, were the captives or pre-Arab populations that did not have a *nisba* (genealogical name), and certainly not one of the names of the noble tribes (see also above, on Kuwait). The Bayādir (Persian *bī-dar*, "without property"?) are agricultural laborers, and the term may be a Sasanian category for the people who manned their irrigation agriculture. In Ibādī areas, bayādir tend to assimilate to Arab tribes: they adopt nisbas and are allowed to intermarry, and their agricultural labor is not considered degrading. In northern Oman, bayādir are more nearly like bayāsira, looked down upon as dependents or clients (*mawālī* in early Islamic terminology). In Dhofār and the Hadramaut, which broke away from Ibādī influence in the eleventh century, a strong hierarchy developed, with saintly families mediating between armed tribes and agriculturalists looked down on, with strong marriage barriers between the different strata (see Bujra 1971 and Kelly 1976). Wilkinson's suggestion is that Ibādīs do not recognize families with *baraka* (charisma), and so stratification based on descent status could not develop. Such speculations are worth further exploration.

Modern Political Ideologies

Religious ideologies remain potent forces, but with the rise of modern economies and secular education, political ideologies have also come to the fore, albeit within settings quite different from the original European homes of these ideologies. The pressures toward constitutional rule, admission of men of middle- and lower-class background to positions of power, and the organization of labor have included organizations such as the Movement of Arab Nationalists (Kuwait, Oman, Yemen); the CNU (Committee for National Union) (Bahrain), and its partial successor, the Front of Progressive Forces (including communists and Baathists); the National Front in Iran (including Tudeh communists, republical nationalists, and religious conservatives); the Arabian Peninsula People's Union (Saʿūdī Arabia); the Popular Front for the Liberation of Oman and the Arab Gulf (Oman, and to a minor extent Bahrain).

The Bahrain case is one of the simpler ones. The CNU provided the leadership for the 1954–56 labor strikes in the oil industry. With newspaper support, demands were for improved working conditions, unions, government reform, a lessened British role, and individual freedoms. The CNU briefly gained recognition from the shaikh to negotiate for the workers, and while this recognition was later withdrawn, the agitation eventually achieved the drafting of a labor ordinance in 1958. As soon as the government regained full control, in 1956, the CNU was suppressed, its press closed, and three of its leaders exiled. Nakhleh, who chronicles the history of subsequent strikes both inside and outside the oil industry (1965, 1968, 1970, 1971, 1972), argues that the refusal of the authorities to be more flexible toward their workers has driven labor to politicize its demands. Every labor strike becomes a political crisis: demands for better pay, conditions, and benefits rapidly become joined to calls for freedom of speech, assembly, press, release of political prisoners, removal of expatriates, and overthrow of the government. Labor leaders and journalists who support them regularly are jailed or exiled.

So far, most of the oil industries in the Gulf have successfully prevented the development of open union negotiations and often retracted offers of other forms of contractual arbitration procedures. The two most liberal states seem to be Qatar and Kuwait: Qatar allows workers committees to help handle grievances; Kuwait allows unions, but only for persons employed in the same job at least five years; no non-Kuwaiti may be an officer. Very little study of labor organization has been allowed or made public. Pauling (1964) speaks of studies and consequent policy changes by Aramco, in an attempt to stabilize their labor force and teach industrial discipline. Between 1945 and 1959, Aramco employed an average of 11,728 Saʻūdīs; to maintain this work force, more than 56,000 Saʻūdīs were hired over the fifteen-year period. Economic bonuses had little effect on this volatility, but in 1953 a Saʻūdī Test for Job Assignment had a positive effect on selecting workers who would remain on the job. No details are given, but Pauling stresses the problems of social and psychological adjustment in training preindustrial labor. It seems, however, that Aramco gave up trying to use bedouin labor and, instead, started to employ Shīʻī, a minority and hence, perhaps, more docile.

Much of the Gulf labor force is imported, and it is argued that the workers are given little security to keep them docile and difficult to organize by leftists. High barriers on eligibility for citizenship and ownership of property by aliens characterize all the Gulf states. They fear that to liberalize labor negotiation procedures and citizenship requirements would lead to the takeover of the political arena by foreigners. In 1975, there were as many Yemenis working in Saʻūdī Arabia as there were Saʻūdī adult males, and as much as a quarter or a third of the total population was foreign; in the next five years, the foreign population was expected to double. Of Qatar's labor force, 40,000 of the 48,000 members are non-Qatari. Over a third of the UAE total population is foreign, 64 percent of Abū Dhabī's population, and over half of Kuwait's; three-quarters of the labor force in these places is foreign. Only 20 percent of Bahrain's total population, but 37 percent of its labor force, is foreign. Iran before the revolution had well over 60,000 foreigners, and Iraq has some 30,000 Egyptians alone. Normal abuses of this kind of guest labor are best documented for Kuwait: illegal aliens having to pay a percentage of their earnings to contractors so as not to be deported; crowding; deportation for minor scrapes with the law; lack of access to the welfare system. State education in Kuwait is free, but only 10 percent of the student body may be non-Kuwaiti; in the university these places are largely reserved for citizens of the Emirates.

If an analysis of the working-class situation leads to questions of control and conservatism on the part of the ruling strata, the analysis of the rising new professional class leads to questions of constitutional change and replacement of shaikhly family rule by technocrats. Rugh (1973) provides a summary of changes in the elite of Saʻūdī Arabia. In the 1950s, only one ministerial post was not held by a royal prince or a protégé of the family: the Minister of Commerce was from a Jeddah merchant family. In 1960, King Sa'ūd gave five ministerial posts to commoners educated abroad (four in Cairo and one in Texas); five posts were held by princes and one by a member of the al-Shaikh family descended from the founder of Wahhābism. In 1969, under King Faisal, of 189 top bureaucratic posts (grade 2 and up), 45 had Western training, 111 had Arabic secular training, and only 31 had traditional religious education. In 1970–71, the Grand Mufti of the al-Shaikh family died and was replaced by a minister of justice from the ranks of the Jeddah judges. Only the Ministry of Education was still held by an al-Shaikh family member, but his two deputies were American educated (one a B.A. degree, the other a doctorate).

The smaller Gulf states are also undergoing a transition from rule by shaikh families, sometimes in concert with merchant families (as in Kuwait), to more technocratically trained elites, but they are further behind. The UAE has retained Jordanian, Sudanese, and Iraqi judges until local ones can be trained, Abū Dhabī relies heavily on Indian and Pakistani administrators, and Qatar's teachers are largely Egyptian.

One index of change is pressures toward constitutional rule and away from the more informal consultation by shaikhs through daily or occasional *majlis* (audiences). The majlis of the governor of Hofuf have shown a shift, with the shift in social power from a predominance of tribal chiefs to a predominance of merchants. In Kuwait, a parliament existed from 1962 to 1975, when pressures from Palestinian agitation threatened its stability. In Bahrain, strikes and demonstrations since the 1950s gradually expanded the representation of Shī'ītes and commoners in the top ranks of government; in 1972 and 1973, elections were held for a constituent assembly to draw up a constitution and then for a national assembly; the latter was dissolved in 1975, when the government failed in its attempt to pass a security law. Qatar in 1970 became the first of the Emirates to have a written constitution, but the assembly was not instituted. All of these consultative forms have had extremely limited power and autonomy, yet their very existence in a hostile environment (of rulers reluctant to delegate power) serves as an indicator of shifts in social power. A more sensitive index would be a careful analysis of the circles and clubs to which active members of society belong and which form a kind of shadow-influence network. In Sa'ūdī Arabia, while three named opposition groups have existed since 1956—the National Liberation Front (pro-Soviet in 1956), the Arabian Peninsula People's Union (pro-Nasser, it claimed responsibility for a series of bombings in 1966–67 of Tapline, the U.S. military headquarters in Riyadh, two palaces, and a Sa'ūdī airbase near Yemen), the Popular Democratic Party (formed in 1970 by Baathists and Nasserites)—they have been ineffective; more effective is the constant pressure of notable and merchant families in the Hijāz (anti-Wahhābī puritanism, pro-liberalization) and the slowly growing cadre of educated professionals. Discontent at various other levels is occasionally expressed: a three-week strike in the oil fields in 1953 yielded shorter hours and higher pay; an antiroyal demonstration greeted King Sa'ūd when he visited Dammān in 1956; in 1969, the commander of the Dharān airbase and 2,000 others were arrested in a security clamp down; and in 1970 thirty people were arrested in the Eastern Province, including the dean of the Petroleum College.

Of the countries bordering on the Gulf before 1979, only Iraq had seen a social revolution in the class origin of the rulers: even in the 1920s the nationalists who exercised much influence often came from the middle or lower-middle classes, educated in Istambul; since 1958, the leadership has been strongly middle class by both criteria of one's father's occupation and one's own education. Thirty-six percent of the 177-member top elite were educated abroad, 28 percent were educated at the Military Academy, and 22 percent at the Baghdad Law College (Marr 1975). Yet Iraq has had difficulty undertaking the radical reforms called for in its Baathist ideology. Part of the problem again is control. Iraq is divided into three ethnic groups: 55 percent are Shī'ī, 25 percent are Sunnī, and 20 percent are Kurds. The Sunnīs dominate the political arena, having controlled half the political posts since 1958 and 80 percent of the top posts. This dominance is a perpetuation of the favoritism shown by the Ottomans to their coreligionists in the last century. The regime thus is an authoritarian one with ethnic competition complicating party alliances and the dislocations of modernization.

Iran has three times attempted a bourgeois revolution. In 1906, an alliance of liberals, radicals, and religious leaders was able to gain a constitution. The achievement of a republic was blocked in 1921, in part by the religious leaders. In 1952–53, the National Front alliance was briefly able to drive the shah from the country, but failed to achieve a nationalized oil industry or a restoration of republican ideals. In 1977–79, an alliance of students, radicals, two guerila organizations, the National Front, the religious hierarchy, the bazaar, the oil workers, the bank staffs, the civil service, and virtually every other sector of society drove the shah from the country again. Of the many causes of the revolution, two of the patterns discussed for other Gulf countries may be noted clearly in Iran. First, the growth of an educated, technocratic middle class, anxious for political participation: of 401 directors-general in the bureaucracy in 1970, only 2 percent had less than a secondary education, 90 percent had at least a B.A., and 20 percent had a Ph.D. Among parliament members, by 1941–63, 36 percent had B.A.s; in the 1963–67 parliament fully a third were educated abroad, as were 90 percent of the cabinet ministers between 1965 and 1974. Second, Iran showed in an exaggerated way, growing much worse with the post-1973 oil revenue increases, the vicious circle in an authoritarian modernizing monarchy of destroying local initiative and self-reliance on which self-sustaining economic growth depends in the name of speeding development and protecting against reaction by innovation from above.

Finally, there is the case of Oman and the Dhofār rebellion. Against a sultan opposed to any progress, the revolutionary movement attempted a wide range of development initiatives: two schools with 850 students by 1973, one-quarter of them female; the organization of agricultural cooperatives, with modern agricultural techniques; a clinic manned by a Syrian doctor; local-level councils to mediate disputes; a mass-education campaign stressing socialism, the need for revolutionary struggle, equality of women; as well as fighting a militant guerila war. The leadership seems to have been university educated in Beirut, Kuwait, and Egypt; others had foreign guerila training; much of the social support came from the many Dhofārīs who could find work in the Gulf but not at home. This is not the place to review the story of how the rebellion was competitively supported by the Russians and the Chinese, then crushed with the support of Saʿūdī Arabia, Jordan, and Iran; but rather to point out a measure of political consciousness and a pool of emigrant labor (some 30,000 Omanis are listed in the Kuwait and Bahrain censuses alone) on which the new sultan (the son, incidentally, of a Qāra mother from Dhofār) can call if he is responsive to their demands.

One thing that a survey of leftist oppositional groups teaches us is the relative weakness of the middle classes, who provide the intelligentsia for these groups, as well as the weakness of the working-class organizations that are supposed to provide the rank and file. More detailed studies than have yet been attempted are required to illuminate the contradictions and dialectical adjustments between ideological positions and status and social power. Lenczowski, for instance, commented in 1947 about the Iranian Tudeh, both in opposition and those who had seized power in Azarbaijan, that their demands were liberal, not revolutionary: liberal labor legislation, legalization of unions, better peasant conditions, free education and health care, equality for minorities and women, judicial reform, constitutional government; but not nationalization of property nor collectivization. In Azarbaijan, only absentee landlords were expropriated; there was no general land reform. One strategy of those in power to remain in power is to coopt the most pressing demands of critics: thus the White Revolution of the Shah promised land reform, state farms, collectivization, nationalization of forests and water resources, expansion of health care and education, equality for minorities and women. In Iraq, some of the contradictions are clearest: a ruling alliance of Baathists and communists is but a thin veneer over sharp ethnic group competition. The original Baath hope to use a generalized Islam as less religion than a rallying slogan of pan-Arabism (formulated by Michel Aflaq, a Greek Orthodox Christian) is rejected in Iraq, as the Sunnī Islam of the dominant politicians from the area around Takrīt; similarly, the communists are split into a pro-Moscow faction, and a Shīʿī southern supported, "pro-Peking" faction. In Oman, the PLOAG was militantly atheistic, thereby alienating much potential support.

Neither political ideology nor education nor health are simple tools to progress. Just as ideologies are complicated and hedged by the status and organizations of their carriers, so education and health are not simply indexed by growing numbers of children in school, or hospital beds and doctors. In the case of education, Iran perhaps again provides the most developed example: the oldest system of modern secular education (begun slowly in the late nineteenth and early twentieth centuries, and greatly expanded in the 1930s and again in the 1960s), the system with the greatest number of students, and the system first to experience overexpansion of academic degree holders and underdevelopment of technical and managerial personnel. The educational system was reorganized in 1965 to better fit it to labor force requirements. Statistics on development of educational facilities are available, but little qualitative evaluation of what is learned. Nor has much attention been paid to the effect of the large number of students trained at foreign universities (some 30,000 students study at U.S. colleges and universities alone), especially the effect of the political system in cushioning and slowing but also adopting new ideas and initiatives.

The political system until 1978–79 consisted of a monarch, who claimed a tradition going back to pre-Islamic times (thereby attempting to by-pass the 'ulamā as protectors of tradition), a barely acknowledged constitution and parliament (thereby by-passing an imperfect, to say the least, election system, on the theory of dealing directly with the people), and a patronage network of competing power centers (strong men who had their own groups of followers who could be shifted about by the Shah in a game of chess). Such a system absorbed people into the patronage net without allowing them to restructure the system: influence of new people was diffused until they were tested and became part of the system. The bureaucracy is not simply a bureaucracy but has Persian rules of play.

Health care, like education, has dual goals. There are the first line objectives: literacy in the case of education. In the case of health care, eradication of endemic diseases: malaria, tuberculosis, bilharzia, dysenteries, plague (earlier in the century), cholera, high infant mortalities (Iran's figure is 104/1000 live births, Sa'ūdī Arabia's 152/1000). But after these important and critical first objectives are under control, if not yet fully achieved, there are other goals having to do with alleviation of stress and enhancing the quality of life. Until 1949, Kuwait only had one hospital, run by American missionaries; by 1967 Kuwait had 547 doctors, a ratio of one per every 690 inhabitants, one of the highest in the world. Sa'ūdī Arabia in the 1950s began a crash hospital building program, so that by 1964 it had 67 hospitals, 157 clinics, and 243 dispensaries, with 510 doctors and 540 nurses. After the 1970 coup Oman immediately began building 4 hospitals to supplement the 2 run by American missionaries and the one old charity hospital. In Iran, again the problem was less the number of doctors and facilities than their distribution; in an attempt to get some more doctors into rural areas, doctors were imported from Pakistan and the Philippines. The public standard of sanitation in all these places is beginning to rise dramatically. Having paid tribute to these most important initiatives and accomplishments, let us finally turn to more qualitative aspects of culture and mental health in the Gulf.

Human Development and Community

Among the most crucial and least well described, let alone analyzed, elements of life in the Gulf region are notions of personhood and cultural meaning. In the superficial account that we do have, such things are recognized as critical, but they are apprehended only in the misleading terms of either national character ("why Arabs or Persians are 'lazy', 'deceitful', 'individualist to the point of lacking responsibility', 'nepotistic'," etc.), or social evolution (how the Middle East is emerging from tribalisms, feudalisms, etc.), or cultural mosaics (primordial fractious and fanatic ethnic and religious loyalties). Such things are repeatedly invoked by planners who want to transform the labor force, and political scientists who seek out bases of legitimacy that might hold a state together. Anthropological accounts will not offer global or complete answers, but they can help refine understanding and thereby provide the basis for better communication.

Three interrelated issues may serve as illustrative foci: notions of community and hierarchy; notions of propriety, of gender definition, and of self and other; and notions of illness and restoration to health.

Community and Hierarchy

Popular imagery of the Middle East tends to stress Islam and tribalism as sources of strong egalitarianism and individualism, and imperial court traditions and urban wealth distinctions as sources of hierarchy. These are at best first approximations. Court and urban linguistic forms encourage duels of wit and repartee that allow for the equality of all human beings and the reranking of players according to skill or moral stature. Thus the folklore and occasional reality of lower-class men who become prime ministers, and the counterpoint ideology of being *darvīsh*, that is, not observing ordinary etiquette and status-assertion rules. It is possible, if not very enlightening, to argue that repartee comes from a tribal heritage, where it served as a primary means of creating honor and social order, and darvīsh from Islamic Sūfism; more challenging and realistic is to recognize that forms of social interaction are highly context-restricted, and that what marks a true Middle Eastern sophisticate is an ability to handle a large range of interaction styles. Similarly, Islam and tribalism cannot be forced easily into simple egalitarianism: tribal societies of the Arabian peninsula and surrounding areas ranked themselves by purity of blood and respectability of ancestry into endogamous lineage groups; early Islam utilized distinctions of family leadership (be it 'Alid or Quraish) versus commoner followership, immediate converts versus later converts, and Arabs versus non-Arabs; and medieval Islam adopted both the ancient (Zoroastrian, Greek, and Hindu) notions of four endogamous strata of society, and the tribal notion of marrying only status equals (*kafā'a*). Again, this is not to debunk the egalitarian claims of Islam, only to temper idealistic visions with historical context and reality.

Ritual forms often provide access to notions of community and hierarchy, for the same ritual can have different meanings and uses in different contexts. Thus, Goodell contrasts the observance of Ramadān in Rahmatābād village and in Byzun town (Khūzistān, Iran). In the village, one that prospered after being land-reformed, the fast is not taken seriously and no one fasts for more than a week: what is important is a clean heart; let those who do not have to work fast—the bureaucrats and shopkeepers who sit all day. In the depressed town of Byzun, a labor center for peasants thrown off the land, people take the fast with deadly seriousness, as an unpleasant spiritual and physical cleansing ordered by the Omnipotent who controls one's fate and therefore whom one must obey if one expects any mercy. Similarly, Goodell contrasts three readers of the Qur'ān during a wake. The mulla from the town read the Qur'ān as "a sermon in plainsong . . . a lesson in piety and a call to the purity and strength of Shī'ī religion for which he is the agent. Outside of the community, yet with us, not as one of us but as a teacher, a guardian, he preached the holy poetry with a twinge of the townsman's ubiquitous self-consciousness, *showing* the Koran's beauty, *urging* devotion to it" (1977:360). Next she describes two villagers, friends of the deceased, reading in "such a muted, mellow expression that one could not understand any words, but the listener sensed a oneness, a pouring out of sorrow and faith like liquid over the bent heads. . . . This villager seemed . . . unaware at all of where he himself stopped and the community around him began, of chanting, of listening " (ibid.). Finally, she describes the health corpsman, an officious young man doing his national service:

When the deputy of the State took the holy book in hand and clasped it resolutely, he grasped the preeminence of loudspeaker and podium as well—indeed a vast piazza lay before him, like Red Square, filled with the masses awaiting his word . . . his chant reviewed the troops . . . the Arabic poetry now barked out in perfectly measured military cadences. . . . Only Mehrabani of the three readers ever stopped to ask for the correct pronunciation of a word (which he inquired of the mullah, but only after the full passage had been beaten out; then he would go back and repeat it as though we had hung on some important details of his command—as though the words . . . had to be spelled out for meticulous letter-of-the-law fulfillment!). On he goose-stepped through the Koran, lifting aloft, brilliantly ordering, putting everything precisely in its place (ibid.: 361–62).

Similar contrastive analysis have not been done for rituals in the Gulf, but a number of illustrative contrasts can be cited from nearby areas to indicate what needs to be done. Peasant feasting systems, for instance, can be used as egalitarian devices to redistribute food to the poor, engage members of the community in a rotating network of obligations and thereby also provide pressures to resolve minor disputes. On the Iranian plateau, this is what the Zoroastrian village feasting system of *gahambars*, *Khairats*, and *sofrehs* successfully seems to do, and the Muslim village *rauzehs* less successfully intend to do. By contrast, the feasting system of the villages of Nūristān in Eastern Afghanistan is a competitive means of gaining prestige and establishing a hierarchy within the village.

Similar hierarchical patterns developed at times among urban Zoroastrians: here the attempt is by giving feasts to the less well off; the rich tried to create clients and moral control over the community.

Community rituals in places that have differentiated classes or status groups are often used to mark and reinforce the stratification system. Thus Bujra (1971) describes how the major rituals of Ramadān in the town of Huraida are held in the mosque of the leading descent group, with a secondary ritual held in the mosque of the second-ranked group; how visiting patterns during the rituals provide ways of confirming the ranking system. Similarly, in Shī'ī passion plays (*ta'ziya*) commemorating the martyrdom of Imām Husain, parts are usually given out in ways congruent with status roles. M. Good (1977) further points out that in the town of Marāgheh processions during the Muharram celebrations mark the position and relative importance of the different participating status groups. By contrast, certain ritual settings deny the rankings of the outside society: thus the traditional Iranian gymnasium (*zūrkhāna*) has an elaborate ritual setting in which precedence is given to sayyids (as marks of respect not to them but to their ancestor, the Prophet), to those who have the longest experience in the zūrkhāna, and to those with the greatest skill. The egalitarian nature of the zūrkhāna is symbolized by the tiny door through which traditionally one entered, so that even the greatest and largest athlete should have to humbly bend and squeeze through.

Sayyid status, not as in the zūrkhāna, but directly appropriated as a claim to special consideration and authority, has been a major hierarchical technique in the Middle East. Sūfī saints and their followers are a frequent, if minor case. More important are cases such as in Yemen, where sayyids were able to become the ruling class. Bujra describes for Huraida how—at least in oral tradition—the Sāda (plural of sayyid) mediated disputes in Huraida and were asked to remain to keep the peace among the tribes and between the tribes and the agricultural folk. A ranked society of Sāda, Mashā'ikh (settled, but with religious claims), Gabā'il (tribesmen), and Masākīn (weak agriculturalists) evolved. A very similar stratified society arose in Baluchistan without a sayyid ruling class. One legend tells that Adam had four sons; one day a wind raised Adam's cloak and exposed his private parts; one son felt shame and thus became the ancestor of the rulers (hākim); two sons laughed and were made the peasants and slaves (hizmatkār, ghulām); and one son said nothing and became a tribal pastoralist (balūch). slavery was only abolished in Baluchistan in the 1920s and in Sa'ūdī Arabia in 1962, and education, as already indicated, is slowly changing the bases of stratification.

In sum, Zoroastrian, Greek, Hindu, Byzantine, and medieval Islamic traditions provide a model of the properly functioning society as hierarchical, with four social strata, each performing a unique task necessary for the maintenance of the whole. The Islamic notion of a community of believers (umma) was always contextually restricted by sectarian considerations and the requirements of statecraft. Only at the hajj are these largely overridden. In a cosmopolitan world, including significant non-Muslim groups, the notion of umma itself is sectarian. Sūfism provided a counterpoint with less stress on community and more on individual righteousness. Above all, even in the Gulf area itself, there was enough intellectual ferment to generate social support for new Islamic movements in addition to the major sects: e.g., the Mahdist movement called Zikrism in Baluchistan, the Shaikhīs in al-Hasā and on the Iranian plateau, Bābism that shook Iran in the nineteenth century before becoming the more quietistic Bahā'ism.

Style, Gender, and Self

If little attention has yet been paid to the pragmatics of ritual, even less has been paid to the codes and rules of interpersonal relations. Phrases like the "economy of honor," the "theater of hospitality," the "paradox of the Arabians' dual lives" (interior and exterior; in their domestic setting, passing with ease abroad), and play for prestige serve well as first approximation evocation and can be attached to anecdotes out of a contemporary *Thousand and One Nights*:

(The Arabian) approach to life is so intensely personal . . . the goal is not to get the job done, or even to acquire a fortune; rather it is to win prestige in other men's eyes and achieve a fame tantamount to a state of grace . . . the regular economy was largely subordinate to an economy of honor . . . no one ever moves business forward at the expense of social rituals . . . their theater of hospitality is probably the most vital of Arabian art forms. It provides an occasion for making grand, Gatsby-like gestures, from which they derive enormous pleasure. . . . When the hijacked Lufthansa jet landed in Dubai this fall, there was little to do while the negotiations went on except surround the plane with troops; Prince Muhammad bin Rashid, the United Arab Emirates' Minister of Defense, used the occasion to treat the hostages to champagne and to send a birthday cake aboard for one of the stewardesses. . . . There are many attractions to life abroad, but I suspect what is most important to the Saudis is that they are offstage for a while, relieved of the demanding role of being Saudis before an audience of other Saudis. At home they are under intense pressure to maintain the appearance of self-effacing modesty and avoid any conspicuous display of self . . . the thought of killing (time) has never crossed their minds . . . the result is chaos. . . . The Saudis, however, are inured to the disorder, and amid loose cash, dust, and confusion, they come and go like so many chevaliers (Iseman 1978: 49–51).

The burden of being Sa'ūdī before other Sa'ūdīs is in part a political burden imposed by the public order of Wahhābism. Similarly, in regard to Iran, Western political scientists speak of cynicism in a system designed to be insecure for everyone except those at the very top (Zonis 1971), and describe intricate personalistic networks or webs of influence (Bill 1972) in which one works behind the scenes using the "three *p* s": *pul* (money), *parti* (pull, Arabic *wasta*), and *pur rūhi* (assertiveness). Mention has already been made of the circles and clubs that help compose these webs.

One linguist has collected examples of interactions in an attempt to illustrate the rules of linguistic countering, beginning with the elaborate politeness forms (*ta'āruf*) but pursuing usages to far more subtle levels, including basic phonemic and morphemic shifts (Beeman 1976). The Culture and Personality Circle, through a series of taped discussions and examples, has elaborated a dualistic notion of Persian self: in a corrupt world one must maintain a masque of cynicism and the attendant skills of indirection, ambiguity, and constant testing of others; but for self-respect, one must simultaneously protect an internal sense of purity, honesty, and directness (Bateson et al. 1977). Hence, the enormous concern to find true friends who will not disappoint you and with whom you can be this true self. The true self can be spoken of in two traditional ways: one is by using the darvīsh notion to devalue the rules of the artificial, insincere, and corrupt outer world; the other is the language of sexual honor: *nāmūs*, or that honor that is jeopardized by attacks on a man's womenfolk.

Modern Westerners have been fascinated by Middle Eastern rules of modesty, honor, and segregation of women. Sa'ūdī Arabia, with its occasional executions for improper sexual relations, its prohibition of women to drive automobiles, and its segregation even of university women from men, remains the center of this sort of attention; but veiling and the liberation of women have become symbolic measures of progress also in other countries, for westernized Middle Easterners as well as Westerners. In Iran, there has been increasing public education of girls since the 1920s, state pressure for the unveiling of women since 1928, admission to the university since 1940, enfranchisement since 1963, admittance into the literacy corps since 1968, granting of expanded legal rights to initiate divorce suits and making polygamy a possible ground for divorce since 1967, women members of majlis, senate, cabinet and, in 1976, the creation of a cabinet post for women's affairs. The contradictory pressures on young women to become educated, unveiled, active members of the labor force (supported by state propaganda and the state-funded Women's Organization, which provides literacy courses, vocational training, legal and family planning counsel) or to become good, modest Muslim women (supported by the 'ulamā and traditional family pressures) are enormous. They lead to a variety of interesting compromises, such as the reasonable question why veiling should in any way stop one from activities such as going to the university, working in an office, or driving a car.

The politics of women's liberation is a fascinating subject in its own right and has received attention in Egypt and North Africa (especially Algeria), but minimally in the Gulf states. In Kuwait, for instance, there are two women's organizations, one lobbying for greater freedom, the other for support of the traditional feminine protectedness. The leader of the former points out that educated women tend not to be her greatest supporters, because having been privileged they do not realize how difficult things are for the less privileged. The University of Kuwait opened in 1966 with separate facilities for women, and by 1969 nearly half of the student body were women, as were nearly half the returning degree holders from abroad; 41 percent of secondary school students were girls. Even more impressive is that many mothers of university women have been attending adult education classes since 1961. In Sa'ūdī Arabia, things are more difficult: the first schools for girls had to be opened by force in 1960. But by 1966, there were 50,870 girls in elementary schools, 81 in secondary schools, and 116 in teacher training schools; by 1978 there were said to have been 500,000 girls in school.

Anthropologically, more interesting even than either the statistics of gradual educational and occupational mobility for women or the politics of women's liberation are the cultural modes of engendering the world. Again, the most work has been done in North Africa, e.g., by Bourdieu on Kabyle society where, in good structuralist fashion, male/female notions are made to fall together with dry/wet, flat/swelling, hot/cold, and other oppositions, to generate rich contemplative devices for making the world pregnant with meaning. For Iran, all that has been established so far is that women and female symbols go together in a general sort of way with the management of emotions: divination always begins from one's mother's name, women have their own curing rituals, and many female legendary figures are central to religious practice and folk belief. That biological femininity and cultural definitions of the same need not be identical everywhere is brought home by the Fallers's (1976) suggestion that professional Turkish women are more independent and self-confident than their European counterparts because the greater separation of male and female worlds socializes them to be independent (with support from female networks) and treats women in the male world as sexually neutral.

But perhaps the most striking ethnographic observation comes from Oman, where segregation of the sexes is strict, that there is a third sexual category of male transvestites (khanīth). Nearly one in fifty adult males of Suhār town fit into this category: they move freely among women behind purdah, seeing their faces, eating with them, joining them at wedding celebrations; they dress in intermediate clothing, neither male nor female. They serve as prostitutes but eventually may marry and become men. Wikan hypothesizes that they are not allowed to dress fully as women (those who try are imprisoned and flogged), because that would imply an equivalence of prostitution and women and would thereby dishonor womanhood. The essence of womanhood is honor, to be protected by her menfolk. For a man to use a female prostitute always runs the risk of affronting another man's honor (especially where the prostitute may be a married woman, rather than a strict professional). To use a male prostitute is to affront no one's honor; it is to seek sexual release, not to demonstrate power over women. Wikan contrasts the ideals of Omani manhood (beautiful manners, dealing with one's sexual drives as correctly as possible) with the Mediterranean Don Juan complex, where dominance over women is important. Inveighing against the popular cliché that Muslims necessarily are oppressed, subjugated, and unhappy, this woman anthropologist suggests that "the Omani woman has an honoured and respected place in her society. She derives confidence from her knowledge that the man wins honor by treating her gracefully" (1977:316).

The above accounts raise a variety of interesting questions that require some examination of socialization and pressures within the family. No such studies exist. Hansen (1961, 1963, 1968) gives a few general comments on a Bahrainī Shīʿī village: that girls are taught to veil from age six, may go to Qurʾān schools until age ten, systematically put on veils in the village lanes by age twelve, are never excluded from female sexual banter, never go to the town to shop, veil laxly in the largely endogamous village, but should they go outside the village are heavily masked and veiled. The subject of homosexuality in Iran has been the subject of an anecdote collection by the Culture and Personality Circle and others, but the dynamics are still poorly understood, with comments ranging from traumatic seductions of youths (especially by the father), to suggestions that many males are so introduced to sex, but that, unlike in the West, homosexuality does not form a subculture apart from the constant male homosexual risqué banter, that most homosexuals are primarily heterosexuals, homosexuality having generally more to do with friendship than sex. Others have speculated on the connections between repression in the family and political violence in the freedom of student politics. Sexual dynamics in religious processions have been similarly noted (M. Good 1977). It has been suggested for Oman and Kurdistan, where segregation is strict, that the marriage night can be traumatic for grooms as well as for brides. Suicide studies in Iran indicate that at highest risk are students and young married women.

Given these glimmerings of a physics of emotion, perhaps one can understand why veiling as a symbol is both overrated and underrated in the West. It is overrated for it is not itself necessarily at issue: in Iran, the veil was outlawed in 1935–36 and when it was again allowed, it had been modified so as not to afford anonymity. Indeed, the veil is a moral device that is manipulable to reflect status, intimacy, religiosity, flirtatiousness, as well as modesty. It is underrated because the emotional contradictions of rules of propriety and demands of modernity, sexual repression and extroverted assertion make an unveiled woman provocative, and so many women want the protection and security of the veil, against the wishes of their husbands.

In sum, the goal is not psychosexual speculation, but rather to describe Middle Eastern behavior patterns in terms that the participants find compelling. First, approximation descriptions depend on metaphors and anecdotes. A second step is recognition of stylistic rules of interpersonal behavior and the cultural terminology in which they are expressed. A third step is to try to grasp the complicated and contradictory pressures that propel individuals, and among which they attempt to steer themselves.

Dances of Illness and Health

From the pragmatics of ritual, and the codes of interpersonal relations, one needs to penetrate further into the ways of regulating psychic health. The so-called *zār* cult of the Gulf is one such important way. The zār cult is known from Ethiopia and Egypt and is closely cognate with the curing rituals of Morocco practiced by the Hamādsha, but the best description so far comes from the Gulf, by the Iranian writer and physician Ghulām Husain Sa'īdī. Sa'īdī writes particularly of the world of poor fishermen and what is left of the old pearling crews, describing how relations between the spirit world and human beings are mediated by the drumming and singing "plays" (*bāzī*) of the *zār, jinn, parī, dīv, ghūl, nobān,* and *mashāyikh* (the various species of spirit):

The Gulf coasts of Iran are favorable striking grounds for psychic disorders and madness. Living on them means a constant exposure and vulnerability to all sorts of fears, anxieties and deprivations. It means a perpetual confrontation with the terrors of thirst, hunger, drowning, ever present sickness, death, exhaustion, and monotony. Sunk into a pervasive state of despondency, the coastal dwellers are forced into a constant preoccupation with themselves. No other shelter or source for security seems accessible to them, facing the hardships of their lives, but the warmth, closeness and affection they can provide each other individually, or as groups. These have been the grounds through which the beliefs and rituals of the "People of the Air" have so quickly penetrated the populations living on the Southern coasts of Iran . . . (The spirits) are everywhere, searching for human hosts who are suffering from fatigue and despair, whether on land or sea. Whenever the inhabitants of a region are more ridden with anxieties and fears, the Winds (al-e hava) assemble in their greatest numbers (E. T. Kaveh Safa-Isfahani, ms 1976).

The idiom of interaction between the anxieties or despondencies of the human beings and the spirits is one of possession. The spirits "mount" their human hosts. The hosts must then be cured by participating in a play (*bāzī*) orchestrated by a Mama or Baba. First, the patient is isolated, rubbed with ointments, and an attempt is made to frighten the jinn from his body. Cult members then gather for the bāzī. The patient is made to drink some blood from a sacrificial animal, there are drumming and tambourines and chanting. The spirit will respond to a particular tune. The patient falls into a trance, and through him the Mama or Baba can talk to the spirit and negotiate a *modus vivendi*. This *modus vivendi* consists of asking the patient to do certain things, make certain gifts, and observe certain taboos. From an outsider's point of view there are two important transformations that occur in the life of the patient by means of the bāzī. One is what psychiatrists call *abreaction*; that is, an image of conflict is suggested to a patient, which he is encouraged to merge with his own emotional conflicts in such a way that, as the image is manipulated by the psychiatrist or Mama, his emotional conflicts are brought to a temporary or more permanent resolution. The second thing that happens to the patient, which is an important support for the abreaction, is that he enters into a cult. He is not cured in the sense that he is returned to his previous state before he fell ill. Rather he is given a new social membership, he is given new daily activities such as observing taboos, and the community is also alerted to treat him in a slightly different way.

It is significant that not all people are equally vulnerable to the spirits. Those with greater economic security, merchants, captains of large boats, and so on, are rarely afflicted. Saʿīdī puts it this way: "They possess the economic resources to guard themselves against all evils and misfortunes; they do this through making pledges, giving charities, and alms of bread." The richer and more secure people, however, do not undermine the cults: they are financial supporters, at least in indirect ways: pledges, charities, alms. The fact that many—both rich and poor—may be skeptics and nonparticipants is not in itself a sociologically destructive force toward the cults. Only today, as the entire economic basis of life and the associated social organization undergo change, are the zār cults likely to decline or change in form. Previous Iranian government attempts to outlaw them merely drove them underground. But today mid-level oil company foremen from Dubai will skeptically dismiss stories of the zār and parī, only to fondly recall experiences from their youth when the spirits were potent.

The spirits exist on both sides of the Gulf and originate in both Africa and India, as well as Arabia—i.e., throughout the entire Gulf trade network. In Oman and Socotra, where Wahhābi religious reforms failed to penetrate, the spirit world is close to the surface. On the Iranian plateau, jinn and parī exist, as do diviners, but there are no elaborated cults of the zār form; the spirits are rather used as individual paths of seeking mental health care (psychological comfort) or aid in decision-making. The plateau villages appear more sober and are built around an egalitarian ideology of exchange, implemented through feasting, communal land-holding in some areas and water-sharing, and intended not to level all to the same income, but to ensure that everyone survives. Shrines surrounding the plateau villages and pilgrimages seem to draw sacred circles around communities, possibly in contrast to a more linear pattern of pilgrimages in the Gulf to certain *qadamgāhs* ("footprints") of saints and holy men. All this, however, remains metaphorical and speculative until some research is done. Indeed, the only work on projection done in the Middle East, using dreams and the spirit world, is Crapanzano's excellent research among the urban poor of Morocco.

Some psychiatric work, of variable quality, has been done more directly in Iran and the Gulf. Parhad (1965), analyzing 210 men and 204 women treated during the first five months of a psychiatric clinic in Kuwait, indicates that most came from the lower classes, and that males and females differ in the symptoms used to express conflicts. Seventy percent of the males were dependent and feminine in character, while 90 percent of the women had aggressive personalitics, i.e., the reverse of the cultural norm and child-rearing system. Males tended to have gastrointestinal symptoms, while women had musculoskeletal symptoms (shifting vague pains, headaches, high blood pressure). Parhad then goes on to postulate typical psychodynamic pressures, beginning in childhood and, for women, intensifying at marriage until a son is born. Most psychiatric reports from the region are even vaguer and more speculative than Parhad. Ihsan and B. al-Issa (1970) and their colleague Bazzoui (1970) remark on the low incidence in Iraq of suicide (but give no evidence) and the relative absence among depressives of mood changes or feelings of guilt, as is the common pattern in the West. Bazzoui suggests that there is a slow change in personality formation among Iraqis, from a tribal system in which one is enmeshed in a rich emotional web of support and sanctioned by feelings of shame before other kin, to a more individualistic conscience-ridden or guilt-driven personality. He cites changes in patterns of mourning from the wailings and the therapeutic ventilation of resentment against being abandoned (by the diseased) and fearing loneliness, to the more Western mode of "dignified repression." Such suggestions of guilt-versus-shame cultures stem from the 1950s and were not very successful as explanatory devices. What is needed is more material in cultural context, and thereafter epidemiological surveys.

B. Good (1976, 1977) has shown what might be done through a semantic analysis of illness terms in Western Iran, including survey material on the incidence of different types of illness in native terms. He thereby illuminates the use of heart palpitations, for instance, frequently complained of by women (as noted by Parhad) and normally passed off by doctors as anemia, as an expression of mapable social stresses, grounded in traditional conceptions of physiology and health. M. Good (1977) has followed this up by illustrating how these traditional concerns affect birth control procedures, especially the concerns with balance and cleanliness of blood, with the relative moisture of the uterus (women are but vessels in which the seed is deposited, but the vessel can be hospitable or not), and with the use of hot and cold foods to adjust the body's economy. The confluence of social stresses and cultural notions can be indexed by good suicide and homicide studies. Gharagozlu-Hamadani (1972) points out that a major reason given by young women who attempt suicide is lack of ability to vent aggression and anger, and consequent turning of the rage against themselves: an expression of the unproven wife's frustrations.

Epidemiological studies need, however, to be pursued with care, first to ensure one is using culturally appropriate categories, and second to control for biases in counting. Insanity is highly stigmatized in Sa'ūdī Arabia, with the result that the mental hospital at Taif becomes a dumping ground for unwanted relatives. On the other hand, as several authors point out, in the Middle East, as long as a person is not violent, sexually indecent, or unable to control motor coordination, he or she does not pose a serious problem. Hallucination and delusion can be passed off as eccentricity and, sometimes, if it takes the proper form, religiosity. Traditional curing systems often make use of this sliding continuum between insanity and religious inspiration (viz., Turkish play between *deli*, "insanity," and *veli*, "saint"; or the Arabic distinction between *junūn*, "insane," and *lā'sab*, "nerves," or *wahm*, "imagination"; or Persian *dīvāna*, "insane," and *nārahatī*, "distress," or *'asabī*, "nerves": a Sudanese curing mosque, described by Baasher (1962), for instance, gives the *mawhūmūn* (neurotics with imagination) some religious instruction for a few days; the *majnūnūn* (psychotics) are isolated, often physically restrained, while fed liquids and solids, and read prayers: in effect, allowing the psychotic episodes to run their course, and allowing the patients to return home during remissions.

Dealing with the abnormal can provide one access to cultural understanding: by seeing where things break down, one often can understand the dynamics and pressures of a society. One is more interested in patterned abnormality for this than for idiosyncratic disturbances. But other access routes to sociocultural definition are equally important. Artistic forms, such as dance and theater, can be informative in this way. Comic theater in Iran (*rūhauzī*) often deals with common problems of status, sexuality, marriage, occupational roles, by inverting common expectations and thereby exposing them to reconsideration or affirmation. Dance works in a more subconscious way: it is the form taken by zār-type cures, but Brooks (1977) argues that it also can be a modeling device of and for the realities, say, of nomadic life. In a paper comparing several Bakhtiārī dances, he shows how each models a different aspect of Bakhtiārī life, and how dance forms have changed over time, along with changes in existential conditions. For instance, the widely distributed stick dance (in which one male attempts to strike the shins of a second) once was done with two small sticks in the hands of each participant (see the 1924 film "Grass") and today is done with one small stick for the attacker, and one large stick for the defender, the better both to attack and to defend, reflecting, he suggests, the intensification of individual need for aggressiveness and defensiveness vis-à-vis a more intrusive state and outside world. Dance forms have been described as important celebratory events in Oman (especially a sword dance) and al-Hasā (where villages have dance squares). But no attempts have been made to deal with them in any systematic way as communication or cultural modeling devices.

Conclusions

Given the simplistic writing about the peoples of the Gulf region—especially the naïve deductions about how they must think and behave because they happen to be Muslim or Arab or Marxist or Wahhābī or nomadic or citizens of oil-rich countries—perhaps the single most important conclusion to be drawn from this review is a sense of the complex but ordered variation of life styles and outlooks in the area. A second conclusion, of course, is that to flesh out the picture, empirical research is needed, especially on the cultural features addressed in the section "Human Development and Community." Third, it would nevertheless appear, even from what we do know, that standard anthropological perspectives are fruitful: that is, looking for ecological-economic bases for existence, ideological differences by class, religious and ethnic group, community organization, the pragmatics of ritual, codes of interpersonal relations, and means of psychic and cultural symbolization.

Selected Bibliography

Abu-Hakima, Ahmad Mustafa. 1965. *History of Eastern Arabia, 1750–1800*. Beirut.

Alavi, Bozorg. 1955. *Kämpfendes Iran*. Berlin.

Ansari, Mostafa. 1974. "The History of Khuzistan, 1878–1925." Ph.D. dissertation, University of Chicago.

Anthony, John Duke. 1975. *Arab States of the Lower Gulf*. Washington, D.C.

Baasher, T. 1962. "Some Aspects of the History of the Treatment of Mental Disorders in the Sudan." *Sudan Medical Journal*, New Series, 1(1), issue 44.

Bateson, M. C.; J. W. Clinton; J.B.M. Kassarjian; H. Safavi; M. Soraya. 1977. "Safa-yi Batin: A Study of the Interrelations of a Set of Iranian Ideal Character Types," in L. C. Brown and N. Itzkowitz, eds., *Psychological Dimensions of Near Eastern Studies*. Princeton.

Bazzoui, Widad. 1970. "Affective Disorders in Iraq." *British Journal of Psychiatry* 117: 195–203.

Beeman, William O. 1976. "Stylistic Variation in the Language of Iranian Interaction and Its Socio-Cultural Meaning." Ph.D. dissertation, University of Chicago.

Bill, James. 1972. *The Politics of Iran*. Columbus, Ohio.

Brooks, David, 1977. "Bakhtiārī Dance." Paper prepared for the Festival of Popular Traditions, Isfahan, Iran, 12–18 October 1977.

Bujra, Abdulla. 1971. *The Politics of Stratification*. Oxford.

Cole, Donald P. 1975. *Nomads of the Nomads: The Al Murrah of the Empty Quarter*. London.

Fallers, Lloyd A. and Margaret C. 1976. "Sex Roles in Edremit," in J. Peristiany, ed., *Mediterranean Family Structure*, Cambridge.

Fischer, Michael M. J. 1973. "Zoroastrian Iran between Myth and Praxis." Ph.D. dissertation, University of Chicago.

———. 1980. *Iran: From Religious Dispute to Revolution*. Cambridge, Mass.

Gharagozlu-Hamadani. 1972. "Psychiatric Evaluation of One Hundred Cases in Suicidal Attempts in Zhiraz, Iran." *International Journal of Social Psychiatry* 18 (2): 140–44.

Good, Byron. 1976. "The Heart of What's the Matter." Ph.D. dissertation, University of Chicago.

———. 1977. "The Heart of What's the Matter: The Semantics of Illness in Iran." *Culture, Medicine, and Psychiatry* 1:1.

Good, Mary-Jo DelVecchio. 1977. "Social Hierarchy and Social Change in a Provincial Iranian Town." Ph.D. dissertation, Harvard University.

Goodell, Grace. 1977. "The Elementary Structures of Political Life." Ph.D. dissertation, Columbia University.

Halliday, Fred. 1974. *Arabia without Sultans*. London.

———. 1977. "Labor Migration in the Middle East." MERIP Report No. 59.

Hansen, Henry Harold. 1961. "The Pattern of Women's Seclusion and Failing in the Shi'a Village." *Folk* 3: 22–42.

———. 1963. "Growing Up in Two Different Muslim Areas." *Folk* 5: 143–56.

———. 1968. *Investigations in a Shi'a Village in Bahrain*. Copenhagen.

Hopwood, Derek, ed. 1972. *The Arabian Peninsula: Society and Politics*. London.

Iseman, Peter. Feb. 1978. "The Arabian Ethos." *Harper's* 256 (1533): 37–56.

al-Issa, Ihsan and B. 1970. "Psychiatric Problems in a Developing Country: Iraq." *International Journal of Social Psychiatry* 16 (1): 15–22.

Kelly, J. B. 1970. "A Prevalence of Furies," in Derek Hopwood, ed., *The Arabian Peninsula*.

————. 1976. "Hadramaut, Oman, Dhar: The Experience of Revolution." *Middle Eastern Studies* 12(2): 213–30.

Lenczowski, G. 1947. "The Communist Movement in Iran." *Middle East Journal* 1(1): 29–45.

Long, David. 1976. *The Persian Gulf.* Boulder, Col.

Lorimer, J. G. 1915. *Gazetteer of the Persian Gulf.* 2 vols. Calcutta.

Marr, P. A. 1975. "The Political Elite in Iraq," in G. Lenczowski, ed., *Political Elites in the Middle East.* Washington, D.C.

Miles, S. B. 1916–66. *The Countries and Tribes of the Persian Gulf.* London.

Nakhleh, Emile. 1976. *Bahrain: Political Development in a Modernizing Society.* Lexington, Mass.

Parhad, Luther. 1965. "The Cultural-Social Conditions of Treatment in a Psychiatric Out-patient Department in Kuwait." *International Journal of Social Psychiatry* 11 (1): 14–19.

Pauling, Norman. 1964. "Labor Separations in an Underdeveloped Area: A Case Study of Worker Adjustment to Change." *American Journal of Economics and Sociology* 23(4): 419–34.

Rugh, William. 1973. "Emergence of a New Middle Class in Saudi Arabia." *Middle East Journal* 27 (1): 7–20.

Sa'idi, Gholam Husain. 1976. "Inhabitants of the Air (Al-e Hava)." E. T. Kaveh Safa-Isfahani. Mimeo.

Sergeant, R. B. 1969. "The Zaydis," in A. J. Arberry, ed. *Religion in the Middle East.* Cambridge.

Steensgaard, Niels. 1973. *The Asian Trade Revolution of the Seventeenth Century.* Chicago.

Vidal, Federico Schmid. 1964. "The Oasis of al-Hasa." Ph.D. dissertation, Harvard University.

Wikan, Unni. 1977. "Man Becomes Woman: Transsexualism in Oman as a Key to Gender Roles." *Man* 12(2): 304–11.

Wilkinson, J. C. 1972. "Origins of the Omani State," in Derek Hopwood, ed., *The Arabian Peninsula.*

Zonis, M. 1971. *The Political Elite of Iran.* Princeton.

Appendixes

KIMBRIEL MITCHELL
AND STAFF

The Persian Gulf

The Persian Gulf lies along a northwest axis between southwest Iran and the Arabian peninsula at 24° N to 30° 30' N and at 48° E to 55° 30' E. It is 239,000 square kilometers in extent and 8,630 cubic kilometers in volume. It is 990 km long and 338 km at its widest from Bandar Maqām in Iran to Ra's al-Sila at the western section of the Sabkha Matti on the coast of the United Arab Emirates (UAE). The narrowest stretch of the Persian Gulf, the Strait of Hormuz, is 56 km across. The length of the coastline of the Gulf is 3,340 km.

Bathymetric Character

The Persian Gulf is a nearly landlocked epicontinental basin, the average depth of whose waters is only 35 meters. The deeper water is off the Iranian shore, the shallower off the Arabian, and especially the UAE, part of the Gulf. The area of 20 meters or less in depth closely follows the coast of the UAE to Abū Dhabī city, from where it extends across the Gulf above Qatar to Ra's Tanūra on the Sa'ūdī coast; there it narrows and keeps to the coast until Kuwait Bay. Then it broadens to take in most of the head of the Persian Gulf. The 20-meter strip is thin all along the shore of Iran, and the 30- to 40-meter region follows the contour of the 20-meter area farther out in the Gulf. Deeper water, up to 80 meters, lies off the Iranian coast. In the vicinity of Shaikh Shu'aib Island, it is nearly 100 meters deep. The deepest point, near Ra's Musandam in the Strait of Hormuz, is up to 110 meters in depth. The Gulf's bathymetric axis lies near the Iranian littoral; thus its bathymetric form is asymmetrical. The tilt of the floor on the Arabian side is a moderate 35 cm/km, that on the Iranian side a steep 175 cm/km.

Climate

The climate of the region is arid and subtropical. Essentially continental and cut off from the climatic influence of the Indian Ocean, its seasonal fluctuations are marked. In summer there is little cloud cover or rain. The *khamsīn*, a wind from the south, brings dust and sand. Mirages on the Arabian littoral, haze, and dust storms are frequent. Thunderstorms and fogs are rare, and squalls and waterspouts occur in the autumn, which, like spring, is brief. Summer air temperatures average about 32° C, but they can rise to over 45° C and sink to 22° C. Mean relative humidity stands at about 60%, but can be higher at places (Bushire and Bahrain, for instance) and minimal inland. The Arabian littoral is slightly less humid than the Iranian coast. Winter air temperatures average around 16° C to 6° C. Winters are colder in the northern part of the Gulf than in the south. Mean relative humidity in the winter measures 72%, and most of the Gulf's rainfall comes between November and April in sudden storms. The Arabian side receives no more than 125 mm annually, while parts of the Iranian coast receive up to 275 mm.

The northwesterly *shamāl* blows in the winter, but it is most prevalent during May to June and from October to December.

Water Temperature and Salinity

Water temperatures in the Gulf also vary seasonally. Surface water temperatures fluctuate as much as 18° C between summer and winter. In cold weather, they are 14° C to 18° C off the Arabian side and 20° C to 22° C off the Iranian coast. In hot weather, they average 31° C to 33° C, with the water off Iran 2° C to 3° C cooler. At their hottest, surface water temperatures may reach nearly 40° C along the shore of the United Arab Emirates, a temperature not surpassed in waters elsewhere in the world. Temperatures are higher in summer and lower in winter closer to the shore than farther out.

The water of the Persian Gulf is quite saline. This is due to high air temperatures and the consequently high rate of evaporation which, at 135 mm a year, exceeds most of the area's usual annual rainfall. Another factor is the comparatively inconsequential flow of fresh water into the Gulf, mainly from the Shatt al-'Arab and from lesser rivers in Iran, reflecting the general aridity of the large catchment area of the region.

In contrast to the average salinity of the oceans of 34% to 35%, the rates of salinity in the Persian Gulf are 37% to 38% at the Strait of Hormuz, 38% to 39% in the area around Bushire and Khārg Island, 39% to 40% off the Iraqi and Kuwaiti coasts, and 42% to 43% in Kuwait and Bahrain bays. Salinity can reach 50% off the Sabkha Matti west to Qatar, up to 60% along the eastern section of the Abū Dhabī coast, and between 60% to 70% in the Gulf of Salwa. These latter places are those with the most extreme temperatures in the summer and winter. The salinity of the northwestern Gulf varies more than that of the southeast; the air is colder than water in winter, particularly in the higher latitudes of the northwest, so that evaporation is increased. Also, winter sees the lowest rate of fresh water inflow from the Shatt al-'Arab and other rivers.

Water Density, Currents, Tides

The excess of evaporation over river discharge and rain is made up for by the flow of water into the Gulf from the Indian Ocean. It moves in a counterclockwise current along the Iranian coast, becomes denser—salinity increases with depth—sinks to the bottom while mixing in part with the water of the Arabian side, then flows out under incoming water. In winter, evaporation and low water temperatures causes high water density. The Gulf's water has the highest specific gravity of the world's seas, and the water of the Persian Gulf is wholly replaced every 2½ to 3 years.

At the Strait of Hormuz, the current of water from the Indian Ocean enters the Gulf at 6 to 7 km per hour. Except here and at the river mouths, the entrance to lagoons, and between islands, the tidal currents in the Persian Gulf are weak, averaging about 3 km per hour. Currents along the bottom of the Gulf move at some 50 cm per second (1.8 km per hour) and at 60 cm per second off Abū Dhabī. The range between high and low tides is 1½ meters around Qatar, 2½ meters in the northwest of the Gulf, and 3½ meters in the southeast. At times, winds can create difficult conditions, notably in the eastern Persian Gulf when they blow against the direction of currents; they have been known to reverse local currents and the flow of water from the mouths of rivers. Strong onshore winds can cause flooding by increasing the level of coastal water by up to 3 meters. Waves in the Persian Gulf rarely exceed 3 meters and are somewhat higher in the south than in the north.

Selected Bibliography

Crisp, D. J. "Prospects of Marine Science in the Gulf Area: The Background Paper." In *Division of Marine Sciences*, UNESCO. "Marine Sciences in the Gulf Area," report of a consultative meeting, Paris 11–14 November, 1975. UNESCO technical papers in marine science, no. 26, pp. 19–38.

Emery, K. O. "Sediments and water of Persian Gulf." *Bulletin of the American Association of Petroleum Geologists* 40, 10 (1956): 2354–83.

Evans, G. "Persian Gulf." In R. W. Fairbridge (ed.), *The Encyclopedia of Oceanography*. Encyclopedia of Earth Sciences Series, vol. 1. New York, 1966.

Grasshoff, K. "Review of Hydrographical and Productivity Conditions in the Gulf Regions." In *Division of Marine Sciences*, UNESCO. "Marine Sciences in the Gulf Area." Report of a consultative meeting, Paris 11–14 November 1975. UNESCO technical papers in marine science, no. 26, pp. 39–62.

National Oceanographic Data Center. *A Summary of Temperature-Salinity Characteristics of the Persian Gulf*. General Series. Publication G-4. Washington, D.C., 1964.

Purser B. (ed.). *The Persian Gulf—Holocene Carbonate Sedimentation and Diagenesis in a Shallow Epicontinental Sea*. Berlin, 1973.

Sugden, W. "The hydrology of the Persian Gulf and its significance in respect to evaporitic deposition." *American Journal of Science* 261 (1963): 741–55.

APPENDIX B

Climate and Oceanography

Iran

Iran lies within subtropical latitudes. The characteristics of its climate, which is so distinctive as to be called "Iranian," are those of the regime of the inner basins: an extreme range of diurnal and seasonal temperatures, vigorous northerly winds, great aridity, very low and variable rainfall, and a high rate of evaporation. Iran's second climate is that of the Caspian littoral and of the Elburz and Zagros mountains, where there is adequate rainfall. The Caspian coast is distinguished by its year-round dampness, its mild temperatures and cloudy, rainy weather in winter, and its considerable heat in summer. A high rate of humidity prevails on the southern Gulf coast, where winters are mild, summers quite hot, and rainfall always inadequate. The ample rainfall on the northern side of the Elburz decreases steadily toward the eastern end of that mountain range. Semidesert conditions prevail in the southeastern Zagros. The main controlling climate factors are the country's high altitude and the high mountains around its rim that prevent moist air from reaching the interior.

Mean daily summer (July) temperature for Azerbaijan and pockets of the Zagros and the eastern highlands range from 15° C to 20° C. In the inner basins, their periphery, and the southern Zagros they range from 25° C to 30° C. Mean daily summer temperatures stand at over 30° C in southwestern Iran and at over 40° C in the Jaz Muriān. Autumn, like spring, is a short season. Average temperatures in winter (January) are below —15° C in the upper Elburz, below 0° C in much of the northwest, and no more than 5° C in the rest of northern Iran. They reach 10° C to 15° C in Khūzistān, 15° to 20° C on the Persian Gulf coast, and over 20° C on the Makrān coast. Mean annual daily temperatures range from less than 5° C in the higher elevations of the mountains to 10° C to 20° C for most of the country, to over 20° C in the south. The absolute range of temperature in Iran is above 50° C. The average national range is 20° C to 25° C.

Humidity. Iran is a country of comparatively low humidity. The coasts become oppressively damp in summer. The northeastern highlands experience a relative humidity of about 50%. Most of the interior records about 40% relative humidity, while the air in Khūzistān is almost dry. In winter, all the coasts save those of Makrān and the northeast register a relative humidity of 80% or more. Khūzistān and many inland stations have 70% to 80% relative humidity. Humidity can drop by over 30% in the interior in the afternoon.

Rain. Rainfall is heaviest in the north and northwest. The western Caspian coast and the Tālish hills sometimes receive more than 2,000 mm annually. The central and eastern Caspian areas receive 1,000 and 600 mm, respectively. In all these places, the rainy season extends from September to April, with September and October being the rainiest months. The northeast records about 200 mm, but a pocket between Gurgān and Mashhad has double this amount. Save for the strip from Kirmānshāh north to the Soviet frontier, which is watered by 600 to 800 mm, Azerbaijan receives about 300 mm a year. The higher reaches of the Zagros southeast to Shīrāz have an annual rainfall of 400 mm. In the mountains of the north, heavy snows are frequent from November to April. The yearly average of rain for the southwest is under 300 mm. The districts peripheral to the desert basins, in which is included Tehran, record no more than 200 mm a year. The overall period of rainfall is from October to May. The wettest months in the south are December and January, while March and April are the rainiest in the north. Annual rainfall varies widely within as well as between regions. Summers are dry.

Winds and Clouds. Winter winds blow from the north and northeast in northern Iran and from the west in the south. The northwesterly *shamāl* blows in the summer. The most notorious wind is the "Wind of the 120 days," which blows continuously from May to September in the southeast and can reach a velocity of 100 km per hour. Iran is a relatively cloudless country; most of the 180 cloudless days in the north and the 230 cloudless days in the south occur in summer and autumn. The Caspian coast is the cloudiest and foggiest area of Iran. Dust storms and mirages are frequent, particularly in the south and east in summer.

Iraq

Iraq's climate is arid, subtropical, and continental, with a Mediterranean element in the mountains of the northeast. Its summers are dry and quite hot. Absolute maxima can reach 50° C, but in the mountains the temperature can be over 10° C cooler. At night, however, the temperature is much lower. Both spring and autumn are short. Winter temperatures, while mild, are colder than usual for a country at Iraq's latitude. This is due to the cold winds that blow southward from central Asia and Anatolia. Absolute minima can sink to —5° C at Basra and below —10° C in the west and north. On the other hand, temperatures in the south can rise to 25° C to 30° C. At over 20° C the average annual range of temperature is quite wide. The range between day and night temperatures is less in the winter than in the summer. Low summer humidity, except around

TABLE B–1. AVERAGE TEMPERATURE, RELATIVE HUMIDITY,
AND ANNUAL RAINFALL IN IRAQ

City		Temperature (°C)			Relative humidity (%)	Rainfall (mm)
		Maximum	Mean	Minimum		
Baghdad	January	16	10	4	69	144
	August	43	34	25	23	
Basra	January	19	13	7	76	140
	August	41	34	26	44[a]	
Rutba	January	13	8	1	66	110
	August	39	30	21	26	
Mosul	January	13	8	3	80	375
	August	43	33	22	30	

[a] A mean relative humidity of about 57% is more typical of Basra for most of the year.
Sources: A. H. al-Shalash, *Climate of Iraq* (Amman: The Co-operative Printing Presses Workers Society, 1966). Meteorological Office, *Tables of Temperature, Relative Humidity and Precipitation for the World*, Part V—*Asia* (London: HMSO, 1966).

the Persian Gulf and the marshlands, mitigates the seasonal heat. Humidity is generally high in the winter.

The amount of average annual rainfall declines from over 1,000 mm in the mountains of Kurdistan, much of it received in the form of winter snows, to less than 100 mm in the western desert. The area of transition from districts with plentiful rain to those with a meager amount is small and at Baghdad less than 150 mm of rain falls in an average year. From year to year, the amount of rainfall is quite variable. The rainy season is from November to April; December to February is the wettest time.

The main wind of Iraq is the dry northwesterly *shamāl*, which blows particularly from June to October and also in the winter. The *sharqī* is a damp southeasterly wind that comes in the winter, often bringing rain. Dust storms can occur at any time during the year, but especially in the summer, when mirages are common.

Kuwait

Arid, subtropical Kuwait has very hot summers. Average daily temperatures stand at 35° C, and absolute maxima can go above 50° C. Kuwait experiences high relative humidity for only a few weeks in August and September. Otherwise, the mean relative humidity is about 45%. Winter temperatures average 13° C, but absolute minimum temperatures can fall to 0° C and below. Relative humidity averages 68%, but can often top 90%. The annual range of temperature is over 20° C. As a rule, temperatures farther inland are somewhat more extreme and the humidity is lower.

Kuwait receives its mean annual rainfall of 110 mm mostly in sudden squalls that occur from November to April, but there are occasional thunderstorms in the early spring. The summer months are rarely relieved by clouds. The northwesterly *shamāl* is the principal wind and brings sand and dust storms during much of the year, especially in summer. The *samūm* from the southwest is also frequent.

Sa'ūdī Arabia

Sa'ūdī Arabia has a desert, continental climate with great heat, low humidity, and minimum rain. Subject to Indian Ocean monsoons, southern 'Asīr province is a distinct climatic region; its higher reaches have a mountain climate, its middle levels a steppe climate, and its lower areas a desert climate.

Average summer temperatures vary from 20° C to 32° C in 'Asīr to 28° C to 32° C in the north to 34° C to 36° C in the south and east, but the absolute maxima can rise to over 50° C in the deserts. Mean winter temperatures vary from about 10° C to 18° C in 'Asīr and 7° C to 12°C in the north and northwest, to 15° C in central Sa'ūdī Arabia and 20° C in the south. They stand at more than 20° C in the southern Red Sea coast. The temperature often falls below 0° C in the center and north, bringing occasional frost and snow, and the absolute minima descend to −12° C. Sa'ūdī Arabia experiences a wide diurnal and seasonal temperature range. The mean annual range is 15° C for the Red Sea coast. Mean relative humidity is low (under 40%) in the interior; along the coasts, however, relative humidity can reach well above 80%.

Save for 'Asīr, Sa'ūdī Arabia receives no more than 75 mm to 85 mm of rain each year, and many places go for several years without rainfall. When rain does come, mostly between November and April, it is usually in sudden storms. 'Asīr receives a yearly average of 300 mm to 320 mm of rain, all of it in the summer from the southwest monsoon.

The northwesterly *shamāl* occurs during much of the year, but particularly from June to September, when it causes dust storms. Sometimes a wind blows from the south and southwest, the *khamsīn*, which also causes dust storms. Fogs sometimes occur along the coast, mainly in winter, and mirages are common in summer.

Bahrain

The subtropical climate of Bahrain is hot and humid. Summer temperatures average 36° C and maxima can reach 47° C, but there is a notable fall in temperature at night. Winters are mild, with average temperatures of 17° C, and readings as low as 5° C have been recorded. The annual range of temperature is between 15° C and 20° C. Bahrain's humidity is oppressive. The rest of the year is dry and cloudless. The *shamāl* blows in summer as well as in January and February. The *ghawth* occurs irregularly in winter. The *barra* is a cool northerly wind that comes in June.

Qatar

Qatar's subtropical desert climate is very hot in the summer. The maximum average temperature in August is 45° C; the minimum is 25° C; and the mean is 37° C. Relative humidity reaches 90% along the coast, but plummets below 30% a few miles inland. Winters are mild; the average minimum temperature for January is 7° C, and the average maximum is 26° C. The mean temperature is 15° C. Relative humidity remains high at about 80%. The annual range of temperature is around 20° C.

Annual rainfall amounts to 75 mm, which, as elsewhere in the Gulf, falls mostly in abrupt squalls in November and the winter months. The principal winds are the northwesterly *shamāl* and the southeasterly *sharqī*. The *shamāl* sometimes brings rain in the winter, as does the *sharqī*, which brings hot and dry air in the summer. Occasionally, the easterly *ghawth* blows in summer.

The United Arab Emirates

The United Arab Emirates lies within the subtropical, arid climatic zone. Its summers are very hot and humid. Temperatures average 32° C and the absolute maxima can exceed 45° C. Average relative humidity on the coast is consistently over 85%. In winter, temperatures average 18° C; they can fall to 5° C. Relative humidity averages about 75%. The desert and mountains are much less humid than the coast, where diurnal temperatures are of a lesser range than those of the interior. The annual temperature of the UAE is around 15° C.

Save for occasional showers in September at al-'Ain oasis, rain falls between November and April, half of it coming in January and February. The annual average rainfall is 75 to 80 mm. Ra's al-Khaima receives roughly 115 mm of rain each year on average and up to 200 mm; morning fogs occur several days each month from February to June. Winds along the coast of the UAE are frequent. The most notable wind is the *khamsīn*, which blows from the south in the summer and brings sandstorms.

Oman

Several aspects of the climate of Oman distinguish it from the climate of other states of the region. The proximity of the Indian Ocean mitigates temperatures on the southern Dhofār coast. The average summer temperature there (Salāla) is 26° C and the mean winter temperature is 23° C. These are some 6° C below and above comparable temperatures for summer and winter elsewhere in the Gulf; they also have the lowest annual temperature range of the area. Absolute summer maxima temperatures register no more than 35° C, and absolute winter minima do not fall below 15° C. Relative humidity at Salāla averages 85% in summer and 62% in winter.

The average summer temperature at Muscat is 33° C, with the absolute maxima reaching over 40° C. Maximum temperatures here and at Salāla occur from May to July, earlier than at other places in the Gulf. Winter temperatures average 22° C, and mean minimum temperatures here, as at Salāla, go no lower than 17° C. The average relative humidity is 68% in summer and 62% in winter. The interior of Oman, however, records greater extremes of temperature and much lower relative humidity.

Unlike the other Gulf countries, and northern Oman too, the Dhofār coast receives its maximum rainfall in July and August rather than in the winter; 44 mm of Salāla's annual rainfall of 108 mm comes in these months, when there is the *kharīf* ("autumn") or southwesterly monsoon. No month passes without rain, but the winter is virtually dry. At Muscat, however, 55 mm of its annual rainfall of over 100 mm comes at this time. June, September, and October are usually dry. The occurrence of rain in the Sultanate from year to year is quite erratic, and in some years the Jabar Mountains, and particularly the Jabal Akhdar, have received over 300 mm of rain. As noted elsewhere, the Rub' al-Khālī can go for years without a trace of rain. Wind in northern Oman comes mainly from the east in summer, but at times the *gharbī*, a westerly wind from the Rub' al-Khālī, blows; at other times of the year, the *shamāl* prevails.

Selected Bibliography

Al-Blehed, A. S. "A Contribution of Climatic Studies on Saudi Arabia." M. Sc. thesis, Durham University, 1957.

Allison, T. R. *The Climate of Kuwait.* Kuwait, 1963.

al-Shalash, A. H. *Climate of Iraq.* Amman, 1966.

Bahrain, Statistical Bureau, Ministry of Finance and National Economy. *Statistical Abstract.* Annual issues.

Banerji, B. N. *Meteorology of the Persian Gulf and Mekran.* Calcutta, 1931.

Dānishgāh-i. Tehran. *Climatic Atlas of Iran.* Tehran, 1965.

Fenelon, K. G. *The United Arab Emirates.* 2nd edition. London, 1976.

Ganji, M. H. "Climate." In W. B. Fisher (ed.), *The Cambridge History of Iran.* Vol. 1. *The Land of Iran.* Cambridge, 1968.

Hawley, D. F. *The Trucial States.* London, 1970.

Mellen, W. P. *The Climate of Arabia, Iraq, and Persia.* California Institute of Technology, 1942.

Meteorological Office. *Tables of Temperature, Relative Humidity and Precipitation for the World.* Part V. *Asia.* London, 1966.

Sultanate of Oman. Development Council, Technical Secretariat National Statistical Department. *Statistical Year Book,* Fourth Issue, 1975. Muscat, November 1976.

U.S. Army Air Force, Weather Division. *Climate of Southwestern Asia.* Report 410. Washington, D.C., 1945.

APPENDIX C

Natural Regions

Iran

Iran is 1,645,000 square kilometers in area and extends from 25°N to 39°N and from 44°E to 64°E. It is bordered by the Soviet Union (2,300 km) and the Caspian Sea (644 km) on the north, Afghanistan (850 km) and Pakistan (830 km) on the east, the Gulf of Oman and the Persian Gulf (combined frontage: 1,880 km) on the south and southwest, and by Iraq (1,280 km) and Turkey (470 km) on the west.

Iran is like a high, irregular, quadrangular bowl in structure, with broad high mountains, the Zagros, along its western and southwestern rim. The Elburz, a high and narrow mountain, extends across its north central side, and lower, broken uplands form its eastern periphery. The interior plateau of the country consists of forbidding basins of silt, pebbles, and sand, which, having no drainage to the sea, have salt lakes or depressions at their lowest points. The largest of these basins are the Dasht-i Kavīr and the Dasht-i Lūt. There is a lowland plain southwest of the Zagros in Khūzistān. Narrow plains lie along the coasts of the Caspian Sea, the Persian Gulf, and the Gulf of Oman. The largest body of water in Iran, Lake Rizā'iyya, is salty. Half the country lies at 1,000 meters or more above sea level.

In Azerbaijan, the Zagros Mountains begin and are typified by rolling, steppe-like plateaus, largely bare and stony and over 1,500 meters high. Here too are volcanic peaks such as Mt. Sahand (3,702 m) and Mt. Savalān (4,269 m). Numerous streams have eroded gorges or sinuous valleys through these plateaus, particularly in the higher, western part of the region. In the northeast, the Soviet frontier cuts across the low Mūghān steppe. The main drainage basins are those of the Aras and Qizil Uzun rivers, which flow to the Caspian Sea, and that of Lake Rizā'iyya. About 1,300 meters above sea level and 140 km in length from north to south and 45 km wide, it is not more than 7 meters deep, even after spring rains. Black, salty mud lies around its fringes. Further away, more fertile soil is cultivated. The Rizā'iyya basin is bounded by mountains and a plateau to the south. Azerbaijan is an important farming area because, although much of the area is rough country, many valleys have fertile soil at their lower levels; moreover, the rainfall is usually adequate and dependable. The Zagros Mountains proper begin in the vicinity of Hamadān and Kirmānshāh. Some 350 km in width, they range southeastward for over 1,200 km. The eastern side of the Zagros is higher and more compact and austere than the western side. The northwestern end receives more rain; thus it is more covered with vegetation than the southeastern end, where desert conditions prevail and few streams flow perennially. At approximately a line from Bushire to Shīrāz, the mountains, which to the north have been straight and tight-packed parallel ranks of "hog's backs," start to change character. They become more loosely bunched and their ranks arched; their trend changes from northwest to southeast to west to east. Some streams and rivers have carved gorges through the northwestern Zagros, while others follow an intricate course around the ends of mountain ridges.

The main river basins of the northwestern Zagros are those of the Sadmara (lower down, the Karkha), Diz, Kārūn, Marun, and Zuhra (Hindīān) rivers. In its upper reaches, the Sadmara flows through high plains and hills. Further down it cuts through mountains and broad, grassy valleys before it reaches the Zagros foothills west of Khurramābād, from where it courses southward into marshes near the Iraqi border. Apart from the highland valleys where the tributaries of the Diz rise, the Diz basin is comprised of bare and steep mountains cut by many gorges. There is little pasturage. The Diz joins the Kārūn River north of Ahvāz. The Kārūn flows southeastward from its source in the high Zagros, then turns northwestward, the direction of its tributaries, until it slices through the mountains at Bard-i Qamchi. From there it runs through the Zagros foothills and on to the plain of Khūzistān at Shustar. It reaches Khurramshahr, where it joins the Shatt al-'Arab. The 850 km long Kārūn is the widest and only navigable river in Iran. Verdant plains that support grazing and farming are found along the upper Kārūn basin, and lower down its reaches are mountain valleys, which are wooded in places. The Marun River and its main tributary, the Ala, flow southwestward across the general trend of the mountains before they converge south of Rām Hormuz. The Marun's water disperses into marshes northwest of Bandar Shāhpur. The upper Zuhra River drains a high plain around Ardakān, 80 km northwest of Shīrāz. It receives the Khairābād River on its westerly course and from where it cuts through the hills and flows south into the Persian Gulf it is known as the Hindīān River. Much of the terrain of the Marun-Zuhra region is rugged and complex, rendering access difficult.

In the southwestern Zagros, the main river basins are formed by the Shāhpur, Mand, Khamir, and Shūr rivers. The relief of the area through which the Shāhpur flows is lower and less pronounced than that of the Zuhra to the northwest. Broad valleys lie between dome-like mountains where the Shāhpur and the Daliki, a tributary, rise to the west of Shīrāz. These streams, heavily diminished by irrigation, flow southwestward and perpendicular to the coast. Northeast of Bushire they fuse, becoming the Hilla Rūd, which empties into the Gulf. The Mand rises west of Shīrāz, flows along a plain between the mountains, then cuts through them southwest of Asmāngird, where it is joined by a tributary, the Fasā. Before it arrives at the Tangistān coast, it winds through desolate country, picking up more tributaries all the while. The Rūd Khamir is a lesser river that courses eastward and reaches the Persian Gulf opposite Qishm Island. The upper region of the Rūd Shūr basin is shaped like a fan, as its tributaries come from west, north, and east. This salt river drains a district of desert plains and rugged hills without soil. A notable feature of the area are pink salt plugs, hundreds of meters in height, which can be seen along much of the course of the Rūd Shūr. The coast from Bushire to the Rūd Shūr is fronted by the hills and plain of the Khūzistān mountains at only several kilometers inland. At places they come directly onto the coast.

From the Sirwān (Diyāla) River on the Iraqi border in the north, 800 km to below Dilam at the head of the Gulf, lies the 50 to 65 km wide strip of foothills that are the southwestern extension of the Zagros. A few fertile valleys and small tracts of woods are located at its northern end. In the south, the red, white, and sometimes green, hills are bare and angular and slashed by gullies. The Khūzistān plain is situated west of these hills from Diz to the Iraqi frontier and south to the Persian Gulf. This tract is a flatland, mostly of alluvial silt. Swamps near the Gulf and marshes and sandhills farther inland give way to firmer soil in the northern part of the plain, which is divided from the southern part by hills northwest of Ahvāz. From Abādān Island to the Hindian River, the coast consists either of mud flats or marshes. From the Hindīān to Bushire it is low and sandy, except for swamps around Bushire Bay.

The Elburz Mountains and a subsidiary range in the west, the Tālish hills, lie between Āstārā in eastern Azerbaijan and Jājarm in western Khurasan province. The Elburz are from 50 to 130 km wide; they rise quickly from plains to their north and south.

The Tālish hills run 175 km southeast along the southwestern Caspian coast. Much of this range rises to over 2,100 meters. Numerous streams fed by abundant rainfall have cut ravines through the hills on their way to the Caspian Sea. The most notable one, the Kangan Rūd, has created a fertile plain. There is extensive woodland on the northeastern side of the Tālish. Many valleys afford either pasturage or cultivation. This range ends where several streams, including the Qizil Uzun and the Shāh Rūd, meet at Manjīl, become the Safīd Rūd, and cut through a valley to the sea.

The Elburz, between the Safīd Rūd and the Harāz Rūd, has two sections. On the west are two ridges of mountains, through which flows the Shāh Rūd. The northern ridge is higher and broader than the ridge 30 km south of it; this area has many gorges and terraces. In the east are three ridges that are separated by the Rūd Nūr and Rūd Lār. At the eastern end of the middle ridge is Mount Demāvand. This peak is 5,774 meters high and overlooks the Harāz Rūd, which flows through the mountains to the coast, receiving the waters of the Nūr River and the Lār River. In contrast to the amply watered, verdant slopes of the Elburz fronting the Caspian Sea, the intermontane valleys are rough and mostly barren. There are few people and little vegetation or farming except in the more open valleys. About 50 km west of the town of Dāmghān the mountains narrow and decrease in height to less than 3,000 meters. Also the trend of the Elburz changes from west to east to southwest to northeast. East of Shāhrūd the mountains dwindle to a high plateau on which is located Jājarm.

North of the Elburz is the Caspian lowland. It is 650 km long and 25 to 35 km wide, although foothills come close to the sea at places. The littoral was formed by the falling away of the sea, which is now some 27 meters below sea level, from the hills. From the shore to the mountains are sand dunes, some lagoons and marshes, then plains and wooded foothills near which are the main towns. The Caspian plain is hot, humid, and quite rainy. It has extensive vegetation and is heavily cultivated by its large population. Conditions are more arid in the east, where the coast north of Bandar Shāh to the Soviet border gives onto a flat steppe that recedes over 160 km inland. Through this plain flows the Gurgān River. The Atrak River to the north forms part of the Soviet-Iranian border.

South of the Elburz is a piedmont zone where Tehran is located. This soon gives way to the major natural feature of inner Iran, the vast desert basins. Once large lakes, these sinks are flat or gently terraced and have no drainage to the sea; most of them lie at about 900 meters above sea level. Encircling mountains close off the circulation of moist air currents inland, so they receive little rain. Summers are extremely hot, but at night one is aware of the large daily variation in temperature. Even in the northwest of the inner basin region, where there is an appreciable supply of water from the Elburz, extreme heat causes a high rate of evaporation.

The largest basin, the Dasht-i Kavīr (a *kavīr* is a tract of viscous, salty slime or mud) lies southeast of the Elburz. Besides *rīg* (sand dunes) and *kavīr*s, it has *shatt*s, deep channels of salty flowing mud that are treacherous because they are covered by a hard crust of salt. In the northwest are salt domes. Lesser sumps north and west of the

Dasht-i Kavīr have a *namakzār* (salt lake) at their lowest part. Gravel and silt, as well as sand and boulders, are found at higher levels. From Kavīr Masīlā in the west to Bijistān Kavīr in the east, the whole region is known as the Dasht-i Kavīr.

The southern Lūt is located southeast of the Dasht-i Kavīr and is bounded by the southeastern Zagros to the west, the eastern uplands of Iran to the east, and by a narrow mountain chain to the south. On the lowest, western side (250 meters above sea level) of this long oval sink is a *namakzār* over 160 km long from northwest to southeast and up to 40 km wide. Eighty km to the east is a mass of sand dunes of an even larger area. Between these bodies of water and sand is the Shar-i Lūt, where dust storms have eroded ridges and channels in a former lake bed which resemble the ruins of ancient cities. Hot, windy, dry, and salty, the southern Lūt is the most desolate region of Iran; there is some farming between its fringes and the surrounding mountains, where water is available. Further basins are located southwest of the Dasht-i Kavīr. The Ardistān-Yazd basin, which lies along the periphery of the eastern Zagros, is distinguished by tracts of sand and *kavīr*. A second congeries of long and narrow salt basins, which also have *kavīr*s, lies to the southwest between Isfahān and Sīrjān. This series is completely enclosed by the mountains at about 1,500 meters and is 600 meters higher than the Ardistān-Yazd basin. Further within the Zagros, at an even greater height, is the Nīrīz basin.

Eastern Iran. This area east of the Elburz Mountains, the inner basins, and the southern Zagros, is over 1,500 km long from north to south; its mean width is about 320 km. Irregular upland massifs separated by troughs over 1,000 meters above sea level make up the definite if less pronounced eastern rim of the country.

Trending northwest to southeast along the Soviet frontier is a set of ridges on whose western end is the Köpet Dāgh; on the east are the Hazār Masjid mountains. The Atrak River flows west and the Kashaf River east between this ridge group and another parallel massif 80 km to the southwest. This second ridge system has the Kūh-i 'Alī chain on its west, the Kūh-i Binālūd in its center, and the Pusht-i Kūh on its southeast. At over 3,000 meters above sea level, the Kūh-i Binālūd peaks are hundreds of meters higher than the other mountains of the region. Both these sets of ridges are 500 to 550 km long and about 65 km wide. Proximity to the Caspian Sea gives their narrow western valleys more rain, hence vegetation (including some woods) and more auspicious conditions for cultivation than the more eastern valleys receive. Each ridge group has gorges and cliffs on its Atrak valley side. Sizable dry and sandy plains with *namakzār*s lie south of the Kūh-i 'Alī and Kūh-i Binālūd ranges.

The Nīshāpūr plain separates the latter range from the Kūh-i Surkh mountains farther south; 250 to 350 km from east to west, about 80 km wide and 2,400 meters high, they are mostly desolate. Their southern side is quite steep and eroded by gullies. The central Kūh-i Surkh contains a high, rolling plateau; eastward is the slender and dome-like Kūh-i Bizak mountain range. Streams from the north- and southwest of the Kūh-i Surkh drain to *kavīr*s farther west. The Kūh-i Khvāf forms the southeastern extension of the Kūh-i Surkh. East of it is the Harī Rūd, whose course turns north out of Afghanistan and makes up the northern section of the Iran–Afghanistan frontier. Before the Qā'in-Birjand highlands are reached, a plain is encountered on which there is a series of sumps from northwest to southeast. The largest is Bijistān Kavīr; next in size is Namaksār-i Khvāf, on the border with Afghanistan.

The Qā'in-Birjand highlands are some 400 km long from northwest to southeast and are up to 240 km wide in the middle. In the north, where the mountains trend in a northwest to southeast direction, there is undulating highland; there are grasses, trees, and patches of cultivation on ridges and in gullies above the 1,200 meter level. Lower down on the plains are sand dunes and *kavīr*. The mountains in the south trend west-northwest to east-southeast and are quite austere. The towns of Birjand and Qā'in have grown up where there is a relative abundance of arable land and pasturage. Southeast of where the mountains taper to a ridge and plateau below Neh is the Helmand basin of the Sīstān lowland, although only one-ninth of this basin lies within Iran. However, as this area is the lowest part, no more than 450 meters above sea level, it receives the drainage of the silt-laden water that flows from the mountains of Afghanistan and Iran after the thaw of snow in the spring. The main feeding river is the Helmand, after which is named the Hāmūn-i Helmand (Lake Helmand). Depending upon annual rainfall, this shallow lake can reach 3,000 sq km in extent. Before the spring waters come, it diminishes to 1,100 sq km. Another 750 to 800 sq km of it becomes swamp. Since it has drainage, the Hāmūn-i Helmand is a fresh water lake. This property renders the Sīstān basin an important area for farming and pasturage. From the lake outward are mud and silt, then sand and clay, and finally sand hills, pebbles, and stones.

Southwest of the Sīstān district is a 450 km long tract of northwest-to-southeast tending mountains known after its principal range, the Kūh-i Taftān. The most notable features of this region are the Zāhidān plateau in the north, and the fertile Khāsh valley in the south, which stands at 1,200 meters above sea level. On the southwest the high, broken, and narrow Kūh-i Basmān mountain chain joins the Kūh-i Taftān to the Zagros Mountains farther west. The Kūh-i Basmān separates the southern Lūt from the Jaz Muriān basin to its south. This basin is over 300 km long and is about 100 km wide. At its lowest point is the salty, seasonal Hāmūn Muriān that is fed by *wādī*s, but principally by the Rūd Halīl from the west and the Rūd Bampur from the east. These *wādī*s and other streams have gullies around the southern perimeter of the basin. Ranged around the lake are plains and terraces of silt and sand dunes. There are low hills and sandy tracts in the eastern Jaz Muriān and eroded islets of rock and rugged hills in the west. Cultivation is carried out along the upper reaches of the basin and along the rivers, particularly at Īrānshahr and Bampūr.

The southern rim of the Jaz Muriān is formed by the Bashāgird hill range, about 120 km from the Makrān coast. These drab green hills are the watershed of Baluchistan; they begin 65 km west of Mīnāb and stretch 400 km to the Pakistan frontier. Peaks of their western section, where there are gaps giving access to the north, reach up to 2,100 meters. The eastern Bashāgird range flattens out into a broad plateau of hill ranges and plains drained by *wādī*s and rivers flowing south.

At places in the midst of the closely packed hills south of the Bashāgird range are small bench-like plains and irregular masses of colored loaf-shaped rocks. Extending for 80 km to the Makrān coast are east-to-west trending outcroppings of red and brown hills shaped like saucers, many of them cliffed. Between them are terraced valleys and plains through which streams course to the coast. Here and there are isolated groups of rocks of most curious shapes, and fingers of hills reach to the coast of western Makrān and divide it into five sections; the coastal plain retreats farther into the interior northwest of Chāh Bahār. Northwest of Jāsk on the Bīābān coast of the Strait of Hormuz are bare, sharp-crested, hill ridges of sandstone whose alignment, contrary to the rest of the hills of Makrān, is from north to south. The Makrān coast is low and sandy, with occasional swamps in the west. Farther east, hills come close to the shore and there are cliffed caps.

Iraq

Iraq lies between 29° 05′ N and 37° 22′ N and 38° 45′ E to 48° 45′ E. Its total area is 438,446 km, including half of the Neutral Zone with Kuwait and its territorial waters. Iraq is bordered on the north by Turkey for 305 km; on the east, by Iran for 1,515 km;

on the south by Kuwait for 254 km and by Sa'ūdī Arabia for 895 km; and on the west by Jordan for 147 km and Syria for 603 km. Its coastline on the Persian Gulf is 58 km long.

Iraq's main geographical regions are the western and southern deserts, which are part of the Arabian plateau; upper Mesopotamia, which includes the Jazīra, the land between the Tigris and Euphrates rivers above Baghdad, and the Assyrian plains and foothills; and lower Mesopotamia, the alluvial plain comprising the area from the Euphrates at Fallūja in the north to the Khor Zubair in the southeast to the Iranian frontier. All of the latter area is less than 100 meters above sea level. Mesopotamia is the trough between the Arabian plateau and the mountain area of Kurdistan in the northeast. The deserts of Iraq, including the Jazīra, form about 260,000 sq km. The alluvial plain covers some 93,000 sq km, and the plains and foothills area with the mountain region comprise about 80,000 sq km. The main rivers are the Tigris, whose length in Iraq is 1,418 km, and the Euphrates, whose length is 1,213 km. The confluence of these two rivers is at Qarmat 'Alī, where begins the 110 km long Shatt al-'Arab. The length in Iraq of other important rivers is: the Greater Zāb, 150 km; the Lesser Zāb, 250 km; and the Diyāla, 300 km. The only river with its entire course within the country is the Adhaim; its length is 230 km.

Mountains of Kurdistan

The mountain region of Iraqi Kurdistan forms the southern periphery of the Taurus and the western periphery of the Zagros mountain ranges. It lies northwest of a line from where the Tigris enters Iraq from Turkey, southeast through Mosul and Kirkūk to the Iranian frontier below Halabja. In the far north, the tributaries of the Khābūr Sū River cut gorges through mountains along the Turkish frontier. These, and other tributaries which flow east to west (the trend of the mountains of the district), drain the grassy but treeless plain of Zakhō. The western Khābūr Sū forms a part of the frontier and joins the Tigris at Maghāra. The Jabal Bakhair and Tang-i Darā ranges form the southern watershed of the Khābūr basin.

The main mountain area is farther east in the basin of the Greater and Lesser Zāb rivers. The mountain massifs here are barriers, as there are few passes between them save for gorges carved out by tributary rivers. The principal gorges of the Greater Zāb basin are the Rukuchuk northeast of Barzan and the Bekhme west of Ruwandiz. To their west are three ranges. Linki Dāgh-Chīya-ī Shīrīn is mostly precipitous and rocky, but there is woodland on its southern side, and the valley of the Greater Zāb to its south is flat enough for farming. Next is the Ghara Dāgh-Piris Dāgh range. It is 65 km long, 3 to 5 km wide, about 2,000 meters high, and consists of twin ridges; its lower slopes are wooded. The third and southernmost range is Chiyākira Dāgh-Aqra Dāgh-Berat Dāgh. Along it are cliffs and plateaus, as well as narrow ridges. The Khazir Sū River rises here, cuts between Chiyākira Dāgh and Aqra Dāgh, and flows south to meet the Greater Zāb in the Assyrian hills.

East of the Rukuchuk and Bekhme gorges, the mountains trend northwest to southeast and reach their greatest height, over 3,500 meters, along the Iranian border. This area, in which are located the country's major forests, is drained by the Barasgird and Dubor rivers, tributaries of the Greater Zāb. North of Ruwandiz is a small fertile plain called Dasht-i Diyāna. Southeast of the Rukuchuk gorge stands Baradost Dāgh, a steep, bare ridge with caves; below its southwestern face the Greater Zāb and a tributary meet and turn southwest through the Bekhme gorge. Ruwandiz is situated at the eastern end of this ridge. The main ranges between this town and the Erbil plain to the southwest are Kandīl Dāgh (on the Iranian frontier), Karokhi Dāgh, Bejan Dāgh,

Harīr Dāgh, Khatī Dagh, and Sefīn Dāgh. Many fruit and nut trees and vines grow on these mountains, and the soil in this district is fertile and heavily cultivated where possible.

The basin of the Lesser Zab lies to the east and southeast of Khoi Sanjaq. The river itself, where it is part of the frontier, gathers tributary waters from the south and east and follows a path northwestward before it slices through the Kūh-i Resh-Kurkur Dāgh range. The Lesser Zāb then strikes south and forces a way through the Habal Sultān and Pīr-i Mukurun ranges farther west. The principal features of the basin are woodlands and green valleys in the southeast and the Pizhder and Rania plains north of the Lesser Zab. The fan-shaped Pizhder plain is cultivated; to the west across the Kūh-i Resh, the Rania plain is marshy in its lower sections due to numerous streams and poor drainage.

Four ranges define the configuration of the Diyāla river basin. Between the Azmar Dāgh and the Baranand Dagh is the 70 km long Sulaimāniyya plain, which is 15 km wide in the northwest and 35 km wide in the southeast. This fertile tract is watered by the Tanjero River. Northeast of where it joins with the Diyāla River is the Halabja plain, an eastern extension of the Sulaimāniyya plain The high, dark green Avromān Dāgh range, along which runs the frontier for a distance, defines the northeast boundary of the Diyāla basin. The Cham-i Dawana, a tributary that flows southeastward into the Diyāla on its southwesterly course toward the Assyrian foothills, drains a valley between the Baranand Dāgh and the wooded Qarā Dāgh ranges; the latter range is the southeastern extension of the Baziān range.

Upper Mesopotamia

The hills and plains of Assyria, the eastern part of upper Mesopotamia, lie between the mountains of the northeast and the Tigris River. They are divided into sections by the Greater and Lesser Zāb rivers. The wooded hills of the north below the Jabal Bakhair-Aqra Dāgh ranges have ridges and plateaus in their midst, but there are fertile valleys with orchards and vineyards in places, and the southern extensions of these hills are often grassy, though in many places cut by ravines. The plains of Mosul consist of rich, undulating steppeland that slopes from over 600 meters in the north to 200 meters above sea level in the south. Many streams and watercourses traverse it; the main river is the southerly flowing Khazir Sū, which merges with the Greater Zāb north of Quwair. Prominent hills are Jabal Maqlūb and Jabal Zirqa Bardaresh.

Central Assyria, whose mountain boundary in the northeast is formed by the Safīn Dāgh and Habbal-Sultān Dāgh, contains the plains of Khoi Sanjaq, Erbil, and Qaraj. The Khoi Sanjaq plain has few trees. It is crisscrossed by many streams, and there is farming on some of its plateaus. The northern part of Erbil plain is stony, but elsewhere it is heavily cultivated. The grassy Avana Dāgh and dark Jabal Qara Chauq hill ranges separate Erbil and Qaraj plains. The latter is mostly flat but its arable soil lacks adequate watering.

Southern Assyria is bounded by the Baziān mountain range and the Iranian frontier. Foremost among the many rivers flowing through it are the Diyāla and Adhaim; the soil is good in places, but many of the plains and plateaus are suitable only for pasturage. Jabal Hamrīn, the principal hill range, is red-colored, slender, and treeless. It follows a southeasterly direction from Fat-ha gorge, about 25 km south of where the Lesser Zāb meets the Tigris, 200 km to Deli 'Abbās and beyond. The Jabal Hamrīn's bare southwestern slope rises more steeply than its northern face, and the overall effect is that of a steppe.

The Jazīra

The land between the Tigris and Euphrates rivers from north of Baghdad to the Syrian border is called the Jazīra (island). Save for hills in the north and cultivated tracts along the rivers, it is a desert plateau descending from a height of 450 meters in the northeast and 250 meters in the northwest to 80 meters above sea level near Baghdad. In the northern Jazīra west of Mosul are low east-to-west tending hill ranges, the most prominent of which, Jabal Sinjar, is 80 km long, some 12 km wide, and 1,500 meters at its highest. North of these hills, the Jazīra is drained by the perennial Wādī Murr. Jutting northwest from Qaiyāra near the Tigris to Tell ʿAfar is a string of little hills, with Jabal Qaiyāra on the southeast and Jabal Shaikh Ibrāhīm on the northwest. Farther to the south and parallel to the Tigris is a brace of narrow, rough hill ranges, Jabal Makhūl and the short Jabal Khanūqa, which are northwestern extensions of Jabal Hamrīn.

The steep-banked Wādī Tharthar is the main watercourse of the Jazīra. It rises in the Jabal Sinjar, gathers subsidiary *wādī*s north of Hadar, and pursues a southerly course 210 km to the Umm Rahal, a salt depression northeast of Hit that is fringed by cliffs. West of Takrīt is the Tharthar depression. The land east of Wādī Tharthar is known as Wādiyān al-Hasabiyyāt, that to the west as al Burayza. A curious feature of the southern part of the latter area is hollow domes of gypsum bulging out of the soil, many of which are covered by gravel. Western al-Burayza is drained by the upper reaches of Wādī ʿAjīj before its course passes across the frontier into Syria. Milha Ashkar is the main *sabkha* or salt flat (the Arabic term equivalent to Persian *namakzār*) of the region.

Lower Mesopotamia. Lower Mesopotamia between the Tigris and Jabal Hamrīn is a desert, except in its southern part where the Tigris and Diyāla rivers converge. The banks of these rivers and the area of the Khalis canal are heavily cultivated. West of the Adhaim River, which flows south into the Tigris, are sandhills and the shallow Lake Shari. The land east of the Tigris away from its cultivated banks from Baghdad to Kūt is also a desert, but canals from the Diyāla project southward into this district and support some farming. In the east is the Hōr al-Shubaika wasteland. This is flooded in winter and, although never deep, can spread over a wide area and sometimes join with Suwaiqiyya marsh north of Kūt. East of the Hōr al-Shubaika the country is riven by streams from foothills on the Iranian frontier.

West of Fallūja, a few kilometers below the Euphrates, is Lake Habbāniyya, which takes the waters of that river if flooding is imminent. Farther south is a saline alluvial depression, Abū Dibbis. Various canals irrigate the land east of the Euphrates between Fallūja and Musaiyib. At the Hindiyya barrage south of Musaiyib the Hilla Canal, the old bed of the Euphrates, takes some of the river's water for distribution above and below Dīwāniyya, but very little water returns from it through creeks to the Euphrates below Sāmarrā. South of the small town of Kifl the Euphrates splits into two courses. These, the Shatt al-Shāmiyya on the east and the Kūfa channel on the west, disperse their water into the Shāmiyya marshes. Having regained a single channel farther south at Shināfiyya, the Euphrates again divides into two courses, the Shatt al-Sabīl and the Shatt al-ʿAtshān, which combine west of Sāmarrā. Further canals siphon off the Euphrates waters from above Nāsiriyya to below Sūq al-Shuyūkh, east of which the river disperses into the Hōr al-Hammār. This lake extends roughly 110 km from east of Sūq al-Shuyūkh to the confluence of the Tigris and Euphrates at Qarmat ʿAlī; its average width is perhaps 15 km, but its northern boundary, which is bordered by low land liable to flooding, is indistinct. In this district grow tall reeds and grasses. The ground south of Hōr al-Hammār rises to the Shāmiyya or Syrian desert.

Away from the intensely irrigated river banks, the terrain between the Tigris and Euphrates from Baghdad to the Shatt al-Gharrāf is in large part wasteland or marshes that dry up in the summer. Some of the irrigated areas suffer from salinity. Southwest of Kūt is the Hōr Dalmaj, a permanent marsh, and in the south are empty, saline, alluvial flats. The Shatt al-Gharrāf branches southwards from the Tigris at Kūt for 160 km and ends in marshes above Nāsiriyya; occasionally it floods the irrigated land along its banks. East of the Shatt al-Gharrāf lies more salty, alluvial land. The Shatt Dumaila, a former channel of the Tigris, departs from that river east of Kūt, follows a south-easterly course, and feeds into Hōr Sanniyya, which lies west of the Tigris from 'Alī Gharbī to south of Amāra; the tract to its west and that to the east of the Tigris is often flooded. Toward the Iranian border is a barren plain, patches of which are sandy, and stream beds run southwestward from hills on the frontier. East of the Tigris below Amara is a salty wasteland flooded by the Hōr al-Hawiza, which stretches south to Qarmat 'Alī.

Along the Shatt al-'Arab from Qarmat 'Alī to the Persian Gulf are extensive date groves. Flanking the river's right bank is a large mud flat; between this and Basra there lies a district of irrigated areas, creeks, and swamps, these latter being the source of the Khōr Zubair, a channel 30 km long that flows southward into the Khōr 'Abdullāh; then westward begins the desert.

The Deserts of the West and South

Wādiyān, the western desert, is bounded by the Euphrates, the Syrian, Jordanian, and Sa'ūdī Arabian borders, and by the southern desert, which lies east of a line southwest from Najif. In the far west, Wādiyān is over 600 meters above sea level. Many *wādī*s traverse its bare, stony surface from west to east. In the north is Wādī Haurān, which is 350 km long from its source at Jabal 'Anaiza to where it comes to the Euphrates below Hadītha. Wādī Ghadaf crosses central Wādiyān, and in the south is Wādī Ubaiyid, which originates well to the west of Iraq in Sa'ūdī Arabia. The main oases of the region are Shithātha and Rahhāliyya to the west of Karbalā.

The western part of the southern desert is called al-Hajara, rocky and strewn with stones and boulders; elsewhere are depressions and small scattered ridges. *Wādī*s tending northeastward to the Euphrates are balked by a ridge of sand up to 20 km wide that runs parallel to the river from Shināfiyya to southeast of Sūq al-Shuyūkh. Their waters feed a narrow *sabkha*, the Rahab, on the northwestern side of this sand strip.

The Haniya ridge between Busaiya and the Neutral Zone separates al-Hajara from al-Dibdiba, the eastern section of the southern desert, much of which is sandy and covered by bushes. The Shāmiyya south of the Hōr al-Hammār has been noted. A steppe called al-Rāha lies west of Khōr Zubair, and immediately north of the Kuwaiti frontier is Jabal Sanam, a small hill range 100 meters high. Near the al-Ratak bluffs farther west is the beginning of Wādī Bātin. The Euphrates sand strip is prevented from reaching it by the Makhāzima ridges parallel to the *wādī*, and numerous wells are found in the area. Both al-Hajara and al-Dibdiba continue southward into Sa'ūdī Arabia.

Kuwait

Kuwait lies at the northwestern corner of the Persian Gulf. Its mainland territory stretches from 20° 45' N to 30° 05' N and from 46° 30' E to 48° 30' E and comprises an area of 16,918 sq km, with Warba, Būbiyān, and other islands adding a further 900 sq km.

Kuwait borders Sa'ūdī Arabia on the south for 250 km and Iraq on the north and west for 240 km, and it fronts the Persian Gulf for 195 km.

The main feature of the country is Kuwait Bay, a 40 km indentation in the coastline. The sandy southern side of the bay, where Kuwait City is located, has three coves, and to the west of the innermost part of the bay is the oasis of Jahrā. The northeast to southwest-trending Jabal al-Zōr hills lie a few kilometers inland of its northwestern shore. Farther east and along the Khōr al-Sabiya there is swamp and marshland.

Northern Kuwait is a hard, stony desert, traversed from west to east by low ridges that end at a trough at Rawdatain where water gathers in winter. The Wādī Bātin, which forms the western frontier, is one of the few spots with pockets of scrub, and elsewhere in the west are mud pans and stretches of gravel. Sandy, undulating southeastern Kuwait is lower than the northwest, and only a few isolated hills, some reaching up to 300 meters, break the monotony of its treeless plain. Vegetation is found along the shallow, 15 km wide al-Shaqq valley, which extends from near Jahrā southward to form the western boundary of the Partitioned Zone with Sa'ūdī Arabia. Paralleling the coast 8 km in the interior is the 125 meter high Ahmadī ridge, after which is named the town and oil port; and the sandy coast is interspersed with *sabkha*s and gravel.

Bahrain

Bahrain, an archipelago of 33 islands[1] 662 sq km in area, lies in the western Persian Gulf between Qatar and Sa'ūdī Arabia. Bahrain Island is 565 km in extent and is located at 50° 27′ E to 50° 38′ E and between 25° 47′ N and 26° 14′ N. It is 48 km long from north to south and 16 km at its widest, and its shape is that of a sea horse.

The southern half of the island is desert, with low and level land with sand and salt flats and marshes. Inland of the partly cultivated western coast, the land rises 50 meters to a light-colored plateau cut by *wādī*s. Inward-facing escaprments overlook a depression 20 km long and 6.5 km wide, in whose middle is dark Jabal Dukhān, 122 meters high, its name, "Smoke Mountain," being due to the fact that in summer it is often shrouded in haze. The limestone rock of the plateau is covered by sand in places, but much of it is strewn with gravel, which was used millenniums ago to make the thousands of tumuli in the north. Manāma lies at the northeastern tip of the island, and to its west is a 5 km wide strip of cultivation, the fruits and vegetables grown here being watered by abundant springs and artesian wells.

Sa'ūdī Arabia

Sa'ūdī Arabia, the largest state bordering the Persian Gulf, is located from 34° 30′ E to 56° E and between about 16° N and 32° N. Its estimated area of 2,150,000 to 2,260,000 sq km comprises four-fifths of the Arabian peninsula. The approximate length of its frontiers is: Kuwait, 235 km; Iraq, 895 km; Jordan, 705 km; Gulf of Aqaba and Red Sea, over 1,700 km; Yemen Arab Republic, perhaps 650 km; People's Democratic Republic of South Yemen, 750 km; and the sultanate of Oman, 705 km. Sa'ūdī Arabia's borders with the latter three states are not fully demarcated. The United Arab Emirates and Qatar share about 530 km and 29 km, respectively, of boundary with Sa'ūdī Arabia, which has about 365 km of coastline on the Persian Gulf. In 1969, the Sa'ūdīs and Kuwaitis partitioned their Neutral Zone, each administering half, and Sa'ūdī Arabia and Iraq agreed to divide equally their Neutral Zone in 1975. Offshore boundaries exist with

1. For islands other than Bahrain, see Appendix D.

Iran, Bahrain, and Qatar. The country is a plateau sloping west to east, with four main geographical regions: Hijāz, 'Asīr, Najd, and the Eastern Province, formerly called al-Hasā.

Hijāz

The Hijāz ("barrier") a mostly mountainous region, lies in northwestern Sa'ūdī Arabia, and forms the northern section of an escarpment that parallels the Red Sea coast south into Yemen. The mountains rise from 1,500 meters around Tabūk to 2,100 to 2,400 meters in the Midian district, then descend to under 1,000 meters near Mecca, where there is a gap south of which begins 'Asīr. The Hijāz range is steep and bare on its western side; wādīs have cut high and narrow valleys along it. Among the more prominent wādīs, some of which provide routes into the interior, are Kamra, Sooi, Dama, Hanra, and al-Hamad, near which is Medina, the largest oasis in the region. Oases are found particularly where fertile soil has been deposited by wādīs and where springs are adequate. Other oases with some agriculture lie along the Wādī Fātima that flows from near Mecca to the Red Sea below Jidda, the main port of the coast. The arid, sandy littoral plain of the Hijāz is less than 15 km wide, and mountains sometimes abut upon it; from Yanbū' to south of Jidda the coast attains its greatest width, over 50 km in places. Some coastal towns (al-Wajh and Rābigh, for instance) are sited along sharms, deep inlets, and there are many reefs lying offshore.

'Asīr

South of Mecca begin the mountains of 'Asīr, which quickly rise to over 2,500 meters near Tā'if and to over 2,700 meters farther south. These too are precipitous on their Red Sea side and are incised by wādīs, among them Yamlamlam, Lith, and Taiya. Rain is more plentiful in 'Asīr, and along the upper reaches of the roughly 50 km wide Tihāma coastal plain lies the most fertile land of Sa'ūdī Arabia, where many grains, vegetables, and fruits are grown. Further inland the mountains are terraced for cultivation, and at their higher levels are the country's only forests, mainly of juniper. Nowhere along the Tihāma coast, however, is there a suitable natural harbor.

Najd

The relief of the eastern side of the Hijāz and 'Asīr escarpment is less abrupt and cut up than the western side, and there are more open valleys. The mountains give way to the broad, eroded, stony Najd plateau, on which are dispersed occasional sandy tracts and small ridges. From an elevation of 1,500 meters in the west, Najd slopes eastward to the Dahnā, where it is only 600 meters above sea level. The mountains are the source of important eastward-flowing wādīs, such as Rīma and Sirra in the north and Bīsha and Dawāsir in the south. These and other wādīs have given rise to oases towns, from Abu Sa'ūd (formerly Najrān) and Qal'at Bīsha to Buraida, and provide places for pasturage in the western highlands of the plateau. Ranging down much of western Najd are harras, large expanses of solidified lava strewn with sharp rocks and boulders; the main ones are Harrat al-Uwairid, Harrat Khaibar, Harrat Rāhat, and Harrat Buqūm.

Northern Najd is the southern extension of the Syrian Desert. Along it from west to east are Wādī Sirhān, al-Harra (lava field), al-Hamad, a flat and dark plateau with gravel, and then al-Wādiyān, through which flow many wādīs into Iraq. Some places in northern Najd, which forms part of the Syrian Desert, have grass and scrub. Farther southeast is al-Hajara; this rocky flatland is flanked on the continent by Wādī Bātin. To the south is the Nafūd, a desert of some 60,000 sq km, at its greatest extent over 325 km from east to west and 270 km wide, and lying 700 to 800 meters above sea level. Ridges of dunes up to 130 meters high stretch for many kilometers and are variably aligned due to erratic local winds, but crescent-shaped dunes are seen in the northwest. Grazing is available for a short time after winter rains, and the Jawf oasis is located on the northern periphery. The desert is encompassed by eroded rock ridges, except in the east, where stony tracts are enclosed by strips of sand, the Nafūd Dāhī and the Dahnā, which curve south over 900 km to the Rub' al-Khālī.

The Jabal Shammar lies along the southern perimeter of the desert and is a massif some 1,400 meters above sea level in the west and 700 meters high in the east. Numerous oases, such as Hā'il, lie in the Jabal Shammar and to the southeast in the Qasīm district. where there is important pasturage. Here is the northern end of Jabal Tuwaiq escarpment, which describes a flat arc 800 km south almost to the Rub' al-Khālī, and is 800 to 1,100 meters high, with the crest of its westward-looking cliff face rising up to 300 meters above the Nafūd Dāhī. Sundry oases are located near it, particularly to the northwest of Riyadh. A notable *wādī*, that of Hanīfa, starts in central Najd, gathers tributaries, cuts through Jabal Tuwaiq near Kharj oasis, then makes a path toward the Persian Gulf. A vale is formed where the Jabal Tuwaiq tapers east to another, lesser escarpment; this cliff is the western periphery of a ridge called al-Biyād that parallels on the west the 35 mile wide Dahnā sand strip, the border of Najd.

The 650,000 sq km of the Rub' al-Khālī sand desert encompasses the entirety of southeastern Sa'ūdi Arabia. It is some 1,250 km long and 450 km wide; its elevation decreases from over 900 meters east of 'Asīr to 150 meters above sea level on the frontier with the United Arab Emirates. Its dunes are over 200 meters high in the west, where there are patches of quicksand; in the east are *sabkha*s and sand flats, as well as long sand dunes. Often not receiving rain for years at a time, it is almost completely arid.

Eastern Province

This region is about 300 km wide. Al-Dibdiba, a plain of sand and gravel transected by Wādī Bātin, lies in the north. Al-Summān is an eroded stony plateau 150 km wide flanked on the west by the Dahnā and on the east by low, broken scarps and sand dunes. Tracts of the low-lying coastal plain are oil fields and Hufūf, the center of al-Hasā oasis, whose many springs make it an important agricultural center. East of Hufūf, the Jafūra, a finger of gravelly desert, points north from the Rub' al-Khālī. The coastline is comprised of sand, salt marshes, and gravel, and north of the oil port of Dammam is found Qatīf oasis.

Qatar

Qatar is a desolate peninsula jutting northward into the western Persian Gulf. It lies between 50° 45' E and 51° 40' E and from 24° 30' N to 26° 10' N; it is 85 to 90 km at its widest and 165 km long; its estimated area is 10,360 sq km. Qatar borders Sa'ūdi Arabia for some 29 km and the United Arab Emirates for about 19 km on the south, and its coastline is roughly 360 km long.

At the base of the peninsula are *sabkha*s and sand dunes. Low hills are Ta's al-Dawain and Umm Sa'īd in the southeast, and the Jabal Naqiyyān sandhills run along the southeastern coast north of Khōr al-Udaid. Depressions, escarpments, and low hills break up the flat, stony limestone desert plateau that covers much of Qatar and descends gently from west to east. There are tracts of gravel and marl, and the middle of the country, where there rises a swell, is covered by a cobble conglomerate. Southwest of

Dōha rises the Jabal al-Tawār. Other distinctive features are narrow-necked crevices (*duhlān*) that have been formed by water filtering through to underground cavities that have caused the surface to break. Among these are Dahl al-Madhlam, Dahl al-Safar, and Dahl al-Haman.

Along the west coast is the 55 km long and 5 km wide Jabal Dukhān range of sandhills that reaches over 75 meters high. Wells are numerous. Rainwater collects into pools at al-Siliyya, al-Majīda, and Rashīd. The main *wādī*s are Muhairab, al-Maida, al-Banāt, and al-'Uqda. Northern Qatar is quite low and, unlike the south, has some natural vegetation; Bū Hasā is an important oasis 1 km northeast of Lusail. Jabal al-Fuwairāt, near the northeast coast, is the most prominent hill. The coastline is low and consists of sand, gravel, and *sabkha*s; and there are numerous small bays, lagoons, and inlets.

The United Arab Emirates

The United Arab Emirates lie between 22° 50' N to 26° N and from 51° E to 56° 25' E, bordering Qatar on the northwest for 19 km, Sa'ūdī Arabia on the west, south, and southeast for approximately[2] 530 km, and Oman on the southeast and northeast for over 450 km. The UAE front on the Persian Gulf for over 695 km and on the Gulf of Oman for about 90 km. Forming the country's overall area of 75,110 sq km are (from southwest to northeast): Abū Dhabī, 64,700 sq. km; Dubai, 3,880 sq km; Sharja, 2,590 sq km; 'Ajmān, 260 sq km; Umm al-Qaiwain, 780 sq km; Ra's al-Khaima, 1,700 sq km; and, on the Gulf of Oman, Fujaira, 1,200 sq km. 'Ajmān, which forms an enclave in the territory of Sharja, possesses small pockets of land in the Western Hajar Mountains at Manāma and Masfūt. Sharja has important settlements at Dibba, Khōr Fakkān, Kalba on the Gulf of Oman, and in the mountains. Umm al-Qaiwain possesses a small oasis at Falaj al-Mu'allā. Ra's al-Khaima has a sizable holding in the Western Hajar to the southwest of Fujaira.

Abū Dhabī

The westernmost district, Abū Dhabī, has the Khōr al-'Udaid on its west and the *sabkha* of Matti to the east. It consists mostly of dark sand dunes, stony hillocks, and pebbly tracts. The treacherous and lifeless *sabkha* of Matti extends along the coastal embayment for 60 km and recedes up to 100 km inland, and to the east of this salt marsh is the Dhafra region. Near the coast are areas of gravel and *sabkha* that give way to ridges and red sand in the interior. At places, hardy vegetation offers grazing for animals. The Liwā series of some thirty oases, 100 km from the coast and 160 km southwest of Abū Dhabī City, extends 65 km from west to east. These oases lie in depressions overlooked by sand dunes and possess good soil, with water available several meters below the surface; to the south is the Rub' al-Khālī.

Sandy desert mitigated by scrub prevails throughout the rest of Abū Dhabī save on the plain of Jawf. This is the northwestern extension of the Zahīra of Oman. On its west is al-'Aīn oasis, which lies 160 km east of Abū Dhabī City. Adequate water from the Western Hajar is available for the good soil of the oasis, seven of whose ten settlements belong to Abū Dhabī; the others, including Buraimī, are possessed by Oman. South of al-'Ain is a group of hills called Jabal Hafīt, which is a spur of the Jajar. The coast is low and sandy with low hills and cliffs in places. Farther north there are lagoons, creeks, and sand.

---

2. The UAE–Saudi frontier has not been definitely demarcated.

The Northern Emirates

As the Oman promontory dwindles to the Musandam peninsula and the UAE coastline trends northeastward, sands and mountains converge. Between them, with stretches of shingle to the west, is a thin and nearly continuous strip of plain whose soil is the gravel outwash brought by *wādī*s from the mountains. The Wādī Samainī is the southern perimeter of this plain, whose 30 to 35 km long southern section is known as Madām. It is enclosed on the west by the Jabal Samainī, a range of hills independent of the Hajar that rise up to 600 meters. Madām has some woodland, as does the plain of Dhaid to which it is connected by the stony Gallah Mahāfidh plateau. Dhaid is 25 km square, with sand hills to the west and mountains to the east, and its main *wādī* is Wādī Hām. Encroaching sand constricts passage north to Jīrī plain, which is 25 km from north to south and is 10 to 12 km wide, with dark and mostly sandy soil and a moderate amount of vegetation. The northernmost plain, Sīr, lies 10 km north and south of Ra's al-Khaima town and is at most 9 km wide; it is cultivated, with date groves.

The Western Hajar Mountains occupy the northeast of the United Arab Emirates. They are 25 to 30 km wide, and range some 150 km south from the UAE–Oman frontier on the Persian Gulf to those states' southern border below Masfūt, and then continue farther south into Oman. Some peaks reach up to 2,500 meters. There is cultivation at a few oases, and vegetation grows along *wādī*s such as Sījī and Hām, but otherwise the Hajar is barren. The mountains come directly onto the eastern (Gulf of Oman) coast, which is called Shamailiyya, and villages are only found where there are small indentations along the littoral. Only in the vicinity of Fujaira do the mountains recede inland.

Oman

Oman is located between 16° 40′ N and 26° 20′ N and from 51° 50′ E to 59° 40′ E. As its frontiers with its neighbors are not clearly defined, Oman's territory is estimated at between 272,000 and 300,000 sq km. The approximate length of its boundaries is: People's Democratic Republic of South Yemen, 307 km; Sa'ūdī Arabia, 705 km; and the United Arab Emirates, 452 km. Its coastline, fronting the Gulf of Oman and Arabian Sea, totals nearly 1,700 km and, with its littoral along the Strait of Hormuz, about 1,864 km.

Peninsular Oman

Cut off from the rest of the country by the United Arab Emirates is the Musandam peninsula and Ru'ūs al-Jibāl promontory, which are about 2,000 sq km in area. Here are steep, desolate mountains, the northern extension of the Western Hajar. They form cliffs on the coast, where bases have been eroded by waves in many places, and Jabal al-Harīm, 25 km south of Khasab, is the highest peak at 2,057 meters. There are a few date groves where valleys give onto small sandy bays. Ra's Musandam is deeply indented by inlets, some of which are up to 15 km long. The heat and humidity of this district are extremely disagreeable in summer.

The Batīna

The Batīna plain extends along the coast of the Gulf of Oman from the UAE frontier in the northwest 250 km to Sīb in the southeast. It is 35 km at its widest, where the Western Hajar Mountains arch away from the coast, and 10 km wide at either end;

in the north are scattered trees and hills of gravel. Batīna is in large part a tract of sand and gravel, some of its outwash from the many *wādi*s that course northeastward down it to the coast, and it is heavily cultivated along a narrow (2 to 3 km) strip several kilometers from the shore for virtually its entire length. Water is obtained for irrigation from underground channels (*aflāj*) tapping water from the Western Hajar.

The Hajar Mountains

Inland of and parallel to the Batīna rise the Western Hajar Mountains. These lie along a northwest-to-southeast axis 270 km from the border with the UAE to the Sumail Gap about 50 km south-southwest of Sīb, with the watershed of the mountains about 65 km from the coast. This range and its foothills stretch up to 40 km toward the coast and 25 km west toward the interior, but its limit on the inner side is less distinct. The overall height of the range is 1,300 meters, but the peaks of the northwest are lower. The Western Hajar are mostly dark, sharp-edged, and without soil; many valleys run perpendicular to the mountains and are quite steep and narrow.

The highest pinnacles are those of the Jabal Akhdar ("Green Mountain"), a 35 km wide massif occupying 80 km at the eastern end of the Western Hajar, many of whose peaks reach over 2,000 meters. The highest, Jabal Shamm to the west of Rustāq, reaches 3,018 meters. As its name suggests, the Jabal Akhdar receives more rain than other areas and has grassy areas and woods, so that some of its valleys support irrigation farming. A plateau high in the mountains cut by ravines falls away precipitously toward the east, and it declines more gently toward inner Oman. Jutting northeast from Jabal Akhdar in the direction of Sīb is a slender ridge 45 km long and 2,200 meters at its highest. Around Sumail Gap, the divide between the Western and Eastern Hajar and the traditional route from the coast to the interior, are many dark, rocky hills.

The roughly 55 km wide Eastern Hajar Mountains describe an arc from east of the Sumail Gap southeast for 200 km to Jabal Khamīs, a small semidetached range aligned from north to south. The mountains' average elevation is 1,900 meters, but they are 1,000 meters lower in the east; the watershed is 80 km from the coast in the northwest and 35 km from the littoral near Sūr. This range is as forbidding as much of the Western Hajar but, unlike the latter, it impinges upon much of the coast as cliffs. The main *wādi*s are Tayin, Banī Jabir, Falāíj, and Banī Khālid.

The Zahīra

The Zahīra plain is bounded by the Western Hajar on the northeast; Jabal Kōr, an outlier of the Western Hajar, and inner Oman on the east; Umm al-Samīm *sabkha* on the southwest; and the Rub' al-Khālī on the west. The small plain of Jawf, on which are located the three villages of the Buraimī Oasis, the UAE frontier, and Jabal Hafīt form its northern perimeter. Zahīra is about 160 km from northwest to southeast and 80 km from northeast to southwest. From a height of 1,000 meters near the mountains, it slopes southwestward to the Rub' al-Khālī, where it is under 100 meters above sea level. The Zahīra consists largely of stretches of sand and gravel, with sand dunes in the west, gravel hills in the east and southeast, and occasional patches of scrub. The main outliers of the Western Hajar located northwest of Ibrī are Jabal Abyad, Jabal Wahba, and Khatmat Dhank. Jabal Kōr is 25 km long from north to south and some of its peaks exceed 2,300 meters. Jabal Aswad and Jabal Fahd are small isolated clusters of hills lying south of Ibrī. Springs and groundwater from the mountains allow cultivation by irrigation at settlements along the upper courses of *wādi*s in the hill fringe, the principal *wādi*s being Dhank, Sawmahan, and al-'Ain.

Inner Oman

The heart of Oman is inner Oman, or Oman proper. This central plateau area slopes southward from the Jabal Akhdar in the direction of the Rub' al-Khālī and Jiddat al-Harāsīs. It is bounded by the Zahīra and Jabal Kōr on the west and the Sharqiyya to the east. As in Zahīra, there is some oasis farming at the periphery of the mountains. The land around Bahla and Nizwa is called the Jawf or "basin," a rocky plain with numerous hills. Below Izkī, the flatter land is characterized by low gravel hills. Otherwise, inner Oman is austere and empty save for a few patches of scrub. The major *wādīs* are Aswad, Bahla, Kalbu, Kabīr, Halfain and Sumail, and Wādī Andam may be considered the division between Oman proper and the Sharqiyya.

The Sharqiyya and Ja'alān

Inland of the Eastern Hajar is the Sharqiyya ("Eastern Province"), which is girdled by inner Oman, the Ja'alān district in the southeast, and the Ramlat al-Wahiba sands to the south. Much of it is sandy, with stony ground as well as sand in the hills and valleys of the north; ridges and scattered scrub are found in the south. There are oases, and Ibra is the main *wādī*. Ja'alān curves around Jabal Khamīs, reaching from the inner hills of the Eastern Hajar and southeast Sharqiyya 80 km to the coast from above Suwayh to al-Ashkhira.

Most of the district is a sandy plain, but there are scattered trees in the west and tracts of gravel hills, particularly east of Jabal Khamīs. The main villages are situated along Wādī al-Bathā, whose course cuts east-southeast into Ja'alān, then runs due east to the coast south of Jabal Khamīs.

The Southeast

From Ramlat al-Wahiba and Umm al-Samīm to the border of the People's Democratic Republic of Yemen, the rest of Oman is a desert save for the small mountain and coastal area of western Dhofār. The Ramlat al-Wahiba is a lake of sand dunes stretching down the southeast coast of Oman for 160 km south of Ja'alān; 100 km to the southwest of it is a *sabkha* in which ends the course of several *wādīs* from inner Oman. Jiddat al-Harāsīs is the large stony region of sand and gravel that comprises the country from the Gulf of Masīra to the Kuria Muria Bay inland to the Rub' al-Khālī, the fringe of whose vast sand ocean lies within western Oman.

Dhofār

This plateau in southwestern Oman is some 100,000 sq km in extent and begins at Rās Sharbithāt, the eastern point of the Kuria Muria Bay. The hard expanse of the Jiddat al-Harāsīs in the northeast gives way along the coast north of Ra's Nūs to Jabal Samhān. This narrow range lies 60 km between western Kuria Muria Bay and Mirbāt. North of the latter place its grassy slopes link with the densely wooded mountains of the Jabal Qāra, the main range of Dhofār, which rises 1,500 meters above sea level. Farther to the west, and lying partly within the PDRY, is Jabal al-Qamar.

From Mirbat 180 km west to the border and up to 25 to 30 km inland, Dhofār catches the rain of the southwest monsoon. The most fertile area is the 50 km of coastline around Salāla, whose alluvial soil is given over to cultivation, with date groves plentiful. No more than 8 km from the shore begin the foothills of the Jabal Qāra, on whose grass and scrub cattle graze, and 25 km to the interior the mountains give way to hills and plains of gravel and sand. Farther north the Wādī Muqshin skirts the southern limit of the Rubʿ al-Khālī.

Selected Bibliography

Al-Feel, M. R. *Iraq. Geographic Study, Social and Economic Development*. Baghdad, 1964.

The American University. *Area Handbook for Iran*. DA Pam. No. 550-68. Washington, D.C., 1971.

———. *Area Handbook for Iraq*. Washington, D.C., 1971.

———. *Area Handbook for Saudi Arabia*. 2nd ed. DA Pam. No. 550-51. Washington, D.C. 1971.

———. *Area Handbook for the Peripheral States of the Arabian Peninsula*. DA Pam. No. 550-92. Washington, D.C., 1971.

Belgrave, J.H.D. *Welcome to Bahrain*. 9th ed. Manama, 1975.

Brice, W. C. *South-West Asia*. London, 1966.

Cressey, G. B. *Crossroads: Land and Life in Southwest Asia*. Chicago, 1960.

Dickson, H.R.P. *Kuwait and Her Neighbours*. London, 1956.

Fisher, W. B. *The Middle East*. 6th ed. London, 1971.

Great Britain, Admiralty, Naval Intelligence Division. *Iraq and the Persian Gulf*. B.R. 524 Geographical Handbook Series. London, 1944.

———. *Persia*. B.R. 525 Geographical Handbook Series.

———. *Western Arabia and the Red Sea*. B.R. 527 Geographical Handbook Series. London, 1946.

Harris, G. L. *Iraq*. New Haven, 1958.

Hawley, D. F. *The Trucial States*. London, 1970.

Hay, R. *The Persian Gulf States*. Washington, D.C., 1959.

Hazard, H. *The Arabian Peninsula*. 3rd ed. New York, 1970.

Johnstone, T. M., and Wilkinson, J. C. "Some geographical aspects of Qatar." *Geographical Journal* 126, 4 (Dec. 1960): 442–50.

The Kingdom of Saudi Arabia. London, 1977.

Lipsky, G. *Saudi Arabia*. London, 1959.

Longrigg, S. H., and Stoakes, F. *Iraq*. London, 1958.

Lorimer, J. G. *Gazetteer of the Persian Gulf, Oman, and Central Arabia*. Calcutta, 1908.

Meigs, P. *Geography of Coastal Deserts*. Paris, 1966.

Qatar, Press and Publication Department, Ministry of Information. *Qatar Year Book*. Doha, 1976.

Rentz, G. *A Sketch of the Geography, People and History of the Arabian Peninsula*. Dhahran, 1960.

Republic of Iraq, Central Statistical Organization, Ministry of Planning. *Annual Abstract of Statistics 1976*. Baghdad, n.d.

Shaw, R. *Kuwait*. London, 1976.

Sultanate of Oman, *Oman*. Muscat, 1972.

Tomkinson, M. *The United Arab Emirates*. London and Hammamet, 1975.

APPENDIX D

Persian Gulf Islands

Iran

In the mouth of Khōr Ghazlān at the head of the Persian Gulf lie Dara and Bumah Islands. These and other islands are virtually extensions of the coastal mud flat. The most important of these islands is 65 km long, Ābādān Island. The Shatt al-'Arab lies to its west and the Khōr Bahmanshīr to its east. It is low and has some date groves along its banks, Ābādān refinery and port are located in the northwest. Khārg Island lies 58 km northwest of Bushire; 8 km by 3 km in size, it is covered by barren, dark brown, flat-topped hills that end in cliffs on the northern and southern coasts. The west coast has cliffs and also sand and rocky points. There is a small cultivated plain and a village on the sandy east coast, and the island is fringed by a reef. Its eastern side is now the site of a major oil terminal. Two miles to the northeast is a low sandy islet with some grass called Khārgū. The major island in Bushire Bay is 6.5 km long, narrow, and divided by a channel into two parts: Shaikh Sa'd on the north and Abbask to the south. Shaikh Sa'd has a rocky strip on its western and on its northern side where there is a village. Elsewhere it is low and swampy, as is Abbask. A smaller island, Muharraq, lies near by.

Some 136 km southeast of Bushire is a low-lying 7 km by ½ km islet called Nakhīlū. Between it and the Tangistān coast is a small, round island, Umm al-Karam. Further southeast, off the Shibkūh coast are the islands of Shaikh Shu'aib, Hindarabī, and Qais. Shaikh Shu'aib is 24 km from east to west and 3 km wide. It is encircled by reefs and pearl banks and has cliffs along much of its coast. Low brown hills along the island are flanked by small plains at both ends. Water is available from wells, but there is little cultivation or vegetation; the villages are located in the east. Several hundred meters from Shaikh Shu'aib is Shatvar islet. Hindarabī is 7 km by 3 km and, except for the fact that it is flat in the interior and has date trees and some cultivation of grains in the north, it much resembles Shaikh Shu'aib. Light brown Qais Island measures 23 km by 7 km. From a low, sandy coast with rocky patches and cliffs on both ends there rises a plateau 35 meters high; villages, date trees, and some cultivation are found on the north side of the island, and goats and sheep are grazed on the plateau. Vegetation is scarce, but water is obtainable. Qais has a reef and pearl banks around it.

At 46 km southwest of Linga is the inhabited Farūr Island. An ellipse 7 km by 5 km, it has coastal cliffs and bare, dark volcanic hills; a reef lies west of the island. At 17 km to the south-southwest is Nabī Farūr, a kilometer in diameter and sandy, with a dark, saddle-shaped hill on its eastern side and reefs off the western and southern shores. Sirrī is situated 42 km due south of Farūr; 6½ km by 2 km, it has a steep, sandy coast and dark hillocks. Small settlements on its northern and southern coasts grow grain and melons, and there is a date grove. Bell-shaped Abū Mūsā, 38 km to the east of Sirrī, is 5 km long and nearly an equal distance wide at its broader, southwestern end; on it are reddish hills of iron oxide and in the west is a ridge. The island is used by fishermen.

Tunb lies northwest of Abū Mūsā and due east of Farūr; it is 3 km in diameter, and brown and sandy with some grass and water. Nabī Tunb lies 14 km to its east-northeast and is 3 km by 1 km. Unlike Tunb, Nabī Tunb has no inhabitants except sea birds; it is barren, waterless, and topped by low, dark hills.

Qishm Island lies off the coast between Linga and Bandar 'Abbās and is the largest island in the Persian Gulf, 108 km from northeast to southwest and 16 km wide on average. Two prominent points jut from its middle: Lāft on the north and Khārgū on the south. The coast is mostly stony, but there are sandy bays on the southeastern and western coasts, and mud flats fringe the western part of the northern shore. Hills are scattered across the island, with the higher peaks (up to 400 meters) in the southwest. Qishm is sandy and barren on its southern side, where, in the east, deposits of salt are mined, but in the north the land is more fertile, and villagers raise livestock and grow dates, melon, grains, and vegetables.

Hanjām Island lies 1½ km southwest of Ra's Khārgū and measures 9 km by 3 km, consisting mostly of dark, rough, empty hills. Two villages and small date groves are located near wells in the southwest, and salt is mined. Shoals lie to the east of the island.

Hormuz Island, which is 18 km southeast of Bandar 'Abbās, was once the main emporium of the Persian Gulf; 9 km by 7 km, it comprises salt hills streaked with the colors of many minerals. Higher, white peaks lie in the middle of the island, and iron oxide is mined. The southern side of Hormuz is cliffed, and a small plain in the north, where Hormuz village is located, dwindles to a low point. There are shoals east and west off the island. At 22 km south-southwest of Hormuz is Lārak, 10½ km by 7 km, with barren hills rising to over 150 meters and southern and western sandy coasts. There is a fishing village on the north coast, which is encircled by a reef.

Kuwait

Low-lying Warba Island is separated from Iraq by the narrow Khōr Shatana. It is triangular in shape, its southeast-facing "base" being 13 km long and its "height" 5 km; it is covered by rough grasses and reeds. Būbiyān Island lies southeast across a channel from Warba and is separated from the mainland of Kuwait by the Khōr al-Sabiya. Low, level, and bare, with swampy shores, Būbiyān is 43½ km long and 24 km wide. Its northwest is partly flooded at high tide, and a mud flat extends southeast of it. Situated on this flat are Failaka, Jazīrat Maskān, and Doha. Sandy, low Failaka is 11 km by 5 km; it has a saint's tomb and shrine on it and is of considerable archeological interest. There are a few trees in the center and villages with date groves in the northwest. Maskān and Doha are both quite small; the latter has scrub on it and is a breeding ground for birds. These three islands lie east of Kuwait Bay, within which are two islets west of Kuwait City—Qurain and Umm al-Naml. Three other small islets belong to Kuwait; Kubbar, 36 km east of Mīnā al-Ahmadī, is low, sandy, and has brushwood. Qaru lies 38 km northeast of Mīnā Saud and is also low and has grass in places; birds breed on it. Umm al-Marādim 27 km southeast of Mīnā Sa'ūd and 6 meters high has scrub; like Kubbar, it is surrounded by reefs on three sides.

Sa'ūdī Arabia

At an average of about 115 km off the northern part of the east coast of Sa'ūdī Arabia lie the small and sandy islets Farsī, 'Arabī, Harqūs, Qaran, and Kuraiyin. At the north of Musallamiyya Bay lies Jinna Island. Light in color, it is 55 meters high and low in the west, with a fort. Sandbanks extend off the north and east. Low, sandy Musallamiyya Island lies in the inner bay, and 25 km southeast of Jinna is low-lying

Abū ʿAlī, 27 km long from east to west and narrow. South of Abu ʿAlī across a narrow channel is sandy al-Batīna, 13 km in length and also narrow. The islets Janna and Juraid are located a few kilometers to the east. Tarūt Island lies on a reef 7 km northeast of Qatīf and is 10 sq km in area; it has springs, and there are date groves in the east and a town and fort in the south. Zakhūniyya Island lies 23 km southeast of ʿUqair; it measures 6 km by 3 km and is bare and sandy. To its east is the small Idhaim islet.

Bahrain

(For Bahrain Island, see Appendix C.) Muharraq Island is located 2 km northeast of Manāma City and is joined to it by a causeway. It is 5 km wide and is shaped like a magnet, with a spur jutting southwest from its right prong. Bahrain airport lies on its low, flat, sandy surface, and it has date plantations and cultivated tracts. Muharraq is the main town, with Hidd located in the southeast. Tadpole-shaped Sitra Island is 7 km long, with its "head" only 4 km south-southeast of Manāma. Date groves and fertile land are found in the north, but the south has *sabkha*s and ends in a sandy point. A bridge spans the shallow channel that separates it from the east coast of Bahrain and on an oil jetty out from Sitra town on the island's eastern side. A carriageway between Manāma and Sitra is under construction. Northwest of Sitra in the indentation of northeastern Bahrain is small Nabī Sālih, an inhabited island mostly covered with date groves, with cultivation in the west. On sandy Umm Hasan Island, 4 km off the northwest coast of Bahrain, and 5½ km by 4 km in area, are several peaks and a spring, and a *sabkha* in the east. There is some pasturage and cultivation; dates are grown. Lesser islands of the Bahrain archipelago near Umm Hasan are Raqa, Jidda, Umm al-Saban, Libainat al-ʿĀliya, Sahaila, and Libainat al-Safliyya. Yūsuf islet lies farther south. Islets in the vicinity of Muharraq Island all lie on reefs; these are Jurdī, Khasaifa, Sajāh, Naim, Suluta, Khulafat, and Abū Shāhin. Farther east are Umm Shajar and Umm Shiyara. The islets Qasrain and Qasr ibn Tarīf are near Sitra. There is a maze of reefs and shoals about the Bahrain archipelago, some of which are exposed at low tide; the most formidable of these reefs are Fasht al-Dibal east-southeast of Muharraq, and Fasht al-Jarim north of Bahrain. Hawar and lesser islands off the coast of Qatar also belong to Bahrain. Hawar is 16 km long from north to south and 3 km wide; north of it is Rubadh Island and to its south is Janan islet. Sawad and North and South Ajaira lie between it and the coast of Qatar.

Qatar

Two small islets lying off western Qatar are ʿAnaibar, 18 km from the head of Dōhat al-Salwa, and Abū Falita in the Dōhat al-Husain. Just off the northern tip of Qatar is Ra's Rakan, and to its east are Qarradh and Umm Tais. Northeast of Dōha (96 km) lies Halūl Island, which is 5 km in circumference; much of it is flat—it is a haunt for sea birds for nesting and an important oil storage center. Reefs and shoals are scattered offshore. At 35 km north of Dōha lies Muqaiyar islet. ʿUlyā lies 1 km and Sifliyya 6 km north of the capital. The islets of Bushairiyya (also called Mishiriyyat) and al-Ashat are located east and south of Umm Saʿīd. Other islets are Ibruk, Dawākhil, and Shrao, a nesting place for birds.

The United Arab Emirates

Islands, as well as reefs, shoals, and pearl banks, abound off the western part of the coast of Abū Dhabī. Five kilometers northwest of Ra's al-Hazra, which forms the southeastern tip of Khōr al-Dhuwaihin, lies a small group of islets called Ghara, and 25 km to the northeast of these is Qafai Island. Farther to the northeast is Makhāsib. Near the east coast of Ra's Mushairib is the islet of Naita. Farther away are several islets known as Faraijdāt. At 25 km east-southeast of Ra's Mushairib are the islands of Yasat 'Ālī and Yasat Saflī, and to their southwest Judaira and Muhammaliyya. Umm al-Halab lies due west of Yasat 'Ālī, and between Jabal Dhanna and Jabal Baraka farther east are the islands of Kashat and Zabut.

At 9 km north of Jabal Dhanna lies the 11 km by 8 km Yās Island. On its southern side is a sandy plain with scrub and an inlet; there are cliffs on the northern and western coasts, and inland are volcanic hills up to 150 meters high. The east coast is low save for a bluff, and reefs encircle much of Yās. A short distance to the north-northeast is the islet of Rashīd, and northwest of Yās are Ghasha, Umm al-Kurkum, Yabr, and Umm Qasr. Hilly Dalma Island is 40 km northwest of Jabal Dhanna; 8 km by 5 km, it has a plain on its south that dwindles to a low, sandy point, and there is a village and a few wells. Reefs girdle it, except on the south.

Farther out in the Gulf are Arzana Island and five neighbors. Arzana measures 3 km by 1½ km. Hills over 65 meters high in the north give way to a flat, low plain in the south, and only the water to the south of it is free of reefs. Daiyina islet lies to the northwest; it is low and has scrub. Shura'awa rises 13 meters above sea level farther northwest; between the center of the islet, which is low, and a sandy shore are hummocks. Hills in the north and a plain in the south comprise the small area of Das Island, which now has a gas liquefaction plant on it. Warnan is south of Das, and Zirko Island is 35 km to the southeast; the latter is 5 km by 3 km and has a peak of 155 meters height. It is bare, except for a little brushwood at its sandy southern end, and is a breeding place for birds.

Numerous small islets lie between Yās and Bazam al-Gharbī. Close to the coast are Sawāmī, Thumariyya, al-Hamar, al-Isha (farther offshore), Bū Shi'āya, and Dagalla. Bazam al-Gharbī is the westernmost island of Fasht al-Bazm; this reef lies some 25 to 35 km offshore and stretches eastward for 75 km. Khōr Bazam (Khōr = "channel") is 7 km wide at Bazam al-Gharbī and 2 km wide at Khōr Qantar in the east. From west to east the main islands are, first, Fiyya and Marrāwa, which are sometimes dry, are separated by a sand and coral strip and partly covered by mangroves. Next are Junaina, Halat al-Mubarraz, and Halat Hā'il, which are farther out on the reef; then Abu'l Abyad, the largest island, which has sand dunes in the west. Al-Salālī, the easternmost island, has a hill in the northeast but elsewhere is low. East of al-Salālī is Khōr Qantar, which stretches 13 km northeast toward Abū Dhabī City. The islands off it are Qantar and Umm al-Majārib, which have mangroves on them, as do other islands cut off from the mainland by creeks, such as Rufayq, Qasabī, Halat al-Bahrānī, and Futaisa. The coast to the northeast of Abū Dhabī City is irregular and indefinite with sand bars, shallow channels, and inlets. The main islands are Sadiyat, Hayl, Fahd, Umm al-Mar, and Ramhan. Sadiyat is a center for experimental farming and Umm al-Nār is of archeological interest. Sīr Bū Nu'air Island lies 84 km north-northwest of Abū Dhabī City; 4 km by 3 km in size, it is low and sandy on the southeast, with volcanic hills to the west. The island, bare save for a little brushwood, has deposits of salt, sulphur, and also iron oxide, which latter have been mined.

The next "island" off the coast of the United Arab Emirates, Zōra, lies between Sharja and Umm al-Qaiwain; 5 km long and thin in shape, it is formed by a creek and is fordable at low tide. Six kilometers long, desolate Siniyya is the insular extension of the sandpit on which Umm al-Qaiwain is located. It forms the outer part of a lagoon in which are located several islets, among them Ghubba. At 17 km southwest of Ra's al-

Khaima is al-Hamrā, a low-lying, inhabited island that is 3 km long and has red sand dunes in the southwest. Between Ra's al-Khaima and al-Shamm lies Hulayla Island.

Oman

The Musandam peninsula begins at Khōr Maqlūb. At its entrance is the island of Saghīr, and just to the north-northeast is Jazīrat Shamm. A short distance off the northwest of the peninsula is Jazīrat al-Ghanam; 4 km by 1 km, it is over 180 meters high in the south, where there are cliffs. The small cliffy islets, Abū Sīr and Kūn (or al-Khail), lie west to east between Rās Sharā'ita on the northwest and Ra's al-Rāb on the northeast of Ra's Musandam. Northeast of this latter point is found Musandam Island; roughly triangular in shape, it measures 3 km on each side, is 270 meters high, and is precipitous except for coves on its eastern side. To the north is small and rocky Sawik islet. At 13 km north of Musandam Island is the group of three small islets known al-Salama wa-Banāt-hā (Salama and her daughters) or the Quoins. Al-Salāma (Great Quoin) is 2 km long and 1 km wide; reefs lie north of it. Fanakū (Gap Island) is 3 km east of al-Salāma. A peak rises in its middle and around its edge are cliffs. Didamar (Little Quoin) close off the south of Fanakū is wedge-shaped. Jazīrat Umm al-Faiyārīn lies east of Ghubbat Shabus in the southeastern Musandam peninsula. East of Lima on the coast of Ru'ūs al-Jibāl is found Jazīrat Lima.

The Jazā'ir Suwādī group of islets lies off Ra's Suwadi on the Batīna coast between Barka and Masna'a. The largest islet, Jabal 'Add, is about 2 km by 1 km and over 80 meters high, and six lesser islets lie west of it; overall, this group is about 3 km in length. The series of desolate islets called Daimaniyyāt is 20 km long and lies 15 km offshore between Sīb and Barka. The westernmost island is Jūn, which is 2 km long, narrow, and some 30 km high on the west. In the middle of the chain is a string of seven light brown cliffed islets averaging 10 meters in height. Kharāba islet forms the eastern end of the Daimaniyyāt group.

Masīra is the main island off the southeastern coast of Oman. It is 66 km long from northeast to southwest, 17 km at its widest, and 7 km wide at its "waist." Much of it is rocky, and the Jabal Hamrā' rises over 250 meters in the northeast. In the southwest, there is a chain of low hills called Jabal al-Khuwayrāt. Masīra is inhabited. Several kilometers off the island's western coastal embayment is Jazīrat Shaghaf. From northeast to southwest, the other islands of the Masīra channel are Ma'āwil, Sifa, al-Hār, Umm al-Kids, and Qa'ad al-Kalbān. Nearby in Ghubbat Hashīsh are the islets Abb and Mahot, and farther south along the coast of the Gulf of Masīra lies Hamar al-Nafūr. The 80 km long Kuria Muria island chain lies 60 km northeast of Ra's Nūs. West to east the islands are named al-Hasikiyya, al-Sawdā, al-Hallāniyya, Gharzaut, and al-Qibliyya. Al-Hallāniyya is 14½ km from east to west and 9 km at its widest (eastern) end. It is rocky in the northeast, and there are small sandy plains in the east and west; the highest hill reaches 500 meters above sea level. The other islands are mostly rocky; and 8 km off the coast southeast of Mirbāt is the small Setima Muqsi.

Selected Bibliography

Great Britain, Hydrographic Office. *Persian Gulf Pilot.* 10th ed. London, 1955.
———. *Red Sea and Gulf of Aden Pilot.* 9th ed. London, 1944.
Great Britain, Admiralty, Naval Intelligence Division. *Iraq and the Persian Gulf.* B.R. 524 Geographical Handbook Series, September 1944.
———. *Persia,* B.R. 525 Geographical Handbook Series, September 1945.

D. Survey. War Office and Air Ministry; later D. Survey, Ministry of Defence; later D Mil. Survey, Ministry of Defence, United Kingdom. "World 1:5000,000" Series 1404 Edition 1-GSGS. Sheets 548-A, 547-B, 444-C, 444-D, 444-A, 445-B, 445-C, 547-A, 547-D, 547-C, 548-D, 563-B, 563-C, 670-B, and 670-D.

U.S. Navy, Hydrographic Office. *Sailing Directions for the Persian Gulf*, no. 158. Washington, D.C., 1952.

APPENDIX E

Mineral Resources

Iran

Iran is the only country of the Persian Gulf whose non-oil mineral resources compare at all in significance with its large hydrocarbon deposits. The most important mineral present is copper, of which there are several billion tons. Deposits are found north of Tabrīz, particularly at Ahar, and others are mined at Isfahān, Tārum, Zanjān, Sabzavār, and Hamadān. In the past decade, valuable finds have been made around Zāhīdān, Nidul, Yazd, Anārak, and Kirmān. Sar Chashma is the major deposit at the latter place. Within an area of 0.2 km by 2.3 km there are about 70 million tons of ore with a high copper content of 1.12%. Estimates of the total amount of this standard of ore exceed 800 million tons, and there is another 500 million tons of lesser grade ore. As yet, Iran must import most of its annual requirement of 35,000 tons of copper. By the early 1980's when the country's yearly need will be perhaps 85,000 tons, Sar Chashma is expected to yield as much as 200,000 tons of blister copper a year.

Chromite is found at Mashhad, Shāhrūd, and Sabzāvar in the northeast, and also at Sīrjān, Isfandaqa, Shīrāz, and Dawlatābād. About 250,000 metric tons have been mined annually in recent years; most of it is for export. New discoveries have been made at Bāfq and Mīnāb. Iran is now thought to have one of the world's largest reserves of chromite, with at least 7 million tons of 35% to 50% pure chromite ore.

The principal iron deposits lie at Shamsābād, Khumain near Isfahān, Simnān, Qum, Mahallāt, Kirmān, and Arāk. Large deposits are found at Ghoghart near Bāfq, where proven reserves total 600 million tons (with another probably 400 million tons), and at Pul-i Gawhar, whose high-grade reserves are thought to amount to more than 200 million tons. Only about 10% of Iran's estimated 1 to 1.6 billion tons of coal reserves is lump coal; the rest is found as grit. Major fields are situated in the Elburz Mountains north of Tehran and around Shāhrūd, the Kirmān region, Qazvīn, eastern Khurāsān, and from Kāshān to Suh. The output of coal was one million metric tons in 1972–73. It has never been an important fuel, but the development of industry is leading to a greater demand for it (for copper and iron, see Appendix K). This, in turn, will bring the application of mechanized mining methods to seams that have only been worked on the surface.

Lead-zinc ores are mined at Bāfq, Dāmghān, Khumain, Tabas, Rāvanj near Qum, and Nā'īn. Valuable deposits are located at Khushk near Bāfq, Mihrābād, Angūrān in Azerbaijan, and in areas of Ardistān. Iran's deserts have plentiful supplies of salt. Sulphur, of which the country is an exporter, is mined at Bandar 'Abbās, Lār, and Simnān. There are deposits of manganese at Rabāt Karīm, Dawlatābād, Mīnāb, and Ardistān. Nickel is mined at Anārak, and islands such as Qishm and Hurmuz have iron oxide. The huge deposits at Nīshāpūr enable Iran to be the world's preeminent producer of turquoise. There are gold veins at Mahallāt, Maima, and Dilījān; further deposits have been discovered in Khurāsan. Uranium is found at Kirmān, Yazd, Hamadān, Khvāja Murādī, and Isfahān. In 1976, discoveries were made at Shāhrūd, Dāmghān, and Simnān, and also in Sīstān and Baluchistan. There is small-scale mining of antimony and magnesite. Deposits of barite are also worked. Tin and tungsten are found at Arāk, and asbestos and alumina are worked at Merman. Other alumina deposits are sited at Arāk, and recently some 500 million tons of high-standard alumina were located at the Takistān area south of Qazvīn. An important quantity of phosphates has been discovered.

Molybdenum and silica are among other minerals found at Sar Chashma. Mica and silicates and also arsenic are available in Azerbaijan and near Isfahān. Gypsum and limestone deposits are widespread. Marble and alabaster are quarried at Yazd, Marāgha, and Shīrā. Iran also has amounts of bauxite, cobalt, fluorspar and borax, and emeralds, topazes, sapphires, and other valuable stones are found.

In terms of world production and reserves, Iran's nonhydrocarbon mineral resources (save for copper and chromite) are small. For the country itself, however, the mining of mineral resources is a valuable and expanding part of its economy.

Iraq

The major non-oil minerals of Iraq are sulphur and phosphates. The main sulphur deposit at Mishraq south of Mosul is being developed, and phosphate deposits at Akashat, close to the Syrian border, are being worked. Other minerals found in the north are chromite, copper, lead and zinc, and iron ore. Limestone, gypsum, low quality coal, salt, and dolomite are also present.

Kuwait, Bahrain, Qatar

These states have no mineral resources of note, other than oil and gas, and are the only countries of the Persian Gulf region not presently conducting mineral surveys.

Sa'ūdī Arabia

Many minerals are present in the Arabian Shield, but as yet few have been assessed for their commercial viability. Iron deposits are found along the Red Sea coast at places such as Wādī Sawāwīn, Wādī Fātima, and Jīzān, where the estimated amounts of ore are several hundred thousand tons with 25 to 9% iron; 48 million tons with 46% iron; and over 100,000 tons with more than 50% iron, respectively. Overall accessible reserves are about 400 million tons. At least eight other deposits are being investigated. There are old copper mines at 'Aqīq, al-'Amir and Samrān. Other copper deposits have been found at Katum-Talah, al-Masāni' (south of Jidda), Jabal Sayyid, and at other places on the Red Sea coast and northeast of the Arabian Shield. Nuqra, Jabal Sayyid, al-Wajh, Mahd al-Dhahab (280 km northeast of Jidda), and other tracts northeast of the Shield have prospects of gold. Silver has been found at the site of ancient mines at Sidriyya, Jabal Samrān, and Samra. Nuqra and Jabal Sayyid have quantities of silver.

Finds of nickel have been made in 'Asīr at Kutum-Talah and Wādī Qatan. An estimated 40 million tons of magnesite have been discovered at Jabal Rukhām; at Zarghat several million tons can be exploited. A belt of some 10,000 tons of barite has been found in the vicinity of Rābigh; there are also veins at Umm Jirād. There is zinc at Masāni‘, Kutum-Talah, Jabal Sayyid, and at Nuqra. Lead is found at Nuqra, and at other places along the Red Sea littoral. Exploration has revealed sizable phosphate deposits at Thaniyyāt (northeast of Tabūk) and at other localities northeast of the Arabian Shield. Small amounts of tungsten have been discovered and there are sizable deposits of gypsum along the Red Sea and also southeast of Riyadh, near which is found high quality limestone. Eastern Sa‘ūdī Arabia has ample amounts of lesser quality limestone. Clay for industrial purposes is obtained at al-Khārj, al-Sarāt, and elsewhere. Salt is mined at Jīzān and Abqā’iq has large deposits. Large quantities of marble lie west of Riyadh, and some is already being mined. The rare metals niobium, yitrium, and zircon occur around Jabal Sayyid and al-Ghurayyāt, and Sa‘ūdī Arabia is reported to contain promising amounts of uranium. Large-scale exploration for more minerals is under way, and geological mapping continues.

The United Arab Emirates

At present the only non-oil minerals being worked in the UAE are those for building purposes, such as limestone chips, cement, brick clays, and stone aggregate. These materials and marble are found in the mountains of Ra's al-Khaima. Uranium, iron ores, and copper have been located in Fujaira, and deposits of chrome estimated at 5,000 metric tons each have been found at Masfūt and Manāma. Traces of platinum, asbestos, magnesium, bauxite, and nickel have been discovered. The quality of these and other minerals, among them manganese, phosphates, sulphur and fluorite, and the nonmetallic resources magnesite and gypsum, has yet to be fully determined.

Oman

Copper is the most important non-oil mineral resource of Oman. Present proven reserves come to 18 million tons, most of it located in the Western Hajar Mountains between Buraimī and Suhār. It is planned that by 1979, three mines will be producing 3,000 to 3,500 tons of copper a day from rock with a high copper ore content of 2.1%. The development of a copper smelter and port facilities for the export of copper at Suhār is a possibility. Their remoteness makes the discovery of further copper deposits difficult, but prospecting continues.

Both coal and manganese have been located in the mountains of the Sharqiyya near Sūr. The estimated potential reserves of the coal seams is 10 million tons. High standard asbestos has been discovered in the northern Western Hajar Mountains, and deposits of possibly exploitable amounts of chrome, magnesite, nickel, iron ore, lead, and zinc also have been located there. The Hajar also contain useful deposits of marble, while there and in Dhofār is found limestone of very good quality. In Dhofār, mineral surveys have revealed the presence of phosphate deposits.

The Omani government hopes that continued exploitation will uncover further mineral wealth that can complement the country's declining oil deposits, and minerals, together with agriculture and fishing, are seen as a more lasting source of national prosperity. An important prerequisite for exploiting the country's mineral wealth is the development of an adequate infrastructure.

Selected Bibliography

al-Otaiba, M. S. *Petroleum and the Economy of the United Arab Emirates*. London, 1977.

Economist Intelligence Unit. *Quarterly Economic Review of Iraq*. Annual Supplement 1977. London, 1977.

————. *Quarterly Economic Review the Arabian Peninsula: Shaikdoms and Republics.* Annual Supplement 1976. London, 1976.

Financial Times. "Country Reports on the States of the Persian Gulf, 1975–77." London, 1975–77.

Harrison, J. V. "Minerals." In W. B. Fisher, ed., *The Cambridge History of Iran.* Vol. 1, *The Land of Iran.* Cambridge, 1968.

Hawley, Donald. *Oman and Its Renaissance.* London, 1977.

————. *The Trucial States.* London, 1970.

Iran, Ministry of Information. *Iran.* 2nd ed. Tehran, 1971.

Iran. A MEED Special Report. February 1977.

Iran Almanac and Book of Facts 1977. 16th ed. Tehran, 1977.

Kingdom of Saudi Arabia, Directorate General of Mineral Resources, Ministry of Petroleum and Mineral Resources. *Mineral Resources Activities.* Jiddah, 1976.

The Middle East and North Africa 1976–77. 23rd ed. London, 1976.

Oman. A MEED Special Report. June 1976.

Profile of Iran, The Mining Industry of Iran. Vol. 2, no. 2. Iranian Embassy, Washington, D.C., February 1977.

Saudi Arabia. A MEED Special Report. December 1976.

United Arab Emirates. A MEED Special Report. July 1977.

APPENDIX F

Flora

Iran

Iran is a botanical transition area between Europe, Asia, and Africa. The primary kind of flora is the Irano-Turanian species that dwells on steppes and in the mountains, where there is a wide range of temperature and low rainfall. In eastern Azerbaijan there are Euro-Siberian (alpine) elements. Deciduous hyrcanian vegetation, with a Mediterranean admixture of low bushes and shrubs, prevails along the Caspian side of the Elburz Mountains, where conditions are warm, rainy, and humid. The northwestern half of the Zagros Mountains has strips of forests of deciduous and evergreen trees. The Nuba-Sindian and Sudanian subspecies of the Saharo-Sindian species of vegetation is found along and inland of the Persian Gulf and Makrān coasts, respectively. There are Indo-Himalayan elements in northeastern Iran. (Iran has a goodly number of plants that are endemic.) Forests and grasslands were once more extensive than they are today. They have been diminished by the search for fuel and timber and extensive grazing.

Some three-quarters of Iran is either arid or semiarid. Preeminent shrubs in this Irano-Turanian zone are thorn cushions, wormwood, cotoneaster, and various milk vetch species. Sage, thyme, thistles, and buckthorn are also widespread. Some shrubs and plants give off usable substances; among these are gum arabic, colcynth, and liquorice. Camelthorn yields manna. Absinthe, rue, sesame, and poppy are found. Henna, saffron, and indigo are seen in many places. Many of the shrubs and plants of Iran are either prickly or spiny. In particularly arid or salty regions there are many halophytic (salt-resisting) and xerophytic (drought-resisting) plants and shrubs. Among these are the bean-caper, saxaul, figwort, tamarind, and the members of the goosefoot family. At higher elevations in the mountains there are grasses, many herbs, and mint and clover in places. Grasses and reeds grow around marshland, such as in Sīstān.

Many kinds of flowers grow wild. Besides the rose, which is the most popular flower in Iran, there are orchids, crocuses, geraniums, irises, dwarf yellow hollyhocks, buttercups, gladioli, tulips, and grape-hyacinths.

Trees comprising the hyrcanian forest of the Caspian area are oaks, elms, honey locusts, walnut trees, maples, beeches, nettles, lindens, hazels, wild pear and plum trees, poplars, elders, and hornbeams. Vines and creepers, among them ivy, are present. Christ's thorns, box trees, medlars, and pomegranates form scrub in open places. Oak forests occupy small areas of the northwestern Zagros. At other places in this range are poplars, willows, plane trees, elms, almond and pistachio trees, junipers, hawthorns, cypresses, various wild fruit trees, peanut trees, celtises, walnut, and mulberry trees.

Many of the plants, shrubs, and trees found in the arid parts of inner Iran will also be found in districts along the Persian Gulf. Among trees are the kunar, tamarisk, crown of thorns, tamarind, willow, hawthorn, date palm, myrtle, poplar, and cypress. Reeds, rushes, grasses, mangroves, oleander, salsola, acacia, mimosa, and terebinth grow along the coast, as do bougainvillea and jasmine.

Iraq

In Iraq, the transition is made from the Irano-Turanian region in the north to the Saharo-Sindian area of the south. Some Mediterranean and Alpine species are found in the mountains of Kurdistan. At the lower levels of these mountains are brambles, mint, watercress, buttercups, and brooklime. Reeds and grasses grow along rivers and there are grapevines. Also seen is Christ's thorn, maidenhair (a fern), and oleander. The main trees are willows, planes, and ashes. Some oaks can be found at higher levels in the far northeast where there are also hawthorns, junipers, terebinths, maples, wild pear trees, and a few pines. The bean trefoil is found here, as are many herbs of the daisy family. At over 2,500 meters there are globe thistles, spurges, milk vetches, and other members of the thorn cushion family. Much of the forest area of the mountains has been denuded and only scrub remains.

Among shrubs and herbs found in the plains and foothills of the north and east are members of the sage and daisy families. There is also mugweed, St. John's wort, stork's bill, phiomis, milkweed, thyme, flax, asphodel, and rootstock. In the upper Mesopotamian plains are the caper, members of the goosefoot family, boxthorn, several grasses, dwarf sedge, groundsel, feverfew, and other herbs. Farther south there is milkweed, tufted grasses, stork's bill, and plantain, as well as some shrubs also present in the north. Along the banks of the lower Tigris and Euphrates rivers may be found willows and poplars, mulberry trees, tamarisks and boxthorns, liquorice plants, grasses and bulrushes. Sedges, reeds, knotgrasses, pimpernels, geraniums, vetches, and spurges are seen around marshes. The date palm is the preeminent tree of southern Iraq. Other notable flora are the acacia, kunar, mimosa, and colocynth. In the desert region of the south and west are found salsola and wormwood bushes and members of the goosefoot and daisy families; the low shrub, 'arfaj, is most representative of the latter family. Other typical vegetation are milfoil; zizyphus; shōk (a low and thorny plant); haram, which is a shrub; and sabha, a grass.

Other Arab States of the Gulf

Kuwait, Sa'ūdī Arabia, Bahrain, Qatar, the United Arab Emirates, and Oman come within the Saharo-Sindian floristic region. Wide strips along the Persian Gulf (and also along the Arabian Sea and Gulf of Oman) are said to fall within the Sudanian subregion. Inland from the Persian Gulf is a Saharan-Arabian element. The flora of these states is poor in species and characterized primarily by its xerophytism and halophytism (see above).

In Kuwait, the main trees are the date, kunar, tamarisk, and *sidr*, whose fruit resembles apples. Among shrubs are *'arfaj*, *'awsaj*, *hamdh*, and boxthorn. The colocynth are seen. *Russi* and *thamsin* are grasses. Sa'ūdī Arabia has many of these, and also shrubs such as *andal*, *rasnad*, *tarfah*, and *rimth*; others are *ghada*, auphorbia, and Abal Artah. Among the grasses are *qasba*, *thamsin* and Subat. *Arad* and *ujrum*, like *namdh* and *rimah*, are salty bushes. Further bushes and shrubs are senna, *harm*, *hamdh*, and *abl*, which is useful for firewood. Among other flora are truffles, camomile, plants such as *su'adam* and aloe, iris, and members of the mustard family. Prominent trees are the date palm, kunar, *markh*, acacia, mimosa, arak, carob, and *dawm* (gingerbread tree). Forests of juniper and wild olive form thin strips on the mountains of southern 'Asīr province, where indigo, wild figs, and myrrh grow. In western Sa'ūdī Arabia, mangroves thrive at places along the coast and *nabq* and *sayal* trees, capers, *rattaf* (a thistle), rue, oraches, and members of the euphorbia group are present.

Bahrain has a few grasses, mangroves, date palms, and kunar trees, but little other vegetation. Qatar is limited to several hardy grasses, palm and lotus trees, a few thorny bushes and stunted bushwood. In the United Arab Emirates there are mangroves, varieties of acacia, dwarf tamarisks, and tamarinds. Among the shrubs are *hams*, *haram*, *hamdh*, *sahkar*, *abal*, and *qasad*. *Arta* and *qufa* are grasses, and *rimth*, *halam*, and the wild castor oil plant are typical plants. Many of the other plants, grasses, and shrubs found along the western Gulf are found as well in the UAE. This applies also to Oman, which has flora not found elsewhere in the lower Gulf. There are frankincense, *mulūkh*, and *tishgart* trees. *Surra* is a small flowering tree; it is a thorny tree with black berries. In *wādīs* and valleys, oleander, sedge, bulrushes, and grasses grow, as do *sawga* (a flower with an orange blossom), and such seasonals as celandine and speedwell. The camel thorn, varieties of acacia and the purple-flowered *ashgar* are seen in more open places. Oman also supports *nasal* (a rush), lavender, calotropis, screwpine, *mara'aha* (a plant bearing a fruit like a lime), capers, worts, turnsoles, henna, wars, and indigo. Among the plentiful vegetation of Jabal Akhdar is included the thorn apple, euphorbia, Oman violet, cotton plants, asparagus, wild potatoes, honeysuckle, the juniper tree, primula, thistles, and grasses. Roses, hollyhocks, marigolds, coconut palms, and pomegranate trees grow in Dhofār.

Selected Bibliography

Blakelock, R. A. "The Rustam Herbarium Iraq," *Kew Bulletin* 2–7, various numbers (1948–53).
———. "Notes on the Flora of Iraq," *Kew Bulletin* 7–11 (1952–57).
Blatter, E. "Flora Arabica." In *Records of the Botanical Survey of India*, vol. 8, parts 1–6. Calcutta, 1919–36.
Bobek, H. "Vegetation." In W. B. Fisher, ed., *The Cambridge History of Iran*. Vol. 1, *The Land of Iran*. Cambridge, 1968.
Dickson, H. R. P. *Kuwait and Her Neighbours*. London, 1956.
Dickson, V. "Plants of Kuwait, Northeast Arabia," *Journal of the Bombay Natural History Society* 40 (1938): 528–38.
Great Britain, Admiralty, Naval Intelligence Division. *Iraq and the Persian Gulf*. B. R. 524 Geographical Handbook Series. London, 1944.
———. *Persia*. B. R. 525 Geographical Handbook Series. London, 1945.

————. *Western Arabia and the Red Sea*. B. R. 527 Geographical Handbook Series. London, 1946.

Guest, E., and Townsend, C., eds. *Flora of Iraq*. 2 vols. Baghdad, 1965.

Hawley, D. F. *Oman and Its Renaissance*. London, 1977.

————. *The Trucial States*. London, 1970.

Lorimer, J. G. *Gazetteer of the Persian Gulf, Oman, and Central Arabia*. Vol. 2, *Geographical and Statistical*. Calcutta, 1908.

Parsa, A. *Flore de l'Iran*. 5 vols. Ministère de l'Education, Museum d'Histoire Naturelle de Teheran. Tehran, 1948–52.

Schwartz, O. "Flora des tropischen Arabiens." In *Mitteilungen aus dem Institut für allgemeine Botanik in Hamburg* 10 (1939): 1–193.

APPENDIX G

Fauna

Iran

Mammals. Iran's roughly 130 species of mammals represent the meeting of animals from many varied areas, as well as the presence of numerous endemic species. About 69 kinds of mammals derive from the Palaearctic region; 23 kinds are endemic and 18 kinds are of Indian origin, while the remaining 20 are of African or mixed species.

The southern Zagros Mountains were the habitat of the lion, which has been hunted to extinction. Hyrcanian tigers live in the forests of the Caspian area, but their number is dwindling as these woodlands are cleared. Panthers can be found in many places, but the cheetah and the caracal, a kind of lynx, verge on extinction. Leopards remain in evidence. Jungle cats live in the south and desert cats are distributed in the northeast and in the southern Zagros. The polecat is seen in Sīstān, brown bears reside in the Elburz Mountains, and a smaller, dark brown bear has its home in the Zagros.

Wolves, hyenas, and jackals are distributed across much of Iran. The southern and eastern parts of the country are the habitat of three kinds of fox. There are badgers in the Caspian area. Otters swim the rivers of this district and also the rivers of the Zagros. Several kinds of Indian mongoose are found in southern parts, while the porcupine is more generally dispersed. The ratel is seen around Rām Hormuz and other places, and the beech marten lives in the Zagros.

The Sind wild goat has its quarters in southeastern Iran, while to the north is found the Persian wild goat. There are three varieties of wild sheep: the urial of the southwest, the Lāristān sheep of the southern coastal area, and the red sheep located in Khurāsān. Onagers or wild asses live around the desert fringes, and wild boar are found in less arid places.

As well as the rodents already mentioned, squirrels, hares, various sorts of mice, including the dormouse, and shrews live in Iran. Hamsters and voles are found in northern Iran, and jerboas and gerbils dwell mainly in desert areas. The pika, or mouse-hare, is found in the high mountains in the vicinity of Quhrūd. Baluchi hedgehogs are located in the hills and mountains of Baluchistan. There are various kinds of bat in southern

Iran and on islands such as Qishm. Besides the above animals, Iran has all the usual domestic animals.

Birds. The birds of Iran derive from the Palaearctic realm, save for a few from the Ethiopian and oriental regions in the southwest and southeast, respectively. Over 450 species have been recorded in Iran, the fact that it is on a migratory route from Europe and Asia to Africa being relevant here. Among the resident birds are the:

sparrow (various kinds)	ringed plover	babbler
nightingale	lapwing (several kinds)	pelican (several kinds)
shrike	owl (several kinds)	sandgrouse (several kinds)
sunbird	flycatcher	small green bee-eater
hoopoe	grebe (a few kinds)	nightingale
bustard (several kinds)	lanner	Mesopotamian crow
eagle (seven kinds)	kestrel	coot
vulture	partridge (various kinds)	purple gallinule
alpine swift	lark (many kinds)	brown-necked raven

Among the many birds that breed in Iran are rooks, jackdaws, great spotted cuckoos, starlings, magpies, various kinds of herons, masked booties, buntings, some kinds of warblers and waders, swifts, woodpeckers, various pigeons, wagtails, several kinds of ibis, flamingoes and storks, tropical birds, many kinds of tern, crab plovers, and Socotra cormorants. Some of the migrants and visitors that come to Iran for either summer or winter are the:

finch	bunting	golden oriole
pipit	swan	goose
duck	chat	red-necked phalarope
snipe	woodcock	red-rumped swallow
gull (many kinds)	Persian shearwater	crake
rail	curlew	redshank
bee-eater (several kinds)	pratincole	yellow wagtail
waxwing	roller	

Iraq

Birds. The birds of Iraq are also mostly of the Palaearctic realm. Resident are the:

babbler	pelican	bulbul
scrub warbler	coot	Iraqi crow
sparrow	partridge (several kinds)	crested lark
sandgrouse	tern	hoopoe
plover	curlew	heron
rock dove	kingfisher	flamingo
spoonbill	wren warbler	cormorant
grey hypercoliuse	lapwing (several kinds)	
little grebe	kestrel	

There are a fair number of migrants and seasonal visitors, including the:

chaffinch	corncrake	great crested grebe
song thrush	goose	lark
wader (numerous kinds)	duck	snipe
spotted flycatcher	bee-eater (several European kinds)	osprey

wagtail	nightjar	linnet
stork	swift	Persian robin
marsh harrier	hoopoe	starling
black kite	swallow	goldfinch
shrike (several kinds)	falcon (several kinds)	owl (several kinds)

Among the birds that breed in Iraq are Egyptian nightjars, greybacked warblers, Persian bee-eaters, avocets, Indian ring-doves, black-winged stilts, and Indian rollers.

Arab States of the Persian Gulf

Mammals. The western and southern Persian Gulf region is a continuation of the transition zone between the fauna of Europe, Asia, and Africa. Despite the great heat and aridity, some 140 kinds of mammal exist in these countries. Twenty-one Palaearctic species live in northern Iraq; there, and in the lower Gulf region, may be found 24 Saharo-Sindian mammals, 18 Indo-Asiatic kinds, 15 indigenous species, 10 tropical-Ethiopian breeds (mostly in Oman), and some 50 pluriregional mammals.

The lion, ostrich, wild ass, and oryx have become extinct in Iraq. Among the wild cats to be found are the Indian jungle cat and the Eastern wildcat. Wolves, foxes, jackals, hyenas, and Marica's gazelle are seen, the latter in the desert. A few bears, wild sheep. goats, and pigs live in the mountains. There are martens, honey badgers, otters, and mongooses. Hares, gerbils, porcupines, mice, and muskrats are present, as is the flying squirrel. There are also numerous varieties of bats. The unwanted locust is present.

Save for bears, martens, otters, the flying squirrel, specific breeds of wildcat, and a few others, most of the mammals found in Iraq are also located in the other Arabian littoral states. Varieties of gazelle, *tahr*s (a kind of goat), oryxes, and ibexes have come close to extinction. Leopards and possibly cheetahs have been killed off, save in Oman, where the former, and also panthers, still exist. In that country is found the black hedgehog as well. Present in small numbers are the civet, lynx, sand cat, Arabian coney, deer, hedgehog, and the wild ass. Baboons inhabit 'Asīr province in southwestern Sa'ūdī Arabia. All the familiar domestic animals are also found.

Birds. Birds from both the Palaearctic and Ethiopian realms are present in these countries. Resident are the following:

magpie	wader	dove
flamingo	Francolin partridge	babbler
sparrow	courser	raven
thrush	bifasciated lark	osprey
swift	nightingale	gull
wagtail	water pipit	Egyptian vulture
warbler	silverbill	red-wattled lapwing
tern	Indian roller	bittern
crab plover	heron	egret
crow	owl	curlew
Arabian see-see	bustard	hawk
great gray shrike	eagle	pigeon
wheater	falcon	coot

There are several subvarieties of many of these birds. Among the numerous migrants are the following:

bustard
duck
goose
snipe
sand grouse
pied flycatcher
bluethroat
spoonbill
dotterel
stock dove
oystercatcher
red-rumped swallow
chiffchaff

kingfisher
cormorant
sanderling
woodcock
greenshank
black redstart
wryneck
black kite
tropic bird
scops owl
swift
whimbrel

blue-cheeked bee-eater
water-rail
nightingale
kestrel
sand martin
tawny pipit
cuckoo
pallid harrier
ortolan bunting
great reed warbler
hoopoe
honey buzzard

Fish. There are more than 200 species of fish in the Persian Gulf, of which some 150 are edible. The major ones are the:

captain's daughter
sea horse
pipe fish
mullet
porcupine fish
parrot fish
cuttle fish
rock cod
hamour
trunk fish
dolphin
sea bass
reef fish
devil ray
flat fish
sea perch
blue fish
garrupa

flying fish
saw fish
black pomfret
silver pomfret
sword fish
chicken grunt
bull dog fish
gar fish
seer fish
white bait
cat fish
sucking fish
Indian rorquel
plaice
silver croaker
sea eel
sail fish
snapper

Indian salmon
sardine
tuna
lady fish
turbot
sole
porpoise
Indian shad
sharks
wrass
bombay duck
milk fish
horse mackerel
Red Sea bream
white truffle
angel fish
barracuda
jelly fish

Whales are occasionally found in the Persian Gulf, as are green and hawksbill turtles. The dugong, a large herbivorous sea mammal, is present. Among the crustaceans are shrimp, oysters, crabs, prawns, lobsters, and clams.

There are numerous fish in the streams and rivers of Iran and Iraq. In northwestern Iran are found the gudgeon, catfish, brine-shrimp, carp, chub, and bleak. Barbel and carp are found elsewhere and roach, bream, sturgeon, "Caspian herrings," and the Caspian salmon are the main fish of the Caspian Sea. Among the fish to be found in the Tigris, Euphrates, and other Iraqi rivers are the carp, barbus, catfish, the "spiny eel," loaches, a small fish related to the minnow, and "toothed carps."

Selected Bibliography

Allouse, B. E. *The Avifauna of Iraq.* Iraq Natural History Museum Publication No. 3. Baghdad, 1953.

Blegvad, H., and Loppenthin, B. "Fishes of the Persian Gulf." In K. Jessen and H. R. Sparck, eds. *Danish Scientific Investigations in Iran.* Copenhagen, 1944.

Dickson, H.R.P. *Kuwait and Her Neighbours.* London, 1956.

Great Britain. Admiralty: Naval Intelligence Division. *Iraq and the Persian Gulf.* B.R. 524 Geographical Handbook Series. London, 1944.

———. *Persia.* B.R. 525 Geographical Handbook Series. London, 1945.

———. *Western Arabia and the Red Sea.* B.R. 527 Geographical Handbook Series. London, 1946.

Harrison, D. L. *The Mammals of Arabia.* 3 vols. London, 1964–72.

Hawley, D. F. *The Trucial States.* London, 1970.

Lane, Maj. W. H. "The game fishes of the Persian Gulf." *Journal of the Bombay Natural History Society* 24, 4 (October 1916): 722–48 (part 1); and 25, 1 (March 1917): 121–35 (part 2).

Lorimer, J. G. *Gazetteer of the Persian Gulf, Oman, and Central Arabia.* Vol. 2, *Geographical and Statistical.* Calcutta, 1908.

McIvor, Lt. I. *Notes on Sea-Fishing in the Persian Gulf,* in *Selections from the Records of the Government of India Foreign Department No. 181, Report on the Administration of the Persian Gulf Political Residency and Muscat Political Agency for Year 1880–1881,* pp. 44–67, by Ross, E. C., Lt. Col. Calcutta, 1881.

Meinertzhagen, R. *Birds of Arabia.* London and Edinburgh, 1954.

Members of the Expeditionary Force 'D'. "A Survey of the Fauna of Iraq." Reprinted from the *Journal of the Bombay Natural History Society.* Bombay, 1923.

Misonne, X. de. "Mammals." In W. B. Fisher, ed., *The Cambridge History of Iran.* Vol. 1. *The Land of Iran.* Cambridge, 1968.

Read, S. J. "Ornithology." In W. B. Fisher, ed., *The Cambridge History of Iran.* Vol. 1, *The Land of Iran.* Cambridge, 1968.

Ticehurst, C. B. "The birds of Mesopotamia." *Journal Bombay Natural History Society* 28 (1923), parts 1, 2, 3.

———. "Birds of the Persian Gulf Islands." *Journal Bombay Natural History Society* 30 (1925), part 3, pp. 725–33.

White, A. W., and Berwani, M. A. *Common Sea Fishes of the Arabian Gulf and Gulf of Oman.* Trucial States Council, Vol. 1. Dubai, 1971.

APPENDIX   H

Demography

The countries of the Persian Gulf, especially Iran and Iraq, have a long urban tradition. Cities such as Nineveh, Ur, Babylon, Ctesiphon, Persepolis, Ecbatana, and Pasargadae formed the core of ancient empires and civilizations. Important cities on the coast of the Persian Gulf were the Chaldean port of Gerrha (near 'Uqair in Sa'ūdī Arabia) and Dilmun, probably situated in Bahrain. These cities were located near plentiful sources of water, whether rivers or oases, and/or on trade routes between Asia and the Mediterranean, and their rise and decline were probably due to political change and shifts in the patterns of trade.

The most important influence upon the cities of the Gulf region and beyond in the past two millenniums has been Islam. Essentially an urban religion, it is the foundation of Arab culture and an essential element of Iranian life. Medieval Islamic towns, as those of earlier times, were local centers of exchange. Farmers brought in produce and obtained goods and services. Mosques were the focal point of religion and also places where justice was meted out and learning cultivated. Some cities (Mecca, Mashhad, Karbalā) had revered shrines and were the object of pilgrimages. Others (Muscat, Baghdad) were on international trade routes. One after another Sīrāf, Qais, Hormuz, and, in the eigthteenth and early nineteenth centuries, Muscat, were the principal ports of the Persian Gulf. All performed administrative and defensive functions (particularly Tabrīz for defense). As the main concentration point of wealth and the only form of government until this century, cities were economically dominant and politically preeminent.

Although their location, climate, culture, and history made for differences, cities were similar in their Islamic physical and social structures. Most were walled for ready defense, and inside the city walls was a fortress (and in larger cities the ruler's palace) where administrative tasks were performed. The main mosque of the city was the tallest building and its dome and minaret formed a landmark. Nearby were public baths and perhaps a hospital. The *sūq* (Persian: *bāzār*) was the market place, in the confines of which many small shops were densely packed. Larger places had caravanserais—inns where merchants could stay with their beasts, store their wares, and meet and deal with one another. Most cities were largely unplanned. Narrow, twisting, shaded streets, some with the houses almost meeting over the roadways, formed a labyrinth leading away from the mosque. Residential quarters were often given over to a particular tribe, sect, trade, or people. Houses were a response to hot and often windy weather, and to the Islamic stress upon the family and its privacy. Walled and constructed of mud brick, with no windows on the ground floor, they looked inward to a narrow courtyard. In parts of Iran and Iraq, many houses were built with an underground room (*sardāb*) ventilated by a wind tower (*bādgīr*) where a family went to avoid the great heat of the day. At night families slept on the flat roof of the house. Rooms were divided into those only for the family (the *haramlik*, to use the Turkish term) and those into which visitors could be received (the *salāmlik*). Generations of a family built their quarters next to the houses of their kinsmen wherever possible, and groups of houses formed a cellular structure.

Islamic cities lacked a corporate life distinct from that of the state. Wealthy merchants of good family, and religious scholars and lawyers (the *'ulamā'* and *fuqahā*) who filled various religious offices, such as interpreting the law, had high status. They were distinguished from craftsmen and shop-owners, to whom Islam accorded a respectable middle-class standing, and from peasants, laborers, and others. What defined people was their identification with their village, craft, or perhaps sect or school of law, groupings of which were organized into their own quarters, as noted above. A communal group, consisting of rich and poor alike, was the primary administrative unit. A *shaikh* or headman responsible for collecting taxes, keeping public order, and representing his community dealt with a ruler and his officials, who were often set off from the people and in some instances were of foreign origin. In the smaller towns of the Persian Gulf, rulers were usually local *shaikh*s, directly accessible to their subjects. It has been suggested that as cities were composites of smaller communities, which were the main foci of loyalty, and that as they had no function that was not met in villages, the Islamic idea of the city was diffuse. One element that tended to set cities off from villages was the presence of craft groups, not however to be compared in their constitution with those of medieval Europe.

Many of the traditional forms and rhythms of Islamic cities have continued well into the present century. But the long period of relative stability and prosperity experienced by many cities ended after the twelfth and thirteenth centuries. In Iraq and Persia, wars, invasions, plagues, famines, fires, earthquakes, a marked decline in agricultural productivity, and the damaging shift in trade due to the European maritime intrusion (beginning in the sixteenth century), caused a general decline in urban life and the size of city populations. Baghdad, for instance, which had perhaps half a million inhabitants in the twelfth century, numbered no more than 20,000 by the 1830s. Arabia from the eighteenth to the early twentieth century was severely disrupted by the Wahhābī movement. In the Persian Gulf of the seventeenth and eighteenth centuries, Bandar 'Abbās and, subsequently, Bushire, were important European trading posts. But the main city and trading center of the region was Muscat. Oman was briefly occupied by the forces of Nādir Shāh of Persia in the 1730s. This brief maritime resurgence was just as much a manifestation of the desire of the Arabs of the Persian littoral who manned the Shah's navy to enhance their trade position as it was a Persian imperialist urge. The Ottoman-Persian conflict was felt in the Gulf, particularly at Basra in the latter part of the century. The rise of new towns along the southeastern Arabian littoral was the cause of further turmoil as they came to challenge Oman's trade predominance. These small ports of the "pirate coast" were eventually controlled by Britain and a perpetual maritime truce imposed. Save for Basra and, to a lesser extent, Bushire, most towns of the Persian Gulf depended more upon fishing, pearling, and shipbuilding for their livelihood than upon trade. Kuwait and Dubai were slowly acquiring a tradition as entrepôts in the nineteenth and early twentieth centuries.

European activity, mainly in the form of the exploitation of the region's oil resources, has been the essential factor behind the regenertaion and expansion of the towns of the Persian Gulf in the twentieth century. With little to offer European markets, except for one or two special goods (carpets from Iran and pearls from the Gulf, for instance), the countries of the region lacked the economic and financial resources to develop until oil began to come on stream in significant quantities after World War II. Centralization has been another important factor. New revenues have been concentrated upon capital cities, since these are where regimes with a heightened nationalist sense have built up the seat of political and economic power. In Iran and Iraq, the central positions of Tehran and Baghdad were well established before oil revenue became important. A secondary factor has been national and international migration. The Arab-Israeli conflict has caused hundreds of thousands of Palestinians and Jordanians to emigrate to Kuwait, Sa'ūdī Arabia, and elsewhere, and the Kurdish conflict has been behind the move of many Kurds to the cities of northern Iraq. But the main impetus of migration in the Persian Gulf region has been economic in nature. A poor living, with few prospects, has "pushed" many off the land to the city, whose "pull" has been the enticement of relatively well-paid jobs. It could be said that the requirements of the expanding cities and ports of the Gulf have created a small regional city-state economy that draws its manpower from a rural hinterland stretching from the Yemen republics and Somalia to India.

Tehran

From an Iranian viewpoint, Tehran's history is short. Located at the southern periphery of the western Elburz Mountains, Tehran was made the national capital in 1786 by Āqā Muhammad Khān Qājār. He wished to be near his tribal base of power and his Caspian provinces, but also to keep a safe distance from the Russians in the northwest and the Turkomans in the northeast. Also, Tehran was located where the east to west trade routes turned north to the Caspian and south along the desert basin.

From an area of about 7.5 square kilometers, with perhaps 20,000 people in 1800, Tehran expanded to 20 square kilometers, with a population of over 140,000 by 1880 during the region of Nāsir al-Dīn Shāh. His main accomplishment was to begin the modernization of the city. Broad avenues and new city walls were built, factories were set up in the south, and post offices, hospitals, and administrative buildings were erected as the city grew. By 1900 it had reached 200,000 and was the preeminent city of Persia.

The rapid expansion of Tehran began only after 1925, when Riza Shah founded the Pahlavī dynasty. Long, geometrically planned boulevards were built through the city, and many old houses were torn down. Greater economic stability and commercial prosperity gave rise to new industry in the south, and new government ministries were built in the city center, which was being vacated by wealthy merchants in favor of the small suburbs to the north, where building was increasing. When the city's walls were knocked down in 1937, Tehran had 500,000 inhabitants. Tehran had grown, at over 5 percent a year, to 4.5 million people in a built-up area of 470 square kilometers in 1976. Tehranis comprise over 13 percent of the national population. Some 43 percent of the capital's population are migrants. These have been attracted by prospects for higher living standards through employment in construction and industry, to which sectors Tehran contributes roughly half of all national activity. Utilities and all manner of services from health to education are concentrated here. All this expansion has been possible due to the government's expenditure of well over one-third of national development funds upon the capital in recent years.

There are many differences between northern and southern Tehran. The north is closer to the Elburz Mountains. It is notably cooler in summer, receives much more rain, and has a better water supply than the south. Here live wealthy and socially prominent Iranians from many parts of the country and most foreigners resident in the capital. The main residential area is from 'Abbāsābād and Shamīrān to Khiyābān-i Shāhrizā. Farther south is the modern business district where the offices of major national and international companies are located. Here too are hotels and western-style stores. Along and around Firdawsī, Hāfiz, and Sa'dī streets are found government ministries and foreign embassies. The bazaar lies within the limits of the old (nineteenth-century) part of the city. Its maze of streets is the beginning of the low-income, high-density district stretching south to the railway station and including Javādiyya and Nazīrābād. The northeastern, eastern, and western parts of the city are also densely populated. Being the principal industrial areas of Tehran, they are also the places with the most migrants.

Difficult problems beset Tehran. The city's housing shortage is chronic. There has been no unified plan to regulate the building of homes and offices or to guide expansion. Land speculation has been rife. A moratorium on new building in Tehran was declared in 1977, but while the construction industry faced a depression, no effective solution seemed at hand. Traffic congestion is severe. The transportation system is inadequate and inefficient. Severe pollution is caused by the city's one million cars, three-quarters of the national total, and roads are poorly maintained; however, an underground transportation network is planned. Other problems are an imminent shortage of water (before a new dam is completed) and the lack of a sewage system. The authorities have come to feel that there is an overconcentration of industry in the Tehran area. New industries are not being allowed to locate within 120 kilometers of the capital.

There are two ranks of primate city in Iran. Tehran occupies the first, national rank. The second rank is taken by cities that are primate within their region, but with which Tehran shares several characteristics. Many are still traditional, but as they slowly modernize and new factories spring up, migrants come into the older and now poorer central districts of these cities and tend to congregate by class and income groups rather than by race or religion as in the past. These areas are characterized by high levels of density, illiteracy, and fertility. The standard of housing and amenities is poor. Local authorities have built roads through these core areas in numerous cities. As in Tehran, wealthy citizens once resident in the central area have moved to new suburbs. Another trend is the decline of the bazaars. In the larger cities, higher order services have followed their likely customers to the suburbs, while in smaller cities lower-order services have moved from the bazaar to the new avenues. This confirms the physical separation of city-dwellers on socioeconomic lines. Industry, too, has developed on the periphery of cities, but the economic importance of the bazaar remains.

A spread of low- as well as high-income modern housing at the fringes is noticeable in many cities. As in the capital, planning and controls are limited and the government has been forced to take action to control speculation and mitigate the housing shortage. In Iran, urban policies have not been well conceived or coordinated, and administrators have been inadequate in numbers and training.

Iran

In 1976, the third national census of Iran recorded 33,591,875 inhabitants. The national population density was 20.8 people per square kilometer. North and northwestern Iran, from the head of the Persian Gulf through Tehran to the Caspian coast, contained much of the population. As a good 85 percent of the people of Iran live on no more than about one-third of the land, the "virtual" national population density is above 50 people per square kilometer. The ratio of people to cultivable land is about 200 per square kilometer. The most heavily inhabited rural areas, the Caspian littoral and southern Elburz, Azerbaijan and the northwestern Zagros Mountains, are those with the best-watered agricultural land, and those are also the regions with the highest urban densities.

Past and present population statistics must be treated with caution. Earlier figures were based on rough estimates or very limited government surveys. More recently, the censuses of 1956 and 1966 underestimated population. Also, the sources of data, such as registration offices, cannot yet be fully relied upon. Although the government's collection and processing of information is improving, conflicts of statistics among various ministries and among them and other sources still occur, and there is much deliberate obstruction and falsification. Thus, the figures presented below should be regarded as a general indication rather than as an accurate profile of the people of Iran.

Wars, invasions, natural disasters, famines, and epidemics have long caused fluctuations in the population. Thus, cholera and famine reduced an estimated 10 million Iranians in 1850 to as few as 6 million by 1875. From 9.86 million in 1900, the population rose at an annual rate of .08 percent to 11.86 million in 1926. Growing at 1.5 percent a year, it stood at 14.55 million by 1940. Improving living conditions after World War II were reflected in a yearly rate of increase of 2.2 percent that brought the number of Iranians to 20.38 million in 1956, the year of the census that recorded 18.95 million. Ten years later, the population had grown by 2.9 percent annually to approximately 26 million according to the 1966 census. (The government's later adjustments suggest that there were 19.1 million in 1956 and 26.1 million in 1966.) The yearly growth rate continued its rise and averaged 3.07 percent over the decade ending in 1976, when 33.59 million Iranians were enumerated. Were this high growth rate to continue, the national population would double several years before 2000,

In the past two decades, the crude birth rate per thousand has declined from 48.5 in 1956 to 46.5 in 1966 and 42.9 in 1976. The fertility rate is estimated at 200 children for every thousand women. The crude death (and infant mortality) rate has declined even more sharply due to the provision of better and more widespread health services. From 22.2 per thousand in 1956, it dropped to 17.8 per thousand in 1966 and 12.6 per thousand in 1976. The infant mortality rate was 102 per thousand in 1976. Both birth and death rates are much higher in rural areas than in cities. The prospect of a continued large increase in the population and the strains that it would exact upon society and the economy has caused the government to emphasize birth control programs. The average life expectancy in the mid-1970s was 51 years.

Unlike most countries, there were more males than females in Iran—17,277,656 (51.1 percent) males to 16,314,219 (48.9 percent) females in 1976. For every hundred females there were 105.9 males. This ratio has narrowed since 1966, when there were 107.3 males for every hundred females. Presently, only Gīlān Province has more women than men. It is probable, however, that some females were not counted in the 1976 census. According to a 1973 estimate, the only age groups in which females exceeded males were the 30 to 44 and 60+ country-dwellers. Even in these they had only a slight majority. The gap between the number of males and females was wider in urban than in rural areas. This is explained largely by the fact that more men than women migrate to cities in search of work. Between 1956 and 1966 the percentage of those under 15 years of age increased from 42 percent to 46 percent of the population, while the 15 to 64 age group dwindled from 54 percent to 50 percent, and those over 65 remained at 4 percent of the population. By 1975, the population had matured somewhat, as 51.5 percent were aged from 15 to 64 compared to 45.5 percent under 15. The mature segment gained most against the over-65 element, which now constituted 3 percent of the population.

For the first four decades of the century, about 78 percent of the people lived in the countryside and 22 percent in cities and towns. In 1956, 69 percent were rural and 31 percent were urban, and in 1966, 61 percent were country-dwellers, while 39 percent lived in urban areas. The 1976 census counted 8,185,219 males and 7,530,120 females in

TABLE H–1. POPULATION OF IRAN, 1976

Province	Population (000)	Total pop. (%)	Surface (000 km²)	Density[a]
Khurāsān	3,267	9.72	314	10.4
Kirmān	1,088	3.24	194	5.6
Sīstān and Balūchistān	659	1.96	183	3.6
Fārs	2,021	6.02	134	15.0
Isfahan	1,975	5.88	95	20.8
Central Province	6,921	20.60	92	75.2
Simnān	486	1.45	82	5.9
E. Azarbaijan	3,195	9.51	67	47.7
Hurmuzdgān	463	1.38	67	7.0
Khūzistān	2,177	6.48	65	33.5
Yazd	356	1.06	57	6.2
Māzandarān	2,384	7.10	47	50.2
W. Azarbaijan	1,405	4.18	44	32.0
Luristān	925	2.75	31	29.8
Bushire	345	1.03	28	12.4
Kurdistan	782	2.33	25	31.3
Zanjān	579	1.72	22	26.3
Hamadān	1,087	3.24	20	54.3
Kirmānshāhān	1,016	3.02	19	53.5
Ilam and Push-i Kūh	244	0.73	18	13.6
Chahārmahāl and Bakhtīyārī	394	1.17	15	26.3
Gīlān	1,578	4.70	15	100.5
Bayir Ahmadī and Kūh Gīlūyeh	245	0.73	14	17.5
Total	33,592	100.00	1,648	20.8

[a] Separate calculation.
Source: Iran Statistics, Banque Etebarate Iran Publications (Tehran, 1976).

urban areas and 9,092,438 males and 8,784,099 females in rural areas. Thus, only 53.2 percent of the Iranian people are now rural, compared to 46.8 percent who are urban. Since 1966, the rural population has grown from 165 million to its present total of 17.9 million at a modest .85 percent annually. The country people are distributed over 48,000 villages with less than 250 inhabitants and 18,000 villages with more than that number. In contrast, the people of the cities and towns have increased from 10.56 million in 1966, by a rate of 4.77 percent annually, to their current number of 15.7 million. One indicator of the rapid urbanization of Iran is the rise of the number of towns—places with over 5,000 people plus administrative centers called "urban areas"—from 223 in 1966 to 365 ten years later. By the early 1980s, a majority of Iranians will be urban.

In 1976, there was only one city of more than a million people—Tehran. Isfahān, Mashhad, and Tabrīz each had grown to over half a million, and five other cities had more than 200,000 people. Thirteen had over 100,00 inhabitants; their aggregate population was 1,984,386. There were 20 cities of between 50,000 and 100,000; they contained 1,461,590 people. The cities of between 100,000 and 200,000 grew at almost 4.8 percent a year. This was less than the 5 percent annual growth rate of cities between 50,000 and 100,000 and more than the 4.3 percent yearly growth rate of cities over 200,000. Overall, the number of cities of more than 50,000 and less than 50,000 increased from 196 in 1966 to 323 in 1976, comprising 4,443,255 people. Their average year's rate of increase was a remarkable 9.9 percent, 3.9 percent higher than the total annual urban growth rate during 1966–76. It could be concluded that Iran is indeed becoming urban but, more specifically, that the movement of the people is toward relatively smaller urban areas. Nonetheless, in 1976 Tehran alone had some 28.5 percent of the total urban population. With the eight other cities over 200,000, it held 51 percent of all city-dwellers. The 42 cities of over 50,000 in 1976 contained 11.27 million people, 71.9 percent of those residing in urban areas, whereas, in 1966 only 27 cities held 70 percent of the urban population.

Although natural increases and the expansion of limits in some cities has added to urban growth, the most significant cause of the large increase in cities and towns has been migration. In the first half of the century, some 60 percent of the movement of people within Iran entailed migration *between* cities, while 40 percent of all migration was from the countryside to cities. In the past 25 years, this trend has been reversed as the nation has launched into industrial development. By 1972, 3,853,000 migrants, 90 percent of the nationwide total of 4,275,000, who lived in urban areas had come from rural areas. A large number came from the provinces of Eastern Azerbaijan, Isfahān, and Gīlān to the Central Province and Khūzistān Province. Many of the principal migrants had left circumstances of under- or unemployment in agriculture for work or a job offering higher

TABLE H–2. ESTIMATED URBAN AND RURAL POPULATION OF IRAN BY AGE GROUP AND SEX, 1973

Age	Urban		Rural		Total		Grand total
	Male	Female	Male	Female	Male	Female	
0–14	3,087	2,953	4,473	4,199	7,560	7,152	14,712
15–29	1,667	1,528	2,529	2,363	4,196	3,891	8,087
30–44	1,248	1,080	1,185	1,187	2,433	2,267	4,700
45–59	625	577	730	695	1,355	1,272	2,627
60+	394	337	390	398	784	735	1,519
Total	7,021	6,475	9,307	8,842	16,328	15,317	31,645

Source: Iranian Statistical Center.

TABLE H-3. POPULATION OF MAIN CITIES OF IRAN

City	1966	1976	Annual growth (%)
Tehran	2,980,041	4,496,159	4.2
Isfahān	424,045	671,825	4.7
Mashhad	409,616	670,180	5.1
Tabrīz	403,413	598,576	3.9
Shīrāz	296,865	416,408	4.4
Ahvāz	206,375	329,006	4.8
Ābādān	272,962	296,081	0.8
Kirmānshāh	187,930	290,861	4.5
Qum	134,292	246,831	6.3
Total	5,315,539	8,015,927	4.3

Sources: Iran Statistics, Banque Etebarate Publications (Tehran, 1976); Iran Almanac and Book of Facts (16th ed.; Tehran: Echo Glen, 1977).

wages in cities where, besides the prospect of job opportunities, there were much more extensive social services. Over half of all migrants were secondary migrants—wives, children, and other dependents. Other reasons for migration were job transfer, marriage, and, to a lesser extent, education. Tehran has been the main destination of migrants, since it is the economic hub of the country. But growing disamenity to Tehranis caused by a heavy strain on all services, and the economic necessity to encourage regional economic development, have prompted the government to stimulate the expansion of provincial economic "poles." By 1977 there were signs that migrants were moving to other cities at a higher rate than to the capital. Seasonal migration is the way of life for some tribes, mainly of the Zagros region, who may number half a million. Many tribes have become sedentary in recent years due to the requirements of modernization, the effects of land reform, and government pressure.

In 1975, 22.6 million Iranians of working age, i.e., over ten years of age, comprised 67.6 percent of the total population. The economically active numbered 9.38 million, 41.5 percent of those of working age. This compared unfavorably with the percentages of the economically active segment to those of working age in 1956 and 1966, which were 47.5 percent and 46.1 percent, respectively. Also, the percentage of active to total population has fallen. In 1956, it was 32 percent, in 1966 it was 30.4 percent, and in 1975 it stood at

TABLE H-4. NUMBER AND PERCENTAGE OF PEOPLE EMPLOYED IN ECONOMIC SECTORS IN IRAN, 1972

Sector	Number (000)	Percent
Agriculture	3,535	39.8
Services	2,730	30.7
Industry and mining	1,789	20.1
Oil	50	0.6
Construction	699	7.9
Utilities	80	0.9
Total	8,883	100.0

Source: Iran Almanac and Book of Facts 1977 (16th ed.; Tehran: Echo Glen, 1977).

28.1 percent. These figures manifest the increasing youthfulness and dependency of the population. An important consequence of urban migration is the steady decline of agricultural manpower, from 56.3 percent of all those employed in 1956 to 46.2 percent in 1966 and 39.8 percent in 1972. The sectors benefiting from this shift have been industry and services. By 1977 there were shortages of labor, especially in the category of skilled workers. One relatively untapped source is the women of Iran, who comprised only 12.5 percent of all economically active people in the country in 1972.

Iraq

The population of Iraq in 1976 was estimated at 11,505,000, excluding Iraqis abroad. The national population density was 27 people per square kilometer. Excluding the least populated governorates of al-Anbar, Karbalā, and Muthannā, in whose combined area of 191,602 square kilometers lived 832,000 people, or 4.3 per square kilometer, the average density was 44 per square kilometer. The average national density in relation to cultivated area is estimated at 155 per square kilometer. The central provinces continue to grow faster than the northern and, particularly, the southern provinces.

At the height of Iraq's economic prosperity, from the eighth to the thirteenth century, perhaps upwards of 15 million people defended an extensive irrigation network. The Mongol invasions of the thirteenth century hastened the decline of the irrigation system. The population dwindled quickly and remained small under Ottoman domination. By 1870 there were about 1.3 million "Iraqis," and then an average annual growth

TABLE H–5. THE POPULATION OF IRAQ AND ITS DENSITY, 1976

Governorate	Population (000)	Area (sq km)	Density/ sq km
Nineveh	1,158	41,320	28
Salāh al-Dīn	356	21,326	17
Ta'mim	439	9,426	47
Diyāla	663	19,047	35
Baghdad	3,036	5,023	604
Anbar	405	89,540	5
Babylon	565	5,503	103
Karbalā	243	52,856	5
Najaf	354	26,834	13
Qādisiyya	395	8,569	46
Muthannā	184	49,206	4
Dhū-Qār	617	13,668	45
Wāsit	409	17,922	23
Maysān	419	16,774	25
Basra	897	19,702	46
Autonomous Region:			
Dohuk	217	6,374	34
Irbīl	493	14,428	34
Sulaimāniyya	656	16,482	40
Total	11,505	434,000[a]	27

[a] This excludes half the Neutral Zone and territorial waters, which comprise 4,446 square kilometers.
Source: Republic of Iraq Ministry of Planning, Central Statistical Organization, *Annual Abstract of Statistics, 1976.*

rate of 2.1 percent brought the population to 2.25 million by 1905. It declined to 2 percent over the next thirty years; in 1935, three years after Iraq's independence, there were 3.605 million people. Between 1935 and 1947, when the number of inhabitants stood at 4.816 million, the average annual growth rate was 2.8 percent. This rose to 3.1 percent during the next decade, at the end of which, in 1957, there were 6.34 million Iraqis. By 1965, a yearly average annual growth rate of 3.5 percent had brought the population to 8.097 million. The yearly rate of growth declined to 3.3 percent during the next five years. From a 1970 total of 9.440 million, the population increased to its 1975 level of 11.124 million at an average rate of 3.36 percent a year. This rate of growth is quite high by world standards. It is estimated that only twenty-one years are required for the 1975 population to double itself. By 2000 it could total over 24 million. As Iraq is considered underpopulated, there seems little likelihood that action will be taken soon to curb this high growth, brought about by rising standards of living and health and by the consequent decline of the rate of mortality, particularly among infants.

Of the 11.505 million Iraqis in 1976, 5.795 million (50.4 percent) were male and 5.710 million (49.6 percent) were female. Out of these, 5.52 million (48.0 percent) were under 15 compared with 44.8 percent under 15 in 1957; 5.399 million (46.9 percent) were aged from 15 to 59, and 47.7 percent were of like age in 1957, when 7.5 percent of the population was over 60. In 1976, only 586,000 (5.1 percent) were more than 60. In aggregate, the Iraqi population is becoming more youthful. This trend will continue as the large under-15 group comes to maturity.

The most significant demographic trend in Iraq is the rapidly increasing urbanization of the population. (In Iraq, any settlement over 5,000 people, plus administrative centers, is considered an urban area.) Iraqi government and United Nations figures indi-

TABLE H–6. VITAL STATISTICS OF IRAQ, 1973–75 (PER 000)

	Rural	Urban	National
Crude birth rate	47.0	39.6	42.6
Crude death rate	12.8	9.1	10.6
Rate of natural increase	34.3	30.5	32.0
Growth rate	11.6	41.7	32.0
Infant death rate	104.5	76.3	88.7
General fertility rate	220.8	182.8	198.1

Source: Republic of Iraq Ministry of Planning, Central Statistical Organization, *Annual Abstract of Statistics, 1976.*

TABLE II–7. POPULATION OF IRAQ BY AGE GROUP AND SEX, 1976 (PER 000)

Age group	Male	Female	Total	% of total population
0–14	2,800	2,720	5,520	48.0
15–29	1,493	1,448	2,941	25.5
30–44	743	737	1,480	12.9
45–59	482	496	978	8.5
60+	277	309	586	5.1
Total	5,795	5,710	11,505	100.0

Source: Republic of Iraq Ministry of Planning, Central Statistical Organization, *Annual Abstract of Statistics, 1976.*

cate that 4.162 million (51.3 percent) were urban and 3.935 million (48.7 percent) were rural in 1965. By 1970, 5.452 million people (57.8 percent) were classified as urban and 3.987 million (42.2 percent) as rural. Urban Iraqis were estimated at 6.875 million (61.8 percent) and rural Iraqis at 4.249 million (38.2 percent) in 1975.

Baghdad remains the first city of Iraq, and is the location of half the country's industry. It had 1,056,000 inhabitants in 1957 and 1,745,000 in 1965. The capital's population increased at an annual rate of 6.6 percent over the next nine years and the estimated number of Baghdadis was 2.8 million in 1974. Baghdad governorate, with 3,036,000 people, held 27.4 percent of the national population in 1976. Mosul, with 179,646 people in 1957 and 243,111 in 1965, grew at 28 percent a year to some 857,000 by 1974. Refugees from the Kurdish conflict and the development of the oil industry account for much of this phenomenal growth rate. Nineveh, the governorate in which it is located, had a population of 1,158,000 in 1976, 10 percent of all Iraqis. Basra, the third largest city, had 164,623 people in 1957. It grew to 313,327 in 1965 and, at an average annual rate of over 15 percent, to about 854,000 by 1974, when it held most of the people of the governorate. Its main attraction to newcomers is its oil industry and port. These three "urban" governorates contained 44.2 percent of all Iraqis.

Directly related to urbanization is large-scale rural migration to the towns. This gathered momentum after World War II and had reached a level of concern to the government by the late 1950s. A severe shortage of agricultural manpower meant that arable land was going uncultivated. Since 1958, however, the republican government's land reform activities have themselves been a cause of migration, because their erratic implementation has caused insecurity and dissatisfaction. Also, jobs in the growing industrial and commercial sectors in cities, where social services are more accessible, have more attraction than anything that the countryside can offer. Indicative of this strong urban influx are the migration rates for urban and rural areas, which were 11.2 per thousand and −22.7 per thousand respectively for 1973–75.

The rural population is distributed into two main regions. Roughly 30 percent live in the foothills and lower levels of the mountains of the northeastern provinces, such as Sulaimāniyya, Diyāla, and Salāh al-Dīn, where there is adequate rain to cultivate cereal crops. Some 70 percent live on the irrigated alluvial plain of of Tigris and Euphrates rivers, from Hīt and Sāmarrā in the north to the region of Dīwāniyya in the south. The four southern provinces, Dhū-Qār, Maysān, Muthannā, and Basra have

TABLE H–8. ESTIMATED EMPLOYMENT OF
MANPOWER IN IRAQ, 1973

Sector	Number	% of work force
Agriculture	1,540,400	50.8
Services	330,000	10.7
Commerce	164,000	5.3
Transport	162,000	5.3
Manufacturing	170,000	5.4
Construction	73,000	2.4
Mining	18,500	0.6
Electricity, gas, & water	14,300	0.5
Others	380,000	12.4
Unemployed	200,100	6.6
Total	3,052,700	100.0

Source: Europa Yearbook 1976–77.

experienced low growth due to urban migration. After the end of the Kurdish conflict in 1975, the government settled some Kurds in other parts of Iraq. By 1977, some were being allowed to return to their homeland.

A sizable number of the 43.5 percent of Iraqis of working age (15–60) are either seasonally or self-employed. Some are members of a family and work without pay. Many who have migrated to the cities are unemployed. Many children are illegal members of the work force. Perhaps not much more than 50 percent of the economically active population are fully employed. In the mid-1960s, nearly 75 percent of all working Iraqis were engaged in agriculture; 8 percent in services, 6 percent in industry, 3 percent in trade, and about a further 8 percent were in occupations such as transport. By 1973, only 51 percent of the economically active were involved in agriculture.

Kuwait

The population of Kuwait was 1,093,900 at the end of 1976. Of this total 518,100 (47.3 percent) were Kuwaitis and 575,800 (52.7 percent) were non-Kuwaitis. In only one year, the population had increased by almost exactly 10 percent over its 1975 total of 994,837. Excluding the uninhabited areas of Būbiyān and Warba islands, there were 64.5 people per square kilometer in 1976. With some 1,050,000 people packed into little more than 1,000 square kilometers of the country's 16,918 square kilometers, Kuwait is indeed a modern city-state. When the very thinly populated desert areas are left aside, the virtual density of the governorates per square kilometer is: capital, 1,039, Hawālī, 1,048, and Ahmadī, 625. The distribution of the population is characterized by two related trends. In many areas, citizens and immigrants live apart from one another. Hawālī is the extreme example. Also, Kuwaitis have become suburban, while non-Kuwaitis reside in the inner city and the older, less planned and more crowded suburbs.

Before the first census of 1957, the population of Kuwait was not known with any certainty. There were an estimated 50,000 inhabitants, including 13,000 Bedouin, around 1907, perhaps 60,000 in the 1930s, and some 160,000 in the early 1950s. Between 1957, when it was assessed at 206,473, and 1965, when it amounted to 467,339, the population grew at almost 16 percent a year. Between 1965 and 1970, the country experienced an annual rate of growth of 12 percent, and from 1970 to 1975 a yearly increase rate of 6.9 percent brought the population from 737,908 to 994,201. Kuwait's growth rate has long been one of the highest in the world, and were the population to expand at this rate, much less its rate of increase for 1976, it would double within a decade.

Immigration is the primary cause of Kuwait's high growth. The large-scale movement into the country began in the 1950s, when the government began to use its growing income from oil to build a modern welfare state. Iraqis, Iranians, and Omanis were the main immigrant groups in the first years after World War II. By 1957, Iraqis (28 percent), Iranians (21 percent), and Jordanians and Palestinians (16 percent) migrating from Israeli-occupied territories were the largest elements of the foreign population in Kuwait. By 1975, the latter group comprised almost two-fifths of the foreign nationals in Kuwait. Political differences are one salient factor behind the relative decline of the number and absolute drop in the percentage of Iraqis in Kuwait. The relatively slow rise of the reported local number of Iranians accounts for the lower percentage of that nationality present in Kuwait. Syrians and, especially, Egyptians have increased in number in recent years. Many of these are professionals.

Youthfulness is the leading characteristic of the population. Compared to 41.5 percent in 1957, about 50 percent of all Kuwaiti citizens have been under 15 since 1965. The immigrant population is gradually gaining in youth: 28 percent were under 15 in 1965 and 39.7 percent in 1975. Children, rather than adolescents, form the bulk of young people. In 1975, adolescents formed only a little more than 10 percent of Kuwaiti nationals and 7.2 percent of all immigrants.

A fairly even balance between the sexes is kept throughout the entire age structure of Kuwaiti citizens, but females exceed males only in the 15 to 29 age bracket. The slight preponderance of males over females in the under-15 non-Kuwaiti age group widens in the 15 to 19 group. Here, women are outnumbered by almost 4 to 3. This disparity increases in the 20 to 39 range, in which there are 3 men for every 2 women, and is at its widest in the 40 to 49 bracket, in which there are about 5 men for every 2 women. This is accounted for by the sizable number of single men and married men away from home who have come to work in Kuwait temporarily before returning to their own country. It is in the 20 to 49 age category that Kuwaiti men are heavily outnumbered—2 to 1—by non-Kuwaiti men. Notably, as some immigrants have settled on a more permanent basis in recent years, there has been a marked increase in the number

TABLE H–9. POPULATION OF KUWAIT BY GOVERNORATE AND SELECTED LOCALITIES, 1975

Governorate	Kuwaitis	Non-Kuwaitis	Total	Area (sq km)	Density (sq km)
Capital	154,242	122,114	276,356	11,230.0	25
Kuwait City	11,777	66,339	78,116	7.6	10,278
Suburbs	55,775	142,465	198,240	11,222.4	18
Desert	10,442	918	12,360	10,964.4	1
Hawālī	230,472	346,117	576,589	550.0	1,048
Hawālī	9,816	120,749	130,565	6.4	20,401
Salīmiyya	16,764	97,179	113,943	10.2	11,171
Ahmadī	86,738	54,518	141,256	5,138.0	27
Ahmadī	9,927	9,210	19,137	59.2	323
Fahāhīl	11,455	20,962	32,417	11.2	2,819
Total	471,452	522,749	994,201[a]	16,918	59

[a] Excluding 636 Kuwaitis abroad.

Source: Kuwait Ministry of Planning, Central Statistical Office, *Annual Statistical Abstract, 1976.*

TABLE H–10. FOREIGN NATIONALS IN KUWAIT, 1975

Nationality	Number	% of total population	% of foreign population
All Arabs	419,187	42.1	80.2
Jordanian/Palestinian	204,178	20.5	39.0
Egyptian	60,534	6.1	11.6
Iraqi	45,070	4.5	8.6
Syrian	40,962	4.1	8.0
Other Arabs	67,843	6.9	13.0
Non-Arabs	103,562	10.4	19.8
Iranian	40,842	4.1	8.0
Indian	32,105	3.2	6.1
Pakistani	23,016	2.3	4.4
All others	2,599	0.8	1.3
Total	522,749	52.5	100.0

Source: Kuwait Ministry of Planning, Central Statistical Office, *Annual Statistical Abstract, 1976.*

TABLE H–11. POPULATION OF KUWAIT BY AGE GROUP, SEX,
AND NATIONALITY, 1975

Age group	Sex	Kuwaitis	Non-Kuwaitis	Total
0–14	M	118,071	106,043	224,114
	F	115,371	101,422	216,793
Total (%)		233,442 (23.4%)	207,465 (20.9%)	440,907 (44.3%)
15–29	M	59,577	83,209	142,786
	F	65,108	57,844	122,952
Total (%)		124,685 (12.6%)	141,053 (14.1%)	265,738 (26.7%)
30–49	M	40,461	101,356	141,817
	F	37,394	47,001	84,395
Total (%)		77,855 (7.7%)	148,357 (15.0%)	226,212 (22.7%)
50+	M	18,491	16,560	35,051
	F	17,615	9,314	26,929
Total (%)		36,106 (3.7%)	25,874 (2.6%)	61,980 (6.3%)
Grand Total	M	236,600	307,168	543,768
	F	235,488	215,581	451,069
Total[a] (%)		472,088 (47.5%)	522,749 (52.5%)	994,837 (100%)

[a] Percentages do not agree with Grand Total due to rounding off.
Source: Kuwait Ministry of Planning, Central Statistical Office, *Annual Statistical Abstract, 1976.*

of women per thousand immigrants and in the number of children in consequence. Both the Kuwaiti and non-Kuwaiti population falls off quickly after 40. Only 6.3 percent of the country's inhabitants are over 50.

The large proportion of dependents in the population is borne out by the country's vital statistics. In 1974, the birth rate for Kuwaitis was 54.4 per thousand, the death rate 7.1 per thousand, and the rate of natural increase an extremely high 4.73 percent. For every thousand of the non-Kuwaiti populace, the birth rate was 39.8 and the death rate 3.7. The rate of natural increase was 3.61 percent. Both Kuwaitis and non-Kuwaitis take full advantage of the state's high standard national health service. One manifestation of its effectiveness is Kuwait's infant mortality rate which, at 44.3 per thousand births in 1974, is less than half the infant mortality rate of Iraq and Iran. The lower birth rate among non-Kuwaitis is due to the imbalance of the sexes, and the very low

TABLE H–12. NUMBER EMPLOYED IN ECONOMIC
SECTORS IN KUWAIT, 1975

Sectors	Kuwaitis	Non-Kuwaitis
Agriculture	3,983	3,531
Mining	1,779	3,080
Industry	2,258	22,209
Construction	1,756	30,500
Utilities	2,034	5,237
Trade	6,327	33,232
Transport/Communications	4,567	11,118
Services	64,265	102,537
Other	2	
Total	86,971	211,444

Source: Kuwait Ministry of Planning, Central Statistical Office, *Annual Statistical Abstract, 1976.*

non-Kuwaiti death rate is due to the small number of aged immigrants. With no pressure to curb their natural increase—indeed, there is political and economic incentive to maintain high growth—Kuwaitis should continue to increase at over 3 percent a year. The country's average life expectancy is 67.2 years.

Of the 238,000 Kuwaitis over 15, 86,971 (36.4 percent) were economically active in 1975. Of the 315,284 non-Kuwaitis over 15, 211,444 (67 percent) were active. In both groups, no more than 12 percent were women. The high percentage of active nonnationals attests to both Kuwait's need for foreign labor and the attractiveness of its wages and social services. The vast preponderance of immigrants in the industrial, construction, and trade sectors indicates Kuwaitis' dislike for manual labor in favor of services, which occupied 73.7 percent of the economically active citizens.

Sa'ūdī Arabia

The census of 1974 recorded a Sa'ūdī population of 7,012,642. This was more than double the 3,302,330 recorded by the officially repudiated census of 1962–63. The government's tacit assumption is that there are about 6.2 million people. A more realistic estimate is between 5 and 5.5 million. This includes some 1.5 million foreigners, upwards of a million of whom are Yemenīs. The kingdom's nominal density was 3.2 people per square kilometer. More Sa'ūdīs, however, were concentrated in cities or relatively small farming areas.

There were 5,128,655 (73.1 percent of the population) settled inhabitants and 1,883,987 (26.9 percent) nomads. Of the sedentary population, 2,705,356 (52.8 percent), or 38.7 percent of all Sa'ūdīs, were resident in cities of more than 30,000. Cities have registered remarkable growth since 1962–63, when an urban population of 800,000, 24 percent of the population, was enumerated. The main cause of this increase has been urban migration due to the development of the nation's economy and industry as the revenue from the oil sector expands and to the improved transportation network.

Besides being the country's principal non-oil industrial centers, Riyadh is the administrative capital, Jidda the business capital, and Mecca the religious capital of Sa'ūdi Arabia. Dammām is the preeminent example of oil-linked growth, having expanded to 128,000 from about 45,000 in 1965. The other cities of over 30,000 are Tabūk, 74,825; Buraida, 69,940; al-Mubarraz, 54,325; Khamīs Mushait, 49,581; al-Khubar, 48,817; Najrān, 47,501; Hā'il, 40,502; Jīzān, 32,812; and Abhā, 30,150.

The location of the smaller cities, as well as the larger ones, was mainly a response to the availability of water for farming. The same is true for the settled rural population. It is concentrated in three north-to-south strips forming an axis across the country with the main cities at its core. The first, somewhat discontinuous strip extends from the Jīzān district of southern 'Asīr, the most densely populated area of the country, to the vicinity of Mecca, Tā'if, and Jidda north to Medina. The second extends north-

TABLE H–13. POPULATION OF THE MAJOR CITIES OF SA'ŪDĪ ARABIA

City	Population	City	Population
Riyadh	666,840	Medina	198,186
Jidda	561,104	Dammām	127,844
Mecca	366,801	Hufūf	101,271
Tā'if	204,857		

Source: Kingdom of Sa'ūdī Arabia, Central Department of Statistics, *The Statistical Indicator*, First Issue, 1976.

west from Riyadh through the Qasīm district to Hā'il. The third lies along the coast of Eastern Province from Hufūf to Qatīf. By definition, the Bedouin have no fixed location, but the authorities have been trying to sedentarize them. It is hoped that their settlement, some in new agricultural villages, will accelerate in the coming years.

Since the census of 1974 is not available, there is no detailed account of the national age structure or of the kingdom's vital statistics. United Nations figures suggest that Sa'ūdīs increased at a rate of almost 3 percent annually from 1970 to 1975. The crude birth rate was estimated at 49.5 per thousand and the crude death rate at 20.2 per thousand. The fertility rate was high at 220.8 per thousand, but the infant mortality rate was also quite high. The average life expectancy in Sa'ūdī Arabia is 45 years. About 44.8 percent of the population is under 14; 52.5 percent is between 15 and 64; and 2.7 percent is over 65.

One of the most pressing problems faced by the country is the acute shortage of manpower; particularly of skilled manpower. Of the 1,600,000 work force in 1975, only 314,000 were listed as non-Sa'ūdīs. But many of the 1,286,000 "Sa'ūdī" workers were in fact Yemenis. It is estimated that a further 500,000 foreigners will be needed for a labor force of 2,331,000 by 1980; 1,518,000 of this projected total will be Sa'ūdīs, but only 48,000 will be women. Differences in outlook and behavior tend to cause friction between Sa'ūdīs and the growing number of immigrants. A recent trend in Sa'ūdī Arabia and other states of the Persian Gulf has been the employment of South Korean and Filipino labor.

Bahrain

The population of Bahrain in late 1975 was 266,078, and the national population density was 400 per square kilometer. (The findings of a census taken in 1976 were not available in mid-1977.) According to the census of 1971, the national population was 216,078; 178,193 (82.5 percent) were citizens and 37,885 (17.5 percent) were foreigners. Some 78.1 percent of the inhabitants were urban, over half of these in Manāma town, and 21.9 percent were rural. Most people lived in northeastern Bahrain; lesser numbers dwelt on Muharraq and Sitra islands. Most nonnationals resided in the capital, notably around Mīnā Salmān.

Since 1941, the year of the first census, which counted 89,970 inhabitants, the population has grown at a high rate. Increasing by 2.6 percent a year, it totaled 109,650 by 1950. An average annual growth rate of 3 percent brought the population to 143,135 by 1959; a steady yearly increase between 1959 and 1971 of 3.3 percent took it up to 182,203 in 1965 and 216,078 in 1971. Between 1971 and 1975, the number of inhabitants grew at 5.6 percent a year.

Between 1941 and 1971, an average of 18.2 percent of the population was foreign. The government's controls on immigration have been due to the modest size of Bahrain and its economy and to its interest in maximizing the benefit to Bahrainis as the economy develops. Contrary to the earlier pattern of gradual increase, the number of immigrants showed both an absolute and relative decline between 1965, when 38,389 foreigners comprised 21.1 percent of the population, and 1971 (for which figures, see above). An important factor behind this decline was the development of the oil industry in the native countries of immigrants, for instance, in Oman and the then Trucial States. As of 1971, the main foreign groups were Omanis, 10,785; Indians, 6,657; Pakistanis, 5,377; Iranians, 5,097; British, 2,901; Yemenis, 1,538; Jordanians/Pakistanis, 1,338; Sa'ūdīs, 1,332; other Arabs, 2,008; all others, 852.

Both the youthful demographic character of and the high rate of natural increase among Bahrainis is indicated by the fact that the under-15 age group comprised 47.1

percent of all nationals in 1971; 48 percent were in the economically active 15 to 59 age group and only 4.9 percent were over 60. The Bahraini population declined quite steeply in number from the lower to the higher age groups. Men outnumbered women in all but the 30 to 44 age group, but this was due to the likely under-reporting of women. The age profile of the immigrants showed that the largest groups were the 15 to 29 and 30 to 44 elements who came for work; these accounted for 62.9 percent of all foreigners. Men exceeded women by a ratio of 3 to 1, excluding the under-15 group, which comprised 23.8 percent of all immigrants. The size of this contingent, which was fairly evenly balanced between males and females, revealed a high birth rate among immigrants resident with their families. Only 13.3 percent of the foreign population was over 45, and only a little more than 2.9 percent were over 60.

The labor force in 1971 was 60,301, 28 percent of the total population. Of the economically active, 37,950 Bahrainis made 63.3 percent, and of these, all but 1,848 were men, comprising about 86 percent of the Bahraini male population between 15 and 60. Of all non-nationals (just under 60 percent) 22,351 non-Bahrainis were economically active; this number was composed of 90 percent of the males between 15 and 60, who made up 36.7 percent of the overall working population.

Unlike most Arab states of the Persian Gulf, there was a fairly even balance throughout the occupations between nationals and nonnationals. With a good educational system, Bahrain has a plentiful supply of skilled manpower. Projections suggest a sur-

TABLE H–14. POPULATION OF BAHRAIN BY URBAN-RURAL
LOCATION AND NATIONALITY, 1971

	Bahrainis	Non-Bahrainis	Total
Manāma division	59,496	29,903	89,399
Manāma town	58,884	29,901	88,785
Rural	612	2	614
Muharraq Island	45,774	3,766	49,540
Muharraq town	34,112	3,620	37,732
Hidd town	5,172	97	5,269
Rural	6,490	49	6,539
Jiddhāfs division	19,065	456	19,521
Jiddhāfs town	10,743	409	11,152
Rural	8,322	47	8,369
Northern division (Rural)	10,454	160	10,614
Western division (Rural)	8,355	334	8,869
Central division	13,946	282	14,228
Isa town	7,285	216	7,501
Rural	6,661	66	6,727
Sitra division	11,263	60	11,323
Sitra town	6,624	41	6,665
Rural	4,639	19	4,658
Riffa division	9,766	2,867	12,633
Riffa town	9,171	1,560	10,731
Awālī town	24	960	984
Rural	571	347	918
Other islands	74	57	131
Total	178,193	37,885	216,078
Urban	132,015	36,804	168,819
Rural	46,178	1,081	47,259

Source: State of Bahrain, Ministry of Finance and National Economy Statistical Bureau, Statistics of the Population Census, 1971.

TABLE H–15. POPULATION OF BAHRAIN BY AGE GROUP, SEX, AND NATIONALITY, 1971

Age group	Sex	Bahrainis	Non-Bahrainis	Total
0–14	M	43,258	4,894	48,152
	F	43,088	4,400	47,488
Total (%)		86,346 (39.9%)	9,294 (4.3%)	95,640 (44.2%)
15–29	M	21,244	9,047	30,291
	F	21,039	3,250	24,289
Total (%)		42,283 (19.6%)	12,297 (5.6%)	54,580 (25.2%)
30–44	M	12,109	8,948	21,057
	F	12,760	2,597	15,357
Total (%)		24,869 (11.5%)	11,545 (5.4%)	36,414 (16.9%)
45–59	M	8,584	2,889	11,473
	F	7,151	795	7,946
Total (%)		15,735 (7.2%)	5,684 (1.8%)	19,419 (9%)
60+	M	4,577	764	5,341
	F	4,383	301	4,684
Total (%)		8,960 (4.1%)	1,065 (0.5%)	10,025 (4.6%)
Grand Total				
	M	89,772	26,542	116,314
	F	88,421	11,343	99,764
Total[a] (%)		178,193 (82.5%)	37,885 (17.5%)	216,078 (100%)

[a] Percentages do not add up due to rounding off.
Source: State of Bahrain, Ministry of Finance and National Economy Statistical Bureau, *Statistics of the Population Census, 1971.*

TABLE H–16. ECONOMICALLY ACTIVE POPULATION BY SECTOR AND NATIONALITY

Sector	Bahrainis	Non-Bahrainis	Total
Agriculture, fishing	2,995	995	3,990
Mining, manufacturing	5,614	2,850	8,464
Utilities	1,480	225	1,705
Construction	5,639	4,765	10,404
Trade	4,851	2,855	7,706
Transportation/communication	5,067	2,676	7,743
Finance, business	740	344	1,084
Services	10,930	7,458	18,388
Other	634	183	817
Total	37,950	22,351	60,301

Source: State of Bahrain, Ministry of Finance and National Economy Statistical Bureau, *Statistics of the Population Census, 1971.*

plus of skilled labor in the 1980s. This could lead to a decline in foreign workers or, possibly, to some Bahrainis emigrating to nearby states.

Qatar

The population of Qatar is about 200,000. The nominal national density is 19 people per square kilometer. About 160,000 live in the capital, Dōha. The rest reside at Dukhān, Umm Sa'īd, and a few small towns elsewhere along the coast. The annual rate of growth is over 3 percent for Qataris and 5 percent for foreigners. The country's growth from

12,000 in 1940 to its present level has been due mostly to immigration. Qatar's oil- and gas-based economy requires many more people to man it than can be supplied from what are probably no more than 50,000 native Qataris. (Other estimates suggest that there are 60,000 citizens.)

The bulk of the three-quarters of the population that is foreign is comprised of Pakistanis and Iranians. These are manual laborers and craftsmen. Some Yemenis are present, and Egyptians, Lebanese, and other "northern" Arabs fill professional jobs. A few Westerners have senior executive and managerial posts. Of Qatar's work force of about 45,000, over 38,000 are nonnationals. The percentage of foreigners in the work force is likely to become even higher in the near future, as there will not be enough Qataris to fill more than one-third of new job openings.

The United Arab Emirates

According to the census of 1975, the population of the United Arab Emirates was 655,937. (At the end of 1977 the UAE recorded 862,000 inhabitants, 71 percent of whom were male.) The number of inhabitants in each Emirate was: Abū Dhabī, 235,662; Dubai, 206,861; Sharja, 88,188; Ra's al-Khaima, 57,282; 'Ajmān, 21,566; Umm al-Qaiwain, 16,879; and Fujaira, 26,498. The nominal population density was 8.4 people per square kilometer. The huge increase in the population from its 1968 total of 180,184, including some 74,000 nonnationals, and the great imbalance between males and females, 400,000 to 255,000, has been due to immigration stimulated by the UAE's need for labor as its economy develops. Foreigners comprise about 500,000 to 525,000, three-quarters of whom are Pakistanis, Indians, and Iranians. The rest are mostly Arabs and a few Europeans. While the local inhabitants increase at a rate of 2.5 percent to 3 percent annually, the overall growth of the UAE is 22 percent. Thus the percentage of foreigners rapidly climbs. The prospect of a new industrial town at Ruwais and another industrial complex at Jabal 'Alī means that there is little likelihood of the immigrant population reaching a "plateau" in the next five to ten years.

Most of the population of Abū Dhabī and Dubai is urban. Abū Dhabī and Dubai cities have the heaviest need for labor and are thus the main residences of immigrants, most of them men between 20 and 40. The northern Emirates have far fewer immigrants and are much less urbanized. There the balance between the sexes is more even, and successive age groups decline in number instead of "bulging" in the middle range.

The economically active, nearly all men, comprise 43 percent of the population. This high percentage is due to over two-thirds of the nonnationals being workers, who form over 80 percent of the labor force. Construction, then government service and agriculture are the major economic activities; these are followed by services, transport, and trade. Iranians and Pakistanis are mostly manual laborers; Indians tend to be clerks and traders; the Arabs are professionals and government officials. Europeans occupy a managerial role. The pattern of labor varies in different Emirates. The northern Emirates have many jobs in fishing and agriculture.

Oman

The official government estimate of the population of Oman is 1.5 million. The United Nations has suggested that there were half that number in 1974. Yet others estimate a more likely figure of about 600,000, which would give a nominal national population density of about 2 people per square kilometer. Some 80,000 reside in the capital area of Muscat, Matra, and Sīb. Perhaps another 40,000 live in Salāla. Other concentrations are along the Batīna coastal plain (as at Sohar) and in inner Oman around towns such as Nizwa.

Oman has a plentiful supply of manpower compared to its neighbors. About 75 percent of the work force is employed in agriculture. Few Omanis are literate or skilled, however, and this is a severe impediment to the nation's development. While several score thousand nationals migrate abroad, where there is a demand for unskilled labor, an estimated 60,000 Indians and Pakistanis are resident in Oman. A majority are craftsmen or semiskilled construction workers. Indians are essential to the national health service. Westerners occupy many executive posts in the economy. Foreigners, concentrated in the Capital region, which has been the prime focus of the national development drive, are the main factor behind the trebling of the area's population in the 1970s. Oman's reliance upon foreign manpower will continue until more local people become educated and acquire skills.

Selected Bibliography

Bahrain, Statistical Bureau, Ministry of Finance and National Economy. *Statistics of the Population Census 1971.*

Bahrambegin, H. "Tehran: An Urban Analysis." M.A. thesis, Durham University, 1972.

Brown, L. C., ed. *From Medina to Metropolis.* Englewood Cliffs, N.J., 1973.

Clark, B. D., and Costello, V. F. "The urban system and social patterns in Iranian cities." *Transactions, Institute of British Geographers* 59 (1975): 99–128.

Clarke, J. I. *The Iranian City of Shiraz.* Department of Geography Research Papers, Series No. 7. Durham University, 1963.

Clarke, J. I., and Clarke, B. D. *Kermanshah: An Iranian Provincial City.* Center for Middle Eastern and Islamic Studies, Publication No. 1, Department of Geography Research Papers, Series No. 10. Durham University, 1969.

Clarke, J. I., and Fisher, W. B., eds. *Populations of the Middle East and North Africa.* London, 1972.

Costello, V. F. *Kashan.* London and New York, 1976.

Economist Intelligence Unit. *Quarterly Economic Review of Saudi Arabia, Jordan.* Annual Supplement 1977. London, 1977.

———. *Quarterly Economic Review, the Arabian Peninsula: Shaikhdoms and Republics.* Annual Supplement 1976. London, 1976.

Fenelon, K. G. *The United Arab Emirates.* 2nd ed. London and New York, 1976.

Financial Times. "Country Reports on the United Arab Emirates, 1975–77." London, 1975–77.

Ibrahim, S. E. "Urbanization in the Arab world." *Population Bulletin of the United Nations Economic Commission for Western Asia* (1974): 74–124.

Iran Almanac and Book of Facts 1977. 16th ed. Tehran, 1977.

Iran Statistics. Banque Etebarate Iran Publications. Tehran, 1976.

Kingdom of Saudi Arabia. Ministry of Finance and National Economy Central Department of Statistics. *The Statistical Indicator.* First Issue, 1976 A.D. Dammām, n.d.

———. *Ministry of Planning Second Development Plan.* Riyadh, 1975.

Kuwait, Central Statistical Office, Ministry of Planning. *Annual Statistical Abstract 1976.*

Planhol, X. de. "Geography of Settlement." In Fisher, W. B., ed. *The Cambridge History of Iran.* Vol. 1, *The Land of Iran.* Cambridge, 1968.

Qatar Today. Press and Publications Department, Ministry of Information Qatar. Dōha, n.d.

Qatar. A Meed Special Report. April 1977.

Republic of Iraq. Central Statistical Organization, Ministry of Planning. *Annual Abstract of Statistics 1976.* Baghdad, n.d.

Shiber, S. G. *Recent Arab City Growth.* Kuwait, 1967.

Statistical Centre of Iran, Plan and Budget Organization. *Population Growth of Iran.*
    Serial No. 624. Tehran, 1976.
The Middle East and North Africa 1976–77. 23rd ed. London, 1976.
United Nations. *Statistical Yearbook 1976.* New York, 1977.
United Nations Secretariat. "Selected World Demographic Indicators by Region and
    Country or Area, 1970–75." *Population Bulletin of the United Nations,* No. 8, 1976.
    New York, 1977.

APPENDIX I

Education

Although most of the Persian Gulf states have a tradition of learning spanning millenniums, modern education in the area is of comparatively recent date. It had been introduced into Iran in the second half of the nineteenth century, into Iraq toward the end of Ottoman rule, and into the other states after World War II. Thus, all Persian Gulf states are still in the process of overcoming the legacy of their past, which bequeathed them a high rate of illiteracy. The diversification in the scope and character of the areas' educational structures reflects the demographic, socioeconomic, political, and cultural differences between the various states. A powerful stimulus to the growth of modern education was given by the acute shortage of skilled indigenous manpower to meet the requirements imposed by the modernization of the Gulf states. The financial means for this educational expansion were provided by oil royalties. Despite the results hitherto achieved, all governments of Persian Gulf states feel the need for a further expansion of the educational system to keep pace with the requirements of an industrial and urban society undergoing a process of rapid development. To this end, generous allocations for expenditure on education were made, amounting in some cases to 23 percent of the budget.

Several of the Persian Gulf states are still in the process of transition from a religious-type Muslim education to a secular education in both the humanities and the sciences. In some of the countries under review, both educational systems coexist. The degree to which the traditional religious-type education has been giving way to secular education can provide some of the criteria according to which the progress of modernization of any given society may be gauged.

Iran

Historical Background. Traditional education was based upon Islam, which puts value upon "knowledge" (*'ilm*) as defined within very specific areas. This traditional education involved primary schooling at *maktabs* or *kuttābs*, religious schools where children learned by rote large parts of the Qur'ān and were taught reading, writing, and arithmetic. At a higher level, Islamic theology, philosophy, and law, as well as history, geography, and something of the classical literatures were taught at *madrasas*. Education was open only to boys.

The first modern schools were set up by European and American missionaries in the mid-nineteenth century mainly for Christian minorities. Increasing contacts with

European influences led to the creation of the *Dār al-Funūn* Polytechnic in 1855. There the sons of leading families learned physics, medicine, military studies, and other subjects. Later, the liberal arts were introduced. Soon a few Persians began to go to Europe for their higher education. Several military schools were formed in the 1880s, and the first girls' school opened in 1896. In an effort to modernize the government, institutions connected with various ministries, such as Economics, Foreign Affairs, and Agriculture, were created around the turn of the century to train cadres for the civil service. Articles of the Constitutional Law of 1907 made modern education compulsory and the Fundamental Law of the Ministry of Education (1911) affirmed the need for universal education, teacher training, and adult education, and for setting up state schools. However, a modern and comprehensive school system had not been created by the time of the accession of Riẓā Shah to the throne in 1925.

As part of his drive to consolidate the government's power and to press for reforms, elementary schools were integrated into a centralized, state-controlled structure. The new, standardized curriculum for elementary and secondary schools followed the French model of education. Owing to expanded administrative needs, priority was given to secondary and university education. The University of Tehran was created in 1934. Other measures were the founding of technical and teacher-training colleges, the launching of anti-illiteracy and adult education programs, and the establishment of military schools. The educational prospects for girls were broadened, but the prevailing conservatism of society still retarded major advances.

In 1940, there were 34 kindergartens, 2,331 primary schools, 321 high schools, 32 vocational schools, and one university. Although the number of elementary and secondary schools was more than triple the 1923 level, and although four times as many students attended school in 1940 as in 1923, still no more than 15 percent of school-age children were enrolled. Education had thorny problems with which to contend. As noted, society was still, to a considerable extent, traditional and conservative. Also, a degree of political and economic instability remained. More specifically, there was an inadequate number of teachers, due in part to the low pay and standing given to teachers, and this rendered universal compulsory education impracticable. Education continued to be elitist, and traditional teaching and learning prevailed. Teaching materials were of a low standard and facilities were scarce. The secondary school curriculum, although useful for future civil servants, was of less pertinence to more specialized or technical occupations.

The numerical expansion of the education system after World War II was rapid. By 1959 there were 286 kindergartens, 9,289 primary schools with over a million students, 1,163 high schools with over 225,000 pupils, 146 vocational schools, and more than five universities, which included 11,000 students at the University of Tehran and several thousand at new (see below) provincial universities. There were some 45,000 teachers. The pace of reform, on the other hand, was slow. Many private schools were formed because the government could not meet the demand for elementary education. But the high school curriculum was changed, and institutes of higher learning were created, such as the Ābādān School of Technology and the Institute for Public Administration; universities were set up at Tabrīz, Mashhad, Isfahān, and Shīrāz. Iran received aid from the United States to increase the efficiency of the school system, and American universities participated in projects concerning public administration, teacher training, and agricultural education. These changes did little to relieve the chronic problems that beset education in Iran. In the early 1960s, still less than 40 percent of all villages had a school. A new problem was the incapacity of the universities to take in more than a fraction of students applying. Shortages of trained manpower were evident in many areas.

The Revolution of the Shah and People. The "White Revolution" of 1963 was the watershed of Iranian education. An educated citizenry was essential for the modernization of society and for sustained economic development. The need to teach peasants in isolated country areas still governed by a feudal structure was particularly important. To this end, the Sixth Point of the "White Revolution" called for the formation of the Literacy Corps. This organization consisted of selected high school graduates who had been drafted for military duty. They trained for six months and then served in a village for eight months. Besides teaching children and adults, they organized youth groups, assisted rural cooperatives, led the building and repair of roads, schools, mosques and other public works, and also promoted village councils. The presence of women corps members slowly enlarged the role and outlook, as well as the education, of village women. A National Committee for the Eradication of Illiteracy had undertaken to extend reading and writing skills in urban areas since 1965. Provincial towns have benefited from educational radio and television, which started in the 1960s. The Reconstruction and Development Corps was created to spread modern agricultural knowledge and techniques.

The other major educational innovation of the "White Revolution" was the "new system of education," which was introduced in the early 1970s. This system restructured education from six years each of elementary and secondary schooling, to five years of primary education, three years of intermediate or "guidance" schooling, and four years of high school. In the last two years of high school, students in the theoretical or vocational streams specialize in a specific area. This new structure is designed to enable better control of standards and curricula, and is also intended to give more appropriate opportunities and individual guidance to students in light of their abilities. The "new system" has brought in its wake changes in curricula, textbooks, and teacher training. Except in Literacy Corps classes, one practice that remains unchanged is the separate teaching of boys and girls prior to university. At this level, advances such as student participation and reformed curricula to meet student needs have been monitored by the Rāmsar Educational Conference that has met yearly since 1968. This conference also assesses past experience and suggests new reforms. For the better management of university affairs and research institutions, a Ministry of Science and Higher Education was created in 1967.

The 15th Point of the "White Revolution" stipulated that all higher education would be free for those students who gave two years service to the government for each year of education. Among other measures stimulating educational development was the 1970 law for educational councils. This devolved broad responsibility for education and funding, expansion and teacher recruitment from the government and local councils. In 1971 and 1972, the Shah decreed the introduction of compulsory primary education in many regions. Free elementary education was introduced in 1974.

Profile. By 1976–77 there were 7,738,000 students of all kinds in Iran. Of this total, 175,000 were in kindergarten, 4,488,000 were in primary school, 1,284,000 were in junior high school, 884,000 were high school students, 152,000 were taking technical and professional training, 44,000 were involved in teacher training, and others, such as those in technical institutes, amounted to 751,000. In 1976 there were 44,432 schools and 233,135 teachers.

Higher education comprises 21 universities, 80 institutes of higher learning, and 115 other state-accredited institutions. In aggregate, these enrolled some 152,000 students, while a further 55,000 were engaged in study abroad. The oldest universities are the University of Tehran, the University of Azerbaijan at Tabrīz, the University of Isfahān, the Āryāmihr University of Technology in Tehran, Firdawsī University at Mashhad, Jundī-Shāhpūr University in Ahvāz, the National University of Iran and the Teachers' Training University, both in Tehran, and Pahlavi University at Shīrāz. Eight universities have been created since 1973: the University of Baluchistan, Rāzī University in Kirmānshāhān, Farah University, the University of Gīlān, Iran Free University, Riżā Shah Kabīr

University in Māzandarān, Kirmān University and Bū-'Alī University in Hamadān. In 1977–78, the University of Shawkat al-Mulk 'Alam' in Birjand and merchant navy schools at Chāhbahār were due to be set up. Among the most notable colleges and institutes are the Ābādān Institute of Technology, the College of Hygenic Sciences, the Higher Institute of Technology, the College of Hygienic Sciences, the Higher Institute of Tele-communications Training, and Tehran Polytechnic.

Iran has a broad scientific research program. Among the leading centers are the Institute of Hydro-Sciences and Water Resources Technology, the Institut Pasteur, which is concerned with microbiology, biochemistry, and epidemiology, the Plant Pests and Disease Research Institute, the International Scientific Research Institute, and the Rāzī State Institute, which stimulates biological research and the study of animal diseases. The National Research Laboratory conducts important medical research.

Much of the country's research—which is not, however, easy to quantify or assess—is done at universities. Research institutes attached to the University of Tehran include those for geophysics, water resources, social research, psychology, and economics. The Institute of Nuclear Science and Technology has a nuclear reactor and conducts research into nuclear physics, radiobiology, electronics, and nuclear chemistry. The Geotechnical Institute of Iran is located at Pahlavi University, where research in astrophysics is also carried on. Jundī-Shāhpūr University has institutes for medical research and for the study of agriculture and human genetics. Research centers at Azerbaijan University are active in the fields of astronomy, rural studies, and studies of the human environment. Āryāmihr University of Technology has research units for water and energy, biochemical engineering, and it also conducts investigations into various problems associated with steel. The National Iranian Oil Company researches into oil, and the government conducts studies on subjects such as economic planning, transport, agriculture, and water resources.

Education plays a key part in Iran's growth into a modern industrial society. The government spent more than the planned $8.2 billion upon it during the Fifth Plan for its quantitative expansion and qualitative improvement and achieved impressive results. Nonetheless, education is by nature an "investment" slow to yield its "return." Difficulties remain, such as pockets of illiteracy in rural areas, the barrier of dialect, resistance to change, and a disinclination to engage in technical or vocational work, areas for which required manpower is lacking. In the light of the growth of the student population at a million new students a year, the present shortage of qualified teachers and the heavy strain upon school facilities will likely become more acute.

These problems will not prevent the government from pressing ahead with its goals for the Sixth Plan, among the most important of which are the achievement of universal primary education, the reduction of adult illiteracy, and a sizable expansion of vocational training. These are to meet rising expectations, as well as to fill gaps in the economy. Although job opportunities are plentiful enough to challenge and satisfy most young Iranians now, there is some doubt for the future. None will be more aware than the Shah himself of the possible consequences of overqualified people chasing relatively scarce jobs at the end of the century in an Iran with dwindling oil revenues and a declining economy.

Iraq

Historical Background. Primary and secondary schools run by the Ottoman government were in operation at the end of the nineteenth century, but since Turkish was the language of administration and education in the Ottoman empire, courses were naturally in Turkish. Education was most active in the Christian and Jewish communities. An American missionary school was present in Basra before World War I. Education for most children meant memorizing the Qur'ān and learning the rudiments of reading and writing at local town or village *kuttābs* under religious teachers.

The number of schools and their standards rose in the 1920s and 1930s. Girls' education was introduced, which, as for boys, was free and nominally compulsory. Schools were set up for Kurds and other minorities, and teaching there was in the local languages. The cycle of schooling was six years of primary, three years of intermediate, and two years of secondary education. Most intermediate and secondary schools were located in the principal towns. By 1941 there were some 90,000 children in 755 state primary schools. Roughly, 14,000 were enrolled in 56 intermediate and secondary schools.

At a higher level, colleges were set up to teach medicine, pharmacy, and law. A law school existed from the Ottoman era. Also created were a higher institute for teachers' training and a teachers' college for women, as well as a police and a military college. An agricultural college opened in 1926, but small success forced its closure in 1931. An engineering college began in 1944. Some Iraqis studied at universities abroad. The main vocational schools were institutions for engineering, technical subjects, and health. Women attended schools of nursing, home arts, and midwifery. Several teacher-training schools and an agricultural officer-training center offered courses, and a commercial school was established by al-Ma'had al-'Ilmī, a literary-cultural society for adults that was taken over by the state.

In the early 1950s, the Development Board launched a heavy school building program that by 1957 had more than doubled the number of schools and enrolled children. Also, in 1951, the government decentralized its authority over schools. Four colleges were formed: for agriculture, dentistry, physical education, and veterinary medicine. A college of arts and science created in 1949 was later split into two faculties. By 1956, when these and other colleges totaled 13, they were merged into the University of Baghdad. The number of literary centers also continued to rise.

Numerous shortcomings had yet to be corrected. Although slowly shifting toward a more practical outlook, primary education remained quite academic, and the curriculum did not provide children with knowledge that was readily understandable and of use. Also, the imbalance between cities, with fewer children and more schools, and the country was not appreciably changed. Girls' schooling still lagged behind. Overall, less than one-third of all school-age children were enrolled in primary school. Teachers, although usually in adequate supply, needed better training. As in all professional lines of work in the Middle East, recruiting teachers to run schools in remote areas was difficult. Technical training was not sufficiently available.

Postrevolutionary governments saw the need for trained manpower to create a

TABLE I-1. EDUCATION IN IRAQ

Level	Students		Teachers		Schools	
	1976–77[a]	*1965–66*	*1976–77*	*1965–66*	*1976–77*	*1965–66*
Kindergarten	51,840	15,307	2,291	479	276	124
Primary	1,947,182	964,327	70,799	44,028	8,156	3,538
Secondary	555,184	255,810	19,573	7,231	1,320	585
Vocational	28,363	7,626	1,906	677	82	45
Technical	21,186	4,389	737	221	43	21
University	81,498	2,222	4,008		8[b]	4

[a] The figures are provisional.

[b] This includes the 15,571 enrolled students and 695 teachers of the Foundation of Technical Institutes, the University of Technology, and two religious colleges.

Source: Republic of Iraq Ministry of Planning, Central Statistical Organization, *Annual Abstract of Statistics 1976.* Baghdad, 1977.

modern society and economy and pressed ahead with the extension of education. Textbooks and curricula were revised to be more practical. Secondary schools added an extra year to their course of study and offered mathematics as a possible subject to specialization, in addition to the choice of scientific or literary work. French was made the second foreign language, after English, to be taught in schools from 1970. In 1974–75, the government declared education from kindergarten to university to be free. All private schools were nationalized. From 1975, emphasis was given to providing more facilities to the Kurdish autonomous region, where Kurdish was the language for teaching.

In the late 1960s, universities were set up at Basra, Mosul, and Sulaimāniyya and were subsequently expanded, particularly their faculties of medicine, science, and engineering. There are also al-Mustansiriyva University and the University of Technology (founded in 1974) in Baghdad. A considerable number of students still go abroad for higher learning. Vocational and technical education have been encouraged and industrial institutes for the study of oil technology, textiles, and mechanical engineering have opened. The Foundation of Technical Institutes was created in 1972 and is attached to the Ministry of Higher Education and Scientific Research. Included among it are centers for technology, administration, and medicine in Baghdad, an institute of technology in Basra, a technical institute in Sulaimāniyya, and also centers for practical arts and agricultural technical studies.

Research. The main scientific research bodies are the Department of Scientific and Industrial Research (under the Directorate General of Industry) and the Foundation of Scientific Research, units of which investigate oil production, natural resources, biology, agriculture, and date farming. The Nuclear Research Institute, which is under the auspices of the Iraqi Atomic Energy Commission, has a nuclear reactor for scientific uses and is active in such fields as nuclear and solid state physics and chemistry. Other institutes research into geology, oil, cancer, and endemic diseases. There is also an agricultural research station. Research units affiliated with Baghdad University are concerned with education and psychology, medicine, economics, administration, and urban and regional planning. Medical technology and business administration are the subject of research centers at Sulaimāniyya University.

Perspective. An inadequate number of educated cadres and skilled manpower, which the government prefers not to relieve by importing foreign labor, has held up national development. This has necessitated a large increase of investment in the expansion of the educational system, for which $149 million was allocated in 1976, $282 million in 1977, and $411 million in 1978. As the country begins to attain 100 percent primary school enrollment, increasing student numbers have strained the supply of teachers and school facilities, notably at the secondary level. To remedy this shortage, hundreds of new schools are to be built and a new teacher-training institute is to be completed by 1979. The trend in secondary education is in the direction of training half of all students for vocational jobs and half for academic work. Education and training is being more linked with current and planned projects, such as the iron and steel industry, mechanics, building, and chemistry. Expansion at universities such as Baghdad and Basra emphasizes the sciences and engineering. Education in the late 1970s was being shifted much more toward a practical and technical orientation, its purpose being not only more directly to aid Iraq's economic advance but also to extend Baathist ideology.

Kuwait

Primary and Secondary Schooling. The Mubārakiyya, which existed between 1912 and 1931, was the only alternative to *kuttāb*s until a group of Palestinian teachers opened several small schools under state control in 1936. The following year girls' education started. By 1950, when oil income had begun to accrue to the country, there were some 6,300 students in 26 schools with 294 teachers. Education, including books, food, and clothes, was free and was made compulsory for children between the ages of 6 and 14 in 1965. Kindergarten is voluntary. Primary and secondary education both last four years, and optional secondary schooling entails a further four years of study.

In 1965–66 there were some 90,800 students, 5,036 teachers, and 178 schools; ten years later there were almost 202,000 students, some 15,500 teachers, and 326 schools, 45 percent of the 121,000 Kuwaiti students being girls. Nearly 40,000 were Palestinian (with another 15,000 being educated outside the state system). By 1977 there were about 250,000 students and 18,000 teachers. Many teachers are Egyptians or Jordanians, working mainly at the intermediate and secondary levels. Private schools numbered 83, with 46,382 pupils and about 2,250 teachers in 1975–76.

Higher and Other Education Research. Vocational training has been emphasized since the late 1960s. There is a religious institute, a secondary training school for girls, and an institute of public health. Other vocational schools include several commercial institutes, an institute of technology, an institute for applied engineering, schools for industrial training, notably those of the Kuwait Oil Company, and two postsecondary teacher-training institutes.

Kuwait University took its first students in 1966. In 1975–76, students numbered 5,832 and teachers 507, and in 1977 there were about 7,500 students. Roughly 60 percent were Kuwaiti women in their separate college. The rest were largely men from other Gulf states. The university has Faculties of Arts, Science, Medicine, and Engineering. Most Kuwaiti men go to Britain, Egypt, or the United States for their university training, payment for which is provided by the state. Recently, some 26,000 adults a year have been attending education and literacy classes at over 120 education centers. The main Kuwait research organizations are the Institute of Social and Economic Planning, the Kuwait Institute for Scientific Research, which is investigating solar power and arid-area agriculture, the Arab Planning Institute, and the Agricultural Experimental Station.

Ordinary expenditure upon education increased from KD 62 million in 1974–75 to KD 122 million in 1977–78. Within the next few years, 182 schools are to be built and 4,000 teachers trained in order to meet the government's intention of educating all Arab children in the country. A new campus for the university will be constructed at Shuwaikh, and another university devoted to Arab culture is under consideration. Kuwait will remain for some time to come considerably dependent upon foreign teachers, and even its expanded facilities will not fully alleviate the pressure caused by the growing numbers receiving education; neither will there be any reduction in the country's reliance upon expatriates for its technical and economic activity.

Saʻūdī Arabia

Primary and Secondary Schools. Except for the offerings of a few private schools in the Hijāz, education was for boys only and was confined to the traditional form and content of the *kuttāb* until 1924. The Department of Education created in that year set up the first state schools that followed the Franco-Egyptian model of education, with the purpose of training future administrators. Little demand, inadequate money, and a conservative suspicion of the worth of modern education, limited the growth of schools to the main towns until after World War II. There were some 53,000 students (all but a few hundred at the primary level), 2,300 teachers, and 470 schools when the Department of Education was raised to the Ministry of Education in 1954. Its major task was to reform the school system, the curricula, and teaching methods. The cycle of free, voluntary education was changed from six years of primary school and five years of secondary schooling to six years of elementary education followed by three years each of intermediate and secondary school. Students can concentrate upon either literary or scientific training in the final two years of secondary school.

Boys not going into "general" secondary school can enter teacher-training or vocational schools. Four of ten secondary industrial schools proposed in the first development plan were open by 1977. Although enrollment has been below target, nine similar schools are to be built by 1980. The first agricultural technical school has opened at Buraida, and four more are scheduled. The number of secondary schools of commerce is due to be increased from five to nine by 1980. Sixteen secondary teacher-training institutes were in operation in 1975. Five new ones are scheduled. There are science and mathematics centers for teachers at Riyadh and Dammām. Outside the formal school system, vocational centers for the training of artisans are to be expanded from 6 to 18. The Ministry of Defense and the religious colleges each take about 1.5 percent of all enrolled boys and private schools account for another 4.5 percent. The first private primary school for girls began in 1956. Public education for girls started in 1960 at the elementary level and in 1965 at the secondary level. This is the responsibility of the Directorate General of Girls' Schools, now called the Administration of Girls' Education, a body supervised by religious leaders. As Table I–2 indicates, education at the primary and secondary levels, and at higher levels too, has expanded sharply in the 1970s. In 1975–76 there were 1,057,994 students, 51,176 teachers, and over 6,500 schools at all levels.

Higher and Other Education. Further education in the kingdom is directed mainly toward developing professional and technical skills that are sorely needed. The Ministry of Higher Education, created in 1975, is in charge of six universities. The first university to be established, in 1957, was the University of Riyadh, which now has faculties of arts, science, pharmacy, commerce, agriculture, education, medicine, and engineering, with particular emphasis being placed on the latter two; it will be relocated at Dir'iyya near Riyadh by 1985. Created at Medina, in 1961, the religious Islamic University is essentially a center for Islamic studies, as is the Imām Muhammad Ibn Sa'īd Islamic University formed in Riyadh in 1970. The University of Petroleum and Minerals, which opened in Dhahrān in 1963, trains students who will someday direct the nation's oil industry. It has links with American universities and has a high intellectual standard. It is to obtain

TABLE I–2. EDUCATION IN SA'ŪDĪ ARABIA

Level	Students		Teachers		Schools	
	1975–76	*1970–71*	*1975–76*	*1970–71*	*1975–76*	*1970–71*
Kindergarten	15,485	6,058	191,000	439	92	49
Primary	686,108	427,797	34,483	17,435	3,497	1,908
Intermediate	154,488	68,928	8,788	3,339	718	395
Secondary	48,826	19,759	2,616	650	212	87
Teacher-training	14,651	13,726	1,139	851	62	57
Technical education	4,063	848	619	224	21	5
Special education	1,804	1,257	630	250	17	10
Other education	10,791	n.a.	316	n.a.	111	n.a.
Higher education[a]	26,437	8,492	2,133	697	35[b]	19[b]
Adult education	95,341	42,677	7,131	n.a.	1,743	609

[a] In 1977–78, an additional 20,000 Sa'ūdīs went abroad to university.   [b] Faculties.

Source: Kingdom of Sa'ūdī Arabia Ministry of Finance and National Economy, Central Department of Statistics, *The Statistical Indicator,* Second Issue, 1977.

a nuclear reactor. Beginning under private auspices in 1967, King 'Abd al-'Azīz University in Jidda came under state control in 1971. Its faculties are economics and administration, arts, science, the College of Education and the College of the *Sharī'a*. In 1976, King Faisal University opened at Dammām with faculties of architecture, medicine, and agriculture. Others are to be added. Sa'ūdī Arabia has three service academies: King 'Abd al-'Azīz Military Academy, the Internal Security Forces Academy, and King Faisal Air Force Academy, all at Riyadh, and there are military training colleges at Dhahrān and Tā'if. Other prominent institutions are the College of Legislation and the Institute of Education in Mecca, and the College of Islamic Law, the Arabic Language College, and the Higher Institute of Jurisprudence in Riyadh. There are women students at the University of Riyadh, King 'Abd al-Azīz University, and King Faisal University, but, as at other levels of education, they are segregated from men students. Colleges for women are the Girls College of Education in Riyadh, which opened in 1970; two teaching colleges in Jidda, and the Women's Teaching College, also at Riyadh, where a college of arts will soon open.

Under the second plan, five junior colleges are being formed that will replace the present secondary teacher-training institutes. Technical training has become increasingly important. The most notable institutions are the Higher Technical, or Royal, Institute at Riyadh and the Hufūf Technical Training School. There are other centers at Jidda and Medina. New ones will be built at Abhā, Tā'if, and 'Unaiza. Adult education is stressed, especially literacy courses, and the involvement of a growing number of women is encouraged.

Government spending for education has risen from SA 666 million in 1970–71 to SR 15.978 billion in 1976–77 and about SR 8.13 billion in 1977–78. Overall, the second plan anticipates spending some SR 74 billion of SR 498 billion on education. The targets for the end of the plan in 1980 are 1,041,163 elementary students, 4,467 schools; 230,052 intermediate students, 991 schools; 72,486 secondary pupils, 231 schools; 27,437 teacher training students, 60 colleges; 14,405 technical students, 37 institutes; 519,031 adult education students, 3,327 institutes; and 42,965 in university.

Perspective. To develop human resources by education and training is an important goal of the secondary development plan. The government's commitment to this has been impressive. Much remains to be done, however, and there are serious difficulties to be faced. About one-third of all boys and two-thirds of all girls of school age have not yet been enrolled in school, and many of those in school are in crowded classes. Learning materials, usually imported, still tend to be out of date, insufficient in number, and inappropriate for local conditions. Many children still learn by rote, and their enrollment falls off sharply after the end of elementary school.

Teachers are in very short supply. Over half are expatriate Arabs, many from Egypt and Jordan. Teaching is not a lucrative job for young Sa'ūdīs, and higher salaries and status can be more easily obtained in other fields. Many teachers themselves require further education and training. The unitary national curriculum suffers from its being derived from other states and from its rigid approach to subjects. Another impediment is the extreme centralization of the educational system. The obvious policies required here are raising the standard of teacher training and revising the curriculum, but educational development is bound up with Sa'ūdī social attitudes, which have the marked preference for general education and government job-rating rather than technical training and manual labor; this means that the kingdom will not be able to supply its own skilled work force, and so will continue to depend upon foreign labor as an essential element of national economic growth. Women's education is rapidly expanding, but in present circumstances, the short-term consequences would seem to be either a waste of their new skills or the slow beginnings of a redefinition of their place in society. This is part of the basic dilemma of Sa'ūdī education: How to reconcile the requirements of a modernizing society with the traditional values of Islam?

Bahrain

Development. Private schools run by missionaries were open for boys and girls by 1905. *Kuttāb* education prevailed well past the founding of the first modern state school in 1921. The first girls' primary school opened in 1918, and a technical school was created in 1937. Secondary education for boys started in 1940 and for girls ten years later. At the latter time, there were 3,792 boys in 15 schools and 1,763 girls in six schools, with 222 teachers.

Many changes have been made in education since the early 1950s. Vocational training and literacy classes were initiated, as were courses providing teachers with further training. In 1960–61 the cycle of schooling was altered from four years of primary and secondary schooling preceded by two years of kindergarten, to six years of primary school, two years of intermediate, and three years of secondary education. A secondary commercial school was opened in 1965, by which time there were 37,600 children in 82 schools with 1,654 teachers. During the next two years, teacher-training colleges were begun for men and women. A second technical school began work in 1969, the year of the opening of the Gulf Technical College, with the involvement of Britain and Abū Dhabī. Courses in the teachers' colleges were expanded to four years in 1974–75. By 1977, a National Training Development Unit was under way for construction workers, and the Sa'ūdīs had agreed to finance a new technical college.

Profile and Perspective. In 1975–76, 59,497 students, 26,713 of them girls, took advantage of free and voluntary education in 77 primary, 22 intermediate, 13 secondary, and 4 specialized state schools, and there were 2,870 teachers. Private schools accounted for 6,271 pupils and 321 teachers. In 1977, some 150 Bahrainis studied abroad at universities; many were enrolled in Kuwait University.

The government recognizes that if it is to lessen the country's reliance upon foreign labor, it must extend education to the roughly half of school-age Bahrainis who are still not in school. Also, improvements are seen to be necessary in curricula, facilities, teaching methods and materials, and also in teacher and technical training. The dilemma is that to make good a shortage of training manpower, and also to make education compulsory when some 60 percent of all nationals are under twenty years of age, would put immense pressure on the country's administration and finance; already the total allotment for education has amounted to over 20 percent of Bahrain's annual budget expenditure.

Qatar

Primary and Secondary Schools. Modern secular education did not begin until a boys' elementary school with 250 pupils and 6 teachers opened in 1952. The first girls' school started in 1955. By 1966–67 there were 80 schools at all levels, with 13,708 pupils and 789 teachers, and by 1975–76 there were 108 schools, 31,166 students, and 1,971 teachers; in 1974–75, 16 private schools enrolled over 3,500 pupils.

A student's six years of compulsory primary education and three years each of voluntary intermediate and secondary education are free, as are books, meals, transportation, and medical attention. Students are given an allowance as an incentive to attend school, and poor parents are given monthly grants. Most of Qatar's teachers come from other Arab states, and textbooks came from abroad as well, but now the government has prepared its own.

Further Education. In 1956, the newly opened technical school at Dōha was the first school at the secondary level. There followed a school of industry, a religious institute, a teachers' college for men and one for women, a school of commerce, a management institute, and a foreign language institute. Making an important contribution to technical education in Qatar and the Persian Gulf is the Vocational (or Regional) Training Center, which opened in Dōha in 1970; it has some 1,000 students graduating annually, and its facilities are to be enlarged. Two colleges of education, one each for men and women, opened in 1973; these merged in 1976 and will be the nucleus of the University of Qatar, which is due to start early in the 1980s, with a capacity for 2,000 students and comprising colleges of science, technology, maritime navigation, public administration, etc. In 1977, some 800 Qataris studied in foreign universities. Adult education and literacy courses are well attended.

A shortage of skilled manpower hinders Qatar's development plans. To maximize the number of educated Qataris, the government increased its education budget from QR 181.6 million in 1975 to QR 895 million in 1977. Besides expenditure on the new university, future funding will be directed at constructing a further 24 elementary and 14 secondary schools by 1982, when education at all levels will become compulsory.

The United Arab Emirates

Development. There were no modern schools in the Trucial States until 1953. As elsewhere in the Gulf, boys memorized the Qur'ān and learned the rudiments of reading and writing in *kuttābs*. The first school, set up in Sharja, was built by Britain and staffed by Kuwaiti teachers. By the end of the decade, other schools had been established in Khōr Fakkān, Abū Dhabī, and Ra's al-Khaima with British help. These did not include secondary education, as did the school in Sharja, where girls' education was inaugurated and the first trade school in the Trucial States started. There a vocational school for the Trucial Oman Scouts (the region's military defense force) was also set up. Kuwait played an essential role in the early development of education. It built schools in 'Ajmān, Umm al-Qaiwain, and elsewhere and supervised and financed education in all the emirates save Abū Dhabī. Teachers came from Bahrain, Qatar, and Egypt, as well as Kuwait. Modern state education began in Abū Dhabī in 1960 with the opening of three schools. Girls' schools began in 1963, and by 1968–69 there were altogether 17,865 students in Trucial States schools. Primary education for girls was available in all emirates and there was a girls' secondary school in Sharja. Coeducational kindergarten was initiated in Abū Dhabī in 1968. At the beginning of the school year 1972–73, shortly before which primary education had been made compulsory, 40,193 students were enrolled, and by 1976–77 school attendance rose to some 90,000 (including adult students). Almost half of the school population is comprised of nonnationals. There were 185 state schools, 82 for boys, 67 for girls, and 36 coeducational schools at the kindergarten and primary levels. Various private schools operate in Abū Dhabī and Dubai.

Public education is free, and children are provided with a monthly allowance, uniforms, books, transportation, and other necessities. Abū Dhabī conducts several boarding schools for children from remote areas. The pattern of schooling is primary education from 6 years through 11, with English introduced at age 9; intermediate education is from 12 through 14, and secondary education from 15 through 17. At the age of 12, when compulsory education ends, attendance falls off.

Further Education. Teacher-training institutes opened in Dubai and Sharja in 1966, at which time trade schools were operating in these emirates. A trade school opened in Ra's al-Khaima, which now also has an agricultural school and an institute of religious studies, and Dubai has a commercial and industrial college. Although the first government-backed technical institute started in Abū Dhabī only at the end of 1972, the Abū Dhabī Marine Areas Training Center, for work in the oil industry, has been in operation since 1959 and that of the Abū Dhabī Petroleum Company since the mid-1960s. Adult education and illiteracy classes have expanded steadily. In 1976–77, 8,421 men and 2,746 women attended 103 adult education institutes, and 5,209 men and 1,583 women were enrolled in literacy classes.

The pride and summit of education in the United Arab Emirates is the new university at al-'Ain, which opened in late 1977 with nearly 600 students. With the most modern facilities, it offers a free, indeed stipendiary, education to students in subjects ranging from Islamic thought to political science, statistics, and science. A full complement of some 3,000 students will be reached in the early 1980s. In 1976–77, 1,298 men and 267 women studied at universities abroad.

Education has been given an important place in the growth of the UAE. Its development allocation has risen from Dh 14.2 million, or 20 percent of all development allocations, in 1973; to Dh 309.3 million, or 17 percent, in 1976; and Dh 306.5 million, 21 percent, in 1977. Over the next years, as many as 117 schools and 20 kindergartens will be built, with an increasing stress being put upon secondary schools, and 4 junior colleges are planned. Several problems confront education, however, including the inability of the government to spend more than one-quarter of the funds it has earmarked for educational development, difficulties in obtaining land for new schools, and in providing housing for thousands of new teachers.

Oman

Development. Other than in its traditional form of village classes conducted by religious teachers, aimed at learning the Qur'ān, education in Oman before 1970–71 consisted of 3 schools at Muscat, Matraḥ, and Salāla respectively, that went only to the intermediate level. Nine hundred boys attended them and there were no places for girls. One of the immediate aims of the new sultan has been greatly to expand educational opportunities. By 1977 there were 261 schools: 213 were at the primary level, 45 were preparatory, and 3 were secondary. Fifty-eight schools were for girls and 77 elementary schools were coeducational. A total 64,975 children, 18,465 of them girls, were receiving free, voluntary education from 2,900 teachers, most of whom were from Egypt, Jordan, or the Sudan. The advance of education has been especially rapid in Dhofār since the end of the war in 1975, and, by 1977, 5,645 pupils were enrolled in 51 schools. An estimated 55 percent of school-age children are being educated in Oman; the government's target is primary education plus three years for all children by the 1980s.

The cycle of education entails six years of primary school, three years of intermediate school (in which the student takes either general or religious studies), and three years of secondary work, with the further choice of vocational education. The study of the Qur'ān remains an important part of the curriculum at all levels. Textbooks and curricula are being revised so that education is more related to Omani history and life. Emphasis has now been put upon the construction of more secondary schools as a larger number of children move through the school program.

Further Education. To increase the inadequate number and to improve the quality of Omani teachers, in the hope that they will work in inaccessible areas, a teachers' training college was established at Matrah in 1972. Two other such colleges, one each for men and women, were built in 1975, and a further training institute at Qurum was nearing completion in early 1978. The demand for skilled labor has caused much attention to be given to vocational training. The state took over Oman's Petroleum Development Company trade school at Matrah in 1972, and this is now a technical school that offers training in areas ranging from carpentry to electronics and mechanical engineering. The Institute of Public Administration opened in 1973 and provides courses in book-keeping, languages, and secretarial skills. Other schemes starting or under way in 1978 included technical colleges at Sūr, Salāla, and Bohār, an agricultural school at Nizwa, and a girls' preparatory school at Ruwi. General and technical education may be obtained in the armed forces. Adult education has increased markedly since 1970, and more facilities are being erected. Omanis must still travel abroad for university education, and some 600 did so in 1977; but as part of the planned University of Qatar, an agricultural college may be set up at Suhār. Some RO 12.9 million was spent on education between 1971 and 1976, and future expenditure will aim at improving the quality of education within Oman.

Selected Bibliography

Arasteh, R. *Education and Social Awakening in Iran: 1850–1968.* 2nd ed., rev. Leiden, 1969.

Bank Markazi Iran. *Annual Report 1976–77.* Tehran, 1977.

Economist Intelligence Unit. *Quarterly Economic Review of the Arabian Peninsula: Shaikhdoms and Republics Annual Supplement 1977.* London, 1977.

Fenelon, K. G. *The United Arab Emirates.* 2nd ed. London and New York, 1976.

Financial Times. Country Reports on the States of the Persian Gulf, 1976–78. London, 1976–78.

Great Britain, Admiralty: Naval Intelligence Division. *Iraq and the Persian Gulf.* B.R. 524 Geographical Handbook Series. London, 1944.

Hawley, Donald. *Oman and Its Renaissance.* London, 1977.

The Kingdom of Saudi Arabia. London, 1977.

Kingdom of Saudi Arabia, Ministry of Finance and National Economy, Central Department of Statistics. *The Statistical Indicator.* 2nd ed. Riyadh, 1977.

Kingdom of Saudi Arabia, Ministry of Planning. *Second Development Plan.* Riyadh, 1975.

Kingdom of Saudi Arabia, Research and Statistical Departments, Saudi Arabian Monetary Agency. *Annual Report 1977.* Riyadh, 1977.

Matthews, R. D., and Akrawi, M. *Education in Arab Countries of the Near East.* Washington, D.C., 1949.

The Middle East and North Africa 1977–78. 23rd ed. London, 1977.

Nakhleh, E. A. *Bahrain.* London, 1976.

Qatar, Press and Publication Department, Ministry of Information. *Qatar Year Book 1976.* Dōha, n.d.

Qubain, F. I. *Education and Science in the Arab World.* Baltimore, 1966.

———. *The Reconstruction of Iraq: 1950–57.* London, 1958.

Rumaihi, M. C. *Bahrain.* London and New York, 1976.

State of Kuwait, Ministry of Planning, Central Statistical Office. *Annual Statistical Abstract 1976.* Kuwait, 1976.

Szyliowicz, J. S. *Education and Modernization in the Middle East.* Ithaca, 1973.

United Arab Emirates, The Department of Press and Publications, Ministry of Information and Culture. *Partners for Progress: A Report on the United Arab Emirates
1971–76*. Abū Dhabī, n.d.

Wassie, W. W. A. *Education in Saudi Arabia*. Basingstoke, 1970.

The World of Learning 1977–78. 28th ed. London, 1977.

APPENDIX J

Transportation and Communication

Iran

The Shah Muhammad Riẓā Pahlavi used his country's oil wealth vastly to expand
the effort begun by his father to make Iran a modern state. A major problem was an
inability to handle efficiently the large imports of heavy machinery, raw materials,
equipment, and foodstuffs, but this is now being relieved by a steady development of
the country's transportation network.

Transportation. Of the more than 60,000 km of roads, about 16,000 km were paved
by 1976. By 1977–78 a further 6,000 km will be ready for use. Over 10,000 km of main
and secondary roads are under construction. One element is an artery that will link
Turkey and Iraq with Pakistan as part of the Asian Highway, which already joins the
former countries with Afghanistan. Other important new roads will be expressways from
Tehran to Sāva via Qum, from Tehran to Mashhad, and from Qum to Bandar Shāhpūr
that will provide another link to the ports of the Persian Gulf. Among the major reasons
for this large building program is the five-fold increase in the volume of traffic in Iran
since 1970. In little more than ten years, the number of private cars has risen from
103,000 to 1.8 million, buses from 12,500 to 35,000, and trucks from 49,000 to 105,000.

The length of the principal railway lines in 1975–76 was 4,519 km. Among the most
important routes are the 1,392 km Trans-Iranian Railway, which runs from Gurgān to
Bandar Shāhpūr via Tehran, the 736 km Tehran to Tabrīz line, and the recently completed Qum–Zāhīdān line that joins India and Pakistan with Turkey and Europe. New
lines are to be built between Kirmān and Bandar 'Abbās and between Zāhīdān and
Sarakhs via Mashhad. Double lined and electrified railways will be constructed from
Tehran to Tabrīz and from Khurramshahr by way of Isfahān to Mashhad. Overall, Iran
expects to have 10,000 km of rail lines by 1986. An estimated 4 million passengers used
Iranian railways in 1974–75, while, in 1973, 4.45 million tons of freight were carried. An
underground transportation system will be built in Tehran.

The main ports of Iran lie on the Persian Gulf; these are Khurramshahr, 70 km
up the Shatt al-'Arab; Bandar Shāhpūr, which lies up Khōr Mūsā; Bushire; and Bandar
'Abbās. Chāhbahār, on the Gulf of Oman, is primarily a naval facility. These ports and
the Caspian Sea ports of Bandar Pahlavī and Nawshahr had a total nominal capacity
of over 5 million tons in 1975. Due to a huge volume of imports, however, some 12 million tons of freight were being handled by shift working. The heavy flow of imports con-

tinues and the government is aiming at a nominal capacity of 28 million tons by 1978 and at least 50 million tons by 1980. Khurramshahr, where the draught is only 8 meters, is having 3 berths added to its present 9 berths. Bandar Shāhpūr had 10 berths in operation by 1977. Twenty more, including 4 berths for containers, are to be added by 1980, when its capacity will reach 25 million tons. Bandar 'Abbās is being greatly enlarged: 22 berths, including container and roll on–roll off facilities are being added to its current 6 and will give it a capacity of 24 million tons by 1980. Four new jetties will be added at Bushire and 3 at Chāhbahār by 1979. In 1975–76, 2,000 merchant vessels visited Iranian ports, while 4,500 tankers called at Māhshahr and Khārg, the country's main oil terminals. The Āryā National Shipping Lines, the merchant fleet of Iran, possesses 26 vessels and plans to expand to 60 ships. The National Iranian Tanker Company has 7 crude-oil tankers with a deadweight tonnage capacity of 670,000 tons; it too will expand. The total number of Iran's merchant marine is 154 vessels, with a capacity of 1,047,000 tons deadweight. On Lake Rizā'iyya and the Kārūn River there are passenger and cargo services.

Iran's international airports are located at Tehran, Isfahān, Shīrāz ,and also at Ābādān and Bandar 'Abbās. The principal domestic airports are at Tabrīz, Kirmanshāh, Mashhad, Yazd, and 13 other cities. Most of these airports are being improved, and a new airport is being built outside Tehran that will be operating by the early 1980s. The Iran National Airlines Corporation (Iran Air) flies to major world capitals from Peking to New York. In 1975–76, its fleet of 26 planes carried 2,100,000 passengers, of whom 600,000 were on international flights. Over 20 foreign airlines provide services to Iran. Pārs Air is the domestic carrier.

Communications. The country's radio and television services are controlled by National Iranian Radio and Television, a semiautonomous government body. The NIRT's radio service is broadcast in all the main languages and dialects, but with a strong emphasis on the modern form of Persian; the Voice of Iran broadcasts abroad in ten different languages. There were five million radios in Iran in 1975. There were two television stations (and channels) in Tehran, where color was introduced in 1975, and stations in thirteen other cities. These only reach a little more than half of the population, however. Nearly one million of the two million television sets in Iran in 1975 were in the region of Tehran.

Over 20 daily and weekly newspapers are published in Tehran. Prominent among these papers are *Ittilā'āt* and *Kayhān*. There also are published 27 weekly and over 44 monthly magazines, and there are upwards of 80 provincial papers. The 2 news agencies of Iran are the International Press Agency of Iran and the Pars News Agency. By 1975 there were 1,844 post offices in the country and by 1976 there were 688,396 telephones. Some 600 new post offices are planned and two million telephones will be in use by 1977. Iran has telex and wireless telegraph links domestically and with Europe. There is a wireless telephone link between Tehran and Tabrīz and between Tehran and Baghdad, Europe and America.

Iraq

The transportation system of Iraq, centered around Baghdad, generally follows the course of the Tigris and Euphrates rivers. Important routes also extend to the northeast and to the oil fields. Since the mid-1960s, the government has stressed the development of roads, railways, airports and ports as a vital part of the infrastructure of a growing economy. Efficient transportation and communications are even more essential now that enhanced oil revenues enable more extensive economic modernization.

Transportation. In 1975, there were 11,869 km of paved roads: 6,566 km were main roads and 5,293 km were secondary routes. The most important roads are from Baghdad to Rutba (and thence into Syria and Jordan), 555 km; Mosul and Tel Kuchuh on the Syrian frontier, 521 km; Kirkūk, Irbil, Zakhō, and into Turkey, 544 km; and Amāra, Basra, and Safwān on the Kuwait border, 595 km. Baghdad is now also connected with Iran by a road via Sulaimāniyya. Since 1970, over $100 million has been designated for the improvement and extension of the roads of Iraq. One planned new road will be from Kirkūk to Rutba, a distance of 475 km. In 1975, 80,549 private cars, 35,010 taxis, 42,543 trucks and vans, and 14,894 buses—172,997 vehicles in all—used the roads.

Besides acquiring more, and more modern, rolling stock and equipment, the pre occupation of the Iraqi government concerning the railway network has been to extend the standard-gauge rail line, which ran only from the Syrian border via Mosul 529 km to Baghdad, down to Basra and Umm Qasr. Until the Baghdad–Basra section (569 km) was finished in 1971, only a narrow (meter) gauge line went south, as well as from Karbalā and Musayyib via Baghdad 461 km to Irbil via Khānaqīn and Kirkūk. In 1976, Iraq had 1,695 km of track; 1,129 km were standard gauge and 566 km narrow gauge. The number of passengers in 1972–73 was 3.519 million, and the amount of freight carried was 5.122 million tons. Iraq plans to build another 1,100 km of rail line by 1980, with tracks going from Basra to Umm Qasr, Kirkūk to Hadītha and elsewhere. Longer-term intentions are to forge rail links with Kuwait, Iran, and Sa'ūdī Arabia. An underground railway is to be built for Baghdad.

The main ports of Iraq are Basra, 107 km up the Shatt al-'Arab from the head of the Persian Gulf, and Umm Qasr, on an inlet located 11 km up Khōr Zubair from Barba Island. The Raqal wharves at Basra can handle 12 ships, while a further 7 can be accommodated at buoys. Nearby, at Abū Fulūs, there is a berth for fertilizer products, and at Multiyya there are 2 berths for oil goods and one silo berth. In 1974, 1,393 ships were handled at Basra; 1,945,000 tons of freight were imported and 1,090,000 tons were exported. Umm Qasr came into operation in the early 1970s, and can take 3 ships. In 1976, it dealt with 104 vessels; imports were 65,000 tons and exports were 189,000 tons. The Iraqi government has been most concerned to secure the approach to Umm Qasr, presently controlled by Kuwait. In 1978, the government announced that in the next several years 28 new berths would be built, bringing the total number of berths to 52 and the country's cargo handling capacity up to 6.5 million tons a year. Overall in 1976, Iraqi ports handled 1,793 ships, total exports were 1,279,000 tons, and total imports were 3,430,000 tons. The deep-water loading terminals for loading oil are at Fāō and Khōr al-'Amāya; the former can deal with 4 ships and the latter 3. In 1974, 41,153,017 tons of crude oil were shipped from these two places. There were 110 large merchant vessels in 1977, including those of the Iraqi Maritime Transport Company. River transport between Baghdad and Basra is of some local importance.

International airports are at Basra and at Baghdad, where another airport is being built. Mosul airport is being readied for international as well as its present national service. Kirkuk has a civil airport and also an airfield for the Iraq Petroleum Company. Seventeen foreign airlines offer services to Iraq. The national airline, Iraqi Airways, flies to most Middle Eastern countries, North Africa, Europe, India, Pakistan, and Thailand. It had a fleet of 26 planes in 1977.

Communications. Iraq's two radio stations are controlled by the Iraqi Broadcasting and Television Establishment, which is part of the Ministry of Information. Both these stations have foreign as well as domestic services. There were 2,700,000 radio sets in 1973. Iraq's 6 television stations are also run by the IBTE. Stations at Muthannā and Umm Qasr are being built. There were 520,000 television sets in Iraq in 1974. At present there are 6 daily and 8 weekly newspapers and over 20 periodicals available. The Iraqi News Agency operates at home and abroad. By 1976 there were 170,089 telephones in use and 367 postal and telegraph offices in the country. Iraq has wireless telegraph and telephone links abroad.

Kuwait

Transportation. Adequate roads and ports have been an important element of Kuwait's oil-based economy. There are nearly 2,000 km of asphalt roads in the country. The main roads are from the Iraqi border to Jahrā, where begins a divided highway that runs along southern Kuwait Bay through Kuwait City and Sālimiyya to Mīnā al-Ahmadī. It also extends 10 km to Kuwait airport. Other principal roads join the oil fields with ports on the coast. A four-lane highway under construction will improve the present route along the coast to Sa'ūdī Arabia and inland to Riyadh. Of the 223,788 motor vehicles registered in 1974, 166,194 were privately owned. Perhaps as many as 350,000 vehicles were on the road in 1978.

Three kilometers west of Kuwait City is Shuwaikh. This port can handle 20 ships; it dealt with 1,780,000 tons of freight from 1,167 ships in 1974 and handled 3.8 million tons of export in 1976. Possibly 44, or even more, berths are being added and a repair yard for small ships is being built. Shu'aiba port, which has 5 berths, services the Shu'aiba industrial zone south of Fahāhīl. It will be expanded by 10 berths by 1980, thus raising its cargo-handling capacity from 1.2 million tons to 3.5 million tons a year. Nearby is Mīnā al-Ahmadī. This port is the country's main oil terminal and can accommodate the largest oil tankers. Its loading platform is over 30 km offshore. Close by is another oil port, Mīnā al-'Abdullāh. Overall, Kuwait controlled 226 merchant ships in 1977, the two shipping companies of Kuwait being Kuwait Oil Tankers Company S.A.K. and Kuwait Shipping Co. S.A.K.; the former owns 7 ships amounting to 1,167,000 deadweight tons and a further 3 tankers of nearly six million tons capacity have come into operation. Five more tankers are on order. The latter company, largely government-owned, has 47 vessels totaling 920,000 tons. In 1976, it merged with the United Arab Shipping Company, in which five other states of the Persian Gulf were involved.

Kuwait's expanding international airport is served by over 20 foreign lines besides the national airline, Kuwait Airways Corporation, which has a fleet of 14 planes and flies to all the main Arab and European states and to Karachi and Delhi.

Communications. The Kuwait Broadcasting Station broadcasts in Arabic, English, and Urdu in short and medium wave and in FM stereo. There were 210,000 radios in 1974. The government-run Television Service of Kuwait broadcasts in Arabic and in color. It reaches other states in the Gulf, besides the 130,000 television receivers in Kuwait. There are 8 daily newspapers, along with 20 weekly periodicals. The government operates the postal and telephone system, which linked 130,000 telephones in 1975. Kuwait has wireless communications abroad and a second earth satellite station has come into operation.

Sa'ūdī Arabia

Transportation. Over the past two decades, Sa'ūdī Arabia has improved greatly its transportation and communication systems. Many obstacles remain in the mid- and late-1970s, for the very pace of its economic advance has put heavy pressure on its infrastructure, particularly the ports.

In 1955, Sa'ūdī Arabia had only several hundred kilometers of paved roads; ten years later it had over 3,000 kilometers of paved roads, mainly in the Jidda–Mecca–Medina region and in the oil fields in the east. Since 1965, road building has been given emphasis, and by 1977 there were 16,638 km of surfaced roads, including the trans-Arabian highway that links Dammām with Jidda via Riyadh, Tā'if, and Mecca. The Sa'ūdīs hope to double their paved roads by the early 1980s. There were 11,867 km of feeder roads in 1976. There were 177,412 private cars, 140,842 goods vehicles, and 17,605 buses in 1975. The cumulative number of registered vehicles amounted to 774,443 at the end of 1976.

The Sa'ūdī government railroad links Riyadh with Dammām on the Persian Gulf. It is a single track, standard gauge line 563 km in length with a further 170 km of spur lines and sidings. It may be extended to Jidda, Medina, and Yanbū'. In recent years, it has carried 200,000 passengers and 1,150,000 tons of freight .The Damascus to Medina railway, which was partly rebuilt after World War I and then abandoned in 1924, is being considered for reconstruction.

Sa'ūdī Arabia must import a wide range of consumer and industrial goods to build a modern economy. As over 90 percent of these come by sea, the ports of Sa'ūdī Arabia are quite congested. By 1977, however, this condition had been much relieved. Work is going ahead to expand and extend the facilities of all Sa'ūdī ports, of which the chief ones are Jidda and Yanbū' al-Bahr on the Red Sea and Dammām on the Persian Gulf. Lesser ports are at Jīzān on the Red Sea and Jubail on the Gulf. Ra's Tanūra is the oil terminal of ARAMCO. The kingdom had 57 berths with a tonnage-handling capacity of 16.1 million tons annually at its disposal in 1977; by 1980 it plans to have available 105 berths with a capacity of 35.3 million tons a year.

Jidda is the most important port of Sa'ūdī Arabia; it handles a large volume of freight and, being the port of Mecca, is the place of entry for many pilgrims. It has 27 berths with an annual capacity of 8.2 million tons, and more than 20 berths will be added in the next several years. Roadstead facilities are provided at Yanbū' and at Jīzān, where berths will be constructed. Yanbū', the port for Medina, is being enlarged and modernized. Local ports on the Red Sea are al-Wajh, Rābigh, and Muwaih.

Dammām port lies 11 km offshore and is connected to the coast by a railway causeway. It had 24 berths in 1977 and could handle 6.5 million tons of cargo yearly. As with Jidda, it will be expanded significantly by the early 1980s, when it could have at least 30 berths. A new 25-berth port is to be developed at Jubail. Local ports are al-Khubar, al-Qatīf, and 'Uqair. New port facilities are to be built at Ra's al-Shair and Rās al-Mirhāb on the Persian Gulf and at Thawar on the Red Sea. The number of the Sa'ūdī merchant fleet came to 119 in 1977.

International airports are at Jidda, Riyadh, and Dhahrān. A second airport is being constructed at Jidda, which will cater to pilgrims, and Riyadh airport is being expanded and modernized. At Dhahrān a new runway will be added, and the airports at Medina and Bisha are being enlarged. A new airport will be built at Abhā, and other local fields will be extended. Sa'ūdī Arabia is visited by 17 foreign airlines. The national airline, Saudia, has a fleet of 50 planes and flies to the capitals of Western Europe, most Arab states, and to the Indo-Pakistan continent. It also connects all principal Sa'ūdī cities.

Communications. The Sa'ūdī Arabian Broadcasting Service operates radio stations at Jidda, Riyadh, Dammām, and Abhā under the auspices of the Ministry of Information. The home service broadcasts in English as well as Arabic, while the overseas service broadcasts in four foreign languages. ARAMCO radio broadcasts in English from a station al-Dhahran. In 1975, there were some 245,000 radio sets in the country. Television stations of the Sa'ūdī Arabian Government Television Service broadcast in Arabic only from Riyadh, Medina, Jidda, Dammām, Abhā, and al-Qasīm. Other stations and relay points are under construction, and a French color television system is being installed. Dhahrān-HZ-22-TV is the English-language television service of ARAMCO. There were 130,000 television sets in Sa'ūdī Arabia in 1975. Of the 9 daily papers in the country, 2 are in English, and there are 16 weeklies and periodicals. Sa'ūdī Arabia has 2 news agencies, the Sa'ūdī Press Agency and the BETA Company. The chief cities are linked by a telephone network that had about 200,000 lines in 1977 and is projected to have 670,000 lines by 1980. The international radio telegraph and radio telephone services are constantly being improved, as is the postal system, which has ever 300 offices. The country now has a 5,500 line telex service in Jidda, Riyadh, Mecca, Medina, Yanbū', and Tā'if. Four communication satellites are in operation and 6 more are planned.

Bahrain

Transportation. Being a major entrepôt of the Persian Gulf, Bahrain has quite good transportation and communications facilities. Paved roads connect all the main towns, and bridges join Muharraq and Sitra islands with Bahrain Island. Dual highways are being built. A causeway will be built joining Bahrain with Sa'ūdī Arabia. There were 32,807 motor vehicles in use in 1975.

Mīnā Salmān at Manāma has berths for 6 ships and 2 slipways for vessels up to 1,000 tons. It handles 700 ships a year. Storage and refrigeration facilities are available. It will be expanded to 12 berths and its capacity is to be trebled. A major project under way is the construction of an extensive dry-dock facility south of Muharraq Island that will be able to service ships up to 500,000 tons deadweight in 4 berths. This project, sponsored by OAPEC, was in operation by 1977. Oil is loaded into tankers from a terminal on Sitra Island. In 1977, Bahrain had a merchant fleet of 28 ships, and many shipping services come to Bahrain and link it with the Gulf, Europe, Asia, and America. Bahrain airport on Muharraq Island can take the largest aircraft, including the Concorde; it handled over 26,000 aircraft and more than 1.1 million passengers in 1975. A new terminal for jumbo jets was opened in 1971, and further expansion is being undertaken, with emphasis upon cargo. Fifteen international airlines use Bahrain Airport. Bahrain owns Gulf Air, along with Qatar, the United Arab Emirates, and the Sultanate of Oman. This line's fleet of 31 planes serves the Gulf area, nearby Arab capitals, Karachi, Bombay, Athens, and London, and flies over a million passengers a year.

Communications. The state-owned and state-run Bahrain Broadcasting Station transmits in Arabic only. There are about 100,000 radio sets in Bahrain. RTV Bahrain was nationalized in 1975; it has broadcast in color since 1973. The only daily newspaper is the Awālī Daily News, which is published in English by the Bahrain Petroleum Company. There are 10 weekly papers, however, and 3 monthly periodicals. Bahrain had over 18,887 telephone lines with 37,316 stations in 1977, and communications abroad are excellent. A worldwide telephone and telex service is in operation, as is an earth satellite station.

Qatar

Transportation. All modes of transport have been seriously congested in recent years, but, gradually, bottlenecks are being overcome. Qatar has 960 km of paved roads, running from Dukhān and Umm Bāb to Dōha and from Umm Sa'īd to al-Wakra, where a divided highway extends to Dōha and north to al-Khōr. Another main road leads farther north to Ruwais. Qatar has road links with Sa'ūdī Arabia, and eventually will be joined with the UAE. It has 2 main ports. Dōha has 4 berths along a quay that is joined to Dōha proper by a causeway; 4 new berths were added in 1977. Between 1975 and 1976, the volume of cargo handled at this port rose from 770,000 tons to 1.2 million tons. Umm Sa'īd harbor is the main oil terminal for Qatar and will have 9 new wharves built. A new port may be built at Jazīrat al-'Ulyā. There are lesser ports at Zakrit and Ruwais. Qatar intends to start a national shipping company and a new airport will be built near Dōha. The number of Qatar's merchant ships in 1977 was 15. The present international airport at Dōha, which is being improved, is served by 14 international lines besides Gulf Air, of which Qatar has partial ownership; Gulf Helicopters also operates in Qatar.

Communications. The Radio Qatar government service broadcasts in both Arabic and English. Qatar Television broadcasts in color, and a second channel is planned. The country's press consists of *al-'Arab,* a daily newspaper; *Gulf News* and *'Urūba,* which are weeklies; and *al-Dōha,* a monthly periodical published by the Ministry of Information. There were 24,500 telephones in service in 1977, and by 1978 some 30,000 were scheduled. Qatar has a telex service and radio telephone connections with Europe and America, and an earth satellite communications station is in operation.

The United Arab Emirates

Transportation. The UAE's economy is expanding rapidly, and its members, with Abū Dhabī and Dubai in the forefront, have made strenuous efforts to provide necessary transportation and communications facilities. By 1976 there were 800 km of paved roads in the UAE, the major roads being those joining Liwā oasis with Abū Dhabī, from where a divided highway leads to al-'Ain and to Dubai. Further paved roads lead through Sharja, 'Ajmān, and Umm al-Qaiwain to Ra's al-Khaima and Rams. Paved roads extend from Sharja to al-Fujaira, from Dibba to Khōr Fakkan, and also Oman, and from Tarīf westward to Qatar. A bridge joins Abū Dhabī island to the mainland. Dubai has twin bridges and a tunnel under its creek. There were 49,104 motor vehicles in the UAE by 1975.

Many of the emirates are increasing the capacity of their ports, which are their most important economic gateway. Dubai, the leading entrepôt of the Gulf, handled 3.2 million tons of freight in 1975, all save 100,000 tons being imports. Its Port Rashīd is the largest port of the Middle East, with 16 deep-water berths. Twenty-two further berths will be added, and work is in progress on 3 dry docks, one of which will be able to handle a million-ton tanker, and 7 repair berths. Another 20 berths are in progress. A much larger port is to be built at Jabal 'Alī to service the planned industrial area. Port Zaid, Abū Dhabī, has 18 berths, 12 being deep-water berths and 6 shallow-water berths. In 1975, 1,050,000 tons of exports were handled. An industrial port will be built at Ruwais. Six berths are scheduled for completion at Sharja's Port Khālid by 1978, and Sharja plans a container port at Khōr Fakkān on the coast of the Gulf of Oman. 'Ajmān is building a dry dock for smaller ships. The harbor at Ra's al-Khaima town is shallow, but a deeper harbor is being constructed at Khōr Khuwair that will have 8 berths. Eight shipping lines call at the ports of the UAE. The UAE merchant fleet totaled 85 vessels in 1977.

There are four international airports in the United Arab Emirates at Dubai, Abū Dhabī, Ra's al-Khaima, and Sharja; Dubai, the largest airport, handled almost a million passengers and 13,400 tons of cargo in 1977. New airports for Abū Dhabī and Dubai, which will be completed in the 1980s, will replace the present airports, and a new airport will be built at al-'Ain. Gulf Air Dubai flies to London, Cairo, Athens, Bombay, and various cities around the Persian Gulf, while Gulf Air Sharja schedules more local flights. The UAE is served by over 20 international airlines.

Communications. Radio stations of the Voice of the United Arab Emirates broadcast from Abū Dhabī, Dubai, Ra's al-Khaima, and Sharja. There were 150,000 radio sets and 80,000 televisions in the UAE by 1976, with color television stations in Abū Dhabī and Dubai. Four newspapers operate daily. The *Gulf Weekly Mirror* is among the 3 weekly papers, and there are 5 monthly journals. The UAE is a member of the Gulf News Agency, begun in collaboration with Sa'ūdī Arabia, Iraq, Kuwait, and Bahrain in 1976, the year the Emirates News Agency was established. By 1977 there were 48,500 telephones. The telephone networks of the UAE are to be unified. There are direct dialing facilities to Bahrain, Qatar, and Oman. In 1978, the UAE planned to increase its 70,000-line telephone network by 200,000 lines. In Dubai, an earth satellite station provides international telephone, telegraph, and telex services; another earth satellite station was completed in Ra's al-Khaima and a third opened in Abū Dhabī in mid-1978.

Oman

Transportation. No Gulf state has thrown itself more vigorously into the task of development since 1970 than has Oman. Road building has incurred large expenditure. Besides a network of over 5,500 km of graded roads linking the main towns of the sultanate, there were some 789 km of paved roads in northern Oman by 1974, compared to 5 km of asphalt roads in 1970. The most important of these go from Buraimī to Suhār and then on to Muscat, while other routes go from Muscat to Nizwa and via Izkī to the oil fields in western Oman. In Dhofār, paved roads run from Raisūt to Ṭaqa via Salāla. Many more asphalt roads are being built, for instance, between Sūr and Muscat. By 1975 there were about 21,000 vehicles in Oman, of which 5,300 were private and 9,925 commercial.

Port construction at Matrah was completed in 1974 and has 10 deep-water berths; in 1975 it handled over one million tons of cargo, nearly all of which were imports. Raisūt harbor near Salāla has 8 berths for smaller vessels; 4 berths for bigger ships will be constructed. The main oil terminal at Mīnā al-Fahal services large tankers at offshore loading buoys, and dealt with 685 ships in 1974. This port and Riyām have facilities for receiving refined oil products. Lesser ports exist at Salāla, Khabūra, Mirbāt, Sūr, and Suhār, the latter two of which will be developed. Four international shipping lines visit Oman regularly. Oman had 10 merchant vessels in 1977.

Sīb International Airport is the chief airport of Oman, and is used by 10 international airlines, including Gulf Air, and by 2 cargo lines, one of which is Cargo Oman. Internal services fly to Buraimī, Nizwa, Suhār, and Salāla, where the airport is being improved to an international standard.

Communications. The 2 radio stations of Oman are Radio Oman and Radio Salāla; the latter broadcasts in the Dhofārī local languages as well as the Arabic. A color television station began operation near Muscat late in 1974, and a year later a color television station began broadcasting in Dhofār; all these stations are under government auspices. There are 4 weekly newspapers, of which 2 are in English. Most of the 7 periodicals are illustrated magazines. Automatic telephone services operate in Muscat, Matrah, Mīnā al-Fahal, and Bait al-Falaj, and by 1975 over 3,000 lines had been installed; a new telephone service will provide 16,000 lines. Radio, telephone, telex, and telegraph facilities link Muscat and Salāla. An international telephone service is in operation, as is a high frequency radio-telephone link with Bahrain. International telex and cable services are available, and an earth satellite station is in operation.

Selected Bibliography

Economist Intelligence Unit. *Quarterly Economic Review of Iran Annual Supplement 1977*. London, 1977.
————. *Quarterly Economic Review of Iraq Annual Supplement 1977*. London, 1977.
————. *Quarterly Economic Review of Saudi Arabia, Jordan, Annual Supplement 1977*. London, 1957.
————. *Quarterly Economic Review, The Arabian Peninsula; Shaikhdoms and Republics Annual Supplement 1976*. London, 1976.
Fallon, N. and Bricault, G. *Development Projects and Street Maps of the Arab World and Iran*. London, 1976.
Financial Times. Country Reports on the States of the Persian Gulf. London, 1975–77.
Iran Almanac and Book of Facts 1977. 16th ed. Tehran, 1977.
Republic of Iraq, Ministry of Planning: Central Statistical Organization. *Annual Abstract of Statistics 1976*. Baghdad, n.d.
The Middle East and North Africa 1976–77. 23rd ed. London, 1976.
The Middle East Yearbook 1977. London, 1976.
Paxton, J., ed. *The Statesman's Yearbook 1977–78*. 114th ed. London, 1977.
Qatar, Press and Publication Department: Ministry of Information. *Qatar Year Book 1976*. Dōha, n.d.
United Arab Emirates. The Department of Press and Publications, Ministry of Information and Culture. *Partners for Progress. A Report on the United Arab Emirates 1971–1976*. Abu Dhabi, n.d.
Whitaker's Almanac. 109th ed. London, 1976.

APPENDIX K

Industrial Development

Iran

Development. The government of Rizā Shah Pahlavi began an industrialization program upon which it spent 20 percent of its budget in the 1930s. Many of the large state-owned concerns processed agricultural produce; others made cement, matches, glass, chemicals, bricks, tiles, and paint. Most of "industry" consisted of small handicraft workshops that made carpets and other woven goods. By the late 1930s, industry added about 5 percent annually to the Gross Domestic Product (GDP).

Manufacturing industry made little headway in the decade after World War II. The FIRST DEVELOPMENT PLAN (1948–55) was crippled by a severe loss of income after the nationalization of the oil industry. Most of private investment was drawn into construction, and productivity was erratic. The government's expenditure upon industry went toward sugar mills, textile factories, a cement plant, and a cotton cloth factory.

SECOND PLAN. The stress of the second development plan (1955–62) upon agriculture and infrastructure did not prevent the rapid growth of private industry. Stimulated by increased government spending, tax concessions, and a liberal credit policy, private investment doubled from $60 million to $120 million between 1956 and 1960. The privately owned Industrial Mining and Development Bank of Iran was opened in 1959 and came to play an important part in the sector's growth. A still slender base of financial, technical and managerial resources restricted private operations to a medium to small scale, however. The key public projects were textile and cement factories and a fertilizer plant. By 1960–61 a recession set in due to the state's actions to reduce the high rate of inflation by cutting expenditure and credit. Industry's development allocation was nearly halved. By this time there were some 70,000 industrial establishments and 4,430 factories, about half of which were located in Tehran and on the Caspian coast. Textiles and food processing accounted for over 60 percent of industrial output. Manufacturers produced a widening range of goods and contributed about 9 percent to the GDP, but remained inefficient.

THIRD PLAN. The purposes and "philosophy" of industry were articulated at the beginning of the Third Plan (1962–68). One element of the Shah's "White Revolution" of 1962 entailed profit-sharing in industry and the return of state enterprises to the private sector. (This was due to cost overruns, inefficiency, and the need to fund agricultural reform.) The government wished to confine itself to subsidizing and protecting industry, taking an active part only in large capital projects for which private resources were insufficient. Private industry, as well as foreign investment and technical aid, would be promoted so as to increase the volume of consumer goods and reduce imports. Long-term development strategy realized that Iran's oil resources were finite. Alternative sources of production would be needed to create a modern, self-supporting state. Industry, the only means to increase and sustain national wealth on a broader and more permanent basis, would be built with oil revenues and in time replace them.

Taking a larger part in industrialization in the Third Plan than it anticipated, the government led the way out of recession and laid the groundwork for the country's sustained burst of industrial growth of the latter 1960s and the 1970s. At the center of government activity was an agreement with the Soviet Union in 1965 to build a steel mill at Isfahān and a machine tool plant at Arāk. Arrangements with Czechoslovakia in 1965 and Romania in 1967 called for the construction of a machine tool plant and tractor plant, respectively. Other large state schemes involved three petrochemical complexes and an aluminum smelter. From Rls. 7 billion in the Second Plan, government spending for industry rose to Rls. 17.1 billion in the Third Plan. This, however, was only 60 percent of planned expenditure, and, as a measure of industry's as yet relative insignificance, only 8.4 percent of total disbursements for development.

Expanding oil revenues, increased government spending, and growing market demand stimulated private industry. In the early years of the plan, it had completed factories for tires, plastic goods, radios and televisions, pharmaceuticals, and bricks and tiles. New investment concentrated upon automobile assembly plants—one was for the Iran National Peykan car—diesel engine plants, steel rolling mills, and factories for glass and sugar-beet processing. A proportion of 16.3 percent of total private investment went into manufacturing industries. Much of this investment was carried out by industrial development banks, most notably Industrial and Mining Development Bank of Iran (IMDBI). This and other banks, such as the Industrial Credit Bank, followed the state's development policy by showing preference for large, modern firms whose products reduced imports. Major recipients of loans were companies making textiles, electric machinery, basic metals, transport equipment, and those producing foodstuffs. The regime also nudged industry toward more capital-intensive enterprises. Otherwise high tariffs were removed in the case of imports of heavy machinery. Some producers took advantage of tax concessions and/or subsidies. A licensing system for companies was set up that channeled development in favored directions, and in 1967 the Industrial Development and Renovation Organization was founded with the purpose of investing in industries and mines for their renovation and of providing technical assistance. Important financial and technical participation was afforded by foreign interests.

By 1967–68 manufacturing industry contributed 13 percent to the GDP. Construction added 5.4 percent, utilities 2 percent, and mining and quarrying 0.3 percent. The annual rate of growth of manufacturing during the Third Plan period was 12.6 percent at constant prices. Indicative of its expansion were the output figures for three major industries (1955–56 figures in parentheses): cotton textiles, 450 million meters (74 million meters); refined sugar, 320,000 tons (75,000 tons); and cement, 1,800,000 tons (131,000 tons). The production of electric power had risen from 1.24 billion kilowatt hours in 1962–63 to 4.5 billion kilowatt hours by 1968. Industry was comprised of some 530,000 establishments with 1,990,000 employees. Only 500 concerns had more than 50 workers.

FOURTH PLAN. The development of industry was the government's principal area of concentration during the Fourth Plan (1968–69/72–73). The consumer goods industry was to be further expanded and the domestic production of capital goods embarked upon for purposes of import substitution. At the core of the state's capital-intensive heavy industrial ambitions were iron and steel and petrochemical projects. These took three-quarters of all public disbursements to industry during the plan. Other elements of industrial policy were the encouragement of firms to use domestic goods to add value to products before they were exported, and the extension of tax measures to companies locating at least 120 km away from Tehran. Obligatory government licensing was used to promote the regionalization of industry. Provincial "poles" were formed to attract new ventures, thereby spreading the country's oil wealth and reducing the flow of people to the congested capital.

In 1970, the government announced a shift in its industrial policy, the intended effect of which was to stimulate greater activity in the private sector. There was to be less state participation in industry. No new state-owned ventures were to be started for the rest of the plan period. A majority of shares in joint stock companies and in new public and private undertakings was to be held privately. The government wanted the private sector to play the exclusive role in providing ancillary services to heavy industry. Emphasis was put upon the distinctive and necessary activity of private enterprise, the priority to be given it in financing expansion, and the need for its greater productivity and profitability.

For all this, the government was the source of Rls. 113 billion of Rls. 145 billion ($1.91 billion) of all industrial capital formed during the Fourth Plan. This was 22.3 percent of total government development expenditure of $6.69 billion. Besides iron and steel and petrochemicals, the state invested in factories for mechanical and electrical equipment, basic metals, and transportation vehicles. Private industry was active in tire-making, chemicals, and electrical machinery. During the plan period, manufacturing (and mining's) share of total gross domestic fixed capital formation rose from 13.7 percent to 16.2 percent. The value added of the sector realized an average annual growth rate of 13.8 percent. Manufacturing and mining contributed 16.5 percent to the GNP by 1972–73.

In terms of productivity, the production index (1967–68 = 100) stood at 194 in 1972–73. Output of capital goods rose at a rate of some 28 percent a year, while durable consumer goods grew at 15.5 percent a year and nondurables grew at 14.8 percent a year. The slowest annual growth was registered by nonbuilding intermediate materials at 11.4 percent. Per capita productivity rose from 100 in 1967–68 to 136 in 1972–73, when there were 1,890,000 employees in manufacturing and mining and 2,730,000 workers in the entire industrial sector.

FIFTH PLAN. The necessity to establish industry as the secure base of the nation's long-term economic well-being was the basic premise of the Fifth Plan (1973–74/77–78).

The great accession of new oil wealth after 1974 made possible a much larger industrialization program, but this posed problems as well as opportunities.

The main response of the state to its new wealth was to make arrangements with
the leading industrial nations of the West and with Japan for large, heavy industrial
projects in areas such as steel and petrochemicals, refineries, and nuclear reactors. But,
as the rate of inflation quickened, financing proved difficult. A few projects were postponed, while others were delayed or fell behind schedule due to cost overruns, as the
government and foreign companies argued over differences about the terms of contracts.
Demand soared as a large amount of money was injected into the economy. The costs
of production rose steeply due to scarcities of skilled labor, materials, land, utilities, and
water. The country's infrastructure was incapable of bearing the heavy pressure put
upon it. Imports burgeoned, while numerous domestic factories often operated well
below capacity and lost money. High price rises, especially for rents, caused labor unrest
as wages "chased" prices, while productivity grew at a relatively slow rate. Potential
investors were also deterred from labor-intensive industries by the government's requirement that firms give their workers annual bonuses even when the firms were losing
money and that they also provide profit-sharing schemes.

The regime wished to encourage private investment from foreign and domestic
sources, particularly in heavy industry beyond the smelting process, where private operations would be more efficient. Social and political considerations, however, compelled
it to take measures that tended to discourage industrial ventures other than in development and construction, for which enormous demand ensured high profits. Profit margins
in industry were reduced by price controls introduced to control inflation. Beset by rising
costs, many companies (particularly those more tightly budgeted foreign businesses) had
their earnings so cut that they faced losses. In other areas, foreign and domestic firms
were wary of government interference, which might cause a reduction of management
control and a loss of returns. In 1975, a program was announced whereby 320 companies were to sell 49 percent of their shares to their employees and the public. This
was designed to lessen the concentration of economic power and to give workers a
greater interest in their company. Another object was to promote the growth of
a capital market that would facilitate industrial investment. As for foreign investors,
their involvement in industry had percentage limits according to the nature of the selected industry. Although the government proved fair and flexible in following through
with its shares policy, the increased liquidity obtaining from the scheme tended to be
invested abroad rather than in new ventures at home, and investors remained cautious
about new undertakings.

Further government actions pertinent to industry were the tightening of credit from
1976 and efforts to shift private investment away from construction, which absorbed
nearly half of all commercial credit. By 1977, controls had been put on building permits. At the same time, the government continued to support the important credit banks.
It also set up a new investment organization to assist private industry. Campaigns against
waste and inefficiency were launched, and the Shah reminded his people of the need for
harder work and higher productivity. The benefits to industry of an improving infrastructure were becoming clear, and this helped plans for new provincial industrial zones.
By early 1978 there were indications that export and import regulations might be
relaxed.

By no means were all the troubles in industry due to economic growing pains or
to government interference. Indeed, company tax levels were generally low and the
central authority favored companies making healthy but not exorbitant profits. However, many businesses remained poorly managed, as well as inefficient. Many had not
adjusted to the relatively more austere conditions prevailing toward the end of the

plan period. This was due to previous years of easy effort for large rewards, an attitude preferring quick gains over longer-term rewards, and to an uncompetitive market. Further factors were a five-year tax holiday for new firms, an expectation of ready state financial support and high tariff protection in some cases.

Investment and Productivity. With high technology and heavy industries spotlighted, manufacturing and mining industries were to receive $6.6 billion, the largest element of the original Fifth Plan's total fixed capital investment of $20.6 billion. The revised plan allotted manufacturing and mining $11.56 billion of $69.6 billion for fixed capital formation.

Although it still received the largest share of the state's budget funds—Rls. 414 billion of Rls. 2,847 billion—this shrank relatively as more credits were devoted to other sectors, most notably Iran's overburdened infrastructure. Metallurgical industries, petrochemicals, and chemicals took over half of government development funds for industry, while handicrafts experienced the fastest increase in funding. Investment fell off in 1976–77 as oil income lagged, but by 1977–78 allocations for manufacturing and mining were Rls. 133.7 billion.

Private investment also recorded significant gains during the plan. In 1973–74, the Ministry of Industry and Mines granted 483 permits for new establishments with Rls. 36 billion of capital. One hundred and twenty new units started operations with Rls. 753 billion of capital. By 1976–77, which experienced a vigorous recovery after a decline of investment in the previous year, 824 licenses were extended for firms with Rls. 64.8 billion of capital, and 313 firms with Rls. 36.1 billion of capital began work. Of the entire industrial sector, the most dramatic increases of private and public investment were in construction.

Construction was by far the largest target of private investment. Lesser areas were in food, cellulose, rubber, beverages, metal products, textiles, chemicals, and machinery. The flow of foreign capital into the Center for the Attraction and Protection of Foreign Investment, which totaled Rls. 4.04 billion in 1973–74 and Rls. 4.5 billion in 1974–75,

TABLE K–1. MANUFACTURING AND MINING'S SHARE OF DOMESTIC FIXED CAPITAL FORMATION IN IRAN (CURRENT PRICES)

	1973–74	1974–75	1975–76	1976–77
Rls. billion	56.0	119.5	195.6	236.2
% Annual growth	25.0	113.4	64.5	20.8
% Total GDFCF	14.1	21.4	19.3	16.8

Source: Bank Markazi Iran Annual Reports.

TABLE K–2. STATE PAYMENTS TO THE MANUFACTURING AND MINING INDUSTRIES IN IRAN (RLS. BILLION)

	1973–74	1974–75	1975–76	Change (%)	1976–77	Change (%)
Manufacturing	17.01	35.031	65.024	85.7	71.784	10.5
Mining	6.50	15.201	18.353	20.7	11.820	35.6
Industrial credits	1.75	28.770	20.000	30.5	10.750	46.2
Total	25.26	79.002	103.395	30.9	94.444	8.7

Source: Bank Markazi Iran Annual Reports.

decreased by 11.6 percent in 1975–76 to Rls. 3.98 billion. The following year, foreign investment rose 64.4 percent to Rls. 6.54 billion. Over 60 percent of this amount was invested in metallurgy and petrochemicals.

Despite inflation, government cutbacks, and recession, industry could boast of significant growth. During the first four years of the plan, its value added amounted to over Rls. 2,000 billion (approximately $28.6 billion). In just three years, industry's value added grew by two-thirds. Its share of the GDP (at constant prices) rose from 13.7 percent in 1973–74 to 18.2 percent in 1976–77. Each subsector realized solid advances, with construction well in the lead. But manufacturing and mining, the core of Iran's economic program that is intended to take over from oil as the prime source of national wealth, contributed only 11.6 percent to the GDP by 1977.

By 1976–77, the value of selected industries was Rls. 236 billion (3.37 billion) at constant 1969–70 prices. Its annual growth rate was 15.7 percent in 1975–76 and 13.8 percent in 1976–77. The most valuable industries were automobiles, Rls. 54.7 billion; spinning and weaving, Rls. 27.2 billion; electric and nonelectric appliances, Rls. 22.3 billion; basic metals, Rls. 20.1 billion; and tobacco, sugar, vegetable shortening, radios and televisions, telephones, and cement.

The indices of the selected manufacturing industries (1969–70 = 100) revealed that production kept pace with industrial growth during the Fifth Plan. It rose from 213.6 in 1974–75 to 284.9 in 1976–77. Output per person expanded more modestly from 151.3 in 1974–75 to 183.3 two years later. Due to a tight labor market, the employment index rose only from 140.9 to 155.5 between 1974–75 and 1976–77, while wages and benefits per person increased from 211.2 to 365.6. In 1976, Iran had over 8,000 major factories and plants that employed over 450,000, out of a total work force of 2.4 million, in mining and manufacturing.

TABLE K–3. PUBLIC AND PRIVATE SECTOR INVESTMENT IN CONSTRUCTION IN IRAN (RLS. BILLION AT CONSTANT 1974–75 PRICES)

	1973–74	1974–75	1975–76	Change (%)	1976–77	Change (%)
Investment	285.7	341.2	522.7	53.2	612.0	17.1
Public	186.8	228.1	357.4	56.7	399.9	11.9
Private	98.9	113.1	165.3	46.2	212.1	28.3

Source: Bank Markazi Iran Annual Reports.

TABLE K–4. IRAN'S INDUSTRIAL VALUE ADDED, ITS GROWTH AND SHARE OF GDP UNDER THE FIFTH PLAN[a] (RLS. BILLION)

	1974–75			1975–76			1976–77		
	Value added	Change (%)	GDP (%)	Value added	Change (%)	GDP (%)	Value added	Change (%)	GDP (%)
Industry	436.8	22.5	14.0	535.8	17.0	17.0	653.8	22.0	18.2
Manufacturing and mining	312.9	18.3	10.2	364.2	16.4	11.6	418.1	14.8	11.6
Construction	98.2	34.1	3.2	141.6	44.2	4.5	202.3	42.9	5.7
Water and power	25.7	19.4	0.6	30.0	16.7	0.9	33.4	11.3	0.9

[a] Most recent figures at 1974–75 constant prices.
Source: Bank Markazi Iran Annual Reports.

Survey of Major Industries. METALLURGY. Ample supplies of iron ore, the essential role of steel in industrialization, burgeoning domestic demand, and costly and rising imports put the expansion of the steel industry at the center of the government's development plans. Iran's first successful Soviet-built steel mill came into full operation in 1976. Located at Isfahān and owned by the National Iranian Steel Company, this complex uses a conventional blast furnace and produces over 600,000 tons of steel a year. By 1977–78 it was to reach 1.9 million tons annual capacity and be enlarged to 4 million tons or more in the 1980s. Another mill that will be constructed by the Soviets is under consideration. Owned and controlled by the National Iranian Steel Industries Company (NISIC), four high-technology gas reduction steel plants are in preparation that are intended to add some 8.2 million tons to the country's output by the mid-1980s. The first stage of the steel complex at Ahvāz has been commissioned; when two other stages are ready by 1978–79, it will have a capacity of 2.5 million tons a year. An Italian interest is involved in setting up a steel works producing 3 million tons a year at Bandar 'Abbās, and the British Steel Corporation (BSC) is managing and technically servicing a gas reduction plant at Isfahān, the yearly capacity of which will be 1.2 million tons. The BSC is also engaged in the construction of a cold rolling mill. West German companies will erect a steel mill, the yearly output of which will be 1.5 million tons, and NISIC and a French interest will build a mill for the production of special steels; its capacity will be 70,000 tons annually. Negotiations are under way for more steel mills; in all, ten are planned. Iran is aiming at a yearly production target of 15 million tons by 1987, and as a start some $5 billion will be spent for this purpose between 1976 and 1980. Until the new mills come into production during the next decade, the country will be heavily reliant upon imports. Even then, virtually all output will be needed for domestic consumption. Private firms are prominent in areas such as rolling and pipes.

Copper has become the country's prime metal resource. The government expects to spend about $600 million for the development of crushing, concentration, smelting, and purification facilities at the Sar Chashma mine near Kirmān. Large-scale extraction will begin early in the Sixth Plan, and soon afterward an electrolytic refinery will start opera-

TABLE K-5. PRODUCTION OF SELECTED INDUSTRIES IN IRAN

Industry (units)	1974–75	1975–76	Change (%)	1976–77	Change (%)
Automobiles and jeeps (000)	73	90	22.4	102	14.1
Vans (number)	21,272	52,216	51.4	41,847	29.9
Trucks (number)	8,415	10,942	30.0	13,475	23.1
Buses (number)	1,989	2,388	20.1	2,574	7.8
Other vehicles (number)	4,359	5,354	22.8	8,247	54.0
Cigars and cigarettes (million)	14,389	15,314	6.4	15,591	1.8
Tobacco (tons)	6,044	5,563	8.0	5,987	7.6
Refrigerators (000)	309	437	41.4	513	17.4
Vegetable shortening (000 tons)	244	255	4.5	269	5.5
Granulated sugar (000 tons)	531	564	6.2	598	6.0
Cement (000 tons)	4,628	5,421	17.1	5,955	9.9
Nonalcoholic beverages (million)	800	978	22.3	1,410	44.0
Radios (000)	351	345	−1.7	242	−29.9
Televisions (000)	326	352	8.0	295	−16.2

Source: Bank Markazi Iran Annual Reports.

tions; it will be followed by a metallurgical plant, the initial yearly output of which will be 150,000 tons of blister copper. Other projects include plants to produce nickel sulphate and to extract precious metals, a wire bar and rod casting factory, and possibly a brass mill or electrical components plant. Copper and copper products are expected to become Iran's main foreign export income earner after oil. Exports will decline somewhat as copper emerges as a basic industry, supplying a secondary one whose products will be wires, plates, pipes, and alloys.

In 1973, an aluminum smelter producing 50,000 tons a year came into operation at Arāk. Over two phases, its output will be expanded to 300,000 tons annually, and an extrusion and a rolling mill are also in hand. A Soviet-Iranian agreement calls for the construction of an aluminum plant with an annual capacity of 500,000 tons a year. Plans are afoot for building concentrating, smelting, and alloy plants to meet growing domestic needs for lead, zinc, and chromite.

PETROCHEMICALS. This industry has a cheap and plentiful supply of raw materials. Despite the cancellation of several projects, and the financial problems encountered by others, the state organization responsible for petrochemicals, the National Petrochemical Company (NPC), aims at a large expansion of capacity both to keep up with domestic needs and to win large export earnings. Investment plans for the sector are ambitious; over $3 billion of new facilities will be commissioned by 1980, and over $10 billion is projected for expenditure during the Sixth and Seventh Plans.

The five main petrochemical plants in operation are sited at Bandar Shāhpūr (fertilizers and sulphur), Khārg Island (sulphur and liquified petroleum gas), Ābādān (plastics, caustic soda, and detergents), Shīrāz (fertilizers), and Ahvāz (carbon black). In 1976–77, these complexes produced 800,000 tons of ammonia products, phosphatic and compound fertilizers, soda ash, and nitric and sulphuric acids; 600,000 tons of sulphur; 40,000 tons of polyvinylchloride; 30,000 tons of STPP; 16,000 tons of carbon black; and 12,000 tons of detergent alkylate. When its expansion is completed, by 1978–79, the yearly capacity of the plant at Shīrāz will be 440,000 tons of ammonia, 550,000 tons of urea, 120,000 tons of ammonium nitrate, and 110,000 tons of nitric acid. The Bandar Shāhpūr complex will double its annual capacity to 660,000 tons of ammonia and its production of urea will reach 742,000 tons yearly. Their augmented production will do little more than meet local demand, however.

Japanese firms figure prominently in new petrochemical projects. Inflation of costs from $600 million to $2.5 billion have delayed completion of the Iran–Japan Petrochemical Company's plant at Bandar Shāhpūr until 1980–81. Of its three parts, a chloralkali unit will turn out 550,000 tons of chlorine and caustic soda; an olefins unit will have a yearly capacity of 500,000 tons of ethylene and propylene; and a third, aromatics unit will produce 450,000 tons of benzene and xylenes. In March 1977, the first stage of the Iran–Japan Petrochemical Company's plant, also at Bandar Shāhpūr, was commissioned. When its second part is ready by 1980, the complex will have an annual capacity of 40,000 tons of DOP plasticizer and over 20,000 tons of phthalic anhydride. The National Petrochemical Company is going ahead with plans for a wholly owned aromatics unit at Ābādān, producing 800,000 tons a year. It also has plans for a wholly owned core unit. The Iran–Japan Petrochemical Company signed contracts with a Japanese firm for a caustic soda plant producing 250,000 tons a year and a vinyl chloride monomer unit producing 150,000 tons a year; both will be located at Bandar Shāhpūr. Letters of intent have been signed with European companies for further petrochemical projects.

While the NPC concerns itself with providing petrochemical feedstocks and basic intermediates, several private sector groupings are engaged in secondary activities. The Persepolis Industrial Resins Company and its British partner will produce resins and molding compounds. The Polyacryl Iran Corporation, one of whose members is DuPont, is building a $450,000 factory that will turn out 42,000 tons of polyester and acrylic fibers yearly. The Irano-Gharb organization is pursuing plans to construct a polystyrene plant. The Shirkat-i Aliaf Company manufactures Nylon-6. The NPC considers that more private firms could be involved in petrochemicals with advantage. For itself, there are doubts that with its higher-priced products it can establish a competitive position for Iran in the international market without state subsidies.

AUTOMOBILES. Despite difficulties such as power cuts, the automobile industry expanded considerably during the Fifth Plan. Production, that is assembly, of all vehicles rose from 77,400 in 1973–74 to over 168,000 in 1976–77, in which year domestically produced vehicles accounted for over 80 percent of the market. In the coming years, the target is to more than double current production.

The largest of Iran's dozen automotive "manufacturers" is Iran National, formed in 1963 with Rootes, now Chrysler UK. Its Peykan car, a version of the Hillman Hunter, was first produced in 1967 and is the country's most popular car. Over 60 percent of its components are manufactured locally. Iran National (IN) is preparing a foundry for the production of engines. It plans a second smaller model and aims at manufacturing an all-Iranian car. In late 1977, an agreement was concluded with Peugeot–Citroën for the production of as many as 100,000 cars a year by the early 1980s. The French company will supply some 60 percent of the components for Peugeot sedans, but this will decrease when IN gets ready a $375 million production factory. Sapya Citroën, maker of an Iranian version of the Citroën Dyane called the Hyane, are second to IN. Its Renault 5TL recently came on the market. General Motors has a 45 percent share in Iran Chevrolet, which introduced its cars in 1974. Other makes will be put on the market. General Motors also has a share of General Motors Iran, which is to introduce models of the Cadillac, Chevrolet, and Buick cars and end assembly of the Opel Commodore. The government is negotiating for the entry of the Volkswagen line into Iran.

The Khavar Industrial Group (Daimler–Benz) is the predominant manufacturer of trucks. Other makers are Volvo, Mack, and British Leyland. The government's import of a large quantity of trucks in 1976 resulted in a surfeit in 1977. Assembly plants, such as British Leyland's in Tehran, worked well below capacity. Mazda and Nissan small vans also are produced domestically. Daimler–Benz and British Leyland produce diesel engines at Tabriz. The Iran Tractor Company will begin to make diesel engines in 1978. In a joint venture with the government, Massey–Ferguson has taken charge of the Tabriz tractor plant and intends to produce 25,000 tractors a year by the 1980s. Another joint venture will make trailers for commercial vehicles; output will initially be 3,000.

Other Industries. The machine tool plant at Tabriz has a capacity to produce 30,000 tons a year of pumps, drilling equipment, compressors, electric motors, industrial valves, and other articles; in 1976–77 it made 20,000 tons of goods. A project is under way both to diversify and to increase its output. The heavy engineering establishment at Arāk, with a capacity of 30,000 tons a year, turned out only 8,000 tons of boilers, cast iron parts, transport and pressure equipment, and other goods in 1976–77; its capacity is now being enlarged for the manufacture of cranes, prefabricated houses and equipment for sugar processing. There have been talks with European firms concerning the construction of new machine tool plants that would produce goods such as locomotives, presses, and parts for cars and other vehicles. Other factories make articles ranging from ball-bearings, electric meters and transformers for television sets, refrigerators, and gas ranges. New plants will be set up to produce ships and light aircraft.

The center for cotton and woolen textiles is Isfahān, but cotton materials are also made in Gurgān and Māzandarān, where jute and silk are produced as well; Tabrīz is important for its woolen goods. The output of cotton, linen, and artificial textiles was 570 million meters in 1976–77, but 130 million meters had to be imported. Domestic woolen products supplied 17.5 million meters of the 18 million meters consumed. Production of hand-woven carpets, the most valuable export item after oil, averages 1.75 million meters a year.

The tire industry produced some 43,000 tons of tires in 1976–77. This was well below available capacity of 70,000 tons annually. Another tire factory is being built south of Tehran that will add 40,000 tons a year capacity. In 1976–77, 110,000 tons of writing paper was produced, but the 230,000 tons output of paper and cardboard was 160,000 tons short of demand for the year. Adding to the production of the country's main paper factory in Khūzistān will be a new wood processing and paper manufacturing plant in Gīlān, with a capacity of 150,000 tons a year. A further factory will be built in Māzandarān. Work on a $1.2 billion ordnance factory, postponed in 1976, seemed likely to resume in 1978.

MINING. The broadening of the country's industrial base has necessitated the development of the mining sector. As recently as the early 1960s, Iran was thought to be poor in mineral resources. But these resources had been neither explored nor surveyed. and known deposits were located in remote areas, with poor transportation making access difficult. By the end of the Fourth Plan, mining produced $94 million of ore and contributed 0.4 percent to the GDP, and there were 555 mines with 21,343 workers. The sector made significant advances during the Fifth Plan; public and private investment increased, and the number and variety of projects accelerated, with particular attention being given to the exploitation of heavy metals. Of some 700 mines operating in 1977, more than two-thirds extracted nonmetallic minerals such as coal and construction aggregates; the rest worked metal ores such as iron and copper. All rights to the exploitation of these latter minerals, as well as to uranium and fossil fuels, have been nationalized. Iranian control over all facets of production has not, however, precluded resort to foreign capital and expertise.

Coal, iron, copper, alumina, and bauxite are the most important minerals for industry. Coal is necessary as the raw material for coke, an essential ingredient for steel, and much of the several million tons of coal a year required for this growing steel industry will come from two mines at Kirmān. New mines will be worked in Khurāsān, where a new colliery will be built. At present there are about 45 largely small-scale coal mines, employing 25,000 of Iran's 46,000 mine workers.

The main iron mines are the Ghoghart mine near Bāfq and the Gul-i Gawhar deposit near Sīrjān. These and other mines supply about one million tons a year to the steel mill at Isfahān. At Gul-i Gawhar, a mine and concentrator works will be set up that could eventually service new steel mills with 4 or 5 million tons of iron a year; at present, large amounts of iron ore must be imported. Plans for lead and zinc, much of the output of which is now exported, and for alumina and bauxite have been noted elsewhere. Exploration for uranium has a high priority, as this will be needed for future nuclear power stations. Important deposits have been located recently, one being in the Kalardasht area of the Elburz Mountains. The development of phosphates is also likely.

Many of Iran's mineral needs are still supplied by imports. But as some needs are imported because local supply cannot yet meet demand, so some are exported because there is as yet little domestic demand for them. The government's mining objectives will tie in with plans for building factories that produce finished goods using local materials, thus cutting imports and adding value to exports.

REFINERIES. All refineries are under the control of the National Iranian Oil Company. Among the world's biggest refineries is that at Ābādān, the capacity of which is 487,000 barrels a day, but an accident badly damaged facilities in October 1977 just as an expansion project was under way to increase capacity to 600,000 b/d. Two refineries in Tehran produce 200,000 b/d. Their output will be expanded to over 240,000 b/d, but even further enlargements will be needed to meet demand. Other refineries are located at Kirmānshāh and Shīrāz. There is a topping plant at Masjid-i Sulaimān and a lubricating oil plant near the capital. Small private companies produce lubricants. Run by the National Iranian Gas Company, a refinery for natural gas liquids, with a daily capacity of 33,000 barrels, operates at Bandar Māh Shahr.

High demand and the government's wish to add value before export are the reasons for plans for a large expansion of refining capacity. Total investment in oil refineries in the Fifth Plan was set at $14 billion. Foreign firms are constructing a 200,000 b/d refinery at Isfahān, while one is being set up at Tabrīz with an 80,000 b/d capacity. Further facilities will be established on Lavan (Shaikh Shu'aib) Island. Construction of an INCO-Shell lubricating oil plant is under way. Of three 500,000 b/d export refineries under consideration in the early 1970s, only plans for one have survived; questions about feasibility, rising prices, and problems with financing mean that the refinery could be completed by the mid-1980s at the earliest. That Iran remained interested in export refineries was indicated by talks with Japanese firms in late 1977. Iran has not been successful in becoming involved in downstream operations in Europe or America, but is a joint partner in refineries in India and Africa.

Two gas liquification facilities will be built. A Japanese-Iranian company will put up a liquid natural gas (LNG) plant on the Kangan coast whose capacity will be 2.5 million tons a year for export to Japan. A Norwegian firm takes a prominent part in a project agreed upon early in 1978 to build a floating LNG complex that will have a capacity of 630 million cubic feet a day. A 100 million cubic feet a day scheme will be put up on Qishm Island, and a gas refinery and a distribution network is being built in northern Iran.

CONSTRUCTION. Construction is the most buoyant industry in Iran. The number of housing units rose from 1,623,000 in urban areas and 2,725,000 in rural areas in 1970 to 2,174,000 in cities (1977) and 2,929,000 in rural areas (1976). During the first four years of the Fifth Plan, 219,000 construction permits were issued in the private sector in all urban areas (in Tehran, 46,535); 357,334 structures were started (42,909), and 296,438 structures were finished (35,760). There was a virtual standstill in new construction in 1974–75 and in new completions in 1975–76.

Rising income and a rapidly growing urban population has stimulated a demand for housing that the construction industry has not been able to meet. In Tehran, for instance, there were only some 720,000 houses for some 4.6 million people in 1977, leaving a shortage of 300,000 houses. The dearth of middle- and low-income housing is particularly acute. The inadequate supply has been due to a shortage of land within city limits, shortages of skilled labor and construction materials, high costs of imported equipment and materials and of transport. There has also been lack of competition among contractors, rising consulting fees, and inflated cost estimates of projects. The housing shortfall led to at least a trebling of the price of land, building costs, and rents during the plan period. In 1976–77, the price of urban land rose by 78 percent. In some areas, workers have found that over half of their income must go for rent alone.

The government has acted to ease the housing problem. Since 1976 it has subjected building projects to a predetermined "base" of production costs. It has given the relatively more efficient private sector a larger responsibility for housing. By direction of the Shah, the state is offering large tracts of its land for moderate cost building. This is an attempt to reduce land and property speculation. It increased expenditure upon housing in its 1977–78 budget by 50 percent over the previous year's level. Thus, in the past two years it will have invested over $2 billion in housing. Much of this is being spent for houses for workers in state industries, and the government will also extend funds for low-cost housing loans. In order to increase the level of building, the government intends to relax house construction regulations. Housing has high priority in the Sixth Plan; 150,000 houses will be put up by the public sector and up to 85,000 by the private sector.

CONSTRUCTION MATERIALS. Inadequate supplies of quarry and produced materials have caused long delays and brought about inflated prices on the black market. Cement production from the ten factories in operation, at 5.96 million tons in 1976–77, was well over a million tons below national consumption. Numerous plants are coming into production; the largest being established are a factory at Hamadān, producing 700,000 tons a year, and a day unit at Isfahān, producing 20,000 tons, and it is hoped that national output will reach 9 million tons in 1978. Some 8.5 million bricks were reported produced in 1975–76, but only about 10 percent came from modern, mechanized kilns; new kilns are now being set up. Iran's tile factories have been expanding and can now put out 300 million tiles a year. By 1976 some 76,000 tons of glass was being produced, but imports were still needed.

POWER. At the end of the Fourth Plan, the public and private sectors produced 6,870 million KwH and 2,683 KwH, respectively. By 1976–77 the Ministry of Energy produced 14,211 million KwH, and private sources generated 3,024 million KwH. The overall output of 17,235 million KwH was 9.8 percent above the total 1975–76 production of 15,700 million KwH. However, while generation of electricity increased by 22 percent since 1974–75, consumption was rising by 18 percent to 20 percent a year. Thus, even had the Riżā Shah dam, with a capacity of 750 MW, come into operation by the summer 1977, the country would still have faced a power shortage. Too low an estimate of the rate of consumption and a lack of physical capacity to expand because of intrastructural difficulties and a shortage of resources left Iran 600 MW to 1,000 MW short of the power it needed in 1977, when installed generating capacity was 3,900 MW. Oil is the source of about 71 percent of national energy generation; gas 18 percent; hydroelectricity supplies 5 percent; and the rest comes mostly from coal.

Industrialization and the drive to bring electricity to all of Iran will make tremendous demands upon the national power grid that is being set up. The government is giving increasing attention to power in its budgets. During the past two years, its allocation of $4.83 billion for power has been the largest single item of the economic section of the budget. The goal of the program for energy generation was 4,814 MW by the end of the Fifth Plan, and is 16,351 MW by the end of the Sixth Plan, 37,216 MW by the end of the Seventh Plan, and 56,019 MW at the end of the Eighth Plan. Hydroelectric power is projected to contribute 15,000 MW to the latter figure, while steam power will add 9,300 MW.

The key role in the expansion of power-generation capacity, however, will be played by nuclear energy, which is expected to supply 23,000 MW by 1993. The government's rationale for turning to nuclear power is that oil, production of which will start to decline in the next decade, is too important to be burnt as a fuel. Even though Iran has the second largest reserve of natural gas in the world, gas is considered best used for the secondary recovery of oil and for industrial purposes. It is to replace oil as the major source of energy only until the planned nuclear reactors come on stream in the 1980s and 1990s.

By 1978 a West German firm was under contract to build six reactors; two, with a capacity of 1,200 MW each, were already being set up. A French company was at work on two reactors of 900 MW each, and Iran wanted four more from France in an oil barter deal. Political and technical considerations obstructed implementation of the 1975 agreement between Iran and the United States that the latter would supply eight nuclear power stations. Many difficulties face the realization of a significant nuclear power capacity in Iran; construction, infrastructure, maintenance, long distances for power transmission, and fuel supplies will be very costly, especially in light of falling oil revenues. Moreover, the country's ability to "absorb" these new stations and to provide for safety against earthquakes is uncertain.

Perspective. The growth of Iranian industry and its capacity to produce a broad range of goods has been impressive. However, much remains to be done for it to achieve self-sufficiency, let alone to embark on a large-scale export drive that will be essentially to maintain and increase the level of national wealth. By 1977–78 the country still imported about half of its manufactured goods. Carpets and textiles remained preeminent among Iran's small volume of non-oil exports. Roughly two-thirds of industry produced nondurable consumer goods. The durable goods industries were largely assembly plants dependent upon imports, pharmaceuticals, and chemicals being an example. The contribution of the capital goods industries, upon which the government concentrated, was as yet quite small.

The state remains the main impetus behind industrialization. It wants to give more responsibility to the private sector, but whether the latter can and will take a larger role and make good-quality products at internationally competitive prices is uncertain. As it embarks upon the Sixth Plan, Iran lacks the personnel, skills, outlook, and resources to become a mature industrial state. Only an impossibly high rate of sustained growth can solve the central problem of Iranian industry: to broaden its base as the oil revenues for accomplishing this process decline.

Iraq

Development. Prerevolutionary Iraq gave little attention to industrialization. The Industrial Bank was created in 1946 with the purpose of providing loans for and participating in new ventures, as well as providing technical and other aid. The plans of the Development Board, established in 1950, and of the Ministry of Development, founded in 1953, neglected industrial expansion in favor of agriculture and river control. Of the roughly ID 177 million of actual disbursements for development between 1951 and 1958, only ID 15 million were used for industry. In the mid-1950s there were no more than 80 manufacturing companies proper. These were concerned mostly with processing food and with chemicals, textiles, cement, tailoring, and beverages. Based mostly in Baghdad and Basra, large industries concentrated upon utilities, construction, and quarrying. Changes in the 1929 Law for the Encouragement of Industries, made in 1950, exempted imports of industrial equipment and raw materials from customs duties, while tariffs protected local industries from foreign goods. In 1954 there were 22,460 industrial establishments employing 90,291 workers, but only 294 firms had more than 20 employees.

The revolution of 1958 dealt a severe blow to the private sector. Loss of confidence was manifested in the flight of a substantial amount of capital abroad. Much of industry was nationalized by 1964, as the government increased its involvement, which had already been important before 1958. The General Establishment for Industry (GEI) was set up to manage most state-owned ventures and carry out renovations. It antagonized private companies by much interference. From 1965, however, there resulted, due to governments more favorable to private enterprise, a change of industrial policy and a reorganization of the GEI. Known as the State Organization of Industry after 1967, it was put under the Ministry of Industry. It authorized the formation of private firms with capital not exceeding ID 250,000 and promised to develop mixed-sector industry and with the Industrial Bank to provide investment assurance for foreign capital. The consequences of these changes of policy were insignificant. Private undertakings were restricted to medium-

and small-scale operations in such areas as food processing and consumer goods. Neither mixed-sector projects nor foreign capital were forthcoming. Indeed, by mid-1968, when the socialist Baath party came to power, the private sector was overseen by the state and required to correlate its production with the government's industrial plans. Public investment in industry in the 1960s amounted to some ID 152.8 million of actual disbursements.[1] This was 20.8 percent of all disbursements for development and about 40 percent of funds allocated to the sector. Indicative of the public sector's expansion was its share of all industrial investment. This rose from 52.9 in 1953 to 76.3 percent in 1969.

Diversifying Iraq's industrial output in the 1960s were new factories for electrical equipment, plastics, aluminum goods, radios, televisions, refrigerators, and metal products. Plants for sulphur extraction and for sugar and oil refining, fertilizers, and textiles were also in hand. Plans were initiated for a petrochemical complex. Overall development was slow, due fundamentally to domestic and international political turmoil rather than to lack of investment funds (although the 1967 Arab-Israeli war indirectly caused a brief drop in outlays). Other hindrances besides restrictions upon private industry were a lack of technical and managerial expertise and of skilled labor. Also, the domestic market was small and export possibilities were doubtful. Industry remained characterized by its small scale, heavy reliance upon imports, and its concern largely with processing raw materials and agricultural produce, refining oil, and making a few consumer goods; cement was the main manufactured export commodity. By the end of the decade, manufacturing contributed about 9 percent to the GDP, to which the total industrial sector added some 14 percent. National power-generating capacity was approximately 750,000 KwH.

The sharp rise in the country's income after the oil nationalization measures of 1972 and the quadrupling of oil prices in 1973 (when Law 157 was passed that exempted selected industries from import and other regulations) gave much stimulation to industrial expansion. Compared to the original total planned investment expenditures of ID 973 million, the revised development plan for 1970–71 through 1975 allocated ID 839 million to industry alone. Of this sum, ID 619.9 million was disbursed. ID 290.2 million was expended in 1975 as oil revenues became available. Gross domestic fixed capital formation (GDFCF) in industry rose from ID 81 million (at constant 1969 prices) in 1973 to ID 236.6 million in 1975, or 34.3 percent of total GDFCF.

In public industrial projects, which received over 90 percent of all industrial investment, particular emphasis was put on oil-related, petrochemical, chemical, textile, and electrical equipment factories. This was in accord with the goals of the plan of 1970–74/75 to strengthen the commodity-producing sectors so as to diversify the economy away from its dependence upon oil revenues and to substitute their products for imports. Among prominent projects (see below for details) were refineries, an iron and steel mill, a ship repair yard, a petrochemical complex, an aluminum rods and extension plant, cement factories and a paper plant; and other factories were to be expanded. Although the government suffered a temporary decline in revenue in 1972–73 due to the dispute with the IPC, and in 1975 owing to the fall of oil exports, it has held fast to its policy of minimizing reliance upon foreign loans. The main source of politically acceptable credit has been the Soviet Union and other East European states. More recently, important economic agreements have been concluded with France and Japan.

The Development Plan of 1975–80. The fundamental government goals for the plan are the completion of current projects and the full use of present capacity in order to

1. This includes an *allocation* of ID 28.7 million in 1963–64.

increase industrial productivity. A growth rate of at least 12 percent a year is aimed at. The enlargement of those industries with an export potential, especially ones processing raw materials, is very important. Also, the regime wants to expand manufacturing in the provinces and to work toward greater local and national self-sufficiency, and collaboration with other Arab states is envisaged.

INVESTMENT. In the first three years of the plan, about $9.6 billion of a total development budget to date of some $23.2 billion has been allocated for industry. This is the largest single allocation of the budget; however, probably less than 50 percent of this amount will be disbursed. Although industry is the main target for investment of the plan, which, as approved in 1977, anticipates injecting into it one-third of its funds, other sectors are receiving larger annual increases of funds. Iraq continues to rely very heavily upon its oil revenues and tends to eschew foreign aid for its industrialization. If lagging oil consumption abroad compels it to look for overseas credit, it will approach countries, such as Japan, that do not present political difficulties. As for its sizable imports, the government prefers to trade with Arab or socialist states so long as these can supply it with goods of high quality.

MAJOR NEW PROJECTS. Much of the funds for industrial development will continue to go to petrochemicals and chemicals, iron and steel, and automobiles. Fully half of the sector's funds are being devoted to industries related to hydrocarbons. These are at the heart of the regime's aim to increase the value added of oil products before they are exported. A $2 billion credit from Japan lies behind four major petrochemical schemes. A consortium of companies will build a $2.26 billion petrochemical plant at Basra whose annual capacity will be 700,000 tons of ethylene. A 3.3 million ton a year liquefied petroleum gas plant costing $420 million will be constructed at Rumaila. Adding to Iraq's present facilities to produce soda ash, urea, and sodium chloride will be a $570 million plant at the Khōr al-Zubair industrial complex near Basra, which is intended to make some 730,000 tons of ammonia and over 1.1 million tons of urea a year. An extension of the present Japanese-built urea plant has an annual capacity of 300,000 tons of nitrogenous fertilizer and 500,000 tons of urea. Under construction is a billion dollar petrochemical complex at Basra; when completed by its American-West German contractors in the early 1980s, its yearly capacity will be 150,000 tons of polyethylene and polyvinyl chloride and 40,000 tons of caustic soda. Most of Iraq's fertilizer output will be exported. This is also the prospect for the products of the chemical fertilizer complex at al-Qā'im in western Iraq; at present being built by a Belgian firm, this will use phosphates from the mines at Akashat to produce each year some 400,000 tons of phosphoric acid, over 1.5 million tons of sulphuric acid, and 1.1 million tons of phosphate-based fertilizer.

Further large projects consist of an oil export refinery producing 15 million tons a year under construction by a Japanese company at Khōr al-Zubair, which will cost $1.9 billion and double Iraq's refining capacity, which will be, when expansion of the refinery at Basra is finished, about 14.5 million tons a year. A further refinery producing 15 million tons a year is a possibility. On a smaller scale, Italy is building an LPG plant with a capacity of 200,000 tons a year, and other schemes are for a gas cylinder plant, a lubrication oil and asphalt works, a hexane plant, and several topping plants. A second rayon factory is being built and a dioctyl phthalate plant to produce 12,000 tons a year is under construction. Presently in operation are an ethylene plant at Basra and a sulphur recovery factory at Kirkūk, both of which have an annual capacity of 120,000 tons.

The creation of an iron and steel industry is the centerpiece of a Franco-Iraqi economic agreement worth some $2.8 billion. A French concern is constructing a steel mill at Khōr al-Zubair, to produce 400,000 tons a year. Two sponge iron works being built will supply the mill with 400,000 tons of concentrated iron ore annually and will also export a further 1.5 million tons. At present, the automobile industry consists of several assembly factories, but in an effort eventually to manufacture its own vehicles, Iraq, in cooperation with French interests, is setting up a factory for the production of car parts and an assembly plant at Suwaira; production targets for the early 1980s are 50,000 cars and 17,000 trucks. A ship repair yard will be established that in time will have facilities to build small ships, and a port complex will be erected at Khōr al-Zubair that could cost $500 million. Several aluminum plants are to be built, but a scheme for a smelter is said to have been postponed.

In response to rising demand and to the government's goal of providing a basic level of national welfare, both the consumer goods and food-processing sectors are to be expanded. There will be new factories for shoes and tanning, carpet-making and textiles. In the area of light engineering, a factory is being constructed at Baʻqūbā for the manufacture of washing machines, locks, spark plugs, and fans. A tire plant is under way at Dīwāniyya, and several new paper mills have been established. Other plants will manufacture such goods as meters and telephone and electric cables. In order to meet the anticipated rise in agricultural output, the government intends to expand food processing on a broad front. Plans will be made for grain mills, sugar refineries, bakeries, canning plants, dairies, and for vegetable oil, match, and cigarette factories. Further facilities for bakeries, beverages, and liquid sugar will be erected. Various smaller ventures are being started by state organizations and the Industrial Bank.

Two other essential areas for development are construction and electricity generation. An inadequate supply of construction materials has held back the building industry and has contributed to inflation. Measures are being taken to augment the supply of goods, ranging from cement and bricks to plywood, glass, and prefabricated buildings. Seven new cement plants are to begin operations by 1978. These will increase national output from about 3.3 million tons by 1977 to over 5 million tons. Further plants coming into production will raise output to 12 million tons a year by 1980. It is hoped that increased production will enable cement to regain its recently lost position as one of the country's major exports. The government intends to begin work on 46,000 new houses in 1978 and to complete 20,000.

An expanding power generating capacity is essential for new industries and the on-going electrification of rural Iraq. Capacity was 1,250 MW in 1977 and is to be increased to 4,000 MW by 1980. The Soviet Union has been active in constructing power stations; it will build a new 840 MW station at Nāsiriyya and a Japanese company will construct one near Basra, with a capacity of 800 MW. Talks have been held with France concerning the acquisition of nuclear power stations. In mining, abundant phosphate supplies are being exploited and large sulphur deposits are being developed with Polish technical aid. An estimated 1.1 million new jobs will be created by 1980. As Iraq does not intend to rely upon expatriate labor, it is providing for big increases in national educational facilities, particularly for vocational training.

Profile. Iraq has not in recent times had a strong handicraft tradition like that of Iran, and it remains a small producer of a limited range of manufactured goods. Productivity, while rising over the years, has been erratic. Recently, industry has been running at a loss and operating as much as 30 percent below capacity. Nonetheless, as industrialization has increased, the value of the industrial output of large industries has more than doubled since 1972, when it stood at ID 235.8 million. In 1976 it was ID 559 million, ID 404.7 million of which was added by the public sector and ID 154.4 million of which was contributed by the private sector. The value of production of small industries rose from ID 59.8 million in 1972 to ID 278.3 million in 1975. In the construction industry in 1975, 23,370 private residential buildings were completed at a cost of ID 52.8 million. In 1976 the government issued 49,891 building permits for buildings costing ID 181.3 million. Of this, ID 146,594 million was for the construction of 31,221 new houses. In 1976, 4,645 million kilowatt hours of electricity were generated.

In the past several years, the contribution of industry to Gross Domestic Product has been steady at over 15 percent. Its growth has only just kept pace with the rest of the economy. The private sector was a significant contributor to the industrial sector, accounting for almost half of manufacturing's value added in 1974 and ID 105.5 million (44.2 percent) of its ID 238.5 million added in 1975. It generated ID 81.1 million of ID 91.3 million of value added in construction in 1975.

TABLE K-6. INDEX OF INDUSTRIAL PRODUCTION IN IRAQ
(1962 = 100)

	1965	1970	1974	1975	1976
Foodstuffs, beverages, and tobacco	113.5	117.6	175.9	216.0	288.1
Textiles	121.1	186.5	268.0	255.4	286.1
Clothes and shoes	128.6	227.7	303.5	313.6	350.4
Oil refining	121.4	163.3	215.0	315.7	403.3
Chemical industries	151.0	238.7	310.3	342.7	371.9
Cement and construction materials	122.1	137.5	182.4	196.5	240.2
Miscellaneous	102.7	186.3	330.3	353.7	407.1
General index	119.4	156.2	221.7	263.3	324.9

Source: Republic of Iraq Ministry of Planning, Central Statistical Organization, *Annual Abstract of Statistics, 1976.*

TABLE K-7. OUTPUT OF PRINCIPAL MANUFACTURED GOODS IN IRAQ, 1975

Commodity (unit)	Quantity	Commodity (unit)	Quantity
Processed dates (ton)	58,006	Bricks (million)	1,045
Vegetable oil (ton)	88,574	Cement (000 tons)	2,385
White sugar (ton)	156,541	Refrigerators (number)	39,630
Soft drinks (000 bottles)	770,218	Air coolers (number)	32,729
Various textiles (000 meters)	79,889	Televisions (number)	24,856
Leather shoes (000 pair)	2,720	Automobiles (number)	152
Soaps (tons)	26,280	Trucks (number)	1,798
Glass (tons)	11,752	Tractors (number)	2,269

Source: Republic of Iraq Ministry of Planning, Statistical Organization, *Annual Abstract of Statistics, 1976.*

TABLE K-8. VALUE OF OUTPUT OF SELECTED
INDUSTRIES IN IRAQ (ID 000)

Industry	Year 1975	1976
Food manufacturing	105,510	140,836
Chemical industry oil products	73,831	102,232
Textiles	51,155	62,296
Nonmetallic mineral products	35,444	45,540
Tobacco/cigarettes	36,455	30,547

Source: Republic of Iraq Ministry of Planning, Statistical Organization, *Annual Abstract of Statistics, 1976.*

Increasing industrialization has caused a marked expansion of employment since the early 1970s. The manufacturing industry comprised 1,384 "large" (i.e., over ten workers) establishments in 1976; these had 131,196 employees. The 227 large public companies employed 93,464, while 1,157 big private concerns employed 37,732. In 1975, 39,275 small establishments retained 101,993 workers. In construction, there were 73,004 workers in the public sector, 27,658 workers in the private sector, and 20,305 workers were in the employ of the state electricity and water services. Overall, there were roughly 375,000 persons employed in industry, including about 20,000 in mining. This represented probably more than 10 percent of the national work force. Some 50 percent of those in industry work in Baghdad, Basra, and Mosul.

Perspective. Unlike many Gulf states, Iraq is not too populous to be able to live off its agricultural production. However, the development of a diversified industry is seen as the only way to raise significantly the living standard of the people from a low level, a political imperative for a government always nervous about its viability and control. Large amounts of oil revenue have been devoted to quickening the pace of industrialization, making industry the prime sector for investment.

Rapidly growing domestic demand has caused the government to accent import substitution as well as to accelerate the quest for greater self-sufficiency and self-reliance. But industry, which as yet produces only a narrow range of goods for local consumption, faces many difficulties. Among these are an inadequate infrastructure and a shortage of trained manpower, although the government has attempted to lure back highly trained expatriates. Particularly acute is the heavy flow of illiterate and unskilled country people into the cities, where there is insufficient work for them. Their prospects cannot be good in light of the trend in industry toward high technology and capital-intensive projects, such as hydrocarbons. Low productivity is chronic, and the state is disinclined to enourage foreign involvement.

The government directs industry. Its plans for the sector, subject to quick shifts in policy, have been made largely on an *ad hoc* basis. Nonetheless, once a scheme is embarked upon, it is usually carried through, if with a longer lead-time than anticipated. No regime, however, can control the world oil market, so the flow of oil income will remain the main determinant of how fast industry can develop. Neither will the government be able to avoid increasing its short-term reliance upon foreign goods and services for industry.

TABLE K–9. INDUSTRIAL VALUE ADDED AND SHARE OF GDP[a] IN IRAQ (MILLION ID AT 1969 CONSTANT PRICES)

	1973			1974[b]			1975[c]		
	Value added	Change (%)	GDP (%)	Value added	Change (%)	GDP (%)	Value added	Change (%)	GDP (%)
Industry	210.6	11.7	15.5	225.0	6.9	15.0	276.8	23.0	15.6
Manufacturing	143.5	8.2	10.6	153.7	7.1	10.2	182.4	18.7	10.4
Construction	51.1	20.0	3.8	52.7	3.1	3.5	69.2	31.1	4.0
Power & water	16.0	16.8	1.1	18.6	16.3	1.3	23.4	25.8	1.2

[a] Factor cost.
[b] Revised.
[c] Provisional.
Source: Republic of Iraq Ministry of Planning, Statistical Organization, *Annual Abstract of Statistics, 1976.*

All in all, industry looks certain to remain the main focus of national development into the 1980s.

Kuwait

Oil Processing and Related Industries. After World War II, the refining and processing of oil, and later gas, took over from pearling and shipbuilding as the main nonextraction industry and represented the first step toward industrial diversification. At Mīnā Ahmadī is located the Kuwait Oil Company's 285,000 b/d export refinery. Another plant will raise the refinery's output of bitumen from 100,000 tons a year to 350,000 tons a year in 1978. The Kuwait National Petroleum Company's advanced hydrogen technology refinery at Shu'aiba has a daily capacity of 180,000 barrels, which is being enlarged. The refinery of the state-owned Wafra Kuwait Oil Company (formerly the American Independent Oil Company) at Mīnā 'Abdullāh has a capacity of 144,000 b/d. There is also a 35,000 b/d desulphurizer. A 30,000 b/d refinery for bunkering fuels at Khafjī is operated by the Arabian Oil Company. The capacity for a lubricating oil blending plant is being augmented from 20,000 to 30,000 tons yearly, and a lubricating oil production complex to produce 400,000 tons a year is a possibility.

The production capacity of the Kuwait Oil Company's liquefied petroleum gas facility at Mīnā Ahmadī is 300,000 b/d. Adding to its output will be a new $1.2 billion three-train gas-gathering and liquefaction complex at Shuaiba industrial zone, which when completed by 1979 will be able to produce yearly 28.4 million barrels of propane, 17.5 million barrels of butane, and 14.7 million barrels of natural gasoline. A large part of its total annual production of 3.6 million tons is intended for export. This plant will use the 38 percent of Kuwait's associated gas that presently is flared off. (Gas fuels most of industry; the rest goes to reinjection in oil fields and to domestic uses.) This, however, will be an inadequate supply for the plant, but as resort to lifting the level of the country's crude oil production seems unacceptable, the productivity of the LPG plant is likely to be restricted.

The Petrochemical Industries Company (PIC), now wholly government-owned, was established in the mid-1960s. It laid the foundation for the country's petrochemical industry in the form of the Kuwait Chemical Fertilizer Company, whose facilities in production by 1967 consisted of a sulphuric acid plant with a yearly capacity of 132,000 tons, an ammonia plant with like capacity, an ammonium sulphate plant of 165,000 tons a year capacity, and a urea plant with an annual capacity of 132,000 tons. The PIC inaugurated a urea complex, producing 462,000 tons a year, in 1972, and since then facilities for producing 580,000 tons a year of ammonia have been added.

The PIC is now pursuing plans for petrochemical ventures, the federation of some of which will derive from the LPG complex. An $800 million olefins plant is foreseen that could turn out up to 350,000 tons a year of ethylene and 550 million tons of related products; these, in turn, would be used for plastics and synthetic-rubber-making factories. The PIC is also involved in an aromatics plant that could cost as much as $1 billion and produce yearly 1.6 million tons of benzol, 6.6 million barrels of gasoline, and 2.6 million barrels of fuel oil, as well as 543,000 barrels of heavy aromatics and other products. Another company is setting up a melamine works to produce 15,000 tons a year. These projects for the expansion of the petrochemical industry, for which $2.63 was to have been allotted in the development plan of 1976–77/80–81, face the prospect of cost inflation, overcapacity, and a "soft" market, besides doubts about the capacity of the LPG plant. The question of the availability of feedstock was no doubt behind the collapse of Kuwait's participation in a petrochemical facility on the Black Sea coast of Romania.

Other Industries: Development and Profile. In the early 1960s, the government led the move to expand industries other than oil. As a start to reducing reliance upon hydrocarbons, the state set up joint-sector companies for activities necessary for the economy but too large for private capital alone. Among these was the National Industries Company. Today it runs cement product factories, a quarry, and plants for bricks, batteries, and asbestos-cement pipes, and is part-owner of a metal pipe plant, a prefabricated buildings firm, and a cement works that is undergoing major enlargement. The jointly owned Kuwait Flour Mills Company produces 110,000 tons of flour annually. The plant at Shuwaikh for the production of hydrochloric acid, salt, caustic soda, and chlorine is, however, wholly state-owned.

Important for the promotion of industry has been the provision of industrial zones, principally at Shu'aiba and also at Shuwaikh and Ahmadī. Besides laying on necessary infrastructure at these places, the government has passed laws giving further encouragement to prospective industries. Laws passed in the mid-1960s required that all companies have at least 50 percent Kuwaiti ownership. Many firms were exempted from import tariffs on a large range of goods and materials and from taxes, and import duties were waived and limited protection extended against competing imports, while low-interest government loans were made available to some ventures. Also new firms had to be licensed by the Industrial Development Board, which was set up to assist the development of industry. Among companies benefiting from these measures have been those for construction materials, foodstuffs, furniture, light engineering, printing, industrial gases, soft drinks, fish processing, paper and leather goods, clothing, oil equipment, and chemicals. In terms of exports, output, value added, and number of workers, the latter is the largest manufacturing industry in Kuwait.

Giving added impetus to the advancement of industry is the Industrial Bank of Kuwait, established in 1974 with 49 percent state participation. Its objects are to provide medium- and long-term loans for new or expanding industries and to promote new joint ventures in Kuwait, such as paper recycling and glass wool factories, or in the Gulf, where it is backing a glass bottling plant with Sa'ūdī Arabia and Bahrain. Also among its purposes are to bring in foreign expertise and technology when these are necessary and to develop a local capital and money market.

Kuwait's industrial and domestic users could draw upon 1,568 MW of power-generating capacity in 1977. The two main groups of power stations are located at Shu'aiba and Shuwaikh. A new station is under construction the first stage of which will lift national capacity to 2,168 MW in 1978, and by 1980, when its second stage comes into operation, Kuwait should have a total generating capacity of some 2,550 MW. National capacity may be lifted to 5,000 MW in the 1990s. Most of the country's 60 million gallons of water consumed each day is distilled. Water supply will rise to 78 million gpd in 1978 and to over 100 gpd in the early 1980s.

In 1973–74, manufacturing added KD 75 million (3.5 percent) to the Gross Domestic Product (compared to 68.5 percent for oil). Utilities and construction between them added another KD 64 million (3 percent) to GDP. In the late 1960s and early 1970s, industrial production grew at about 11 percent a year. Between 1972 and 1975, it increased at an average annual rate of 15 percent. The value of industrial output rose from KD 23.8 million in 1968 to KD 148.2 in 1974, while industrial value added increased from KD 8.8 million to KD 80 million. Manufacturing is said to have added 5 percent to GDP in 1975–76. Of 3,050 manufacturing establishments in 1973, with 22,090 workers, only 310 had over 10 employees and only 26 had over 100 workers. Of 378 construction firms with 11,600 workers, only 103 had over 10 workers. Eighteen utilities companies employed 230 people. The non-oil industry, consisting mostly of non-Kuwaitis, accounted for a little more than 10 percent of the national work force. Manufacturing accounted for some 8.2 percent of the labor force in 1975.

Perspective. Shortages of manpower, a small market, a scarcity of all raw materials save hydrocarbons, the high cost of imports, and, more recently, high project costs and other inflation have not stopped Kuwait from pushing toward the feasible limits of industrialization. The government has almost always been guided by a realistic appraisal of what local industry can and cannot achieve economically. Thus, light industry for import substitution and capital-intensive, heavy, oil-related industries have been encouraged, and projects such as smelters and nuclear reactors have not been taken up. Taken as a general indicator of current priorities, the (now cancelled) 1976–77/80–81 development plan confirms the emphasis on industry. As noted above, oil and gas processing was to take KD 764 million of the KD 909.5 million for industry. The non-oil sector was to receive the remaining KD 144 million, with KD 125 million to be used by increasingly active private interests. Although its direct investment has been small, the state continues to be the essential factor for the success of industry. With a realism that comprehends more than national needs, it now calls for a coordinated regional industrial policy.

Sa'ūdī Arabia

Development. Traditional "industry" consisted of small handicraft workshops for making mats, pottery, soap, furniture, and other household goods. Other activities were dyeing, tanning, date packing, and metal working. Pearling, fishing, and shipbuilding were also important. The beginnings of modern industry were stimulated by the operations of the Arab American Oil Company (ARAMCO). Local ventures were set up to provide the goods and services it needed, and some were helped by ARAMCO's Local Industrial Development Center founded in 1946.

The largest demand was for construction and construction materials. By the early 1960s, there were about 200 firms in the latter category to meet the growing requirements of the government and the private sector for new buildings and facilities. Cement plants were in operation in Jidda and Hufūf by 1965, and there were 11 cement pipe factories and over 170 brick works, of which only 3 were mechanized. Other enterprises produced gypsum, made lime and tiles, and cut marble. There were also industries for bottling industrial gases, manufacturing pipes and spare parts, producing ice, printing, and repairing vehicles. Dairies, soft drink bottling plants, bakeries, and factories for salt extraction and the production of macaroni were in production as well. Many of these were located at the seat of ARAMCO's operations in Eastern Province. The most important nonextraction industry was the refinery at Ra's Tanūra that produced some 100,000 barrels a day by 1964.

By then, the government had realized that even its vast oil reserves were limited and that it would be necessary to gradually reduce dependence upon oil by widening the base of the Sa'ūdī economy through industrial development. The core of the country's industrial policy is the promotion of *laissez faire*. For entrepreneurs who have won a government contract or who propose to set up on their own, the state decreed a program for the Protection and Encouragement of National Industries in 1963. This provided industrialists with land or rents at nominal prices, exempted them from customs duties on a wide range of imported goods, and set tariffs upon the import of competing goods. Other measures on behalf of industry have been the provision of liberal foreign investment laws and the infrastructure and vocational training. Begun in 1967, the Industrial Studies and Development Center has aided industry by making feasibility and market studies.

Late in 1962, the semiautonomous General Petroleum and Mineral Organization was created with the purpose of managing completely the country's oil and mineral resources, from exploration right through to marketing. To encourage the exploration for non-oil minerals it formulated a mining code in 1963 that, while asserting exclusive government ownership of all mineral deposits, offered generous incentives to local and foreign investors to exploit resources by way of concessions. Petromin's "brief" extended to other industries, and by 1965 it was involved in the Sa'ūdī Arabian Fertilizer Company, whose daily production capacity was to be 1,100 tons of urea, 600 tons of ammonia, and up to 30 tons of liquid sulphur. Other activities, undertaken mostly with foreign interests, included a polyvinyl chloride plant, a steel rolling mill whose output was planned at 45,000 tons annually, and the country's second refinery with a daily capacity of 12,000 barrels. These and match and soap factories had started production by the end of the decade. Industries in hand were a grain mill, a glass factory, and a refrigerator assembly plant.

Manufacturing, other than refining, which contributed about 6 percent, added some 1.9 percent to GDP in the late 1960s. All non-oil industry—manufacturing, construction, utilities, and mining—comprised about 8 percent of GDP.

FIRST PLAN. During the First Plan (1970–75), four bodies were created to advance industrial development. The General Investment Fund was set up in 1971 to finance investment and purchase shares in government and semigovernment sponsored commercial projects. Foreign investors were allowed all the benefits afforded domestic investors. Those projects with at least 25 percent Sa'ūdī participation were exempted from taxes for five years after their operations began. Created in 1974 with the purpose of stimulating private industry, especially in the area of power generation, the Sa'ūdī Industrial Investment Fund was empowered to provide low-interest, long-term loans for up to 50 percent of the cost of a project. Construction was favored by the establishment in the same year of the Construction Financing Program that gives loans to Sa'ūdī contractors for up to five years for the purchase of material and equipment. The Real Estate Development Fund was designed to promote private and commercial construction with loans covering as much as 70 percent of costs. Industry benefited by tariff reforms in 1973 and 1974, under which reductions of levels of tariffs or exemptions from them were passed for many goods. A 20 percent tariff was pegged to protect locally made products. During the plan, the government stated its intention to proceed with the establishment of major industrial zones with necessary infrastructure at Jidda, Riyadh, and Dammām. Among further inducements to attract more foreign capital was the promise of free repatriation of capital and a revision of the mining law in 1973, giving overseas interests further incentives.

Allocations for industry in the first plan were quite small. They comprised less than half of one percent of both the government's ordinary and projects budget. Between 1970 and 1974, 261 licenses for new private industries were issued. Over half were for food products, chemicals, pharmaceuticals, wood and paper, and 79 licenses were provided for foreign-owned operations. The total number of establishments licensed by the end of 1975 was 639. The 466 wholly-owned Sa'ūdī concerns were capitalized at SR 3.675 million, and SR 571 million of foreign capital was invested in the remainder. The most numerous industries were in metal and metal products, with 185 establishments. The construction and building materials industry was the second largest and, at SR 1.227 billion, had the largest capital value of the sector. New industries that were set up included paints, plastics, detergents, and shoes; these and most of the other factories in Sa'ūdī Arabia are located in Jidda, Riyadh, and Dammām.

Cement, construction, and power generation were the most important private sector activities. Construction contributed some 27 percent to all private economic endeavor in 1975 and 80 percent of all private industrial operations. Construction added SR 4.362 billion, or 3 percent, to GDP at market prices in 1974–75. The rest of industry added SR 1.410 billion, or 0.9 percent, to GDP. The output of cement increased from 667,000 tons in 1970 to 1,125,000 tons in 1975 and 1,118,900 in 1976, while the country's power-generating capacity of 2,013 million KwH was almost three times its 1970 level of 699 million KwH. It increased to 2,778.4 million KwH in 1976. In 1975 377,000 b/d was refined at the Ra's Tanūra refinery. Two small refineries, at Jidda and Riyadh, produced 55,000 b/d between them. Oil refining contributed SR 7.495 billion, or 5 percent, to GDP in 1974–75. A lubricating oil plant was in operation and an asphalt plant was also in production. The number of employees in industry rose from 36,000 in 1970 to 46,000 in 1975. Sa'ūdī desalination plants produced 70,000 cubic meters of water a day in early 1978. This was to reach 114,000 cubic m/d by later 1978 and 400,000 cubic m/d (30 million gallons) by 1981.

SECOND DEVELOPMENT PLAN. The goals of the second development plan of 1975–80 related to industry are the maintenance of a high rate of economic growth, the reduction of dependence upon oil, and the development of human resources and the national infrastructure. Industrial growth will contribute to the diversification of the economy, lessening the impact of outside influence while beginning to provide cost advantages from local production. The country's relative advantage in hydrocarbons is to be capitalized upon by the expansion, with the help of foreign capital, of oil- and gas-related industries, particularly petrochemicals, fertilizers, and also refining. Basic metals and industries essential to the national welfare will receive special emphasis. Dispersion of industry to regions is to be carried through so as to increase and also spread employment and income. The enlargement of the role of the private sector in manufacturing is envisaged. Some of the areas upon which the government would like to see it concentrate are cement, agricultural equipment, food processing, and household and commercial equipment. Numerous and generous tax and other incentives, among them the virtually free provision of infrastructure at industrial zones and freedom of capital movement from currency controls, are to be provided for domestic and foreign investors. Training programs are to be increased and a large number of foreign workers are to be brought in.

The plan anticipates spending on the order of SR 50 billion[2] upon hydrocarbon-based industry. In order to deal more efficiently with the many new projects, a Ministry of Industry and Electricity was set up late in 1975 that took responsibility for industry from Petromin in all sectors save for the production, refining, and selling of oil and gas. The responsibility for all heavy non-oil industry has been given to the Sa'ūdī Arabian Basic Industries Corporation, which has a fund of SR 10 billion. The Industrial Development Corporation was created to participate in manufacturing industry, especially in essential areas where not enough private capital is forthcoming and to continue with foreign interests for major projects. In July 1976, the Sa'ūdī Investment Banking Corporation was instituted with the purpose of providing another source for medium- and long-term industrial loans. In 1975–76, the government allocated SR 841.8 million in its budget expenditure and SR 586.7 million in its projects budget for industry, electricity, and commerce. Of major projects, the largest project in the plan was a gas-gathering and treatment system. Initially designed with a capacity to produce 1.6 billion cubic feet a day, its scale has now been reduced, and at present the only element of this system in operation is a 210,000 b/d NGL complex. Most of the gas system (and other projects mentioned below) will not be ready until the mid-1980s. Besides their going to export terminals and power stations, the products of the gas system will feed as many as five petrochemical plants; three of these last are to be sited at the Jubail industrial estate on the Persian Gulf and, upon completion, would have a capacity of 1.5 million tons a year of ethylene-based products. Another plant here is a possibility. Pipelines will take gas to a petrochemical works at the Yanbū' industrial complex on

2. Project costs have risen steeply since this figure was proposed.

the Red Sea, which is intended to produce yearly up to 500,000 tons of polyethylene, styrene, and glycol. In the area of refining, the capacity of the refinery at Jidda will be expanded from 40,000 b/d to 210,000 b/d, and that at Riyadh will be enlarged from 15,000 b/d to 115,000 b/d. The output of both will be for internal consumption. Two new export refineries are to be built, one at Jubail, the other at Yanbūʿ, whose combined capacity will be about 500,000 b/d. The country's second lubricating oil plant came into operation at Jidda in 1978. A steel mill with a yearly capacity of 800,000 tons is to be constructed at Jubail industrial center, whose gas-fuel direct reduction process will turn out sponge iron. Saʿūdī policy is to embark upon these projects on a 50–50 basis with foreign partners, so that these interests will be committed to their smooth functioning and to the easing of possible marketing difficulties. The government plans to build new industrial estates at Qasīm, Hufūf, and Mecca. Construction will remain very active as the housing budget has been enormously increased. Housing has been expanded in many cities, and by 1977 100,000 houses had been built, as compared to 42,000 projected for the course of the active Second Plan; current projects entail the construction of several new cities. The state is standardizing the national electricity supply, and the Public Electricity Corporation, founded in 1976, is extending electrification throughout the country.

By way of the Industrial Studies and Development Center, which has provided a list of feasible industries and has carried out market research, and by way of licensing and the granting of loans from the various development banks, the government has pointed the direction for private enterprise to take. Only very recently have entrepreneurs in Saʿūdī Arabia and elsewhere in the Persian Gulf thrown off somewhat the attitude that industry is difficult, expensive, undignified, and unrewarding relative to trading or property speculation and development.

In the first eighteen months of the plan, 451 licenses were granted for new industries. The main large private industrial projects are a vehicle assembly plant, a fertilizer complex, steel and asbestos cement pipes factories, steel products works, and cement factories. The vehicle plant, a Saʿūdī-West German venture, began trial production in 1977, its intended capacity being 6,000 heavy trucks a year. The largest proposed scheme is a $100 million phosphate fertilizer complex based in northwestern Saʿūdī Arabia that will produce 700,000 tons a year, but the prospects for its construction were uncertain in early 1978. Two steel goods factories planned in conjunction with foreign interests will, when completed, turn out steel billets, reinforcing bars, iron sheets, and other articles. Three cement plants, at Jidda, Riyadh, and Hofūf, with a current aggregate capacity of 3,900 tons a day, are being expanded to an overall daily capacity of 11,400 tons of cement. New cement factories are intended for Jīzān, Buraida, and Yanbūʿ; each will have a daily capacity of 3,000 tons. Saʿūdī and Bahraini interests plans a cement works at Abqāʿiq to produce 5,000 tons a day, and the Kuwaiti government will participate with Saʿūdī investors in the construction of a cement factory, to produce 7,000 tons a day, to be constructed in the Partitioned Zone. Building materials, metal products, food processing, and beverages account for much of private manufacturing's growth, but mineral and chemical concerns are also growing in importance.

Perspective. The inherent difficulties faced by an immature economy with large financial resources at its disposal have plagued Saʿūdī Arabia and have caused it to reduce the scope of its industrial ambitions as conceived in 1974–75. Projects for a protein plant and for fertilizer complexes have been dropped due to uncertainties about world market demand. Plans for an aluminum smelter were shelved in 1977, mainly because of doubts about its ability to compete with two other smelters in the Gulf. Vehicle assembly plants were put aside due to the small and uncertain domestic market. Cost and general inflation, partly imported, partly owing to an overburdened infrastructure, were behind the scaling down of the gas system, as is the fact that the country's short-term level of oil production will not be as high as recently anticipated. Lack of trained manpower has been a serious impediment to the construction of new projects and has reduced the level of output of factories in operation. The government has not allayed its qualms about importing large amounts of manpower. Harsh technical operating conditions also present formidable difficulties, such as those encountered by the Sa'ūdī Arabian Fertilizer Company.

By 1977–78, industry's prospects seemed on a sounder footing. Inflation was decreasing, the expanding infrastructure, which has recently been given priority over industry, was coping well with the enormous flow of imports, and the planned petrochemical and refinery schemes were in progress. Sa'ūdī Arabia found that it lacked the resources and market for large-scale light industry and that the initially foreseen range of heavy industry had not proved feasible. Despite this, it has now embarked on a sensible and sustainable course of industrial development.

Bahrain

Development. Modern industry began with the discovery of oil in the early 1930s, coinciding with the decline of pearling and shipbuilding. A few years later a refinery began operations, and its present daily capacity is 260,000 barrels. There is also a 50,000 b/d hydrodesulphurizer, and in the 1950s a ship repair yard and a paper factory were constructed.

As it was the first Gulf state to reap the benefits of oil, so Bahrain is the first to be confronted with the relatively imminent exhaustion of its oil resources. In conjunction with keeping its role as a main entrepôt and, more recently, as the leading banking center of the region, Bahrain has striven to expand the non-oil industrial base of its economy. One step toward this end has been the creation of an industrial free zone at Mīnā Salmān. This provides local and foreign investors with free land and with gas at low prices; here, entrepreneurs are exempted from duties on the import of industrial equipment and materials.

Another measure was the establishment of the Development Bureau for New Industry. Its major success has been the $225 million aluminum smelter completed in 1972, whose capacity in 1978 was being expanded from 120,000 tons to 150,000 tons a year; with 2,300 Bahraini employees, it is the largest single employer after construction and oil. Derivative industries comprise an aluminum atomizer plant with an annual capacity of 3,000 tons and a privately owned aluminum cable factory that started production in 1978. The largest new project is the Arab Ship Repair Yard; opened late in 1977, it was built for the Organization of Arab Petroleum Exporting States and has a broad range of facilities to service very large crude oil carriers of up to 500,000 tons. Doubts about its success concern the lack of necessary manpower and low-priced competitors outside the Gulf. Political factors, however, weigh heavily in its *raison d'être* and preservation.

Other industries manufacture soft drinks, signs, tiles, concrete blocks, nails, matches, wood products, consumer and industrial plastic goods, air conditioners, clothing, system-built houses, and oil well equipment. There are also dairies, bakeries, and a shrimp-processing plant. A flour mill is being enlarged and another is to be built. Bahrain is building a cement plant in conjunction with Sa'ūdī Arabia. Despite a mild recession, the construction industry has remained active, especially in the area of hotel building. A new power station coming into operation in 1980 will add 200 MW to the country's present capacity of 176 MW. It is estimated that non-oil industry may contribute about 5 percent to the GDP.

Perspective. Bahrain has followed its industrialization policy successfully and is continuing to expand the range of its manufactures. Of the 1978–79 development budget, $151 million of $696 million will be allocated to industry. In the near future, it will build a $70 million gas-processing plant to produce 280,000 tons a year of natural gas liquid (NGL). A large NGL project is a possibility and would form the core of a petrochemical industry. The fate of this scheme will depend not only upon the government's assessment of its economic and market viability but also upon whether the state wants and the country can support more heavy industry, in the light of static oil revenues and a small, if skilled, manpower base. The likelihood of several more industrial estates being built to attract light manufacturing and engineering companies and construction materials firms indicates that the main thrust of development will be toward light industry. Favorable feasibility studies for welding electrodes, aluminum sheets, and furniture factories confirm this, as does the formation of a company for light industry. Light industries and service industries should benefit from the construction of a causeway between Sa'ūdī Arabia and Bahrain.

Qatar

Initial Development. Oil extraction replaced fishing and pearling as the main industry after World War II. The first nonextraction project was a small refinery that came on stream in 1954. The first factory, for making cement, began production in 1969, with a yearly capacity of 100,000 tons, and, in order to meet growing demand, its output was raised to 266,000 tons in 1974. A further expansion was completed in 1977 that lifted its capacity to 366,000 tons annually, and by 1979 yet another addition will boost the cement plant's capacity to 566,000 tons a year.

By 1973, a fertilizer complex was in operation at Umm Sa'īd, which has become the location of heavy industry in Qatar. This plant's initial daily capacity of 900 tons of ammonia and 1,000 tons of urea was doubled in 1978, and in recent years it has operated at about 80 percent of capacity. A 6,000 b/d refinery that started production at Umm Sa'īd in 1973 will have its capacity increased to 15,000 b/d. In April 1977, a fire destroyed the country's first natural gas liquids complex (NGL 1). Completed only two years earlier, its export capacity was 400,000 tons of propane, 250,000 tons of butane, and 150,000 tons of natural gasolines. Among light industries established by 1973 were a private flour mill that is now being enlarged, a soft drink bottling plant, a factory for retreading tires, and a shrimp-processing plant.

Industrial Strategy and Profile. In 1972–73, the government studied Qatar's economic prospects and decided to launch upon a development of heavy industry that was ambitious for so small a state. The country's plentiful hydrocarbon resources would be used, it was planned, to fund and to fuel export-oriented projects that would diversify its sources of wealth, thereby reducing dependence upon oil and gas alone. Also, light industry would be expanded. Besides the enlargement of present factories, as noted above, there are major new schemes for a petrochemical complex, an iron and steel mill, and a natural gas liquefaction plant, all to be located at Umm Sa'īd, where a large amount of funds is being expended on housing and infrastructure. Responsibility for coordinating the industrial program is held by the Technical Center for Industrial Development (TCID). Allocation for these schemes was QR 1.495 million in 1976 (almost five times the industrial allocation for the previous year) and QR 1.580 million in 1977. These amounts comprised about 34 percent and 25 percent of total allocations for 1976 and 1977, respectively. The more than halving of industry's development allocation for 1978—$434 million, down from $704 million—was due partly to recession, but also to the fact that a good part of the new scheme's construction costs had already been paid.

Main Projects. The natural gas liquids project being completed in 1980 by Japanese interests was initially designed to produce 1,100 tons of propane, 900 tons of benzene, and 900 tons of natural gasolines daily, but its capacity is being doubled to make up for the lost output of NGL 1. The costliest of the new projects, at more than $500 million, is a petrochemical complex being built by French and other firms. When in production in 1979, it will supply yearly 300,000 tons of ethylene, 140,000 tons of polyethylene, and 130,000 tons of plastic products. (Qatar also has a stake in a petrochemical complex in France.) The iron and steel mill was due to begin work in 1978, and 300,000 tons of its yearly production of 400,000 tons will be for export. Despite budget cutbacks late in 1977, the government decided to go ahead with plans for a $380 million 150,000 b/d oil refinery.

In the area of light industry, a plastics factory making hoses, pipes, and sacks opened in 1978. In view of the sluggish growth of the economy, the director of the TCID said that the state would give more attention to the development of smaller industrial concerns. An area southwest of Dōha has been set aside for small, mostly private consumer industries. Likely enterprises are for food processing, tanning, and the making of paints, metal containers, leather goods, and industrial detergents; a paper mill is also a possibility.

The government has been active in construction and housing. Many modern buildings have been added to a rapidly expanding Dōha. The price of land and rents is high, so that the state has taken steps to build low-cost housing. By 1977, 1,500 such houses had been put up and 600 more were planned. Private industry had made little contribution to housing up to 1977, owing to the greater profitability of speculation and to a dearth of workers and materials.

Qatar's electricity generating capacity is about 200 MW. This is due to rise to 500 MW at the end of 1978, with the expansion of the station at Ra's Abū 'Abbūd and with the completion of a new plant at Ra's Abū Fartas, where further increases are planned. The Umm Sa'īd industrial area is to have a 450 MW capacity. It will produce 8 million gallons of water a day for industrial uses. The national production of distilled water will rise from 11 million gallons per day to 39 million gallons per day by the end of 1978, much of this increase coming from the Ra's Abū Fartas plant.

As elsewhere in the Gulf, Qatar has had to contend with inflation, insufficient labor and infrastructures, and a lack of non-oil resources in the course of building its industry. Although the prospects for industry cannot be fully assessed until the major new projects come into production, in several years' time, the vulnerability of the country's export-oriented industries to world market vagaries, and the likelihood of their dubious competitiveness without subsidization, already seems indicated. In 1977–78, the government's decision to stimulate light industry and to cancel a large aluminum smelter project suggested that it clearly recognized the limits as well as the needs of domestic industry. A sign that in the future Qatari industry might be able to expand its potential was the creation and establishment at Dōha in 1977 of the Gulf Organization for Industrial Consultation, whose purpose is to encourage joint planning among member states.

The United Arab Emirates

Abū Dhabī. Oil has been the catalyst of industrial development in the UAE, and this first began in Abū Dhabī. The slow start to the building of infrastructures after oil revenues began flowing in the mid-1960s was given much impetus by the coming to power of Shaikh Zāyid in 1966. A five-year development plan ran from 1968 to 1972, and 59.4 million Bahraini dinars out of a total budget allocation of BD 296 million was devoted to industry. This was the second largest sectoral allocation after infrastructure and went primarily toward power stations and water plants. The government took the lead in industrial activity, which meant in practice construction, and it was followed vigorously by the private sector—to the detriment of manufacturing, of which it had no experience and which promised only slow and arduous financial returns. At the height of building activity in 1969, some 12,000 of the then Trucial States' work force of 29,000 were engaged in construction. After a recession in 1970–71, activity in this area again grew rapidly, especially when the large increase in national income after 1973 led to a much greater demand for new buildings of all kinds; but another recession in 1976–77 caused a marked downturn in construction work, and numerous structures were left unfinished.

DEVELOPMENT: MONEY AND POLICY. Government spending on the expansion of industry and power has increased by almost 2,700 percent since 1972, when it was 40.3 million dirhams, or 2.3 percent of development expenditure, to Dh. 1.113 billion, or 6.1 percent of expenditure, in 1976. But the contribution of manufacturing to the GDP has remained quite small; it added no more than 2 percent to the GDP in 1974, while construction added 11.5 percent. By 1976, construction and public works added 7.3 percent to the GDP and, with oil, accounted for 73.3 percent of the total GDP, whereas manufacturing and power contributed only 0.9 percent to the GDP.

The objectives for industry of the new three-year plan that was to start in 1977 are further to diversify production, to encourage private enterprises, and to promote import substitution. Stress is upon oil- and gas-related industries, other high technology ventures, and the use of local raw materials, as in the building industry. The commitment to new industry is evidenced by the plan's budget, in which $3.3 billion of a total $8.7 billion is designated for industrial projects. Related development expenditures for the plan are about $1.83 billion for utilities and $3.4 billion for infrastructure. On a long-term basis, as much as $22 billion could be spent to develop Ruwais, the intended center of the emirate's heavy industry. As in the other emirates, most of the current and new development projects are a joint government (or Abū Dhabī National Oil Company) and foreign operation. In 1977, the drafting of a bill was in hand to offer new incentives to potential investors, and by 1978 the government had decreed that all industry must have at least a 51 percent local ownership. Of benefit to light industries has been the UAE Development Bank, set up in 1974. As contributor of most of the funds for the federal budget, Abū Dhabī is an indirect backer of industrial growth in those emirates that take advantage of federal outlays for development.

MAJOR PROJECTS. The most important projects existing and in the course of building are those using or treating hydrocarbons. Abū Dhabī's first oil refinery, whose capacity is 15,000 b/d, opened at Umm al-Nār near Abū Dhabī City in 1976; there are now plans to increase its capacity to 50,000 b/d, so as to meet the UAE's domestic needs and to build a 120,000 b/d export refinery at Ruwais, for which a $500 million contract has been given. A $550 million plant for the annual production of 2.2 million tons of liquefied natural gas and up to one million tons of liquefied petroleum gas came into production on Das Island in 1977, but was troubled by technical problems. Initial agreements have been signed for the construction of a $1.2 billion NGL complex at Ruwais that will produce 114,000 b/d of LPG and 71,000 b/d of natural gasoline. From this one billion cubic feet a day of dry gas will be on hand; difficulties with financing have held up this project, however. A nitrogen fertilizer works to produce 535,000 tons a year is proposed for Ruwais as well. An LPG bottling plant producing 28 tons a day is located near Umm al-Nār; its capacity is to be increased to 53 tons daily.

Enormous needs for cement led to the setting up of a cement factory producing 250,000 tons a year at al-'Ain; its capacity is to be tripled and another cement plant is to be built there. A brick factory with a yearly capacity of 40 million bricks began work at al-'Ain in 1977. A gypsum factory is also present. Other enterprises in operation in Abū Dhabī include ice plants, printing presses, a furniture factory, and an iron reinforcing bar plant whose yearly capacity of over 20,000 tons is to be increased. A paper bag factory started operation in 1978, and a PVC pipe plant, a flour mill producing 200 tons a day, and grain silos are being erected. A compost fertilizer plant at Musaffali industrial area that has a daily capacity of 450 tons will also be expanded. Schemes likely to be followed up involve the production of tires, bricks, steel pipes, and chemicals. A study of industry gives high priority to the establishment of plants for building materials, glass and metal products, wire, aluminum and plastic products, asbestos sheets, batteries, vegetable oil, carbon black, paint, soap, cigarettes, and animal feeds. Abū Dhabī had about 320 MW of power-generating capacity in 1977, and some 200 MW of further power should be on hand by 1978, with additions of 370 MW being prepared. Abū Dhabī had distillation plants with a capacity of 30 million gallons per day in 1978, and a further 39 million gallons per day were due on stream by the end of the year.

Dubai. Dubai earned its living from its port and its entrepôt trade before it began receiving oil revenues in the late 1960s. Its new income has been spent primarily upon infrastructure. More recently, it has embarked upon heavy industrial expansion as a complement to its trading role and to the existing light industries. Among these are factories for metal products, bricks and tiles, dairy goods, and soft drink plants. Other factories make paints and varnishes, asbestos cement pipes, soap, gas cylinders, and bottled gas. There are also a privately owned flour mill producing 30,000 tons a year, facilities for producing prefabricated houses and assembling offshore oil platforms, and a steel fabrication plant.

NEW PROJECTS. The most important new scheme is an aluminum smelter to produce 135,000 tons a year and costing over $600 million. Its annual capacity may be enlarged to 180,000 tons. It is being constructed at the Jabal 'Alī industrial zone, which, with its port, has become the focal point of the emirate's industry and will require the construction of a new city to house its workers. An aluminum extrusion plant is also being set up. Fueling these and other projects will be a $400 million natural gas complex producing yearly as much as 370,000 tons of propane, 260,000 tons of butane, and over 2 million barrels of condensate. A cement plant producing 500,000 tons a year was ready for production in 1978. A cable-making factory will be put up at Jabal 'Alī, and other likely projects there are an iron and steel mill and a 150,000 b/d oil refinery. An important addition will be a supertanker dry dock capable of handling ships of 500,000 tons and more. Also, a second, smaller steel fabrication plant is to be built. Dubai had 320 MW of power-generating capacity by 1978, and a further 860 MW with a distilled water capacity of 40 million gallons per day is planned.

Dubai's industrialization program is more diversified than Abū Dhabī's because it lacks its neighbor's abundant stocks of gas upon which to base development.

Sharja. Besides infrastructural work, Sharja has used its oil revenues for a cement plant producing 220,000 tons a year, a ready-mixed concrete works, an air conditioner assembly factory, and factories producing nylon ropes and cement bags. A marble cutting works has long been in operation. A tile works and a radiator remanufacturing plant have come into production, as have several prefabricated house factories, and a steel building components factory is projected. The National Industries and Development Company, in which the government is a participant, is the main body for the promotion of joint-sector industry in Sharja. The emirate's power-generating capacity is about 106 MW.

Ra's al-Khaima. The largest factory is the cement plant at Khōr Khuwair that produces 250,000 tons a year. Its yearly capacity is soon to be increased to over one million tons. Other industries make steel pipes and steel reinforcing rods. A fish-meal plant with an intake capacity of 350 tons a day began production in 1977, but its future was uncertain in 1978. Quarrying is important. Sulphur-free rock is exported to Abū Dhabī and Sa'ūdī Arabia. A lime kiln and a pharmaceutical plant were expected to begin operation by the end of 1978, and a 100,000 b/d oil refinery is a possibility. Over 300 MW will be added to Ra's al-Khaima's current power-generating capacity of 115 MW.

Umm al-Qaiwain, 'Ajmān, and Fujaira. A fish-processing plant and an asbestos cement works will be set up in Umm al-Qaiwain. Present factories in 'Ajmān, which is constructing a fish-meal plant, are concerned with cutting marble and bottling mineral water, and there is also a small dry dock and repair yard. An Italian company is to build a factory for the manufacture of glass, fertilizer, and other goods. A cement plant to produce 300,000 tons a year is under construction, and an explosives and also a bedding factory will be erected. Fujaira may build a fish-processing plant.

Perspective. The quest for diversification of industry in the UAE so as to reduce dependence upon oil is beset by difficulties, not the least of which is the relative absence of natural resources other than oil and gas. The most fundamental problem is that of manpower. If the UAE, that is, mainly Abū Dhabī and Dubai, are to fulfill their industrial ambitions, a very large number of foreign workers will be needed whose presence could raise political tensions. Small local markets and the problematic competitiveness of its export industries must also be contended with; taken altogether, these difficulties have caused several large projects to be dropped. In view of these considerations, light industry seems attractive for the UAE. It too could face pitfalls, however, as each emirate has developed largely on an *ad hoc* basis and with little reference to and some rivalry with the others. The other emirates, for instance, resist Abū Dhabī's attempt to federalize its 51 percent local ownership law. Also, while the bottlenecks, inflation and lack of utilities experienced in the latter 1970s promised to ease somewhat, it was not sure that coordination of the public sector with the still small private sector would increase. But as property becomes less of an attraction, private capital seems likely to give industry more attention, once the credit squeeze of 1977–78 eases.

Oman

Development and Contribution to Economy. Save for oil extraction and some construction, there was no modern industry in Oman before 1970. Traditional activities were metal working, weaving, dyeing, wood carving, and boat building. The new regime of Sultan Qābūs gave first priority for the use of growing oil revenues to the erection of social and economic infrastructure. However, feasibility studies were made for asbestos goods plants, metal, plastic, and glass products factories, oil and sugar refineries, and a steel rerolling mill. Two large projects that were to form the core of a petrochemical industry were a gas liquefaction complex and a fertilizer plant. Overspending, due to the need for rapid development and the heavy financial demand exacted by the insurgency in Dhofār, resulted in the abandonment of these schemes in 1974.

Construction has been the most active sector in the state's effort to build a modern country. It added RO 20.4 million (about 16 percent) to the GDP at market prices in 1971. Its contribution of RO 89.2 million in 1975 and RO 96 million in 1976[3] accounted for 12 percent if the GDP. Not until 1976, when their value was RO 3 million and RO 5 million, respectively, did manufacturing and power combined contribute as much as

3. The figures for 1976 are estimates.

1 percent to the GDP. By then, light industries whose main purpose was import substitution had come into operation to produce bricks and asbestos cement, aluminum and plastic articles, furniture, soft drinks, and industrial gases. By 1978, two date processing plants producing 10,000 tons a year, a private dairy products factory, a private flour mill with an annual capacity of 45,000 tons, and several fish-meal factories were working, as were a pipes factory and a privately owned paint factory with a yearly capacity of 1.2 million liters.

Work was in progress on a cement plant, to produce a million tons a year, in which there was Kuwaiti participation. Agreement had been reached whereby Sa'ūdī Arabia would provide $100 million for a $120 million copper smelter near Suhār that would have an annual capacity of 20,000 tons, most of it for export. Prospects for either an oil refinery or topping plant and for a $250 million petrochemicals complex with Kuwaiti participation were good. Petroleum Development Oman was to set up two gas liquids plants, whose combined daily capacity was projected at over 6,000 barrels. Oman had a power-generating capacity of perhaps over 345 MW by 1977, but new power stations were being brought into operation and a rural electrification scheme was nearing completion.

Perspective. In several ways, 1976–77 was a turning point for industry. Although the economy continued to grow, its rate of increase was slower as the government spent more cautiously. As a result, there was a slump in construction work. But other changes were afoot in this sector. The state began to give more contracts to local firms, or those with local partners, so as to keep more development funds in the country. Also, such new building activity as there was concentrated not upon the capital area but upon the Dhofār region.

Another change was the start of systematic planning in the form of a five-year development plan from 1976 to 1980. Projections for a substantial increase in manufacturing, notably copper and cement, indicated that the government was beginning to shift its primary concern from infrastructural to selective industrial development. Much of the responsibility for expanding revenue-generating schemes has been given to the private sector. Thus, out of private projects anticipated in the plan at RO 420 million, some RO 145 million is for housing and construction, RO 23 million is for cement and copper each, and RO 50 million is for manufacturing. In light of the low level of private investment in 1976 (RO 3 million), it was uncertain that even in a more benign economic climate private enterprise would meet its expectations. The creation of the Oman Development Bank and tax concessions for firms with at least 51 percent Omani involvement were among measures taken to stimulate private activity. The most fundamental uncertainty, however, was how much of a future there was for industry in an Oman whose oil income would soon decline and whose market and manpower resources were small. In the late 1970s, industry complemented modestly the country's agricultural and fishing activities.

Selected Bibliography

al-Otaiba, M. S. *Petroleum and the Economy of the United Arab Emirates.* London, 1977.

American University. *Area Handbook for Iran.* DA Pam. No. 550–68. Washington, D.C., 1971.

———. *Area Handbook for Iraq.* DA Pam. No. 550–31. Washington, D.C., 1971.

———. *Area Handbook for Saudi Arabia.* 2nd ed. DA Pam. No. 550–51. Washington, D.C., 1971.

———. *Area Handbook for the Peripheral States of the Arabian Peninsula.* DA Pam. No. 550–92. Washington, D.C., 1971.

Bharier, J. *Economic Development in Iran, 1900–1970.* London, 1971.

Central Bank of Iraq. *Annual Reports.*

Central Bank of Oman. *Al-Markazi Special Edition.* Oman, 1976.

Economist Intelligence Unit. *Quarterly Economic Review of Iran.* Annual Supplement. London, 1977.

———. *Quarterly Economic Review of Iraq.* Annual Supplement. London, 1977.

———. *Quarterly Economic Review of The Arabian Peninsula: Shaikhdoms and Republics.* Annual Supplement. London, 1977.

Fenelon, K. G. *The United Arab Emirates.* 2nd ed. London and New York, 1976.

Hawley, Donald. *Oman and Its Renaissance.* London, 1977.

Industrial Mining and Development Bank of Iran. *Annual Reports.*

Iran Almanac and Book of Facts 1977. 16th ed. Tehran, 1977.

Jalal, F. *The Role of Government in the Industrialization of Iraq 1950–1965.* London, 1972.

Kachachi, S. *Industrial Development Strategy and Policies: The Experience of Iraq, 1950–1972.* Vienna, 1973.

Kingdom of Saudi Arabia, Ministry of Finance and National Economy, Central Department of Statistics. *Statistical Year Book.* A.H. 1395 eleventh issue. Dammām, n.d.

Kingdom of Saudi Arabia, Ministry of Planning. *Second Development Plan.* Riyadh, 1975.

Langley, K. M. *The Industrialization of Iraq.* Cambridge, Mass., 1961.

McLachlan, K. S. "The Iranian Economy, 1960–1976." In H. Amirsadeghi, ed., *Twentieth Century Iran.* London, 1977.

———. Unpublished paper on the economy of Iraq, 1977.

The Middle East Annual Review. Saffron Walden, England, 1978.

Middle East Economic Digest. Weekly issues for 1977 and 1978.

Middle East Economic Survey. Weekly issues for 1977 and 1978.

The Middle East and North Africa, 1977–78. 23rd ed. London, 1977.

Qatar, Press and Publications Department, Ministry of Information. *Qatar Year Book, 1976.* Dōha, n.d.

Republic of Iraq, Ministry of Planning, Central Statistical Organization. *Annual Abstract of Statistics, 1976.* Baghdad, n.d.

Saudi Arabian Monetary Agency. *Annual Reports.*

State of Kuwait, Ministry of Planning, Central Statistical Office. *Annual Statistical Abstract, 1976.* Kuwait, 1976.

United Arab Emirates, The Department of Press and Publications, Ministry of Information and Culture. *Partners for Progress.* Abū Dhabī, n.d.

APPENDIX L

Agriculture, Fishing, and Pearls

Iran

Land, Water, and Productivity. Of Iran's 164,800,000 hectares (ha) of land, roughly 17.3 million ha (10.5 percent) were cultivated in 1975–76: 6.1 million ha were irrigated, and 11.2 million ha were dry-farmed. About another 3.50 percent of the land, some 5.75

million ha, is potentially cultivable. A further 11 million ha (6.6 percent) comprises permanent pasturage; while forests and woodlands take up 18 million ha, or 11 percent, of the land. In 1972–73, 55.15 percent of farmland came under annual cultivation, 7.59 percent was used for permanent and fodder cropping, and 37.26 percent lay fallow.

Low average annual rainfall (325 mm) subject to large fluctuations, extremes of seasonal temperatures in most places, droughts and floods, and poor or shallow soils are constraints upon agriculture. About half the country receives less than the minimum 250 mm of rain needed for productive dry-farming. In the northwest, where there is adequate rainfall, rugged terrain presents difficulty. The estimated 400 billion cubic meters of rain and snow received each year are very unevenly distributed: 37 percent falls on the Caspian littoral area and the upper reaches of the Elburz and Zagros mountains, which comprise 67,000 square kilometers, or 4 percent, of Iran; 77 percent waters 567,000 sq km, or 33 percent, of the country; and the east and south, over a million sq km, receive the remaining 21 percent. A great problem is the high rate of summer evaporation that takes 270 billion cubic meters of Iran's water. Forty billion cu m are absorbed into the ground and 90 billion cu m become flowing water. Each year, some 10 billion cu m are used for dry-farming, while 42 billion cu m go to irrigation. By the end of the Fourth Plan in 1972, twelve dams contained 16.36 billion cu m of water. It is expected that by the end of the Fifth Plan, a further 11 dams now in various stages of completion will hold another 10 billion cu m of water. The 45,000 qanāts (underground irrigation channels) in use provide over 15 billion cu m of water.

Wheat, barley, cotton, rice, beans and peas, sugar beets, and the produce of fruit and nut trees are the most important crops. The major wheat and barley growing areas are in Azerbaijan, Gurgān, Khurāsān, and Khūzistān, and the coastal tracts of the Persian Gulf; these occupy some 45 percent of the total cultivated area of Iran. The output of wheat has more than doubled since 1950, while the production of barley has increased by over 1½ times. The amount of rice grown mainly along the Caspian coast and Khūzistān has trebled, and sugar beet output has risen by a factor of 75 since that time. The output of cotton, which is grown in the eastern Caspian lowlands, has increased over 1,000 percent. Many fruits are grown in Azerbaijan and Khurāsān. Nut crops are specialties in Azerbaijan, the Caspian coast, and the central-southern Zagros. Vineyards are widespread, but dates are confined mostly to the southern coast. Other valuable crops are tobacco and tea. The estimated 1975–76 output of sugar, grown in Khūzistān, was 1.1 million tons.

Iran was virtually self-sufficient in foodstuffs in the early 1960s. But rising population

TABLE L-1. MAJOR CROPS OF IRAN, THEIR AREA
(1972–73) AND PRODUCTION (1974–76)

		000 tons	
	000 hectares	1974–75	1975–76
Wheat	5,469	4,700	5,500
Barley	1,446	863	1,400
Cotton	309	715	470
Rice	377	1,313	1,430
Sugar beet	146	4,300	4,670
Tea	24.6	96	80

Source: K. S. McLachlan, R. M. Burrell et al., The Developing Agriculture of the Middle East (London, 1976), p. 28. Sample census of Agriculture, 1972/73 Statistical Centre. Economist Intelligence Unit Quarterly.

and income have caused a demand that now quite outstrips the supply of agricultural produce: farm output grows at about 3 percent a year (the rate of population increase), consumption increases at 12.5 percent a year. In 1975–76, 1.4 million tons of wheat had to be imported, despite increased production. Sugar imports were very heavy, and rice and barley also had to be purchased abroad. Total imports of food for the year, comprising 13.3 percent of total imports, cost $1.6 billion, over 4½ times the level of imports for 1973–74. Some forecasts suggest that relative domestic food supply capacity will deteriorate further, leading to imports in the early 1980s worth $4 billion.

Imports of 100,000 tons of red meat in 1975–76—domestic output was 560,000 tons—and of dairy products signify the slow growth of the livestock sector relative to other agricultural sectors and to national demand. In the early 1960s, there were some 28 million sheep, 5.2 million cattle, and 14 million goats. By 1976–77, the estimated number of livestock was 28 million sheep, 5.3 million cattle, and 14 million goats. The number of poultry was 80 million; pigs, 60,000; camels, 100,000; horses and mules, 360,000. The traditional raisers of livestock, nomadic and transhumant tribal herders, have dwindled in number. They have been affected by governmental pressure to settle, by poor rainfall, by various modernization schemes, and by the economic lure of the cities. The prospect for the near future is for even heavier imports of meat and dairy goods, but government projects for livestock improvement and range management will bring at least a modest increase in the number of the animal population. Fishing in Iran has never been of much economic importance, save for caviar, of which over 200 tons annually is exported. The estimated catch of fish in 1976–77 was 5,500 tons in the Caspian Sea and 8,900 tons in the Persian Gulf.

Structure and Policy. Iranian agriculture has undergone much evolution since the passing of the Land Reform Act in 1962. The consequence of this bill was the distribution to peasants of much land that had been held by large landowners. The functions of cooperatives that were started were to act as a means of transferring land to its new owners, to enable the better combining of resources, to facilitate the distribution of seeds and the maintenance of machinery and the irrigation network, and to enable the people to take advantage of various health, education, credit, and extension services offered by the government. Widespread ownership, however, led to the fragmentation of the land into holdings too small to be farmed by modern methods. After 1968, the government's support of the cooperatives waned, and its new object became the amalgamation of these units for more efficient productivity. This was carried through by 1976, when there were 2,859 cooperatives with 2.9 million people, compared to 8,900 cooperatives with 1.25 million people in 1969.

In the late 1960s, policy shifted toward the formation of farm corporations to be owned by farmer-shareholders and run by government officials. The reasoning behind this change of outlook, which became definitive by 1973, and for the intermediate step of forming rural production cooperatives that left ownership in the hands of the peasants, can be seen in the figures for farm holdings and productivity. In 1972–73, nearly 84 percent of all farms, i.e., 2,122 of 2,533 farms, were under 11 hectares in size; they occupied 40 percent of the land but produced only 20 percent of a year's market output. Then 404 farms between 11 and 100 ha (16 percent of all farms) occupied about 48 percent of all farmland and contributed about 75 percent of all market produce. Seven holdings over 100 ha (0.3 percent of all farms) took up some 12 percent of the cultivated land and produced 6 percent of all farm goods for market. Corporations are thought necessary so that collectivized farms can take full advantage of capital-intensive mechanization, centralized management, and improved and extended irrigation networks. By late 1975, there were 65 farm corporations comprising 180,000 ha and 24 rural production cooperatives occupying 37,000 ha. To date, the real accomplishments of these corporations and production cooperatives are uncertain. The government has planned to increase the number of corporations to 143 by 1978; they are to work 420,000 ha.

Since 1973, the government, in collaboration with foreign companies, has started up agro-industries on reclaimed land. These farms of usually more than 5,000 ha use intensive mechanization and sophisticated techniques for specialized crops. By 1976, over 100 agreements for agro-industrial farms were operating. So far, however, their achievements have been indifferent.

The 320,000 farms of more than 20 ha have been the primary object of a government credit extension scheme begun in 1974 to stimulate productivity. This is a response to the fact that many farmers have stoutly resisted the introduction of modern ideas and techniques. Especially in the private sector, many are curbing their investment due to uncertainty about whether state intervention will compel them to merge their land into larger units. The productivity of their farms suffers not only for this reason but also because they see the government's food-pricing policy, in its effort to restrain rising food costs, denying them profits. As for smaller holdings, legislation has been passed that empowers the government to enforce their conversion to production cooperatives or corporations.

Goals and Problems. Large-scale collectivization, increased mechanization and irrigation, the development of modern practices, particularly for using water resources, and an efficient infrastructure are the objectives of Iranian agricultural policy in the last quarter of the century. These are intended to insure a large and steady increase of the production of food, with grains being given emphasis over meat, so as to make the country more self-sufficient. In the coming decade, the target rate for agricultural growth is 7 percent a year; agriculture's share of the GNP is expected to decline from 14 percent in 1974–75 to about 8 percent in the early 1980s.

Many difficulties must be faced in the quest for greater self-sufficiency. Until recently, national development plans have concentrated on industrialization. Having been relatively ignored, agriculture has not been able to meet the demand created by the new industrial wealth. The Fifth plan has given agriculture higher priority, but, although 5.6 billion Rls. has been allocated for the development of agricultural and water resources, no more than 40 percent of this amount had been spent in the first three years of the plan, even when financing for capital-intensive projects has been essential. The questionable real increases in productivity from corporations injected with funds and machines has been noted. As for mechanization, the target for 1978 is 68,000 tractors and 2,000 combines in Iran. Until domestic output of farm machinery rises and mechanized agriculture becomes more widespread and familiar, heavier imports of machinery, as well as food, must be expected. Some of the present loss of productivity can be made good, however, by improving storage and distribution facilities and by more efficient use of available labor and machinery.

There are broader and less tangible problems too. Greater mechanization will cause a larger degree of under- and unemployment in the countryside. Agricultural rationalization is deemed necessary, but it will bring large social-demographic changes that will entail hardship. Over two million people who live in villages of under 250 people will receive no government assistance, and their need for a livelihood will compel them to move to larger farming centers. Lack of trained agricultural cadres to manage and administer the farm corporations and to teach the peasants new ideas, new ways, and new techniques is also a difficulty that can be overcome only slowly. Despite all these problems, the government will press ahead vigorously with its agricultural program so as to best take advantage of its oil revenue before this begins to decline.

Iraq

Twenty million hectares of Iraq's total land area of 43.5 million ha is desert and 23.5 million ha are capable of cultivation (but much of it only at a prohibitive cost; 7.54 million ha is a more realistic figure). Presently, 5.55 million ha are used for cultivation, but only about 40 percent—2.23 million ha—is actually planted in a year; some 2.42 million ha lie fallow. Also, 230,000 ha are pasture; 51,800 ha comprise woodland, while fruit and nut trees and vines take up 128,000 ha; the rest is uncultivable. Some 2.9 million ha are irrigated and 2.75 million ha are rain-fed.

Water and Production. The northern and northeastern governorates, which comprise half the country's farmland, receive over 350 mm of rain each year and are thus primarily rain-fed. The alluvial plain of central and southern Iraq receives less than 200 mm of rain annually. There, the waters of the Tigris and Euphrates rivers are crucial; the former irrigates ½ million ha and the latter waters ¾ million ha. These rivers rise in the mountains of southeastern Turkey, where the annual rainfall governs their discharge in Iraq. Including tributaries in Iraq, this discharge is estimated at an average of 84.5 billion cu m yearly. A perennial threat to agriculture is that there will be either a surfeit or deficit of rain in the mountains, resulting either in spring floods that ruin irrigation works and inundate farmland, or droughts that deny water for growing crops. Large year-to-year fluctuations of the water supply are an unfortunate fact. The water-flow of the Tigris and Euphrates rivers totaled 54 billion cu m in 1962; 112 billion cu m in 1969; and 35.5 billion cu m in 1974.

Besides such serious natural problems as salination, silting of irrigation channels, and poor drainage, there is the man-made problem of excessive and inefficient use of river water and the consequent inadequacy of the drainage system; 59 billion cu m of water on average was used and has been used recently to cultivate an area not appreciably larger than that farmed in the 1940s with only 19 billion cu m a year. Reliance upon this large volume of water, almost 70 percent of the total river flow, renders agriculture quite vulnerable to a deficit of water in drought years, reduces opportunities for more intensive cropping, and impedes maintenance (much less the reclamation) of agricultural land. In fact, overirrigation causes the loss of 25,000 to 30,000 ha a year due to salinity and alkalinity. The expanding cities and industries are also making much heavier demands for water. A difficulty with a political dimension is how Turkey, Syria, and Iraq can most equitably and efficiently share the waters of the Euphrates. Iraq has recently claimed a shortfall of 2.260 million cu m, as against its traditional use of 11,700 million cu m, due to the Syrian dam at Lake Asad.

Wheat, barley, and dates are the major crops of Iraq, but rice, cotton, cane sugar,

TABLE L–2. MAJOR CROPS OF IRAQ, THEIR AREA AND PRODUCTION, 1975–76

Crop	Cultivated area (000 donums)	Output (tons)	Crop	Cultivated area (000 donums)	Output (tons)
Wheat	6,070.0	1,312,400	Cane sugar	12.0	128,125
Barley	2,399.0	579,300	Sugar beet	12.2	72,178
Rice	212.7	163,360	Maize	81.9	54,980
Cotton	107.4	33,890	Dates	n.a.	371,980

Source: Republic of Iraq, *Annual Abstract of Statistics, 1967.*

sugar beet, and maize are also important. Wheat and barley are low-yield winter crops, taking 70 percent to 75 percent of a year's cultivated land. Until the early 1960s, barley was more important than wheat. Dates are a very important export crop. Rice is a high-yielding summer crop, but its annual output is susceptible to much fluctuation (as is that of other crops, wheat and barley for instance), and production was very poor in 1974 and 1975. Sorghum, maize, and millet are important summer crops, and melons, tomatoes, cucumbers, eggplants, and onions are among summer vegetables; root and leaf crops, lentils, vetch, and beans are grown in the winter; tobacco, sesame, and liquorice are also grown, while vineyards and almond and walnut trees are found in the northeast.

Livestock, much of it owned by nomads, accounts for almost half of the value of the agricultural sector. In the past several decades, the livestock population has risen, but recent figures show a marked decline in some categories, notably sheep, camels, buffaloes, horses, and asses. As of 1976, there were 1,804,235 cattle, 8,400,939 sheep, 2,989,270 goats, 145,535 buffaloes, 52,352 camels, 69,140 horses, 459,244 asses, and 13,934,705 chickens. Much remains to be done to provide for adequate fodder supplies and veterinary services so that downturns in the number of livestock can be avoided. Fishing in Iraq is on a small scale; in 1975 the total amount of sold river fish was 9,773 tons (compared to 20,868 tons in 1972), while the total amount of sea fish caught was 6,159 tons. Sea fishing as a state industry is being expanded with the aid of the Soviet Union.

Iraqi agriculture has registered halting growth, but this has by no means been adequate to supply a rapidly growing population experiencing rising incomes and expectations. Poor yearly rainfall and other factors outlined below retard the production of foodstuffs and animal products and thus the amount of surplus in some commodities for export. Thus, in 1974, a year of below-average rain, food imports, much of them consisting of grain, meat, and sugar, amounted to $623 million, or 26.3 percent of all imports. Better rain in the next year kept food imports down to $650.7 million, 15.5 percent of total imports. This requirement to buy abroad puts a severe strain on the country's foreign reserves and points to the necessity for the rapid development of agriculture on all fronts.

Policy and Structure. Since the revolution of 1958, the government's agricultural policies have emphasized water management and land reform. The former entails controlling the spring flood water of the rivers, storing it for use in the summer, and then distributing it for irrigation. Among important recent projects have been the Warrar barrage on the Euphrates near Ramādī. This channels excess water into Lake Habbāniyya and the Abū Dibbis depression. The Wādī Tharthar project diverts the flood water of the Tigris from a barrage at Sāmarrā via a canal to the Wādī Tharthar depression, which has a storage capacity of 70 billion cu m of water. Now however, there are new uses for this water and the depression will be prevented from filling up. Schemes for irrigation and drainage are the Kirkūk-Hawija-Adhāyim, Amāra, and Gharrāf systems. There are drainage networks at Hawija, Karbalā, and Shanifiyya, but drainage facilities cannot cope with the extension of irrigation works.

Land reform has been carried out to distribute the large holdings of big landowners— in 1958, 2 percent of all landowners possessed 68 percent of all farmland—to landless peasants. Maximum limits set to ownership were no more than 1,000 donums of irrigated land or 2,000 donums of rain-water land, and 30 to 60 donums of irrigated land or 60 to 120 donums of dry land were to go to each peasant. In 1970, the ceiling on holdings of irrigated land was reduced to 400 donums.

The main vehicle of reform has been the cooperative society. Its purpose is to supply seeds, to take care of irrigation, credit and administration, and to arrange for fertilizers and machinery. The number of cooperatives has risen from 74 in 1965 to 845 in

1971 and to 1852 in 1976, covering 21.94 million donums with 296,502 members. The setting-up of collective farms is now being stressed, as they will benefit most from large-scale mechanization. From 22 in 1971, their number had risen to 79 in 1975–76, comprising 634,099 donums with 9,857 members. Other, private forms of agricultural production are the share tenancy, in which a farmer gives a landowner a share of his crop in return for the use of facilities; private ownership and working of the land by a farmer; and plantation farming, which involves the hiring of labor by a tenant or owner.

Although well-intentioned, governmental reform policies have both encountered and caused much difficulty. Much more land has been expropriated by the government than has been redistributed. Land has been rented to farmers, but not efficiently and much has been ill-used by farmers uncertain of the future of their holdings as agrarian policies have shifted. Lack of government aid in providing services for agricultural extension, credit, and marketing have also retarded development. Moreover, governments have rarely spent more than 50 percent of funds allocated for the agricultural sector. Other severe impediments have been a lack of trained personnel, low use of fertilizers, and a low level of mechanization. In 1973 there were 9,000 tractors and 1,600 combines in use. Urban migration poses a threat to productivity, and shortages of manpower have been acutely felt at harvest time.

Development. The main emphasis of the government's agricultural development plan for 1976–80, on which over $11 billion may be spent, is to complete land reform. When this is attained, it will take in 3.7 million ha, or 64 percent, of all land presently cultivated. All farmland coming under the reform, and some private land, will be turned into cooperatives, while other cooperatives will become collectives. By 1980, collectives could comprise 200,000 ha; state farms could encompass 125,000 ha. The long-term concern with irrigation, reclamation of land from saline areas, and with water control, diversion, and storage is sustained. Major irrigation schemes are at Kirkūk, where 500,000 ha will eventually come under irrigation, and at Mosul, where up to 750,000 ha will be reached by improved or extended irrigation. The 225,000 ha Abū Ghuraib project is located near Baghdad. Foreign organizations will play an important part in these and other undertakings, such as the Lower Khalis project and the Himrīn dam on the Diyāla River. Plans for increased water storage are intended to add 625,000 ha to the total irrigated area. Another important project is in the Tharthar district, where a canal will be constructed to feed some of the water of the Tigris into the Euphrates in anticipation of future shortages due to diversions up-river in Syria and Turkey. These works are part of a drive of 36 works made to bring the permanent area of cultivation up to 4.25 million ha.

Mechanized, capital-intensive cultivation is being taken up, mainly on government-run farms and reclaimed areas. By 1980 it is hoped that 32,000 tractors and 7,000 combines may be in use. Several rural-based machinery centers are to be established. The government has recognized that mechanization is vital for agricultural progress and intends that all land will be farmed by mechanized means by the end of the century. (In the light of its past performance, this intention and others must be viewed skeptically.) Improvement of the livestock sector will be concentrated upon, so as to reduce the country's volume of imports. The practice of modern breeding is to be expanded and veterinary services are to be improved. Poultry and other livestock production will be expanded, and dairy farms are to be begun. New villages will be formed to settle the migratory tribes. Kurdistan is being reintegrated into the agricultural economy, and land reform and several small irrigation projects have been initiated there. A large number of agricultural cadres will be trained, and large increases in the production of major crops are expected.

Despite its importance to the economy, the development of agriculture has been relatively ignored in favor of industry until quite recently. As the rest of the economy grows, agriculture's share in the GDP has fallen from 15.5 percent in 1971 to about 7.5 percent in 1975. Annual water supplies remain erratic despite the construction of costly water control projects. Rural conditions continue depressed; there is an inadequate base of machinery, skill, knowledge, necessary services, and infrastructure. Current productivity tends to be static with fluctuations or, at best, experiences very slow growth. The prospect of increasing output on presently farmed areas, much less of bringing new districts into cultivation, is diminished by a lack of manpower as many people migrate to the cities. The government's development program aspires to significant advances for agriculture, but few substantive changes will be made that will directly affect the lot of most farmers or augment productivity. Basically, old solutions remain for old problems that are becoming more acute.

Kuwait

A harsh climate, little water, and saline soil are inimical to extensive agriculture in Kuwait. The total cultivable area is estimated at 27,000 donums, 3 percent of the country. Another 67,000 donums are considered pasture land. There are 518 farms. The main sources of water are the 50 million gallons a day produced from desalination plants, 5 million gallons daily of fresh water from underground sources at Raudatain, and the traditional wells and oases, as at Jahrā.

Vegetables, mainly tomatoes, radishes, cucumbers, and melons, and crops, largely clover and alfalfa, take up 6,000 donums, and orchards and woodlands another 1,000 donums. In 1976 there were produced an estimated 16,000 tons of vegetables and melons and 1 million tons of fruit. Local produce provides 13 percent of the country's vegetables. Date palms are also cultivated. The traditional agricultural activity has been animal husbandry, but this has been in relative decline in recent years, as many nomads have migrated to the capital. The estimated livestock population in 1976 was 9,000 cattle and 111,000 sheep, as well as 6,000 camels and 86,000 goats. There were more than 5,740,000 chickens in 1975. Some 6 percent of Kuwait's milk supply, 20 percent of its eggs, and 45 percent of its poultry are supplied locally. All other foods must be imported. Fishing is a more important sector, and some 10,000 tons of fish are caught annually; much of the roughly 5,000 tons exported each year consists of shrimp and prawns.

Although agriculture contributes no more than 0.03 percent to the Gross Domestic Product, and involves no more than 2 percent of the economically active population, the government encourages its expansion in order to cope with the demands of a rapidly growing population. It has established an experimental farm which, besides dealing with trees and shrubbery for the parks of Kuwait City, has sections devoted to poultry and dairy farming and also to hydroponics—the growing of plants in chemical solution without recourse to soil. An important experiment has been the irrigation of crops with treated effluent. The government subsidizes the purchase of seeds and machinery and offers technical advice to farmers. Private farming and the raising of livestock are encouraged. Greater self-sufficiency is hoped for in cattle, poultry, and vegetables, but large imports will remain vital.

Sa'ūdī Arabia

The cultivated area of Sa'ūdī Arabia is 525,000 hectares, 0.3 percent of the total land area. In 'Asīr, 404,000 ha are rain-fed and 121,000 ha are irrigated at oases. According to a survey of the Ministry of Agriculture for 1973–74, there were 10,347,743 donums of total cultivable land; 3,152,531 donums were for temporary crops; 6,074,041 donums were "other cultivable land"; 799,949 donums were being used for permanent crops; and 1,121,171 donums were lying fallow. It has been suggested that with judicious irrigation practices and improved water distribution and drainage, cultivable land could be doubled. An estimated 210 million ha are used for grazing. Woodland is said to cover 16 million donums, but only a much smaller area is of value for forestry. There are 85,000 to 90,000 farms in Sa'ūdī Arabia; over 60,000 are under 10 donums in size.

Water and Crops. The kingdom's water resources are scarce. Many *wādīs*, however, are flooded by rainwater from the mountains in winter. Dams at Abhā and Wādī Jīzān in 'Asīr and at Medina, Riyadh, Tā'if, and elsewhere, over 20 in all by 1976, have been built to contain and store this water. The one exception to the country's dearth of water is the springs at al-Hasā and Qatīf oases in Eastern Province. These and other underground sources supply 1.85 billion cu m of water yearly for irrigation. By 1980, 2.5 billion cu m annually will be demanded. As farming consumes the largest amount of water, desalination of sea water is being stressed, so that conflicting demands for water from growing industries and cities can be minimized. It is hoped to increase the expected capacity of desalination plan in 1977, 135,000 cu m a day to 400,000 cu m daily by 1980.

The main crops of Sa'ūdī Arabia are wheat, dates, alfalfa, sorghum, tomatoes, millet, melons, and vegetables. Rice is an important crop, and onions, citrus fruits, and grapes are grown in sizable quantities. The output of crops is subject to large fluctuations. As of winter 1972 there were 1,237,770 sheep, 755,210 goats, 185,920 cattle, 58,652 camels, 99,076 asses; and 331,315 poultry. The rearing of livestock remains mostly on traditional lines, and this has caused the overgrazing and destruction of pasturage. Fishing remains on a small and local scale. In 1973, trawlers based at Dammām caught 11,000 tons of shrimp, and other fishermen caught 20,100 tons of fin fish.

Problems and Development. The government's agricultural goals as set out in the second Five Year Plan (1975–80) call for a raising of the income and living standards of the rural population, the release of surplus labor to other sectors, and the reduction of dependence on imports of foodstuffs. The latter task alone is formidable: total food imports in 1975 were 350 percent above their 1971 level; they comprised over 40 percent of major Sa'ūdī imports. Ambitious production targets have been set, and overall agricultural output is expected to increase by over 4 percent annually (compared to about 3.6 percent a year for 1970–75).

Numerous problems must be faced if these objectives are to be realized. A particular concern is to reduce present inefficient uses of water and to adapt more economical irrigation. At al-Hasā, for instance, work is under way to reclaim 20,000 ha by removing

TABLE L-3. PRODUCTION OF CROPS IN SA'ŪDĪ ARABIA, 1971–72

Crop	Tons	Crop	Tons
Wheat	38,954	Dates	187,846
Alfalfa (1970–71)	180,000	Tomatoes	110,950
Sorghum	52,360	Melons	453,646
Millet	17,244		

Sources: Kingdom of Sa'ūdī Arabia, Ministry of Finance and National Economy, *Statistical Yearbook, 1394* and *The Statistical Indicator, 1396*, Kingdom of Sa'ūdī Arabia, *Development Plan, 1975–80.*

swampy areas, repairing springs and wells, and improving drainage and irrigation so as to reduce salinity. At the al-Faisal Typical Project at Haradh 4,000 ha have been converted to sprinkler irrigation. The government intends to increase the amount of irrigated land by 50,000 ha to 171,000 ha. This new tract will be farmed by modern methods and be subjected to rigorous water usage. More flood drainage and irrigation projects will be launched.

Annual crop output remains low because most farmers do not observe modern agricultural practices. One means of increasing output is to expand the amount of farmed land, and 42,500 ha of public land have been distributed (but as yet, little of this has been developed). Other means are special economic incentives, as well as expanded credit from the Agricultural Bank. Subsidies of 50 percent are being offered on fertilizers and animal feeds, and subsidies of 45 percent are given for purchases of farm machinery and irrigation pumps. New dairy or poultry farms are eligible for a 30 percent subsidy. The government is encouraging greater self sufficiency in "inputs" such as seeds and machinery—there were only 750 tractors in the country in 1973; the production, processing, and marketing of food in the private sector also is backed. Agricultural research and surveys, training programs, and information services are being increased. Many schemes, from experimental dairy farming to land reclamation, are receiving foreign assistance.

The government's aim in the 1970s has been to expand the agricultural sector so as to diversify the economy and increase national wealth. But in relative terms, the sector has declined. Its contribution to the Gross Domestic Product has declined from 6 percent in the late 1960s to 1 percent by 1974–75. Even its absolute advance from a money value of Rls. 881 million in 1967–68 to Rls. 1,392 million by 1974–75 was dwarfed by the advances in other sectors. As for allocations for agriculture in the country's development budgets, Rls. 399 million was provided in 1968–69 and Rls. 1,721 million was set aside in 1976–77. But in terms of total budget allocations, agriculture's share has fallen from 15.5 percent to 2.3 percent. Although agriculture will derive benefit from the Rls. 34 billion provided for desalination projects in the second Five Year Plan, its direct allocation, Rls. 3.84 billion, is less than 1 percent of the total budget allocation. (There is a limit, of course, to how much the sector can absorb.)

The problems of Sa'ūdī agriculture also have a human dimension. Increasing numbers of farmers and nomads have been attracted by the much higher economic rewards and living conditions in relation to agriculture that are available in cities and towns as a result of the oil-fueled economic boom. On the other hand, those nomads who do not go to the cities remain indifferent to a settled agricultural life. Since 1970, the agricultural labor force is officially estimated to have declined from 40 percent to 28 percent of the national work force. This is the government's wish. But expenditure of funds for developing water resources and increasing the amount of cultivable land and number of livestock will not be fully justified if there is insufficient manpower to translate more money into enhanced output. Agriculture has a very limited resource base, and even with a vigorous rate of growth, its prospect is to fall farther behind in supplying the country with food, especially as the number of foreign workers grows; greater demand will inevitably entail more imports.

Bahrain

Bahraini agriculture suffers the same climatic drawbacks as the agricultural sectors of the rest of the states of the Persian Gulf. It does, however, have an adequate supply of water from springs for the cultivated district of the north. Here there are 500 hectares of date palms, another 500 ha for alfalfa, 300 ha for vegetables such as tomatoes, cabbage, egg plant, onions, carrots, and melons, and 100 ha for fruits such as figs, grapes, mangoes, bananas, and pomegranates. Another 4,000 ha is considered pasturage. In 1976, an estimated 19,000 metric tons of fruits and 10,000 metric tons of melons and vegetables were produced. Wasteful flood irrigation has resulted in a falling water table and increasing salinity of the soil that has put over 500 ha out of use. Other problems are the drift of manpower off the land, an increasing demand for water from other sectors, and the possible urbanization of some farming areas.

Cattle-breeding and fishing are important, but the latter has been in decline due to the economic attractions and requirements for manpower of oil production. There were an estimated 5,000 cattle, 4,000 sheep, 8,000 goats, and 1,000 camels in 1976. A dairy farm is under way on Muharraq and there are 17 commercial poultry farms. The number of chickens was estimated at 172,000 in 1976. Much of the annual catch of 3,500 tons of fish is made by non-Bahraini dhows. The trawlers of the Bahrain Fishing Company catch shrimp and prawns, much of which is for export.

Agriculture contributes only a small amount to the economy and most food will always have to be imported. Nonetheless, the government has taken action to stimulate its growth. Besides maintaining an experimental farm at Budaiya, it provides food subsidies and essential agricultural services. It encourages farmers to form cooperatives for more efficient production, has set up an agricultural credit fund, and has sought UN assistance. Land reclamation could be a means of further development.

Qatar

Less than one percent of the land of Qatar is cultivated, but significant advances have been made since the early 1960s, when there were only 119 farms cultivating 1,604 donums. By 1974, 450 farms had 1,300 ha in use. Their main crops were tomatoes, spinach, okra, aubergines, onions, lettuce, marrows, eggplants, and melons. Dates, figs, grapes, and citrus fruits are grown, and other fruits have been introduced. In 1974, Qatar's output of vegetables was 18,342 tons; 25,520 tons of alfalfa were grown. Wheat is also being grown. By 1975, some 1,500 ha were being farmed that produced about 21,000 tons of vegetables. Qatar exports vegetables such as tomatoes, but it is still an importer of various other vegetables and most other foods. The 80-hectare research-and-trials station at Rawdat al-Khail has been an important factor in Qatar's agricultural progress.

Besides an increase in crop yields, the agricultural development begun in 1970 has also aimed at an enlargement of Qatar's livestock population. By 1974 there were 5,616 cattle, 36,380 sheep, 42,315 goats, 8,148 camels and 68,600 chickens. In 1975, the government began a poultry farm at Umm Qarn, 50 km north of Dōha. This is intended to produce 12 million eggs a year from 15,000 hens, which would meet 80 percent of the country's needs for poultry. The second dairy farm of Qatar is being set up by the government and will have 500 cows. A government sheep farm for 13,000 head is to be started in the south, and both the dairy and sheep farms are to grow their own fodder. Shrimp and prawns meant primarily for export are the main focus of the Qatar National Fishing Company, which has a modern fleet of six refrigerated trawlers that it now also intends to use to catch other kinds of fish. The current annual catch is about one million tons. Qatar is the headquarters of a UN project to survey fishery resources in the Persian Gulf.

Water is the most fundamental problem facing Qatari agriculture. Of the 10.5 million gallons of water consumed every day, 3.2 million gallons come from natural sources. These are being overused; the water table is falling and the water is becoming more salty. The government intends to rely solely on desalinated water for agricultural and other purposes by 1979. At a later time, 32 million gallons a day will be processed from sea water. Recycled effluents will also be used. The need to settle the Bedouin is also important; training programs have been set up with UN assistance, but sedentarization is slow. The government provides various services and farm equipment. A difficult climate and lack of adequate resources make the government's goal of agricultural self-sufficiency unlikely, and heavy outlays of funds for imports and also food subsidies will continue.

The United Arab Emirates

Agriculture in the United Arab Emirates faces the severe problems of high temperatures, low rainfall, and often strong winds. Gypsum and limestone encrust the poor soil, which has become quite saline in places in the course of irrigation. The water supply is quite limited, and much of it is brackish.

Farming Areas and Projects. No more than 5 percent of the UAE is arable. Of the 20,500 ha that are suitable for agriculture, 15,006 ha are now farmed at some time during the year, 4,000 ha of this latter area being irrigated. Ra's al-Khaima is the foremost farming area of the UAE, and greater rainfall than in the other emirates and ground water from the mountains enable 15 percent of its land to be cultivated; accordingly, it produces half the country's fruit, vegetables, cereals, and livestock. Among the main crops are dates, cucumbers, and alfalfa. The important Agricultural Trials Station at Diqdaqa tests many varieties of fruits and vegetables; the more successful kinds are grown on its nearly 160 ha of land. Here there is also a herd of Friesian dairy cattle. On Sadiyat Island is located the Abū Dhabī Arid Lands Research Station, whose ton of vegetables a day supplies nearby Abū Dhabī City. The crops here are watered by controlled drip feeding, which has saved large amounts of water. Overall, the UAE produces 55,000 tons of vegetables annually.

Cattle and dairy farms are in operation at al-'Ain, where a government research station is experimenting with varieties of wheat on part of its 500-hectare holding. The new Malāqit dam will raise the level of the ground water, which will be used to reclaim and irrigate arable land. Other important agricultural areas in the UAE are Liwā Oasis, Mulaiha, and the UAE's segment of the Batīna coast. Poultry farms are being set up in Sharja and Umm al-Qaiwain.

The United Arab Emirates also emphasizes afforestation, and the planting of over 200 million trees in 32,000 ha by 1976 has been intended to reduce the erosion of soil and to protect crops against sand and wind. The highways from Abū Dhabī City to al-'Ain and from al-'Ain to Dubai are now lined with trees, and seedlings are being planted at Tarīf and Jabal Dhanna. Abū Dhabī intends to develop a 6,000-hectare afforestation scheme, and Liwā Oasis will be the site of a future afforestation project.

Fishing in the UAE is in transition from traditional to modern methods and equipment. Assistance is being given by UN agencies and foreign companies; in 1974 the catch of fish was said to be 60,000 tons.

Development. The most rigorous constraint upon the agricultural development of the UAE will remain its limited water resources. If the present heavy rate of usage continues, the country will face a crisis within a decade. Efficient management of present resources and the exploitation of little-tapped supplies at al-'Ain and Liwā Oases will be essential if farming in the emirates is to expand. Other important requirements will be increased governmental technical, financial, and educational assistance to farmers. Also, more people must be persuaded to return to the land and the sedentarization of the Bedouin continues to be important. The UAE relies considerably in foreign technology and expertise for its agricultural development. Its prospects are for future self-sufficiency in perhaps a few crops, but heavy reliance on imports for a broad range of agricultural produce.

Oman

Of the 36,000 to 39,000 ha under cultivation, 38.3 percent is along the Batīna plain. The other major farming areas are in Oman proper (18.9 percent), the Za-hīra (10 percent), and the Western Hajar Mountains (10.6 percent). In 1974, the main home and export crops, dates (52,000 tons produced) and limes (1,700 tons), used 37.1 percent and 9.9 percent, respectively, of arable land. Alfalfa (124,800 tons) took 15.4 percent and onions (6,800 tons) 10.2 percent. Among other crops grown in Oman are tobacco, wheat, tomatoes, sugar cane, chickpeas, bananas, coconuts (in Dhofār), citrus fruits, mangoes, and melons. The number of livestock in 1974 was 216,800 goats, 72,600 sheep, 117,500 cattle, of which some 50,000 were raised in Dhofār, and 15,500 camels. The annual catch of fish is about 70,000 tons.

Achievements and Problems. There have been positive gains in agriculture since 1970. Thirteen government production and experimental farms, the main ones at Rumais, Salālā, Suhār, and Wādī Quraiyāt, and 27 extension centers are now helping Omanis to use improved varieties of seeds and more modern methods of farming. (In 1975, over 600 tons of fertilizer were distributed, compared with less than 100 tons in 1972.) Poultry and dairy farms have been started, and beef cattle are being bred in Dhofār. A concession to a foreign consortium has started the systematic exploitation of the country's rich fishery resources. Overall, agricultural production has risen 3 percent a year since 1971.

Omani agriculture does face serious problems, however; increased national income from oil has stimulated a demand for food that cannot be met by the 75 percent of the labor force that is engaged in agriculture. Imports of foodstuffs have risen 4½ times since 1971, and amounted to $80 million in 1975. There has been a decline in the level of the water table of the Batīna plain, and its supply has also become more salty. Many people have been drawn from the land by the promise of better paid work and easier living in the expanding cities at home and abroad, so that much needed farm labor is lacking.

Development. The government recognizes that the sultanate's oil resources will last no more than perhaps a generation, and it now stresses the long-term importance of agriculture. It is giving much greater prominence to it in development plans than recently, when the need to build hospitals, schools, and an infrastructure took precedence, and agriculture received only 2.2 percent of annual expenditure. The current Five Year Plan involves the spending of many times the $3 million devoted to agriculture between 1972 and 1975.

Other objectives are to augment presently cultivated land by 8,000 ha and to expand output by over 160 percent over recent levels. The range of produce will be widened, and particular attention will be given to enlarging the volume of fruit and vegetables and the number of livestock. Farmers along the Batīna are being encouraged to move their holdings closer to the mountains so as to reduce the absorption of salt into the *aflāj* (underground water channels), the local equivalent of the Iranian *qanāts*. Processing factories are being planned for country areas in an effort to arrest the rural exodus. The development of the fishing industry is being given a high priority, since it has much export, and hence income-generating, potential. As foreign companies train Omanis in fishing techniques, a modern trawling fleet will be acquired; also, onshore facilities will be improved and new plants will be built.

All these targets and schemes will take time, and Oman cannot immediately hope to arrest an increase in its food imports. Nonetheless, self-sufficiency in as many farm goods as possible and an enlargement of the country's agricultural export volume remain the fundamental goals. Improved water usage continues to be essential to the steady advance of the sector. Large quantities of water, some in tables close to the surface, remain untapped, as in the Sharqiyya. Were the run-off of rain water into *wādīs* to be contained and used, arable land in northern Oman could be enlarged 2½ times. The enduring and potential importance of agriculture and fishing assure them a central place in the development of Oman's economy.

Pearls and Pearl Fishing

There are three kinds of pearl-yielding oysters, which also produce mother of pearl. The *mahhāra* grows to 2 to 9 inches in diameter and provides most of the pearls of the Persian Gulf. The best quality of pearls formed by the *zanniyya* are inferior to those of the *mahhāra*. The *zanniyya* and the *sadaifiyya*, which is 6 to 8 inches in diameter, rarely produce pearls. But when the *sadaifiyya* does yield a pearl, it is both large and of very good quality.

Oysters thrive in the shallow, salty waters of the Gulf. The floor of the places where they are found—the best beds lie at a depth of 5 to 10 meters but some are at as low a depth as 60 meters—consists of coral with a thin covering of sand or of hard mud and shells. The main pearl banks of the Persian Gulf lie in the embayment of the coast of the United Arab Emirates south of a line from Dubai City to the islands of Sīr Bū Nu'air and Dās and then to Qatar. The main pearling area here is the Great Pearl Bank. Other banks stretch around Qatar up to 50 km offshore. The best pearl tract lies from northeast of Bahrain to Abū 'Alī Island. It has traditionally accounted for 35 percent of the pearls of the region. The smaller and relatively less productive banks off the steeper coast of Iran lie around Khārg Island and between Kangān and Lingeh. The *mahhāra* is found in most of these places. The *zanniyya* is located particularly off Ra's al-Khaima and the islands of Hind'arabī, Shaikh Shu'aib, and Qais. The *sadaifiyya* occurs around the above islands and also off Ra's al-Khaima and Dās, Zirkō, and Qarnain islands. Within these areas, oyster beds shift from year to year.

Pearl fishing was the main source of wealth of the states of the lower Gulf until the introduction of Japanese cultured pearls and the world economic depression in the 1930s. Early in the century, the pearling industry involved more than 70,000 men in 4,500 boats whose efforts in the main season from May to September brought forth pearls whose export value was over \$1,400,000 (over \$6,700,000 in 1907). By the late 1940s, when oil was becoming the main industry and offering less demanding work, the value of pearl exports was only some \$200,000, provided by perhaps 10,000 men in some 530 boats. By the early 1972s, however, only a few dozen boats were engaged in operations. Recently, the Bahraini government has been trying to promote a revival of pearling. (A concise recent discussion of pearling is found in M. S. Al-Otaiba, *Petroleum and the Economy of the United Arab Emirates* [London, 1977]).

Selected Bibliography

Beaumont, P., Blake, G. H., and Wagstaff, J. M. *The Middle East: A Geographical Study*. London, 1976.

Bowen, R. "The Pearl Fisheries of the Persian Gulf." *Middle East Journal* 5 (1951): 161–80.

Economist Intelligence Unit. *Quarterly Economic Review of Iran*. London, 1977.

————. *Quarterly Economic Review of Iraq*. London, 1977.

————. *Quarterly Economic Review of Saudi Arabia, Jordan*. London, 1977.

————. *Quarterly Economic Review of The Arabian Peninsula: Shaikhdoms and Republics*. London, 1976.

1976 F.A.O. Production Yearbook. Vol. 30. Rome, 1977.

Financial Times. "Country Reports on the States of the Persian Gulf, 1975–77." London, 1975–77.

Fisher, W. B. *The Middle East*. 6th ed. London, 1971.

"Focus on Kuwait." *Progress International*. May 1975.

"Focus on Saudi Arabia." *Progress International*. n.d.

Iran. A MEED Special Report. n.p., 1977.

Kingdom of Saudi Arabia, Ministry of Information. *Agriculture and Water*. Riyadh, n.d.

The Kuwaiti Digest 5 (April–June 1977.)

Lorimer, J. G. "The Pearl and Mother-of-Pearl Fisheries of the Persian Gulf." *Gazetteer of the Persian Gulf, Oman, and Central Arabia*. Calcutta, 1915.

McLachlan, K. S., Burrell, R. M., Hoyle, S., and Parker, C. *The Developing Agriculture of the Middle East*. London, 1976.

The Middle East and North Africa, 1976–77. 23rd ed. London, 1976.

The Middle East Annual Review, 1977. Saffron Waldon, England, 1977.

The Middle East Yearbook, 1977. London, 1977.

Qatar, Press and Publication Department, Ministry of Information. *Qatar Year Book, 1976*. Dōha, n.d.

Republic of Iraq. Central Statistical Organization, Ministry of Planning. *Annual Abstract of Statistics, 1976*. Baghdad.

Sultanate of Oman. Development Council, Technical Secretariat National Statistical Department. *Statistical Year Book*. Fourth issue. Muscat, 1976.

Sultanate of Oman. Ministry of Information and Culture. *Agriculture and Fisheries* (n.d., n.p.).

United Arab Emirates. The Department of Press and Publications, Ministry of Information and Culture. *Partners for Progress: A Report on the United Arab Emirates, 1971–76*. Abū Dhabī, n.d.

Index